Contemporary Authors®

NEW REVISION SERIES

Explore your options!
Gale databases offered in
a variety of formats

DISKETTE/MAGNETIC TAPE

Many Gale databases are available on diskette or magnetic tape, allowing systemwide access to your most-used information sources through existing computer systems. Data can be delivered on a variety of mediums (DOS-formatted diskette, 9-track tape, 8mm data tape) and in industry-standard formats (comma-delimited, tagged, fixed-field).

CD-ROM

A variety of Gale titles are available on CD-ROM, offering maximum flexibility and powerful search software.

The information in this Gale publication is also available in some or all of the formats described here. Your Gale Representative will be happy to fill you in.

ONLINE

For your convenience, many Gale databases are available through popular online services, including DIALOG, NEXIS, DataStar, ORBIT, OCLC, Thomson Financial Network's I/Plus Direct, HRIN, Prodigy, Sandpoint, HOOVER, The Library Corporation's NLightN, and Telebase Systems.

A number of Gale databases are available on an annual subscription basis through GaleNet, a new online information resource that features an easy-to-use end-user interface, the powerful search capabilities of BRS/SEARCH retrieval software and ease of access through the World-Wide Web.

For information, call

GALE
1-800-877-GALE

Contemporary Authors®

A Bio-Bibliographical Guide to
Current Writers in Fiction, General Nonfiction,
Poetry, Journalism, Drama, Motion Pictures,
Television, and Other Fields

JEFF CHAPMAN
PAMELA S. DEAR

Editors

NEW REVISION SERIES
volume 51

GALE

DETROIT · NEW YORK · TORONTO · LONDON

Jeff Chapman and Pamela S. Dear, *Editors, New Revision Series*

John D. Jorgenson, *Pre-Manuscript Coordinator*
Thomas Wiloch, *Sketchwriting Coordinator*

Brigham Narins, Deborah A. Stanley, Aarti Dhawan Stephens,
Kathleen Wilson, and Janet Witalec, *Contributing Editors*

Polly A. Vedder, *Associate Editor*

George H. Blair and Daniel Jones, *Assistant Editors*

Suzanne Bezuk, Bruce Boston, Gary Corseri, Ellen French, Lane A. Glenn, Joan Goldsworthy,
Lisa Harper, Anne Janette Johnson, Elizabeth Judd, Anne Killheffer, Jane Kosek, Doris Maxfield,
Jim McWilliams, Robert Miltner, Julie Monahan, John Mort, Ryan Reardon, Bryan Ryan, Kenneth R. Shepherd,
Pamela L. Shelton, Arlene True, Denise Wiloch, Michaela Swart Wilson,
and Tim Winter-Damon, *Sketchwriters*

Tracy Arnold-Chapman, Jane Kosek, Doris Maxfield, Emily J. McMurray,
Trudy Ring, and Geri Speace, *Copyeditors*

James P. Draper, *Managing Editor*

Victoria B. Cariappa, *Research Manager*

Barbara McNeil, *Research Specialist*

Michele P. Pica, Norma Sawaya, and Amy Terese Steel, *Research Associates*

Alicia Noel Biggers and Julia C. Daniel, *Research Assistants*

○™ This book is printed on acid-free paper that meets the minimum requirements
of American National Standard for Information Sciences-
Permanence Paper for Printed Library Materials, ANSI Z39.48-1984.

Library of Congress Catalog Card Number 81-640179

ISBN 0-8103-9342-5
ISSN 0275-7176

Printed in the United States of America.

Gale Research, an International Thomson Publishing Company.
ITP logo is a trademark under license.
10 9 8 7 6 5 4 3 2 1

Contents

Indexing note: All *Contemporary Authors New Revision Series* entries are indexed in the *Contemporary Authors* cumulative index, which is published separately and distributed with even-numbered *Contemporary Authors* original volumes and odd-numbered *Contemporary Authors New Revision Series* volumes.

As always, the most recent *Contemporary Authors* cumulative index continues to be the user's guide to the location of an individual author's listing.

Contemporary Authors
was named an
"Outstanding
Reference Source" by
the American Library
Association Reference
and Adult Services
Division after its 1962
inception.
In 1985 it was listed by
the same organization
as one of the
twenty-five most
distinguished reference
titles published in the
past twenty-five years.

Preface

The *Contemporary Authors New Revision Series* (*CANR*) provides completely updated information on authors listed in earlier volumes of *Contemporary Authors* (*CA*). Entries for individual authors from *any* volume of *CA* may be included in a volume of the *New Revision Series*. *CANR* updates only those sketches requiring significant change.

Authors are included on the basis of specific criteria that indicate the need for significant revision. These criteria include bibliographical additions, changes in addresses or career, major awards, and personal information such as name changes or death dates. All listings in this volume have been revised or augmented in various ways. Some sketches have been extensively rewritten, and many include informative new sidelights. As always, a *CANR* listing entails no charge or obligation.

How to Get the Most out of *CA*: Use the Index

The key to locating an author's most recent entry is the *CA* cumulative index, which is published separately and distributed with even-numbered original volumes and odd-numbered revision volumes. It provides access to *all* entries in *CA* and *CANR*. Always consult the latest index to find an author's most recent entry.

For the convenience of users, the *CA* cumulative index also includes references to all entries in these Gale literary series: *Authors and Artists for Young Adults, Authors in the News, Bestsellers, Black Literature Criticism, Black Writers, Children's Literature Review, Concise Dictionary of American Literary Biography, Concise Dictionary of British Literary Biography, Contemporary Authors Autobiography Series, Contemporary Authors Bibliographical Series, Contemporary Literary Criticism, Dictionary of Literary Biography, DISCovering Authors, DISCovering Authors: British, DISCovering Authors: Canadian, DISCovering Authors: Modules, Drama Criticism, Hispanic Literature Criticism, Hispanic Writers, Junior DISCovering Authors, Major Authors and Illustrators for Children and Young Adults, Major 20th-Century Writers, Native North American Literature, Poetry Criticism, Short Story Criticism, Something about the Author, Something about the Author Autobiography Series, Twentieth-Century Literary Criticism, World Literature Criticism,* and *Yesterday's Authors of Books for Children.*

A Sample Index Entry:

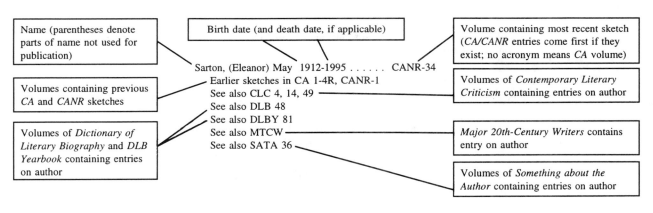

For the most recent *CA* information on Sarton, users should refer to Volume 34 of the *New Revision Series,* as designated by "CANR-34"; if that volume is unavailable, refer to CANR-1. And if CANR-1 is unavailable, refer to CA 1-4R, published in 1967, for Sarton's First Revision entry.

How Are Entries Compiled?

The editors make every effort to secure new information directly from the authors. Copies of all sketches in selected *CA* and *CANR* volumes previously published are routinely sent to listees at their last-known addresses, and returns from these authors are then assessed. For deceased writers, or those who fail to reply to requests for data, we consult other reliable biographical sources, such as those indexed in Gale's *Biography and Genealogy Master Index,* and bibliographical sources, such as *National Union Catalog, LC MARC,* and *British National Bibliography.* Further details come from published interviews, feature stories, and book reviews, and often the authors' publishers supply material.

* Indicates that a listing has been compiled from secondary sources believed to be reliable but has not been personally verified for this edition by the author sketched.

What Kinds of Information Does an Entry Provide?

Sketches in *CANR* contain the following biographical and bibliographical information:

- **Entry heading:** the most complete form of author's name, plus any pseudonyms or name variations used for writing

- **Personal information:** author's date and place of birth, family data, educational background, political and religious affiliations, and hobbies and leisure interests

- **Addresses:** author's home, office, or agent's addresses as available

- **Career summary:** name of employer, position, and dates held for each career post; resume of other vocational achievements; military service

- **Membership information:** professional, civic, and other association memberships and any official posts held

- **Awards and honors:** military and civic citations, major prizes and nominations, fellowships, grants, and honorary degrees

- **Writings:** a comprehensive, chronological list of titles, publishers, dates of original publication and revised editions, and production information for plays, television scripts, and screenplays

- **Adaptations:** a list of films, plays, and other media which have been adapted from the author's work

- **Work in progress:** current or planned projects, with dates of completion and/or publication, and expected publisher, when known

- **Sidelights:** a biographical portrait of the author's development; information about the critical reception of the author's works; revealing comments, often by the author, on personal interests, aspirations, motivations, and thoughts on writing

- **Biographical and critical sources:** a list of books and periodicals in which additional information on an author's life and/or writings appears

Related Titles in the *CA* Series

Contemporary Authors Autobiography Series complements *CA* original and revised volumes with specially commissioned autobiographical essays by important current authors, illustrated with personal photographs they provide. Common topics include their motivations for writing, the people and experiences that shaped their careers, the rewards they derive from their work, and their impressions of the current literary scene.

Contemporary Authors Bibliographical Series surveys writings by and about important American authors since World War II. Each volume concentrates on a specific genre and features approximately ten writers; entries list works written by and about the author and contain a bibliographical essay discussing the merits and deficiencies of major critical and scholarly studies in detail.

Available in Electronic Formats

CD-ROM. Full-text bio-bibliographic entries from the entire *CA* series, covering approximately 100,000 writers, are available on CD-ROM through lease and purchase plans. The disc combines entries from the *CA, CANR,* and *Contemporary Authors Permanent Series* (*CAP*) print series to provide the most recent author listing. It can be searched by name, title, subject/genre, and personal data, and by using boolean logic. The disc will be updated every six months. For more information, call 1-800-877-GALE.

Magnetic Tape. *CA* is available for licensing on magnetic tape in a fielded format. Either the complete database or a custom selection of entries may be ordered. The database is available for internal data processing and nonpublishing purposes only. For more information, call 1-800-877-GALE.

Online. The *Contemporary Authors* database is made available online to libraries and their patrons through online public access catalog (OPAC) vendors. Currently, *CA* is offered through Ameritech Library Services' Vista Online (formerly Dynix), and is expected to become available through CARL Systems. More OPAC vendor offerings will follow soon.

GaleNet. *CA* is available on a subscription basis through GaleNet, a new online information resource that features an easy-to-use end-user interface, the powerful search capabilities of the BRS/Search retrieval software, and ease of access through the World-Wide Web. For more information, call Melissa Kolehmainen at 1-800-877-GALE, ext. 1598.

Suggestions Are Welcome

The editors welcome comments and suggestions from users on any aspects of the *CA* series. If readers would like to recommend authors whose entries should appear in future volumes of the series, they are cordially invited to write: The Editors, *Contemporary Authors,* 835 Penobscot Bldg., Detroit, MI 48226-4094; call toll-free at 1-800-347-GALE; fax to 1-313-961-6599; or e-mail at conauth@gale.com.

CA Numbering System and Volume Update Chart

Occasionally questions arise about the *CA* numbering system and which volumes, if any, can be discarded. Despite numbers like "29-32R," "97-100" and "150," the entire *CA* series consists of only 128 physical volumes with the publication of *CA New Revision Series* Volume 51. The following charts note changes in the numbering system and cover design, and indicate which volumes are essential for the most complete, up-to-date coverage.

CA **First Revision**	• 1-4R through 41-44R (11 books) *Cover:* Brown with black and gold trim. There will be no further First Revision volumes because revised entries are now being handled exclusively through the more efficient *New Revision Series* mentioned below.
CA **Original Volumes**	• 45-48 through 97-100 (14 books) *Cover:* Brown with black and gold trim. • 101 through 150 (50 books) *Cover:* Blue and black with orange bands. The same as previous *CA* original volumes but with a new, simplified numbering system and new cover design.
CA **Permanent Series**	• *CAP*-1 and *CAP*-2 (2 books) *Cover:* Brown with red and gold trim. There will be no further *Permanent Series* volumes because revised entries are now being handled exclusively through the more efficient *New Revision Series* mentioned below.
CA **New Revision Series**	• *CANR*-1 through *CANR*-51 (51 books) *Cover:* Blue and black with green bands. Includes only sketches requiring extensive changes; **sketches are taken from any previously published *CA, CAP,* or *CANR* volume**.

If You Have:	You May Discard:
CA First Revision Volumes 1-4R through 41-44R **and** *CA Permanent Series* Volumes 1 and 2	*CA* Original Volumes 1, 2, 3, 4 and Volumes 5-6 through 41-44
CA Original Volumes 45-48 through 97-100 **and** 101 through 150	**NONE:** These volumes will not be superseded by corresponding revised volumes. Individual entries from these and all other volumes appearing in the left column of this chart may be revised and included in the various volumes of the *New Revision Series*.
CA New Revision Series Volumes *CANR*-1 through *CANR*-51	**NONE:** The *New Revision Series* does not replace any single volume of *CA*. Instead, volumes of *CANR* include entries from many previous *CA* series volumes. All *New Revision Series* volumes must be retained for full coverage.

A Sampling of Authors and Media People Featured in This Volume

Peter Ackroyd

An English novelist, biographer, critic, and poet, Ackroyd is known for works concerning the influence of the past on contemporary art and life. Acclaimed for both his fiction and nonfiction, Ackroyd's writings include the Whitbread Award and Goncourt Prize-winning *Hawksmoor,* and the Heinemann Award-winning biography *T. S. Eliot: A Life.*

Isabel Allende

One of Latin-America's most prominent authors, Allende is a Chilean novelist. Written in a style reminiscent of magic realism, her works explore the social and political tumult of South America and include such novels as *The House of the Spirits* and *Of Love and Shadows.* Allende was named "Feminist of the Year" in 1994.

A. R. Ammons

Winner of the 1993 National Book Award for Poetry for his collection *Garbage,* and the 1995 Ruth Lilly Poetry prize, Ammons is widely regarded as a major American poet. In such works as *Collected Poems: 1951-1971,* he explores the complex relationship between nature and humankind.

Thomas Berger

Author of *Little Big Man,* which some critics consider a modern masterpiece, Berger is an American novelist and short story writer. Nominated for the Pulitzer Prize in 1984 for his novel *The Feud,* he has been favorably compared to such satirists as Mark Twain and H. L. Mencken.

Marion Zimmer Bradley

A prolific American science fiction and fantasy writer, Bradley is widely known for her *Darkover* novels, which trace the evolution of the planet Darkover. Her works often address such themes as communication, feminism, and utopian ideals. Among her non-*Darkover* novels is *The Mists of Avalon,* a retelling of the Arthurian legend from the viewpoint of the women involved.

E. L. Doctorow

Known for the gravity of his philosophical themes and the variety and versatility of his prose, Doctorow is a highly respected American novelist, dramatist, short story writer, and essayist. His novels, including *The Book of Daniel,* *Ragtime,* and *Billy Bathgate,* often center on figures and periods from America's past. He has been the recipient of many awards, including the National Book Critics Circle Award and the American Book Award.

Horton Foote

A highly regarded American dramatist and screenwriter, Foote received the 1995 Pulitzer Prize for Drama for *The Young Man from Atlanta,* which, like his other works, focuses on social change in the rural South. Foote established himself as a successful screenwriter during the 1960s when he adapted Harper Lee's *To Kill a Mockingbird,* which garnered him an Academy Award for best screenplay. He won a second Academy Award in 1983 for *Tender Mercies.*

Ruth Prawer Jhabvala

Jhabvala's novels about life in India are often rooted in the conflict between Western materialism and the spirituality of Indian traditions. She received the Booker Prize in 1975 for her novel *Heat and Dust,* and has been acclaimed for her screenplays, garnering an Academy Award for her film adaptation of E. M. Forster's *A Room with a View.*

Mark Mathabane

Mathabane is best known for his autobiography *Kaffir Boy: The True Story of a Black Youth's Coming of Age in Apartheid South Africa,* in which he recounts his early life of dire poverty and fear in a township near Johannesburg. His most recent book, *African Women,* presents the life stories of his mother, sister, and grandmother.

W. S. Merwin

Merwin is a highly acclaimed American poet, translator, and dramatist, whose works include *The Carrier of Ladders,* which won the 1971 Pulitzer Prize for Poetry, and *Travels,* which received the Lenore Marshall/*Nation* Poetry Prize. Thematically, Merwin's poetry focuses on humankind's separation from nature. Many critics consider him among the most influential of contemporary poets.

Czeslaw Milosz

A Lithuanian-born poet, critic, essayist, novelist, and translator, Milosz won the Nobel Prize for Literature in 1980. Hailed as the foremost Polish poet of this century, Milosz focuses on themes of spiritual survival. His works include *The Captive Mind* and *The Seizure of Power.*

V. S. Naipaul

Born in Trinidad, Naipaul is an English novelist and essayist. His works often center on the Caribbean and focus on characters who feel estranged from the societies to which they ostensibly belong. Known for their precise prose and wry wit, Naipaul's works, including *A House for Mr. Biswas* and *The Mimic Men,* have received much critical praise. His novel *In a Free State* received the Booker Prize in 1971.

Gloria Naylor

Recipient of the American Book Award for best first fiction in 1983 for her novel, *The Women of Brewster Place,* Naylor is an African-American novelist whose works focus on the lives and experiences of African-American women. Naylor's first four novels, which include *Linden Hills, Mama Day,* and *Bailey's Cafe,* are a "quartet" reflecting the diversity of the African-American experience.

Elaine Hiesey Pagels

Pagels is a scholar of religious studies whose works focus on the beliefs of the early Christian church. In *The Gnostic Gospels,* for instance, she explains some of the beliefs of the gnostic sect and tells the story of its losing struggle against the orthodox Christian church. Her most recent work, *The Origin of Satan,* looks at the ways in which central Christian beliefs about sexuality and evil evolved from differing traditions within Christianity.

James Purdy

Purdy is an American novelist, dramatist, short story writer, and poet whose works present a bleak picture of human nature as obsessed with destructive, materialistic concerns. Written in a style that blends fantasy, realism, and black humor, his novels, which include the PEN/Faulkner award nominated *On Glory's Course,* have received high praise from such literary figures as Dorothy Parker and Gore Vidal.

Judith Rossner

Best known for *Looking for Mr. Goodbar,* Rossner is an American novelist and short story writer. Her novels, which include *To the Precipice* and *His Little Women,* focus on human motivation and conflict in contemporary urban America. Many critics laud Rossner for her concern with deep psychological truths and the fluid prose of her works.

Susan Sontag

Though best known as one of America's leading intellectuals and critics, Sontag is also a novelist, short story writer, director, and author of screenplays. Sontag's essays, including the National Book Award-nominated collection *Against Interpretation, and Other Essays,* are considered an important part of the modern critical canon.

Scott Spencer

An American novelist, Spencer is best known for *Endless Love,* a story of obsessive love between two adolescents. Praised for their intense prose, Spencer's novels often focus on psychological conflict and characters whose unchecked desires place them at odds with the rest of the world.

Gloria Steinem

Steinem emerged in the late 1960s as one of the leading organizers of the women's movement. Co-founder and editor of *Ms.* magazine, Steinem's articles and essays, published in such collections as *Outrageous Acts and Everyday Rebellions,* focus on a variety of topics ranging from Marilyn Monroe to the pervasive importance of self-esteem.

Somtow Sucharitkul

Sucharitkul is a Thai science fiction and horror writer. Among his science-fiction works are *Starship and Haiku,* which describes a post-holocaust society, and the "Inquestors" series, a saga of virtually immortal humans. Sucharitkul has also written several novels under the pseudonym S. P. Somtow, including *Vampire Junction,* a horror-love-fantasy story.

John Updike

One of the most prominent and celebrated American authors, Updike is best known for his tetralogy on the life of Rabbit Angstrom, collectively published for the first time as *Rabbit Angstrom: The Four Novels* in 1995. Considered a chronicler of middle-class American life, Updike has received numerous literary awards, including Pulitzer Prizes for *Rabbit Is Rich* and *Rabbit at Rest.*

Contemporary Authors®

NEW REVISION SERIES

*Indicates that a listing has been compiled from secondary sources believed to be reliable but has not been personally verified for this edition by the author sketched.

ABBOTT, Lee K(ittredge) 1947-

PERSONAL: Born October 17, 1947, in Panama Canal Zone; son of Lee Kittredge (in the military) and Elaine (a homemaker; maiden name, Kelly) Abbott; married Pamela Jo Dennis (a bookstore manager), December 20, 1969; children: Noel Lee-Kittredge, Kelly Glenn. *Education:* New Mexico State University, B.A., 1970, M.A., 1973; attended Columbia University, 1970; University of Arkansas, M.F.A., 1977.

ADDRESSES: Home—71 Rockwell Way, Worthington, OH 43085. *Office*—Department of English, Ohio State University, 164 West 17th Ave., Columbus, OH 44106. *Agent*—Elaine Markson, Elaine Markson Literary Agency, Inc., 44 Greenwich Ave., New York, NY 10011.

CAREER: Case Western Reserve University, Cleveland, Ohio, assistant professor, 1977-82, associate professor, 1983-87, professor of English, 1987-89, Samuel B. & Virginia C. Knight Professor of Humanities, 1988-89; Ohio State University, professor of English, 1989—, director of Master of Fine Arts program in creative writing, 1993—. Visiting professor at Colorado College, 1984, and Washington University, St. Louis, MO, 1985; Gladys Louise Fox Visiting Professor at Rice University, 1988.

MEMBER: Associated Writing Programs.

AWARDS, HONORS: Fellow of National Endowment for the Arts, 1979 and 1985; St. Lawrence Award for Fiction from *Fiction International,* 1981, for *The Heart Never Fits Its Wanting;* O. Henry Prize from Doubleday & Co., 1984, for "Living Alone in Iota";

Prize for Fiction from *Story Quarterly,* 1985, for "Youth on Mars"; National Magazine Award from Graduate School of Journalism at Columbia University, and Editors Choice Award from Wampeter-Doubleday, both 1986, both for "Time and Fear and Somehow Love"; Pushcart Prize from Pushcart Press, 1986, for "X," and 1989, for "The Era of Great Numbers"; Major Artist Fellowship, Ohio Arts Council, 1991-92; Governor's Award for the Arts, Ohio Arts Council, 1993; Syndicated Fiction Award, 1995.

WRITINGS:

SHORT STORIES

The Heart Never Fits Its Wanting, North American Review Press (Cedar Falls, IA), 1980.
Love Is the Crooked Thing, Algonquin Books (Chapel Hill, NC), 1986.
Strangers in Paradise, Putnam (New York City), 1987.
Dreams of Distant Lives, Putnam, 1989.
Living After Midnight (novella and stories), Putnam, 1991.

Work represented in anthologies, including *Best American Short Stories,* 1984 and 1987. Contributor to magazines, including *Atlantic, Epoch, Harper's, Georgia Review, Missouri Review,* and *Southern Review.*

WORK IN PROGRESS: The Lost History of Everything, stories, for Putnam.

SIDELIGHTS: All of Lee K. Abbott's story collections to date are set in New Mexico, but his stories vary widely. He writes about bank robbers, soldiers in Vietnam, college professors, and rock and roll bands, with a wit and style that prompted reviewer Amy Hempel to call him "something of a linguistic hellion." Hempel wrote in the *New York Times Book Review:* "Mr. Abbott's enthusiastic wordplay is a great deal of fun," yet when he "stows the be-bop speed rap for a little peace and quiet, he writes quietly powerful stories." Hempel particularly enjoyed "Having the Human Thing of Joy," the story of a man who discovers his wife's infidelity and reminisces about his mother, and "The Final Proof of Fate and Circumstance," a tale related by a father to his son, which ends the collection *Love Is the Crooked Thing.*

William Ferguson, also of the *New York Times Book Review,* described the characters of *Strangers in Paradise:* "We see them either at home, driven to various kinds of excess by the pressures of love and sports . . . or confused and frightened abroad. . . . Plots tend to overlap, . . . as if several fields of force were being directed at a single invisible core of meaning, in a prose at once exuberant and inventive."

Abbott told *CA:* "I only write stories (well, with one exception, it was an accident of sudden and unwelcome insight)—all of them short as love with a stranger, all of them dense as 'heavy water.' I like the form, which is probably a wishy-washy way of admitting that meaning—between margins, at least—yields itself between fifteen and fifty pages. I'm not smart enough to find my way beyond that, another admission I'm too dumb to keep to myself. In addition, I like the big news of small places, the compression and the speed, the whoop-de-do of novels without all that darn typing. Last, I like to get to the end of things, those two or three moments where the blood is let and time backs up on itself like a sea wave, that instant—odd as a night on Neptune—where truth comes rising up loud and bright and cold."

BIOGRAPHICAL/CRITICAL SOURCES:

PERIODICALS

New York Times Book Review, March 16, 1986; February 15, 1987.
Virginia Quarterly Review, autumn, 1986.

ACKROYD, Peter   1949-

PERSONAL: Born October 5, 1949, in London, England; son of Graham and Audrey (Whiteside) Ackroyd. *Education:* Clare College, Cambridge, M.A., 1971; attended Yale University, 1971-73.

ADDRESSES: Home—London, England. *Agent*—Anthony Sheil Associates Ltd., 43 Doughty St., London WC1N 2LF, England.

CAREER: Writer.

MEMBER: Royal Society of Literature (fellow).

AWARDS, HONORS: Somerset Maugham Award, 1984, for *The Last Testament of Oscar Wilde;* Prix Goncourt, Whitbread Award, and fiction prize from *Guardian,* all 1985, all for *Hawksmoor;* Heinemann Award for nonfiction, Royal Society of Literature, 1985, for *T. S. Eliot: A Life.*

WRITINGS:

POETRY

Ouch, Curiously Strong Press (London), 1971.
London Lickpenny (also see below), Ferry Press (London), 1973.
Country Life (also see below), Ferry Press, 1978.
The Diversions of Purley, and Other Poems (contains poems from *London Lickpenny* and *Country Life*), Hamish Hamilton (London), 1987.

NOVELS

The Great Fire of London, Hamish Hamilton, 1982.
The Last Testament of Oscar Wilde, Harper (New York City), 1983.
Hawksmoor, Hamish Hamilton, 1985, Harper, 1986.
Chatterton, Grove (New York City), 1988.
First Light, Grove, 1989.
English Music, Random House (New York City), 1992.
The House of Doctor Dee, Hamish Hamilton, 1993.
Dan Leno and the Limehouse Golem, Sinclair-Stevenson (London), 1994, published in United States as *Elizabeth Cree: A Novel of the Limehouse Murders,* Doubleday (New York City), 1995.

NONFICTION

Notes for a New Culture: An Essay on Modernism, Barnes & Noble (New York City), 1976.

Dressing Up: Transvestism and Drag: The History of an Obsession, Simon & Schuster (New York City), 1979.

Ezra Pound and His World, Scribner (New York City), 1981.

T. S. Eliot: A Life, Simon & Schuster, 1984.

(Editor) *PEN New Fiction,* Quartet Books (London), 1984.

Dickens, Sinclair-Stevenson, 1990, HarperPerennial (New York City), 1992.

Introduction to Dickens, Sinclair-Stevenson, 1991, Ballantine (New York City), 1992.

Blake, Sinclair-Stevenson, 1995.

OTHER

Short story "The Inheritance" published in the anthology *London Tales,* edited by Julian Evans, Hamish Hamilton, 1983. Author of introductions to *Dickens' London: An Imaginative Vision,* Headline (London), 1987, and *Frank Auerbach: Recent Works,* by Frank Auerbach, Marlborough (New York City), 1994. Literary editor of *Spectator,* 1973-77, managing editor, 1977-81; chief book reviewer, London *Times,* 1986—. Contributor of book reviews to periodicals, including the *New York Times Book Review.*

WORK IN PROGRESS: A biography of Thomas More and a novel in which English poet John Milton travels to colonial America.

SIDELIGHTS: Considered an accomplished, versatile writer, Peter Ackroyd has authored works ranging from poems to novels, criticism to biography. He was published first as a poet; his first book, *London Lickpenny,* prompted a *Times Literary Supplement* reviewer to deem him "a delicate and insistent stylist" whose words "[make] not only an odd poetry, but a poetry out of the oddness of the world." Ackroyd came to literary prominence, however, as a biographer, and his well-received volumes on literary giants T. S. Eliot and Charles Dickens were complimented by his novels which frequently fictionalize the lives of famous historical personalities such as Oscar Wilde and Thomas Chatterton. Glen M. Johnson, writing in the *Dictionary of Literary Biography,* explained that "as his career has developed, Ackroyd has sought 'a new way to interanimate' biography and fiction." In addition to fusing history and fiction, his novels also consider the nature of time and art, often involving the protagonist in situations that transcend time and space. Ackroyd once told *CA:* "My own interest isn't so much in writing historical fiction as it is in writing about the nature of history as such. . . . I'm much more interested in playing around with the idea of time."

Ackroyd's 1976 publication *Notes for a New Culture: An Essay on Modernism,* in which the author condemns the British intellectual traditions of empiricism and positivism, established the writer as a brash, literary upstart for suggesting that the foundations of twentieth-century philosophy were staid and uninspiring. Ackroyd also dismissed literary realism as an outmoded, invalid concept and defined language as self-referential. Critics later noted that his novels also reflect his disdain for conventional form and narrative. With his next book, *Dressing Up: Transvestism and Drag: The History of an Obsession,* Ackroyd traced cross-dressing from Greek times to the present and delineated its use in theaters around the world from Japanese No drama to Elizabethan-era productions, and even provided accounts of transvestism's famous practitioners, including the Roman emperor Caligula.

In 1982 Ackroyd published his first novel, *The Great Fire of London,* which revolves around the film production of Charles Dickens's novel *Little Dorrit.* Ackroyd's tale presents itself as a continuation of the Dickens novel, which concerns a young girl's trials and tribulations in Victorian England. Beginning with a summary of Dickens's work, *The Great Fire of London* then introduces its own cast of Dickensian characters, including Spenser Spender, a filmmaker who plans the adaptation of *Little Dorrit;* Sir Frederick Lustlambert, a bureaucrat who arranges the film's financing; and Rowan Phillips, a Dickens scholar who has written the film's script. Another important figure is Little Arthur, an adult so named because he ceased growing at age eight. Little Arthur is proprietor of an amusement park near Marshalsea Prison, a key setting in *Little Dorrit.* When Arthur's park closes, he loses his grasp on reality and commits murder. Once apprehended, he is sentenced to Marshalsea Prison, where Spender is filming his adaptation. Spender's insistence on realism eventually sparks the disaster of the novel's title, a raging inferno resulting from a mishap on the film set.

Galen Strawson, in his review of *The Great Fire of London* in the *Times Literary Supplement,* described Ackroyd's novel as an extension of Dickens's *Little Dorrit.* "Ackroyd is clearly intrigued by the idea of past fiction working great changes in present (fictional) reality," Strawson wrote, "and he misses few chances to make further connections and to elaborate the network of coincidences." Strawson was also impressed with Ackroyd's insights into human nature, writing that "he is continually alive . . . to that hidden presence in many people's lives which he calls 'the vast sphere of unremembered wishes,' and to the effects it has on their conscious thoughts and actions."

Ackroyd followed *The Great Fire of London* with *The Last Testament of Oscar Wilde,* a novel purporting to be Wilde's autobiography, written during the final months of the author's life when he was living in Paris, where he had fled in self-imposed exile after serving two years in a British prison for indecency. Many critics praised Ackroyd's duplication of Wilde's own writing style and commended the work for its compelling insights into the notorious Irish writer. Toronto *Globe and Mail* critic William French, for instance, declared that Ackroyd "does an uncanny job of assuming Wilde's persona." Similarly, London *Times* reviewer Mary Cosh, who called Ackroyd's novel "a brilliant testament in its own right," lauded Ackroyd for fashioning a well-rounded portrait of Wilde. Cosh wrote: "Not only does Peter Ackroyd exert a masterly command of language and ideas that credibly evokes Wilde's sharp wit in epigram or paradox, but he captures the raw vulnerability of the man isolated behind his mask."

When *The Last Testament of Oscar Wilde* was published in 1983, Ackroyd was already working on the biography *T. S. Eliot: A Life.* In researching the poet's life, Ackroyd encountered imposing obstacles: he was forbidden by Eliot's estate from quoting Eliot's correspondence and unpublished verse, and he was allowed only minimum citations of the published poetry. Critics generally agreed, however, that Ackroyd nonetheless produced a worthwhile account of the modernist poet. As A. Walton Litz wrote in the *New York Times Book Review:* "Given all these restrictions, Peter Ackroyd has written as good a biography as we have any right to expect. He has assimilated most of the available evidence and used it judiciously." Rosemary Dinnage, who wrote of *T. S. Eliot* in the *New York Review of Books,* also praised Ackroyd's difficult feat, observing that he "illuminates Eliot's poetry and criticism more acutely than many a ponderous academic volume." And *Newsweek*'s Paul Gray contended that Ackroyd's biography "does more than make the best of a difficult situation; it offers the most detailed portrait yet of an enigmatic and thoroughly peculiar genius." In the end, Ackroyd acknowledged that his inability to quote Eliot's letters or work made for a better book

because "I had to be much more inventive about how I brought him to life," he told *CA.*

In searching for a subject for his next biography, which eventually became *Dickens,* Ackroyd told *CA* that he sought "to choose someone who would be a difficult subject, as Eliot was, so I chose the opposite extreme. With Dickens, there have been so many biographies that it's an equal challenge to do something different. It's always the challenge of doing a subject that attracts me." Unlike Eliot, many other biographies of Dickens existed, so Ackroyd's intent was not to provide the definitive account of the writer's life, but rather to "rescue the character" of Dickens, as Verlyn Klinkenborg wrote in the *Smithsonian* and thereby "[cross] the boundary between Dickens' fiction and his life." Klinkenborg further asserted that "[Ackroyd] does this not only to show how the novels illuminate the life, but also to understand the transforming powers of Dickens' imagination." Yet James R. Kincaid of the *New York Times Book Review* lamented that *Dickens* utilizes none of the twentieth-century conventions for understanding biography: "post-structuralist suspicions have made no inroads, and even Freud causes no alarm." Despite this, Kincaid allowed that *Dickens* sets itself apart from other biographies on the author and "demands our attention precisely (and only) because it is so open to the strange." An undeniably popular writer in his own time, Dickens wrote of the tragedies of Victorian England and rose to great prominence and wealth, all the while remaining a secretive, prolific writer who, even as he exposed the horrors of the Industrial Age, benefitted from them enormously. In addition, Ackroyd surmises that Dickens's long relationship with the young Ellen Ternan was not sexual, a conclusion at odds with nearly all other Dickens biographers. Ackroyd proposes that Dickens was a man capable of such a platonic friendship and that those who cannot consider this possibility are constricted by their own thinking.

After several more novels, Ackroyd returned to biography with *Blake,* an account of William Blake, the visionary poet and artist who lived from 1757 to 1827. A London native, Blake's life appeared outwardly unremarkable. He was happily married, lived modestly, and worked hard. But many of Blake's contemporaries considered him insane; he spoke of his grandiose visions and hallucinations as if they were commonplace, often astounding acquaintances by relating his conversations with devils and angels. Blake was an engraver by trade whose illustration style was composed of intricate scenes of battling angels and fallen men, and he boldly compared his writing to John Milton's *Paradise Lost*. Because "Ackroyd does Blake the considerable service of taking his visions as seriously and soberly as he did," stated a reviewer in the *Economist,* Blake "has found the gentlest of biographers." In addition, Ackroyd's knowledge of London history serves to accentuate the biography, continued the reviewer, since he is familiar with the places that Blake would have known and are the most likely locales for some of his prose. Charles Moore of the *Spectator* commented that Blake's eccentricities, one of which he called a "magnificent lack of embarrassment," were in fact the result of what Ackroyd deemed the "peculiar kind of lucidity which springs from those who have nothing left to lose."

Winner of the Prix Goncourt and the Whitbread Award, *Hawksmoor* fuses the detective and horror story genres. One of the work's two principal characters is Nicholas Hawksmoor, a police detective trying to solve a series of grisly murders at various eighteenth-century churches in London. Alternating with the account of Hawksmoor's progress are chapters on eighteenth-century London architect Nicholas Dyer. Dyer adheres to certain demonic principles and consecrates his churches with human blood sacrifices to please Satanic creatures. Dyer's nemesis is renowned architect Christopher Wren, his superior, who contends that science and rational thought will bring an end to superstition. Hawksmoor is also faithful to rationalism, and when he fails to perceive the connection between the two sets of murders he finds himself slowly going insane.

Ackroyd told *CA* that "the whole point of the novel was the transition between the two epochs," a bridge he accomplished by "enter[ing] the language of the period." And like Ackroyd's earlier novels, *Hawksmoor* impressed critics as a daring, technically innovative work. *Newsweek*'s Peter S. Prescott called it "a fascinating hybrid, a tale of terrors that does double duty as a novel of ideas." Similarly, *Time*'s Christopher Porterfield, who noted that Ackroyd possessed "a gift for historical pastiche," acknowledged "the eerie interplay between the earlier age and our own" and commended *Hawksmoor* as "a fictional architecture that is vivid, provocative, and as clever as . . . the devil." Another of the novel's many enthusiasts was Joyce Carol Oates, who wrote in the *New York Times Book Review* that *Hawksmoor* was "primarily a novel of ideas, a spirited debate between those who believe . . . that 'the highest

Passion is Terrour' and those who believe . . . that the new science of rationalism and experimental method will eventually eradicate superstition." Oates deemed Ackroyd a "virtuoso" and lauded *Hawksmoor* as "an unfailingly intelligent work of the imagination."

Ackroyd executed another multiple-narrative story with *Chatterton,* a novel revolving around seventeenth-century poet Thomas Chatterton, who committed suicide when he was seventeen. In Ackroyd's novel, Chatterton appears through an autobiographical document that suggests he may have faked his death. The document is owned by Charles Wychwood, a minor poet obsessed with an old portrait whose subject might have been Chatterton. The painting, however, is dated 1802, thus serving as further indication that Chatterton might not have died in 1770. Another story line concerns the creation of an actual painting, Henry Wallis's *The Death of Chatterton.* But this painting, too, is misleading, for Wallis finished it in 1856, long after Chatterton's death, and relied on another young man, writer George Meredith, to represent Chatterton. Further discrepancies of authenticity and originality abound in the novel—a writer steals plots from second-rate Victorian novels, and an artist's secretary completes his employer's canvases. And even Chatterton confesses to chicanery of a sort, having attributed his own poems to fictitious fifteenth-century clergyman Thomas Rowley.

With *Chatterton,* Ackroyd strengthened his reputation as a unique and compelling storyteller. Dennis Drabelle, in his review for the *Washington Post Book World,* called Ackroyd's work a "witty, tricky new novel," and "a contrivance of the highest order." Denis Donoghue, writing in the *New York Times Book Review,* was similarly enthusiastic, describing *Chatterton* as "a wonderfully vivid book" and "superb." London *Times* reviewer Victoria Glendinning praised the novel as "agile and entertaining." She added, "In *Chatterton* [Ackroyd] has at least three balls in the air, and [he] keeps them up there."

With the novel *English Music,* critics were divided on the success of Ackroyd's time-twisting and reality-bending plot. An involved story regarding Timothy Harcombe and his spiritualist father's wish that he learn everything possible about English culture— "English music," he calls it—the novel traverses time and a multitude of ideas that wind their way through fantasy and reality. It is the story of the wandering soul that critic Chris Goodrich of the *Los Angeles*

Times Book Review compared to James Joyce's *Ulysses,* "though one written very, very small" but concluded that the book "rarely seems more than an academic exercise." Michael Levenson of the *New Republic* summarized the novel's theme: "Life on the margins is the universal norm. The center is an optical illusion."

John McAleer of Chicago *Tribune Books* further explained *English Music* as a narrative look at Ackroyd's world view: "his work is so autobiographical that intrusion of self gives fictional texture to his biographies and biographical texture to his fiction." Tim's father instructs him in all matters of music, literature, art, and architecture which comprise English culture, leading Tim to understand that the past and the present are fused through these traditions—"There is no past and no future, Tim, just the two of us listening to the music," the father tells his son. Roz Kaveney, writing for *New Statesman and Society,* called this all "a bathetic celebration of Heritage," and Levenson stated that though the book rightly purports "that identity develops inside a language, which unfolds inside a tradition, which bears the ancient traces of nation," he nevertheless concluded that Ackroyd's assertion that "National greatness issues from a changeless identity" is "sad" and "banal."

The interconnectedness of time past, present, and future is also central to Ackroyd's next book, *The House of Doctor Dee,* a historical novel concerning the Elizabethan-era intellectual John Dee, a purported practitioner of black magic and alchemy. Dee alternates narrative duties with Matthew Palmer, the modern-day inheritor of Dee's house in London whose curiosity sparks an investigation into the house's lurid history. Much of the book's detail concerns the milieu of fifteenth-century London's buildings and history, one of Ackroyd's favorite subjects. *Spectator* reviewer Francis King noted the differing styles of the two narrators—Dee writes in an Elizabethan-dialect that reminds King of Ben Jonson, and Matthew writes in a more modern voice—and called the contrast "fascinating." As Matthew learns more about the house's previous owner, paranormal occurrences abound—not the least of which is Matthew's discovery that he is embroiled in an ancient plot concerning an immortal homunculus. Soon Dee's and Matthew's paths cross, and as they become aware of each other through visions and research both are eventually redeemed in "a timeless London," stated Eric Korn of the *Times Literary Supplement,* "for time can be deconstructed by any magician or novelist."

Multiple narratives again are the crux of *Dan Leno and the Limehouse Golem.* In 1881, a seedy district in London suffers a gruesome series of murders, which some residents believe is the work of a golem. Exhibiting Ackroyd's penchant for infusing his fiction with historical figures, the suspects include Karl Marx, George Gissing, and Dan Leno, one of the era's popular comedians. But a diary hints that the killer is John Cree, whose wife Elizabeth, a former vaudeville cross-dresser, has been hanged for poisoning him. David Sexton of the *Spectator* proclaimed that Ackroyd "manages these parallel narratives expertly. . . . He just loves to feel all London's past coming up behind him."

"I never doubt I can *do* anything," Johnson quoted Ackroyd as saying, "But . . . I'm in a constant state of agony over whether I'm any good or not." Calling poetry his main interest and ambition, Ackroyd once told *CA:* "Some of the cadences and the images and the ideas and the perceptions and even the very phrases which occurred in my poetry have recurred in the fiction. It's not as if I've lost the poetry; it's just been transformed into another context." He further stated, "I think of myself primarily as a novelist. The other activities are marginal but related—certainly I think my novels and biographies are connected, although not in ways I myself could interpret. I leave that to the critics."

BIOGRAPHICAL/CRITICAL SOURCES:

BOOKS

Contemporary Literary Criticism, Gale (Detroit), Volume 34, 1985, Volume 52, 1989.
Dictionary of Literary Biography, Volume 155: *Twentieth-Century Literary Biographers,* Gale, 1995.

PERIODICALS

America, January 19, 1985.
Antioch Review, summer, 1985.
Books, September-October, 1993, p. 8; summer, 1995, p. 22.
Chicago Tribune Book World, November 18, 1984.
Christian Science Monitor, February 1, 1985; February 25, 1991, p. 13.
Economist, September 29, 1984; November 11, 1995.
Globe and Mail (Toronto), January 7, 1984.
Guardian Weekly, September 12, 1993, p. 28.
London Review of Books, November 17, 1983; December 22, 1994, pp. 20-22.

Los Angeles Times Book Review, December 2, 1984; February 14, 1988; October 25, 1992, pp. 3, 11.

Maclean's, February 17, 1986.

New Republic, December 17, 1984; January 18, 1993, pp. 29-32.

New Statesman, March 19, 1976; November 30, 1979; January 29, 1982; October 12, 1984; September 27, 1985.

New Statesman and Society, September 9, 1994, p. 39.

Newsweek, November 26, 1984; February 24, 1986.

New Yorker, March 25, 1985; November 23, 1992, pp. 142-3.

New York Review of Books, April 30, 1981; December 20, 1984.

New York Times, August 21, 1995, p. B3.

New York Times Book Review, December 16, 1984; January 19, 1986; January 17, 1988; January 13, 1991, pp. 1, 24; October 11, 1992, p. 7.

New York Times Magazine, December 22, 1991, pp. 27-36.

Observer (London), August 29, 1993, p. 51; September 11, 1994.

Publishers Weekly, December 25, 1987, pp. 59-60.

Smithsonian, January, 1993, pp. 131-2.

Spectator, September 29, 1984; September 28, 1985; September 11, 1993, p. 27; September 10, 1994; September 23, 1995, p. 36-7.

Time, December 3, 1984; February 24, 1986.

Times (London), April 14, 1983; September 27, 1984; September 26, 1985; February 19, 1987; June 8, 1987; September 3, 1987.

Times Literary Supplement, May 3, 1974; December 7, 1979; August 28, 1981; January 29, 1982; April 15, 1983; September 21, 1984; November 30, 1984; September 27, 1985; September 11, 1987; September 10, 1993, p. 20; September 9, 1994, p. 21.

Tribune Books (Chicago), November 1, 1992, p. 6.

Voice Literary Supplement, December, 1984; December 1992, p. 6.

Washington Post Book World, December 9, 1984; February 16, 1986; January 24, 1988.*

*   *   *

ADAM, Peter   1929-

PERSONAL: Born August 3, 1929, in Berlin, Germany; immigrated to England. *Education:* Attended Antioch College; Sorbonne, University of Paris, M.A.; University of Berlin, Ph.D.

ADDRESSES: Home—55 Milson Rd., London W14 0LH, England.

CAREER: British Broadcasting Corporation, London, England, director, 1967—; writer, 1967—.

AWARDS, HONORS: Gold Star Award, Houston Film Festival; British Academy award nomination, for *George Gershwin Remembered;* Best Arts Documentary of the Year Award, British Academy of Film and Television Arts, 1989, for *Art of the Third Reich.*

WRITINGS:

Eileen Gray, Architect-Designer: A Biography, Abrams (New York City), 1987.

Art of the Third Reich (based on his two-part television documentary film of the same name [also see below]), Abrams, 1992.

Not Drowning but Waving (autobiography), Deutsch (London), 1995.

Also author of *Alfred Eisenstaedt,* Abbeville, and *Andre Kertesz,* Abbeville.

TELEVISION SERIES

Architecture at the Crossroads, British Broadcasting Corp. (BBC-TV), 1985.

The Stage Management of Power (part one of *Art of the Third Reich*), BBC-TV, 1988.

The Propaganda Machine (part two of *Art of the Third Reich*), BBC-TV, 1988.

Also author of *George Gershwin Remembered* and of other television scripts.

SIDELIGHTS: "During the 12 nightmare years of Adolf Hitler's rule," writes *Wall Street Journal* contributor Helen Dudar, "the only contemporary art allowed on the walls of the museums and public buildings of Germany were pictures delivering the canny imagery of Nazi ideology: soothing family kitchen scenes; clean, sturdy farm folk in the fields; young, richly muscled defenders of the Reich, all of them blond with short noses." "At the same time," states Gordon A. Craig in the *New York Times Book Review,* "since National Socialism was supposed to be the final realization of the Greek ideal, there was a new vogue of mythological painting." "Naked but carefully unaphrodisiac German women," Craig continues, ". . . posed as Greek goddesses, as in Adolf Ziegler's 'Judgment of Paris' . . . in which the goddesses are clearly too virginal for their known reputations and Paris is obviously thinking of something else, perhaps his chances of becoming an SS *Gruppenfuhrer.*"

Since the end of World War II, this Nazi art has been concealed from the public. "Anyone hoping to see the collection," Dudar explains, "must either have a degree in art history or a persuasive claim to a need to know." In *Art of the Third Reich,* film producer Peter Adam brings many of these forgotten relics of the Nazi era to light in order to show how the National Socialists manipulated *all* the art forms in order to spread their myth of Aryan superiority. "The visual arts," declares London *Observer* contributor Richard Overy, "became tools of indoctrination, expressions of Hitler's preoccupation with race and empire."

According to Willibald Sauerlaender in the *New York Review of Books,* one of the points Adams makes in his book is that "in an ironic reversal of the situation in 1937, Nazi art is now banned, while so-called 'degenerate' art has once again found its legitimate place in public collections." "Certainly nothing is wrong in principle with the landscapes, portraits, still lifes, and figurative paintings that people of conservative tastes like to hang on their walls," Sauerlaender continues. "In an open society, there can be no moral or aesthetic obligation for any citizen to like modern art, and it is absurd to believe that an abstract painting is by definition more democratic than a view of a lake, a cow, or a bunch of flowers." In many ways, says Adam, this popular appeal is one of the things that makes Nazi art so frightening. "Adam consistently maintains that what is most terrifying about Nazi art," states Brooks Adams in *Art in America,* "is how banal it all looks. In this he follows Hannah Arendt's classic hypothesis about the banality of evil. As he observes in his conclusion, 'What is frightening about all these works of art is not so much what was Fascist about them, but what was normal, a normality which pleased so many.'"

While critics recognize the value of Adam's study, some disagree with his conclusion that art was in fact dead in Germany while the Third Reich was in power. Adam, according to *New Statesman and Society* contributor Peter Campbell, claims that the official Nazi artists lacked "'driving force, the energy which could only come from conflict and from a burning desire to break with old habits.'" He declares that ". . . the official support system that

removed Velasquez or Rubens from 'abrasiveness' did them no harm." Robert Dassanowsky-Harris writes in the *American Book Review,* "Despite the copious examples of kitsch, imitation, and doctrinaire work in his book, can Adam truly conclude . . . that there was no 'real art' in Germany between 1933 and 1945. . .[?] Even with the smoke of Auschwitz hanging in memory, the answer must be no." Nonetheless, Overy concludes, "Adam's book is a plea for cultural diversity and cultural toleration and is all the more valuable for that."

BIOGRAPHICAL/CRITICAL SOURCES:

PERIODICALS

American Book Review, April-May, 1993, pp. 14, 20.
American Record Guide, September-October, 1994, p. 278.
Art in America, October, 1992, pp. 47, 49, 51.
Art Journal, spring, 1993, pp. 94-95, 97, 99.
British Journal of Photography, March 25, 1983.
Central European History, March, 1992, pp. 361-64.
New Statesman and Society, May 29, 1992, p. 41.
New York Review of Books, April 21, 1994, pp. 16-18.
New York Times Book Review, June 21, 1992, pp. 13-14.
Observer (London), May 17, 1992, p. 54.
Times Literary Supplement, May 5, 1995, p. 26.
Wall Street Journal, June 15, 1992, p. A11.

*   *   *

ALDRIDGE, (Harold Edward) James   1918-

PERSONAL: Born July 10, 1918, in White Hills, Victoria, Australia; son of William Thomas (a newspaper publisher) and Edith (Quayle) Aldridge; married Dina Mitchnik, 1942; children: two sons. *Education:* Attended London School of Economics and Political Science; attended Oxford University, 1939. *Avocational interests:* Trout-fishing.

ADDRESSES: Home—21 Kersley St., London SW11, England. *Agent*—Curtis Brown, Ltd., 162-68 Regent St., London W1R 5TB, England.

CAREER: Writer. *Sun,* Melbourne, Australia, office boy and file clerk, 1934-37, reporter, 1937-38; *Herald,* Melbourne, reporter, 1937-38; *Daily Sketch* and

Sunday Dispatch, London, England, feature writer, 1939; freelance war correspondent for Australian Newspaper Service and North American Newspaper Alliance in Finland, Norway, Greece, the Middle East, and the Soviet Union, 1939-44; *Time* and *Life* correspondent in Teheran, Iran, 1944.

MEMBER: British Sub-Aqua Club.

AWARDS, HONORS: Rhys Memorial Prize, 1945; International Organization of Journalists Prize, 1967; Lenin Memorial Peace Prize, 1972; Australian Children's Book Council Book of the Year Award, 1985; *Guardian* Children's Fiction Prize, 1987, for *The True Story of Spit MacPhee;* World Peace Council Gold Medal.

WRITINGS:

FICTION; FOR YOUNG ADULTS

The Flying Nineteen, Hamish Hamilton (London), 1966.
My Brother Tom, Hamish Hamilton, 1966, also published as *My Brother Tom: A Love Story,* Little, Brown (Boston), 1967.
A Sporting Proposition, Little, Brown, 1973, also published as *Ride a Wild Pony,* Penguin (New York City), 1976.
The Marvelous Mongolian, Little, Brown, 1974.
The Broken Saddle, MacRae Books (London), 1983.
The True Story of Lilli Stubeck, Hyland House (South Yarra, Australia), 1984, Penguin, 1986.
The True Story of Spit MacPhee, Viking (London), 1986.
The True Story of Lola MacKellar, Viking, 1992.

FICTION; FOR ADULTS

Signed with Their Honour, Little, Brown, 1942.
The Sea Eagle, Little, Brown, 1944.
Of Many Men, Little, Brown, 1946.
The Diplomat, Bodley Head (London), 1949, Little, Brown, 1950.
The Hunter, Little, Brown, 1951.
Heroes of the Empty View, Knopf (New York City), 1954.
I Wish He Would Not Die, Doubleday (New York City), 1958.
Gold and Sand (short stories), Bodley Head, 1960.
The Last Exile, Doubleday, 1961.
A Captive in the Land, Hamish Hamilton, 1962.
The Statesman's Game, Doubleday, 1966.

Mockery in Arms, M. Joseph (London), 1974, Little, Brown, 1975.
The Untouchable Juli, Little, Brown, 1975.
One Last Glimpse, Little, Brown, 1977.
Flying, Pan Books (London), 1979.
Goodbye Un-America, Little, Brown, 1979.

NONFICTION

Underwater Hunting for the Inexperienced Englishman, Allen & Unwin (London), 1955.
Cairo: Biography of a City (travel), Little, Brown, 1969.
(With Paul Strand) *Living Egypt* (travel), Horizon Press (New York City), 1969.

OTHER

The 49th State (play), produced in London, 1946.
One Last Glimpse (play), produced in Prague, 1981.

Contributor to the anthology *Winter's Tales 15,* edited by A. D. Maclean, Macmillan, 1969, St. Martin's, 1970. Also author of scripts for *Robin Hood* television series, and of articles for *Playboy.*

ADAPTATIONS: Ride a Wild Pony was filmed by Disney in the late 1970s.

SIDELIGHTS: After spending ten years as a journalist and twenty-five years as a writer of international suspense novels for adults, Australian author James Aldridge began writing fiction for young adults in 1966. Most of his young adult novels take place in the fictional town of St. Helen, Australia, which closely resembles the real town of Swan Hill, on the banks of the Murray River near Aldridge's birthplace. Though he has lived most of his life elsewhere, Aldridge told Michael Stone in *Twentieth-Century Young Adult Writers* that he revisits his childhood home in his novels because "I can't escape Australia, and I don't want to."

Three of Aldridge's publications for young adults—*A Sporting Proposition* (also published as *Ride a Wild Pony*), *The Marvelous Mongolian,* and *The Broken Saddle*—are "considered among the finest horse stories written by an Australian," according to Stone. *A Sporting Proposition* takes place during the Great Depression. It tells the story of thirteen-year-old Scott Pirie, the poor son of Scotch immigrants, whose main joy in life is his Welsh pony, Taff. Scott loses Taff, and he soon learns that the pony has been adopted by Josie, the handicapped daughter of a wealthy family, and renamed Bo. The whole town takes sides during their ensuing fight over ownership of the pony. They take the matter to court, but it is finally resolved when Scott's lawyer devises a "sporting proposition" that everyone can agree to. In a review for *Library Journal,* Margaret Wimsatt called *A Sporting Proposition* "an atmospheric tale, professionally told." The story was adapted for a Disney movie in the 1970s.

The Marvelous Mongolian, Aldridge's next book for young adults, also describes the love two young people share for a horse. Tachi, a wild Mongolian stallion, is taken from his home in the mountains to a game preserve in England, where scientists hope he will help establish new herds of wild horses. Although he becomes attached to a Welsh pony mare named Peep, Tachi is unhappy in captivity. He finally escapes from the game preserve with Peep and makes his way across the continent to Mongolia, enduring numerous dangers along the way. His incredible journey is followed anxiously by Kitty Jamieson, an English girl whose grandfather is in charge of the game preserve, and Baryut Mingha, a Mongolian boy who saw Tachi in the wild. They write letters to each other whenever they receive word about Tachi's whereabouts. A *Publishers Weekly* reviewer praised the book as "a remarkable and charming animal story for young and old alike."

Like *A Sporting Proposition,* Aldridge's third horse story, *The Broken Saddle,* is also set in Australia during the Great Depression. Eric Thompson comes from a poor family. His father was forced to move far away to get a job driving cattle, and Eric must perform odd jobs for neighbors in order to help put food on the table. On one return visit, his father brings Eric a pony. At first Eric and the willful pony are inseparable, but as they become involved in more formal activities like saddle-riding and performing in gymkhanas, their relationship begins to grow more distant. After Eric breaks his leg in a riding accident, his mother sells the pony to pay for food. Although he is sad when he sees his now-docile pony being ridden by a wealthy girl, Eric learns from the experience. A reviewer for *Junior Bookshelf* praised Aldridge for avoiding sentimentality, calling *The Broken Saddle* "a powerful story . . . written with such skill as to make it compulsive reading."

Aldridge's next three books for young adults tell the "true story" of a series of unusual and sometimes mysterious characters. *The True Story of Lilli Stubeck,* published in 1984, describes the life of a girl who arrives in St. Helen with her disreputable family at the age of seven. When the family leaves town, they sell Lilli to a wealthy old lady, Miss Dalgleish, as a servant. Miss Dalgleish decides to turn Lilli into a civilized young woman. Outwardly Lilli's appearance and manners improve, but when her ill mother returns with her younger brother, Lilli begins to revert back to her old ways. In the end, she manages to establish her own identity and leave a distinct impression on the town. A reviewer for *Growing Point* called Aldridge's work "a remarkable tale which calls upon the reader for close attention and sympathy and will reward this kind of approach handsomely."

Aldridge received the *Guardian* Children's Fiction Prize for his next book, *The True Story of Spit MacPhee.* It follows the adventures of an eleven-year-old orphan boy, Spit, who lives with his mentally ill grandfather along the banks of the Murray River. Although his grandfather is sometimes prone to violent fits, the two manage to build a satisfying, independent life for themselves. When his grandfather burns down their home and is taken away to die, two families from town fight to decide what happens to Spit. Betty Arbuckle, an Evangelical Christian, wants to send Spit to the Bendingo Boys' Home, where he can be civilized and turned into a proper boy. Meanwhile, Grace Tree, the Catholic mother of one of Spit's friends, wants to adopt Spit and take care of him. During the ensuing court battle, the entire town is divided along religious lines. "Work of this quality is rare indeed," according to a *Junior Bookshelf* reviewer. "Aldridge has given us a very fine story, tough, penetrating, and profoundly honest."

Aldridge's 1992 book, *The True Story of Lola MacKellar,* slowly unravels the mystery of Lola's background. The story begins when the wealthy Eyre family brings five-year-old Lola to their estate, but then leaves her in the care of their hired hands, the Scobies. The Eyres pay for Lola's room and board, but they also tell the Scobies to keep her far away from their house and their young daughter, Josie. Several years later, the two girls meet and become friends anyway, and Lola helps Josie recover from polio. The mystery reaches its peak when Lola's biological mother suddenly appears at the estate, accompanied by Lola's twin sister, and asks her to leave the only home she has known and return with them to Germany. A *Junior Bookshelf* reviewer called the novel "story-telling at its best," noting that "the secrets of Lola's background are divulged at tantalizing intervals holding the reader's attention up to the final revelation of her true past and the settling of her future."

Summing up Aldridge's work for young adults, Stone commented: "Through his novels James Aldridge seeks to answer age-old questions that have concerned humanity since Plato and Aristotle: how people ought to live in communities and how best to organize their political and social life. Aldridge is concerned with the betterment of life through the search for moral and religious understandings."

BIOGRAPHICAL/CRITICAL SOURCES:

BOOKS

Twentieth-Century Young Adult Writers, St. James Press (Detroit), 1994, p. 11.

PERIODICALS

Booklist, September 1, 1974, p. 33.
Growing Point, September, 1986.
Junior Bookshelf, February, 1983, p. 36; December, 1986, p. 228; April, 1993, p. 72.
Kirkus Reviews, June 15, 1966, p. 602; April 1, 1967, p. 435; February 15, 1979, p. 204.
Library Journal, October 15, 1969, p. 3643; August, 1973, p. 2330.
Newsweek, June 18, 1979.
New York Times Book Review, March 14, 1976, p. 32; July 10, 1977, p. 45; July 1, 1979, p. 12.
Publishers Weekly, March 25, 1974, p. 49; November 18, 1974, p. 46; April 3, 1975, p. 63.
School Librarian, May, 1993, p. 72.
School Library Journal, September, 1987, p. 133.
Times Educational Supplement, May 1, 1987, p. 31.
Times Literary Supplement, March 24, 1966, p. 250; July 16, 1970, p. 768; September 20, 1974; October 10, 1975; February 6, 1987, p. 145.

*　　*　　*

ALEXANDER, Charles
　See HADFIELD, (Ellis) Charles (Raymond)

ALEXANDER, R(obert) McNeill　1934-

PERSONAL: Born July 7, 1934, in Lisburn, Northern Ireland; son of Robert Priestley (an engineer) and Janet (an author; maiden name, McNeill) Alexander; married Ann Elizabeth Coulton (an adult education teacher), July 29, 1961; children: Jane Coulton, Robert Gordon. *Education:* Cambridge University, B.A., 1955, Ph.D., 1958, M.A., 1959; University of Wales, D.Sc., 1969.

ADDRESSES: Home—14 Moor Park Mount, Leeds LS6 4BU, England. *Office*—Department of Biology, University of Leeds, Leeds LS2 9JT, England.

CAREER: University of Wales, University College of North Wales, Bangor, assistant lecturer, 1958-61, lecturer, 1961-68, senior lecturer in zoology, 1968-69; University of Leeds, Leeds, England, professor of zoology, 1969—.

MEMBER: Royal Society (fellow), Society for Experimental Biology (president, 1995—), Institute of Biology (fellow), American Society of Zoologists (honorary member), Zoological Society of London (secretary, 1992—).

AWARDS, HONORS: Scientific Medal from Zoological Society of London, 1969; Linnean Medal from Linnean Society of London, 1979; Maybridge Medal, International Society for Biomechanics, 1991.

WRITINGS:

Functional Design in Fishes, Hutchinson (London), 1967, 3rd edition, 1974.
Animal Mechanics, Sidgwick & Jackson (London), 1968, 2nd edition, 1983.
Size and Shape, Edward Arnold (Baltimore, MD), 1971.
The Chordates, Cambridge University Press (New York City), 1975, 2nd edition, 1981.
Biomechanics, Chapman & Hall (London), 1975.
The Invertebrates, Cambridge University Press, 1979.
Locomotion of Animals, Blackie & Son (London), 1982.
Optima for Animals, Edward Arnold, 1982.
Elastic Mechanisms in Animal Movement, Cambridge University Press, 1988.
The Dynamics of Dinosaurs and Other Extinct Giants, Columbia University Press (New York City), 1989.
Animals, Cambridge University Press, 1990.

The Human Machine, Columbia University Press, 1992.
Exploring Biomechanics: Animals in Motion, Scientific American Library (New York City), 1992.
Bones: The Unity of Form and Function, Macmillan (New York City), 1994.

Contributor to scientific journals.

EDITOR

(With Geoffrey Goldspink) *Mechanics and Energetics of Animal Locomotion,* Chapman & Hall, 1977.
The Collins Encyclopaedia of Animal Biology, Collins (London), 1986.
The Mechanics of Animal Locomotion, Springer (New York City), 1992.

SIDELIGHTS: R. McNeill Alexander told *CA:* "My principle research interest is the mechanics of animal movement, especially walking and running of people and other large mammals, and of dinosaurs. My books treat animal structure and movement as problems in engineering."

*   *   *

ALLEN, Roger M(ichael) A(shley)   1942-

PERSONAL: Born January 24, 1942, in Tavistock, Devon, England; came to the United States in 1968; son of William Ivor (a tobacco company manager) and Doreen Mabel Lily (Chappell) Allen; married Mary D. North (a teacher), November 25, 1972; children: Timothy, Marianna. *Education:* Lincoln College, Oxford, B.A., 1965, M.A., 1968, D.Phil., 1968.

ADDRESSES: Home—6346 Sherwood Rd., Philadelphia, PA 19151. *Office*—Department of Asian and Middle Eastern Studies, University of Pennsylvania, Philadelphia, PA 19104.

CAREER: University of Pennsylvania, Philadelphia, assistant professor, 1968-73, associate professor, 1973-84, professor of Arabic language and literature, 1984—. Visiting lecturer at Oxford University, 1976. Organist and choirmaster at St. Mary's Episcopal Church in Philadelphia, 1974—.

MEMBER: Middle East Studies Association of North America, American Oriental Society, American Association of Teachers of Arabic (president, 1977-78).

AWARDS, HONORS: American Research Center fellow in Egypt, 1970-71, 1975-76; Lindback Foundation Distinguished Teaching Award, 1972.

WRITINGS:

(Translator from the Arabic with Akef Abadir) Nagib Mahfuz, *God's World: An Anthology of Short Stories,* Bibliotheca Islamica, 1973.
(Contributor) Leonard Binder, editor, *The Study of the Middle East: Research and Scholarship in the Humanities and the Social Sciences,* Wiley (New York City), 1976.
(Translator from the Arabic) Mahfuz, *Mirrors: A Novel,* Bibliotheca Islamica, 1977.
(Editor and translator from the Arabic) Yusuf Idris, *In the Eye of the Beholder: Tales of Egyptian Life from the Writings of Yusuf Idris,* Bibliotheca Islamica, 1978.
The Arabic Novel: An Historical and Critical Introduction, Syracuse University Press (Syracuse, NY), 1982, second edition, 1995.
(Translator from the Arabic with Adnan Hayder) Jabra Ibrahim Jabra, *The Ship,* Three Continents (Washington, DC), 1985.
(Editor) *Modern Arabic Literature,* Ungar (New York City), 1987.
(Translator from the Arabic) Abd al-Rahman Munif, *Endings,* Quartet Books, 1988.
Critical Perspectives on Yusaf Idris, Three Continents, 1994.
(Coeditor) *Sex and Gender in Modern Arabic Literature,* Saqi (London), 1994.
(Editor with Salma al-Jayyusi) *Modern Arabic Drama: An Anthology,* Indiana University Press (Bloomington), 1995.

Contributor to numerous scholarly journals, including *Journal of Arabic Literature, Mundus Artium,* and *Muslim World.* Editor of *Edebiyat,* 1976-86; *Twentieth Century Encyclopedia of World Literatures,* 1978—; *Journal of Arabic Literature,* member of editorial board, 1989—, managing editor, 1996—; Arabic literature editor, guest editor of *Nimrod,* 1982, and *Translation,* 1983; member of editorial board, *World Literature Today,* 1991—.

WORK IN PROGRESS: The Arabic Literary Tradition, to be published by Cambridge University Press, 1996; *Cambridge History of Arabic Literature: The*

Post-Classical Period, coediting with Donald Richards, to be published by Cambridge University Press, 1998.

SIDELIGHTS: In his book *The Arabic Novel: An Historical and Critical Introduction,* Roger M. A. Allen traces the history of the novel in the Arab world from its origins in 1913 to its later stages of development. Allen's account is divided into two periods, the first covering Arabic literature's growth up to 1939, and the second (which he terms "the period of maturity") from 1939 to the present. Among the novels Allen features are Muhammad Husayn Haykal's *Zaynab* (the book that initiated the genre in 1913), al-Tayyib Salih's *Season of Migration to the North,* and 1988 Noble Prize-winner Nagib Mahfuz's *Chatter on the Nile.* Allen reviews the historical and political events surrounding the emergence of each of these novels and shows the significance of such events in the rise of Arabic literature.

Allen's *Modern Arabic Literature* brings together a collection of critical essays on seventy-four modern Arab litterateurs, providing bio-bibliographical information and a critical survey of selected works by each author. "This work," Allen told *CA,* "allows Western readers to assess for the first time the development of modern criticism in the Arab world." With his translation of *Endings* by the Saudi novelist Abd al-Rahman Munif, Allen continues, "English readers are introduced for the first time to a new and thoroughly original voice in modern Arabic fiction, one who invokes the insights of a social scientist and the narrative techniques of a traditional story-teller in his depictions of life in a desert community."

Allen told *CA:* "The combination of two careers, as a professor of Arabic literature and as a professional church musician, is important to the way of life within which I do much of my writing. I regard the introduction of treasures from Arabic literature— whether from the medieval or modern periods—as increasingly important to a Western world which knows terrifyingly little about cultures other than its own. My most recent work on the novel in Arabic is illustrative of this desire to make the literature of the Arab world accessible to a broader Western audience. It is particularly gratifying to me therefore that, through an article in *World Literature Today,* I was able to play a role in nominating Nagib Mahfuz to the Nobel Prize committee. That event ensures that my long-term goal will now begin to be achieved."

BIOGRAPHICAL/CRITICAL SOURCES:

PERIODICALS

Times Literary Supplement, September 10, 1982.
World Literature Today, spring, 1983, spring, 1988.

*   *   *

ALLENDE, Isabel   1942-

PERSONAL: Surname is pronounced "ah-*yen*-day"; born August 2, 1942, in Lima, Peru; daughter of Tomas (a Chilean diplomat) and Francisca (Llona Barros) Allende; married Miguel Frias (an engineer), September 8, 1962 (divorced, 1987); married William Gordon (a lawyer), July 17, 1988; children: (first marriage) Paula (deceased), Nicolas, Scott (stepson). *Education:* Graduated from a private high school in Santiago, Chile, at age 16.

ADDRESSES: Office—116 Caledonia St., Sausalito, CA 94965. *Agent*—Carmen Balcells, Diagonal 580, Barcelona 08021, Spain.

CAREER: United Nations Food and Agricultural Organization, Santiago, Chile, secretary, 1959-65; *Paula* magazine, Santiago, journalist, editor, and advice columnist, 1967-74; *Mampato* magazine, Santiago, journalist, 1969-74; television interviewer for Canal 13/Canal 7 (television station), 1970-75; worked on movie newsreels, 1973-75; Colegio Marroco, Caracas, Venezuela, administrator, 1979-82; writer. Guest teacher at Montclair State College, NJ, 1985, and University of Virginia, 1988; Gildersleeve Lecturer, Barnard College, 1988; teacher of creative writing, University of California, Berkeley, 1989.

AWARDS, HONORS: Best Novel of the Year, Chile, 1983; Author of the Year and Book of the Year, Germany, 1984; Grand Prix d'Evasion, 1984; Radio Television Belge: Point de Mire Award, Belgica, 1985; Best Novel, Mexico, 1985; Quality Paperback Book Club New Voice Award, 1986, for *The House of the Spirits;* Premio Literario Colima, Mexico, and Author of the Year, Germany, both 1986; XV Premio Internazionale I Migliori Dell'Anno, Italy, Mulheres Award for best foreign novel, Portugal, Quimera Libros, Chile, and Book of the Year, Switzerland, all 1987; *Los Angeles Times* Book Awards finalist for fiction, 1987, for *Of Love and Shadows;*

Eva Luna was named one of *Library Journal*'s Best Books of 1988; Before Columbus Foundation Award, 1988; member of Academia de la Lengua, Chile, 1989; named Professor of Literature Honoris Causae, University of Chile, 1991; XLI Bancarella Literary Award, Independent Foreign Fiction Award, and Brandeis University Major Book Collection Award, all 1993; Marin Women's Hall of Fame, Condecoracion Gabriela Mistral, Chile, Chevalier dans l'Ordre des Arts et des Lettres, France, and Feminist of the Year, Feminist Majority Foundation, all 1994; named Honorary Citizen of the city of Austin, and member of the Academia de Artes y Ciencias, Puerto Rico, both 1995; "Read About Me" literary award, and Critics Choice Award, both 1996; Books to Remember Award, American Library Association, 1996; received honorary degrees from New York State University, 1991, and Dominican College and Bates College, 1994.

WRITINGS:

NOVELS

La casa de los espiritus, Plaza y Janes (Barcelona), 1982, translation by Magda Bogin published as *The House of the Spirits,* Knopf (New York City), 1985.
De amor y de sombra, Plaza y Janes, 1984, translation by Margaret Sayers Peden published as *Of Love and Shadows,* Knopf, 1987.
Eva Luna, Plaza y Janes, 1987, translation by Peden published under same title, Knopf, 1988.
Cuentos de Eva Luna, Plaza y Janes, 1990, translation by Peden published as *The Stories of Eva Luna,* Atheneum (New York City), 1991.
El plan infinito, Plaza y Janes, 1991, translation by Peden published as *The Infinite Plan,* HarperCollins (New York City), 1993.
Paula, Plaza y Janes, 1994, translation by Peden published under same title, HarperCollins, 1995.

OTHER

Civilice a su troglodita: Los impertinentes de Isabel Allende (humor), Lord Cochran (Santiago), 1974.
La gorda de porcelana (juvenile; title means "The Fat Porcelain Lady"), Alfaguara (Madrid), 1983.

Author of plays, including *El Embajador,* 1971, *La Balada del Medio Pelo,* 1973, and *Los Siete Espejos,* 1974. Also author of stories for children. Contributor to *Paths of Resistance,* edited by William

Zinsser, Houghton (Boston), 1989. Author of weekly newspaper column for *El Nacional* (Caracas), 1975-84. Contributor to newspapers and periodicals, including *Discurso Literario* and *Revista Iberoamericana.*

Allende's works have been translated into more than twenty-seven languages.

ADAPTATIONS: Eva Luna and *Stories of Eva Luna* were adapted for the theater; *The House of the Spirits* was adapted for the theater and also as a motion picture starring Meryl Streep, Glenn Close, and Jeremy Irons, Miramax, 1994; *Of Love and Shadows* was adapted as a motion picture starring Antonio Banderas and Jennifer Conley.

SIDELIGHTS: One of Latin America's prominent writers, Isabel Allende began her career as a novelist after working for several years in her native Chile as a journalist. She has combatted both personal tragedy and political upheaval during the course of her career. Inspired by feminist convictions and personal insight into the cultures of Latin America and the United States—where she has lived since 1988—Allende has displayed a talent for creating fascinating stories, engaging characters, and memorable imagery. Her books have been consistent best-sellers, both in Spanish and translation, in the United States and abroad.

The 1973 assassination of her uncle, President Salvador Allende—performed as part of a military coup against Chile's ruling socialist government—had a profound effect on Allende. "I think I have divided my life [into] before that day and after that day," she told *Publishers Weekly* interviewer Amanda Smith. "In that moment, I realized that everything was possible—that violence was a dimension that was always around you." While the Allende family did not at first believe that a dictatorship could last in Chile, they were soon forced to flee to Venezuela for safety. Although an established journalist in her native country, Allende found it difficult to find work in Venezuela and did not write for several years. Word that her nearly one-hundred-year-old grandfather, who had remained in Chile, was near death finally inspired her to begin setting her thoughts down on paper again. "My grandfather thought people died only when you forgot them," the author explained to Harriet Shapiro in *People.* "I wanted to prove to him that I had forgotten nothing, that his spirit was going to live with us forever." Allende wove memories of her family and her country into a letter to her grandfather—a letter that ultimately became her first novel, *The House of the Spirits,* published in 1982. "When you lose everything, everything that is dear to you . . . memory becomes more important," she explained to *Mother Jones* contributor Douglas Foster. With *The House of the Spirits,* she added, "[I achieved] the recovery of those memories that were being blown by the wind, by the wind of exile."

Following three generations of the Trueba family's domestic and political conflicts, *The House of the Spirits* "is a novel of peace and reconciliation, in spite of the fact that it tells of bloody, tragic events," claims *New York Times Book Review* contributor Alexander Coleman. "The author has accomplished this not only by plumbing her memory for the familial and political textures of the continent, but also by turning practically every major Latin American novel on its head." Allende's grand scope and use of fantastic elements and characters have led many critics to place *The House of the Spirits* in the "magic realism" tradition within Latin American writing, comparing it specifically to Nobel Prize-winner Gabriel Garcia Marquez's *One Hundred Years of Solitude.* "Allende has her own distinctive voice, however," notes a *Publishers Weekly* reviewer, and though "her prose lacks the incandescent brilliance of the master's, it has a whimsical charm, besides being clearer, more accessible and more explicit about the contemporary situation in South America." In contrast, *Village Voice* contributor Enrique Fernandez believes that "only the dullest reader can fail to be distracted by the shameless cloning from *One Hundred Years of Solitude.* . . . Allende writes like one of the many earnest minor authors that began aping Gabo after his success, except she's better at it than most." Although agreeing that Allende's work owes a debt to Marquez, the *Washington Post Book World*'s Jonathan Yardley concludes that "she is most certainly a novelist in her own right and, for a first novelist, a startlingly skillful, confident one."

The political realities behind *The House of the Spirits* act as counterpoint to the novel's magic realism. *Times Literary Supplement* reviewer Antony Beevor states that whereas the early chapters seem "to belong firmly in the school of magical realism," a closer reading "suggests that Isabel Allende's tongue is lightly in her cheek. It soon becomes clear that she has taken the genre to flip it over. The metaphorical house, the themes of time and power, the *machista* violence and the unstoppable merry-go-round of history: all of these are reworked and then examined from the other side—from a woman's perspective." Other critics, however, fault Allende for trying to combine the magical and the political. Richard Eder of the *Los Angeles Times* feels that the author "rarely manages to integrate her magic and her message," while *Nation* contributor Paul West claims that the political story is "the book Allende probably wanted to write, and would have had she not felt obliged to toe the line of magical realism." Other critics maintain that the contrast between the fantastic and political segments is effective, as Harriet Waugh of the *Spectator* explains: "[The] magic gradually dies away as a terrible political reality engulfs the people of the country. Ghosts, the gift of foretelling the future and the ability to make the pepper and salt cellars move around the dining-room table cannot survive terror, mass-murder and torture." "*The House of the Spirits* does contain a certain amount of rather predictable politics, but the only cause it wholly embraces is that of humanity, and it does so with such passion, humor and wisdom that in the end it transcends politics," asserts Yardley, who concludes that *The House of the Spirits* "is also a genuine rarity, a work of fiction that is both an impressive literary accomplishment and a mesmerizing story fully accessible to a general readership."

With 1984's *Of Love and Shadows,* Allende "proves her continued capacity for generating excellent fiction," according to *Detroit Free Press* contributor Anne Janette Johnson. "She has talent, sensitivity, and a subject matter that provides both high drama and an urgent political message." The novel begins "matter-of-factly, almost humorously," comments Charles R. Larson in the *Detroit News,* with the switching of two identically named babies. The story becomes more complicated, however, when one of the babies grows up to become the focus of a journalist's investigation. Soon after a reporter and photographer expose the murder of the girl as political, they are forced to flee the country. "And so," Larson observes, "Allende begins with vignettes of magical realism, only to pull the rug out from under our feet once we have been hooked by her enchanting tale. What she does, in fact, is turn her story into a thriller." "Love and struggle a la 'Casablanca'—it's all there," Gene H. Bell-Villada states in the *New York Times Book Review.* "Ms. Allende skillfully evokes both the terrors of daily life under military rule and the subtler form of resistance in the hidden corners and 'shadows' of her title." But while political action comprises a large part of the story, "above all, this is a love story of two young people sharing the fate of their historical circumstances, meeting the challenge of discovering the truth, and determined to live their life fully, accepting their world of love and shadows," Marjorie Agosin declares in the *Christian Science Monitor.* With *Of Love and Shadows,* Agosin concludes, "Allende has mastered the craft of being able to intertwine the turbulent political history of Latin America with the everyday lives of her fictional characters caught up in recognizable, contemporary events."

Rosemary Sullivan, however, feels that Allende is not so successful in blending magical and realistic elements in *Of Love and Shadows.* Sullivan remarks in the Toronto *Globe & Mail* that "Allende has some difficulty getting her novel started because she has to weave two stories separately, and seems to be relying initially too much on her skills as a journalist." *New York Times* critic Michiko Kakutani similarly relates that the book is "more literal in a way that points up the author's tendency to cast everything in terms of white and black, good and evil, love and shadows." This leads to what Beevor perceives as a lack of "emotional distance," finding that the author's characters, "in spite of their lack of depth, are all perfectly convincing until she burdens them with interior monologues, giving them superfluous roles in a Greek chorus." Johnson, however, believes that Allende's characters, "major and minor, brim with the vagaries of human nature. Allende hops from one personality to another . . . with a gentle grace that is quite endearing. When her tale descends to horror, which inevitably it must, she never relinquishes the warm, confiding tone, like that used between old friends." "One of [the book's] many strengths is that Allende sees no person and no issue in simplistic terms," Yardley notes, concluding that Allende's "work contains depths of empathy and compassion rarely found in fiction that embraces a political cause."

"Fears that Isabel Allende might be a 'one-book' writer, that her first success . . . would be her only one, ought to be quashed by *Eva Luna,*" asserts Abigail E. Lee in the *Times Literary Supplement.* "The eponymous protagonist and narrator of this . . . novel, has an engaging personality, a motley collection of interesting acquaintances and an interesting angle on political upheavals in the unnamed Latin American republic in which she lives." Born illegitimate and later orphaned, Eva Luna becomes a scriptwriter and storyteller, involved with a filmmaker—Rolf Carle, an Austrian emigre haunted by his Nazi father—and his subjects, a troop of revolutionary guerrillas. "In *Eva Luna,* Allende moves

between the personal and the political, between realism and fantasy, weaving two exotic coming-of-age stories—Eva Luna's and Rolf Carle's—into the turbulent coming of age of her unnamed South American country," Elizabeth Benedict summarizes in *Chicago Tribune Books.* Switching between the stories of the two protagonists, *Eva Luna* is "filled with a multitude of characters and tales," states *Washington Post Book World* contributor Alan Ryan. Allende's work is "a remarkable novel," Ryan elaborates, "one in which a cascade of stories tumbles out before the reader, stories vivid and passionate and human enough to engage, in their own right, all the reader's attention and sympathy."

Commenting on the novel's abundance of stories and characters, *New York Times Book Review* contributor John Krich argues that "few of the cast of characters emerge as distinctive or entirely believable. Too often, we find Eva Luna's compatriots revealed through generalized attributions rather than their own actions. . . . Is this magic realism a la Garcia Marquez or Hollywood magic a la Judith Krantz? We can only marvel at how thin the line becomes between the two, and give Ms. Allende the benefit of the doubt." London *Times* writer Stuart Evans, however, praises Allende's "range of eccentric or idiosyncratic characters who are always credible," and adds: "Packed with action, prodigal in invention, vivid in description and metaphor, this cleverly plotted novel is enhanced by its flowing prose and absolute assurance." "*Eva Luna* is a great read that *El Nobel* [Garcia Marquez] couldn't hope to write," claims Dan Bellm in the *Voice Literary Supplement,* for the women "get the best political debate scenes, not the men." Lee also sees a serious political side to Allende's third novel, noting the author's juxtaposition of feminism and politics: "In all the depictions of women and their relationships with men . . . one feels not a militant or aggressive feminism—rather a sympathetic awareness of the injustices inherent in traditional gender roles." Ryan concludes: "Reading this novel is like asking your favorite storyteller to tell you a story and getting a hundred stories instead of one . . . and then an explanation of how the stories were invented . . . and then hearing the storyteller's life as well."

Allende continues in a similar vein with *The Stories of Eva Luna,* published in 1991. Positing her protagonist Eva Luna as a modern-day Scheherazade, Allende's central character spins tales to her boyfriend to help him distance himself from the ever-present realities he confronts as a television newscaster. Allende grounds several of her stories in the political upheaval common to Latin America, while others focus on the inner lives of women whose optimism persists even in the light of such modern-day turmoil. *People* reviewer Ralph Novak finds that Allende has "gracefully spun" the collection of stories from her novel *Eva Luna,* "transplanting Scheherazade's sense of fable and magic to Latin America."

Allende's 1993 novel *The Infinite Plan* takes place in California and follows the lives of its three main characters—Gregory Reeves, Carmen Moralez, and Gregory's sister, Judy—over a span of forty years. When Reeves, the son of a touring preacher marketing a pseudo-religion dubbed "The Infinite Plan," falls ill during a stop on the touring circuit, his father decides to stop travelling and put down roots. The Reeves family settles in a house in the barrio of East Los Angeles. For Reeves, as well as his sister, this new place within the fabric of a Hispanic community is the closest he will ever come to a stable life—his adult life will be scarred by his service overseas during the Vietnam War and an endless pursuit of wealth and security. It is while growing up in the barrio that Reeves meets Moralez, an energetic Latina with a lust for life, who dresses in full, colorful flamenco dress and works as a jewelry designer. Meanwhile, his sister Judy begins what becomes a series of failed marriages, through which she gains the children she treasures. Reeves, Judy, and Moralez become part of the fabric of numerous other characters: visiting old lovers, witnessing births and deaths, and encountering emotional upheavals running the gamut from angry fights and divorce to love affairs.

While praising Allende's first novel, Kate Kellaway notes in the London *Observer* that "in *The Infinite Plan* each narrative detail is a bubble blown for its own sake—popping prettily but to no purpose. . . . What was charming in Chile (clairvoyants, psychics, oddballs) seems bogus and tawdry in America. What was fresh and off-beat has turned into fatiguingly dependable eccentricity." Writing in the *New Statesman & Society,* Kathryn Hughes laments that "in her rush to get this over-schematic saga to pan out, she ignores the very pleasures of the journey that made her earlier work such a satisfying experience." However, Patricia Hart praises the novel in *World Literature Today.* Asserting that the work exhibits "all the exuberant strengths and endearing weaknesses" of

Allende's fiction, Hart maintains that while "readers may struggle a bit to suspend disbelief at certain points, . . . the mosaic of outrageous anecdote, flamboyant and varied detail, and shrewd insight into the struggles of being human more than [overcome] our skepticism." The challenges to which the author has set herself in *The Infinite Plan*—adopting a male viewpoint rather than that of a woman and writing about a country with which she has only a limited familiarity—are not lost on some critics. "We could say that *The Infinite Plan* is not as elegant as *The House of the Spirits* and less assured than the 'Eva Luna' books," Robert Bly writes in the *New York Times Book Review,* "but it has more vision and ambition. Ms. Allende's ambit is large; she offers pity and terror. Her novel, more the house of bodies than of spirits but informed by spirits, calls for grief over the damage the United States has inflicted on itself during the last decades."

Allende's encounter with personal tragedy is the subject of 1995's *Paula,* written while she attended the bedside of her twenty-eight-year-old daughter Paula, who was fatally ill with porphyria—a hereditary metabolic abnormality—and lay in a coma in a Madrid hospital. A collage of memories—of her brothers, mother and grandparents, the reforms in Chilean politics that led to the death of her uncle in 1973, her feminist beliefs, her first marriage, and the building of a successful career in a patriarchal culture—fills the somber frame of Allende's portrait of her daughter's last days. Despite deeming *Paula* Allende's "best work to date," Suzanne Ruta in the *New York Times Book Review* comments on the seeming preoccupation of the novelist with her own life rather than that of her daughter's: "Mrs. Allende's literary breakthroughs, her divorce and remarriage dominate the second half of the book. It could have been called 'Isabel.'" However, such introspection is necessary to the work in the opinion of other critics. "The sad frame for these stories, the long bedside spells in the hospital in Madrid, and then in California when Isabel brings the dying Paula to her house in California, and the day of her death when Isabel accepts her daughter's presence as a spirit while bidding farewell to her body, are in themselves important to the book," explains Doris Grumbach in the *Los Angeles Times.* "They are poignant elegies to a great maternal love." Allende commented to John Boudreau in the *Los Angeles Times*: "When I write, it is as if I'm in a maze, a labyrinth. You never get over the confusion, because life is chaos and confusion. But somehow you get to see the pattern of your life. Then things become more bearable."

BIOGRAPHICAL/CRITICAL SOURCES:

BOOKS

Allende, Isabel, *Diez cuentos de Eva Luna: con guia de comprension y repaso de gramatica,* edited by Kenneth M. Taggart and Richard D. Woods, introduction by Marjorie Agosin, McGraw-Hill (San Francisco, CA), 1994.

Coddou, Marcelio, editor, *Los libros tienen sus propios espiritus: Estudios sobre Isabel Allende,* Universidad Veracruzana (Jalapa, Mexico), 1986.

Contemporary Literary Criticism, Gale (Detroit), Volume 39, 1986, Volume 57, 1989.

Dictionary of Literary Biography, Volume 145: *Modern Latin-American Fiction Writers, Second Series,* Gale, 1994, pp. 33-41.

El Amor: grandes escritores latinoamericanos, Ediciones Intituto Movilizador de Fondos Cooperativos (Buenos Aires), 1991.

Hart, Patricia, *Narrative Magic in the Fiction of Isabel Allende,* Fairleigh Dickinson University Press (Rutherford, NJ), 1989.

Rojas, Sonia Riquelme, and Edna Aguirre Rehbein, editors, *Critical Approaches to Isabel Allende's Novels,* P. Lang (New York City), 1991.

Wittig, Wolfgang, *Nostalgie und Rebellion: zum Romanwerk von Gabriel Garcia Marquez, Mario Vargas Llosa und Isabel Allende,* Konigshausen & Neumann (Wurzburg), 1991.

PERIODICALS

Boston Globe, April 25, 1993, p. 14.
Chicago Tribune, May 19, 1985.
Chicago Tribune Books, October 9, 1988.
Christian Science Monitor, June 7, 1985; May 27, 1987; June 10, 1993, p. 14.
Detroit Free Press, June 7, 1987.
Detroit News, June 14, 1987.
Globe & Mail (Toronto), June 24, 1985; June 27, 1987.
Los Angeles Times, February 10, 1988; May 31, 1993, p. E1.
Los Angeles Times Book Review, June 16, 1985; May 31, 1987; June 6, 1993, p. 13; April 30, 1995, pp. 3, 8.
Mother Jones, December, 1988.
Nation, July 20-27, 1985.
New Statesman & Society, July 5, 1985; July 2, 1993, pp. 38-39.
Newsweek, May 13, 1985.
New York Review of Books, July 18, 1985.

New York Times, May 2, 1985; May 20, 1987; February 4, 1988.
New York Times Book Review, May 12, 1985; July 12, 1987; October 23, 1988; May 2, 1993, p. 13; May 21, 1995, p. 11.
Observer (London), July 4, 1993, p. 62 *People,* June 10, 1985; June 1, 1987; March 4, 1991; May 2, 1994; June 5, 1995.
Publishers Weekly, March 1, 1985; May 17, 1985.
Review, January/June, 1985.
Spectator, August 3, 1985.
Time, May 20, 1985.
Times (London), July 4, 1985; July 9, 1987; March 22, 1989; March 23, 1989.
Times Literary Supplement, July 5, 1985; July 10, 1987; April 7-13, 1989.
US News and World Report, November 21, 1988.
Village Voice, June 7, 1985.
Voice Literary Supplement, December, 1988.
Washington Post Book World, May 12, 1985; May 24, 1987; October 9, 1988; May 23, 1993, p. 6.
World Literature Today, spring, 1993, pp. 335-36.

*   *   *

ALLIN, Craig Willard 1946-

PERSONAL: Born October 3, 1946, in Two Harbors, MN; son of Willard S. (a minister) and Beverly J. Allin; married Kathleen Joy Armstrong, May 30, 1968 (divorced, 1976); married Elizabeth Anne Sparks (an attorney), October 8, 1977. *Education:* Grinnell College, B.A., 1968; Princeton University, M.A., 1970, Ph.D., 1976. *Politics:* Democrat. *Avocational interests:* Backpacking, bicycling, camping, canoeing, movies, photography, politics, sports.

ADDRESSES: Home—218 Second Ave. N., Mount Vernon, IA 52314-1303. *Office*—Department of Politics, Cornell College, 600 First St. W., Mount Vernon, IA 52314-1098.

CAREER: Cornell College, Mount Vernon, IA, assistant professor, 1972-79, associate professor, 1979-85, professor of political science, 1985—, chair of department, 1979-89, 1995—. Visiting assistant professor at Duke University, 1978. Member of joint legislative internship committee of Iowa General Assembly, 1974-84. Has presented papers and delivered lectures at numerous conferences, convocations, and symposia, 1982—; has appeared on radio broadcasts. Founding member, Joint Internship Committee of the Iowa State Legislature, 1974—. Lisbon-Mount Vernon (IA) Ambulance Service, member, 1973-87, chief, 1976-87, member of board of directors, 1991—, president of board of directors, 1995—; certified emergency medical technician, 1974-87; certified emergency rescue technician, 1979-87; active in Lisbon-Mount Vernon local government. Manuscript and grant referee.

MEMBER: American Political Science Association, American Association of University Professors, Policy Studies Organization, National Parks and Conservation Association, Sierra Club, Wilderness Society, Wilderness Watch, Iowa Conference of Political Scientists, Phi Beta Kappa.

AWARDS, HONORS: University House fellow, University of Iowa, 1982-83; Presidential fellow, Cornell College, 1989-90.

WRITINGS:

The Politics of Wilderness Preservation, Greenwood Press (Westport, CT), 1982.
(Editor and contributor) *International Handbook of National Parks and Nature Preserves,* Greenwood Press, 1990.

Contributor to books, including *Federal Lands Policy,* edited by Phillip O. Foss, Greenwood Press, 1987; *Outdoor Recreation Policy,* edited by John D. Hutcheson, Jr., Greenwood Press, 1990; and *Preparing to Manage Wilderness in the Twenty-First Century,* edited by Patrick C. Reed, University of Georgia (Athens), 1990. Contributor to encyclopedias, including *Encyclopedia of Environmental Science,* Chapman & Hall (New York City), *Encyclopedia of Conservation and Environmentalism,* Garland Publishing (New York City), and *World Book Encyclopedia,* World Book (Chicago). Contributor of articles to periodicals, including *Journal of Politics, American Historical Review, Cornell Magazine, Pacific Historical Review, Parks and Recreation, Chicago Tribune,* and *Policy Studies Review.*

WORK IN PROGRESS: "When I get an opportunity to work on it, my long-term project is a book tentatively entitled *Wilderness Management: History, Politics, and Policy.* In the course of this research I have travelled more than 60,000 miles and spent more than 500 hours interviewing land managers,

legislators, academicians, and interest group representatives"; articles on wilderness issues.

SIDELIGHTS: Craig Willard Allin once told *CA:* "I discovered the Boundary Waters wilderness of Minnesota at age thirteen. That visit whetted an appetite for wild country that persistently beckons me to experience the American wilderness. My books and research are a result of that interest and the conviction that one should mix business with pleasure at every opportunity.

"Preservation politics has run nearly full circle in the United States. Early Americans confronted a continental wilderness and set about taming it. With the birth of the nation, the federal government became a partner in the conquest, squandering its birthright to further industrial development and economic expansion. Today wilderness has become a scarce commodity outside of Alaska, and policymakers have responded with legislation to preserve a few fragments of what remains.

"I have attempted to trace the genesis and development of the wilderness issue in American politics from the early era of resource abundance to the present age of scarcity. Wilderness is a natural resource like coal, oil, fertile soil, pure water, and clear air. Economic growth tends to deplete all these resources, but wilderness is the first to go.

"In recent decades the growing appreciation of wilderness scarcity among policymakers and the public has forced the nation to come to grips with a question first posed by Aldo Leopold, 'whether a still higher "standard of living" is worth its cost in things natural, wild, and free.' Personally I am skeptical.

"In 1964 Congress passed the Wilderness Act 'to secure for the American people of present and future generations the benefits of an enduring resource of wilderness.' By 1995 Congress had placed more than 90 million acres in the National Wilderness Preservation System, and we can reasonably anticipate the addition of 10 to 30 million more acres before the process of designation comes to its inevitable end. The resulting wilderness system will embrace about five percent of the total land surface of the United States. The decision to conserve has come none too soon, for the time is rapidly approaching when the only wilderness that will remain is the wilderness that has been purposefully preserved. When that time comes, 100 million acres will not seem too much."

BIOGRAPHICAL/CRITICAL SOURCES:

PERIODICALS

American Historical Review, June, 1983.
Conservationist, September-October, 1983.
Current Geographical Publications, January, 1983.
Science, October 1, 1982.

*   *   *

ALTHER, Lisa   1944-

PERSONAL: Born July 23, 1944, in TN; daughter of John Shelton (a surgeon) and Alice Margaret (Greene) Reed; married Richard Philip Alther (a painter), August 26, 1966; children: Sara Halsey. *Education:* Wellesley College, B.A., 1966. *Politics:* None. *Religion:* None.

ADDRESSES: Office—c/o Watkins-Loomis, Inc., 133 East 35th St., New York, NY 10016.

CAREER: Atheneum Publishers, New York, NY, secretary and editorial assistant, 1967; freelance writer, 1967—. Writer for Garden Way, Inc., Charlotte, VT, 1970-71. Member of board of directors of Planned Parenthood of Champlain Valley, 1972.

MEMBER: PEN, National Writers' Union, Authors Guild, Authors League of America.

WRITINGS:

NOVELS

Kinflicks, Knopf (New York City), 1976.
Original Sins, Knopf, 1981.
Other Women, Knopf, 1984.
Bedrock, Knopf, 1990.
Five Minutes in Heaven, Dutton (New York City), 1995.

OTHER

(Author of introduction) Flannery O'Connor, *A Good Man Is Hard to Find,* Women's Press, 1980.

Also contributor to *Homewords,* edited by Douglas Paschell and Alice Swanson. Contributor of articles and stories to national magazines, including *Vogue, Cosmopolitan, Natural History, New Society, Yankee, Vermont Freeman, New Englander, New York Times Magazine,* and *New York Times Book Review.*

SIDELIGHTS: Lisa Alther's *Kinflicks* made publishing news when, instead of a small press run, her first novel boasted an initial printing of 30,000 hardback copies; it quickly ascended to the best-seller lists and was widely and favorably reviewed. Some critics compared it to J. D. Salinger's *Catcher in the Rye.* This comparison stems largely from the similarity between the novels' protagonists as Ginny Babcock, in her search for a meaningful existence, emerges as a female Holden Caulfield. Like Salinger's character, Ginny is a survivor, and while the story of how adolescents survive is now a familiar one, Alther's graphic depiction of Ginny's Tennessee teens, her flight north, and subsequent return south to her mother's deathbed rescues the novel from predictability. As a *New Yorker* critic explains: "A number of other excellent writers have covered various parts of the turf covered here," but "no other writer has yet synthesized this material as well as Miss Alther has. In fact, it would not be an exaggeration to say that her cynical, clear-eyed, well-heeled, disaster-prone heroine, Ginny Babcock, can easily take her place alongside Holden Caulfield as a symbol of everything that is right and wrong about a generation." Furthermore, notes Valentine Cunningham in the *New Statesman,* "her account is often to be caught uproariously in the rye."

In her second novel, *Original Sins,* Alther covers much the same territory she did in her first book, only this time there are five protagonists. "*Kinflicks* followed a single heroine from her Tennessee upbringing through a series of wacky encounters up North with the countercultures of the '60s," Paul Gray explains in *Time.* "*Original Sins* quintuples its predecessor, offering five main characters, all Southerners, who try to grow up in a region and a country that are changing even faster than they are."

Alther chronicles the relocation of three of the five to the North while painting a broad social history of the sixties and seventies. Women's liberation, Vietnam, black power, civil rights, and the counterculture are among her subjects, and the portrait that emerges is unsatisfactory to some. Several critics charge that in her attempt to cover so much ground, Alther has sacrificed her characters' individuality. "The reader is haunted by the thought that the central characters, with the exception, perhaps, of the obstinately individualistic Emily, exist chiefly in order to illustrate differently developing states of political consciousness, as their progress from childhood to maturity is traced in often absorbing but sometimes oppressive detail," remarks a *Times Literary Supplement* reviewer.

Whereas her first novel is a burlesque satire bordering on farce, *Original Sins* "is a protest novel of a conventional sort, a compound of outrage and doctrine," according to Mark Schechner. "It is an all-out assault on the South for its rigidly maintained double standards on matters of race, sex, and class and for its failures to live up to its deficiencies," he continues in his *New Republic* review.

Critics fault Alther's use of dialect and what some refer to as a didactic tone. "The essential problem with those nearly 600 pages," Susan Wood writes in the *Washington Post Book World,* "is that they present every cliche you've ever heard about the South or about the political movements of the last two decades as though they are really, truly true: that is, with no sense of the complexities of individual lives, with no sympathy for the characters." Wood adds that such characters, like stick figures, are difficult to perceive as real people. Gray suggests that "Alther takes risks that sometimes fail. She is willing to sacrifice plausibility for comic effect, to put her characters through paces that occasionally seem dictated rather than inevitable. But such lapses are more than offset by the novel's page-turning verve and intelligence." Alther "gives generously, both to her readers and to the children of her imagination," Gray concludes. Cyra McFadden maintains in her *Chicago Tribune Book World* review that Alther's "excesses are those of overflowing talent and high spirits," and proclaims *Original Sins* "a thoroughly endearing book."

Other Women examines how women relate to each other in various roles—as friends, lovers, and patient-to-therapist. Caroline Kelley is a doctor's ex-wife who gives up on men for women, and after a disappointing affair with a female friend, seeks aid in psychotherapy. Suspense builds around the question of what her sexual preference will be after analysis. Caroline and therapist Hannah Burke are "believable characters with real problems and realistic attitudes," notes Merle Rubin in the *Los Angeles Times.* According to critics, elements in the novel identified as problematic are balanced against its positive features. Isabel Raphael of the London *Times,* for example, takes particular delight in Alther's portrait of

Caroline's parents, two self-sacrificing people who give so much of themselves to others that they have little left to offer their own children. In addition, says Raphael, *Other Women* has "some sharp insights and a disarmingly fluent style."

Alther's novel *Bedrock* continues her satirical look at contemporary American life. Chronicling the whirlwind life of middle-aged Clea Shawn—a wealthy woman who decides to leave a hectic cosmopolitan existence for a small town in Vermont—the novel presents a humorous portrait of small-town American life. As Barbara Rich explains in the *Women's Review of Books, Bedrock*'s Vermont "is replete with characters so off-the-wall their very names bring a grin to the lips and a therapeutic, circulatory chuckle to the heart." Clea, too, is a comic figure, according to Jane Marcus in the *Nation:* "In Clea Shawn, Lisa Alther has created one of the most spoiled, overprotected and privileged heroines in recent serious fiction." Other critics were less enthusiastic. Writing in the *New York Times Book Review,* Tracy Cochran claims that Alther "never really brings her rural characters to life—and never achieves the humor and humanity that made *Kinflicks* so appealing." Merle Rubin, in a review for the *Los Angeles Times Book Review,* explains that "what Alther is doing is juxtaposing contrasting sets of stereotypes, over and over. Neither the story nor the characters are interesting enough in the first place to bear retelling."

Five Minutes in Heaven is a novel about a friendship between two women, Jude and Molly, which grows into a lesbian relationship. Following Molly's early death, Jude moves on to sexual liaisons with a gay man and another woman. Critical reaction to *Five Minutes in Heaven* has been mixed. A *Publishers Weekly* critic considers it "a work of admirable ambition but only tepid interest," and Jeannine Delombard argues in the *New York Times Book Review* that compared to the works of other women authors, Alther's "accounts of Jude's pansexual escapades seem tame, even quaint." However, Donna Seaman in *Booklist* calls Alther "candid and genuinely inquisitive" as she "ponders the ambiguity of sexual relationships and the 'cultural cacophony' that accompanies them."

BIOGRAPHICAL/CRITICAL SOURCES:

BOOKS

Contemporary Literary Criticism, Gale (Detroit), Volume 7, 1977, Volume 41, 1987.

PERIODICALS

Booklist, March 1, 1995, p. 1139.
Chicago Tribune Book World, June 14, 1981; December 9, 1984.
Harper's, May, 1976.
Lambda Book Report, January, 1992, p. 43.
Los Angeles Times, June 4, 1981; December 20, 1984.
Los Angeles Times Book Review, July 29, 1990, p. 5.
Ms., May, 1981.
Nation, April 25, 1981; August 27, 1990, p. 212-13.
New Republic, June 13, 1981.
New Statesman, August 27, 1976; May 29, 1981.
New Statesman & Society, August 17, 1990, p. 36-7.
New Yorker, March 29, 1976; May 4, 1981.
New York Review of Books, April 1, 1976.
New York Times, March 16, 1976; December 10, 1984.
New York Times Book Review, March 14, 1976; May 3, 1981; November 11, 1984; June 3, 1990, p. 23; June 18, 1995.
People, June 18, 1990, p. 26.
Publishers Weekly, February 27, 1995, p. 84.
Time, March 22, 1976; April 27, 1981; May 21, 1990, p. 82.
Times (London), February 28, 1985.
Times Literary Supplement, June 26, 1981; August 17, 1990, p. 868.
Village Voice, March 8, 1976; December 18, 1984.
Washington Post Book World, March 28, 1976; May 31, 1981.
Women's Review of Books, March, 1985, p. 14; July, 1990, p. 25-6.*

* * *

AMMONS, A(rchie) R(andolph)   1926-

PERSONAL: Born February 18, 1926, in Whiteville, NC; son of Willie M. and Lucy Della (McKee) Ammons; married Phyllis Plumbo, November 26, 1949; children: John Randolph. *Education:* Wake Forest College (now University), B.S., 1949; University of California, Berkeley, studies in English, 1950-52.

ADDRESSES: Office—Department of English, Cornell University, Ithaca, NY 14853.

CAREER: Poet and painter. Elementary school principal in Hatteras, North Carolina, 1949-50;

Friederich & Dimmock, Inc. (manufacturer of biological glassware), Atlantic City, NJ, executive vice president, 1952-61; Cornell University, Ithaca, NY, teacher of creative writing, 1964-69, associate professor, 1969-71, professor of English, 1971—, Goldwin Smith Professor, beginning in 1973. Wake Forest University, Winston-Salem, NC, visiting professor, 1974-75. *Military service:* U.S. Naval Reserve, 1944-46; served in South Pacific.

AWARDS, HONORS: Scholarship in poetry, Bread Loaf Writers' Conference, 1961; John Simon Guggenheim fellowship, 1966; American Academy of Arts and Letters traveling fellowship, 1967; Levinson Prize, 1970; D.Litt., Wake Forest University, 1972, and University of North Carolina at Chapel Hill; National Book Award in Poetry, 1973, for *Collected Poems, 1951-1971,* and 1993, for *Garbage;* Bollingen Prize, Yale University, 1974-75; MacArthur Prize fellowship, 1981-86; American Book Award nomination and National Book Critics Circle Award, 1982, for *A Coast of Trees: Poems;* North Carolina Award for Literature, 1986; National Institute of Arts and Letters Award; Rebekah Johnson Bobbit National Prize for Poetry, 1994; Ruth Lilly Poetry Prize, 1995.

WRITINGS:

POETRY

Ommateum, with Doxology, Dorrance (Bryn Mawr, PA), 1955.
Expressions of Sea Level, Ohio State University Press (Columbus, OH), 1964.
Corsons Inlet: A Book of Poems, Cornell University Press (Ithaca, NY), 1965.
Tape for the Turn of the Year (book-length poem not included in later collections), Cornell University Press, 1965.
Northfield Poems, Cornell University Press, 1966.
Selected Poems, Cornell University Press, 1968.
Uplands, Norton (New York City), 1970.
Briefings, Norton, 1971.
Collected Poems, 1951-1971, Norton, 1972.
Sphere: The Form of a Motion, Norton, 1973.
Diversifications: Poems, Norton, 1975.
For Doyle Fosso, Press for Privacy (Winston-Salem, NC), 1977.
Highgate Road, Inkling X Press, 1977.
The Snow Poems, Norton, 1977.
The Selected Poems, 1951-1977, Norton, 1977, expanded edition, 1987.
Breaking Out, Palaemon, 1978.

Six-Piece Suite, Palaemon, 1978.
Selected Longer Poems, Norton, 1980.
Changing Things, Palaemon, 1981.
A Coast of Trees: Poems, Norton, 1981.
Worldly Hopes: Poems, Norton, 1982.
Lake Effect Country: Poems, Norton, 1982.
Sumerian Vistas: Poems, 1987, Norton, 1987.
The Really Short Poems of A. R. Ammons, Norton, 1991.
Garbage, Norton, 1993.
The North Carolina Poems, North Carolina Wesleyan College Press (Rocky Mount, NC), 1994.

OTHER

(Author of foreword) Don Boes, *The Eighth Continent,* Northeastern University Press (Boston, MA), 1993.

Contributor to *Hudson Review, Poetry, Carleton Miscellany,* and other periodicals. Poetry editor, *Nation,* 1963.

SIDELIGHTS: A. R. Ammons once told the *Winston-Salem Journal and Sentinel:* "I never dreamed of being a Poet poet. I think I always wanted to be an amateur poet." But critics have long recognized him as a major American poet. The measure of critics' esteem is implied by the stature of the poets to whom they compare Ammons. Tracing his creative genealogy, they are apt to begin with Ralph Waldo Emerson and Henry David Thoreau and work chronologically forward through Walt Whitman, Ezra Pound, Robert Frost, Wallace Stevens, and William Carlos Williams. Of those poets, Harold Bloom feels that the transcendentalists Emerson and Whitman have influenced Ammons the most. Bloom contends in his book *The Ringers in the Tower: Studies in Romantic Tradition* that "the line of descent from Emerson and Whitman to the early poetry of Ammons is direct, and even the Poundian elements in [Ammons's poem] 'Ommateum' derive from that part of Pound that is itself Whitmanian." "Ommateum" refers to an insect's compound eye, and accurately presages the inclusiveness that marks Ammons's canon and the works of earlier transcendentalists.

Daniel Hoffman, writing in the *New York Times Book Review,* agrees that Ammons's poetry "is founded on an implied Emersonian division of experience into Nature and the Soul," adding that it "sometimes consciously echo[es] familiar lines from Emerson, Whitman and [Emily] Dickinson." While inheriting both the emancipation from strict metrical forms won by Emerson and the multiplicity of alternatives recognized by Whitman, Ammons brings to poetry a fidelity to the details of nature and a contemporary, conversational tone. Thus Ammons has revitalized a significant portion of traditional American literature. According to Bloom, Ammons "illuminates Emerson and all his progeny as much as he needs them for illumination."

While they acknowledge Ammons's debt to other writers, reviewers find that he has forged a style that is distinctly his own. Jascha Kessler writes in *Kayak,* "[Ammons] makes his daily American rounds about lawn and meadow, wood, hill, stream, in an easy, articulate, flat, utterly uneventful expository syntax. Altogether unlike Thoreau's sinewy, exacting, apothegmatic prose, and unlike that suavely undulant later Stevens from whom he borrows some of his stanza structures or envelopes, transmogrifying the Master of Imagination into a freshman-text writer who uses the colon for endless, undigestible linkages, never daring Stevens' comma, or venturing Thoreau's period." Other critics join Kessler in objecting to Ammons's sparse punctuation, but David Kirby defends Ammons, writing in the *Times Literary Supplement* that "his short lines, his overall brevity, his avoidance of punctuation marks other than the occasional comma and that quick stop-and-go colon are hallmarks of his minimalism, his exquisitely unencumbered technique."

Peter Stevens believes that Ammons's punctuation and form serve his intents well in some cases, poorly in others. Writing in the *Ontario Review,* he argues that the "ongoing flux" in *Tape for the Turn of the Year* (a long poem composed on an adding machine tape) works as "an almost perfect method to allow his notion of organic form to function," but that "no such wedding of form and content" occurs in another long poem, *Sphere: The Form of a Motion.* In the latter work, says Stevens, "the looseness that Ammons believes in derives from the use of a form the poet has tried before. [The poem is] written in three-or four-line stanzas. . . . Breathing space is provided by commas and colons only. Such a form fits snugly into Ammons' concern with flux and motion, and yet somehow the form seems too arbitrary."

Ammons is concerned with change both in nature and in daily life. In the poems "Cascadilla Falls," "The Wide Land," "Poetics," and many others, Ammons articulates the tension between the individual's sense of self as bound to particulars of space and time, and the sense of self as part of a larger continuum—an identity man learns from nature. William Logan notes in the *Chicago Tribune Book World* that in these interests, Ammons's work is "reminiscent of Frost on one side and Williams on the other, and in the work of both men, as in the [some] dozen books of their heir, intellect copes with its surroundings." According to Robert Shaw in *Poetry,* Ammons does more than describe; he forces the reader to involve himself. "The interest in an Ammons poem," he writes, "is less in the thing perceived than in the imaginative effort of the perceiver." Richard Howard explains further in his *Alone with America: Essays on the Art of Poetry in the United States since 1950* that "Ammons rehearses a marginal, a transitional experience[;] he is a littoralist of the imagination because the shore, the beach, or the coastal creek is not a *place* but an *event,* a transaction where land and water create and destroy each other, where life and death are exchanged, where shape and chaos are won and lost." This is clearly stated in "Corson's Inlet" (published in *The Selected Poems, 1951-1971*), a loosely-formed poem where line lengths vary in order to imitate "the few sharp lines" and "the disorderly orders" of nature. While acknowledging that any poem lends an order to its materials, the poet celebrates "that there is no finality of vision, / that I have perceived nothing completely, / that tomorrow a new walk is a new walk."

M. L. Rosenthal feels that although Ammons shares Stevens's desire to intellectualize rather than simply describe, he falls short of Stevens's success. Rosenthal writes in *Shenandoah:* "Ammons does have certain advantages over Stevens: his knowledge of geological phenomena and his ability to use language informally and to create open rhythms. . . . What he lacks as compared to Stevens, is a certain passionate confrontation of the implicit issues. . . . There is a great deal of feeling in Ammons; but in the interest of ironic self-control he seems afraid of letting the feeling have its way [as Stevens does]." *Partisan Review* contributor Paul Zweig agrees that "unlike [T. S.] Eliot or Stevens, Ammons does not write well about ideas." He feels that "only when his poem plunges into the moment itself does it gain the exhilarating clarity which is Ammons' best quality." Zweig asserts that Ammons's strength is in his form.

"At first glance," he writes, "Ammons . . . seems to be a maverick, working vigorously against the limitations of the plain style. . . . Yet his best poems are closer to the plain style than one might think. It is when one hears William Carlos Williams in the background of his voice that the poems work clearly and solidly."

Though shorter than the poems in his other books, the poems in *A Coast of Trees: Poems* are remarkably inclusive. Robert Phillips writes in the *Hudson Review* that the volume contains some of the poet's best work. The poem "Rapids," for example, begins "with a case for the superiority of autumn over spring and end[s] in the nature of the universe 100-million years from now—all within 12 lines!" Helen Vendler, writing in the *New Republic,* calls the poem "Easter Morning" "a new treasure in American poetry, combining the blankest of losses with the fullest of visions." Of the other poems in the book, she writes, "The poems enable us to watch this poet going about the business of the universe, both its 'lost idyllic' and its present broken radiance. He has been about this business for years now, but I notice in reading this new collection how much more secure his language has become. . . . Now the scientific world in Ammons is beautifully in balance with the perceptual one, and the tone is believably, and almost perfectly, colloquial." Phillips concludes, "In this tidy book there is less abstraction, more people, and a continuation of Ammons' explorations of light, color and radiance. It is a fine place to begin for any reader not yet familiar with this poet who is determined to capture the shape and flow of the universe and to untell its dreams." Though some critics gave the book negative reviews, others gave it high praise. *A Coast of Trees: Poems* was nominated for the National Book Award and won the National Book Critics Circle Award in 1982.

Sumerian Vistas, published in 1988, further develops the theme of transcendental unity found in Ammons's other work. In many poems that address the writing process, the poet relates that writing is an ordering process while nature is a continuum in flux. Alice Fulton comments in a *Poetry* review, "Poetry and epitaphs are seen as efforts to fix time, while nature is read as a script of motion, a text of regeneration. . . . Sumeria is invoked [in the title] as a metaphor of inception. It was there that writing first developed, and antiquity serves as a backdrop for explorations of beginning and closure, of generative cycles." The relationship between time and flux, the personal and the nonpersonal, the holy and the profane is explored in these poems. At times, these polarities meet and paradoxically remain in balance; Ammons's metaphor for these times is "a ridge, . . . a *line* where two upward sloping surfaces meet," relates Fulton. As in his other poems, Ammons points out the comforting aspects of nature. Fulton observes, "Nature consoles because it has designs without having designs on us. In fact, Ammons goes to nature precisely because it lets him 'miss anything personal / in the roar of sunset.' In contrast to human cruelty, which frightens since it is 'like one's own mercilessness,' nature's cruelty is mitigated by its impersonality."

"Though Ammons's vistas do not deny age,. . . his tone has not changed: it still has the spring and backlash and curiosity of his young voice," Helen Vendler comments in the *New Yorker*. She adds that the poet's distinctive voice accounts for the success of these poems. "It is Ammons' entrancing Southern storytelling voice that carries us along in his narratives of natural fact," she says, referring to a long poem about finding a dead mole in a neglected watering can. The poem begins, "I noticed last fall's leaves in the / can and thought well that will improve / the juice but I thought it did smell / funny." When the narrator finds the dead mole under the leaves, he says, "mercy: I'd just had / lunch: squooshy ice cream: I nearly / unhad it." Vendler comments, "There has been nothing like this in American poetry before Ammons—nothing with this liquidity of folk voice."

Critics find echoes of other poetic voices in Ammons's *Sumerian Vistas*. David McDuff observes in *Stand,* "Taking W. C. Williams' dictum ['No ideas but in things'] one step further, Ammons shows that things may possess the quality of ideas, and ideas those of things." In short statements called "Tombstones," the poet sees "through layers of memory, emotion and experience to reveal the spiritual cohesion that lies behind the observed reality, and the elemental forces that unite the animate and inanimate phenomena of the world with the processes of human existence." The reviewer also sees a connection between the poems in *Sumerian Vistas* and Robinson Jeffers's vision of sinful man fallen from grace, yet Ammons emphasizes man's place as a part of nature and the poet's role as "an interpreter of the cosmic will."

Bloom suggests that while readers may indeed hear other voices in the background, Ammons's poems are uniquely valuable because of the personal voice that not only borrows from but also adds to the poetic tradition. Bloom writes: "Ammons's poetry does for me what Stevens's did earlier, and the High Romantics [Bloom's term for William Blake, William

Wordsworth, Samuel Coleridge, Percy Bysshe Shelley, John Keats, and Lord Byron] before that; it helps me to live my life. If Ammons is, as I think, the central poet of my generation, because he alone has made a heterocosm, a second nature in his poetry, I deprecate no other poet by this naming. . . . He has emerged as an extraordinary master, comparable to the Stevens of *Ideas of Order* and *The Man With the Blue Guitar*." Bloom concludes that as one tracks Ammons through the body of his work, one finds "by not only a complete possibility of imaginative experience, but by a renewed sense of the whole line of Emerson, the vitalizing and much maligned tradition that has accounted for most that matters in American poetry."

Ammons's transcendental, everyman concerns shine and coalesce with what may prove to be his finest effort: the National Book Award winner of 1993, *Garbage*. The title, suggested when Ammons drove by a Florida landfill, is characteristically flippant and yet perfectly serious. "*Garbage* is a brilliant book," says David Baker in the *Kenyon Review*. "It may very well be a great one . . . perhaps even superior to his previous long masterwork, *Tape for the Turn of the Year*." Once again evoking an Emersonian view of nature, Baker notes, "Ammons discovers that nature everywhere is composed of the decadent and entropic, the aged, the tired" and also shows that matter transforms and renews itself, turning "garbage into utility, decay into new life." As Robert B. Shaw shows in *Poetry,* however, Ammons's transcendent meditations are always seasoned with "jokes, slang, ironies, L'l Abnerisms."

Elizabeth Lund of the *Christian Science Monitor* criticizes Ammons for his tendency to jump "unexpectedly from one image or idea to another." And yet this very disjointedness may be a strength, suggests David Kirby in his *Southern Review* essay, since Ammons's poetry "does not communicate everything it finds" and because poetry in general "is less subject than fiction to a demand for clarity." It is even through the illogical ideal of "not making sense," Kirby argues, that Ammons is able to communicate "under the world of sameness . . . what is different." *New York Times* reviewer Edward Hirsch articulates what may be the consensus regarding *Garbage*. He sees the poem as a brilliant summation of the poet's life's work, "an American testament that arcs toward praise, a poem of amplitude that confronts our hazardous ends and circles around to saying, 'I'm glad I was here, / even if I must go.'"

BIOGRAPHICAL/CRITICAL SOURCES:

BOOKS

Ammons, A. R., *The Selected Poems, 1951-1971*, Norton, 1955.

Ammons, A. R., *Sumerian Vistas: Poems, 1987*, Norton, 1987.

Authors in the News, Volume 1, Gale (Detroit), 1976.

Bloom, Harold, *The Ringers in the Tower: Studies in Romantic Tradition*, University of Chicago Press (Chicago), 1971.

Bloom, Harold, *Figures of Capable Imagination*, Seabury-Continuum, 1976.

Bloom, Harold, editor, *A. R. Ammons*, Chelsea House (New York City), 1986.

Contemporary Literary Criticism, Gale, Volume 2, 1974; Volume 3, 1975; Volume 5, 1976; Volume 8, 1978; Volume 9, 1978; Volume 25, 1983; Volume 57, 1990.

Dictionary of Literary Biography, Volume 5: *American Poets since World War II*, Gale, 1980.

Holder, Alan, *A. R. Ammons*, Twayne (New Haven, CT), 1978.

Howard, Richard, *Alone with America: Essays on the Art of Poetry in the United States since 1950*, Atheneum (New York City), 1969, enlarged edition, 1980.

Waggoner, Hyatt H., *American Visionary Poetry*, Louisiana State University Press (Baton Rouge, LA), 1982.

PERIODICALS

Book Week, February 20, 1966.

Chicago Tribune Book World, July 26, 1981; June 12, 1983.

Christian Science Monitor, December 30, 1993, p. 13.

Contemporary Literature, winter, 1968.

Diacritics, winter, 1973.

Hudson Review, summer, 1967; autumn, 1981; summer, 1994, pp. 313-314.

Kayak, summer, 1973.

Kenyon Review, fall, 1994, pp. 161-171.

Los Angeles Times Book Review, May 16, 1982.

Nation, April 24, 1967; January 18, 1971.

New Republic, April 25, 1981.

New Yorker, February 15, 1988.

New York Times, November 10, 1972.

New York Times Book Review, December 14, 1969; May 10, 1981; January 17, 1982; September 4, 1983; December 12, 1993, p. 30.

Ontario Review, fall-winter, 1975-76.

Partisan Review, Volume 41, number 4, 1974.

Pembroke Magazine, Number 18 (special Ammons issue), 1986.

Poetry, April, 1969; November, 1973; January, 1988; May, 1994, pp. 97-107.

Prairie Schooner, fall, 1967.

Shenandoah, fall, 1972.

Southern Review, autumn, 1994, pp. 869-880.

Stand, autumn, 1988.

Time, July 12, 1971.

Times Literary Supplement, April 24, 1981; October 23, 1981; May 25, 1984.

Washington Post, April 25, 1995, p. D2.

Winston-Salem Journal and Sentinel, December 1, 1974.

*   *   *

ANAYA, Rudolfo A(lfonso)   1937-

PERSONAL: Born October 30, 1937, in Pastura, NM; son of Martin (a laborer) and Rafaelita (Mares) Anaya; married Patricia Lawless (a counselor), July 21, 1966. *Education:* Attended Browning Business School, 1956-58; University of New Mexico, B.A. (English), 1963, M.A. (English), 1968, M.A. (guidance and counseling), 1972.

ADDRESSES: Home—5324 Canada Vista N.W., Albuquerque, NM 87120. *Office*—Professor Emeritus, Department of Language and Literature, University of New Mexico, Albuquerque, NM 87131.

CAREER: Public school teacher in Albuquerque, NM, 1963-70; University of Albuquerque, Albuquerque, NM, director of counseling, 1971-73; University of New Mexico, Albuquerque, associate professor, 1974-88, professor of English, 1988-93, professor emeritus, 1993—. Teacher, New Mexico Writers Workshop, summers, 1977-79; lecturer, Universidad Anahuac, Mexico City, Mexico, summer, 1974; lecturer at other universities, including Yale University, University of Michigan, Michigan State University, University of California, Los Angeles, University of Indiana, and University of Texas at Houston; guest lecturer in foreign countries, including Italy, Spain, Portugal, France, and Germany; established the Premio Aztlan, a one-thousand dollar literary prize rewarding new Hispanic writers, with wife Patricia, 1992.

MEMBER: Modern Language Association of America, American Association of University Professors, National Council of Teachers of English, Trinity Forum, Coordinating Council of Literary Magazines (vice president, 1974-80), Rio Grande Writers Association (founder and first president), La Compania de Teatro de Albuquerque, Multi-Ethnic Literary Association, Before Columbus Foundation, Santa Fe Writers Co-op, Sigma Delta Pi (honorary member).

AWARDS, HONORS: Premio Quinto Sol literary award, 1971, for *Bless Me, Ultima;* University of New Mexico Mesa Chicana literary award, 1977; City of Los Angeles award, 1977; New Mexico Governor's Public Service Award, 1978; National Chicano Council on Higher Education fellowship, 1978-79; National Endowment for the Arts fellowships, 1980; Before Columbus American Book Award, Before Columbus Foundation, 1980, for *Tortuga;* New Mexico Governor's Award for Excellence and Achievement in Literature, 1980; literature award, Delta Kappa Gamma (New Mexico chapter), 1981; D.H.L., University of Albuquerque, 1981; Corporation for Public Broadcasting script development award, 1982, for *Rosa Linda;* Award for Achievement in Chicano Literature, Hispanic Caucus of Teachers of English, 1983; Kellogg Foundation fellowship, 1983-85; Mexican Medal of Friendship, Mexican Consulate of Albuquerque, NM, 1986; PEN-West Fiction Award, 1993, for *Alburquerque;* Erna S. Fergusson Award for exceptional accomplishments, University of New Mexico Alumni Association, 1994; Art Achievement Award, Hispanic Heritage Celebration, El Fuego Nuevo Award, Association of Mexican American Educators, and Excellence in the Humanities Award, New Mexico Endowment for the Humanities, all 1995; honorary Doctor of Humane Letters from University of Albuquerque, Marycrest College, University of New England, and California Lutheran University; honorary Ph.D. from College of Santa Fe.

WRITINGS:

NOVELS

Bless Me, Ultima (also see below), Quinto Sol (Berkeley, CA), 1972, new hardcover edition, Warner Books (New York City), 1994.
Heart of Aztlan, Editorial Justa (Berkeley, CA), 1976.
Tortuga, Editorial Justa, 1979.

The Legend of La Llorona, Tonatiuh/Quinto Sol International (Berkeley, CA), 1984.
Alburquerque, University of New Mexico Press (Albuquerque), 1992.
Zia Summer, Warner Books, 1995.
Jalamanta, a Message from the Desert, Warner Books, 1996.
Rio Grande Fall, Warner Books, 1996.

EDITOR

(With Jim Fisher, and contributor) *Voices from the Rio Grande,* Rio Grande Writers Association Press, 1976.
(With Antonio Marquez) *Cuentos Chicanos: A Short Story Anthology,* University of New Mexico Press, 1980.
(With Simon J. Ortiz) *A Ceremony of Brotherhood, 1680-1980,* Academia Press (Albuquerque), 1981.
Voces: An Anthology of Nuevo Mexicano Writers, University of New Mexico Press, 1987.
(With Francisco Lomeli) *Aztlan: Essays on the Chicano Homeland,* El Norte (Albuquerque), 1989.
Tierra: Contemporary Fiction of New Mexico, Cinco Puntos, 1989.

PLAYS

The Season of La Llorona (one-act), first produced in Albuquerque, NM, at El Teatro de la Compania de Alburquerque, October 14, 1979.
Who Killed Don Jose, first produced in Albuquerque, NM, by La Compania at Menaul High School Theatre, July, 1987.
The Farolitos of Christmas, first produced in Albuquerque, NM, by La Compania at Menaul High School Theatre, December, 1987.
Ay, Compadre, first produced in Albuquerque, NM, at Su Teatro, Denver an La Casa, 1995.

Author of *Billy the Kid, Death of a Writer,* and *Matachines;* also author of unproduced play *Rosa Linda,* for the Corporation for Public Broadcasting.

OTHER

(With Carlos and Jeff Penichet) *Bilingualism: Promise for Tomorrow* (screenplay), Bilingual Educational Services (Los Angeles), 1976.
(Author of introduction) Sabine Ulibarri, *Mi abuela fumaba puros,* Tonatiuh International (Berkeley, CA), 1978.

(Translator) *Cuentos: Tales from the Hispanic Southwest, Based on Stories Originally Collected by Juan B. Rael,* edited by Jose Griego y Maestas, Museum of New Mexico Press (Santa Fe), 1980.

The Silence of the Llano (short stories), Tonatiuh/Quinto Sol International, 1982.

The Adventures of Juan Chicaspatas (epic poem), Arte Publico (Houston, TX), 1985.

A Chicano in China (nonfiction), University of New Mexico Press, 1986.

The Farolitos of Christmas: A New Mexican Christmas Story (juvenile), New Mexico Magazine (Santa Fe), 1987, new edition with illustrations by Edward Gonzales published as *The Farolitos of Christmas,* Hyperion (New York City), 1995.

Lord of the Dawn: The Legend of Quetzacoatl, University of New Mexico Press, 1987.

Selected from "Bless Me, Ultima," Literary Volumes of New York City, 1989.

(With others) *Man on Fire: Luis Jimenez = El hombre en llamas,* Albuquerque Museum, 1994.

The Anaya Reader (collection), Warner Books, 1995.

Maya's Children (juvenile), Hyperion, 1996.

Author of booklet "Autobiography," TQS Publications, 1991. Also author of unpublished and unproduced dramas for the Visions Project, KCET-TV (Los Angeles). Contributor of short stories, articles, essays, and reviews to periodicals in the United States and abroad, including *La Luz, Bilingual Review-Revista Bilingue, New Mexico Magazine, La Confluencia, Contact II, Before Columbus Review, L'Umano Avventura, 2 Plus 2,* and *Literatura Uchioba;* contributor to *Albuquerque News.* Editor, *Blue Mesa Review;* associate editor, *American Book Review,* 1980-85, and *Escolios;* regional editor, *Viaztlan* and *International Chicano Journal of Arts and Letters;* member of advisory board, *Puerto Del Sol Literary Magazine.*

Anaya's works have been translated into Italian, French, German, Russian and Japanese. His manuscript collection is housed at the Zimmerman Library, Special Collections, University of New Mexico, Albuquerque.

SIDELIGHTS: Best known for his first novel, *Bless Me, Ultima,* Rudolfo A. Anaya writes about his New Mexican background and his fascination with the oral tradition of Spanish *cuentos* (stories). Anaya is, William Clark writes in *Publishers Weekly,* "one of the founding fathers of Chicano literature." The mystical element within the folk tales which inspire Anaya has had a significant influence on his novels,

but he also focuses thematically on loss of faith. As Anaya explains in his *Contemporary Authors Autobiography Series* entry, his education at the University of New Mexico caused him to question his religious beliefs, and this, in turn, led him to write poetry and prose in order to "fill the void." "I lost faith in my God," Anaya writes, "and if there was no God there was no meaning, no secure road to salvation. . . . The depth of loss one feels is linked to one's salvation. That may be why I write. It is easier to ascribe those times and their bittersweet emotions to my characters."

Bless Me, Ultima, "a unique American novel that deserves to be better known," in *Revista Chicano-Riquena* contributor Vernon Lattin's opinion, leans heavily on Anaya's background in folklore in its depiction of the war between the evil Tenorio Trementina and the benevolent *curandera* (healer) Ultima. Some critics, such as *Latin American Literary Review*'s Daniel Testa, praise Anaya's use of old Spanish-American tales in his book. "What seems to be quite extraordinary," avers Testa, " . . . is the variety of materials in Anaya's work. He intersperses the legendary, folkloric, stylized, or allegorized material with the detailed descriptions that help to create a density of realistic portrayal."

Bless Me, Ultima is a *bildungsroman* of a young boy named Antonio, who grows up in a small village in New Mexico around the time of World War II. Most of Antonio's maturation is linked to his struggles with religious faith and in choosing between the nomadic way of life of his father's family, and the agricultural lifestyle of his mother's. Many reviewers of *Bless Me, Ultima* laud Anaya for his depiction of these dilemmas in the life of a young Mexican-American. For example, in *Chicano Perspectives in Literature: A Critical and Annotated Bibliography,* authors Francisco A. Lomeli and Donaldo W. Urioste call the work "an unforgettable novel . . . already becoming a classic for its uniqueness in story, narrative technique and structure." *America* contributor Scott Wood remarks: "Anaya offers a valuable gift to the American scene, a scene which often seems as spiritually barren as some parched plateau in New Mexico." *Bless Me, Ultima* sold over 300,000 copies in 21 printings before appearing in a new hardcover edition in 1994.

Anaya's next novel, *Heart of Aztlan,* is a more political work about a family that moves from a rural community to the city, but like its predecessor, Anaya mixes mystical elements with the book's social concern for the Chicano worker in capitalist America. Clemente Chavez, Anaya's protagonist, is forced to sell his small farm in New Mexico after his land is found depleted and useless—incapable of supporting his family. This results in what Charles R. Larson summarizes in *World Literature Today* as "the systematic destruction of the family unit once the rootedness to the land has been severed." The myth of Aztlan, "a sustaining force in the face of oppression . . . is within the [Hispanic] people themselves," notes Marvin A. Lewis in *Revista Chicano-Requena,* and Clemente leads his "people in a nonviolent confrontation with the evil forces that have had such a profound effect upon their lives."

Reaction to *Heart of Aztlan* has been somewhat less enthusiastic than for *Bless Me, Ultima.* Lewis observes in *Revista Chicano-Riquena* that "on the surface [*Heart of Aztlan*] is a shallow, romantic, adolescent novel which nearly overshadows the treatment of adult problems. The novel does have redeeming qualities, however, in its treatment of the urban experience and the problems inherent therein, as well as in its attempt to define the mythic dimension of the Chicano experience." Larson feels *Bless Me, Ultima* involves "mythological layerings paralleling the story's surface narrative, an aspect also true of *Heart of Aztlan,* though not as successfully employed here. Still there is much to admire in Anaya's recent work." Carter Wilson, however, in *Ploughshares,* argues that *Heart of Aztlan* is "more patiently wrought [than *Bless Me, Ultima*] and, in that sense at least, a better piece of fiction. It is as though in the first book it was necessary for Anaya to establish lineage, lay specific claim to the heritage which would enable him to do what he was bound to do."

Anaya's 1979 novel *Tortuga* continues in the mythical vein of the author's earlier works. The novel concerns a young boy who must undergo therapy for his paralysis and wear a body cast, hence his nickname "Tortuga," which means turtle. "Tortuga," however, also "refers . . . to the 'magic mountain' (with a nod here to Thomas Mann) that towers over the hospital for paralytic children," according to Angelo Restivo in *Fiction International.* While staying at the Crippled Children and Orphans Hospital, Tortuga becomes more spiritually and psychologically mature, and the novel ends when he returns home after his year-long ordeal. As with Anaya's first two novels, *Tortuga* is a story about growing up; indeed, *Bless Me, Ultima, Heart of Aztlan,* and *Tortuga* form a loosely-tied trilogy depicting the

Hispanic experience in America over a period of several decades. Anaya once told *CA:* these novels "are a definite trilogy in my mind. They are not only about growing up in New Mexico, they are about life."

Anaya's early novels attempt to find answers to life's questions from the perspective of his own personal cultural background. "If we as Chicanos do have a distinctive perspective on life," he tells Juan Bruce-Novoa in *Chicano Authors: Inquiry by Interview,* "I believe that perspective will be defined when we challenge the very basic questions which mankind has always asked itself: What is my relationship to the universe, the cosmos? Who am I and why am I here? If there is a Godhead, what is its nature and function? What is the nature of mankind?" These questions echo the doubts that Anaya has struggled with for a majority of his life—doubts which he finds closely linked with American mythology. Anaya explains to Bruce-Novoa that literature, "certainly Chicano literature," reflects the "mythos" of a people. This mythos, in turn, has as its base the philosophical positions that define a culture's worldview. For Anaya, his stuggle with doubt is tied to the mythology of the Americas: "In a real sense, the mythologies of the Americas are the only mythologies of all of us, whether we are newly arrived or whether we have been here for centuries. The land and the people force this mythology on us. I gladly accept it; many or most of the American newcomers have resisted it."

With *Alburquerque,* Anaya changed direction, emphasizing "contemporary social issues" and writing in a "more accessible style," William Clark explains in *Publishers Weekly. Alburquerque,* taken from the original spelling of present-day Albuquerque, tells of Abran Gonzalez, a young boxer searching for the truth about his family heritage after learning that he is adopted. After receiving a letter from his birth mother who is dying in a hospital in Albuquerque, Gonzalez begins to search for the truth about his family. According to Feroza Jussawalla in *World Literature Today,* the novel involves "a quest for knowledge" while portraying "many cultures intersecting at an urban, power-and politics-filled crossroads." David H. Jackson in *Small Press* claims that the story is a "portentous, dubiously-plotted pastiche," although "there are wonderful descriptions of New Mexico's natural beauty" and "some of the characters . . . reach and find the reader." Calling *Alburquerque* an "exhilarating fiesta" and a "splendid reading experience," Kevin Mcilvoy in the *Los Angeles Times Book Review* concludes that the novel is "a cleansing, blessing journey of simple steps through old and complex paths."

Anaya's 1995 novel *Zia Summer* is a murder mystery focusing on the death of Alburquerque (Anaya again uses the original spelling) politician Frank Dominic's wife Gloria. Private detective Sonny Baca, Gloria's cousin, seeks to find the killer in the midst of various ethnic and class conflicts. As *Washington Post Book World* contributor Tom Miller notes, *Zia Summer*'s cast of characters is fleshed out with "a Japanese computer tycoon with whom Gloria has a satisfying affair; Turco, Gloria's drug smuggling brother, . . . Sonny's three appealingly impish and elderly neighbors who represent the simple, unadorned life our hero [Sonny] knows is passing from this scene," and Raven, a cult leader who doubles as an environmentalist. Although Robert Franklin Gish, writing in the *Bloomsbury Review,* finds that "spotting the murderer early on is no mystery," he nonetheless believes that *Zia Summer* shows Anaya to be "a maturing author full of the juices of literary creativity and endurance." Miller argues that *Zia Summer* fails as suspense due to the reader's ability to judge each character quickly and easily, but concludes that the novel is well-paced, with dialogue that comes "naturally and convincingly," and that Anaya has created a strong, "easygoing and amiable" character in Sonny Baca. The *New York Times Book Review*'s Marilyn Stasio finds that *Zia Summer* is a narrative of "stories within stories," and that in Anaya's "incantatory voice, they are all magical."

BIOGRAPHICAL/CRITICAL SOURCES:

BOOKS

Bruce-Novoa, Juan, *Chicano Authors: Inquiry by Interview,* University of Texas Press (London and Austin, TX), 1980.

Chicano Literature: A Reference Guide, Greenwood Press (Westport, CT), 1985.

Contemporary Authors Autobiography Series, Volume 4, Gale (Detroit), 1986.

Contemporary Literary Criticism, Volume 23, Gale, 1983.

Dictionary of Literary Biography, Volume 82: *Chicano Writers, First Series,* Gale, 1989.

Gonzales-Trujillo, Cesar A., editor, *Rudolfo A. Anaya: Focus on Criticism,* Massachusetts Bay Press (Wellesley Hills), 1989.

Kanellos, Nicolas, editor, *Understanding the Chicano Experience through Literature,* Mexican American Studies, University of Houston (Houston, TX), 1981.

Lomeli, Francisco A. and Donaldo W. Urioste, *Chicano Perspectives in Literature: A Critical and Annotated Bibliography,* Pajarito, 1976.

Vassallo, Paul, editor, *The Magic of Words: Rudolfo A. Anaya and His Writings,* University of New Mexico Press, 1982.

PERIODICALS

America, January 27, 1973.

American Book Review, March-April, 1979.

Bloomsbury Review, April, 1991, p. 7; July, 1992, p. 5; November-December, 1995, pp. 22-23.

Booklist, May 15, 1995, p. 1610.

Fiction International, Number 12, 1980.

Hispanic, September, 1994, p. 90.

La Luz, May, 1973.

Latin American Literary Review, spring-summer, 1978.

Library Journal, July, 1992, p. 119.

Los Angeles Times Book Review, August 30, 1992, p. 8.

Multicultural Review, October, 1992, p. 60.

Nation, July 18, 1994, p. 98.

New York Times Book Review, November 29, 1992, p. 22; July 2, 1995, p. 15.

Ploughshares, Volume 4, number 3, 1978, pp. 190-97.

Publishers Weekly, May 25, 1992, p. 36; March 21, 1994, p. 24; April 10, 1995, p. 56; June 5, 1995, pp. 41-42.

Review of Contemporary Fiction, fall, 1992, p. 201.

Revista Chicano-Riquena, spring, 1978; summer, 1981.

School Library Journal, December, 1992, p. 36.

Small Press, fall, 1992, pp. 63-64.

University of Albuquerque Alumni Magazine, January, 1973.

University of New Mexico Alumni Magazine, January, 1973.

Washington Post Book World, May 14, 1995, p. 5.

Western American Literature, fall, 1991, p. 285; summer, 1993, p. 190.

World & I, August, 1994, p. 324.

World Literature Today, spring, 1979; winter, 1994, p. 125.

B

BACON, R(onald) L(eonard) 1924-

PERSONAL: Born in 1924 in Melbourne, Australia.

ADDRESSES: Home—3/5a McIntyre Rd., Mangere Bridge, Auckland, New Zealand.

CAREER: Teacher and writer. Favona Primary School, Auckland, New Zealand, principal.

AWARDS, HONORS: Russell Clark Award, New Zealand Library Association, 1978, for *The House of the People;* New Zealand Picture Story Book of the Year Award, for *The Fish of Our Fathers.*

WRITINGS:

CHILDREN'S FICTION

The Boy and the Taniwha, illustrated by Para Matchitt, Collins (London), 1966, International Publications Service (New York City), 1976.

Rua and the Sea People, illustrated by Matchitt, Collins, 1968, International Publications Service, 1976.

Again the Bugles Blow, illustrated by V. J. Livingston, Collins, 1973, International Publications Service, 1973.

The House of the People (Maori legend), illustrated by Robert Jahnke, Collins, 1977.

Hatupatu and the Bird Woman (Maori legend), illustrated by Stanley J. Woods, Collins, 1979.

The Fish of Our Fathers (Maori legend), illustrated by Jahnke, Waiatarua, 1984.

Creation Stories, illustrated by Jahnke, Shortland, 1984.

Maui Stories, illustrated by Cliff Whiting, Shortland, 1984.

Maori Legends: Seven Stories, illustrated by Philippa Stitchbury, Shortland, 1984.

The Home of the Winds (Maori legend), illustrated by Jahnke, Waiatarua, 1985.

Hemi Dances, illustrated by Sandra O'Callaghan, Waiatarua, 1985.

Hotu-Puku, illustrated by Frank Bates, Waiatarua, 1985.

Little Pukeko and the Tiki, illustrated by Bates, Waiatarua, 1985.

Maui and Kuri, illustrated by Bates, Waiatarua, 1985.

Ruru and the Green Fairies, illustrated by Bates, Waiatarua, 1985.

A Legend of Kiwi, illustrated by Steven Dickinson, Waiatarua, 1987.

Hemi and the Whale, illustrated by O'Callaghan, Waiatarua, 1988.

The Bone Tree, illustrated by Mark Wilson, SRA, 1994.

Also author of *The Green Fish of Ngahui,* 1989; *The Banjo Man,* illustrated by Kelvin Hawley, 1990; *The Clay Boy,* illustrated by Chris Gaskin, 1990; *A Mouse Singing in the Reeds,* 1990; and *Three Surprises for Hemi,* 1990.

READERS FOR CHILDREN

Wind, illustrated by Philippa Stitchbury, Ashton (Shoreham-by-Sea, West Sussex), 1984.

The Bay, illustrated by Sandra Morris, Ashton, 1986.

Jessie's Flower, illustrated by Liz Dodson, Shortland, 1986.

The Greatest, illustrated by Bryan Pollard and Margaret McGrath, Shortland, 1987.

Let's Make Music, illustrated by Deirdre Gardiner, Shortland, 1987.

In My Bed, illustrated by Morris, Shortland, 1988.

In My Room, illustrated by Glenda Jones, Shortland, 1988.

Just Me, illustrated by Kelvin Hawley, Shortland, 1988.

Off to Work, illustrated by Hawley, Shortland, 1988.

Our Dog Sam, illustrated by Helen Funnell, Shortland, 1988.

Save Our Earth, illustrated by Rodney McRae, Shortland, 1988.

The Scarecrow, illustrated by Isabel Lowe, Shortland, 1988.

Weaving, illustrated by Heidi Fegan, Shortland, 1988.

Grandma's Bicycle, illustrated by Philip Webb, Shortland, 1988.

CHILDREN'S NONFICTION

Codes and Messages, Shortland, 1987.

Games and Their Past, illustrated by Ian McNee and Rachel Jones, Shortland, 1987.

(With Carol Hosking) *Rainy Day Ideas!,* illustrated by Jones, Shortland, 1987.

Weaving, illustrated by Fegan, Shortland, 1988.

ADULT BOOKS

In the Sticks (novel), illustrated by David More, Collins, 1963.

Along the Road (novel), illustrated by More, Collins, 1964.

Auckland: Gateway to New Zealand, photographs by Gregory Riethmaier, Collins, 1968.

Auckland: Town and Around, photographs by Riethmaier, Collins, 1973.

Publishing a Book, photographs by Richard Redgrove, Shortland, 1987.*

*   *   *

BANGLEY, Bernard K.   1935-

PERSONAL: Born November 27, 1935, in Suffolk, VA; son of James H. (a fire chief) and Ethel (a secretary; maiden name, Modlin) Bangley; married Anna Hollowell (a water colorist), February 1, 1958; children: David, Diane, Jennifer. *Education:*

Hampden-Sydney College, B.A., 1959; Union Theological Seminary, Richmond, VA, M.Div., 1962.

ADDRESSES: Office—Quaker Memorial Presbyterian Church, P.O. Box 4056, Lynchburg, VA 24502.

CAREER: Ordained Presbyterian minister, 1962; pastor of Presbyterian churches in Ararat, VA, 1962-66, and Rockbridge Baths, VA, 1967-77; First Presbyterian Church, Lynchburg, VA, associate pastor, 1977-80; Pine Shores Presbyterian Church, Sarasota, FL, pastor, 1981-84; Quaker Memorial Presbyterian Church, Lynchburg, pastor, 1984—. Lecturer in psychology at Virginia Military Institute, 1971-73.

AWARDS, HONORS: Grants from Virginia Foundation for the Humanities and Public Policy.

WRITINGS:

(Editor and translator) *Growing in His Image,* Harold Shaw (Wheaton, IL), 1983.

Bible Basic: Bible Games for Personal Computers, Harper (New York City), 1983.

Spiritual Treasure, Paulist Press (Ramsey, NJ), 1985.

Forgiving Yourself, Harold Shaw, 1986.

Christian Classics in Modern English, Imitation of Christ, Harold Shaw, 1991.

If I'm Forgiven, Why Do I Still Feel Guilty?, Harold Shaw, 1992.

Getting Along when You Feel Like Getting Even, Harold Shaw, 1993.

FILMS

Descent (clay animation), Atlantis Films, 1973.

What Mean These Stones?, Virginia Foundation for the Humanities and Public Policy, 1976.

Portrait of a Farmer, Virginia Foundation for the Humanities and Public Policy, 1977.

Echoes from the Garden (biography), Virginia Foundation for the Humanities and Public Policy, 1979.

OTHER

Also composer of music, including "Requiem," performed in Lexington, VA, winter, 1977. Contributor to magazines.

If I'm Forgiven, Why Do I Still Feel Guilty? has been translated into Spanish.

WORK IN PROGRESS: The Prodigal, a seventy-minute musical drama, lyrics by Dean Foster, 1996.

SIDELIGHTS: "Writing is in my blood," Bernard K. Bangley told *CA.* "I have honestly enjoyed the steady discipline of writing imposed by the ministry. I have also been grateful for a lifetime of reading in fields that range widely."

BIOGRAPHICAL/CRITICAL SOURCES:

PERIODICALS

Hampden-Sydney Record, winter, 1973.
National Observer, February, 1975.
Roanoke Times, July 15, 1973.

*   *   *

BARON, J. W.
  See KRAUZER, Steven M(ark)

*   *   *

BATEY, Mavis   1921-

PERSONAL: Born May 5, 1921, in London, England; daughter of Frederick (a civil servant) and Lilian (Day) Lever; married Keith Batey (an academic); children: Elizabeth, Christopher, Deborah. *Education:* Attended University of London, 1937-39. *Religion:* Church of England.

ADDRESSES: Home—West House, Barrack Lane, Aldwick, West Sussex PO21 4ED, England.

CAREER: Worked at Bletchley as cryptographer until 1946; Oxford University, Oxford, England, tutor in external studies, 1972-92. Trustee of Lewis Carroll Birthplace Trust.

MEMBER: Garden History Society (president).

AWARDS, HONORS: Veitch Memorial Medal, 1986; named member of Order of the British Empire, 1987; Gold Medal, Royal Horticultural Society.

WRITINGS:

Alice's Adventures in Oxford, Pitkin (London), 1978.
Oxford Gardens, Avebury (Surrey, England), 1982, Scolar Press (Aldershot, Hants, England), 1986.

(With Sandra Raphael, Christopher Thacker, and Denis Wood) *Of Oxfordshire Gardens,* illustrations by Meriel Edmunds, Oxford Polytechnic Press (Oxford), 1982.
Oxford and Cambridge Gardens, Macmillan (London and New York City), 1988.
(With David Hambert) *The English Garden Tour,* John Murray (London), 1990.
The Adventures of Alice, Macmillan, 1991.
Arcadian Thames, Barn Elms (London), 1994.
Regency Gardens, Shire (Risborough, Aylesbury, Bucks, England), 1995.
Jane Austen and Landscape, Barn Elms, 1996.

Also author of *The Story of the Privy Garden at Hampton Court.* Contributor to *Country Life, Garden History,* and *Oxoniensia.*

WORK IN PROGRESS: Further work on Lewis Carroll.

SIDELIGHTS: Mavis Batey told *CA:* "My chief work has been in conservation, for the Council for the Protection of Rural England, English Heritage, the Oxford Civic Society, the Oxford Preservation Trust, the Garden History Society, and many historic garden trusts. I am also much involved in adult education, particularly American summer schools in Oxford."

Oxford Gardens provides not only a history of the gardens at Oxford University but also a glimpse of the men and women who created them. London *Times* critic Ruth Stungo comments that Batey "covers all aspects of the life of the university which have influenced garden history in its widest sense." The author not only concentrates on the Commonwealth and Restoration periods, when creativity in garden design was at its height, but she also examines the decline of the Oxford garden and the ideas of designers like Capability Brown, whose plans were never realized. Stungo concludes: "For anyone with an interest in garden history or the history of Oxford, this is an essential book."

Of Oxfordshire Gardens is a collection of essays in which Batey and her coauthors point out the importance Oxford has held in garden history because of its many gardens and the prominent designers who worked there. They present information on gardens now vanished, with an emphasis on the eighteenth century, and they discuss the impact of these decorative gardens on the writers and artists of the day. John Buxton of the *Times Literary Supplement* deems it "a delightfully produced and elegantly adorned book for the relaxed perusal of anyone who has delighted in gardens anywhere."

Batey commented: "I am very used to giving lectures illustrated by slides which are closely related to the text. I see [my] new books as a development of this. My work continues to be largely associated with conservation and restoration, often trying to reach a wider public through education. *The Story of the Privy Garden at Hampton Court* explains the new restoration and is sold as a guide book. *Regency Gardens* was the result of research for the restoration of the grounds of the Brighton Pavilion. [*Jane Austen and Landscape*] combines my interest in literature and landscape—and a great admiration for Jane Austen: it related fact and fiction in the gardens and landscapes of her novels."

BIOGRAPHICAL/CRITICAL SOURCES:

PERIODICALS

Times (London), September 20, 1986.
Times Literary Supplement, July 20, 1982.

*   *   *

BEAGLE, Peter S(oyer)   1939-

PERSONAL: Born April 20, 1939, in New York, NY; son of Simon and Rebecca (Soyer) Beagle; married Enid Elaine Nordeen, May 8, 1964 (divorced July, 1980); married Padma Hejmadi, September 21, 1988; children (first marriage): Vicki, Kalisa, Daniel, Nordeen. *Education:* University of Pittsburgh, B.A., 1959; Stanford University, graduate study, 1960-61.

ADDRESSES: Home—2135 Humboldt Ave., Davis, CA 95616. *Agent*—McIntosh & Otis, Inc., 310 Madison Ave., New York, NY 10017.

CAREER: Writer.

MEMBER: American Civil Liberties Union (vice chair, Santa Cruz chapter, 1968-69).

AWARDS, HONORS: Scholastic Writing Scholarship, 1955; Wallace Stegner Writing fellow, 1960-61; Guggenheim Foundation Award, 1972-73; guest of

honor, Seventh World Fantasy Convention, 1981; Mythopoeic Fantasy Award for best novel, 1987; Locus Award for best novel, 1993.

WRITINGS:

FICTION

A Fine and Private Place (also see below), Viking (New York City), 1960.
The Last Unicorn (also see below), Viking, 1968 (published in England as *The Last Unicorn: A Fantastic Tale,* Bodley Head (London), 1968).
Lila the Werewolf (chapbook; also see below), Capra Press (Santa Barbara, CA), 1974, revised edition, 1976.
The Fantasy Worlds of Peter S. Beagle (contains *A Fine and Private Place, The Last Unicorn, Lila the Werewolf,* and "Come, Lady Death"), Viking, 1978.
The Folk of the Air, Del Rey, 1987.
The Innkeeper's Song, Penguin (New York City), 1993.
The Unicorn Sonata, Turner Publications (Atlanta), 1996.
The Magician of Karakosk, and Others (short fiction), Penguin (New York City), 1997.

SCREENPLAYS

The Zoo (television script), Columbia Broadcasting System, 1973.
The Dove, E.M.I., 1974.
The Lord of the Rings, Part One, United Artists, 1978.
The Last Unicorn, Marble Arch/Rankin-Bass, 1982.

Also author of the television script, *The Greatest Thing That Almost Happened,* 1977, and of the story and teleplay, "Sarek," an episode for *Star Trek: The Next Generation.*

OTHER

I See by My Outfit, Viking, 1965.
The California Feeling, with photographs by Michael Bry and Ansel Adams, Doubleday (New York City), 1969.
(With Harry N. Abrams) *American Denim: A New Folk Art,* Warner (New York City), 1975.
(With Pat Derby) *The Lady and Her Tiger,* Dutton (New York City), 1976.
The Garden of Earthly Delights, Viking, 1981.

(Editor with Janet Berliner) *Peter S. Beagle's Immortal Unicorn,* HarperCollins (New York City), 1995.

(With Derby) *In the Presence of Elephants,* Capra Press (Santa Barbara), 1995.

Also author of opera libretto, *The Midnight Angel,* 1993. Work has appeared in anthologies, including *New Worlds of Fantasy,* edited by Terry Carr, Ace Books (New York City), 1967; *New Worlds of Fantasy #3,* edited by Carr, Ace Books, 1971; *Phantasmagoria,* edited by Jane Mobley, Anchor Books (New York City), 1977; *The Fantastic Imagination: An Anthology of High Fantasy,* edited by Robert H. Boyer and Kenneth J. Zahorski, Avon (New York City), 1977; *Dark Imaginings: A Collection of Gothic Fantasy,* edited by Boyer and Zahorski, Dell (New York City), 1978. Work also appears in a volume of *Prize Stories: The O. Henry Awards.* Author of introduction to *The Tolkien Reader,* Houghton (Boston), 1966; *Adventures of Yemima, and Other Stories,* by Abraham Soyer, translated by Rebecca Beagle and Rebecca Soyer, Viking, 1979; *The Best of Avram Davidson,* by Avram Davidson, Doubleday, 1979; and *Adventure in Unhistory,* by Davidson, Owlswick Press, 1993.

Contributor of articles and fiction to periodicals, including *Holiday, Seventeen, Today's Health, Saturday Evening Post, Venture, West, Atlantic, Ladies' Home Journal,* and other publications.

ADAPTATIONS: Erik Haagensen and Richard Isen created a musical comedy based on Beagle's novel entitled *A Fine and Private Place,* Samuel French, 1992.

SIDELIGHTS: Peter S. Beagle's highly regarded fantasy fiction has wrought comparisons to J. R. R. Tolkien, C. S. Lewis, Thomas Malory, and Lewis Carroll. He is, as William H. Archer of *Best Sellers* notes, "a writer whose work speaks so eloquently [that he] needs no comparison." These accolades have been garnered on the basis of a relatively small body of work: several novels, a novella, and a short story.

A Fine and Private Place, Beagle's first novel, is set in a Bronx cemetery and concerns Jonathan Rebeck, a bankrupt druggist who has given up on the world to live in an isolated mausoleum. Rebeck lives on food stolen by a talking raven and spends his days playing chess and taking walks. He also talks to the ghosts of the recently deceased, but only for a short while; the ghosts soon forget their lives and, by forgetting, drift into their final sleep. Two such ghosts are Michael Morgan and Laura Durand, who meet in the cemetery, fall in love, and seek to avoid the oblivion that is their fate. Michael and Laura's relationship is echoed in the friendship between Rebeck and Mrs. Gertrude Klapper, a widow who visits her husband's grave in the cemetery. When it becomes necessary for Rebeck to leave the cemetery to resolve the dilemma of the two ghostly lovers, Mrs. Klapper provides the support he needs to do so.

"The idea with which Beagle seems to have begun," Granville Hicks writes in *Saturday Review,* "is that the distinction between living and not living is less than clear-cut. His concern is not with life after death but with death in life." To illustrate his point, Hicks quotes the character Morris Klapper, who tells Rebeck: "We are all ghosts. We are conceived in a moment of death and born out of ghost wombs. . . . For ghosts there can only be one battle: to become real." A contributor for *Kirkus Reviews* writes that Beagle's "conclusion that life is our portion, not to be embraced reluctantly, develops convincingly out of the fascinating intricacy of the plot."

A Fine and Private Place was received enthusiastically by critics, especially the portrayal of vivid characters, both living and dead. Speaking of the characters, Hicks claims that "Rebeck lives so close to death that it was quite a trick to give him substance, as Beagle succeeds in doing. . . . And there is the raven, one of the most entertaining characters in recent fiction and by no means one of the least credible." In an evaluation of *A Fine and Private Place* in *Fantasy Literature: A Core Collection and Reference Guide,* it is noted that "the main characters are memorable, but so are the support characters. . . . The delightful humor of the book . . . springs largely from the speech and mannerisms of the characters. Yet characters retain their deeper sides." Harold Jaffe of *Commonweal* thinks that "the allegorical truth of the characters [and] their situations developed leisurely, emanated naturally without violating the integrity of the fiction."

Beagle's writing style itself also found critical appreciation. Orville Prescott of the *San Francisco Chronicle* praises Beagle's "smooth, precise, graceful prose, bright with wit and sparkling with imaginative phrases." Darrell Schweitzer of the *Science Fiction Review* calls the book "immaculately written." In *Fantasy Literature,* Beagle's style is described as "truly a thing of beauty. Beagle always hits the right note, whether recording a dialogue between a raven and a squirrel or describing a scene of tender emotion between Michael and Laura."

Critics were also impressed with the maturity of Beagle's writing, even though he was only nineteen when he wrote *A Fine and Private Place*. Hicks remarks that "for so young a writer, Beagle is amazingly sure of himself." Edmund Fuller of the *New York Times Book Review* holds that "Beagle makes a striking debut on several counts. With the first two paragraphs of *A Fine and Private Place* a style is established [and] a personality registered. [The book] has wit, charm, and individuality with a sense of style and structure notable in a first novel." Virginia Peterson of the *New York Herald Tribune Book Review* writes that *A Fine and Private Place* "leaves you with considerable admiration for its young author," while C. W. Mann of *Library Journal* judges it "an excellent first novel."

Several observers thought the novel's only flaws were its length and its tendency to move too slowly. As Prescott phrases it: "[The novel] doesn't go fast enough. Its basic idea might have been adequate for a short story or a novelette. Extended to novel length, it seems too slight. . . . But such unevenness of quality is easy to forgive, considering how often Beagle is delightfully amusing."

Beagle did not publish his second novel, *The Last Unicorn,* until 1968. But it, too, received scholarly attention as well as considerable critical praise. Raymond M. Olderman, writing in his *Beyond the Waste Land,* calls the book "a magnificent romance with a sweetly sorrowful happy ending." A *Fantasy Literature* reviewer states that "if there were a 'ten best' list of modern fantasy, *The Last Unicorn* would certainly be on it."

The novel tells the story of the world's last unicorn and her quest to discover the fate of the rest of her species. She is aided in her quest by Schmendrick the Magician, a bumbling wizard who performs simple tricks ineffectively but who can, on rare occasions, perform feats of true magic, and by Molly Grue, a peasant woman who has been searching for true wonder and finds it in the unicorn. The three of them discover that King Haggard, ruler of a waste land, has imprisoned the unicorns with the help of the Red Bull, a creature who inspires fear and forgetfulness. King Haggard has captured the unicorns because he

enjoys their beauty and wishes to possess all of it. At the novel's end, the unicorns are set free and the waste land becomes fertile once more.

As with *A Fine and Private Place, The Last Unicorn* is concerned with a kind of death in life. Olderman believes that Beagle's unicorn "is the dream we have forgotten how to see, the thing whose absence makes our world a waste land; she is renewal and rebirth, the lost fertility and potency of life." Comparing *The Last Unicorn* to other novels dealing with a waste land theme, Olderman finds the book concerned with moving "out of the waste land and into the magic of life, as in [*A Fine and Private Place*] where the main character literally moves out of a cemetery to rejoin the living."

Other critics have different interpretations of the novel's theme. In an article for *Critique: Studies in Modern Fiction,* Don Parry Norford examines the ideas of reality and illusion presented in *The Last Unicorn.* He believes that the book presents such pairs of opposites as "the immortal and mortal, joy and sorrow, [and] life and death [which are] equally real halves of the same whole: you cannot have one without the other." What happened in King Haggard's realm, according to Norford's reasoning, is the separation of these halves by the removal of the unicorns from the world. The result of this separation is the creation of a waste land. At the novel's end, with the freeing of the unicorns to live in the world of man, this separation is overcome and the waste land becomes fertile again.

By blending high romance with low comedy and humorous anachronism, Beagle draws comparisons between King Haggard's waste land kingdom and our own world. "Always the miraculous is juxtaposed with the mundane," Jaffe explains. "In this way the fable on the stage is fused with the seemingly unfabulous existence of the audience. On the one hand, Beagle is saying that the same magic as there is in his tale exists in our sloganized lives. But to the cynics he may also be saying that if we think unicorns and wizards are unreal, we should examine the 'verities' of our own lives."

In an article for *Extrapolation,* R. E. Foust examines Beagle's use of comedy and anachronism from a different perspective. After defining fantasy as "a vision ruled by possibility—the latent possibility of endless and repeatable transformation," Foust notes that a reader's initial acceptance of a fantasy world is most important to the creation of this vision of possibility. Beagle continually jolts his readers out of this acceptance of his world through the use of comedy or anachronism. This jolt, Foust maintains, "returns the readers to their extra-fictive reality, thus allowing them to once again adjust to the world of fantasy [and] re-engage the text in the active process of re-creating the fabulous world." Thus, the important initial acceptance of the fantasy world is continuously repeated throughout the novel.

Foust notes that Beagle's book is reflexive in other ways as well. The characters, for instance, call attention to themselves and the story by their very actions and words. At one point, Schmendrick exclaims to Molly, "Haven't you ever been in a fairy tale before?," and then explains to her how such a tale is structured. Beagle's language, too, becomes noticeable by the mixing of slang terms or bits of commercials with the language of high romance. Foust explains, though other writers have utilized similar devices, Beagle's purposes differ from theirs. "John Barth, Donald Barthelme, and Robert Coover, have used the technique to 'demythologize' their stories." Beagle uses it, Foust argues, to place "the mythical realm within the same range of reader acceptability as the realistic." This allows *The Last Unicorn* to express the "hope of transformation" that is the "essence of all fantasy art" and which "represents the best future hope of the novel to raise itself transformed from the ashes of its current despair."

As with *A Fine and Private Place,* Beagle enjoyed critical admiration for his writing in *The Last Unicorn.* Hicks calls Beagle "a true magician with words, a master of prose and a deft practitioner in verse." Echoing this sentiment, Archer also calls Beagle "a magician with words" and describes *The Last Unicorn*'s charms as "arising in part from [Beagle's] deft deployment of mood, shading of comedy into tragedy, of horror into humor, while blending the irrational with poetry or with dream."

Other reviewers noticed a blending of forms as well. Norman Stein of *Book World* finds the book "neither quite fairy tale, myth, dream, or nightmare." George Cohen of the *Chicago Tribune* writes that *The Last Unicorn* "is a bedtime story, a fairy tale, but like *Alice in Wonderland,* it is much more complex. It is rich in language and meaning, an adventure on a grand scale." Lin Carter complains that he "cannot in the least explain my reaction to [*The Last Unicorn*], which seems like an ingenious and entertaining but fairly ordinary fantasy novel when you examine its components. . . . When these components

are assembled between a single set of covers, however,. . . I am helplessly lost in a story that sweeps me along with breathless urgency and stunning beauty." Carter concludes that *The Last Unicorn* "is in a class all by itself—one of the inexplicable curiosities of modern fantasy."

Beagle's most well-known short fiction consists of the novella *Lila the Werewolf* and the story "Come, Lady Death." *Lila the Werewolf,* originally published as "Farrell and Lila the Werewolf," is the story of a young man who discovers that his lover becomes a werewolf at every full moon. Cohen calls it a "crazy, wonderful short story." Schweitzer notes that the story's "linkage between lycanthropy and sex is one of the more interesting variants on the subject I've seen," while Cohen concedes that the relationship between Farrell and Lila is "a bizarre affair to say the least." "As far as I know," Beagle writes of the story in his introduction to *The Fantasy Worlds of Peter S. Beagle,* "I was just spinning a tale, as always, and the equating of womanhood with lycanthropy, or sexual needs with blood and death, was entirely dictated by the story and the characters. But I wonder now, and I never used to."

Beagle's short story, "Come, Lady Death," is set in eighteenth-century London where a bored society lady invites Death to her party to liven things up. "Again Beagle manages to create genuinely living characters," Schweitzer observes, "and avoid all the cliches that usually turn up in such stories." Beagle claims that he wrote the story in college "to see whether I could sneak it past Frank O'Connor [his English professor], who hated all fantasy."

For economic reasons, during the 1970s and most of the 1980s Beagle spent most of his time writing screenplays. "In those days, thanks to a miraculous Hollywood agent who has become my protective older sister over the years, although she's ten years younger than I am, it was possible finally for me to do one or two film things a year and write fiction for the rest of the time," he wrote *CA.* "Today there is much less money available for anyone who does not write serial-killer scripts, so I am writing a lot more fiction than I used to, and *almost* living off it. Even so, I've been very lucky in the sense that I've made my living in one way or another off my writing. That's almost impossible. . . . I don't live off my fiction, and if it hadn't been for my nonfiction and my screen work, I would have been in trouble. . . . I'm genuinely concerned about what is happening to the structure of publishing in America," Beagle continues. "I'm very alarmed that a lot of good writers are going to be driven away from it in the coming years by economics and, worse, by lack of any real recognition. That frightens me and angers me when I think of people who are as good as I am—let alone my wife, Padma Hejmadi, who is better—who haven't been anywhere near as lucky."

After a long stint as a screenwriter—including the 1982 screen version of his own novel *The Last Unicorn*—Beagle returned to fantasy in 1987 with *The Folk of the Air,* which is set in southern California in modern times. Joe Farrell, who Beagle created for *Lila the Werewolf,* is back once again as the main character—a musician who arrives in California and moves in with an old friend from college, Ben. He soon takes up with a former girlfriend, Julie, who is a member of the League for Archaic Pleasures (a version of the real-life Society for Creative Anachronism), and Ben and Joe become involved with the many strange League members. "Among other things," writes Suzy McKee Charnas in the *Los Angeles Times Book Review,* "the book is a sympathetic study of characters who suffer from various sorts and degrees of discomfort in our time, and who long for real or imagined ages past."

Conflict ensues when a teenage witch named Aiffe succeeds in summoning a young man named Bonner who involves the characters in a duel of magic. Once again, reviewers celebrated Beagle's style. Beagle, states Jonas in the *New York Times Book Review,* "knows how to use language to keep the reader from peering too closely at the machinery of a tale. . . . The plot unfolds at a languorous but inexorable pace that seems entirely appropriate to the matters at hand." "Beagle's language is rich, his deployment of it deft and fluid, and his eye for detail wonderfully keen," says Charnas. "Scenes set at the doings of the League sparkle with wry, affectionate humor, and the magic . . . is wild and disorienting, as magic should be." "Beagle's wonderful prose is what carries his work," declares Charles de Lint in *Fantasy Review,* "and it has been sorely missed these last two decades."

In 1993, Beagle again fulfilled reader's expectation with *The Innkeeper's Tale.* Unlike *The Folk of the Air, The Innkeeper's Tale* is set in a preindustrial society in which power is manipulated by wizards and magicians. The story's viewpoint flips between the various characters: three different women, "a young man consumed by love, the innkeeper, his servants, and a 'fox' who is sometimes a 'man' but

who turns out to be neither," explains Jonas in the *New York Times Book Review.* Beagle sums up the moral of his story, Jonas states, in a "characteristically complex" statement: "'Love each other from the day we are born to the day we die, we are still strangers every minute, and nobody should forget that, even though we have to.'" Beagle explained that he writes fantasy because "the fantastic turn of vision suits both my sense of the world as a profoundly strange and deceptive place, and my deepest sense of poetry, which is singing."

BIOGRAPHICAL/CRITICAL SOURCES:

BOOKS

Beagle, Peter S., *The Fantasy Worlds of Peter S. Beagle,* Viking, 1978.

Beagle, interview with Jean W. Ross, *Contemporary Authors New Revision Series,* Volume 4, Gale (Detroit), 1981, pp. 49-54.

Carter, Lin, *Imaginary Worlds: The Art of Fantasy,* Ballantine (New York City), 1973.

Contemporary Literary Criticism, Volume 7, Gale, 1977.

Dictionary of Literary Biography Yearbook: 1980, Gale, 1981.

Olderman, Raymond M., *Beyond the Waste Land: A Study of the American Novel in the Nineteen-Sixties,* Yale University Press (New Haven, CT), 1972.

Tymn, Marshall B., Kenneth J. Zahorski, and Robert H. Boyer, *Fantasy Literature: A Core Collection and Reference Guide,* Bowker (New York City), 1979.

PERIODICALS

Algol, spring, 1977.

Analog Science Fiction/Science Fact, April, 1994, pp. 166-68.

Best Sellers, April 1, 1968; September, 1976.

Books and Bookmen, October, 1968.

Book World, April 7, 1968.

Chicago Tribune, June 5, 1960; November 26, 1978.

Christian Century, August 31, 1960.

Christian Science Monitor, May 9, 1968.

Commonweal, June 28, 1968.

Critique: Studies in Modern Fiction, Volume 19, number 2, 1977.

Extrapolation, fall, 1979; spring, 1980.

Fantasiae, November/December, 1979.

Fantasy Review, April, 1987, p. 33.

Galaxy, April, 1961; June, 1977.

Hollins Critic, April, 1968.

Kirkus Reviews, March 15, 1960.

Library Journal, May 1, 1960; June 1, 1960; February 15, 1968.

Locus, June 30, 1976; February, 1994, p. 36-37, 38.

Los Angeles Times Book Review, February 1, 1987, pp. 1, 9; January 13, 1991, p. 10.

New Worlds, December, 1968.

New York Herald Tribune Book Review, May 29, 1960.

New York Times Book Review, June 5, 1960; March 24, 1968; September 23, 1979; January 18, 1987, p. 33; November 14, 1993, p. 74.

San Francisco Chronicle, June 2, 1960.

Saturday Review, May 28, 1960; March 30, 1968.

Science Fiction Review, February, 1978; March-April, 1979.

Time, May 23, 1960.

Today's Health, October, 1974.

*　　*　　*

BECKETT, Kenneth A(lbert)　1929-
(Keith Bower)

PERSONAL: Born January 12, 1929, in Brighton, England; son of Albert Henry (a tax inspector) and Gladys (a secretary; maiden name, Bower) Beckett; married Gillian Tuck (a writer and editor), August 1, 1973; children: Keith Christopher. *Education:* Royal Horticultural Society School of Horticulture, diploma, 1953.

ADDRESSES: Home and office—Bramley Cottage, Stanhoe, King's Lynn, Norfolk PE31 8QF, England.

CAREER: Brighton Parks Department, apprentice, 1943-47, improver, 1949-51; St. Louis Botanic Garden, St. Louis, MO, horticulturist, 1954; John Innes Research Institute, Bayfordbury, England, technical assistant, 1955-63; Glasgow Botanic Garden, Glasgow, Scotland, assistant curator, 1963-65; *Gardeners' Chronicle,* London, technical editor, 1965-69; freelance writer, 1969—. *Military service:* British Army, 1947-49.

MEMBER: International Dendrology Society, Royal Horticultural Society (committee member), Botanical Society of the British Isles, British Pteridological Society, Hardy Plant Society, Hebe Society, European Bamboo Society, Alpine Garden Society, Australian Plant Society, Plant Life.

AWARDS, HONORS: Veitch Memorial Medal, Royal Horticultural Society, 1987, for advancement of the science and practice of horticulture; Lyttel Trophy, Alpine Garden Society, 1995.

WRITINGS:

(With Tom Stobart) *Reader's Digest Pocket Guide to Herbs* (booklet), Reader's Digest Association (London), 1971.

(Editor) *The Gardener's Bedside Book,* Arco (New York City), 1973.

The Love of Trees, Octopus (New York City), 1975.

(With wife, Gillian Beckett, and Roy Hay) *Dictionary of House Plants,* Rainbird, 1975.

(With G. Beckett) *Illustrated Encyclopaedia of Indoor Plants,* Doubleday (New York City), 1976.

Illustrated Dictionary of Botany, Tribune Books, 1977.

Green Fingers Encyclopaedia, Orbis Books (Maryknoll, NY), 1978, revised edition published as *The Concise Encyclopedia of Garden Plants,* Orbis Books, 1983.

Amateur Greenhouse Gardening, Ward, Lock, 1979.

(With G. Beckett) *Planting Native Trees and Shrubs,* Jarrold, 1979.

(Editor and contributor) *The Love of Gardening,* Cassell (London), 1980.

The Complete Book of Evergreen Trees, Shrubs, and Plants, Van Nostrand (New York City), 1981, also published as *The Complete Book of Evergreens,* Ward, Lock, 1981.

Growing Hardy Perennials, Biblio Distribution (Totowa, NJ), 1981.

(Editor with G. Beckett) J. Rhia and R. Subik, *The Illustrated Encyclopedia of Cacti and Other Succulents,* Octopus, 1981.

Gardening under Glass, Octopus, 1982.

Growing under Glass, Simon & Schuster (New York City), 1982.

(With David Carr and David Stevens) *The Contained Garden: A Complete Illustrated Guide to Growing Plants, Flowers, Fruits, and Vegetables Outdoors in Pots,* Viking (New York City), 1983.

Climbing Plants, Croom Helm, 1983.

(Editor and coauthor) *The Healthy Garden,* Orbis Books, 1984.

The R. H. S. Encyclopedia of House Plants, Century Hutchinson (London), 1987.

Evergreens: A Wisley Handbook, Cassell/The Royal Horticultural Society, 1990.

Encyclopedia of Alpines (two volumes), AGS Publications (London), 1993, 1994.

BOOKLETS

Let's Grow Chrysanthemums, Charles Letts (London), 1976.
Let's Grow Dahlias, Charles Letts, 1976.
Let's Grow Handy Bulbs, Charles Letts, 1976.
Let's Grow House Plants, Charles Letts, 1976.
Let's Grow Gladioli, Charles Letts, 1976.
Let's Grow Lilies, Charles Letts, 1976.
Let's Grow Sweet Peas, Charles Letts, 1976.
Let's Grow Roses, Charles Letts, 1976.
Let's Grow Plants in Window Boxes, Charles Letts, 1976.

"THE GARDEN LIBRARY" SERIES

Herbs, Ballantine (New York City), 1984.
Annuals and Biannuals, Ballantine, 1984.
Roses, Ballantine, 1984.
Flowering House Plants, Ballantine, 1984.

"AURA GARDEN HANDBOOKS" SERIES

Alpines, Marshall Cavendish (Freeport, NY), 1985.
Conifers, Marshall Cavendish, 1985.
Fuchsias, Marshall Cavendish, 1985.
Colourful Shrubs, Marshall Cavendish, 1985.
Lawns, Marshall Cavendish, 1985.

OTHER

Contributor to numerous encyclopedias on plants and gardening. Also contributor of horticulture articles to magazines, sometimes under pseudonym Keith Bower. Former editor, *News Bulletin* of the Botanical Society of the British Isles, *Bulletin* of the Hardy Plant Society, and *Yearbook* of the International Dendrology Society.

SIDELIGHTS: Kenneth A. Beckett told *CA:* "I began writing articles on plants in 1955 because I wanted to share my enthusiasm with fellow gardeners. It was never my intention to write books, but as soon as I became a freelance writer and consultant I was asked by the Reader's Digest Association to act as a technical adviser during the compilation of their (now best selling) book, *Encyclopaedia of Garden Plants and Flowers.* This opened my eyes to the possibilities of book authorship and when Octopus Books Ltd. asked me to write a general book on trees I was keen to have a go. *The Love of Trees* was my first book. It was not horticultural and gave me the opportunity to concentrate on the plants and their homelands, a particular interest of mine.

"Over the years I have been asked more and more to write and edit encyclopaedic gardening books. This certainly puts my knowledge to the test and gives quite a lot of satisfaction, though the work can be very repetitive, tedious and mentally tiring. The books I have enjoyed writing most of all concentrate on the plants in detail and are on subjects of my own choice, for example, *Climbing Plants* and *The Complete Book of Evergreen Trees, Shrubs, and Plants.* But though of my own choosing, the books were commissioned and given a word number total to work to. The latter book was one of a series of eight so-called 'complete' guides and so I was landed with an impossible title for a book which could not be complete with just 60,000 words. Such titles are an embarrassment to author and publisher alike!

"To earn a living writing gardening books and articles, one has to do what the publisher asks, no more and no less. It would be a real luxury to sit down and write a series of books on the plants and places seen on my travels about the world, but no publisher is interested and one has to admit that such a project would never be financially viable in our monetarist society!"

Beckett participated in a plant-hunting expedition to Chile in 1971 and 1972 and has also visited New Zealand, Australia, Hawaii, Tahiti, Easter Island, Japan, Turkey, Costa Rica, Canada, and the United States.

BIOGRAPHICAL/CRITICAL SOURCES:

PERIODICALS

Globe and Mail (Toronto), May 19, 1984.
Los Angeles Times Book Review, August 5, 1984; August 12, 1984; September 27, 1987.

*   *   *

BECKHAM, Stephen Dow   1941-

PERSONAL: Born August 31, 1941, in Coos Bay, OR; son of Ernest Dow (a teacher, logger, and salesperson) and Anna M. (Adamson) Beckham (a teacher); married Patricia Joan Cox (a music teacher), August, 1967; children: Andrew Dow, Ann-Marie C. *Education:* University of Oregon, B.A., 1964; University of California, Los Angeles, M.A., 1966, Ph.D., 1969. *Politics:* Democrat. *Religion:* Baptist.

ADDRESSES: Home—1389 Southwest Hood View Lane, Lake Oswego, OR 97034-1505. *Office*—Department of History, Lewis and Clark College, Portland, OR 97219.

CAREER: Long Beach State College (now California State University, Long Beach), Long Beach, CA, lecturer in history, 1968-69; Linfield College, McMinnville, OR, assistant professor, 1969-72, associate professor of history, 1972-76; Lewis and Clark College, Portland, OR, associate professor, 1977-81, professor, 1981-92, Pamplin Professor of History, 1992—. Consultant to Coos, Lower Umpqua, and Siuslaw Indian Tribes, 1972—, Small Tribal Organization of Western Washington, 1973, 1980—, Chinook Indian Tribe, 1978—, Cow Creek Band of Umpqua Tribe of Indians, 1979—, and to Cowlitz Indian Tribe, 1978—. Member of board of advisers, National Trust for Historic Preservation, 1977-83; member of Oregon advisory committee on historic preservation, 1977-84; board member, John and LaRee Caughey Foundation, Los Angeles, 1984—, and Native American Arts Council, Portland Art Museum, 1988-90. Expert witness in federal courts in Oregon and Washington in a number of cases concerning Indian tribes.

MEMBER: American Historical Association, Organization of American Historians, Western History Association.

AWARDS, HONORS: Grant from National Endowment for the Humanities, 1972; faculty enrichment grant, Canadian government, 1986; Oregon Preservationist of the Year award, 1986; national award for contributions in American history, Daughters of the American Revolution, 1986; Oregon Professor of the Year award, 1992; Eugene Asher Distinguished Teaching Award, American Historical Association, 1995.

WRITINGS:

Requiem for a People: The Rogue Indians and the Frontiersmen, University of Oklahoma Press (Norman), 1971.

The Simpsons of Shore Acres, Arago Books, 1971.

Lonely Outpost: The Army's Fort Umpqua, Oregon Historical Society (Portland, OR), 1971.

Coos Bay: The Pioneer Period, 1851-1890, Arago Books, 1973.

(Editor and author of introduction) *Tall Tales from Rogue River: The Yarns of Hathaway Jones,* Indiana University Press (Bloomington), 1974.

(Contributor) William Loy and Allan Stuart, editors, *Historical Atlas of Oregon,* University of Oregon Press, 1976.

The Indians of Western Oregon: This Land Was Theirs, Arago Books, 1977.

Identifying and Assessing Historical Cultural Resources, Forest Service, U.S. Department of Agriculture, 1978.

(With Rick Minor and Kathryn Anne Toepel) *Cultural Resource Overview of the BLM Lake District, South-Central Oregon: Archaelology, Ethnography, History,* Department of Anthropology, University of Oregon (Eugene), 1980.

(With Minor and Toepel) *Cultural Resource Overview of BLM Lands in Northwestern Oregon: Archaeology, Ethnography, History,* Department of Anthropology, University of Oregon, 1980.

(With Minor and Toepel) *Prehistory and History of BLM Lands in West-Central Oregon: A Cultural Resource Overview,* Department of Anthropology, University of Oregon, 1981.

(With Minor and Toepel) *Native American Religious Practices in the Coastal Zone of Oregon,* Department of Anthropology, University of Oregon, 1984.

(Coeditor with Harriet Duncan Munnick) *Catholic Church Records of the Pacific Northwest,* Volume 6: *Grand Ronde Indian Reservation, 1860-1898,* Binford & Mort (Portland, OR), 1987.

Lewis and Clark College, Lewis and Clark College, 1991.

(Editor) *Many Faces: An Anthology of Oregon Autobiography,* Oregon State University Press (Corvallis), 1993.

Hoffman Construction Company: Seventy-five Years of Building, Hoffman Corporation, 1995.

Also author of *Land of the Umpqua: A History of Douglas County, Oregon,* 1986, and of television series "This Land Was Theirs: The Indians of the Oregon Coast," produced by Columbia Broadcasting System and Oregon Educational Broadcasting Co., 1971-72. Author or coauthor of eighty-six cultural resource consultant studies in Pacific Northwest archaeology, ethnohistory, and history for federal and state agencies, 1974—, including Army Corps of Engineers, Forest Service, Bureau of Land Management, Bureau of Reclamation, U.S. Coast Guard, and the Oregon State Historic Preservation Office. Author or coauthor of petitions for federal acknowledgement by the Bureau of Indian Affairs for the Chinook Indian Tribe and the Cowlitz Indian Tribe, 1981—. Contributor to *Handbook of the American Indian,* edited by William Sturtevant, *First*

Oregonians, 1991, and *Native America in the Twentieth Century: An Encyclopedia,* 1995. Also contributor to professional journals and numerous exhibits, interpretive centers, and museums.

SIDELIGHTS: Stephen Dow Beckham told *CA:* "As a teacher I have always felt that I should ask of myself what I ask of my students. I believe that my role in the classroom is, in part, to set an example as well as to display enthusiasm and commitment to the subjects I teach. I believe in getting into history: researching it, reflecting on it, and, if need be, putting on my boots and hiking to where it happened. To teach and write about the past requires the expenditure of time and energy and the marshalling of multiple resources and approaches to bring it alive. Knowledge of the past helps us understand who we are, where we have been, and where we ought to be. It is a mirror to human accomplishment, aspiration, and frailty. My life's work has been concerned with linking past to present through teaching, researching, and writing. It is an enterprise I much enjoy."

Beckham also told *CA:* "In the mid-1980s I made a shift in my approach as a teacher to move from the classroom into larger venues. Earlier experience in writing and narrating television programs, in part, influenced this decision. My goals were to integrate textual and visual information with objects of material culture and to interpret the past using multiple sources and experiences. This focus led to selection as guest curator in 1988 by the Center for Book, Library of Congress, to inaugurate an exhibit format for the 'States of the Nation Project.' Working with the LC exhibit staff, I selected and wrote the 'Uncle Sam in the Oregon Country' exhibit which subsequently had a sixteen-month tour throughout Oregon and was featured nationally in a half-hour video program on educational television.

"In 1990 I began background research and scripting of the Department of the Interior's National Historic Oregon Trail Interpretive Center at Flagstaff Hill, Baker City, Oregon. This project has led to numerous subsequent assignments to work in structuring themes and storylines, mounting textual, visual, and object research, writing panel copy, and writing outlines for audio-visual programs or scripting media productions. Work on interpretive centers for the Department of the Interior/BLM, U.S. Forest Service, county and regional museums, the World Forestry Center, and the Hong Kong Museum of History have expanded my audience from a few hundred students a year to hundreds of thousands of visitors to interpretive facilities.

"Throughout my career I have consistently affirmed teaching as my primary calling. It has been a special pleasure each year to encounter new generations of eager students. To challenge, prod, encourage, nurture and share with others those things which have captured my curiosity has truly been a privilege. I have attempted to bring these enthusiasms to lectures, books, articles, interpretive panels, and media pieces."

*　　*　　*

BEER, Jeanette (Mary Scott)

PERSONAL: Born in Wellington, New Zealand; immigrated to United States, naturalized citizen; daughter of Alexander Samuel (a lawyer) and Una Doreen (a teacher; maiden name, Castle) Scott; married Colin Gordon Beer (a university professor), June 27, 1959; children: Stephen James Colin, Jeremy Michael Alexander. *Education:* Victoria University of Wellington, B.A., 1954, M.A. (with first class honors), 1955; University of Poitiers, Diplome d'etudes francaises, 1957; Oxford University, B.A., 1958, M.A. (with first class honors), 1962; Columbia University, Ph.D., 1967. *Religion:* Anglican.

ADDRESSES: Home—256 West Hudson Ave., Englewood, NJ 07631. *Office*—Department of Foreign Languages and Literatures, Purdue University, West Lafayette, IN 47907.

CAREER: Victoria University, Wellington, New Zealand, assistant lecturer in French, 1956; lecturer at University of Montpellier, Montpellier, France, 1958-59; Oxford University, Oxford, England, Commonwealth fellow and Olwen Rhys memorial fellow of Lady Margaret Hall, 1956-58, Una Goodwin research fellow of St. Anne's College, 1959-60; University of Otago, Dunedin, New Zealand, lecturer in French, 1962-64; Barnard College, New York City, instructor in French, 1966-68; Columbia University, New York City, faculty scholar and Woodbridge Honorary fellow, 1967; Fordham University, New York City, assistant professor, 1968-69, associate professor, 1969-76, professor of French, 1977-80, director of Medieval Studies Program, 1972-80, associate dean of Thomas More College, 1972-73; Purdue University, West Lafayette, IN, professor of

French, 1980—, head of Department of Foreign Languages and Literatures, 1980-83, fellow of Center for Humanistic Studies, 1986, 1990, 1994. Chair of Inter-University Doctoral Consortium Project for Medieval and Renaissance Studies, 1979-80; National Endowment for the Humanities, member of national board of consultants, 1979—, assistant director of Division of Fellowships and Seminars, 1983-84; member of review panel of Indiana Committee for the Humanities, 1986. Broadcaster on WRVR Radio and WFUV Radio.

MEMBER: International Arthurian Society, International Courtly Literature Society, American Association of Teachers of French, Anglo-Norman Text Society, Medieval Academy of America, Modern Language Association of America, senior member of Oxford University, Societe Guilhem IX, Societe Rencesvals, Columbia University Graduate Faculties Alumni Association, Columbia University Medieval Seminar (associate).

AWARDS, HONORS: Postgraduate scholar in arts, New Zealand, 1956; National Endowment for the Humanities grant, 1973-80, fellowship, 1980; fellow of Indiana Committee for the Humanities, 1985; grant from American Philosophical Society, 1986.

WRITINGS:

Villehardouin: Epic Historian, Droz, 1968.
A Medieval Caesar, Droz, 1976.
Medieval Fables: Marie de France, A. H. & A. W. Reed (Wellington), 1981, Dodd (New York City), 1983.
Narrative Conventions of Truth in the Middle Ages, Droz, 1981.
"Master Richard's Bestiary of Love" and *"Response,"* illustrations by Barry Moser, University of California Press (Berkeley), 1986.
Medieval Translators and Their Craft, Medieval Institute (Kalamazoo, MI), 1990.
Early Prose in France, Medieval Institute, 1992.
(Coeditor) *Translation and the Transmission of Culture between 1300 and 1600,* Medieval Institute, 1995.

General editor of *Teaching Language through Literature,* 1971-88, and of *Romance Languages Annual,* 1991—. Associate editor of *Purdue Studies in Romance Literatures,* 1991—. Contributor to *Dictionary of the Middle Ages* and *Medieval Latin Studies—Introduction and Bibliographical Guide* (forthcoming).

Contributor of articles and reviews to language and literature journals, including *Allegorica, Cahiers de civilisation medievale, Chaucer Yearbook, Classical and Modern Literature, Encomia, French Review, Mosaic, New Zealand Journal of French Studies, Parergon, Romance Philology, Revue des langues romanes,* and *Speculum.*

WORK IN PROGRESS: Richard de Fournival's *"Bestiare d'amour"* and the Anonymous *"Response."*

*   *   *

BELFIGLIO, Valentine J(ohn)   1934-

PERSONAL: Surname is pronounced "Bell-*feel*-yo"; born May 8, 1934, in Troy, NY; son of Edmond L. (a pharmacist) and Mildred (Sherwood) Belfiglio; married Jane M. Searles, May 27, 1957 (divorced October, 1969); children: Valentine E. *Education:* Union University, B.S., 1956; University of Oklahoma, M.A., 1967, Ph.D., 1970. *Politics:* Republican. *Religion:* Roman Catholic. *Avocational interests:* Gourmet cooking, bridge, golf, sailing, travel (Europe and the Orient).

ADDRESSES: Home—704 Camilla Lane, Garland, TX 75040. *Office*—Department of History and Government, Texas Woman's University, Denton, TX 76204.

CAREER: Hospital unit training officer in U.S. Air Force, 1959-67, retired as a captain; University of Oklahoma, Norman, instructor in political science, 1967-70; Texas Woman's University, Denton, assistant professor, 1970-77, associate professor, 1977-87, professor of history and government, 1987—. *Military service:* Texas State Guard; major.

MEMBER: International Studies Association, American Political Science Association, Mensa.

WRITINGS:

The Essentials of American Foreign Policy, Kendall-Hunt (Dubuque, IA), 1971.
The United States and World Peace, McCutchan (Berkeley, CA), 1971.
American Foreign Policy, University Press of America (Lanham, MD), 1979, 2nd edition, 1983.

The Italian Experience in Texas, Eakin (Austin, TX), 1983.

The Best of Italian Cooking, Eakin, 1985.

Alliances, Ginn Custom (Lexington, MA), 1986.

Go for Orbit, Eakin, 1987.

Pride of the Southwest, Eakin, 1991.

Honor, Pride, Duty: A History of the Texas State Guard, Eakin, 1995.

Circumstantial Evidence in Support of an Encounter between Indian Texans and Ancient Romans, South Texas Studies, The Victoria College, 1995.

Contributor to newspapers and professional publications, including *International Studies, International Problems, Strategic Digest, Rocky Mountain Social Science Journal, Asian Survey,* and *Asian Studies.*

WORK IN PROGRESS: The preparation of biographical sketches of prominent Italo-Texans for the revised version of *The Handbook of Texas,* for Texas State Historical Society.

SIDELIGHTS: Valentine J. Belfiglio told *CA:* "The broad masses of the people can be moved to immediate action by the power of the spoken word. But the power of the written word is more long-lasting and can inspire the opinion-shaping elite of society to act, centuries after the Angel of Death has embraced the author."

* * *

BELL, Janet
  See CLYMER, Eleanor

* * *

BELL, Quentin (Claudian Stephen)   1910-

PERSONAL: Born August 19, 1910, in London, England; son of Clive (an art critic) and Vanessa (a painter; mainden name, Stephen) Bell; married Anne Olivier Popham, February 16, 1952; children: Julian, Virginia, Cressida. *Education:* Attended Leighton Park School; University of Durham, M.A., 1954.

ADDRESSES: Home—Cobbe Place, Beddingham, Sussex, England. *Office*—University of Sussex, Falmer, Brighton, Sussex, England.

CAREER: Painter, sculptor, potter, author, and art critic. University of Newcastle, King's College, Newcastle, England, lecturer in art education, 1952-57, senior lecturer, 1957-59; University of Leeds, Leeds, England, senior lecturer, 1959-61, professor of fine art, 1961-67, head of department of fine art, 1959-67; University of Sussex, Brighton, England, professor of history and theory of art, 1967-75; emeritus professor of history and theory of art, 1975—. Slade Professor of Fine Art, Oxford University 1964-65; Ferens Professor of Fine Art, University of Hull, 1965-66. Worked in the Political Warfare Executive, 1941-43; chairman of Lewes Divisional Labour Party, 1948-52; panel member, National Council for Diplomas in Art and Design, 1962; member of National Advisory Committee on Art Education, 1967.

MEMBER: Royal Society of Arts (fellow), Reform Club.

WRITINGS:

(Editor) Julian H. Bell, *Essays, Poems, and Letters,* Hogarth Press (London), 1938.

On Human Finery, Hogarth Press, 1947, revised and enlarged, Schocken Books (New York City), 1976.

(With Alison Gernsheim and Helmut Gernsheim) *Those Impossible English,* Crown (New York City), 1952.

The Political Notions of the Member for Lewes, Firle, 1952.

(Translator of commentaries with J. H. Bell) Stephane Mallarme, *Poems,* Vision Press, 1952.

The True Story of Cinderella, Faber (Winchester, MA), 1957, Barnes, 1960.

The Schools of Design, Routledge & Kegan Paul (Boston), 1963.

Ruskin, Oliver & Boyd (England), 1963, 2nd edition, Braziller (New York City), 1978.

Victorian Artists, Harvard University Press (Cambridge), 1967.

Bloomsbury, Weidenfeld & Nicolson (London), 1968, Basic Books (New York City), 1969.

Virginia Woolf: A Biography, Harcourt (New York City), 1972, 2nd edition, Hogarth, 1990.

The Art Critic and the Art Historian, Cambridge University Press (London), 1974.

A Demotic Art, University of Southampton (Southampton, England), 1976.

Vanessa Bell's Family Album, Norman and Hobhouse (London), 1981.

(Editor with Agelica Garrett) *Virginia Bell's Family Album,* Norman and Hobhouse, 1981.

A New and Noble School: The Pre-Raphaelites, Macdonald (London), 1982.

Techniques of Terracotta, Chatto and Windus (London), 1983.

The Brandon Papers (novel), Harcourt (San Diego, CA), 1985.

Charleston: Past and Present, Harcourt, 1987.

Bad Art (essays), University of Chicago Press (Chicago), 1989.

Bloomsbury Recalled, Columbia University Press (New York City), 1996.

Also author of introduction to *The Diary of Virginia Woolf,* edited by Anne Olivier Bell, Harcourt, 1977, and of foreword to *Virginia Woolf: A Centenary Perspective,* edited by Eric Warner, St. Martin's Press (New York City), 1984. Regular contributor to *Listener,* 1951—. Contributor of articles to magazines and journals.

SIDELIGHTS: As the nephew of Virginia Woolf, Quentin Bell is best known for a biography of his famous aunt, titled *Virginia Woolf: A Biography,* as well as a chronicler of the Bloomsbury group of which Woolf was a prominent member. Leonard Woolf, a founding member of the group, describes Bell's *Bloomsbury,* as an account of "sound intelligence," both "judicious and entertaining." Angus Wilson states that Bell "has taken on the difficult task of writing about the cultural aristocracy of which his parents were such eminent members. It is a remarkable juggling feat, in which reasoned criticism is modified with inner light and natural personal prejudice with a fine if markedly academic objectivity."

Besides his familial connections, Bell's writings also reflect his interest in the visual arts, as both a creator and historian. *Bad Art* collects essays written over a period of twenty years. The *New York Times Book Review* terms the collection "an intellectual autobiography" and describes Bell's style as conversational. In an article for the *Georgia Review,* Harold Fromm calls the essays "engaging" and "genial," and praises what he terms Bell's "great openness to new ideas and new experience, and a tendency to take things casually, gracefully, and amusingly." Through all these essays, Fromm observes, Bell steers toward the middle ground, avoiding polemical and extreme statements. However, Fromm continues, the book suffers from a lack of organization and a "bold and unifying central subject." Nevertheless Fromm finds

some connections between the various essays, one of which is a discussion of what determines good art. "To illustrate this principle, Bell makes the . . . point . . . that copies of great paintings, no matter how technically skilled, lack the distinctive quality of the original because they are unable to reproduce the sentiment or emotional state that lay behind their creation," Fromm writes. The essays collected in *Bad Art* also examine such subjects as the practice of using live models in art classes, the relationship of art to societal norms and values, form and content, and Bell's own artistic development. Peter Conrad notes in the *Observer* that *Bad Art* "is at its best in its memories of Bloomsbury—the superb essay on Sickert, for example." William Feaver, commenting on the same essay, writes in the *Times Educational Supplement,* "Writing about Sickert, about Sickert's outlandish stances and set opinions, Bell fairly wriggles with delight."

Despite his close links to British literary history, Bell displays an ability to view his lineage with a jocular eye. In the farcical novel, *The Brandon Papers,* he pokes fun at Bloomsbury biographers, particularly those with a feminist perspective. The story begins when the collected papers of one Lady Brandon, supposedly an intimate of Virginia Woolf, land in the author's hands. In reviewing the papers and researching the subject's background, Bell portrays Lady Brandon as a saintly suffragist who could do no wrong. "Some critics may feel that Mr. Bell's irreverent satire on feminist hagiography reveals an indelible misogynist stripe, but I think the rest of the novel argues otherwise," writes Angeline Green in the *New York Times Book Review.* Instead, Green notes that the novel is more of a "cautionary tale" that says, "Let the biographer beware who approaches her/his subject with the blunt weapon of a fixed agenda."

Roy Fuller comments that "there are some clever and amusing touches in *The Brandon Papers* . . . but as a whole it is a fair notion fatally flawed." The problem as Fuller sees it are the excerpts from Lady Brandon's unfinished novel and the memoirs of her associate, Lady Alcester, both of which he calls "unconvincing." A brief review in the *Virginia Quarterly Review* calls *The Brandon Papers* "an interesting though implausible tale."

In *Bloomsbury Recalled,* Bell returns to the familiar ground of his family and the Bloomsbury circle to write what Janet Malcolm describes in the *New York Times Book Review* as an "autobiography" that functions as "a kind of extended footnote to the work of other chroniclers of Bloomsbury." Malcolm notes that Bell's tone is that of a "detached observer," but laments that this "has resulted in a certain sacrifice of tautness in Mr. Bell's narrative." His "anecdotes and observations . . . bob about somewhat aimlessly," Malcolm concludes. As with Bell's other writings on the subject, *Bloomsbury Recalled* is rich with candid portraits of both major and minor figures in the Bloomsbury group. He also writes about his early life and, according to a *Publishers Weekly* review, "conveys a sense of the emotional strain of growing up in 'a multi-parent family'" in which he and his sister lived in the same house as his father, mother, and his mother's lover.

BIOGRAPHICAL/CRITICAL SOURCES:

BOOKS

Dictionary of Literary Biography, Volume 155: *Twentieth-Century British Literary Biographers,* Gale, 1995.

PERIODICALS

Georgia Review, fall, 1989, pp. 611-15.
Listener, February 28, 1985, p. 27.
New Statesman and Society, August 27, 1982, p. 19.
New Yorker, November 18, 1985, p. 174.
New York Times Book Review, October 13, 1985, p. 14; June 11, 1989; March 3, 1996, pp. 14-5.
Observer (London), February 24, 1985; February 5, 1989, p. 42.
Publishers Weekly, January 15, 1996, pp. 450-51.
Times Educational Supplement, February 24, 1989, p. B7.
Virginia Quarterly Review, spring, 1986, p. 55.

*   *   *

BERGER, Arthur Asa   1933-

PERSONAL: Born January 3, 1933, in Boston, MA; son of Simon (an owner of a home for the aged) and Frances (Savel) Berger; married Phyllis Wolfson, June 25, 1961; children: Miriam Frances, Gabriel. *Education:* University of Massachusetts—Amherst, B.A., 1954; University of Iowa, M.A., 1956; University of Minnesota, Ph.D., 1965. *Politics:* Democrat. *Religion:* Jewish.

ADDRESSES: Home—118 Peralta Ave., Mill Valley, CA 94941. *Office*—Department of Broadcast and Electronic Communication Arts, San Francisco State University, San Francisco, CA 94132.

CAREER: San Francisco State University, San Francisco, CA, 1965—, began as assistant professor, became associate professor of social sciences, currently professor in the department of broadcast and electronic communication arts. Annenberg School of Communications, University of Southern California, Los Angeles, visiting professor, 1984-85. San Francisco correspondent, *Il Confronto* (Milan, Italy). Former member of board of directors, Committee on Children's Television. *Military service:* U.S. Army, 1956-58.

AWARDS, HONORS: Fulbright fellow at University of Milan, Italy, 1963-64; grant to attend Comparative Popular Culture Research Seminar, East-West Center, 1976.

WRITINGS:

(With S. I. Hayakawa and Arthur Chandler) *Language in Thought and Action,* Harcourt (San Diego, CA), 1968, 4th edition, 1978.
Li'l Abner: A Study in American Satire, Twayne (Boston, MA), 1970, University Press of Mississippi (Jackson), 1994.
Pop Culture, Pflaum/Standard (Fairfield, NJ), 1973.
The Comic-Stripped American: What Dick Tracy, Blondie, Daddy Warbucks, and Charlie Brown Tell Us about Ourselves, Walker & Co. (New York City), 1974.
(Editor) *About Man: An Introduction to Anthropology,* Pflaum/Standard, 1974.
The TV-Guided American, Walker & Co., 1976.
Television as an Instrument of Terror, Transaction (New Brunswick, NJ), 1979.
(Editor) *Film in Society,* Transaction, 1980.
Media Analysis Techniques, Sage (Beverly Hills, CA), 1982, reprinted, 1991.
Signs in Contemporary Culture: An Introduction to Semiotics, Longman (New York City), 1984.
(Editor) *Television in Society,* Transaction, 1986.
(Editor) *Media USA: Process and Effect,* Longman, 1988, second edition, 1991.
Seeing Is Believing: An Introduction to Visual Communication, Mayfield Publishing (Palo Alto, CA), 1989.
(Editor) *Political Culture and Public Opinion,* Transaction, 1989.

Agit-Pop: Political Culture and Communication Theory, Transaction, 1989.

Scripts: Writing for Radio and Television, Sage, 1990.

Media Research Techniques, Sage, 1991.

Reading Matter: Multidisciplinary Perspectives on Material Culture, Transaction, 1991.

Popular Culture Genres: Theories and Texts, Sage, 1992.

An Anatomy of Humor, Transaction, 1993.

Improving Writing Skills: Memos, Letters, Reports, and Proposals, Sage, 1993.

Blind Men and Elephants: Perspectives on Humor, Transaction, 1995.

Cultural Criticism: A Primer of Key Concepts, Sage, 1995.

Essentials of Mass Communication Theory, Sage, 1995.

Manufacturing Desire: Media, Popular Culture and Everyday Life, Transaction, 1995.

Also author of *The Evangelical Hamburger,* 1970. Editor of "Classics in Communications" reprint series, Transaction. Contributor to *Information and Behavior,* edited by Brent D. Ruben, Transaction, 1987, and *The Semiotic Web: A Yearbook of Semiotics,* 1987. Television columnist, *Focus.* Contributor of articles to *International Journal of Visual Sociology, Journal of Popular Culture, Nation, Proteus, San Francisco Chronicle,* and other periodicals, and of cartoons to *Army Times* and European publications. Film and television review editor, *Society;* editor, *International Series in Visual Sociology* and *American Behavioral Scientist;* consulting editor, *Humor* and *Journal of Communication.*

Media Analysis Techniques has been translated into Italian, Chinese, and Korean.

WORK IN PROGRESS: The Art of Comedy Writing.

SIDELIGHTS: Arthur Asa Berger told *CA:* "I am interested in popular culture (and other kinds of communication), its relation to art and society, our psyches, the political order, etc. Within this broad field I've some special interests: television, humor, terror, and the role language plays in ordering the world for us. I've kept a notebook-journal since 1956 and hope to use it to do something on journal-writing and creativity. I am also an artist and illustrator. In recent years, I've become increasingly interested in humor and have been doing a good deal of writing on the subject."

BERGER, John (Peter)   1926-

PERSONAL: Born November 5, 1926, in London, England; son of S. J. D. and Miriam (Branson) Berger; divorced; children: two sons and one daughter. *Education:* Attended Central School of Art and Chelsea School of Art, London. *Politics:* Marxist.

ADDRESSES: Office—Quincy, Mieussy, 74440 Taninges, France; c/o Weidenfeld & Nicolson, 11 St. John's Hill, #H-11, London SW 11, England.

CAREER: Worked as a painter and teacher of drawing; has exhibited his work at the Wildenstein, Redfern, and Leicester Galleries, London, England; art critic and writer. Has made numerous television appearances. Actor in films, including *Walk Me Home. Military service:* British Army, 1944-46, served in the Oxford and Buckinghamshire Infantry.

AWARDS, HONORS: Booker Prize, 1972, and James Tait Black Memorial Prize, 1973, both for *G;* New York Critics Prize for the Best Scenario of the Year, 1976, for *Jonah Who Will Be 25 in the Year 2000;* Prize for Best Reportage from the Union of Journalists and Writers, Paris, 1977, for *A Seventh Man: A Book of Images and Words about the Experience of Migrant Workers in Europe.*

WRITINGS:

FICTION

A Painter of Our Time, Secker & Warburg (London), 1958, expanded edition, Pantheon (New York City), 1989.

The Foot of Clive, Methuen, 1962.

Corker's Freedom, Methuen, 1964.

G, Viking (New York City), 1972.

Pig Earth (part one of a trilogy; also see below), Writers and Readers Publishing Cooperative (London), 1979, Vintage Books (New York City), 1992.

Once in Europa (part two of a trilogy; also see below), Pantheon, 1987.

Lilac and Flag: An Old Wives' Tale of a City (part three of a trilogy; also see below), Pantheon, 1990.

Into Their Labours (trilogy; contains *Pig Earth, Once in Europa,* and *Lilac and Flag: An Old Wives' Tale of a City*), Pantheon, 1991.

To the Wedding, Pantheon, 1995.

NONFICTION

Renato Guttuso, translation from the original English manuscript by Wolfgang Martini, Verlag der Kunst, 1957.

Permanent Red: Essays in Seeing, Methuen, 1960, published as *Toward Reality: Essays in Seeing,* Knopf (New York City), 1962.

The Success and Failure of Picasso, Penguin (London), 1965, Vintage International (New York City), 1993.

A Fortunate Man: The Story of a Country Doctor, photographs by Jean Mohr, Holt (New York City), 1967.

Art and Revolution: Ernst Neizvestny and the Role of the Artist in the U.S.S.R., Pantheon, 1969.

The Moment of Cubism, and Other Essays, Pantheon, 1969.

Selected Essays and Articles: The Look of Things, edited by Nikos Stangos, Penguin, 1972, published as *The Look of Things: Essays,* Viking, 1974.

Ways of Seeing (based on a television series), Penguin, 1972, Viking, 1973.

A Seventh Man: A Book of Images and Words about the Experience of Migrant Workers in Europe, photographs by Mohr, Penguin, 1975, published as *A Seventh Man: Migrant Workers in Europe,* Viking, 1975.

About Looking (essays), Pantheon, 1980.

Une autre facon de raconter photographs by Mohr, F. Maspero (Paris), 1981, published as *Another Way of Telling,* Pantheon, 1982.

And Our Faces, My Heart, Brief as Photos, Pantheon, 1984.

The Sense of Sight: Writings (essays), edited by Lloyd Spencer, Pantheon, 1985, published in England as *The White Bird: Writings,* Chatto & Windus (London), 1985.

Keeping a Rendezvous (essays), Pantheon, 1991.

TRANSLATOR

(From the German, with Anya Bostock) Bertolt Brecht, *Poems on the Theatre,* Scorpion (Buckhurst, U.K.), 1961, published as *The Great Art of Living Together: Poems on the Theatre,* Granville Press (London), 1972.

(From the German, with Bostock) Bertolt Brecht, *Helene Weigel, Actress,* Veb Edition (Leipzig), 1961.

(From the French, with Bostock) Aime Cesaire, *Return to My Native Land,* Penguin, 1969.

SCREENPLAYS

Marcel Frishman, New Yorker Films, 1958.

City at Chandigarh (documentary), New Yorker Films, 1966.

(With Alain Tanner) *La Salamandre* (title means "The Salamander"), New Yorker Films, 1971.

(With Tanner) *Le Metier du Monde* (title means "The Middle of the World"), New Yorker Films, 1974.

(With Tanner) *Jonas qui aura 25 ans en l'an 2000,* translation by Michael Palmer, published as *Jonah Who Will Be 25 in the Year 2000,* North Atlantic Books (Berkeley, CA), 1983.

Also author, with Timothy Neat, of *Play Me Something.*

OTHER

Poems in Voix (poems), Maspero (Paris), 1977.

(With Nella Bielski) *Question de geographie* (play; produced at Theatre National de Marseille, 1984), J. Laffitte (Marseille), 1984, published in England as *A Question of Geography,* Faber (London), 1987.

(With Bielski) *Le dernier portrait de Francisco Goya: le peintre joue aujourd'hui* (play), Champ Vallon (Seyssel, France), 1989.

Contributor to books, including, *Artists and Writers: Ways of Seeing Art in Small Countries,* Duncan of Jordanstone College of Art (Dundee), 1981, and *About Time* (based on a television series directed by Michael Dibb and Christopher Rawlence), edited by Rawlence, J. Cape in association with Channel 4 Television Co. (London), 1985. Author of introduction, *Prison Paintings,* by Michael Quanne, J. Murray (London), 1985. Also contributor to periodicals, including *Nation* and *New Statesman.*

SIDELIGHTS: John Berger, known primarily as an author of art criticism and fiction, is also a poet, essayist, translator, playwright and screenwriter. Assessing the writer's achievements in a *New York Times Book Review* piece, Robert Boyers proclaims that in all his work, Berger has shown "great vividness of imagination and extraordinary clarity of intention. . . . To read Mr. Berger over the last 30 years has been to feel oneself in the presence of an intelligence utterly unmoved by literary or political fashion and unfailingly committed to its own clear vision of what is decent and important, in art and in life."

Berger began his working life as an artist and teacher, exhibiting his work at galleries in London including Wildenstein, Redfern, and Leichester. During this period, he also served as art critic for such prominent periodicals as *New Statesman, New Society, Punch* and the *Sunday Times.* Some of his early essays were collected and published in *Permanent Red: Essays in Seeing,* a book whose title reflects the author's dedication to Marxist philosophies. According to *Dictionary of Literary Biography* contributor G. M. Hyde, Berger's criticism is unique in that it avoids "the given historical categories of art criticism in favor of an existential engagement with the historical moment of the artist and the work of art." Berger's interest in the relationship between art and politics is further illustrated in *The Moment of Cubism, and Other Essays.* Berger contends that the revolutionary art form of cubism presaged the political and economic revolution in Russia. The "moment of cubism," according to Berger, was that brief period in which artists reached an understanding of the changes occurring in the outside world and reflected this understanding in their paintings.

Berger's nonfiction began to take on a more mixed-media appearance, including essays, criticism, poetry, and prose commentary. In 1982, Berger collaborated with photographer Jean Mohr (and aided by Nicholas Philibert) on *Une autre facon de raconter,* published as *Another Way of Telling.* Suzanne Muchnic in the *Los Angeles Times Book Review* called *Telling* the "most original photography book to appear in recent months." Edward W. Said in the *Nation* argues that the photographs are "extraordinary both as pictures and as accompaniment to the text." Said comments that the book's basic premise is "an argument *against* linear sequence— that is, sequence construed by Berger as the symbol of dehumanizing political processes . . . engaged in the extinction of privacy, subjectivity, free choice." A *Newsweek* reviewer concludes that *Another Way of Telling* will "certainly be widely read and hotly debated."

And Our Faces, My Heart, Brief as Photos, notes Peter Schjeldahl in the *New York Times Book Review,* is "a series of prose meditations and poems on themes of loss and love, both individual and historical." Containing some passages of art criticism as well, *And Our Faces* reflects the eclectic nature of Berger's work. "Modern history, as Berger sees it, no longer guarantees the present's incorporation into the past, but hastens the present towards a future which never comes," argues London *Observer* re-

viewer Peter Conrad. For Conrad, Berger's "reflection on the twin determinants of our fate, time and space" is "high-minded rather than inspired," but also "noble and moving." Michael Ignatieff in the *Times Literary Supplement* notes that "Time and Death are grand and risky themes," but concludes that *And Our Faces* is "among the most finished of Berger's works because it is the most serene, the one least troubled by the impulse to instruct or convert."

As his career progressed, Berger's essays drifted away from pure art criticism, becoming increasingly involved with the processes of seeing and thinking. In *The Sense of Sight: Writings,* for example, he includes his impressions of some of the world's great cities, peasant art, and the work of such artists as Goya, Rembrandt, and Amedeo Modigliani. Reviewing the book in *Time,* Otto Friedrich calls it the work of "a resourceful mind passionately at work." He praises Berger for his "vivid prose" and his avoidance of "windy academic generalities." Friedrich summarizes: "He not only sees more than most people do but seizes what he sees, twisting and probing until it yields up its meaning."

Berger's 1991 collection *Keeping a Rendezvous* includes essays, poems and meditations mostly concerning visual art. But as John Barrell notes in the *London Review of Books,* "none of them is about art alone: they place the paintings, the sculptures, the films, the photographs they discuss in the context of geography, sexuality, the nature of time, the rise of multinationals, the collapse of totalitarian Communism." Barrell argues that Berger values the visual arts "for their ability, as he believes, to put us in touch with the pre-verbal" but concludes that Berger is not clear upon how this is accomplished or why "that should be a particularly good thing for art to do." *Times Literary Supplement* reviewer Roger Moss comments that *Keeping a Rendezvous,* like *Into Their Labours,* is "a consistent meditation on what might save us, on the possibility of paradise. This alone makes them a welcome antidote to the infectious cynicism that has come to characterize so much English left-wing writing." Geoff Dyer in *Guardian Weekly* concludes that although "Berger's answers are becoming increasingly spiritual, they are still rooted in a visceral sense of the needs and hopes of the oppressed. . . . It is exactly this recognition and quality that gives Berger's own books their gravity and grace."

Berger's fiction has also attracted a great deal of critical attention and debate. *Corker's Freedom,*

Berger's 1964 novel, was praised in England upon its initial publication released in the United States nearly twenty years later, it was again acclaimed as a "contemporary masterwork," in the words of Douglas Glover, contributor to the *Washington Post Book World. Corker's Freedom* describes one day in the life of a sixty-four-year-old man who decides to strike out on his own, leaving the home he has shared for years with his invalid sister. This adventure, the greatest ever to occur in the man's life, quickly comes to a miserable end. Glover calls *Corker's Freedom* "an exhilarating achievement, wise, unsettling, and alive with a sense of humanity that is flawed, doomed, yet oddly indomitable." Joyce Reiser Kornblatt, in a retrospective review of *Corker's Freedom* in the *New York Times Book Review,* calls the book "a valuable antecedent to the greater novels that followed it," and concludes that Berger is "one of the most intelligent writers alive."

Berger followed *Corker's Freedom* with *G*—the tale of a modern Don Juan, presented in what Gerald Marzorati describes in the *New York Times Magazine* as a "brilliant, late-modernist" style. Berger's fascination with the impact that social structures have on the individual is reflected in the character G, the protagonist of the novel, who is essentially apolitical though profoundly affected by the historical events of his time. Duncan Fallowell in *Books and Bookmen* calls *G* "terribly good" and also "terribly pretentious." Fallowell concludes that Berger's "undoubted power to move the reader is too frequently undersold by the author himself." Leo Baudy in the *New York Times Book Review* argues that *G* "belongs to that other tradition of the novel, the tradition of George Eliot, [Leo] Tolstoy, D. H. Lawrence and Norman Mailer, the tradition of fallible wisdom, rich, nagging and unfinished. To read [*G*] is to find again a rich commitment to the resources and possibilities of the genre." Arnold Kettle in the *New Republic* comments that although *G* "isn't an easy book to deal with," it is a "fine, humane and challenging book." Though not embraced by all critics, *G* nevertheless won the prestigious Booker Prize in 1972 and secured Berger's reputation as a novelist of the first order.

In the early 1970s, Berger moved to the Giffre River valley in France to make his home in a peasant village, where he began work on what some commentators consider his greatest work, the trilogy *Into Their Labours.* In the first volume of this trilogy, *Pig Earth,* Berger created a portrait of the ancient lifestyle of the French peasant class. "Fiction or anthropology? The publisher's catalogue heading lists both, but it is difficult to categorize this rich melange of story, fable, and social document—with poems interspersed between the chapters," reports William Wiser in the *New York Times Book Review.* Wiser concludes that as Berger "faithfully records the seasons of the pig earth and searches for the French peasant in himself, he reveals something elemental in us all." Kenneth A. Cook in the *Washington Post Book World* claims that Berger "evokes with remarkable economy a peasant world as resilient to history, as sensual and as unpredictable as the village of Macondo built so lavishly by [Gabriel] Garcia Marquez."

Once in Europa, the second part of Berger's *Into Their Labours* trilogy, shows the intrusion of the modern world into the old ways, and the swift crumbling of centuries-old traditions that follows. *Progressive* reviewer Saul Landau finds the stories "beautiful and painful" and credits Berger with painting "the characters and landscapes like a Goya with words, conjuring up horrifying yet real images of devastating change." Sean French in the *New Statesman* comments that *Once in Europa* traces "the end of peasant life from the inside. This momentous, inevitable process haunts everything in this volume." French finds the collection of stories "a very strong collection indeed," noting the "intense sensual detail of Berger's writing." Richard Critchfield in the *New York Times Book Review* argues that a "sense of loss—both of loved people and a whole way of life . . . haunts this second volume" of Berger's trilogy. Hoping Berger will gain a wider readership in America with this volume, Critchfield calls Berger "one of the most gifted and imaginative [of] contemporary writers."

In *Lilac and Flag: An Old Wives' Tale of a City,* the author focuses on the final degradation of the village people who have attempted to start new lives in the city. This culminating novel of Berger's trilogy received mixed reviews. Guy Mannes-Abbott in the *New Statesman* argues that throughout the trilogy, "the stories get longer as they approach the challenge of the modern, until they fracture into the complexity of [*Lilac and Flag*]." Mannes-Abbott comments that the "simple, but not simplistic, life [Berger] records slides into idealisation," but concludes that *Lilac and Flag* is "a unique piece of fiction." Robert Boyers in the *New York Times Book Review* argues that although Berger's "characteristic eye for telling physical detail and his feeling for the poetry of everyday life" are evident in *Lilac and Flag,* the book is burdened by its "fragmentariness and dreaminess." Boyers concludes: "one wonders how a writer of his experience and sophistication can have gone so wrong."

To the Wedding, Berger's 1995 novel, depicts two young lovers whose relationship continues even after the woman, Ninon, reveals that she is HIV-positive. The story culminates with the couple's wedding. A writer for *Kirkus Reviews* comments: "While the tragedy of AIDS has spawned many poignant works in the last decade, few have achieved the level of emotional, psychological, and physical harmony found here." Donna Seaman in *Booklist* agrees that Berger avoids "melodrama and overanalysis . . . [and] has gone straight to the heart of the matter." Joanna M. Burkhardt in *Library Journal* notes that royalties from *To the Wedding* will be donated to aid those with HIV and AIDS, and calls the novel "bittersweet."

Berger's eclectic approach has led some reviewers to consider him a difficult, albeit intelligent and original, author. Summarizing Berger's career, Edward W. Said in *Nation* writes: "Berger is not easy to digest partly because he has a great deal to say in his stream of essays, books of criticism, film scripts and novels, and partly because he says it in unusual ways. . . . His knowledge of art history, philosophy and literature, like his acute political sense, is sophisticated without being heavy or obtrusive. The best thing about him, though, is his relentless striving for accessible truths about the visual arts—their ambiguity, memorial enchainments, half-conscious projections and irreducibly subjective force."

BIOGRAPHICAL/CRITICAL SOURCES:

BOOKS

Contemporary Literary Criticism, Gale (Detroit), Volume 2, 1974, Volume 19, 1981.
Dictionary of Literary Biography, Volume 14: *British Novelists since 1960,* Gale (Detroit), 1983.
Dyer, Geoff, *Ways of Telling: The Work of John Berger,* Pluto Press (London), 1986.
Papastergiadis, Nikos, *Modernity as Exile: The Stranger in John Berger's Writing,* Manchester University Press (Manchester, U.K.), 1993.
Weibel, Paul, *Reconstructing the Past: G and The White Hotel, Two Contemporary "Historical" Novels,* P. Lang (Bern), 1989.

PERIODICALS

Antioch Review, fall, 1992.
Atlantic, May, 1969, pp. 99-101.
Booklist, May 1, 1995.
Books and Bookmen, September, 1972.
Book World, June 9, 1968.
Commonweal, July 11, 1969.
Guardian Weekly, February 16, 1992.
Harper's Magazine, December, 1992, pp. 56-59.
Kirkus Reviews, August 15, 1993; March 1, 1995, pp. 246-47.
Library Journal, October 1, 1993; May 1, 1995.
Listener, June 12, 1975, p. 788.
London Magazine, March, 1980, p. 92.
London Review of Books, April 9, 1992, p. 3.
Los Angeles Times Book Review, March 13, 1983, p. 6.
Minnesota Review, fall, 1980, pp. 123-26.
Nation, September 4, 1967, pp. 181-82; December 4, 1982, pp. 595-97.
New Republic, October 7, 1972; March 15, 1975; June 26, 1976, pp. 26-27; July 26, 1976.
New Statesman, May 5, 1967; February 28, 1969; June 15, 1979, p. 876; September 8, 1989, p. 34; February 1, 1991, p. 36.
Newsweek, September 6, 1982, pp. 76-77.
New Yorker, April 19, 1976.
New York Review Of Books, April 6, 1967; November 30, 1972, pp. 40-43; February 5, 1976.
New York Times, August 26, 1980, pp. 513-14; November 24, 1987.
New York Times Book Review, November 6, 1969; September 10, 1972; January 11, 1976, pp. 19-20; September 21, 1980, pp. 14, 39; January 31, 1982; May 13, 1984, p. 18; April 5, 1987, pp. 9-10; August 19, 1990, p. 20; December 20, 1992; January 6, 1993; November 7, 1993, p. 15; February 27, 1994, p. 8.
New York Times Magazine, November 29, 1987, pp. 39, 46, 50, 54.
Observer (London), December 16, 1984, p. 19; January 19, 1986, p. 48; January 23, 1993.
Observer Review, April 30, 1967.
Progressive, June, 1988, pp. 30-31.
Publishers Weekly, November 22, 1993, pp. 44-45; January 23, 1995; March 6, 1995.
Punch, August 6, 1980.
School Library Journal, September, 1992.
Time, July 21, 1986, p. 73.
Times Literary Supplement, May 25, 1967; June 12, 1969; June 9, 1972, pp. 645-46; December 7, 1979, p. 104; January 4, 1985, p. 7; May 22, 1992.

Village Voice, August 27-September 2, 1980, p. 32.
Washington Post Book World, October 12, 1980, p.
    7; November 1, 1981; February 27, 1994, p. 6.*

*   *   *

BERGER, Thomas (Louis)   1924-

PERSONAL: Born July 20, 1924, in Cincinnati, OH;
son of Thomas Charles and Mildred (Bubbe) Berger;
married Jeanne Redpath (an artist), June 12, 1950.
Education: University of Cincinnati, B.A. (honors),
1948; Columbia University, graduate study, 1950-
51.

ADDRESSES: Office—P. O. Box 11, Palisades, NY
10964. *Agent*—Don Congdon Associates, 156 Fifth
Ave., New York, NY 10010.

CAREER: Novelist, short story writer, playwright.
Librarian, Rand School of Social Science, 1948-51;
staff member, *New York Times Index,* 1951-52; associate editor, *Popular Science Monthly,* 1952-53; film
critic, *Esquire,* 1972-73; writer in residence, University of Kansas, 1974; Distinguished Visiting Professor, Southampton College, 1975-76; lecturer, Yale
University, 1981, 1982; Regents' Lecturer, University of California, Davis, 1982. *Military service:*
U.S. Army, 1943-46.

AWARDS, HONORS: Dial fellowship, 1962; Richard
and Hinda Rosenthal Award, National Institute of
Arts and Letters, and Western Heritage Award, both
1965, both for *Little Big Man;* Ohioana Book Award,
1982, for *Reinhart's Women;* Pulitzer Prize nomination, 1984, for *The Feud;* Litt.D., Long Island University, 1986.

WRITINGS:

NOVELS

Crazy in Berlin, Scribner (New York City), 1958.
Reinhart in Love, Scribner, 1962.
Little Big Man, Dial (New York City), 1964.
Killing Time, Dial, 1967.
Vital Parts, Baron, 1970.
Regiment of Women, Simon & Schuster (New York
    City), 1973.
Sneaky People, Simon & Schuster, 1975.
Who Is Teddy Villanova?, Delacorte (New York
    City), 1977.

Arthur Rex: A Legendary Novel, Delacorte, 1978.
Neighbors, Delacorte, 1980.
Reinhart's Women, Delacorte, 1981.
The Feud, Delacorte, 1983.
Nowhere, Delacorte, 1985.
Being Invisible, Little, Brown (Boston), 1987.
The Houseguest, Little, Brown, 1988.
Changing the Past, Little, Brown, 1989.
Orrie's Story, Little, Brown, 1990.
Meeting Evil, Little, Brown, 1992.
Robert Crews, Morrow (New York City), 1994.

OTHER

Other People (play), first produced at Berkshire
    Theatre Festival, 1970.
Granted Wishes (short stories), Lord John
    (Northridge, CA), 1984.

Also author of *The Burglars,* a play published in *New
Letters,* fall, 1988. Contributor to numerous magazines, including short stories in *Gentleman's Quarterly, American Review, Penthouse, Playboy, Saturday Evening Post,* and *Harper's.*

A collection of Berger's papers is at the Mugar
Memorial Library, Boston University. Berger's
works have been published in fifteen foreign languages.

ADAPTATIONS: The film adaptation of *Little Big
Man,* starring Dustin Hoffman, was released in 1970;
the film adaptation of *Neighbors,* starring John
Belushi, was a Universal Studios release in 1981; the
film adaptation of *The Feud* was released in 1990 and
broadcast on the Public Broadcasting Service (PBS)
in 1992.

SIDELIGHTS: "Thomas Berger belongs, with Mark
Twain and [H. L.] Mencken and Philip Roth, among
our first-rate literary wiseguys," writes John Romano
in the *New York Times Book Review.* "Savvy and
skeptical, equipped with a natural eloquence and a
knack for parody, he has been expertly flinging mud
at the more solemn and self-important national myths
for more than 20 years." Other critics agree with this
assessment of Berger's talent, rating him as one of
the leading American satiric novelists. Brom Weber
of *Saturday Review* writes that Berger is "one of the
most successful satiric observers of the ebb and flow
of American life after World War II. His prolificacy
promises a continued development of the tragicomic
mode of vision." Writing in the *National Review,*

Guy Davenport calls Berger "the best satirist in the United States, the most learned scientist of the vulgar, the futile, and the lost, and the most accurate mimic in the trade." In a later *National Review* piece, Davenport elaborates his praise, calling Berger "a comedian whose understanding of humanity is devilishly well informed and splendidly impartial. Nothing is exempt from the splash of his laughter. The result is an amazing universality."

Berger, who often says he writes to celebrate the creative possibilities of language, works with a variety of traditional kinds of fiction. Critics have especially emphasized the comic social commentary in the books; and in at least two of his novels— *Killing Time* and *Sneaky People*—Berger makes serious comments on modern society. But Berger's forte is the kind of mock-heroism found in his best-known novel, *Little Big Man*. Some critics state that the movie version produced in 1970, which was a box-office success, did not do justice to the novel. Michael Harris opines in the *Washington Post Book World* that "*Little Big Man,* unfortunately obscured by the movie, is nothing less than a masterpiece. American history itself provided Berger with his types—a set of buckskin-fringed waxworks bedizened with legend—and in blowing the myths up to ridiculous proportions he paradoxically succeeded in reclaiming history." Gerald Green, writing in *Proletarian Writers of the Thirties,* believes that "the glory of *Little Big Man* lies in the way Berger imposes his comic view of life on a deadly accurate portrait of the Old West. . . . It is the truest kind of humor, a humor that derives from real situations and real people."

Although *Little Big Man* was not an immediate success when it was first published in 1964, "its reputation has spread and solidified since then," according to R. V. Cassill of the *New York Times Book Review.* "Now a great many people understand that it was one of the very best novels of the decade and the best novel ever written about the American West. On the strength of this prodigious work alone, the author's reputation can rest secure." *Atlantic*'s David Denby believes the book to be "probably as close as sophisticated men can come to a genuine folk version of the Old West. Its central character, Jack Crabb, is not so much a hero as an Everyman—an essentially passive recorder of vivid experience. American history happens to him, runs over him, and fails to break him. . . . Crabb himself is decent, competent, hopeful, and neither outstandingly courageous or weak; life is sordid, absurd, and as Crabb always

survives, surprisingly persistent in its ability to make him suffer. . . . Crabb just wants to survive."

Another Berger character who is, more than anything else, a survivor is Carlo Reinhart, protagonist of *Crazy in Berlin, Reinhart in Love, Vital Parts,* and *Reinhart's Women.* Jib Fowles comments in *New Leader* that both "Reinhart and Crabb were people that Berger obviously liked having around. . . . Reinhart was neither a comedian nor a scapegoat, but he was never far from things comic or painful. . . . Like most of us, Reinhart could not qualify as a hero or anti-hero; he got through, and Berger set it all down in wry and superbly-told accounts." Unlike Crabb, Reinhart lives in the twentieth century and the four books in which he appears take him from his youthful days in World War II (*Crazy in Berlin*) to his middle years in the late 1970s (*Reinhart's Women*). A *Newsweek* reviewer notes that "Berger loves Carlo Reinhart, and he makes us love him, and he does this without resorting to tricks. . . . Reinhart is an unlikely hero: fat, 'bloated with emptiness,' scorned by women and animals, looked through as though he were polluted air, in debt, a voyeur, 'redundant in the logistics of life,' he nonetheless is a splendid man. He is novel, quick to forgive and hope."

The reviewers' opinions on the effectiveness of the Reinhart series and of the individual books differ. Writing in the *National Review,* Davenport believes that the Reinhart saga "stands well against all contenders as the definitive comic portrait of our time." Cassill expresses both the quality and the problems of the series in the *New York Times Book Review:* "There are so very many fine things in all the Reinhart novels and such a heroic unfolding conception that one hates to mention the difficulties of taking them in. Yet, trying to gather Reinhart whole into the mind is like trying to embrace a whale and finding not only that the stretch is terrific but that somehow it isn't quite the same whale when your hands feel their way to the other side of it. . . . Yet, the whole ambiguous carcass is so imposing and looms so enticingly amid the deep waters of the recent past that there is really no choice for the serious reader except to go after it with Ahab's passions."

Who Is Teddy Villanova? is Berger's exploitation of what the *New York Times'* John Leonard calls "the pulp detective story, in which, of course, nothing is as it seems and nothing ever makes any sense. The story, moreover, is populated entirely by people who talk like books, usually, but not always, 19th-century books by such Englishmen as Thomas Babington Macaulay and John Ruskin." Writing in the *New York Times Book Review,* Leonard Michaels comments on Berger's style, comparing it to that of S. J. Perelman—"educated, complicated, graceful, silly, destructive in spirit, and brilliant—and it is also something like Mad Comics—densely, sensuously detailed, unpredictable, packed with gags. Beyond all this, it makes an impression of scholarship—that is, Berger seems really to know what he jokes about. This includes not only Hammett and Chandler, but also Racine, Goethe, Ruskin, Elias Canetti, New York and the way its residents behave. . . . His whole novel . . . is like a huge verbal mirror. Its reflections are similar to what we see in much contemporary literature—hilarious and serious at once."

Having exposed the humor of American life from the Old West in *Little Big Man* to the twentieth century in the Reinhart series, Berger turns in *Arthur Rex* to a parody of ancient myth and literature. The *New Republic*'s Garrett Epps calls the book "a massive retelling of the Camelot legend" and says that *Arthur Rex* "may be Berger's most ambitious book, at least in size and literary scale." Commenting in the *New York Times Book Review* on Berger's method in the retelling of this morality tale, John Romano explains that he paints his mythical landscapes "in his droll, relentlessly straight-faced prose, so as to empty them of romance, and let the brutal/crummy facts stare out. His pages swarm with bawdy puns and slapstick and bookish in-jokes; but even at his most absurd, his intrinsic tone is that of a hard-nosed realist who won't let the myths distort his essentially grouchy idea of the way things are."

In *Neighbors,* his tenth novel, Berger returns to the present suburban neighborhood and, according to the *New York Times*' Christopher Lehmann-Haupt, "parodies all the rituals of neighborliness—the competitiveness, the bonhommie, the striving for civility in the face of what seems to be barbarism—and compresses into a single day a lifetime of over-the-back-fence strife." Paul Gray of *Time* calls *Neighbors* "a tour de force, [Berger's] most successfully sustained comic narrative since *Little Big Man.* . . . Like the best black humor of the 1960s, *Neighbors* offers a version of reality skewed just enough to give paranoia a good name." Berger agrees with Gray's assessment; in a *New York Times Book Review* interview, he told Richard Schickel: "As my tenth novel, begun at the close of my twentieth year as a published novelist, it is appropriately a bizarre celebration of whatever gift I have, the strangest of all my

narratives. . . . A poor devil named Earl Keese is tormented by the newcomers in the house next door—who, however, may be essentially better sorts than he. The morality of this work, like that of all my other volumes, will be in doubt until the end of the narrative—and perhaps to the end of eternity, now that I think about it."

Berger explains that in *Neighbors* he is paying homage to "[Franz] Kafka, who has always been one of my masters. It was Kafka who taught me that at any moment banality might turn sinister, for existence was not meant to be unfailingly genial." Several reviewers note the debt to Kafka. As Frederick Busch explains in the *Chicago Tribune Book World,* "Kafka has made it clear to us that a middle-class household can breed nightmares *that become true.*" Writing in the *Washington Post,* Joseph McLellan comments that "Berger's debt to Kafka is evident in the slippery way the book's realities keep shifting, the constant confrontation with uncertainty. . . . There is also a trace of Kafka in the way identities tend to dissolve and shift, and in the constant recurrence of absurdity as a basic plot ingredient. In his exploration of these elements, Berger takes an honorable place in the lineage not only of Kafka but of [novelists James] Joyce and [Vladimir] Nabakov."

Writing in the *New York Times Book Review,* Thomas Edwards believes that *Neighbors* "raises yet again the embarrassing question of why Thomas Berger isn't more generally recognized as one of the masters of contemporary American fiction." Isa Kapp writes in the *New Republic:* "It is a mystery of literary criticism, that Thomas Berger, one of the most ambitious, versatile, and entertaining of contemporary novelists, is hardly ever mentioned in the company of America's major writers. He is a wit, a fine caricaturist, and his prose crackles with Rabelaisian vitality." Edwards postulates, "No doubt the trouble has something to do with obtuse notions that funny writing can't really be serious, that major talents devote themselves to 'big' subjects and elaborate fictional techniques, that Mr. Berger is too eclectic and unpredictable to be important. . . . But *Neighbors* proves once again that Thomas Berger is one of our most intelligent, witty and independent-minded writers, that he knows, mistrusts and loves the texture of American life and culture as deeply as any novelist alive, and that our failure to read and discuss him is a national disgrace."

In *The Feud,* reports *New York Times Book Review* contributor Anne Tyler, "a gigantic sprawl of disasters [is] triggered by the smallest of events." The owner of a hardware store sees a fire hazard in a customer's unlit cigar; discussion over this perceived threat ends when Reverton, the owner's cousin, forces the customer to apologize at gunpoint. The gun, it turns out, is harmless, but the series of revenges that follow are not; businesses, lives and futures are destroyed before the novel's end. Berger makes the story comic as well as sad; thus, the usual conventions of the feud novel gain new life from Berger, say reviewers. "What makes Thomas Berger's version so fresh is the innocent bewilderment of most of the people involved," Tyler notes. Garrett Epps, writing in the *Washington Post Book World,* concurs: "In presenting this pageant of ignorance, rage, and deceit, Berger is harsh but never cruel. In all their variety, his novels have consistently presented a serious view of humanity as a race utterly spoiled by something that looks a lot like Original Sin. This merciless vision frees Berger somehow to love even his less prepossessing creations."

Critics find *The Feud* remarkable for a number of reasons. As Epps sees it, Berger "taps into" the hidden fire of human hostility "and turns it into something cleansing and safe. That he makes it look easy only adds to the achievement." *New York Times* reviewer Lehmann-Haupt offers, "For all its slapstick comedy and manic plot machinery, what *The Feud* rather surprisingly adds up to is an ugly portrait of middle America in the 1930's. I can't quite figure out how Mr. Berger has achieved such a realistic mood using such anti-realistic techniques." With similar admiration, *Chicago Tribune Book World* contributor Howard Frank Mosher remarks, "Berger has once again written a novel that spoofs a literary tradition while simultaneously becoming its best contemporary example."

Critical assessments of *Nowhere* and *Being Invisible* generally rate them both as limited successes in comparison to Berger's other novels. A cross between a spy-thriller and an updated *Gulliver's Travels, Nowhere* allows Berger to joke about private eyes while examining human nature, remarks David W. Madden in the *San Francisco Review of Books.* Lehmann-Haupt of the *New York Times* finds it a courageous attempt "to poke fun at every excess of the world from the cold war to racial prejudice," a text troubled by the same kinds of excesses it ridicules. More important to Madden is Berger's "ability of consistently exploring new fictional possibilities" while at the same time returning to characters and

themes seen in his earlier novels. "There is a certain type of scene that no writer does better than Mr. Berger: the depiction of the instant when the most routine social encounter becomes—suddenly and without provocation or warning—pure hell; the simplest exchange of banalities turns sour, then surly, then rancorous, then violent," and accordingly, *Being Invisible* has its "moments of random brutality," writes Francine Prose in the *New York Times Book Review.* The fact that Fred Wagner, the non-hero of *Being Invisible,* can disappear at will gives his story some "marvelous ironies," including Fred's distaste "for the voyeurism, the petty crime, the guilty, secret delights" available to him when he vanishes, Prose relates. In this "fantasy of the white male as victim," as it is described by *Los Angeles Times* reviewer Carolyn See, Fred is "outnumbered by jerks—pushy, stupid, self-satisfied," notes Prose. Fred's blandness beside them becomes a problem for Berger, say reviewers. Fred does not rise beyond "the strictly mundane; no fabulistic soarings are permitted him, no flights, no dizzying privy perspectives on the great world," explains *Times Literary Supplement* reviewer John Clute. However, he points out, "If *Being Invisible* was meant to give modest pleasure and then disappear, it may then be reckoned a success, even in the hour of its passing."

Though *Being Invisible* lacks some of the depth of character achieved in other novels, Fred's world—"one in which total strangers will humiliate you for the fun of it," or kill you for a piece of cheap jewelry—is familiar to Berger fans, Prose adds. Balancing her dissatisfaction with Berger's cartoon-like characters and the disparaging view of female behavior presented in the book, Prose applauds Berger for providing another thought-provoking view of the contemporary world: "As our Government works to persuade us that life is good, that everything is all right, it's an enormous *relief* to hear Mr. Berger's voice sneering, shrill, combative, insisting that life isn't all right or likely to be, that strangers will just as soon kill you as give you the time of day. It is a sign of the times that we feel such affection for Thomas Berger's dogged, cranky courage, and for the denizens of his unwelcoming and chaotic corner of the fictional world."

Many critics feel, as does MacDonald Harris of the *Washington Post Book World,* that Berger excels when observing a quarrel "from the sidelines" in *Neighbors* and *The Feud.* "In *The Houseguest,*" says Harris, Berger "takes up the Quarrel again, and treats it in a way that is more complicated, more subtle, and more odd than anything in his previous work." The antagonist, in this case, is a charming visitor who gradually takes control of a well-to-do family's household. At first, his hosts, the Graves family, do not resist, because he serves them as handyman and gourmet cook. But after the outsider steals from them and tricks their daughter into having sex with him, they decide to kill him. He not only survives their violent attacks, but wins a place in the Graves household by providing the amenities which they have grown to expect.

Harris finds *The Houseguest* the most interesting of Berger's novels "because it seems to suggest something more subtle going on under the surface," perhaps an allegorical significance that points to relations between the privileged and underprivileged in America. Since neither class under Berger's gaze behaves admirably, it is clear that "Berger will not take sides," Art Seidenbaum relates in the *Los Angeles Times Book Review*. Seidenbaum calls this a weakness, but other critics find it consistent with the view of humanity expressed in Berger's other books. In *The Houseguest,* says Harris, Berger remains "ready to strain our credence with . . . the loutish realism of his events. His humor is Rabelaisian: larger than life, improbable and always on the edge of vulgarity; his penchant for stripping off the dirty underwear of life is unrelenting."

Like *Arthur Rex,* Berger's novel *Orrie's Story* harkens back to an ancient myth, updates it, and provides its author a forum for his modern concerns. This time Berger's source is the *Oresteia,* the Greek tragedy which recounts the story of Orestes. The story has been told many times before, by Aeschylus, Sophocles, and Euripides in ancient times and by numerous others in more modern days. The ancient tragedy is a tale of murder and revenge, justice and redemption. A wife kills her husband; a son, Orestes, kills his mother; he flees from the Furies, but finds justice and redemption in the big city. For Berger, it offers a fitting framework for his dark comic satire. He includes all of the characters, only the names have been slightly altered, the setting and events updated, and the themes slightly twisted.

Berger's play with one of the classics does not succeed, according to *Washington Post Book World* editor Nina King. She writes that "*Orrie's Story* is decidedly unsteady. It is also grim, colorless, flat." King also argues that the events in the novel do not develop in any purposeful way. "In *The Oresteia,* cause leads inexorably to effect, fate must work itself

out, and 'men shall learn wisdom—by affliction schooled.' In *Orrie's Story* randomness is all." Yet, Michael Harris finds more to the novel. *Orrie's Story* resembles those earlier comedies of mutual incomprehension, *Sneaky People* and *The Feud,* in which the omniscient author reveals that all of his characters are riddled with lust and chicanery *and* with a wacky but genuine innocence," he notes in the *Los Angeles Times Book Review.* "Every one of them is a type, right down to his or her innermost fantasies." And, by connecting these modern characters and their stories with those of Greek tragedy, Berger draws the parallels. "What he did with types," concludes Harris, "he can do with archetypes just as well."

Meeting Evil represents Berger's attempt to push his audience, readers and critics alike, to see his dark writing in a new light. As Laurel Graeber explains in a *New York Times Book Review* interview, "Thomas Berger is always annoyed that the public finds his novels funny." Berger told Graeber, "I think some people dismiss me as a clown who makes fun of serious things. . . . I've been trying in recent years to be grimmer and grimmer and grimmer. . . . I wanted to write a book no one could call comic." "The result," Graeber points out, " is *Meeting Evil,* his 18th novel." John Felton, an ordinary guy with a wife, two children, and a job in real estate, makes the mistake of answering the doorbell during breakfast one morning. At the door, John finds Richie, a motorist in need of help, or so we think. What John does not know is that he is at this moment "meeting evil." With one seemingly innocent request after another, Richie lures John toward a slippery slope that ends in destruction and death.

As Louis B. Jones points out in the *New York Times Book Review,* the author "throws a nice guy together with a scoundrel for a daylong crime spree, and thereby submits niceness to a daylong test." Jones continues, "In a trip by turns scary and farcical, intended to examine the nature of evil itself, Mr. Berger arrives at a . . . paradox of our century: that innocence consorts, mysteriously, with evil." This may occur because each person comprises both good and evil, an idea that emerges in *Meeting Evil* as Berger raises the possibility that Richie is just the darker side of John. Joseph Coates remarks upon this quality in his *Chicago Tribune Books* review. He also notes Berger's ability to keep characters and readers struggling with this issue. "To the last line and beyond, this brilliant and troubling book keeps in suspense the question of 'who was the greater criminal to the other'—a question Richie typically forces John to face and resolve, if either he or we can."

From the moment that John meets evil at his doorstep the events of the day rush ever more maddeningly toward their climax. This characteristic draws both positive and negative evaluations from reviewers. "A ferocious storyteller, [Berger] exhibits his usual inventiveness and narrative dexterity, constantly teasing and subverting our expectations," comments *New York Times* reviewer Michiko Kakutani. "He seems so intent on building the suspense of his story, however, that he gives only the most perfunctory attention to the social details and moral implications of his story." The result, according to Kakutani, is that the novel "lacks the social and emotional resonance of Mr. Berger's finest work. In the end, it's less a philosophical mystery than a fairly ordinary if entertaining thriller." Jones sees the same elements in a different light. "*Meeting Evil* is a novel intended not to be savored but crashed through, with characters and readers stumbling over every obstacle." He believes that "the plot gets nicely complicated in the end, and the entire contraption claps together in a great, unpredictable, satisfying calamity."

Robert Crews is another of Berger's updates of a literary classic. This time he creates a Robinson Crusoe story for the 1990s. Robert Crews is a middle-aged man who has never had to worry about money, thanks to his inherited wealth. As a result, he has spent an aimless life in a drunken stupor feeling sorry for himself. A fishing trip with those who pass for his friends comes to an abrupt end when the small plane carrying the fishing party goes down in a lake somewhere in a north country forest. Crews is the only survivor. "Just as in the original tale," suggests Thomas M. Disch in the *Washington Post Book World,* there is a strong didactic component. "The moral of Berger's story is drawn from the most successful theology of the present time, the recovery movement." The struggle for survival in nature proves just what Crews needs. He slowly and painfully develops the skills to sustain himself. He eventually meets another, his Friday, a woman escaping from her abusive husband.

Crews's newfound skills and redemption come too easily for some reviewers. For Philip Graham of *Chicago Tribune Books,* Crews "mysteriously develops a woodsman's competence too quickly, leaving behind decades of heavy drinking with no apparent ill effects." Writes James Knudsen in *World Litera-*

ture Today, "Although the narrator steps in to tell us that Crews has changed form his old ways, we never come to understand *how* he changed." Knudsen still admits that "despite its problems, *Robert Crews* is immaculately written and entertaining." Graham tempers his praise more. "Though *Robert Crews* is often engaging," he concludes, "it is also depressingly short on ambition, a minor work by a major talent."

Stuart Dybek finds that *Robert Crews* fits well with Berger's previous books, "a body of work that has established Mr. Berger as an American original and an American classic." This and his other novels demonstrate that Berger "is a writer with a voracious appetite for all manner of tales, legends and picaresque adventures, and a measure of his importance as a novelist is the ingenuity with which he has roamed world literature, collecting and integrating these storytelling resources into the modern American novel, a feat he has accomplished without recourse to self-consciously avant-garde techniques." Berger is, in the words of Coates, "the laureate of the ludicrous tragedy, the chronicler of complicated nonentities, and that may be why he gets less attention than his talent deserves." Coates continues, "He taps into a level of mental minutiae in his characters that appalls us by its continuous and irredeemable pettiness—trivial thoughts, minor but idiot miscalculations, weakly shameful motives that are our common human climate but that we continually repress for the sake of self-esteem."

BIOGRAPHICAL/CRITICAL SOURCES:

BOOKS

Cohen, Sarah Blacher, editor, *Comic Relief,* University of Illinois Press (Champaign), 1978.

Contemporary Literary Criticism, Gale (Detroit), Volume 3, 1975, Volume 5, 1976, Volume 8, 1978, Volume 11, 1979, Volume 18, 1981, Volume 38, 1986.

Dictionary of Literary Biography, Volume 2: *American Novelists since World War II,* Gale, 1978.

Dictionary of Literary Biography Yearbook: 1980, Gale, 1981.

Landon, Brooks, *Thomas Berger,* Twayne, 1989.

Madden, David, editor, *Proletarian Writers of the Thirties,* Southern Illinois University Press (Carbondale), 1968.

Madden, David W., editor, *Critical Essays on Thomas Berger,* G.K. Hall (New York City), 1995.

Mitchell, Burroughs, *The Education of an Editor,* Doubleday (New York City), 1980.

Schulz, Max F., *Black Humor Fiction of the Sixties: A Pluralistic Definition of Man and His World,* Ohio State University Press (Columbus), 1973.

Thompson, Raymond H., *The Return from Avalon: A Study of Arthurian Legend in Modern Fiction,* Greenwood Press, 1985.

Wallace, Jon, *The Politics of Style: Language as Theme in the Fiction of Berger, McGuane, and McPherson,* Hollowbrook (Durango, CO), 1992.

PERIODICALS

American Book Review, March-April, 1982.

Antaeus, Number 61, 1988.

Armchair Detective, Number 14, 1981.

Atlanta Journal-Constitution, October 7, 1990, p. N10.

Atlantic, March, 1971; September, 1973.

Audience, Volume 2, number 4, 1972.

Best Sellers, November 1, 1964; October 1, 1967; April 15, 1970.

Books and Bookmen, July, 1968.

Book Week, October 25, 1964.

Boston Globe, June 21, 1992, p. 108; February 23, 1994, p. 27.

Bulletin of Bibliography, Volume 51, number 2.

Centennial Review, Number 13, 1969.

Chicago Tribune Book World, April 13, 1980; September 27, 1981; December 18, 1981; May 29, 1983; May 20, 1984; May 19, 1985; June 16, 1985.

Commentary, July, 1970.

Confrontation, spring/summer, 1976.

Detroit News, October 18, 1981.

Globe and Mail (Toronto), July 20, 1985.

Guardian Weekly (Manchester), April 17, 1971.

Harper's, April, 1970.

Hollins Critic, December, 1983.

Life, March 27, 1970.

Listener, July 11, 1974.

Los Angeles Times, May 11, 1987; June 15, 1992, p. E5.

Los Angeles Times Book Review, November 1, 1981; May 15, 1983; May 19, 1985, p. 12; April 3, 1988, p. 12; September 24, 1989, p. 2; November 11, 1990, p. 6.

Ms., August, 1973.

Nation, August 20, 1977; May 3, 1980; June 11, 1983.

National Review, November 14, 1967; April 21, 1970; October 10, 1975.

New Leader, November 6, 1967; November 12, 1973; May 23, 1977.

New Republic, October 7, 1978; April 26, 1980; May 23, 1983.

Newsweek, April 20, 1970; December 21, 1970.

New Yorker, October 21, 1967; July 8, 1985, p. 73.

New York Review of Books, May 26, 1977.

New York Times, September 20, 1967; March 31, 1970; March 18, 1977; April 1, 1980; September 28, 1981; May 2, 1983; April 29, 1985, p. 17; April 2, 1987, p. 23; June 2, 1992, p. C16.

New York Times Book Review, October 11, 1964; September 17, 1967; March 29, 1970; May 13, 1973; April 20, 1975; March 20, 1977; April 17, 1977; November 12, 1978; April 6, 1980; September 27, 1981; June 6, 1982; June 20, 1982; May 8, 1983; February 24, 1985, p. 34; April 7, 1985, p. 24; May 5, 1985; April 2, 1987; April 12, 1987, p. 9; April 17, 1988, p. 12; August 27, 1989, p. 12; October 7, 1990, p. 12; July 12, 1992, p. 7; March 6, 1994, p. 7.

Observer (London), May 5, 1968; February 6, 1986, p. 26; July 17, 1988, p. 43.

Philological Quarterly, Volume 62, number 1, 1983.

Punch, May 15, 1968; April 16, 1986, p. 44.

San Francisco Review of Books, summer, 1985, p. 16; January, 1988, p. 34.

Saturday Review, March 21, 1970; July 31, 1973; May-June, 1985.

South Dakota Review, Volume 4, number 2, 1966.

Studies in American Humor, spring, 1983; fall, 1983.

Studies in Medievalism, Volume 2, number 4, 1983.

Time, December 21, 1970; April 7, 1980; October 12, 1981; May 23, 1983; June 17, 1985, p. 76; April 27, 1987, p. 80; April 11, 1988, p. 73; September 11, 1989, p. 82.

Times (London), January 12, 1984.

Times Literary Supplement, September 3, 1982; February 10, 1984; February 21, 1986, p. 198; June 17, 1988, July 22, 1988, p. 802; August 4, 1989, p. 851; April 27, 1990, p. 456.

Tribune Books (Chicago), April 12, 1987, p. 7; April 3, 1988, p. 3; November 19, 1989, p. 6; November 25, 1990, p. 6; July 12, 1992, p. 6; February 13, 1994, p. 5.

Wall Street Journal, February 5, 1979.

Washington Post, April 8, 1970; April 14, 1980; September 14, 1981.

Washington Post Book World, April 20, 1975; September 17, 1978; June 27, 1982; May 15, 1983; August 26, 1984; July 7, 1985, p. 9; April 19, 1987, p. 4; April 17, 1988; September 3, 1989, p. 4; September 16, 1990, p. 15; October 14, 1990, p. 6; June 14, 1992, p. 6; January 30, 1994, p. 3.

Western American Literature, Volume 8, numbers 1-2, 1973; Volume 22, number 4, 1988.
World Literature Today, spring, 1995, p. 360.
Yale Review, winter, 1981.

*   *   *

BERGMAN, David (L.)   1950-

PERSONAL: Born March 13, 1950, in Fitchburg, MA; son of Stanley (an art director) and Rita (a teacher; maiden name, Fergenson) Bergman. *Education:* Kenyon College, B.A., 1972; Johns Hopkins University, M.A., 1974, Ph.D., 1977.

ADDRESSES: Home—3024 North Calvert St., Apt. C5, Baltimore, MD 21218. *Office*—Department of English, Towson State University, Towson, MD 21204. *Agent*—Irene Skolnick, 121 West 27th St., Suite 601, New York, NY 10001.

CAREER: Towson State University, Towson, MD, professor of English, 1978—.

AWARDS, HONORS: George Elliston Poetry Prize, 1985; finalist, Lambda Literary Award, 1995.

WRITINGS:

(With Patricia Plante) *The Turtle and the Two Ducks: Animal Fables From La Fontaine* (juvenile), Crowell (New York City), 1981.
(With Daniel Mark Epstein) *The Heath Guide to Poetry,* Heath (Lexington, MA), 1983.
(With Epstein) *The Heath Guide to Literature,* Heath, 1984, 3rd edition, 1992.
Cracking the Code (poems), Ohio State University Press (Columbus), 1985.
The Story: Readers and Writers of Fiction, Macmillan (New York City), 1988.
(Editor) John Ashbery, *Reported Sightings: Art Chronicles, 1957-87,* Knopf (New York City), 1989.
Gaiety Transfigured: Gay Self-Representation in American Literature, University of Wisconsin Press (Madison), 1991.
(Editor) *Camp Grounds: Style and Homosexuality,* University of Massachusetts Press (Amherst), 1993.
Care and Treatment of Pain (poems), Kairos Editions (Lawrence, KS), 1994.

(Editor) *The Violet Quill Reader: The Emergence of Gay Writing after Stonewall,* St. Martin's (New York City), 1994.
(Editor) *Men on Men 5: The Best Gay Short Fiction,* Dutton/Penguin, 1994.
(Editor) Edmund White, *The Burning Library: Essays,* Knopf, 1994.

Editor, *Men on Men;* member of editorial board, *American Literary History.*

WORK IN PROGRESS: The Violet Quill: Gay Writing between Stonewall and AIDS, for St. Martin's.

SIDELIGHTS: David Bergman told *CA:* "My work has been extremely varied. I am a poet, a critic, a scholar, and an editor. As a critic and scholar, I am engaged in bringing the literature of the past, which might be forgotten or overlooked, to my readers' attention. As the editor of *Men on Men,* I work hard to bring the fiction of young writers to the public. As a poet and essayist, I try to add something worthwhile to the language. As varied as these activities are, they seem to me bound up with one another. Writing does not exist in a vacuum; the creation and appreciation of literature requires both a sense of the vital past and the emerging present and that the work most likely to be preserved in the future is one that has as complete a sense as possible of the resources of language, history, and culture."

*   *   *

BERNSTEIN, Michael Andre   1947-

PERSONAL: Born August 31, 1947, in Innsbruck, Austria; immigrated to Canada, 1956, naturalized citizen, 1956; son of John Vladimir (a diplomat) and Marion (Sklarz) Bernstein; married Jeanne Wolff von Amerongen (a clinical psychologist), November 3, 1980; children: Anna-Nora. *Education:* Princeton University, B.A., 1969; Oxford University, B.Litt., 1973, D.Phil., 1975.

ADDRESSES: Home—44 Highgate Road, Kensington, CA 94707. *Office*—Department of English, University of California, Berkeley, CA 94720.

CAREER: University of California, Berkeley, assistant professor, 1975-81, associate professor, 1981-87, professor of English and comparative literature, 1987—.

AWARDS, HONORS: Danforth fellowship, 1969-75; fellowships from Association of Commonwealth Universities, 1969-73, Canada Council, 1973-75, American Council of Learned Societies, 1977-78 and 1981, and University of California, 1977-89; Koret Israel Prize, 1989; President's Research in the Humanities fellowship, 1991; Guggenheim Memorial fellowship, 1993; American Academy of Arts and Sciences (fellow), 1995.

WRITINGS:

The Tale of the Tribe: Ezra Pound and the Modern Verse Epic, Princeton University Press (Princeton, NJ), 1980.

Prima della Rivoluzione (poems; title means "Before the Revolution"), National Poetry Foundation/University of Maine Press (Orono, ME), 1984.

Bitter Carnival: Ressentiment and the Abject Hero, Princeton University Press, 1992.

Foregone Conclusions: Against Apocalyptic History, University of California Press (Berkeley, CA), 1994.

Contributor to numerous books, including *George Oppen: Man and Poet,* edited by B. Hatlen, National Poetry Foundation/University of Maine Press, 1981; *Ezra Pound and History,* edited by Marianne Korn, National Poetry Foundation/University of Maine Press, 1985; *Bakhtin: Essays and Dialogues on His Work,* edited by Gary Saul Morson, University of Chicago Press (Chicago, IL), 1986; *Ruth Francken: Antlitze,* edited by Wolfgang Horn, Kunsthalle Nuernberg (Nuernberg, Germany), 1986; *Ezra Pound: Modern Critical Views,* edited by Harold Bloom, Chelsea House (New Haven, CT), 1987; *Politics and Poetic Value,* edited by Robert von Hallberg, University of Chicago Press, 1987; *Rethinking Bakhtin: Extensions and Challenges,* edited by Morson and Caryl Emerson, Northwestern University Press (Evanston, IL), 1989; Shimon Attie, *Die Schrift an der Wandt,* Edition Braus (Heidelberg, Germany), 1993, translation published as *The Writings on the Wall: Projections in Berlin's Jewish Quarter,* Edition Braus, 1994; and *World War II: Fifty Years Later,* edited by Alvin Rosenfeld, Indiana University Press (Bloomington, IN), 1995.

Also contributor of critical essays, poems, and reviews to various American and European journals, including *Via, Poetics and Theory of Literature, University Publishing, St. Andrews Review, Yale Review, Critical Inquiry, Sagetrieb, Yeats Annual, TriQuarterly, New Orleans Review, Times Literary Supplement, New Republic, Modern Philology,* and *Modernism/Modernity.*

WORK IN PROGRESS: Progressive Lenses, a novel.

SIDELIGHTS: Michael Andre Bernstein told *CA:* "I consider all of my writing, from my volume of poetry to my three critical works as well as my novel-in-progress to be part of the same constellation of concerns, and in that sense, even part of the same project. The intersection of the imagination with history, and the search for an ethical language that engages moral issues without being moralistic is at the heart of my work.

"My writing stresses that in our culture it is not the attractiveness of extreme risk nor the darkest teachings of violence and domination that are repressed. Exactly these issues have long constituted an enormous, if not actually the major, portion of our intellectual conversation about history as well as about the human psyche. What *is* repressed, though, is the value of the quotidian, the counter-authenticity of the texture and rhythm of our daily routines and decisions, the myriad of minute and careful adjustments that we are ready to offer in the interest of a habitable social world. It is those adjustments, the moment-by-moment way we experience our lives and make our plans that most grip my imagination and inspire all of my writing."

BIOGRAPHICAL/CRITICAL SOURCES:

PERIODICALS

Times Literary Supplement, March 6, 1981.

*   *   *

BIERHORST, John (William)   1936-

PERSONAL: Born September 2, 1936, in Boston, MA; son of John William and Sadie Belle (Knott) Bierhorst; married Jane Elizabeth Byers (a graphic designer), June 25, 1965; children: Alice Byers. *Education:* Cornell University, B.A., 1958.

ADDRESSES: Home—Box 10, West Shokan, NY 12494.

CAREER: Writer. Former concert pianist; became attracted to the study of Native American cultures during a botanical field trip to Peru in 1964; subsequently visited pre-Columbian sites in Yucatan and Mexico.

MEMBER: American Folklore Society, American Anthropological Association.

AWARDS, HONORS: Grants from Center for Inter-American Relations, 1972 and 1979, National Endowment for the Humanities, 1979 and 1986, and National Endowment for the Arts, 1986. American Library Association notable book citations for *In the Trail of the Wind: American Indian Poems and Ritual Orations, Black Rainbow: Legends of the Incas and Myths of Ancient Peru, The Girl Who Married a Ghost: Tales from the North American Indian, A Cry from the Earth: Music of the North American Indians, The Whistling Skeleton: American Indian Tales of the Supernatural, The Sacred Path: Spells, Prayers, and Power Songs of the American Indians, Spirit Child: A Story of the Nativity,* and *The Naked Bear: Folktales of the Iroquois.*

WRITINGS:

A Cry from the Earth: Music of the North American Indians, Four Winds (Bristol, FL), 1979.
(Translator) *The Glass Slipper: Charles Perrault's Tales of Times Past,* Four Winds, 1981.
(Translator) *Spirit Child: A Story of the Nativity,* Morrow (New York City), 1984.
A Nahuatl-English Dictionary, Stanford University Press (Stanford, CA), 1985.
The Mythology of North America, Morrow, 1985.
The Mythology of South America, Morrow, 1988.
The Mythology of Mexico and Central America, Morrow, 1990.
Codex Chimalpopoca: The Text in Nahuatl with a Glossary and Grammatical Notes, University of Arizona Press (Tucson), 1992.
(Translator) *History and Mythology of the Aztecs: The Codex Chimalpopoca,* University of Arizona Press, 1992.
The Way of the Earth: Native America and the Environment, Morrow, 1994.
Mythology of the Lenape: Guide and Texts, University of Arizona Press, 1995.

EDITOR

The Fire Plume: Legends of the American Indians, Dial (New York City), 1969.
The Ring in the Prairie: A Shawnee Legend, Dial, 1970.

In the Trail of the Wind: American Indian Poems and Ritual Orations, Farrar, Straus (New York City), 1971.
Four Masterworks of American Indian Literature: "Quetzalcoatl," "The Ritual of Condolence," "Cuceb," "The Night Chant," Farrar, Straus, 1974.
Songs of the Chippewa, Farrar, Straus, 1974.
The Red Swan: Myths and Tales of the American Indians, Farrar, Straus, 1976.
(And translator) *Black Rainbow: Legends of the Incas and Myths of Ancient Peru,* Farrar, Straus, 1976.
The Girl Who Married a Ghost: Tales from the North American Indian, Four Winds, 1978.
The Whistling Skeleton: American Indian Tales of the Supernatural, Four Winds, 1982.
(And translator) *The Sacred Path: Spells, Prayers, and Power Songs of the American Indians,* Morrow, 1983.
The Hungry Woman: Myths and Legends of the Aztecs, Morrow, 1984.
(And translator) *Cantares Mexicanos: Songs of the Aztecs,* Stanford University Press, 1985.
(And translator) *The Monkey's Haircut and Other Stories Told by the Maya,* Morrow, 1986.
The Naked Bear: Folktales of the Iroquois, Morrow, 1987.
Doctor Coyote: A Native American Aesop's Fables, Macmillan (New York City), 1987.
Lightning Inside You and Other Native American Riddles, Morrow, 1992.
The Woman Who Fell from the Sky: The Iroquois Story of Creation, Morrow, 1993.
On the Road of Stars: Native American Night Poems and Sleep Charms, Macmillan, 1994.
The White Deer and Other Stories Told by the Lenape, Morrow, 1995.

OTHER

Also editorial associate for *The Norton Anthology of World Masterpieces, Expanded Edition,* edited by Maynard Mack, Norton (New York City), 1995; editorial advisor for the Smithsonian Series of Studies in Native American Literatures, 1990—.

BIOGRAPHICAL/CRITICAL SOURCES:

PERIODICALS

Los Angeles Times Book Review, March 11, 1984.
New York Times Book Review, January 31, 1982; September 1, 1985; November 22, 1987; October 2, 1988.

Times Literary Supplement, April 18, 1986.
Washington Post Book World, March 14, 1982.

*   *   *

BIRCH, Bruce C(harles) 1941-

PERSONAL: Born December 3, 1941, in Wichita, KS; son of Lauren (a machinist) and Marjory (Roberts) Birch; married Susan Halse; children: Jeremy, Rebecca; stepchildren: Ehren, Anna. *Education:* Southwestern College, B.A., 1962; Southern Methodist University, B.D. (with honors), 1965; Yale University, M.A., 1967, M.Phil., 1968, Ph.D., 1970.

ADDRESSES: Home—328A S. Jefferson St., Middletown, MD 21769. *Office*—Department of Old Testament, Wesley Theological Seminary, 4500 Massachusetts Ave. NW, Washington, DC 20016.

CAREER: Ordained clergymember of United Methodist Church, 1963. Iowa Wesleyan College, Mount Pleasant, IA, instructor, 1968-69, assistant professor of religion, 1969-70; Erskine College, Due West, SC, assistant professor of Bible and religion, 1970-71; Wesley Theological Seminary, Washington, DC, assistant professor, 1971-73, associate professor, 1973-76, professor of Old Testament, 1976—; Palmer Lecturer at University of Puget Sound, 1976.

Chair of National Interseminary Council, 1964-76; chair of national faculty advisory committee, Bishop's Call for Peace and Self-Development of Peoples, 1974-80. Member of board of directors, Washington International College, 1971-74, and International Program for Human Resources Development, 1975-85. Member of United Methodist Board of Ordained Ministry, 1975-84, North American regional committee, St. George's College, Jerusalem, 1976—, and General Board of Church and Society, United Methodist Church, 1980-88.

MEMBER: Society of Biblical Literature (president of Chesapeake Bay region, 1975-76; chair of section on Old Testament theology, 1980-88; cochair of section on Feminist Hermeneutics of the Bible, 1989-93), American Academy of Religion.

AWARDS, HONORS: Woodrow Wilson fellow, 1965-66, 1967-68; research fellow, Association of Theological Scholars, 1977-78.

WRITINGS:

(With Larry Rasmussen) *Bible and Ethics in the Christian Life,* Augsburg (Minneapolis, MN), 1976, revised edition, 1989.
The Rise of the Israelite Monarchy: The Growth and Development of First Samuel, 7-15 (monograph), Scholars Press (Missoula, MT), 1976.
(With Rasmussen) *Predicament of the Prosperous,* Westminster (Philadelphia, PA), 1978.
Singing the Lord's Song: A Study of Isaiah 40-55, Board of Global Ministries, 1981.
What Does the Lord Require? The Old Testament Call to Social Witness, Westminster, 1985.
Let Justice Roll Down: The Old Testament Ethics and Christian Life, Westminster/John Knox, 1991.
To Love As We Are Loved: The Bible and Relationships, Abingdon (Nashville, TN), 1992.

Contributor to *New International Standard Bible Encyclopedia.* Also contributor to various books, including *Living Simply: An Examination of Christian Lifestyles,* edited by D. Crean, Seabury (New York City), 1981; *Social Themes of the Christian Year,* edited by D. Hessel, Geneva Press, 1983; *Wesleyan Theology Today,* edited by T. Runyon, Kingswood, 1985; *A Guide to Contemporary Hermeneutics,* edited by D. McKim, Eerdmans (Grand Rapids, MI), 1986; *The Congregation: Its Power to Form and Transform,* edited by C. Ellis Nelson, John Knox (Atlanta, GA), 1988; *Canon, Theology, and Old Testament Interpretation,* edited by Gene M. Tucker (and others), Fortress (Philadelphia), 1988; and *The Bible Book by Book,* edited by B. Anderson, Macmillan (New York City), 1988. Also contributor of articles and reviews to theology journals.

WORK IN PROGRESS: Hosea, Joel, Amos: The Westminster Companion to the Bible 1 and 2 Samuel, The New Interpreters Bible, and (with others) *The Old Testament: A Theological Introduction.*

BIOGRAPHICAL/CRITICAL SOURCES:

PERIODICALS

United Methodist Reporter, February 20, 1976.
U.S. News and World Report, February 9, 1976.

BISSET, Donald   1910-1995

PERSONAL: Born August 30, 1910, in London, England; died August 10, 1995; married wife, Nancy, 1946 (divorced); children: one son. *Education:* Attended Warehousemen, Clerks, and Drapers School, Addington, Surrey, England. *Avocational interests:* Horseback riding.

CAREER: Author and illustrator of children's books. Radio, television, and stage actor; appeared with the National Theatre and Royal Shakespeare Theatre companies; appeared in the television film *Henry VIII,* New York City, and in *The Great Waltz,* Drury Lane Theatre, London, both 1971. *Military service:* British Royal Artillery, 1940-46; became lieutenant.

WRITINGS:

CHILDREN'S FICTION; SELF-ILLUSTRATED

Anytime Stories, Faber & Faber (Winchester, MA), 1954, Transatlantic (Albuquerque, NM), 1955.
Sometime Stories, Faber & Faber, 1957.
Next Time Stories, Methuen (New York City), 1959.
This Time Stories, Methuen, 1961.
Another Time Stories, Methuen, 1963.
Talks with a Tiger, Methuen, 1967.
Nothing, Benn, 1969.
Time and Again Stories, Methuen, 1970.
Tiger Wants More, Methuen, 1971.
Father Tingtang's Journey, Methuen, 1973.
The Adventures of Mandy Duck, Methuen, 1974.
"Oh Dear," Said the Tiger, Methuen, 1975.
The Lost Birthday, Progress Publishers, 1976.
The Story of Smokey Horse, Methuen, 1977.
This Is Ridiculous, Beaver Publications (Beaverton, OR), 1977.
The Adventures of Yak, Methuen, 1978.
What Time Is It When It Isn't?, Methuen, 1980.
Johnny Here and There, Methuen, 1981.
The Joyous Adventures of Snakey Boo, Methuen, 1982.
Sleep Tight, Snakey Boo!, Methuen, 1985.

CHILDREN'S FICTION

Little Bear's Pony, illustrated by Shirley Hughes, Benn, 1966.
Hullo Lucy, illustrated by Gillian Kenny, Benn, 1967.
Kangaroo Tennis, illustrated by Val Biro, Benn, 1968.

Benjie the Circus Dog, illustrated by Biro, Benn, 1969.
Upside Down Land, Progress Publishers, 1969.
Barcha the Tiger, illustrated by Derek Collard, Benn, 1971.
Yak and the Sea Shell, illustrated by Lorraine Calaora, Methuen, 1971.
Yak and the Painted Cave, illustrated by Calaora, Methuen, 1971.
Yak and the Buried Treasure, illustrated by Calaora, Methuen, 1972.
Yak and the Ice Cream, illustrated by Calaora, Methuen, 1972.
Jenny Hopalong, illustrated by Collard, Benn, 1973.
Yak Goes Home, illustrated by Calaora, Methuen, 1973.
The Happy Horse, illustrated by David Sharpe, Benn, 1974.
Baby Crow Learns to Fly, Benn, 1975.
Hazy Mountain, illustrated by Hughes, Kestrel, 1975.
(With Michael Morris) *Paws with Numbers,* illustrated by Tony Hutchins, Intercontinental Books, 1976.
Paws with Shapes, illustrated by Hutchins, Intercontinental Books, 1976.
Journey to the Jungle, Beaver Publications, 1977.
The Hedgehog Who Rolled Uphill, Methuen, 1982.
Just a Moment!, Methuen, 1987.
Ogg, illustrated by Amelia Rosato, Methuen, 1987.
Upside Down Stories, Puffin (New York City), 1987.
Please Yourself, Methuen, 1991.

OTHER

Also author of *Cornelia and Other Stories,* 1980. Writer for the animated television series *Yak,* 1971.

Bisset's books have been translated into sixteen languages.

SIDELIGHTS: "All my books are modern fairy stories—animistic in concept—and, on the surface, nonsensical, but nevertheless they have meanings (varied)," British children's author and illustrator Donald Bisset told Stephanie Nettell in *Twentieth-Century Children's Writers.* This formula led to a successful career during which Bisset produced nearly forty children's books. Nettell praised Bisset's "spiky little childlike drawings," engaging use of language, and appealing characters, concluding that "innocence is the essential quality of all Donald Bisset's work—a pure, shining, quite unselfconscious innocence that finds a delighted response in a small child's mind and has an extraordinary *cleansing* effect in an adult's." Liz Waterland described the reaction of a group of young children to Bisset's *Upside Down Stories* in *Books for Keeps:* "They fell about with laughing and then fought to read them themselves. A palpable hit!"

Bisset's work includes many collections of nonsense animal stories for very young children, one of which is *The Hedgehog Who Rolled Uphill.* In addition to the title character, this book features an elephant who has trouble sleeping and a crocodile who loves to sing. "The author's lively style makes the book ideal for reading aloud," according to a *British Book News* reviewer. Writing in the *Times Educational Supplement,* Will Harris noted that Bisset's stories "somehow capture the freshness and illogicality and zest of a child's imagination."

The Joyous Adventures of Snakey Boo, which features illustrations by Bisset, is told in short episodes that incorporate jokes, puzzles, and rhymes. The title character is a snake who is the captain of a steamboat, *Foley Bridge,* which really wants to be a houseboat. Snakey Boo's crew consists of a number of other animals with funny problems and habits. In a review for the *Times Literary Supplement,* Nettell stated that Bisset's "voice speaks from the page as captivatingly as his drawings." Bisset continued the adventures of Snakey Boo in 1985 with *Sleep Tight, Snakey Boo!*

BIOGRAPHICAL/CRITICAL SOURCES:

BOOKS

Twentieth-Century Children's Writers, 4th edition, St. James Press (Detroit), 1995.

PERIODICALS

Books for Keeps, January, 1986, p. 14; March, 1988, p. 17.
British Book News, autumn, 1982, p. 18; March, 1986, p. 27; June, 1987, p. 11.
Growing Point, May, 1981, p. 3875; April, 1983, p. 73.
Junior Bookshelf, August, 1980, p. 172; October, 1981, p. 193.
Times Educational Supplement, June 18, 1982, p. 28.
Times Literary Supplement, January 31, 1986, p. 126.*

BLAKE, Gerald H(enry) 1936-

PERSONAL: Born February 1, 1936, in Southampton, England; son of Geoffrey Thomas (a master mariner) and Grace (Dibben) Blake; married Brenda Jane Peach (a college lecturer), April 17, 1965; children: Robert, Carolyn, Julia. *Education:* St. Edmund Hall, Oxford, B.A. (with honors), 1960; Oxford University, M.A., 1960; University of Southampton, Ph.D., 1964. *Avocational interests:* Travel, rowing, maritime museums.

ADDRESSES: Home—Principal's House, Collingwood College, University of Durham, Durham DH1 3LT, England. *Office*—International Boundaries Research Unit, University of Durham, Mountjoy Centre, Durham DH1 3UR, England.

CAREER: St. John's College, Johannesburg, South Africa, schoolteacher, 1960-61; University of Durham, Durham, England, lecturer, 1964-75, reader, 1975-94, professor, 1994—, principal of Collingwood College and director of International Boundaries Research Unit, 1987—. Justice of the peace for county of Durham, 1972—. *Military service:* Gold Coast Regiment, 1954-56; became second lieutenant.

MEMBER: British Society for Middle Eastern Studies (fellow), Royal Geographical Society (fellow).

WRITINGS:

(With P. Beaumont and J. M. Wagstaff) *The Middle East: A Geographical Study,* Wiley (New York City), 1976, Fulton, 2nd edition, 1988.
(With A. D. Drysdale) *The Middle East and North Africa: Political Geography,* Oxford University Press (New York City), 1985.
(With J. C. Dewdney and J. K. Mitchell) *Cambridge Atlas of the Middle East and North Africa,* Cambridge University Press (New York City), 1987.
(Editor) *Maritime Boundaries and Ocean Resources,* Croom Helm, 1987.
(Editor with R. N. Schofield) *Arabian Boundaries, 1853-1957,* 30 volumes, Archive Editions (Buckinghamshire, England), 1988.
Maritime Boundaries (volume 5 of "World Boundaries" series), Routledge (London and New York City), 1994.
(Editor with M. A. Pratt and others) *The Peaceful Management of Transboundary Resources,* Graham and Trotman, 1995.

WORK IN PROGRESS: Edited edition of Captain Kelly's diary (Sudan-Uganda Boundary Commission, 1913).

SIDELIGHTS: Gerald H. Blake told *CA:* "The Middle East is one of the world's most vital regions, and one of the most misunderstood. My books have sought to highlight some of the geographical realities which underpin political events in the area. My latest research concerns the origins and evolution of land and maritime boundaries between states: while many are the product of an earlier imperial age, others remain to be drawn, especially at sea."

*   *   *

BLAKE, Olive
  See SUPRANER, Robyn

*   *   *

BLAKELY, Allison   1940-

PERSONAL: Born March 31, 1940, in Clinton, AL; son of Ed Walton (a farmer) and Alice Blakely (a seamstress); married Shirley Ann Reynolds (a nutritional scientist), July 5, 1968; children: Shantel, Andrei. *Education:* University of Oregon, B.A., 1962; University of California, Berkeley, M.A., 1964, Ph.D., 1971.

ADDRESSES: Home—1 Sunnyside Road, Silver Spring, MD 20910. *Office*—Department of History, Howard University, Washington, DC 20059.

CAREER: Stanford University, Stanford, CA, instructor in history, 1970-71; Howard University, Washington, DC, assistant professor, 1971-77, associate professor, 1977-87, professor of history, 1987—. Member of test development committee of Educational Testing Service, 1984-88; member of board of directors of National History Day, Inc., College Park, MD. *Military service:* U.S. Army, 1966-68; became captain; received Bronze Star and Purple Heart.

MEMBER: World History Association, American Historical Association, American Association for the Advancement of Slavic Studies, American Association for Netherlandic Studies, Association for the Study of Negro Life and History, Phi Beta Kappa (member of governing Senate).

AWARDS, HONORS: Andrew Mellon fellow, 1976-77; Fulbright fellow, 1985-86; Ford Foundation fellow, 1987-88; American Book Award, 1988.

WRITINGS:

Russia and the Negro: Blacks in Russian History and Thought, Howard University Press (Washington, DC), 1987.
Blacks in the Dutch World: The Evolution of Racial Imagery in a Modern Society, Indiana University Press (Bloomington), 1994.

Contributor to books, including *Latin American Populism in Comparative Perspective,* edited by Michael Conniff, University of New Mexico Press (Albuquerque), 1982; and *Modern Encyclopedia of Russian and Soviet History.* Also contributor to history and black studies journals.

WORK IN PROGRESS: A book on the history of democracy in Russia.

SIDELIGHTS: Allison Blakely told *CA:* "My research and writing have centered on topics which I consider very important, but which have been neglected. This is true of Russian populism, which I view as the prototype for twentieth-century revolutionary movements. The role and significance of blacks in European history and culture is also neglected. Russia and the Netherlands are both countries of global importance which have been omitted in previous studies of this subject."

*   *   *

BLANE, Howard T(homas)   1926-

PERSONAL: Born May 10, 1926, in De Land, FL; son of Chesley Thomas and Olive (van Heest) Blane; married Eleanor Peckham (an illustrator), December 27, 1958 (divorced, 1989); children: Benjamin Thomas, Eva Ann. *Education:* Harvard University, A.B. (cum laude), 1950; Clark University, M.A., 1951, Ph.D., 1957. *Politics:* Independent. *Religion:* None.

ADDRESSES: Office—Research Institute on Addictions, 1021 Main St., Buffalo, NY 14203-1016.

CAREER: Massachusetts General Hospital, Boston, research assistant, 1953-54; Children's Medical Center, Boston, clinical research psychologist, 1954-56; Massachusetts General Hospital, research fellow, 1956-57, assistant psychologist, 1957-62, associate psychologist, 1962-70; Harvard University, Medical School, Boston, instructor, 1957-61, research associate, 1961-65, associate, 1965-67, assistant professor of psychology, 1968-70; University of Pittsburgh, Pittsburgh, PA, associate professor, 1970-72, professor of education and psychology, 1972-86, research professor of epidemiology, 1978-86; Research Institute on Addictions, Buffalo, NY, director, 1986—; State University of New York at Buffalo, research professor of psychology, 1986—, research professor of psychiatry, 1989—, research professor of social and preventive medicine, 1995—.

Psychotherapist in private practice, 1957-70, 1980-85. Assistant in social work, Simmons College, 1955-58. Field supervisor of research training program for social scientists, Massachusetts Division of Alcoholism, 1961-70; visiting research fellow at Social Science Research Institute, University of Hawaii, 1968-69. Vice president and board member, Health Education Foundation, Washington, DC, 1975—; member of educational advisory council, Distilled Spirits Council of the United States, Washington, DC, 1976-79; associate director, National Clearinghouse for Alcohol Information, 1979-80. Manuscript reviewer for Allyn & Bacon, Plenum Press, and University Park Press, all 1976—. Consultant to mental health organizations.

MEMBER: American Psychological Association (fellow), American Psychological Society (fellow), American Association for the Advancement of Science, Research Foundation for Mental Hygiene (member, board of directors, 1986—), Jellinek Memorial Fund (member, board of directors, 1994—), Research Society on Alcoholism, New York Academy of Science, Sigma Xi.

AWARDS, HONORS: Recipient of grants from various organizations, including National Institute of Mental Health, National Science Foundation, National Institute on Alcohol Abuse and Alcoholism, National Institute of Justice, Robert Wood Johnson Foundation, and Dupont-Merck Pharmaceutical Company.

WRITINGS:

The Personality of the Alcoholic: Guises of Dependency, Harper (New York City), 1968.
(With M. E. Chafetz and M. J. Hill) *Frontiers of Alcoholism,* Science House, 1970.
(Editor with Chafetz) *Youth, Alcohol, and Social Policy,* Plenum (New York City), 1979.
(Editor with K. E. Leonard) *Psychological Theories of Drinking and Alcoholism,* Guilford (New York City), 1987.

Contributor to various books, including *The Child: A Book of Readings,* edited by Jerome M. Seidman, Rinehart (Boulder, CO), 1958; *Current Studies in Psychology,* edited by F. J. McGuigan and A. Calvin, Appleton-Century-Crofts (Norwalk, CT), 1958; *Human Development: Selected Readings,* edited by M. L. Haimowitz and N. R. Haimowitz, Cromwell, 1960; *The Clinical Interpretation of Psychological Tests,* edited by J. Muller, Little, Brown (Boston), 1966; *Clinical Research in Alcoholism,* edited by J. O. Cole, American Psychiatric Association (Washington, DC), 1968; *Alcoholism,* edited by R. J. Catanzaro, Thomas, 1968; *Recent Advances in Studies of Alcoholism,* edited by N. Mello and J. Mendelson, National Institute of Mental Health, 1971; *Prevention of Alcohol Problems,* by R. Room, University of California Press (Berkeley), 1976; *Alcoholism: Development, Consequences, and Interventions,* edited by N. J. Estes and M. E. Heinemann, Mosby (St. Louis, MO), 1977, 3rd edition, 1986; *Controversies in the Addictions Field,* edited by R. C. Eng, Kendall-Hunt (Dubuque, IA), 1990; and *Recent Developments in Alcoholism,* edited by M. Galanter, Plenum, 1993.

Coeditor of Substance Abuse Series, Guilford Press, 1979—. Editorial reviewer for over a dozen medical journals since 1966, including *American Psychologist, Journal of Nervous and Mental Disease,* and *Science. Journal of Studies on Alcohol,* field editor, 1983-84, member of editorial board, 1983-92, associate editor, 1992—; member of editorial advisory board, *Alcohol Health and Research World,* 1986-89.

WORK IN PROGRESS: "Working on the second edition of *Psychological Theories of Drinking and*

Alcoholism to bring readers up-to-date on the exciting advances that have occurred in this field during the past decade."

*   *   *

BLAU, Francine D(ee)   1946-

PERSONAL: Born August 29, 1946, in New York, NY; daughter of Harold (an educator) and Sylvia (Goldberg) Blau; married Richard Weisskoff, August, 1969 (divorced, June, 1972); married Lawrence M. Kahn (a college professor), January 1, 1979; children: (second marriage) Daniel Blau Kahn, Lisa Blau Kahn. *Education:* Cornell University, B.S., 1966; Harvard University, M.A., 1969, Ph.D., 1975.

ADDRESSES: Home—Ithaca, NY. *Office*—School of Industrial and Labor Relations, Cornell University, 265 Ives Hall, Ithaca, NY 14853-3901.

CAREER: Yale University, New Haven, CT, visiting lecturer in economics, spring, 1971; Trinity College, Hartford, CT, instructor in economics, 1971-74; Ohio State University, Columbus, research associate at Center for Human Resource Research, 1974-75; University of Illinois, Urbana-Champaign, assistant professor, 1975-78, associate professor, 1978-83, professor of economics and labor and industrial relations, 1983-94, associate of Center for Advanced Study, 1988; Cornell University, School of Industrial and Labor Relations, Ithaca, NY, Frances Perkins Professor of Industrial and Labor Relations, 1994—, research director, 1995—, co-director of Institute for Labor Market Policies, 1995—. Research associate, National Bureau of Economic Research, Inc., Cambridge, MA, 1988—; visiting fellow, Australian National University, Canberra, 1993.

Has given keynote addresses, delivered lectures, and presented papers at symposia, annual meetings, and conferences; conference organizer and panelist. Testified before New York City Human Rights Commission, 1975, subcommittee on Civil and Constitutional Rights of the Judiciary Committee of the U.S. House of Representatives, 1983, and Select Committee on Children, Youth, and Families of the U.S. House of Representatives, 1986; consultant to U.S. Commission on Civil Rights, Equal Employment Opportunity Commission, and Agency for International Develop-

ment. Referee for more than twenty-five periodicals; grant reviewer for National Science Foundation, National Institute of Education, Social Science research Council, and Social Sciences and Humanities Research Council of Canada. Consultant to numerous government and private organizations.

MEMBER: American Economic Association (vice-president, 1993), National Academy of Sciences (member of panel on Technology and Women's Employment, 1983-86; member of panel on Pay Equity Research, 1985—), Industrial Relations Research Association (member of executive board, 1987-89; president-elect, 1995), Population Association of America, Midwest Economics Association (vice president, 1983-84; member of executive committee, 1990-93; president, 1991-92), Phi Kappa Phi, Pi Gamma Mu, Pi Delta Epsilon.

AWARDS, HONORS: Grants from U.S. Department of Labor's Employment and Training Administration, 1977-78, 1979-80; Ford Foundation grant, 1988-89, 1990-92; University of Illinois at Urbana-Champaign, named best graduate instructor in Economics Department, 1981, Kinkead Research Fellowship, 1991-92, 1992-93; University of Illinois, named best faculty teacher in undergraduate instruction in Economics Department, 1976, Burlington Northern Faculty Achievement Award, 1993, for outstanding teaching and research.

WRITINGS:

(With Adele Simmons, Ann Freedman, and Margaret Dunkle) *Exploitation from Nine to Five: Report of the Twentieth Century Fund Task Force on Women and Employment,* Lexington Books (Lexington, MA), 1975.

Equal Pay in the Office, Lexington Books, 1977.

(With husband, Lawrence M. Kahn) *Race and Sex Differences in the Probability and Consequences of Turnover,* Employment and Training Administration, U.S. Department of Labor, 1979.

(With Kahn) *The Determinants and Consequences of Obtaining Unionized Employment,* Employment and Training Administration, U.S. Department of Labor, 1980.

Occupational Segregation and Labor Market Discrimination: A Critical Review, National Academy of Sciences (Washington, DC), 1982.

(With Heidi Hartmann and others) *Computer Chips and Paper Clips: Technology and Women's Em-*

ployment, National Academy Press (Washington, DC), 1986.

(With Marianne A. Ferber) *The Economics of Women, Men and Work,* Prentice-Hall (Englewood Cliffs, NJ), 1986, 2nd edition, 1992.

Contributor to numerous books, including *Contemporary Brazil: Issues in Economic and Political Development,* edited by H. Jon Rosenbaum and William Tyler, Praeger (New York City), 1972; *Women: A Feminist Perspective,* edited by Jo Freeman, 3rd edition, Mayfield, 1984; *Women's Studies Encyclopedia,* edited by Helen Tierney, Greenwood Press (Westport, CT), 1988; and (with Kahn) *Differences and Changes in Wage Structures,* edited by Lawrence Katz and Richard Freeman, University of Chicago Press (Chicago), 1995. Contributor of numerous articles and reviews to periodicals, including *American Economic Review, Quarterly Journal of Economics, Industrial and Labor Relations Review, Southern Economic Journal, Journal of Human Resources, Economic Inquiry,* and *Journal of Economic Literature.* Co-editor, *Journal of Labor Economics,* 1992-95; associate editor, *Journal of Economic Perspectives,* 1994—; member of editorial board, *Social Science Quarterly,* 1978-94, *Signs: Journal of Women in Culture and Society,* 1979—, *Women and Work,* 1983—, *Industrial Relations,* 1989—, and *Feminist Economics,* 1994—; consulting editor, *Women's Studies Encyclopedia,* 1985—.

WORK IN PROGRESS: Research on trends in the male-female pay gap, occupational segregation, wage inequality, and international comparisons.

SIDELIGHTS: Francine D. Blau once told *CA:* "An important motivating factor in much of my research has been a desire to better understand the causes of sex and race inequality in the labor market. Such an understanding is crucial to the formulation of social policies that can lessen these inequities."

*   *   *

BLOM, Karl Arne   1946-
   (Bo Lagevi)

PERSONAL: Born January 22, 1946, in Naessjoe, Sweden; son of Karl Axel (a hotel owner) and Ester (Skoeld) Blom; married Karin Ann-Marie Gyllen (a nurse), June 29, 1969; children: Karl Anders Bertil, Kristina Magdalena, Katarina Elisabet. *Education:* University of Lund, B.A., 1972. *Politics:* "Liberal, cosmopolitan, anti-Communist." *Religion:* Catholic.

ADDRESSES: Home and office—Smaaskolevaegen 22, S-224 67 Lund, Sweden. *Agent*—Lennart Sane, Hollaendareplan 9, S-37434 Karlshamn, Sweden; Norstedts foerlag, P.O. Box 2052, S-10312 Stockholm, Sweden.

CAREER: Author and translator; freelance writer, 1970-75.

MEMBER: International Association of Crime Writers (president, 1994-97), Crime Writers Association of Scandinavia, Union of Swedish Authors, Swedish Academy of Detection, Society of Detective Story Writers of Skane (honorary chair), Mystery Writers of America, Crime Writers Association (England), Poe Club (Denmark).

AWARDS, HONORS: Sherlock Award from *Expressen* (newspaper), 1974, for *The Moment of Truth.*

WRITINGS:

Sanningens oegonblick, AWE/Gebers, 1974, translation by Erik J. Friis published as *The Moment of Truth,* Harper (New York City), 1977.
Smartgransen, AWE/Gebers, 1978, translation by Joan Tate published as *The Limits of Pain,* Ram Publishing (Salt Lake City, UT), 1979.

IN SWEDISH

Naagon borde soerja (title means "Somebody Should Mourn"), AWE/Gebers, 1971.
Naagon aer skyldig (title means "Somebody Is Guilty"), AWE/Gebers, 1972.
Naagon slog tillbaka (title means "Somebody Hit Back"), AWE/Gebers, 1973.
Ett gammalt mord (title means "An Old Murder"), Gleerups, 1974.
(Editor) *Brottpunkter* (title means "Murderous Points"), Lindqvist, 1975.
Vaaldets triumf (title means "Triumph of Violence"), AWE/Gebers, 1975.
Resan till ingenstans (stories; title means "Journey into Nowhere"), Zindermans, 1975.
Lund, Hermods, 1975.

(Editor) *Skaanska Brottstycken* (title means "Pieces of Crimes"), Bra Deckare, 1976.

Kortaste straaet (title means "Second Best"), Lindqvist, 1976.

Noedhamm (title means "Harbor of Refuge"), Lindqvist, 1976.

Lyckligt lottade (title means "The Happy People"), AWE/Gebers, 1976.

(Under pseudonym Bo Lagevi) *Allt vad du gjort mot naagon* (title means "All the Things You Did"), B. Wahlstroem, 1976.

Noedvaern (novel; title means "Self-Defense"), Zinderman, 1977.

40 [degrees] Kallti Solen (stories; title means "40 Degrees Cold in the Sun"), Zindermans, 1977.

Frihetssoekarna (title means "Searchers of Freedom"), AWE/Gebers, 1977.

(Under pseudonym Bo Lagevi) *Utan personligt ansvar* (title means "Without Personal Responsibility"), B. Wahlstroem, 1977.

Det var en gang (title means "Once upon a Time"), AWE/Gebers, 1978.

Mannen i granden (title means "The Man in the Alley"), AWE/Gebers, 1979.

Bristningspunkten (title means "The Breaking Point"), AWE/Gebers, 1979.

Kvinnan pa bussen (title means "The Woman on the Bus"), AWE/Gebers, 1980.

Noedvandigt Ont (title means "Justified Evilness"), AWE/Gebers, 1980.

Mordanglarna (title means "The Murderous Angels"), AWE/Gebers, 1981.

Med andra ogon (title means "A Point of View"), AWE/Gebers, 1981.

Nattbok (title means "Nightbrook"), AWE/Gebers, 1982.

Ingenmansland (title means "No Man's Land"), AWE/Gebers, 1982.

Utvagen (title means "The Way Out"), AWE/Gebers, 1983.

Aterresan (title means "The Way Out"), AWE/Gebers, 1983.

Aendamalet (title means "The Purpose"), AWE/Gebers, 1984.

Oevertaget (title means "The Advantage"), AWE/Gebers, 1985.

Madonna, AWE/Gebers, 1986.

Krigsbarn (title means "Child of War"), AWE/Gebers, 1987.

Skuggan av en stoevel (title means "The Shadow of a Boot"), AWE/Gebers, 1988.

Siste turisten i Europa (title means "The Last Tourist in Europe"), AWE/Gebers, 1989.

Svarta aenglar i Berlin (title means "Black Angels in Berlin"), AWE/Gebers, 1990.

Lilla Marlene (title means "Little Marlene"), AWE/Gebers, 1991.

Stormcentrum (title means "The Center of the Storm"), Norstedts, 1992.

Noedslakt (title means "Slaughter of Necessity"), Norstedts, 1993.

Ingenstans i Sverige (title means "Nowhere in Sweden"), Norstedts, 1994.

Offerlamm (title means "Sacrificial Lamb"), Norstedts, 1995.

TRANSLATOR INTO SWEDISH

Jack Higgins, *Bikten* (title means "A Prayer for the Dying"), Lindqvist, 1975.

Emilie Gaboriau, *Den lille mannen i Batignolles* (title means "The Little Man in Batignolles") Lindqvist, 1975.

Arthur Conan Doyle, *En studie i roett* (title means "A Study in Scarlet"), AWE/Gebers, 1977.

Hanning Hjuler, *Raattorna* (title means "The Rats"), Bra Deckare, 1977.

Doyle, *Silverblaesen* (title means "The Memoirs of Sherlock Holmes"), AWE/Gebers, 1977.

Det tomma huset (title means "The Return of Sherlock Holmes"), AWE/Gebers, 1978.

Den doende detehtiven (title means "His Last Bow"), AWE/Gebers, 1978.

Den krypande mannen (title means "The Casebook of Sherlock Holmes"), AWE/Gebers, 1978.

Translator into Swedish of numerous mystery novels written by Stanley Ellin, R. R. Irvine, Loren Singer, Joe L. Hensley, Newton Thornburg, Lawrence Treat, and Hillary Waugh.

OTHER

Author of material for television series and several books on historic topics. Contributor of articles and stories to magazines.

SIDELIGHTS: Karl Arne Blom once wrote *CA:* "So far most of what I have written is crime novels . . . because this is the kind of novel by which you can best describe and try to analyze time, society, and human beings. I try to tell about our time—people as they are now and the problems people are facing in a Swedish so-called welfare society. My other novels and most of my short stories are efforts to describe the surrealistic and absurd realities of life.

"I regard the mystery genre as not inferior to so-called real literature. In my opinion a crime novel, a mystery, or whatever it happens to be, can be as good a book as any book of fiction. . . . A good mystery or crime novel is like an iceberg. You see what's on the surface and a lot of things are hidden.

"My first three books deal with crime and murder and violence. But the first one is also a book about how lonely people can be when they are apparently among many others. The second one is about the economic problems students are facing, and the third one is about unemployment among students with degrees. From there on I have dealt with the basic elements of violence among people, with violence in our time and how violence has become almost a natural way of expressing oneself."

*   *   *

BLUM, William (Henry)   1933-

PERSONAL: Born March 6, 1933, in Brooklyn, NY; son of Isadore (a factory worker) and Ruth (maiden name, Katz) Blum; married Adelheid Zoefel (a translator); children: Alexander. *Education:* City College (now City College of the City University of New York), B.B.A., 1955. *Politics:* Socialist.

ADDRESSES: Home—5100 Connecticut Ave. NW #707, Washington, DC 20008.

CAREER: Accountant in New York City, 1955-60; International Business Machines Corp., New York City, computer systems analyst and programmer, 1960-64; U.S. State Department, Washington, DC, computer systems analyst and programmer, 1964-67; *Washington Free Press,* Washington, DC, founder, editor, and columnist, 1967-69; freelance journalist in the United States, South America, and Europe, 1970-76; Radio Station KPFA, Berkeley, CA, business manager and news writer, 1976-80; *Daily Californian,* Berkeley, CA, general manager and writer, 1981-82; writer, 1982—.

MEMBER: National Writers Union.

WRITINGS:

The CIA: A Forgotten History—U.S. Global Interventions since World War II, Zed (Burbank, CA), 1986.

Killing Hope: U.S. Military and CIA Interventions since World War II, Common Courage (Monroe, ME), 1995.

Contributor to Barbara Rogers, *For Men Only,* Pandora Press, 1988. Also contributor of articles to periodicals, including *Covert Action Quarterly, Los Angeles Times, National Catholic Reporter, People's Almanac, San Francisco Chronicle,* and *To the Point.*

SIDELIGHTS: William Blum told *CA:* "My political writing is aimed principally at dispelling the myths—particularly the anti-Communism and anti-socialism myths—that all Americans are raised to believe. This is a formidable task, for I have to do battle with no less than a lifetime of indoctrination of my potential audience."

*   *   *

BLY, Carol(yn)   1930-
(Joanna Campbell, Ann Reynolds)

PERSONAL: Born April 16, 1930, in Duluth, MN; daughter of C. Russell and Mildred (Washburn) McLean; married Robert Bly (a poet and translator), June 24, 1955 (divorced June, 1979); children: Mary, Bridget, Noah, Micah. *Education:* Wellesley College, B.A., 1951; graduate study at University of Minnesota, 1954-55. *Politics:* Democrat. *Religion:* Episcopalian.

ADDRESSES: Home—Rt. 2, Box 546, Sturgeon Lake, MN 55783 (summer); 1668 Juno Ave., St. Paul, MN 55116. *Agent*—Georges Borchardt, 136 East 57th St., New York, NY 10022.

CAREER: Fifties (magazine), Madison, MN, manager, 1958-59; Sixties Press and *Sixties* (magazine), Madison, manager, 1960-70; *Seventies* (magazine), Madison, manager, 1970-71; Custom Crosswords, Sturgeon Lake, MN, proprietor, 1978—. Humanities consultant and theme developer for American Farm Project, sponsored by National Endowment for the Humanities and National Farmers Union, 1978-81; humanities consultant for Land Stewardship Project, 1982—; project director and writer for "A Lifeline to High School Students," sponsored by Project Impull, 1983. Visiting writer in Basic Arts Program of Duluth, MN, school system, 1982; COMPAS writer in residence of senior writing program, 1982—; associated with University of Minnesota creative writing program, 1986—. Instructor of ethics and literature, University of Minnesota, 1989—. Cofounder of Prairie Arts Center, Madison, 1971; founder and charter teacher of the Loft Writing Exchange, 1993. Member of Chamber of Commerce of Madison, 1971-78. County chairperson of Countryside Council, Marshall, MN, 1975-78. Lay reader in Episcopal Church, 1975-79; member of board of diocesan publications for Episcopal Church, MN, and of Episcopal City Services, Minneapolis, MN.

Lecturer at Institute on Man and Science, Renssalaerville, NY, and at Rural Institute, Marshall; teacher at The Loft, Minneapolis, 1979-82, Upper Midwest Writers Conference, Bemedji, MN, 1980 and 1981, Metropolitan University, 1982, Hamline University, 1983, 1986-87, and summer workshop instructor at University of Minnesota, 1983, 1992—, and at Northland College, 1992—. Lecturer at Carleton College, Mankato State University, University of Minnesota, Minneapolis, Duluth, and Morris, Assumption College, University of Wisconsin, Syracuse University, Indiana University, University of Delaware, University of Iowa, and others; lecturer for Minnesota Council of Teachers of English, Duluth school system, and community organizations.

MEMBER: Minnesota Independent Scholars' Forum (board member, 1982-84); Horizon 100; The Loft (board member, 1991-94); Episcopal Community Services (board member, 1978-79). Cochair of the Collaborative of Teachers and School Social Workers.

AWARDS, HONORS: Grant, Minnesota State Arts Board, 1980, 1990; fellowship, Bush Foundation, 1981, 1991; certificate of honor, South Dakota Council of Teachers of English, 1985; award, Friends of America Writers, 1991, for *The Tomcat's Wife and Other Stories;* Doctor of Humane Letters, Northland College, 1992; "Friend of School Work" award, Minnesota School Social Workers' Association, 1994; award, Seabury-Western Theological Seminary, for distinguished Christian service; Ramsey County Women's political caucus founding feminist.

WRITINGS:

(Translator from Danish) Anders Bodelson, *One Down,* Harper (New York City), 1970.

(With Joe Paddock and Nancy Paddock) *Soil and Survival* (humanities handbook), Sierra Club Books (San Francisco), 1981.
Letters from the Country (essays), Harper, 1981.
Backbone: Short Stories by Carol Bly, Milkweed Editions, 1985.
(With J. Paddock and N. Paddock) *Soil and Survival* (essays), Sierra Books, 1986.
Bad Government and Silly Literature, Milkweed Editions, 1986.
The Passionate, Accurate Story, Milkweed Editions, 1990.
The Tomcat's Wife and Other Stories, Harper, 1991.

Also translator of poems and of story "New Directions," by Gunter Eich. Contributor of essays to Minnesota Public Radio's, *View from the Loft,* and *Brick* magazines and anthologies. Contributor of short stories to the *New Yorker, American Review, Ploughshares, Twin Cities* and anthologies. Contributor of poems, under the pseudonyms Joanna Campbell and Ann Reynolds, to *Poetry Northwest* and *Coastlines.* Also contributor to "At the Edge of Town: Duluth," a CD-ROM project, and Yale Divinity School/Trinity Church literature and spirituality video project, 1995.

ADAPTATIONS: Rachel River, a film based on three of Bly's short stories by Cantor Films, Ltd., was shown on American Playhouse (1990) and won awards at the Toronto Film Festival.

WORK IN PROGRESS: Changing the Bully Who Rules the World, an anthology of stories, poems, and essays, for Milkweed Editions, 1996; *The Lucky Predator and Other Essays.* Also designing coursework for the collaborative teaching of literature in elementary and high schools.

SIDELIGHTS: Carol Bly, writes Noel Perrin in the *New York Times Book Review,* "wants the farmers and small town merchants of America to live with passion, to have a sense of greatness in their lives, to take themselves as seriously as a Beethoven or a Thoreau." She insists that her peers find and enjoy their individual inner lives in spite of the fact that small-town thinking generally precludes the investigation of personal potential. After living in a rural situation for over twenty-five years, Bly concluded that the sense of community in a small town inhibits people's natural, critical judgments. Suspicious of emotion or argument, the small towner, the author suggests, resembles a "malignant mix of repression and hypocrisy." According to Mark Kramer's *Atlan-*

tic review of Bly's *Letters from the Country,* "Bly develops with keen perception the connections between spiritual malaise and dullness of character and culture. And she delineates, with exquisite accuracy, her neighbors' shared sense of the sacredness of family, of holidays, of country, a sense that seems to paralyze their evaluative instincts."

The lack of critical discussion of important topics, such as the effects of government scandals or even dismissing a preacher, alarms the author. Townspeople, she believes, bridle their ideas and pen up their frustrations as peacekeeping measures, which is dangerous. Rosellen Brown explains in the *New Republic* that as "residents of an inescapable community, few dare to make the saving distinctions that would allow them to be critical of one another and of their institutions, or of local and national politics, for fear of strewing their dooryards with corpses." According to Bly, unarticulated feelings are explosives while total small talk and perpetual niceties are deadly to humans who thrive on the thought process and dissenting opinions. "Positive thinking," Bly states, "is [a] kind of naivete. People who practice or commend it are interested in feeling no pain and in preserving a high. Sometimes a whole culture wishes to preserve this high: then its art and doctrines turn not into positive thinking but into positive pretending."

By denying their evaluative instincts, small towners often fail to realize their inner lives, maintains Bly. Recognizing that every individual possesses "an ethical and esthetic nature," the author insists that this inner life be experienced, though it is threatened by the small-town mentality of women's groups and shared opinions. "Few novelists," states Brown, "have distilled as accurately and poignantly as Bly the essences of small-town life—its dense configuration of satisfactions and impoverishments, the contradictory pleasures of community and isolation, and, perhaps the most elusive element, the difficulty of coming to a full exercise of individual capacity without seeming an alien, even a threat, to one's neighbors."

In order to raise rural consciousness, Bly published essays in Minnesota Public Radio's magazine, later collecting the essays in book form. The result, *Letters from the Country,* explores topics such as the ordeal of holidays and family gatherings, artists in small towns, and agrarian literature. Practical sug-

gestions show rural readers how to become energized and aware of their inner selves. For example, Bly suggests the appointment of a "mail order servant" in a small town, a position she once held. As a public employee, the mail order servant peruses reference sources, including *Books in Print,* and orders material for the town's enrichment.

Letters from the Country, says Brown, "is an engaging mixture of specific, practical advice for rural improvement (self-and otherwise) and a sympathetic fiction writer's vision of a diminished sector of American life." "It's a clarion call, fine silver notes, meant to resound along a thousand Main Streets," writes Perrin.

Bly has garnered similar praise for her work *Backbone.* "Each of the five stories in this collection has heft to it," notes Tess Gallagher in the *New York Times Book Review.* "With a novel's amplitude, her stories present self-reliant individuals held in a web of communal interdependence. Their very resourcefulness grants them a solitary dignity, even as it holds them captive to the general good. . . . What the reader will remember is Carol Bly's spiritual and moral intelligence as glimpsed through the valor of these vibrant characters."

In a 1991 compilation of stories, *The Tomcat's Wife and Other Stories,* Bly depicts the lives, full of disappointments, of some rural Minnesotans. Louis B. Jones, in a *New York Times Book Review* assessment, lauds that "every story in the collection, each for its own sake, is recommended" and, in reference to the appealing nature of the volume, states that "poison in fine pharmaceutical doses is medicinal." *San Francisco Chronicle* reviewer Sherri Hallgren finds that the book contains "eight multilayered, richly textured stories" and that "Bly goes to the core of human nature in a way that is quiet and efficient and dead sure. And also surprising. In each one, she moves around the obvious story, choosing paths that, while unexpected, are inevitably right."

Bly told *CA:* "I am interested in (and am exploring) the ways in which the new psychology of stage development and moral imagination can be brought to bear in the peace movement. I think writers and nonbehavioristic psychotherapists may link arms in this work. I am organizing conferences and giving talks about this."

BIOGRAPHICAL/CRITICAL SOURCES:

BOOKS

Lifshin, Lyn, editor, *Ariadne's Thread: A Collection of Contemporary Women's Journals,* Harper, 1982.

PERIODICALS

Atlantic, June, 1981.
Border Crossings, July, 1990, pp. 11-17.
Christian Science Monitor, June 3, 1981.
Iowa Review, fall 1992, pp. 1-17.
Nation, December 26, 1981.
New Republic, June 20, 1981.
New York Times Book Review, May 24, 1981; January 27, 1985; March 31, 1991.
San Francisco Chronicle, May 5, 1991.

*   *   *

BOICE, James Montgomery   1938-

PERSONAL: Born July 7, 1938, in Pittsburgh, PA; son of G. Newton (an orthopedic surgeon) and Jean (Shick) Boice; married Linda Ann McNamara, June 9, 1962; children: Elizabeth Anne Dawson, Heather Louise, Jennifer Sue. *Education:* Harvard University, A.B. (with high honors), 1960; Princeton Theological Seminary, B.D., 1963; University of Basel, D.Theol. (insigni cum laude), 1966.

ADDRESSES: Home—1935 Pine St., Philadelphia, PA 19103. *Office*—Tenth Presbyterian Church, 1701 Delancey Pl., Philadelphia, PA 19103.

CAREER: Licensed in the Presbytery of Pittsburgh, PA, 1963. *Christianity Today,* Washington, DC, member of editorial staff, summers, 1962, 1963, assistant editor, 1966-68; Tenth Presbyterian Church, Philadelphia, PA, pastor, 1968—; City Center Academy, Philadelphia, principal, 1983-87, chair of board of trustees, 1983—. Speaker on "The Bible Study Hour," radio program originating in Philadelphia, 1969—. Chair of Philadelphia Conference on Reformed Theology, 1974—. President of Evangelical Ministries, Inc., 1985—.

MEMBER: Alliance of Confessing Evangelicals.

WRITINGS:

Witness and Revelation in the Gospel of John, Zondervan (Grand Rapids, MI), 1970.
Philippians: An Expositional Commentary, Zondervan, 1971.
The Sermon on the Mount, Zondervan, 1972.
How to Really Live It Up, Zondervan, 1973, published as *How to Live the Christian Life,* Moody (Chicago), 1982.
The Last and Future World, Zondervan, 1974.
How God Can Use Nobodies, Victor Books (Wheaton, IL), 1974, published as *Ordinary Men Called by God,* 1974.
Commentary on the Gospel of John, five volumes, Zondervan, 1975-79.
(Contributor) Frank E. Gaebelin, editor, *The Expositor's Bible Commentary,* Zondervan, 1976.
Can You Run Away from God?, Victor Books, 1977.
Our Sovereign God, Baker Book (Grand Rapids, MI), 1977.
The Sovereign God, Inter-Varsity Press (Downers Grove, IL), 1978.
God the Redeemer, Inter-Varsity Press, 1978.
Awakening to God, Inter-Varsity Press, 1979.
(Editor) *Making God's Word Plain,* Tenth Presbyterian Church, 1979.
The Epistles of John, Zondervan, 1980.
Does Inerrancy Matter?, Tyndale (Wheaton, IL), 1980.
God and History, Inter-Varsity Press, 1981.
(Editor) *Our Savior God,* Baker Book, 1981.
The Parables of Jesus, Moody, 1983.
The Christ of Christmas, Moody, 1983.
The Minor Prophets, two volumes, Zondervan, 1983-86.
Genesis, three volumes, Zondervan, 1983-87.
Standing on the Rock, Tyndale, 1984.
The Christ of the Empty Tomb, Moody, 1985.
Christ's Call to Discipleship, Moody, 1986.
(Editor) *Transforming Our World: A Call to Action,* Multnomah (Portland, OR), 1988.
Daniel: An Expositional Commentary, Zondervan, 1989.
Ephesians: An Expositional Commentary, Zondervan, 1989.
Joshua: We Will Serve the Lord, Revell (Old Tappan, NJ), 1989.
Nehemiah: Learning to Lead, Revell, 1990.
Romans: An Expositional Commentary (four volumes), Baker Book, 1992-96.
The King Has Come, Christian Focus Publications, 1992.

Amazing Grace, Tyndale, 1993.
Mind Renewal in a Mindless Age, Baker Book, 1993.
Psalms: An Expositional Commentary (one volume of three), Baker Book, 1994.
Sure I Believe, So What!, Christian Focus Publications, 1994.
Hearing God When You Hurt, Baker Book, 1995.

Contributor to religious periodicals.

*   *   *

BOND, William J(oseph)   1941-

PERSONAL: Born October 23, 1941, in Winchester, MA; son of Edmond Charles (a laborer) and Mary Ellen (Costello) Bond; married Janet Lupico (a retailer), November 18, 1967; children: Paul Greg, Marie Christine. *Education:* Burdett College, A.A., 1966; Salem State College, B.S., 1968, M.A.T., 1972.

ADDRESSES: Home and office—67 Melrose Ave., Haverhill, MA 01830.

CAREER: Raytheon Co., Andover, MA, senior analyst, 1968-70; Humphrey Browning McDougall Advertising, Boston, MA, manager, 1970-74; Newark Boxboard Co., Newark, NJ, controller, 1974-76; Career Publishing/Consulting Co., Haverhill, MA, president, 1976—; Northern Essex College, Haverhill, instructor in business, 1976-84; American Business Institute, Boston, instructor in business accounting, 1984-86; Bavarian Strudel Shoppe, Salem, NH, founder and owner, 1986—. Instructor at Middlesex Community College, 1977-81, University of New Hampshire, 1980-82, New Hampshire College, 1982—, and Hesser College, 1982—. Guest on radio and television programs. *Military service:* U.S. Army, 1960-62.

MEMBER: American Management Association, Massachusetts Business Educators.

WRITINGS:

Secrets to Success in Your Job, Career Publishing, 1977.
1001 Ways to Beat the Time Trap, Fell (New York City), 1982.
Ten Best Home Businesses, CBI Publishing (Boston, MA), 1983.

199 Ways to Build Your Career, New American Library (New York City), 1983.
Riding the Success Express at Work, Madonna Publishing, 1983.
Managing Career Skills Successfully, Ashley Books (Port Washington, NY), 1988.
The Joy of Success, Ballantine (New York City), 1988.
199 Timewasters and How to Avoid Them, Fell, 1989.
Homebased Mail Order, McGraw-Hill (New York City), 1990.
Homebased Newsletter Publishing, McGraw-Hill, 1992.
Homebased Catalog Marketing, McGraw-Hill, 1993.
You Can Do It Just Try, Best Business, 1993.
Managing Your Priorities from Start to Success, Irwin (Homewood, IL), 1995.
Homebased Specialty Consulting, McGraw-Hill, 1995.

Author of columns "Time Management Views" in *Executive Review,* 1974 and "Time Means More Money at Work" in *Florida Business Digest;* also author of syndicated column "Time Factors." Contributor to business and accounting journals. Founding editor of newsletter *New Career Ways.*

SIDELIGHTS: William J. Bond told *CA:* "I am interested in helping other people grow in their lives, especially in their jobs and careers. I write about my own experiences in the world of work, and the experiences of others around me. My teaching and writing blend together harmoniously and give me numerous ideas for other books. I run my own seminars on 'time management' and home business at colleges and universities.

"I have never been more excited about my writing than during the nineties. I finally connected to my readers. I enjoy getting letters from my readers and seeing my books in the bookstores. I finally feel my message is getting out to people all over the world now. Never give up on your writing. Once you choose, establish it, keep working at it."

BIOGRAPHICAL/CRITICAL SOURCES:

PERIODICALS

Haverhill Gazette, June 19, 1982.
Lawrence Eagle Tribune, December 28, 1981.
New Jersey Essex Journal, October 14, 1982.

BONNER, Terry Nelsen
  See KRAUZER, Steven M(ark)

* * *

BOOTH, Irwin
  See HOCH, Edward D(entinger)

* * *

BOULDING, Elise (Biorn-Hansen)   1920-

PERSONAL: Born July 6, 1920, in Oslo, Norway; daughter of Joseph (an engineer) and Birgit (Johnsen) Biorn-Hansen; married Kenneth Ewart Boulding (a professor), August 31, 1941; children: John Russell, Mark David, Christine Ann, Philip Daniel, William Frederic. *Education:* Douglass College, B.A., 1940; Iowa State College, M.S., 1949; University of Michigan, Ph.D., 1969. *Religion:* Society of Friends.

ADDRESSES: Home—624 Pearl St., Boulder, CO 80302.

CAREER: University of Colorado, Boulder, lecturer, 1967-68, assistant professor, 1968-69, associate professor, 1969-73, professor of sociology, 1971-78; Dartmouth College, Hanover, NH, professor of sociology and chair of department, 1979-85, professor emerita, 1985—. Women's International League for Peace and Freedom, international chair, 1967-70; U.N. University, advisor to Human and Social Development program, 1977-80, council member, 1980-85, consultant to Household Gender and Age project, 1982-87; member of international jury of the UNESCO Peace Prize for Peace Education, 1982-87; Exploratory Project on Conditions for a Just World Peace, 1984-90, cochair, 1988-89; International Peace Research Association, secretary-general, 1988-91, foundation president, 1989—, secretary and project director of Commission on Peace Building in the Middle East, 1991-94; Parenting Center, Boulder, CO, chair, 1988-93. Participant in numerous projects, including Congressional Commission on Proposals for the National Academy of Peace and Conflict Resolution, 1979-80; American Friends Service Committee Corporation, 1987-94; World Order

Models Project: The International Commission for a Just World Peace, 1984-87; The Coming Global Civilization Project, 1988-92; Union of International Associations, 1990—; and Committee for the Quaker United Nations Office, 1995—.

MEMBER: International Peace Research Association, International Sociological Association (secretary, 1970-73; cochair, 1973-77), American Association for the Advancement of Science (member of executive committee, 1970-72), American Sociological Association (chair of committee on status of women in the profession, 1970-72, and committee on sociology of world conflicts, 1972-74; chair of Section on the Sociology of World Conflicts, 1980-82, committee on World Sociology, 1983-84), Consortium on Peace Research, Education and Development (secretary, organizing committee, 1970, chair, 1972-74), UNESCO (U.S. National Commission for UNESCO, 1978-84, member, Social Science Committee, 1978-84), International Studies Association, World Future Studies Federation, World Future Society.

AWARDS, HONORS: Danforth fellow, 1965-67; Distinguished Achievement Award, Douglass College, 1973; Ted Lentz International Peace Research Award, 1976; Woman of Conscience Award, National Council of Women, 1980; Jessie Bernard Award, American Sociological Association, 1981; Award for Distinguished Scholars and Practitioners in the Field of International Interchanges, International Society for Educational, Cultural and Scientific Interchanges, 1982; Athena Award, University of Michigan Alumnae Council, 1983; Woman Who Made a Difference Award, National Women's Forum, 1985; Mary Rhodes Award, Sisters of Loretto, 1985; Adin Ballou Peace Award, Unitarian Universalist Peace Fellowship, 1986; Institute for Defense and Disarmament Award for a Lifetime of Work for Peace and Democracy, Peace Studies Association Award, and Nobel Peace Prize nomination, all 1990; Jack Gore Memorial Peace Award, 1992; Hall of Distinguished Alumni, Rutgers College, 1994.

WRITINGS:

(Translator) Fred Polak, *Image of the Future,* two volumes, Oceana Press, 1961, one volume abridgment, Jossey-Bass/Elsevier (San Francisco, CA), 1972 (originally published as *De Toekomst is Verleden,* W. De Haan N. V. [Utrecht], 1953).

(With Daniel Marshall) *From a Monastery Kitchen,* Harper, 1976, revised edition, 1989.

(With Shirley A. Nuss, Dorothy Lee Carson and Michael Greenstein) *Handbook on International Data on Women,* Halsted Press (New York City), 1976.

The Underside of History: A View of Women through Time, Westview (Boulder, CO), 1976, revised edition, Sage (Beverly Hills, CA), 1992.

Women in the Twentieth Century World, Sage, 1977.

Children's Rights and the Wheel of Life, Transaction Press (New Brunswick, NJ), 1979.

(With L. Robert Passmore and Robert Scott Gassler) *Bibliography on World Conflict and Peace,* Westview, 1979.

(With husband, Kenneth E. Boulding, and Guy M. Burgess) *The Social System of the Planet Earth,* Addison-Wesley (Reading, MA), 1980.

(With Jane Lilleydahl, Elizabeth Moen, and Rise Palm) *Women and the Social Costs of Development: Two Colorado Case Studies,* Westview, 1981.

(With Lillydahl, Moen, Yount, Scott-Stevens and Gallon) *Quality of Life, Expectations of Change, and Planning for the Future in an Energy Production Community: A Report to the People of Meeker and Walden,* University of Colorado Press (Boulder), 1982.

Building a Global Civic Culture: Education for an Interdependent World, Teachers College Press (New York City), 1988.

One Small Plot of Heaven: Reflections of a Quaker Sociologist on Family Life, Pendle Hill (Wallingford, PA), 1989.

(With K. Boulding) *The Future: Images and Processes,* Sage, 1995.

EDITOR

(With Robert L. Kahn) *Power and Conflict in Organizations,* Basic Books (New York City), 1964.

(With Robert Chen and Stephen Schneider) *Social Science Research and Climate: An Interdisciplinary Appraisal,* D. Reidel (Netherlands), 1983.

(With Clovis Brigagao and Kevin Clements) *Peace Culture and Society: A Transnational Dialogue,* Westview, 1991.

New Agendas for Peace Research: Conflict and Security Reexamined, Lynne Reinner (Boulder, CO), 1992.

Studies in the Interconnectedness of Peace in the Middle East and the World: Perspectives from Europe, Africa, and Latin America, IPRA/Research Institute for Social Studies of the Hungarian Academy of Sciences (Budapest), 1993.

Building Peace in the Middle East: Challenges from States and Civil Society, Lynne Reinner, 1994.

OTHER

Author of numerous pamphlets, including *The Fruits of Solitude for Children,* Pendle Hill, 1963; *Born Remembering,* Pendle Hill, 1975; *The Family As a Way into the Future,* Pendle Hill, 1978; *The Recreation of Relationship, Interpersonal and Global,* Wider (Philadelphia, PA), 1981; *The Family as a Small Society,* Schumacher Society, 1982; and *The Dialectics and Economics of Peace* (occasional paper with K. Boulding), Center for Conflict Analysis and Resolution, George Mason University (Fairfax, VA), 1990. Contributor to numerous books, including *Families under Stress,* by Reuben Hill, Macmillan, 1949; *Images of the Future,* edited by Robert Bundy, Prometheus Books, 1975; *Impact of Technological Change on Women,* edited by Roslyn Dauber and Melinda Cain, Westview, 1980; *Towards a Just World Peace,* edited by Saul Mendlovitz and R. B. J. Walker, Butterworth, 1987; *Peace Action in the Eighties: Sociological Views,* edited by John Lofland and Sam Maulla, Rutgers University Press, 1990; *Conflict Resolution Theory and Practice Integration and Application,* edited by Dennis Sandhole and Hugo van der Merwe, Manchester University Press (England), 1993; *Culture, Development, and Democracy: The Role of the Intellectual,* edited by Selo Soemardjan and Kenneth W. Thompson, United Nations University Press (New York City), 1994; and *Preparing for the Future, Notes and Queries for Concerned Educators,* edited by David Hicks, Adamantine, 1994.

Contributor to annuals and proceedings, and of numerous articles and reviews to journals, including *Marriage and Family Living, Human Relations, War/Peace Report, Bulletin of Atomic Scientists, International Journal of Nonviolence, International Social Science Journal, Japan Christian Quarterly, New Era, Journal of World Education,* and *Contemporary Sociology. International Peace Research Newsletter,* editor, 1963-68, North American editor, 1968-73 and 1984-87; guest editor of *Journal of Social Issues,* January, 1967, and *Journal of Conflict Resolution,* December, 1972; associate editor of *American Sociologist,* 1970-73, and *International Interactions,* 1973—; member of board of editors, *Peace and Change: A Journal of Peace Research,* 1971.

BOWER, Keith
See BECKETT, Kenneth A(lbert)

*   *   *

BOWSER, Eileen   1928-

PERSONAL: Born January 18, 1928, in Columbia Station, OH; daughter of Roy and Florence (Doyle) Putt; married William Patton Bowser, June, 1950. *Education:* Marietta College, B.A., 1950; University of North Carolina, M.A., 1953.

ADDRESSES: Home—23 Bank St., New York, NY 10014.

CAREER: Department of Film, Museum of Modern Art, New York City, member of staff, 1954-76, curator, 1976-93, with responsibility for film collections, acquisitions, cataloging, storage, preservation and access. Federation Internationale des Archives du Film (FIAF), executive committee member, 1969-91, president of Documentation Commission, 1972-81, vice president, 1977-85; DOMITOR, organizing committee member for 3rd Colloquium New York, 1994, and executive committee member. Ernst Lindgren Memorial Lecturer, National Film Archive, London, 1995. Lecturer on film history and archiving in Belgium, Bulgaria, Great Britain, Italy, Japan, Mexico, Spain, Switzerland, Yugoslavia, U.S.S.R., and the United States;

MEMBER: Honorary member of Society of Cinema Studies, DOMITOR, and Federation Internationale des Archives du Film (FIAF).

AWARDS, HONORS: Prix Jean Mitry, Silent Film Festival of Pordenone, 1989; Katherine Singer Kovacs Prize, 1991, for *The Transformation of Cinema: 1907-1915.*

WRITINGS:

(With Iris Barry) *D. W. Griffith: American Film Master,* Museum of Modern Art, 1965.
(Editor and primary author) *Film Notes,* Museum of Modern Art, 1965.
(Editor and author of introduction) *Biograph Bulletins, 1908-1912,* Farrar, Straus (New York City), 1973.
(And coeditor with John Kuiper) *A Handbook for Film Archives,* Federation Internationale des Archives du Film (Brussels), 1980, revised edition, Garland (New York City), 1991.
(With Richard Griffith and Arthur Mayer) *The Movies,* 3rd edition, Simon & Schuster (New York City), 1981.
(And editor) *The Slapstick Symposium,* Federation Internationale des Archives du Film, 1988.
The Transformation of Cinema: 1907-1915 (Volume 2 in series "History of American Cinema"), Scribners (New York City), 1990.

Also author of brochure *Carl Dreyer,* Museum of Modern Art (New York City), 1964. Contributor of articles on film history and archival work to books, including *Pastrone-Griffith* (proceedings of the FIAF symposium of June 6, 1975), Associazione Italiana per le ricerche di Storia Del Cinema (Torino), 1975; *Cinema 1900-1906* (proceedings of the Brighton Symposium, compiled by Roger Holman), FIAF, 1982; *Film Before Griffith,* edited by John Fell, University of California Press, 1983; *Circulating Film Library Catalog,* Museum of Modern Art, 1984; *David Wark Griffith,* Publications de la Sorbonne, L'Harmattan (Paris), 1984; *Les premiers ans du cinema francais,* Actes du V Colloque International de l'Institut Jean Vigo (Perpignan), 1985; and *Le cinema Francais muet dans le monde, influences reciproques,* Symposium de la FIAF Cinematheque de Toulouse/Institut Jean Vigo (Paris), 1988. Also contributor to journals, including *Griffithiana* and *Le revue de la cinematheque.*

*   *   *

BOYD, Malcolm   1923-

PERSONAL: Born June 8, 1923, in New York, NY; son of Melville (a financier) and Beatrice (Lowrie) Boyd. *Education:* University of Arizona, B.A. in English, 1944; Church Divinity School of the Pacific, B.D., 1954; additional study, Oxford University, 1954-55, and Ecumenical Institute of the World Council of Churches, Geneva, Switzerland; Union Theological Seminary, S.T.M., 1956; member of work-study program at the Taize community in France, 1957.

ADDRESSES: Office—St. Augustine by-the-Sea, 1227 Fourth St., Santa Monica, CA 90401.

CAREER: Author, social commentator, and activist. Foote, Cone, & Belding Advertising Agency, Hollywood, CA, copywriter, 1945-46; Republic Pictures and Samuel Goldwyn Productions, writer and producer, 1947-49; Pickford, Rogers, & Boyd, New York City, founder with Mary Pickford and Buddy Rogers, 1949, vice president and general manager, 1949-51. Ordained Episcopal priest, 1955; St. George's Episcopal Church, Indianapolis, IN, rector, 1957-59; Colorado State University, Fort Collins, Episcopal chaplain, 1959-61; Wayne State University, Detroit, MI, Episcopal chaplain, 1961-64; Grace Episcopal Church, Detroit, assistant priest, 1961-64; Church of the Atonement, Washington, DC, assistant pastor, 1964-68, on leave as chaplain-at-large to American universities and colleges, beginning 1965; appointed chaplain of Integrity, 1981; St. Augustine by-the-Sea Episcopal Church, Santa Monica, CA, writer-priest in residence, 1981—; AIDS Commission of the Episcopal Diocese of Los Angeles, chaplain, 1990—. Lecturer, World Council of Churches, 1955, and 1964; national field representative, Episcopal Society for Cultural and Racial Unity, 1965-68. Yale University, Calhoun College, resident fellow, 1968-71, associate fellow, 1971-75; resident guest, Mishkenot Sha'ananim, Jerusalem, 1974. Host of television specials, including *Sex in the Seventies,* CBS-TV, 1975. Member, Los Angeles City/County AIDS Task Force, 1985—.

MEMBER: PEN (president, Los Angeles Center, 1984-87), National Council of Churches (member of film awards committee, 1965), Clergy and Laity Concerned, National Association for the Advancement of Colored People (NAACP), Episcopal Society for Cultural and Racial Unity.

AWARDS, HONORS: Selected by *Life* magazine as one of the "100 Most Important Young Men and Women in the United States," 1962; Integrity Award, 1978, "for contribution to the gay movement and the gay Christian community"; Union of American Hebrew Congregations award, 1980, for "enhancement of better understanding between Christians and Jews"; honorary Doctor of Divinity, Church Divinity School of the Pacific, 1995.

WRITINGS:

Crisis in Communication, Doubleday (New York City), 1957.
Christ and Celebrity Gods, Seabury (New York City), 1958.
Focus: Rethinking the Meaning of Our Evangelism, Morehouse (Wilton, CT), 1960.
If I Go down to Hell, Morehouse, 1962.

The Hunger, the Thirst, Morehouse, 1964.
(Editor) *On the Battle Lines* (essays), Morehouse, 1964.
Are You Running with Me, Jesus? (prayers), Holt (New York City), 1965, revised edition, Beacon Press (Boston), 1990.
Free to Live, Free to Die (secular meditations), Holt, 1967.
(Editor) *The Underground Church,* Sheed & Ward, 1968.
Malcolm Boyd's Book of Days, Random House (New York City), 1968.
The Fantasy Worlds of Peter Stone, and Other Fables, Harper (New York City), 1969.
As I Live and Breathe: Stages of an Autobiography, Random House, 1970.
My Fellow Americans, Holt, 1970.
Human Like Me, Jesus, Simon & Schuster (New York City), 1971.
The Lover, Word Books, 1972.
(With Paul Conrad) *When in the Course of Human Events,* Sheed & Ward, 1973.
The Runner, Word Books, 1974.
Christian: Its Meanings in an Age of Future Shock, Hawthorn (New York City), 1975.
The Alleluia Affair, Word Books, 1975.
Am I Running with You, God? Doubleday, 1978.
Take Off the Masks, Doubleday, 1978, third edition, HarperCollins (New York City), 1993.
Look Back in Joy: Celebration of Gay Lovers, Gay Sunshine (San Francisco), 1981, revised edition, Alyson (Boston), 1990.
Half Laughing/Half Crying: Songs for Myself, St. Martin's (New York City), 1986.
Gay Priest: An Inner Journey, St. Martin's, 1986.
(With Nancy Wilson) *Amazing Grace,* Crossing Press (Trumansburg, NY), 1991.
Edges, Boundaries and Connections, Broken Moon (Tacoma, WA), 1992.
Rich with Years: Daily Meditations on Growing Older, HarperCollins, 1994.

Author of plays, all produced in New York City: *They Aren't Real to Me,* 1962; *The Job,* 1962; *Study in Color,* 1962; *Boy* and *The Community,* produced on a double bill, 1964. Also coauthor of screenplays, including *Are You Running with Me, Jesus?* (with Ervin Zavada), based on Boyd's book of the same title. Contributor to books, including *Christianity and the Contemporary Arts,* Abingdon (Nashville, TN), 1962; *Witness to a Generation,* by Edward Fiske, Bobbs-Merrill, 1967; *You Can't Kill the Dream,* John Knox (Atlanta, GA), 1968; and *Gay Spirit: Myth and Meaning,* edited by Mark Thompson, St. Martin's, 1987. Author of weekly column for *Pittsburgh Courier,* 1963-65; motion picture columnist for *Episcopalian, United Church Herald, Christian Century, Presbyterian Survey,* and *Canadian Churchman.* Contributor of reviews and articles to numerous periodicals, including *Los Angeles Times Book Review, Ms., New York Times, Washington Post, Los Angeles Times, Parade, Advocate,* and *Modern Maturity.* Contributing editor, *Renewal and Integrity Forum;* reviewer of devotional books, *Christian Century,* 1974-81.

Rich with Years: Daily Meditations on Growing Older has been translated into Chinese. The Malcolm Boyd Collection and Archives was established at Boston University in 1973.

ADAPTATIONS: All of Boyd's plays have appeared on television; film adaptations have been made of *The Job, Study in Color,* and *Boy,* and are distributed nationally by the Anti-Defamation League of B'nai B'rith in New York City.

WORK IN PROGRESS: "Two new book projects: an encompassing, spiritual biography and a work about the complexities and triumphs of aging."

SIDELIGHTS: Malcolm Boyd, the "espresso priest" who moved religion into coffeehouses during the 1960s, believes that writers should get involved in social issues. His own life as a civil rights activist, anti-Vietnam War protester, and gay Episcopalian priest reflects this philosophy—both its rewards and risks. Boyd first became nationally known in the mid-1960s when his avant-garde book of prayers *Are You Running with Me, Jesus?* became an unexpected bestseller. But long before that, Boyd had embarked upon a course of social activism that would shape his writing and influence his career. Boyd's willingness to act on his beliefs has often generated controversy. However, as Mark Henry reports in the *Los Angeles Times,* Boyd never went looking for causes. Instead, Boyd told Henry, "I participated in the life of my time."

Between 1945 and 1951, Boyd worked as a writer and director in advertising and motion pictures in Hollywood. In 1949, along with Mary Pickford and Buddy Rogers, Boyd formed Pickford, Rogers, & Boyd, Inc., an agency that packaged shows for radio and television. Respect for his reputation in the media field spread throughout Hollywood to such an

extent that, in 1949, Boyd was elected the first president of the Television Producers Association of Hollywood.

In 1951, to the amazement of many of his associates, Boyd gave up his promising career and enrolled in the Church Divinity School of the Pacific in preparation for a career in the Episcopal ministry. In an interview with Helen Dudar for the *New York Post,* Boyd commented: "It's too complex to explain briefly, but in a somewhat simplified form, this is what happened. I was involved in mass media from a standpoint of taking and exploiting, and I became totally dissatisfied with it. My life had little meaning beyond each day." After his theological studies, which included a year of training at Oxford University and a year of study under Reinhold Niebuhr at the Union Theological Seminary, Boyd began the first assignment of what many people consider a very controversial religious career and life.

In 1978, dissatisfied with the charade he had been living, Boyd dropped the mask that had been hiding his homosexuality and openly declared himself a gay priest. His autobiographical book, *Take off the Masks,* documents the rewards—and costs—of his coming out. "Suddenly, upon announcing that I was gay, I knew that in a strange sense I had lost my life," Boyd wrote. "But I knew that in the deepest recesses of my soul," he continued, "I had chosen life, with its unpredictable valleys and mountains, its tests and glories, over the plastic death of security, withdrawal, monochrome rigidity, and the refusal to risk." The repercussions of Boyd's decision proved to be deep and long-lasting. There was a backlash from the conservative arm of the Episcopal clergy, and some members demanded his expulsion from the priesthood. Though he never abandoned his ministry, Boyd did sever his ties with organized religion for a time.

Yet the book also received strong support from others. *Christian Century* critic E. J. Curtin applauded *Take off the Masks* as "a testament to truth and courage, an angry, sad, joyful challenge to those who buy the social lie and seek to escape from freedom. Those who seek titillation should look elsewhere. This is a very sensitive story of one man's religious and sexual liberation." *Library Journal* contributor G. M. Gerdes also commended Boyd's honesty and his straightforward approach, which "avoids melodrama, sentimental piety, and defensiveness as he reveals the flesh and soul of a mediamyth we thought we knew." Boyd also received scores of letters from readers whose own lives had mirrored his experience in some way.

Even with the support he received, Boyd experienced a personal crisis during the late 1970s and early 1980s. Pulled in conflicting directions, uncertain as to how to support himself financially, he considered abandoning his ministry to return to motion picture and television work. Instead Boyd decided to work for change from within. "I'm angry toward the Episcopal church for many things, but that [is] all the more reason to remain a priest and work for change," he told Henry. "The people who are going to change anything are the ones who have to be inside it. And they change a lot just being there."

Over time, Boyd has found a niche for himself within the clergy. In 1981, he was invited to be writer-priest in residence at St. Augustine by-the-Sea Episcopal Church in Santa Monica, California. In addition to preaching every third week, Boyd works to support gay and lesbian causes and to educate the public about AIDS, serving as chaplain to the AIDS Commission of the Episcopal Diocese of Los Angeles. Still a prolific writer, Boyd served as president of the Los Angeles Center of PEN from 1984 to 1987 and in that capacity he developed a special concern for imprisoned writers under authoritarian regimes. As he once told *CA:* "I think it's essential to be part of the community of one's time. One has to know what's happened in the world, and one has to feel the pain of it and to cry and to laugh. Unless one is willing and able to do this, art moves into a vacuum."

Boyd further commented: "I have been able to go public with much of my deeply personal life and feelings; therefore, that has not been a deliberate, thought-out act like opening a door and walking into a room. It's something I've done in the creative process. So I can look over my shoulder at that and not exactly understand it. One reason that, creatively, it was very important to come out is that, both as a priest and a writer, it seemed such a contradiction not to be able to share something this basic. In fact, it seemed a betrayal of the whole creative process. Several reviewers have referred to me as 'Holden Caulfield in a collar' or a 'balding Holden Caulfield'—they keep bringing Holden into it. And I'm quite aware of Holden in myself.

"In a way I'm not an earthling. I'm very detached. I can feel: It's all been a mistake; I don't belong here; I don't understand it at all. Yet I've done the best I could; I've tried very hard and rather successfully to come to terms with the earth and body, mind and soul and who I am. And to communicate. It's important to hear each other. And you can do that if you are able to put the issues away a little bit and say, Here's a person. Who is this person? And also be willing to share something with that person. I've loved having one-on-one encounters with people who, at the outset, seemed to hate me for one reason or another. I observed a lot of hate in the civil rights and peace movement. And when that hate could go, and I changed from pure stereotype into a person in someone else's eyes, then we could laugh, we could eat together, take a walk, focus together on certain things."

BIOGRAPHICAL/CRITICAL SOURCES:

BOOKS

Boyd, Malcolm, *As I Live and Breathe: Stages of an Autobiography,* Random House, 1970.
Boyd, *Take Off the Masks,* Doubleday, 1978, third edition, HarperCollins, 1993.

PERIODICALS

Advocate, September 8, 1976; November 30, 1977; June 28, 1978; August 7, 1984; April 2, 1985; June 11, 1985; November 12, 1985; January 7, 1986; March 18, 1986; August 4, 1987; December 22, 1987.
Catholic World, February, 1969.
Christian Century, January 30, 1974; July 1, 1974; October 2, 1974; December 11, 1974; September 24, 1975; February 4, 1976; March 3, 1976; April 14, 1976; May 25, 1977; April 19, 1978; May 9, 1979; April 2, 1980; October 22, 1980; December 2, 1987.
Christian Science Monitor, July 8, 1966; November 5, 1968; January 22, 1970.
Gay Sunshine, autumn/winter, 1980.
Library Journal, July, 1978.
Los Angeles Times, January 30, 1966; September 14, 1966; June 8, 1967; May 26, 1968; July 4, 1968; February 27, 1970; July 25, 1971; October 8, 1972; February 18, 1973; December 16, 1973; January 20, 1974; December 25, 1974; June 15, 1975; August 1, 1975; June 10, 1979; October 7, 1979; November 18, 1979; January 20, 1980; May 11, 1980; June 29, 1980; August 29, 1980; October 19, 1980; October 26, 1980; November 16, 1980; February 22, 1981; March

23, 1984; April 3, 1984; April 13, 1984; April
14, 1984; July 21, 1985; October 3, 1985; January 22, 1986; January 26, 1986; February 16,
1987; July 4, 1987; September 11, 1987; December 7, 1987.

New York Post, February 10, 1961.

New York Times, June 7, 1961; August 14, 1964;
March 23, 1966; April 9, 1966; November 13,
1966; July 28, 1968; June 22, 1969; January 11,
1970; October 24, 1971; February 17, 1972;
August 27, 1972; February 1, 1973; August 5,
1973; December 25, 1974; September 1, 1985.

New York Times Book Review, March 26, 1967;
September 17, 1967; January 25, 1976; December 20, 1985; October 12, 1986.

U.S. Catholic, November, 1969.

Village Voice, November 23, 1967.

Washington Post, March 23, 1965; April 4, 1965;
August 10, 1965; May 29, 1966; March 26,
1967; September 24, 1967; June 1, 1968; May
2, 1973; September 9, 1973; January 20, 1974;
April 14, 1974.

* * *

BOYD, William 1952-

PERSONAL: Born March 7, 1952, in Accra, Ghana;
son of Alexander Murray (a physician) and Evelyn (a
teacher; maiden name, Smith) Boyd; married Susan
Wilson (a magazine editor), 1975. *Education:* University of Nice, diploma in French studies, 1971;
University of Glasgow, M.A. (with honors), 1975;
postgraduate study at Jesus College, Oxford, 1975-
80.

ADDRESSES: Home—London, England. *Agent*—The
Agency, 24 Pottery Lane, Holland Park, London
W11 4LZ, England.

CAREER: Novelist and screenwriter. Lecturer in
English at St. Hilda's College, Oxford, 1980-83.

MEMBER: Royal Society of Literature (fellow),
Chevalier de l'Ordre des Arts et Lettres.

AWARDS, HONORS: Whitbread Literary Award for
best first novel from Booksellers Association of
Great Britain and Ireland, 1981, and Somerset
Maugham Award from Society of Authors, 1982,
both for *A Good Man in Africa;* John Llewelyn Rhys
Memorial Prize and Booker McConnell Prize nomi-

nation from National Book League, both 1982, both
for *An Ice-Cream War;* James Tait Black Memorial
Book Prize, 1991, for *Brazzaville Beach; Los Angeles Times* Book Prize for fiction, 1995, for *The Blue
Afternoon.*

WRITINGS:

FICTION

A Good Man in Africa (novel; also see below),
Hamish Hamilton (London), 1981, Morrow
(New York City), 1982.

On the Yankee Station and Other Stories, Hamish
Hamilton, 1981, expanded edition published as
On the Yankee Station: Stories, Morrow, 1984.

An Ice-Cream War (novel), Hamish Hamilton, 1982,
Morrow, 1983.

Stars and Bars (novel; also see below), Morrow,
1985.

The New Confessions (novel), Morrow, 1988.

Brazzaville Beach (novel), Morrow, 1990.

The Destiny of Nathalie "X" and Other Stories,
Sinclair Stevenson, 1994.

The Blue Afternoon (novel), Knopf (New York City),
1995.

SCREENPLAYS

*School Ties: "Good and Bad at Games" and "Dutch
Girls"* (television screenplays; *Good and Bad at
Games* first broadcast by Channel Four Television, 1984; *Dutch Girls* first broadcast by ITV,
1985), Hamish Hamilton, 1985, Morrow, 1986.

Scoop (based on Evelyn Waugh's novel), ITV, 1986.

Stars and Bars (based on novel of same title), Columbia, 1988.

Tune In Tomorrow (based on *Aunt Julia and the
Scriptwriter,* by Mario Vargas Llosa), Cinecom,
1990.

Mister Johnson (based on a novel by Joyce Cary),
Avenue Pictures, 1991.

Chaplin, Carolco, 1992.

A Good Man in Africa (based on novel of same title),
Gramercy, 1994.

OTHER

Television critic for *New Statesman,* 1981-83; fiction
reviewer for London *Sunday Times,* 1982-83. Contributor of stories and reviews to periodicals, including *Harper's, Books and Bookmen, London Magazine, Times Literary Supplement, Washington Post,*

New York Times Book Review, London Review of Books, New Republic, Daily Telegragh, and *Spectator.*

SIDELIGHTS: British novelist and critic William Boyd has found a wide readership for his work on both sides of the Atlantic. Boyd's darkly humorous fiction addresses subjects from expatriation to modern mathematical theory, reflecting the author's own view that life's events are completely unpredictable and even the most banal folk can be buffeted by fate. *Time* magazine reviewer Martha Duffy called Boyd "an intellectual who wears his learning lightly, when he does not toss it aside completely." Likewise, *New Statesman & Society* correspondent Boyd Tonkin noted that the author's books "spice the old narrative virtues with exotic locales and a mildly modernist flavour drawn from recent culture, science and politics. The results give post-imperial English writing its nearest equivalent to Somerset Maugham." *Washington Post Book World* columnist Jonathan Yardley maintained that Boyd "has firmly established himself as a writer of impressive, original achievement. He writes more often than not about the conflict of alien cultures, but he invariably does so in ways that are unpredictable and imaginative; he is heir to an established tradition of English comic fiction, yet within it he is clearly his own man; he is a biting satirist and social commentator, yet he regards his characters with an affection that is too rare in such fiction. There's hardly a writer around whose work offers more pleasure and satisfaction."

With the publication of his comic first novel, *A Good Man in Africa,* Boyd won acclaim as one of England's brightest young literary talents. Favorably compared with the writings of Evelyn Waugh and Tom Sharpe and particularly to Kingsley Amis's novel *Lucky Jim,* the book earned two of Britain's top literary prizes, the Whitbread and Somerset Maugham awards. The novel's protagonist, Morgan Leafy, is a British junior diplomat in a dusty outpost of post-colonial West Africa whose misadventures— stemming from his fondness for alcohol and women and his frustrated career ambitions—are comically exacerbated by his foreign environment. Charged with removing a corpse protected by a tribal taboo before the arrival of royal visitors (and beset by romantic entanglements as well), the Englishman manages to bumble his way from one humiliating experience to another. "Leafy wants to improve his life, and his ambitions are endearingly average," wrote Mona Simpson in the *New York Times Book Review.* "Of course, as a comic hero Leafy gets nothing of the sort."

Many reviewers allowed that, as a rollicking farce, *A Good Man in Africa* succeeds admirably. "It lack[s] depth, perhaps, but not finesse or wit," Anne Tyler commented in the *Detroit News.* "William Boyd's control of a fairly complicated plot reveals him as a most accomplished *farceur,*" remarked A. N. Wilson in a *Spectator* critique, "and he puts Morgan through his paces with all the assurance of a circus trainer making a poodle jump through hoops."

For his second award-winning novel, *An Ice-Cream War,* Boyd again chose Africa as his principal setting, this time the East African front of World War I where British and German colonial armies waged parochial, but brutal, combat. Against this historical backdrop the author explored the stories of six characters swept up in the conflict, including an American expatriate sisal farmer, his German officer neighbor, a young British military officer, and his artistic younger brother. It is through the experiences of the last, Felix Cobb, that Boyd most conspicuously advances his theme that war is "chaotic and absurd"; securing a commission to find his captured brother, the young intellectual learns firsthand the utter senselessness of war and a chestthumping terror of death in battle. "It is the romance of *war* that Boyd wants to destroy, and the hideous chaos of the war in Africa . . . is recreated with . . . a fine balance of satire, black comedy and horror," Harriett Gilbert reported in a *New Statesman* review.

Commending the novel's historical detail, critics professed even greater praise for the sureness and skill with which Boyd developed his ambitious theme and complex narrative. "This book boasts a rich, expansive tableau," commented Michiko Kakutani, writing in the *New York Times.* "Using an almost cinematic technique, Mr. Boyd cuts back and forth between the exploits of different characters, building narrative suspense with brisk assurance." "The scenes and characters shift with admirable dispatch," commented Robert Towers in the *New York Review of Books.* "All display the narrator's firm hand." Reviewers also noted that Boyd tempered the exuberance and tendency to overwrite seen in his earlier novel; Towers observed that, this time, the "style is that of a writer confident enough of his effects to refrain from belaboring the obvious." Kakutani concluded: "*An Ice-Cream War* . . . represents Mr. Boyd's discovery of his own voice—an elastic voice that is capable not only of some very funny satire but also of seriousness and compassion."

The single weakness detected by some critics in Boyd's historical drama lies in the realm of character development. Kakutani noted that "the only real problem is that Mr. Boyd's narrative fluency lets him get away with a handful of characters, who seem like two-dimensional exiles from an old English comic novel." Towers held a similar opinion: "Boyd's panoramic approach involves certain shortcuts in characterization that preclude any real subtlety or inwardness. Whatever is ultimately mysterious or unpredictable in the human personality is largely missing—and yet we hardly notice its absence, so effective are the strong, quick outlines he provides." And *New York Times Book Review* critic Michael Gorra determined: "The book draws four separate narrative strands together in a successful conclusion on a stage that is by implication as large as Africa itself. In attempting to create that stage, however, Mr. Boyd tends to lose sight of his characters. . . . That abundance doesn't free Mr. Boyd from the obligation to bring his characters' individual psychologies into sharp focus."

Yet other critics—like *New Republic* reviewer Jack Beatty—felt that Boyd's characters "are endowed with a subtle psychology." And Gorra acknowledged that "in its treatment of its central theme, [*An Ice-Cream War*] fulfills the ambition of the historical novel at its best: to comprehend the past, not as a colorful backdrop to a costume drama, but as the controlling force in the lives of its characters." Jonathan Yardley reiterated the evaluation in the *Washington Post Book World:* "As is appropriate to its large subject, *An Ice-Cream War* is populous and far-ranging. It is not dominated by a single protagonist . . . but by a number of individuals each of whom for a time comes front and center; the war, which is always there, is its real protagonists. It takes the great themes raised by the war and translates them into the terms of ordinary lives, thereby rendering them more immediate and understandable. . . . These people are participants in what Boyd calls 'the utter randomness and total contingency of events.' Few contemporary novelists have grasped this essential, inescapable truth more firmly than Boyd, and even fewer have described it with such wit and understanding."

Boyd's early collection of short stories, *On the Yankee Station,* was expanded and reissued for publication in the United States following the appearance of his two novels. Containing fifteen stories that vary widely in subject matter and narrative technique, the book was perceived by critics as the work of a gifted young writer experimenting with his craft. Not that the stories display "faltering" or "rough edges," asserted Tyler; "some writers arrive full-blown." Reviewing the collection for the *Spectator,* Paul Ableman agreed. "The feeling of apprentice work derives not from their quality but from their variety," he stated. "Here is a collection of short stories which are, with one exception, formidably accomplished. . . . They reveal no sign of beginner's fumbling. . . . The impression they convey is of an aspiring author exploring his talent by setting it a variety of literary challenges."

Largely traditional narratives, the stories portray innocents and misfits struggling in an indifferent world: a faded child-star-turned-parking-attendant who dreams of meeting a celebrity, a young boy tortured by his mother's adulteries, a bullied soldier obsessed with revenge. *Los Angeles Times Book Review* critic Malcolm Boyd described *On the Yankee Station* as a look "at life's underside instead of its smiling face." Kakutani related that "the incongruous attachments formed by these characters . . . end either in predictable violence or, occasionally, in more surprising glimpses of redemption." She added: "For the most part, though, Mr. Boyd's people are not an overly introspective lot: Instead of looking into their own souls for answers, they tend to project their needs and frustrations outward to the world at large." Andrew Motion reiterated this assessment when writing for the *Times Literary Supplement.* "Boyd does not show his characters receiving impressions," he commented. "They exist primarily in terms of narrative event: for all the frequency with which circumstances conspire against them, they seldom form a speculative or philosophical attachment to their worlds. The greatest virtue of this narrative method is a certain kind of readability—Boyd's stories race along, confident and competent. The disadvantage, though, is a degree of sameness."

But again, all critics did not share disappointment in Boyd's characters. "Boyd's people run true; they are believable in their strengths and weakness," maintained Virginia Curtin Knight, reviewing *On the Yankee Station* for the *Detroit Free Press.* "Bringing readers into the souls of such characters is . . . a technical *tour de force,*" applauded *Washington Post Book World* critic Joseph McLellan. And most reviewers agreed that, regardless of flaws, the stories showcase the obvious skills of a major developing talent. "Nothing in this accomplished collection is less than diverting," wrote Patricia Craig in a review for the *Times Literary Supplement*. "Even when his subject is slight," a second *Washington Post Book World* critic concluded, "Boyd's prose always gives pleasure."

In his third novel, *Stars and Bars,* Boyd returned to the comic tradition of the hapless Englishman abroad, introducing Henderson Dores, a timid, proper London art appraiser who takes a new job with a Manhattan auction house, eager to lose his inhibitions and reserve in the bold, impetuous world of America. Frequently daunted by New York City manners and conventions, the Englishman surrenders all comprehension when he travels to a backwater Georgian hamlet to purchase the art collection of a reclusive southern millionaire. The millionaire's lunatic family, strong-arm rival art dealers, an ex-wife fiancee, a mistress, and a nymphetic stepdaughter-to-be confound Dores's ill-fated mission; finally stranded on Park Avenue wearing only a cardboard box, perceived as a madman by fellow pedestrians, he abdicates his responsible self to an irrational world—and feels sudden kinship. "This 'America' by which he has hoped to be liberated," observed Yardley in another *Washington Post Book World* critique, "turns out to be a far more complex and difficult place than he bargained for."

Reviewing *Stars and Bars* for the *New York Times Book Review,* Caroline Seebohm determined that Boyd's "talent in evoking a place, which worked so well in his earlier two novels, serves him brilliantly here." Yardley concurred, lauding the author's sense of "the American landscape, both physical and psychological" and contending that Boyd "recreates American speech with the aplomb of a born mimic." Writing in the *Village Voice Literary Supplement,* Lawrence Klepp also commended Boyd's "ear for American idiom" and "command of backwater American geography and character," adding, "Occasionally the plot yields entertainingly sour observations of American life." But while Boyd pokes fun at "American food, accents, adolescents, motels with their conventions, hotels with interior forests and lakes," opined *Newsweek* reviewer Peter S. Prescott, he never loses sight of his "primary target," the transplanted Englishman who cannot assimilate. "Can this British author get all this American arcana right?" the critic pondered. "Alas, he can."

Welcoming Boyd's return "to what he does best—the comic novel," John Nicholson announced in the London *Times* that "*Stars and Bars* made me laugh out loud." *Los Angeles Times Book Review* critic Florence King repeated the compliment, maintaining that Boyd is "funnier than Evelyn Waugh." Some reviewers, however, did express confusion concerning the novel's final "revelation" episode; "the theme of Henderson's fresh start is never fully developed," wrote David Montrose in a critique for the *Times Literary Supplement.* "The 'new clarity' with which he views the world at the end remains, for the reader, a lingering fog," seconded Seebohm. Still, Klepp suggested that although Dores's "liberating illumination" may leave "most readers . . . in the dark . . . they will be left in good humor . . . for this is still a consistently entertaining and almost dauntingly intelligent novel."

While still a doctoral candidate at Oxford University Boyd became fascinated and inspired by the *Confessions* of Jean-Jacques Rousseau. In his novel *The New Confessions,* a Scottish expatriate filmmaker named John James Todd looks back over a life than spans much of the twentieth century. Once again war is presented as a metaphor for the chaos that can engulf anyone at any time, and the central character's paranoia is fanned by the McCarthy-era sweep of Hollywood in search of communists in the film industry. "I wanted this to be like a life," Boyd explained in the *Washington Post.* "I wanted the graininess, the texture of life, with the blind alleys and circlings that a real life has. I wanted [the character] to seem like a real person. That type of genial egomaniac is his own worst enemy."

New Republic reviewer Thomas R. Edwards maintained that with the publication of *The New Confessions,* "I would expect Boyd to become popular with intelligent general readers in America. . . . *The New Confessions* has its problems of scale and focus. But it's a novel that can be read with pleasure for its story, and also one that grows in the mind as you think about it afterward, the most ambitious and the best work this interesting writer . . . has yet produced." In the *Los Angeles Times Book Review,* Ronald Gottesman observed that in this novel "Boyd has created an important and complex character in a vividly evoked series of settings. He has told a tale that we cannot not believe in (in spite of its many astonishing turns). He has written a subtle and provocative history of our time. Boyd is no longer a young writer of promise; with this book, he takes his place as a major novelist."

Boyd's next novel, *Brazzaville Beach,* won the James Tait Black Memorial Book Prize. Once again set in an unnamed African nation torn by civil war, the story follows a scientist named Hope Clearwater as she observes chimpanzee behavior and ruminates on her unsuccessful marriage to a troubled mathematician. Hope's discovery that groups of chimpanzees in the game reserve are actually waging war upon each other threatens to refute the many popular publications of the reserve's leading scientist. "Strong or interesting characters give *Brazzaville Beach* its color, impetus, and bite, but Hope is its dynamo," wrote Michael Bishop in the *Washington Post Book World.* "She sets things going—from her courtship of John Clearwater, who attracts her because he has a cast of mind beyond her own understanding, to the necessary dismantling of a great primatologist's self-deluding theories about the chimpanzees at Grosso Arvore Research Project, a group of which has fallen into a pattern of cannibalistic wilding." The critic concludes that *Brazzaville Beach*'s "people convince, its contrapuntal story unfolds with a complex inevitability that does not preclude surprises, and its intellectual music, honestly grounded in the workaday lives of its characters, resonates from the earth up rather than from the sky down."

A number of American critics offered similar praise for *Brazzaville Beach.* Kakutani, in a *New York Times* piece, commended the work for its "sure storytelling" and "terrific sense of drama," praising the author for his "ability to build emotional suspense into the narrative structure." *New York Times Book Review* correspondent Blanche d'Alpuget wrote: "William Boyd is a champion storyteller. His prose style is intelligent, vigorous, and pleasant." In *Newsweek,* Peter S. Prescott described the work as "that rare breed of novel that's both intelligent and entertaining."

The Blue Afternoon, published in 1995, weaves a story through the interaction of a confident and successful woman with the man who claims to be her natural father. The heart of the novel offers the flashback memories of the father, Salvador Carriscant, who worked as a physician in the Philippines. In her *New York Times* review, Kakutani praised *The Blue Afternoon* as "a pitch-perfect story of love and redemption, a story that is as moving as it is entertaining, as dexterously wrought as it is compelling. . . . Part detective story, part love story, part historical epic, *The Blue Afternoon* is a novel that fulfills all the promise of Mr. Boyd's earlier books, a novel that attests to the full maturation of his talents."

Although he was born in Africa and educated in Scotland and England, Boyd described himself in a *Publishers Weekly* interview with Amanda Smith as leading "a rather banal life in a way, nothing out of the ordinary." He now lives in London and supports himself solely by writing—novels, journalism, screenplays, and criticism. "All my fiction is about luck and destiny, so-called, and how you cope with it, how you come to terms with it," he said. "It's to do with the comic tradition in the sense that things are crazy and totally unpredictable and nobody knows what's going to happen, so what sort of attitude do you have in the face of this kind of indifferent and random universe? I think that the comic absurd is the only way to cope with it. . . . In my heroes' case it's usually to do with recognizing that the universe is utterly indifferent to the fate of individuals. Once you realize that, all sorts of choices and dilemmas don't come any easier, but there's some sort of perverse logic there working."

BIOGRAPHICAL/CRITICAL SOURCES:

BOOKS

Contemporary Literary Criticism, Gale, Volume 28, 1984, Volume 53, 1989, Volume 70, 1992.

PERIODICALS

Detroit Free Press, August 26, 1984.
Detroit News, August 12, 1984.
London Review of Books, September 23, 1993, p. 22.
Los Angeles Times Book Review, March 27, 1983; August 26, 1984; May 26, 1985; June 19, 1988, p. 2, 8.
New Republic, April 25, 1983; June 13, 1988, pp. 32-34.
New Statesman, January 30, 1981; September 17, 1982.
New Statesman & Society, September 24, 1993, p. 24.
Newsweek, January 14, 1985; May 6, 1985; July 8, 1991, p. 59.
New Yorker, April 12, 1982; April 25, 1983; October 15, 1984; May 20, 1985.
New York Review of Books, June 2, 1983; October 10, 1991, p. 33-4.
New York Times, April 5, 1983; May 21, 1983; July 2, 1984; August 9, 1986; April 27, 1988, p. 24C; May 31, 1991, p. 29C; April 11, 1995, p. 2B.

New York Times Book Review, April 25, 1982; February 27, 1983; August 5, 1984; April 14, 1985; June 23, 1991, p. 14.

Observer (London), September 12, 1982.

Publishers Weekly, April 29, 1988, pp. 56-57.

Spectator, February 28, 1981; August 8, 1981; November 28, 1981; September 11, 1982; December 18, 1982; January 1, 1983; October 6, 1984.

Time, July 30, 1984; May 20, 1985; June 24, 1991, p. 64.

Times (London), October 28, 1981; February 28, 1983; September 20, 1984; September 28, 1987.

Times Literary Supplement, January 30, 1981; July 17, 1981; September 17, 1982; October 22, 1982; September 21, 1984.

Village Voice Literary Supplement, September, 1984; May, 1985.

Washington Post, May 31, 1988.

Washington Post Book World, March 20, 1983; July 10, 1983; August 5, 1984; April 28, 1985; November 24, 1985; June 2, 1991, p. 1, 14.

*   *   *

BRADLEY, Marion Zimmer   1930-
(Lee Chapman, John Dexter, Miriam Gardner, Valerie Graves, Morgan Ives, Elfrida Rivers)

PERSONAL: Born June 3, 1930, in Albany, NY; daughter of Leslie (a carpenter) and Evelyn (a historian; maiden name, Conklin) Zimmer; married Robert A. Bradley, October, 1949 (divorced, 1963); married Walter Henry Breen (a numismatist), June, 1964 (divorced); children: (first marriage) David Stephen Robert; (second marriage) Patrick Russell Donald, Moira Evelyn Dorothy. *Education:* Attended New York State College for Teachers (now State University of New York at Albany), 1946-48; Hardin-Simmons College, B.A., 1964; additional study at University of California, Berkeley. *Politics:* None. *Avocational interests:* Supports Merola, an opera apprentice program.

ADDRESSES: Home—Berkeley, CA. *Office*—P.O. Box 72, Berkeley, CA 94701. *Agent*—Scovil Chichak Galen Literary Agency, 381 Park Ave. S., #1020, New York, NY 10016.

CAREER: Writer, editor, and musician.

MEMBER: Authors Guild, Science Fiction Writers of America, Alpha Chi.

AWARDS, HONORS: Hugo Award Nomination, 1963; Nebula Award Nomination, 1964 and 1978; Invisible Little Man Award, 1977; Leigh Brackett Memorial Sense of Wonder Award, 1978, for *The Forbidden Tower;* Locus Award for best fantasy novel, 1984, for *The Mists of Avalon.*

WRITINGS:

SCIENCE FICTION/FANTASY

The Door through Space [bound with *Rendezvous on Lost Planet* by A. Bertram Chandler], Ace Books (New York City), 1961.

Seven from the Stars [bound with *Worlds of the Imperium* by Keith Laumer], Ace Books, 1962.

The Colors of Space, Monarch (New York City), 1963, revised edition, illustrated by Barbi Johnson, Donning (Norfolk, VA), 1983, illustrated by Lee Moyer, Donning, 1988.

Falcons of Narabedla [and] *The Dark Intruder and Other Stories,* Ace Books, 1964.

The Brass Dragon [bound with *Ipomoea* by John Rackham], Ace Books, 1969.

(With brother, Paul Edwin Zimmer) *Hunters of the Red Moon,* DAW Books (New York City), 1973.

The Parting of Arwen (short story), T-K Graphics, 1974.

The Endless Voyage, Ace Books, 1975, expanded edition published as *Endless Universe,* 1979.

The Ruins of Isis, illustrated by Polly and Kelly Freas, Donning, 1978.

(With P. E. Zimmer) *The Survivors,* DAW Books, 1979.

The House between the Worlds, Doubleday (New York City), 1980, revised edition, Del Rey (New York City), 1981.

Survey Ship, illustrated by Steve Fabian, Ace Books, 1980.

The Mists of Avalon, Knopf (New York City), 1982.

The Web of Darkness (also see below), illustrated by V. M. Wyman and C. Lee Healy, Donning, 1983.

Web of Light (also see below), illustrated by C. Lee Healy, Donning, 1983.

(Editor and contributor) *Greyhaven: An Anthology of Fantasy,* DAW Books, 1983.

Night's Daughter, Ballantine (New York City), 1985.

(With Vonda McIntyre) *Lythande* (anthology), DAW Books, 1986.

The Fall of Atlantis (includes *Web of Light* and *Web of Darkness*), Baen Books (Riverdale, NY), 1987.

The Firebrand, Simon & Schuster (New York City), 1987.

Warrior Woman, DAW Books, 1988.

(With Andre Norton and Julian May) *The Black Trillium,* Doubleday, 1990.

The Forest House, Viking (New York City), 1994.

Lady of the Trillium, Bantam (New York City), 1995.

(With Norton and Mercedes Lackey) *Tiger Burning Bright,* Morrow (New York City), 1995.

GOTHIC FICTION

(Under pseudonym Miriam Gardner) *The Strange Woman,* Monarch, 1962.

Castle Terror, Lancer (New York City), 1965.

Souvenir of Monique, Ace Books, 1967.

Bluebeard's Daughter, Lancer, 1968.

Dark Satanic, Berkley Publishing (New York City), 1972.

Drums of Darkness: An Astrological Gothic Novel, Ballantine, 1976.

The Inheritor, Tor Books, 1984.

Witch Hill, Tor Books, 1990.

Ghostlight, Tor Books (New York City), 1995.

"DARKOVER" SCIENCE FICTION SERIES

The Sword of Aldones [and] *The Planet Savers,* Ace Books, 1962, *The Sword of Aldones,* with introduction by Richard A. Lupoff, Gregg Press (Boston), 1977, *The Planet Savers,* introduction by Bradley, Gregg Press, 1979, published as *Planet Savers: The Sword of Aldones,* Ace Books, 1984.

The Bloody Sun, Ace Books, 1964, revised edition, Ace Books, 1979, with introduction by Bradley, Gregg Press, 1979.

Star of Danger, Ace Books, 1965, with introduction by Bradley, Gregg Press, 1979.

The Winds of Darkover [bound with *The Anything Tree* by Rackham], Ace Books, 1970, with introduction by Bradley, Gregg Press, 1979.

The World Wreckers, Ace Books, 1971, with introduction by Bradley, Gregg Press, 1979.

Darkover Landfall, DAW Books, 1972, with introduction by Theodore Sturgeon, Gregg Press, 1978.

The Spell Sword, DAW Books, 1974, with introduction by Bradley, Gregg Press, 1979.

The Heritage of Hastur (also see below), DAW Books, 1975, with introduction by Susan Wood, Gregg Press, 1977.

The Shattered Chain (also see below), DAW Books, 1976, with introduction by Bradley, Gregg Press, 1979.

The Forbidden Tower, DAW Books, 1977, with introduction by Bradley, Gregg Press, 1979.

Stormqueen!, DAW Books, 1978, with introduction by Bradley, Gregg Press, 1979.

(Editor and contributor) *Legends of Hastur and Cassilda,* Thendara House Publications (Berkeley, CA), 1979.

(Editor and contributor) *Tales of the Free Amazons,* Thendara House Publications, 1980.

Two to Conquer, DAW Books, 1980.

(Editor and contributor) *The Keeper's Price and Other Stories,* DAW Books, 1980.

Sharra's Exile (also see below), DAW Books, 1981.

Children of Hastur (includes *The Heritage of Hastur* and *Sharra's Exile*), Doubleday, 1981.

Hawkmistress!, DAW Books, 1982.

(Editor and contributor) *Sword of Chaos,* DAW Books, 1982.

Oath of the Renunciates (includes *The Shattered Chain* and *Thendara House*), Doubleday, 1983.

Thendara House (also see below), DAW Books, 1983.

City of Sorcery, DAW Books, 1984.

(Editor, contributor, and author of introduction) *Free Amazons of Darkover: An Anthology,* DAW Books, 1985.

(Editor and contributor) *Red Sun of Darkover,* DAW Books, 1987.

(Editor and contributor) *The Other Side of the Mirror and Other Darkover Stories,* DAW Books, 1987.

(Editor and contributor) *Four Moons of Darkover,* DAW Books, 1988.

The Heirs of Hammerfell, DAW Books, 1989.

(Editor) *Domains of Darkover,* DAW Books, 1990.

(Editor) *Renunciates of Darkover,* DAW Books, 1991.

(Editor) *Leroni of Darkover,* DAW Books, 1991.

(Editor) *Towers of Darkover,* DAW Books, 1993.

(With Mercedes Lackey) *Rediscovery: A Novel of Darkover,* DAW Books, 1993.

Marion Zimmer Bradley's Darkover (short stories), DAW Books, 1993.

Exile's Song, DAW Books, 1996.

NOVELS

(Under pseudonym Lee Chapman) *I Am a Lesbian,* Monarch, 1962.

(Under pseudonym Morgan Ives) *Spare Her Heaven,* Monarch, 1963.

(Under pseudonym Miriam Gardner) *My Sister, My Love,* Monarch, 1963.

(Under pseudonym Miriam Gardner) *Twilight Lovers,* Monarch, 1964.

(Under pseudonym Morgan Ives) *Knives of Desire,* Cornith (San Diego, CA), 1966.

(Under pseudonym John Dexter) *No Adam for Eve,* Cornith, 1966.

The Catch Trap, Ballantine, 1979.

Also author of novels as Valerie Graves and under other undisclosed pseudonyms.

CRITICISM

Men, Halflings, and Hero Worship, T-K Graphics, 1973.

The Necessity for Beauty: Robert W. Chamber and the Romantic Tradition, T-K Graphics, 1974.

The Jewel of Arwen, T-K Graphics, 1974.

OTHER

Songs from Rivendell, privately printed, 1959.

A Complete, Cumulative Checklist of Lesbian, Variant, and Homosexual Fiction, privately printed, 1960.

(Translator) Lope de Vega, *El Villano en su Rincon,* privately printed, 1971.

In the Steps of the Master (teleplay novelization), Tempo Books, 1973.

Can Ellen Be Saved? (teleplay novelization), Tempo Books, 1975.

(With Alfred Bester and Norman Spinrad) *Experiment Perilous: Three Essays in Science Fiction,* Algol Press, 1976.

The Ballad of Hastur and Cassilda (poem), Thendara House Publications, 1978.

(Editor) *Sword and Sorceress* (annual anthology), Volumes 1-14, DAW Books, 1984-97.

The Best of Marion Zimmer Bradley, edited by Martin H. Greenberg, Academy Chicago (Chicago, IL), 1986, revised edition published as *Jamie and Other Stories: The Best of Marion Zimmer Bradley,* Academy Chicago, 1991.

Contributor, sometimes under name Elfrida Rivers and other pseudonyms, to anthologies and books, including *Essays Lovecraftian,* edited by Darrell Schweitzer, T-K Graphics, 1976. Also contributor to periodicals, including *Magazine of Fantasy and Science Fiction, Amazing Stories,* and *Venture.* Editor of *Marion Zimmer Bradley's Fantasy Magazine,* 1988—.

SIDELIGHTS: Marion Zimmer Bradley is author of one of the best-loved series in science fiction and fantasy; her "Darkover" novels have not only inspired their own fan magazines, known as "fanzines," but also a series of story collections in which other authors set their tales in Bradley's universe. A lost colony rediscovered after centuries of neglect by Earth's "Terran Empire," Darkover has developed its own society and technology, both of which produce internal and external conflicts. Darkover fascinates so many readers because it is a world of many contradictions; not only do the psychic abilities of the natives contrast with the traditional technologies of the empire, but a basically repressive patriarchal society coexists, however uneasily, with such groups as an order of female Renunciates, the "Free Amazons." Consisting of over twenty books and spanning many years of the world's history, "the Darkover novels test various attitudes about the importance of technology, and more important, they study the very nature of human intimacy," claims Rosemarie Arbur in *Twentieth-Century Science Fiction Writers.* The critic explains that "by postulating a Terran Empire the main features of which are advanced technology and bureaucracy, and a Darkover that seems technologically backward and is fiercely individualistic, Bradley sets up a conflict to which there is no 'correct' resolution." The permutations of this basic conflict have provided Bradley with numerous opportunities to explore several themes in various ways.

For example, Susan M. Shwartz observes in *The Feminine Eye: Science Fiction and the Women Who Write It,* one theme in particular provides a foundation for the Darkover novels: "For every gain, there is a risk; choice involves a testing of will and courage." Unlike some fantasy worlds where struggles are easily decided, "on Darkover any attempt at change or progress carries with it the need for pain-filled choice," Shwartz comments. While Bradley provides her characters with ample avenues of action "in the Darkover books, alternatives are predicated upon two things . . . sincere choice and a willingness to pay the price choice demands." For example, Shwartz continues, "in *The Shattered Chain,* the payment for taking an oath is the payment for all such choices: pain, with a potential for achievement. In Bradley's other books, too, the price of choice is of great importance."

The Shattered Chain is one of Bradley's most renowned Darkover novels and, as Arbur describes it in her study *Marion Zimmer Bradley,* the novel "is one of the most thorough and sensitive science-fiction explorations of the variety of options available to a self-actualizing woman; not only does it present us with four strong and different feminine characters who make crucial decisions about their lives but its depth of characterizations permits us to examine in detail the consequences of these decisions." The novel begins as a traditional quest when Lady Rohana, a noblewoman of the ruling class, enlists the aid of a tribe of Free Amazons to rescue a kidnapped kinswoman from a settlement where women are chained to show that they are possessions. But while the rescue is eventually successful, it is only the beginning of a series of conflicts. Rohana's experiences force her to reevaluate her life, and both the daughter of the woman she rescues and a Terran agent who studies the Amazons find themselves examining the limits of their own situations. "In terms of its structure, plot, characterization, and context within the series," Shwartz argues, *The Shattered Chain* "is about all the choices of all women on Darkover and, through them, of all people, male and female, Darkovan and Terran."

Bradley also emphasizes two other themes. As Laura Murphy states in the *Dictionary of Literary Biography:* "The first is the reconciliation of conflicting or opposing forces—whether such forces are represented by different cultures or by different facets of a single personality. The second," the critic continues, "closely related to the first, is alienation or exile from a dominant group." While these ideas are featured in Bradley's Darkover series, they also appear in the author's first mainstream best seller, *The Mists of Avalon.* "Colorfully detailed as a medieval tapestry, *The Mists of Avalon* . . . is probably the most ambitious retelling of the Arthurian legend in the twentieth century," Charlotte Spivack maintains in *Merlin's Daughters: Contemporary Women Writers of Fantasy.* The critic adds that this novel "is much more than a retelling. . . . [It] is a profound revisioning. Imaginatively conceived, intricately structured, and richly peopled, it offers a brilliant reinterpretation of the traditional material from the point of view of the major female characters," such as Arthur's mother Igraine; the Lady of the Lake, Viviane; Arthur's half-sister, the enchantress Morgaine; and Arthur's wife, Gwenhwyfar.

In addition, Bradley presents the eventual downfall of Arthur's reign as the result of broken promises to the religious leaders of Avalon. While Arthur gained his crown with the aid of Viviane and the Goddess she represents, the influence of Christian priests and Gwenhwyfar led him to forsake his oath. Thus not only does Bradley present Arthur's story from a different viewpoint, she roots it "in the religious struggle between matriarchal worship of the goddess and the patriarchal institution of Christianity, between what [the author] calls 'the cauldron and the cross,'" writes Spivack. In presenting this conflict, Bradley "memorably depicts the inevitable passing of times and religions by her use of the imagery of different simultaneous worlds, which move out of consciousness as their day ebbs," remarks Maude McDaniel in the *Washington Post.* "Bradley also compares head-on the pre-Christian Druidism of Britain and the Christianity that supplants it, a refreshing change from some modern writers who tend to take refuge at awkward moments in cryptic metaphysics."

According to Carrol L. Fry in the *Journal of Popular Culture,* Bradley "reverses the traditional Arthurian lore to criticize institutional Christianity. She levels much of that criticism at her perception . . . of the church's misogyny." In her article, Fry traces parallels between the beliefs of modern Neo-Paganism and the Druidism Bradley presents in *The Mists of Avalon.* "Priests repress femininity," Fry explains, "and Igraine, Morgaine's mother, confesses that she allowed her daughter to go to Avalon because she would fare better with the Goddess 'than in the hands of the black priests who would teach her to think that she was evil because she was a woman.' Igraine had been a priestess herself and knows the changes the Romans brought." "Morgaine gets most of the powerfully feminist lines," Fry continues, "while Gwenhwyfar, despite her infidelity, represents the repressed woman who denies the power of the feminine." "Bradley uses the timeless matter of Arthur as the basic story line and she intertwines the Neo-Pagan monomyth with it in symbiotic fashion," the critic concludes. "The result is a richly ironic narrative, but also a powerful feminist statement."

Despite critical praise for Bradley's fresh approach to Arthurian legend, McDaniel finds *The Mists of Avalon* too motionless in its treatment of the Arthurian legend: "It all seems strangely static," the critic writes, "set pieces the reader watches rather than enters. Aside from a couple of lackluster jousts, everything is intrigue, jealousy and personal relationships, so that finally we are left with more bawling than brawling." *Science Fiction Review* contributor Darrell Schweitzer concurs, for while he finds *The*

Mists of Avalon "certainly an original and quite well-thought-out version," he faults the novel for changes which are "all in the direction of the mundane, the ordinary." The critic explains: "Most of the interesting parts happen offstage. Alas, for whatever reason the women, Morgaine in particular, just aren't that central to the whole story. They aren't present at the crucial moments."

Maureen Quilligan, however, believes that Bradley's emphasis on Morgaine and the other female characters is both effective and appropriate; as she writes in the *New York Times Book Review,* by "looking at the Arthurian legend from the other side, as in one of Morgaine's magic weavings, we see all the interconnecting threads, not merely the artful pattern. . . . *The Mists of Avalon* rewrites Arthur's story so that we realize it has always also been the story of his sister, the Fairy Queen." By presenting another side, the critic adds, "this, the untold Arthurian story, is no less tragic, but it has gained a mythic coherence; reading it is a deeply moving and at times uncanny experience." "In short," concludes Beverly Deweese in a *Science Fiction Review* article, "Bradley's Arthurian world is intriguingly different. Undoubtedly, the brisk pace, the careful research and the provocative concept will attract and please many readers. . . . [But] overall, *Mists of Avalon* is one of the best and most ambitious of the Arthurian novels, and it should not be missed."

Bradley employs similar themes and approaches in reworking another classic tale: *The Firebrand,* the story of the fall of Troy and of Kassandra, royal daughter of Troy and onetime priestess and Amazon. As the author remarked in an interview with *Publishers Weekly*'s Lisa See, in the story of Troy she saw another instance of male culture overtaking and obscuring female contributions: "During the Dorian invasion, when iron won out over bronze, the female cult died," Bradley explained. "The Minoan and Mycenaean cultures were dead overnight. But you could also look at [that period of history] and say, here were two cultures that should have been ruled by female twins—Helen and Klytemnestra. And what do you know? When they married Menelaus and Agamemnon, the men took over their cities. I just want to look at what history was really like before the women-haters got hold of it. I want to look at these people like any other people, as though no one had ever written about them before." The result of Bradley's reconstruction, as *New York Times Book Review* contributor Mary Lefkowitz describes it, is that Kassandra "becomes active, even aggressive; she

determines the course of history, despite the efforts of her father, her brothers and other brutal male warriors to keep her in her place." "The dust of the war fairly rises off the page," notes a *Publishers Weekly* reviewer, "as Bradley animates this rich history and vivifies the conflicts between a culture that reveres the strength of women and one that makes them mere consorts of powerful men."

Bradley returns to ancient Britain with *The Forest House,* the story of the love between the erstwhile British priestess Eilan and the Roman officer Gaius Marcellius. The pair conceive a child before their respective families separate them, and Eilan in particular is caught between her feelings for Gaius, her position in the Forest House as High Priestess of the Great Goddess, and her problems with the competing influences of the Druids. "An aging priestess, mentor of Eilan," explains a critic for *Kirkus Reviews,* ". . . tells the sad story of lovers' deaths, and takes the child Gawen (of mingled ancestry, presaging a new British people) to the vale of 'Afallon.'" "History and legend collide," declares Carolyn Cushman in *Locus,* "and though history dominates, by the end the mythic elements grow to hint satisfactorily at the Arthurian wonder to come."

Despite this emphasis on female viewpoints in *The Firebrand* and her other fiction, Bradley is not a "feminist" writer. "Though her interest in women's rights is strong," elaborates Murphy, "her works do not reduce to mere polemic." Arbur similarly states that Bradley "refuses to allow her works to wander into politics unless true concerns of realistic characters bring them there. Her emphasis is on character, not political themes." "Bradley's writing openly with increasing sureness of the human psyche and the human being rendered whole prompted Theodore Sturgeon to call the former [science fiction] fan 'one of the Big ones' currently writing science fiction," Arbur relates in *Twentieth-Century Science Fiction Writers.* "That she has extended her range" beyond science fiction and into "mainstream" fiction, the critic concludes, "suggests that Sturgeon's phrase applies no longer only to the science-fiction writer Marion Zimmer Bradley continues to be, for she has transcended categories."

BIOGRAPHICAL/CRITICAL SOURCES:

BOOKS

Alpers, H. J., editor, *Marion Zimmer Bradley's Darkover,* Corian, 1983.

Arbur, Rosemarie, *Leigh Brackett, Marion Zimmer Bradley, Anne McCaffrey: A Primary and Secondary Bibliography,* G. K. Hall, 1982.

Arbur, *Marion Zimmer Bradley,* Starmont House, 1985.

Breen, Walter, *The Gemini Problem: A Study of Darkover,* T-K Graphics, 1975.

Breen, *The Darkover Concordance: A Reader's Guide,* Pennyfarthing Press, 1979.

The Darkover Cookbook, Friends of Darkover, 1977, revised edition, 1979.

Dictionary of Literary Biography, Volume 8: *Twentieth-Century American Science Fiction Writers,* Gale, 1981.

Lane, Daryl, editor, *The Sound of Wonder,* Volume 2, Oryx, 1985.

Magill, Frank, editor, *Survey of Science Fiction Literature,* Volume 1, Salem Press, 1979.

Magill, editor, *Survey of Modern Fantasy Literature,* Volume 1, Salem Press, 1983.

Paxson, Diana, *Costume and Clothing as a Cultural Index on Darkover,* Friends of Darkover, 1977, revised edition, 1981.

Roberson, Jennifer, *Return to Avalon,* DAW Books, 1996.

Spivack, Charlotte, *Merlin's Daughters: Contemporary Women Writers of Fantasy,* Greenwood Press, 1987.

Staicar, Tom, editor, *The Feminine Eye: Science Fiction and the Women Who Write It,* Ungar, 1982.

Twentieth-Century Science Fiction Writers, St. James Press, 1986.

Wise, S., *The Darkover Dilemma: Problems of the Darkover Series,* T-K Graphics, 1976.

PERIODICALS

Algol, winter, 1977/1978.

Booklist, February 15, 1993, p. 1011; January 15, 1994, p. 875; March 15, 1995, p. 1313.

Entertainment Weekly, May 20, 1994, p. 57.

Fantasy Review of Fantasy and Science Fiction, April, 1984.

Journal of Popular Culture, summer, 1993, pp. 67-80.

Kirkus Reviews, February 1, 1994, pp. 81-82.

Library Journal, December, 1990, p. 167; December 15, 1991, p. 117; March 15, 1992, p. 129; June 15, 1992, p. 106; March 15, 1993, p. 111; May 15, 1993, p. 100; June 15, 1993, p. 104; March 15, 1994, p. 104; June 15, 1994, p. 99; May 15, 1995, p. 99.

Locus, April, 1994, p. 29.

Los Angeles Times Book Review, February 3, 1983.

Mythlore, spring, 1984.

New York Times Book Review, January 30, 1983; November 29, 1987.

Publishers Weekly, September 11, 1987; October 30, 1987; March 15, 1993, p. 74; February 28, 1994, p. 72; February 27, 1995, p. 91.

San Francisco Examiner, February 27, 1983.

Science Fiction Review, summer, 1983.

Washington Post, January 28, 1983.

West Coast Review of Books, number 5, 1986.

* * *

BRAILSFORD, Frances
See WOSMEK, Frances

* * *

BRANIGAN, Keith   1940-

PERSONAL: Born April 15, 1940, in Slough, Buckinghamshire, England; son of Arthur Allan (a clerk) and Constance Gladys (a homemaker; maiden name, Saunders) Branigan; married Kuabrat Sivadith, June 20, 1965; children: Alun, Holly, Tania. *Education:* University of Birmingham, B.A., 1963; Ph.D., 1966.

ADDRESSES: Home—Sheffield, England. *Office*—Department of Prehistory and Archaeology, University of Sheffield, Sheffield S10 2TN, England.

CAREER: University of Birmingham, Birmingham, England, research fellow, 1965-66; University of Bristol, Bristol, England, lecturer in archaeology, 1966-67; University of Sheffield, Sheffield, England, professor of prehistory and archaeology, 1976—. Director of Archaeology in Education; chair of British Universities Archaeology Committee, 1980-86.

MEMBER: Prehistoric Society (vice president, 1980-83), Society for the Promotion of Roman Studies, Society of Antiquaries of London (fellow).

WRITINGS:

Copper and Bronzeworking in Early Bronze Age Crete, P. Arstroem, 1968.

The Foundations of Palatial Crete: A Survey of Crete in the Early Bronze Age, Praeger (London), 1970, published as *Pre-Palatial: The Foundations of Palatial Crete: A Survey of Crete in the Early Bronze Age,* Benjamins North America (Philadelphia, PA), 1988.

The Tombs of Mesara: A Study of Funerary Architecture and Ritual in Southern Crete, 2800-1700 B.C., Duckworth (London), 1970.

Latimer: Belgic, Roman, Dark Age, and Early Modern Farm, Bristol Chess Valley Archaeological and Historical Society, 1971.

Town and Country: The Archaeology of Verulamium and the Roman Chilterns, Spurbooks (London), 1973.

Reconstructing the Past: A Basic Introduction to Archaeology, David & Charles (Newton Abbot, Devon, England), 1974.

Aegean Metalwork of the Early and Middle Bronze Ages, Clarendon Press (Oxford, England), 1974.

Atlas of Ancient Civilizations, John Day, 1976.

Prehistoric Britain: An Illustrated Survey, Spurbooks, 1976.

(Editor with P. J. Fowler) *The Roman West Country: Classical Culture and Celtic Society,* David & Charles, 1976.

The Roman Villa in Southwest England, Moonraker Press (Surrey, England), 1977.

Gatcombe: The Excavation and Study of a Romano-British Villa Estate, 1967-1976, British Archaeological Reports (Oxford), 1978.

(Editor) *Rome and the Brigantes: The Impact of Rome on Northern England,* Department of Prehistory and Archaeology, University of Sheffield (Sheffield, England), 1980.

Roman Britain: Life in an Imperial Province, Reader's Digest Association (London), 1980.

(With Michael Vickers) *Hellas: The Civilizations of Ancient Greece,* McGraw (Maidenhead, Berks, England), 1980.

(Editor) *Atlas of Archaeology,* St. Martin's (New York City), 1982.

Prehistory, Kingfisher (London), 1984.

The Catuvellauni, Alan Sutton (Glouchester, England), 1986.

Archaeology Explained, Focus Info, 1988.

(With M. J. Dearne) *Romano-British Cavemen,* Oxbow, 1992.

Dancing with Death: Life and Death in Southern Crete c.3000-2000 B.C., Benjamins North America, 1993.

(Editor with others) *Lexicon of the Greek & Roman Cities & Place Names in Antiquity, c.1500 B.C.- A.D. 500,* Benjamins North America, 1993.

(With P. Fasto) *Barra: Archaeological Research on Ben Tangaral,* Sheffield Academic Press, 1995.

General editor of series "Peoples of Roman Britain," Duckworth, 1973—.

WORK IN PROGRESS: Research on prehistoric and early historic upland settlement in eastern Crete.

SIDELIGHTS: Keith Branigan has been praised by critics for his ability to explain a difficult, technical, and often dry subject to the educated general reader. A. M. Snodgrass writes in the *Times Literary Supplement,* "*Aegean Metalwork of the Early and Middle Bronze Ages* is the Plain Man's Guide to Aegean prehistory . . . a book which can be understood without wide background knowledge or preconceptions." It is a detailed book, nonetheless. The critic continues, "This is the modern approach at its best: let us see the *entire* picture of the evidence available."

Of *Town and Country: The Archaeology of Verulamium and the Roman Chilterns,* a *Times Literary Supplement* reviewer reports: "The story-line is simple and uncluttered with the provisos that normally beset archaeological writing. It is a straight forward description of life among the upper echelons of Roman society."

Branigan once told *CA:* "By the age of eight I had decided I wanted to be an archaeologist. I never consciously worked toward it, but suddenly at the age of eighteen the opportunity was there in front of me and I grabbed it. It was the same, I suppose, with writing. I always enjoyed writing essays, and I had an English master who encouraged me, so when I was offered a contract to write a book I didn't hesitate a minute. I really enjoy writing, particularly those books that try to reach out and introduce new people to the sheer enjoyment of archaeology. But archaeology is one of the fastest moving subjects under the sun—so much new evidence every year, so many new theories to read and digest—that it becomes increasingly difficult to keep up with it all *and* find time to write.

"My greatest thrill in archaeology was excavating an Early Minoan communal tomb (from about 2500 B.C.) in southern Crete in the early 1970s. Although it had been looted by modern tomb robbers there was much to learn from it about the fascinating people who had built and used it."

BIOGRAPHICAL/CRITICAL SOURCES:

PERIODICALS

Times Literary Supplement, October 12, 1973; January 10, 1975.

*   *   *

BRASCH, Rudolph   1912-

PERSONAL: Born November 6, 1912, in Berlin, Germany; son of British citizens, Gustav and Hedwig (Mathias) Brasch; married Liselott Le Buchbinder, February 16, 1952. *Education:* Attended University of Berlin, 1931-35; University of Wurzburg, Ph.D. (summa cum laude), 1936; Jewish Theological Seminary, Berlin, Rabbi (with highest honors), 1938.

ADDRESSES: Home—14 Derby St., Vaucluse, Sydney, New South Wales, Australia.

CAREER: Rabbi of Progressive synagogues in London, England, 1938-48, and Dublin, Ireland, 1946-47; Johannesburg, South Africa, rabbi and director of public relations, 1948-49; Temple Emanuel, Woollahra, New South Wales, Australia, chief minister, 1949-79. University of Sydney, guest professor, 1952-53; visiting rabbi in Montgomery, AL, 1980; University of Hawaii, visiting professor, 1981. Lecturer on cruise ships. Life vice president and chair of ecclesiastical board, Australian and New Zealand Union for Progressive Judaism; member of governing body, World Union for Progressive Judaism; director of education, Liberal Education Board of New South Wales; justice of the peace and civil marriage celebrant, for Australia. *Military service:* Padre to Civil Defence during London blitz; received Coronation Medal (Queen Elizabeth II) for his work.

MEMBER: Royal Australian Historical Society, Society of Religious History (founding member), Rotary Club (Sydney).

AWARDS, HONORS: D.D., Hebrew Union College-Jewish Institute of Religion, Los Angeles, 1959; named Officer of the British Empire, 1967; Order of Australia, 1979; Peace Media Medal, Australian Association of the United Nations, 1979; made lieutenant-colonel in the Alabama militia.

WRITINGS:

(With Lily M. Montagu) *A Little Book of Comfort for Jewish People in Times of Sorrow,* [London], 1948.
The Star of David, Angus & Robertson (London), 1955.
The Eternal Flame, Angus & Robertson, 1958.
General Sir John Monash (biography), Royal Australian Historical Society, 1959.
How Did It Begin?, Longmans, Green (London), 1965, McKay (New York City), 1966.
Mexico: A Country of Contrasts, McKay, 1966.
Judaic Heritage, McKay, 1969.
The Unknown Sanctuary: The Story of Judaism, Its Teachings, Philosophy, and Symbols, Angus & Robertson, 1969.
How Did Sports Begin?: A Look at the Origins of Man at Play, McKay, 1970, reprinted, HarperCollins (London and New York City), 1995.
How Did Sex Begin?: The Sense and Nonsense of the Customs and Traditions that Have Separated Men and Women since Adam and Eve, McKay, 1973, Angus & Robertson, 1995.
The Supernatural and You!, Cassell (London), 1976.
Strange Customs and How They All Began, McKay, 1976, Fontana (London), 1991.
Australian Jews of Today and the Part They Have Played, Cassell, 1977.
There's a Reason for Everything, Fontana, 1982, HarperCollins, 1988..
Mistakes, Misnomers and Misconceptions, Fontana, 1983, Collins, 1988.
Thank God I'm an Atheist, Fontana, 1987, Collins, 1988.
Permanent Addresses (Australians Down Under), Collins, 1987, Angus & Robertson, 1995.
Even More Permanent Addresses (More Australians Down Under), Collins, 1989.
The Book of the Year, Collins, 1991.
A Book of Comfort, Collins, 1991.
The Book of the Year Collection, HarperCollins, 1993.
A Book of Good Advice, Angus & Robertson, 1993.
A Book of Friendship, Angus & Robertson, 1994.
That Takes the Cake, Angus & Robertson, 1994.
Christmas Customs and Traditions, Angus & Robertson, 1995.
The Book of Anniversaries, Angus & Robertson, 1995.

A Book of Forgiveness, Angus & Robertson, 1995.
Circles of Love, Angus & Robertson, 1996.

Also author of *The Midrash Shir Ha-shirim Zuta,* 1936, *The Jewish Question Mark,* 1945, and *The Symbolism of King Solomon's Temple,* 1954. Contributor to *This Is Australia,* Hamlyn (London), 1975, 1977, and 1982, and to *The Australian Beef Eater's Diary,* 1977. Scriptwriter for Australian Broadcasting Commission. Also author of column "Religion and Life," in Australia's *Sun-Herald.* Contributor to *Mankind* and *Commentary* (both United States), and to other magazines and newspapers in Australia, Europe, and Africa. Editor, *Progressive Jew,* Johannesburg, 1948-49.

Some of Brasch's works have been translated into German and Japanese.

SIDELIGHTS: Rudolph Brasch is a master of twelve languages, among them Babylonic-Assyrian (Cunei-form), Syriac, Arabic, and Persian. From his early days, he has been active in inter-faith relations; in Ireland he stayed at a Franciscan monastery; in London he conducted a Hindu-Jewish service; in South Africa he addressed Bantus and held a Dutch Reformed-Jewish service; in Australia he has spoken in the Unitarian and Catholic churches of Sydney and at the Inland Mission Church at Alice Springs in the heart of the interior. He is a regular broadcaster and telecaster as a world authority on the origins of customs, superstitions, and phrases.

*   *   *

BROOKS, Terry   1944-

PERSONAL: Born January 8, 1944, in Sterling, IL; son of Dean Oliver (a printer) and Marjorie Iantha (a homemaker; maiden name, Gleason) Brooks; married Barbara Ann Groth, April 23, 1972 (marriage ended); married Judine Elaine Alba (a bookseller), December 11, 1987; children (first marriage): Amanda Leigh, Alexander Stephen. *Education:* Hamilton College, A.B., 1966; Washington and Lee University, LL.B., 1969.

ADDRESSES: Home—Seattle, WA.   *Office*—c/o Ballantine/Del Rey, 201 East 50th St., New York, NY 10022.

CAREER: Called to the Bar of Illinois; Besse, Frye, Arnold, Brooks & Miller, P.C. (attorneys), Sterling, IL, partner, 1969-86; writer, 1977—.

MEMBER: Authors Guild, American Bar Association, Trial Lawyers of America, Illinois State Bar Association.

AWARDS, HONORS: Best Young Adult Books citation, American Library Association, 1982, for *The Elfstones of Shannara;* Best Books for Young Adults citations, *School Library Journal,* 1982, for *The Elfstones of Shannara,* and 1986, for *Magic Kingdom for Sale—Sold!*

WRITINGS:

"SHANNARA" FANTASY NOVELS

The Sword of Shannara, Random House (New York City), 1977.
The Elfstones of Shannara, Ballantine/Del Rey (New York City), 1982.
The Wishsong of Shannara, Ballantine/Del Rey, 1985.
The First King of Shannara, Ballantine/Del Rey, 1996.

"THE HERITAGE OF SHANNARA" FANTASY NOVELS

The Scions of Shannara, Ballantine/Del Rey, 1990.
The Druid of Shannara, Ballantine/Del Rey, 1991.
The Elf Queen of Shannara, Ballantine/Del Rey, 1992.
The Talismans of Shannara, Ballantine/Del Rey, 1993.

"MAGIC KINGDOM OF LANDOVER" FANTASY NOVELS

Magic Kingdom for Sale—Sold!, Ballantine/Del Rey, 1986.
The Black Unicorn, Ballantine/Del Rey, 1987.
Wizard at Large, Ballantine/Del Rey, 1988.
The Tangle Box: A Magic Kingdom of Landover Novel, Ballantine/Del Rey, 1994.

OTHER

Hook: A Novel, Fawcett Columbine (New York City), 1992.
Witches' Brew, Ballantine/Del Rey, 1995.

WORK IN PROGRESS: A new fantasy novel.

ADAPTATIONS: The Sword of Shannara was recorded on cassette, Caedmon, 1986; *The Scions of Shannara* and *The Druid of Shannara* are also available in audio versions.

SIDELIGHTS: The first novel in Terry Brooks' long-running fantasy series set in the mythical world of Shannara, *The Sword of Shannara,* received an ambivalent reception from *Dune* author Frank Herbert. Herbert praised Brooks' "free-rolling ability to tell a grand story," but felt that "*The Sword of Shannara* is a distinctly split work. . . . [Brooks] spends about half of this book trying on J. R. R. Tolkien's style and subject matter. The debt to Tolkien is so obvious that you can anticipate many of the developments. In spite of that, you're held by the numerous hints at what will happen if and when Brooks reverts to his own style. This he does somewhere around Chapter 20." Through the years Brooks' critical reception has not greatly improved. In fact, as a *People* magazine interview noted, "most critics ignore his work." But Brooks' fantasy/adventure stories have all been bestsellers, and reviewers have found his sense of humor appealing. Brooks' "Magic Kingdom of Landover" series, which began in 1986 with *Magic Kingdom for Sale—Sold!,* was praised by Jackie Cassada of *Library Journal* for its "welcome touches of humor" and "endearing characters," while Roland Green of *Booklist* noted in his review of the generally well-received *The Tangle Box* that Brooks has a "surer touch with humorous fantasy than with the saga." *Kirkus Reviews* reviewers found the Shannara series "glum and mediocre" and wondered at its "large-selling appeal" but also found *The Tangle Box* to be a "solid entertainment for series fans, and useful comic relief." *Publishers Weekly* critic Sybil Steinberg perhaps best summed up the reactions to all of Brooks' work in noting, of *Witches' Brew,* that the novel seems "cobbled together," but that "the familiar characters remain as appealing as when they first appeared."

BIOGRAPHICAL/CRITICAL SOURCES:

PERIODICALS

Atlantic, May, 1977.
Booklist, September 15, 1987; September 1, 1988; December 15, 1991; March 15, 1994.
Kirkus Reviews, October 15, 1987; February 1, 1990; January 1, 1992; March 15, 1994; February 1, 1995.
Library Journal, February 15, 1990; February 15, 1992; April 15, 1994; March 15, 1995.
Locus, October, 1992.
New York Times Book Review, April 10, 1977.
People, May 10, 1993.
Publishers Weekly, September 25, 1987; August 19, 1988; January 19, 1990; December 20, 1991; January 18, 1993; April 4, 1994; February 20, 1995.
Washington Post Book World, May 1, 1977.*

*   *   *

BROWN, Judith K.

PERSONAL: Married Maurice F. Brown (a professor), 1957 (deceased); children: Frederick W. K., Mathilde Charlotte. *Education:* Cornell University, B.S., 1952; Harvard University, M.Ed., 1954, Ed.D., 1962; London Institute of Education, certificate in child development, 1955; postdoctoral study at Radcliffe College, 1967-69.

ADDRESSES: Office—Department of Sociology and Anthropology, Oakland University, Rochester, MI 48309-4401.

CAREER: Oakland University, Rochester, MI, lecturer, 1964-66, assistant professor, 1969-75, associate professor, 1975-83, professor of anthropology, 1983—. Stanford University, Institute for Research on Women and Gender, Stanford, CA, visiting scholar, 1989; Bryn Mawr College, Department of Anthropology, Bryn Mawr, PA, visiting research associate, 1993.

MEMBER: Association for Anthropology and Gerontology, American Anthropological Association (fellow), Current Anthropology (associate), Society for Psychological Anthropology, American Association of University Professors.

AWARDS, HONORS: Postdoctoral fellowship from Bunting Institute of Radcliffe College, 1967 and 1968; Oakland University faculty research grants, 1970 and 1981; Educational Development Fund small grant award, 1982; National Institute of Health Division of Human Development and Aging, research grants, 1990-93.

WRITINGS:

EDITOR AND CONTRIBUTOR

(With Virginia Kerns) *In Her Prime: A New View of Middle-Aged Women,* Bergin & Garvey (South Hadley, MA), 1985, enlarged second edition, University of Illinois Press (Urbana), 1992.
(With Dorothy Counts and Jacquelyn Campbell) *Sanctions and Sanctuary: Cultural Perspectives on the Beating of Wives,* Westview (Boulder, CO), 1992.

Contributor of articles to collections, including *Toward an Anthropology of Women,* Monthly Review Press (New York City), 1975; *Sex Differences: Social and Biological Perspectives,* Anchor Books (New York City), 1976; *Handbook of Cross-Cultural Human Development,* Garland Publishing (New York City), 1981; and *Women's Age Hierarchies* (special edition of the *Journal of Cross-Cultural Gerontology*), edited by Brown and Jeanette Dickerson, 1994. Contributor of articles and book reviews to scholarly journals, including *Current Anthropology, Ethos, Anthropos,* and *American Anthropologist.*

WORK IN PROGRESS: Research on relationships between mothers-in-law and daughters-in-law in various cultures.

BIOGRAPHICAL/CRITICAL SOURCES:

PERIODICALS

American Anthropologist, September, 1986.
Newsweek, February 14, 1983.

*   *   *

BRUNVAND, Jan Harold   1933-

PERSONAL: Born March 23, 1933, in Cadillac, MI; son of Harold N. (a civil engineer) and Ruth (Jorgensen) Brunvand; married Judith Darlene Ast (a librarian), June 10, 1956; children: Erik, Amy, Dana, Karen. *Education:* Michigan State University, B.A., 1955, M.A., 1957; attended University of Oslo, 1956-57; Indiana University, Ph.D., 1961.

ADDRESSES: Home—1031 1st Ave., Salt Lake City, UT 84103. *Office*—Department of English, University of Utah, Salt Lake City, UT 84112.

CAREER: University of Idaho, Moscow, assistant professor of English, 1961-65; Southern Illinois University at Edwardsville, associate professor of English, 1965-66; University of Utah, Salt Lake City, associate professor, 1966-71, professor of English and folklore, 1971—. Visiting assistant professor at Indiana University, summer, 1965. Member of Utah Folk Arts Advisory Panel, 1976—. Has appeared on morning programs and talk shows, including *Late Night with David Letterman. Military service:* U.S. Army, Signal Corps, 1962-63.

MEMBER: American Association of University Professors, American Folklore Society (fellow; president, 1985), California Folklore Society, International Society for Contemporary Legend Research.

AWARDS, HONORS: Fulbright scholar in Norway, 1956-57, grant for Romania, 1970-71; Guggenheim fellow, 1970-71; International Research and Exchanges Board in Romania, fellow, 1973-74, 1981; fellow of Committee for the Scientific Investigation of Claims of the Paranormal.

WRITINGS:

A Dictionary of Proverbs and Proverbial Phrases from Books Published by Indiana Authors before 1890, Indiana University Press (Bloomington), 1961.
The Study of American Folklore (instructor's manual available), Norton (New York City), 1968, 3rd edition, 1986.
A Guide for Collectors of Folklore in Utah, University of Utah Press (Salt Lake City), 1971.
Norwegian Settlers in Alberta, Canadian Centre for Folk Cultural Studies, 1974.
Folklore: A Study and Research Guide, St. Martin's (New York City), 1976.
Readings in American Folklore, Norton, 1979.
The Vanishing Hitchhiker: American Urban Legends and Their Meanings, Norton, 1981.
The Choking Doberman and Other "New" Urban Legends, Norton, 1984.
The Mexican Pet: More "New" Urban Legends and Some Old Favorites, Norton, 1986.
Curses! Broiled Again! The Hottest Urban Legends Going, Norton, 1989.

The Baby Train and Other Lusty Urban Legends, Norton, 1993.

(Author of introduction and commentary) *The Big Book of Urban Legends,* Paradox Press, 1994.

American Folklore: An Encyclopedia, Garland, 1996.

Contributor to books, including *The Western Folklore Conference: Selected Papers* (monograph), edited by Austin E. Fife and J. Golden Taylor, Utah State University Press (Logan), 1964; *Forms upon the Frontier* (monograph), edited by Austin E. Fife, Alta Fife, and Henry H. Glassie, Utah State University Press, 1969; *Popular Culture and Curricula,* edited by Ray B. Browne and Ronald J. Ambrosetti, Bowling Green University (Bowling Green, OH), 1970; *American Folk Legend: A Symposium,* edited by Wayland D. Hand, University of California Press (Berkeley), 1971; *Folklore Today: Festschrift for Richard W. Dorson,* edited by Glassie, Linda Degh, and Felix J. Olinas, Indiana University Press, 1976; and *Subject and Strategy: A Rhetoric Reader,* 2nd edition, edited by Paul Escholz and Alfred Rosa, St. Martin's, 1981.

Author of column "Urban Legends," distributed by United Features Syndicate, 1987-92. Contributor of over a hundred articles and reviews to folklore journals and to newspapers. Assistant editor of *Midwest Folklore,* 1959-60, book review editor, 1961-64; associate editor of *Journal of American Folklore,* 1963-67 and 1973-76, book review editor, 1967-73, editor, 1976-80.

WORK IN PROGRESS: General editor of *The Study of American Folklore,* fourth edition, for Norton.

SIDELIGHTS: Jan Harold Brunvand, professor of English and folklore at the University of Utah, has written five books to date on what he calls the "urban legend." Urban legends, though often sworn to be true by their tellers, are largely unsubstantiated modern-day stories which criss-cross the globe mainly by word of mouth. Stories include the woman tourist in Mexico who, upon finding a cute little dog, sneaked the dog back to the States only to be told by her veterinarian that the dog was actually a sewer rat. Another legend involves a cat who exploded after being placed in the microwave oven as a means of drying it off. According to Brunvand, some of these legends are grounded in the past and they often take slightly different forms as they move from region to region, but no matter what their origin or form, they are pure fiction. However, it is not uncommon for these stories to be picked up by the media and printed or reported as truth, making them seem all the more valid.

Brunvand's books relate many known urban legends, providing some explanation as to what they mean and why they arose. In a conversation with *U.S. News and World Report* contributor Alvin P. Sanoff, Brunvand maintained that "urban legends fill a need people have to tell each other stories, to know the latest that's going on. . . . These stories are the folklore of the mostly educated, white middle class. . . . In an urbanized society, these stories provide a common bond. They are a means by which strangers can easily communicate with one another." Additionally, in a *Time* review, Donald Morrison observes: "Why do such stories survive, even flourish, in an age of science and cynicism? Many of them, says Brunvand, serve as cautionary tales, sermonettes on the evils of, say, parking in deserted lanes or buying cheap imported goods. Others are inspired by suspicion of change—of microwave ovens or fast-food restaurants. Writes Brunvand: 'Whatever is new and puzzling or scary, but which eventually becomes familiar, may turn up in modern folklore.'" Some of these legends are even viewed as part of ongoing racial or cultural stereotyping, like stories involving Southeast Asian immigrants to the United States capturing and eating people's pets.

Although *Times Literary Supplement* critic Mark Abley feels that Brunvand's first collection on urban legends, *The Vanishing Hitchhiker: American Urban Legends and Their Meanings,* is weak in terms of explaining the implications and the significance of urban legends, *New York Times* reviewer Christopher Lehmann-Haupt claims Brunvand's third collection, *The Mexican Pet: More "New" Urban Legends and Some Old Favorites,* "offers enough material to suggest a number of conclusions." According to Lehmann-Haupt, in *The Mexican Pet* "Brunvand includes new versions of beliefs and stories discussed in his earlier books, so that we may judge for ourselves how apocryphal stories evolve. He also attempts here to establish the provenance of several legends, particularly those that have been circulated by the media. . . . *The Mexican Pet* is enlightening in several respects. By seeing new permutations of old stories, we become convinced that what we once took as gospel is indeed nothing more than plausible fabrication." *New York Times Book Review*'s Gahan Wilson, in a review of *The Baby Train and Other*

Lusty Urban Legends, cautions against dismissing these stories completely, arguing that the purpose of these stories is to "remind us that life is wonderful and mysterious after all." Wilson concludes, however, that Brunvand is "a bona fide scholar" on a "sincere, if slightly wacky, educational mission."

BIOGRAPHICAL/CRITICAL SOURCES:

BOOKS

Brunvand, Jan Harold, *The Vanishing Hitchhiker: American Urban Legends and Their Meanings,* Norton, 1981.

PERIODICALS

Chicago Tribune Book World, July 17, 1986.
Choice, May, 1969; May, 1982.
Columbia Journalism Review, March, 1982.
Detroit Free Press, July 6, 1984.
Journal of American Folklore, January, 1969; July, 1978; October, 1978.
New York Times, July 21, 1986.
New York Times Book Review, July 6, 1986; May 30, 1993.
Smithsonian, November, 1992.
Time, November 9, 1981.
Times Literary Supplement, August 13, 1982.
U.S. News and World Report, September 22, 1986.

C

CAMPBELL, Joanna
   See BLY, Carol(yn)

* * *

CARMICHAEL, Fred   1924-

PERSONAL: Born February 1, 1924, in Pelham, NY; son of Cyril and Edith (Nichols) Carmichael; married Patricia Wyn Rose (a theater director), May 31, 1952. *Education:* Educated in England and Pelham, NY; attended Feagin School of Drama, New York, NY, 1941-43.

ADDRESSES: Home—West Rd., Dorset, VT 05215. *Agent*—Samuel French, Inc., 45 West 25th St., New York, NY 10010.

CAREER: Playwright, producer in summer stock, and actor. Producer at Dorset Playhouse (summer theater), Dorset, VT, 1949-76, and of Champlain Festival Pageant for Fort Edward, NY; actor on television and stage, appearing with two companies on U.S. tours.

MEMBER: Actors' Equity Association, American Federation of Television and Radio Artists, Screen Actors Guild, Dramatists Guild.

AWARDS, HONORS: Out of Sight . . . Out Murder won the Vermont State Playwright's Contest.

WRITINGS:

ONE-ACT PLAYS; ALL PUBLISHED BY BAKER CO. (LUBBOCK, TX)

Florence Unlimited, 1952.
Green Room Blues, 1956.
Four for the Money, 1960.
Dear Millie, 1962.
There's a Fly in My Soap, 1973.
Foiled by an Innocent Maid, 1978.
The Three Million Dollar Lunch, 1981.

THREE-ACT PLAYS; ALL PUBLISHED BY SAMUEL FRENCH (NEW YORK CITY)

More Than Meets the Eye, 1954.
Inside Lester, 1955.
The Night Is My Enemy, 1956.
Petey's Choice, 1957.
Luxury Cruise, 1958.
The Pen Is Deadlier, 1959.
Exit the Body, 1961.
The Robin Hood Caper, 1962.
Dream World, 1963.
Any Number Can Die, 1964.
The Best Laid Plans, 1966.
All the Better to Kill You With, 1967.
Surprise, 1968.
Victoria's House, 1969.
Done to Death, 1971.
Mixed Doubles, 1972.
Who Needs a Waltz, 1973.
Hey, Naked Lady, 1974.
Last of the Class, 1975.
Whatever Happened to Mrs. Kong, 1976.
Don't Step on My Footprint, 1978.

Exit Who?, 1982.
Out of Sight . . . Out Murder, 1983.
Murder on the Rerun, 1985.
Said the Spider to the Spy, 1987.
Home Free, 1991.
Hot Property, 1992.
Murder Is the Game, 1993.
Coming Apart, 1994.
Damsel of the Desert, 1995.
I Bet Your Life, 1995.

OTHER

Author of scripts for seven half-hour historical shows presented daily each summer at Old Sturbridge Village in Massachusetts; has written material for television and radio comedians, including a record album, *The Other Side of Lee Tully;* also author of a television play, *Tea Pastries and Blank Cartridges,* produced in Germany. Editor of ship's newspaper on Home Lines cruises plying South America and the Caribbean for two months each winter, 1952-66.

WORK IN PROGRESS: A play.

SIDELIGHTS: Fred Carmichael once told *CA:* "In writing plays, both one-act and three-act, one must not forget the amateur market and the dinner theaters. They are a great source of revenue for playwrights. Of course it is exciting when one gets long runs and T.V. adaptations of one's shows, but the backbone of my royalties is in the hundreds and hundreds of community theaters and high schools which perform one or two evenings with a show. Don't forget them. Europe and the Orient have also proved to be a marketable source for plays. It always amazes me at royalty time to see the number and diversification of places where the shows are performed."

*   *   *

CARTLEDGE, Paul 1947-

PERSONAL: Born March 24, 1947, in London, England; son of Marcus Raymond (a banker) and Margaret (Oakley) Cartledge; married Judith Portrait (a lawyer), July 21, 1976; children: Gabrielle. *Education:* Oxford University, B.A. (with first class honors), 1969, D.Phil., 1975.

ADDRESSES: Home—Cambridge, England. *Office*—Clare College, Cambridge University, Cambridge CB2 1TL, England.

CAREER: New University of Ulster, Coleraine, Northern Ireland, lecturer in classics, 1972-73; Trinity College, Dublin, lecturer in classics, 1973-78; University of Warwick, Coventry, England, lecturer in classical civilization, 1978-79; Cambridge University, Cambridge, England, lecturer in ancient history, 1979—, fellow and director of studies in classics at Clare College, 1981—, reader in Greek History, 1993—.

MEMBER: Society for the Promotion of Hellenic Studies, Society of Antiquaries of London (fellow).

AWARDS, HONORS: Leverhulme grant, 1982.

WRITINGS:

Sparta and Lakonia: A Regional History, 1300-362 B.C., Routledge & Kegan Paul (London), 1979.
(Editor with F. D. Harvey, and contributor) *Crux: Essays in Greek History Presented to G. E. M. de Ste. Croix,* Duckworth (London), 1985.
Agesilaos and the Crisis of Sparta, Duckworth, 1987.
(With A. J. S. Spawforth) *Hellenistic and Roman Sparta,* Routledge & Kegan Paul, 1988.
(Editor with P. C. Millett and S. C. Todd, and contributor) *NOMOS: Essays in Athenian Law, Politics and Society,* Cambridge University Press (Cambridge, England), 1990.
Aristophanes and His Theatre of the Absurd, Bristol Classical Press (Bristol, England) and Duckworth, 1990.

Contributor to classical studies journals and newspapers.

WORK IN PROGRESS: Classical Greece: A Social and Economic History, Duckworth; *A History of Greek Political Thought,* Cambridge University Press.

SIDELIGHTS: Simon Hornblower writes in the *Times Literary Supplement* that Paul Cartledge's *Sparta and Lakonia: A Regional History, 1300-362 B.C.* is in many ways the best book available on the ancient city of Sparta. Hornblower finds the book both a "densely documented" archaeological study and "a vigorous political and social history of Classical Sparta." The author's "major achievement,"

Hornblower concludes, "is to bring out the importance of Sparta's *perioikoi,* that is, the members of the communities which were controlled by Sparta but were not reduced by her to serfdom."

Cartledge once told *CA:* "Though my professional preoccupation is with ancient Greece, the history I write has to be meaningful to people living in societies with radically different economic, social, religious, and political structures. Comparative study of contemporary non-Western societies and Mediterranean village communities is therefore vital to my work. Equally important is a sense of place: hence my extensive travel and archaeological field work in Greece, especially in the region around Sparta in the southern Peloponnese."

BIOGRAPHICAL/CRITICAL SOURCES:

PERIODICALS

Times Literary Supplement, February 15, 1980.

*   *   *

CASTILLO, Ana   1953-

PERSONAL: Born June 15, 1953, in Chicago, IL; daughter of Raymond and Rachel Rocha Castillo; children: Marcel Ramon Herrera. *Education:* Northern Illinois University, B.A., 1975; University of Chicago, M.A., 1979; University of Bremen, Ph.D., 1991.

ADDRESSES: Office—c/o Susan Bergholz, 17 W. 10th St. #5, New York, NY 10011.

CAREER: Writer, 1975—. Instructor in ethnic studies at Santa Rosa Junior College, Santa Rosa, CA, 1975; writer in residence, Illinois Arts Council, 1977; lecturer in history, Northwestern University, 1980-81; poet-in-residence, Urban Gateways of Chicago, 1980-81; instructor in women's studies, San Francisco State University, 1986-87; visiting professor of creative writing and fiction, California State University at Chico, 1988-89; instructor, Department of English, University of New Mexico, 1989, 1991-92; professor of bilingual creative writing, Mount Holyoke College, 1994.

AWARDS, HONORS: American Book Award, Before Columbus Foundation, 1986, for *The Mixquiahuala Letters;* honored by Women's Foundation of San Francisco for "pioneering excellence in literature," 1987; "Women of Words" honoree, San Francisco Women's Foundation, 1988; California Arts Council fellowship for fiction, 1989; National Endowment for the Arts fellowship for poetry, 1990; New Mexico Arts Commission Grant, 1991; Carl Sandburg Literary Award in Fiction for *So Far from God,* 1993; Mountains and Plains Booksellers Award for *So Far from God,* 1994.

WRITINGS:

Zero Makes Me Hungry (poetry), Scott, Foresman (Chicago), 1975.
i close my eyes (to see) (poetry), Washington State University Press (Pullman), 1976.
Otro canto (poetry), Alternativa Publications (Chicago), c. 1977.
The Invitation, privately printed, 1979, revised edition, La Raza (San Francisco), 1986.
Women Are Not Roses, Arte Publico (Houston, TX), 1984.
The Mixquiahuala Letters (novel), Bilingual Press (Binghamton, NY), 1986.
(Editor with Cherrie Moraga) *This Bridge Called My Back,* ISM Press (San Francisco, CA), 1988, Spanish translation by Castillo and Norma Alarcon published as *Este puente, mi espalda: Voces de mujeres tercermundistas en los Estados Unidos,* 1988.
My Father Was a Toltec: Poems, West End Press (Albuquerque, NM), 1988, reprinted as *My Father was a Toltec and Selected Poems 1973-1988,* Norton (New York City), 1995.
Sapogonia: An Anti-Romance in 3/8 Meter (novel), Bilingual Press (Tempe, AZ), 1990.
So Far from God (novel), Norton (New York City), 1993.
Massacre of the Dreamers: Essays on Xicanisma, University of New Mexico Press (Albuquerque, NM), 1994.

Contributor to numerous anthologies, including *The Third Woman: Minority Woman Writers of the United States,* Houghton (Boston), 1980; *Cuentos Chicanos,* University of New Mexico Press, 1984; *Nosotras: Latina Literature Today,* Bilingual Press, (Binghamton, NY), 1986; *English Con Salsa,* Macmillan (New York), 1994; *More Light: Father and Daughter Poems,* Harcourt (San Diego, CA), 1994; *Daughter of the Fifth Sun,* Riverhead Books, Putnam (New York City), 1995; *Latinas,* Simon & Schuster (New York City), 1995; and *Tasting Life*

Twice, Avon (New York City), 1995. Contributor to periodicals, including *Revista Chicano-Riquena, Spoon River Quarterly, River Styx,* and *Maize.*

Ana Castillo's manuscripts are housed at the University of California, Santa Barbara.

SIDELIGHTS: Ana Castillo is a highly respected Chicana poet, novelist, and essayist. Her writing explores the tribulations of womanhood and offers sociopolitical comment. The style of her work is often based on established oral and literary traditions, yet at the same time it is highly innovative. She is "the most daring and experimental of Latino novelists," according to *Commonweal* contributor Ilan Stavans, who further noted that her "desire to find creative alternatives and to take risks is admirable."

Born and raised in Chicago, Castillo credits the rich storytelling tradition of her Mexican heritage as the foundation for her writing. She wrote her first poems when she was nine years old, following the death of her grandmother. In high school and college, Castillo was active in the Chicano movement and used her poetry to express her political sentiments. Her first published volumes of verse— *Otro Canto, The Invitation,* and *Women Are Not Roses*—"examine the themes of sadness and loneliness in the female experience," according to *Dictionary of Literary Biography* contributor Patricia De La Fuente. "[They speak] for all women who have at one time or another felt the unfairness of female existence in a world designed by men primarily for men." Castillo expressed her feminist concerns in another form in *Massacre of the Dreamers: Essays on Xicanisma.* This book explores the Chicana experience and the historical and social implications of Chicana feminism. It is a "provocative" collection, according to Marjorie Agosin in *Multicultural Review,* who praised Castillo as "lyrical and passionate" and "one of the country's most provocative and original writers."

Castillo's first novel, *The Mixquiahuala Letters,* is described by De La Fuente as "a far-ranging social and cultural expose." Through the device of letters exchanged over a ten-year period between Teresa, a California poet, and her college friend Alicia, a New York artist, *The Mixquiahuala Letters* explores the changing role of Hispanic women in the United States and Mexico during the 1970s and 1980s and the negative reaction many conservative Hispanic and

Anglo men felt toward this liberation. Castillo created three possible versions of Teresa's and Alicia's story—for the "Conformist," the "Cynic," and the "Quixotic"—by numbering the letters and supplying varying orders in which to read them, each with a different tone and resolution. Her next novel, *Sapogonia: An Anti-Romance in 3/8 Meter,* tells the tale of Maximo Madrigal, the male narrator, and his obsession with Pastora Ake, the only woman he is unable to conquer. De La Fuente declared: "Castillo hits her full-fledged and sophisticated stride in an intricately woven tale of the destructive powers of male-female relationships."

So Far from God is Castillo's most widely reviewed book, and according to some reviewers, it has the greatest mass appeal of any of her novels. The lengthy narrative follows the life of one strong Latina woman, Sofi, and her four daughters. Esperanza, the eldest, graduates from college and becomes a television newscaster but finds her life empty and unhappy despite her success; Caridad, the beauty of the family, squanders her life in a series of one-night stands; Fe, seemingly the most "normal" sister, goes into a year-long trance when her fiance leaves her; and the youngest, known as La Loca ("The Crazy One"), dies on her third birthday, only to be magically resurrected and regarded thereafter as a saint. Castillo's customary social comment is supplied through the voice of the narrator, who describes herself as "highly opinionated."

Barbara Kingsolver stated in the *Los Angeles Times Book Review* that *So Far from God* belongs to the genre of magic realism, frequently identified with prominent South American writers like Gabriel Garcia Marquez and Isabel Allende; yet, in Kingsolver's view, Castillo's book stands apart from theirs because of its humor and readability. "Give it to people who always wanted to read *One Hundred Years of Solitude* but couldn't quite get through it," she advised. According to Stavans, "the novel's intent is original: to parody the Spanish-speaking *telenovela,* e.g., the popular television soap operas that enchant millions in Mexico and South America." Yet Stavans criticized the novel as the least successful of all Castillo's works. "The experimental spirit is absent here," he complained. "The terrain is overtly sentimental and cartoonish. . . . With an overabundance of stereotypes and its crowded cast of theatrical characters, *So Far from God* stumbles from the outset. . . . The novel is uneven, conventional, and often annoying." Still, he expressed his strong belief that "in due time, [Castillo's] creativity will match her passion to experiment and the outcome will be formidable."

Ray Gonzalez agreed in the *Nation* that *So Far from God* is overcomplicated, stating: "Castillo's novel takes on too much. It is full of stories told by too many characters who fade in and out of the vague plot." *Belles Lettres* contributor Irene Campos Carr also admitted that "the author's tendency to try to include *everything* in this book seems forced, and at times become intrusive," but her overall assessment was favorable. She summarized: "The story . . . catches the reader in a net of surprises as the narra-tor carefully details folklore, new Mexican recipes, home remedies, and more."

BIOGRAPHICAL/CRITICAL SOURCES:

BOOKS

Binder, Wolfgang, editor, *Contemporary Chicano Poetry II: Partial Autobiographies: Interviews with Twenty Chicano Poets,* Palm & Enke (Erlangen, Germany), 1985, pp. 28-38.
Dictionary of Literary Biography, Volume 122: *Chicano Writers,* Gale (Detroit), 1992, pp. 62-65.
Horno-Delgado, Asuncion, and others, editors, *Breaking Boundaries: Latina Writings and Critical Readings,* University of Massachusetts Press (Amherst, MA), 1989, pp. 94-107.
Navarro, Marta A., *Chicana Lesbians: The Girls Our Mothers Warned Us About,* Third Woman (Berkeley, CA), 1991, p. 113.

PERIODICALS

Belles Lettres, fall, 1993, pp. 52-53.
Bloomsbury Review, November-December, 1995, pp. 5, 13.
Choice, May, 1987.
Commonweal, January 14, 1994, pp. 37-38.
Hispania, May, 1988.
Los Angeles Times, May 16, 1993, pp. 1, 9.
Multicultural Review, March, 1995, p. 69.
Nation, June 7, 1993, pp. 772-73.
New York Times Book Review, October 3, 1993, p. 22.*

CATANZARITI, John   1942-

PERSONAL: Born June 1, 1942, in New York, NY; son of Dominick and Rose Catanzariti; married Rosemary Bellofatto in 1965; children: Jason, Tracie. *Education:* Queens College of the City University of New York, B.A., 1964, M.A., 1973.

ADDRESSES: Office—"The Papers of Thomas Jefferson," Princeton University Library, Princeton, NJ 08544.

CAREER: Queens College of the City University of New York, Flushing, NY, associate editor, 1970-80, coeditor, 1980-81, editor and project director of "The Papers of Robert Morris," 1981-86; Princeton University, Princeton, NJ, senior research historian and editor of "The Papers of Thomas Jefferson," 1987—.

MEMBER: Massachusetts Historical Society, Institute of Early American History and Culture, Association for Documentary Editing.

WRITINGS:

(Associate editor) *The Papers of Robert Morris, 1781-1784,* University of Pittsburgh Press (Pittsburgh, PA), Volume 1, 1973, Volume 2, 1975, Volume 3, 1977, Volume 4, 1978.
(Editor with E. James Ferguson) *The Papers of Robert Morris, 1781-1784,* University of Pittsburgh Press, Volume 5, 1980, Volume 6, 1984.
(Editor) *The Papers of Robert Morris, 1781-1784,* Volume 7, University of Pittsburgh Press, 1988.
(Editor) *The Papers of Thomas Jefferson,* Princeton University Press (Princeton, NJ), Volume 24, 1990, Volume 25, 1992, Volume 26, 1995.

Contributor to *American Writers before 1800: A Biographical and Critical Dictionary,* Volume 2, edited by James A. Levernier and Douglas R. Wilmes, Greenwood Press (Westport, CT), 1983. Also contributor to *Prologue: Quarterly of the National Archives,* and the Massachusetts Historical Society *Proceedings.*

*   *   *

CHAPMAN, Lee
See BRADLEY, Marion Zimmer

CHASE, Philander D(ean) 1943-

PERSONAL: Born March 10, 1943, in Elkin, NC; son of Vern Warren and Marion (Wagner) Chase; married Jeanne Sheaffer (a counselor), September 18, 1971. *Education:* North Carolina State University, B.A., 1965; Duke University, M.A., 1968, Ph.D., 1973.

ADDRESSES: Home—223 Old Lynchburg Rd., Charlottesville, VA 22903. *Office*—"Papers of George Washington," Alderman Library, University of Virginia, Charlottesville, VA 22901.

CAREER: University of Virginia, Charlottesville, assistant editor of "Papers of George Washington," 1974-89, associate editor, 1989-92, editor, 1992—.

MEMBER: American Historical Association, Association for Documentary Editing, Institute for Early American History and Culture, Southern Historical Association.

AWARDS, HONORS: Fellow of National Historic Publications and Records Commission, 1973-74; Phillip M. Hamer Award for documentary editing from Society of American Archivists, 1978, for *The Diaries of George Washington;* distinguished alumnus, North Carolina State University, College of Humanities and Social Sciences, 1994.

WRITINGS:

(Assistant editor) *The Diaries of George Washington,* six volumes, University Press of Virginia (Charlottesville), 1976-79.
(Assistant editor) *The Papers of George Washington: Colonial Series,* ten volumes, University Press of Virginia, 1982-94.
(Editor) *The Papers of George Washington: Revolutionary War Series,* University Press of Virginia, Volume 1: *June-September 1775,* 1985, Volume 2: *September-December 1775,* 1987, Volume 3: *January-April 1776,* 1988, Volume 4: *April-June 1776,* 1991, Volume 5: *June-August 1776,* 1993, Volume 6: *August-October 1776,* 1994.

Contributor to history journals.

WORK IN PROGRESS: The Papers of George Washington: Revolutionary War Series, Volume 7: *October 1776-January 1777,* University Press of Virginia, in 1996.

CHEEVER, Susan 1943-

PERSONAL: Born July 31, 1943, in New York, NY; daughter of John (an author) and Mary (a poet and teacher; maiden name, Winternitz) Cheever; married Robert Cowley (an editor), 1967 (divorced); married Calvin Tomkins II (a writer) 1981 (divorced); married Warren James Hinckle III, 1989; children: (second marriage) Sarah Liley, (third marriage) Warren James Hinckle IV. *Education:* Brown University, B.A., 1965.

ADDRESSES: Agent—Andrew Wylie, Wylie, Aitken & Stone, 250 West 57th St., New York, NY 10107.

CAREER: Taught English at the Colorado Rocky Mountain School and the Scarborough School, 1965-69; affiliated with *Queen* magazine, London, England, 1969-70; *Tarrytown Daily News,* Tarrytown, NY, reporter, 1971-72; *Newsweek,* New York City, 1974-78, began as religion editor, became lifestyle editor; writer. Instructor in creative writing, Hoffstra University, 1980; professor, Marymount Manhattan College; instructor in Bennington Writing Seminars, Bennington College.

MEMBER: Authors Guild (member of council), PEN American Center.

AWARDS, HONORS: Guggenheim fellowship, 1983; nomination for National Book Critics Circle Award in biography/autobiography, 1984, for *Home before Dark;* Lawrence L. Winship Book Award, *Boston Globe,* 1986, for *Home before Dark.*

WRITINGS:

NOVELS

Looking for Work, Simon & Schuster (New York City), 1980.
A Handsome Man, Simon & Schuster, 1981.
The Cage, Houghton (Boston), 1982.
Doctors and Women, C. N. Potter (New York City), 1987.
Elizabeth Cole, Farrar, Straus (New York City), 1989.

OTHER

Home before Dark (biographical memoir of father, John Cheever), Houghton, 1984.
Treetops: A Family Memoir, Bantam (New York City), 1991.

A Woman's Life: The Story of an Ordinary American and Her Extraordinary Generation, Morrow (New York City), 1994.

Contributor to numerous periodicals, including *Architectural Digest, Harper's Bazaar, New Choices for Retirement, New Yorker* and *New York Times Book Review.*

SIDELIGHTS: Susan Cheever, the daughter of the late Pulitzer Prize-winning author John Cheever, is an acclaimed writer in her own right. Though she began her career as a journalist, she later turned to fiction and biography. Her novels frequently explore the lives of contemporary women, dissatisfied with their marriages and careers, who are searching for more fulfillment in their lives. She is also the author of several memoirs, including one on her father.

In her first novel, *Looking for Work,* Cheever "paints the cheery saga of a spoiled, upper-middle-class brat who marries the wrong guy . . . has an affair, and finally gets ready for a steady job," writes Elizabeth Fox-Genovese in the *Antioch Review.* The story of Salley Gardens "is the one that so many writers regard as the story of our time," comments a reviewer for the *Atlantic,* "the demise of a marriage, told by a young wife who mistakenly assumed that she should and could find meaning in her life by helping her husband live his." In following her heroine's life from marriage to divorce to her eventual landing of a job on the staff of *Newsweek,* Cheever creates a novel that "belongs to a tradition of realism which sets itself the task of illuminating the way we all live now," observes Cheryl Rivers in *Commonweal.*

The view of contemporary American life offered in *Looking for Work* is, in the words of *New York Times Book Review* contributor Robert Kiely, "very much like a certain kind of Hollywood film; brisk, bouncy, sharply focused, filled with primary colors and abrupt transitions. . . . [The] novel is easy to read. Nothing drags, nothing lingers, no one mopes." But this ease, argues *Newsweek*'s Jean Strouse, detracts from the overall impact of the book. "By merely *telling* us how Salley feels instead of giving those feelings dramatic life," writes Strouse, "Cheever has created something less than a novel." *New York Times* book reviewer Christopher Lehmann-Haupt offers a similar assessment: *Looking for Work* "is not really much of a story. . . . Nor has Miss Cheever found a metaphor to tie her narrative together." All the same, Lehmann-Haupt does admit that "Cheever

shows considerable promise. She strikes a note of amusing rue that manages to avoid self-pity."

Though some critics faulted *Looking for Work* for its story, Cheever earned praise for its technical features. According to Susan Kennedy in the *Times Literary Supplement,* "Cheever enlivens [the] well-trodden literary topography [of New York, Europe, and San Francisco] with some good descriptive writing; indeed, it is her unobtrusive technical assurance, her respect for the just use of words, that keeps the novel together." Rivers, too, finds that Cheever's inventive writing raises this novel above the level of cliche: "She plays with style, abruptly changing pace, mood, and vision. She is capable of intimate, wry commentary and of showy descriptions of events." Beyond this, continues the reviewer, "Cheever's very real accomplishment in *Looking for Work* is the vividness with which she has observed the familiar plight of her heroine and the gentle affection with which she draws her cast of characters. She has avoided turning her characters into parodies; her belief in her characters allows us to believe in them and to care about their predicaments." Cheever succeeds in the end in showing the reader that "love, marriage, and even sex no longer have the redemptive qualities so widely advertised in popular culture, common sense, and our own psyches," concludes Rivers.

Cheever's second novel, *A Handsome Man,* focuses on a vacation in Ireland, shared by Hannah Bart, a divorcee in her thirties, her older lover, Sam, his teenage son, Travis, and Hannah's younger brother, Jake. "The work depends almost entirely upon the shifting dynamics between Hannah, Sam, and Travis," comments Susan Currier in the *Dictionary of Literary Biography Yearbook.* "Cheever moves the reader smoothly from one character's mind and feelings to another's, though Hannah's remains the dominant perspective." When revealing this young woman's character, in the opinion of *Washington Post* contributor Michele Slung, Cheever captures the interest of her readers: "Hannah is a real woman come alive on these pages. Both her doubts and her wisecracks ring true. But," adds the reviewer, "Sam and Travis added to Hannah make for a human equation that has less verisimilitude."

The novel "is meant as a study in the forms of selfishness afflicting lovers, father and son, the young and the not-so-young," observes Judith Chernaik in the *Times Literary Supplement.* Yet, in the end, concludes the reviewer, it "is marred by a pervading slickness, a tendency to slip into woman's-magazine banality." As Joyce Shaffer puts it in a *New Republic* review, "It is like a faded color photograph: a brief moment of reality is accurately reproduced, but there is no movement or excitement." Slung attributes the novel's shortcomings to its having to compete with its own setting. Cheever's "prose, when it is good . . . is seductive and tightly phrased," she writes, "but it is not always strong enough to fight off the scene-stealing proclivities of things Irish."

"No youthful protagonist in search of either lover or work animates [*The Cage,* Cheever's third novel]," observes Currier. "It is a more tightly structured book than the first two, with a darker vision of a middle-aged couple trapped in mutual disappointment and destruction." The cage referred to in the book's title was once used to house the menagerie kept by Judith Bristol's late father on the grounds of his New Hampshire estate. Restoring this long-neglected pen has become a sort of therapy for Julia's husband, Billy, during the couple's summer vacation at the estate. The cage also plays a central part in the couple's final confrontation. This story of conflict simmering beneath the calm exterior of suburban America is reminiscent of the world of the author's father, John Cheever, a point on which Richard Eder comments in his *Los Angeles Times Book Review* article: "Susan Cheever has chosen deliberately, with some courage and less prudence, to start in her father's territory and walk her own wilder track out of it."

Cheever's detailed account of the uneventful surface features of suburban life is at the center of much of the criticism devoted to this book. "One of the problems with *The Cage*—which seems not so much a novel as an extended story or even a television script . . .—is that it is mostly surface," comments Sheila Ballantyne in the *New York Times Book Review,* "embroidered with glittery and often repetitive detail." But *New Statesman* contributor Bill Greenwell finds those same features one of the novel's primary virtues. "What Cheever achieves with startling clarity is a surface naturalism, with a powerful eye for telling, insignificant detail and a feeling for the petty emotions of jealousy and depression." These mundane events are the pieces that build slowly toward the book's climax, he believes. "The novel's conclusion is masterly. As the final pages turn, the reader recalls a succession of brilliant images, sewn into the subtext, by which we have been prepared for the ending. Cheever is exceptionally talented," concludes Greenwell, "this novel superbly compulsive."

Although Cheever's first three novels all draw upon her experiences, none is as personal as her fourth novel, *Doctors and Women.* Its central character, Kate, like the author, has lost a father to cancer. But Kate's fictional life is affected by a number of other complications: her mother is hospitalized with cancer; she is unhappy in her marriage; and, she is "fascinated by the charismatic power doctors seem to exercise over the lives of their patients," explains Susan Kenney in the *New York Times Book Review.* Her story offers, in the words of *Los Angeles Times Book Review* contributor Linsey Abrams, "a coming-of-age novel, all the more interesting because it documents that *second* coming of age, in one's 30s, when one chooses the life one is actually living over the fantasy lives that, like fiction, run parallel to it."

The novel had its genesis, Cheever told *CA,* in the events of her father's illness. She was struggling to make sense of his battle with cancer when she became intrigued with the doctors attending to his and other cancer patients' day-to-day crises. She decided to learn more about these men, researching their professional duties and their personal lives. The information she gathered, intended originally for a nonfiction work, became instead the basis for this novel. "It is clear that Ms. Cheever has not only done her research, but also been there; her accounts of medical procedure and hospital ambience are authentic right down to the contents of IV bags and bulletin boards," writes Kenney. "Written in graceful prose, these scenes have the power and authority we associate with the best nonfiction."

In fact, it is in the arena of nonfiction that Cheever has enjoyed her greatest success, both in examining her personal concerns and in making a name for herself. After John Cheever's death from cancer, the younger Cheever decided to edit the log she was keeping of her thoughts. Her original intent was to distill this written mourning into a short memoir of the man she knew—father and author.

When she turned for supplementary material to her father's private journals—thirty volumes written over several decades—as she explained to Curt Suplee in a *Washington Post* interview, "I learned a lot of things I hadn't known before—how different life was for my father than we had imagined, how the humor he used was just transmuted pain." Her first reaction was to give up the memoir entirely, but as she explained to Suplee, "I knew that articles and a biography were going to be written. And I decided it'd be better if I presented these things myself, in context." The resultant book, *Home before Dark,* notes Suplee, "is a frank but frankly loving biographical memoir."

Yet, as Brigitte Weeks writes in the *Washington Post Book World,* "*Home before Dark* is much more than Susan Cheever's memoir of her famous author father: it is a portrait of the artist as a young man, a middle-aged man, an old man, a sick man. It is, in fact, one of the most moving and intimate books I have read in years." In looking back, Cheever follows her family's history from her grandfather's downfall during the Depression through her father's rise from struggling writer in the close quarters of the big city to respected author surrounded by the comforts of a suburban estate. This family history provides the backdrop for her close examination of John Cheever, the man, the author, and the father.

"The book seems to omit few unpleasant, even sordid details in its depiction of John Cheever as a tortured father, writer and man," suggests John Blades in the *Chicago Tribune,* "telling of his turbulent marriage, his long and frustrating struggle to make a living as a writer, his alcoholism, his paternal inadequacies, his aristocratic pretensions and his confused sexual life." Though faulted by a number of reviewers for these revelations—what was considered by some a daughter's betrayal of her father—Cheever also received commendations for her sensitive handling of a subject so close to home. Weeks, for one, remarks that "the wonder of this book is the astonishing combination of dispassion and compassion with which Susan Cheever portrays her father." Eliot Fremont-Smith, writing in the *Village Voice,* describes Cheever's memoir in the following words: "She is not intrusive, only truthful; so this intimate, disturbing book is an act of mourning and forgiveness, of ultimate respect." And, he takes exception to some of the criticism of the book. "This is a deeply responsible and touching book," he concludes. "Those who find it shameful or lacking in respect know only the price of courage, not its necessity."

Beyond the insights it offers into the father's work, *Home before Dark* provides evidence of the daughter's personal and professional development. In this book, writes Lehmann-Haupt, "we get to know a man we scarcely dreamed existed behind the elegant facade. It is a painful discovery, but it is to Miss Cheever's credit that she persevered. Not only

has she finally identified her father, but in doing so she has faced up to the challenge of identifying herself." In his review, Kaplin touches upon the special effort required of the younger Cheever in writing this book: "*Home Before Dark* clearly demanded from its author more courage and force of heart than will be required of any biographer of John Cheever." Concludes Charles Champlin in the *Los Angeles Times Book Review,* "If the reader is touched, it is not by the mannered style but by the candor and insight that have gone before. There will be full-dress biographies of Cheever and his work in due course. All will be the more knowing for his daughter's paining portrait."

A Woman's Life: The Story of an Ordinary American and Her Extraordinary Generation was Cheever's attempt to remove the name and the notoriety from her own life and examine, as she told Robert S. Boynton in *New York,* "an average woman, *my* age, who is trying to juggle two kids, a job, and a husband!" The woman in question, known as Linda Green in the quasi-biography, is indeed a composite of the women who were raised in the 1950s and 1960s. Though she was a high school cheerleader, Green rejects her traditional upbringing by turning to a hippie lifestyle of drugs and communal living with her young husband, experiments with open marriage, and wanders Europe. After weathering divorce and remarriage to a domineering, conservative man, at 47 years of age she juggles a job as a teacher with her roles as a suburban housewife raising two children. Although she criticizes the novel for its "lapse into cliche and . . . a missionary feminism," Marie Arana-Ward praises *A Woman's Life* in the *Washington Post Book Review* as "ultimately valuable for its essential truth about human relationships and for its rare grasp of the texture of the American woman's lot." While complementing the work for its "finely tuned observation of human foibles," Kathleen Norris questions, in the *New York Times Book Review,* whether Green is "an Everywoman. Ms. Cheever's keen novelist's eye allows us a fascinating glimpse into one individual life, but her book is also a cautionary tale about the dangers of making broad generalizations about our own experience or that of a generation."

The world of Susan Cheever's writing is a personal world, one which focuses on the people, places, and concerns that reside close to home. As she told Boynton, "I write to bear witness, whether about my three failed marriages or my crazy family. If I have any usefulness on this planet, it is to tell the story of my life and 'to tell the truth truly,' as Emerson said."

BIOGRAPHICAL/CRITICAL SOURCES:

BOOKS

Cheever, Susan, *Home before Dark,* Houghton, 1984.
Contemporary Literary Criticism, Gale (Detroit), Volume 18, 1981, Volume 48, 1988.
Dictionary of Literary Biography Yearbook: 1982, Gale, 1983.

PERIODICALS

American Spectator, January 1982; February 1985.
Antioch Review, spring 1980.
Atlantic, January 1980.
Boston Globe, April 22, 1991, p. 34.
Chicago Tribune, October 21, 1984.
Chicago Tribune Book World, January 13, 1980; February 10, 1980; April 12, 1981.
Commonweal, July 4, 1980.
Esquire, February 1985.
Globe and Mail (Toronto), June 20, 1987.
Los Angeles Times, November 24, 1985, p. 26.
Los Angeles Times Book Review, October 3, 1982; October 24, 1984; May 17, 1987.
New Republic, May 16, 1981; November 12, 1984.
New Statesman, February 4, 1983.
New York, July 25, 1994, p. 28.
New York Review of Books, December 20, 1984.
New York Times, December 17, 1979; October 11, 1984; October 15, 1984.
New York Times Book Review, January 6, 1980; October 3, 1982; October 21, 1984; July 17, 1994, pp 10-11.
Newsweek, January 14, 1980; October 22, 1984.
People, November 5, 1984.
Publishers Weekly, November 2, 1984; January 18, 1991.
Spectator, February 2, 1985.
Time, December 24, 1979.
Times Literary Supplement, February 22, 1980; September 4, 1981; February 22, 1985; June 3, 1988.
Tribune Books (Chicago), May 3, 1987.
Village Voice, October 30, 1984.
Washington Post, July 19, 1981; October 15, 1984.
Washington Post Book World, October 7, 1984; June 26, 1994, pp. 1, 8.

CHRISTIE, Ian R(alph) 1919-

PERSONAL: Born May 11, 1919; son of John Reid and Gladys Lilian Christie. *Education:* Oxford University, B.A., M.A., 1948.

ADDRESSES: Home—10 Green Lane, Croxley Green, Hertfordshire, England.

CAREER: University of London, University College, London, England, assistant lecturer, 1948-51, lecturer, 1951-60, reader, 1960-66, professor of modern British history, 1966-79, Astor Professor of British History, 1979-84, dean of arts, 1971-73, chair of department, 1975-79. *Military service:* Royal Air Force, 1940-46; became acting flight lieutenant.

MEMBER: British Academy (fellow), Royal Historical Society, Historical Association.

WRITINGS:

The End of North's Ministry, 1780-1782, Macmillan (London), 1958.
Wilkes, Wyvill, and Reform, Macmillan, 1962.
Crisis of Empire: Great Britain and the American Colonies, 1754-1783, Norton (London and New York City), 1966.
(Editor) *Essays in Modern History Selected from the Transactions of the Royal Historical Society,* Royal Historical Society (London), 1968.
Myth and Reality in Late-Eighteenth Century British Politics and Other Papers, Macmillan, 1970.
(Editor) *The Correspondence of Jeremy Bentham,* Volume 3, Athlone (London), 1971.
(With B. W. Labaree) *Empire or Independence, 1760-1776,* Norton, 1976.
(With Lucy M. Brown) *Bibliography of British History, 1789-1851,* Clarendon Press (Oxford), 1977.
Wars and Revolutions: Britain, 1760-1815, Harvard University Press (London), 1982.
Stress and Stability in Late Eighteenth-Century Britain: Reflections on the British Avoidance of Revolution, Clarendon Press, 1984.
The French Revolution and British Popular Politics, Cambridge University Press (Cambridge), 1991.
The Benthams in Russia, 1780-1790, Berg Publishers (Oxford), 1993.
British "Non-Elite" M.P.s, 1715-1820, Clarendon Press, 1995.

Contributor to numerous books, including *The Connoisseur Period Guide,* edited by Ralph Edwards and

L. G. G. Ramsey, Crown (Watford), Volume 4: *Late Georgian, 1760-1810,* 1956, Volume 5: *Regency, 1810-1830,* 1958; *Handbook for History Teachers,* edited by W. H. Burston and C. W. Green, 1958; *The History of Parliament: The House of Commons, 1754-1790,* three volumes, edited by Sir Lewis Namier and John Brooke, H.M.S.O. (London), 1964; *William III and Louis XIV,* edited by Ragnhild Hatton and J. S. Bromley, Liverpool University Press (Liverpool), 1968; *Red, White, and True Blue: The Loyalists in the Revolution,* edited by Esmond Wright, AMS Press (London), 1976; and (with L. A. Sitnikov) *Istochniki po Istorii Sibiri dosovyetskogo perioda,* Novosibirsk, 1988. Also contributor to history and archaeology journals. Member of editorial board, *The History of Parliament.*

SIDELIGHTS: Ian R. Christie is considered a distinguished and prolific scholar of late eighteenth-century British history. Before retiring from his post as Astor Professor of British History at University College, London, he delivered the Ford Lectures at Oxford in 1983. Extended versions of these lectures were compiled and published as *Stress and Stability in Late Eighteenth-Century Britain: Reflections on the British Avoidance of Revolution.* According to *British Book News* contributor H. T. Dickinson, *Stress and Stability* attempts to explain why the majority of the British population neither revolted *en masse* nor supported radical reformers during an age of popular political revolution. Summarizing Christie's arguments, William Thomas stated in a *Times Literary Supplement* review that "British institutions took the strain of discontent pretty well, and . . . the ruling class defended those institutions with ability and humane good sense." Thomas added, "This is a useful book, the modesty of which tends to veil the prodigious learning which it condenses." Though Dickinson suggested that Christie's arguments could be strengthened by further discussion of conservative forces, he noted that Christie "has certainly succeeded in demonstrating once more those qualities for which he has become famous: prodigious research, an incisive mind, a cool appraisal of motives and achievements, and a brisk, clear style."

Christie told *CA* that he attributed his "commitment to the study and exposition of British constitutional and political history to the years of his military service in World War II, when the issue of overriding importance seemed to be the deference of Western democratic forms of government against the onslaught of tyrannous dictatorships born of European Fascism."

BIOGRAPHICAL/CRITICAL SOURCES:

PERIODICALS

British Book News, January, 1985.
New Statesman, August 21, 1970.
Spectator, August 8, 1970.
Times Educational Supplement, June 1, 1984.
Times Literary Supplement, July 9, 1970; August 6, 1976; September 24, 1982; April 19, 1985.

*   *   *

CINCINNATUS
   See CURREY, Cecil B(arr)

*   *   *

CIRCUS, Anthony
   See HOCH, Edward D(entinger)

*   *   *

CLARE, Ellen
   See SINCLAIR, Olga

*   *   *

CLARK, Mary Higgins   1929-

PERSONAL: Born December 24, 1929, in New York, NY; daughter of Luke Joseph (a restaurant owner) and Nora C. (a buyer; maiden name, Durkin) Higgins; married Warren F. Clark (an airline executive), December 26, 1949 (died September 26, 1964); married Raymond Charles Ploetz (an attorney), August 8, 1978 (marriage annulled); children: Marilyn, Warren, David, Carol, Patricia. *Education:* Attended Villa Maria Academy, Ward Secretarial School, and New York University; Fordham University, B.A. (summa cum laude), 1979. *Politics:* Republican. *Religion:* Roman Catholic. *Avocational interests:* Traveling, skiing, tennis, playing piano.

ADDRESSES: Home—2508 Cleveland Ave., Washington Township, NJ 07675; and 210 Central Park

S., New York, NY 10019. *Agent*—Eugene H. Winick, McIntosh & Otis, Inc., 475 Fifth Ave., New York NY 10017.

CAREER: Writer. Remington Rand, New York City, advertising assistant, 1946; stewardess for Pan American Airlines, 1949-50; radio scriptwriter and producer for Robert G. Jennings, 1965-70; Aerial Communications, New York City, vice president, partner, creative director, and producer of radio programming, 1970-80; David J. Clark Enterprises, New York City, chair of the board and creative director, 1980—. Chair, International Crime Writers Congress, 1988.

MEMBER: Mystery Writers of America (president, 1987; member of board of directors), Authors Guild, Authors League of America, American Academy of Arts and Sciences, American Society of Journalists and Authors, American Irish Historical Society (member of executive council).

AWARDS, HONORS: New Jersey Author Award, 1969, for *Aspire to the Heavens: A Biography of George Washington,* 1977, for *Where Are the Children?,* and 1978, for *A Stranger Is Watching;* Grand Prix de Litterature Policiere (France), 1980; honorary doctorate, Villanova University, 1983.

WRITINGS:

NOVELS

Where Are the Children? (also see below), Simon & Schuster (New York City), 1975.
A Stranger Is Watching (also see below), Simon & Schuster, 1978.
The Cradle Will Fall (also see below), Simon & Schuster, 1980.
Three Complete Novels (also see below; contains *Stillwatch, A Cry in the Night,* and *Weep No More, My Lady*), Wings, 1982.
A Cry in the Night, Simon & Schuster, 1982.
Stillwatch, Simon & Schuster, 1984.
(With Thomas Chastain and others) *Murder in Manhattan,* Morrow (New York City), 1986.
Weep No More, My Lady, Simon & Schuster, 1987.
While My Pretty One Sleeps, Simon & Schuster, 1989.
Loves Music, Loves to Dance, Simon & Schuster, 1991.
All Around the Town, Simon & Schuster, 1992.
I'll Be Seeing You, Simon & Schuster, 1993.
Remember Me, Simon & Schuster, 1994.

Let Me Call You Sweetheart, Simon & Schuster, 1995.
Mary Higgins Clark: Three Complete Novels (contains *Where Are the Children?, A Stranger Is Watching,* and *The Cradle Will Fall*), Wings (New York City), 1995.
Silent Night, Simon & Schuster, 1995.
Moonlight Becomes You, Simon & Schuster, 1996.

SHORT STORY COLLECTIONS

(Editor) *Murder on the Aisle: The 1987 Mystery Writers of America Anthology,* Simon & Schuster, 1987.
(With others) *Caribbean Blues,* J. Curley, 1988.
The Anastasia Syndrome and Other Stories, Simon & Schuster, 1989.
The Lottery Winner: Alvirah and Willy Stories, Simon & Schuster, 1994.
(Editor and author of introduction) *The International Association of Crime Writers Presents: Bad Behavior,* Harcourt Brace (San Diego, CA), 1995.

OTHER

Aspire to the Heavens: A Biography of George Washington, Meredith Press, 1969.
(Contributor) *I, Witness,* Times Books (New York City), 1978.
(Contributor) *Family Portraits,* edited by Carolyn Anthony, Doubleday (New York City), 1989.

Work anthologized in *The Best "Saturday Evening Post" Stories,* 1962. Also author of syndicated radio dramas. Contributor of stories to periodicals, including *Saturday Evening Post, Redbook, McCall's,* and *Family Circle.*

ADAPTATIONS: A Stranger Is Watching was filmed by Metro-Goldwyn-Mayer in 1982; *The Cradle Will Fall* was shown on CBS as a "Movie of the Week" in 1984; *A Cry in the Night* was filmed by Rosten productions in 1985; *Where Are the Children?* was filmed by Columbia in 1986; *Stillwatch* was broadcast on CBS in 1987; *A Cry in the Night,* two stories from *The Anastasia Syndrome,* and *Weep No More, My Lady* were produced by Ellipse. Several of Clark's books have been released on audiocassette, including *While My Pretty One Sleeps,* read by Jessica Walter, Simon & Schuster Audio, 1989, and *Loves Music, Loves to Dance,* read by Kate Burton, Simon & Schuster Audio, 1991.

SIDELIGHTS: Mary Higgins Clark began her writing career as a newly widowed mother of five, and has instilled her passion for suspense stories in her children, including daughter Carol, also a best-selling novelist. Clark's stories "about nice people confronting the forces of evil and vanquishing them," as Patti Doten noted in the *Boston Globe*, have proven so popular that her publisher, Simon & Schuster, signed her to a record-breaking $11.4 million contract in 1989 to produce four novels and a short story collection, and a $35 million contract for five novels and a memoir in 1992.

Clark's success began with her first novel, *Where Are the Children?*, a best seller in 1975 which earned over $100,000 in paperback royalties. She followed that with another thriller, *A Stranger Is Watching,* which earned more than $1 million in paperback rights and was filmed by Metro-Goldwyn-Mayer in 1982. For Clark, this meant financial security. "[The money] changed my life in the nicest way," she told Bina Bernard in *People.* "It took all the choking sensation out of paying for the kids' schools."

The key to Clark's popularity, according to several critics, is her technique. White maintains that Clark "is a master storyteller who builds her taut suspense in a limited time frame," noting that *Where Are the Children?* takes place in one day and *A Stranger Is Watching* in three. Carolyn Banks, moreover, points out in the *Washington Post* that there is a kind of "Mary Higgins Clark formula" that readers both expect and enjoy: "There are no ambiguities in any Clark book. We know whom and what to root for, and we do. Similarly, we boo and hiss or gasp when the author wants us to. Clark is a master manipulator." Although Clark wants to provide her readers with entertainment and romance, she once told *CA:* "I feel a good suspense novel can and should hold a mirror up to society and make a social comment."

Clark's style is to write about "terror lurking beneath the surface of everyday life," observes White. "[She] writes about ordinary people suddenly caught up in frightening situations as they ride a bus or vacuum the living room," as are characters of *Loves Music, Loves to Dance,* who encounter a murderer when they agree to participate in an experiment involving newspaper personal ads. Other stories play on readers' fears of unfamiliar or undesirable situations. For example, Clark explored mental illness in both *Loves Music, Loves to Dance,* in which the killer's behavior is caused by a personality disorder, and *All Around the Town,* in which the main character is afflicted with multiple personality disorder attributed to severe sexual abuse in her childhood. In *I'll Be Seeing You,* Clark's characters find themselves victimized by villains more knowledgeable than they in the issues of genetic manipulation and in-vitro fertilization. Many of the events and details of Clark's stories come from the lives of her friends and family, news events, and even her own experiences. Clark told *New York Times* interviewer Shirley Horner that the burglary which the heroine comes home to in *Stillwatch* was based on break-ins Clark herself has endured. "Everything that a writer experiences goes up in the mental attic," she told Horner.

Writing has become a family affair for the Clarks. Carol Higgins Clark's first novel, *Decked,* appeared on the paperback bestseller list as her mother's *I'll Be Seeing You* was departing the hardcover list after seventeen weeks. Carol's second book, *Snagged,* debuted in hardcover in 1993, and a third, to be titled *Iced,* is in progress. To critics who suggest that Clark may have contributed to the writing of her daughter's books, the elder author's response is, "Not so, we have very different voices," Sarah Booth Conroy noted in the *Washington Post.* Conroy observed that Mary "writes deadly serious novels about the sort of chilling fears that come to women in the middle of the night," while Carol "spoons in a bit of bawdy, a soupcon of slapstick." Carol did, however, exert some influence in her mother's writing: she is responsible for saving two of Clark's most popular characters, Alvirah, a cleaning woman who wins the lottery, and her husband, Willy. When they first appeared in a short story, Alvirah was poisoned and Clark planned to finish her off, but Carol convinced her mother to allow Alvirah to recover. The two have since become recurring characters and are featured in *The Lottery Winner: Alvirah and Willy Stories,* published in 1994.

BIOGRAPHICAL/CRITICAL SOURCES:

BOOKS

Bestsellers 89, Issue 4, Gale (Detroit), 1989.

PERIODICALS

Best Sellers, December, 1984.
Booklist, November 1, 1989, p. 524.
Boston Globe, August 19, 1994, p. 47.
Chicago Tribune, September 20, 1987; June 12, 1988; July 31, 1989.
Chicago Tribune Book World, June 8, 1980.

Cosmopolitan, May, 1989.

Kirkus Reviews, April 1, 1993, p. 390; April 1, 1994, p. 413; October 15, 1994, p. 1363.

Library Journal, April 15, 1969, p. 1792; June 1, 1989, p. 170; March 15, 1990, pp. 35-37.

Los Angeles Times Book Review, November 4, 1984; May 14, 1989; March 3, 1991, p. 10; June 9, 1991, p. 13; May 10, 1992, p. 8.

Newsweek, June 30, 1980.

New Yorker, August 4, 1980.

New York Times, January 22, 1982; July 3, 1987; December 6, 1989; June 4, 1992, p. C18; October 18, 1992, p. 1; August 11, 1993, p. C17.

New York Times Book Review, May 14, 1978; November 14, 1982; December 9, 1984, p. 26; June 28, 1987; June 18, 1989; December 3, 1989, p. 82; March 10, 1991, p. 28; June 16, 1991, p. 16; May 10, 1992, p. 23; May 2, 1993, p. 22.

People, March 6, 1978; August 31, 1992, p. 31.

Publishers Weekly, December 26, 1977, p. 59; September 7, 1984, p. 70; May 19, 1989, pp. 64-65; June 2, 1989, p. 58; September 29, 1989, p. 61; April 5, 1991, p. 138; March 30, 1992, p. 91; October 17, 1994, p. 62; February 27, 1995, p. 89.

Rapport, May, 1993, p. 24.

Reader's Digest, December, 1989, pp. 92-94; July, 1991, pp. 83-86.

School Library Journal, September, 1991, p. 292.

Spectator, August 19, 1978, p. 22.

Voice of Youth Advocates, April, 1990, p. 26.

Washington Post, May 19, 1980; July 17, 1980; October 18, 1982; August 10, 1987; June 7, 1992, p. 8; September 23, 1993, p. C1.

West Coast Review of Books, November, 1982, p. 33.

Wilson Library Bulletin, September, 1987, p. 73.

Writers Digest, April, 1988, pp. 46-47.*

*   *   *

CLARK, William Bedford   1947-

PERSONAL: Born January 23, 1947, in Oklahoma City, OK; son of William B. (a pipeliner) and Florine (Griggs) Clark; married Charlene Kerne (a library development professional), December 22, 1972; children: Mary Frances, Eleanor Kerne. *Education:* University of Oklahoma, B.A., 1969, Louisiana State University, M.A., 1971, Ph.D., 1973.

ADDRESSES: Home—2304 Burton, Bryan, TX 77802. *Office*—Department of English, Texas A & M University, College Station, TX 77843.

CAREER: North Carolina Agricultural and Technical State University, Greensboro, assistant professor of English, 1974-77; Texas A & M University, College Station, 1977—, began as assistant professor, became professor of English.

MEMBER: Society for the Study of Southern Literature, Conference on Christianity and Literature, South Central Modern Language Association, American Literature Association, Robert Penn Warren Circle (president, 1993-95), Phi Kappa Phi.

AWARDS, HONORS: Grants from National Endowment for the Humanities, 1973-74, 1977, 1980; Distinguished Faculty Achievement Award in Teaching, 1990, and University Honors Teacher/Scholar Award, 1993, both from Texas A & M University.

WRITINGS:

(Editor and author of introduction) *Critical Essays on Robert Penn Warren,* G. K. Hall (Boston, MA), 1981.

(Editor with W. Craig Turner) *Critical Essays on American Humor,* G. K. Hall, 1984.

(Editor with Clinton Machann) *Katherine Anne Porter and Texas: An Uneasy Relationship,* Texas A & M University Press (College Station, TX), 1990.

The American Vision of Robert Penn Warren, University Press of Kentucky (Lexington, KY), 1991.

Contributor to *Faulkner and Humor,* edited by Ann Abadie and Doreen Fowler, University of Mississippi (University, MS), 1985. Also contributor of about sixty articles and reviews to literature journals and literary magazines, including *Antioch Review, American Literature, Kenyon Review, Renascence, Sewanee Review, South Atlantic Quarterly, Southern Review,* and *Studies in American Humor.* Editor of *South Central Review,* 1984-87.

WORK IN PROGRESS: Editing the selected letters of Robert Penn Warren and researching the role of Catholicism in American literature and culture.

SIDELIGHTS: William Bedford Clark told *CA:* "For me, literary criticism is not only the exploration of a text but a mode of self-exploration. I am often surprised by the degree to which my own writings represent an implicit autobiography."

*   *   *

CLYMER, Eleanor 1906-
(Janet Bell, Elizabeth Kinsey)

PERSONAL: Born January 7, 1906, in New York, NY; daughter of Eugene (a ship engineer) and Rose (Fourman) Lowenton; married Kinsey Clymer (a journalist and social worker), 1933 (died, 1984); children: Adam. *Education:* Attended Barnard College, 1923-25; University of Wisconsin, B.A., 1928; also attended Bank Street College of Education and New York University.

ADDRESSES: Home—3118 Elm, The Quadrangle, 3300 Darley Rd., Haverford, PA 19041.

CAREER: Writer of children's books, 1943—. Dodd, Mead and Company, New York City, accounts assistant, 1930-32; worked in a doctor's office, for a social work agency, and as a teacher in the early 1930s.

MEMBER: Authors Guild (former chair of the children's book committee), Authors League of America, Wilderness Society, Native American Rights Fund.

AWARDS, HONORS: Woodward School Zyra Lourie book award, 1968, for *My Brother Stevie;* Juvenile Literature Award of Border Regional Library Association, Texas, 1971, for *The Spider, the Cave, and the Pottery Bowl;* Children's Book Award of the Child Study Association of America, 1975, for *Luke Was There;* Sequoyah Book Award of the Oklahoma Library Association, 1978, for *The Get-Away Car.*

WRITINGS:

CHILDREN'S FICTION

A Yard for John, illustrated by Mildred Boyle, McBride, 1943.
Here Comes Pete, illustrated by Boyle, McBride, 1944.
The Grocery Mouse, illustrated by Jeanne Bendick, McBride, 1945.
Little Bear Island, illustrated by Ursula Koering, McBride, 1945.
The Country Kittens, illustrated by Bendick, McBride, 1947.
The Trolley Car Family, illustrated by Koering, McKay (New York City), 1947.
The Latch-Key Club, illustrated by Corinne Dillon, McKay, 1949.
Treasure at First Base, illustrated by Jean MacDonald Porter, Dodd (New York City), 1950.
Tommy's Wonderful Airplane, illustrated by Kurt Wiese, Dodd, 1951.
Thirty-Three Bunn Street, illustrated by Jane Miller, Dodd, 1952.
Chester, illustrated by Ezra Jack Keats, Dodd, 1954.
Not Too Small After All, illustrated by Tom O'Sullivan, F. Watts (New York City), 1955.
Sociable Toby, illustrated by Ingrid Fetz, F. Watts, 1956.
Mr. Piper's Bus, illustrated by Wiese, Dodd, 1961.
Benjamin in the Woods, illustrated by William Russell, Wonder Books, 1962.
Now That You Are Seven, illustrated by Ingrid Fetz, Association Press, 1963.
Harry, the Wild West Horse, illustrated by Leonard Shortall, Atheneum (New York City), 1963.
The Tiny Little House, illustrated by Fetz, Atheneum, 1964.
Chipmunk in the Forest, illustrated by Fetz, Atheneum, 1965.
The Adventure of Walter: A Whale, illustrated by Fetz, Atheneum, 1965.
My Brother Stevie, Holt (New York City), 1967.
The Big Pile of Dirt, illustrated by Robert Shore, Holt, 1968.
Horatio, illustrated by Robert Quackenbush, Atheneum, 1968.
Belinda's New Spring Hat, illustrated by Gioia Fiamenghi, F. Watts, 1969.
We Lived in the Almont, illustrated by David Stone, Dutton (New York City), 1970.
The House on the Mountain, illustrated by Leo Carty, Dutton, 1971.
The Spider, the Cave, and the Pottery Bowl, illustrated by Fetz, Atheneum, 1971.
Me and the Eggman, illustrated by Stone, Dutton, 1972.
How I Went Shopping and What I Got, illustrated by Trina Schart Hyman, Holt, 1972.
Santiago's Silver Mine, illustrated by Fetz, Atheneum, 1973.

Luke Was There, illustrated by Diane de Groat, Holt, 1973.

Leave Horatio Alone, illustrated by Quackenbush, Atheneum, 1974.

Take Tarts as Tarts Is Passing, illustrated by Roy Doty, Dutton, 1974.

Engine Number Seven, illustrated by Quackenbush, Holt, 1975.

Hamburgers—And Ice Cream for Dessert, illustrated by Doty, Dutton, 1975.

Horatio's Birthday, illustrated by Quackenbush, Atheneum, 1976.

Horatio Goes to the Country, illustrated by Quackenbush, Atheneum, 1978.

The Get-Away Car, Dutton, 1978.

Horatio Solves a Mystery, illustrated by Quackenbush, Atheneum, 1980.

A Search for Two Bad Mice, illustrated by Margery Gill, Atheneum, 1980.

Beautiful Soup, illustrated by Hilary Einsel, Houghton (Boston), 1981.

My Mother Is the Smartest Woman in the World, illustrated by Nancy Kincade, Atheneum, 1982.

The Horse in the Attic, illustrated by Ted Lewin, Bradbury (Scarsdale, NY), 1983.

UNDER PSEUDONYM JANET BELL

Sunday in the Park, illustrated by Aline Appel, McBride, 1946.

Monday—Tuesday—Wednesday Book, illustrated by Mary Stevens, McBride, 1946.

UNDER PSEUDONYM ELIZABETH KINSEY

Teddy, illustrated by Bendick, McBride, 1946.

Patch, illustrated by James H. Davis, McBride, 1946.

Sea View Secret, illustrated by Mary Stevens, F. Watts, 1952.

Donny and Company, illustrated by Stevens, F. Watts, 1953.

This Cat Came to Stay!, illustrated by Don Sibley, F. Watts, 1955.

CHILDREN'S NONFICTION

Make Way for Water, illustrated by J. C. Wonsetler, Messner (New York City), 1953.

(With Lillian Erlich) *Modern American Career Women,* Dodd, 1959.

The Case of the Missing Link, illustrated by Robert Reid MacGuire, Basic Books (New York City), 1962.

Search for a Living Fossil: The Story of Coelacanth, illustrated by Joan Berg, Holt, 1963.

(With Ralph C. Preston) *Communities at Work* (textbook), Heath (Lexington, MA), 1964.

Wheels: A Book to Begin On, illustrated by Charles Goslin, Holt, 1965.

The Second Greatest Invention: Search for the First Farmers, illustrated by Lili Rethi, Holt, 1969.

OTHER

Also author, with Lillian M. Gilbreth and Orpha Mae Thomas, of *Management in the Home,* Dodd, 1954.

ADAPTATIONS: Luke Was There was filmed for the *Learning to Be Human* series by the Learning Corporation of America and was broadcast on *Special Treat,* National Broadcasting Company (NBC), 1976.

SIDELIGHTS: Eleanor Clymer is the author of such classic children's books as *The Trolley Car Family, The Latch-Key Club, My Brother Stevie, Luke Was There,* and *The Get-Away Car.* Clymer credits the birth of her own son with inspiring her to turn her hand to fiction. "I wanted to tell stories to little children," she explains in an essay for *Something about the Author Autobiography Series* (SAAS), "like my own son and his friends who were beginning to find their way in the everyday world of family, play, work, pets, familiar things that they experienced and understood. Realistic fiction was for me." The advice of pioneering children's writer Lucy Sprague Mitchell was also important in Clymer's decision to write realistic stories. Mitchell had, in her textbook *The Here and Now Story Book,* encouraged writers to deal with everyday issues for children. Fairy tales and fantasy were both important, Mitchell admitted, but it was more important for a writer to listen to children at play and learn the real-life issues that were important to them. Clymer, a student of Mitchell's at the Bank Street School, took this dictum to heart. "I learned how to listen to children's own stories and language," she recalls in *SAAS,* "and soon I was writing here and now stories of my own."

The first of these stories to be published, *A Yard for John,* is the story of a little boy who wants a place to be able to dig in the earth. Such activity is not allowed in the park, but when his parents are able to buy a country house, John can dig to his heart's content. In rapid succession, Clymer followed this book with *Here Comes Pete, The Grocery Mouse,* and *The Country Kittens,* the last book about two kittens who come to the big city and get an uncommon education in city ways. Ellen Lewis Buell, writing in the *New York Times Book Review,* comments that "this cat's tour of New York is artfully scaled to a kitten's viewpoint, spontaneous and funny."

Because these early books were successful, Clymer was able to work at home and raise her son, whose many interests inspired her later books. His love of baseball, for example, led to *Treasure at First Base,* the story of how one young boy establishes baseball as the favorite sport in his new neighborhood, and solves a historical mystery in the process. Doris M. Blasco in *Library Journal* notes that the book has all the features of a good story: "action, humor . . . real boys who do real things." A *Booklist* critic calls it a "lively story . . . for the middle grades." Clymer's son's interest in photography is reflected in *Chester,* a book about a young boy who desperately wants a camera. The ways Chester sets about attaining this dream create "a fun-filled story," according to a *Booklist* reviewer.

Life in the city inspired other books for Clymer. *The Trolley Car Family* tells of a trolley car driver, put out of work by the advent of city buses, who buys an old trolley car and moves it to the country where his family takes up residence for the summer. Helen Dore Boylston and Jane Cobb, writing in *Atlantic Monthly,* call *The Trolley Car Family* "a warm, goofy book, delightfully written," and Phyllis Fenner, in the *New York Times Book Review,* notes that it is "an unusually nice, folksy story of an amusing American family." *The Latch-Key Club* is another urban story, this one about city kids who, because both parents work, have to look out for themselves after school. When new neighbors move in, the children form a club among themselves. The book is "a warm and richly human account," writes Helen M. Brogan in *Library Journal.* A *Booklist* reviewer comments that *The Latch-Key Club,* told from the social worker's point of view, ran the risk of sounding preachy and tedious, but is instead "lively and entertaining." *Thirty-Three Bunn Street* includes some of the adventures Clymer and her family had when she was eight. It is "the kind of genuine, everyday story most little girls love," writes Jennie D. Lindquist in *Horn Book,* and a *Booklist* writer dubs it "one of the author's best."

Clymer's husband worked for the Department of Welfare and told his wife a variety of stories about the lives of city children he met. Such information allowed her to write from the point of view, in *My Brother Stevie,* of a young African-American girl,

and in *Luke Was There,* from that of a runaway boy. The latter book explores the life of a boy adrift in the city after he has run away from a children's shelter where he was lodged when his mother was hospitalized. As Beryl Robinson writes in *Horn Book,* the story shows "credible and moving insight concerning a child's response to difficult problems." Betty Boegehold, in *Twentieth-Century Children's Writers,* explains that "Clymer never *tells* us; the characters and their actions *show* us."

Realistic social problems form the basis for two other books from this period. *The House on the Mountain* is the story of inner-city African-American children who, while on a picnic in the country, explore an empty house until they are confronted by the racially prejudiced owner. A reviewer for *Publishers Weekly* believes that the story adds "another star to the growing list" of Clymer's "distinguished books." *The Big Pile of Dirt* had its origins in a newspaper story about some children whose playground was a vacant lot full of trash. A load of dirt is accidentally dumped there and instantly provides a real playground for them, until some well-meaning adults propose to clean it up for the children. It is a story, as a critic for *Kirkus Reviews* notes, told in a conversational style to "convey a kid's side of the fence . . . a chronicle that could be a folk ballad."

Clymer's two main themes of city and country are brought together in *The Get-Away Car,* inspired by an actual car Clymer and her husband bought for ten dollars at the beginning of their marriage. The story follows Maggie and her grandmother as they make their way from the city to a cousin's house in the country, taking along with them several neighborhood children. Along the way they help numerous people, and then are in need of help themselves when finally they arrive at the cousin's house to find it in a state of disrepair and with a sale imminent because of delinquent taxes. A "warm and pleasant diversion" is how Karen Harris describes the book in *School Library Journal. The Get-Away Car* won the Sequoyah Book Award of the Oklahoma Library Association.

Over the course of Clymer's long writing career, she has explored a wide range of themes, but she never lost sight of the individual child reading a story. "Mainly," she writes in *SAAS,* "I try to interpret children's feelings, questions, and interest in the world they live in." She once explained how important it was for her to represent real lives of real children: "I feel that children's emotions and their problems in dealing with the adult world are very important, and need interpretation, and not necessarily in terms of everything turning out happily. At the same time I think that a book for children should not paint a picture that is too threatening or hopeless."

BIOGRAPHICAL/CRITICAL SOURCES:

BOOKS

Something about the Author Autobiography Series, Volume 17, Gale (Detroit), 1994.
Twentieth-Century Children's Writers, 4th edition, St. James Press (Detroit), 1995.

PERIODICALS

Atlantic Monthly, December, 1947, p. 144.
Booklist, October 15, 1949, p. 68; July 1, 1950, p. 338; June 1, 1952, p. 324; October 15, 1954, p. 89; January 15, 1984, p. 747.
Bulletin of the Center for Children's Books, February, 1966, p. 96; June, 1967, p. 151; October, 1968, pp. 23-24; January, 1969, p. 75; September, 1969, p. 5; June, 1971, p. 154; July, 1971, p. 167; July, 1972, p. 167; July, 1974, pp. 172-173; September, 1975, p. 5; February, 1979, p. 97; March, 1979, p. 111; December, 1980, p. 167; February, 1983, p. 105; December, 1983.
Horn Book, June, 1952, p. 174; April, 1965, p. 165; October, 1965, p. 497; June, 1967, p. 346; August, 1973, p. 374; April, 1974, p. 147; June, 1974, p. 275; October, 1974, p. 131; April, 1976, p. 151; October, 1976, p. 490; December, 1978, p. 635; April, 1980, p. 161; February, 1981, p. 349; October, 1983, p. 571.
Kirkus Reviews, June 15, 1968, p. 642; September 15, 1978, p. 1016.
Library Journal, November 15, 1949; August, 1950, pp. 1308-1309.
New York Times Book Review, November 16, 1947, p. 36; February 8, 1948, p. 30; May 9, 1965, p. 26; April 23, 1967, p. 26; August 4, 1968, p. 20; November 16, 1975, p. 34.
Publishers Weekly, April 3, 1967, p. 56; July 22, 1968, p. 63; September 16, 1968, p. 71; April 31, 1970, p. 279; March 8, 1971, p. 71; May 10, 1971, p. 43; April 15, 1974, p. 52; September 23, 1974, p. 156; May 26, 1975, p. 59; June 21, 1976, p. 92; August 21, 1978, p. 60; March 21, 1980, p. 69; September 10, 1982, p. 76.

School Library Journal, September, 1975, p. 78; January, 1976, p. 36; September, 1976, p. 97; October, 1978, pp. 130, 143; May, 1980, p. 84; November, 1980, p. 72; November, 1982, p. 78.

* * *

COLE, Richard Cargill 1926-

PERSONAL: Born April 16, 1926, in Kansas City, KS; son of Horace Richard (a postal official) and Iris Verner (a homemaker; maiden name, Cargill) Cole; married Florence Adaline Mason (a homemaker), June 27, 1956; children: Celia Elizabeth Cole Shaw, Paul Richard. *Education:* Hamilton College, B.A., 1950; Yale University, M.A., 1951, Ph.D., 1955. *Politics:* Republican. *Religion:* Presbyterian.

ADDRESSES: Home—217 Crescent Dr., Davidson, NC 28036. *Office*—Department of English, Davidson College, Davidson, NC 28036.

CAREER: Manlius School, Manlius, NY, English teacher, 1951-52; Yale University, New Haven, CT, assistant to dean of freshmen, 1953-54; University of Texas at Austin, instructor in English, 1954-57; Radford College (now University), Radford, VA, associate professor, 1957-59, professor of English, 1959-61; Davidson College, Davidson, NC, professor of English, 1961-93, professor emeritus, 1993—. *Military service:* U.S. Army Air Force, 1944-46; served in Europe; became sergeant.

MEMBER: Phi Beta Kappa.

AWARDS, HONORS: Grant from American Council of Learned Societies, 1975; Robert Warnock research fellow at Yale University, 1975-76; research fellow, Yale Divinity School, 1978; grant from National Endowment for the Humanities, 1985 and 1989.

WRITINGS:

Irish Booksellers and English Writers, 1740-1800, Mansell Publishing (Bronx, NY), 1986.
(Editor) *Robert Colvill's Atlanta and Savannah,* Scholars' Facsimiles and Reprints (Delmar, NY), 1987.
(Editor) *John Singleton's European Journal, 1815-1817,* Peter Lang (New York City), 1987.
Thomas Mante, Writer, Soldier, Adventurer, Peter Lang, 1993.

(Editor) *The General Correspondence of James Boswell, 1766-67,* Yale University Press (New Haven, CT), 1993.

Editor of "The Private Papers of James Boswell," Yale University, 1975—. Contributor to literature and philology journals.

WORK IN PROGRESS: Editing James Boswell's correspondence in the years 1768 to 1769, for Yale University Press and Edinburgh University Press.

SIDELIGHTS: The subject of Richard Cargill Cole's first book is eighteenth-century Irish booksellers and their contribution to the popularity of British authors. He concerned himself not with the publishers who reprinted authorized editions from the British mainland, but with the pirates who produced cheap, unauthorized copies of British titles. Though they were the object of bitter complaints from the London publishing industry, these Irish entrepreneurs were responsible for popularizing the work of authors like Dr. Johnson, Boswell, Goldsmith, and Gibbon by making their work affordable to a wide audience. Reviewer James Raven wrote in the *Times Literary Supplement:* "*Irish Booksellers and English Writers, 1740-1800* is an important contribution to the history of eighteenth-century publishing."

BIOGRAPHICAL/CRITICAL SOURCES:

PERIODICALS

Scotsman, February 5, 1994.
Times Literary Supplement, January 2, 1987.

*   *   *

COLEMAN, Bill
  See COLEMAN, William V(incent)

*   *   *

COLEMAN, Patricia R(egister)   1936-
  (Patty R. Coleman)

PERSONAL: Born November 1, 1936, in Orlando, FL; daughter of Oliver C. (an engineer) and Athena (an accountant; maiden name, Athanasaw) Register;

married William Vincent Coleman (a writer and publisher), November 27, 1974; children: Lisa, Sarah Angela, James Richard. *Education:* University of Georgia, A.A., 1956; Florida State University, B.A., 1974. *Religion:* Roman Catholic.

ADDRESSES: Office—Apartado Postal #330-5, Cuernavaca, Morelos 62051, Mexico.

CAREER: St. Joseph's Church, Macon, GA, director of religious education, 1970-72; Growth Associates (ministerial service), Mystic, CT, co-founder and vice president, 1972—, artistic director of publications, 1980-89. Diocesan associate director of Department of Christian Formation, Savannah, GA, 1971-74. Member of board of directors of Norwich Community Ministries, 1981-83, Martin House, Inc., 1982-83, and the Vermont Association for Mexican Opportunity and Support (VAMOS!), 1986—. Field director of VAMOS!, Mexico, 1989—. *National Catholic Reporter,* correspondent, 1993—.

WRITINGS:

WITH HUSBAND, WILLIAM V. COLEMAN

Mine Is the Morning, ten volumes, Twenty-Third (Mystic, CT), 1974-77, revised edition, 1978.
God Believes in Me, five volumes, Ave Maria Press, 1975.
Confirmed to Courage, Twenty-Third, 1976.
The Saints: Heroes to Follow, Twenty-Third, 1976.
Daybreak, ten volumes, Twenty-Third, 1976-77.
The Church, Twenty-Third, 1977.
God's Own Child, two volumes, Twenty-Third, 1977, revised edition, 1983.
Jesus, Our Brother, Twenty-Third, 1977.
Rediscovering Lent, six volumes, Twenty-Third, 1977.
Morality, Twenty-Third, 1977.
Parish Youth Ministry, Twenty-Third, 1977.
Renewing Your Family's Covenant, Twenty-Third, 1978.
Planning Tomorrow's Parish, two volumes, Twenty-Third, 1978.
Only Love Can Make It Easy, two volumes, Twenty-Third, 1979.
What Is Youth Ministry?, Growth Associates, 1979.
Together with Jesus, six volumes, Twenty-Third, 1979.
Together in Prayer, six volumes, Twenty-Third, 1979.
A Time for Comfort and Hope, Twenty-Third, 1979.

Catholic Prayers and Devotions, Twenty-Third, 1979.

Make Friends with God, Growth Associates, 1980.

A Confirmation Journal, Twenty-Third, 1980.

A Junior High Prayerbook, Twenty-Third, 1980.

Awakening to Jesus, two volumes, Twenty-Third, 1981.

Sex Today, Growth Associates, 1981.

The Youth Ministry Handbook, Growth Associates, 1981.

The Mass Today, Growth Associates, 1982.

No-Pain Learning, Growth Associates, 1982.

You, Your Life and Jesus, Growth Associates, 1982.

Confirm and Renew, two volumes, Growth Associates, 1982.

Be Reconciled, two volumes, Growth Associates, 1982.

Lord, Hear Our Prayer, two volumes, Growth Associates, 1983.

This Is My Body, two volumes, Growth Associates, 1983.

The Mustard Seed People, Growth Associates, 1983.

Our Parish: A Place to Grow, Growth Associates, 1985.

Fifty Youth Things to Do, Growth Associates, 1986.

Whispers of Revelation: Finding the Spirit of the Poor, Twenty-Third, 1993.

OTHER

Radical Images, Growth Associates (Rochester, NY), 1987.

Co-founder and co-editor of *Catholic Youth Ministry, Parish Communication,* and *Radical Option;* co-founder of *Synthesis.* Sometimes publishes under the name Patty R. Coleman.

WORK IN PROGRESS: Capitalism, Corruption and Chaos, which explores the reasons behind the economic, social, ecological and political disaster which has overtaken Mexico and much of Latin America. These same forces are behind the slow erosion of the quality of life and growing social unrest in the U.S. and other developed countries. Unless capitalism is regulated, we will experience a breakdown of our system of government similar to what happened to bureaucratic Communism in the U.S.S.R.

SIDELIGHTS: Patricia R. Coleman told *CA:* "I was an artist when I was drawn into religious education by the renewal of the Catholic church after Vatican Council II. My life work has been to struggle with my husband to develop a contemporary synthesis of religious ideas and contemporary faith for those participating in the diverse community we call 'church.'

"Years ago my husband and I decided that what kept most couples in tension with one another was the dissimilarities of their development. Husbands went one way, wives another. We decided that we would work together on the same projects so that this would not happen to us.

"We struggle with every new idea and wonder together what each new experience means to us. It is hard to define our working time and our family time. It has all merged together, as have we. Sometimes we marvel together at how close our thoughts and values have become. These have, in turn, influenced our children, who grew up in the midst of all our questioning and writing.

"I love being a woman, a wife, and a writer. The older I become, the more I see my many roles merging into one, to be a disciple of the Lord Jesus and to follow him wherever he leads Bill and me. I am confident that, short of death, he will never lead us anywhere except together."

*   *   *

COLEMAN, Patty R.
    See COLEMAN, Patricia R(egister)

*   *   *

COLEMAN, William V(incent)   1932-
    (Bill Coleman)

PERSONAL: Born January 27, 1932, in Waterbury, CT; son of William V. (a chemist) and Ethel (Brennan) Coleman; married Patricia Register (a writer), November 27, 1974; children: Lisa, Sarah Angela, James Richard. *Education:* Saint Bernard College, Rochester, NY, B.A., 1953; Saint Bernard Seminary, B.D., 1955, M.Div., 1957; Fairfield University, M.A., 1965; Florida State University, Ph.D., 1976.

ADDRESSES: Office—Apartado Postal #330-5, Cuernavaca, Morelos 62051, Mexico.

CAREER: Writer. Ordained Roman Catholic priest, 1957; Catholic Diocese of Savannah, GA, rector of St. John's Seminary, 1958-68, director of education, 1968-74; left priesthood, 1974; Growth Associates (ministerial service), Mystic, CT, president, 1975-89; correspondent for National Catholic Reporter, 1993—. Has lectured throughout the United States, Canada, and Europe; Mexican representative of Vermont Association for Mexican Opportunity and Support (VAMOS!), 1989—.

MEMBER: American Education Association, National Association for the Advancement of Colored People, National Association of Public Continuing Adult Education.

WRITINGS:

(With Patricia McLemore) *Personal Morality* (monograph), Twenty-Third (Mystic, CT), 1974.
The Way of the Cross, two volumes, Twenty-Third, 1975.
Finding a Way to Follow: Values for Today's Christian, Morehouse (Wilton, CT), 1977.
Prayer Talk, Ave Maria Press (Notre Dame, IN), 1982.
Special Days, Growth Associates (Rochester, NY), 1984.
Christian Economics, Growth Associates, 1986.
Everyday People, Growth Associates, 1987.

WITH WIFE, PATRICIA R. COLEMAN

Mine Is the Morning, ten volumes, Twenty-Third, 1974-77, revised and enlarged edition, 1978.
God Believes in Me, five volumes, Ave Maria Press, 1975.
Confirmed to Courage, Twenty-Third, 1976.
The Saints: Heroes to Follow, Twenty-Third, 1976.
Daybreak, ten volumes, Twenty-Third, 1976-77.
The Church, Twenty-Third, 1977.
God's Own Child, two volumes, Twenty-Third, 1977, revised edition, 1983.
Jesus, Our Brother, Twenty-Third, 1977.
Rediscovering Lent, six volumes, Twenty-Third, 1977.
Morality, Twenty-Third, 1977.
Parish Youth Ministry, Twenty-Third, 1977.
Renewing Your Family's Covenant, Twenty-Third, 1978.
Planning Tomorrow's Parish, two volumes, Twenty-Third, 1978.
What Is Youth Ministry?, Growth Associates, 1979.

Only Love Can Make It Easy, two volumes, Twenty-Third, 1979.
Together with Jesus, six volumes, Twenty-Third, 1979.
Together in Prayer, six volumes, Twenty-Third, 1979.
A Time for Comfort and Hope, Twenty-Third, 1979.
Catholic Prayers and Devotions, Twenty-Third, 1979.
Make Friends with God, Growth Associates, 1980.
A Confirmation Journal, Twenty-Third, 1980.
A Junior High Prayerbook, Twenty-Third, 1980.
Awakening to Jesus, two volumes, Twenty-Third, 1981.
Sex Today, Growth Associates, 1981.
The Youth Ministry Handbook, Growth Associates, 1981.
The Mass Today, Growth Associates, 1982.
No-Pain Learning, Growth Associates, 1982.
You, Your Life and Jesus, Growth Associates, 1982.
Confirm and Renew, two volumes, Growth Associates, 1982.
Be Reconciled, two volumes, Growth Associates, 1982.
Lord, Hear Our Prayer, two volumes, Growth Associates, 1983.
This Is My Body, two volumes, Growth Associates, 1983.
The Mustard Seed People, Growth Associates, 1983.
Our Parish: A Place to Grow, Growth Associates, 1985.
Fifty Youth Things to Do, Growth Associates, 1986.
Whispers of Revelation: Discovering the Spirit of the Poor, Twenty-Third, 1993.

OTHER

Also author of *Teach Us How to Pray,* two volumes, Twenty-Third, *The Leadership Training Book,* Growth Associates, and *Lent '82, Lent '83, Lent '84, Lent '85, Lent '86, Lent ' 87, Lent '88, Advent '84, Advent '85, Advent '86,* and *Advent '87,* all from Growth Associates. Author of scripts for numerous filmstrips produced by Twenty-Third and over fifty cassette tapes produced by Twenty-third Publications, *National Catholic Reporter,* and Growth Associates. Author of column, "Update," published in *Today's Parish.* Publisher of the newsletters *Catholic Youth Ministry, Parish Communication, Southern Cross,* and *Synthesis;* co-founder and coeditor, *Radical Option.*

WORK IN PROGRESS: Capitalism, Corruption and Chaos, an examination of the economic, social, ecological and political disaster which has overtaken Mexico and much of Latin America.

SIDELIGHTS: William V. Coleman told *CA* that his "life's work is to share the gospel of Jesus with everyday people. I have been able to do that in many ways: writing, speaking, giving retreats, and publishing. Whatever the medium, the message remains the same. Looking back over the years, I understand how my attention has gone more and more to the people of Latin America and their fascinating change. It is [there] that I find hope for our civilization and, indeed, for the world.

"[Recently, I've been] living among the Mexican poor and writing about their plight. I have learned more during the past six years than my books and classes and degrees ever hoped to teach me."

*   *   *

COLLINS, David R(aymond) 1940-

PERSONAL: Born February 29, 1940, in Marshalltown, IA; son of Raymond A. (an educator) and Mary Elizabeth (Brecht) Collins. *Education:* Western Illinois University, B.S., 1962, M.S., 1966. *Politics:* Democrat. *Religion:* Roman Catholic.

ADDRESSES: Home—3403 45th St., Moline, IL 61265. *Office*—Department of English, Moline Senior High School, 3600 23rd Ave., Moline, IL 61265.

CAREER: Teacher of English in Moline, IL, at Woodrow Wilson Junior High School, 1962-83, and Moline Senior High School, 1983—. President of Friends of the Moline Public Library, 1965-67.

MEMBER: National Education Association (life member), Children's Reading Roundtable, Society of Children's Book Writers, Authors Guild, Authors League of America, Juvenile Forum (president, 1975—), Writers' Studio (president, 1968-72), Mississippi Valley Writers Conference (founder; director, 1974—), Illinois Education Association, Illinois Congress of Parents and Teachers (life member), Illinois State Historical Society (life member), Blackhawk Division of Teachers of English (president, 1967-68), Quad City Writers Club, Quad City Arts Council, Phi Delta Kappa, Kappa Delta Pi, Delta Sigma Pi.

AWARDS, HONORS: Outstanding Juvenile Writer Award, Indiana University, 1970; Judson College Writing Award, 1971; Writer of the Year Awards, Writers' Studio, 1971, and Quad City Writers Club, 1972; Alumni Achievement Award, Western Illinois University, 1973; Outstanding Illinois Educator Award, 1976; Junior Literary Guild Award, 1981; Midwest Writing Award, 1982; Gold Key Award, 1983; Catholic Press Writing Award, 1983; National Catholic Book Award, 1984, for *Thomas Merton: Monk with a Mission;* Veterans of Foreign Wars Teacher of the Year Award, 1987-88; Distinguished Alumni Award, Western Illinois University, 1993; Cornelia Meigs Literary Award, 1990; Who's Who Among America's Teachers, 1994; Louise Messer Young Authors Prize, 1994.

WRITINGS:

JUVENILES

Kim Soo and His Tortoise, Lion Press, 1970.
Great American Nurses, Messner (New York City), 1971.
Walt Disney's Surprise Christmas Present, Broadman (Nashville, TN), 1971.
Linda Richards: First American Trained Nurse, Garrard (Easton, MD), 1973.
Harry S. Truman: People's President, Garrard, 1975, reprinted, Chelsea House (New York City), 1990.
Football Running Backs: Three Ground Gainers, Garrard, 1976.
Abraham Lincoln, Mott Media (Milford, MI), 1976.
Illinois Women: Born to Serve, DeSaulniers, 1976.
Joshua Poole Hated School, Broadman, 1976.
George Washington Carver, Mott Media, 1977.
A Spirit of Giving, Broadman, 1978.
Charles Lindbergh: Hero Pilot, Garrard, 1978, reprinted, Chelsea House, 1990.
If I Could, I Would, Garrard, 1979.
Joshua Poole and Sunrise, Broadman, 1980.
The Wonderful Story of Jesus, Concordia (St. Louis, MO), 1980.
The One Bad Thing about Birthdays, Harcourt (San Diego, CA, and New York City), 1981.
Joshua Poole and the Special Flowers, Broadman, 1981.
George Meany: Mr. Labor, St. Anthony Messenger Press (Cincinnati, OH), 1981.
Dorothy Day: Catholic Worker, St. Anthony Messenger Press, 1981.
Thomas Merton: Monk with a Mission, St. Anthony Messenger Press, 1982.

Francis Scott Key, Mott Media, 1982.

(With Evelyn Witter) *Notable Illinois Women,* Quest Publishing (Rock Island, IL), 1982.

Johnny Appleseed, Mott Media, 1983.

Florence Nightingale, Mott Media, 1983.

The Special Guest, Broadman, 1984.

The Long-legged Schoolteacher, Eakin Press (Austin, TX), 1985.

Not Only Dreamers, Brethren Press (Ashland, OH), 1986.

Ride a Red Dinosaur, Milliken Press, 1987.

Probo's Amazing Trunk, Modern Curriculum Press (Cleveland, OH), 1987.

Ara's Amazing Spinning Wheel, Modern Curriculum Press, 1987.

Ursi's Amazing Fur Coat, Modern Curriculum Press, 1987.

Leo's Amazing Paws and Jaws, Modern Curriculum Press, 1987.

Ceb's Amazing Tail, Modern Curriculum Press, 1987.

Hali's Amazing Wings, Modern Curriculum Press, 1987.

The Wisest Answer, Milliken Press, 1988.

Grandfather Woo Comes to School, Milliken Press, 1988.

Country Artist: The Story of Beatrix Potter, Carolrhoda (Minneapolis, MN), 1988.

To the Point: The Story of E. B. White, Carolrhoda, 1988.

Harry S. Truman: Our 33rd President, Garrett Educational, 1988.

Grover Cleveland: Our 22nd and 24th President, Garrett Educational, 1988.

Woodrow Wilson: Our 28th President, Garrett Educational, 1989.

Zachary Taylor: Our 12th President, Garrett Educational, 1989.

Noah Webster—God's Master of Words, Mott Media, 1989.

Jane Addams, Warner Press (Anderson, IN), 1989.

Clara Barton, Warner Press, 1989.

James Buchanan: Our 15th President, Garrett Educational, 1990.

William McKinley: Our 25th President, Garrett Educational, 1990.

Gerald Ford: Our 38th President, Garrett Educational, 1990.

Pioneer Plowman: A Story about John Deere, Carolrhoda Books, 1990.

The Greatest Life Ever Lived, Brethren Press, 1991.

Tales for Hard Times: A Story about Charles Dickens, Carolrhoda Books, 1991.

J. R. R. Tolkien—Master of Fantasy, Lerner Publications (Minneapolis, MN), 1991.

Lee Iacocca—Chrysler's Good Fortune, Garrett Educational, 1992.

Philip Knight—Running with Nike, Garrett Educational, 1992.

Black Rage: The Story of Malcolm X, Dillon Press (Minneapolis, MN), 1992.

M-A-R-K T-W-A-I-N! A Story about Samuel Clemens, Carolrhoda Books, 1993.

Tad Lincoln: White House Wildcat, Discovery Enterprises, 1994.

Shattered Dreams: The Story of Mary Todd Lincoln, Morgan Reynolds, 1994.

Against the Wind: The Story of Arthur Ashe, Dillon Press, 1994.

Eng and Chang: The Original Siamese Twins, Dillon Press, 1994.

William Jefferson Clinton: Our 42nd President, Garrett Educational, 1995.

The Farmer's Friend: A Story about Caesar Chavez, Carolrhoda Books, 1995.

Casimir Pulaski—Soldier on Horseback, Pelican Publishing (Gretna, LA), 1995.

Attack on Fort McHenry, Rigby Educational, 1995.

Got a Penny? The Dorothy Day Story, St. Paul Books and Media, 1996.

You're Never Alone: The Thomas Merton Story, St. Paul Books and Media, 1996.

OTHER

Contributor to periodicals, including *Catholic Boy, Catholic Miss, Junior Discoveries, Modern Woodman, Plays,* and *Vista.*

WORK IN PROGRESS: Numerous biographies for youth; an adult novel.

SIDELIGHTS: David R. Collins told *CA:* "Children are curious, their minds open and flexible. A child is eager to enjoy new adventures. Anyone choosing to write for young readers faces an exciting challenge and a great responsibility. He must remember that his words and ideas may have a lasting effect on his reader's imagination, personality, even his entire character. Young readers deserve the best in reading.

"Why did I decide to write for children? Probably because some of my best childhood adventures were discovered in books. . . . I owe a tremendous debt to the realm of children's literature. Perhaps if I can offer something worthwhile to young readers, part of that debt will be repaid."

COURT, Wesli
  See TURCO, Lewis (Putnam)

*   *   *

COWEN, Emory L(eland)   1926-

PERSONAL: Born April 20, 1926, in New York, NY; son of Philip H. and Rose D. Cowen; married Renee Senna (a teacher), January 28, 1947; children: Richard Jan, Peter Rolf, Lisa Allyson, Andrew Philip. *Education:* Brooklyn College (now of the City University of New York), A.B. (cum laude), 1944; Syracuse University, A.M., 1948, Ph.D., 1950.

ADDRESSES: Home—32 Aberthaw Rd., Rochester, NY 14610. *Office*—Center for Community Study, University of Rochester, 575 Mt. Hope Ave., Rochester, NY 14620.

CAREER: University of Rochester, Rochester, NY, assistant professor, 1950-55, associate professor, 1955-60, professor of psychology, 1960—, professor of psychiatry, 1967—, professor of education, 1973-84, director of Undergraduate Counseling Service, 1956-61, director of clinical psychology training program, 1956-69, directory of primary mental health project, 1958-91, assistant chair of psychology department, 1960-63, associate chair of psychology department, 1963-69, associate in psychiatry, 1960-67, director of Center for Community Study, 1969—. Consultant to Veterans Administration, 1955—; New York State Board of Examiners in Psychology, member, 1962-68, vice-chair, 1963-64, chair, 1964-66. Member of National Science Foundation visiting scientist program; member of psychology training subcommittee for National Institute of Mental Health, 1964-68. *Military service:* U.S. Navy, 1944-46; became lieutenant junior grade.

MEMBER: American Psychological Association (fellow; member of committee on advisory services for training and accreditation, scientific affairs committee, executive committee, 1973-77, nominations committee, 1976-77, chair of fellowship committee, 1973-74), Eastern Psychological Association, New York State Psychological Association (past member of board of directors and clinical research committee), Genessee Valley Psychological Association (past president), Sigma Xi, Psi Chi.

AWARDS, HONORS: National Institute of Mental Health special senior research fellow at Institut de Psychologie, Universite de Paris, 1961-62; Research Award, American Personnel and Guidance Association, 1962; research award, Phi Delta Kappa, 1977; Creative Community Program Award, New York State Division of Youth, 1978; COMPEER Award, Community Volunteer Service, 1979; Outstanding Research Contribution Award (Senior Category), New York State Psychological Association, 1979; Award for Distinguished Contributions to Psychology in the Public Interest, American Psychological Association, 1989; Seymour B. Sarason Award for Community Research and Action, American Psychological Association, 1995.

WRITINGS:

(With R. P. Underberg, R. T. Verrillo, and F. G. Benham) *Adjustment to Visual Disability in Adolescence,* American Foundation for the Blind (New York City), 1961.
(Editor with E. A. Gardner and M. Zax, and contributor) *Emergent Approaches to Mental Health Problems,* Appleton (New York City), 1967.
(With Zax, D. R. Beach, and others) *Follow-Up Study of Children Who Participated in a Preventive Mental Health Program* (monograph), U.S. Office of Education (Washington, DC), 1967.
(With J. Rappaport and J. M. Chinsky) *Innovations in Helping Chronic Patients: College Students in a Mental Hospital,* Academic Press (New York City), 1971.
(With Zax) *Abnormal Psychology: Changing Conceptions,* Holt (New York City), 1972, 2nd edition, 1976.
(With R. P. Lorion) H. H. Barten and L. Bellak, editors, *Progress in Community Mental Health,* Volume 3, Grune (New York City), 1975.
(With R. V. Isaacson, L. D. Izzo, and others) *New Ways in School Mental Health: Early Detection and Prevention of School Maladaptation,* Human Sciences, Inc. (New York City), 1975.
(With E. L. Gesten) B. B. Wolman, J. Egan, and A. O. Ross, editors, *Handbook of Treatment of Mental Disorders in Childhood and Adolescence,* Prentice-Hall, 1978.
(With Gesten, R. Flores de Apodaca, M. H. Rains, and R. P. Weissberg) M. W. Kent and J. E. Rolf, editors, *The Primary Prevention of Psychopathology, Volume 3: Social Competence in Children,* University Press of New England (Hanover, NH), 1979.

(With Gesten) M. Gibbs, J. R. Lachenmeyer, and J. Segal, editors, *Community Psychology Theoretical and Empirical Approaches,* Gardner Press (New York City), 1980.

(With Gesten and Weissberg) R. H. Price and P. Politzer, editors, *Evaluation and Action in the Social Environment,* Academic Press, 1980.

(With A. D. Hightower) S. M. Auerbach and A. L. Stolberg, editors, *Crisis Intervention with Children and Families,* Hemisphere Publications (New York City), 1987.

(With J. L. Pedro-Carroll) J. P. Vincent, editor, *Advances in Family Intervention, Assessment and Theory: Volume IV,* JAI Press (Greenwich, CT), 1987.

(Editor with Price, Lorion, and J. Ramos-McKay) *Fourteen Ounces of Prevention: A Casebook of Exemplary Prevention, Promotion and Intervention Alternatives,* American Psychological Association (Washington, DC), 1988.

(With Hightower) T. B. Gutkin and C. R. Reynolds, editors, *Handbook of School Psychology,* second edition, Wiley (New York City), 1989.

(With Hightower, Pedro-Carroll, and W. C. Work) Lorion, editor, *Protecting the Children: Strategies for Optimizing Emotional and Behavioral Development,* Haworth Press (New York City), 1990.

(With Work and P. A. Wyman) Kessler and Goldston, editors, *The Present and Future of Prevention Research: Essays in Honor of George Albee,* Sage Publications (San Francisco, CA), 1992.

(With Hightower, Work, Pedro-Carroll, Wyman, and W. G. Haffey) *Prevention, Young Children and the Schools: The Primary Mental Health Project Story,* American Psychological Association, 1995.

(With Hightower) M. C. Roberts, *Model Programs in School Mental Health,* Lawrence Erlbaum (Hillsdale, NJ), 1995.

(With Work and Wyman) S. Luthar, J. Burack, J. Weisz, and D. Cicchetti, editors, *Developmental Psychopathology: Perspectives on Risk and Disorder,* Cambridge University Press (New York City), 1996.

Contributor to numerous books, including *A Psychology of Exceptional Children and Youth,* edited by W. M. Cruickshank, Prentice-Hall (Englewood Cliffs, NJ), 1955, 2nd edition, 1963; *Psychological Research and Rehabilitation,* edited by L. H. Lofquist, American Psychological Association, 1963; *Children as Teachers: Theory and Research on Tutoring,* edited by V. L. Allen, Academic Press, 1976; *International Encyclopedia of Neurology, Psychiatry, Psychoanalysis and Psychology,* edited by Wolman, Brunner-Mazel (New York City), 1979; *Volunteers and Children with Special Needs,* edited by W. Cunningham and D. Mulligan, National School Volunteer Program, Inc. (Arlington, VA), 1980; *The Social Psychology of Psychological Problems,* edited by M. P. Feldman and J. Orford, Wiley (Chichester, England), 1980; *Concepts of Primary Prevention: A Framework for Program Development,* edited by Goldston and M. L. Shore, California Office of Prevention (Sacramento, CA), 1988; and *Handbook of Community Psychology,* second edition, edited by Rappaport and E. Seidman, Wiley, 1995. Contributor to professional journals. Advisory editor of *Journal of Consulting and Clinical Psychology,* 1967-76; associate editor of *American Journal of Community Psychology,* 1972-83, consulting editor, 1977-85, guest editor, 1980-82; advisory editor of *Journal of Primary Prevention,* 1979—; advisory editor of *Journal of Preventive Psychiatry,* 1980—.

*   *   *

CURREY, Cecil B(arr)   1932-
(Cincinnatus)

PERSONAL: Born November 29, 1932, in Clarks, NE; son of Cecil Chalmers (a store manager) and Edith Estelle (Barr) Currey; married Laura Gene Hewett (a school psychologist), August 14, 1952; children: Samuel Bowman, Anne Estelle, Laura Alise. *Education:* Attended Nebraska Central College, 1950, and Friends Bible College, Haviland, KS, 1951-52; Fort Hays Kansas State College (now Fort Hays State University), A.B., 1958, M.Sc., 1959; graduate study at University of Nebraska, 1959-60, and Municipal University of Omaha, 1961-62; University of Kansas, Ph.D, 1965. *Politics:* Unaffiliated. *Religion:* Congregationalist.

ADDRESSES: Home—3330 Lake Crenshaw Rd., Lutz, FL 33549. *Office*—Department of History, University of South Florida, Tampa, FL 33620.

CAREER: Ordained minister of Congregational Church; pastor in Downs, KS, 1957-59, and Ashland, NE, 1960-62; Nebraska Wesleyan University, Lincoln, 1964-67, began as assistant professor, became associate professor of history; University of South Florida, Tampa, associate professor, 1967-71, professor of history, 1971—. Vietnam history consultant and technical advisor. Has appeared on television and radio on matters dealing with military analysis of topical events as well as his own work on over 240 occasions. *Military service:* U.S. Army, Medical Service Corps, 1953-55. Army National Guard, 1965-79; served as chaplain; became colonel; U.S. Army Reserve, 1979-92; retired.

MEMBER: American Historical Association, Organization of American Historians, Florida College Teachers of History (executive council, 1968-70, vice-president and program chair, 1980, president, 1981), Association of Third World Studies, Phi Kappa Phi, Phi Alpha Theta, Phi Delta Kappa, Pi Gamma Mu.

AWARDS, HONORS: S & H Lectureship Fund grant, 1966, 1967; Library Travel grant, University of South Florida, Tampa, 1969; distinguished alumni award, Fort Hays State University, 1975; Outstanding Teaching Award, Mortar Board Society, University of South Florida, 1978; State of Florida Distinguished Service Medal for outstanding meritorious service, 1982; General Fund grant, 1985, Faculty Research and Development Program grant, College of Social and Behavioral Sciences, 1985, 1990, Research and Creative Scholarship grant, 1985, 1990, all from University of South Florida; National Geographic Society grant, 1988; Meritorious Service Medal for outstanding meritorious service, Department of Army, 1991; Travel grant, University of South Florida, 1994; Teaching Incentive Program Award, University of South Florida, 1995.

WRITINGS:

Road to Revolution: Benjamin Franklin in England, 1765-1775, Doubleday (New York City), 1968, revised edition, Peter Smith (Glouchester, MA), 1978.

Code Number 72: Ben Franklin, Patriot or Spy?, Prentice-Hall (Englewood Cliffs, NJ), 1972.

The Craft and Crafting of History, Omni/Burgess (Sarasota, FL), 1975.

Reason and Revelation: John Duns Scotus on Natural Theology, Franciscan Herald Press (Chicago, IL), 1977.

Guide to Images of America (text to university television course based on Alistair Cooke's PBS television series "America"), Kendall-Hunt (Dubuque, IA), 1980.

(Under pseudonym Cincinnatus) *Self-Destruction: The Disintegration and Decay of the United States Army during the Vietnam Era* (Military Book Club selection), Norton (New York City), 1981.

Follow Me and Die: The Destruction of an American Division in World War II (Military Book Club selection), Stein & Day (Briarcliff Manor, NY), 1984.

With Wings As Eagles: A History of Army Aviation, Department of the Army (Fort Rucker, AL), 1984.

Edward Lansdale: The Unquiet American, Houghton (Boston, MA), 1989.

(Editor with others) *The Chaplain and the Chaplain Assistant,* Government Printing Office (Washington, DC), 1989.

(With Israel Drazin) *For God and Country: A Constitutional Challenge to the Military Chaplaincy,* Ktau Publishing (Baltimore, MD), 1994.

Red Dragon Rising: A Biography of General Vo Nguyen Giap, Brassey's (McLean, VA), 1996.

Contributor to books, including, *The Birth of America,* edited by Raymond Friday Locke, Mankind Publishing (Melrose, CA), 1971; *Makers of American Diplomacy: From Benjamin Franklin to Henry Kissinger,* two volumes, edited by Frank Merli and Theodore Wilson, Scribner's (New York City), 1974; *The International Military Encyclopedia,* edited by John P. Sloan, Academic International Publishing (Gulf Breeze, FL), 1983; *Vietnam Reconsidered: Lessons from a War,* edited by Harrison E. Salisbury, Harper, 1984; *The Dictionary of Christianity in America,* edited by Daniel G. Reid, InterVarsity Press (Downers Grove, IL), 1990; Edward G. Lansdale, *In the Midst of Wars,* expanded edition, Fordham University Press (Bronx, NY), 1991; *American, France and Vietnam: Cultural History and Ideas of Conflict,* edited by Jon Roper and Phil Melling, Gower (London), 1991; *Tet, 1968,* edited by William Head and Marc J. Gilbert, Greenwood (Westport, CT), 1996; *The Vietnam War: An Encyclopedia,* edited by Spencer C. Tucker, Garland (New York City), 1996. Also contributor to numerous newspapers and periodicals, including, *Viet Nam Generation, Conflict Quarterly, Military Review, St. Petersburg Times, Italian Quarterly, New York Times,* and *Soldiers Magazine.* Also writer, producer, and director of a television play, "The Stamp Act, 1765," broadcast by a number of Nebraska television stations to commemorate the bicentennial of that event.

WORK IN PROGRESS: Long Binh Jail: An Oral History of the United States Army Vietnam Installation Stockade.

SIDELIGHTS: Upon its publication in 1981, *Self-Destruction: The Disintegration and Decay of the United States Army during the Vietnam Era* attracted a great deal of attention, partly because it contained pointed criticism of the political and military systems in America and partly because of the mystery surrounding its author. The book was published under the name Cincinnatus, the name of a fifth-century Roman soldier who "left his farm, was made dictator long enough to save Rome, and then renounced his title and returned to the farm," as Michael Getler relates in the *Washington Post*. At the time the book was published, several claims were made about the author, claims which eventually were discovered to be inaccurate and which added to the controversy surrounding the book. Some months after its appearance, the book was revealed to have been written by Cecil B. Currey, a historian and professor who had served in the Army Medical Service Corps, the Army National Guard, and the Army Reserve. Because Currey's position was chaplain and because he had not served in Vietnam, some reviewers questioned his qualifications for writing this book and his reasons for using a pseudonym.

In a letter to *CA*, Currey commented on the attention given *Self-Destruction:* "The book was published to much controversy because members of the media failed in their own responsibilities to check their facts and sources. It began when Military Book Club wrote the brochure without checking with anyone at the publishing house and described Cincinnatus as one who had served in Vietnam. That was then taken up by authors of news articles and endlessly repeated. Reporters read other reporters' stories and each new 'assumption' became incorporated as 'fact' in the next story. Both my editor, Eric Swenson, and I made every effort to short-circuit such mistakes and inferences with letters and phone calls. It was like chasing feathers from a torn pillow in a high wind."

He continued, "The only claims about the author by me or the publisher appeared on the dust jacket which described me as a 'military man' (inasmuch as for thirty years I had served either as an enlisted man in the Active Army and Army Reserve or as an officer in the National Guard or Army Reserve); a 'field grade officer' (I was at the time holding the rank of lieutenant colonel); a 'graduate of the United States Army's Command and General Staff College' (my certificate of graduation from the course is dated 1975); 'assigned to the Pentagon' (my duty, whenever I served on active duty, was to work in the Office of the Chief of Chaplains in the Pentagon); and the holder of three degrees (I hold the A.B., M.A., and Ph.D.). From this simple claim came all that followed as reporters tried to embellish what they knew with what seemed to them likely or probable. The scandal of it all lay not with author or publisher but with reporters who failed to fulfill the high responsibilities of their own calling!

"Even after Michael Getler wrote the article in the *Washington Post* naming me as author, reporters could not get their facts straight. My rank was listed in various places ranging from captain to major general (I was a lieutenant colonel); I became a graduate of the Army War College (I have never attended there); my date of commissioning was printed variously as 1962-1963-1964-1965 (it was 3 December 1965); someone described me as an Episcopal clergyman (my faith is Congregational); and I was elevated from *working* in the Office of the Chief of Chaplains to *being* the active Army Chief of Chaplains. Stories about me as Cincinnatus contained at least *thirty* different errors of fact—all of which could have been easily checked but which 'newshounds' were too indifferent to worry about."

In explaining his use of the pseudonym Cincinnatus, Currey told *CA:* 'The simple fact of the matter is that both Swenson and I believed the message was so important some way must be found to make the military listen to it. There was no other reason. Previous books of the same genre inevitably suffered from official military complaints about the failings of the authors—repeated use of the *argumentum ad hominem* to discredit a book by discrediting the author. We sought to avoid that by publishing pseudonymously. Think for a moment of all those who have done so. James Madison of Virginia wrote some of the 'Federalist' essays as 'Publius' in order to convince New Yorkers to ratify the Constitution. Benjamin Franklin wrote as 'Silence Dogood' on a number of occasions. Samuel Clemens was 'Mark Twain.' Charles Lutwidge Dodgson, as Lewis Carroll, brought the world 'Alice in Wonderland.' All felt what they had to say outweighed the ego satisfaction to be gained from seeing their own name in print. So did I!

"Lastly, I would add that despite the initial furor, the Army later decided the book was valuable and today it is on one of the Army Training and Doctrine Command professional reading lists for officers who wish to stay abreast of current doctrine."

BIOGRAPHICAL/CRITICAL SOURCES:

PERIODICALS

Los Angeles Times, March 27, 1981.
New York Times, May 3, 1981.
Washington Post, May 2, 1981.

D

DALLAS, Ruth
  See MUMFORD, Ruth

*   *   *

DANIELS, Olga
  See SINCLAIR, Olga

*   *   *

DAVIS, David Brion   1927-

PERSONAL: Born February 16, 1927, in Denver, CO; son of Clyde Brion (a writer) and Martha (a writer and painter; maiden name, Wirt) Davis; married Toni Hahn (an attorney), September 9, 1971; children: (first marriage) Jeremiah, Martha, Sarah; (second marriage) Adam, Noah. *Education:* Dartmouth College, A.B. (summa cum laude), 1950; Harvard University, A.M., 1953, Ph.D., 1956; Oxford University, M.A., 1969; Yale University, M.A., 1970. *Politics:* Democrat.

ADDRESSES: Home—733 Lambert Rd., Orange, CT 06477. *Office*—Hall of Graduate Studies, Yale University, New Haven, CT 06520.

CAREER: Dartmouth College, Hanover, NH, instructor in history and Ford Fund for the Advancement of Education intern, 1953-54; Cornell University, Ithaca, NY, assistant professor, 1955-58, associate professor, 1958-63, Ernest I. White Professor of History, 1963-69; Yale University, New Haven, CT,

professor of history, 1969-72, Farnham Professor of History, 1972-78, Sterling Professor of History, 1978—. Fulbright lecturer in India, 1967, and at universities in Guyana and the West Indies, 1974. Lecturer at colleges and universities in the United States, Europe, and the Middle East, 1969—. Commissioner, Orange, CT, Public Library Commission, 1974-75; associate director, National Humanities Institute, Yale University, 1975. *Military service:* U.S. Army, 1945-46.

MEMBER: American Historical Association (member of Pulitzer Prize and Beveridge Prize committees), Organization of American Historians (president, 1988-89, member of executive board, 1987-92), Society for American Historians, American Antiquarian Society, Institute of Early American History and Culture (member of council), American Philosophical Society, American Academy of Arts and Sciences, British Academy, Phi Beta Kappa.

AWARDS, HONORS: Guggenheim fellow, 1958-59; Anisfield-Wolf Award, 1967; Pulitzer Prize, 1967, for *The Problem of Slavery in Western Culture;* National Mass Media Award, National Conference of Christians and Jews, 1967; Center for Advanced Study in the Behavioral Sciences fellow, 1972-73; Albert J. Beveridge Award, American Historical Association, 1975; National Book Award for history, 1976, for *The Problem of Slavery in the Age of Revolution, 1770-1823;* Bancroft Prize, 1976; Henry E. Huntington Library fellow, 1976; Litt.D., Dartmouth College, 1977; National Endowment for the Humanities, research grants, 1979-80 and 1980-81, and fellowship for independent study and research, 1983-84; Fulbright traveling fellow, 1980-81; L.H.D., University of New Haven, 1986; corresponding fellow, Massachusetts Historical Society, 1989; Presidential Medal for Outstanding Leadership and Achievement, Dartmouth College, 1991; corresponding fellow, British Academy, 1992.

WRITINGS:

Homicide in American Fiction, 1798-1860: A Study in Social Values, Cornell University Press (Ithaca, NY), 1957.

The Problem of Slavery in Western Culture, Cornell University Press, 1967.

(Editor) *Ante-bellum Reform,* Harper (New York City), 1967.

The Slave Power Conspiracy and the Paranoid Style, Louisiana State University Press (Baton Rouge), 1969.

Was Thomas Jefferson an Authentic Enemy of Slavery?, Clarendon Press (Oxford, England), 1970.

(Editor) *The Fear of Conspiracy: Images of Un-American Subversion from the Revolution to the Present,* Cornell University Press, 1971.

The Problem of Slavery in the Age of Revolution, 1770-1823, Cornell University Press, 1975.

(With others) *The Great Republic: A History of the American People,* Little, Brown (Boston, MA), 1977, revised edition, 1985.

(Editor) *Antebellum American Culture: An Interpretive Anthology,* Heath (Lexington, MA), 1979.

Slavery and Human Progress, Oxford University Press (New York City), 1984.

Slavery in the Colonial Chesapeake (pamphlet), Colonial Williamsburg (Williamsburg, VA), 1986.

From Homicide to Slavery: Studies in American Culture, Oxford University Press, 1986.

Revolutions: Reflections on American Equality and Foreign Liberations, Harvard University Press (Cambridge, MA), 1990.

(Coauthor) *The Antislavery Debate: Capitalism and Abolitionism as a Problem in Historical Interpretation,* edited by Thomas Bender, University of California Press (Berkeley), 1992.

OTHER

Author of the pamphlet *The Emancipation Moment,* 1984. Contributor to books, including *The Stature of Theodore Dreiser,* edited by Alfred Kazin and Charles Shapiro, Indiana University Press (Bloomington), 1955; *Twelve Original Essays on Great American Novels,* edited by Shapiro, Wayne State University Press (Detroit, MI), 1958; *Perspectives and Irony in American Slavery,* edited by Harry

Owens, University of Mississippi Press (University, MS), 1976; *Slavery and Freedom in the Age of the American Revolution,* edited by Ira Berlin and Ronald Hoffman, University of Virginia Press (Charlottesville, VA), 1983; and *British Capitalism and Caribbean Slavery,* edited by Barbara Solow and Stanley L. Engerman, Cambridge University Press (New York City), 1987. Contributor to professional journals and other periodicals, including *New York Times Book Review, Times Literary Supplement, New York Review of Books, Washington Post Book World, New Republic, American Historical Review, Journal of American History, American Jewish History, New England Quarterly, Yale Review,* and *Reviews in American History.*

WORK IN PROGRESS: The Problem of Slavery in the Age of Emancipation, 1815-1890, for Oxford University Press.

SIDELIGHTS: "David Brion Davis ranks high among the elite historians of New World slavery," remarks M. I. Finley in the *New York Times Book Review.* Davis's series, "The Problem of Slavery," has won numerous awards, including a Pulitzer Prize and a National Book Award. His books on slavery have been praised for their scholarship, lucidity, and especially for their new insights into a much-analyzed institution.

In a *New York Times Book Review* article, J. H. Plumb calls the Pulitzer Prize-winning *The Problem of Slavery in Western Culture* "one of the most scholarly and penetrating studies of slavery" and states that Davis displays "his mastery not only of a vast source of material, but also of the highly complex, frequently contradictory factors that influenced opinion on slavery." In this book, according to George M. Fredrickson in the *New York Review of Books,* Davis is concerned "mainly with the changes that had to occur in Western views of the nature of man and his relationship to society and authority before antislavery ideas could emerge." For example, he discusses "the role of original sin as a justification for slavery and how the modification and dilution of this traditional Christian doctrine in the eighteenth century had raised troublesome questions about black servitude."

In *The Problem of Slavery in the Age of Revolution, 1770-1823,* Davis continues this analysis with a study of "how ideas antithetical to slavery could win acceptance and become the basis of practical policies that served the broader needs of dominant groups,"

Fredrickson writes. To do this, Davis compares the American antislavery movement with that in Great Britain and other countries at the same time. Fredrickson feels that it is clear from Davis's account "that the British antislavery movement had much greater success in this period than the American, even though both countries legislated against the international slave trade in the same year (1807)." To account for this dichotomy, "Davis undertakes a detailed analysis of the relationship of antislavery to dominant ideologies in both the United States and Great Britain." The result, according to Plumb is "a rich and powerful book [that] will, I am sure, stand the test of time—scholarly, brilliant in analysis, beautifully written."

Slavery and Human Progress approaches the issue of slavery from a perspective different from that of the author's previous work. "The most striking characteristic of this richly learned book is Davis's sensitivity to ambiguities and ambivalences," writes William H. McNeill in the *Washington Post Book World.* The work explores one particular issue, the similarity in rhetoric and reasoning of both the pro-and anti-slavery forces. "The scope of the study is awe-inspiring," comments *Los Angeles Times Book Review* contributor Larry May, covering "slavery in the Western world from biblical times to the present." Finley finds this scope somewhat limiting: "From this reading [Davis] has distilled a lively but superficial account of the rhetoric. . . . The account is superficial because genuine explanation is persistently avoided and often even the importance or typicality of the people he cites is not discussed." J. Morgan Kousser, writing in the *Times Literary Supplement,* echoes this assessment, commenting that the book lacks "a straight-forward discussion of the ideas of progress and slavery." Nevertheless, the critic concedes that "as perceptive as he is learned and diligent, [Davis] offers illuminating comments on a whole range of topics."

BIOGRAPHICAL/CRITICAL SOURCES:

PERIODICALS

Los Angeles Times Book Review, November 25, 1984.
Nation, April 26, 1975.
New York Review of Books, October 16, 1975.
New York Times Book Review, February 9, 1975; February 3, 1985; October 5, 1986.
Times (London), January 24, 1985.
Times Literary Supplement, February 1, 1985.
Washington Post Book World, October 21, 1984.

DAVIS, Philip J.   1923-

PERSONAL: Born January 2, 1923, in Lawrence, MA; son of Frank and Annie (Shrager) Davis; married Hadassah Finkelstein (a historical writer), January 2, 1944; children: Abigail, Frank, Ernest, Joseph. *Education:* Harvard University, B.S., 1943, Ph.D., 1950.

ADDRESSES: Home—175 Freeman St., Providence, RI 02906.   *Office*—Department of Applied Mathematics, Brown University, Providence, RI 02912.

CAREER: National Bureau of Standards, Washington, DC, mathematician, 1952-58, chief of numerical analysis section, 1958-63; Brown University, Providence, RI, professor of applied mathematics, 1963—.

MEMBER: Mathematical Association of America.

AWARDS, HONORS: Guggenheim fellow, 1956-57; math award from Washington Academy of Sciences, 1960; Chauvenet Prize from Mathematical Association of America, 1963; American Book Award from Association of American Publishers, 1983, for *The Mathematical Experience;* Lester R. Ford Prize, 1983, George Polya Prize, 1987, and Hedrick Award, 1990, all from the Mathematical Association of America.

WRITINGS:

The Lore of Large Numbers, Random House (New York City), 1961.
Interpolation and Approximation, Blaisdell Publishing, 1963.
The Mathematics of Matrices: A First Book of Matrix Theory and Linear Algebra, Blaisdell Publishing, 1965, 2nd edition, Xerox College Publishing, 1973.
(With Philip Rabinowitz) *Numerical Integration,* Blaisdell Publishing, 1967.
(With William G. Chinn) *3.1416 and All That* (essays), Simon & Schuster (New York City), 1969, 2nd edition, Birkhauser-Boston (Cambridge, MA), 1985.
The Schwarz Function and Its Applications (monograph), Mathematical Association of America (Washington, DC), 1974.
(With Rabinowitz) *Methods of Numerical Integration,* Academic Press (New York City), 1975, 2nd edition, 1984.

Circulant Matrices, Wiley (New York City), 1979, new edition, Chelsea Publishing (New York City), 1994.

(With Reuben Hersh) *The Mathematical Experience,* introduction by Gian-Carlo Rota, Birkhauser Boston, 1981, students' edition, 1995.

The Thread: A Mathematical Yarn, illustrations by Elisa M. Nazeley, Birkhauser Boston, 1983.

(With Hersh) *Descartes' Dream: The World According to Mathematics,* Harcourt (New York City), 1986.

(Editor with David Park) *No Way: The Nature of the Impossible,* W. H. Freeman (New York City), 1987.

Thomas Gray: Philosopher Cat, illustrated by Marguerite Dorian, Harcourt, 1988.

Spirals: From Theodorus to Chaos, A. K. Peters (Wellesley, MA), 1993.

Thomas Gray in Copenhagen: In Which the Philosopher Cat Meets the Ghost of Hans Christian Andersen, illustrated by Dorian, Copernicus Books, 1995.

Some of Davis's works have been translated into Swedish, Italian, Japanese, German, Spanish, Chinese, Hungarian, Portuguese, Czechoslovakian, French and Dutch.

WORK IN PROGRESS: A new edition of *Numerical Integration* with Philip Rabinowitz and Ronald Cools, for Academic Press.

SIDELIGHTS: In their award-winning *The Mathematical Experience* Philip J. Davis and Reuben Hersh describe for general readers the workings of the contemporary mathematical community. Looking at what mathematicians do and who they are, the authors focus on a fundamental in science: Do mathematical theorems and structures exist independent of the human mind? Exploring this timeless argument of discovery versus invention (with as many different labels), Davis and Hersh ultimately take the anthropocentric view that mathematics is a human invention.

While praising Davis and Hersh for discussing topics not usually found in books for general readers, *New York Review of Books* critic Martin Gardner took issue with their basic belief that "mathematics is a humanistic study." As a mathematical realist, Gardner argued: "Why do mathematical theorems fit the universe so accurately that they have enormous explanatory and predictive power? . . . If mathematical concepts have no locus outside human culture,

how has nature managed to produce such a boundless profusion of beautiful models of mathematical objects?" Gardner insisted that mathematical advancement, like most other scientific progress is a mixture of creativeness and innovative thinking, and he contended that the authors' stance was more confusing than illuminating in explaining mathematics to a lay audience.

Reviewing *The Mathematical Experience* for the *Times Literary Supplement,* Roger Penrose confessed Platonistic leanings as well. "How can it be that such childishly simple ingredients can have such power and unexpected application?" he similarly proposed. Still, his opposition to the views of Davis and Hersh did little to dampen his enthusiasm for their "sometimes witty . . . frequently instructive . . . compelling and stimulating" book, which allows lay readers to familiarize themselves with activities of "professional working mathematicians," judged the critic. "Nothing quite like this book has been written about mathematics, and it may well become a sort of classic," a reviewer for the *New Yorker* agreed. Writing in *Harper's,* Hugh Kenner was heartened by the success of *The Mathematical Experience*—a "new *kind* of popular book" that indicates a reading public "with a fair capacity to ponder abstraction." "That's a powerful sign," the critic declared.

Davis and Hersh collaborated again to write *Descartes' Dream: The World According to Mathematics.* Reflecting on the increasing mathematization of the world since Rene Descartes ushered in the Age of Science with his methods of reason in the seventeenth century, the authors focus on the relationship that has evolved between humankind and the mathematics humans have created. Today "we take it as a given that objective reality can be measured, counted, quantified and analyzed by the tools of mathematics," noted Lee Dembart in the *Los Angeles Times.* "But Davis and Hersh find the mathematization of reality both wrong and harmful. . . . Reason, math and logic can do only so much. To follow them further is to invite catastrophe."

Assessing *Descartes' Dream* in the *New Statesman,* Peter Wilsher found Davis and Hersh "particularly good . . . on the application of mathematics to questions of social policy and its weaknesses when faced with the swirling complexity of real events and real people." A fan of the volume, Dembart remarked that "part of the pleasure of their book is the ease with which they convey complicated ideas, their masterful grasp of their material and the balanced tone of their argument." Dembart pronounced *Descartes' Dream* "just as wonderful" as the pair's first collaborative effort. *New York Times Book Review* critic Daniel Gorenstein described the authors' approach as "speculative rather than analytical . . . more concerned with presenting diverse points of view than with attempting to reach definitive conclusions." The reviewer continued: "Mr. Davis and Mr. Hersh raise important questions about man's ability to adapt to an increasingly computerized world but unfortunately their discussion is often too superficial or fragmented to give adequate guidance."

BIOGRAPHICAL/CRITICAL SOURCES:

PERIODICALS

Christian Science Monitor, May 14, 1982.
Globe and Mail (Toronto), April 11, 1987.
Harper's, October, 1981.
Los Angeles Times, November 11, 1986, July 21, 1987.
New Statesman, December 12, 1986.
New Yorker, March 9, 1981.
New York Review of Books, August 13, 1981.
New York Times Book Review, October 5, 1986.
Times Literary Supplement, May 14, 1982, February 13, 1987.

*   *   *

DAWKINS, Richard   1941-

PERSONAL: Born March 26, 1941, in Nairobi, Kenya; immigrated to England in 1949; son of Clinton John (a farmer) and Jean Mary Vyvyan (Ladner) Dawkins; married Marian Stamp, August 19, 1967 (divorced, 1984); married Eve Barham, June 1, 1984; children: Juliet Emma. *Education:* Balliol College, Oxford, B.A., 1962, M.A., 1966, D.Phil., 1966. *Religion:* None. *Avocational interests:* Computer programming.

ADDRESSES: Home—74 Hawkswell Gardens, Oxford OX2 7JW, England. *Office*—Department of Zoology, New College, Oxford University, Oxford OX1 3BN, England.

CAREER: University of California, Berkeley, assistant professor of zoology, 1967-69; Oxford University, Oxford, England, lecturer in zoology and fellow of New College, 1970-90, reader in zoology, 1990-

95, Charles Simonyi Reader in public understanding of science, 1995.

AWARDS, HONORS: Royal Society of Literature Prize, 1987, and *Los Angeles Times* Book Prize in current interest, 1987, both for *The Blind Watchmaker: Why the Evidence of Evolution Reveals a Universe without Design;* Michael Faraday Award of the Royal Society of London, 1990; Nakayama Prize for Human Sciences, 1994; D.Litt., University of St. Andrews, Scotland, 1995.

WRITINGS:

The Selfish Gene, Oxford University Press (New York City), 1976.
The Extended Phenotype: The Gene as the Unit of Selection, W. H. Freeman (New York City), 1982.
(Editor) *Oxford Surveys in Evolutionary Biology 1984,* two volumes, Oxford University Press, 1985.
The Blind Watchmaker: Why the Evidence of Evolution Reveals a Universe without Design, Norton (New York City), 1986.
River Out of Eden, Basic Books (New York City), 1995.
Climbing Mount Improbable, Norton, 1996.

Honorary editor of *Animal Behaviour,* 1974—.

SIDELIGHTS: A zoologist at Oxford University, Richard Dawkins "has already established himself as a biological guru" with the publication of three books detailing and expanding upon Darwinian theory, according to *Times Literary Supplement* contributor Stephen R. L. Clark. Seeing a decline in the popular acceptance of Darwin's theories, Dawkins "has been concerned to convince the literate public that they must now take evolutionary theory seriously as the context within which to think about ourselves and the world," writes Clark. Although some critics consider his theoretical explanations technical and involved, Dawkins strives to bring his theories to an audience of lay readers through comprehensible analogies and clear writing.

In *The Selfish Gene,* Dawkins "gently and expertly debunks some of the favourite illusions of social biology about altruism," writes Peter Medawar in the *Spectator.* The critic also remarks that the work is "a most skilful reformulation of the central problems of social biology in terms of the genetical theory of natural selection." "Building on a beautifully chosen set of analogies," describes Douglas R. Hofstadter in the *Washington Post Book World,* ". . . Dawkins shows how, in the end, spectacularly complex organizations can have the properties we attribute to ourselves, all as a consequence of aimless chemical reactions. This is one of the coldest, most inhuman and disorienting views of human beings I have ever heard," continues Hofstadter, "and yet I love it! It is so deep an insight, to bridge the gap between the lifeless and the living, the chemical and the biological, the random and the teleological, the physical and the spiritual."

In contrast, John Pfeiffer finds the significance of Dawkins's evolutionary theories somewhat elusive: "Dawkins is somewhat ambiguous when it comes to considering how all this applies to human beings," he writes in the *New York Times Book Review.* "[He is] perhaps swayed by his own eloquence." *New York Times* critic Christopher Lehmann-Haupt, conversely, finds Dawkins's writing more than adequate to his task: "It is not the theory of *The Selfish Gene* that is so arresting as the marvelous lucidity with which Mr. Dawkins applies it to various behavior mechanisms that have hitherto been misunderstood." Pfeiffer also admits that Dawkins "demonstrates a rare and welcome ability to make formidably technical findings come alive." A *New Yorker* reviewer expresses a similar opinion: "What makes [*The Selfish Gene*] accessible is the brilliance and wit of Mr. Dawkins' style. It is a splendid example of how difficult scientific ideas can be explained by someone who understands them and is willing to take the trouble." In 1989 Dawkins produced a second edition of *The Selfish Gene,* which included extensive new endnotes as well as two new chapters.

Of his second book, *The Extended Phenotype: The Gene as the Unit of Selection,* Dawkins tells *CA:* "I suppose most authors have one piece of work of which they would say 'It doesn't matter if you never read anything else of mine, please at least read *this.*' For me, it is *The Extended Phenotype.* In particular, the last four chapters constitute the best candidate for the title 'innovative' that I have to offer. The rest of the book does some necessary sorting out on the way."

Dawkins once again investigates aspects of Darwinian theory in *The Blind Watchmaker: Why the Evidence of Evolution Reveals a Universe without Design.* Lee Dembart of the *Los Angeles Times* calls the work "a clear, logical, rational book that is the antidote to silliness. . . . [The book] cuts through the

nonsense about the origin and development of life and leaves it for dead," continues Dembart. "He demonstrates beyond a shadow of a doubt that evolution is the only possible explanation for the world we see around us." In this work, Dawkins refutes the argument that the complexity of life cannot be random, thus implying a designer or creator. The author uses Darwin's idea of small mutational variation to "demonstrate that it (and it alone) is competent to explain the enormous diversity of living things in all their extremes of complexity and specialization," writes David Jones in the London *Times.* Like the author's previous work, Jones finds that *The Blind Watchmaker* "is brillant exposition, tightly argued but kept readable by plentiful recourse to analogies and examples."

Because of its controversial topic and method of exposition, this book has inevitably drawn its share of criticism. Rose, writing in the *New Statesman,* finds the author's work self-contradictory: "There is much which is good and not merely clever about this book. But Dawkins' greatest problem is his continual tendency to allow himself to be dragged over the top by the very vigour of his own writing." While Dawkins "provides an excellent account of why and how reductionism fails," remarks Rose, ". . . he can't resist beginning a chapter . . . [with] beautiful and fallacious writing, not only profoundly reductionist, but, as he would himself put it, 'deeply superficial.'" Clark not only disputes Dawkins's methods, he argues against his theory as well, claiming that the work lacks "any argument for the claim that the god of hard metaphysical theism either is or ought to be conceived as something inordinately complex." The critic continues: "Dawkins cannot simply ignore theological and philosophical discussion of what it would mean to speak of God's design, or God's existence."

While Clark disagrees with many of Dawkins' theories and faults the author for omitting what he feels are important considerations, he still thinks the book works on a specific level. "What Dawkins does successfully is very good: *The Blind Watchmaker* is as clear, as enthralling, as convincing an account of neo-Darwinian theory as I have read. . . . His opposition to dogmatic vivisectionists and his appreciation of the marvellous diversity and ingenuity of the world are very welcome." Dembart summarizes his own impression of the work: "The book is beautifully and superbly written. It is completely understandable, but it has the cadence of impassioned speech. Every page rings of truth," continues the critic. "It is one of the best science books—one of the best any books—I have ever read." Explaining the origin of this "passion" for truth, Dawkins remarked that his "early interest in evolution was really as a sort of alternative to religion, and an explanation for the way things are," the author remarked to Sarah Duncan in the London *Times*. While "other biologists start out as bird watchers or bug hunters," said Dawkins, "I started with a curiosity about why things exist."

BIOGRAPHICAL/CRITICAL SOURCES:

PERIODICALS

Chicago Tribune, November 20, 1986.
Los Angeles Times, November 25, 1986.
Los Angeles Times Book Review, December 28, 1986; October 25, 1987.
New Statesman, November 19, 1976; April 16, 1982; November 14, 1986.
New Yorker, April 11, 1977.
New York Times, March 17, 1977.
New York Times Book Review, February 27, 1977; December 14, 1986.
Saturday Review, February 19, 1977.
Science, May 13, 1977; December 10, 1982.
Spectator, January 15, 1977.
Times (London), October 3, 1986; December 11, 1986.
Times Literary Supplement, February 4, 1977; July 20, 1984; September 26, 1986.
Washington Post Book World, December 2, 1979.

*   *   *

DEE, Johnny
  See KRAUZER, Steven M(ark)

*   *   *

de HAMEL, Joan Littledale   1924-

PERSONAL: Born March 31, 1924, in London, England; immigrated to New Zealand, 1955; daughter of Humphrey Rivers (a medical practitioner) and Eleanor (Littledale) Pollock; married Francis de Hamel (a professor of medicine), April 24, 1948;

children: Michael, Christopher, William, Richard, Quentin. *Education:* Lady Margaret Hall, Oxford, B.A. (with honors), 1944, M.A., 1949. *Religion:* Church of England. *Avocational interests:* Art (especially French art), history, literature, education, botany, ornithology, animal behavior, oral history.

ADDRESSES: Home—25 Howard St., Macandrew Bay, Dunedin, New Zealand. *Agent*—Ray Richards, 3/43 Aberdeen Rd., Castor Bay, Auckland, New Zealand; and A. P. Watt Ltd., 20 John St., London WC1N 2DL, England.

CAREER: Writer. St. Nicholas School (girls' preparatory school), Hemel Hempstead, Hertfordshire, England, assistant mistress, 1944-45; Francis Holland School, London, head of languages, 1945-48; Dunedin Teachers College, Dunedin, New Zealand, lecturer in French, 1967-79. Angora goat breeder, 1985—.

MEMBER: New Zealand Society of Authors.

AWARDS, HONORS: Esther Glen Medal, New Zealand Library Association, 1979, for *Take the Long Path;* Reed Memorial Award, 1985, for *Hemi's Pet.*

WRITINGS:

CHILDREN'S FICTION

(Self-illustrated) *X Marks the Spot,* Lutterworth (Cambridge, England), 1973.
Take the Long Path, illustrated by Gareth Floyd, Lutterworth, 1978.
Hemi's Pet, illustrated by Christine Ross, Methuen (London), 1985, Houghton (Boston), 1987.
The Third Eye, Viking (New York City), 1987.
Hideaway, Penguin (New York City), 1992.

Also author of scripts, including *To Chartres in Three Hours,* produced by the British Broadcasting Corp. (BBC), *Mr. Timms and Mr. Mott,* produced by the BBC, and *The Chaubord Omelette,* produced by New Zealand Broadcasting Corp. Contributor to magazines. Editor of *Polyglot. Hemi's Pet* has been published in Afrikaans, Sesotho, Xhosa, and Maori.

SIDELIGHTS: From her first children's book, *X Marks the Spot,* Joan Littledale de Hamel has shown a concern for the social and environmental problems faced by New Zealanders. Her fiction has dealt with the lives of the country's indigenous people and the problems facing its endangered species.

X Marks the Spot tells the story of three children who are lost in the New Zealand bush following a helicopter crash. Thrilled at first by the landscape and the freedom their situation permits, the children are forced to confront the bush's perilous reality after losing their backpacks and supplies. With only a gun and some matches remaining, the children must make difficult decisions to survive. In the course of their adventures, the children also deal with a group of poachers who are pursuing a rare species of parrot.

The children from *X Marks the Spot* return in *The Third Eye* as teenagers in world that is becoming increasingly complex. A large company is attempting to develop lands which once belonged to New Zealand's indigenous people, the Maori. A dispute arises over the rights of the Maori to determine the land's future. "Young readers . . . will realise that serious themes are explored within this well crafted adventure," remarks Margery Fisher in *Growing Point.*

Hideaway is a story of intrigue involving a young girl, Becky, and a Russian sailor who has jumped ship. Becky hides the boy in a ramshackle hut and begins a routine of bringing food to his hiding place. In addition to providing for the mysterious youth, Becky raises a young goat abandoned by its mother, and confronts her cousin Chloe's increasing rebelliousness at home. These themes are interwoven, *School Librarian* reviewer Sandra Bennett explains, "providing suspense until eventually all problems are resolved at the same time."

De Hamel has also authored a picture book, *Hemi's Pet,* in which a young Maori boy enters his sister in his school pet show. The other students protest but Hemi argues that she meets the criteria for a pet: he loves her and cares for her. The judges are convinced, and Hemi is awarded the prize for most original pet. "Refreshing and warm, this is a delightful story," asserts Cathy Woodward in *School Library Journal.*

De Hamel once commented: "I wrote for myself from early childhood, for money after marriage, and sold most of it. I immigrated to New Zealand in 1955 and turned mostly to radio writing. When my fifth son was at kindergarten, I began my first full-length novel, and in 1978, at last, became a full-time writer."

A seasoned traveler, the author has explained that her stories are based on her own real-life adventures.

"*X Marks the Spot* was based on my personal experiences, lost in the bush. At the time, this was NO JOKE, and, indeed, all my books are based on true NO JOKE events in my life. *Take the Long Path* was inspired by watching a penguin that had been savaged by a shark. *The Third Eye* came from a terrifying adventure in limestone caves. The heart-rending plight of a motherless kid goat inspired *Hideaway.*

"My books are built up from diary notes, on-the-spot jottings, and by digging deep into childhood memories, adding extras, fiddling everything around," de Hamel notes. She adds that "this takes time. I am a very slow writer."

BIOGRAPHICAL/CRITICAL SOURCES:

BOOKS

Gilderdale, Betty, *Introducing Twenty-one New Zealand Children's Writers,* Hodder & Stoughton (London), 1991, pp. 43-47.
Twentieth-Century Children's Writers, 4th edition, St. James Press (Detroit), 1995, pp. 283-284.

PERIODICALS

Booklist, April 1, 1987, p. 1203.
Growing Point, May, 1989, pp. 5155-5163.
Junior Bookshelf, December, 1978, p. 309.
Magpies, September, 1993, p. 31.
Publishers Weekly, April 10, 1987, p. 94.
School Librarian, August, 1993, p. 120.
School Library Journal, June-July, 1987, p. 81.

*   *   *

DEMPSEY, Hugh Aylmer   1929-

PERSONAL: Born November 7, 1929, in Edgerton, Alberta, Canada; son of Otto L. and Lily (Sharp) Dempsey; married Pauline S. Gladstone, September 30, 1953; children: L. James, Louise, John, Leah, Lois. *Education:* Educated in primary and secondary schools in Edmonton, Alberta. *Religion:* Anglican.

ADDRESSES: Home—95 Holmwood Ave. NW, Calgary, Alberta, Canada T2K 2G7.

CAREER: Edmonton Bulletin, Edmonton, Alberta, Canada, reporter and editor, 1949-51; Government of Alberta, Edmonton, publicity writer, 1951-56; Glenbow Foundation, Calgary, Alberta, archivist, 1956-57; Glenbow-Alberta Institute, Calgary, technical director, 1967-70, director of history, 1970-80; Glenbow Museum, Calgary, assistant director, 1980-86, associate director of collections, 1986-89. Retired, 1991. Lecturer at Canadian Universities. Lifetime director of Calgary Exhibition and Stampede, 1989—; member of Alberta Records Publication Board, 1981—.

MEMBER: Canadian Historical Association (chair of archives section, 1961-62), Canadian Museums Association (executive member, 1968-70), Indian-Eskimo Association of Canada (executive member, 1960-65), Champlain Society (member of council, 1972-74), Historical Society of Alberta (executive member, 1952—; vice president, 1955-56; president, 1956-57), Indian Association of Alberta, Fort Calgary Preservation Society (executive member, 1969-75), Kainai Chieftainship.

AWARDS, HONORS: Annual award from Historical Society of Alberta, 1963; Alberta Achievement Award, 1974, 1975; L.L.D. from University of Calgary, 1974; Order of Canada, 1975; Alberta Non-Fiction Award, 1975, for *The Best of Bob Edwards;* Alberta Theater Products Award, 1983; Canadian Historical Association Award of Merit, 1987; Alberta Museum Assocaition Award of Merit, Sir Frederick Haultain Award, and Alberta Booksellers award, all 1991.

WRITINGS:

Historic Sites of Alberta, Government of Alberta, 1952.

Crowfoot: Chief of the Blackfeet, University of Oklahoma Press (Norman), 1972, expanded edition, 1989.

A History of Rocky Mountain House, Department of Indian Affairs and Northern Development (Ottawa, Ontario), 1973.

William Parker, Mounted Policeman, Hurtig, 1973.

Charcoal's World, Western Producer Prairie Books, 1978.

Indian Tribes of Alberta (monograph), Glenbow-Alberta Institute, 1978.

Hutterites: The Hutterite Diamond Jubilee, Glenbow-Alberta Institute, 1978.

Red Crow, Warrior Chief, University of Nebraska Press (Lincoln), 1980.

Christmas in the West, Western Producer Prairie Books, 1982.

History in Their Blood, Douglas & McIntyre, 1982.

Big Bear: The End of Freedom, Douglas & McIntyre, 1984.

The Gentle Persuader: James Gladstone, Western Producer Prairie Books, 1986.

Treaty Seven, Indian and Northern Affairs, 1987.

(With Lindsay Moir) *Bibliography of the Blackfoot,* Scarecrow Press (Metuchen, NJ), 1989.

Treasures of the Glenbow Museum, Glenbow Museum (Calgary, Alberta), 1991.

Calgary; Spirit of the West, Glenbow Museum and Fifth House (Saskatoon, Saskatchewan), 1994.

The Amazing Death of Calf Shirt and Other Blackfoot Stories, Fifth House, 1994.

The Golden Age of the Canadian Cowboy, Fifth House, 1995.

EDITOR

The Big Chief of the Prairies (biography of Father Lacombe), Palm Publishers, 1953.

Thomas Edmund Wilson, *Trailblazer of the Canadian Rockies,* Glenbow-Alberta Institute, 1972.

A Winter at Fort Macleod, McClelland & Stewart (Toronto, Ontario), 1974.

Men in Scarlet, McClelland & Stewart, 1974.

The Best of Bob Edwards, Hurtig, 1975.

The Wit and Wisdom of Bob Edwards, Hurtig, 1976.

Robert Terrill Rundle, *The Rundle Journals, 1840-1848,* Historical Society of Alberta, 1977.

(And author of introduction) *My Tribe, the Crees,* Glenbow Museum, 1979.

The Best from Alberta History, Western Producer Prairie Books, 1981.

The CPR West, Douglas & McIntyre, 1984.

Claude Gardiner, *Letters from an English Rancher,* Glenbow Museum, 1988.

Heaven is Near the Rocky Mountains; Journals and Letters of Thomas Woolsey, 1855-1864, Glenbow Museum, 1989.

(And author of introduction) Everett Soop, *I See My Tribe is Still Behind Me,* Glenbow Museum, 1990.

Former author of column "Tawasi," in the daily *Edmonton Bulletin.* Contributor to national and international journals, including *Journal of American Folklore, Plains Anthropologist,* and *Journal of the Washington Academy of Science.* Editor of *Canadian*

Archivist, 1963-66; associate editor of *Alberta History,* 1953-58, editor, 1958—; Northern and Canadian editor of *Montana Magazine of History.*

OTHER

Also director of the documentary film *Okan, Sun Dance of the Blackfoot.*

WORK IN PROGRESS: Tom Three Persons.

SIDELIGHTS: While associated with the Government of Alberta, Hugh Aylmer Dempsey was responsible for historical work, including a historic highway sign program and historic sites research. His interest in history developed alongside his work with and research on Canadian Indians. His wife is a Blood Indian and in 1967 Dempsey was made an honorary Blood chief. Beginning with work for the Indian Association of Alberta, he assisted attempts to organize locals on Blackfoot and Peigan Reserves. Much of his writing concerns the Indian tribes of Alberta.

*   *   *

DENTINGER, Stephen
  See HOCH, Edward D(entinger)

*   *   *

de ROO, Anne Louise   1931-

PERSONAL: Born in 1931 in Gore, New Zealand; daughter of William Fredrick (a health inspector) and Amy Louisa (Hayton) de Roo. *Education:* University of Canterbury, Christchurch, New Zealand, B.A., 1952.

ADDRESSES: Home—38 Joseph St., Palmerston North, New Zealand. *Agent*—A.P. Watt & Son, 26-28 Bedford Row, London WC1R 4HL, England.

CAREER: Dunedin Public Library, Dunedin, New Zealand, library assistant, 1956; Dunedin Teacher's College, Dunedin, librarian, 1957-59; Church Preen, Shropshire, England, governess and part-time gardener, 1962-68; part-time secretary in Barkway, Hertfordshire, England, 1969-73; medical typist in Palmerston North, New Zealand, 1974-78; writer, 1978—.

AWARDS, HONORS: ICI Bursary, 1981.

WRITINGS:

JUVENILE

The Gold Dog, Hart-Davis (London), 1969.
Moa Valley, Hart-Davis, 1969.
Boy and the Sea Beast, illustrated by Judith Anson, Hart-Davis, 1971, Scholastic (New York City), 1974.
Cinnamon and Nutmeg, Macmillan (London), 1972, Nelson, 1974.
Mick's Country Cousins, Macmillan, 1974.
Scrub Fire, Heinemann (London), 1977, Atheneum (New York City), 1980.
Traveller, Heinemann, 1979.
Because of Rosie, Heinemann, 1980.
Jacky Nobody, Methuen (Auckland, New Zealand), 1983.
The Bats' Nest, Hodder & Stoughton (Auckland), 1986.
Friend Troll, Friend Taniwha, illustrated by R. H. G. Jahnke, Hodder & Stoughton, 1986.
Mouse Talk, Church Mouse Press (Palmerston North, New Zealand), 1990.
The Good Cat, Church Mouse Press, 1990.
Hepzibah Mouse's ABC, Church Mouse Press, 1991.
Sergeant Sal, Random Century (Auckland), 1991.
Hepzibah's Book of Famous Mice, Church Mouse Press, 1993.

PLAYS

The Dragon Master, music by John Schwabe, first produced in Palmerston North, New Zealand, 1978.
The Silver Blunderbuss, music by Schwabe, first produced in Palmerston North, 1984.

NOVELS

Hope Our Daughter, Church Mouse Press, 1990.
Becoming Fully Human, Church Mouse Press, 1991.
And We Beheld His Glory, Church Mouse Press, 1994.

SIDELIGHTS: Anne Louise de Roo's novels for young people often illustrate how the rugged terrain of her native New Zealand has shaped the country's history and culture. Nature is profound, beautiful, and often dangerous in her works of historical fiction as well as in her contemporary dramas. At the same time, de Roo's stories emphasize the strength and adaptability of New Zealand's indigenous people, European immigrants, and their descendants as they cope with the wilderness and learn to live with each other. While de Roo once told *CA* that she is delighted by the idea that her novels introduce New Zealand to children in other parts of the world, she asserted that she is "a New Zealand writer, principally concerned with the building up in a young country of a children's literature through which children can identify themselves and their roots, whether European or Maori."

De Roo wrote her first five books during the twelve years she lived in England. *Boy and the Sea Beast,* set on North Island, was inspired by the true story of two famous dolphins in New Zealand: Pelorous Jack and Opo. After saving Thunder, the dolphin, from exploitation, the boy in the novel must release the him to live freely in the wild. According to Tom Fitzgibbon, a contributor to *Twentieth-Century Children's Writers,* "*Boy and the Sea Beast* marks a stage when a new direction enters [de Roo's] work. Up to this point, it is clear that de Roo is technically very effective but, while the quality of suspense is strong, the solution to the action comes too easily and character is subordinated to the need for a happy ending. This is much less so in *Boy and the Sea Beast.*"

The main character of de Roo's 1972 novel *Cinnamon and Nutmeg* lives on a dairy farm in the hot bushland near the side of a mountain in New Zealand. Tessa is a tomboy who doesn't get along well with her older sister and feels neglected by her father. She occupies herself by reading the books her witty Aunt Helen left at the farm. When Tessa finds Nutmeg, a wild baby goat whose mother has been killed by a gun shot, and Cinnamon, an orphaned Jersey purebred calf, she finds solace in secretly nurturing the animals. Although, according to a *Bulletin of the Center for Children's Books* reviewer, *Cinnamon and Nutmeg* contains an "all-threads-tied" conclusion, the story is "satisfying and logical."

The characters from *Cinnamon and Nutmeg* reappear in *Mick's Country Cousins.* Mick, who is half-Maori, is sent to live with his cousins on their farm. He has led a troubled life—his father has abandoned the family, his mother has not been able to control her sons, and his brother, Kevin, has been sent to a detention center for delinquent boys. Mick's arrival at the farm does not solve these problems—at first he

is convinced he is only accepted as a farm hand and not as a member of the family. Barbara Britton argues in the *Times Literary Supplement* that *Mick's Country Cousins* is "an extremely good novel, full of comprehension of difficult feelings."

As de Roo once explained to *CA,* the years she spent abroad allowed her to return to New Zealand "with a new perspective and a new and deeper appreciation of the natural beauty of New Zealand's forests, mountains and sea." This "deeper appreciation" is reflected in *Scrub Fire.* According to Patricia Manning in *School Library Journal,* de Roo evocatively describes the "flora and fauna" in the New Zealand wilderness in great detail in this novel, "lend[ing] credence to her tale." Thirteen-year-old Michelle, who reluctantly accompanies her younger brothers on a camping trip led by her aunt and uncle, is horrified when her Uncle Don's attempt at wilderness cooking sets the scrub on fire. The group scatters as the fire spreads, and although Michelle spends some time in the wilderness alone, she is soon reunited with her two brothers who use survival tactics during the twelve days they are lost to reach safety. By the time the children are rescued, as a critic for *Kirkus Reviews* remarked, Michelle is "a bigger and better person."

De Roo once told *CA* that in addition to writing dramatic novels and historical fiction, she sometimes needs to "branch out . . . into the realms of fantasy and fairy tale." She continued: "The theatre is a lifelong love and much of my spare time is devoted to amateur theatre, which is particularly strong in a small country with little scope for professional theatre. The spoken word, its sounds and possibilities, has always fascinated me, from youthful poetry writing onwards, and even in books, the dialogue is the part in which I always feel most at home."

BIOGRAPHICAL/CRITICAL SOURCES:

BOOKS

Twentieth-Century Children's Writers, 4th edition, St. James Press (Detroit), 1994, pp. 295-96.

PERIODICALS

Bulletin of the Center for Children's Books, December, 1974, p. 60; January, 1981, p. 91.
Junior Bookshelf, February, 1975, p. 60; August, 1979, p. 216.
Kirkus Reviews, January 15, 1974, p. 55; November 1, 1980, p. 1394.
School Library Journal, November, 1980, p. 72.

Times Educational Supplement, September 27, 1985, p. 28.

Times Literary Supplement, December 4, 1969, p. 1394; December 6, 1974, p. 1376; July 18, 1980, p. 806.*

*   *   *

DEXTER, John
  See BRADLEY, Marion Zimmer

*   *   *

DIXON, Bernard   1938-

PERSONAL: Born July 17, 1938, in Darlington, England; son of Ronald and Grace (Peirson) Dixon; married Margaret Helena Charlton, 1963 (marriage ended, 1987); children: two sons, one daughter. *Education:* King's College, Durham, B.Sc., 1961; University of Newcastle-upon-Tyne, Ph.D., 1964.

ADDRESSES: Home—130 Cornwall Rd., Ruislip Manor, Middlesex HA4 6AW, England.

CAREER: University of Newcastle-upon-Tyne, Newcastle-upon-Tyne, England, research microbiologist, 1961-65; *World Medicine,* London, England, assistant editor, 1965-66, deputy editor, 1966-68; *New Scientist,* London, deputy editor, 1968-69, editor, 1969-79; *Omni* magazine, London, European editor, 1979-82; *Science 80* Magazine, London, editor, 1980-86; European editor for *Bio/Technology,* 1985—, and *Scientist* newspaper, 1986-90; editor, *Medical Science Research,* 1989—.

MEMBER: British Association for the Advancement of Science (vice president of general section), Association of British Science Writers (member of committee, 1969—; chair, 1971-72), Society for General Microbiology, Institute of Biology (fellow), Institute of Biotechnology (fellow, 1987).

AWARDS, HONORS: Luccock Research Fund fellowship, 1961-64, Frank Schon fellowship from Marchon Products, 1964-65; special award from the Medical Journalists' Association, 1978; Glaxo travelling fellowship, 1980.

WRITINGS:

(Editor) *Journeys in Belief,* Allen & Unwin (London), 1968.
What Is Science For?, Harper (New York City), 1973.
Magnificent Microbes, Atheneum (New York City), 1976, published in England as *Invisible Allies: Microbes and Man's Future,* Temple Smith, 1976.
Beyond the Magic Bullet, Harper, 1978.
Medicine and Care, Heinemann (London), 1981.
(With Geoffrey Holister) *The Ideas of Science,* Basil Blackwell (London), 1986.
Genetically Engineered Organisms in the Environment: Scientific Issues, American Society for Microbiology (Washington, DC), 1986.
Health and the Human Body, Perseus Press (Pacific Palisades, CA), 1987.
From Creation to Chaos, Sphere Books (London), 1991.
Power Unseen: How Microbes Rule the World, W. H. Freeman (Oxford, England), 1994.

Also contributor to books, including David Patessa and Richard Ryder, *Animal Rights,* Centaur (Cheshire, England), 1979; *The Book of Predictions,* edited by David Wallechinsky and others, Morrow, (Suffolk and New York City), 1980; *The DNA Story,* edited by James D. Watson and John Tooze, W. H. Freeman, 1981; and *From Biology to Biotechnology,* edited by Colette Kinnon, UNESCO, 1982. Also contributor to *Development of Science Publishing in Europe,* 1980. Contributor to scientific and popular journals. Correspondent for *World Medicine,* 1968-83, *Spectator,* 1971-79, *British Medical Journal,* 1985—, *Tiede* (Finland), 1985—, *Biotec* (Italy), 1985—, and the *Independent,* 1989—.

SIDELIGHTS: In his book *What Is Science For?,* Bernard Dixon explores the scientific research process, including the education of scientists, the financial factors, the outside pressures for results in research, and the internal competition. Dixon also examines how these elements affect the final scientific result. A critic for the *Times Literary Supplement* remarks that "scientifically educated, [Dixon] is gifted with an admirable sense of history. He writes most readably, drawing on an abundance of recent illustration; and he deals with a complex subject both in depth and in extent in a way seldom achieved in a book of this modest length." Roger Williams writes in *Encounter:* "Dixon does a convincing job of showing how more than most things science manages to be 'all things to all men,' from deadly genie to rescuing angel, from the purely utilitarian to the purely cultural. And his prescription for restoring a symbiosis between science and society is something one can only applaud."

In *Beyond the Magic Bullet,* Dixon explains his ideas concerning the medical concept of etiology, the theory that specific germs cause specific diseases. According to Harold M. Schmeck, Jr., writing in the *New York Times,* Dixon believes that this hypothesis has "outlived much of its usefulness. . . . He insists that the 'specific cause' idea tells far less than the whole story and, in any case, is largely irrelevant to some of the most important public-health problems of the late twentieth century." Schmeck reports that Dixon "says that too slavish an adherence to the science of specific etiology has spawned a monstrous overuse of antibiotic drugs; the public perception that there must be an available cure for every human ill, real or imagined, and the spending of many hundreds of millions of American dollars in a war against cancer that has yet to conquer anything."

Dixon's 1994 book, *Power Unseen: How Microbes Rule the World,* is an assembly of 75 three-page "short stories" about various unusual microbes and the people who discovered and study them. Philip Morrison in the *Scientific American* agues that *Power Unseen* is "science in practice, biodiversity itself packaged along with a critical look at the nature of evidence . . . as edifying as it is entertaining."

BIOGRAPHICAL/CRITICAL SOURCES:

PERIODICALS

Economist, May 15, 1976.
Encounter, January, 1974.
New Statesman, October 26, 1973.
Newsweek, August 2, 1976.
New York Times, January 9, 1979; May 1, 1979.
Scientific American, August, 1994.
Times Literary Supplement, October 12, 1973.

*   *   *

DOCTOROW, E(dgar) L(aurence) 1931-

PERSONAL: Born January 6, 1931, in New York, NY; son of David R. (a music store proprietor) and Rose (a pianist; maiden name, Levine) Doctorow; married Helen Esther Setzer (a writer), August 20, 1954; children: Jenny, Caroline, Richard. *Education:* Kenyon College, A.B. (with honors), 1952; Columbia University, graduate study, 1952-53.

ADDRESSES: Home—New Rochelle, NY. *Office*—c/o Random House, 201 East 50th St., New York, NY 10022; and Department of English, New York University, New York, NY 10003-6607.

CAREER: Former script reader, Columbia Pictures Industries, Inc., New York City; New American Library, New York City, senior editor, 1959-64; Dial Press, New York City, editor-in-chief, 1964-69, vice president, 1968-69; University of California, Irvine, writer in residence, 1969-70; Sarah Lawrence College, Bronxville, NY, member of faculty, 1971-78; New York University, New York City, Glucksman Professor of English and American Letters, 1982—. Creative writing fellow, Yale School of Drama, 1974-75; visiting professor, University of Utah, 1975; visiting senior fellow, Princeton University, 1980-81. *Military service:* U.S. Army, Signal Corps, 1953-55.

MEMBER: American Academy and Institute of Arts and Letters, Authors Guild (director), PEN (director), Writers Guild of America East, Century Association.

AWARDS, HONORS: National Book Award nomination, 1972, for *The Book of Daniel;* Guggenheim fellow, 1973; Creative Artists Service fellow, 1973-74; National Book Critics Circle Award and Arts and Letters award, 1976, both for *Ragtime;* L.H.D., Kenyon College, 1976; Litt.D., Hobart and William Smith Colleges, 1979; National Book Award, 1986, for *World's Fair;* L.H.D., Brandeis University, 1989; Edith Wharton Citation, 1989-91; PEN/Faulkner Award, National Book Critics' Circle Award, William Dean Howells Medal, and National Book Award nomination, all 1990, all for *Billy Bathgate.*

WRITINGS:

NOVELS

Welcome to Hard Times, Simon & Schuster (New York City), 1960, published in England as *Bad Man from Bodie,* Deutsch (London), 1961).
Big as Life, Simon & Schuster, 1966.

The Book of Daniel (also see below), Random House (New York City), 1971.

Ragtime (Book-of-the-Month Club selection), Random House, 1975.

Loon Lake, Random House, 1980.

World's Fair, Random House, 1985.

Billy Bathgate (Book-of-the-Month Club main selection), Random House, 1989.

The Waterworks, Random House, 1994.

E. L. Doctorow: Three Complete Novels (contains *Billy Bathgate, World's Fair* and *Loon Lake*), Wings Books (New York City), 1994.

OTHER

(Contributor) Theodore Solotaroff, editor, *New American Review 2,* New American Library (New York City), 1968.

Drinks before Dinner (play; first produced Off-Broadway at Public Theater, November 22, 1978), Random House, 1979.

American Anthem, photographs by Jean-Claude Suares, Stewart, Tabori (New York City), 1982.

Daniel (screenplay; based on author's *The Book of Daniel*), Paramount Pictures, 1983.

Lives of the Poets: Six Stories and a Novella, Random House, 1984.

The People's Text: A Citizen Reads the Constitution, Nouveau Press (Jackson, MS), 1992.

Jack London, Hemingway, and the Constitution: Selected Essays, 1977-1992, Random House, 1993.

ADAPTATIONS: Welcome to Hard Times was filmed in 1967 by Metro-Goldwyn-Mayer; *Ragtime* was filmed in 1981 by Milos Forman; *The Book of Daniel* was filmed by Paramount in 1983; the screenplay for *Billy Bathgate* was written by Tom Stoppard, filmed in 1991 by Robert Benton and starred Dustin Hoffman.

SIDELIGHTS: E. L. Doctorow is a highly regarded novelist and playwright known for his philosophical probings, the subtlety and variety of his prose style, and his unusual use of historical figures in fictional works.

Doctorow's first novel, *Welcome to Hard Times,* was inspired, he tells Jonathan Yardley of the *Miami Herald,* by his job as a reader for Columbia Pictures, where he "was accursed to read things that were submitted to this company and write synopses of them." "I had to suffer one lousy Western after another," continues Doctorow, "and it occurred to

me that I could lie about the West in a much more interesting way than any of these people were lying. I wrote a short story, and it subsequently became the first chapter of that novel." The resulting book, unlike many Westerns, is concerned with grave issues. As Wirt Williams notes in the *New York Times Book Review, Welcome to Hard Times* addresses "one of the favorite problems of philosophers: the relationship of man and evil. . . . Perhaps the primary theme of the novel is that evil can only be resisted psychically: when the rational controls that order man's existence slacken, destruction comes. [Joseph] Conrad said it best in *Heart of Darkness,* but Mr. Doctorow has said it impressively. His book is taut and dramatic, exciting and successfully symbolic." Similarly, Kevin Stan, writing in the *New Republic,* remarks: "*Welcome to Hard Times* . . . is a superb piece of fiction: lean and mean, and thematically significant. . . . He takes the thin, somewhat sordid and incipiently depressing materials of the Great Plains experience and fashions them into a myth of good and evil. . . . He does it marvelously, with economy and with great narrative power."

After writing a Western of sorts, Doctorow turned to another form not usually heralded by critics: science fiction. In *Big as Life,* two naked human giants materialize in New York harbor. The novel examines the ways in which its characters deal with a seemingly impending catastrophe. Like *Hard Times, Big as Life* enjoyed much critical approval. A *Choice* reviewer, for example, comments that "Doctorow's dead pan manner . . . turns from satire to tenderness and human concern. A performance closer to James Purdy than to [George] Orwell or [Aldous] Huxley, but in a minor key." In spite of reviewers' praise, however, *Big as Life,* like *Welcome to Hard Times,* was not a large commercial success.

The Book of Daniel, Doctorow's third book, involves yet another traditional form, the historical novel. It is a fictional account based on the relationship between Julius and Ethel Rosenberg and their children. The Rosenbergs were Communists who were convicted of and executed for conspiracy to commit treason. As with *Welcome to Hard Times* and *Big as Life,* Doctorow has modified the traditional form to suit his purposes. The work is not an examination of the guilt or innocence of the Rosenbergs, but, as David Emblidge observes in *Southwest Review,* a look at the central character Daniel's psychology and his attempts to deal with the trauma he suffered from his parents' deaths. Thus many critics argue that the book, unlike typical historical novels, is largely independent of historical fact. Jane Richmond, writing in *Partisan Review,* believes that "if Julius and Ethel Rosenberg had never existed, the book would be just as good as it is." In like manner, Stanley Kauffmann remarks in the *New Republic:* "I haven't looked up the facts of the Rosenberg case; it would be offensive to the quality of this novel to check it against those facts."

Many critics were impressed with the achievement of *The Book of Daniel.* Kauffmann terms it "the political novel of our age, the best American work of its kind that I know since Lionel Trilling's *The Middle of the Journey.*" Peter S. Prescott of *Newsweek* adds that *The Book of Daniel* "is a purgative book, angry and more deeply felt than all but a few contemporary American novels, a novel about defeat, impotent rage, the passing of the burden of suffering through generations. . . . There is no question here of our suspending disbelief, but rather how when we have finished, we may regain stability." Richmond calls it "a brilliant achievement and the best contemporary novel I've read since reading Frederick Exley's *A Fan's Notes.* . . . It is a book of infinite detail and tender attention to the edges of life as well as to its dead center."

In *Ragtime,* Doctorow again forays into historical territory. The novel interweaves the lives of a white, upper-middle-class, privileged family, a poor immigrant family, and the family of a black ragtime musician with historical figures such as I. P. Morgan, Harry Houdini, Henry Ford, and Emma Goldman. Particularly intriguing to readers is that Doctorow shows famous people involved in unusual, sometimes ludicrous, situations. In the *Washington Post Book World,* Raymond Sokolov notes that "Doctorow turns history into myth and myth into history. . . . [He] continually teases our suspicion of literary artifice with apparently true historical description. . . . On the one hand, the 'fact' tugs one toward taking the episode as history. On the other, the doubt that lingers makes one want to take the narrative as an invention." Sokolov argues that Doctorow "teases" the reader in order to make him try "to sort out what the author is doing. That is, we find ourselves paying Doctorow the most important tribute. We watch to see what he is doing."

Newsweek's Walter Clemons also finds himself teased by *Ragtime*'s historical episodes: "The very fact that the book stirs one to parlor-game research is amusing evidence that Doctorow has already won

the game: I found myself looking up details because I wanted them to be true." In addition, George Stade, in the *New York Times Book Review,* expresses a belief similar to Sokolov's. "In this excellent novel," Stade writes, "silhouettes and rags not only make fiction out of history but also reveal the fictions out of which history is made. It incorporates the fictions and realities of the era of ragtime while it rags our fictions about it. It is an anti-nostalgic novel that incorporates our nostalgia about its subject."

David Emblidge, however, provides a more somber view of Doctorow's use of history. He contends that there is a motif common to *Welcome to Hard Times, The Book of Daniel,* and *Ragtime:* "This motif is the idea of history as a repetitive process, almost a cyclical one, in which man is an unwilling, unknowing pawn, easily seduced into a belief in 'progress.'" Doctorow intertwines historical figures and fictional characters to mock a romantic theory of history, the critic hypothesizes. "Again the point of view," Emblidge continues, "in political terms, is that history . . . is far from progressive evolution toward peace among men. *Ragtime* is an indictment of the recurrent malignancies of spirit beneath the period's chimerical technological progress and social harmony." Emblidge even finds that ragtime music, which superimposes melodic improvisation on "fundamental repetition," "becomes symbolic of the historical process: endless recurrence under a distracting facade of individualistic variation."

Not all critics admire Doctorow's manipulation of history. In *Books and Bookmen,* Paul Levy maintains that *Ragtime* "falsifies history. [Sigmund] Freud, [Carl] Jung, Emma Goldman, Henry Ford, Pierpont Morgan, Stanford White and Harry Houdini simply did not perpetrate the grotesqueries they are made to commit in its pages. That is all. There is no problem. The characters in *Ragtime* that bear those famous names are not historical personages; they are merely pawns in Doctorow's particularly dotty and tasteless game of chess." On the other hand, Doctorow denies the need for historical accuracy. In a *Publishers Weekly* interview he suggests that the figures represent "images of that time" and are used "because they carried for me the right overtones of the time." When asked if some of the incidents actually occurred, Doctorow declined to answer directly: "What's real and what isn't? I used to know but I've forgotten. Let's just say that *Ragtime* is a mingling of fact and invention—a novelist's revenge on an age that celebrates nonfiction."

Ragtime's political content also generates debate. Several reviewers believe that *Ragtime* presents a simplistic leftist viewpoint. Hilton Kramer of *Commentary,* for instance, contends that "the villains in *Ragtime,* drawn with all the subtlety of a William Gropper cartoon, are all representatives of money, the middle class, and white ethnic prejudice. . . . *Ragtime* is a political romance. . . . The major fictional characters . . . are all ideological inventions, designed to serve the purposes of a political fable." Similarly, Jeffrey Hart, writing in the *National Review,* objects that Doctorow judges his revolutionary and minority characters much less harshly than the middle and upper-class figures, which results in "what can be called left-wing pastoral," a form of sentimentality.

In spite of some protest on political and historical grounds, *Ragtime* garnered copious praise. "*Ragtime,*" Eliot Fremont-Smith of the *Village Voice* comments, "is simply splendid. . . . It's a bag of riches, totally lucid and accessible, full of surprises, epiphanies, little time-bombs that alter one's view of things, and enormous fun to read." Clemons finds that "*Ragtime* is as exhilarating as a deep breath of pure oxygen." In the *New Republic,* Doris Grumbach remarks that "*Ragtime* is a model of a novel: compact because it is perfectly controlled, spare, because a loose end would have detracted from the shape it has, completely absorbing, because once in, there is no possible way out except through the last page." Kauffmann, in a *Saturday Review* critique, adds that "*Ragtime* is a unique and beautiful work of art about American destiny, built of fact and logical fantasy, governed by music heard and sensed, responsive to cinema both as method and historical datum, shaken by a continental pulse."

The prose style of *Ragtime* is especially hailed. Yet at least a few readers denigrate *Ragtime*'s writing. In the *Village Voice,* Greil Marcus calls it "all surface." Jonathan Raban, writing in *Encounter,* feels that *Ragtime* "is chock-a-block with glittering, unexamined conceits. . . , little firecrackers that glow with suggestive, but finally fraudulent brilliance, because they can be pursued no further than the sentences which encapsulate them." In contrast, Grumbach notes: "My enthusiasm for [*Ragtime*] is based primarily on the quality of the prose, an ingenious representation in words and sentences of Scott Joplin's rag rhythms." "Like ragtime," remarks R. Z. Sheppard of *Time,* "Doctorow's book is a native American fugue, rhythmic, melodic and stately. . . . Its lyric tone, fluid structure and vigorous rhythms

give it a musical quality that explanation mutes." Moreover, Kauffmann finds that the book is written "exquisitely. . . . The 'ragtime' effect is fundamentally to capture a change in the rhythm of American life, a change to the impelling beat of a new century." That many reviewers focus on the power of *Ragtime*'s prose, that some describe it as absorbing and lucid would be no surprise to Doctorow. For, as he explains to John F. Baker in the *Publishers Weekly* interview, in writing *Ragtime* he "was very deliberately concentrating on the narrative element. I wanted a really relentless narrative, full of ongoing energy. I wanted to recover that really marvelous tool for a novelist, the sense of motion." Furthermore, Doctorow tells Jonathan Yardley: "I don't think a writer can ignore seventy years of optical technology. . . . You can't ignore the fact that children grow up now and see a commercial which in thirty seconds or a minute has five or eight scenes and tells a whole story. . . . People understand things very rapidly today, and I really want to keep one step ahead of them." Doctorow also remarks to Yardley that "in a certain sense [*Ragtime*] was an act of exploration, to find out what it itself was about. I did that with *Daniel,* too. [In] the first two books I was very calculating, and I think that was a mistake. I learned to trust the act of writing and not to impose the degree of control that could kill whatever might happen."

In *Loon Lake,* Doctorow continues to experiment with prose style and to evoke yet another period in American history, the Depression. The novel's plot revolves around the various relationships between an industrial tycoon, his famous aviatrix-wife, gangsters and their entourage, an alcoholic poet, and a young drifter who stumbles onto the tycoon's opulent residence in the Adirondacks. The novel works on several levels with "concentrically expanding ripples of implication," according to Robert Towers in the *New York Times Book Review.* For the most part, however, it is Doctorow's portrait of the American dream versus the American reality which forms the novel's core. As Christopher Lehmann-Haupt of the *New York Times* explains, *Loon Lake* "is a complex and haunting meditation on modern American history."

Time's Paul Gray believes that "Doctorow is . . . playing a variation on an old theme: The American dream, set to the music of an American nightmare, the Depression." Lehmann-Haupt infers a similar correlation and elaborates: "This novel could easily have been subtitled *An American Tragedy Revisited.* . . . *Loon Lake* contains [several] parallels to, as well as ironic comments on, the themes of [Theodore] Dreiser's story. . . . Had Dreiser lived to witness the disruptions of post-World War II American society—and had he possessed Mr. Doctorow's narrative dexterity—he might have written something like *Loon Lake.*"

Doctorow's extraordinary narrative style has generated much critical comment. "The written surface of *Loon Lake* is ruffled and choppy," Gray remarks. "Swatches of poetry are jumbled together with passages of computerese and snippets of mysteriously disembodied conversation. Narration switches suddenly from first to third person, or vice versa, and it is not always clear just who is telling what." A reviewer for the *Chicago Tribune* finds such "stylistic tricks" distracting. "We balk at the frequent overwriting, and the clumsy run-on sentences," he reports. "We can see that Doctorow is trying to convey rootlessness and social unrest through an insouciant free play of language and syntax. . .; the problem is that these eccentricities draw disproportionate attention to themselves, away from the characters and their concerns."

Doctorow, seemingly in anticipation of such criticism, defends his unconventional narrative approach in a *New York Times Book Review* interview with Victor S. Navasky: "[In *Loon Lake*] you don't know who's talking so that's one more convention out the window. That gives me pleasure, and I think it might give pleasure to readers, too. Don't underestimate them. People are smart, and they are not strangers to discontinuity. There's an immense amount of energy attached to breaking up your narrative and leaping into different voices, times, skins, and making the book happen and then letting the reader take care of himself."

While some reviewers note certain structural flaws in *Loon Lake,* they praise the novel's overall literary significance and indicate that it is something of a milestone in Doctorow's career. "*Loon Lake* is not as elegantly formed as *Ragtime,*" Stade comments in the *Nation,* ". . . but it is even more ambitious particularly in its mixture of styles and in its reach for significance." Gray echoes this assessment when he writes: "Doctorow may try to do too much in *Loon Lake.* . . . But the author's skill at historical reconstruction, so evident in *Ragtime,* remains impressive here; the novel's fragments and edgy, nervous rhythms call up an age of clashing anxiety. *Loon Lake* tantalizes long after it is ended." Moreover, Stade finds that *Loon Lake* contains "a tone, a mood,

an atmosphere, a texture, a poetry, a felt and meditated vision of how things go with us" that is only hinted at in Doctorow's four previous novels. And the *Chicago Tribune* reviewer, despite his earlier criticism, concludes: "*Loon Lake* is highly interesting—for its relationship among the other novels . . . in Doctorow's developing portrayal of modern America; for its echoes of and associations with other fiction. . .; for its maverick theorizing about capitalism vs. socialism vs. individuality; and its intrinsic picturesqueness and dramatic power. At its best, this straining, challenging book becomes an unpleasantly accurate synthesis of the American experience; a fractious, swaggering song of ourselves."

Doctorow's play, *Drinks before Dinner,* seems to have been created through an analogous act of exploration. In the *Nation,* he states that the play "originated not in an idea or a character or a story but in a sense of heightened language, a way of talking. It was not until I had the sound of it in my ear that I thought about saying something. The language preceded the intention. . . . The process of making something up is best experienced as fortuitous, unplanned, exploratory. You write to find out what it is you're writing." In composing *Drinks before Dinner,* Doctorow worked from sound to words to characters. Does this "flawed" method of composition show a "defective understanding of what theater is supposed to do?" wonders Doctorow. His answer: "I suspect so. Especially if we are talking of the American theater, in which the presentation of the psychologized ego is so central as to be an article of faith. And that is the point. The idea of character as we normally celebrate it on the American stage is what this play seems to question."

Doctorow's experiment garners a mixed response from drama critics. In the *Village Voice,* Michael Feingold observes that in *Drinks before Dinner* Doctorow "has tried to do something incomparably more ambitious than any new American play has done in years—he has tried to put the whole case against civilization in a nutshell." According to Feingold, the intent is defeated by a "schizoid" plot and "flat, prosy, and empty" writing. "I salute his desire to say something gigantic," Feingold concludes; "how I wish he had found a way to say it fully, genuinely, and dramatically." Richard Eder of the *New York Times* responds more positively: "Mr. Doctorow's turns of thought can be odd, witty and occasionally quite remarkable. His theme—that the world is blindly destroying itself and not worrying about it—is hardly original, but certainly worth saying. And he finds thoughtful and striking ways of saying it, even though eventually the play becomes an endless epigram, a butterfly that turns into a centipede." "Still, a play of ideas is rare enough nowadays," Eder observes, "and Mr. Doctorow's are sharp enough to supplement intellectual suspense when the dramatic suspense bogs down."

Doctorow's *World's Fair* and *Billy Bathgate* are both set in 1930s-era New York and have received wide critical acclaim. *World's Fair,* considered by many reviewers to be autobiographical, relates a boy's experiences in New York City during the Depression and ends with his visit to the 1939 World's Fair. Although *World's Fair* received a National Book Award, many critics view the author's next novel, *Billy Bathgate,* as an even greater achievement. The story of fifteen-year-old Billy Behan's initiation into the world of organized crime is a "grand entertainment that is also a triumphant work of art," according to *Washington Post Book World* contributor Pete Hamill. A number of reviewers especially appreciate Doctorow's ability to avoid cliched characters: "Even the various gangsters [in *Billy Bathgate*] are multidimensional," Anne Tyler remarks in the *New York Times Book Review.* The completion of *Billy Bathgate* was also a milestone for its author. Discussing *Billy Bathgate* in the *Washington Post,* Doctorow reveals that he felt he had been "liberated by it to a certain extent. . . . Certain themes and preoccupations, that leitmotif that I've been working with for several years. I think now I can write anything. The possibilities are limitless. I've somehow been set free by this book."

Doctorow turned to nonfiction in 1993, gathering his commissioned work on literature and politics in *Jack London, Hemingway, and the Constitution: Selected Essays, 1977-1992.* For almost the first time in his career, Doctorow drew mixed reviews. For instance, writing in the *National Review,* Donald Lyons calls the collection "a salad bar of limp banalities" and the *New Republic*'s Andrew Delbanco, ordinarily a champion of Doctorow's work, believes that "many of Doctorow's points border on cant." The British critic Stephen Fender, however, writing for the *Times Literary Supplement,* feels that Doctorow's essays yield great insights into his historical fiction, and finds Doctorow's comments on Theodore Dreiser and Jack London to be "trenchant and illuminating."

Yet even Fender saved his highest praise for *The Waterworks,* Doctorow's 1994 novel, marveling at the author's ability to adapt his style to his material,

employing "the balanced periods and formal address of Victorian prose." The novel is set in an 1871 New York City caught up in the Industrial Revolution. The story tells of a missing book reviewer, Martin Pemberton, sought after by his editor and a policeman not corrupted by the Boss Tweed machine, who become a sort of Holmes and Watson team sifting through clues and making scientific deductions. But this "only serves to get us into the city," notes Mark Shechner in the *Chicago Tribune,* "a gaslit phantasmagoria of ambition and squalor." The waterworks itself, on the site of what is now the New York Public Library, is the wild, near-gothic setting where the mystery of Pemberton's disappearance is resolved.

"Boss Tweed's New York is material that any novelist-cum-urban historian might long to dirty his hands with," Shechner continues. "But since his one great novel, *The Book of Daniel,* Doctorow had adopted a clean hands strategy, side-stepping character development in favor of special effects." But Delbanco feels that Doctorow is not really interested in conventional realism, suggesting that the author is committed to "a kind of allegorical romance" in the tradition of Nathaniel Hawthorne and Edgar Allan Poe. Ted Solotaroff takes much the same view, writing in the *Nation* that "Hints and glints of Poe are embedded in [the novel's] twinned interests in mystery and science, its detective-story format, its necrological overlay, its protagonist" and that Herman Melville, too, "haunts the book's pages." Solotaroff goes on to praise Doctorow as "a remarkable writer" whose novels, viewed together, "form a highly composed vision of American history." Similarly, writing in the *Los Angeles Times Book Review,* Jonathan Franzen states that "what makes Doctorow our most exciting historical novelist, aside from sheer talent and audacity, is his perception that history can only be reconstructed, never re-experienced." He concludes that the considerable success of *The Waterworks* derives both from its old-fashioned qualities and its postmodern assumptions, inviting us "to peer back to the verge of modern industrial society—and show us ourselves peering forward."

BIOGRAPHICAL/CRITICAL SOURCES:

BOOKS

Authors in the News, Volume 2, Gale (Detroit), 1976.
Bestsellers 89, Issue 3, Gale, 1989.
Concise Dictionary of American Literary Biography: Broadening Views, 1968-1988, Gale, 1989.

Contemporary Literary Criticism, Gale, Volume 6, 1976, Volume 11, 1979, Volume 15, 1980, Volume 18, 1981, Volume 37, 1986, Volume 44, 1987, Volume 65, 1990.

Dictionary of Literary Biography, Gale, Volume 2: *American Novelists since World War II,* 1978, Volume 28: *Twentieth-Century American-Jewish Fiction Writers,* 1984.

Dictionary of Literary Biography Yearbook: 1980, Gale, 1981.

Fowler, Douglas, *Understanding E. L. Doctorow,* University of South Carolina Press (Columbia), 1992.

Johnson, Diane, *Terrorists and Novelists,* Knopf (New York City), 1982.

Levine, Paul, *E. L. Doctorow,* Methuen (New York City), 1985.

Morris, Christopher D., *Models of Misrepresentation: On the Fiction of E. L. Doctorow,* University Press of Mississippi (Jackson), 1991.

Parks, John G., *E. L. Doctorow,* Continuum (New York City), 1991.

Trenner, Richard, editor, *E. L. Doctorow: Essays and Conversations,* Ontario Review (New York City), 1983.

PERIODICALS

America, May 13, 1989, p. 457.
American Literature, March, 1978.
American Scholar, winter, 1975/1976.
Atlantic Monthly, September, 1980.
Best Sellers, June 1, 1966; August 15, 1971.
Booklist, April 15, 1994; October 1, 1994, p. 238.
Books and Bookmen, June, 1976.
Chicago Tribune, September 28, 1980.
Choice, November, 1966.
Christian Science Monitor, June 13, 1994, p. 13.
Commentary, October, 1975; March, 1986.
Connoisseur, May, 1989, p. 50.
Detroit Free Press, February 19, 1989.
Detroit News, November 10, 1985.
Drama, January, 1980.
Economist, August 20, 1994, p. 70.
Encounter, February, 1976.
Entertainment Weekly, June 17, 1994, p. 46; July 15, 1994, p. 58.
Esquire, June, 1994, p. 148.
Glamour, March, 1989, p. 190.
Globe and Mail (Toronto), March 11, 1989.
Hudson Review, summer, 1986.
Insight on the News, March 6, 1989, p. 62.
Journal of Popular Culture, fall, 1979.
London Magazine, February, 1986.

Los Angeles Times Book Review, November 24, 1985; March 5, 1989; June 19, 1994, p. 1.
Maclean's, March 6, 1989, p. 58; July 25, 1994, p. 54.
Manchester Guardian, February 23, 1986.
Miami Herald, December 21, 1975.
Midstream, December, 1975.
Midwest Quarterly, autumn, 1983.
Modern Fiction Studies, summer, 1976.
Nation, June 2, 1979; September 27, 1980; November 17, 1984; November 30, 1985; April 3, 1989, p. 454; June 6, 1994, pp. 784-790.
National Catholic Reporter, May 12, 1989, p. 33.
National Review, August 15, 1975; March 14, 1986; May 5, 1989, p. 52; December 27, 1993, p. 72.
New Leader, December 16-30, 1985; June 6, 1994, p. 35.
New Republic, June 5, 1971; July 5, 1975; September 6, 1975; September 20, 1980; December 3, 1984; March 20, 1989, p. 40; July 18, 1994, pp. 44-48.
New Statesman & Society, September 15, 1989, p. 37; June 17, 1994, p. 40.
Newsweek, June 7, 1971; July 14, 1975; November 4, 1985; February 13, 1989, p. 76; June 27, 1994, p. 53.
New York, September 29, 1980; November 25, 1985; February 20, 1989, p. 63.
New Yorker, December 9, 1985; March 27, 1989, p. 112; June 27, 1994, p. 195.
New York Herald Tribune, January 22, 1961.
New York Review of Books, August 7, 1975; December 19, 1985; March 2, 1989, p. 3; June 23, 1994, p. 10.
New York Times, August 4, 1978; November 24, 1978; September 12, 1980; November 6, 1984; October 31, 1985; February 9, 1989; November 4, 1993, p. C24.
New York Times Book Review, September 25, 1960; July 4, 1971; July 6, 1975; September 28, 1980; December 6, 1984; November 10, 1985; February 26, 1989, p. 1; December 3, 1989, p. 69; June 19, 1994, p. 1.
Partisan Review, fall, 1972.
People, March 20, 1989, p. 33; July 4, 1994, p. 28.
Playboy, February, 1989, p. 22; July, 1994, p. 34.
Progressive, March, 1986; August, 1989, p. 38.
Publishers Weekly, June 30, 1975; June 27, 1994, pp. 51-52.
Saturday Review, July 17, 1971; July 26, 1975; September, 1980.
South Atlantic Quarterly, winter, 1982.
Southwest Review, autumn, 1977.
Spectator, May 28, 1994, p. 33.

Springfield Republican, September 18, 1960.

Time, July 14, 1975; September 22, 1980; December 18, 1985; February 27, 1989, p. 76; June 20, 1994, p. 66.

Times Literary Supplement, February 14, 1986; May 27, 1994, p. 20.

Tribune Books, July 10, 1994, p. 3.

USA Today, July, 1989, p. 96.

Village Voice, July 7, 1975; August 4, 1975; December 4, 1978; November 26, 1985.

Wall Street Journal, February 7, 1986.

Washington Post, April 6, 1990.

Washington Post Book World, July 13, 1975; September 28, 1980; November 11, 1984; November 17, 1985; February 19, 1989; June 5, 1994, pp. 1, 9.

World Literature Today, winter, 1995, pp. 138-139.

*   *   *

DODD, Lynley (Stuart)   1941-

PERSONAL: Born July 5, 1941, in Rotorua, New Zealand; daughter of Matthew Fotheringhan (a forester) and Elizabeth Sinclair (a secretary; maiden name, Baxter) Weeks; married Anthony Robert Fletcher Dodd, January 2, 1965; children: Matthew Fletcher, Elizabeth Anne. *Education:* Elam School of Art, diploma, 1962; further study at Auckland Teachers College, 1962.

ADDRESSES: Home and office—Edward Avenue, R.D. 3, Tauranga, New Zealand.

CAREER: Queen Margaret College, Wellington, New Zealand, art mistress, 1963-68; freelance author and illustrator, 1968—.

MEMBER: PEN International.

AWARDS, HONORS: Esther Glen Medal, New Zealand Library Association, 1975, for *My Cat Likes to Hide in Boxes;* Choysa Bursary for Children's Writers, jointly from New Zealand Literary Fund and Quality Packers Ltd., 1978; New Zealand Book Award for illustrations, 1981, for *Druscilla;* New Zealand Children's Picture Book of the Year Award, 1984, for *Hairy Maclary from Donaldson's Dairy,* 1986, for *Hairy Maclary's Scattercat,* and 1988, for *Hairy Maclary's Caterwaul Caper;* Third Prize in the AIM Children's Picture Book of the Year Award, for *Hairy Maclary's Rumpus at the Vet,* 1990; The New Zealand 1990 Commemorative Medal "in recognition of services to New Zealand"; Third Prize in the AIM Children's Picture Book of the Year Award, for *Slinky Malinki,* 1991; AIM Children's Picture Book of the Year Award, for *Hairy Maclary's Showbusiness,* 1992.

WRITINGS:

SELF-ILLUSTRATED CHILDREN'S BOOKS

(With Eve Sutton) *My Cat Likes to Hide in Boxes,* Hamilton, 1973, Era, 1984.

The Nickle Nackle Tree, Hamilton, 1976, Era, 1985.

Titimus Trim, Hamilton, 1979, Hodder & Stoughton (London), 1979.

The Smallest Turtle, Mallinson Rendel, 1982, Gareth Stevens, 1985.

The Apple Tree, Mallinson Rendel, 1982, Gareth Stevens, 1985.

Hairy Maclary from Donaldson's Dairy, Mallinson Rendel, 1983, Gareth Stevens, 1985.

Hairy Maclary's Bone, Mallinson Rendel, 1984, Gareth Stevens, 1985.

Hairy Maclary's Scattercat, Mallinson Rendel, 1985, Gareth Stevens, 1988.

Wake Up, Bear, Mallinson Rendel, 1986, Gareth Stevens, 1986.

Hairy Maclary's Caterwaul Caper, Mallinson Rendel, 1987, Gareth Stevens, 1989.

A Dragon in a Wagon, Mallinson Rendel, 1988, Gareth Stevens, 1989.

Hairy Maclary's Rumpus at the Vet, Mallinson Rendel, 1989, Gareth Stevens, 1990.

Slinky Malinki, Mallinson Rendel, 1990, Keystone, 1990.

Find Me a Tiger, Mallinson Rendel, 1991, Gareth Stevens, 1992.

Hairy Maclary's Showbusiness, Mallinson Rendel, 1991, Keystone, 1991.

The Minister's Cat ABC, Mallinson Rendel, 1992, Gareth Stevens, 1994.

Slinky Malinki, Open the Door, Mallinson Rendel, 1993, Gareth Stevens, 1994.

Schnitzel von Krumm's Basketwork, Mallinson Rendel, 1994, Gareth Stevens, 1994.

Sniff-Snuff-Snap!, Mallinson Rendel, 1995.

ILLUSTRATOR

Jillian Squire, *Pussyfooting,* Millwood Press, 1978.

Clarice England, *Druscilla,* Hodder & Stoughton, 1980.

Also illustrator of several educational readers for Price Milburn, 1974-83.

SIDELIGHTS: Lynley Dodd told *CA:* "I was brought up in small, isolated forestry settlements. There were few children in the neighborhood, but for those few there was unlimited space for play, and miles of pine trees in any direction provided plenty of scope for imagination. I have always had pen and drawing paper ready—most times I have had an illustrating assignment of some sort in hand. I have also done a little cartooning. At the arrival of my first baby I took on work for a correspondence school, illustrating fortnightly sets for seven-to nine-year-olds."

Dodd's work as a writer began with Eve Sutton's suggestion that they collaborate on a children's book, *My Cat Likes to Hide in Boxes,* a picture book based on Dodd's family cat. It was after this collaboration that Dodd became fascinated with picture books. She also had two small children at the time who were active consumers of children's books, so she decided to try writing her own. The book that came out of this effort was *The Nickle Nackle Tree,* which a reviewer in *Publishers Weekly* calls, "just the thing to lift the spirits in the bleak, lifeless winter months."

"I now write as well as illustrate my own picture books," Dodd told *CA.* "I find being able to plan the whole book from the outset exciting and rewarding. The idea is roughed out first and fit into the format and length required. Then a 'dummy' is made, a complete miniature mock-up of the finished book. This gives the publisher a good indication of plan and serves as a working model for me when I come to do final illustrations."

The lead character in Dodd's *Hairy Maclary from Donaldson's Dairy* is perhaps the most popular she has created. Hairy Maclary is a small, black, scruffy terrier-type dog who inhabits a canine community that includes such friends as Hercules Morse, Muffin McLay, Bitzer Maloney, Bottomley Potts, the dachshund Schnitzel von Krumm, and the dogs' arch-enemy, the fierce tomcat Scarface Claw. *Hairy Maclary from Donaldson's Dairy* became the first in a series for which Dodd is best known around the world, and especially in her native New Zealand. Colin Mills states in a review in *Books for Keeps* that with the combination of Dodd's text and pictures, youngsters will learn a great deal "about sound, stress, intonation and the patterning of language."

"Since Hairy Maclary came on the scene, books have been a full-time occupation and I seem to spend as much time answering letters as in the actual writing and illustration," Dodd commented. "I take part in the New Zealand Book Council's Writers in Schools' scheme—a worthwhile activity as it keeps me in touch with the 'consumers.' It's a two-way thing; the children are able to put a face to the name on the books and the feedback I get, plus the fun of sharing the books with large numbers of children, is stimulating and a spur to new ideas, as well as a way to keep myself on track."

Dodd has been praised for creating animal characters with distinctly individual personalities, as well as for her ability to conjoin text and pictures. Two of Dodd's memorable creations from the Hairy Maclary series went on to become leading characters themselves. The dachshund is the star of *Schnitzel von Krumm's Basketwork,* in which Schnitzel finds that the basket he sleeps in has been replaced with a stylish new one. Schnitzel goes off in search of a bed as cozy and comfortable as his old one. *School Librarian* critic Carol Woolley praises the book as a "charming tale for any dog lover" and notes that its rhyme and rhythm "carry the story along swiftly."

"Writing for children is an exacting business," Dodd commented. "Beginning as an illustrator and only later trying my hand at writing text as well, I know only too well the truth of the saying, 'The fewer the words, the harder the job.' It's exasperating to hear, from those who should know better, 'I'd like to try writing—I think I'll start with a children's book.' One hopes the results never reach the children! (However I may have overdone the 'blood, sweat and tears' bit in my school talks, as a recent comment from a child's letter shows, 'I might just be an author when I grow up, unless I get a better job.')"

"Hard work, yes, but enormous satisfaction too. To travel halfway around the world and find a Glasgow audience of five-to seven-year-olds, muffled to the eyebrows against snow outside and draughts inside, happily chanting the results of one's labours at a desk 12,000 miles away, is to reap the reward that makes it all worthwhile."

BIOGRAPHICAL/CRITICAL SOURCES:

PERIODICALS

Booklist, December 1, 1988, p. 646.
Books for Keeps, January, 1986, p. 13; November, 1993, p. 10; July, 1994, p. 6.
Junior Bookshelf, October, 1983, p. 206.
Magpies, November, 1991, p. 26.

Publishers Weekly, January 23, 1978, p. 373.

School Librarian, February, 1992, p. 15; February, 1993, pp. 14-15; November, 1994, p. 145.

School Library Journal, August, 1991, p. 144; February, 1992, p. 15.

Times Educational Supplement, July 29, 1988, p. 21; January 7, 1994, p. 33.

*   *   *

DORFF, Elliot N. 1943-

PERSONAL: Born June 24, 1943, in Milwaukee, WI; son of Sol (a civil engineer) and Anne (a teacher; maiden name, Nelson) Dorff; married Marlynn Wertheimer; children: Tammy, Michael, Havi, Jonathan. *Education:* Columbia University, A.B. (summa cum laude), 1965, Ph.D., 1971; Jewish Theological Seminary of America, M.H.L., 1968, Rabbi, 1970.

ADDRESSES: Home—125 N. Ledoux Rd., Beverly Hills, CA 90211. *Office*—Department of Graduate Studies, University of Judaism, 15600 Mulholland Dr., Los Angeles, CA 90077.

CAREER: University of Judaism, Los Angeles, CA, assistant professor, 1971-76, associate professor, 1976-85, professor of philosophy, 1985—, professor in residence at Camp Ramah, 1972-91, dean of graduate studies, 1974-85, provost, 1980-94, coordinator of Earl Warren Institute of Ethics and Human Relations, 1984—, rector, 1994—. Lecturer at University of California, Los Angeles, 1974-90, Fuller Theological Seminary, 1976, 1977, and University of Southern California Law Center, 1987; visiting professor at University of California, Los Angeles, 1990—; visiting associate professor at University of California, Irvine, 1976. Member of National Youth Commission, United Synagogue of America, 1971—; member of Conservative Movement Committee on Jewish Law and Standards, 1984—, and Commission on Conservative Philosophy, 1985—. Member of Board of Rabbis of Southern California. Member of board of directors of American Jewish Committee of Los Angeles, 1972-74; Hillel Council, 1974-76, and Jewish Family Service, 1985—; member of Los Angeles Priest-Rabbi Dialogue, 1974—, co-chair, 1990—; coordinator of Los Angeles Chevrah, 1982-85; member of Commission on Spirituality, Council on Jewish Life, Jewish Federation Council of Greater Los Angeles, 1983-90; chair of Jewish Hospice Commission, 1985-90; member of Ethics Committee of University of California, Los Angeles, Medical Center, 1988—, and of Hillary Rodham Clinton's Health Care Task Force, spring, 1993.

MEMBER: International Association of Jewish Lawyers and Jurists, Academy for Jewish Philosophy (chair, 1992-94), American Academy of Religion, American Philosophical Association, Association of Jewish Studies (member of board of directors, 1982-85), Jewish Law Association (chair, 1992-94), Rabbinical Assembly, Religious Education Association, Society for Values in Higher Education, Phi Beta Kappa.

WRITINGS:

Jewish Law and Modern Ideology, United Synagogue of America (New York City), 1970.

(With Sheldon Dorph and Victoria Kelman) *A First Course in Hebrew Bible Study,* Bureau of Jewish Education (Los Angeles), 1977.

Conservative Judaism: Our Ancestors to Our Descendants, United Synagogue of America, 1977.

(With Arthur Rosett) *A Living Tree: The Roots and Growth of Jewish Law,* State University of New York Press (Albany) and The Jewish Theological Seminary of America (New York City), 1988.

(Editor and contributor) *Willing, Learning and Striving: A Course Guide to Emet Ve-Emunah, Sources and Approaches for Teaching Adults,* Jewish Theological Seminary, Rabbinical Seminary (New York City) and United Synagogue of America, 1988.

Mitzvah Means Commandment, United Synagogue of America, 1989.

Knowing God: Jewish Journeys to the Unknowable, Jason Aronson (Northvale, NJ), 1992.

(With Louis Newman) *Contemporary Jewish Ethics and Morality: A Reader,* Oxford University Press, 1995.

"This Is My Beloved, This Is My Friend": A Rabbinic Letter on Intimate Relations, Rabbinical Assembly, 1995.

Also contributor to numerous books, including *Issues in the Jewish-Christian Dialogue: Jewish Perspectives on Covenant, Mission, and Witness,* edited by Helga Croner and Leon Klenicki, Paulist Press (Ramsey, NJ), 1979; *Slow Down and Live: A Guide to Shabbat Observance and Enjoyment,* edited by Stephen Garfinkel, United Synagogue Youth (New York City), 1982; *The Poor Among Us: Jewish Tradition and Social Policy,* American Jewish Committee (New York City), 1986; *Three Faiths: One God,* edited by John Hick, Macmillan (New York City) and State University of New York, 1988; *Teaching about World Religions: A Teacher's Supplement,* edited by Alfred Wolf, Houghton (Boston, MA), 1991; and *Shalom Bayit: A Jewish Response to Child Abuse and Domestic Violence,* edited by Ian Russ, Sally Weber, and Ellen Ledley, Shalom Bayit Committee of the University of Judaism and Jewish Family Service of Los Angeles (Los Angeles), 1993. Also contributor of numerous articles to periodicals.

WORK IN PROGRESS: An Anthology of readings on contemporary Jewish theology for Oxford University Press; a book on Jewish medical ethics for the Jewish Publication Society.

SIDELIGHTS: Elliot N. Dorff told *CA:* "My work has concentrated on Jewish ethics, law and theology. In ethics, I have written on theoretical subjects (e.g., the methodology by which one can access the Jewish tradition for moral guidance, the relationships between Jewish law and ethics) and on specific moral issues, including poverty, war, sex, and especially, bioethics. My papers on end-of-life issues and on human sexuality have become the official positions of Judaism's Conservative Movement, the largest in America. In Law, I have written about both the philosophy of Jewish law (e.g., the bases of authority of the law, the covenantal nature of Jewish law) and specific discussions in Jewish law. In theology, I have written about my own approach to Jewish theology, with special attention to epistemological matters, and about topics in, and the theological bases for, interfaith relations."

*　　*　　*

DOWN, Goldie M(alvern)   1918-

PERSONAL: Born June 26, 1918, in Sydney, Australia; daughter of Herbert William (an insurance inspector) and Violet Marion (Knox) Scarr; married David Kyrle Down (a clergyman), September 8, 1946; children: Kendall, Glenda, Michele, Teddy, Richley, another daughter (adopted). *Education:* Attended Avondale College (New South Wales, Australia), 1940-42.

ADDRESSES: Home—2 Neridah Ave., Mount Colah 2079, Australia.

CAREER: Secretary in Australia, 1943-44; Seventh-Day Adventist missionary with her husband, in India, 1953-73; teacher of creative writing to adult students, principally at government evening colleges, 1976—; freelance writer.

AWARDS, HONORS: Second prize in *Write Now* competition, Review & Herald, for *Fear Was the Pursuer.*

WRITINGS:

Missionary to Calcutta, Review and Herald, 1958.
Twenty-One Thousand Miles of Adventure, Southern Publishing, 1964.
God Plucked a Violet, Southern Publishing, 1968.
If I Have Twelve Sons, Southern Publishing, 1968.
Their Kind of Courage, Review and Herald, 1973.
No Forty Hour Week, Southern Publishing, 1977.
Kerri and Company, Review and Herald, 1978.
More Lives Than a Cat, Southern Publishing, 1979.
You Never Can Tell When You May Meet a Leopard, Review and Herald, 1980.
Fear Was the Pursuer, Review and Herald, 1981.
Missionaries Don't Cry, Review and Herald, 1981.
Like Fire in His Veins, Review and Herald, 1982.
We Gotta Tell Them, Edie, Review and Herald, 1982.
Saga of an Ordinary Man, Pacific Press, 1984.
Feed Me Well, Ilona, Pacific Press, 1985.
Wings Over New Guinea, Pacific Press, 1988.
The Adventures of a Watercop, Eben Press, 1991.
There's No Magic Formula, Longman Cheshire, 1991.
When Father Disappeared, Eben Press, 1994.
(With Wintley Phipps) *The Power of a Dream,* Zondervan (Grand Rapids, MI), 1994.
Paper in the Mud, Eben Press, 1995.

Contributor of numerous stories and articles to church and health periodicals.

WORK IN PROGRESS: A biography of Rev. Dr. Gordon Moyes, head of Sydney Wesley Centre and well-known radio and television speaker; a compilation of stories of pioneers of Seventh-day Adventist Church in Australia and the South Pacific.

SIDELIGHTS: Goldie M. Down told *CA* that she and her family have spent twenty years in India as missionaries. All five Down children completed their primary and secondary education in India by correspondence, before they returned to Australia for their tertiery education. All her children write well, and two are published authors themselves. Down claims she is a compulsive writer, specializing in non-fiction. She hopes that those who read her writings will not only be entertained but inspired. Down reports that she loves teaching creative writing to adults and is especially proud of *There's No Magic Formula,* her textbook for beginning writers.

*   *   *

DOYLE, Charles (Desmond)   1928-
   (Mike Doyle)

PERSONAL: Born October 18, 1928, in Birmingham, England; son of Charles and Mary (Carroll) Doyle; married Helen Merlyn Lopdell, November 26, 1952 (deceased); married Doran Ross Smithells, July 28, 1959 (divorced); married Rita Jean Brown, October 9, 1993; children: (second marriage) Aaron William, Patrick Haakon, Kegan Ross, Mary Elizabeth Katharine. *Education:* Victoria University College, University of New Zealand (now Victoria University of Wellington), B.A., 1956, M.A. (honors), 1958; Wellington Teachers' College, Diploma of Teaching, 1955; University of Auckland, Ph.D., 1968. *Politics:* "Social democrat and green." *Avocational interests:* Taoism, T'ai Chi, tennis, open form poetry, the music of Hayden, Mozart, and C.P.E. Bach, the history of art, especially 19th-and 20th-Century Western.

ADDRESSES: Home—641 Oliver Street, Victoria, British Columbia, Canada.

CAREER: University of Auckland, Auckland, New Zealand, lecturer, 1961-66, senior lecturer in English and American literature, 1966-68; University of Victoria, Victoria, British Columbia, associate professor, 1968-76, professor of English and American literature, 1976-93, professor emeritus/adjunct professor, 1993—. Visiting fellow in American studies, Yale University, 1967-68. *Military service:* Royal Navy.

MEMBER: League of Canadian Poets, Canadian Union of Writers, Canadian Association of University Teachers.

AWARDS, HONORS: UNESCO creative artist's fellowship, 1959; American Council of Learned Societies fellow at Yale University, 1967-68; Canada Council grants, 1971, 1972, fellowship, 1974-75; Social Sciences and Humanities Research Council of Canada fellowship, 1982-83.

WRITINGS:

POETRY

A Splinter of Glass: Poems, 1951-56, Pegasus, 1956.
(With James K. Baxter, Louis Johnson, and Kendrick Smithyman) *The Night Shift: Poems on Aspects of Love,* Capricorn Press, 1957.
Distances: Poems, 1956-61, Paul's Book Arcade (Hamilton, New Zealand), 1963.
Messages for Herod, Collins, 1965.
A Sense of Place, Wai-te-Ata Press, 1965.
Earth Meditations: 2, Alldritt, 1968.
Noah, Soft Press, 1970.
Intimate Absences: Selected Poems, Beach Holme, 1993.

POETRY UNDER PSEUDONYM MIKE DOYLE

Abandoned Sofa, Soft Press, 1971.
Earth Meditations: One to Five, Coach House Press, 1971.
Earth Shot, Exeter Books, 1972.
Preparing for the Ark, Weed/Flower Press, 1973.
Planes, Seripress, 1975.
Stone-dancer, Oxford University Press, 1976.
A Steady Hand, Porcupine's Quill, 1983.

NONFICTION

(Editor) *Recent Poetry in New Zealand,* Collins, 1965.
R.A.K. Mason, Twayne, 1970.
James K. Baxter, Twayne, 1976.
(Editor) *William Carlos Williams: The Critical Heritage,* Routledge & Kegan Paul, 1980.
William Carlos Williams and the American Poem, Macmillan, 1982.
(Coeditor) *The New Reality: The Politics of Restraint in British Columbia,* New Star, 1984.
(Editor) *Wallace Stevens: The Critical Heritage,* Routledge & Kegan Paul, 1985.
(Coeditor) *After Bennett: A New Politics for British Columbia,* New Star, 1986.

Richard Aldington: A Biography, Southern Illinois University Press, 1989.

(Editor) *Richard Addington: Reappraisals,* University of Victoria Press, 1991.

OTHER

Contributor to anthologies, including *Twentieth Century New Zealand Poetry,* edited by Vincent O'Sullivan, Oxford University Press, 1970; *Contemporary Poetry of British Columbia;* edited by J. M. Yates, Sono Nis, 1970; *New Zealand Poetry: An Introduction,* edited by F. M. McKay, New Zealand University Press, 1970; and *New Zealand Writing since 1945,* edited by Vincent O'Sullivan and MacD. P. Jackson, Oxford University Press, 1983. Also contributor of poetry to periodicals, and critical essays to books and professional journals.

*   *   *

DOYLE, Mike
  See DOYLE, Charles (Desmond)

E

EDWARDS, Bronwen Elizabeth
See ROSE, Wendy

*   *   *

EL-BAZ, Farouk   1938-

PERSONAL: Born January 1, 1938, in Zagazig, Egypt; son of El-Sayed (an educator) and Zahia (Hammouda) El-Baz; married Catherine Patricia O'Leary; children: Monira, Soraya, Karima, Fairouz. *Education:* Ain Shams University, B.S., 1958; University of Assiut, graduate study, 1958-60; University of Missouri School of Mines and Metallurgy (now University of Missouri—Rolla), M.S., 1961, Ph.D., 1964; Massachusetts Institute of Technology, graduate study, 1962-63. *Religion:* Muslim.

ADDRESSES: Home—213 Silver Hill Rd., Concord, MA 01742. *Office*—Center for Remote Sensing, Boston University, 725 Commonwealth Ave., Boston, MA 02215.

CAREER: University of Assiut, Assiut, Egypt, instructor in geology, 1958-60; University of Missouri—Rolla, instructor in geology, 1963-64; University of Heidelberg, Institute of Mineralogy and Petrography, Heidelberg, Germany, instructor in mineralogy, 1964-65; Pan American-UAR Oil Co., Cairo, Egypt, exploration geologist, 1966-67; Bellcomm, Inc., Washington, DC, member of technical staff, 1967-69, supervisor of lunar exploration, 1969-72; Smithsonian Institution, National Air and Space Museum, Washington, DC, director of Center for Earth and Planetary Studies, 1973-82; Litton Industries, Itek Optical Systems, Lexington, MA, vice-president for international development, 1982-86; Boston University, Boston, MA, director of Center for Remote Sensing, 1986—. Consultant to Dover Publications, Time-Life Books, and National Geographic Society.

MEMBER: International Astronomical Union, World Aerospace Education Organization, American Association for the Advancement of Science, Geological Society of America, American Association of Petroleum Geologists, American Geophysical Union, National Geographic Society for Photogrammetry and Remote Sensing, Missouri Academy of Science, Explorers Club, Sigma Xi.

WRITINGS:

Say It in Arabic, Dover, 1968.
(With Walter Haentzschel and G. C. Amstutz) *Coprolites: An Annotated Bibliography,* Geological Society, 1968.
(With L. J. Kosofsky) *The Moon as Viewed by Lunar Orbiter,* National Aeronautics and Space Administration, 1970.
(With Amstutz and others) *Glossary of Mining Geology,* Springer Verlag, 1970.
Astronaut Observations from the Apollo-Soyuz Mission, Smithsonian Institution, 1977.
(With H. Masursky and G. W. Colton) *Apollo over the Moon: A View from Orbit,* National Aeronautics and Space Administration, 1978.
Egypt as Seen by Landsat, Dar Al-Maaref (Cairo), 1978.

(With D. M. Warner) *Apollo-Soyuz Test Project Summary Science Report,* Volume II: *Earth Observations and Photography,* National Aeronautics and Space Administration, 1979.

(With T. A. Maxwell) *Desert Landforms of Southwest Egypt: A Basis for Comparison with Mars,* National Aeronautics and Space Administration, 1982.

(Editor with M. H. Hassan) *Physics of Desertification,* Martinus Nijhoff, 1986.

(Editor with Hassan and V. Cappellini) *Remote Sensing and Resource Exploration,* World Scientific, 1989.

(Editor with R. M. Makharita) *The Gulf War and the Environment,* Gordon and Breach, 1994.

Also author of *Deserts and Arid Lands,* 1984, and compiler of *Geology of Egypt: An Annotated Bibliography,* 1984. Contributor to magazines and journals, including *National Geographic, Explorers Journal,* and *Smithsonian.*

WORK IN PROGRESS: Remote Sensing in Archaeology, a review of the utility of space-age, remote sensing techniques in archaeological investigations; *Apollo and I,* a personal narrative of involvement in the training of astronauts and the selection of landing sites for the Apollo mission to the moon; *Desert Wisdom,* a review of knowledge of the dry lands gained by studying satellite images and field excursions in all the major deserts of the world.

SIDELIGHTS: Farouk El-Baz told *CA* that he involves the space program in his writing because he believes in its value and long-term benefits: "observations from space, particularly photography, will help us better utilize the Earth for the benefit of mankind, especially in deserts and semiarid lands."

*   *   *

ELIAS, John L(awrence)   1933-

PERSONAL: Born December 23, 1933, in Asheville, NC; son of F. George (a pharmacist) and Josephine (a dressmaker; maiden name, Anastasi) Elias; married Eleanor J. Flanigan (a professor), March 18, 1972; children: Rebecca, Rachel. *Education:* St. Charles College, B.A., 1955; St. Charles Seminary, M.Div., 1959; Temple University, Ed.D., 1974. *Politics:* "Democrat-Socialist." *Religion:* Roman Catholic.

ADDRESSES: Home—32 Spring Garden Drive, Madison, NJ 07940. *Office*—School of Religious Studies, School of Education, New York, NY 10023.

CAREER: High school teacher in Easton, PA, 1959-64, and in Bethlehem, PA, 1964-66; Trenton State College, Trenton, NJ, assistant professor of education, 1972-77; Fordham University, New York City, associate professor of religion and religious education, 1977-82, professor of religion and education, 1982—. Visiting professor to University of Birmingham, 1983-84, and St. Mary's College, 1984-85.

MEMBER: Society for Educational Reconstruction (member of executive board, 1976-79), Religious Education Association (board of directors, 1995—), American Educational Studies Association, Association of Professors and Researchers in Religious Education.

WRITINGS:

Psychology and Religious Education, Catechetical Communications, 1975, 3rd edition, Robert E. Krieger, 1983.

Conscientization and Deschooling: Freire's and Illich's Proposals for Reshaping Society, Westminster, 1976.

(With Sharan Merriam) *Philosophical Foundations of Adult Education,* Robert E. Krieger, 1980, revised edition, 1995.

The Foundations and Practice of Adult Education, Robert E. Krieger, 1982, revised edition, 1993.

Studies in Theology and Education, Robert E. Krieger, 1986.

Moral Education: Secular and Religious, Robert E. Krieger, 1989.

Paulo Freire: Pedagogue of Liberation, Robert E. Krieger, 1994.

Philosophy of Education: Classical and Contemporary, Robert E. Krieger, 1995.

Contributor to education journals and inspirational magazines.

WORK IN PROGRESS: A history of education in the United States; historical perspectives on Catholic education.

BIOGRAPHICAL/CRITICAL SOURCES:

PERIODICALS

Adult Education Quarterly, summer, 1977.
Christian Century, November 16, 1977.

Educational Studies, winter, 1981.
Lifelong Learning, January, 1978.

*   *   *

ELLIS, Bret Easton   1964-

PERSONAL: Born March 7, 1964, in Los Angeles, CA; son of Robert Martin (a real estate investment analyst) and Dale (a homemaker; maiden name, Dennis) Ellis. *Education:* Bennington College, B.A., 1986. *Avocational interests:* Piano, playing keyboards in bands, reading, sculling.

ADDRESSES: Agent—Amanda Urban, International Creative Management, 40 W. 57th St., New York, NY 10019.

CAREER: Writer.

MEMBER: Authors Guild, PEN, Writers Guild of America.

WRITINGS:

Less Than Zero, Simon & Schuster (New York City), 1985.
The Rules of Attraction, Simon & Schuster, 1987.
American Psycho, Vintage (New York City), 1991.
The Informers, Knopf (New York City), 1994.

Contributor of articles to periodicals, including *Rolling Stone, Vanity Fair, Wall Street Journal, Vogue, American Film,* and *Interview.*

ADAPTATIONS: Less Than Zero, directed by Marek Kanievska and starring Robert Downey, Jr., Jami Gertz, and James Spader, was released by Twentieth Century-Fox in 1988.

SIDELIGHTS: In 1985 twenty-one-year-old Bret Easton Ellis jolted the literary world with his first novel, *Less Than Zero.* Many reviewers' reactions to the book echoed that of *Interview* magazine's David Masello, who called it "startling and hypnotic." Eliot Fremont-Smith of the *Voice Literary Supplement* pronounced the book "a killer"—and, like other critics, was impressed not only with the novel itself but also with its author's youth. "As a first novel, [*Less Than Zero*] is exceptional," John Rechy declared in the *Los Angeles Times;* it is "extraordinarily accomplished," a *New Yorker* critic concurred. *Less Than*

Zero, wrote Larry McCarthy in *Saturday Review,* "is a book you simply don't forget." A college undergraduate at the time of novel's publication, Ellis has been hailed by more than one critic as the voice of the new generation. Upon the publication of his third novel, *American Psycho,* Ellis again attracted attention, this time for writing a story so disturbing and violent that Matthew Tyrnauer of *Vanity Fair* called Ellis "the most reviled writer in America, the Salman Rushdie of too much, too fast."

The somewhat-autobiographical *Less Than Zero* grew out of a writing project Ellis began at Bennington College under his professor, writer Joe McGinniss. "That first draft was written very hurriedly, in a period of eight weeks," Ellis told *CA.* "The real writing, I think, came in the *rewriting* process." Comprised of vignettes about his high school experiences in a wealthy section of Los Angeles, the book centers on Clay, an eighteen-year-old freshman at an eastern college who returns to Los Angeles for Christmas vacation. Drugs, sex, expensive possessions, and an obsession with videotapes, video games, and music videos fill the lives of Clay and his jaded peers. Events others might find horrifying— hard-core pornography, a corpse in an alley, and a girl who is kidnapped, drugged, and raped—become passive forms of entertainment. At the outset, Ellis was afraid the novel would not be published at all. "[Simon & Schuster] was harshly divided on it," he told *CA.* "There was a group who really wanted to pick it up and there was a group who were vehement about not wanting to publish it at all. . . . It was a strange, slow process."

The novel's grim subject matter is related in a detached, documentary-style prose, leading *New York Times* reviewer Michiko Kakutani to state that *Less Than Zero* was "one of the most disturbing novels [she had] read in a long time." *Time* magazine's Paul Gray, asserted that "Ellis conveys the hellishness of aimless lives with economy and skill," while Alan Jenkins of the *Times Literary Supplement* found that "at times [the novel] reproduces with numbing accuracy the intermittent catatonic lows of a psychophysical system artificially stimulated beyond normal human endurance." This tone took Ellis a while to develop: "At first it was hard to become so blase and so passive. But once I started getting into that character's head and his patterns of speech, then the writing came a lot easier," he told *CA.*

Some critics drew comparisons between *Less Than Zero* and J. D. Salinger's *Catcher in the Rye,* the

1950s classic of disaffected youth. But Anne Janette Johnson, writing in the *Detroit Free Press,* explained that such comparisons could not extend "beyond the fact that both [novels] concern teenagers coming of age in America. Salinger's now-famous narrator [Holden Caulfield] had feelings—anger, self-pity, desire. The youths in [*Less Than Zero*] are merely consuming automatons, never energetic enough to be angry or despairing." *Less Than Zero* reminded Johnson more of the nihilistic "lost generation" of American authors in the 1920s and 1930s like Ernest Hemingway and F. Scott Fitzgerald; for other critics, the novel brought to mind Jack Kerouac and similar "beat generation" writers of the 1950s. And Kakutani found echoes of Raymond Chandler, Joan Didion, and Nathanael West in Ellis's evocation of Los Angeles.

Reviewers agreed, nonetheless, on the novel's indebtedness to the early 1980's rise of the music video and MTV. The book's characters constantly refer to songs and artists. Additionally, Ellis divides *Less Than Zero* into brief scenes in much the same way that MTV is fragmented into videos that last only three or four minutes. Fremont-Smith reported that Ellis called *Less Than Zero* "a very visual book" in which he employed a deliberately "staccato pace [and] the rapid layering of image upon image." Even before critics dubbed the book "the first MTV novel," according to Fremont-Smith, Ellis's publisher revealed that the author was "anxiously awaiting the first review that tabs him as the first voice of the video generation." Ellis admitted to *CA* that television "contributed to this generation's short attention span," but movies and books—novelist Joan Didion in particular—were his primary influences as a young writer: "I don't see how any writer born after the 1940s or 1950s can *not* have been influenced by films. At least for me, they've made more of an impression and their influence has been a lot stronger than the influence of TV."

Ellis's second novel, *The Rules of Attraction,* continued in the vein of *Less Than Zero;* as R. Z. Sheppard of *Time* magazine noted, "the village of the damned goes East." *Rules* is set at Camden College, a fictional East Coast school which bears a striking similarity to Bennington College in Vermont, where Ellis earned his degree. Despite the academic setting, many reviewers noted the absence of the usual rigors of higher education. Richard Eder announced in the *Los Angeles Times Book Review* that "we actually catch a glimpse of one professor . . . and he is asleep on his office couch and reeks of pot." What is present, however, are "drunken parties, drugs, sex, shoplifting, [and] pop music," according to Campbell Geeslin in *People.* The three main characters, Paul, Sean, and Lauren, are involved in a frustrating love triangle: Paul, a homosexual, desires the bisexual Sean; Sean meanwhile longs to deepen his involvement with Lauren, who is pining after someone else. *New York Times Book Review* contributor Scott Spencer stated that these characters "live in a world of conspicuous and compulsive consumption—consuming first one another, and then drugs, and then anything else they can lay their hands on."

Spencer praised Ellis for "portraying the shallowness of [his characters'] desires," but objected to what he deemed the author's gratuitous use of brand names which served no higher function than to glamorize the narrative. Spencer also surmised that Ellis is a potentially adept satirist, but that in *The Rules of Attraction* "his method of aping the attitudes of the burnt-out works against him. . . . One closes the book feeling that this time out the author has stumbled over the line separating cool from cold. Where we ought to be saying, 'Oh my God, no,' we are, instead, saying, 'Who cares?'" *Newsweek* reviewer David Lehman also found Ellis's authorial skill to be somewhat deficient, and he concluded that "like *Less Than Zero, The Rules of Attraction* is more effective as a sociological exhibit than as a work of literary art." Conversely, Geeslin called Ellis's writing "exceedingly effective" and concluded: "If college these days is like this, it's a miracle that anyone survives, much less graduates."

A very minor character from *The Rules of Attraction*—Sean's older brother Patrick—became the central figure in Ellis's third novel, *American Psycho.* Like Ellis's other protagonists, Patrick Bateman is young, greedy, wealthy, and devoid of morals. A Wall Street executive who shops at the most expensive stores and dines at the trendiest restaurants, Patrick also enjoys torturing, mutilating, and murdering people at random, mostly from New York City's underclass. His crimes are described in the same emotionless detail that he devotes to his observations on food, clothing, and stereo equipment. Though he drops many hints of his covert activities to friends and authorities, he is never caught, and none of the victims seems to be missed.

Ellis has stated that he intended *American Psycho* to be a satirical black comedy about the lack of morality in modern America, and some critics agree that he achieved this aim. Other commentators, however, accused him of pandering to readers' most base desires by producing a novel with all the artistic worth of a low-budget horror movie. Man, woman, child, and animal all meet grisly ends at the hands of Bateman, and the book's violence towards women in particular prompted one chapter of the National Organization of Women to organize a boycott not only of the book itself, but of all books by its publisher, Vintage, and its parent company, Random House.

Some critics saw little literary merit in the book. In a *Washington Post* review, Jonathan Yardley called *American Psycho* "a contemptible piece of pornography, the literary equivalent of a snuff flick" and urged readers to forego the experience. Andrew Motion echoed Yardley's sentiments in the London *Observer,* calling the book "deeply and extremely disgusting. . . . [S]ensationalist, pointless except as a way of earning its author some money and notoriety." Similarly, Albert Manguel of *Saturday Night* also reported that his reaction to the book was not as the author intended: "not intellectual terror, which compels you to question the universe, but physical horror—a revulsion not of the senses but of the gut, like that produced by shoving a finger down one's throat." John Leonard of the *Nation,* however, argued that "There is no reason this couldn't have been funny: if not Swiftian, at least a sort of *Bonfire of the Vanities* meets *The Texas Chainsaw Massacre. . . .* Ellis has an ear for the homophobic and misogynistic fatuities of his social set. . . . When Patrick tells people that he's 'into murders and executions,' what they hear him say is 'mergers and acquisitions.'"

Likewise, other reviewers gave Ellis high marks for what they saw as the work's serious intent and technical skill. Henry Bean voiced such an opinion in the *Los Angeles Times Book Review: American Psycho* is "a satire, a hilarious, repulsive, boring, seductive, deadpan satire of what we now call . . . the Age of Reagan. The miracle of Bret Easton Ellis is that without a plot, without much in the way of characters and with a throwaway nonstyle that renders the luxurious, the erotic and the grotesque in the same uninflected drone. . ., he nevertheless makes it virtually impossible to stop reading. . . . Ellis is, first and last, a moralist. Under cover of his laconic voice, every word in his three novels to date springs from grieving outrage at our spiritual condition." Similarly, British novelist Fay Weldon called the novel "brilliant" in a *Washington Post* review, stating that "Ellis is a very, very good writer. He gets us to a 'T.' And we can't stand it. It's our problem,

not his. *American Psycho* is a beautifully controlled, careful, important novel that revolves about its own nasty bits."

Other unlikely proponents of the book include Gore Vidal, who Tyrnauer quotes as remarking, "I thought it was really rather inspired. . . . These nutty characters, each on his own track—and the tracks keep crossing. It was a wonderfully comic novel." Director David Cronenberg considered making a film version, and author Michael Tolkin argued, as Tyrnauer reports, that "There was a massive denial about the strengths of the book. . . . People scapegoated the violence, but that wasn't his sin. He made a connection between the language of fashion writing and serial murder."

Still another group of critics walked a middle ground between the two critical extremes. Allowing that Ellis had been sincere in his attempt to write a serious book, they nonetheless found him lacking the skills required to successfully complete his ambitious mission. Mim Udovitch summarized this point of view in a *Village Voice* article, calling *American Psycho* "more serious (and less compelling) text than the critical focus on blood and guts gives it credit for. . . . It seeks to explode rather than perpetuate the myth of isolationist privilege that enjoys such high regard among the would-be isolationist privileged. . . . The book's truly irredeemable drawback is that laudable as Ellis's great lurch forwards is in thematic terms, he remains an amateurish formalist and a downright lousy stylist."

The debate over Ellis's style continued with his 1994 publication, *The Informers*. A novel constructed from loosely related short pieces which take place once again in Los Angeles and concern rich and beautiful college students, the book displayed the deadpan prose and scenes of horror on which Ellis's reputation had been built. The book contains graphic depictions of vampirism and murder on par with those in *American Psycho,* but violence is not the novel's focus. A multitude of friends and acquaintances, mostly tan, blonde, and sleeping with each other, find their lives uprooted by several random murders and mutilations of their relatives and peers. As it turns out, two of these young trendy types, Dirk and Jamie, are vampires. But once again Ellis focuses on the emptiness of the 1980s and on characters consumed with style and materialism who have contempt for any real analysis of their lives. "*The Informers* is full of scintillating chitchat," wrote Leonard in the *Nation.* "What Ellis has digitized, instead of a novel, is a video. He channel-surfs—from bloody bathroom to bloodier bedroom; from herpes to anorexia," he continued.

For Neal Karlen, reviewer for the *Los Angeles Times Book Review, The Informers* represented "a further slide down for an author who long ago had it." Karlen dismissed the book as full of "a rancid phoniness" and characterized all of Ellis's later work as being "opaque and bitter, devoid of both humanity and meaning" because "Ellis apparently has not learned the lesson of empathy, either on the page or in life." Conversely, for *New York Times Book Review* contributor George Stade, *The Informers* was "spare, austere, elegantly designed, telling in detail, coolly ferocious, sardonic in its humor." Stade concluded that Ellis himself was "a covert moralist and closet sentimentalist, the best kind, the kind who leaves you space in which to respond as your predispositions nudge you, whether as a commissar or hand-wringer or, like me, as an admirer of his intelligence and craft." Richard Stern of the *Chicago Tribune Book World* concurred, calling Ellis "another of the talented post-Hemingway, post-*Stranger* minimalists . . . whose stories spell out the farce and desperation under the fantastic gadgetry of modern wealth."

In Tyrnauer's interview with Ellis, he noted that "a certain slangy level of ironic detachment informs even his most serious statements—and not everybody gets it. 'I am an incredibly moralistic person. . . . A lot of people totally mistake the books in some cases as advocating a certain behavior or as glorifying a certain form of behavior.'" Commenting on his role as a spokesperson for his generation, he told *CA* that "I . . . don't believe that there's one or two spokespeople for a generation, one collective voice who's going to speak for the whole lot. . . . What you have to do when you're asked to be on a panel like that or write a magazine article about it is just feel safe enough about your own opinion and go ahead and state it. You shouldn't feel burdened or pressured knowing that there are two million kids out there who might have differing opinions."

BIOGRAPHICAL/CRITICAL SOURCES:

BOOKS

Contemporary Literary Criticism, Gale (Detroit), Volume 39, 1986, Volume 71, 1992.

PERIODICALS

Advocate, January 29, 1991, pp. 78-79.
Chicago Tribune, September 13, 1987.
Chicago Tribune Book World, August 14, 1994, p. 3.
Christian Science Monitor, March 19, 1991, p. 13.
Commentary, July, 1991, pp. 52-54.
Detroit Free Press, August 18, 1985.
Detroit News, August 11, 1985.
Film Comment, December, 1985; May-June, 1991, pp. 55-56.
Interview, June, 1985.
Los Angeles Times Book Review, May 26, 1985; September 13, 1987; March 17, 1991, pp. 1, 5; August 21, 1994, pp. 3, 8.
Mademoiselle, June, 1986.
Nation, April 1, 1991, pp. 426-28; September 5-12, 1994, pp. 238-41.
National Review, February 14, 1986; June 24, 1991, pp. 45-56.
New Republic, June 10, 1985.
Newsweek, July 8, 1985; September 7, 1987, p. 72; November 26, 1990, p. 85; March 4, 1991, pp. 58-59; March 25, 1991, pp. 65-66.
New York, December 17, 1990, pp. 32-37; August 8, 1994, pp. 71-2.
New Yorker, July 29, 1985.
New York Review of Books, May 29, 1986.
New York Times, June 8, 1985; November 17, 1990, p. A13; November 18, 1990, p. 17; December 5, 1990, p. 27; December 10, 1990, pp. C13, C18; March 6, 1991, pp. C13, C18; March 10, 1991, section 2, pp. 1, 20-21; March 11, 1991, p. C18.
New York Times Book Review, June 16, 1985; June 22, 1986; September 13, 1987, pp. 14-15; December 16, 1990, pp. 3, 16; September 18, 1994, p. 14.
Observer, April 21, 1991, p. 61.
People, July 29, 1985; September 28, 1987.
Rolling Stone, September 26, 1985; April 4, 1991, pp. 45-46, 49-51.
Saturday Night, July-August, 1991, pp. 46-47, 49.
Saturday Review, July-August, 1985.
Time, June 10, 1985; October 19, 1987; October 29, 1990, p. 100; April 22, 1991, p. 94.
Times Literary Supplement, February 28, 1986.
Vanity Fair, March, 1991, pp. 154-59, 220-21; August, 1994, pp. 94-7, 124-5.
Village Voice, February 25, 1991, pp. 65-66.
Voice Literary Supplement, May, 1985.
Wall Street Journal, March 6, 1991, p. A7.
Washington Post, February 27, 1991, pp. B1, B3; April 28, 1991, pp. C1, C4.
Writer's Digest, December, 1986.

EMERSON, Earl W. 1948-

PERSONAL: Born July 8, 1948, in Tacoma, WA; son of Ralph W. and June (Gadd) Emerson; married Sandra Evans, April 25, 1968; children: Sara, Brian, Jeffrey. *Education:* Attended Principia College, 1966-67, and University of Washington, Seattle, 1967-68.

ADDRESSES: Home—North Bend, WA. *Agent*—Dominick Abel, Dominick Abel Literary Agency Inc., 146 West 82nd St., Suite 1B, New York, NY 10024.

CAREER: Seattle Fire Department, Seattle, WA, lieutenant, 1978—. Guest of honor, Left Coast Crime Convention, 1992.

MEMBER: Mystery Writers of America, Private Eye Writers of America.

AWARDS, HONORS: Shamus Award, 1985, for *Poverty Bay.*

WRITINGS:

MYSTERY NOVELS

The Rainy City, Avon (New York City), 1985.
Poverty Bay, Avon, 1985.
Nervous Laughter, Avon, 1986.
Fat Tuesday, Morrow (New York City), 1987.
Black Hearts and Slow Dancing, Morrow, 1988.
Deviant Behavior, Morrow, 1988.
Help Wanted: Orphans Preferred, Morrow, 1990.
Yellow Dog Party, Morrow, 1991.
Morons and Madmen, Morrow, 1993.
The Portland Laugher, Ballantine (New York City), 1994.
The Vanishing Smile, Ballantine, 1995.*

*   *   *

ENGEL, J. Ronald 1936-

PERSONAL: Born March 17, 1936, in Baltimore, MD; son of John A. (an accountant) and Beatrice (a housewife; maiden name, McGee) Engel; married Joan Helen Gibb (a teacher and writer), September 7, 1957; children: John Mark, Kirsten Helene. *Education:* Johns Hopkins University, B.A., 1958;

Lombard College, B.D., 1964; University of Chicago, M.A., 1971, Ph.D., 1977. *Politics:* Democrat.

ADDRESSES: Home—Box 717, Beverly Shores, IN 46301. *Office*—Meadville/Lombard Theological School, 5701 South Woodlawn Ave., Chicago, IL 60637.

CAREER: Ordained Unitarian-Universalist minister; minister of Second Unitarian-Universalist church in Chicago, IL, 1965-68; Meadville/Lombard Theological School, Chicago, assistant professor, 1970-77, associate professor, 1977-83, professor of social ethics, 1983—. Lecturer at University of Chicago, 1978—.

MEMBER: American Academy of Religion, Society of Christian Ethics, American Studies Association, World Conservation Union (chair, Ethics Working Group, 1984—).

AWARDS, HONORS: Melcher Book Award from Unitarian-Universalist Association, and award from Geographic Society of Chicago, both 1984, for *Sacred Sands: The Struggle for Community in the Indiana Dunes.*

WRITINGS:

Sacred Sands: The Struggle for Community in the Indiana Dunes, Wesleyan University Press (Middletown, CT), 1983.
(Editor) James L. Adams, *Voluntary Associations: Socio-Cultural Analyses & Theological Interpretation,* Exploration Press (Chicago, IL), 1986.
(Coeditor) *Ethics of Environment and Development,* University of Arizona Press (Tucson), 1991.
(Coauthor) *Ecology, Justice and Christian Faith,* Greenwood Press (Westport, CT), 1995.

Contributor to theology and environmental ethics journals.

WORK IN PROGRESS: Research on environmental ethics and world faiths; research on democratic faith in America.

SIDELIGHTS: Sacred Sands by J. Ronald Engel has been praised as a history, not only of the Indiana Dunes, but of the social, political, and scientific movements that were born there. The Dunes pageant of 1917 introduced a liturgical movement, or a civil religion, that was centered in the Dunes. One of the goals of the movement was the environmental and ecological production of the area, which survives as the Indiana National Dunes Seashore. Eugene Kennedy wrote in the *Chicago Tribune,* that "Professor Engel does a thorough job of presenting a story that is now largely unknown . . . by most residents of the Midwest." He referred to the work as a "pleasant and splendid book."

Engel told *CA:* "The motivation for my writing, as well as my academic research and teaching, is rooted in my conviction that a new world faith (variously called the 'religion of democracy' and 'ecological' or 'evolutionary humanism') has arisen in the modern world. To give that faith definition and institutionalization is an important task. In *Sacred Sands: The Struggle for Community in the Indiana Dunes,* I show the interplay between the models of scientific research that established the science of ecology in America through field studies in the Dunes, and the symbols of the progressive reform movement and artistic renaissance centered in Chicago and focused on the Dunes as a 'sacred landscape.'"

BIOGRAPHICAL/CRITICAL SOURCES:

PERIODICALS

Chicago Tribune, January 30, 1983.

*   *   *

ESTEP, W(illiam) R(oscoe), Jr. 1920-

PERSONAL: Surname is pronounced "*Eas*-tep"; born February 12, 1920, in Williamsburg, KY; son of William Roscoe and Rhoda Mae (Snyder) Estep; married Edna McDowell, December 23, 1942; children: William Merl, Alice Ann (died, 1947), Rhoda MacDonald, Mary Morgan, Lena Gipson, Martin Andrew (died, 1969). *Education:* Berea College, B.A., 1942; Southern Baptist Theological Seminary, Th.M., 1945; Southwestern Baptist Theological Seminary, Th.D., 1951; additional study at Union Theological Seminary, 1958, La Escuela de Idiomas, Costa Rica, 1959, University of Basel, 1967, University of Zurich, 1967-68, Concordia Seminary, 1970, and Oxford University, 1974. *Avocational interests:* Photography, electronics, music, golf, fishing, gardening.

ADDRESSES: Home—1 York Dr., Fort Worth, TX 76134. *Office*—P.O. Box 22037, Fort Worth, TX 76122.

CAREER: Baptist minister; pastor of churches in Kentucky, Oklahoma, and Texas. Los Angeles Baptist Seminary, Los Angeles, CA, professor of church history, 1946-47; Union Baptist Seminary, Houston, TX, professor of church history, 1951-53; Southwestern Baptist Theological Seminary, Fort Worth, TX, professor of church history, 1954-94. Teacher, extension department, Baylor University, 1952-53; guest professor, Seminario Bautista Internacional Teologico, Cali, Colombia, 1959-60, International Baptist Theological Seminary, Ruschlikon, Switzerland, 1967-68, Spanish Baptist Seminary, Madrid, 1975, Southern Baptist Theological Seminary, and Seminario Bautista, Trujillo, Peru, 1989; senior lecturer for the Southwest Commission on Religious Studies, 1988-89, Summer Institute of Theological Education, Ruschlikon, 1991, Hong Kong Baptist Theological Seminary, 1994-95, and Canadian Southern Baptist Seminary, 1995.

MEMBER: American Society of Church History, Conference on Faith and History, Southern Baptist Historical Society, Society for Reformation Research, Texas Baptist Historical Society, Phi Kappa Phi.

AWARDS, HONORS: Distinguished Service Award, Christian Life Commission, Baptist General Convention, 1994; Distinguished Service Award, The Historical Commission, Southern Baptist Convention, 1994.

WRITINGS:

La Fe de Los Apostoles, Editorial Verdad, 1962.
The Anabaptist Story, Broadman (Nashville, TN), 1963, revised edition, Eerdmans (Grand Rapids, MI), 1975, revised and enlarged, Eerdmans, 1995.
(Contributor) *Baptist Advance,* Broadman, 1964.
(Contributor) *Baptists and Christian Unity,* Broadman, 1966.
(Contributor) *Colombia: Land of Conflict and Promise,* Convention Press, 1968.
And God Gave the Increase: A Centennial History of the First Baptist Church of Beaumont, 1872-1972, First Baptist Church of Beaumont, 1972.
(Editor) *Anabaptist Beginnings: 1523-1533,* de Graaf (Netherlands), 1976.

(Editor) *The Lord's Free People in a Free Land,* School of Theology, Southwestern Baptist Theological Seminary, 1976.

(Editor) *Balthasar Hubmaier: Anabaptist Theologian and Martyr,* Judson (Valley Forge, PA), 1978.

(Editor) *The Reformation: Luther and the Anabaptists,* Broadman, 1979.

The Reformation and Protestantism, Caribe Press, 1981.

Renaissance and Reformation, Eerdmans, 1986.

The Gaston Story, Hanson Printing, 1987.

(Contributor) Robinson B. James, editor, *The Unfettered Word: Southern Baptists Confront the Authority-Inerrancy Question,* Word Books (Waco, TX), 1987.

Revolution within the Revolution: The First Amendment in Historical Context, 1612-1789, Eerdmans, 1990.

(Contributor) Paul Basden and David Dockery, editors, *The People of God: Essays on the Believers' Church,* Broadman Press, 1991.

(Contributor) Paul Towes, editor, *Mennonites and Baptists: A Continuing Conversation,* Kindred Press (Winnipeg, Manitoba; and Hillsboro, KS), 1993.

Whole Gospel—Whole World: Sesquicentennial History of the Foreign Mission Board of the Southern Baptist Convention, 1845-1995, Boardman and Holman, 1994.

Also contributor to *Encyclopedia of Southern Baptists,* 1956, 1970, 1971, and 1981, *The Concept of the Believer's Church,* 1969, *God and Caesar: Case Studies in the Relationship between Christianity and the State,* 1971, *Adult Life and Work Lesson Annual,* 1973, *Baptist Relations with Other Christians,* 1974, *Evangelical Dictionary of Theology,* 1984, *Dictionary of Christianity in America,* 1990, *The Mennonite Encyclopedia,* V, 1990, *The Brethren Encyclopedia,* 1983, *Encyclopedia U.S.A.,* 1983. Contributor of articles to religious periodicals and professional journals, including *Christianity Today, Mennonite Quarterly Review, Grace Theological Journal, Review and Expositor,* and *Baptist History and Heritage.* Editor, *Southwestern Journal of Theology,* 1963-67.

SIDELIGHTS: W. R. Estep, Jr. once told *CA:* "For me, writing is hard work. I never would have gone into it simply from the sheer joy of literary production. Recognizing, however, that the pen is not only 'mightier than the sword' but longer lasting than the spoken word and that books outlast classroom lec-

tures, I began to write in order to convey a message which I felt my discipline had to offer to a twentieth-century audience.

"My serious attempt at writing history was motivated by a desire to let the message found particularly in sixteenth-century Anabaptism speak to my own generation. Subsequently, I became involved in all sorts of writing projects as editor, translator, and contributor to encyclopedias, as well as author. However, there has always been the desire that my writing would help the reader to achieve a greater degree of self-understanding in translating the proven values of the past into positive action in the present. As I reflect upon my writing career, perhaps the overall motivation has been to challenge the reader to live a more meaningful life. Perhaps my goals have been too ambitious and my purpose has not been fully attained. In short, I suppose I have attempted to extend my teaching career by writing."

He adds: "My motivation for adding yet another book to an already overcrowded field on the Renaissance and Reformation was mixed. After having taught courses on the Reformation more than twenty-five years I felt compelled to share some of the insights I had gleaned. I wished to place the Anabaptists within the context of Reformation, showing both their dependence upon certain insights of the reformers and the uniqueness of the Anabaptist contribution to the shape of contemporary Protestantism. I also tried to give the Spanish Reformation more attention than it generally has received in such works. Further, I attempted to show that the spiritual sources that eventually precipitated the Reformation also brought about the initial impulse toward a Catholic revival.

"All of the above may appear nothing more than the work of a revisionist church historian. However, I like to think of my work filling out the picture of movements which has been left incomplete at a number of points. If history does indeed help with self-identity, then those who read this narrative history should benefit thereby, and if history is, indeed, the midwife of values this work may help stimulate a return to the spiritual foundations of the Reformation which could in turn spark a dynamic and fruitful revival in the last decade of the twentieth century."

Commenting on the state of contemporary literature, Estep writes: "I feel that the book shelves are cluttered with trash. I also feel that we are doing the students in high schools and universities a terrible disservice by neglecting the great masters of the past for contemporary fads which major on sexual fantasies. It is time that we were getting back to the classic examples of literary excellence for the sake of our students."

Estep speaks Spanish and German and has a reading knowledge of Greek, Hebrew, Latin, French, and Portuguese. Some of his books have been translated into Portuguese, Spanish, Italian, Serbo-Croate, and Korean.

*   *   *

EVEREST, Allan S(eymour) 1913-

PERSONAL: Born October 9, 1913, in South Shaftsbury, VT; son of Charles Seymour (a merchant) and Clara (Hawkins) Everest; married Elsie Hathaway Lewis, October 10, 1942; children: Martha. *Education:* University of Vermont, Ph.B., 1936; Columbia University, M.A., 1937, Ph.D., 1948.

ADDRESSES: Home—5057 South Catherine St., Plattsburgh, NY 12901.

CAREER: Green Mountain Junior College, Poultney, VT, instructor in social science, 1938-41; State University of New York College at Plattsburgh, professor of American history, 1947-83, professor emeritus, 1983—. *Military service:* U.S. Army Air Forces, 1941-46; became captain.

MEMBER: New York State Historical Association, Clinton County Historical Association (former president), Phi Beta Kappa, Pi Gamma Mu.

WRITINGS:

Morgenthau, the New Deal and Silver: A Story of Pressure Politics, King's Crown Press, 1950, reprinted, Da Capo Press, 1973.
British Objectives at the Battle of Plattsburgh, Moorsfield Press, 1960.
(Editor) David Sherwood Kellogg, *Recollections of Clinton County and the Battle of Plattsburgh, 1800-1840,* Clinton County Historical Association, 1964.
Pioneer Homes of Clinton County, 1790-1820, Clinton County Historical Association, 1966.

(Editor) Kellogg, *A Doctor at All Hours: A Private Journal of a Small-Town Doctor's Varied Life, 1886-1909,* Greene, 1970.
Our North Country Heritage: Architecture Worth Saving in Clinton and Essex Counties, Tundra Books (Plattsburgh, NY), 1972.
(Editor) Charles Carroll, *The Journal of Charles Carroll of Carrollton,* Champlain-Upper Hudson Bicentennial Committee, 1976.
Moses Hazen and the Canadian Refugees in the American Revolution, Syracuse University Press (Syracuse, NY), 1976.
Run across the Border: The Prohibition Era in Northern New York, Syracuse University Press, 1978.
Henry Delord and His Family, George Little Press, 1979.
The War of 1812 in the Champlain Valley, Syracuse University Press, 1981.
Briefly Told: Plattsburgh, New York, 1784-1984, Clinton County Historical Association, 1984.
(Coauthor) *Clinton County, A Pictorial History,* Donning (Norfolk, VA), 1988.
The Military Career of Alexander Macomb and Macomb in Plattsburgh, Clinton County Historical Association, 1989.
Pliny Moore: North Country Pioneer of Champlain, New York, Clinton County Historical Association, 1990.
Point au Fer on Lake Champlain, Clinton County Historical Association, 1992.

SIDELIGHTS: Allan S. Everest has traveled extensively in the British Isles, Western Europe, and Canada and has twice taught at English universities.

*   *   *

EYERLY, Jeannette (Hyde) 1908- (Jeannette Griffith)

PERSONAL: Born June 7, 1908, in Topeka, KS; daughter of Robert C. (a railroad executive) and Mabel (Young) Hyde; married Frank Rinehart Eyerly (a newspaper editor), December 6, 1932; children: Jane Kozuszek, Susan Pichler. *Education:* Attended Drake University, 1926-29; University of Iowa, A.B., 1930. *Politics:* Independent. *Religion:* Roman Catholic. *Avocational interests:* Family, friends, flowers, children, reading, public libraries, playing Scrabble.

ADDRESSES: Home—3524 Grand Ave., Apt. 3203, Des Moines, IA 50312. *Agent*—Curtis Brown, Inc., 10 Astor Pl., New York, NY 10003.

CAREER: Writer and lecturer. Des Moines Public Library, Des Moines, IA, publicity director, 1930-32; Des Moines Child Guidance Center, IA, member of board of directors, 1949-54, president, 1953-54; Des Moines Adult Education Program, IA, creative writing teacher, 1955-57. St. Joseph Academy Guild, member of board of directors, 1954-57, president, 1957. Member of acquisition committee, Des Moines Art Center, 1960-63. Polk County Mental Health Center, member of board of directors, 1968-78, president, 1977-78, 1982—. Iowa Commission for the Blind, member of board, 1977-80, chair, 1978-79.

MEMBER: Authors League of America, Iowa Center of the Book of the Library of Congress (charter member).

AWARDS, HONORS: Susan Glaspell Award, 1965, for *Gretchen's Hill;* Christopher Award, 1969, for *Escape from Nowhere; Radigan Cares* was selected as one of the Child Study Association's Books of the Year, 1970; *Someone to Love Me* selected "Book for Reluctant Reader," American Library Association, 1987; Polk County (Iowa) Mental Health Center was renamed "The Eyerly/Ball Community Health Services Building," 1995, in her honor.

WRITINGS:

NOVELS

(With Valeria Winkler Griffith under joint pseudonym Jeannette Griffith) *Dearest Kate,* Lippincott (Philadelphia), 1961.
More Than a Summer Love, Lippincott, 1962.
Drop-Out, Lippincott, 1963.
The World of Ellen March, Lippincott, 1964.
Gretchen's Hill, Lippincott, 1965.
A Girl Like Me, Lippincott, 1966.
The Girl Inside, Lippincott, 1968.
Escape from Nowhere, Lippincott, 1969.
Radigan Cares, Lippincott, 1970.
The Phaedra Complex, Lippincott, 1971.
Bonnie Jo, Go Home, Lippincott, 1972.
Goodby to Budapest: A Novel of Suspense, Lippincott, 1974.
The Leonardo Touch, Lippincott, 1976.
He's My Baby, Now, Lippincott, 1977.
See Dave Run, Lippincott, 1978.

If I Loved You Wednesday, Lippincott, 1980.
The Seeing Summer, Lippincott, 1981.
Seth and Me and Rebel Make Three, Lippincott, 1983.
Angel Baker, Thief, Lippincott, 1984.
Someone to Love Me, Lippincott, 1987.

OTHER

(With Lee Hadley and Annabelle Irwin) *Writing Young Adult Novels,* Writer's Digest (Cincinnati), 1988.

Wrote syndicated weekly newspaper column, "Family Diary," with Valeria Winkler Griffith, under joint pseudonym Jeannette Griffith. Contributor to *Ladies' Home Journal, McCall's,* and other periodicals.

ADAPTATIONS: He's My Baby, Now was adapted as an *ABC Afterschool Special* titled *Schoolboy Father,* 1978; *The Seeing Summer* was adapted as a short classroom play.

WORK IN PROGRESS: A young-adult novel, *The Education of Adams Henry;* a book of verse, *Animalographies: An ABC Book for Adults.*

SIDELIGHTS: In her novels for young adults, Jeannette Eyerly writes of the many possible troubles teenagers face, including pregnancy, abortion, suicide, mental illness, crime, alcoholism, and divorce. By dealing with these subjects openly Eyerly hopes to give young people guidance.

This hope was evident in Eyerly's first novel, *More Than a Summer Love.* She notes in her essay for the *Something About the Author Autobiography Series* (*SAAS*) that *More Than a Summer Love,* "though a romance, had a point, one in which I firmly believe: that if a boy and girl really love each other, neither will endanger the other's future by a too-early marriage." Eyerly's next book also offered guidance about a serious subject: dropping out of school. "*Drop-Out* was among the first books, if not *the* first, to reflect the 'real-life' situations of young adults," Eyerly once explained. She notes in *SAAS* that when writing *Drop-Out* she had a very tangible goal: "to dissuade potential dropouts by reading a good story, rather than by threats and lectures." Eyerly points out in *SAAS* that *Drop-Out* "is often cited as the turning point between the 'gumdrop' [novels in which the teen heroine always gets the boy of her dreams in the end] and the 'anything goes' novels of the eighties."

In 1966 Eyerly dealt with illegitimacy and adoption in *A Girl Like Me,* the story of Robin, who discovers that her friend, Cass, is about to give birth to an illegitimate baby. Robin, who has been tempted to have sex with her own boyfriend, also learns that she was the child of an unwed mother before her parents adopted her. *A Girl Like Me* is described by a contributor in *Kirkus Reviews* as "somewhat more than a do-good soap opera from one of the better writers for teenage girls," and "a quite realistic and candid story" by a reviewer in *Bulletin of the Center for Children's Books.*

Death seems to stalk the heroine of Eyerly's next novel, *The Girl Inside.* After Chris loses her mother, her father, and the legal guardian who takes care of her, she must learn to cope with sorrow and loss. Though a reviewer in *Bulletin of the Center for Children's Books* states that *The Girl Inside* has the "faint air of a carefully fictionalized case history," *Horn Book* contributor Ruth Hill Viguers believes that the character of Chris was "exceptionally well drawn."

The issue of drug use was addressed by Eyerly in *Escape from Nowhere.* Teenaged Carla feels that nothing is going right in her life: she has an uncommunicative, alcoholic mother, and an absent father. When she tries to escape her loneliness by smoking marijuana with a friend, the friend ends up institutionalized while Carla, after being arrested, finds herself on probation. A critic in *Bulletin of the Center for Children's Books* states that "the family situation seems contrived," adding that "the writing style sustains an insubstantial plot built around the message." Jane Manthorne, however, writing in *Horn Book,* finds that *Escape to Nowhere* "sounds convincingly like Carla's confession rather than an adult's morality lesson." In 1969 *Escape from Nowhere* was awarded the Christopher Medal as the outstanding young adult novel of the year.

Teen pregnancy and the plight of the unwed father were themes of two of Eyerly's novels. The fatherless teenage boy Charles, who impregnates his girlfriend in *He's My Baby, Now,* decides that he does not want to sign the papers to put the infant up for adoption. A reviewer in the *Bulletin of the Center for Children's Books* observes that although the story is not entirely convincing, "it may appeal to readers since most books about premarital pregnancy focus almost exclusively on the mother." Joan Scherer Brewer declares in *School Library Journal* that Charles' tale "is sure to twang a responsive chord in his contemporaries." A pregnant teenager's plight is detailed again in *Someone to Love Me,* in which fifteen-year-old Patrice chooses to keep her baby. Cynthia J. Leibold, writing in *School Library Journal,* praises the "well constructed narrative" and "realistic actions and characteristics personified in Patrice." According to a reviewer in *Bulletin of the Center for Children's Books,* however, *Someone to Love Me* is "a 'problem novel' with a fairy-tale ending, which is presented as happy, but is in fact very sad."

In *Angel Baker, Thief,* Angel tries shoplifting in an effort to get accepted by a clique at her new school. *School Library Journal* contributor Valerie A. Guarini finds that the "characterization is excellent, particularly that of Angel, a teenage girl who desperately wants to be accepted by her peers." Reviewing *Angel Baker, Thief* in *Voice of Youth Advocates,* Luvada Kuhn states, "The conflict between Angel's conscience and her need to be accepted makes for a dramatic conclusion."

Reflecting on her career, Eyerly writes in *SAAS,* "I have sometimes wondered what it would be like to have writing as one's only occupation." She continues, "Though I've occasionally been wistful, I've never been envious. I think of myself as a wife, a mother, a grandmother, and a sister. . . . Add to that the roles of friend, breadmaker, volunteer worker for this or that good cause, teacher, lay psychiatrist . . . the list goes on and on—and, of course, includes author, which I wanted to be all along.

"The curious thing is that had I not been all of the above, I could never have been an author at all, for in one guise or another they have been the source of what I write about."

BIOGRAPHICAL/CRITICAL SOURCES:

BOOKS

Something about the Author Autobiography Series, Volume 10, Gale (Detroit), 1990, pp. 87-102.

PERIODICALS

Books and Bookmen, January, 1977.
Book World, May 4, 1969.
Bulletin of the Center for Children's Books, January, 1967, p. 73; October, 1968, p. 25; September, 1969, pp. 6-7; December, 1970, p. 58; February, 1975, p. 92; September, 1977, p. 14; December, 1984, p. 64; February, 1987, p. 105.

Commonweal, November 11, 1966; May 23, 1969.

Grade Teacher, January, 1971.

Horn Book, August, 1968, p. 428; April, 1969, p. 195.

Kirkus Reviews, September 1, 1965, p. 904; August 15, 1966, p. 841; September 1, 1972, p. 1034; July 15, 1974, p. 749; January 1, 1976, p. 12; January 15, 1981, p. 79.

Library Journal, January 15, 1965, p. 387; January 15, 1966, p. 424; October 15, 1971, p. 3475.

New York Times Book Review, November 6, 1966; November 9, 1969; November 12, 1972; May 1, 1977.

Publishers Weekly, October 23, 1991, p. 62.

Saturday Review, November 13, 1971.

School Library Journal, January 15, 1971, p. 275; May, 1977, p. 69; October, 1978, p. 154; October, 1980, p. 154; August, 1982, p. 115; January, 1985, p. 84; April, 1987, p. 109.

Voice of Youth Advocates, October, 1983, p. 200; February, 1985, p. 325.

F

FAINLIGHT, Ruth (Esther) 1931-

PERSONAL: Born May 2, 1931, in New York, NY; daughter of Leslie Alexander and Fanny (Nimhauser) Fainlight; married Alan Sillitoe (an author), November 19, 1959; children: David Nimrod, Susan (adopted). *Education:* Attended schools in United States and England; studied two years at Birmingham and Brighton Colleges of Arts and Crafts, England.

ADDRESSES: Home—14 Ladbroke Terrace, London W11 3PG, England. *Office—European Judaism,* 80 East End Rd., London N3 2SY, England.

CAREER: Poet, writer, translator, and librettist. Vanderbilt University, Nashville, TN, poet in residence, 1985, 1990.

AWARDS, HONORS: Cholmondeley Award for Poetry, Society of Authors, 1994.

WRITINGS:

POETRY

Cages, Macmillan (London), 1966, Dufour (Chester Springs, PA), 1967.
18 Poems from 1966, Turret Books (London), 1967.
To See the Matter Clearly, Macmillan, 1968, Dufour, 1969.
(Contributor with Ted Hughes and Alan Sillitoe) *Poems,* Rainbow Press (London), 1971.
The Region's Violence, Hutchinson (London), 1973.
21 Poems, Turret Books, 1973.
Another Full Moon, Hutchinson, 1976.
Sibyls and Others, Hutchinson, 1980.
Climates, Bloodaxe Books (Newcastle, England), 1983.

Fifteen to Infinity, Hutchinson, 1983, Carnegie-Mellon University Press (Pittsburgh, PA), 1987.
Selected Poems, Hutchinson, 1987.
The Knot, Hutchinson, 1990.
Sibyls, Gehenna (Searsmont, Maine), 1991.
This Time of Year, Sinclair-Stevenson (London), 1994.
Selected Poems, Sinclair-Stevenson, 1995.

Contributor of poetry to anthologies, including, *The Poetry Anthology,* edited by Hine and Parisi, Houghton (Boston, MA), 1981; *Bread and Roses,* Virago (London), 1982; *The Oxford Book of Dreams,* edited by Stephen Brook, Oxford University Press (England), 1983; *The Bloodaxe Book of Contemporary Women Poets,* Bloodaxe Books, 1985; *Voices in the Gallery,* Tate Gallery (London), 1986; *The Poetry Book Society Anthology,* Hutchinson, 1988, new edition, 1991; *Fire the Sun,* Longman (London), 1989; *The Bedford Introduction to Literature,* St. Martins Press (New York City), 1990; *Images of Women in Literature,* Houghton, 1991; *The Carnegie Mellon Anthology of Poetry,* Carnegie-Mellon University Press, 1993; and *Reflecting Families,* BBC Education (London), 1995. Also selector and author of introduction of *Selected Poems of Harry Fainlight,* Turret, 1987; and Harry Fainlight, *Journeys,* Turret, 1992. Poetry editor, *European Judaism,* London.

Fainlight's poems have been translated into French, Portugese, and Hebrew.

SHORT STORIES

Daylife and Nightlife, Deutsch (London), 1971.
Dr. Clock's Last Case, Virago, 1994.

Contributor of short stories to anthologies, including, *Penguin Modern Stories,* edited by Judith Burnley, Penguin (London), 1971; *Works in Progress 4* (Literary Guild of America), Doubleday (New York City), 1971; *Bananas,* edited by Emma Tennant, Quartet (London), 1977; *12 Stories by Famous Women Writers,* edited by D. Val Baker, W. H. Allen (London), 1978; *New Stories 4* (Arts Council Anthology), edited by E. Feinstein and F. Weldon, Hutchinson, 1979; *The Parchment Moon,* edited by Susan Hill, Michael Joseph (London), 1990; *The Penguin Book of Modern Women's Short Stories,* edited by Hill, Penguin, 1991; *Caught in a Story,* edited by Christine Park and Caroline Heaton, Vintage (London), 1992; and *The Picador Book of the Beach,* edited by Robert Drew, Picador (Chippendale, Australia), 1993.

TRANSLATOR

(With husband, Alan Sillitoe) Lope de Vega, *All Citizens Are Soldiers,* Macmillan, 1969.

Sophia de Mello Breyner, *Navigations* (English section of tri-lingual edition), Imprensa Nacional-Casa da Moeda (Lisbon, Portugal), 1983.

de Mello Breyner, *Marine Rose* (selected poems), Black Swan Books (Redding Ridge, CT), 1988.

Contributor of translations of poetry by de Mello Breyner to anthologies, including, *The Other Voice,* Norton (New York City), 1976; *The Contemporary World Poets,* Harcourt (San Diego, CA, and New York City), 1976; *Contemporary Portuguese Poetry,* Carcanet (London), 1978; *Literature from the World,* Scribner (New York City), 1981; and *Anthology of World Literature by Women, 1875-1975,* Longman, 1989.

LIBRETTO

The Dancer Hotoke (chamber opera), composed by Erika Fox, (commissioned by the Royal Opera House, for *The Garden Venture*), 1991.

The European History (based on Fainlight's poem of the same name), composed by Geoffrey Alvarez, (commissioned by the Royal Opera House, for *The Garden Venture*), 1993.

Mad Dogs and Englishmen, composed by Robert Jan Stips, (commissioned by Channel 4, for series *War Cries*), 1995.

WORK IN PROGRESS: "Having published three books in the last two years, nothing is scheduled for the immediate future. But, all being well, I hope to have a new collection of poems ready in about a year."

SIDELIGHTS: Ruth Fainlight told *CA:* "I enjoy travel, both the plunge into the totally exotic—such as my visits to India and Japan, and the slower sort, by which I mean living somewhere for a while. So far I have done this in France, Spain, Morocco and Israel. Having been based in England for so long—since the age of 15—it would be sophistical to add that country to my list.

"My chief interest is human behavior—which, apart from literature, its best describer and explainer, means the study of history, anthropology, religion (etc. etc. etc.). I am also a reader of books about every area of science I am capable of understanding—having had no scientific education at all.

"I attended art school as a girl, then later was a student at art college, and though I rarely draw now, painting and sculpture remain important pleasures and have been the source of many poems. Work as a librettist is recent but, since the age of twelve—when I hurried home on Saturday afternoons from the art classes for school children at the Corcoran Gallery in Washington D.C. to listen to that week's broadcast from the Metropolitan Opera House—I have been an opera lover.

"I am either writing a poem or waiting with a variety of emotions for the next poem to announce itself. Other forms of writing—stories, translation, libretti—can divert me for a while, but if too much time passes without work on a poem, I feel uneasy. Everything that happens to me, whatever I read or hear about, can become material for a poem. The more I learn and the longer I live, the more apparent becomes the connections between the past, the present and, who knows?, perhaps the future; between all living beings and their environment; between the individual and society and between one person and another. But the medium of poetry is language: poems are made with words. Poetry is the relationship between writer and language and finally, that relationship is what involves me most deeply."

BIOGRAPHICAL/CRITICAL SOURCES:

BOOKS

The Bloodaxe Book of Contemporary Women Poets, Bloodaxe (Newcastle, England), 1985.

How to Write Poetry, Arco (New York City), 1991.

PERIODICALS

Hudson Review, summer, 1987.
London Review of Books, February 2, 1984.
New Statesman, March 12, 1976; May 9, 1980.
Poetry, February, 1978.
Times Literary Supplement, April 8, 1977; May 23, 1980; April 13, 1984.

*   *   *

FARRER, Claire R(afferty) 1936-

PERSONAL: Born December 26, 1936, in New York, NY; daughter of Francis Michael (a welder) and Clara Anna (a nurse; maiden name, Guerra) Rafferty; married Donald Nathanael Farrer (a psychologist), February 2, 1957 (divorced, 1973); children: Suzanne Claire. *Education:* University of California, B.A., 1970; University of Texas, M.A., 1974, Ph.D., 1977. *Politics:* Democrat. *Religion:* Quaker.

ADDRESSES: Office—California State University, Chico, CA 95929-0400.

CAREER: San Jose State University, San Jose, CA, worked in personnel office, 1956; International Business Machines Corporation (IBM), San Jose, statistical analyst, 1956-57; Jennings Radio Manufacturing Co., San Jose, statistical consultant, executive secretary, 1957-58; Washington State University, Pullman, clerk, 1958-59, executive secretary, 1959-61; *Otero County Star,* Alamogordo, NM, columnist, 1963-65; Unitarian Universalist Fellowship, Alamogordo, founder, administrator, 1964-71; Zia School, Alamogordo, curriculum consultant and teacher, 1966-68, 1970-71; Smithsonian Institution, Washington, DC, conducted survey, 1973-74; ethnographic analyst, Texas Joint Senate-House Committee on Prison Reform, 1974; ethnographic researcher, Mescalero Apache Indian Reservation, 1974-75; National Endowment for the Arts, Washington, DC, administrator of Folk Arts program, 1976-77; School of American Research, Santa Fe, NM, resident scholar, 1977-78; University of Illinois at Urbana-Champaign, assistant professor of anthropology, 1978-85; California State University, Chico, professor of anthropology, 1985—.

Field research at Mescalero Apache Indian Reservation, 1972-75, 1977, 1978—. Has presented papers at professional meetings. Fund raiser for Otero County Child Care Center, 1967-71. Member of Interdisciplinary Committee on Folk Curriculum, University of Illinois, 1978-85. Consultant on several advisory boards; consultant on film *Geronimo's Children,* broadcast by the British Broadcasting Corporation, 1976.

MEMBER: American Anthropological Association (fellow), American Astronomical Association—History Division, American Ethnological Society, American Folklore Society, American Society for Ethnohistory, Royal Anthropological Society, Southwestern Anthropological Association, California Scholastic Federation, Western Writers Association, Writers Guild, Phi Kappa Phi, Sigma Xi.

AWARDS, HONORS: Whitney M. Young, Jr., memorial fellowship, 1974-75; Weatherhead resident fellowship, School of American Research, 1977-78; University of Illinois grant, 1979; American Philosophical Society grant, 1983; American Council of Learned Societies grants, 1984, 1987; Belgian National Science Foundation grant, 1989-90; California State University, Chico, Outstanding Professor award, 1993-94.

WRITINGS:

(Editor) *Women and Folklore: Images and Genres,* University of Texas Press, 1976, revised edition, Waveland Press, 1986.
(Editor with Edward Norbeck) *Forms of Play of Native North Americans,* West Publishing, 1979.
Play and Interethnic Communication: A Practical Ethnography of the Mescalero Apache, Garland (New York City), 1990.
Living Life's Circle: Mescalero Apache Cosmovision, University of New Mexico Press (Albuquerque), 1991.
(Editor with Ray A. Williamson) *Earth and Sky: Visions of the Cosmos in Native American Folklore,* University of New Mexico Press, 1992.
Thunder Rides a Black Horse: Mescalero Apaches and the Mythic Present, Waveland Press (Prospect Heights, IL), 1994.

Contributor to books, including, *The Anthropological Study of Play: Problems and Prospects,* edited by David F. Lancy and B. Allan Tindall, Leisure Press, 1976; *Southwestern Indian Ritual Drama,* edited by Charlotte J. Frisbie, University of New Mexico

Press, 1980; *Play and Context,* edited by Alyce T. Cheska, Leisure Press, 1981; *Betwixt and Between: Patterns of Masculine and Feminine Initiation,* edited by Louise Carus Mahdi, Steven Foster, and Meredith Little, Open Court, 1987; and *Women's Studies Encyclopedia,* edited by Helen Tierney, Greenwood (New York City), 1989.

Also author of "Graded Supplementary Reading Materials for the Children of the Bent-Mescalero School" (twenty-four stories concerning Mescalero Apache history). Book review editor and author of quarterly column, "New and Noteworthy," *Western Folklore,* 1985-89. Contributor of numerous articles to journals, including *Parabola, The World and I, Archaeoastronomy,* and *Canadian Journal of Native Studies.* Co-founder and coeditor of first issue, *Folklore Feminists Communication;* editor of *Women and Folklore,* special issue of *Journal of American Folklore;* reader for several refereed journals.

WORK IN PROGRESS: Reflections: Words to Live by While Having Cancer (seeking publisher); *Kaleidescopic Vision and the Rope of Experience; Cross-Cultural Religion* (under contract); a fiction tetralogy; poetry; short stories; further research on Mescalero Apache society and culture, folklore of women and children, cross-cultural aesthetics, shamanism, and ethnoastronomy.

SIDELIGHTS: Claire R. Farrer told *CA:* "I am an old-fashioned cultural anthropologist interested in ethnography and folklore, in its widest sense. I am particularly attracted to desert and maritime people as well as expressive behavior. I am led by serendipity often-times—a quixotic but fascinating guide. I write to see what I am thinking."

*   *   *

FAULKNOR, Cliff(ord Vernon)   1913-
(Pete Williams)

PERSONAL: Born March 3, 1913, in Vancouver, British Columbia, Canada; son of George Henry and Rhoda Anne Faulknor; married Elizabeth Harriette Sloan, August 21, 1943; children: Stephen Edward Vernon, Noreen Elizabeth. *Education:* University of British Columbia, B.S.A. (with honors), 1949. *Politics:* "A little right of centre." *Religion:* Protestant.

ADDRESSES: Home—403-80 Point McKay Cr. NW, Calgary, Alberta T3B 4W4, Canada.

CAREER: Affiliated with Royal Bank of Canada, beginning 1929; also worked with lumber companies, and as an assistant ranger for British Columbia Forest Service; British Columbia Department of Lands and Forests, Land Utilization Research and Survey Division, Victoria, BC, Canada, land inspector, 1949-54; *Country Guide* (national farm monthly), Calgary, Alberta, Canada, associate editor, 1954-75; McKinnon, Allen & Associates, Calgary, accredited appraiser, 1976—; member of Alberta Land Compensation Board, 1978—. *Military service:* Canadian Army, Water Transport, 1939-45; became sergeant.

MEMBER: Agricultural Institute of Canada, Appraisal Institute of Canada, Writers' Union of Canada, Canadian Farm Writers' Federation, Alberta Farm Writers' Association (past president).

AWARDS, HONORS: Awards from Canadian Farm Writers Federation, 1961, 1962, 1968, 1969, 1973, 1974, and 1975; Pacific Northwest Writers Conference award, 1963, for short story; Canadian Children's Book Award, Little, Brown, 1964, for *The White Calf; Pen and Plow* was named best nonfiction book by an Alberta writer, 1976; Vicky Metcalf Award, 1979, for contributions to Canadian literature.

WRITINGS:

YOUNG ADULT FICTION

The White Calf, illustrated by Gerald Tailfeathers, Little, Brown (Boston, MA), 1965.
The White Peril, Little, Brown, 1966.
The In-Betweener, Little, Brown, 1967.
The Smoke Horse, McClelland & Stewart (Toronto), 1968.
West to Cattle Country, McClelland & Stewart, 1975.
Johnny Eagleclaw, John LeBel Enterprises, 1982.

OTHER

The Romance of Beef, Public Press, 1967.
Pen and Plow, Public Press, 1976.
Turn Him Loose!, Western Producer Prairie Books, 1977.
Alberta Hereford Heritage, Advisor Graphics, 1981.

Contributor to anthologies, including *Chinook Arch,* Co-op Press, 1967; *Western Profiles,* Alberta Education, 1979; *Transitions,* Alberta Education, 1979; and *The Alberta Diamond Jubilee Anthology,* Hurtig,

1979. Former columnist, under pseudonym Pete Williams, for *Country Guide;* former freelance columnist for *Victoria Times.* Contributor of articles and short stories to numerous magazines and newspapers, including *Toronto Star Weekly, Liberty, Canadian Geographic Journal,* and *Cattlemen.*

WORK IN PROGRESS: Dog of Destiny, a juvenile book.

SIDELIGHTS: Cliff Faulknor's adventure stories for young adults are noted for their action-based plots and accurate historical details. The author's best known work, the trilogy beginning with *The White Calf,* portrays the coming of age of a young Blackfoot Indian brave during the middle of the nineteenth century, just as the encroachment of whites into Indian territory begins to pose a threat to their way of life.

As *The White Calf* opens, Eagle Child, age twelve, finds an orphaned albino buffalo calf, a creature so rare that tribal legend holds it as a symbol of good luck. While Eagle Child spends the summer of his twelfth year learning the skills necessary to become a brave, he also raises the calf until the time when it can be set free to roam with the herd. Critics note that the calf symbolizes Eagle Child's journey to manhood. Janice R. Scott writes in a *Library Journal* review that the details of Blackfoot ways, including hunting buffalo and performing rituals, would likely "appeal to adventure-minded boys." A reviewer in *Times Literary Supplement* highlights the realistic portrayal of Faulknor's Indian characters. "In a simple prose with no false note," according to the critic, Faulknor presents characters who are "alive and real," offering "exciting" descriptions of hunting, inter-tribal warfare, and performances of tribal rituals.

"The events are exciting, and the details of Blackfoot life are authentic, but [*The White Calf*] suffers a little from the presence of two heroes"—Eagle Child and his brother War Bonnet—according to John Robert Sorfleet in *Twentieth-Century Children's Writers.* Its sequel, *The White Peril,* however, offers the advantages of the earlier book, including excitement and realistic detail, claims Sorfleet, without introducing the possible problem of reader-identification presented by dual heroes. In *The White Peril,* which takes place five years after the earlier book, Eagle Child's buffalo has become a rogue killer that must be destroyed, and the increasing presence of white settlers threatens the survival of the tribe. While a

critic in *Kirkus Reviews* feels that "the theme of the disintegration of the tribe is stronger than the story can support," and complains of the lack of a sympathetic central character, Sorfleet comments: "The book contains a realistic admixture of sadness and joys, with the coming of the whites viewed from an Indian perspective."

In what Sorfleet calls "a fitting conclusion to the trilogy," *The Smoke Horse* brings Eagle Child to full manhood when he learns the quality of mercy. Faulknor relies again on the action of hunting and fighting scenes to fill out a story that Sorfleet dubs "well-crafted and gripping, with many flashes of Faulknor's subtle humour and adept dialogue." Of the highly praised historical background of his adventures, Faulknor told *Twentieth-Century Children's Writers:* "As for the story setting and background information, I research this very carefully. And if I am dealing with the past, my story must be true to the history of that period, and the setting must be as it was during that period."

Faulknor once commented: "When I was a youth, I could idle away a whole summer's day on some beach without a twinge of conscience, just listening to the music of the waves or watching galleon-like cumulus clouds moving across the sky. Later, I was somehow inveigled into taking what is often referred to as 'higher education' and soon fell prey to the work ethic demon. In that grinding process and the various careers which followed, the boy on the beach was lost. But I found him again, or at least a part of him, when I began to write adventure stories for juveniles. I did not plan any of these stories. My daily journalistic chores gave me about all the planning I could stomach. With my juveniles, I just sat down at my typewriter and put my characters into motion. If any new ones appeared I tossed them into the pot and stirred. The characters themselves did the rest. As they went about their lives they took me with them. I recommend this as a cure to those who feel that they are growing old in heart."

BIOGRAPHICAL/CRITICAL SOURCES:

BOOKS

Twentieth-Century Children's Writers, 4th edition, St. James Press (Detroit), 1995.

PERIODICALS

Books in Canada, December, 1982, p. 11.

Kirkus Reviews, May 15, 1965, p. 499; October 1, 1966, p. 1054.

Library Journal, October 15, 1965, p. 4615; June 15, 1967, p. 2449.

Times Literary Supplement, November 24, 1966, p. 1069; March 14, 1968, p. 263.

*   *   *

FISCHER, John Martin   1952-

PERSONAL: Born December 26, 1952, in Cleveland, OH; son of Joseph (a physician) and Armeda (Schutte) Fischer. *Education:* Stanford University, B.A., 1975, M.A., 1975; graduate study at Oxford University, 1978-79; Cornell University, M.A., 1980, Ph.D., 1982.

ADDRESSES: Home—821 South University Dr., Riverside, CA 92507. *Office*—Department of Philosophy, University of California, Riverside, CA 92521.

CAREER: Cornell University, Ithaca, NY, assistant professor, summer, 1981; Yale University, New Haven, CT, assistant professor, 1981-85, associate professor of philosophy, 1985-88; University of California, Riverside, associate professor, 1988-90, professor, 1990—.

MEMBER: American Philosophical Association, Phi Beta Kappa.

AWARDS, HONORS: Henry Rushton Fairclough Prize, Department of Classics, Stanford, 1975; Cornell University Graduate Fellowship, 1976-77; Cornell Continuing Humanities Fellowship, 1977-78; Cornell Program on Science, Technology, and Society Fellowship, 1978-79; National Endowment for the Humanities Fellowship for Independent Study and Research, 1983-84, 1994-95; Center for Ideas and Society, University of California, Riverside, Residential Fellowship, 1991.

WRITINGS:

(Editor) *Moral Responsibility,* Cornell University Press (Ithaca, NY), 1986.

(Editor) *God, Foreknowledge and Freedom,* Stanford University Press (Stanford, CA), 1989.

(Editor) *The Metaphysics of Death,* Stanford University Press, 1989.

(Editor with M. Ravizza) *Ethics: Problems and Principles,* Harcourt (San Diego, CA), 1991.

(Editor, with Ravizza) *Perspectives on Moral Responsibility,* Cornell University Press, 1993.

The Metaphysics of Free Will: An Essay on Control, Basil Blackwell (Oxford, England), 1994.

Contributor to books, including *Responsibility, Character, and the Emotions: New Essays on Moral Psychology,* edited by Ferdinand Schoeman, Cambridge University Press, 1987; *Divine and Human Action: Essays in the Metaphysics of Theism,* edited by Thomas Morris, Cornell University Press, 1988; and *The Encyclopedia of Ethics,* edited by Lawrence C. Becker, Garland Publishing, 1992. Also contributor to periodicals, including *Ethics, Philosophical Review, Philosophical Studies, Journal of Social Philosophy,* and *Journal of Philosophy.*

WORK IN PROGRESS: An Introduction to Free Will, for Westview Press, and *Responsibility and Control: A Theory of Moral Responsibility,* for Cambridge University Press, both with M. Ravizza.

*   *   *

FLORES, Janis   1946-

PERSONAL: Born January 12, 1946, in Fort Benton, MT; daughter of J. Eldon (an airline dispatcher) and Dorothea (a legal secretary; maiden name, Dickens) Overholser; married Raynaldo G. Flores (a horseshoer), January 13, 1968. *Education:* Immaculate Heart College, Los Angeles, CA, B.A., 1968; St. Luke Hospital, Pasadena, CA, license in medical technology, 1969. *Avocational interests:* Reading, riding and training four Arabian horses, training her dogs, sewing. "I love animals and belong to several wildlife and other organizations, among them Defenders of Wildlife."

ADDRESSES: Home—1200 Ferguson Rd., Sebastopol, CA 95472. *Agent*—Emilie Jacobson, Curtis Brown Ltd., Ten Astor St., New York, NY 10003.

CAREER: Live Oak Laboratory, Arcadia, CA, medical technologist, 1969-72; Biskind Laboratory, Santa Rosa, CA, supervisor, 1972-76; Empire Laboratory, Santa Rosa, supervisor, 1976-79; full-time writer.

MEMBER: Author's Guild, Novelists Inc., California Writers Club.

WRITINGS:

NOVELS

Hawkshead, Doubleday (New York City), 1976.
Peregrine House, Doubleday, 1977.
Gyrfalcon Hall, Ace Books (New York City), 1977.
Bittersweet, Bantam (New York City), 1978.
Cynara, Ace Books, 1979.
High Dominion, Signet (New York City), 1981.
Loving Ties, Fawcett (New York City), 1986.
Running in Place, Fawcett, 1987.
Divided Loyalties, Fawcett, 1989.
Above Reproach, Fawcett, 1990.
Touched by Fire, Fawcett, 1991.
Siren Song, Fawcett, 1993.

Also author of various contemporary romances, 1981-95.

*   *   *

FONTANA, Biancamaria   1952-

PERSONAL: Born September 10, 1952, in Milan, Italy; daughter of Giuseppe (a manager) and Luciana (a manager; maiden name, Garrone) Fontana. *Education:* Universita degli Studi-Milan, Ph.D., 1974; Cambridge University, Ph.D., 1983.

ADDRESSES: Home—24 Avenue Servan, 1006 Lausanne, Switzerland. *Office*—Faculty of Social and Political Sciences, BFSH2, University of Lausanne, 1015 Lausanne, Switzerland; also (for correspondence) King's College, Cambridge CB2 1ST, England.

CAREER: Fondazione l'Einaudi, Turin, Italy, fellow in the history of ideas, 1977-79; Cambridge University, Cambridge, England, fellow of King's College, 1979-84; freelance writer and translator, 1984-86; University of Edinburgh, Edinburgh, Scotland, visiting fellow at the Institute for Advanced Study, 1986; European University Institute, Florence, Italy, fellow, 1986-87; University of Lausanne, Switzerland, professor of the history of political ideas, 1991—; Centre de Recherche d'Epistemologie Applique (CREA) of the CNRS, Paris, France, 1994—; writer.

WRITINGS:

I Principi di Economic Politica di J. S. Mill (title means "Principles of Political Economy"), two volumes, Utet, 1983.
Rethinking the Politics of Commercial Society: The Edinburgh Review, 1802-1832, Cambridge University Press (New York City), 1985.
The Political Writings of Benjamin Constant, Cambridge University Press, 1987.
Benjamin Constant and the Post-Revolutionary Mind, Yale University Press (New Haven, CT), 1991.
(Editor) *The Invention of the Modern Republic,* Cambridge University Press, 1994.

WORK IN PROGRESS: Dangerous Liaisons: Captain Laclos and His Novel.

SIDELIGHTS: Reviewer Peter Mandler informed readers of the *Times Literary Supplement* that Biancamaria Fontana's book *Rethinking the Politics of Commercial Society: The Edinburgh Review, 1802-1832* represents "a major contribution to a crucial historical project." Fontana's book is a study of the Scottish philosophers of the *Edinburgh Review* and their reaction to the French Revolution and its aftermath. The author contends that the revolution and the Napoleonic wars forced these Scotsmen to relocate in London, the capital of the empire, where they could play an active role in guiding Great Britain's politicians and lawmakers. She emphasizes that their efforts to reform the political system were eminently successful. For this, the critic wrote, "she demonstrates a [broad] appreciation of what mattered in early nineteenth-century politics" and an unusually shrewd "grasp of the Edinburgh point of view."

BIOGRAPHICAL/CRITICAL SOURCES:

PERIODICALS

Times Literary Supplement, May 2, 1986.

*   *   *

FOOTE, Horton   1916-

PERSONAL: Born March 14, 1916, in Wharton, TX; son of Albert (a merchant and cotton farmer) and Hallie (Brooks) Foote; married Lillian Vallish (a theatrical producer), June 4, 1945 (died August 5, 1992); children: Barbara Hallie, Albert Horton,

Walter Vallish, Daisy Brooks. *Education:* Studied at Pasadena Playhouse School of Theatre, 1933-35, and Tamara Daykarhanova School of Theatre, 1937-39.

ADDRESSES: Home—505 N. Houston St., Wharton, TX 77488. *Agent*—Barbara Hoegenson Agency 19 W. 44 St., Suite 1000, New York, NY 10036.

CAREER: Writer for stage, screen, and television. Actor in Broadway plays, including *The Eternal Road, The Fifth Column, The Coggerers,* and *Texas Town,* 1932-42; King Smith School of Creative Arts, Washington, DC, workshop director, 1944; Productions, Inc. (a semi-professional theatre), Washington, DC, manager and instructor in playwriting and acting, c. 1945-49. Writer of dramatic teleplays for Columbia Broadcasting Company (CBS), National Broadcasting Company (NBC), American Broadcasting Company (ABC), Public Broadcasting Service (PBS), and British Broadcasting Corp. (BBC); contributor of scripts to dramatic television series, including *Kraft Playhouse, DuPont Show of the Week,* and *Playhouse 90.*

MEMBER: Writers Guild of America, Authors Guild, Dramatists Guild, Ensemble Studio Theatre (executive board member), Texas Institute of Letters, Fellowship of Southern Writers.

AWARDS, HONORS: Emmy Award nomination, 1958, for *Old Man;* Academy Award (Oscar) for best screenplay, Academy of Motion Picture Arts and Sciences for best screenplay, and Writers Guild of America Screen Award, both 1962, both for *To Kill a Mockingbird;* Academy Award (Oscar) for best screenplay, Academy of Motion Picture Arts and Sciences, and Writers Guild Award for best original screenplay, both 1983, and Christopher Award, all for *Tender Mercies;* Academy Award (Oscar) nomination for best screenplay, Academy of Motion Picture Arts and Sciences, 1985, for *The Trip to Bountiful;* Capestolo Award, 1987; Dickinson College Arts Award, William Inge Lifetime Achievement Award, and Evelyn Burkey Award, Writers Guild, all 1989; Alley Theatre Award, Headliners' Club Award, both 1991; Torch of Hope Award, Barbara Barondess Theatre Lab Alliance, 1992; Laurel Award, Writers Guild East Beverly Hilton Hotel, 1993; Lontinkle Award, Texas Institute of Letters, 1994; Lucille Lortel Award, 1995; Pulitzer Prize for Drama, 1995, for *The Young Man from Atlanta;* American Academy of Arts and Letters literature award, Outer Critics Circle Special Achievement Award, Heartland Film Festival Lifetime Achieve-

ment Award, all 1995; Theatre Hall of Fame inductee, 1996; honorary degrees received from Drew University, Austin College, Spalding University, and American Film Institute.

WRITINGS:

PUBLISHED PLAYS

Only the Heart (also see below; three-act; produced in New York City at Bijou Theatre, 1944), Dramatists Play Service (New York City), 1944.

The Chase (also see below; three-act; produced on Broadway, 1952), Dramatists Play Service, 1952, published as a novel under same title, Rinehart, 1956.

The Trip to Bountiful (also see below; adapted from his teleplay of the same title; three-act; produced on Broadway, 1953), Dramatists Play Service, 1954.

A Young Lady of Property (also see below; adapted from his teleplays of the same titles; contains *The Dancers* [produced in Los Angeles at Fiesta Hall, 1963], *A Young Lady of Property, The Old Beginning, John Turner Davis* [produced in New York City, 1958], *Death of the Old Man,* and *The Oil Well*), Dramatists Play Service, 1954.

The Traveling Lady (also see below; adapted from his teleplay of the same title; three-act; produced on Broadway, 1954), Dramatists Play Service, 1955.

The Midnight Caller (also see below; adapted from his teleplay of the same title; one-act; produced in New York City, 1958), Dramatists Play Service, 1959.

Harrison, Texas: Eight Television Plays, Harcourt (New York City), 1959.

Three Plays (also see below; contains *Roots in a Parched Ground* and two plays based on stories by Faulkner, *Old Man* and *Tomorrow*), Harcourt, 1962.

Tomorrow (also see below; based on story by William Faulkner; produced Off-Broadway, 1985), Dramatists Play Service, 1963.

The Roads to Home (also see below; adapted from his teleplay of the same title; three one-act plays; contains *Nightingale, The Dearest of Friends,* and *Spring Dance;* produced in New York City at Manhattan Punch Line Theatre, 1982), Dramatists Play Service, 1982.

Blind Date (one-act; part of "Marathon '86;" produced in New York City at Ensemble Studio Theatre, 1986), Dramatists Play Service, 1986.

Selected One-Act Plays of Horton Foote, edited by Gerald C. Wood, Southern Methodist University Press (Dallas, TX), 1988.

The Man Who Climbed the Pecan Trees (produced in Los Angeles, CA, at Loft Theatre, 1988), Dramatists Play Service, 1989.

Habitation of Dragons (also see below; produced at Pittsburgh Playhouse, 1988), Dramatists Play Service, 1993.

4 New Plays (also see below; contains *The Habitation of Dragons* [also see below; adapted from his teleplay], *Night Seasons* [produced in New York City at Signature Theatre Company, 1994], *Dividing the Estate* [produced in Princeton, NJ, at McArthur Theatre, 1989], and *Talking Pictures* [produced in New York City at Signature Theatre Company, 1994]), Smith and Kraus (Newbury, VT), 1993.

The Tears of My Sister, The Prisoner's Song, The One-Armed Man, The Land of the Astronauts, Dramatists Play Service, 1993.

The Young Man from Atlanta (produced in New York City, by Signature Theatre Company), published in *American Theatre* magazine, September, 1995.

UNPUBLISHED PLAYS

Wharton Dance, American Actors Theatre, New York City, 1940.

Texas Town, produced in New York City at Weidman Studio, 1941, produced Off-Broadway, 1942.

Out of My House, produced in New York City, 1942.

Two Southern Idylls (double-bill; contains *Miss Love* and *The Girls*) produced in New York City at Neighborhood Playhouse, 1945.

Celebration (one-act), produced in New York City at Maxine Elliott Theatre, 1948.

In a Coffin in Egypt, produced Off Broadway, 1980.

The Old Friends, produced Off Broadway, 1982.

The Road to the Graveyard (one-act; part of "Marathon '85"), produced in New York City at Ensemble Studio Theatre, 1985.

Also author of plays produced Off-Broadway, including *Arrival and Departure.*

"ORPHANS' HOME" CYCLE

Roots in a Parched Ground (also see below; adapted from his teleplay *The Night of the Storm,*), Dramatists Play Service, 1962.

On Valentine's Day (also see below; produced Off-Broadway, 1980), Dramatists Play Service, 1987.

1918 (also see below; produced Off-Broadway, 1982), Dramatists Play Service, 1987.

Convicts (also see below), produced in New York City at Ensemble Studio Theatre, 1983.

Courtship (also see below; produced in Louisville, KY, by Actors' Theatre, 1984), Dramatists Play Service, 1984.

Cousins (also see below), produced in Los Angeles at Loft Theatre, 1984.

Lily Dale (also see below), produced Off-Broadway, 1986.

The Widow Claire (also see below), produced Off-Broadway, 1986, published in *The Best Plays of 1986-1987,* Dodd (New York City).

"Courtship," "Valentine's Day," and "1918": Three Plays from "The Orphans' Home" Cycle (also see below under the title *The Story of a Marriage,* 1987), Grove Press (New York City), 1987.

"Roots in a Parched Ground," "Convicts," "Lily Dale," and "The Widow Claire" (also see below), Grove Press, 1988.

The Death of Papa (also see below), Dramatists Play Service, 1989.

"Cousins" and "The Death of Papa": Two Plays from "The Orphans' Home" Cycle, Grove Press, 1989.

SCREENPLAYS

Storm Fear (based on a novel by Clinton Seeley), United Artists, 1956.

To Kill a Mockingbird (also see below; based on the novel by Harper Lee), Universal, 1962, published as *The Screenplay of "To Kill a Mockingbird,"* Harcourt, 1964.

Baby, the Rain Must Fall (based on his teleplay, *The Traveling Lady*), Columbia, 1965.

Tomorrow (based on a story by Faulkner), Filmgroup, 1973.

Tender Mercies (also see below), Universal, 1983.

1918 (based on his play of the same title), Cinecom International, 1984.

On Valentine's Day (based on his play of the same title), Angelika Films, 1985.

The Trip to Bountiful (also see below; based on his teleplay of the same title), Island Pictures, 1985.

"To Kill a Mockingbird," "Tender Mercies," and "The Trip to Bountiful": Three Screenplays, Grove Press, 1989.

Convicts (based on his play of the same title), Management Company Entertainment Group, 1991.

Of Mice and Men (based on the novel by John Steinbeck), Metro-Goldwyn-Mayer, 1992.

Lily Dale (based on his play of the same title), Products Entertainment Group, 1996.

Also author of screenplay, *Spring Moon*, based on the novel by Bette Bao Lord, 1987, and *Courtship*, based on his play of the same title.

TELEVISION PLAYS

Only the Heart, NBC, 1947.
Ludie Brooks, CBS, 1951.
The Travelers, NBC, 1952.
The Old Beginning, NBC, 1953.
The Oil Well, NBC, 1953.
The Midnight Caller, NBC, 1953.
Trip to Bountiful, NBC, 1953.
The Rocking Chair, NBC, 1953.
Expectant Relations, NBC, 1953.
Tears of My Sister, NBC, 1953.
Young Lady of Property, NBC, 1953.
John Turner Davis, NBC, 1953.
Death of the Old Man, NBC, 1953.
The Dancers, NBC, 1954.
Shadow of Willie Greer, NBC, 1954.
Roads to Home, ABC, 1955.
Flight, NBC, 1956.
Drugstore: Sunday Noon, ABC, 1956.
The Traveling Lady, CBS, 1957.
Member of the Family, CBS, 1957.
Old Man (based on a novel by Faulkner), CBS, 1959, Hallmark Hall of Fame, 1996.
Tomorrow, CBS, 1960.
The Shape of the River, CBS, 1960.
The Night of the Storm, CBS, 1960.
The Gambling Heart, NBC, 1964.
The Displaced Person (based on a story by Flannery O'Connor), PBS, 1977.
Barn Burning (based on a story by Faulkner), PBS, 1980.
Keeping On, PBS, 1983.
The Story of a Marriage (based on his plays *Courtship, On Valentine's Day,* and *1918*), PBS, 1987.
The Habitation of Dragons, TNT, 1992.

OTHER

Author of the book for *Gone with the Wind* (a musical version of Margaret Mitchell's novel), produced on the West End, 1972, produced in Los Angeles at Dorothy Chandler Pavilion, 1973.

ADAPTATIONS: The Chase was adapted to film by Lillian Hellman for Columbia Pictures in 1966.

SIDELIGHTS: "From the beginning," Horton Foote once wrote, "most of my plays have taken place in the imaginary town of Harrison, Texas, and it seems to me a more unlikely subject could not be found in these days of Broadway and world theatre, than this attempt of mine to recreate a small Southern town and its people. But I did not choose this task, this place, or these people to write about so much as they chose me, and I try to write of them with honesty." While the Wharton, Texas, native admits the unlikelihood of his rural settings among the contemporary fares of Broadway and Hollywood, his lean style is equally improbable. At a time when the sensational and carnal preside over a great portion of the popular dramatic arts, Foote continues to stress the subtle and the intimate. "What seems remarkable about Foote's career," wrote Charles Champlin in the *Los Angeles Times*, "is that across all the media and amid all the conflicts of art versus commerce, in which art is always the long-odds underdog, he has produced a coherent body of work. . . . It is most often an intimate, loving, perceptive exploration of ordinary people and their often extraordinary resilience, courage, persistence and wisdom in the face of trials, disappointments and dreams that have had to be deferred or abandoned."

Foote began his theatrical career as an actor, studying first in California, then in New York, where he was cast in several Off-Broadway plays during the late 1930s. It was while performing with the American Actors Company between 1939 and 1942 that Foote realized his talent as a dramatist, and in 1942 his play *Texas Town* was produced in New York City. For several years during the 1940s Foote operated a production company in Washington, DC, and managed to get two more works produced in New York, *Out of My House* (1942) and *Only the Heart* (1944). "It is impossible not to believe absolutely in the reality of his characters," wrote Brooks Atkinson in his review of *Texas Town* for the *New York Times*. Of *Out of My House*, Atkinson commented: "Foote pulls himself together in a vibrant and glowing last act that is compact and bitterly realistic." Foote's early plays—emotionally restrained dramas emphasizing character development and set within the social context of the rural South—established a recognizable pattern that he has rarely wavered from.

In the late 1940s, while still writing for the stage, Foote also began working in television. He adapted many of his own dramas for such showcases as *Playhouse 90* and *Kraft Playhouse,* and occasionally adapted the work of other Southern writers to television, including William Faulkner's *Old Man* and *Tomorrow.* In all, Foote adapted more than thirty dramas for television. His book *Harrison, Texas,* a collection of eight television plays written and produced between January, 1953, and March, 1954, elicited reviewer praise. "Television is in redemptive hands as long as it can work with art like this," wrote a *Saturday Review* critic.

In Foote's acclaimed 1953 teleplay, *The Trip to Bountiful,* an elderly widow longs to escape the cramped Houston, Texas, apartment she shares with her unsupportive son and his lazy wife. The widow eventually journeys to her small-town birthplace, only to find desolation instead of a sentimental homecoming. Prompted by *Bountiful*'s television success, Foote adapted it for the theatre, and it ran on Broadway that same year. In 1985, a film version earned Foote an Oscar nomination for best screenplay.

In 1956, Foote's play *The Chase* was published as a novel and received critical acclaim for its dramatic power and strong characterizations. Anthony Boucher made these comments: "Sharply effective as a melodrama of violence, it is also powerful as a novel of character, probing deeply into many lives . . . and studying the inherent moral and psychological problems of violence." While *Commonweal*'s W. J. Smith found the book's lengthy epilogue to be ineffective, he was enthusiastic about the story itself: "The characterizations are excellent, the action is fast and suspenseful and the ramifications of the plot neatly interlocked. The novel attains a level beyond that of the mere thriller—psychological melodrama, perhaps, describes it better."

With the demise of live television in the late 1950s, Foote moved his dramatic efforts to the movie screen. His adaptation of Harper Lee's novel *To Kill a Mockingbird* won the 1962 Academy Award for best screenplay, and Gregory Peck received the award for best actor for his portrayal of Atticus Finch, a lawyer and father. Concentrating on the lives of Finch's two children in depression-era, rural Alabama, the film reveals the prevailing bigotry of a small town as the children watch their father defend in court a black man falsely accused of rape. The film culminates in a guilty verdict, but not until the children witness the harmful consequences of prejudice and learn through their father's noble efforts the value of integrity. Bosley Crowther lauded the film's "feeling for children." In the *New York Times* he wrote: "There is . . . so much delightful observation of their spirit, energy, and charm. . . . Especially in their relations with their father."

Following the success of *Mockingbird,* Foote wrote such screenplays as *Baby, the Rain Must Fall* and an adaptation of Faulkner's *Tomorrow.* But he withdrew into semi-retirement during the 1970s to live on a farm in New Hampshire with his family. His eventual reemergence in Hollywood came at the suggestion of a friend, actor Robert Duvall, who requested a screenplay from the writer. The result was *Tender Mercies,* the 1983 movie that won Foote a second Academy Award for best screenplay and Duvall an Oscar for best actor.

The film portrays a famous country singer who succumbs to alcoholism and loses his career and marriage. Eventually he finds solace with a young widow and her son in a Texas roadside motel. True to Foote's enduring, subtle style, "the excitement of *Tender Mercies* lies below the surface," wrote David Sterritt in the *Saturday Evening Post.* "It's not the quick change of fast action, the flashy performances or the eye-zapping cuts. Rather, it's something much more rare—the thrill of watching characters grow, personalities deepen, relationships ripen and mature. It's the pleasure of rediscovering the dramatic richness of decency, honesty, compassion and a few other qualities that have become rare visitors to the silver screen." Vincent Canby wrote in the *New York Times* that "Foote's screenplay . . . doesn't overexplain or overanalyze. It has a rare appreciation for understatement, which is the style of its characters if not of the actual narrative." Canby called Foote's *Tender Mercies* "the best thing he's ever done for films."

Even before his successful return to the screen, Foote had begun work on a nine-part dramatic series called *The Orphans' Home.* Based on the life of his own father in the early twentieth century, the cycle follows several generations of the Robedaux family and depicts their hardships amid the decline of the plantation aristocracy in southern Texas. Critical response to the series, which included the filmed *1918, On Valentine's Day,* and *Convicts,* has been divided between opponents and proponents of Foote's typically subdued style. Writing in the *National Review,* Chilton Williamson, Jr. thought Foote "trivializes life into a banal serenity," while Canby argued that

Foote's characters, "being so resolutely ordinary, become particular." Canby called *1918* a "writer's movie. . . . One that, for better or worse, pays no attention to the demands for pacing and narrative emphasis that any commercially oriented Hollywood producer would have insisted on. The very flatness of its dramatic line is its dramatic point."

In 1992 Foote provided the screenplay for the Metro-Goldwyn-Mayer film adaptation of John Steinbeck's *Of Mice and Men.* The same year, Lillian, his wife of forty-seven years, died. For a short time the prolific writer produced no new work and there was speculation that age, illness, and the loss of his long-time partner may have finally ended his career. Then in 1994 he was given a rare opportunity when an Off-Off-Broadway playhouse proposed an entire season devoted to his work. The tiny, seventy-five-seat Signature Theatre Company in lower Manhattan dedicated each of its first three seasons to the plays of a single American dramatist. Romulus Linney, Lee Blessing, and Edward Albee had all been thus honored, and Foote became the fourth playwright whose works were featured. Two previously produced plays, *Talking Pictures* and *Night Seasons,* along with two world premieres, *The Young Man from Atlanta* and *Laura Dennis,* were produced.

In an *American Theatre* magazine interview Foote described his year with the Signature company. "It was a wonderful experience and satisfying on every count," he said. "I don't know how many playwrights get that opportunity. . . . At the Signature, we had not always the best conditions, everyone had to kind of make do—but the theatre somehow managed to create a good feeling that permeated the whole experience." As a whole, the season met with mixed critical response. *New York Times* reviewer Ben Brantley noted, "These performances show that even Mr. Foote's lesser works provide a visceral richness actors thrive on. Being able to focus on that quality for the last several months has been a luxury for New York theatergoers." This same quality, however, irked others. John Simon complained in *New York,* "Foote's specialty is putting tiny lives under the microscope and making them, paradoxically, loom even less large than they are."

The experience, however, gained the multiple Academy Award-winning Foote an honor that had long eluded him: the Pulitzer Prize for drama for the play staged as Signature's third production, *The Young Man from Atlanta.* Set in Houston, Texas in 1950, the play has all the markings of a Foote script: a small cast of leading characters, intimate settings, and action accented with details of ordinary life. At the same time it resonates with stylistic echoes of Arthur Miller, Tennessee Williams, and William Inge—Foote's theatrical contemporaries.

The plot focuses on Will and Lily Dale Kidder, an elderly couple nearing retirement and faced with a series of crises that challenge their faith in God, country, and themselves. Their only son, Bill, has drowned himself in a Florida lake. Lily Dale desperately turns to the church for solace, while Will grapples with his thirty-seven-year-old son's suicide and the uncomfortable news that it might have been the result of a homosexual affair he was having with a grifter ten years his junior.

To compound their problems, Will is fired from his job at the Sunshine Southern Wholesale Grocery, where he has worked for nearly forty years, and replaced by a younger colleague he trained in the business. Lily Dale has been secretly giving money from the couple's savings to their son's friend, Randy Carter, the "young man from Atlanta" in the play's title. When Carter appears in Houston, Will refuses to see him or talk to him, knowing that he is linked to his son's death. Lily Dale, however, is comforted by the stories the young man tells about her boy. Though central to the play, Carter never appears on stage. Rather, he remains an intangible presence for the Kidders as they try to restore order and hope to their lives. In the end their fate is unknown. As the lights fade to black, Will holds his wife and assures her that everything will be all right.

The Pulitzer garnered by *The Young Man from Atlanta* is an indication of the play's success with critics. Competition was especially keen in 1995, with such luminaries as August Wilson, David Mamet, and Terrence McNally all nominated for the award. *Chicago Tribune* critic Richard Christiansen, who served as chairman for the Pulitzer's five-person jury, observed, "This is a small drama with large emotional impact, its force gathered by the piling up of the many details of daily life that Foote has marshaled to show the extent of the Kidders' domestic tragedy." Frank Rich, reviewer for the *New York Times,* also noted the play's emotional force. He wrote, "Months after seeing this play, I can still hear [Will's] gruff voice swell unexpectedly on the line 'I just want my son back,' keeping company with the rest of us who have known inconsolable grief." Another *New York Times* critic, Vincent Canby, observed, "*The Young Man from Atlanta* doesn't soothe or lift any hearts. It's tough, one of Mr. Foote's most serious and scathing works."

For all the attention it received in its first year, Foote's Pulitzer-winning play was not widely exposed to audiences. Rich noted, "To be exact, only 1,700 people saw *The Young Man from Atlanta* during its four weeks at [the Signature]—fewer than see *Show Boat* in a single night." The author himself, though, was unconcerned with numbers. "You have to learn the lessons poets have learned," he told the *Christian Science Monitor.* "T. S. Elliot—when he had the Criterion Magazine, I think the most subscriptions he ever had were 1,500 subscribers, but it had an enormous influence. And his poems, and [Ezra] Pound's, they all found a way to do their work. And that's all you can ask, is to be allowed to do your work."

BIOGRAPHICAL/CRITICAL SOURCES:

BOOKS

Contemporary Literary Criticism, Volume 51, Gale (Detroit), 1989.
Dictionary of Literary Biography, Volume 26: *American Screenwriters,* Gale, 1984.

PERIODICALS

America, May 10, 1986.
American Theatre, September, 1995.
Atlanta Journal and Constitution, April 19, 1995.
Chicago Tribune, May 14, 1985; February 7, 1986; January 8, 1987; February 23, 1995; May 7, 1995.
Christian Science Monitor, March 22, 1995.
Commonweal, March 16, 1956; February 26, 1988, pp. 110-115; January 13, 1995.
Los Angeles Times, March 4, 1983; April 3, 1983; April 3, 1984; April 17, 1984; June 12, 1985; December 23, 1985; March 15, 1986; December 13, 1987.
National Review, June 14, 1985; June 6, 1986.
New Republic, March 31, 1986.
Newsday, November 21, 1986.
New York, May 26, 1986; January 5, 1987; April 6, 1987; November 21, 1994; February 27, 1995.
New Yorker, December 29, 1986.
New York Herald Tribune Book Review, February 6, 1956.
New York Times, April 30, 1941; January 8, 1942; December 7, 1942; April 5, 1944; April 16, 1952; November 4, 1953; October 28, 1954; February 19, 1956; April 12, 1982; February 8, 1983; March 4, 1983; March 13, 1983; April 21, 1985; April 26, 1985; April 28, 1985; May 27, 1985; December 20, 1985; April 11, 1986; April 13, 1986; May 4, 1986; May 13, 1986; August 15, 1986; October 8, 1986; October 17, 1986; November 21, 1986; December 18, 1986; April 5, 1987; December 2, 1989; December 3, 1989; October 2, 1994; January 30, 1995; March 14, 1995; April 6, 1995; April 19, 1995; April 23, 1995.
New York Times Magazine, February 9, 1986.
San Francisco Chronicle, February 26, 1956.
Saturday Evening Post, October, 1983.
Saturday Review, February 18, 1956.
Time, April 14, 1986.
TV Guide, April 4, 1987.
Washington Post, February 8, 1983; April 29, 1983; January 31, 1985; April 25, 1986.

—Sketch by Lane Glenn

*   *   *

FREEMAN, Roger A(nthony Wilson)   1928-
(Roger Anthony Freeman)

PERSONAL: Born May 11, 1928, in Ipswich, England; married Jean Margaret Blain; children: Sarah, Emma, Daniel. *Religion:* Church of England.

ADDRESSES: Home—May's Barn, May's Lane, Dedham, Colchester, Essex CO7 6EW, England.

CAREER: Farmer; F. F. C. Freeman & Sons (family enterprise), Colchester, Essex, England, partner, 1959—. Historical advisor and presenter in documentary films, including *Wing and a Prayer: Utah Man;* historical and technical advisor to *Memphis Belle,* Warner Bros., 1990. Advisor to air museums and moderator for airwar symposia; lecturer and broadcaster.

WRITINGS:

NONFICTION

(With others) *U.S. Army and Air Force Fighters,* Harleyford (London), 1961.
The Mighty Eighth, Doubleday (London), 1970, Motorbooks International (Osceola, WI), 1992.

Republic Thunderbolt, Ducimus, 1970.

American Bombers, Volume I, Profile, 1972.

Mustang at War, Doubleday, 1974.

The U.S. Strategic Bomber, Macdonald & Jane's (London), 1975.

Camouflage and Markings: U.S.A.A.F., Ducimus, 1975.

B-17 Fortress at War, Scribner, 1977.

Airfields of the Eighth: Then and Now, Battle of Britain Prints, 1978.

Thunderbolt: A Documentary History, Scribner, 1978, Motorbooks International, 1991.

B-26 Marauder at War, Ian Allan (Surrey), 1978.

Mighty Eighth War Diary, Macdonald & Jane's, 1981, Motorbooks International, 1990.

B-24 Liberator at War, Ian Allan, 1983.

B-17 Flying Fortress, Jane's Publishing, 1983.

Mighty Eighth War Manual, Jane's Publishing, 1984, Motorbooks International, 1991.

Combat Profile: Merlin Mustang, Ian Allan, 1988.

The Hub: Fighter Leader, Airlife (Shrewsbury), 1988, published in the United States as *Zempke's Wolfpack.*

Combat Profile: B-17 Fortress, Ian Allen, 1989, Motorbooks International, 1990.

Experiences at War: The British Airman, Arms & Armor, 1989.

Zempke's Stalag, Smithsonian, 1990.

U.S. Strategic Airpower Europe: 1942-1945, Arms & Armour, 1990.

U.S. Tactical Airpower Europe: 1942-1945, Arms & Armour, 1991.

Experiences at War: The American Airman in Europe, Arms & Armour, 1991.

Britain at War, Cassell, 1991.

The Mighty Eighth in Colour, Arms & Armour, 1992, Specialty (Ocean, NJ), 1992.

The Friendly Invasion, EATB & Lavenham Press, 1992.

The Royal Air Force of World War Two in Colour, Arms & Armour, 1993.

Britain: The First Colour Photographs, Blandford (Dorset), 1994, published in the United States as *Britain: The First Color Photograph Images of Wartime Britain,* Sterling (New York City), 1995.

Airfields of the Ninth: Then and Now, After the Battle, 1994.

(With Steve Birdsall) *Claims to Fame: The B-17 Flying Fortress,* Arms & Armour, 1994, Sterling, 1995.

The Ninth Air Force in Colour, Arms & Armour, 1995.

Author of twelve monographs on U.S. Army Air Force aircraft markings during World War II, Ducimus, 1971-73.

OTHER

(Under name Roger Anthony Freeman) *I Mind the Time* (fiction), Cassell, 1988.

As I Was A-Saying (fiction), Malthouse (Oxford), 1993.

Author of television and military documentaries. Contributor to magazines.

WORK IN PROGRESS: Two historical and one fiction book in preparation; two novels completed but unpublished.

*   *   *

FREEMAN, Roger Anthony
  See FREEMAN, Roger A(nthony Wilson)

*   *   *

FRIEDLANDER, Albert H(oschander)   1927-

PERSONAL: Born May 10, 1927, in Berlin, Germany; came to United States in 1940; son of Alex (a textile broker) and Sali (Hoschander) Friedlander; married Evelyn Philipp (a pianist), July 9, 1961; children: Ariel Judith, Michal Sali, Noam Ilana Alexandra. *Education:* University of Chicago, Ph.B., 1946; Hebrew Union College—Jewish Institute of Religion, Cincinnati, OH, B.H.L., 1950, Rabbi, 1952, D.D., 1977; Columbia University, Ph.D., 1966. *Politics:* Democrat.

ADDRESSES: *Home*—Kent House, Rutland Gardens, London SW7 1BX, England. *Office*—Leo Baeck College, 80, East End Rd., Finchley, London, England.

CAREER: Rabbi, United Hebrew Congregation, Fort Smith, AR, and civilian chaplain, Camp Chaffee, AR, both 1952-56; Temple B'nai Brith, Wilkes-Barre, PA, rabbi, and Wilkes College, instructor in philosophy, both 1956-61; Columbia University, New York City, chaplain and student counselor, 1961-66; Jewish Center of the Hamptons, East

Hampton, Long Island, NY, 1961-65; Wembley Liberal Synagogue, London, rabbi, 1966-71; Leo Baeck College, London, lecturer, 1966-71, director, 1971-82, dean, 1982—; Westminster Synagogue, London, rabbi, 1971—. Visiting professor at Emory University, summer, 1975, Kirchliche Hoschschule, 1988, and University of Basel, 1993; guest lecturer at University of Berlin, summers, 1981, 1982, and other various universities. Broadcaster, "Meditations" and "Words of Faith," British Broadcasting Corporation (BBC) World Service, 1967—.

MEMBER: World Union for Progressive Judaism (member of American board, 1964-66; member of European board, 1967—; vice president, 1983-95), Central Conference of American Rabbis (chair of committee on art and literature, 1961-66), World Conference of Religions for Peace (honorary international president, 1994—), Rabbinic Conference.

AWARDS, HONORS: Interfaith Gold Medal (Sir Sigmund Sternberg Award), presented by Cardinal Hume, 1990; Officers Cross of the German Legion of Merit, presented by President Weizsaecker, 1993.

WRITINGS:

Early Reform Judaism in Germany: An Introduction, published in two parts, Union of American Hebrew Congregations (New York City), 1954-55.

Isaac M. Wise: The World of My Books, American Jewish Archives, 1954.

Reform Judaism in America: The Pittsburgh Platform, Union of American Hebrew Congregations, 1958.

(Translator) Leo Baeck, *This People Israel* (original title, *Dieses Volk*), Holt (New York City), 1968.

Leo Baeck: Teacher of Theresienstadt, Holt, 1968.

Leo Baeck: Leben und Lehre, Deutsche Verlags-Anstalt (Germany), 1973.

Glaube nach Auschwitz, Kaiser Verlag, 1980.

(With Friedrich-Wilhelm Marquardt) *Das Schweigen der Christen und die Menschlichkeit Gottes-Glaeubige Existenz nach Auschwitz,* Kaiser Verlag, 1980.

Versoehnung mit der Geschichte, Neske Verlag, 1985.

The Death Camps and Theology within the Jewish-Christian Dialogue (lecture), Diocese of London, 1985.

(Coauthor with Wolfhart Pannenberg) *Der christliche Glaube und seine juedisch-christliche Herkunft,* Evangelische Kirche in Deutschland (Hanover, Germany), 1986.

(With Elie Wiesel) *The Six Days of Destruction,* Pergamon (Elmsford, NY), 1988.

Ein Streifen Gold: Auf Wegen zur Versoehnung, Kaiser Verlag, 1989.

A Thread of Gold: Journeys towards Reconciliation, SCM Press, 1990.

Die Sechs Tage der Schoepfung und der Zerstoerung, Herder, 1992.

Riders towards the Dawn, Constable (London), 1993.

(With Walter Homolka) *Von der Sintflut ins Paradies,* Wissenschaftliche Buchgesellschaft, 1993.

(With Homolka) *The Gate to Perfection,* Berghahn Books, 1994.

Das Ende der Nacht: Juedische und Christliche Denker nach dem Holocaust, Guetersloh Verlag, 1995.

EDITOR

The Words They Spoke: Statements from the Speeches and Writings of Early Leaders of Reform Judaism, Union of American Hebrew Congregations, 1954.

Never Trust a God over Thirty: New Styles in Campus Ministry, introduction by Paul Goodman, McGraw (New York City), 1967.

Out of the Whirlwind: A Reader of Holocaust Literature, Doubleday (New York City), 1968.

Meir Gertner: An Anthology, B'nai B'rith Hillel Foundation (Washington, DC), 1977.

Georg Salzberger: Leben und Werk, W. Kramer Verlag, 1982.

(And translator) *The Five Megillot,* Central Conference of American Rabbis (New York City), 1983.

CONTRIBUTOR

M. Kaempchen and G. Sartory, editors, *Nahe der Nabe des Rades,* Herderbuecherei (Freiburg, Germany), 1985.

James Luther Adams, Wilhelm Pauck, R. L. Shinn, editors, *The Thought of Paul Tillich,* Harper (New York City), 1985.

A. A. Cohen and P. Mendes-Flohr, editors, *Contemporary Jewish Thought,* Scribner (New York City), 1987.

P. B. Clarke, editor, *The World's Religions,* Reader's Digest Press (New York City), 1993.

OTHER

Terezin Kaddish (libretti; music by R. Senator), first produced at Canterbury Cathedral, 1986.

Also author of libretti, including *The Binding,* 1965, *The Two Brothers,* 1971, *The Harp and the Lovers,* 1974, *The Burning City,* 1975, *The Five Scrolls,* 1975, *Wedding Song,* 1981, and *Children of Theresienstadt,* 1982.

Contributing editor, *Jews from Germany in the United States,* 1955. Member of editorial staff, 1967-76, and editor, 1976—, of *European Judaism* magazine; member of editorial staff of *Dialog der Religionen,* 1991—. Coeditor of "Littman Library Series," Oxford University Press, 1989-93.

Author of monographs, including *Jews and God,* 1972, *Jewish Views of Suffering,* 1974, and *Leo Baeck's Theology of Suffering,* 1974. Author of radio broadcasts, including "Martin Luther und die Juden," published in two anthologies. Contributor to *Dictionary of Pastoral Care,* Society for Promoting Christian Knowledge, 1987. Contributor to periodicals, including *Saturday Review, Dimensions, American Judaism, Encounter, Reconstructionist, Der Monat, Der Spiegel,* and *Christian Jewish Relations.* Author of regular columns in London's *Times, Independent,* and *Guardian.*

SIDELIGHTS: "It is to Albert [H.] Friedlander's credit that, despite his profound love for his late teacher, he does not permit emotion to interfere with objective scholarly appraisal," states Alan W. Miller in his review of *Leo Baeck: Teacher of Theresienstadt* in *Saturday Review.* He further describes Friedlander's work as a "sensitive and thoughtful exploration of the tension between the mind and the man."

Friedlander told *CA* his motivation encompasses "the need to communicate, to preserve and to transmit the past, to enlarge the role of the rabbi in contemporary life."

BIOGRAPHICAL/CRITICAL SOURCES:

PERIODICALS

Christian Century, September 3, 1969.
New Republic, March 15, 1969.
Saturday Review, January 11, 1969.

*   *   *

FRINGS, Manfred S. 1925-

PERSONAL: Surname rhymes with "rings"; born February 27, 1925, in Cologne, Germany; U.S. citi-

zen; son of Gottfried (a teacher) and Maria (Over) Frings; married Karin Muckes, 1985; children: one. *Education:* University of Cologne, Ph.D., 1953, and staatsexamen in English and Philosophy, State Teacher Training Diploma, postdoctoral study, 1953-55. *Religion:* Roman Catholic.

ADDRESSES: Office—Department of Philosophy, University of New Mexico, Albuquerque, NM 87131.

CAREER: University of Detroit, Detroit, MI, assistant professor of philosophy, 1958-61; Gymnasium of Monchen-Gladbach, Monchen-Gladbach, Germany, school master, 1961-62; Duquesne University, Pittsburgh, PA, associate professor of philosophy, 1962-66; DePaul University, Chicago, IL, associate professor, 1966-68, professor of philosophy, 1968-93, professor emeritus, 1993—; University of New Mexico, Albuquerque, adjunct professor of philosophy, 1995—. Initiator of Heidegger Conference, 1966—.

MEMBER: American Association of University Professors, American Philosophical Association, Husserl Society (secretary, 1971-72), Max Scheler Society (president).

AWARDS, HONORS: Fulbright grant, 1958-59; American Council of Learned Societies grant, 1973; Deutsche Forschungsgemeinschaft research grant, 1979-80, 1987-88.

WRITINGS:

(Editor) *Readings in the Philosophy of Science,* University of Detroit Press (Detroit), 1960.
Max Scheler: A Concise Introduction into the World of a Great Thinker, Duquesne University Press (Atlantic Highlands, NJ), 1965.
Person und Dasein: Zur Frage der Ontologie des Wertseins, Nijhoff (Dordrecht, The Netherlands), 1969.
Zur Phaenomenologie der Lebensgemeinschaft, Anton Hain, 1970.
(Contributor) *Linguistic Analysis and Phenomenology,* Macmillan (New York City), 1972.
(Cotranslator) Max Scheler, *Formalism in Ethics and Non-Formal Ethics of Values,* Northwestern University (Evanston, IL), 1973.
(Contributor) *Grundprobleme der Grossen Philosophen,* Vandenhoeck & Ruprecht, 1973.
(Translator) Scheler, *Problems of a Sociology of Knowledge,* Routledge & Kegan Paul (Boston, MA), 1980.

(Editor) Martin Heidegger, *Parmenides,* Klostermann, 1982.
(Translator) Scheler, *Person and Self-Value,* Nijhoff, 1987.

Contributor to numerous international journals.

SIDELIGHTS: "I believe that writing a book should be a creative process coming from one's own imagination, preferably from the spur of the moment," Manfred S. Frings told *CA.* "Having been born with perfect pitch, I am at heart a musician. I improvised and created music (piano) from my fourth year of life. I am completely self-taught, playing almost exclusively Chopin. I also took twelve years of violin lessons. I have tried to convey intuition in music to writing. At times it works, but only for a short while. I feel that at those moments I might have reached the essence of writing which I hold should have only a minimum of planning ahead. In philosophy this is very difficult to do and yields mostly fragments or jottings whose meanings coincide with their phases in time, or at the fitting moment of the time-flux. Strangely enough, I have always been enamored with Formula I racing also."

Frings received a private audience with Pope John Paul II on March 6, 1980, concerning the philosophy of Max Scheler.

*   *   *

FROMMER, Harvey   1937-

PERSONAL: Born October 10, 1937, in Brooklyn, NY; son of Max and Fannie (Wechsler) Frommer; married Myrna Katz (a writer, teacher, and freelance editor), January 23, 1960; children: Jennifer, Freddy, Jan. *Education:* New York University, B.S., 1957, M.A., 1961, Ph.D., 1974. *Religion:* Jewish. *Avocational interests:* Gardening.

ADDRESSES: Home—791 Oakleigh Rd., North Woodmere, NY 11581.

CAREER: United Press International (UPI), Chicago, IL, sportswriter, 1957-58; New York public schools, New York City, high school English teacher, 1960-70; City University of New York, New York City Technical College, professor of writing and speech, 1970—. Adjunct professor of journalism, Adelphi University, 1982-84; adjunct professor of history,

New York University, 1984. Visiting professor of liberal studies, Dartmouth College, 1992, 1994, and Wesleyan University, 1994-95. Has appeared on television and radio talk shows as a sports nostalgia and trivia expert. Historical consultant to broadway play *The First,* 1983. Guest curator and executive producer of "Stars of David: Jews in Sports" exhibit at B'nai B'rith Klutznik Museum, Washington, DC, 1991. *Military service:* U.S. Army, 1958-59.

MEMBER: Association of American University Professors.

AWARDS, HONORS: City University of New York, Salute to Scholars Award, 1984; United States Olympic Committee, Olympic Book of the Year, 1984, for *Olympic Controversies; Spitball Magazine,* Autobiography of the Year nomination, 1988, for *Throwing Heat: The Autobiography of Nolan Ryan.*

WRITINGS:

A Baseball Century: The First 100 Years of the National League, Macmillan (New York City), 1976.
(With Ron Weinmann) *A Sailing Primer,* Atheneum (New York City), 1978.
The Martial Arts: Judo and Karate, Atheneum, 1978.
Sports Lingo: A Dictionary of the Language of Sports, Atheneum, 1980.
Sports Roots: How Nicknames, Namesakes, Trophies, Competitions, and Expressions Came to Be in the World of Sports, Atheneum, 1980.
The Great American Soccer Book, Atheneum, 1980.
New York City Baseball: The Last Golden Age, 1947-1957, Macmillan, 1980.
The Sports Dates Book, Ace (New York City), 1981.
Rickey and Robinson: A Dual Biography, Macmillan, 1982.
Baseball's Greatest Rivalry: The New York Yankees vs. the Boston Red Sox, Atheneum, 1982.
Baseball's Greatest Records, Streaks, and Feats, Atheneum, 1982.
Jackie Robinson, F. Watts (New York City), 1984.
National Baseball Hall of Fame, F. Watts, 1985.
Baseball's Greatest Managers, F. Watts, 1985.
Olympic Controversies, F. Watts, 1985.
City Tech: The First Forty Years, Technical College Press, 1986.
(With Red Holzman) *Red on Red: The Autobiography of Red Holzman,* Bantam (New York City), 1987.
Primitive Baseball: The First Quarter-Century of the National Pastime, Atheneum, 1988.

(With Nolan Ryan) *Throwing Heat: The Autobiography of Nolan Ryan,* Doubleday (New York City), 1988.

150th Anniversary Album of Baseball, F. Watts, 1988.

Growing Up at Bat: 50th Anniversary Book of Little League Baseball, Pharos, 1989.

(With Tony Dorsett) *Running Tough: The Autobiography of Tony Dorsett,* Doubleday, 1989.

(With Don Strock) *Behind the Lines: The Autobiography of Don Strock,* Pharos, 1991.

(With Holzman) *Holzman on Hoops,* Taylor (Dallas), 1991.

Shoeless Joe and Ragtime Baseball, Taylor, 1992.

Baseball in the Big Apple, Taylor, 1995.

New York Yankees Encyclopedia, Macmillan, in press.

WITH WIFE, MYRNA KATZ FROMMER

Basketball My Way—Nancy Lieberman, Scribner (New York City), 1982.

Sports Genes, Ace, 1982.

(Editor) *The Games of the Twenty-Third Olympiad: Los Angeles 1984 Commemorative Book,* International Sport Publications, 1984.

It Happened in the Catskills, Harcourt (San Diego), 1991.

It Happened in Brooklyn, Harcourt, 1993.

Growing Up Jewish in America, Harcourt, 1995.

Contributor of articles and reviews to professional journals and periodicals, including *New York Times, New York Daily News, Los Angeles Times, Yankees Magazine, United Features, Library Journal, Golf Digest, St. Louis Post-Dispatch, Queens Magazine,* and *Newsday.*

SIDELIGHTS: In 1974 Harvey Frommer wrote his doctoral dissertation in English on the influence of sports on television and of television on sports. His efforts to have the work published resulted in the opportunity to write *A Baseball Century,* the official centennial history of the National League.

Frommer told *CA:* "Sports and work and writing fascinate me; gardening acts as a release. I am involved all the time with one of these or another. I have written almost thirty books on sports and look forward to doing many more. I also have hopes of expanding my writing into other fields—gardening,

travel, and institutional history. In 1986 *City Tech: The First Forty Years* was published. I spent three years on the project—the story of New York City Technical College of the City University of New York, an educational, cultural history.

"I enjoy my dual careers—as professor of writing and speech and as sports author and lecturer. My family functions as support and critic. My wife Myrna is at times my coauthor and always my editor; my daughter and two sons are involved in the world of sports, and we have been able to share anecdotes and good times playing and viewing games—especially baseball. I still find myself anchored in my own childhood world of games and fanhood. Perhaps that is what inspired *New York City Baseball* and *Rickey and Robinson*—both books deal with the golden heroes of my growing up years, when the world we all knew was very different.

"I received the 'Salute to Scholars Award' from the Chancellor of the City University of New York in 1984 and was invited by the government of Mexico in 1983 to tour that nation and write about its sports. Together with my wife Myrna, I have expanded my publications to include travel writing. We have been guests of the governments of England (1986), Jamaica (1987), Finland (1987), Scotland (1988), Greece (1988), Barbados (1990), Dominican Republic (1990) Curacao (1990-91), and Spain (1993-5), invited to research and write those nations' history and culture.

"It was my *Contemporary Authors* listing that was of critical help in my being selected in a national search of 500 sports authors to be the editor and major author of the Official Olympic Book in 1984. So far that has been the crown jewel of my career. I take great satisfaction when I realize how far a poor kid from a seedy neighborhood in Brooklyn came in the United States of America. I dream now of other journeys, other accomplishments, other big and significant books for the future—in sports, in oral cultural history, in other areas."

BIOGRAPHICAL/CRITICAL SOURCES:

PERIODICALS

Chicago Tribune Book World, June 6, 1982.
Los Angeles Times Book Review, May 23, 1982; October 2, 1983; May 12, 1985.
New York Times, April 13, 1980.

New York Times Book Review, June 15, 1980; February 15, 1988; May 8, 1988.
Washington Post Book World, July 18, 1982.

* * *

FROST, Erica
   See SUPRANER, Robyn

G

GALENSON, Walter 1914-

PERSONAL: Born December 5, 1914, in New York, NY; son of Louis P. (a certified public accountant) and Libby (Mishell) Galenson; married Marjorie Spector (a professor), June 27, 1940; children: Emily, Alice, David. *Education:* Columbia University, A.B., 1934, Ph.D., 1940.

ADDRESSES: Home—4600 Connecticut Ave. N.W., Apt. 423, Washington, DC 20008. *Office*—School of Industrial and Labor Relations, Cornell University, Ithaca, NY 14850.

CAREER: Hunter College (now Hunter College of the City University of New York), New York City, assistant professor of economics, 1938-41; economist with U.S. Office of Strategic Services, 1942-44, and U.S. Foreign Service, 1944-46; Harvard University, Cambridge, MA, assistant professor of economics, 1946-51; University of California, Berkeley, professor of economics, 1951-66; Cornell University, Ithaca, NY, 1966—, began as professor of economics, currently professor emeritus.

MEMBER: Association for Comparative Economic Studies.

AWARDS, HONORS: Fulbright fellow, 1950; Guggenheim fellow, 1954-55.

WRITINGS:

Rival Unionism in the United States, American Council on Public Affairs, 1940.

Labor in Norway, Harvard University Press (Cambridge, MA), 1949.

Unemployment Compensation in Massachusetts, State of Massachusetts, 1950.

The Danish System of Labor Relations, Harvard University Press, 1952.

The CIO Challenge to the AFL, Harvard University Press, 1960.

(With S. M. Lipset) *Labor and Trade Unionism: An Interdisciplinary Reader,* Wiley (New York City), 1960.

Trade Union Democracy in Western Europe, University of California Press (Berkeley), 1961.

(With F. G. Pyatt) *The Quality of Labor and Its Impact on Economic Development,* International Labour Office (Washington, DC), 1964.

A Primer on Employment and Wages, Random House (New York City), 1966.

(With Nai-Ruenn Chen) *The Chinese Economy under Communism,* Aldine (Hawthorne, NY), 1969.

The Labor Force and Labor Problems, Fontana, 1975.

Labor in the Twentieth Century, Academic Press (San Diego, CA), 1978.

Economic Growth and Structural Change in Taiwan, Cornell University Press (Ithaca, NY), 1979.

The International Labor Organization, University of Wisconsin Press (Madison), 1981.

The United Brotherhood of Carpenters, Harvard University Press, 1983.

A Welfare State Strikes Oil: The Norwegian Experience, University Press of America (Lanham, MD), 1986.

New Trends in Employment Practices, Greenwood Press (Westport, CT), 1991.

Labor and Economic Growth in Five Asian Countries, Praeger (New York City), 1992.

Trade Union Growth and Decline, Praeger, 1994.

EDITOR

Comparative Labor Movements, Prentice-Hall (Englewood Cliffs, NJ), 1952.

Labor Productivity in Soviet and American Industry, Columbia University Press (New York City), 1955.

Labor and Economic Development, Wiley, 1959.

Labor in Developing Economies, University of California Press, 1962.

(With Alexander Eckstein and T. C. Liu) *Economic Trends in Communist China,* Aldine, 1968.

Foreign Trade and Investment: The Newly Industrializing Asian Countries, University of Wisconsin Press, 1985.

China's Economic Reform, The 1990 Institute, 1993.

Contributor to economics journals.

*   *   *

GARBINI, Giovanni   1931-

PERSONAL: Born October 8, 1931, in Rome, Italy; son of Vittorio and Margherita (Virgili) Garbini; married Maria Enrica Mognaschi (a teacher), August 23, 1956; children: Paolo, Enrica. *Education:* Attended University of Rome, 1950-54. *Religion:* Roman Catholic.

ADDRESSES: Home—Via Piave 41, Rome, Italy 00187.

CAREER: University of Rome, Rome, Italy, associate professor of Semitic epigraphy, 1957-68; Oriental Institute, Naples, Italy, professor of Semitic philology, 1964-77; Superior Normal School, Pisa, Italy, professor of Semitic philology, 1977-82; University of Rome, Rome, Italy, professor of Semitic philology, 1982—. Member of Accademia nazionale dei Lincei (Rome), "corrispondente," 1983, "nazionale," 1990. Has taken part in archaeological expeditions at Ramat Rahel (Jerusalem), Tas Silg (Malta), Motya (Sicily), Monte Sirai (Sardinia), and in northern Yemen. *Military service:* Italian Army, officer, 1955-56.

WRITINGS:

Il Semitico di Nord-Ovest, Oriental Institute (Naples), 1960.

Le Origini della Statuaria Sumerica, University of Rome Press (Rome), 1962.

The Ancient World, McGraw (New York City), 1966.

Le Lingue semitiche: Studi di storia linguistica, Oriental Institute, 1972, 2nd enlarged edition, 1984.

Storia e problemi dell'epigrafia semitica, Oriental Institute, 1979.

I Fenici: Storia e religione, Oriental Institute, 1980.

Storia e idelogia nell'Israele antico, Paideia Ed. (Brescia), 1986, English edition, SCM Press (London), 1988.

Venti anni di epigrafia punica nel Magreb (1965-1985), National Council for Researches (Rome), 1986.

Il Semitico nordoccidentale: Studi di storia linguistica, University of Rome Press, 1988.

Cantico dei cantici, Paideia Ed., 1992.

Aramaica, University of Rome Press, 1993.

(With Olivier Durand) *Introduzione alle lingue semitiche,* Paideia Ed., 1994.

La religione dei Fenici in Occidente, University of Rome Press, 1994.

WORK IN PROGRESS: A book on the history and culture of the Philistines.

*   *   *

GARDNER, Miriam
    See BRADLEY, Marion Zimmer

*   *   *

GAY, Carlo T(eofilo) E(berhard)   1913-

PERSONAL: Born July 12, 1913, in Villar Pellice, Torino, Italy; son of Lino Renato (a physician) and Letizia (Malan) Gay; married Claudia Boyd, July 4, 1948; children: Oliver Robin. *Education:* Institute of Oriental Languages of Naples, diploma in Amaric, 1938; University of Naples, Ph.D. (economics), 1940. *Avocational interests:* Mountaineering, speleology, exploration, and photography.

ADDRESSES: Home—80-71 Grenfell St., Kew Gardens, New York, NY 11415.

CAREER: Dalmine (steel pipe manufacturers), Milan, Italy, executive, 1940-55, vice-president of subsidiary Dalminter, Inc., and president of Canadian subsidiary Dalminter Ltd., New York City, 1955-61; researcher and writer on art and history of ancient Mexico, 1962-95. *Military service:* Italian Army, Alpine Corps, 1933-35; became lieutenant.

MEMBER: Royal Anthropological Institute of Great Britain, New York Academy of Sciences.

AWARDS, HONORS: Fellowships from Fondation Etudes et Recherches, Basel, Switzerland, 1983-87, Fondazione dell'Istituto Bancario, San Paolo di Torino, Italy, 1990-91, and Istituto Italiano per gli Studi Filosofici, Naples, Italy, 1993-95.

WRITINGS:

Guerrero: Stone Sculpture from the State of Guerrero, Mexico (exhibition catalogue), edited by Elayne H. Varian, Finch College Museum of Art, 1965.

Mezcala Stone Sculpture: The Human Figure, Museum of Primitive Art, 1967.

Chalcacingo, Akademische Druck u. Verlagsanstalt, 1971.

Xochipala: The Beginnings of Olmec Art, Art Museum, Princeton University Press (Princeton, NJ), 1972.

(With Frances Pratt) *Ceramic Figures of Ancient Mexico: Guerrero, Mexico, Guanajuato, Michoacan,* Akademische Druck u. Verlagsanstalt, 1979.

Mezcala Architecture in Miniature, Academie Royale de Belgique, 1987.

Mezcala: Ancient Stone Sculpture from Guerrero, Mexico, Balsas Publications, 1992.

Ancient Ritual Stone Artifacts: Mexico, Guatemala, Costa Rica, Academie Royale de Belgique, 1995.

Contributor to *Natural History, Archaeology, Antike Welt, Raggi, Primitifs,* and *Almogaren.*

WORK IN PROGRESS: Further research on Olmec culture and related lithic traditions indigenous to the Middle Balsas River region in Guerrero, Mexico; research on the stone-tool industries of the Lower and Middle Paleolithic of Europe and Africa; research on "cupules" dating from the Middle Paleolithic to the present. Books in preparation include a comprehensive study of the Chontal lithic traditions of Guerrero.

BIOGRAPHICAL/CRITICAL SOURCES:

PERIODICALS

American Antiquity, April, 1990, p. 434.
Christian Science Monitor, February 9, 1973.
Corriere della Sera, April 15, 1967.
El Financiero, April 27, 1992.
El Sol de Mexico, May 6, 1971.
L'Europeo, December, 1967.
Life, May 12, 1967.
New York Times, April 14, 1967; April 23, 1967; April 21, 1992.
Siempre, June 28, 1967.

*   *   *

GEISLER, Norman L(eo)   1932-

PERSONAL: Born July 21, 1932, in Warren, MI; son of Alphonso H. (a factory worker) and Bertha (Rottmann) Geisler; married Barbara Jean Cate (a pianist), June 24, 1955; children: Ruth, David, Daniel, Rhoda, Paul, Rachel. *Education:* Wheaton College, Wheaton, IL, B.A., 1958, M.A., 1960; Detroit Bible College (now William Tyndale College), Th.B., 1964; Loyola University, Chicago, IL, Ph.D., 1970. *Politics:* Republican. *Avocational interests:* Collecting rocks and fossils, wood working.

ADDRESSES: Office—Southern Evangelical Seminary, 5801 Pineville-Matthews Rd., Charlotte, NC 28226-3447.

CAREER: Ordained minister, 1956. Pastor of Dayton Center Church, Silverwood, MI, 1955-57, River Grove Bible Church, River Grove, IL, 1958-59, and Memorial Baptist Church, Warren, MI, 1960-63; Detroit Bible College, Detroit, MI, instructor, 1959-62, assistant professor, 1963-66, chair of Bible-Theology department, 1965; Trinity College, Deerfield, IL, assistant professor of Bible, 1967-69, associate professor of philosophy, 1970-71; Trinity Evangelical Divinity School, Mundelein, IL, visiting professor of philosophy of religion, 1969-70, chair of department, 1970-79; Dallas Theological Seminary, professor of systematic theology, 1979-88; Research Center, Liberty University, dean, 1989-91; Southern Evangelical Seminary, Charlotte, NC, dean, 1992—. Interim pastor in Michigan, Illinois, and Texas, 1965—. International lecturer at universities, churches, retreats, and pastors' conferences. Member of Mundelein High School Board of Education, beginning 1971.

MEMBER: American Philosophical Association, Evangelical Theological Society, Evangelical Philosophical Society (president, 1976), American Academy of Religion, American Scientific Affiliation, Alumni of Detroit Bible College (president, 1961-62).

AWARDS, HONORS: Outstanding Educator of America, 1975; Choice Evangelical Book of the Year, *Christianity Today,* 1975, for *Philosophy of Religion;* elected member of Wheaton Scholastic Honor Society, 1977; Alumnus of the Year, William Tyndale College, 1982.

WRITINGS:

(Coauthor) *General Introduction to the Bible,* Moody (Chicago, IL), 1968, revised edition, 1986.

Christ: The Theme of the Bible, Moody, 1968.

Ethics: Alternatives and Issues, Zondervan (Grand Rapids, MI), 1971.

The Christian Ethic of Love, Zondervan, 1973.

(With Winfried Cordvan) *Philosophy of Religion,* Zondervan, 1974, revised edition, Baker Book (Grand Rapids, MI), 1988.

(With William E. Nix) *From God to Us,* Moody, 1974.

Christian Apologetics, Baker Book, 1976.

A Popular Survey of the Old Testament, Baker Book, 1977.

The Roots of Evil, Zondervan, 1978.

To Understand the Bible, Look for Jesus, Baker Book, 1979.

Introduction to Philosophy: A Christian Perspective, Baker Book, 1980.

Options in Contemporary Christian Ethics, Baker Book, 1981.

The Creator in the Courtroom: "Scopes II," foreword by Duane T. Gish, Mott Media (Milford, MI), 1982.

Miracles and Modern Thought, Zondervan, 1982.

Is Man the Measure: An Evaluation of Humanism, Baker Book, 1982.

Cosmos: Carl Sagan's Religion for the Scientific Mind, Quest Publishing (Rock Island, IL), 1983.

The Religion of the Force, Quest Publishing, 1983.

(With William D. Watkins) *Perspectives: Understanding and Evaluating Today's World Views,*

Here's Life (San Bernardino, CA), 1984, revised edition published as *A Handbook on World Views,* Baker Book, 1988.

False Gods of Our Time, Harvest House (Eugene, OR), 1985.

Christianity under Attack, Quest Publishing, 1985.

(With J. Yutaka Amano) *The Reincarnation Sensation,* Tyndale (Wheaton, IL), 1986.

(With J. Kerby Anderson) *Origin Science: A Proposal for the Creation-Evolution Controversy,* Baker Book, 1987.

To Drink or Not to Drink: A Sober Look at the Question, revised edition, Quest Publishing, 1987.

Signs and Wonders, Tyndale, 1988.

The Battle for the Ressurection, Thomas Nelson (Nashville, TN), 1989.

Christian Ethics: Options and Issues, Baker Book, 1989.

The Infiltration of the New Age, Tyndale, 1989.

Knowing the Truth About Creation, Servant Press (Ann Arbor, MI), 1989.

Matters of Life and Death, Baker Book, 1989.

Worlds Apart: A Handbook on World Views, Baker Book, 1989.

Apologetics in the New Age, Baker Book, 1990.

Civil Disobedience: When Is it Right?, Quest Publishing, 1990.

Gambling: A Bad Bet, Revell (Old Tappan, NJ), 1990.

The Life and Death Debate, Greenwood Press (Westport, CT), 1990.

When Skeptics Ask, Victor Books (Wheaton, IL), 1990.

In Defense of the Resurrection, Quest Publishing, 1991.

Thomas Aquinas, Baker Book, 1991.

When Critics Ask, Victor Books, 1992.

Answering Islam, Baker Book, 1993.

An Encyclopedia of Christian Evidences, Victor Books, 1996.

EDITOR

Inerrancy, Zondervan, 1980.

Decide for Yourself: How History Views the Bible, Zondervan, 1981.

Biblical Errancy: Its Philosophical Roots, Zondervan, 1981.

Contributor to *What Augustine Says,* Baker Book, 1982. Also contributor to philosophical and religious periodicals.

GELMAN, Mitch(ell Barry) 1962-

PERSONAL: Born March 21, 1962, in New York, NY; son of Stephen M. (a journalist) and Rita (a writer; maiden name, Golden) Gelman. *Education:* Attended London School of Economics and Political Science, 1982-83; University of California, Berkeley, B.A. (with highest honors), 1985; attended National University of Singapore, 1985-86.

ADDRESSES: Home—Seattle, WA. *Office*—ESPN-ET.SportsZone.com, 13810 Southeast Eastgate Way, Suite 400, Bellevue, WA 98005.

CAREER: Journalist. Part-time reporter for *Los Angeles Herald-Examiner,* 1981, and *Time* magazine's London bureau, 1982-83; *New York Newsday,* New York City, crime and political reporter, 1986-95; ESPNET.SportsZone.com, Bellevue, WA, feature editor, 1995—.

MEMBER: Phi Beta Kappa.

AWARDS, HONORS: Nellie Bly Cub Reporter Award, New York Press Club, 1989; Pulitzer Prize for Spot News Reporting, 1992.

WRITINGS:

Great Quarterbacks of Pro Football, Scholastic (New York City), 1981.
Crime Scene: On the Streets with a Rookie Police Reporter, Times Books (New York City), 1992.

THE *"PLAY IT YOUR WAY"* SERIES

Can You Win the Pennant? Pocket Books (New York City), 1983.
Pro Football Showdown, Pocket Books, 1983.
Super Bowl Sunday, Pocket Books, 1984.
World Series Pressure, Pocket Books, 1984.
Opening Day, Pocket Books, 1985.
Defending Champions, Pocket Books, 1985.

SIDELIGHTS: Mitch Gelman told *CA:* "After nearly ten years as a reporter on the streets of New York City, I am excited about stepping into cyberspace. With ESPNET.SportsZone, I hope to help bring indepth and entertaining journalism to the world wide web. The next wave of communications is upon us, and it is very exciting."

GENG, Veronica 1941-

PERSONAL: Born January 10, 1941, in Atlanta, GA; daughter of Charles Emil and Rosina (Butter) Geng. *Education:* Received B.A. from University of Pennsylvania.

ADDRESSES: Agent—Andrew Wylie, 250 West 57th St., Suite 2106, New York, NY 10107.

CAREER: Freelance writer and editor. *New Yorker,* New York City, writer and fiction editor, 1977-92. Movie critic for *Soho News,* 1980-81.

WRITINGS:

(Editor) *In a Fit of Laughter: An Anthology of Modern Humor* (for young people), introduction by Steve Allen, Platt (New York City), 1969.
Partners (satire collection), Harper (New York City), 1984.
Love Trouble Is My Business, Harper, 1988.

Contributor to periodicals, including *Harper's, Ms., New York Review of Books, New York Times Book Review, New Republic,* and *New York Observer.*

SIDELIGHTS: Called "the cleverest *New Yorker* humorist to come along since Woody Allen" by *National Review* contributor Terry Teachout, Veronica Geng exhibits her talent for social satire in *Partners,* a collection of twenty-nine parodies—many first appearing in the *New Yorker.* Using contemporary rhetoric to lampoon current mores and popular culture, Geng comments on such emblems of our age as the how-to book, the tell-all memoir, and the politician's newsletter. "Her strength is mimicking other styles," observes Ellen Stein, reviewing *Partners* for *Ms.* "[Geng] hoists her subjects on their own non sequiturs," Grace Lichtenstein agrees in the *Washington Post.* "She has what all real satirists have: an ear with perfect pitch."

Writing in the *New York Times,* Christopher Lehmann-Haupt determines that "the wit of many of the . . . pieces in *Partners* . . . begins with the author's unlikely coupling of subjects." "Often," he continues, "these are as pungent in conception as they are in execution"; "Record Review," for example, "is a deft parody of a hip discographer with nothing less than the Watergate tapes as its subject." In the critique for the *Los Angeles Times Book Review* Elaine Kendall advances a similar evaluation. "Though Geng is extremely particular about targets, she's wonderfully eclectic, impaling the innocuous with the same skillful glee she lavishes on the truly evil and pernicious," states the reviewer. "Where she does this in the same brief essay, the effect is particularly hilarious."

While noting in Geng's satiric pieces "a particularly *New Yorker* brand of humor that is as dry and smooth as a good martini," Stein regretfully points out that "we rarely, if ever, hear Geng's own voice." "Geng's style is particularly opaque, never revealing the author's attitude toward her subjects other than a general amusement at society's foibles," elaborates the reviewer. "Personally, I prefer my satire a bit more Swiftian, where one senses the passion and moral outrage beneath the stance of ironic detachment." Lichtenstein, too, admits that Geng's pastiches reveal "no new sensibility" or convey "no great political thrust." "Still, 'Partners' is fun," Lichtenstein concludes, deeming its stylish, daring sendups to be "first-class."

To *Newsweek* reviewer Ron Givens it is "Geng's beautifully calibrated sense of style," particularly, that distinguishes her from other parody writers. While "mak[ing] you laugh out loud," the critic relates, "[Geng] has refined her wit to the point where it's, well, erudite. . . . [It's] just right for educated funny bones." And Lehmann-Haupt maintains that Geng's clever burlesques slyly achieve their satiric ends. "Miss Geng is lethal," he writes. "She wields what Mary Wortley Montagu once called 'a polished razor keen' that wounds 'with a touch that's scarcely felt or seen.'"

BIOGRAPHICAL/CRITICAL SOURCES:

PERIODICALS

Antioch Review, winter, 1985.
Christian Science Monitor, November 1, 1985.
Los Angeles Times Book Review, August 26, 1984.
Ms., October, 1984.
National Review, September 20, 1985.
Newsweek, September 17, 1984.
New York Times, July 6, 1984.
New York Times Book Review, July 15, 1984.
Washington Post, September 4, 1984.

GERBER, Merrill Joan 1938-

PERSONAL: Born March 15, 1938, in Brooklyn, NY; daughter of William (an antique dealer) and Jessie (Sorblum) Gerber; married Joseph Spiro (a college teacher), June 23, 1960; children: Becky Ann, Joanna Emily, Susanna Willa. *Education:* Attended University of Miami, 1955; University of Florida, B.A., 1959; Brandeis University, graduate study, 1959-60, M.A., 1981. *Religion:* Jewish.

ADDRESSES: Home—542 Santa Anita Ct., Sierra Madre, CA 91024.

CAREER: Former editor, Houghton Mifflin Co., Boston, MA; lecturer at many writers' conferences, including those at University of California, University of Florida, and Pasadena City College; has taught creative writing at California State University, Los Angeles, University of Redlands, and Pasadena City College, Pasadena, CA; currently teaches fiction writing at the California Institute of Technology.

AWARDS, HONORS: Stanford University creative writing fellowship, 1962-63; residency grant, Yaddo Writers' Colony, 1981; Andrew Lytle Fiction Prize, *Sewanee Review,* 1985, for "At the Fence"; short fiction award, *Fiction Network,* 1985, for "Hairdos"; O. Henry Award, Doubleday and Co., Inc., 1986, for "I Don't Believe This"; Pushcart Editors' Book Award for literary distinction, 1990, for *King of the World;* Harold U. Ribalow Prize, *Hadassah* magazine, for best English-language book of fiction on a Jewish theme, 1992, for *The Kingdom of Brooklyn.*

WRITINGS:

NOVELS

An Antique Man, Houghton (Boston), 1967.
Now Molly Knows, Arbor House (New York City), 1974.
The Lady with the Moving Parts, Arbor House, 1978.
King of the World, Pushcart (Wainscott, NY), 1990.
The Kingdom of Brooklyn, Longstreet Press, 1992.

SHORT STORIES

Stop Here, My Friend, Houghton, 1965.

Honeymoon, University of Illinois Press (Champaign), 1985.

Chattering Man: Stories and a Novella, Longstreet Press, 1991.

This Old Heart of Mine: The Best of Merrill Joan Gerber's Redbook Stories, Longstreet Press, 1993.

YOUNG ADULT

Please Don't Kiss Me Now, Dial (New York City), 1981.

Name a Star for Me, Viking (New York City), 1983.

I'm Kissing as Fast as I Can, Fawcett (New York City), 1985.

The Summer of My Indian Prince, Fawcett, 1986.

Also Known as Sadzia! The Belly Dancer!, Harper (New York City), 1987.

Marry Me Tomorrow, Fawcett, 1987.

Even Pretty Girls Cry at Night, Crosswinds, 1988.

I'd Rather Think About Robby, Harper, 1988.

Handsome as Anything, Scholastic (New York City), 1990.

OTHER

Old Mother, Little Cat: A Writer's Reflections on Her Kitten, Her Aged Mother . . . and Life (nonfiction), Longstreet Press, 1995.

Contributor to books, including *Prize Stories: The O. Henry Awards 1986,* edited by William Abrahams, Doubleday (New York City), 1986. Also contributor of short stories to periodicals, including *Mademoiselle, New Yorker, Redbook, Sewanee Review, McCall's, Ladies' Home Journal, Woman's Day,* and *Family Circle.* Also contributor of articles on writing to the *Writer* and *Writer's Digest.*

WORK IN PROGRESS: *Glimmering Girls.*

SIDELIGHTS: Merrill Joan Gerber has published more short stories in *Redbook* than any other contributor.

BIOGRAPHICAL/CRITICAL SOURCES:

PERIODICALS

Los Angeles Times, May 7, 1988.

Los Angeles Times Book Review, December 18, 1985.

New York Times Book Review, December 15, 1985.

Washington Post Book World, November 17, 1985.

*   *   *

GHOSH, Dipali 1945-

PERSONAL: Born November 27, 1945, in Calcutta, India; daughter of Rajkumar and Anima Mukherji; married Amalendu Ghosh (an accountant), January 31, 1975. *Education:* Bombay University, B.A., 1967; Shreemati Nathibai Damodar Thackersey Women's University, B.Lib.Sc., 1968; University of North London, postgraduate diploma in librarianship, 1980. *Religion:* Hindu.

ADDRESSES: *Home*—10 St. Alphage Court, Colindeep Lane, Colindale, London NW9 6BU, England. *Office*—Oriental and India Office Collections, British Library, Orbit House, 197 Blackfriars Road, London SE1, England.

CAREER: Bombay Labour Institute, Bombay, India, librarian, 1968; Government Institute of Printing Technology, Bombay, librarian, 1968-70; Victoria Jubilee Technical Institute, Bombay, assistant librarian, 1970-75; British Library, Department of Oriental Collections, London, in various posts, 1975-85, curator, 1986—, and Oriental and India Office Collections.

WRITINGS:

Translations of Bengali Works Into English, Mansell (London), 1986.

Translations of Hindi Works Into English: A Bibliography, Munshiram Manoharlal Publishers (New Delhi), 1995.

Contributor of articles to journals and periodicals.

WORK IN PROGRESS: *Tulsidas; Indian Political Literature in Bengali, 1857-1947; Catalogue of Hindi Manuscripts in the Oriental and India Office Collections.*

SIDELIGHTS: Dipali Ghosh told *CA:* "The aim of compiling these bibliographies is to help students, research workers and all those who are interested in Hindi and Bengali literatures but cannot read the original languages to find out which works have been translated into English. To date no general bibliographies have been giving adequate information about the large number of translations from Hindi or

Bengali that were published during the nineteenth and early twentieth centuries, but attempts have been made in these bibliographies to give comprehensive information as far as possible."

* * *

GORDON, John (William) 1925-

PERSONAL: Born November 19, 1925, in Jarrow, County Durham, England; son of Norman (a teacher) and Margaret (Revely) Gordon; married Sylvia Ellen Young, January 9, 1954; children: Sally, Robert. *Education:* Educated in Jarrow and Wisbech, England.

ADDRESSES: Home—99 George Borrow Rd., Norwich, Norfolk NR4 7HU, England.

CAREER: Isle of Ely and Wisbech Advertiser, Wisbech, England, reporter, 1947-49, subeditor, 1949-51; *Bury Free Press,* Bury St. Edmunds, Suffolk, England, chief reporter, then subeditor, 1951-58; *Western Evening Herald,* Plymouth, England, subeditor, 1958-62; *Eastern Evening News,* Norwich, Norfolk, England, columnist and subeditor, 1962-73; *Eastern Daily Press,* Norwich, subeditor, 1973-85; writer. *Military service:* Royal Navy, 1943-47.

WRITINGS:

JUVENILE FICTION

The Giant under the Snow, Hutchinson (London), 1968, Harper (New York City), 1970.
The House on the Brink, Hutchinson, 1970, Harper, 1971.
The Ghost on the Hill, Kestrel (London), 1976, Viking (New York City), 1977.
The Waterfall Box, Kestrel, 1978.
The Spitfire Grave and Other Stories, Kestrel, 1979.
The Edge of the World, Atheneum (New York City), 1983.
Catch Your Death and Other Ghost Stories, illustrated by Jeremy Ford, Hardy, 1984.
The Quelling Eye, Bodley Head (London), 1986.
The Grasshopper, Bodley Head, 1987.
Ride the Wind, Bodley Head, 1989.
Blood Brothers, Signpost (Birmingham, England), 1989.
Secret Corridor, Blackie & Son (London), 1990.
The Burning Baby and Other Ghosts, Walker, 1992, Candlewick, 1993.
Gilray's Ghost, Walker, 1995.

OTHER

Ordinary Seaman (memoir), Walker, 1992.

Contributor to anthologies, including *The Thorny Paradise,* edited by Edward Blishen, Kestrel, 1975; *The Year's Best Horror Stories,* edited by Karl Edward Wagner, DAW (New York City), 1985; *Twisted Circuits,* edited by Mick Gower, Hutchinson, 1987; and *Electric Heros,* edited by Gower, Bodley Head, 1988. Contributor to periodicals.

Gordon's works have been translated into Japanese, Danish, Swedish, German, and Norwegian.

WORK IN PROGRESS: A young adult novel.

SIDELIGHTS: John Gordon's novels and short stories for children and young adults seek to shorten the gap between fantasy and reality. The "other" worlds his characters stumble into exist simultaneously with the real world they live in on a daily basis. Drawing from the history of the Fen Country in England, where he grew up, Gordon populates his tales with ghosts and creatures from the past, leading readers through several suspenseful twists and turns before revealing all. "Gordon has confidently mastered the art of holding his reader in suspense, often delaying a climax until the byways of a carefully engineered plot have been explored," maintains *Junior Bookshelf* reviewer G. Bott.

Gordon first started writing fiction while working as a newspaper editor. His first published story, *The Giant under the Snow,* follows a group of children, including Jonk, as they cross over from their modern world to a parallel dimension. In this "other" world of ancient magic, there are witches and invading Leathermen, and the children learn how to fly. In the end, the evil forces must deal with a prehistoric giant that rises from under the snow. Dennis Hamley, writing in *Twentieth-Century Children's Writers,* observes that *The Giant under the Snow* "formed a stunning debut for a writing career which flourishes and constantly surprises."

This first children's book was followed with a young adult novel which was set in Peckover House in Wisbech, England—a house Gordon had visited himself. *The House on the Brink* concerns the home's owner, Mrs. Knowles, and a teenage boy, Dick Dodds. Both observe and are affected differently by what appears to be a blackened log which rises out of the fen, seeming to move closer and closer to the house with each sighting. "Few authors have a more convincing way of suggesting the cohesions and moods of the young teens than John Gordon," writes *Growing Point*'s Margery Fisher. "His dialogue is brilliantly elliptical, comic and perceptive, and he moves so confidently from real to surreal that the reader makes the transition without realizing it." Hamley asserts that *The House on the Brink* "is a riddling, difficult, memorable book close to the status of classic."

Gordon also writes short stories that often include supernatural elements. Many of these have been collected in several volumes, including *The Spitfire Grave and Other Stories, Catch Your Death and Other Ghost Stories,* and *The Burning Baby and Other Ghosts.* "Like most novelists who are masters of construction, Gordon is equally at home in the short story," observes Hamley, adding that Gordon's collections "contain narratives which, in their uncompromising spareness, are disturbing, even shocking." One story concerns a young boy who plans his own suicide after his father takes his life. Another has the spirit of a drowned boy luring another boy into the same icy pool of water. The stories in *The Burning Baby and Other Ghosts* include everything from an unborn baby coming back to haunt its murderer to a ten-year-old being smothered and fed to eels.

Robert Protherough, in his *School Librarian* review of *The Burning Baby and Other Ghosts,* explains that "the stories grip from the beginning and raise the reader's curiosity." In addition, the critic notes, "Gordon writes vividly, the characters and settings are firmly realised, and the dialogue is convincing." Deborah Stevenson similarly points out in the *Bulletin of the Center for Children's Books* that "Gordon is skilled at spare but meaningful characterization as well as the occasional doomsday sentence." As Hamley concludes: "These stories push to the very edge the power of imagination to work in real, tangible settings."

Gordon once told *CA* about the connection between his writing and his dreams: "Stories are dreams in disguise. There are dreams hidden in all my stories. They are necessary, but they must remain hidden because they are mine and mean nothing to anybody else. The stories that surround them are meant to make you have similar dreams, your *own* dreams, which will again be secret. Stories are a way of sharing secrets too deep to mention."

BIOGRAPHICAL/CRITICAL SOURCES:

BOOKS

Twentieth-Century Children's Writers, 4th edition, St. James Press (Detroit), 1995, pp. 392-94.

PERIODICALS

Bulletin of the Center for Children's Books, September, 1977; October, 1993, p. 44.
Growing Point, May, 1982, p. 3893; January, 1988, pp. 4906-7.
Horn Book, October, 1983, p. 581.
Junior Bookshelf, June, 1980, p. 142; June, 1984, p. 138; February, 1988, p. 57; April, 1989, pp. 80-81.
School Librarian, March 30, 1984, p. 335; August, 1989, p. 114; November, 1992, p. 158.
School Library Journal, January, 1984, pp. 75-76.
Signal, May, 1972.
Times Literary Supplement, March 30, 1984, p. 335; April 7, 1989, p. 379.
Voice of Youth Advocates, February, 1984, p. 343.
Wilson Library Bulletin, May, 1994, p. 98.

*   *   *

GOULD, Peter R(obin) 1932-

PERSONAL: Born November 18, 1932, in Coulesdon, England; son of Ralph Graham and Helene (Hanson) Gould; married Johanna Stuyck, July 10, 1956; children: Katherine, Richard, Andrew. *Education:* Colgate University, B.A. (summa cum laude), 1956; Northwestern University, M.A., 1957, Ph.D., 1960. *Avocational interests:* Reading, travel, gardening, walking, wine.

ADDRESSES: Home—921 Oak Ridge Ave., State College, PA 16801. *Office*—306 Walker Building, Pennsylvania State University, University Park, PA 16802.

CAREER: Syracuse University, Syracuse, NY, assistant professor, 1960-63; Pennsylvania State University, University Park, PA, assistant professor, 1963-64, associate professor, 1964-68, professor, 1968-86, Evan Pugh Professor, 1986—. Visiting lecturer at numerous universities in the United States, Canada, the Caribbean, and Europe. Chair of numerous professional conferences. Consultant to various governmental agencies, universities, and private firms. Member of numerous committees at Pennsylvania State University. *Military service:* British Army, Infantry (Gordon Highlanders), 1951-53, became lieutenant.

MEMBER: Social Science Research Council, Amnesty International, Greenpeace, Phi Beta Kappa.

AWARDS, HONORS: Ford Foundation fellowship, 1959-63; National Science Foundation grants, 1965-84; award for meritorious contribution, American Association of Geographers, 1975; faculty research medal, Pennsylvania State University, 1981; D.Sc. (honoris causa), Universite Louis Pasteur, Strasbourg, 1982; Prix International de Geographie, medaille d'or, 1993.

WRITINGS:

The Development of the Transportation Pattern in Ghana (monograph), Department of Geography, Northwestern University (Evanston, IL), 1960.
(Editor) *Africa: Continent of Change,* Wadsworth (Belmont, CA), 1961.
On Mental Maps, Michigan Inter-University Community of Mathematical Geographers, 1966.
Spatial Diffusion, Association of American Geographers (Washington, DC), 1969, published as *Spatial Diffusion: The Spread of Ideas and Innovations in Geographic Space,* Learning Resources in International Studies (Croton-on-Hudson, NY), 1975.
(With E. J. Taaffe, N. Ginsburg Burton, F. Lukermann, and P. L. Wagner) *Geography,* Prentice-Hall (Englewood Cliffs, NJ), 1970.
(With Ronald Abler and John S. Adams) *Spatial Organization: The Geographer's View of the World,* Prentice-Hall, 1971.
(With G. Tornqvist, S. Nordbeck, and B. Rystedt) *Multiple Location Analysis,* Gleerup (Lund, Sweden), 1972.
(With Rodney White) *Mental Maps,* Penguin (New York City), 1974, 2nd edition, Allen & Unwin (London), 1986.
People in Information Space: The Mental Maps and Information Surfaces of Sweden, Gleerup, 1975.
(With G. Olsson) *A Search for Common Ground,* Pion (London), 1982.
(With A. Pires, I. Boura, J. Gaspar, and R. Jacinto) *Estrutura agraria e inovacao na cova da beira,* Comissao de Coordenacao da Regiao Centro (Coimbra, Portugal), 1983.

(With J. Johnson and G. Chapman) *The Structure of Television,* Volume I: *Television, the World of Structure,* Volume II: *Structure, the World of Television,* Pion, 1984.
The Geographer at Work, Routledge & Kegan Paul (London), 1985.
(With R. Golledge and H. Couclelis) *A Ground for Common Search,* Santa Barbara Geographical Press, 1988.
Fire in the Rain: The Democratic Consequences of Chernobyl, Polity Press (Oxford, England), 1988.
The Slow Plague: A Geography of the AIDS Epidemic, Blackwell (London), 1993.
(With A. Cliff, A. Hoare, and N. Thrift) *Diffusing Geography,* Blackwell, 1995.
(With A. Bailly) *Le Pouvoir des Cartes,* Economica (Paris), 1995.

Contributor of articles to over fifty books. Has delivered over eighty papers to international conferences and meetings. Contributor of over one-hundred sixty articles to periodicals, including *Atlantic* and *Harper's.* Consulting editor to journals, including *Environment and Planning, Geographical Analysis, L'Espace Geographique, Geografia, Journal of Geography in Higher Education, Journal of Geography, Geografiska, Sistema Terra, The AIDS Leader,* and *Mappemonde.*

Some of Gould's works have been translated into French, Italian, and Japanese.

WORK IN PROGRESS: A work on the diffusion of the news of the 1755 Lisban earthquake and its intellectual impact; a book of collected essays and articles for Syracuse University Press, expected in 1996.

SIDELIGHTS: Peter R. Gould's book *Mental Maps,* co-written with Rodney White, analyzes perception of place, i.e. how people perceive geographic locales other than their own. A reviewer for the *Times Literary Supplement* writes that "the authors' approach, full of zest and zeal, is not of theoretical interest alone. It has implications for planners and policymakers, administrators and educationists."

BIOGRAPHICAL/CRITICAL SOURCES:

PERIODICALS

Choice, October, 1974.
Lambda Book Report, November, 1993, p. 47.

Nature, September 6, 1990, p. 30; November 25, 1993, p. 377.
New Scientist, July 21, 1990, p. 56.
New Statesman & Society, May 11, 1990, p. 40.
Reference and Research Book News, December, 1993, p. 51.
Third World Resources, July, 1994, p. 8.
Times Literary Supplement, June 14, 1974.

*   *   *

GRABAR, Oleg   1929-

PERSONAL: Born November 23, 1929, in Strasbourg, France; immigrated to United States, 1951, naturalized citizen, 1960; son of Andre and Julie (Ivanova) Grabar; married Terry Ann Harris, June 9, 1951; children: Nicolas Howard, Anne Louise. *Education:* Harvard University, B.A. (magna cum laude), 1950; University of Paris, Licence d'Histoire, 1950; Princeton University, Ph.D., 1955.

ADDRESSES: Home—43 Maxwell Ln., Princeton, NJ 08540. *Office*—School of Historical Studies, Institute for Advanced Study, Princeton, NJ 08540.

CAREER: University of Michigan, Ann Arbor, instructor, 1954-55, assistant professor, 1955-59, associate professor, 1959-64, professor of Islamic art, 1964-69; Harvard University, Cambridge, MA, professor of fine arts, 1969-79, Aga Khan Professor, of Islamic Art, 1979-89; Institute for Advanced Study, Princeton, NJ, professor of historical studies, 1990—. American School of Oriental Research, director in Jerusalem and Jordan, 1960-61, vice president, 1968-75; director of Michigan-Harvard excavations in Syria, 1964-71.

MEMBER: College Art Association of America (director, 1968-72, 1981-85), Archaeological Institute of America, Mediaeval Academy of America, American Academy of Arts and Sciences (councilperson, 1982-86), American Philosophical Society, Middle Eastern Studies Association, German Archaelogical Institute, honorary member of British Academy and Austrian Academy.

WRITINGS:

Coinage of Tulunids, American Numismatic Society (New York City), 1957.

Persian Art Before and After the Mongol Conquest, University of Michigan Museum of Art (Ann Arbor), 1959.
Islamic Architecture and Its Decoration, Faber & Faber (Winchester, MA), 1967.
Sasanian Silver: Late Antique and Early Medieval Arts of Luxury From Iran, University of Michigan Museum of Art, 1967.
The Formation of Islamic Art, Yale University Press (New Haven, CT), 1973, revised and enlarged edition, 1987.
The Alhambra, Harvard University Press (Cambridge, MA), 1978.
City in the Desert, Harvard University Press, 1978.
(With Sheila Blair) *Epic Images and Contemporary History,* University of Chicago Press, 1980.
(Editor) *Muqarnas: An Annual on Islamic Art and Literature,* Yale University Press and E. J. Brill, 10 Volumes, 1983-90.
The Illustrations of the Maqamat, University of Chicago Press, 1984.
(With Richard Ettinghausen) *The Art and Architecture of Islam, 650-1250,* Penguin (New York City), 1987.
The Great Mosque of Isfahan, New York University Press, 1988.
The Mediation of Ornament, Princeton University Press (Princeton, NJ), 1993.

Contributor to scholarly journals. Editor of *Arts Orientalis,* 1957-71.

WORK IN PROGRESS: Research on early medieval Jerusalem and Islamic Sicily.

BIOGRAPHICAL/CRITICAL SOURCES:

PERIODICALS

Los Angeles Times Book Review, March 13, 1988.
Washington Post Book World, February 14, 1988.

*   *   *

GRADWOHL, David M(ayer)   1934-

PERSONAL: Born January 22, 1934, in Lincoln, NE; son of Bernard Sam (a lawyer) and Elaine (Mayer) Gradwohl; married Hanna Rosenberg (a social worker), December 29, 1957; children: Steven, Jane, Kathryn. *Education:* University of Nebraska, B.A. (with highest distinction), 1955; graduate study at

University of Edinburgh, 1955-56; Harvard University, Ph.D., 1967. *Politics:* Liberal. *Religion:* Jewish.

ADDRESSES: Home—2003 Ashmore Drive, Ames, IA 50014. *Office*—Department of Anthropology, 319 Curtiss Hall, Iowa State University, Ames, IA 50011.

CAREER: Iowa State University, Ames, instructor, 1962-66, assistant professor, 1966-67, associate professor, 1967-72, professor of anthropology, 1972—, coordinator of anthropology, 1968-75, chair of American Indian Studies Program, 1981-85, faculty adviser to American Indian Rights Organization. Field worker and archaeological field supervisor in South Dakota and Nebraska for Nebraska State Historical Society, 1952-59; conducted field work in Nebraska, Wyoming, and Montana for University of Nebraska State Museum, 1953; archaeological field worker in Scotland, 1955, and at Stonehenge, 1956; director of Red Rock Reservoir Archaeological Project, 1964—, Ames Reservoir Archaeological Project, 1971—, and Saylorville Reservoir Archaeological Project, 1967—. Member of Iowa advisory committee of National Register of Historic Sites and Places, 1969-88; member of advisory committee of Office of the State Archaeologist of Iowa, 1983—; member of Iowa Conservation Commission's Ledges State Park Task Force, 1977-81; member of Iowa's First Farmers Committee, a joint project of Iowa Natural Heritage Foundation and Living History Farms, 1979-88. *Military service:* U.S. Army, 1957-59; served in Europe.

MEMBER: American Anthropological Association (fellow), Current Anthropology (associate), Society for American Archaeology, American Interprofessional Institute, American Culture Association, Society for Historical Archaeology, Conference on Historic Sites Archaeology, National Association for Ethnic Studies, Association for Gravestone Studies, United Native American Student Association, Plains Anthropologist (member of board of directors, 1969-72; vice-president, 1971; president, 1972), Plains Anthropological Society (member of board of directors, 1987-91), Association of Iowa Archaeologists (fellow; chair, 1977-78), Iowa Archaeological Society (member of board of trustees, 1966-69, 1971-74), Missouri Archaeological Society, Nebraska State Historical Society, Nebraska Jewish Historical Society (charter member), Nebraska Association of Professional Archaeologists (fellow; charter member), Phi Beta Kappa, Sigma Xi, Phi Kappa Phi, Alpha

Kappa Delta, Sigma Gamma Epsilon, Delta Sigma Rho.

AWARDS, HONORS: Fulbright fellow in Scotland, 1955-56; Woodrow Wilson fellow, 1955-56; grants from National Science Foundation, 1961-62, U.S. Army Corps of Engineers, 1976—, National Park Service, 1977—, and National Endowment for the Humanities, 1985—; 2nd place in adult division, Iowa Poetry Association contest, 1990; Charles C. Irby Distinguished Service Award, National Association for Ethnic Studies, 1990; Amoco Foundation Award for Career Achievement in Undergraduate teaching, 1992; Award for Outstanding Leadership with Respect to Diversity in the Area of Multicultural Education, Iowa State University, Office of Minority Student Affairs, 1994; 5th place award, Arcadia Poetry Press, 1995.

WRITINGS:

(Editor with Gretchen M. Bataille and Charles L. P. Silet, and contributor) *The Worlds between Two Rivers: Perspectives on American Indians in Iowa,* Iowa State University Press (Ames), 1978.

(With Nancy M. Osborn) *Exploring Buried Buxton: Archaeology of an Abandoned Iowa Coal Mining Town with a Large Black Population,* Iowa State University Press, 1984.

(With Nancy M. Osborn) *Blacks and Whites in Buxton: A Site Explored, a Town Remembered,* Media Resources Center, Iowa State University, 1986.

(With Timothy A. Kohler and Gary P. Smith) *Peer Review of the Central and Northern Plains Overview (CNPO),* Arkansas Archaeological Survey (Fayetteville, AR), 1994.

Facing Humanity: Selections from the Feinberg Mask Collection, Koch Brothers (Des Moines, IA), 1995.

Contributor to books, including *Aspects of Upper Great Lakes Anthropology: Papers in Honor of Lloyd A. Wilford,* edited by Eldon Johnson, Minnesota Historical Society (St. Paul), 1974; (with Hanna Rosenberg) *Persistence and Flexibility: Anthropological Studies of American Jewish Identities and Institutions,* edited by Walter P. Zenner, State University of New York Press (Albany), 1988; *Archaeology of Eastern North America,* edited by James B. Stoltman, Mississippi Department of Archives and History (Jackson), 1993; *Fragile Giants: Landscapes, Environments and Peoples,* edited by Connie

Mutel and Mary Swander, University of Iowa Press, 1994; *Tomorrow Never Knows,* Watermark (Owings Mills, MD), 1995; and *Treasured Poems of America, Fall 1995,* Sparrowgrass Poetry Forum (Sistersville, WV), 1995. Also contributor to *Plains Indian Studies: A Collection of Essays in Honor of John C. Evans and Waldo R. Wedel.*

Contributor of articles and reviews to scholarly journals. Member of editorial board of *Ethnic Reporter, Explorations in Sights and Sounds,* and *Explorations in Ethnic Studies,* 1987—. Member of advisory board, *Journal of the Iowa Archaeological Society,* 1992—.

WORK IN PROGRESS: A study of Jewish cemeteries in Des Moines; research on the archaeology of Buxton; research on the ethnoarchaeology of Jewish, Latvian-American, and American Indian cemeteries.

SIDELIGHTS: David M. Gradwohl told *CA:* "I am continuing my research projects (prehistoric and ethnoarchaeology), teaching interests (the American Indian, North American archaeology, and cultural continuity and change in the Prairie Plains), and social-activist involvements in American Indian studies. I serve as the faculty adviser to the recently formed American Indian Rights Organization (AIRO) at Iowa State University in addition to participating in the United Native American Student Association (UNASA), which I helped co-found in 1971. Each year on campus we sponsor the Iowa State University American Indian Symposium dealing with social and political issues as well as literary programs and art exhibits.

"Our archaeological work at Buxton, Iowa, resulted in the placement of the townsite on the National Register of Historic Places. Research verified the fact that both blacks and whites enjoyed a relatively high standard of living, had a well-ordered and appointed community, and lived together in a notably harmonious fashion. Our book and audiovisual program are aimed at getting this message across to people today in the hope of creating better interracial and cross-cultural understanding.

"My wife's and my recent ethnoarchaeological studies of Jewish cemeteries continue our research interests in historical traditions and ethnicity. More specifically, the studies show some of the dimensions of *intra*group diversity in regard to theology, national origin, and different sociocultural factors. Ultimately our understanding of the importance of ethnicity and individual identities must take into account *intra*group variations as well as *inter*group differences.

"In addition to my scientific research, writing, and reviews, I am also pursuing my dormant interests in creative writing. Several of my recent publications have intentionally slanted the humanistic dimension of anthropology. Beyond that, I am writing poetry and have published five poems since 1990."

*   *   *

GRAVES, Richard Perceval 1945-

PERSONAL: Born December 21, 1945, in Brighton, England; son of John Tiarks Ranke (a teacher) and Mary (a teacher; maiden name, Wickens) Graves; married Anne Katharine Fortescue, April 4, 1970 (divorced, 1988); children: David John, Philip Macartney, Lucia Mary. *Education:* St. John's College, Oxford, B.A., 1968, M.A., 1972. *Politics:* Social Democrat. *Religion:* Church of England.

ADDRESSES: Agent—Rachel Calder, Tessa Sayle Agency, 11 Jubilee Place, London SW3 3TE, England.

CAREER: Writer. Teacher of English, history, and Latin at private schools in England, 1968-73; Whittington parish councillor, 1973-76; chair of Whittington Youth Club, 1974-79; Oswestry borough councillor, 1977-83.

MEMBER: Society of Authors.

WRITINGS:

Lawrence of Arabia and His World, Scribner (New York City), 1976.
A. E. Housman: The Scholar-Poet, Routledge & Kegan Paul (London), 1979, Scribner, 1980.
The Brothers Powys, Scribner, 1983.
Robert Graves: The Assault Heroic, 1895-1926, Weidenfeld & Nicolson (London), 1986, Viking (New York City), 1987.
Robert Graves: The Years with Laura Riding, 1926-1940, Viking, 1990.
Richard Hughes, Andre Deutsch, 1994.
Robert Graves and the White Goddess (1940-1985), Weidenfeld & Nicolson, 1995.
(Editor) Robert Graves, *Good-bye to All That,* Berghahn Books, 1995.

Editor of *Housman Society Journal,* 1977-80.

SIDELIGHTS: Richard Perceval Graves is an English biographer and literary critic. The one-time teacher of

English, history, and Latin focuses much of his work on his uncle, Robert Graves, but he has also published works on other historical figures, including A. E. Housman and Richard Hughes.

Graves's *A. E. Housman: The Scholar-Poet,* published in 1979, is notable for shedding light on Housman's personal life and for bringing Housman the man to the forefront. According to William Pratt in *World Literature Today,* "Housman is a stern test for the biographer, and Graves has met it handsomely, constructing an honest and good-humored portrait of an exceedingly reticent and aloof figure, whose own family could never fathom him." Joseph Parisi comments in the *Chicago Tribune Book World* that Graves's text on Housman "presents a portrait of not only the sad artist and acerbic scholar, but what Housman's contemporaries were prevented from seeing: the kind, sensuous, many-sided human being."

While reviewers praise Graves for his success in depicting Housman's personal life, some criticize his analysis of Housman's poetry. Whereas James Atlas maintains in the *New York Times Book Review* that the author's estimate of Housman's poetry "seems to me just right," others, like Molly Tibbs in *Contemporary Review,* express some reservations. In the opinion of Tibbs, "the essay on Housman's achievements as a classical scholar . . . is neat, compendious and useful. One is, however, somewhat taken aback by . . . Graves'[s] apologetic attitude to the poetry. He begins his discussion thereof with the discouraging comment that there is much that is morbid and self-pitying. . . . [Graves] expressly wishes to introduce a new generation to the neglected beauties of Housman's poetry, and this cannot be the way to do it." Pratt believes that "it has to be said that if Graves adds much to the understanding of Housman's mind and character, he adds little to the appreciation of his art. In fact, he dismisses some of Housman's finest lyrics as 'inferior work.'" Nevertheless, according to a *New Yorker* reviewer, Graves's "realistic, honest, admiring approach is the best thing that could have happened to Housman's reputation."

In 1986 Graves published the first volume in a proposed multi-volume study of his uncle, the poet and novelist Robert Graves. A detailed examination of the elder writer's early years, *Robert Graves: The Assault Heroic, 1895-1926,* has received extensive critical attention, particularly regarding the family connection between the biographer and his subject. Opinions are divided as to the effect this relationship

has on the book. Commenting in the *New York Review of Books,* for example, John Wain states that the Graves biography "is very much a family job, and none the worse for a certain old-fashioned sense of family loyalty that peeps through its pages. He inherited a vast amount of manuscript material, and . . . it would have been a waste for him not to use it." John Gross concurs in his *New York Times* contribution: "one . . . enjoys the advantages of intimate family knowledge and access to previously unexplored family papers." In turn, Martin Seymour-Smith, once a tutor to Robert Graves's son and the author of the first biography of the poet in 1956, argues in the *London Review of Books* that the virtue of Graves's biography lies in "its meticulous Victorian charm." "What we have here is the first-hand account of a wayward genius from the viewpoint of one who 'loves' him . . . but cannot possibly even begin to understand him," comments Seymour-Smith. Though he finds the book "awful and misleading as an account of the processes of mind of Robert Graves between his birth and 1926," Seymour-Smith concludes that *The Assault Heroic* is "a perfect family record: something that I should have thought, until I read it, impossible of achievement at this over-sophisticated instant in history."

In contrast to these viewpoints, some critics think there might be too much of a family orientation in *Robert Graves: The Assault Heroic.* According to London *Times* commentator Peter Ackroyd, "this particular volume takes some 328 pages to complete a period of Robert Graves's history which, in Martin Seymour-Smith's own . . . biographical account, needed only 130. The recital of family memories does not necessarily make for interesting reading." *Books and Bookmen* contributor Paul O'Prey shares this opinion: "the seemingly endless list of relatives we meet can only be of limited interest to those outside the clan. This concentration on the family seriously unbalances the book. . . . Robert's friendships with . . . Siegfried Sassoon, T. E. Lawrence and Basanta Mallik, which were more important for him after he reached a certain age than were his relationships with his parents, and which are surely more important for us, receive a relatively superficial treatment."

Though the assessment of *Robert Graves: The Assault Heroic* is divided on the matter of how much family detail the author should have included in his study, many critics agree that the book is a lucid and honest portrait of Robert Graves. "His truth of tone and his respectfulness," notes Peter Levi in the *Spectator,* "have produced a full and clear picture with many currents under its surface." Levi ultimately judges the work to be a "wonderful and deeply stirring biography." And according to Gross, "[Richard Perceval] Graves tells his story straightforwardly and unaffectedly; there is no doubt a cleverer book on [Robert] Graves waiting to be written, but it is hard to imagine one that enters into his spirit with keener sympathy or more intuitive understanding." Samuel Hynes, commenting in the *New Republic,* describes *Robert Graves: The Assault Heroic* as "a promising beginning of what may well become the standard life of Graves. . . . It provides a full and sympathetic account of Graves's early worlds, told by an intelligent and informed observer." "Richard Graves is a good writer and a conscientious historian," concludes an *Atlantic Monthly* reviewer. "This is the first volume of what promises to be a splendid biography."

The second volume in Graves's biography of his uncle was 1990's *Robert Graves: The Years with Laura Riding, 1926-1940.* In this volume, Graves focuses on the years Robert spent in Egypt and England with the American poet Laura Riding. As Peter Kemp in the *Times Literary Supplement* notes, Robert Graves left his professorship at the University of Cairo and was soon bewitched by Laura: "[Robert Graves] rapidly became possessed by all her beliefs—outstanding among which was the notion that she was not of mere human stock but somehow embodied the principle of Finality and had brought historical time to a stop." Graves focuses on his uncle's menage a trois with Laura and his wife Nancy Nicholson (eventually turning into a short lived foursome with poet Geoffrey Phibbs), which "was as nothing [compared] to the melodrama to come," according to Kemp. Kemp concludes that no one "interested in [Robert] Graves—or the ludicrous—should miss" *The Years with Laura Riding.*

In 1994 Graves published *Richard Hughes,* a biography of the novelist, poet and playwright. T. J. Binyon in the *Times Literary Supplement* remarks that Graves' biography "answers perhaps all the questions which one might have about Hughes except for the most important: how good a novelist is he?" Hoping that the biography and the re-issuing of Hughes' novels would increase interest in the novelist's work, Binyon calls Graves's *Richard Hughes* an "interesting, extremely readable, sympathetic and solid biography."

BIOGRAPHICAL/CRITICAL SOURCES:

BOOKS

Contemporary Literary Criticism, Volume 44, Gale (Detroit), 1987.

PERIODICALS

Atlantic Monthly, April, 1987.
Books and Bookmen, November, 1986.
Chicago Tribune Book World, June 15, 1980.
Contemporary Review, February, 1980; April, 1983; December, 1994.
Kirkus Reviews, September 1, 1990, p. 1223.
London Review of Books, October 9, 1986; April 5, 1990, p. 10; June 23, 1994, p. 20.
New Republic, June 28, 1980; March 30, 1987.
New Yorker, August 18, 1980.
New York Review of Books, June 25, 1987.
New York Times, March 6, 1987.
New York Times Book Review, May 25, 1980.
Observer (London), September 21, 1986; May 22, 1994, p. 18.
Spectator, March 19, 1983; September 27, 1986; May 28, 1994, p. 31.
Time, July 28, 1980; September 11, 1986.
Times (London), April 4, 1981.
Times Literary Supplement, December 21, 1979; November 21, 1986; August 3, 1990, p. 820; August 19, 1994, p. 5.
Washington Post Book World, June 29, 1980; March 15, 1987.
World Literature Today, spring, 1981.

* * *

GRAVES, Valerie
See BRADLEY, Marion Zimmer

* * *

GREEN, Paul E(dgar) 1927-

PERSONAL: Born April 4, 1927, in Glenolden, PA; son of Joseph (a law book dealer) and Lucy Mae (Gordy) Green; married Elizabeth Ann Weamer; children: three. *Education:* University of Pennsylvania, A.B., 1950, A.M., 1953, Ph.D., 1961.

ADDRESSES: Office—Department of Marketing, Wharton School, Suite 1450, Steinberg Hall-Dietrich Hall, University of Pennsylvania, Philadelphia, PA 19104-6371.

CAREER: Sun Oil Co., Philadelphia, PA, statistician, 1950-53; Lukens Steel Co., Coatesville, PA, commercial research analyst, 1953-54, supervisor of operations research group and senior marketing analyst, 1955-58; E. I. duPont DeNemours & Co., Wilmington, DE, market planning consultant, 1958-62. University of Pennsylvania, Wharton School, Philadelphia, instructor in statistics, 1954-55, deputy director of Management Science Center and associate professor, 1962-65, professor, 1965-71, S. S. Kresge Professor of Marketing, 1971—. Guest lecturer at more than one hundred universities in the United States, Europe, Latin America, the Far East, and Australia/New Zealand. Consultant to private firms, including General Motors, IBM, and American Airlines.

Chair of Institute of Management Sciences' College on Marketing, 1970-71; member of advisory council, Association for Consumer Behavior, 1970-74; American Marketing Association, member of local executive council, 1965-69, Educational Advisory committee on Pharmaceutical Marketing, 1967-68, Parlin Award committee, 1972-79, 1982-87, and board of directors, 1976-78; member of Census Advisory Committee, 1980-83; Academy of Marketing Sciences, member of policy board, 1982-85, advisory board, 1988-90; SEI Center for Advanced Studies in Management, member of advisory board, 1989—.

MEMBER: European Marketing Research Society, American Association for the Advancement of Science, American Marketing Association, Operations Research Society of America, Institute of Management Sciences, American Institute of Decision Sciences (fellow), Society of Multivariate Experimental Psychology, American Statistical Association (fellow), Psychometric Society, Academy of Marketing Sciences, Association of Consumer Research.

AWARDS, HONORS: Award from Alpha Kappa Psi, 1963, 1981, and 1991; silver medal from J. Walter Thompson Agency, 1970; honorable mention in research design contest from American Marketing Association, 1971; first prize in research design competition from American Psychological Association, 1972; Parlin Award for the advancement of science in marketing from American Marketing Association, 1977; Paul D. Converse Award in marketing theory, 1978; distinguished lecturer award from Beta Gamma Sigma, 1978; elected to Attitude Research Hall of Fame, 1981; O'Dell Award, *Journal of Marketing Research,* finalist, 1982, 1987, and winner, 1989; special award from Marketing Science Institute, 1986; finalist for Franz Edelman Award, 1988; Outstanding Marketing Educator Award, Academy of Marketing Science, 1992.

WRITINGS:

(With Wroe Alderson) *Planning and Problem Solving in Marketing,* Irwin (Homewood, IL), 1964.

(With D. S. Tull) *Research for Marketing Decisions,* Prentice-Hall (Englewood Cliffs, NJ), 1966, 5th edition (with Tull and G. Albaum), 1988.

(With P. T. FitzRoy and P. J. Robinson) *Experiments on the Value of Information in Simulated Marketing Environments* (monograph), Allyn & Bacon (Newton, MA), 1967.

(With R. E. Frank) *A Manager's Guide to Marketing Research: Survey of Recent Developments,* Wiley (New York City), 1967.

(With Frank) *Quantitative Methods in Marketing Analysis,* Prentice-Hall, 1967.

(With F. J. Carmone) *Multidimensional Scaling and Related Techniques in Marketing Analysis,* Allyn & Bacon, 1970.

(With V. R. Rao) *Applied Multidimensional Scaling,* Holt (New York City), 1972.

(With Yoram Wind) *Multi-Attribute Decisions in Marketing,* Holt, 1973.

(Editor with Martin Christopher) *Brand Positioning,* EJM Publishers (London), 1973.

Mathematical Tools for Applied Multivariate Analysis, Academic Press (New York City), 1976.

Analyzing Multivariate Data, Dryden (Hinsdale, IL), 1978.

(With P. K. Kedia and R. S. Nikhil) *Electronic Questionnaire Design and Analysis with CAPPA,* Scientific Press (Palo Alto, CA), 1985.

(With Carmone and Scott Smith) *Multidimensional Scaling: Concepts and Applications,* Allyn and Bacon, 1989.

MONOGRAPHS, PUBLISHED BY OMICRON RESEARCH (PHILADELPHIA)

Conjoint Analysis and Buyer Choice Simulation with HYCON, 1985.

(With A. M. Kreiger) *Product Positioning and Preference Analysis with METRIMAP,* 1986.

(With Krieger) *Conjoint Analysis and Computer Simulation with HYSIM,* 1986.

(With C. M. Schaeffer) *Advertising and Concept Testing with ADVAL,* 1987.

(With Krieger and Schaeffer) *Optimal Product Line Design and Positioning with OPTPRO,* 1987.

OTHER

Contributor to numerous books, including *Marketing and the Computer,* edited by Alderson and Shapiro, Prentice-Hall, 1963; *Explorations in Consumer Behavior,* edited by Montrose Sommers and Jerome Kernan, University of Texas Press (Austin), 1968; *Multivariate Procedures in Marketing,* edited by J. N. Sheth, American Marketing Association (Chicago, IL), 1975; *Encyclopedia of the Statistical Sciences,* McGraw (New York City), 1983; and *Marketing Handbook,* second edition, edited by S. Levy, Dartnell (Chicago, IL), in press. Coeditor of a marketing series, Holt, 1967-78.

Contributor of more than a hundred articles to technical journals, including *Business Horizons, Journal of Marketing, Applied Statistics, Management Science, Wharton Quarterly,* and *Journal of Consumer Research.* Associate editor of *Decision Sciences,* 1990; member of editorial board of *Journal of Marketing Research,* 1965—, *Journal of Consumer Research,* 1973-87, *Journal of Business Research,* 1973-75, *Journal of Marketing,* 1978—, *Journal of the Market Research Society* (London), 1981—, *Journal of Classification,* 1984—; *International Journal of Research in Marketing,* 1985-86, *Marketing Science,* 1985-94; and *Journal of the Academy of Marketing Science,* 1991—; referee for *Psychometrika, Journal of the Operations Research Society, Management Science, Academy of Marketing Science, International Journal of Research in Marketing,* and *Decision Sciences.*

WORK IN PROGRESS: Marketing Research, with G. Albaum and S. M. Smith.

*   *   *

GREGORY, J. Dennis
  See WILLIAMS, John A(lfred)

GRIFFITH, Jeannette
  See EYERLY, Jeannette

*   *   *

GRIFFITHS, Helen   1939-
  (Helen Santos)

PERSONAL: Born May 8, 1939, in London, England; daughter of Mary Christine (Selwood) Griffiths; married Pedro Santos de la Cal (a hotel manager), October 17, 1959 (died June 21, 1973); children: Elena, Cristina, Sara. *Education:* Attended Balham and Tooting College of Commerce, London, 1953-56.

CAREER: Novelist and freelance writer. Cowgirl on farm in Bedfordshire, England, 1956; Blackstock Engineering, Cockfosters, Hertfordshire, secretary, 1957-58; Selfridges Department Store, London, employee in record section, 1958-59; Oliver and Boyd Ltd. (publisher), London, secretary, 1959-60; teacher of English as a foreign language, Madrid, 1973-76; parish church secretary in Bath, England, 1984—.

AWARDS, HONORS: Highly commended by Carnegie Medal Award, 1966, for *The Wild Horse of Santander;* Child Study Association book list mention, 1968, for *Stallion of the Sands;* Silver Pencil Award, Holland, 1978, for *Witch Fear.*

WRITINGS:

JUVENILE

Horse in the Clouds, illustrated by Edward Osmond, Hutchinson (London), 1957, Holt (New York City), 1958.

Wild and Free, illustrated by Osmond, Hutchinson, 1958.

Moonlight, illustrated by Osmond, Hutchinson, 1959.

Africano, Hutchinson, 1961.

The Wild Heart, illustrated by Victor Ambrus, Hutchinson, 1963, Doubleday (New York City), 1964.

The Greyhound, illustrated by Ambrus, Hutchinson, 1964, Doubleday, 1966.

The Wild Horse of Santander, illustrated by Ambrus, Hutchinson, 1966, Doubleday, 1967.

Leon, illustrated by Ambrus, Hutchinson, 1967, Doubleday, 1968.

Stallion of the Sands, illustrated by Ambrus, Hutchinson, 1968, Lothrop, 1970.

Moshie Cat: The True Adventures of a Mallorquin Kitten, illustrated by Shirley Hughes, Hutchinson, 1969, Holiday House (New York City), 1970.

Patch, illustrated by Maurice Wilson, Hutchinson, 1970.

Federico, illustrated by Hughes, Hutchinson, 1971.

Russian Blue, illustrated by Ambrus, Hutchinson, 1973, Holiday House, 1973.

Just a Dog, illustrated by Ambrus, Hutchinson, 1974, Holiday House, 1975.

Witch Fear, illustrated by Ambrus, Hutchinson, 1975, published as *The Mysterious Appearance of Agnes,* Holiday House, 1975.

Pablo, illustrated by Ambrus, Hutchinson, 1977, published as *Running Wild,* Holiday House, 1977.

The Kershaw Dogs, illustrated by Douglas Hall, Hutchinson, 1978, published as *Grip: A Dog Story,* Holiday House, 1978.

The Last Summer: Spain 1936, illustrated by Ambrus, Hutchinson, 1979, Holiday House, 1979.

Blackface Stallion, illustrated by Ambrus, Hutchinson, 1980, Holiday House, 1980.

Dancing Horses, Hutchinson, 1981, Holiday House, 1982.

Hari's Pigeon, Hutchinson, 1982.

Jesus, as Told by Mark, illustrated by Jenny Kisler, Scripture Union (Philadelphia), 1983.

Rafa's Dog, Hutchinson, 1983, Holiday House, 1983.

(Under name Helen Santos) *Caleb's Lamb,* Scripture Union, 1984.

The Dog at the Window, Hutchinson, 1984, Holiday House, 1984.

(Under name Helen Santos) *If Only,* Scripture Union, 1987.

OTHER

The Dark Swallows (adult novel), Hutchinson, 1966, Knopf (New York City), 1967.

ADAPTATIONS: The Wild Heart was serialized by the British Broadcasting Corp.

SIDELIGHTS: Helen Griffiths began publishing at age seventeen. That first book, *Horse in the Clouds,* was "all about horses and gauchos," as she describes it in an entry in *Something about the Author Autobiography Series* (*SAAS*), and it set the tone for nearly two dozen books to follow: compassionate animal stories set in foreign lands. Her twin passions—animals and things Spanish—set the course for much of her life, as well, for she married a Spaniard and lived for many years in Spain. Griffiths' central "kindling theme," according to Naomi Lewis in *Twentieth-Century Children's Writers,* is "the lot of animals—those especially linked with man—in a predatory human world."

Griffiths left school at the age of fifteen to work as a cowgirl in Bedfordshire. It was then that she also began to write *Horse in the Clouds,* a story set in Argentina, a country she had never visited. "My ambition," she explains in *SAAS,* "was to write the kind of horse story I'd always wanted to read. I tried to put into it just about everything I'd always wanted to find in a horse story, but never had." When the publishing firm of Hutchinson accepted and published the book, she became something of a celebrity because of her extreme youth. "There were interviews on BBC television and radio," she recalls in *SAAS,* "fan letters, and seventy-five pounds, an incredible sum of money."

Following her marriage to a Spainard in 1959, Griffiths lived for many years in Spain, a country that has been the setting for many of her novels, both contemporary and historical. She has set several books during the Spanish Civil War of the 1930s. In *Leon,* Griffiths creates a "memorable story of the relationship between dog and man," according to Virginia Haviland, writing in *Horn Book.* Ten years later she returned to the historical epoch of the Spanish Civil War, this time taking on the challenge of writing a sympathetic treatment of somebody on the Franco side of the conflict. The result was *The Last Summer: Spain 1936,* a story of a young boy whose father is killed by the revolutionary soldiers and who must ride on his favorite mare to the safety of his mother. Ethel L. Heins, in *Horn Book,* notes that Griffiths' "profound knowledge of Spain and her love of animals" are everywhere evident in this "moving, sensitively told story." A reviewer for *Publishers Weekly* concludes that *The Last Summer* is an "engrossing adventure."

Griffiths also periodically returned to Argentina in her writings. Though she has never visited the country, her portraits were so accurately drawn that when her books were published in Argentina she received fan mail telling her how well she had captured the sense of place. *Stallion of the Sands* tells the story of young Aurelio, who sets out to find his long-missing gaucho father and prove himself to be a gaucho in the process. Though criticized for its lengthy opening told from the horse's point of view, the novel is also "an exciting adventure story," as Mary E. Ballou writes in *Library Journal*. The strength of the book, according to *Kirkus Reviews,* is in "the embrace of 19th century life on the pampas."

Following her husband's death in an auto accident in 1973, Griffiths was forced to provide for her family alone. She taught English in Madrid and concentrated on writing books at a steady pace. Two of her most popular books, *The Mysterious Appearance of Agnes* and *Running Wild,* appeared at this time. The first, originally published in England as *Witch Fear,* was a complete departure for Griffiths: a story told without an animal protagonist. Set in the sixteenth century, the book tells the story of a young autistic girl who wanders out of the forest one day and is adopted by a childless couple. The girl is later suspected of being a witch but in the process of proving her innocence, she begins to heal the trauma leading to her autism. The books is a "powerful story," notes Paul Heins in *Horn Book,* while Elizabeth Jane Howard in *New Statesman* concludes that Griffiths displays "true imaginative power." The book also won the Silver Pencil Award from Holland upon translation into Dutch. *Running Wild* is set in a more familiar setting for Griffiths, telling the story of a Spanish boy who must abandon a litter of puppies. Published as *Pablo* in England, the book brings home the powerful message of—as Paul Heins in *Horn Book* puts it—the "great disparity between nature's way and man's way."

In a book that tested the "loyalty of her animal-lover fans," as a critic for *Publishers Weekly* states, Griffiths explores the world of bullfighting in *Dancing Horses.* Set in Spain after the Civil War, this coming-of-age story traces the dreams of a stableboy who wants to train an unruly Andalusian horse for bullfighting. Charlene Strickland, writing in *School Library Journal,* notes that the book contains "fast-paced action," and Karen M. Klockner in *Horn Book* commends the book as "gracefully written."

Griffiths once explained the motivation behind her books: "I love animals, I have an instinctive feeling for them, so that it is only natural that I should combine my love of writing with my love of animals to produce books about them. I hope that my books in some small way help children to understand and appreciate animals too."

BIOGRAPHICAL/CRITICAL SOURCES:

BOOKS

Something about the Author Autobiography Series, Volume 5, Gale (Detroit), 1988, pp. 147-60.
Twentieth-Century Children's Writers, 4th edition, St. James Press (Detroit), 1995, pp. 417-18.

PERIODICALS

Booklist, September 15, 1966, p. 119; March 15, 1968, p. 867; March 1, 1971, p. 558; April 1, 1971, p. 663; September 1, 1975, p. 40; January 1, 1976, p. 626; February 1, 1978, p. 924; December 1, 1978, p. 616; January 1, 1980, p. 667; November 15, 1980, p. 459; February 1, 1984, p. 813.
Bulletin of the Center for Children's Books, September, 1975, p. 9; April, 1976, p. 124; April, 1984, p. 147.
Horn Book, October, 1967, p. 593; April, 1968, p. 177; February, 1976, p. 50; April, 1978, pp. 165-66; February, 1979, p. 61; April, 1980, p. 173; December, 1980, p. 649; August, 1982, p. 403; February, 1984, p. 53; January, 1985, p. 50.
Junior Bookshelf, April, 1983, p. 81.
Kirkus Reviews, October 15, 1970, p. 1162.
Library Journal, January 15, 1971, p. 268.
New Statesman, November 7, 1975, p. 583.
New Yorker, December 17, 1966, p. 223.
Publishers Weekly, September 28, 1970, p. 80; December 3, 1979, p. 51; June 18, 1982, p. 74.
School Library Journal, September, 1975, p. 103; December, 1975, p. 67; January, 1978, p. 89; January, 1979, p. 61; December, 1979, p. 91; February, 1984, p. 70; February, 1985, p. 84; August, 1986, pp. 36-37.
Times Literary Supplement, November 24, 1966, p. 1091; November 30, 1967, p. 1157; October 3, 1968, p. 1110; June 26, 1969, p. 700; April 2, 1971, p. 391; June 15, 1973, p. 684; December 5, 1975, p. 1450.

*   *   *

GROSS, S(amuel Harry) 1933-

PERSONAL: Born August 7, 1933, in Bronx, NY; son of Max (an accountant) and Sophie (Heller) Gross; married Isabelle Jaffe (a social work supervisor), June 7, 1959; children: Michelle. *Education:* College of the City of New York (now City College of the City University of New York), B.B.A., 1954.

ADDRESSES: Home—115 East 89th St., New York, NY 10128.

CAREER: Accountant, 1956-62; freelance cartoonist, 1962—. Designer of greeting cards and lithograph prints; has written for Public Broadcasting System's "Sesame Street"; former senior contributing artist, and cartoon editor, 1991-92, for *National Lampoon;* cartoon editor for *Parents* magazine, 1993, and *Smoke* magazine, 1995. Works exhibited at Foundry Gallery, Washington, DC, 1983, and Master Eagle Gallery, New York City, 1984 and 1985. Former vice-president and president, Cartoonists Guild. *Military service:* U.S. Army, 1954-56.

MEMBER: Cartoonists Association.

AWARDS, HONORS: Inkpot Award, San Diego Comicon, 1980.

WRITINGS:

CARTOONS

How Gross, Dell (New York City), 1973.
I Am Blind and My Dog Is Dead, Dodd (New York City), 1977.
An Elephant Is Soft and Mushy, Dodd, 1980.
ULK (collection), Nelson Verlag (Germany), 1980.
More Gross, Congdon & Weed (New York City), 1982.
Love Me, Love My Teddy Bear, Perigee (New York City), 1986.
No More Mr. Nice Guy: A New Collection of Outrageous Cartoons, Perigee, 1987.
Your Mother Is a Remarkable Woman, Viking (New York City), 1993.
Grossieretes (collection), Glenat (France), 1993.
Cats by Gross, Ballantine (New York City), 1995.

EDITOR

(And author of foreword) *Why Are Your Papers in Order?: Cartoons for 1984,* Avon (New York City), 1983.
Dogs, Dogs, Dogs: A Collection of Great Dog Cartoons, Harper (New York City), 1985.
Cats, Cats, Cats: A Collection of Great Cat Cartoons, Harper, 1986.
All You Can Eat: A Collection of Great Food Cartoons, Harper, 1987.
(With Jim Charlton) *Books, Books, Books: A Hilarious Collection of Literary Cartoons,* Harper, 1988.
Golf, Golf, Golf: A Collection of Great Golf Cartoons, Harper, 1989.
Movies, Movies, Movies, Harper, 1990.
(With Charlton) *Ho, Ho, Ho: A Stocking-Full of Christmas Cartoons,* Penguin (New York City), 1990.
Moms, Moms, Moms: A Mirthful Merriment of Cartoons, Harper, 1990.
(With Charlton) *Play Ball: An All-Star Lineup of Baseball Cartoons,* HarperCollins (New York City), 1991.
Cat Cartoon-A-Day Calendar, Viking, 1993.
Lawyers, Lawyers, Lawyers: Cartoon Collection, Contemporary Books (Chicago, IL), 1994.
Teachers, Teachers, Teachers, Contemporary Books, 1995.

Contributor to numerous books, including *Best Cartoons of the World,* edited by Bob Abel, Dell, 1969; *Best Cartoons from the New Yorker, 1925-1975,* Viking, 1975; *Jumping Up and Down on the Roof, Throwing Bags of Water on People,* Doubleday (New York City), 1980; *The New Yorker Book of Cat Cartoons,* Knopf (New York City), 1990; *National Lampoon's Truly Tasteless Cartoons,* Contemporary Books, 1992; *That's Sick: National Lampoon's Rudest and Crudest Cartoons,* Contemporary Books, 1994; *National Lampoon's Truly Twisted Cartoons,* Contemporary Books, 1995; and *The 100 Best Comics of the Century,* Metropolis Publishing, 1995.

Also contributor to syndicated newspaper features and numerous periodicals, including the *New Yorker, Esquire, National Lampoon, Cosmopolitan, Saturday Review, Genius,* and *Toppix.*

H-I

HAAKONSSEN, Knud 1947-

PERSONAL: Given name is pronounced "Ca-*nute*"; born July 9, 1947, in Tingsted, Denmark; son of Helmer Daniel (a lawyer) and Laura Eline (a shopkeeper; maiden name, Marquardsen) Haakonssen; married Lis Soerensen (a high school teacher), June 26, 1968 (divorced, 1986); married Lisbeth Mary Gurholt, January 1987; children: (first marriage) Eric Christoph. *Education:* University of Copenhagen, M.A., 1972; University of Edinburgh, Ph.D., 1978.

ADDRESSES: Home—Brookline, MA. *Office*—Department of Philosophy, Boston University, 745 Commonwealth Ave., Boston, MA 02215.

CAREER: Monash University, Melbourne, Australia, senior tutor in philosophy, 1976-79; Victoria University of Wellington, Wellington, New Zealand, lecturer in political theory, 1979-82; Australian National University, Canberra, began as research fellow, became senior research fellow, later became senior fellow in the history of ideas, 1982-94; Boston University, Boston, MA, professor of philosophy and director of Graduate Studies in Philosophy, 1995—. Visiting professor at University of New Brunswick, 1984; visiting fellow at University of Aarhus, 1985, University of Edinburgh, 1986, and Australian National University, Max-Planck Institute for History, Woodrow Wilson International Center for Scholars, University of Manitoba, and McGill University. Lecturer for International Hume Society/National Endowment for the Humanities, 1990.

MEMBER: International Hume Society (member of Executive Committee, 1990-92), Secretariat of the International Association for Philosophy of Law and Social Philosophy (1990-92), International Society for Intellectual History, International Faculty of Danish Research Academy, American Philosophical Association, Australasian Association of Philosophy, American Society of Legal Philosophy, British Society for the History of Philosophy, New Zealand Society for Legal Philosophy (cofounder and past committee member), Edinburgh University Philosophy Society (president, 1974-75), American Society for Eighteenth-Century Studies, British Society for Eighteenth-Century Studies, Deutsche Gesellschaft fuer die Erforschung des achtzehnten Jahrhunderts, Societe francaise d'etude du XVIIIe siecle, Schweizerische Gesellschaft fuer die Erforschung des achtzehnten Jahrhunderts, International Society for Eighteenth-Century Studies, Eighteenth-Century Scottish Studies Society, The Conference for the Study of Political Thought, Lessing Akademie, Wolfenbuettel.

AWARDS, HONORS: Gold medal of the University of Aarhus, 1970; Academy of Social Sciences in Australia fellow, 1992; Royal Danish Academy of Sciences and Letters foreign member, 1995; various Australian, British, Canadian, Danish, and German grants.

WRITINGS:

The Science of a Legislator: The Natural Jurisprudence of David Hume and Adam Smith, Cambridge University Press (Cambridge, England), 1981.

(Editor) *The Liberal Tradition,* Centre for Independent Studies (Sydney, Australia), 1987.

(Editor) *Traditions of Liberalism: Essays on John Locke, Adam Smith and John Stuart Mill,* Centre for Independent Studies, 1988.

(Editor) Thomas Reid, *Practical Ethics: Being Lectures and Papers on Natural Religion, Self-Government, Natural Jurisprudence, and the Law of Nations,* Princeton University Press (Princeton, NJ), 1990.

(Coeditor) *A Culture of Rights: The Bill of Rights in Philosophy, Politics and Law—1791 and 1991,* Cambridge University Press, 1991.

(Editor) David Hume, *Political Essays: 'Cambridge Texts in the History of Political Thought,'* Cambridge University Press, 1994.

(Editor and author of introduction) Dugald Stewart, *Collected Works,* eleven volumes, Thoemmes Press (Bristol, England), 1994.

Moral Philosophy and Natural Law: From Hugo Grotius to the Scottish Enlightenment, Cambridge University Press, 1995.

(Editor) *Enlightenment and Religion: The Case of the Rational Dissenters, 'Ideas in Context,'* Cambridge University Press, 1996.

Also translator into Danish of T. S. Kuhn's *The Structure of Scientific Revolutions,* Bertrand Russell's *Problems of Philosophy,* and selections of K. R. Popper's *Kritisk Rationalisme.* Contributor to history and political science journals.

WORK IN PROGRESS: Editing *The Cambridge History of Eighteenth-Century Philosophy* and *The Edinburgh Edition of Thomas Reid;* research on natural law/natural rights and on the Enlightenment.

*   *   *

HADFIELD, (Ellis) Charles (Raymond) 1909-
(E. C. R. Hadfield; pseudonym, Charles Alexander)

PERSONAL: Born August 5, 1909, in Pietersburg, South Africa; son of Alexander Charles and Marion Francis (Fulford) Hadfield; married Alice Mary Smyth (a writer), October 20, 1945; children: Alexander, John, Caroline; Laura (stepdaughter). *Education:* Attended Blundell's School and St. Edmund Hall, Oxford. *Religion:* Church of England.

ADDRESSES: Home and office—13 Meadow Way, South Cerney, Cirencester, Gloucestershire GLY

6HY, England. *Agent*—David Higham Associates Ltd., 5-8 Lower John St., Golden Square, London W1R 4HA, England.

CAREER: Oxford University Press, London, editor, 1936-38, chief editor of juvenile books, 1938-39, 1945-46; Central Office of Information, London, director of publications, 1946-48, overseas controller, 1948-62; David & Charles (publishers), Newton Abbot, England, director, 1960-64. Councillor, Paddington Borough Council, 1924-35; part-time member, British Waterways Board, 1962-66.

MEMBER: Railway and Canal Historical Society (president, 1960-63), Inland Waterways Association (vice president), Newcomen Society.

AWARDS, HONORS: Companion of Order of St. Michael and St. George, 1954.

WRITINGS:

(With Frank Eyre) *English Rivers and Canals,* World Publishing, 1945.

British Canals: An Illustrated History, Phoenix House (London), 1950, 7th edition, David & Charles (Newton Abbot, England), 1984.

(Under pseudonym Charles Alexander) *The Church's Year,* Oxford University Press (Oxford, England), 1950.

Introducing Canals, Benn (London), 1955.

The Canals of Southern England, Phoenix House, 1955, augmented excerpts published as *The Canals of South West England,* David & Charles, 1967, 2nd edition, 1985, and *The Canals of South and South East England,* David & Charles, 1969.

The Canals of South Wales and the Border, University of Wales Press (Cardiff, England), 1960, 2nd edition, David & Charles, 1967.

(With John Norris) *Waterways to Stratford,* David & Charles, 1962, 2nd edition, 1968.

Canals of the World, Basil Blackwell (Oxford, England), 1964.

The Canals of the West Midlands, 1966, 3rd edition, David & Charles, 1985.

The Canals of the East Midlands, David & Charles, 1966, 2nd edition, 1970.

Canals and Waterways, Raleigh Press, 1966.

(With wife, Alice Mary Hadfield) *The Cotswolds,* Batsford (London), 1966.

Atmospheric Railways: A Victorian Venture in Silent Speed, David & Charles, 1967, 2nd edition, Sutton (Gloucester, England), 1985.

(With Michael Streat) *Holiday Cruising on Inland Waterways,* David & Charles, 1968, 2nd edition, 1971.

The Canal Age, David & Charles, 1968, Praeger (New York City), 1969, 2nd edition, David & Charles, 1981.

(With Gordon Biddle) *The Canals of North West England,* David & Charles, 1970.

(Editor) *Canal Enthusiasts' Handbook, 1970-1971,* David & Charles, 1970.

The Canals of Yorkshire and North East England, David & Charles, 1972-73.

(Editor) *Canal Enthusiasts' Handbook Number 2,* David & Charles, 1973.

(Editor with Hadfield, and contributor) *The Cotswolds: A New Study,* David & Charles, 1973.

Waterways Sights to See, David & Charles, 1976.

(With Hadfield) *Introducing the Cotswolds,* David & Charles, 1976.

Inland Waterways, David & Charles, 1978.

(With Hadfield) *Afloat in America,* David & Charles, 1979.

(With A. W. Skempton) *William Jessop, Engineer,* David & Charles, 1979.

World Canals: Inland Navigation Past and Present, David & Charles, 1986.

Thomas Telford's Temptation, Baldwin (London), 1993.

UNDER NAME E. C. R. HADFIELD

(Editor) *Book of Sea Verse,* Oxford University Press, 1940.

Civilian Fire Fighter, English Universities Press, 1941.

(Compiler) *Book of Animal Verse,* Oxford University Press, 1943.

(With James E. MacColl) *Pilot Guide to Political London,* Pilot Press, 1945.

(With MacColl) *British Local Government,* Hutchinson University Library (London), 1948.

CHILDREN'S BOOKS; UNDER NAME E. C. R. HADFIELD

(With C. H. Ellis) *Young Collector's Handbook,* Oxford University Press, 1940.

(With Alexander D'Agapeyeff) *Maps,* Oxford University Press, 1942, 2nd edition, 1950.

Fire Service To-day, Oxford University Press, 1944, 2nd edition, 1953.

OTHER

Contributor of articles on canals to journals. Editor, *Quaker Monthly,* 1963-69.

WORK IN PROGRESS: Charles Hadfield: Canal Man-and More, "a combined autobiography, written by Hadfield, and critical biography of Charles Hadfield as a canal writer, written by Joseph Boughey," for Sutton, 1998.

BIOGRAPHICAL/CRITICAL SOURCES:

BOOKS

Baldwin, Mark, and Anthony Burton, editors, *Canals, A New Look: Studies in Honour of Charles Hadfield,* Phillimore (Chichester, England), 1984.

*   *   *

HADFIELD, E. C. R.
  See HADFIELD, (Ellis) Charles (Raymond)

*   *   *

HAFEMEISTER, David W(alter)   1934-

PERSONAL: Born July 1, 1934, in Chicago, IL; son of Lester D. (in business) and Alma D. (a homemaker; maiden name, Schmidt) Hafemeister; married Gina Rohlander (a weaver), 1961; children: Andrew, Jason, Heidi. *Education:* Northwestern University, B.S.M.E., 1957; University of Illinois at Urbana-Champaign, M.S., 1960, Ph.D., 1964.

ADDRESSES: Home—553 Serrano, San Luis Obispo, CA 93401. *Office*—Department of Physics, California Polytechnic State University, San Luis Obispo, CA 93407.

CAREER: Argonne National Laboratory, Argonne, IL, Particle Accelerator Division, mechanical engineer, 1957-58; Los Alamos Scientific Laboratory, Los Alamos, NM, physicist and research fellow in physics division, 1964-66; Carnegie-Mellon University, Pittsburgh, PA, assistant professor of physics, 1966-69; California Polytechnic State University,

San Luis Obispo, assistant professor, 1969-72, associate professor of physics, 1972—. Science adviser to U.S. Senator John Glenn, 1975-77; special assistant to undersecretary of state, 1977-78. Visiting scientist at Massachusetts Institute of Technology, 1983-84, and at Lawrence Berkeley National Laboratory, 1985-86. Staff member, Senate Foreign Relations Committee, 1990-92, and Senate Governmental Affairs Committee, 1992-93.

MEMBER: American Association for the Advancement of Science, American Physical Society.

AWARDS, HONORS: Scientific Congressional fellow, 1975-76; fellow of American Association for the Advancement of Science at Office of Strategic Nuclear Policy, U.S. Department of State, 1987—.

WRITINGS:

(With Anthony Buffa and Ronald Brown) *Physics for Modern Architecture,* Paladin, 1983.
(Editor with Dietrich Schroeer) *Physics and Technology of the Nuclear Arms Race,* American Institute of Physics (New York City), 1983.
(Editor with Henry Kelly and Barbara Levi) *Energy Sources: Conservation and Renewables,* American Institute of Physics, 1985.
(Editor with Kosta Tsipis and Penny Janeway) *Arms Control Verification: The Technologies That Make It Possible,* Pergamon (Elmsford, NY), 1986.
Science and Society "Tests," El Corale, 1988.
Nuclear Arms Technologies in the 1990s, American Institute of Physics, 1988.
Physics and Nuclear Arms Today, American Institute of Physics, 1991.
Global Warming: Physics and Facts, American Institute of Physics, 1992.

SIDELIGHTS: David W. Hafemeister's fourth book, *Arms Control Verification: The Technologies That Make It Possible,* is, according to critic Paul Bracken, "a work that gives the educated public insight into the arcane world of the technologies that underlie assessments of whether or not states are living up to the agreements they enter into." *Arms Control Verification* is concerned, not so much with the question of whether an arms control agreement is being violated, but whether such an agreement can be verified by modern technology. Some of the book's contributors are disturbed by the development of such weapons as the cruise missile, the Stealth bomber, and the new, ultra-quiet submarines, which

may be all but impossible to detect. Others consider the difficulty of accurately monitoring nuclear tests. Still other contributors point out that the monitoring devices themselves are capable of being used in an active, hostile manner. Bracken concludes in his *Washington Post Book World* review: "Overall this book is an important contribution to the understanding of arms control and national security because it throws light on obscure areas of technology."

Hafemeister once told *CA:* "In several areas I remain optimistic that improved technologies can monitor arms control treaties. For example, by calibrating nuclear test sites with nuclear explosions it should be possible to measure the difference between test sites and thus improve the monitoring of the Threshold Test Ban Treaty. By employing remote, unattended seismic stations in the Soviet Union, it should be possible to reduce the threshold below 150 kilotons to the region of 1 to 10 kilotons. In the area of Strategic Arms Reduction Treaty or Strategic Arms Limitation Treaty, the advances in mobile missiles and cruise missiles present more difficult challenges than the silos of the past, but by using cooperative means, along with advances in electronics and optics, some of these difficulties can be overcome.

"In my view, science and technology are the driving forces of history, much more so than pan-nationalism and varying economics systems. If we don't look at the implications of these technologies, then we shouldn't be surprised if some negative results surface to haunt us. Our goal should be to refrain from those technologies that can make a bad situation worse."

BIOGRAPHICAL/CRITICAL SOURCES:

PERIODICALS

Washington Post Book World, June 22, 1986.

*   *   *

HALLETT, Judith Peller   1944-

PERSONAL: Born April 4, 1944, in Chicago, IL; daughter of Leonard (an engineer) and Celia (in business; maiden name, Stern) Peller; married Mark Hallett (a neurologist), June 26, 1966; children: Nicholas Leonard, Victoria Claire. *Education:*

Wellesley College, A.B., 1966; Harvard University, M.A., 1967, Ph.D., 1971. *Politics:* Democrat. *Religion:* Jewish.

ADDRESSES: Home—5147 Westbard Ave., Bethesda, MD 20816. *Office*—Department of Classics, University of Maryland at College Park, College Park, MD 20742.

CAREER: Teacher, secondary school level, Latin and ancient civilizations, Phillips Academy, Andover, MA, 1965, Buckingham School, Cambridge, MA, 1967-69, Stone Ridge Academy of the Sacred Heart, Bethesda, MD, 1970-72; Harvard University, Cambridge, MA, teaching fellow, 1969-70; Clark University, Worcester, MA, lecturer, 1972-73, assistant professor of classics, 1973-74; Boston University, Boston, MA, lecturer, 1973, assistant professor of classical studies, 1974-82, assistant dean, academic advising, 1977-79; Brandeis University, Waltham, MA, assistant professor of humanities, 1982-83; University of Maryland, College Park, associate professor, 1983-93, acting equity administrator, arts and humanities, 1988-89, director of graduate studies, department of classics, 1989-94, professor of classics, 1993—, acting chair, department of classics, 1995. Lecturer and presenter at academic conferences, 1968—. Member of Institute for Classical Studies, London, 1975-76.

MEMBER: American Philological Association, Association of Ancient Historians, Women's Classical Caucus (co-chair, 1987).

AWARDS, HONORS: Blegen visiting scholar at Vassar College, 1980; Mellon Foundation Fellowships, Brandeis University and Wellesley College Center for Research on Women, 1982-83; Grant, Classical Association of New England, 1983; Fellowship for College Teachers, National Endowment for the Humanities, 1986-87; Distinguished scholar-teacher, University of Maryland, College Park, 1992-93; Outstanding teacher award, University of Maryland, College Park, 1994.

WRITINGS:

Fathers and Daughters in Roman Society: Women in the Elite Family, Princeton University Press (Princeton, NJ), 1984.

Editor with Marilyn Skinner of *Roman Sexualities.* Contributor to books on classical studies, including *Women in the Ancient World: The Arethusa Papers,* edited by John Peradotto and John P. Sullivan, [Albany], 1984; *The Age of Augustus,* edited by Rolf Winkes [Providence and Louvain-La-Neuve], 1986; and *Feminist Theory and the Classics,* edited by Nancy Sorkin Rabinowitz and Amy Richlin, [New York and London], 1993. Contributor to classical studies and philology journals. Translator for articles in scholarly books and journals. Assistant editor of *Classical World,* 1980-93, associate editor, 1993—.

WORK IN PROGRESS: Breathing beneath the Images: Latin Literary Texts and the Recovery of Elite Roman Women; editing volumes on the personal voice in classical studies and nineteenth and twentieth century American women classicists.

SIDELIGHTS: Judith Peller Hallett told *CA* how she came to specialize in classical studies: "Five inspiring years of Latin in high school; antipathy to concentrating in subjects with massive numbers of majors such as English, history, and sociology; and compatibility with the interdisciplinary focus of classics as it was taught at Wellesley College. But I might well have lost heart with the discipline during my years of graduate study (as the subject was there presented in a narrow and heavily linguistic manner) had the women's movement not come along to awaken my interest in uncovering and recovering the women of classical antiquity."

* * *

HARRISON, James (Thomas) 1937-
(Jim Harrison)

PERSONAL: Born December 11, 1937, in Grayling, MI; son of Winfield Sprague (an agriculturist) and Norma Olivia (Wahgren) Harrison; married Linda May King, October 10, 1959; children: Jamie Louise, Anna Severin. *Education:* Michigan State University, B.A., 1960, M.A., 1964. *Religion:* "Zennist." *Avocational interests:* Hunting, fishing, cooking, wine.

ADDRESSES: Home—Box 135, Lake Leelanau, MI 49653. *Agent*—Phoenix Literary Agency, 315 South F St., Livingston, MT 59047.

CAREER: Writer. Assistant professor of English, State University of New York at Stony Brook, 1965-66. Screenwriter for Warner Brothers and other film companies.

MEMBER: Trout Unlimited, Grouse Society.

AWARDS, HONORS: National Endowment for the Arts grants, 1967-69; Guggenheim fellowship, 1969-70; two awards from National Literary Anthology.

WRITINGS:

UNDER NAME JIM HARRISON, EXCEPT AS INDICATED

POETRY

(Under name James Harrison) *Plain Song,* Norton (New York City), 1965.
Locations, Norton, 1968.
Walking, Pym Randall Press (Cambridge, MA), 1969.
Outlyer and Ghazals, Simon & Schuster (New York City), 1971.
Letters to Yesinin, Sumac Press (Fremont, MI), 1973.
Returning to Earth, Ithaca House (Ithaca, NY), 1977.
Selected and New Poems, 1961-1981, Delacorte (New York City), 1982.
The Theory and Practice of Rivers & New Poems, Clark City Press (Livingston, MT), 1989.
Country Stores, Longstreet Press (Marietta, GA), 1993.

FICTION

Wolf: A False Memoir, Simon & Schuster, 1971.
A Good Day to Die, Simon & Schuster, 1973.
Farmer, Viking (New York City), 1975.
Legends of the Fall (contains three novellas, "Revenge," "The Man Who Gave Up his Name," and "Legends of the Fall"), Delacorte, 1979.
Warlock, Delacorte, 1981.
Sundog: The Story of an American Foreman, Bantam (New York City), 1984.
Dalva, Dutton (New York City), 1988.
The Woman Lit by Fireflies (collection of three novellas), Houghton (Boston), 1990.
Julip (collection of three novellas; includes "Julip," "The Seven-Ounce Man" and "The Beige Dolorosa"), Houghton, 1994.

NONFICTION

Just Before Dark: Collected Nonfiction, Clark City Press, 1991.

OTHER

Author of screenplays, including (with Tom McGuane) *Cold Feet,* 1989; (with Jeffrey Fishkin) *Revenge,* 1990; and (with Wesley Strick) *Wolf,* 1994. Contributor to books, including *Contemporary American Poetry,* edited by A. Poulin, Jr., Houghton, 1971; and *Fifty Modern American and British Poets,* edited by Louis Untermeyer, McKay (New York City), 1973. Contributor of poems, stories, articles, and reviews to periodicals, including *New York Times Book Review, Sports Illustrated, Partisan Review, Esquire, American Poetry Review,* and *Nation.*

ADAPTATIONS: Legends of the Fall was adapted for film in 1994 and starred Anthony Hopkins, Brad Pitt, and Aidan Quinn.

SIDELIGHTS: James Harrison is a writer who has made a name for himself both as a poet and novelist. His efforts include several collections of poems, novellas, short stories, essays, and screenplays. Harrison began his writing career as a poet, publishing his first collection, *Plain Song,* while still in college. While he continued to write and experiment with various forms of poetry, it was with the publication of such works as "Legends of the Fall," and "Revenge" (both of which have been adapted for film) that Harrison gained the most attention. Harrison continues to write in both genres, however, and often, combines both forms in his work to convey images that reflect his concern with nature and the changing environment.

Born in Grayling, Michigan, in 1937, Harrison grew up on his father's farm. Tracing his career in a *Detroit Free Press* interview, Harrison related that he decided to become a writer when he was twelve years old because it offered an exciting alternative to the sedate middle-class life he led on the farm. Years later, however, when he became a full-time writer, Harrison returned to live in rural northern Michigan, and his work reflected many details of his early years on the farm. In a review of *Selected and New Poems, 1961-1981, New York Times Book Review* writer Richard Tillinghast praised Harrison for his knowledge of the natural world, declaring that the author had "few equals as a writer on outdoor life."

Beginning in 1972, Harrison expanded into fiction with the publication of *Wolf: A False Memoir.* Telling the story of Swanson, a man disgusted with the civilized trappings of modern society who moves to the rural outback of northern Michigan, *Wolf* focuses on Swanson's realization of the importance of his past, the traditions of his own family, and the necessity for him to reconnect with these bedrock values. Swanson's goal, Robert E. Burkholder wrote in the *Dictionary of Literary Biography Yearbook 1982,* "is to come to grips with the person he has become after his initiation into the decadence and corruption of modern America."

Legends of the Fall, Harrison's 1979 collection of three novellas, brought him a wider audience for his work. Concerned with the themes of redemption and revenge, *Legends of the Fall* offers violent portraits of men buffeted by fate and obsession, especially the tormented Tristan Ludlow of the title story. Burkholder wrote of that character: "One cannot help but feel that Harrison's tale of Tristan, which might ostensibly seem to be purely an adventure yarn, is an environmental statement that laments the extinction of a species, whether it be the true romantic hero like Tristan or the passenger pigeon. In any case, Tristan is the spiritual grandfather of . . . the other protagonists of Harrison's fiction because he is the elemental man who has successfully fronted the facts of life. Indeed, Tristan is what so many of the other characters yearn to be but cannot—at least not in an age that defines romance as the rape of the land in the name of progress." In a *Washington Post Book World* review of *Legends of the Fall,* Garrett Epps commended the novellas as "beyond question, the work of a gifted and accomplished writer." Epps concluded that in the novellas Harrison "is holding up a view of manhood—self-sufficient, violent, strong, antisocial—that seems to be losing currency in this country."

The success of *Legends of the Fall*—and its thematic similarity to other early fiction by Harrison—perhaps inevitably led to the author's being branded a "macho" writer, or as Roz Kaveney put it in *Books,* "the novelist of American regional male tough-mindedness." Harrison himself was disturbed by this facile categorization of his work, noting in numerous interviews that he personally did not share the philosophies of his characters. In the author's defense, *Great Lakes Review* essayist William H. Roberson wrote: "None of Harrison's work celebrates a masculine self-sufficiency. The male characters are not confident in life. On the contrary, they are all deficient in one aspect or another. . . . A central theme in Harrison's work is man's quest to acquire that intangible element that will bring stability and completeness to his life. In at least two of his works,

Farmer and *Warlock,* a woman eventually satisfies a major portion of that need, no small irony if masculine self-sufficiency is Harrison's intent."

Subsequent Harrison fiction has highlighted strong and quirky female characters, such as the protagonist of *Dalva* and the resourceful Julip of the novella "Julip." Dalva is a part-Sioux businesswoman with a ranching background, and her story is one of coming to terms with her personal past and her family's hidden secrets. *Christian Science Monitor* contributor Michael C. M. Huey described the novel as "a festival of life's poetry." Although Kaveney noted that Harrison can exhibit "sentimentalities and lazinesses," she judged *Dalva* to be "a powerful and inspiring book" and Harrison to be "a fine writer [with] a good eye for both social occasion and the natural world."

The three novellas collected in *Julip,* wrote Kelly Cherry in the *Los Angeles Times Book Review,* "seize us by the hand and take us on three different paths through the world." In the title novella, Harrison writes of a woman trying to get her brother moved from prison—where he is incarcerated for shooting three men—and into a mental hospital. Her efforts on his behalf lead her to a better understanding of the differences between the sexes. In "The Seven-Ounce Man," the character Brown Dog has a run-in with law enforcement over an Indian corpse he is trying to save from scientific examination. The final novella, "The Beige Dolorosa," tells of a professor who leaves academia after a sexual harassment charge, takes up a new life in the American Southwest, and rediscovers himself in the process. According to Cherry, "Rollicking and sad, hilarious and startlingly sweet smart and never cynical, these are stories that remind us no life should be overlooked or taken for granted." Jonis Agee in the *New York Times Book Review* believed that "what makes these novellas work best is the authority of Mr. Harrison's voice, expressed via a curiously old-fashioned, ironic yet earnest narrator who acts as a kind of moral and ethical guide."

Assessing Harrison's work, *Tribune Books* reviewer Alan Cheuse found that the author's career adds up "to one of the most interesting and entertaining bodies of work by any writer of his generation. . . . The novellas in *Legends of the Fall,* particularly the title work, show off a writer at the height of his powers." "Harrison is a consummate story teller—truly one of those writers whose books are hard to put down," noted Judith Freeman in the *Los Angeles Times Book*

Review. "He is unfailingly entertaining but he is much more—a haunting, gifted writer who can't be shoved into any category. . . . His work seems to be getting stronger, and one wonders if he won't finally move beyond the small but passionate following he has built up over the years to receive the wider recognition he deserves."

Despite his success, Harrison shuns media attention that is not focused on his writing. "I've consistently turned down interviews that were based on personality," he told *CA.* "That's why I have a big sign in my front driveway that says, 'Do not stop here without calling. This means *you*.' I don't understand writers who want to be in some publicity-oriented limelight, because it's never based on people who are actually interested in the work." Speaking to Jean W. Ross in the *Dictionary of Literary Biography Yearbook 1982,* Harrison explained his creative process: "I usually start, even on a novel, with a collection of sensations and images. A form is a convenience that emerges out of what I have to say rather than something I impose on the material."

BIOGRAPHICAL/CRITICAL SOURCES:

BOOKS

Contemporary Literary Criticism, Gale (Detroit), Volume 6, 1976, Volume 14, 1980, Volume 33, 1985, Volume 66, 1991.

Dictionary of Literary Biography Yearbook 1982, Gale, 1983.

PERIODICALS

Atlantic, September, 1979.
Best Sellers, September, 1979.
Bloomsbury Review, March, 1989, p. 22.
Booklist, November 1, 1979; March 1, 1994, pp. 1139-1140.
Books, June, 1989, p. 16.
Chicago Sun-Times, July 15, 1979.
Christian Science Monitor, January 27, 1977; September 5, 1979.
Detroit Free Press Magazine, April 16, 1972, pp. 19-20.
Detroit News, December 15, 1981.
Detroit News Magazine, August 17, 1980.
Great Lakes Review, fall, 1982, pp. 29-37.
Harper's, June, 1978.
Kirkus Reviews, February 15, 1994, p. 163.
Listener, February 28, 1980.

Los Angeles Times Book Review, October 25, 1981; April 10, 1988, p. 12; August 19, 1990, pp. 1, 5; August 14, 1994, p. 8.
Nation, July 7, 1979; June 23, 1984, pp. 767-71.
National Review, March 7, 1980.
Newsweek, August 30, 1976; July 9, 1979.
New Yorker, August 30, 1976; July 30, 1979.
New York Times, November 24, 1971; September 13, 1973; July 26, 1976.
New York Times Book Review, July 18, 1971; December 4, 1971; September 9, 1973; October 10, 1976; June 17, 1979; November 22, 1981; December 12, 1982, pp. 14, 31; May 14, 1989, p. 34; September 16, 1990, p. 13; May 22, 1994, p. 41.
Northwest Review, Volume 33, number 2, 1995, pp. 106-19.
Observer (London), July 18, 1993, p. 58.
Paris Review, number 107, 1988, pp. 53-97.
Partisan Review, summer, 1972.
Poetry, July, 1966; February, 1971.
Publishers Weekly, June 25, 1982, p. 114; February 28, 1994, pp. 71-2.
Saturday Review, February 19, 1966; December 18, 1971; December 25, 1971; August 21, 1976; October, 1981.
Time, November 9, 1981.
Times (London), January 7, 1982.
Times Literary Supplement, March 21, 1980; January 15, 1982; March 24, 1989, p. 299.
Tribune Books (Chicago), March 20, 1988, p. 1; May 8, 1994, p. 5.
Virginia Quarterly Review, summer, 1966.
Washington Post, March 2, 1980; March 6, 1988, p. 3.
Washington Post Book World, September 9, 1973; May 13, 1979; July 8, 1979; November 29, 1981; April 17, 1994, p. 7.
Western Humanities Review, spring, 1972.

* * *

HARRISON, Jim
  See HARRISON, James (Thomas)

* * *

HIGGINS, George V(incent)   1939-

PERSONAL: Born November 13, 1939, in Brockton, MA; son of John Thompson and Doris (Montgomery) Higgins; married Elizabeth Mulkerin, September 4, 1965 (divorced January, 1979); married Loretta Lucas Cubberley, August 23, 1979; children: (first marriage) Susan, John. *Education:* Boston College, B.A., 1961, J.D., 1967; Stanford University, M.A., 1965.

ADDRESSES: Home—15 Brush Hill Lane, Milton, MA 02186. *Office*—AA ICM, 40 W. 57th St., New York, NY 10019.

CAREER: Writer. *Journal* and *Evening Bulletin,* Providence, RI, reporter, 1962-63; Associated Press, bureau correspondent in Springfield, MA, 1963-64, newsperson in Boston, MA, 1964; Guterman, Horvitz & Rubin (law firm), Boston, researcher, 1966-67; admitted to the Massachusetts Bar, 1967; Commonwealth of Massachusetts, Office of the Attorney General, Boston, legal assistant in the administrative division and organized crime section, 1967, deputy assistant attorney general, 1967-69, assistant attorney general, 1969-70; U.S. District Court of Massachusetts, Boston, assistant U.S. attorney, 1970-73, special assistant U.S. attorney, 1973-74; George V. Higgins, Inc. (law firm), Boston, president, 1973-78; Griffin & Higgins (law firm), Boston, partner, 1978-82. Instructor in law enforcement programs, Northeastern University, Boston, 1969-71; instructor in trial practice, Boston College Law School, 1973-74, 1978-79; visiting professor, State University of New York, Buffalo, 1988. Consultant, National Institute of Law Enforcement and Criminal Justice, Washington, DC, 1970-71.

MEMBER: Writers Guild of America.

AWARDS, HONORS: The Friends of Eddie Coyle was chosen one of the top twenty postwar American novels by the Book Marketing Council, 1985.

WRITINGS:

NOVELS

The Friends of Eddie Coyle (also see below), Knopf (New York City), 1972.
The Digger's Game, Knopf, 1973.
Cogan's Trade (also see below), Knopf, 1974.
A City on a Hill, Knopf, 1975.
The Judgement of Deke Hunter, Little, Brown (Boston), 1976.
Dreamland, Little, Brown, 1977.
A Year or So with Edgar, Harper (New York City), 1979.

Kennedy for the Defense, Knopf, 1980.
The Rat on Fire (also see below), Knopf, 1981.
The Patriot Game, Knopf, 1982.
A Choice of Enemies, Knopf, 1984.
Penance for Jerry Kennedy, Knopf, 1985.
The Friends of Eddie Coyle, Cogan's Trade, The Rat on Fire, Robinson, 1985.
Imposters, Holt (New York City), 1986.
Outlaws, Holt, 1987.
Trust, Holt, 1989.
Victories, Holt, 1990.
The Mandeville Talent, Holt, 1991.
Defending Billy Ryan, Holt, 1992.
Bomber's Law, Holt, 1993.
The Judgement of Deke Hunter, Holt, 1994.
Swan Boats at Four, Holt, 1995.

The Friends of Eddie Coyle has been translated into Italian, Spanish, French, Danish, Norwegian, Finnish, German, Flemish, and Turkish; *The Digger's Game* has been translated into Spanish and Norwegian; *Cogan's Trade* has been translated into Norwegian.

OTHER

The Friends of Richard Nixon (nonfiction), Little, Brown, 1975.
Style versus Substance: Boston, Kevin White, and the Politics of Illusion, Macmillan (New York City), 1984.
Old Earl Died Pulling Traps: A Story, limited edition, Bruccoli Clark (Columbia, SC), 1984.
Wonderful Years, Wonderful Years, Holt, 1988.
The Progress of the Seasons: Forty Years of Baseball in Our Town, Holt, 1989.
On Writing: Advice for Those Who Write to Publish (or Would Like To), Holt, 1990, Bloomsbury (London), 1991.

Also contributor to *The Best American Short Stories 1973,* edited by Martha Foley, Houghton (Boston), 1973, and *They Don't Dance Much,* edited by James Ross, Southern Illinois University Press (Carbondale), 1975. Columnist, *Boston Herald American,* 1977-79; author of magazine criticism column, *Boston Globe,* 1979-85; author of biweekly television column, *Wall Street Journal,* 1984—. Contributor of essays and short fiction to journals and magazines, including *Arizona Quarterly, Cimarron Review, Esquire, Atlantic, Playboy, GQ, New Republic,* and *Newsweek.*

ADAPTATIONS: The Friends of Eddie Coyle was filmed by Paramount, 1973.

WORK IN PROGRESS: A nonfiction study of Congressional irresponsibility.

SIDELIGHTS: A lawyer who has served as a prosecutor and defense lawyer in both state and federal courts, George V. Higgins has an intimate knowledge of the criminal justice system and the political system. As a novelist, Higgins draws from his experience, creating detailed examinations of crime, justice, and politics. Higgins told Nicholas Shakespeare of the London *Times,* "The disability of much American literature is that it's written by college professors sitting on their big fat rusty-dusties who don't know anything about law, politics, or any subject in which real people make real livings." Higgins has worked with real criminals, real police officers, real lawyers, and real politicians; his fiction has been praised for its authentic depictions of these people and their lives.

As Hugh M. Ruppersburg points out in the *Dictionary of Literary Biography,* "George V. Higgins' work has two notable features: its analysis of the motives underlying human character and behavior, and its reliance on dialogue for the revelation of plot, character, and theme." Although he focuses on characters who live outside the mainstream of society, Higgins demonstrates that these people are plagued by the same ambitions and frustrations as those in more mundane walks of life. He allows each character to speak for himself and then arranges the conversations like the testimony in a trial to convey the larger story. The author uses dialogue so extensively that "the plot of a Higgins novel—suspense, humor and tragedy—is a blurrily perceived skeleton within the monsoon of dialogue," comments Roderick MacLeish in the *Washington Post Book World.* Higgins's novels are spoken, and therefore "lacking in figurative or heavily imagistic language," writes Ruppersburg. "The result is a concrete style, economical and to the point."

His first three novels—*The Friends of Eddie Coyle, The Digger's Game,* and *Cogan's Trade*—established Higgins as "an impressive chronicler of the life style of the small-time hoodlum for whom crime is the only thing that does pay," notes O. L. Bailey in the *New York Times Book Review.* Some reviewers immediately placed his fiction in the crime genre; yet, unlike the traditional crime novelist, Higgins "forgoes sentimentality, private eyes and innocent victims to write exclusively of criminals who work on each other in a community where sin is less talked of than are mistakes," relates Peter S. Prescott in

Newsweek. The author's scrutiny of this often unseen yet real segment of society puts his novels in the company of serious mainstream fiction. Similarly, by uncovering the obscure world of the criminal, Higgins allows its comparison to mainstream society. "Money, family pressures, and the desire for a middle-class life-style motivate the behavior of the criminal as well as the average citizen," indicates Ruppersburg. "Kids grow up," J. D. O'Hara adds in *New Republic,* "customs change, new men take over from the dying or incompetent old men, power changes hands, deals succeed or fail." Yet the tone of this subsociety is different. "The criminal world is . . . realistically depicted as a pitiless jungle where self-preservation depends on constant vigilance, and everyone leads a twitching knife-edge existence," Leo Harris observes in *Books and Bookmen.*

Higgins received immediate critical approval for his writing with the publication of *The Friends of Eddie Coyle,* "one of the best of its genre I have read since Hemingway's 'The Killers,'" claims Christopher Lehmann-Haupt of the *New York Times.* It "is fiction of a most convincing order," according to Harvey Gardner in the *New York Times Book Review.* "The story of Eddie and his hood friends, and of the cops and lawyers who belong in their world as much as the crooks do, is told in short, beautifully-made episodes, full of nicely heard talk." Eddie Coyle is a struggling middleman in Boston's underworld economy whose specialty is dealing guns. "There is nothing glamorous or humorous about Eddie Coyle, and nothing remotely adventurous about the life he leads," Joe McGinniss observes in the *New York Times Book Review.* "It is seamy; it is drab."

The Friends of Eddie Coyle introduced what would become the trademark of Higgins's fiction, a "unique virtuosity in exploiting an uncanny ear for the argot of the underworld," explains Bailey. By using the language of the criminal and emphasizing dialogue, Higgins creates a book that is "flat, toneless, and positively reeking with authenticity," writes McGinniss. "Its dialogue eats at one's nerve endings," adds Lehmann-Haupt. However, not all reviewers praise Higgins's use of dialogue to relate his story. One complaint is that because all these criminals speak the same slang, they sound alike; character distinctions become blurred. McGinniss admits that "all of Eddie's friends . . . seem not so much individuals as facets of the same personality." The reviewer adds, however, "Rather than a weakness, I suspect that this may well be Higgins's main point." In Harris's opinion, *The Friends of Eddie Coyle* "is expressed in dialogue that is perhaps just a shade too good, too redolent of Hemingway . . . and Runyon." Yet Harris finds that Higgins's style "makes a literary tragedy out of a small time crook and his fate." McGinniss concludes, "With *The Friends of Eddie Coyle,* [Higgins has] given us the most penetrating glimpse yet into what seems the real world of crime."

The Digger's Game "confirms that Higgins writes about the world of crime with an authenticity that is unmatched," comments Jonathan Yardley in the *Washington Post Book World.* "In [his first two] novels," adds Yardley, "the central character is an obscure man who has done something fairly stupid but quite understandable, and is trying to pay the price without getting killed in the process." The Digger's mistake is gambling away eighteen thousand dollars in Las Vegas, putting him in debt to a loan shark.

Higgins follows Digger; the things he does and the people he sees while trying to pay his debt tell his story. "Higgins has done more than write a fast, gripping story about Boston's underworld," James Mills notes in *The New York Times Book Review.* "He has created in the Digger a deeply touching character who . . . would be equally moving if he were out of crime and struggling for survival in a bank or an automobile factory." Mills adds, "A lot of writers have taken a shot at the Vegas madness, but none has described it with more humor, sadness and pathos than Higgins."

The critical debate surrounding Higgins's third novel, *Cogan's Trade,* has centered on the author's continued evolution toward a novel told completely through the dialogue of its characters. Understanding is difficult in the opinion of Bailey because the reader must glean information from the conversations of characters who speak in unfamiliar slang. "The flaw in *Cogan,*" he writes in the *New York Times Book Review,* "is that there is not enough of our mother tongue to keep confusion at bay." What prose there is offers primarily physical description and very little interpretation or judgment of the criminal behavior of Higgins's characters. But a *Times Literary Supplement* reviewer maintains that "in Higgins, violence is always committed in cold blood; people are just doing their job, and so the prose can afford to remain disinterested."

Higgins employs dialogue for more than its realistic effect, believe some reviewers. "Like [James] Joyce,

Higgins uses language in torrents, beautifully crafted, ultimately intending to create a panoramic impression," writes Roderick MacLeish. Adds a contributor to the *Times Literary Supplement,* "For all their surface authenticity, the speeches have more in common with dramatic monologues than with conversations that are merely 'overheard'; brutal and obscene though they unquestionably are, their effect is still one of stylization." "He's drawing the fewest possible lines on his canvas in order to conjure up in the reader's imagination the details of the spaces in between," explains Lehmann-Haupt. "Lines that provoke the imagination so actively are what entertaining art is all about." In summary writes MacLeish: "As a novel, *Cogan's Trade* is a brilliant exposition of Higgins's Boston underworld as the flipside of all respectable lives of desperation. As a thriller it is that taut story whose drama is heightened by our own understanding of how it has to end." "*Cogan's Trade* . . . firmly establishes [Higgins] as a novelist of wit, intelligence and disquieting originality," concludes a *Times Literary Supplement* reviewer.

In his fourth novel, *A City on a Hill,* Higgins "has abandoned Boston lowlife for the more complex and intellectually treacherous milieu of Washington politics," Pearl K. Bell comments in the *New Leader.* The United States had entered the Watergate era and Higgins tuned his ear for the power struggles and corruption of the political arena. "In politics as in crime, Higgins' interest lies with those who work in the shadows. He is as concerned as ever with hopes that go unrealized, prospects that never materialize, ambitions that prove excessive," Yardley relates in the *New Republic.* Politics has remained a major concern of Higgins's fiction; it has also been the topic of a nonfiction work, an examination of the Watergate incident entitled *The Friends of Richard Nixon.*

A City on a Hill "may be the definitive novel of Washington at the staff level," Christopher Lydon writes in the *New York Times Book Review,* "the world of driven, dependent campaign hotshots who so quickly become power junkies and then political tramps and almost never leave the capital." Yardley finds that although this novel "contains many perceptive observations about the machinations of politics and political people . . . Higgins does not seem secure of his territory." Yardley adds: "*A City on a Hill* simply does not have the authenticity, the sureness, of the earlier novels. When it does have authenticity, Higgins has moved from Washington back to Boston, to the people he knows."

Higgins concentrates on the people and the city he knows best in another novel of the political scene, *A Choice of Enemies*. The story is that of Bernie Morgan, speaker of the state house, his fall from power, and the people responsible. "Certain [is Higgins's] feeling for the corridor and cloakroom dynamics of Massachusetts politics," writes Charles Champlin in the *Los Angeles Times Book Review*. As a novel, *A Choice of Enemies* received a mixed critical response, primarily because of its form; "all information, personal background, emotion (everything but interior decoration and clothing) is expressed through dialogue," explains *National Review* contributor D. Keith Mano.

Some reviewers believe that with this novel Higgins's continuing experiment with form exceeded its limits. "Every monotonous obscenity, every dropped word, every cliche and catch phrase, has an initial ring of taped reality," Champlin concedes. He adds, however, "Like transcripts, it needs careful pruning or the sound overruns the sense and, even more damaging, grows dull." In his article in the *New York Times Book Review,* Peter Andrews is strongly critical of the book: "*A Choice of Enemies* represents the final collapse of [Higgins's] ongoing experiment in trying to create a kind of gutter prose-poetry as a vehicle for narrative storytelling." Andrews remarks, "The author has told his tale in such an opaque fashion that I could never get a handle on the story."

Higgins responded to his critics in a letter to *CA:* "What I am doing is replacing the omniscient author with the omniscient reader. The requisite suspension of disbelief consists wholly of the reader's agreement that for his money he has gotten not only a batch of search warrants valid everywhere, to listen in on what the characters say, but the remarkable good fortune to attend only those conversations in which they hatch their plots, betray themselves, and doublecross each other. If the reader is acute, the characters will tell him the story, leaving him to judge for himself the morality, ethics and decency of their actions."

Some reviewers do respond favorably to Higgins's efforts. In gradually moving toward a story told entirely by dialogue, "Higgins has pulled off a remarkable transition," writes D. Keith Mano, "from distinctive realist crime writer to serious, long-reach novelist, still distinctive." "Hemming, hawing, tortuous circumlocutions, and the endless maundering excursuses of quotidian conversation are the devices that Higgins expertly uses to build suspense and tension," explains Nick Tosches in the *Village Voice*. And according to Mano, Higgins has overcome one of the faults that weakened his earlier novels: "Where, in *Cogan's Trade* (1974), each voice sounded like the same marvelous Boston Glib Person, here you have differentiation, variety, and social ecumenism." "Higgins is the master of what he does, and *A Choice of Enemies* contains some of the most brilliant and outrageous passages he has ever brought forth," concludes Tosches.

Jerry Kennedy, the protagonist of three of Higgins's novels, lives at the intersection of crime, politics, justice, and middle-class America. Like Higgins, Kennedy is a Boston criminal trial lawyer. *Kennedy for the Defense, Penance for Jerry Kennedy,* and *Defending Billy Ryan* offer the expected insights into criminal behavior and political infighting, but they also examine the role of the criminal trial lawyer in the American justice system. Kennedy "makes his living providing the Constitutionally guaranteed defense for the victims and/or perpetrators of the rampant socio-economic chaos prevalent in various levels of society in and around Boston," observes Tom McNevin in *Best Sellers*. Kennedy defends not by proving his clients innocent; his cases seldom go to trial. The offenders he represents are usually guilty, and more often than not he advises them to plead so.

Higgins explains in a *Time* article: "There is a good reason why 85 to 90 of all criminal cases brought by a competent prosecutor end up in defense pleas; nobody can win them." What Kennedy does is use the various mechanisms of justice to obtain for his clients lesser charges, reduced sentences, and accelerated probations. "Higgins argues that experts like Kennedy fill a vital function in the criminal justice system as indispensable agents of the plea bargaining in whose absence the courts would surely collapse," comments Robert Lekachman in the *Nation*. "Higgins claims further that justice is more likely to be served by the ministrations of cynical, greedy but invariably astute lawyers than by the more formal processes of trial and sentence."

Beyond their portraits of the criminal trial lawyer and the justice system, the Jerry Kennedy novels have gained attention for their characterization. As John Jay Osborn, Jr., notes in the *Washington Post Book World,* "Because the characters ruminate instead of react, there is never much tension. . . . Yet some of what is lost in the way of tension is gained in the careful depiction of character." Jeremiah

Francis Kennedy is a man caught between his desire to lead a relaxed middle-class life-style and his fascination with his work. Kennedy, his colleagues, and clients make *Kennedy for the Defense* "a variegated yarn of third-rate perpetrators, second-class citizens and first-person encounters," *Time* reviewer Peter Stoler remarks. Although they may not be likable, Stoler adds that this "tangled cast is instantly credible and permanently delightful." Evan Hunter echoes Stoler's view. He writes in the *New York Times Book Review:* "George V. Higgins has created a genre of his own, in which the people are so real that it doesn't matter what they're doing or how they go about doing it; just being in their company is pleasure enough."

In *Penance for Jerry Kennedy,* Higgins presents an older Kennedy plagued by difficulties, "a decent, hard-working lawyer who has not lived up to the expectations of his professors, his clients, his colleagues or his wife, and who knows it," says Elaine Kendall in the *Los Angeles Times.* Kennedy commits a mistake that earns him the disfavor of an influential judge and makes him the object of a television reporter's investigation. Kennedy compounds his troubles by drinking to excess. He is at the depths of his personal and professional life. His values are going out of style. "*Penance for Jerry Kennedy* is a novel about a dying breed—lawyers who think on their feet rather than from behind desktop computer terminals and who fight with reasoned words instead of endless streams of documents," Douglas E. Winter remarks in the *Washington Post Book World.* "But Jerry Kennedy is unstoppable," concludes Winter, "the kind of fictional lawyer one meets all too rarely—one whose life and work are made real." Winter, commenting on *Defending Billy Ryan* in *Washington Post Book World,* calls Higgins's third Jerry Kennedy novel "vintage Higgins" and states, "Funny and sad, touching and mad, this is not just another novel by a lawyer but a novel by a writer."

In *Trust* Higgins introduces a new protagonist, Earle Beale, who was once a corrupt basketball player and who is now a corrupt used-car dealer. After running into trouble with the law, Beale is released from prison early due to a technicality, but this raises suspicions that he has become an informer. Sean French writes in *New Statesman & Society,* "Like all of Higgins's novels, *Trust* is funny and shocking. It also continues his creation of a whole society permeated with corruption. His world is a complex web of shady deals that begin with his low-life crooks and end nowhere." Lorenzo Carcaterra notes in *People,*

"Beale is Higgins's most cynical creation since Eddie Coyle ran guns (*The Friends of Eddie Coyle*) and Jerry Kennedy got back Cadillac Teddy's driver's license (*Kennedy for the Defense*)."

Higgins's novel *The Mandeville Talent* centers on the death of James Mandeville, a man who was murdered in Goshen, Massachusetts, twenty three years earlier. Jill, Mandeville's granddaughter, and her husband, Joe Corey, return to the area when Jill is offered a teaching post in a nearby town. Joe, once a young lawyer in a big Manhattan firm, decides to set up a private practice and solve the old murder case. Susan Engberg writes in *People,* "Higgins presents sharp miniportraits of troubled humans facing the barrenness of hard choices. They are led to their destiny by a determined and driven Jim Corey, out to solve a mystery everyone wants left alone."

Higgins's recent novels, including *Bomber's Law,* are considered more thematically complex by some reviewers. According to Robert Worth in *Commonweal,* "Higgins appears to be expanding his interests [in *Bomber's Law*], pressing out against the limits of his genre. The detective novel is based, after all, on violence, and rooted in a Manichean world-order; pursuers and pursued. Now Higgins . . . has written a book in which the cops pursue each other. They do so for reasons that have less to do with law and order than with that great crucible of narrative fiction: character. Crime and punishment recede in *Bomber's Law* into a mosaic of stories about human motive."

Higgins's more recent works of nonfiction include *On Writing: Advice for Those Who Write to Publish (or Would Like To)* and *The Progress of the Seasons: Forty Years of Baseball in Our Town.* In *On Writing* Higgins "develops his insights into the psychology of authorship and the essentials of good writing," states William A. Donovan in *Library Journal.* The latter work traces the history of the Boston Red Sox at Fenway Park and addresses why the Sox haven't won the World Series since 1918.

Higgins has been called by some a crime novelist and by others the creator of a new genre. He has at times been compared to major literary figures of the twentieth century. For Hugh M. Ruppersburg, "his skill in characterization and realistic dialogue, his success at portraying individuals in a crisis of identity, his understanding of the influences which form human character, and his development of a unique, effective novelistic form appropriate to his talents . . . establish George V. Higgins as a writer of considerable stature."

BIOGRAPHICAL/CRITICAL SOURCES:

BOOKS

Contemporary Literary Criticism, Gale (Detroit), Volume 4, 1975, Volume 7, 1977, Volume 10, 1979, Volume 18, 1981.
Dictionary of Literary Biography, Volume II: *American Novelists since World War II,* Gale, 1978.
Dictionary of Literary Biography Yearbook: 1981, Gale, 1982.

PERIODICALS

Best Sellers, August, 1980.
Books and Bookmen, September, 1972.
Christian Science Monitor, September 22, 1992, p. 12; January 21, 1994, p. 17.
Commonweal, March 25, 1994, p. 24.
Library Journal, June 1, 1990, p. 138.
Los Angeles Times, February 28, 1985.
Los Angeles Times Book Review, March 4, 1984.
Nation, April 26, 1980; August 21, 1989, pp. 210-11.
National Review, November 7, 1975; May 18, 1984.
New Republic, March 30, 1974; April 12, 1975.
New Statesman & Society, November 10, 1989.
Newsweek, March 25, 1974; April 28, 1975; September 6, 1976; March 3, 1980; December 13, 1993, p. 62.
New Yorker, June 24, 1974; March 18, 1985.
New York Times, January 25, 1972; March 23, 1973; April 10, 1974; March 14, 1975.
New York Times Book Review, February 6, 1972; February 11, 1973; March 25, 1973; March 31, 1974; March 30, 1975; October 26, 1975; March 2, 1980; February 12, 1984; February 24, 1985; October 12, 1989, pp. 49-53; November 14, 1993, p. 67; September 18, 1994, p. 32; June 18, 1995, p. 20.
People, February 12, 1990, pp. 27, 29; February 3, 1992, pp. 24, 26.
Publishers Weekly, February 17, 1989, p. 64; July 12, 1991, pp. 52-3.
Sewanee Review, spring, 1992, pp. 290-98.
Time, April 1, 1974; April 14, 1975; August 23, 1976; March 31, 1980; November 15, 1993, p. 97.
Times (London), May 16, 1985.
Times Literary Supplement, August 16, 1974; November 7, 1980; March 19, 1993, p. 20.
Tribune Books, September 6, 1992, p. 4.
Village Voice, January 31, 1984.
Washington Post Book World, April 1, 1973; March 31, 1974; March 2, 1980; March 17, 1985; September 20, 1992, p. 5.

*   *   *

HIRSCH, E(ric) D(onald), Jr.   1928-

PERSONAL: Born March 22, 1928, in Memphis, TN; son of Eric Donald (a businessperson) and Leah (Aschaffenburg) Hirsch; married Mary Pope, 1958; children: John, Frederick, Elizabeth. *Education:* Cornell University, B.A., 1950; Yale University, M.A., 1953, Ph.D., 1957.

ADDRESSES: Home—2006 Pine Top Rd., Charlottesville, VA 22903. *Office*—Department of English, University of Virginia, Charlottesville, VA 22901.

CAREER: Yale University, New Haven, CT, instructor, 1956-60, assistant professor, 1960-63, associate professor of English, 1963-66; University of Virginia, Charlottesville, professor, 1966-72, William R. Kenan Professor of English, 1973—, chair of department, 1968-71, 1981-82, director of composition, 1971—. Member of faculty, Northwestern University, School of Criticism and Theory, summer, 1981; Bateson Lecturer, Oxford University, 1983. Trustee and founder, Cultural Literacy Foundation. *Military service:* U.S. Naval Reserve, 1950-54; active duty, 1950-52.

MEMBER: American Academy of Arts and Sciences (fellow), Modern Language Association of America, Keats-Shelley Association, Byron Society, American Rhododendron Society.

AWARDS, HONORS: Fulbright fellow, 1955; Morse fellow, 1960-61; Guggenheim fellow, 1964-65; *Explicator* (magazine) Prize, 1964, for *Innocence and Experience: An Introduction to Blake;* National Endowment for the Humanities senior fellow, 1971-72, 1980-81; Wesleyan University Center for the Humanities fellow, 1973, 1974; Princeton University Council of the Humanities fellow, 1976; Stanford University Center for Advanced Study in the Behavioral Sciences fellow, 1980-81; Australian National University Humanities Research Centre fellow, 1982.

WRITINGS:

Wordsworth and Schelling: A Typological Study of Romanticism, Yale University Press (New Haven, CT), 1960.

Innocence and Experience: An Introduction to Blake, Yale University Press, 1964.

Validity in Interpretation, Yale University Press, 1967.

The Aims of Interpretation, University of Chicago Press, 1976.

The Philosophy of Composition, University of Chicago Press, 1977.

Cultural Literacy: What Every American Needs to Know, Houghton (Boston), 1987.

(With Joseph Kett and James Trefil) *Dictionary of Cultural Literacy: What Every American Needs to Know* (Literary Guild selection), Houghton, 1988, revised edition, 1993.

A First Dictionary of Cultural Literacy: What Our Children Need to Know, Houghton, 1991.

"CORE KNOWLEDGE" SERIES; PUBLISHED BY DOUBLEDAY (NEW YORK CITY)

What Your First Grader Needs to Know, 1991.
What Your Second Grader Needs to Know, 1991.
What Your Third Grader Needs to Know, 1992.
What Your Fourth Grader Needs to Know, 1992.
What Your Fifth Grader Needs to Know, 1993.
What Your Sixth Grader Needs to Know, 1993.

OTHER

Contributor to books, including *From Sensibility to Romanticism: Essays Presented to Frederick A. Pottle,* edited by Harold Bloom and Frederick W. Hilles, Oxford University Press (New York City), 1965; *History as a Tool in Critical Interpretation: A Symposium,* edited by Thomas F. Rugh and Erin R. Silva, Brigham Young University Press (Provo, UT), 1978; and *What Is Literature?,* edited by Paul Hernadi, Indiana University Press (Bloomington), 1978. Also contributor of essays and articles to *American Educator, Times Literary Supplement, Critical Inquiry, College English,* and *American Scholar.*

SIDELIGHTS: After spending a quarter of a century publishing works that have had a "significant impact on recent American literary criticism and theory," according to Brian G. Caraher of the *Dictionary of Literary Biography,* E. D. Hirsch, Jr., published *Cultural Literacy: What Every American Needs to Know,* a book that hit the bestseller lists and raised a storm of controversy. Hirsch argues in the book that many Americans are ignorant of the shared terms and concepts of their society, and that this renders them incapable of participating fully in that society. *Cultural Literacy* brought Hirsch to the attention of a wide reading audience and pushed him into founding the Cultural Literacy Foundation, an organization promoting the teaching of a shared core of knowledge in the nation's schools.

Cultural Literacy begins with a recitation of facts illustrating the degree to which contemporary students are ill-informed. Hirsch quotes studies showing that the majority of high school students do not know when the American Civil War took place, half cannot identify Winston Churchill or Joseph Stalin, three-fourths do not recognize Walt Whitman or Henry David Thoreau, and many are unaware of when Christopher Columbus discovered America. High school students' knowledge of science, geography, the arts, and other subjects is also weak. Such a lack of basic information renders much of what these students read meaningless. They are not illiterate, but they are unable to identify people and places discussed in what they read, and are baffled by historic, scientific, and literary terms or allusions. "That so many people should be stumbling around in this kind of fog," writes John Gross in the *New York Times,* "is an obvious cause for concern. It implies a coarsening in the quality of life, and a drying-up of invaluable common traditions. It makes it harder for us to communicate with one another. For the children of the poor and disadvantaged, it represents a formidable barrier to progress." "Most Americans can make out the words," James W. Tuttleton explains in *Commentary.* "The literacy we need, according to Hirsch, is *cultural* literacy."

As a means of identifying some of the information that cultural illiterates lack, Hirsch includes a 63-page list of 5,000 names, terms, and phrases he considers to be essential to cultural literacy. Compiled with the assistance of two academic colleagues, historian Joseph Kett and physicist James Trefil, the list includes such varied items as "absolute zero," "flapper," "Sherlock Holmes," "critical mass," and "empiricism." A complete and thorough knowledge of each item is not needed, Hirsch explains. To understand a text a reader needs schemata, thumbnail explanations of these terms. David Gates in *Newsweek* defines schemata as "simple, superficial ideas suggested by words." Studies show that these are enough to allow a literate person to comprehend newspapers, books, and other media, and more importantly, to participate in his/her society. According to Tuttleton, Hirsch "points out that the culturally illiterate—and the same goes for those not having a command of standard English—can exercise no effect on discourse concerning social policy." As Hirsch writes in the book: "We will be able to achieve a just and prosperous society only when our schools ensure that everyone commands enough shared background knowledge to be able to communicate effectively with everyone else."

Not all critics have favorable things to say about *Cultural Literacy.* Some critics claim that the book calls for a return to "teaching names, dates and places by rote and providing a context later," as Stefan Kanfer of *Time* puts it. The list of needed cultural information has prompted "accusations of elitism," Charles Trueheart reports in the *Washington Post.* Robert Pattison of *Nation* argues that "a culture index poses a fundamental political question: How far are the wishes of the people to be consulted in determining the nature of culture itself?" But even harsh critics admit that the book raises some serious questions about the failure of American education.

In the *Dictionary of Cultural Literacy: What Every American Needs to Know,* written with Joseph Kett and James Trefil, Hirsch provides definitions of the items listed in his earlier book, along with the definitions of many other terms. "The dictionary is more ambitious and really more important," Hirsch tells Trueheart in the *Washington Post,* "because it will suggest to people who are outsiders in the literate culture, 'What do these characters really know that I'm being excluded from?'" The book is arranged into twenty-three sections which cover the major categories of knowledge, providing definitions of hundreds of terms, ideas, events, and names.

Many of Hirsch's ideas about cultural literacy are derived from his years as a literary critic, during which time he has shown "an enduring concern for *types* and for the *typicality* of expressive and interpretive behavior," according to Caraher. As a critic, Hirsch does not isolate a text from its author. Rather, he focuses his attention on the author's worldview, knowledge, and cultural situation—a critic must enter into the author's perceptual framework. Caraher finds that Hirsch's "most singular contribution to modern American criticism and theory . . . might very well be his persistent iteration of the philosophical inevitability and the heuristic power of *typology.*"

Hirsch's Cultural Literacy Foundation aims at modifying the present grade-school curriculum, focusing more on the necessary background information that will enable students to have a thorough foundation of knowledge. The Cultural Literacy Foundation issues lists and tests for third, sixth, ninth, and twelfth grade students. Hirsch told *CA:* "The Foundation's fundamental aim is to enhance literacy, and to do it by affecting the school curriculum, particularly in the very early grades."

Hirsch summarized: "One theme is consistent: language is saying more than appears on the page, or in the sounds we make. The actual words are able to convey meaning only because of all sorts of implications that are *not* said. The reader must bring those meanings to the words by virtue of background knowledge. That principle, which is one that dates way back to the 1950s and early '60s in my work, forms a principle of continuity with my work on literacy."

BIOGRAPHICAL/CRITICAL SOURCES:

BOOKS

Dictionary of Literary Biography, Volume 67: *Modern American Critics since 1955,* Gale (Detroit), 1988.
Lentricchia, Frank, *After the New Criticism,* University of Chicago Press, 1980.
Ray, William, *Literary Meaning: From Phenomenology to Deconstruction,* Blackwell (Oxford, England), 1984.

PERIODICALS

American Reference Books Annual, 1990, p. 128; 1994, p. 126.
Atlantic, December, 1989, p. 119.
College English, November, 1977.
Commentary, July, 1987.
Journal of Aesthetics and Art Criticism, fall, 1984.
Journal of Reading, May, 1988.
Los Angeles Times Book Review, December 10, 1989, p. 8.
Nation, May 30, 1987.
Newsweek, April 20, 1987.
New York Times, April 17, 1987; June 14, 1987.
New York Times Book Review, March 15, 1987; December 17, 1989, p. 22; November 14, 1993, p. 69.
Partisan Review, fall, 1967.
Pre/Text, spring/fall, 1980.

Time, July 20, 1987.

Virginia Quarterly Review, summer, 1967; winter, 1988.

Washington Post, April 20, 1987.

Wilson Library Bulletin, January, 1990, p. 128; December, 1993, p. 76.

*   *   *

HITE, Molly 1947-

PERSONAL: Born June 26, 1947, in Seattle, WA; daughter of F. Herbert and Patricia G. Hite; married Frank C. Costigliola; children: Joshua, Molly Amanda. *Education:* Seattle University, B.A. (summa cum laude), 1974; University of Washington, Seattle, Ph.D., 1981.

ADDRESSES: Home—117 Stewart Ave., Ithaca, NY 14850. *Office*—Department of English, Cornell University, Ithaca, NY 14853.

CAREER: Cornell University, Ithaca, NY, assistant professor of English, 1982—.

AWARDS, HONORS: Fellow of American Council of Learned Societies, 1984.

WRITINGS:

Ideas of Order in the Novels of Thomas Pynchon, Ohio State University Press (Columbus), 1982.

Class Porn (novel), Crossing Press (Trumansburg, NY), 1987.

The Other Side of the Story, Cornell University Press (Ithaca, NY), 1989.

Breach of Immunity (novel), St. Martin's Press (New York City), 1992.

Contributor of articles and reviews to magazines.

*   *   *

HOCH, Edward D(entinger) 1930-
   (Irwin Booth, Anthony Circus, Stephen Dentinger, Pat McMahon, Mister X, R. E. Porter, R. L. Stevens)

PERSONAL: Surname rhymes with "coke"; born February 22, 1930, in Rochester, NY; son of Earl G.

(a banker) and Alice (Dentinger) Hoch; married Patricia McMahon, June 5, 1957. *Education:* Attended University of Rochester, 1947-49. *Politics:* Liberal Republican. *Religion:* Roman Catholic. *Avocational interests:* "The contemporary motion picture as an art form."

ADDRESSES: Home—2941 Lake Ave., Rochester, NY 14612.

CAREER: Rochester Public Library, Rochester, NY, researcher, 1949-50, member of board of trustees, 1982—; Pocket Books, Inc., New York City, staff member in adjustments department, 1952-54; Hutchins Advertising Co., Rochester, copy and public relations writer, 1954-68; full-time author, 1968—. *Military service:* U.S. Army, Military Police, 1950-51, Post Librarian, 1951-52.

MEMBER: Mystery Writers of America (president, 1982-83), Authors Guild, Crime Writers Association, Science Fiction Writers of America.

AWARDS, HONORS: Edgar Allan Poe ("Edgar") Award of Mystery Writers of America for best mystery short story of 1967, for "The Oblong Room;" guest of honor, Bouchercon 22, 1991.

WRITINGS:

The Shattered Raven, Lancer (Sims, AR), 1969.

The Transvection Machine, Walker & Co. (New York City), 1971.

The Judges of Hades, Leisure Books (Norwalk, CT), 1971.

The Spy and the Thief, Davis Publications (Worcester, MA), 1971.

City of Brass, Leisure Books, 1971.

The Fellowship of the Hand, Walker & Co., 1973.

The Frankenstein Factory, Warner Books (New York City), 1975.

The Thefts of Nick Velvet, Mysterious Press (New York City), 1978.

The Monkey's Clue [and] *The Stolen Sapphire* (juvenile), Grosset (New York City), 1978.

The Quests of Simon Ark, Mysterious Press, 1984.

Leopold's Way, Southern Illinois University Press (Carbondale), 1985.

The Night My Friend, Ohio University Press (Athens), 1991.

Diagnosis: Impossible, Crippen & Landru, 1996.

EDITOR

Dear Dead Days, Walker & Co., 1973.
Best Detective Stories of the Year (annual), Dutton (New York City), 1976-81.
All But Impossible!, Ticknor & Fields (New York City), 1981.
The Year's Best Mystery and Suspense Stories (annual), Walker & Co., 1982-95.

OTHER

Contributor, sometimes under pseudonym, of more than 750 short stories to periodicals, including *Antaeus, Argosy, Black Mask, Ellery Queen's Mystery Magazine* (every issue since 1973), and *Alfred Hitchcock's Mystery Magazine.*

ADAPTATIONS: Fourteen of Edward D. Hoch's stories have been adapted for television, including three for the NBC-TV series "McMillan and Wife."

BIOGRAPHICAL/CRITICAL SOURCES:

BOOKS

Edward D. Hoch Bibliography, Moffatt House (Anchorage, AK), 1991.

PERIODICALS

Armchair Detective, spring, 1990.
Ellery Queen's Mystery Magazine, August, 1976.
New York Times Book Review, June 29, 1968; March 11, 1973.
Rochester Democrat and Chronicle, September 7, 1969.
Writer, April, 1974.

*   *   *

HODGES, Devon Leigh   1950-

PERSONAL: Born February 23, 1950, in Santa Monica, CA; daughter of Kenneth M. Hodges (a consultant) and Shirley Wolfe (a librarian; maiden name, Davis); married Eric Swanson (an economist); children: Tristan, Cecily. *Education:* Attended Reed College, 1968-71; University of California, Berkeley, B.A., 1972; State University of New York at Buffalo, M.A., 1977, Ph.D., 1979.

ADDRESSES: Home—2015 North Lincoln St., Arlington, VA 22207. *Office*—Department of English, George Mason University, 4400 University Dr., Fairfax, VA 22030.

CAREER: University of Wyoming, Laramie, assistant professor, 1979-80; George Mason University, Fairfax, VA, assistant professor, 1981-86, associate professor, 1986-92, professor of English and American studies, 1992—.

WRITINGS:

Renaissance Fictions of Anatomy, University of Massachusetts Press (Amherst), 1985.
(With Janice Doane) *Nostalgia and Sexual Difference,* Methuen (New York City), 1987.
(With Doane) *From Klein to Kristeva,* University of Michigan Press (Ann Arbor), 1992.

WORK IN PROGRESS: Research on narratives of traumatic remembering.

SIDELIGHTS: Devon Leigh Hodges told *CA:* "Anatomies were a fad in Renaissance England. In a wide range of texts—theological, scientific, and literary—Renaissance writers used their pens as scalpels to strip away appearances and expose the truth. In my 1985 book, *Renaissance Fictions of Anatomy,* I make use of contemporary literary theory to argue that the anatomy is a transitional form marking the shift from a metaphorical to an analytical view of the world.

"*Nostalgia and Sexual Difference,* written with Janice Doane, also uses poststructuralist theories of language to analyze representation—in this case, the rhetorical practices associated with nostalgia. In the imaginative past of nostalgic writers, men are men, women are women, and reality is real. In lamenting the 'degeneracy' of the American of the present, these writers often choose to scapegoat the women's movement, especially feminist writing. At issue are basic questions about the authority of women's writing and the power of male discourse to define reality.

"*From Klein to Kristeva,* also written with Janice Doane, charts the development of object-relations theory, a 'mother-centered' form of psychoanalysis that has profoundly influenced recent feminist thought. By making visible a powerful discourse that has constructed us as feminists, as well as defined women as mothers, we hope to give our readers a chance to rethink and renegotiate the meaning of femininity."

*   *   *

HOGARTH, (Arthur) Paul   1917-

PERSONAL: Born October 4, 1917, in Kendal, Westmorland, England; son of Arthur and Janet (Bownass) Hogarth; married Phyllis Daphne Pamplin; married Patricia Douthwaite, February 14, 1959; married Diana Marjorie Cochran, May 4, 1989; children: (first marriage) Virginia; (second marriage) Toby. *Education:* Attended Manchester College of Art, 1936-38, and St. Martin's School of Art, 1938-40. *Avocational interests:* Travel (Hogarth has been to Poland, Czechoslovakia, the USSR, Rhodesia, Central and South America, Australia, Italy, Croatia, China, South Africa, Ireland, Canada, and the United States).

ADDRESSES: Home and office—Hidcote Manor, Hidcote Bartrim, Chipping Campden, Gloucestershire GL55 6LR, England. *Agent*—Tessa Sayle Agency, 11 Jubilee Place, London SW3 3TE, England.

CAREER: Freelance artist and illustrator. London County Council Central School of Arts and Crafts, London, visiting lecturer, 1951-54; Cambridge School of Art, Cambridge, England, senior tutor of drawing, 1959-61; Royal College of Art, London, senior tutor, 1964-70, visiting lecturer in Department of Illustration, Faculty of Graphic Design, 1971-75. Visiting associate professor, Philadelphia College of Art, 1968-69. Art exhibitions at several London locations, including Leicester Gallery, the American Embassy, and bi-yearly at the Kyle Gallery.

MEMBER: Royal Designers for Industry, Royal Academy of Arts, Chartered Society of Designers (fellow), Association of Illustrators (honorary president, 1982), Arts Club (London).

AWARDS, HONORS: Francis Williams Illustration Award, 1982, for *Poems* by Robert Graves; *Yorkshire Post* award for best art book, 1986, for the revised edition of *The Artist as Reporter.*

WRITINGS:

Defiant People: Drawings of Greece Today, Lawrence & Wishart (London), 1953.
Drawings of Poland, Wydawnictwo Artystczno-Graficzne (Warsaw), 1953.
Looking at China, Lawrence & Wishart, 1956.
People Like Us: Drawings of South Africa and Rhodesia, Dobson (Durham), 1958, published as *The Sons of Adam,* Thomas Nelson (Surrey), 1960.
Irish Sketchbook, Verlag der Kunst, 1962.
Creative Pencil Drawing, Watson, 1964, 6th edition, 1979.
The Artist as Reporter, Reinhold (Workingham), 1967, revised and enlarged edition, Gordon Fraser (Devon), 1986.
Creative Ink Drawing, Watson, 1968.
Drawing People, Watson, 1971.
Artists on Horseback: The Old West in Illustrated Journalism, 1857-1900, Watson, 1972.
Drawing Architecture, Watson, 1973.
Paul Hogarth's American Album, Lion and Unicorn Press (London), 1974.
Paul Hogarth's Walking Tours of Old Philadelphia, Barre Publications (New York City), 1976.
Paul Hogarth's Walking Tours of Old Boston: Through North End, Downtown, Beacon Hill, Charleston, Cambridge, and Back Bay, Dutton (New York City), 1978.
Arthur Boyd Houghton, Gordon Fraser, 1982.
Paul Hogarth's Walking Tours of Old Washington and Alexandria, EPM Publications (McLean, VA), 1985.
(With Graham Greene) *Graham Greene Country,* Pavilion Books (London), 1986.
(With Lawrence Durrell) *The Mediterranean Shore: Travels in Lawrence Durrell Country,* Pavilion Books, 1988.

ILLUSTRATOR

Charlotte Bronte, *Jane Eyrova,* Mlada Fronta (Prague), 1953.
Charles Dickens, *Pan Pickwick,* Statni Nakladatelstvi Detske Knihy (Prague), 1956.
Doris Lessing, *Going Home,* M. Joseph (London), 1957.
Arthur Catherall, *Jungle Trap,* Roy, 1958.
Arthur Conan Doyle, *The Adventures of Sherlock Holmes,* Folio Society (London), 1958.
R. Haggard, *King Solomon's Mines,* Penguin (West Drayton, Middlesex), 1958.
P. Knight, *The Gold of the Snow Geese,* Thomas Nelson, 1958.

O. Henry, *Selected Short Stories,* Folio Society, 1960.

Elizabeth Gaskell, *Marie Bartonova,* Mlada Fronta, 1960.

Olive Schreiner, *The Story of an African Farm,* Limited Editions Club, 1961.

Jean Jacques Salomon, *Prehistory: Civilizations before Writing,* Dell (West Yorkshire), 1962.

Brendan Behan, *Brendan Behan's Island,* Geis, 1962.

Behan, *Brendan Behan's New York,* Geis, 1964.

Robert Graves, *Majorca Observed,* Doubleday (London and New York City), 1965.

(And author of introduction and captions) Malcolm Muggeridge, *London a la Mode,* Hill & Wang (London and New York City), 1967.

Alaric Jacob, *A Russian Journey: From Suzdal to Samarkand,* Hill & Wang, 1969.

James D. Atwater and R. E. Ruiz, *Out from Under,* Doubleday, 1969.

Doris Whitman, *The Hand of Apollo,* Follet (New York City), 1969.

Elizabeth Sheppard-Jones, *Stories of Wales: Told for Children,* Academy Chicago (Chicago), 1978.

Siegfried Sassoon, *Memoirs of a Fox-Hunting Man,* Limited Editions Club, 1978.

James Joyce, *Ulysses,* Franklin Library, 1978.

Nigel Buxton, *America,* Cassell, 1979.

Stephen Spender, *America Observed,* Potter (Kenilworth, Warks), 1979.

Graves, *Poems,* Limited Editions Club, 1980.

Sassoon, *Memoirs of an Infantry Officer,* Limited Editions Club, 1981.

Hugh Johnson, *Hugh Johnson's Wine Companion,* Simon & Schuster (New York City), 1984.

Joseph Conrad, *Nostromo,* Folio Society, 1984.

William Trevor, *Night at the Alexandria,* Century Hutchinson (London), 1987.

Peter Mayle, *A Year in Providence,* Hamish Hamilton (London), 1989.

John Betejam, *In Praise of Churches,* John Murray (London), 1996.

OTHER

Contributor to *Penrose Annual* of Hastings House, *Daily Telegraph Magazine, Fortune, Sports Illustrated, House and Garden,* and other periodicals. Art editor, *Contact,* 1950-51.

WORK IN PROGRESS: Drawings on Life, for David & David (Devon), publication expected in 1997.

HOLMES, (Edward) Richard   1946-

PERSONAL: Born March 29, 1946, in Aldridge, Staffordshire, England; son of William (an engineer) and Helen (Jacques) Holmes; married Elizabeth Saxton (a theater designer), August 2, 1975; children: Jessica Helen, Sara Corinna. *Education:* Emmanuel College, Cambridge, B.A., 1968, M.A., 1973; attended Northern Illinois University, 1968-69; Reading University, Ph.D., 1975.

ADDRESSES: Home—Vine House, North St., Ropley, Alresford, Hants SO24 0DF, England. *Office*—Cranfield Security Studies Institute, Royal Military College of Science, Shrivenham, Swindon, Wiltshire SN6 8LA, England.

CAREER: Department of War Studies and International Affairs, Royal Military Academy Sandhurst, Camberley, Surrey, England, senior lecturer, 1969-85, deputy head of department, 1985; served active duty as lieutenant colonel, commanding officer, 2nd Battalion The Wessex Regiment, 1990; codirector of Cranfield Security Studies Institute, 1995; professor of Military and Security Studies at Cranfield University. *Military service:* Territorial Army, 1965-94; became brigadier.

MEMBER: Royal United Services Institute for Defence Studies, Writers Guild.

AWARDS, HONORS: History Scholar, Emmanuel College, Cambridge, 1965-67; bronze award for documentary from the New York International Film and Television Festival, 1980, for *Comrades in Arms? Dunkirk 1940,* and 1986, for *Fighting Spirit* and *Casualty;* Officer of the Order of the British Empire (Military Division), 1988.

WRITINGS:

Borodino 1812, Charles Knight (Croydon, England), 1971.

Bir Hacheim: Desert Citadel, Ballantine (New York City), 1971.

(With Peter Young) *The English Civil War: A Military History of the Three Civil Wars, 1642-1651,* Methuen (London), 1974.

Epic Land Battles, edited by S. L. Mayer, Octopus Books (London), 1976.

(With Christopher Chant and William Koenig) *Two Centuries of Warfare,* Octopus Books, 1978.

(Contributor) John Keegan, editor, *World Armies,* Macmillan (New York City), 1979.

The Little Field-Marshal: Sir John French, J. Cape (London), 1981.

(With Anthony Kemp) *The Bitter End,* Antony Bird (Chichester, West Sussex, England), 1982.

The Road to Sedan: The French Army, 1866-70, Royal Historical Society (London), 1982.

(With Keegan) *Soldiers: A History of Men in Battle* (also see below), Hamish Hamilton (London), 1985, Viking (New York City), 1986.

Firing Line, J. Cape, 1985, published as *Acts of War: The Behavior of Men in Battle,* Free Press (New York City), 1986.

The World Atlas of Warfare, Mitchell Beazley (London), 1988.

Nuclear Warriors: Soldiers, Combat and Glasnost, J. Cape, 1991.

Fatal Avenue: A Traveller's History of the Battlefields of Northern France and Flanders, 1346-1945, J. Cape, 1992.

Riding the Retreat: Mons to the Marne 1914 Revisited, J. Cape, 1995.

Army Battlefield Guide, Her Majesty's Stationery Office (London), 1995.

Reviewer for *Times Literary Supplement.*

TELEPLAYS

Tanks, Southern Television, 1977.

Comrades in Arms? Dunkirk 1940, Southern Television, 1980.

(With Keegan) *Soldiers* (thirteen-episode series), British Broadcasting Corporation (BBC-TV), 1985.

(Presenter) *The War Within,* TVS, 1990.

(Coauthor and presenter) *D-day: The Secret Maps,* BBC-TV, 1994.

Burma: Tales from the Map Room, BBC-TV, 1995.

Also author of *Fighting Spirit* and *Casualty.* Served as military adviser for *The Duellists,* 1976.

WORK IN PROGRESS: Editing and contributing to *Companion to Military History,* for Oxford University Press.

SIDELIGHTS: Richard Holmes's *The Little Field-Marshal: Sir John French* is a biography of John Denton Pinkstone French, a noted British military figure. According to Brian Bond of the *Times Literary Supplement,* "Holmes has been reasonably successful in overcoming the military biographer's chief difficulty; namely how to provide a convincing portrait of a man of action without digressing into de-

tailed narratives of the operations in which he took part. A biographer less interested in military history would doubtless have devoted more space to this subject's philandering and its repercussions on his family, but Holmes is circumspect."

Acts of War: The Behavior of Men in Battle "is about battle, men in battle, the sweat, filth, misery, noise, loneliness, boredom and exhilaration, desperation and heroism of battle . . .," writes Douglas Porch in the *Washington Post Book World.* "It is also about preparation for battle, and about the things soldiers do both on and off the battlefield, things like get drunk, desert, shoot their officers in the back and themselves in the feet, panic, fraternize with the enemy, kill prisoners, pick fights with civilians, and commit most of the deadly sins." As *New York Times* critic Christopher Lehmann-Haupt explains, Holmes was of the opinion that too little research had been completed on the individual's battle experiences, so he "set out to 'redress the balance' by tracing the military experience from induction to discharge. . . . The result is satisfyingly exhaustive. . . . And *Acts of War* is filled with revelations." However, apart from what this critic discerns as repetition in the way Holmes presents his ideas, Lehmann-Haupt believes the book's major flaw "is that we already know most of what Mr. Holmes is trying to tell us, at least about the paramount horror of battle." Military analyst and *New York Times Book Review* contributor Edward N. Luttwak brings up a few complaints regarding *Acts of War.* According to Luttwak, Holmes emphasizes battle too highly in his examination of the military experience. "Battle is a rare experience . . . [and] is therefore the exception, and not the logical culmination, of military endeavor. . . . *Acts of War . . .* obscure[s] this fundamental truth." Luttwak further concludes that Holmes has sacrificed clarity and in-depth analysis for elegance. Having read the Luttwak review, Porch refutes both of Luttwak's complaints by noting, first, that battle is the event toward which armies primarily focus their energies and, second, by expressing his feelings of gratitude that *Acts of War* is not "heavy with theory and psychoanalysis." As Porch remarks: "I for one would place *Acts of War* on the Pentagon's required reading list."

Holmes told *CA:* "*Acts of War* and, to a lesser extent, *Nuclear Warriors: Soldiers, Combat, and Glasnost,* explored the individual's response to the challenge of combat. More recently I have concentrated on the places in which this combat took place, firstly by a general examination of what Charles de Gaulle called the 'fatal avenue,' that strip of territory between Paris and the German border which has seen so much military activity over the centuries. I then narrowed the focus still more, by riding on horseback from Mons in Belgium, where the British army fired its first shots in August 1914, to the river Marne, following the line of the British retreat in late August and early September. I travelled at the right time of year, covered the sorts of daily distances marched by my ancestors, and slept, much as they might have done, in farms, chateaux, or simply on the ground at my horse's feet. Before setting out I had read as many contemporary letters and diaries as possible, using unpublished sources as often as I could, and *Riding the Retreat: Mons to the Marne 1914 Revisited* wove these recollections into the fabric of my own journey.

"*The Companion to Military History* is a major project, with some 700,000 words and 2,500 entries. I was delighted to be offered the opportunity of acting as general editor and major contributor, all the more so because there is currently no Oxford companion to the subject, so I am breaking new ground. However, it is a huge challenge, and judging the relative importance of Arcola and Arrow, Bastion and Bataan, and Cataphract and Catapult is no easy business."

BIOGRAPHICAL/CRITICAL SOURCES:

PERIODICALS

New York Times, March 20, 1986.
New York Times Book Review, March 23, 1986.
Times (London), October 3, 1985.
Times Literary Supplement, November 13, 1981; August 23, 1985; February 5, 1993.
Washington Post Book World, April 13, 1986.

* * *

HUBBARD, J(ake) T(imothy) W(illiam)   1935-

PERSONAL: Born May 23, 1935, in London, England; U.S. citizen; son of Walter Glover (a master printer) and Ada Moubray (Rolland) Hubbard; children: Stephanie, Rufus John, Katherine, Clare. *Education:* Attended Pembroke College, Cambridge, 1955-56; Queen's University at Kingston, B.A. (with honors), 1960; Columbia University, M.Sc., 1961. *Religion:* Anglican. *Avocational interests:* Cross-

country skiing, boat building, history of navigation, colonial history, commercial history.

ADDRESSES: P.O. Box 322, Frontenac Island, Clayton, NY 13624.

CAREER: Reporter for *Winnipeg Free Press* and *Toronto Telegram,* 1958-60; *National Geographic,* Washington, DC, staff writer, 1961; *Business Week,* New York City, staff writer and assistant editor, 1961-63; *Newsweek,* New York City, associate editor, 1963-65; University of Missouri, Columbia, associate professor of journalism, 1965-69; Syracuse University, Syracuse, NY, professor of magazine journalism, 1969—, chair of magazine department, 1969—. President and cofounder of Quadrant Research Associates (editorial consultant firm). *Military service:* British Army, 1953-55; became lieutenant.

MEMBER: Half Crown Club (founding member), Antique Boat Museum, Save the River.

WRITINGS:

Banking in Mid-America, Public Affairs Press (Washington, DC), 1969.
(Contributor) *Bicentennial History of the United States,* U.S. News and World Report (Washington, DC), 1975.
Magazine Editing: How to Acquire the Skills You Need to Win a Job and Succeed in the Magazine Business, Prentice-Hall (Englewood Cliffs, NJ), 1982.
The Race: An Inside Account of What It's Like to Compete in the Observer Singlehanded Transatlantic Race from Plymouth, England, to Newport, Rhode Island, Norton (New York City), 1986.
For Each, the Strength of All: A History of Banking in the State of New York, New York University Press (New York City), 1995.

Contributor to periodicals, including *Newsweek, Business Week, National Geographic,* and *SAIL.*

WORK IN PROGRESS: Researching bank histories.

SIDELIGHTS: J. T. W. Hubbard told *CA:* "I grew up in a cottage on the east coast of England where I came to love the vagaries of the weather, the flow of the tides, and the life of the sailor. In the spring of 1984 I entered my home-finished cutter, *Johan Lloyde,* in the Observer Singlehanded Transatlantic Race (OSTAR). Under the rules, each contestant must sail his or her boat alone, without use of the engine, from Plymouth, England, to Newport, Rhode Island. Of the ninety-two boats that started, only sixty-four arrived in Newport. The others did not make it due to such mishaps as dismasting, capsizing, collision, whale attack, personal injury, and simple failure of nerve. I fought my share of gales and grappled with boarders in a brief stop at the mysterious Azorean isle of Flores in my forty-two day voyage to Newport. But it was the quirky personalities of my fellow entrants that intrigued me most. I became fascinated by the psychological and the mythic dimensions of this Homeric contest and wrote the story of my experiences in a book that eventually became *The Race.*"

OSTAR is staged every four years with competitors ranging from paid professional sailors backed by large corporations to amateurs like Hubbard, a journalism professor at Syracuse University, who built his own thirty-two-foot cutter. Larry Martz, writing for *Newsweek,* commended Hubbard's "engaging, witty account" of his six-week-long transatlantic sail and added that *The Race,* subtitled *An Inside Account of What It's Like to Compete in the Observer Singlehanded Transatlantic Race from Plymouth, England, to Newport, Rhode Island,* is "well told, often funny and honest."

Andrew Mershon, writing, for the *Oregonian,* called *The Race* a "rollicking good tale" while a contributor to *Book Locker,* which goes to the 200,000 members of Boat Owners Association of America, described Hubbard as "undoubtedly the best writer ever to chronicle a major offshore race. . . . His account of his crossing is both funny and philosophical." Les Galloway, writing in the San Francisco *Examiner,* likened *The Race* to the works of Joshua Slocum and Jack London, and noted that it is "an extremely well-written and paced book that can be read like a novel by those not interested in the technical side of ocean racing."

As well as sailing, Hubbard has an interest in banking. In his 1995 volume, *For Each, the Strength of All: A History of Banking in the State of New York,* Hubbard explores the development of the New York banking system and its influence on domestic and international finance. Mike Vogel of *Buffalo News* praised the book as "both enlightening and eminently readable" and concluded that it is a "valuable work that can help any local history enthusiast better

understand why and how cities, towns and villages have been shaped."

BIOGRAPHICAL/CRITICAL SOURCES:

PERIODICALS

Book Locker, fall, 1986.
Buffalo News, September 10, 1995.
Examiner (San Francisco), January 22, 1987.
Newsweek, November 17, 1986.
Oregonian, September 16, 1986.
Wall Street Journal, May 8, 1995.

*   *   *

HUMBER, William   1949-

PERSONAL: Born September 9, 1949, in Toronto, Ontario, Canada; son of Alfred and Betty (Westlake) Humber; married Catherine McConkey (a teacher), August 10, 1974; children: Bradley, Darryl, Karen. *Education:* University of Toronto, B.A. (with honors), 1972; York University, M.Environmental Studies, 1975. *Religion:* Anglican.

ADDRESSES: Home—15 Beech Ave., Bowmanville, Ontario, Canada L1C 3Al. *Office*—Seneca College, 1750 Finch Ave. E., Willowdale, Ontario, Canada M2J 2X5.

CAREER: Seneca College, Toronto, Ontario, program coordinator of continuing education, 1977-83, teacher of Baseball Spring Training for Fans, 1979—, chair of continuing education, 1983—. Public participation officer for North Pickering Project, 1974-76; president of Visual Arts Centre of Newcastle, 1975-76; member of Newcastle Community Services Planning Board, 1983-86; subject specialist for baseball exhibit mounted by the Royal Ontario Museum, 1989; founding vice president of Society for International Hockey Research, 1991; member of board of governors of Canadian Baseball Hall of Fame, 1993-94; member of board of trustees of Ontario Environmental Training Consortium, 1994—. Coach of pennant winning bantam level Bowmanville Glass and Mirror baseball team, 1993-94; presenter at Baseball and Sultan of Swat Conference at Hofstra University, 1995.

MEMBER: North American Society for Sports History, Canadian Association for Sports Heritage, Society of American Baseball Research (secretary, 1982-83), Society for International Hockey Research, British Society for Sports History.

AWARDS, HONORS: Fellow of Central Mortgage and Housing Corp., 1973; international LERN Award for programming excellence in energy training, 1989; awarded first ever Ontario continuing education CONNY award for programming excellence in energy training, 1994.

WRITINGS:

Cheering for the Home Team: The Story of Baseball in Canada, Boston Mills Press (Erin, Ontario), 1983.
Freewheeling: The Story of Bicycling in Canada, Boston Mills Press, 1986.
The History of Central Public School in Bowmanville, Josten's (Topeka, KS), 1989.
Let's Play Ball: Inside the Perfect Game, Lester and Orpen, 1989.
The Baseball Book and Trophy, Somerville House, 1993.
The Kids' Soccer Book and Medallion, Somerville House, 1994.
Diamonds of the North: A Concise History of Baseball in Canada, Oxford University Press (New York City), 1995.
(With John St. James) *All I Thought about Was Baseball: Essays on a Canadian Pastime,* University of Toronto Press (Toronto), 1996.

Television and radio writer. Contributor to *The Canadian Encyclopedia,* 1988; *The Canadian Historical Atlas,* Volume 2, 1990; and *Essays for the Serious Fan,* 1993. Also contributor to magazines, including *Horizon Canada, Athletics, Globe and Mail, Pedal, Toronto Daily Star, Winning, Dugout,* and *Innings.*

WORK IN PROGRESS: A history of Bowmanville, Ontario and a history of sports in Toronto, both for Natural Heritage Press; accounts of village life in Ontario based on the history of a 125-year-old soccer league in Darlington Township and of Canada's participation in the 1928 through 1936 Olympic Games, focusing on the life of Dr. Phil Edwards, a medalist in each of those summer games.

SIDELIGHTS: William Humber told *CA:* "I am interested in the study of sports, not as a record of trivia and numbers (though I say that not disparagingly, for I believe the *Baseball Encyclopedia,* for instance, is a significant existential statement about the worth of men's lives), but as a means of exploring a people's culture through storytelling. In making public presentations on this theme, I make use of theater, music, photography, and so on. I yearn for a return to the organized lyceum movement, with venues throughout North America where I could share my tales, but for now books and magazine articles will suffice."

BIOGRAPHICAL/CRITICAL SOURCES:

PERIODICALS

Globe and Mail (Toronto), December 13, 1986.

*   *   *

HUNT, Nan
See RAY, N(ancy) L(ouise)

*   *   *

HYNDMAN, Donald W(illiam)   1936-

PERSONAL: Born April 15, 1936, in Vancouver, British Columbia, Canada; son of Andrew William (a high school principal) and Joan (MacDonald) Hyndman; married Shirley Boyes, August 25, 1960; children: Karen, David. *Education:* University of British Columbia, B.A.Sc., 1959; University of California, Berkeley, Ph.D., 1964.

ADDRESSES: Home—615 Hastings, Missoula, MT 59801. *Office*—Department of Geology, University of Montana, Missoula, MT 59801.

CAREER: University of Montana, Missoula, assistant professor, 1964-68, associate professor, 1968-72, professor of geology, 1972—. Technical officer of Geological Survey of Canada in British Columbia, summers, 1959-62.

MEMBER: Mineralogical Association of Canada, Geological Association of Canada (fellow), Association of Professional Geologists, Geological Society of America (fellow), American Geophysical Union, Mineralogical Society of America (fellow), Sigma Xi.

WRITINGS:

Petrology and Structure of Nakusp Map-Area, British Columbia, Geological Survey of Canada Bulletin, 1969.

Petrology of Igneous and Metamorphic Rocks, McGraw (New York City), 1972, 2nd edition, 1985.

(With Richard Hazlett) *Roadside Geology of Hawaii,* Mountain Press (Missoula, MT), 1996.

Contributor to journals.

WITH DAVID D. ALT; PUBLISHED BY MOUNTAIN PRESS

Roadside Geology of the Northern Rockies, 1972.

Rocks, Ice, and Water: Geology of Watertow Glacier Park, 1973.

Roadside Geology of Northern California, 1974.

Roadside Geology of Oregon, 1978.

Roadside Geology of Washington, 1984.

Roadside Geology of Montana, 1986.

Roadside Geology of Idaho, 1989.

Northwest Exposure, 1995.

EDITOR WITH ALT; PUBLISHED BY MOUNTAIN PRESS

Keith Frye, *Roadside Geology of Virginia,* 1986.

Bradford B. Van Diver, *Roadside Geology of New Hampshire-Vermont,* 1987.

Halka Cronic, *Roadside Geology of New Mexico,* 1987.

Cathy Connor and Daniel O'Haire, *Roadside Geology of Alaska,* 1988.

David Lageson and Darwin Spearing, *Roadside Geology of Wyoming,* 1988.

Steve Harris, *Fire Mountains of the West,* 1988.

Chronic, *Roadside Geology of Utah,* 1990.

Diver, *Roadside Geology of Pennsylvania,* 1990.

Harris, *Agents of Chaos,* 1990.

Spearing, *Roadside Geology of Texas,* 1990.

Spearing, *Roadside Geology of Louisiana,* 1995.

Paul Gries, *Roadside Geology of South Dakota,* 1996.

*   *   *

INGE, M(ilton) Thomas 1936-

PERSONAL: Surname rhymes with "fringe"; born March 18, 1936, in Newport News, VA; son of Clyde Elmo and Bernice Lucille (Jackson) Inge;

married Betty Jean Meredith, December 28, 1958 (divorced April 20, 1977); married Tonette Long Bond, June 12, 1982 (divorced March 18, 1991); children: (first marriage) Scott Thomas; (stepchildren) Michael Gordon Bond. *Education:* Randolph-Macon College, B.A., 1959; Vanderbilt University, M.A., 1960, Ph.D., 1964.

ADDRESSES: Home—22 Trotter Mill Close, P.O. Box 129, Ashland, VA 23005-0129. *Office*—Blackwell Professor of the Humanities, Randolph-Macon College, Ashland, VA 23005-5505.

CAREER: Irby Studio, Richmond, VA, freelance commercial artist, 1953-55; Virginia State Department of Highways, Richmond, traffic technician, summers, 1956-58; Vanderbilt University, Nashville, TN, instructor in English, 1962-64; Michigan State University, East Lansing, assistant to associate professor of American thought and language, 1964-69; Virginia Commonwealth University, Richmond, associate professor, 1969-73, professor of English, 1973-80, chair of department, 1974-80; Clemson University, Clemson, SC, professor of English and head of department, 1980-82; U.S. Information Agency, Washington, DC, resident scholar in American Studies, 1982-84, and director of Summer Institute in American Studies for Foreign Scholars, 1993-95; Randolph-Macon College, Ashland, VA, Robert Emory Blackwell Professor of the Humanities, 1984—.

Fulbright lecturer in American literature at universities worldwide, including University of Salamanca, Spain, 1967-68, Buenos Aires, Argentina, 1971, Moscow State University, Soviet Union, 1979, University of Leningrad, Soviet Union, 1979, and Charles University, Prague, Czech Republic, University of Helsinki, Finland, Odense University, Denmark, and University of Kiel, Germany, all 1994; visiting associate professor, Vanderbilt University, summer, 1969; lecturer in the U.S. and abroad at numerous other universities, conferences, workshops, and symposia.

MEMBER: American Studies Association, Modern Language Association of America, American Humor Studies Association, European Association for American Studies, Society for the Study of Southern Literature, Popular Culture Association, Ellen Glasgow Society, Melville Society, Mark Twain Circle, Southern Studies Forum, Popular Culture Association in the South, South Atlantic Modern Language Association, Cosmos Club, Phi Beta

Kappa, Omicron Delta Kappa, Pi Delta Epsilon, Lambda Chi Alpha.

AWARDS, HONORS: Research, study, or travel grants from Michigan State University, 1965, 1966, 1968, American Philosophical Society, 1970, American Council of Learned Societies, 1978, Clemson University, 1981, Institute for Southern Studies, South Carolina, 1982, Southern Regional Education Board, 1982, 1984, National Endowment for the Humanities, 1986, 1991, 1992, Newbery Library, 1987, Virginia Foundation for the Humanities, 1987, 1993, and U.S. Information Agency, 1993, 1994, and 1995; outstanding reference work citation, American Library Association, 1979, for *Handbook of American Popular Culture;* named Virginia Cultural Laureate, 1992.

WRITINGS:

(With Thomas Daniel Young) *Donald Davidson: An Essay and a Bibliography,* Vanderbilt University Press (Nashville, TN), 1965.
Publications of the Faculty of the University College: A Bibliography, Michigan State University (East Lansing), 1966.
(With Young) *Donald Davidson,* Twayne (Boston), 1971.
(Author of introduction) George Herriman, *Baron Bean: A Complete Compilation,* Hyperion Press (Westport, CT), 1977.
The American Comic Book, Ohio State University Libraries (Columbus), 1985.
Comics in the Classroom, Smithsonian Institution Traveling Exhibition Service (Washington, DC), 1989.
Great American Comics: 100 Years of Cartoon Art, Smithsonian Institution Traveling Exhibition Service, 1990.
Comics as Culture, University Press of Mississippi (Jackson), 1990.
Faulkner, Sut, and Other Southerners, Locust Hill Press (West Cornwall, CT), 1992.
Dark Laughter: The Satiric Art of Oliver W. Harrington, University Press of Mississippi, 1993.
Perspectives on American Culture: Essays on Humor, Literature, and the Popular Arts, Locust Hill Press, 1994.
Anything Can Happen in a Comic Strip: Centennial Reflections on an American Art Form, Ohio State University Libraries/University Press of Mississippi, 1995.

EDITOR

George Washington Harris, *Sut Lovingood's Yarns,* College and University Press, 1966.
Harris, *High Times and Hard Times, Sketches and Tales,* Vanderbilt University Press, 1967.
Agrarianism in American Literature, Odyssey Press (Indianapolis), 1969.
John Donald Wade, *Augustus Baldwin Longstreet: A Study of the Development of Culture in the South,* revised edition, University of Georgia Press (Athens), 1969.
Honors College Essays 1967-68, Michigan State University Honors College (East Lansing), 1969.
(With others) *The Black Experience: Readings in Afro-American History and Culture from Colonial Times through the Nineteenth Century,* Michigan State University Press (East Lansing), 1969.
William Faulkner, *A Rose for Emily,* C. E. Merrill (Columbus, OH), 1970.
Richmond Croom Beatty, *William Byrd of Westover,* Archon Books (Hamden, CT), 1970.
The Merrill Studies in "Light in August," C. E. Merrill, 1971.
Virginia Commonwealth University Self-Study, Virginia Commonwealth University, 1972.
The Frontier Humorists: Critical Views, Archon Books, 1975.
Ellen Glasgow: Centennial Essays, University Press of Virginia (Charlottesville), 1976.
(With Maurice Duke and Jackson R. Bryer) *Black American Writers: Bibliographical Essays,* two volumes, St. Martin's (New York City), 1978.
(And contributor) *Handbook of American Popular Culture,* three volumes, Greenwood Press (Westport, CT), 1978-81, revised and enlarged three-volume edition, 1989.
Bartelby the Inscrutable: A Collection of Commentary on Herman Melville's Tale, Archon Books, 1979.
(And contributor) *Concise Histories of American Popular Culture,* Greenwood Press, 1982.
(With Edgar E. MacDonald) *James Branch Cabell: Centennial Essays,* Louisiana State University Press (Baton Rouge), 1982.
(With Duke and Bryer) *American Women Writers: Bibliographic Essays,* Greenwood Press, 1983.
Huck Finn among the Critics: A Centennial Selection, U.S. Information Agency (Washington, DC), 1984, revised edition, University Publications of America (Frederick, MD), 1985.
Truman Capote: Conversations, University Press of Mississippi, 1987.

Naming the Rose: Essays on Umberto Eco's "The Name of the Rose," University Press of Mississippi, 1988.

Handbook of American Popular Literature, Greenwood Press, 1988.

A Nineteenth-Century American Reader, U.S. Information Agency, 1988.

Colton Waugh, *The Comics,* University Press of Mississippi, 1991.

(With Sergei Chakovsky) *Russian Eyes on American Literature,* University Press of Mississippi, 1993.

Oliver W. Harrington, *Why I Left America and Other Essays,* University Press of Mississippi, 1993.

William Faulkner: The Contemporary Reviews, Cambridge University Press (New York City), 1994.

OTHER

Contributor to more than fifty books, including *Concise American Composition and Rhetoric,* edited by Donald Davidson, Scribner (New York City), 1964, 5th edition, 1968; *Southern Literary Study: Problems and Possibilities,* edited by Louis D. Rubin, Jr., and C. Hugh Holman, University of North Carolina Press (Chapel Hill), 1975; *Faulkner: International Perspectives,* edited by Doreen Fowler and Ann Abadie, University Press of Mississippi, 1984; and *Author-ity and Textuality: Current Views of Collaborative Writing,* edited by James S. Leonard and others, Locust Hill Press, 1994. Contributor to annuals and dictionaries, including *The Lovingood Papers 1963, 1964, and 1965,* edited by Ben Harris McClary, University of Tennessee Press (Knoxville); *American Literary Scholarship: An Annual 1970, 1971, 1972, and 1973,* edited by J. Albert Robbins, Duke University Press (Durham, NC); *Southern Writers: A Biographical Dictionary,* edited by Robert Bain and others, Louisiana State University Press, 1979; *Dictionary of Literary Biography,* Volume 11: *American Humorists, 1800-1950,* Gale (Detroit), 1982; *American Writers for Children,* 1983; and *The Comic Book Price Guide.*

General editor of "American Critical Tradition" series for Burt Franklin (New York City), 1973-79, research guide series for St. Martin's, 1975-76, reference guide series in popular culture for Greenwood Press, 1978—, "Studies in Popular Culture" series for the University Press of Mississippi, 1987—, and "Cambridge Critical Archives" series for Cambridge University Press, 1991—. Contributor of essays, articles, and reviews to numerous periodicals, including *American Literature, Chronicle of Higher Educa-*tion, *Journal of Popular Culture, Modern Fiction Studies, Notes on Contemporary Literature, Studies in American Humor,* and *Studies in Popular Culture.* Founding co-editor of *Resources for American Literary Study,* 1971-80, and of *American Humor: An Interdisciplinary Newsletter,* 1974-80.

WORK IN PROGRESS: Continuing research for books and articles on Herman Melville, Daniel Carter Beard, Mark Twain, William Faulkner, Walt Disney, American humor, comic art, literature, and popular culture.

SIDELIGHTS: M. Thomas Inge "has become internationally known and widely quoted as a chronicler of American popular culture, particularly the art and history of that unique American invention—the newspaper comic strip," asserts Rob Schultz in *Northside Magazine.* Charles Slack writes in the *Richmond Times-Dispatch* that "Dr. Inge has become a leading voice for the artistic and literary importance of one of America's most maligned art forms." Warren Epstein notes in the *Tampa Tribune* that Inge has remarked that "he wants to lend a heap of academic credibility to comic books and comic strips—the only art forms besides jazz that he said originated in the United States." Slack adds that Inge's "combination of academic respectability and irreverence has made him a cherished source for journalists around the country writing on popular culture."

Inge attributes his adult interest in comics and humor to a childhood love of the genre, yet he obtained his academic and professorial qualifications along traditional routes. After earning his academic degrees, he established credentials through university teaching positions, specializing in American literature—especially author William Faulkner. Eventually, in addition to his writings on "important" fiction and authors, he introduced comic books to his university classes through study and research on American humor and began publishing books on the topic. Comments Bob Eason in the *Randolph-Macon College Bulletin,* "In fact, today [Inge] is considered one of the leading experts on one of America's most underappreciated art forms and cultural icons." Many of his fellow professors and academics have reacted with skepticism to Inge's theories on the literary role of comic humor. Despite his assertions that comics offer a microcosm of American society, that they "have been interesting reflections of social change," as Epstein paraphrases Inge in the *Tampa Tribune,* Don Oldenburg observes in the *Washington Post* that "the criticism hasn't stopped—only now it comes from stuffy colleagues, literary critics and brow-beating dilettantes. 'Not everyone agrees that this is an adult thing to be doing,' he [Inge] confesses, though not sheepishly." Inge nevertheless believes in the social and historical importance of his comic humor research, as Oldenburg quoted Inge's response to his detractors: "I assure them it is not a hobby. . . . My work on comics in the long run will probably be far more important than anything I have to say on William Faulkner."

M. Thomas Inge once told *CA:* "I consider myself primarily a literary and cultural historian with strong interests in editing, bibliography, and criticism. Clarifying events, ascertaining the facts, and establishing the bibliographic record are essential preliminary steps in understanding and appreciating our cultural heritage. My interests range widely through nineteenth-and twentieth-century American literature and culture with specific focuses on American humor, Southern and ethnic writing, twentieth-century fiction, American literature abroad, popular culture, comic art, biography, and intellectual history."

Inge adds: "One of the best kept secrets of the academic life is the sheer pleasure of teaching, research, and writing in combination with each other. Of what value are new ideas without a class with which to share them or the printed page on which to convey them to the larger community of interested readers and scholars? Recent commentators on education have falsely portrayed colleges and universities as places of disillusionment and drudgery, where competence goes unrewarded and mediocrity prevails. Some of my colleagues believe that learning must be made difficult and students should be taxed beyond their limitations as a rite of passage to a degree. All such people overlook the joy in learning and teaching. Sharing an excitement of your own with a class creates a rewarding environment, and discovering interesting things to research and write about can be the highest kind of pleasure. I hope my writing reflects some of these pleasures."

BIOGRAPHICAL/CRITICAL SOURCES:

PERIODICALS

Herald-Progress (Hanover County, VA), November 26, 1992, p. 3.
Huntsville Times, June 22, 1987, p. B1.
News-Leader Plus (Richmond, VA), May 7, 1986, pp. N12-13.
New York Times, November 5, 1989, p. 16.
Northside Magazine (Richmond, VA), June, 1995, p. 18.
Otago Daily Times (New Zealand), July 31, 1993, p. 19.
Randolph-Macon College Bulletin, winter, 1995, pp. 6-7.
Richmond Times-Dispatch, October 18, 1992, pp. G1, G7.
Tampa Tribune, March 21, 1987, p. 10F.
Tribune Books (Chicago), March 29, 1987.
USA Today, January 31, 1990.
Washington Post, April 10, 1991, p. B5.

*   *   *

IVES, Morgan
  See BRADLEY, Marion Zimmer

J

JACKMAN, Robert W(illiam) 1946-

PERSONAL: Born October 31, 1946, in Oamaru, New Zealand; immigrated to United States, 1968, naturalized citizen, 1980; son of David S. (a teacher) and Helen (a teacher; maiden name, Murray) Jackman; married Mary R. Peretz (a professor), September 10, 1968; children: Rachael, Saul. *Education:* University of Auckland, B.A., 1968; University of Wisconsin—Madison, M.A., 1970, Ph.D., 1972.

ADDRESSES: Home—Davis, CA. *Office*—University of California, Davis, CA 95616-8682.

CAREER: Michigan State University, East Lansing, assistant professor, 1972-75, associate professor, 1975-80, professor of political science, 1980-89; University of California, Davis, professor of political science, 1989—. Fellow at Center for Advanced Study in the Behavioral Sciences, Stanford, CA, 1986-87.

AWARDS, HONORS: Guggenheim fellow, 1980-81; Distinguished Faculty Award, Michigan State University, 1988.

WRITINGS:

Politics and Social Equality: A Comparative Analysis, Wiley (New York City), 1975.
(With wife, Mary R. Jackman) *Class Awareness in the United States,* University of California Press (Santa Cruz), 1983.
Power without Force: The Political Capacity of Nation-States, University of Michigan Press (Ann Arbor), 1993.

JACKSON, MacDonald P. 1938-

PERSONAL: Born October 13, 1938, in Auckland, New Zealand; son of Donald Leslie (a teacher) and Margaret (a housewife; maiden name, Pairman) Jackson; married Nicole Philippa Lovett (a librarian), September 2, 1964; children: Cameron, Anna, Juliet. *Education:* University of Auckland, B.A., 1959, M.A., 1960; Merton College, Oxford, B.Litt., 1963.

ADDRESSES: Home—21 Te Kowhai Pl., Remuera, Auckland 5, New Zealand. *Office*—Department of English, University of Auckland, Private Bag 92019, Auckland, New Zealand.

CAREER: University of Auckland, Auckland, New Zealand, junior lecturer, 1960-61, lecturer, 1964-68, senior lecturer, 1969-77, associate professor, 1978-86, professor of English, 1987—.

WRITINGS:

Shakespeare's "A Lover's Complaint": Its Date and Authenticity, University of Auckland (Auckland, New Zealand), 1965.
(Editor) *Poetry Australia: New Zealand Issue,* South Head Press, 1966.
Studies in Attribution: Middleton and Shakespeare, University of Salzburg, 1979.
(Editor) *"The Revenger's Tragedy," Attributed to Thomas Middleton: A Facsimile of the 1607/8 Quarto,* Associated University Presses, 1983.
(Editor with Vincent O'Sullivan) *The Oxford Book of New Zealand Writing since 1945,* Oxford University Press (New York City), 1983.

(Editor with Michael Neill) *The Selected Plays of John Marston,* Cambridge University Press (New York City), 1986.

(Editor) *A. R. D. Fairburn: Selected Poems,* Victoria University Press, 1995.

OTHER

Contributor to numerous books, including *Thirteen Facets,* edited by Ian Wards, New Zealand Government Printer, 1978; *The Cambridge Companion to Shakespeare Studies,* edited by Stanley Wells, Cambridge University Press, 1986; *The Oxford History of New Zealand Literature in English,* edited by Terrg Sturm, Oxford University Press, 1991; and *In the Same Room: Conversations with New Zealand Writers,* edited by Mark Williams and Elizabeth Alley, Auckland University Press, 1992.

Contributor of more than one hundred articles and reviews to academic and literary journals.

WORK IN PROGRESS: Editing William Shakespeare's *Pericles* and *The Complete Works of Thomas Middletown,* both for Oxford University Press.

*   *   *

JACKSON, R(ichard) Eugene   1941-

PERSONAL: Born February 25, 1941, in Helena, AR; son of Howard L. (a steamfitter) and Edna (Warren) Jackson; children: Brandon D. *Education:* Memphis State University, B.S., 1963; Kent State University, M.A., 1964; Southern Illinois University, Ph.D., 1971.

ADDRESSES: Home—1901 Oakleaf Ct., Mobile, AL 36609-7047. *Office*—Drama Department, University of South Alabama, Mobile, AL 36688-0002.

CAREER: Teacher of English, speech, and drama at high school in Antwerp, OH, 1964-65; Wisconsin State University—Eau Claire (now University of Wisconsin—Eau Claire), instructor of drama, 1967-68; San Francisco State University, San Francisco, CA, assistant professor of drama, 1968-70; University of South Alabama, Mobile, assistant professor, 1971-75, associate professor, 1975-78, professor of drama, 1980—, chair of department of dramatic arts, 1978—. Director of numerous local and university

theater productions, including *The Imaginary Invalid, Promises, Promises,* and *Cat on a Hot Tin Roof.*

MEMBER: American Alliance of Theatre and Education, ASSITEJ, Association for Theatre in Higher Education, Dramatists Guild, Southeastern Theatre Conference (chair of children's theater division, 1979-80), Alabama Theatre League, Phi Kappa Phi, Mobile Jaycees.

AWARDS, HONORS: Winner of several local and university contests; first alternate, O'Neill Playwriting Contest, 1973, for *No Way;* winner of Pioneer Drama Service national playwriting contest, 1979, for *Brer Rabbit's Big Secret,* and 1980, for *Snowhite and the Space Gwarfs.*

WRITINGS:

PUBLISHED PLAYS

Ferdinand and the Dirty Knight (two-act comedy; first produced in Kent, OH, at Kent State University, June, 1964), Pioneer Drama Service, 1968.

Little Red Riding Wolf (three-act play; first produced in Mobile, AL, at Pixie Playhouse), I. E. Clark (Schulenburg, TX), 1973.

Who Can Fix the Dragon's Wagon (two-act play; first produced in Eau Claire, WI, at the University of Wisconsin—Eau Claire, November, 1967), I. E. Clark, 1974.

Triple Play (one-act play), Dramatic Publishing, 1974.

The Creepy Castle Hassle (three-act play; first produced in Mobile at Pixie Playhouse), Performance Publishing, 1975.

The Crazy Paper Caper (three-act play; first produced in Mobile at Pillans School Theatre), Performance Publishing, 1976.

Snowballs and Grapevines (one-act play; first produced in Mobile at Bethel Theatre, 1973), published in *Dekalb Literary Arts Journal,* summer, 1976.

The Wonderful Wizard of Oz (three-act play; first produced in Mobile at Pixie Playhouse, 1975), I. E. Clark, 1976.

Rumpelstiltskin Is My Name (two-act play), I. E. Clark, 1977.

(With Susan Snider Osterberg) *Bumper Snickers* (two-act play), I. E. Clark, 1978.

Superkid (three-act play), I. E. Clark, 1980.

A Golden Fleecing (three-act play; first produced in Gulf Shores, AL, at State Park Theatre, June 1, 1980), Pioneer Drama Service, 1980.

Rag Dolls (two-act play), I. E. Clark, 1981.

The Adventures of Peter Cottontail (two-act play; first produced by Children's Musical Theatre in Mobile, summer, 1979), Pioneer Drama Service, 1981.

Unidentified Flying Reject (three-act play), I. E. Clark, 1982.

Coffee Pott and the Wolf Man (three-act play), I. E. Clark, 1982.

Animal Krackers (two-act play; first produced by Children's Musical Theatre in Mobile, October 1, 1981), Pioneer Drama Service, 1983.

Christmas Crisis at Mistletoe Mesa, Pioneer Drama Service, 1987.

School for Nerds, Pioneer Drama Service, 1989.

The Brave Little Tailor, Pioneer Drama Service, 1991.

You're a Grand Old Flag, I. E. Clark, 1992.

The Creepy Crawlers, Eldridge Publishing Company (Franklin, OH), 1994.

Hospital Hijinx, Eldridge Publishing Company, 1994.

Goofus and Doofus, Eldridge Publishing Company, 1995.

Switcheroo, Eldridge Publishing Company, 1995.

Wild Pecos Bill, Eldridge Publishing Company, 1995.

Amazing Grace and Her Jellybean Tree, I. E. Clark, 1995.

PUBLISHED PLAYS; AUTHOR AND LYRICIST

The Sleeping Beauty (two-act musical; first produced by Children's Musical Theatre in Mobile, 1975), Pioneer Drama Service, 1976.

Brer Rabbit's Big Secret (two-act musical; first produced by Children's Musical Theatre in Mobile, October 1, 1978), Pioneer Drama Service, 1979.

Snowhite and the Space Gwarfs (two-act musical; first produced by Children's Musical Theatre in Mobile, October 1, 1980), Pioneer Drama Service, 1980.

Lindy (three-act musical), Performance Publishing, 1981.

The Hatfields and the McFangs (two-act musical; first produced by Children's Musical Theatre in Mobile, October 1, 1981), Performance Publishing, 1982.

Boogie Man Rock (three-act musical), Baker's Plays, 1984.

Popeye the Sailor (full-length musical), Pioneer Drama Service, 1984.

Pinocchio, I. E. Clark, 1985.

Arnold (full-length musical), Pioneer Drama Service, 1985.

Babes in Toyland, I. E. Clark, 1987.

The Hunting of the Snark, I. E. Clark, 1987.

The Life and Adventures of Santa Claus, Pioneer Drama Service, 1988.

The Song of Hiawatha, first produced by Children's Musical Theatre in Mobile, 1988, I. E. Clark, 1988.

The Dancing Snowman, Pioneer Drama Service, 1989.

Christmas with the Three Bears, I. E. Clark, 1990.

Rock 'n' Roll Santa, I. E. Clark, 1990.

The Little Mermaid, Pioneer Drama Service, 1991.

The Secret Garden, I. E. Clark, 1992.

Peter and the Wolf, I. E. Clark, 1993.

Peter Pan in Neverland, I. E. Clark, 1994.

PRODUCED PLAYS

Carbolic Acid Is Not as Sweet as White Ribbons (two-act play; for adults), first produced in Memphis at Memphis Little Theatre, August, 1963.

A Thousand and One Spells to Cast (two-act play; for children), first produced in Kent at Kent State University, 1964.

Sticks and Stones (two-act play; for children), first produced at Memphis Little Theatre, August, 1964.

Mother Goose Follies (two-act play; for children), first produced by Southern Illinois University in Carbondale, September, 1971.

(And lyricist) *The Jumping Off Place,* first produced by Children's Musical Theatre in Mobile, 1985.

(And lyricist) *Wild Pecos Bill,* first produced by Children's Musical Theatre in Mobile, summer, 1985.

(Librettist) *The Cantor of Vilna* (short opera), first produced by Sha'arai Shomayin Temple in Mobile, April, 1986.

OTHER

Also author of *Felicia and the Magic Pinks* (two-act play), first produced in Mobile at Pixie Playhouse. Author of several as yet unpublished and unproduced plays, including *No Way, April, May, June, S/he,* and *Byrds of Prey.* Also author of lyrics for numerous musical plays produced by Children's Musical Theatre, Mobile, AL. Contributor of articles to *Children's Theatre Review.*

WORK IN PROGRESS: "I'm always working on new writing projects."

SIDELIGHTS: R. Eugene Jackson told *CA:* "Teaching theater on the university level is an exciting and fulfilling vocation. Even better, it provides the opportunity for me to write plays and often to see them produced prior to publication. For exercise, fun, and further artistic achievement, I enjoy formal ballroom dancing."

*   *   *

JENNINGS, Coleman A(lonzo)   1933-

PERSONAL: Born November 21, 1933, in Granger, TX; son of Vaudra R. and Elsie (Fox) Jennings; married Lola Hanawalt, 1961; children: Coleman Charles, Adrienne Elise. *Education:* University of Texas at Austin, B.F.A., 1958, M.F.A., 1961; New York University, Ed.D., 1974.

ADDRESSES: Office—Department of Theatre & Dance, University of Texas at Austin, Austin, TX 78712.

CAREER: High school drama and history teacher in Austin, TX, 1960-61; Midland Community Theatre, Midland, TX, children's theater director and teacher of creative drama, 1961-63; University of Texas at Austin, drama faculty, 1963—, chair of department, 1981-93, founder and director of Summer Theatre Pizazz, 1965—. Guest assistant professor at University of Illinois at Urbana-Champaign, summers, 1963-64; visiting assistant professor at New York University, summers, 1968, 1971; visiting lecturer at University of Arkansas at Little Rock, 1978, Trinity University and University of Texas at San Antonio, both 1980. Technical director at Chase Barn Playhouse, Whitefield, NH, summers, 1956-57; technician and assistant manager of Off-Broadway productions, 1958-59. Member of U.S. Commission for UNESCO, 1969-75, member of its executive committee, 1973-75; U.S. representative to Jamaican UNESCO Cultural and Conservation Conference, 1970; member of National Conference on Theatre Education for Public Schools, 1977; member of executive committee of Education Program, National Endowment for the Arts, 1980. Chair of Creative Drama Curriculum Committee of Texas Education Agency, 1969-72; member of Texas Alliance for Arts Education, 1978; member of theater panel of

Texas Commission on the Arts and Humanities, 1978-80; judge of local drama contests. Member of executive committee of Winifred Ward Memorial Scholarship Fund, 1975; member of advisory board of Creative Theatre Unlimited, 1986-90; consultant to Rockefeller Foundation and Performing Arts Repertory Theatre of New York City. *Military service:* U.S. Army, 1953-55, served in Europe as ground control radar operator.

MEMBER: International Association of Theatre for Children and Youth (member of executive committee, 1978-80), American Alliance for Theatre & Education, American Theatre Association, Children's Theatre Association of America (vice-president, 1973-75; president, 1975-77), Children's Theatre Conference of America (member of board of governors, 1965-68), Children's Theatre Foundation of America (member of board, 1995—), Southwest Theatre Conference, Texas Educational Theatre Association (chair of Creative Drama Curriculum Committee, 1965-70, 1990-93; member of board of directors, 1984-86), Texas Non-Profit Theatre Association.

AWARDS, HONORS: Charlotte Chorpenning National Award, Children's Theatre Association of America, 1962, for work at Midland Community Theatre, and 1965, for international exhibit "Children's Theatre in America"; grants from Texas Commission on the Arts and Humanities, 1975 and 1977; Founders Award from Texas Educational Theatre Association, 1986; inducted into the College of Fellows of the American Theatre, Kennedy Center, Washington, DC, 1993.

WRITINGS:

Learning Partners: Reading and Creative Dynamics, Texas Education Agency, 1976.
(Author of biography and play analyses) *Six Plays for Children by Aurand Harris,* foreword by Lowell Swortzell, University of Texas Press (Austin, TX), 1977.
(With Lola H. Jennings) *Creative Drama in the Elementary School,* Texas Education Agency, 1978.

PLAYS

The Honorable Urashima Taro, The Dramatic Publishing Company (Chicago, IL), 1972.
(With Jennings) *Braille: The Early Life of Louis Braille,* The Dramatic Publishing Company (Woodstock, IL), 1989.

(With Jennings) *Johnny Tremain* (adapted from the novel by Esther Forbes), The Dramatic Publishing Company, 1992.

EDITOR OF ANTHOLOGIES

(With Aurand Harris) *Plays Children Love: A Treasury of Contemporary and Classic Plays for Children*, foreword by Mary Martin, Doubleday (New York City), 1981.
(With Gretta Berghammer) *Theatre for Youth: Twelve Plays with Mature Themes*, foreword by Jed Davis, University of Texas Press, 1986.
(With Harris) *Plays Children Love, Volume II: A Treasury of Twenty Contemporary and Classic Plays for Children*, foreword by Carol Channing, St. Martin's (New York City), 1987.

AUTHOR OF FOREWORD, INTRODUCTION, OR PREFACE

(Introduction) *Yankee Doodle*, Anchorage Press (New Orleans, LA), 1975.
(Preface and contributor) *Go Adventuring: A Celebration of Winifred Ward, America's First Lady of Drama for Children*, Anchorage Press, 1977.
(Preface) *Flashback* (play), Anchorage Press, 1980.
(Preface) *I Didn't Know That* (play), Anchorage Press, 1980.
(Foreword) Barbara Salisbury, *Theatre Arts in the Elementary Classroom, Grade Four through Grade Six*, Anchorage Press, 1986.
(Foreword) Salisbury, *Theatre Arts in the Elementary Classroom, Kindergarten through Grade Three*, Anchorage Press, 1986.

OTHER

Also author of computer diskette, *A Bibliographic Research Database Covering the Areas of Creative Drama and Theatre for Young Audiences*, Anchorage Press, 1993. Contributor of articles and reviews to periodicals, including *Children's Theatre Review* and *University Interscholastic Leaguer*. Contributor to *Twentieth-Century Children's Writers*, St. James Press, Ltd. (London, England), 1978. Editor of *Children's Theatre Review*, 1965-67.

WORK IN PROGRESS: Graduate Research: Creative Drama and Theatre for Youth, a computerized database of theses and dissertations written in the United States, from 1923 to the present; research on child actors and the child audience.

BIOGRAPHICAL/CRITICAL SOURCES:

PERIODICALS

Fanfare, February, 1984.

*   *   *

JHABVALA, Ruth Prawer   1927-

PERSONAL: Born May 7, 1927, in Cologne, Germany; came to England, 1939; naturalized British citizen, 1948; naturalized U.S. citizen, 1986; daughter of Marcus (owner of a clothing business) and Eleonora (Cohn) Prawer; married Cyrus S. H. Jhabvala (an architect), 1951; children: Renana, Ava, Firoza. *Education:* Queen Mary College, London, M.A., 1951.

ADDRESSES: Home—400 East 52nd St., New York, NY 10022-6404. *Agent*—Harriet Wasserman, 137 East 36th St., New York, NY 10016.

CAREER: Writer, 1951—.

AWARDS, HONORS: Booker Award for Fiction, National Book League, 1975, and British Academy of Film and Television Arts (BAFTA) award for *Heat and Dust;* Guggenheim fellow, 1976; Neil Gunn international fellow, 1979; MacArthur Foundation fellow, 1986-89; Writers Guild of America Award for best adapted screenplay, 1986, and Academy Award (Oscar) for best screenplay adapted from another medium, 1987, both for *A Room with a View;* Academy Award nomination for best screenplay adaption, 1993, for *Howards End;* New York Film Critics Award, for *Mr. and Mrs. Bridge;* D.Litt., London University.

WRITINGS:

FICTION

To Whom She Will, Allen & Unwin (London), 1955, published as *Amrita*, Norton (New York City), 1956.
The Nature of Passion, Allen & Unwin, 1956, Norton, 1957.
Esmond in India, Allen & Unwin, 1957, Norton, 1958.
The Householder (also see below), Norton, 1960.

Get Ready for Battle, Murray (London), 1962, Norton, 1963.

Like Birds, Like Fishes and Other Stories, Murray, 1963, Norton, 1964.

A Backward Place, Norton, 1965.

A Stronger Climate: Nine Stories, Murray, 1968, Norton, 1969.

An Experience of India (stories), Murray, 1971, Norton, 1972.

A New Dominion, Murray, 1972, published as *Travelers,* Harper, 1973.

Heat and Dust (also see below), Murray, 1975, Harper, 1976.

Autobiography of a Princess, Harper, 1975.

How I Became a Holy Mother and Other Stories, Murray, 1975, Harper, 1976.

In Search of Love and Beauty, Morrow (New York City), 1983.

Out of India: Selected Stories, Morrow, 1986.

Three Continents, Morrow, 1987.

Poet and Dancer, Doubleday (New York City), 1993.

Shards of Memory (also see below) Doubleday, 1995.

SCREENPLAYS

The Householder (based on her novel), Royal, 1963.

(With James Ivory) *Shakespeare Wallah* (produced by Merchant-Ivory Productions, 1966), Grove, 1973.

(With Ivory) *The Guru,* Twentieth Century-Fox, 1968.

Bombay Talkie, Merchant-Ivory Productions, 1970.

Roseland, Merchant-Ivory Productions, 1977.

Hullabaloo over Georgie and Bonnie's Pictures, Contemporary, 1978.

(With Ivory) *The Europeans* (based on the novel by Henry James), Levitt-Pickman, 1979.

Jane Austen in Manhattan, Contemporary, 1980.

(With Ivory) *Quartet* (based on the novel by Jean Rhys), Lyric International/New World, 1981.

Heat and Dust (based on her novel), Merchant-Ivory Productions, 1983.

The Bostonians (based on the novel by James), Merchant-Ivory Productions, 1984.

The Courtesans of Bombay, Channel 4, England/New Yorker Films, 1985.

A Room with a View (based on the novel by E. M. Forster), Merchant-Ivory Productions, 1986.

(With John Schlesinger) *Madame Sousatzka* (based on the novel by Bernice Rubens), Universal, 1988.

Mr. and Mrs. Bridge (based on the novels *Mr. Bridge* and *Mrs. Bridge* by Evan S. Connell), Merchant-Ivory Productions, 1990.

Howards End (based on the novel by Forster), Merchant-Ivory Productions, 1992.

The Remains of the Day (based on the novel by Kazuo Ishiguro), Merchant-Ivory Productions, 1993.

Jefferson in Paris, Merchant-Ivory Productions, 1995.

Also author of screenplay for a forthcoming Merchant-Ivory film based on her novel *Shards of Memory.*

WORK IN PROGRESS: A screenplay about Picasso.

SIDELIGHTS: Although Ruth Prawer Jhabvala has long been celebrated in Europe and India for her fiction and screenplays, it was not until she captured an Academy Award for her film adaptation of E. M. Forster's *A Room with a View* that she began winning widespread attention in the United States for her work. As a German-born, British citizen who lived in India for over twenty years, and in New York for over a decade, Jhabvala brings a unique perspective to her novels and stories of East-West conflict. "With a cool, ironic eye and a feeling for social nuance," asserts Bernard Weinraub in a *New York Times Magazine* article, Jhabvala "[has] developed a series of themes—families battered by change in present-day India, the timeless European fascination with the subcontinent—that were probably both incomprehensible and inconsequential to readers who were not intrigued with India in the first place. And yet," continues the critic, "as Mrs. Jhabvala's work darkened and turned more melancholy, as her detachment grew chilling in her later work, critics began to notice that the writer's India had become as universal as [William] Faulkner's Yoknapatawpha and [Anton] Chekhov's czarist Russia." "Like Jane Austen," notes *Saturday Review* contributor Katha Pollitt, Jhabvala "treats satirically and intimately a world in which conventions are precisely defined and widely accepted, even by those who are most harmed by them."

Jhabvala herself has led a rather unconventional life. She and her family narrowly escaped the Nazi persecution of the Jews, fleeing to relative safety in England in 1939. All her father's relatives died in the Holocaust. Ten years after the family's flight into exile she met the man who became her husband, the architect Cyrus S. H. Jhabvala. After their marriage, the couple left Europe to live in newly independent India. "I was 24," Jhabvala is quoted by David Streitfeld in the *Washington Post Book World,* "and just at the age when one really starts to write seriously. There was so much subject matter for me. I hardly finished a book before I started a new one. I was so full of energy, I immediately wrote as if I were an Indian, from inside." Yet, she adds, she was not truly an Indian writer. "I wasn't even really anything when I was in India, because I was a foreigner there. People are always asking where my roots are, and I say I don't have any."

Indeed, since the appearance of her first work, *Amrita* (published in England as *To Whom She Will*), Jhabvala has been recognized for her cutting portrayals of India's middle class. In *Amrita,* comments Nancy Wilson Ross in the *New York Herald Tribune Book Review,* Jhabvala "has written a fresh and witty novel about modern India. It is not necessary to know anything about the customs and habits of . . . New Delhi—the setting of Mrs. Jhabvala's lively comedy of manners—to enjoy her ironic social commentary." And in a *Times Literary Supplement* review of *A Backward Place,* one critic maintains that while Jhabvala "has not the sustained brilliance that Jane Austen often rises to . . . all the same her many excellent qualities are nearly all Austenish ones, and they make her a most interesting and satisfactory writer." "At least three British reviewers have compared her to Jane Austen," observes J. F. Muehl in his *Saturday Review* account of Jhabvala's debut novel, "and the comparison is not only just; it is inevitable."

Jhabvala's later fiction, while still set in India, has focused more on the differences and resulting conflicts between Eastern and Western cultures, and has led to comparison with the work of yet another great English novelist. For example, a *Washington Post Book World* contributor considers the Booker Prize-winning novel *Heat and Dust* to be "crafted with a technical skill as assured as it is unobtrusive," and, "because of its setting and its theme of Anglo-Indian relationships, reminiscent of E. M. Forster's great novel, *A Passage to India.*" *Heat and Dust* details the story of a young British woman who is journeying through India in imitation of her grandfather's first wife Olivia and contains "social comedy . . . as funny and as sympathetic as it is in Mrs. Jhabvala's earlier novels, even though she has departed from her more usual theme of middle-class Indian life," according to Brigid Allen in the *Times Literary Supplement.* The account presents the parallel experiences of the two women by moving between the journal of the elder and the story of the younger; Pearl K. Bell says in the *New York Times Book Review* that "Jhabvala moves nimbly between the two generations and the divergent points of time and sentiment." The critic elaborates: "Writing with austere emphatic economy, [Jhabvala] does not belabor the parallels between the two levels of narrative—at least not until the end. Like Forster, she renders the barriers of incomprehension and futility that persist between English and Indians with witty precision."

While *New York Review of Books* contributor Frank Kermode agrees that Jhabvala's "two narratives are quite subtly plaited, with magical chiming between the two," he believes that the author writes "impassively, almost incuriously," about her characters' failures. But Julian Barnes finds this distancing appropriate and deliberate, noting in the *New Statesman* that Jhabvala "offers no comment except through the subsequent experiences of the narrator, which gradually flow into a distorted, parallel version of Olivia's life." Barnes adds that "the two halves make up a stylish and gentle exploration of the theme of Anglo-Indian interpenetration, confirming Aziz's prophetic remarks in *A Passage to India* about the relationship between the two nations." Calling *Heat and Dust* "distinguished by a rapier wit and subtlety," Dorothy Rabinowitz likewise concludes in the *Saturday Review* that Jhabvala's novel "is, particularly in its delicate chartings of passion and of the growth of consciousness, a superb story, a gift to those who care for the novel, and to the art of fiction itself."

Although Jhabvala had been securing a name for herself as one of the foremost modern writers about India after the publication of *Heat and Dust,* she was finding it difficult both to remain in and write about her adopted country. Critics began observing an increasing amount of ambivalence toward India in Jhabvala's writing, a change evident in her retrospective collection of stories, *Out of India.* The *New York Times*'s Michiko Kakutani, for example, comments that "bit by bit, . . . the stories in *Out of India* darken, grow denser and more ambiguous. In choosing narrative strategies that are increasingly ambitious," explains the reviewer, "Mrs. Jhabvala gradually moves beyond the tidy formulations of the comedy of manners, and a strain of melancholy also begins to creep into her writing."

Village Voice contributor Vivian Gornick similarly sees a sense of "oppressiveness" in Jhabvala's writing, and speculates that "Jhabvala is driven to separate herself from India." The critic believes that this need undermines the author's work: "That drive deprives her of empathy and, inevitably, it deprives her characters of full humanness." In contrast, Paul Gray claims in his *Time* review that the stories in *Out of India* "do not demystify India; they pay the place tributes of empathy and grace." "Reading [these stories] is like watching a scene through an exceptionally clear telescope," states Rumer Godden in the *New York Times Book Review*. This distance, however, "does not take away from the stories' sureness of touch," Godden continues. "They have a beginning, middle and end, but fused so subtly we drift into them—and are immediately at home—and drift out again."

Some of Jhabvala's more recent works, while eschewing the familiar Indian setting, still explore some of her usual themes, such as the search for spiritual fulfillment. *Three Continents,* for example, relates the story of 19-year-old twins Michael and Harriet Wishwell, heirs to a large fortune who are drawn to the promises of a trio of supposed spiritual philosophers. The twins become obsessed with the Rawul, his consort the Rani, and their "adopted son" Crishi, and turn over control of their lives and fortune to the swindlers. "In its geographical scope, its large and far-flung cast and its relentless scrutiny of both sexual and intellectual thralldom," maintains Laura Shapiro in *Newsweek, Three Continents* "is Jhabvala's most ambitious and impressive work." *Los Angeles Times* reviewer Elaine Kendall similarly calls the novel "perhaps [Jhabvala's] most ambitious work," remarking that it "not only confronts these issues [from her previous work] directly but in a more contemporary context."

Despite these positive assessments of *Three Continents*, some critics fault the author for her narrative method. "The narrative belongs to Harriet," Nancy Wigston notes in the Toronto *Globe and Mail,* "and therein lies much of the frustration of the book. Harriet may not be a phony," the reviewer explains, "but she is somewhat of an airhead . . . [and] her insights are limited." Kendall likewise observes that "while the youth and naivete of the narrator help our credulity, ultimately we're left with an inescapable skepticism." "This is an intelligent but unsatisfactory novel," Anita Brookner asserts in the *Spectator,* "intelligent because the author is and cannot help but be so, unsatisfactory because the effort of staying inside Harriet's stupid head conveys a certain tedium." Victoria Glendinning, however, believes that Harriet's narration provides an added dimension:

"One of the cleverest things about the writing is the way Ruth Prawer Jhabvala shows how on one level Harriet is aware of everything that is happening, while never admitting it to herself," as the critic writes in the London *Times. Three Continents,* she adds, "[is] a book full of urgent messages about the East and West, about the need to belong somewhere, and the sinister pressures of the modern world." "As a meditation on the twin themes of inheritance and family, *Three Continents* is a significant achievement," comments *New York Times Book Review* contributor Peter Ackroyd, concluding that "as a guidebook to the inner recesses of idealism and desire it is undoubtedly a success."

Poet and Dancer, like *Three Continents,* is a non-Indian novel; it is, in fact, set in New York. The novel was inspired by the story of a double suicide, two sisters who killed themselves for no perceptible reason. "I was wondering how this could have happened—it was a very dark deed, a dark relationship," states Jhabvala in a quote reported by Streitfeld. The relationship as Jhabvala depicts it is between two cousins, Angel and Lara. Angel (the poet) has lived her entire life in New York City, while Lara (the dancer) has travelled all over the world. "As the reader might expect," states Claire Messud in the *Times Literary Supplement,* "Angel, to whom Lara appears an exotic and precious butterfly, devotes herself adoringly to her cousin; but Lara proves dangerous and ultimately mad, and the result of their closeness is their mutual destruction." Some critics express puzzlement over Angel's fascination with Lara, who, they feel, is depicted very unsympathetically. A critic writing for *Rapport,* calls their association a "chilling relationship between hunter and prey where the boundary between love and obsession is crossed so many times it is blurred beyond recognition." "There's something lacking in this small, well-made novel," declares *New Statesman and Society* reviewer Wendy Brandmark, "some moral centre, some emotional touchstone. . . . We do not know why we should care about these characters and their destructive search for the perfect life, the perfect art, the perfect love." In *Shards of Memory* Jhabvala explores themes of family and history by detailing the saga of several generations of one multicultural family throughout the twentieth century. Through one man's search for information about his unknown father (by perusing trunks of documents left by the spiritual teacher of his grandparents), the story of the entire family is told. A *Publishers Weekly* contributor commends Jhabvala for her skillful treatment of the complex and sophisticated story "evoking the family's world of shabby bohemian gentility while creating fascinating characters made more credible by her wise portrayal of their emotional states" and her expression of East-West relationships through the characters' natures. The *Nation*'s Molly E. Rauch finds that "the double-time plot can make for a refreshing reclamation of the past". And while noting that the storyline could be aided by a screenplay and that the characters were difficult to track, *New York Times Book Review*'s Barbara Grizzuti Harrison acknowledges that she likes *Shards of Memory* because it deals with family values. She concludes: "The best part of *Shards of Memory,* and the noblest, is the explicit acknowledgment that any configuration of human beings, however unlikely, may be called a family if among or between them there is love—even if it is a kind of love that can only be described but cannot be comprehended by those outside that family's magic circle."

While Jhabvala has been a consistent force on the literary scene, she is also a member of the longest producer-director-writer partnership in film history. Along with Ismail Merchant and James Ivory, Jhabvala has helped create numerous movies that, while not always hits at the box office, have been praised by critics for their consistent literary quality. Their association dates back to 1963, when Ivory and Merchant telephoned the author, then living in India, and asked her to write a screenplay from her fourth novel *The Householder.* "That gave me the opportunity I otherwise would never have had," Jhabvala reveals in a statement recounted by Streitfeld. "I was so lucky. Merchant and Ivory are like a shield for me. I don't have to bother with the things that are so gruesome for other screenwriters, like story conferences."

Although the author was initially reluctant to attempt screenplays, critic Yasmine Gooneratne thinks that the dramatic qualities necessary for films have always been present in Jhabvala's work. Writing in *World Literature Written in English,* Gooneratne states that the author's early novels have "the tight structure of stage plays, and even [contain] casts of characters. The process by which the comparative simplicities of satiric drama yield to the complexity of ironic fiction is hastened, it would appear, through her experience of working repeatedly within the narrow limits of a screenplay." The critic cites the film-like structure of *Heat and Dust* as an example, and adds that "despite the fact that Mrs. Jhabvala's increasing technical skill as a writer of screenplays has

helped her to devise ways and means to make the cinema screen yield workable equivalents for her established fictional techniques, it is probable that her artistry as a fiction-writer still outstrips her achievement as a writer for film. So rapid has her development been, however," Gooneratne continues, "that this is unlikely to be the case for very long." This prediction has proved accurate, for several recent Merchant-Ivory-Jhabvala productions have been popular as well as critical successes.

For example, about *The Bostonians,* the 1984 adaptation of Henry James's novel, Vincent Canby of the *New York Times* remarks that "it's now apparent [that Jhabvala, Merchant and Ivory have] enriched and refined their individual talents to the point where they have now made what must be one of their best films as well as one of the best adaptations of a major literary work ever to come onto the screen." The best, perhaps, until Jhabvala and her collaborators produced the film that earned the author her first Oscar nomination, 1986's *A Room with a View.* Director Ivory and screenwriter Jhabvala "have taken E. M. Forster's 1908 novel and preserved its wit, irony and brilliant observation of character," states Lawrence O'Toole in *Maclean's.* "And they never allow its theme—the importance of choosing passion over propriety—to escape their grasp." Calling the trio's film "an exceptionally faithful, ebullient screen equivalent to a literary work that lesser talents would embalm," Canby notes that "maybe more important than anything else [in the film] is the narrative tone." He explains that Ivory and Jhabvala "have somehow found a voice for the film not unlike that of Forster, who tells the story of *A Room with a View* with as much genuine concern as astonished amusement. That's quite an achievement." Audiences found the film entertaining as well, for *A Room with a View* became one of the most popular Merchant-Ivory-Jhabvala collaborations ever, setting house records at many theaters.

For their next film, *Mr. and Mrs. Bridge,* Jhabvala, Merchant, and Ivory chose a different author, but a similar theme—the foibles of the American, rather than the English, upper-middle class. But Jhabvala's version of Evan S. Connell's two novels "is not social satire as much as a melancholy, delicate and gently funny look at the ordinariness of American life," declares Richard A. Blake in *America.* "In her adaptation, Jhabvala has tried to balance highlights of the Bridges' lives with dailiness," Stanley Kauffmann states in the *New Republic,* "though inevitably there's less of the non-dramatic in the film than in the novels."

The end result, Blake concludes, "is a charming, elegant and literate film, beautifully embellished by finely balanced, sensitive ensemble acting."

Yet "for all the respect [the trio's] films garnered," explains *Newsweek* contributor David Ansen, "there were always detractors who dismissed their works as enervated 'Masterpiece Theatre' gentility." The dichotomy is especially evident in the diversity of critical commentary that greeted the three's version of Forster's *Howards End*—the film that brought Jhabvala her second Oscar nomination. John Simon, writing in *National Review,* terms the movie "inept." Anne Billson states in her *New Statesman and Society* review of the film, "If *Howards End* is supposed to be an indictment of snobbery and greed, it fails, because it revels in the snobbish and greedy way of life." "The qualities of such illustrated English Lit are not cinematic, but are those of the Edwardian theme park," she continues. "This film should be bought up by the National Trust, though it doesn't need to be preserved. It has already been pickled in the formaldehyde of nostalgia." *New Yorker* contributor Terrence Rafferty calls the film well-done, but adds, "those of us who love Forster might miss the sense of strain, the awkward human beauty of his artistic failure." On the other hand, Ansen pronounces *Howards End* "the crowning achievement of [the trio's] careers, the movie that seems to incorporate all they have learned about filmmaking—and life—and raised it to a new plateau." "It's fascinating," he concludes, "that Jhabvala and Ivory have chosen not to include that often quoted epigraph ['only connect'] in their movie. They didn't need to: their images have made the point. Everyone says great books never make great movies. *Howards End* is one grand exception."

In the opinion of *Commonweal* contributor Richard Alleva, Jhabvala, Merchant, and Ivory actually improved on author Kazuo Ishiguro's novel *The Remains of the Day* by making it into a film. Alleva points out that Ishiguro, by seeing his story about a butler whose sense of self-worth rests wholly on his usefulness to his employer only through the butler's eyes, makes the novel "predictable." "It's a stunt," Alleva says, "and you soon learn the mechanics of the stunt." But the "Ruth Prawer Jhabvala film adaptation is not a stunt, just a good movie," the reviewer continues, because it takes the story away from the butler-only point of view and presents the plot in a linear fashion. "The stoic poignancy of the title, *The Remains of the Day,*" he concludes, "is more fully earned by the movie than by the book." Simon en-

joys the film as well, stating in a later review for *National Review* that "*The Remains of the Day* will long remain in your memory as a portrait of heroic futility, heartbreaking fatuity, and purblind doggedness, as they become the downfall of a society, an empire, and, worst of all, a single human soul."

Jhabvala herself sees little overlap between the people who read her books and the people who watch her screenplays. "I think the two audiences are completely different," she once told *CA.* "I suppose people who see films may also read books, but to me it's either one or the other. But I may be wrong. Quite recently my books have been more available in America, and I may be getting more readers. But one doesn't really know about these things".

Yet in some ways, Jhabvala adds, the two forms of writing—fiction and screenplays—enhance each other. "I certainly don't think I could write screenplays very well if I didn't, most of the time, work at creating characters and dialogue and situations of my own in my fiction," she tells *CA* interviewer Jean Ross. "Then whatever I've accumulated of experience in that, I bring to the screenplays. And in writing novels you also get a certain feel for structure which you have to have in constructing a screenplay. But I also think the screenwriting has definitely influenced my fiction. For instance, I think you can see it in *Heat and Dust,* and in *In Search of Love and Beauty* in the way I've juggled scenes and time sequences around. That's something I learned in films. They certainly are mutually enriching, but one is so much more difficult than the other—writing fiction is much harder."

"What I think of first of all in writing a script is how to present the story in the most economical terms possible. That includes the characters and the whole ambience, but the ambience is not going to be my job. What I have to do myself in fiction, like actually dressing the characters and furnishing the rooms, somebody else is obviously doing in the film. But, on the other hand, I have to give them the opportunity to do that. I have to give a sense of how the characters are interacting with their setting and why there should be this particular setting and how it will enhance what is going on in their minds and in the dialogue. So I do have to think about all these things, although I don't actually do them in screenwriting as I do in fiction."

While she has been compared to several classic writers, Jhabvala has achieved a prominent literary standing with her consistently excellent work, and critics no longer need comparisons to describe its quality. "How does one know when one is in the grip of art, of a literary power?" asks Rabinowitz in the *New York Times Book Review.* "One feels, amongst other things, the force of personality behind the cadence of each line, the sensibility behind the twist of the syllable. One feels the texture of the unspoken, the very accents of a writer's reticence." Jhabvala, maintains the critic, "seems to come naturally by a good deal of that reticence." Godden similarly praises the author for her original voice: "Time has proved [her unique]; she has written [numerous works] . . . and I could wager there is not in any of them one shoddy line or unnecessary word, a standard few writers achieve. Each book," Godden continues, "has her hallmark of balance, subtlety, wry humor and beauty." And Weinraub, in assessing Jhabvala's reputation in the literary community, quotes the late novelist C. P. Snow: "Someone once said that the definition of the highest art is that one should feel that life is this and not otherwise. I do not know of a writer living who gives that feeling with more unqualified certainty than Mrs. Jhabvala."

BIOGRAPHICAL/CRITICAL SOURCES:

BOOKS

Agarwal, Ramlal G., *Ruth Prawer Jhabvala: A Study of Her Fiction,* Sterling Publishers (New Delhi), 1990.

Bailur, Jayanti, *Ruth Prawer Jhabvala: Fiction and Film,* Arnold Publishers (New Delhi), 1992.

Contemporary Literary Criticism, Gale (Detroit), Volume 4, 1975, Volume 8, 1978, Volume 29, 1984.

Crane, Ralph J., editor, *Passages to Ruth Prawer Jhabvala,* Sterling Publishers, 1991.

Crane, *Ruth Prawer Jhabvala,* Twayne (New York City), 1992.

Dictionary of Literary Biography, Volume 139: *British Short-Fiction Writers, 1945-1980,* Gale, 1994.

Gooneratne, Yasmine, *Silence, Exile, and Cunning: The Fiction of Ruth Prawer Jhabvala,* Orient Longman (New Delhi), 1983.

Jha, Rekha, *The Novels of Kamala Markandaya and Ruth Jhabvala: A Study in East-West Encounter,* Prestige Books (New Delhi), 1990.

Long, Robert Emmet, *The Films of Merchant Ivory,* Abrams (New York City), 1991.

Pritchett, V. S., *The Tale Bearers: Literary Essays,* Random House (New York City), 1980.

Shahane, Vasant A., *Ruth Prawer Jhabvala,* Arnold-Heinemann (New Delhi), 1976.

Sucher, Laurie, *The Fiction of Ruth Prawer Jhabvala,* St. Martin (New York City), 1988.

Wiley, Mason and Damien Bona, *Inside Oscar,* Ballantine (New York City), 1993.

PERIODICALS

America, May 13, 1995, p. 24.

Christian Science Monitor, January 26, 1956, p. 7; December 8, 1976, p. 32; March 19, 1993, p. 14.

Commonweal, December 17, 1993, p. 14; May 19, 1995, p. 20.

Cosmopolitan, March, 1992, p. 20; November, 1993, p. 18.

Daily Telegraph (London), April 14, 1978, p. 17.

Entertainment Weekly, May 8, 1992, p. 42; June 12, 1992, p. 52; April 16, 1993, p. 48; April 7, 1995, p. 61.

Globe and Mail (Toronto), July 26, 1986; October 17, 1987.

Guardian, November 20, 1975, p. 12.

Indian PEN, Volume 43, numbers 11-12, 1977, pp. 4-8.

Interview, November, 1990, p. 128; March, 1992, p. 40.

Journal of Commonwealth Literature, Volume 20, number 1, 1985, pp. 171-203.

London Review of Books, March 31, 1988, p. 27; March 25, 1993, pp. 22-23; November 30, 1995.

Los Angeles Times, November 9, 1983; September 4, 1987; June 10, 1990, pp. 29-30.

Los Angeles Times Book Review, August 3, 1986, p. 4; March 14, 1993, pp. 3, 9.

Los Angeles Times Magazine, November 28, 1993, pp. 30-34, 62.

Maclean's, March 31, 1986; November 15, 1993, p. 93; April 10, 1995, p. 51.

Midstream, March, 1974, pp. 72-79.

Modern Fiction Studies, winter, 1984.

Nation, September 11, 1995, pp. 244-245.

National Review, December 13, 1993, pp. 61-63; May 1, 1995, p. 84.

New Republic, December 24, 1990, pp. 26-27; March 23, 1992, pp. 26-27; December 6, 1993, pp. 32-33; April 24, 1995, p. 30.

New Review, Volume 2, number 21, 1975, pp. 53-57.

New Statesman, October 31, 1975; April 15, 1983.

New Statesman and Society, May 29, 1992, p. 32; April 9, 1993, p. 56.

Newsweek, April 19, 1976; March 10, 1986; August 24, 1987; March 16, 1992, pp. 66-69; November 8, 1993, p. 78.

New York, November 8, 1993, p. 74; April 17, 1995, p. 106.

New Yorker, May 4, 1992, p. 74; March 22, 1993, p. 106; November 15, 1993, pp. 114-117.

New York Herald Tribune Book Review, January 15, 1956.

New York Review of Books, July 15, 1976; October 8, 1987, pp. 45-46; May 14, 1992, pp. 3-4; December 16, 1993, pp. 39-40.

New York Times, July 17, 1973, p. 31; August 30, 1973; May 15, 1976, p. 14; July 19, 1983; September 15, 1983; August 2, 1984; August 5, 1984; March 7, 1986; May 17, 1986; July 5, 1986; August 6, 1987; September 17, 1987, p. C16; March 8, 1992, pp. 15, 20-21.

New York Times Book Review, January 15, 1956; February 2, 1969; July 8, 1973; April 4, 1976; June 12, 1983; May 25, 1986, pp. 1, 20; August 23, 1987, pp. 3, 13; March 28, 1993, pp. 13-14; July 31, 1994, p. 28; September 17, 1995, p. 12.

New York Times Magazine, September 11, 1983, pp. 106-114; March 28, 1993.

Observer (London), June 17, 1979, p. 61; March 29, 1987, p. 26; October 25, 1987, p. 26.

People, March 17, 1986; September 28, 1987; April 13, 1992, pp. 18-19; April 10, 1995, p. 15.

Playboy, January, 1991, p. 18; December, 1993, p. 30.

Premiere, July, 1991, p. 100.

Publishers Weekly, June 6, 1986; July 17, 1995, p. 217.

Quest, Number 91, 1974, pp. 33-36.

Rolling Stone, January 10, 1991, p. 51; April 2, 1992, p. 41; November 25, 1993, p. 125.

Saturday Review, January 14, 1956; March 1, 1969; April 3, 1976; October 30, 1976.

Sight and Sound, Volume 48, number 1, 1978-79, pp. 15-18.

Signs: Journal of Women in Culture and Society, spring, 1981, pp. 413-435.

Spectator, April 23, 1983; October 24, 1987, pp. 27, 29; April 24, 1993, pp. 28-29; November 20, 1993, p. 37.

Time, May 12, 1986, p. 90; October 6, 1986; November 8, 1993, p. 87; April 10, 1995, p. 82.

Times (London), July 13, 1978, p. 12; July 13, 1981, p. 9; February 4, 1983; April 14, 1983; October 15, 1987.

Times Literary Supplement, May 20, 1965; November 7, 1975; April 16, 1983, p. 20; April 24, 1987, p. 434; November 13, 1987; April 16, 1993, p. 20.

Tribune Books (Chicago), February 28, 1993, p. 6.

Twentieth Century Literature, July, 1969, pp. 89-90.

Vanity Fair, March, 1993, p. 142.

Village Voice, August 2, 1983; May 8, 1986; September 30, 1986.

Vogue, March, 1992, p. 189; March, 1993, pp. 248, 254.

Wall Street Journal, June 19, 1990, p. A18; February 23, 1993, p. A18.

Washington Post, December 9, 1975, p. C2; October 7, 1983; September 22, 1984; April 5, 1986; November 7, 1993, pp. G4-G5.

Washington Post Book World, September 12, 1976; September 18, 1983; May 25, 1986, p. 9; August 23, 1987, p. 3; February 21, 1993, p. 9; March 28, 1993, p. 15.

World Literature Today, autumn, 1993, pp. 824-825.

World Literature Written in English, April, 1978; November, 1979, pp. 368-386.

*   *   *

JOKEMEISTERS
See KRAUZER, Steven M(ark)

K

KELLER, Evelyn Fox   1936-

PERSONAL: Born March 20, 1936, in New York, NY; daughter of Albert and Rachel Fox; children: Jeffrey and Sarah. *Education:* Brandeis University, B.A. (magna cum laude), 1957; Radcliffe College, M.A., 1959; Harvard University, Ph.D., 1963.

ADDRESSES: Office—Massachusetts Institute of Technology, ES1-263B, 77 Massachusetts Ave., Cambridge, MA 02139-4307.

CAREER: New York University, New York City, instructor in physics, 1962-63, assistant research scientist, 1963-66, associate professor of mathematical biology, 1970-72; Cornell University Medical College, New York City, assistant professor, 1963-69; State University of New York College at Purchase, Purchase, NY, associate professor in division of natural science, 1972-82, chair of mathematics board of study, 1972-74; Northeastern University, Boston, MA, professor of humanities and mathematics, beginning in 1982; University of California, Berkeley, professor of rhetoric, women's studies, and history of science, 1988-92; Massachusetts Institute of Technology (MIT), Cambridge, MA, professor of history and philosophy of science, 1992—. Special lecturer in mathematical biology at University of Maryland, 1974; MIT Program in Science, Technology, and Society, visiting fellow, 1979-80, visiting scholar, 1980-84, visiting professor, 1985-86; visiting professor at Northeastern University, 1981-82, and Northwestern University, 1985; member of Institute for Advanced Study, Princeton, 1987-88. Gordon Conference on Theoretical Biology, vice chairperson, 1973, chairperson, 1974; organizer and coordinator of Boston Area Colloquium on Feminist Theory,

1982—. Guest lecturer and consultant at institutions including Rutgers University, Columbia University, Harvard University, Brandeis University, and University of California, Santa Cruz.

MEMBER: American Association for the Advancement of Science, Phi Beta Kappa, Sigma Xi.

AWARDS, HONORS: National Science Foundation, fellowship, 1957-61, visiting professorship for women, 1985; Mina Shaughnessy Scholars Award from Fund for the Improvement of Postsecondary Education, 1981-82; Mellon Fellowship from Wellesley College Center for Research on Women, 1984; Rockefeller Humanities Fellowship, 1985-86; distinguished publication award from Association for Women in Psychology, 1986; senior fellow of Society for the Humanities, Cornell University, 1986-87; honorary degrees, L.H.D., Mt. Holyoke College, 1991, doctorate, University of Amsterdam, 1993, doctorate of humane science, Simmons College, 1995, doctorate of humane letters, Rensselaer Polytechnic Institute, 1995.

WRITINGS:

A Feeling for the Organism: The Life and Work of Barbara McClintock, W. H. Freeman, 1983.
Reflections on Gender and Science, Yale University Press, 1985.
(Editor, with Mary Jacobus and Sally Shuttleworth, and contributor) *Women, Science, and the Body,* Methuen, 1988.

Contributor to various books, including *Working It Out: Twenty-three Women Writers, Artists, Scientists, and Scholars Talk about Their Lives and Work,* edited by Sara Ruddick and Pamela Daniels, Pantheon, 1977; *Discovering Reality: Feminist Perspectives on Epistemology, Metaphysics, Methodology, and Philosophy of Science,* by Sandra Harding and Merrill B. Hintikka, Reidel, 1983; *Machine ex Dea,* edited by Joan Rothschild, Pergamon, 1983; *Nineteen Eighty-four: Science between Utopia and Dystopia,* edited by Everett Mendelsohn and Helga Nowotny, Reidel, 1984; *Competition among Women: A Feminist Analysis,* edited by Helen Longino and Valerie Miner, Feminist Press, 1987; and *Hermeneutics and Psychoanalysis,* edited by S. Messer and R. Woolfolk, Rutgers University Press, in press.

Also contributor of numerous articles to professional journals, including *Science, Nature, Journal of Theoretical Biology, American Journal of Physics,* and *International Journal of Women's Studies,* and of reviews to periodicals, including *Change* and *New York Times Book Review.*

Editor of "Feminist Theory" series for Northeastern University Press; adviser to Harvard University Press. American editor of *Fundamenta Scientiae;* member of editorial board of *Woman's Review of Books, Hypatia,* and *Biology and Philosophy.*

WORK IN PROGRESS: Editing *Keywords in Evolutionary Discourse,* with Elisabeth Lloyd.

SIDELIGHTS: "Evelyn Fox Keller's biography of Barbara McClintock is a welcome and useful addition to the growing literature on the recent history of . . . women's achievements in science," judged Margaret W. Rossiter in the *New York Times Book Review.* McClintock, recipient of the 1983 Nobel Prize for medicine and several other recent prizes and honorary degrees, was largely ignored when, in the early 1950s, she first presented her observations about the mobility or transposition of genes on chromosomes. In *A Feeling for the Organism: The Life and Work of Barbara McClintock,* Keller outlines several factors that may have contributed to the initial rejection of McClintock's ideas: the antifeminist nature of genetic research in that era, the unpopularity of McClintock's subject of study (maize rather than bacteria), and the incomprehension of McClintock's colleagues about her unprecedented conclusions.

Stephen Jay Gould, an acclaimed specialist in geology and evolution, described in the *New York Review of Books* the incompatibility of McClintock's early findings with the accepted notions of the time. James D. Watson and Francis Crick's 1953 discovery of the double helical structure of DNA—double "rows of beads (genes) on strings (chromosomes)," explained Gould—seemed to suggest a rigid, largely immobile structure "subject to change only by substituting one bead for another." McClintock's model of DNA, however, suggested a structure that was "fluid and mobile, changing constantly in quality and quantity," wrote Gould. Such a model did not make sense to researchers in that era, who merely expressed "incomprehension and bewilderment" at the scientist's "revolutionary" proposals. Only in the late 1970s did "McClintock's research findings, though still controversial," related Rossiter, begin "receiving new confirmation from other scientists [who] suddenly observed phenomena very like what Miss McClintock had called 'transposition.'"

"The strength of Keller's fine book," asserted Gould, "lies in her successful attempt to . . . [provide] a rare and deep understanding of a troubling, fascinating, and general tale in the history of science—initial rejection (or, more frustratingly, simple incomprehension) of great insights." Expressing a thought echoed by other reviewers, David Graber noted in the *Los Angeles Times Book Review* that McClintock "was, one suspects, not the easiest of subjects for Keller. How does one write of a person whose whole life has been devoted to work even the specialists did not understand?" He commended Keller, who was "trained in the history, philosophy and psychology of science," as "particularly qualified for the task of explicating Barbara McClintock." *A Feeling for the Organism,* he concluded, "must of necessity be as much genetics as biography, and Keller accomplishes the dual task with intellectual power of her own."

In her second book, *Reflections on Gender and Science,* "Keller analyzes the pervasiveness of gender ideology, investigates how it became established and how it still shapes the course of scientific theory and experimentation, and speculates what science might be like if it were gender free," related Evelyn Shaw in the *New York Times Book Review.* Shaw commended Keller's use of "a wide range of scientific and other literature to bolster her . . . arguments about how the hugely invasive precepts of gender have deformed our concepts of science, kept women from entering the disciplines and undoubtedly shaped the direction of scientific research."

After tracing the history of women's exclusion from scientific pursuits, Keller "pleads for a gender-free science, a pluralistic science, one in which many voices can be heard, one that integrates many visions. The methods of achieving this ideal state," Shaw added, "remain illusory." "Her account is more an invitation to think than a conclusion," observed Ian Hacking in the *New Republic,* noting that, "in general, Keller enters a wise plea for tolerance, cooperation, mutual respect, and more sharing of resources among more competing ideas."

BIOGRAPHICAL/CRITICAL SOURCES:

PERIODICALS

Los Angeles Times Book Review, November 6, 1983.
Nation, November 19, 1983.
New Republic, July 15, 1985; July 22, 1985.
New York Review of Books, March 29, 1984.
New York Times Book Review, October 2, 1983; April 21, 1985.

* * *

KELLERMAN, Jonathan 1949-

PERSONAL: Born August 9, 1949, in New York, NY; son of David (an electrical engineer) and Sylvia (Fiacre) Kellerman; married Faye Marilyn Marder (an author), July, 1972; children: Jesse, Rachel, Ilana. *Education:* University of California, Los Angeles, B.A., 1971; University of Southern California, M.A., 1973, Ph.D., 1974. *Religion:* Jewish. *Avocational interests:* Painting, book collecting, art collecting, playing and collecting guitars.

ADDRESSES: Agent—Barney Karpfinger, 357 W. 20th St., New York, NY 10011-3379.

CAREER: Writer. *Daily Bruin,* University of California, Los Angeles, editorial cartoonist, editor, and political satirist, 1967-71; Children's Hospital, Los Angeles, CA, director of psychosocial program, 1976-80; University of Southern California, Los Angeles, assistant clinical professor, 1978-80, clinical associate professor, 1980-89. Freelance illustrator, 1966-1972.

AWARDS, HONORS: Samuel Goldwyn literary award, University of California, Los Angeles/Metro-Goldwyn-Mayer, 1971, for *Poor Lieber;* Edgar Allan Poe Award for first novel, Mystery Writers of America, and Anthony Boucher Award, both 1986, both for *When the Bough Breaks.*

WRITINGS:

Psychological Aspects of Childhood Cancer, C. C. Thomas (Springfield, IL), 1980.
Helping the Fearful Child: A Parent's Guide to Everyday and Problem Anxieties, Norton (New York City), 1981.
When the Bough Breaks (novel), Atheneum (New York City), 1985, published in England as *Shrunken Heads,* Macdonald & Co. (London), 1986.
Blood Test (novel), Atheneum, 1986.
Over the Edge (novel), Atheneum, 1987.
The Butcher's Theater (novel), Bantam (New York City), 1988.
Silent Partner (novel), Bantam, 1989.
Time Bomb (novel), Bantam, 1990.
Private Eyes (novel), Bantam, 1992.
Devil's Waltz (novel), Bantam, 1993.
Bad Love (novel), Bantam, 1994.
Daddy, Daddy, Can You Touch the Sky?: Poems for Children and Parents to Share, written and illustrated with Jesse Kellerman, Bantam, 1994.
Self-Defense (novel), Bantam, 1995.
The Web (novel), Bantam, 1996.

Also co-author of *Poor Lieber,* an unpublished comic novel. Contributor to anthologies; contributor of stories to *Alfred Hitchcock's Mystery Magazine;* contributor to *Newsweek, Los Angeles Times,* and *Los Angeles Magazine;* contributor of many articles to academic journals.

ADAPTATIONS: When the Bough Breaks was adapted for television in 1986; most of Kellerman's novels have been recorded on audiotape.

SIDELIGHTS: Working as a child psychologist for ten years before becoming a full-time writer, Jonathan Kellerman now bases his popular mystery novels on the experience he gained while in practice. The hero of his first three mysteries, Dr. Alex Delaware, is also a child psychologist and somewhat similar to Kellerman in that they both have worked with cancer-stricken children, a subject about which the author wrote professionally in his first book, *Psychological Aspects of Childhood Cancer.* In addition to his nonfiction and suspense novels, he has also written *Helping the Fearful Child: A Parent's Guide to Everyday and Problem Anxieties* and *Daddy, Daddy, Can You Touch the Sky?: Poems for Children and Parents to Share,* a collection written and illustrated with Kellerman's son Jesse and intended to help children develop stronger identity. But

Kellerman remains best known for his Alex Delaware novels, as well as the highly acclaimed *The Butcher's Theatre,* a novel about serial killings set in Jerusalem.

Kellerman's first published novel, *When the Bough Breaks,* won the Edgar Allan Poe Award and Anthony Boucher Award in 1986 and was later made into a television movie. John Gross evaluated the merits of this book in a *New York Times* article: *When the Bough Breaks* "marks an assured and more than promising debut. Some of the ingredients may have a familiar look—memories of 100 television programs hover somewhere in the background—but they have been whipped together with skill and conviction, and the result is an exceptionally exciting story." In this first novel to feature Alex Delaware, the 33-year-old retired psychologist is introduced while recuperating from the stress of his job. But his new-found, relaxing lifestyle is interrupted when Sergeant Milo Sturgis, a friend of his who is also a gay Los Angeles Police Department homicide detective, enlists the psychologist's help to solve a double homicide. The only witness is an abused and uncommunicative girl from whom Delaware must get testimony.

Because *When the Bough Breaks* was published soon after the highly publicized child molestation case against the McMartin Preschool workers in California, "there is . . . the niggling suspicion that [Kellerman] had cashed in on the most unspeakable crime of the year," wrote *Los Angeles Times Book Review* critic Mary Dryden. But, Dryden assured, "These doubts are quickly dispelled. The reader rapidly will gather that neither the child molesters nor the children themselves are exploited. Further, the author . . . had written and submitted this novel for publication many months before the McMartin case surfaced." The subjects about which Kellerman writes, however, are indeed topical. In addition to the subject of child molestation in his first mystery, he addressed the issues of child abduction in *Blood Test* and child persecution in *Over the Edge,* doing so "with authority and humor, sensitivity and more than considerable skill," said one *Publishers Weekly* reviewer.

Critics have also lauded the author's depiction of life on the West Coast and his skills at characterization. For example, *Newsweek* contributor David Lehman commented that *Blood Test,* which, like the other Delaware novels, is set in Los Angeles, "renders this atmosphere of nouveau depravity and trendy nutti-ness vividly but not ostentatiously. It's a relentlessly intelligent thriller." "Kellerman is also unusually good at making his characters seem [genuinely human]", added Tony Hillerman in a *Washington Post Book World* review, "and at telling a story of multiple murder which holds your attention." One weakness in the author's thrillers, noted by several critics, is his portrayal of the relationship between Delaware and his girlfriend, "who remains thoroughly and stubbornly uninteresting," wrote Dryden. In his review of *Over the Edge,* Gross also expressed a certain disappointment with the book's "gothic superabundance of revelations, and a sentimental finale." Gross qualified, however, that "this is the kind of letdown that readers of mysteries learn to live with, and it doesn't cancel out the excitement of what has gone before."

In *The Butcher's Theater* Kellerman broke away from the Alex Delaware series in Los Angeles and took his readers to Jerusalem. About this move Mort Kamins remarked in the *Los Angeles Times Book Review* that "it's good to see Kellerman break a mold that threatened to straitjacket his creativity. And Jerusalem as a setting was an inspired choice." Having lived in that city in 1968 and 1969, Kellerman was able to write about it from the same kind of experience that lent realism to his earlier novels. In his interview with Brisick, he revealed, "[Jerusalem is] almost a second home to me, and I feel comfortable writing about places that I know." Several reviewers have praised the book for this authenticity. As Edward Hawley asserted in a *Chicago Tribune* article, "The author does a superb job of evoking the sights, sounds and smells of Jerusalem." And Kamins concluded that "Kellerman has written a compelling story full of idiosyncratic characters in a beautifully rendered setting." Within this setting, the author weaves a tale about a serial murderer who targets young Arab women in Jerusalem, a city in which the homicide rate is normally very low. Avoiding the temptation to dwell on the political aspects that such a situation could inspire, Kellerman instead has provided his readers with an action-packed plot which, according to Hawley, "is constructed like a good movie,. . . with episode after episode that keeps the pace moving swiftly."

In 1989 Kellerman returned to the Alex Delaware series with *Silent Partner,* in which an ex-girlfriend apparently commits suicide after calling Delaware for help. His investigation into the mystery surrounding her death reveals links to the pornography underworld. Kellerman's next novel, *Time Bomb,* followed in 1990 and focuses on the psychological background of a schoolyard sniper, prompting Ray Vignovich of the *Library Journal* to compare Kellerman with Ross MacDonald, "as both authors examine the underlying psychological motivations of their characters." Breaking his novel-a-year trend, *Private Eyes* appeared in 1992 to mixed reviews. Marilyn Stasio remarked in the *New York Times Book Review* that by the time a plot has developed, "the reader is already numb from Alex's obsessively fussy descriptions."

Devil's Waltz, called "a superior mystery-thriller" by Charles Champlin in the *Los Angeles Times Book Review,* is a fictional case study of Munchausen's Syndrome by proxy, wherein a girl's parents fabricate her illnesses in order to bask in the attention and concern generated by their repeated trips to the hospital. Champlin complimented the novel by saying, "Kellerman constructs a tense, dank atmosphere of suspicion and doubt. The plot strands tighten like knots." *Booklist* reviewer Emily Melton praised Kellerman's plotting as well, calling it "an awesome performance."

In the eighth Alex Delaware thriller, *Bad Love,* Delaware finds himself a likely target for death when fellow panelists at a psychology conference on corrective therapy start dying in "accidents." A *Booklist* reviewer described *Bad Love* as "macabre enough to induce nightmares in the most sensible readers." Robert Ward agreed and wrote in his review for the *Los Angeles Times Book Review* that "the book generates a good deal of suspense." Other reviewers, such as Robyn Sisman of the London *Observer* noted that the suspense is derailed by tedious descriptions and overly detailed investigations. Tom de Haven of *Entertainment Weekly* wrote that what started out as "a top-of-the-line suspense novel" eventually evolves into "a preposterous TV-style ratings grabber."

In 1995 Delaware issued *Self-Defense,* a novel dealing with the controversial topic of repressed memories. Though deemed melodramatic by some critics, the book received positive reviews from many others. Stasio of the *New York Times Book Review* complimented Kellerman on his ability to tell "an exciting story that is loaded with tension and packed with titillating insights into abnormal psychology." Critics have applauded Kellerman's sense of suspense and his ability to load a book with intricate plots which Dr. Delaware unravels with great finesse. However, several critics have suggested that perhaps Dr. Delaware is *too* smooth. For example, De Haven of *Entertainment Weekly* described Delaware as a "consummate professional," but complained that he was "so consummate that you wish he'd break a sweat once in awhile, get sidetracked or flustered, maybe even lose his temper." Mark Harris elaborated in an *Entertainment Weekly* review; he called the character "a perfect therapist but a drab detective. If he ever had a cranky day, a panicky moment, a fleeting neurosis, it happened when readers weren't looking." Despite the criticisms of his nature, Delaware continues to solve crimes, and each of Kellerman's novels have outsold the previous release. "If you plot a graph line," Kellerman told Catherine M. Nelson in an interview for *Armchair Detective,* "each book has increased over the previous book by twenty, thirty percent." This may be, as Kellerman once told *CA,* because he believes in good storytelling above all: "I think there's an awful lot of emperor's clothing in fiction, stories about nothing. I still like something that has a beginning, a middle, and an end. . . . I'm not trying to make any political points or hype a big message. I just want to tell an engrossing story that captivates the reader."

BIOGRAPHICAL/CRITICAL SOURCES:

BOOKS

Bestsellers 90, Issue 1, Gale (Detroit), 1990.
Contemporary Literary Criticism, Volume 44, Gale, 1987.

PERIODICALS

Armchair Detective, winter, 1993, pp. 9-15, 92-5.
Booklist, October 15, 1992, p. 379; October 15, 1993, p. 395.
Chicago Tribune, May 6, 1988.
Chicago Tribune Book World, April 20, 1986.
Detroit News, April 26, 1987.
Entertainment Weekly, January 14, 1994, p. 46; December 16, 1994, p. 60; January 20, 1995, p. 47.
Library Journal, September 1, 1993, p. 242.
Los Angeles Times, December 2, 1985; March 20, 1986; January 8, 1992, p. E2.
Los Angeles Times Book Review, September 8, 1985; April 26, 1987; March 13, 1988; April 11, 1993, p. 8; February 6, 1994, p. 12.
Newsweek, June 9, 1986.
New York Times, March 12, 1985; April 4, 1986; April 24, 1987; January 13, 1992, p. C16.
New York Times Book Review, February 2, 1992, p. 19; February 21, 1993, p. 24; January 8, 1995, p. 24.

Observer (London), December 5, 1993, p. 22.
Publishers Weekly, January 25, 1985; February 19, 1988.
School Library Journal, November, 1994, p. 98.
Spectator, December 5, 1992, p. 51.
Times (London), December 31, 1987.
Times Literary Supplement, January 30, 1987.
Washington Post Book World, March 16, 1986; July 5, 1987; January 31, 1993, p. 13.*

*   *   *

KEMP, Anthony   1939-

PERSONAL: Born January 31, 1939, in London, England; son of Herbert (an oil company executive) and Vera (Jiminez) Kemp; married Ute Klingenschmidt, July 29, 1967 (marriage ended); married Kimberly Spanswick, July, 1992; children (first marriage): Oliver, Fiona. *Education:* Pembroke College, Oxford, M.A., 1976.

ADDRESSES: Home—Avalon, Chabreville, 16190 Cougeac, France.   *Agent*—Fose and Howard, 4 Bramerton St., London, England.

CAREER: Teacher of English at private schools in Wuerzburg and Nuremberg, West Germany (now Germany), 1962-66; U.S. Army, C.D.M.Z., Kaiserslautern, West Germany (now Germany), civilian quality control official, 1966-70; freelance writer and translator, 1970—; Television South Ltd., Southampton, England, principal program researcher, producer and director, 1982-90. Consultant to Fort Ltd., Newhaven, Sussex, England. *Military service:* Royal Air Force, 1959-62.

MEMBER: Fortress Study Group (founder; chair, 1975-79), Special Forces Club (London).

AWARDS, HONORS: Special Jury Prize, for documentary *The Secret Hunters.*

WRITINGS:

Castles in Color, Arco (New York City), 1977.
(Translator) G. Schomaekers, *The American Civil War,* Blandford (Poole, England), 1978.
The Weapons and Equipment of the Marlborough Wars, Blandford, 1980.
Maginot Line: The Myth and Reality, Stein & Day (New York City), 1981.

The Unknown Battle: Metz, 1944, Stein & Day, 1981.
(With Richard Holmes) *The Bitter End—Singapore 1942,* Anthony Bird (Chichester, England), 1982.
The German Commanders of World War II, Osprey (Huntington, NY), 1982.
The Allied Commanders of World War II, Osprey, 1982.
South Hampshire and the D-Day Landings, Milestone Press (Hordean, England), 1984.
The Secret Hunters (based on his documentary of the same title), Michael O'Mara Books, 1986.
Escape from Berlin, Boxtree, 1987.
Lorraine Album Memorial, Editions Heimdal (Bayeux, France), 1988.
A City at War: Southampton in the Blitz, Ensign Publications (Southampton, England), 1989.
(Ghostwriter) Johnnie Cooper, *One of the Originals,* Pan Books (England), 1991.
The S.A.S. at War—1941-1945, J. Murray (England), 1991.
Witchcraft and Paganism in Britain, Michael O'Mara Books, 1993.
The S.A.S. Savage Wars of Peace—1947 to the Present, J. Murray, 1994.
D-Day and the Invasion of Normandy, Abrams (New York City), 1994, published as *D-Day: The Normandy Landings and the Liberation of Europe,* Thames and Hudson (London), 1994, and as *6 June 1944. Le debarquement en Normandie,* Gallimard (Paris), 1994.
Le Debarquement (volume of children's series, "Passion pour l'histoire"), Gallimard, 1994.
(Principal author and consultant) *Battaille de Normandie,* Gallimard, 1994.
1939-1945. Le Monde en Guerre, Gallimard, 1995.
Pegasus Bridge, Memorial, (Caen et Ouest, France), 1995.

Also author of scripts for films and documentaries, including *Comrades in Arms?,* first broadcast by Southern Television on I.T.V., 1980; *The Cure,* 1982; *Nan Red,* 1984; *The Perfect Lady,* 1986; *The Secret Hunters,* 1986; and *Hanni Sends Her Love,* 1986. Contributor to journals.

WORK IN PROGRESS: Victors' Justice, a film for French television for the fiftieth anniversary of the Nuremberg trials; *Ancient Wisdom,* a book about the history of occult thought in the West, for Blandford Press; *Practical Paganism,* for John Hale.

SIDELIGHTS: Anthony Kemp told *CA:* "In 1990 I abandoned my full-time career in television as I found that the media was being increasingly run by accountants rather than creative people. Shortly afterwards I purchased a ruined farmhouse in the southwest of France where I planned to semi-retire as a fugitive from Thatcher's government. Having moved there and remarried, I found that I was still in demand as a writer, both in Britain and France. For many years I have been writing popular military history and with all the fiftieth anniversaries to celebrate, have not been short of work. As far as French publishers are concerned, I write in English and they translate my texts. Currently, however, I am in the process of changing my subject as I feel that I have said all that I wish to on the subject of the Second World War. My intention now is to concentrate on paganism and the nature-based religions, in which I became interested while researching for a television documentary several years ago.

"I write from an office a couple of miles away from my house, as I feel the need to 'go to work' in the morning. Otherwise there is a temptation to loaf on the terrace and drink wine. I use a word processor—the best thing invented since sliced bread—and still get a kick out of seeing my work in a bookshop. Being interviewed by the media I find difficult as I am not very good at selling myself, and the worst possible thing is being questioned by a presenter who has not read the book."

BIOGRAPHICAL/CRITICAL SOURCES:

PERIODICALS

Globe and Mail (Toronto), February 21, 1987.

*　　*　　*

KEMPTON, (James) Murray 1918-

PERSONAL: Born December 16, 1918, in Baltimore, MD; son of James Branson and Sally (Ambler) Kempton; married Mina Bleuthenthal, June 11, 1942 (divorced); married Beverly Gary; children: (first marriage) Sally Ambler, James Murray, Jr. (died November 26, 1971), Arthur Herbert, David Llewellyn; (second marriage) Christopher. *Education:* Johns Hopkins University, B.A., 1939.

ADDRESSES: Office—Newsday, 2 Park Ave., New York, NY 10016.

CAREER: Worked in New York City as organizer for International Ladies' Garment Workers Union, and as writer for both Young People's Socialist League and Worker's Defense League, 1930s; publicity director for American Labor Party, 1941-42; *New York Post,* New York City, labor reporter, 1942-43; *Wilmington Star,* Wilmington, NC, reporter, 1946-47; *New York Post,* assistant to labor editor, 1947-49, labor editor, 1949-63, columnist, 1949-63 and 1966-69; *New Republic,* Washington, DC, member of editorial staff and columnist, 1963-64; *World-Telegram and Sun,* New York City, columnist, 1964-66; *New York Post,* columnist, 1977-81; *Newsday,* New York City, columnist, 1981—. News commentator for Columbia Broadcasting System (CBS-Radio) feature, *Spectrum,* 1970-77. Visiting instructor of journalism at University of Rome. Delegate to Democratic National Convention, 1968. *Military service:* U.S. Army, 1942-45; became corporal.

MEMBER: American Civil Liberties Union, Committee for Cultural Freedom, League for Industrial Democracy, Adlai Stevenson Institute (fellow), Alpha Delta Phi.

AWARDS, HONORS: Sidney Hillman Foundation Award for reporting, 1950; Page One Award, Newspaper Guild of New York, 1955, for "outstanding writing in the field of civil liberties," 1962, for series on Freedom Riders, and 1982; grant from Fulbright Foundation, 1958; George Polk Memorial Award, 1967, for interpretive reporting, and 1988, for lifetime achievement; L.L.D., Grinnell College, 1973, and Long Island University, 1987; National Book Award in contemporary affairs, 1974, for *The Briar Patch: The People of the State of New York Versus Lumumba Shakur, et al;* American Academy and Institute of Arts and Letters award, 1978; Pulitzer Prize for commentary, 1985; American Society of Newspaper Editors distinguished writing award, 1985; Grammy Award, National Academy of Recording Arts, 1987, for liner notes.

WRITINGS:

Part of Our Time: Some Ruins and Monuments of the Thirties, Simon & Schuster (New York City), 1955.
America Comes of Middle Age: Columns, 1950-1962, Little, Brown (Boston), 1963.
The Briar Patch: The People of the State of New York Versus Lumumba Shakur, et al., Dutton (New York City), 1973.
Rebellions, Perversities and Main Events, Times Books (New York City), 1994.

Contributor to periodicals, including *New York Review of Books, Reporter, Commonweal, Life, Harper's, Atlantic Monthly, Esquire,* and *Playboy.*

SIDELIGHTS: A left-wing newspaper columnist who has won both the Pulitzer Prize as well as Page One Awards and George Polk Memorial Awards, journalism's highest honors, Murray Kempton has long been regarded as one of America's leading journalists. "Although little known by the larger public outside Gotham," notes Mike Dorning in the *Chicago Tribune,* "[Kempton] is considered by many in his craft to be the nation's finest living columnist." In several collections of his newspaper writings, Kempton has offered his views on a variety of current issues facing American society.

Kempton began his career in the 1930s as a labor organizer for the International Ladies' Garment Workers Union, and as a writer with the Young People's Socialist League, the Workers Defense League, and the American Labor Party. Despite the evolution of his beliefs over the years, Kempton still greets cabdrivers, according to Dorning, with "his customary greeting, 'Hello, fellow worker.'" Kempton is, Dorning explains, "unabashedly and invariably, . . . on the side of underdogs. . . . An unreconstructed liberal."

In 1942 Kempton took a job as labor reporter with the *New York Post.* Following a stint in the army during World War II, and a year as a reporter with the *Wilmington Star* in North Carolina, Kempton returned to the *Post,* where he covered the city's labor politics until 1963. He also wrote a column for the newspaper from 1949 until 1969, and from 1977 to 1981. Since 1981 he has worked as a columnist for *Newsday.*

During the McCarthy era of the 1950s, Kempton acquired a reputation as a daring and controversial journalist for his efforts in publicly defending the civil liberties of communists. It was this involvement as well as his former affiliation with a socialist party that led critics to hail his first book, *Part of Our Time: Some Ruins and Monuments of the Thirties,* as a revealing insight into the "Red Decade." R. H. Rovere of the *New Yorker,* for instance, regards the book as "easily the best essay on American Communism and Communists that anyone has done" and calls its author "a journalist of formidable talent and versatility." *New York Times* critic R. L. Duffus concurs: "[The] book is exceedingly well written. It

holds us in some places with a pathos of futility and in others with a drama of achievement." Martin Solow states in the *Nation* that "taken as a whole I found 'Part of Our Time' one of the most stimulating books in many years." He adds however, that "were [the author] to assay further his values today and his values yesterday, he might well find that he need not patronize and deprecate that past."

In *The Briar Patch: The People of the State of New York Versus Lumumba Shakur, et al.,* Kempton examines the controversial Black Panther trial of 1970. The case originally involved twenty-one members of the radical group who were suspected of plotting to blow up several buildings, including a police station, the Bronx Botanical Gardens, and a discount store. Based on flimsy and fabricated evidence, the trial was widely held to be a conspiracy against the left-wing organization. "Put simply," summarizes Andrew Hacker, "the proceeding was an exercise in deception, consciously conceived and cruelly executed." Hacker adds, however, that Kempton "never patronizes his subjects [in *The Briar Patch*] or condescends, a difficult temptation to avoid in view of the bewilderment and incompetence in the Panther case." *The Briar Patch* was recommended by some critics, but was criticized by a reviewer for *Time:* "The language is accurate enough in its grand way, but eventually the reader cares less about the defendants than about the author, gesticulating here and there in a peculiar kind of 18th century jive."

Kempton's writing style is, according to some reviewers, oddly out of sympathy with his usual subject matter. As Walter Goodman explains in the *New York Times Book Review,* Kempton's typical columns "[cloak] a 1930's mood in the locutions of an 1830's Whig" and are marked by "demanding sentences with their rewarding rhythms and riffs, the venturesome allusions, the virtuoso wordplay that [strains] the rules of grammar and [mocks] the rules of journalism schools." Russell Miller in the *Los Angeles Times* calls Kempton's writing "American baroque," while Dorning finds it to be "heavily ornamented with irony, literary references and esoteric vocabulary."

Kempton's usual routine begins with a bicycle ride through New York City in search of the day's subject for his column. Visiting hotel conventions, city hall, police headquarters, the courts, and other likely locales, he scouts for a suitable topic among the real-life activities of New York's inhabitants. "Kempton deals," Miller writes, "in the criminal, the ethically murky and the unforgivable." Over the course of his career, he has often written of the city's murderers, swindlers, crooked politicians, and rapists. "Whatever the politics of the case," writes Goodman, "Mr. Kempton can be counted on to choose the victims over their tormentors. His disgust with the uses of power is not just a sentimental indulgence . . . ; it grows from a conviction that every society is so inherently unjust that all the winners must be suspect." In his foreword to his collection *Rebellions, Perversities and Main Events,* Kempton states: "I write every day for the next and walk wide of the cosmic and settle most happily for the local."

BIOGRAPHICAL/CRITICAL SOURCES:

BOOKS

Kempton, Murray, *Rebellions, Perversities and Main Events,* Times Books, 1994.

PERIODICALS

Atlanta Journal & Constitution, May 7, 1994, p. A16.
Best Sellers, September 15, 1973.
Book Week, November 17, 1963.
Boston Globe, March 20, 1994, p. 18; April 17, 1994, p. A15.
Chicago Tribune, April 27, 1994, sec. 5, p. 1; May 21, 1995, p. 8.
Christian Science Monitor, June 30, 1955; November 5, 1963; September 1, 1994, p. 13.
Commonweal, November 9, 1973.
Harper's, November, 1973.
Los Angeles Times, May 23, 1994, p. E1.
Los Angeles Times Book Review, April 24, 1994, p. 1.
Nation, August 20, 1955.
National Review, January 14, 1964; September 28, 1973.
Newsweek, August 27, 1973.
New Yorker, May 21, 1955; January 18, 1964.
New York Review of Books, November 1, 1973.
New York Times, May 1, 1955; February 28, 1988, p. 47; May 23, 1994, p. B5.
New York Times Book Review, December 8, 1963; August 26, 1973; April 10, 1994, p. 13.
San Francisco Chronicle, July 10, 1955.
Saturday Review of Literature, May 14, 1955; November 16, 1963.

Time, September 10, 1973.
Wall Street Journal, May 13, 1994.
Washington Post Book World, April 17, 1994, p. 5.

*   *   *

KENNY, James Andrew   1933-

PERSONAL: Born October 12, 1933, in Evanston, IL; son of James Valentine (a lawyer) and Ann Freda (Filz) Kenny; married Mary Jane Nelsen (a writer and certified public accountant), January 26, 1957; children: Joseph, Christopher, Theresa, Michael, John Paul, Thomas, Peter, Ann, Elizabeth, Robert, Sharon, Matthew. *Education:* Maryknoll College, B.A., 1954; Loyola University, M.S.W., 1957; University of Maine, Ph.D. (psychology; cum laude), 1962; Indiana University, M.A., 1971, Ph.D. (anthropology), 1974. *Avocational interests:* Travel, camping, swimming, jogging.

ADDRESSES: Home—P.O. Box 305, Rensselaer, IN 47978. *Office*—219 W. Harrison St., Ste. 4, Rensselaer, IN 47978.

CAREER: Chicago Department of Welfare, Chicago, IL, social caseworker, 1955; Cook County Department of Welfare, Chicago, social caseworker, 1956; St. Joseph's College, Rensselaer, IN, associate professor, 1964-72, professor of psychology, 1972-75, chair of department, 1968-75, clinical psychologist, 1964-75; Jasper-Newton Mental Health Center, Rensselaer, director and clinical psychologist, 1975-82. Clinic of Family Medicine, Rensselaer, private practice of clinical psychology, 1973-75, 1982—. Associate professor of anthropology at Indiana University, 1975-76; visiting professor at St. Joseph's College, 1975—. *Military service:* U.S. Air Force, 1957-64; psychiatric social worker at Eglin Air Force Base, 1957-60, and at U.S. Air Force hospital in Wiesbaden, West Germany (now Germany), 1960-62, clinical child psychologist and director of Child Guidance Clinic in Wiesbaden, 1962-64; became captain.

MEMBER: American Psychological Association, Academy of Certified Social Workers, National Association of Social Workers, American Anthropological Association (fellow), Midwestern Psychological Association, Indiana Psychological Association.

AWARDS, HONORS: Edwin G. Kaiser Faculty Scholar Award from St. Joseph's College, 1973; distinguished service award from Indiana Commission on Mental Health, 1977; "Family Talk" was named best syndicated column of 1982 and 1983 by Catholic Press Association.

WRITINGS:

The CHAP Guide to Facilities in Europe, U.S. Air Force in Europe, 1963.

(With wife, Mary Kenny) *When Your Marriage Goes Stale,* Abbey Press (St. Meinrad, IN), 1979.

(With M. Kenny) *Making the Family Matter,* St. Anthony Messenger Press (Cincinnati, OH), 1980.

(Coauthor) *Families Doing Things Together* (cassette series), Abbey Press, 1980.

(With M. Kenny) *Happy Parenting!,* St. Anthony Messenger Press, 1982.

(With M. Kenny) *Whole-Life Parenting,* Crossroad/Continuum (New York City), 1982.

(With Stephen Spicer) *Caring for Your Aging Parent,* St. Anthony Messenger Press, 1984.

(Coauthor) *Caring for the Elderly* (cassette series), Abbey Press, 1986.

(Coauthor) *Helping Children of Divorce* (cassette series), St. Anthony Messenger Press, 1987.

Sex Education for Toddlers to Young Adults, St. Anthony Messenger Press, 1989.

Loving and Learning: A Guide to Practical Parenting, St. Anthony Messenger Press, 1992.

Coauthor of "Family Talk," a weekly column syndicated by Catholic News Service, 1976—. Contributor of nearly fifty articles to professional journals and popular magazines, including *Marriage, Our Family, Columbia, Catholic Digest, Today's Family,* and *Family Digest.*

SIDELIGHTS: Kenny told *CA:* "Everything I had learned in school seemed so far-removed and academic when we had to spend an all-nighter with a sick child or confront a growing adolescent who had had too much to drink. Bit by bit, incident by incident, we put together a childrearing philosophy that is practical, positive, developmental, and above all, effective. I write to stay sane and to find the humor that underlies all great endeavors. Our book *Whole-Life Parenting* gives our thoughts on raising children learned through mistakes, hammered out on the anvil of everyday demands, salted by education, and tempered by the reality of raising twelve children. The

book is dedicated to our children, who have taught us most of what we know and in some cases more than we wanted to learn.

"We lived in Europe for five years, during which time I visited Russia and the Middle East. After returning to the United States, we bought an old school bus which we outfitted with hammocks to sleep twelve, and were frequent campers. I have been a swim coach for several years. I jog-run four miles daily and enjoy road races, which help me keep one step ahead of our twelve children."

*   *   *

KENT, Cromwell
    See SPARSHOTT, Francis (Edward)

*   *   *

KESLER, Jay   1935-

PERSONAL: Born September 15, 1935, in Barnes, WI; son of Herbert E. and Elsie (Campbell) Kesler; married Jane Smith, June 7, 1957; children: Laura, Bruce, Terri. *Education:* Attended Ball State University, 1953-54; Taylor University, B.A., 1958.

ADDRESSES: Home—711 Reade Ave., Upland, IN 46989. *Office*—Taylor University, 500 W. Reade Ave., Upland, IN 46989-1001.

CAREER: Youth for Christ International, Wheaton, IL, director of Marion, Indiana branch, 1955-58, crusade staff evangelist, 1959-60, director of Illinois-Indiana region, 1960-62, director of college recruitment, 1962-63, vice president for personnel, 1963-68, vice president for field coordination, 1968-73, president, 1973-85, and current member of board of directors; Taylor University, Upland, IN, president, 1985—. Chief executive officer, Youth for Christ International's Interdenominational ministry to high school students throughout the United States; copastor, First Baptist Church of Geneva, Geneva, IL, 1972-85; faculty member, Billy Graham Schools of Evangelism; lecturer, Staley Distinguished Christian Scholar lecture program; speaker on daily radio broadcast "Family Forum." Member of board of directors, Brotherhood Mutual Insurance Co.; member of board of directors, *Christianity Today;* member of advisory board, Discovery Network, Inc.

MEMBER: Christian Educators Association International, International Council on Biblical Inerrancy (member of advisory board), Prison Fellowship International (member of board of directors), Venture Middle East (member of advisory board), National Association of Evangelicals Board of Administration (member of board of directors), National Educators Fellowship, Christian Bible Society (member of advisory board), Christian Camps, Inc., Christian Coalition for Colleges & Universities, Evangelical Council for Financial Accountability (member of board of directors), Evangelicals for Social Action (member of advisory board), Project Partner, Independent Colleges and Universities of Indiana (member of board of directors).

AWARDS, HONORS: D.D., Barrington College, 1977, Asbury Theological Seminary, 1984; L.H.D., Taylor University, 1982, John Brown University, 1987; H.H.D., Huntington College, 1983; Angel Award, Religion in Media, 1985.

WRITINGS:

Let's Succeed with Our Teenagers, David Cook (Elgin, IL), 1973.
I Never Promised You a Disneyland, Word, Inc. (Waco, TX), 1975.
The Strong Weak People, Victor Books (Wheaton, IL), 1976.
Outside Disneyland, Word, Inc., 1977.
I Want a Home with No Problems, Word, Inc., 1977.
Growing Places, Revell (Old Tappan, NJ), 1978.
Too Big to Spank, Regal Books (Ventura, CA), 1978.
Breakthrough, Zondervan, 1981.
Family Forum, Victor Books, 1984.
Parents and Teenagers, Victor Books, 1984.
Making Life Make Sense, Tyndale (Wheaton, IL), 1986.
Parents and Children, Victor Books, 1986.
Being Holy, Being Human, Word, 1988.
Ten Mistakes Parents Make with Teenagers (And How to Avoid Them), Wolgemuth & Hyatt, 1988.
Energizing Your Teenager's Faith, Group (Loveland, CO), 1990.
Grandparenting—The Agony and the Ecstasy, Servant (Ann Arbor, MI), 1993.
Raising Responsible Kids, Avon (New York City), 1993.

Restoring A Loving Marriage, Cook, 1993.
Challenges for the College Bound, Baker Books, 1994.

Contributor to numerous evangelical publications, including *Christian Herald, Christianity Today, Focus on the Family, Marriage Partnership, Partnership,* and *Today's Christian Woman.* Also author of column, "I Never Promised You a Disneyland," *Campus Life* (magazine), 1974-75. Member of editorial review committee for *New King James Bible;* member of advisory committee, *Campus Life.*

*   *   *

KESSLER, Herbert L(eon)   1941-

PERSONAL: Born July 20, 1941, in Chicago, IL; son of Ben and Bertha Kessler; married Johanna Zacharias (a writer and editor), April 24, 1976; children: Morisa Kessler-Zacharias. *Education:* University of Chicago, A.B., 1961; Princeton University, M.F.A., 1963, Ph.D., 1965.

ADDRESSES: Home—211 Ridgewood Rd., Baltimore, MD 21210. *Office*—Department of Art, Johns Hopkins University, Baltimore, MD 21218.

CAREER: University of Chicago, Chicago, IL, assistant professor, 1965-68, associate professor, 1968-73, professor of art history, 1973-76, chairperson of department of art and university director of fine arts, 1973-76; Johns Hopkins University, Baltimore, MD, professor of art history and chairperson of department, 1976—, Charlotte Bloomberg Professor of the Faculty of Arts and Sciences, 1984—.

MEMBER: College Art Association of America, Medieval Academy of America (fellow, 1991—), Phi Beta Kappa.

AWARDS, HONORS: Woodrow Wilson fellow, 1961-62; Dumbarton Oaks, junior fellow, 1964-65, senior fellow, 1980-86; Institute of Advanced Studies fellow, Princeton, NY, 1969-70; Guggenheim fellow, 1972-73; American Council of Learned Societies fellow, 1979-80 and 1988-89; American Philosophical Society fellow, 1980; fellow at American Academy in Rome, 1984-85; Medieval Academy of America fellow, 1991—; American Academy of Arts and Sciences fellow, 1995—.

WRITINGS:

French and Flemish Illuminated Manuscripts in Chicago Collections, Newberry Library (Chicago), 1969.

The Illustrated Bibles from Tours, Princeton University Press (Princeton, NJ), 1977.

(With Kurt Weitzmann) *The Cotton Genesis: British Library Codex Cotton Otho B. VI,* Princeton University Press, 1986.

(With Weitzmann) *The Frescoes of the Dura Synagogue and Christian Art,* Dumbarton Oaks (Washington, DC), 1990.

Studies in Pictorial Narrative, Pindar Press, 1994.

*   *   *

KHANSHENDEL, Chiron
See ROSE, Wendy

*   *   *

KINDEM, Gorham A(nders)   1948-

PERSONAL: Born May 28, 1948, in Dickenson, ND; son of Ingolf Bjarne (a minister) and Bette Ann (a homemaker; maiden name, Carlson) Kindem; married Nancy Houston (a teacher), June 19, 1971; children: Peter Anders, Thomas Houston, John Paul. *Education:* Lawrence University, B.A., 1970; Northwestern University, M.A., 1972, Ph.D., 1977. *Avocational interests:* Golf, skating, skiing, reading.

ADDRESSES: Home—301 Hickory Dr., Chapel Hill, NC 27514. *Office*—Department of Communication Studies, Bingham Hall, University of North Carolina at Chapel Hill, Chapel Hill, NC 27599-3280.

CAREER: Allied Film Laboratory, Chicago, IL, color timer, 1972-74; Shaw University, Raleigh, NC, instructor in radio and television, 1976; University of North Carolina at Chapel Hill, assistant professor, 1977-82, associate professor, 1982-88, professor of radio, television, and motion pictures, 1988-93, department chairperson, 1987-92, professor of communication studies, 1993—. Visiting professor at University of Trondheim, 1983-84; visiting associate professor at Duke University, 1987.

MEMBER: Society for Cinema Studies, University Film and Video Association.

AWARDS, HONORS: CINE Golden Eagle Award for documentary film *Chuck Davis, Dancing through West Africa.*

WRITINGS:

Toward a Semiotic Theory of Visual Communication in the Cinema, Arno, 1981.

(Editor) *The American Movie Industry: The Business of Motion Pictures,* Southern Illinois University Press (Carbondale, IL), 1982.

The Moving Image: Production Principles and Practices, Scott, Foresman (Glenview, IL), 1986.

The Live Television Generation of Hollywood Film Directors, McFarland (Jefferson, NC), 1994.

(With Robert Musburger) *Media Production in the Digital Age, An Introduction,* Focal Press (Woburn, MA), 1996.

Associate editor of *Cinema Journal,* 1977-82; member of editorial board, *Journal of Film and Video,* 1982—. Also associated with *Chuck Davis, Dancing through West Africa,* Public Broadcasting Service (PBS-TV), 1988, and *Hungers of the Soul: Be Gardiner, Stone Carver,* UNC Center for Public Television (UNC-TV), 1994.

SIDELIGHTS: Gorham A. Kindem told *CA* that his goal is "to promote film and television as areas of artistic and scholarly study, combing theory and practice, research and creative expression."

*   *   *

KINSEY, Elizabeth
See CLYMER, Eleanor

*   *   *

KITCHEN, Martin   1936-

PERSONAL: Born December 21, 1936, in Nottingham, England; son of John Sutherland (an insurance manager) and Margaret (Pearson) Kitchen; married Brigitte Meyer (a social worker), March 13, 1960 (divorced); married Bettina Franke; children:

(first marriage) Corinna, Susan. *Education:* Attended Magdalen College, Oxford, 1957-59; University of London, B.A. (with honors), 1963, Ph.D., 1966. *Politics:* Social Democrat. *Religion:* Roman Catholic.

ADDRESSES: Home—24B-6128 Patterson Ave., Burnaby, British Columbia, Canada V5H 4P3. *Office*—Department of History, Simon Fraser University, Burnaby, British Columbia, Canada.

CAREER: Simon Fraser University, Burnaby, British Columbia, assistant professor, 1966-69, associate professor, 1969-74, professor of history, 1974—. *Military service:* British Army, 1955-57; became lieutenant.

WRITINGS:

The German Officer Corps, 1890-1914, Clarendon Press (Oxford, England), 1968.
A Military History of Germany, Weidenfeld & Nicolson (London), 1975.
Fascism, Macmillan (London), 1976.
The Silent Dictatorship: The Politics of the German High Command under Hindenburg and Ludendorff, Croom Helm (Beckenham, Kent, England), 1976.
The Political Economy of Germany, 1815-1914, Croom Helm, 1978.
The Coming of Austrian Fascism, Croom Helm, 1980.
(Editor with Volker R. Berghahn) *Germany in the Age of Total War,* Croom Helm, 1981.
British Policy towards the Soviet Union during the Second World War, Macmillan, 1986.
Europe between the Wars, Longman (London, England), 1988.
(With Laurence Aronsen) *The Origins of the Cold War in Comparative Perspective,* Macmillan, 1988.
Europe between the Wars, Longman, 1988.
Nazi Germany at War, Longman, 1994.
A World in Flames: A Concise History of the British Empire and the Commonwealth, Simon Fraser University Press (Burnaby, British Columbia, Canada), 1994.
The Cambridge Illustrated History of Germany, Cambridge University Press (Cambridge, England), in press.

WORK IN PROGRESS: Kaspar Hauser.

SIDELIGHTS: Martin Kitchen writes that his work "Covers a wide range of topics in modern history with a particular emphasis on Germany."

BIOGRAPHICAL/CRITICAL SOURCES:

PERIODICALS

Times Literary Supplement, August 1, 1980; June 26, 1981.

*　　*　　*

KLEINZAHLER, August 1949-

PERSONAL: Born December 10, 1949, in Jersey City, NJ; son of Marvin and Isabel (Resnitzky) Kleinzahler. *Education:* Attended University of Wisconsin—Madison, 1967-70, and University of Victoria, 1973.

ADDRESSES: Home—San Francisco, CA; c/o P.O. Box 842, Fort Lee, NJ 07024.

CAREER: Poet and editor. Visiting Holloway Lecturer at University of California, Berkeley, 1987.

MEMBER: Poetry Society of America.

AWARDS, HONORS: Grants from Canada Council, 1977 and 1979, Ontario Arts Council, 1978, and New Jersey State Council on the Arts, 1980 and 1985; award for younger writers from General Electric Foundation, 1983, for poems in *Sulfur* magazine; award from Bay Area Book Reviewers Association, 1985, for *Storm over Hackensack;* John Simon Guggenheim fellow, 1989; Lila Wallace-*Reader's Digest* Writers' Award, 1991-94.

WRITINGS:

A Calendar of Airs (poems), Coach House Press (Chicago, IL), 1978.
(Editor) *News and Weather: Seven Canadian Poets,* Brick Books, 1982.
Storm over Hackensack (poems), Moyer Bell, 1985.
On Johnny's Time (poems), Pig Press, 1988.
Earthquake Weather, Moyer Bell, 1989.
Red Sauce, Whiskey and Snow (poems), Faber and Faber Limited (London), Farrar, Straus & Giroux (New York City), 1995.

Contributor to magazines and newspapers, including *American Poetry Review, Art International, Chicago Review, Grand Street, Harper's, Independent* (London), *Kenyon Review, Los Angeles Times, London Review of Books, New American Writing, New Yorker, New York Times, Origin, Paris Review, PN Review, Poetry, Sulfur,* and *Three Penny Review.*

SIDELIGHTS: According to Geoffrey O'Brien of the *Village Voice,* August Kleinzahler uses inventive language to write about the small, ordinary things of life. *Storm over Hackensack,* O'Brien writes, is a collection of "handcrafted, sinuous, intensely focused poems" which indicate "both that subject matter still has its uses and that recent death announcements for the personal lyric were slightly premature." Kleinzahler's language, the critic reports, "veers jauntily from video parlor argot to Ovidian tropes," and he "ranges in mood from the goofy to the mournful, but always what concerns him is the shape of what he makes." O'Brien concludes: "Not many writers . . . will have either the wit or the fluent technical inventiveness to follow in Kleinzahler's track."

A reviewer for the *Economist,* discussing the Faber and Faber edition of Kleinzahler's *Red Sauce, Whiskey and Snow,* says of the poems: "[They] twitch and jerk and snap their fingers at you. . . . High and low vocabularies hang out together. They are hectic, pulsing things, ever alive to the music of words when spoken." The reviewer summarizes: "They take us back to Walt Whitman and his inventive recklessness with words. They are expansive, energetic and, from time to time, a touch crazed: an authentically American voice."

BIOGRAPHICAL/CRITICAL SOURCES:

PERIODICALS

Economist, July 8, 1995, p. 82.
Village Voice, August 20, 1985.

*   *   *

KLINGELHOFER, E(dwin) L(ewis) 1920-

PERSONAL: Born October 4, 1920, in Buffalo, NY; son of Benjamin Carl (in business) and Winifred (a homemaker; maiden name, Townson) Klingelhofer; married Jean Elizabeth Merrick (a librarian), January 31, 1946; children: Anne Elizabeth, Jon Merrick. *Education:* State University of New York at Buffalo, B.S., 1946; University of Iowa, Ph.D., 1953.

ADDRESSES: Home and office—P.O. Box 329, North San Juan, CA 95960.

CAREER: California State University, Sacramento, assistant professor, 1953-56, associate professor, 1956-61, professor of psychology, 1961-76; freelance writer and consultant in psychology, 1976—. University of East Africa, visiting professor, 1965-67; University of California, Berkeley, visiting research psychologist, 1970-72; University of Malawi, senior Fulbright lecturer, 1974-75. *Military service:* U.S. Army, 1942-46; became captain.

AWARDS, HONORS: Distinguished Community Service Award from city of Sacramento, California, 1970.

WRITINGS:

Human Behavior in Africa, Greenwood Press (Westport, CT), 1972.
Educational Characteristics and Needs of New Students, Center for Research and Development in Higher Education, University of California, Berkeley, 1972.
(With M. Eric Gershwin) *Asthma: Stop Suffering, Start Living,* Addison-Wesley (Reading, MA), 1987.
Coping with Grown Children, Humana (Totowa, NJ), 1988.
(With Gershwin) *Conquering Your Child's Allergies,* Addison-Wesley, 1988.
(With Gershwin) *Living Allergy Free,* Humana, 1992.
Fly-Fishing California's North Yuba River, Salmo Press, 1993.

WORK IN PROGRESS: A novel; the second edition of *Conquering Your Child's Allergies.*

SIDELIGHTS: E. L. Klingelhofer once told *CA:* "One of my earliest memories is that of wanting to be a writer, but force of circumstance prevented me from doing it. In 1976 I decided that if I was to begin, I had to do it then. I've spent ten years learning the trade, and they have been the best, happiest ones of my life."

KNOKE, David (Harmon) 1947-

PERSONAL: Born March 4, 1947, in Philadelphia, PA; son of Donald Glenn (a carpenter) and Frances (a school teacher; maiden name, Dunn) Knoke; married Joann Margaret Robar, August 29, 1970; children: Margaret Frances. *Education:* University of Michigan, B.A., 1969, M.S.W., 1971, Ph.D., 1972; University of Chicago, M.A., 1970. *Politics:* "Passive observer of the parade." *Religion:* Unitarian Universalist. *Avocational interests:* Walking, reading.

ADDRESSES: Home—7305 Wooddale, Edina, MN 55435. *Office*—Department of Sociology, University of Minnesota, Minneapolis, MN 55455.

CAREER: Indiana University at Bloomington, assistant professor, 1972-75, associate professor, 1975-81, professor of sociology, 1981-85; University of Minnesota, Minneapolis, professor of sociology, 1985—, chairperson of department, 1989-92. Member of advisory committee of National Opinion Research Center's General Social Survey, 1976-89; member of sociology program review board, National Science Foundation, 1981-83; member of sociology advisory panel for Fulbright fellowships, 1993-95. Principal investigator on nine National Science Foundation grants.

MEMBER: International Network for Social Network Analysis, American Sociological Association (chair of Section on Organizations and Occupations, 1992-93), Sociological Research Association, Phi Beta Kappa.

AWARDS, HONORS: National Science Foundation fellowship, 1969-70; research scientist development award, National Institute of Mental Health, 1977-82; Fulbright senior research fellow, Kiel, Germany, 1989; fellow, Center for Advanced study in the Behavioral Sciences, 1992-93.

WRITINGS:

Change and Continuity in American Politics, Johns Hopkins University Press (Baltimore, MD), 1976.

(With Peter J. Burke) *Log-Linear Models,* Sage Publications (Beverly Hills, CA), 1980.

(With James R. Wood) *Organized for Action,* Rutgers University Press (New Brunswick, NJ), 1981.

(With James H. Kuklinski) *Network Analysis,* Sage Publications, 1982.

(With George W. Bohrnstedt) *Statistics for Social Data Analysis,* F. E. Peacock (Itaska, IL), 1982.

(With Edward O. Laumann) *The Organizational State,* University of Wisconsin Press (Madison, WI), 1987.

Organizing for Collective Action, Aldine de Gruyter (Hawthorne, NY), 1990.

Political Networks, Cambridge University Press (New York City), 1990.

(With Bohrnstedt) *Basic Social Statistics,* F. E. Peacock, 1991.

(With Franz U. Pappi, Jeffrey Broadbent and Yukata Tsujinaka) *Comparing Policy Networks,* Cambridge University Press, 1996.

(With Arne Kalleberg, Peter V. Marsden and Joe L. Spaeth) *Organizations in America,* Sage Publications, 1996.

Contributor to social science journals.

WORK IN PROGRESS: Research, with Kalleberg and Marsden, on interorganizational networks in hiring and training workers, with a monograph expected to result.

SIDELIGHTS: David Knoke once told *CA:* "My writing reflects the interplay between abstract theorizing and empirical data analysis, to the extent that where one breaks off and the other begins is obscure. Showing students how to break into this continuous process has been a major challenge in recent years."

*   *   *

KRAUZER, Steven M(ark) 1948-
(J. W. Baron, Adam Lassiter; joint pseudonyms Johnny Dee, JokeMeisters, Owen Rountree,; Terry Nelsen Bonner, a house pseudonym)

PERSONAL: Born June 9, 1948, in Jersey City, NJ; son of Earl (in business) and Bernice Krauzer. *Education:* Yale University, B.A., 1970; University of New Hampshire, M.A., 1974.

ADDRESSES: Home—13 September Dr., Missoula, MT 59802. *Agent*—Ginger Barber, Virginia Barber Literary Agency, Inc., 353 West 21st St., New York, NY 10011.

CAREER: Writer.

MEMBER: Authors Guild, Mystery Writers of America, Writers Guild of America (West).

WRITINGS:

Cocaine Wars (screenplay), New Horizon Picture Corp., 1985.
(With others) *Sweet Revenge* (screenplay), Concorde Pictures, 1987.
Frame Work (novel), Bantam (New York City), 1989.
Brainstorm (novel), Bantam, 1991.
Rojak's Rule (novel), Pocket Books (New York City), 1992.
Kayaking: Waterwater and Touring Basics (nonfiction; a Trailside Series Guide), introduction by John Viehman, W. W. Norton (New York City), 1995.
(With Peter Stark) *Winter Sports: A Complete Guide* (nonfiction), W. W. Norton, 1995.

"HOLT" WESTERN SERIES

God's Country, Fawcett (New York City), 1993.
Winter of the Wolf, Fawcett, 1994.

UNDER PSEUDONYM J. W. BARON

Blaze (western novel), Pinnacle (New York City), 1983.

UNDER HOUSE PSEUDONYM TERRY NELSEN BONNER

The Diggers, Dell/Emerald (New York City), 1983.

UNDER JOINT PSEUDONYM JOHNNY DEE

(With Cheryl Krauzer and Michael J. Sherwood), *You Gotta Be Kidding* (jokebook), St. Martin's (New York City), 1991.

UNDER JOINT PSEUDONYM "THE JOKEMEISTERS"

(With C. Krauzer and Sherwood), *The Jokemeisters* (jokebook), St. Martin's, 1990.

"DENNISON'S WAR" SERIES; ACTION-ADVENTURE NOVELS UNDER PSEUDONYM ADAM LASSITER

Dennison's War, Bantam, 1984.
Conte's Run, Bantam, 1985.
Bell on Wheels, Bantam, 1985.
King of the Mountain, Bantam, 1985.
Triangle, Bantam, 1985.
Snowball in Hell, Bantam, 1986.

"CORD" SERIES OF WESTERN NOVELS; WITH WILLIAM KITTREDGE UNDER JOINT PSEUDONYM OWEN ROUNTREE

Cord, Ballantine (New York City), 1982.
Cord the Nevada War, Ballantine, 1982.
Cord the Black Hills Duel, Ballantine, 1983.
Cord Gunman Winter, Ballantine, 1983.
Cord Hunt the Man Down, Ballantine, 1984.
Cord King of Colorado, Ballantine, 1984.
Cord Gunsmoke River, Ballantine, 1985.
Cord Paradise Valley, Ballantine, 1986.
Cord Brimstone Basin, Ballantine, 1986.

EDITOR WITH KITTREDGE

Great Action Stories, New American Library (New York City), 1977.
The Great American Detective, New American Library, 1978.
Stories into Film, Harper (New York City), 1978.

OTHER

Contributor to books, including *That Awesome Space*, edited by E. Richard Hart, Westwater (Boulder City, NV), 1982. Contributor of articles, stories, and reviews to magazines, including *Armchair Detective, Cavalier, Far West, Rocky Mountain,* and *Triquarterly.* Author of monthly column, "Almanac," *Outside* magazine, 1992-94. Guest editor with Kittredge of *Triquarterly,* number 48, 1980.

BIOGRAPHICAL/CRITICAL SOURCES:

PERIODICALS

Los Angeles Times, February 10, 1986.
Publishers Weekly, November 9, 1984; March 7, 1987.

L

LACKEY, Mercedes R(itche) 1950-

PERSONAL: Born June 24, 1950, in Chicago, IL; daughter of Edward George and Joyce (a homemaker; maiden name, Anderson) Ritche; married Anthony Lackey, June 10, 1972 (marriage ended); married Larry Dixon (an artist and writer), December 10, 1990. *Education:* Purdue University, B.S., 1972. *Politics:* "Esoteric." *Religion:* "Nontraditional." *Avocational interests:* Music, falconry, scuba diving.

ADDRESSES: Agent—Russell Galen, 845 Third Ave., New York, NY 10022.

CAREER: Artist's model, South Bend, IN, 1975-81; Associates Data Processing, South Bend, computer programmer, 1979-82; CAIRS (survey and data processing firm), South Bend, surveyor, layout designer, and analyst, 1981-82; American Airlines, Tulsa, OK, computer programmer, 1982-90.

MEMBER: Science Fiction and Fantasy Writers of America.

WRITINGS:

FANTASY NOVELS

Arrows of the Queen (also see below), DAW Books (New York City), 1987.
Arrow's Flight (also see below), DAW Books, 1987.
Arrow's Fall (also see below), DAW Books, 1988.
Oathbound (also see below), DAW Books, 1988.
Oathbreakers (also see below), DAW Books, 1989.
(With C. J. Cherryh) *Reap the Whirlwind,* Baen (Riverdale, NY), 1989.
Magic's Pawn (also see below), DAW Books, 1989.

Magic's Promise (also see below), DAW Books, 1989.
(With Ellen Guon) *Knight of Ghosts and Shadows,* Baen, 1990.
Magic's Price (also see below), DAW Books, 1990.
By the Sword, DAW Books, 1991.
(With Andre Norton) *The Elvenbane: An Epic High Fantasy of the Halfblood Chronicles,* Tor Books (New York City), 1991.
Winds of Fate (first book of "Mage Winds" trilogy), DAW Books, 1991.
Winds of Change (second book of "Mage Winds" trilogy), DAW Books, 1992.
The Last Herald Mage, Penguin (New York City), 1992.
The Lark and the Wren (first book of "Bardic Voices" series), Baen, 1992.
(With husband, Larry Dixon) *Born to Run* (part of "SERRAted Edge" series), Baen, 1992.
(With Mark Shepherd) *Wheels of Fire* (part of "SERRAted Edge" series), Baen, 1992.
(With Guon) *Summoned to Tourney,* Baen, 1992.
The Last Herald-Mage (contains *Magic's Pawn, Magic's Promise,* and *Magic's Price*), Doubleday Book and Music Clubs, 1992.
(With Josepha Sherman) *Castle of Deception* (part of "Bard's Tale" series), Baen, 1992.
(With Anne McCaffrey) *The Ship Who Searched,* Baen, 1992.
(With Holly Lisle) *When the Bough Breaks* (part of "SERRAted Edge" series), Baen, 1993.
(With Piers Anthony) *If I Pay Thee Not in Gold,* Baen, 1993.
(With Marion Zimmer Bradley) *Rediscovery: A Novel of Darkover,* DAW Books, 1993.
(With Ru Emerson) *Fortress of Frost and Fire* (part of "Bard's Tale" series), Baen, 1993.

Winds of Fury (third book of "Mage Winds" trilogy), DAW Books, 1993.

The Robin and the Kestrel (second book of "Bardic Voices" series), Baen, 1993.

Vows and Honor (contains *The Oathbound* and *Oathbreakers*), Doubleday Book and Music Clubs, 1993.

Queen's Own (contains *Arrows of the Queen, Arrow's Flight,* and *Arrow's Fall*), Science Fiction Book Club, 1993.

Sacred Ground, Tor Books, 1994.

(With Josepha Sherman) *A Cast of Corbies,* Baen, 1994.

(With Dixon) *The Black Gryphon,* DAW Books, 1994.

(With Dixon) *Chrome Circle,* Baen, 1994.

(With Shepherd) *Prison of Souls* (part of "Bard's Tale" series), Baen, 1994.

Storm Warning (first book in "Mage Storms" series), DAW Books, 1994.

(With Dixon) *The White Gryphon,* DAW Books, 1995.

The Eagle and the Nightingales (third book of "Bardic Voices" series), Baen, 1995.

The Fire Rose, Baen, 1995.

Storm Rising, DAW Books, 1995.

Also author of *Lammas Night,* Baen.

OTHER

Burning Water (horror novel; "Diana Tregarde Investigations" series), Tor Books, 1989.

Mercedes Lackey—Live! (cassette), Firebird Arts, 1989.

Children of the Night: A Diana Tregarde Investigation, Tor Books, 1990.

Jinx High (part of "Diana Tregarde Investigations" series), Tor Books, 1991.

(With Guon) *Wing Commander: Freedom Flight* (science fiction), Baen, 1992.

Heralds, Harpers and Havoc Songbook, Firebird Arts (Portland, OR), in press.

Lackey has written lyrics for and recorded nearly fifty songs for Off-Centaur, a small recording company specializing in science fiction folk music.

WORK IN PROGRESS: A novel, *Storm Breaking; Tiger Burning Bright,* with Marion Zimmer Bradley and Andre Norton; *The Silver Gryphon,* with Larry Dixon; *Elvenblood,* with Norton.

SIDELIGHTS: Mercedes R. Lackey proclaims herself a storyteller, and most of her books focus on the genre of fantasy fiction. Her books range from *A Cast of Corbies,* in which an oppressive institution known as the Church censors music and attacks magic, to *Sacred Ground,* in which a female Native American detective must solve a mystery to placate the souls whose resting place has been violated. Despite these diverse plots, Lackey has become identified with certain traits, which reviewer Mary K. Chelton, writing about *The Lark and the Wren* in *Voice of Youth Advocates,* enumerates as "an abused, alienated teenager with latent magical powers, . . . a wonderfully realistic medieval fantasy setting, elves, evil mages, and mature (though not explicit) sexuality."

Lackey is perhaps best known for her fantasy land of Valdemar, featured in such works as *Arrows of the Queen* and *Winds of Fury.* This land is peopled by several intelligent species, including humans and a variety of bird known as Gryphons. *Winds of Fury* tells about the need to reinstate the power of magic in Valdemar and places the heir of the throne, Elspeth, in direct conflict with a political schemer, Ancar of Hardorn, and an evil and manipulative mage, Mornilithe Falconsbane. *The Black Gryphon,* set in ancient times long before the founding of Valdemar, recounts the legendary mage wars and the friendship between Skandragon, the title character, and the Healer Amberdrake. The popularity of the Valdemar cycle has prompted Lackey to announce "that she will keep writing Valdemar stories as long as people want them," reports Chelton in a *Voice of Youth Advocates* review of *Winds of Fury.*

Many of Lackey's novels combine contemporary themes and characters with medieval settings—or, sometimes, fantastic characters with modern settings. *When the Bough Breaks* is an example of the latter: It features an elfish race-car driver, a fifth-grade human teacher, and a sexually abused girl who has developed multiple personalities. Reviewer Elaine M. McGuire states in *Voice of Youth Advocates* that the book's opening is "full of today's realities" and it "succeeds in masterfully blending the real and unreal." *Born to Run* follows a similar pattern in dealing with the topics of child pornography, teenage prostitution, and a teenaged mage who is fascinated by fast cars and rock music. Calling it "part morality tale" and "part fast-action adventure," Diane G. Yates in *Voice of Youth Advocates* says that "this improbable mixture is tied together well." *Summoned to Tourney* takes place in San Francisco and involves psychically summoned creatures called Nightflyers who are capable of eating souls. *Wheels of Fire,* set mostly in Oklahoma, concerns parental abduction of children, fanatical religious cults, religious and political intolerance, racism, violence, and abuse.

Lackey once told *CA:* "I'm a storyteller; that's what I see as 'my job.' My stories come out of my characters; how those characters would react to the given situation. Maybe that's why I get letters from readers as young as thirteen and as old as sixty-odd. One of the reasons I write song lyrics is because I see songs as a kind of 'story pill'—they reduce a story to the barest essentials or encapsulate a particular crucial moment in time. I frequently will write a lyric when I am attempting to get to the heart of a crucial scene; I find that when I have done so, the scene has become absolutely clear in my mind, and I can write exactly what I wanted to say. Another reason is because of the kind of novels I am writing: that is, fantasy, set in an other-world semi-medieval atmosphere. Music is very important to medieval peoples; bards are the chief newsbringers. When I write the 'folk music' of these peoples, I am enriching my whole world, whether I actually use the song in the text or not.

"I began writing out of boredom; I continue out of addiction. I can't 'not' write, and as a result I have no social life! I began writing fantasy because I love it, but I try to construct my fantasy worlds with all the care of a 'high-tech' science fiction writer. I apply the principle of TANSTAFL ('There ain't no such thing as a free lunch') to magic, for instance; in my worlds, magic is paid for, and the cost to the magician is frequently a high one. I try to keep my world as solid and real as possible; people deal with stubborn pumps, bugs in the porridge, and love-lives that refuse to become untangled, right along with invading armies and evil magicians. And I try to make all of my characters, even the 'evil magicians,' something more than flat stereotypes. Even evil magicians get up in the night and look for cookies, sometimes.

"I suppose that in everything I write I try to expound the creed I gave my character Di Tregarde in *Burning Water*—there's no such thing as 'one, true way'; the only answers worth having are the ones you find for yourself; leave the world better than you found it. Love, freedom, and the chance to do some good—they're the things worth living and dying for, and if you aren't willing to die for the things worth living for, you might as well turn in your membership in the human race."

BIOGRAPHICAL/CRITICAL SOURCES:

BOOKS

Authors and Artists for Young Adults, Volume 13, Gale (Detroit), 1994.

PERIODICALS

Booklist, December 15, 1994, p. 740.
Locus, April, 1994, p. 33.
Publishers Weekly, November 1, 1993, p. 70.
Voice of Youth Advocates, April, 1992, pp. 44-45; August, 1992, p. 176; October, 1992, p. 240; April, 1993, pp. 42-43; June, 1993, pp. 102-03; August, 1993, p. 166; December, 1993, pp. 310-11; April, 1994, pp. 37-38.*

*   *   *

LAGEVI, Bo
See BLOM, Karl Arne

*   *   *

LASSITER, Adam
See KRAUZER, Steven M(ark)

*   *   *

LAUMER, (John) Keith   1925-1993
(Anthony Le Baron)

PERSONAL: Surname is pronounced *"law-*mer"; born June 9, 1925, in Syracuse, NY; died January 23, 1993; married Janice Perkinson, February, 1949; children: two. *Education:* Attended University of Indiana, Bloomington, 1943-44, and University of Stockholm, 1948-49; University of Illinois, B.Arch., 1950, B.Sc. in Architecture, 1952.

CAREER: University of Illinois, Urbana, staff member, 1952; U.S. Foreign Service, vice-consul and third secretary in Rangoon, Burma, 1956-59;

freelance writer, 1959-93. *Military service:* U.S. Army, 1943-46, served in Europe; became corporal. U.S. Air Force, 1953-56, 1960-65; became captain.

AWARDS, HONORS: Nebula Award nomination for best novel, Science Fiction Writers of America (now Science Fiction and Fantasy Writers of America), 1965, for *A Plague of Demons;* Hugo Award nomination for best novel, World Science Fiction Society, 1965, for *The Great Time Machine Hoax;* Nebula Award nominations, 1968, for best novelette, for "Once There Was a Giant," and for best novella, for "The Day beyond Forever"; Nebula Award nomination, 1970, and Hugo Award nomination, 1971, both for short story "In the Queue"; Hugo Award nomination for best novella, 1978, for excerpt entitled "The Wonderful Secret" from *The Ultimax Man.*

WRITINGS:

"RETIEF" SERIES

Envoy to New Worlds (short stories), Ace Books (New York City), 1963.
Galactic Diplomat: Nine Incidents of the Corps Diplomatique Terrestrienne (short stories), Doubleday (New York City), 1965.
Retief's War (originally published in three installments in *Worlds of If* magazine), Doubleday, 1966.
Retief and the Warlords, Doubleday, 1968.
Retief: Ambassador to Space; Seven Incidents of the Corps Diplomatique Terrestrienne (short stories), Doubleday, 1969.
Retief's Ransom, Putnam (New York City), 1971, published as *Retief and the Pangalactic Pageant of Pulchritude* (includes novella of the same title), Baen (New York City), 1986.
Retief of the CDT (short stories), Doubleday, 1971.
Retief: Emissary to the Stars (short stories), Pocket Books (New York City), 1975.
Retief Unbound (short story omnibus), Ace Books, 1979.
Retief at Large (short stories), Ace Books, 1979.
Retief and the Rebels, Pocket Books, 1980.
Retief: Diplomat at Arms, Pocket Books, 1982.
Retief to the Rescue, Timescape (New York City), 1983.
The Return of Retief, Baen, 1985.
Retief in the Ruins, Baen, 1986.
Reward for Retief, Baen, 1989.
Retief and the Rascals, Baen, 1993.

SHORT STORY COLLECTIONS

Nine by Laumer (includes "End as a Hero" [also see below]), Doubleday, 1967.
Greylorn (includes "The House in November" [also see below]), Berkley Publishing (New York City), 1968, published in England as *The Other Sky,* Dobson (London), 1968.
It's a Mad, Mad, Mad Galaxy (includes "The Body Builders" [published in *Galaxy,* August, 1966], "The Planet Wreckers," "The Star-Sent Knaves," "The War with the Yukks," and "Goobereality"), Berkley Publishing, 1969.
Once There Was a Giant (originally published in *Fantasy and Science Fiction,* November, 1968), Doubleday, 1971.
Timetracks, Ballantine (New York City), 1972.
The Big Show, Ace Books, 1972.
The Undefeated, Dell (New York City), 1974.
Bolo: The Annals of the Dinochrome Brigade, Berkley Publishing, 1976.
The Best of Keith Laumer, Pocket Books, 1976.
The Galaxy Builder, Ace Books, 1984.
Chrestomathy, Baen, 1984.
The Compleat Bolo, Baen, 1990.
Alien Minds, Baen, 1991.

NOVELIZATIONS

Enemies from Beyond (based on the television series *The Invaders*), Pyramid Publications (New York City), 1966.
The Invaders (based on the television series of the same title), Pyramid Publications, 1967, published in England under pseudonym Anthony Le Baron as *Meteor Man,* Corgi (London), 1968.
The Avengers, No. 5: The Afrit Affair (based on the British television series *The Avengers*), Berkley Publishing, 1968.
The Avengers, No. 6: The Drowned Queen, Berkley Publishing, 1968.
The Avengers, No. 7: The Gold Bomb, Berkley Publishing, 1968.

OTHER

How to Design and Build Flying Models, Harper (New York City), 1960, revised edition, 1970.
Worlds of the Imperium, Ace Books, 1962.
A Trace of Memory, Berkley Publishing, 1963.
The Great Time Machine Hoax, Simon & Schuster (New York City), 1964.
Embassy, Pyramid Publications, 1965.

The Other Side of Time (shorter version published in *Amazing Stories,* April, May, and June, 1965), Berkley Publishing, 1965.

A Plague of Demons, Berkley Publishing, 1965.

(With Rosel George Brown) *Earthblood,* Doubleday, 1966.

Catastrophe Planet, Berkley Publishing, 1966, reprinted with other works as *The Breaking Earth,* 1981.

The Monitors, Berkley Publishing, 1966.

The Time Bender, Berkley Publishing, 1966.

Galactic Odyssey, Berkley Publishing, 1967.

(With Gordon R. Dickson) *Planet Run,* Doubleday, 1967.

The Day before Forever [and] *Thunderhead,* Doubleday, 1968.

Assignment in Nowhere, Berkley Publishing, 1968.

The Long Twilight (abridged edition published as "And Now They Wake" in *Galaxy,* March, April, and May, 1969), Putnam, 1969.

Time Trap, Putnam, 1970.

The World Shuffler, Putnam, 1970.

The House in November (shorter version first published as "The Seeds of Gonyl" in *Worlds of If,* October, November, and December, 1969), Putnam, 1970.

(With others) *Five Fates,* Doubleday, 1970.

The Star Treasure, Putnam, 1971.

Deadfall, Doubleday, 1971, published as *Fat Chance,* Pocket Books, 1975.

Dinosaur Beach, Scribner (New York City), 1971.

Night of Delusions, Putnam, 1972.

The Infinite Cage, Putnam, 1972.

The Shape Changer, Putnam, 1972.

The Glory Game, Doubleday, 1973.

The Ultimax Man (excerpt published as "The Wonderful Secret" in *Analog Science Fiction-Science Fact,* September-October, 1977), St. Martin's (New York City), 1978.

Star Colony, St. Martin's, 1981.

Beyond the Imperium, Pinnacle Books (New York City), 1981.

End as a Hero, Ace Books, 1985.

Rogue Bolo, Baen, 1986.

Zone Yellow, Baen, 1990.

The Stars Must Wait, Baen, 1990.

Judson's Eden, Baen, 1991.

Back to the Time Trap, Baen, 1992.

Bolos, Book 1: Honor of the Regiment, Baen, 1993.

The Unconquerable Bolos, Baen, 1994.

Bolos 3, Baen, 1995.

Also author of "Prototaph," published in *Analog,* March, 1966; "The Plague," published in *Analog,* November, 1970; "The Right to Revolt" and "The Right to Resist," both published in *If,* June, 1971; and "In the Queue," published in *Orbit,* Volume 7. Contributor of more than forty short stories to *Galaxy, Fantasy and Science Fiction, If, Analog,* and other science fiction magazines; contributor of more than thirty articles to periodicals, including *Model Airplane News, American Modeler, Flying Models,* and *Aeromodeller.*

Laumer's manuscripts are housed in collections at University of Syracuse and University of Mississippi.

ADAPTATIONS: The Avengers, No. 5: The Afrit Affair was produced for British television by ITV Productions and subsequently aired on ABC-TV in the United States; *The Monitors* was filmed by Second City in Chicago in 1969; *Deadfall* was released by Twentieth Century-Fox as *The Peeper; Earthblood* has been optioned.

SIDELIGHTS: After his first book appeared in 1960, Keith Laumer wrote dozens more, including works as diverse as a mystery novel and a guide on how to build model airplanes. It was for his science-fiction novels and short stories, however, that Laumer was best known; his works were nominated for many Nebula and Hugo awards, the top prizes in the science-fiction field. Although *Dictionary of Literary Biography* writer Hugh M. Ruppersburg acknowledged that Laumer was "not as well-known as Ray Bradbury, Arthur C. Clarke, or Robert Heinlein," he nonetheless maintained that "his best work rival[ed] theirs" and described Laumer as "one of the prominent figures of the last two decades in science fiction."

Laumer was born in Syracuse, New York, and enlisted in the army at the age of eighteen. From 1943 until 1965 he served in the military and attended college between tours of duty. He did not begin writing full time until he resigned from the armed forces in 1965, after which he concentrated on the science-fiction novels for which he gained popularity.

Ruppersburg detected the influence of Laumer's military career in his writing: "Many of his novels concern war (or the threat of it) and life in the military." Critics found this theme particularly evident in the series of novels and short stories involving Laumer's best-known character, Retief. In a *Publishers Weekly* review of *Reward for Retief,* Penny Kaganoff described this hero as a "conservative James Bond figure amid helpless liberal bureaucrats," whereas another *Publishers Weekly* reviewer characterized the series as "effective broad satires of U.S. foreign policy." Although Ruppersburg considered "invincibility" to be Retief's "primary characteristic," the character was not intended to be a superman, according to Laumer. Instead, Laumer considered Retief, a diplomat in the Corps Diplomatique Terrestrienne, to be "a perfectly normal specimen of Homo sapiens," Ruppersburg quoted. "He does nothing that some other man could not have done. His distinctive trait is that he has fully realized his human potential." What Retief usually does with his "human potential," Ruppersburg claimed, is "outwit and short-circuit" the plans of ne'er-do-well diplomats and government officials and "do the right thing."

Although they form the most popular Laumer series, the Retief stories resemble a "comic strip—stereotyped characters and situations, funny but shallow satire, and plenty of action," according to Ruppersburg. Other reviewers offered similar assessments. One *Publishers Weekly* writer, reviewing *Retief to the Rescue,* referred to the Retief stories as Laumer's "most typical, if not his best work" but also "his most popular, and with good reason."

A frequently noted characteristic of Laumer's novels and stories was his ability to write action sequences. Barbara A. Bannon, for example, wrote in *Publishers Weekly* that *Bolo: The Annals of the Dinochrome Brigade* is filled with "lots of spectacular action," and in another *Publishers Weekly* review, critic Genevieve Stuttaford referred to Laumer as "probably the best writer of action sequences working in SF." Laumer, however, felt that "the action in my books is purely incidental," as Ruppersburg quoted. Laumer found it "more interesting to examine ideas in a dynamic way, rather than in academic discussion."

Ruppersburg further noted that Laumer's later novels "have been distinguished by a clear emphasis on philosophical themes." Themes explored by Laumer include what Bannon referred to in a *Publishers Weekly* review of *The House in November* as "man's essential puniness against the panorama of the universe" and what she termed, in a review of *Dinosaur Beach,* as "the possibilities of man's attempt to explore . . . the natural flow of time." Ruppersburg praised Laumer's stories as "rife with profound themes and exciting action" and added that the author was "a serious writer of serious science fiction."

Preferring universal themes over what he termed "political propaganda," Laumer summarized the concerns of his work in words quoted in *Dictionary of Literary Biography:* "I prefer to address myself to those values which have been important to man ever since he became man, and will continue to be of value as long our species is human. Among these values are truth and beauty, loyalty and justice, kindness and gentleness, [and] ethics and integrity."

BIOGRAPHICAL/CRITICAL SOURCES:

BOOKS

Dictionary of Literary Biography, Volume 8: *Twentieth-Century American Science Fiction Writers,* Gale (Detroit), 1981.
Twentieth-Century Science-Fiction Writers, third edition, St. James Press (Chicago), 1991.

PERIODICALS

National Review, January 12, 1971.
New York Times Book Review, January 30, 1972, p. 24; March 30, 1975, p. 24.
Publishers Weekly, October 31, 1966, p. 88; April 24, 1967, p. 95; November 20, 1967, p. 52; July 28, 1969, p. 56; January 26, 1970, p. 269; June 8, 1970, p. 179; September 14, 1970, p. 68; July 12, 1971, p. 68; July 19, 1971, p. 119; December 6, 1971, p. 52; March 27, 1972, p. 73; October 16, 1972, p. 44; November 13, 1972, p. 42; November 10, 1975, p. 56; February 9, 1976, p. 99; July 5, 1976, p. 86; May 29, 1978, p. 42; October 16, 1981, p. 63; December 24, 1982, p. 50; June 28, 1985, p. 72; January 6, 1989, p. 98.
Times Literary Supplement, November 28, 1968, p. 1346; October 13, 1972, p. 1235; June 14, 1974, p. 644.

OBITUARIES:

PERIODICALS

Locus, March, 1993.

*   *   *

LAWRENCE, R(onald) D(ouglas)   1921-

PERSONAL: Born September 12, 1921, in Vigo, Spain; son of Thomas Edward and Esther

(Rodriguez) Lawrence; married Joan Frances Gray, September 18, 1962 (died June 7, 1969); married Sharon Janet Frise (a teacher), December 16, 1973. *Education:* Educated at private school in Barcelona, Spain, and by a private tutor. *Politics:* None. *Religion:* None.

ADDRESSES: Home and office—RR1, Norland, Ontario, Canada K0M 2L0. *Agent*—Wallace & Sheil Agency, Inc., 177 East 70th St., New York, NY 10021.

CAREER: Writer. *Daily Mirror,* London, England, journalist, 1945-54; trapper, logger, and cattle farmer on homestead in northern Ontario, 1954-57; *Free Press,* Winnipeg, Manitoba, night editor, 1957-61; *Telegram,* Toronto, Ontario, worked as reporter, entertainment and financial editor, and publisher of affiliate suburban weekly newspaper, 1960-70. *Military service:* Fought with anti-Franco forces in Spanish Civil War, c. 1935-37; British Army, Military Intelligence, Tank Corps, 1939-44.

MEMBER: American Society of Mammalogists, Writers Union of Canada, Mark Twain Society (honorary member).

AWARDS, HONORS: Frank H. Kortright awards from Toronto Sportsman's Show, 1967 and 1968, for writings on conservation.

WRITINGS:

Wildlife in Canada, M. Joseph (London), 1966.
The Place in the Forest, M. Joseph, 1967.
Where the Water Lilies Grow, M. Joseph, 1968.
The Poison Makers, Thomas Nelson (Surrey, England), 1968.
Maple Syrup, Thomas Nelson, 1970.
Cry Wild, Thomas Nelson, 1970.
Wildlife in North America: Mammals, Chilton (Radnor, PA), 1974.
Wildlife in North America: Birds, Chilton, 1974.
Paddy: A Naturalist's Story of an Orphan Beaver Rescued, Adopted and Observed, Knopf (New York City), 1976, condensed edition, Reader's Digest Press (New York City), 1978.
The North Runner, Holt (New York City), 1979, condensed edition, Reader's Digest Press, 1979.
Secret Go the Wolves, Holt, 1980, condensed edition, Reader's Digest Press, 1982.
The Zoo That Never Was, Holt, 1981.
Voyage of the Stella, Holt, 1982.
The Ghost Walker, Holt, 1983.

Canada's National Parks, Collins, 1983.
Shark! Nature's Miracle, McClelland & Stewart (Toronto), 1985, Chapters (Shelburne, VT), 1994.
In Praise of Wolves, Holt, 1986.
The Natural History of Canada, Key Porter Books (Toronto), 1988.
The White Puma: A Novel, Holt, 1990.
Wolves, Sierra Club Books (San Francisco, CA), 1990.
Trail of the Wolf, Rodale Press (Rodale, PA), 1993.
The Green Trees Beyond: A Memoir, Holt, 1994.

Contributor to proceedings of Myrin Institute, 1980. General editor, Sierra Club Books for Children, 1994.

Lawrence's books have been translated into thirteen languages and have been published in sixteen countries.

WORK IN PROGRESS: A novel dealing with Communist pressures on the United States from bases in Canada; a book examining the wildlife of Canada and the United States and the measures employed by governmental wildlife agencies of both nations to ensure their conservation.

SIDELIGHTS: R. D. Lawrence, according to *Quill and Quire* contributor Alec Ross, is "one of Canada's most prolific nature writers" and one who "has made a career of describing wild places and their inhabitants—from sharks to mountain lions to wolves." However, Lawrence started out as a soldier, not a writer or naturalist. Born in Spain to an English-Spanish couple, he enlisted at the age of fourteen in the Communist (anti-Franco) forces during the Spanish Civil War. After two years of service, he retreated across the Pyrenees. At the outbreak of World War II, he joined the British army, was seriously wounded in the retreat at Dunkirk, served in North Africa, and participated in the D-Day invasion of Normandy. Lawrence recounts his war experiences in *The Green Trees Beyond: A Memoir.* In that book, according to Ross, Lawrence explains how his fascination with animals helped him keep his sanity after his harrowing experiences. "Lawrence," states Chris Goodrich in the *Los Angeles Times Book Review,* "goes deep into emotionally difficult territory at times, as when he professes never to have felt love until his mid-30's, and then only toward his mortally wounded dog." He immigrated to Canada and ended up homesteading in northern Ontario, eventually becoming a respected writer, conservationist, and biologist. "Since 1966," Ross explains, "he's produced more than two dozen novels and non-fiction books about animals, many of them critically acclaimed."

Lawrence is especially well known for his work with wolves in Ontario and northern Michigan. His 1979 book *The North Runner,* a memoir of his experiences living in northern Ontario, featured a half-wolf hybrid named Yukon. A *New York Times Book Review* critic writes that *The North Runner* contains "sensitive moments, quietly and richly described. . . . Lawrence reveals not a little of his own honesty and also offers insight into the psychology of the lone human." He followed it with *Secret Go the Wolves,* which along with *The North Runner* "won a large and receptive audience for wolves and the wild country of Ontario," according to David M. Graber in the *Los Angeles Times Book Review. In Praise of Wolves* looks at the social organization of a captive wolf pack in the Upper Peninsula of Michigan, while *Trail of the Wolf* presents a basic introduction to wolves for a popular readership.

Lawrence approaches his work with wolves with an emotionalism usually not associated with professional biologists. "Lawrence loves wolves passionately," Graber declares. "There is nothing dispassionate about [*In Praise of Wolves*], nor any other of Lawrence's writings. Also evident is Lawrence's intense desire for physical and 'spiritual' contact with wolves." Lawrence's conservation ideology emerges in *Trail of the Wolf,* where "midway through the book, the author talks about his experience in raising orphaned wolf pups," writes B. T. Aniskowicz in *Nature Canada.* "Lawrence's advice against keeping wolves as pets, and his discussion of Eurasian wolves which ends with an impassioned plea for conservation worldwide, are valuable." Sue Sutton, a contributor to *Quill and Quire,* adds, "Addresses are given for conservation groups and specialty publications in Canada and elsewhere for those interested in pursuing the subject further."

Lawrence told *CA:* "The single most potent motive force is my consuming interest in living things, from mouse to man, and it was on this subject that I wrote a diary of wildlife seen which I later expanded into my first book, *Wildlife in Canada.*

"I began writing about nature as a child; I explored nature as a child, but perhaps the greatest influence in my life, and writings, comes from Henry David Thoreau. At fourteen I read *Walden* and was deeply impressed by one of Thoreau's sentences: 'In wildness is the preservation of the world.'

"Over the years I have received, and continue to receive, thousands of letters from readers of my work; this is the greatest stimulation that I obtain from my writings. The knowledge that so many people share my passion for life lived in mutual respect and toleration keeps me elevated during those times (which are now occurring with greater frequency) when the insanity of man's politics begins to debase and depress me."

BIOGRAPHICAL/CRITICAL SOURCES:

PERIODICALS

Atlantic Monthly, June, 1986, p. 83.
Canadian Historical Review, September, 1989, pp. 285-87.
Christian Science Monitor, June 19, 1990, p. 14.
Library Journal, April 15, 1990, p. 122; June 15, 1994, p. 75.
Los Angeles Times, December 27, 1990, p. E2.
Los Angeles Times Book Review, June 29, 1986, pp. 1, 6; August 28, 1994, p. 7.
Nature Canada, spring, 1994, pp. 53-54.
New York Times, April 21, 1990, p. A14.
New York Times Book Review, July 24, 1977; July 22, 1979; June 22, 1986, p. 27.
Publishers Weekly, March 23, 1990, p. 64; May 9, 1994, p. 56.
Quill and Quire, May, 1993, p. 27; August, 1994, p. 27.
Washington Post Book World, April 17, 1979; June 8, 1986, pp. 6-7.*

*   *   *

LEARY, David E.   1945-

PERSONAL: Born May 5, 1945, in Los Angeles, CA; son of Thomas G. and Betty (Elliott) Leary; married Marjorie Bates, June 11, 1972; children: Emily, Elizabeth, Matthew. *Education:* San Luis Rey College, B.A., 1968; San Jose State College (now University), M.A., 1971; University of Chicago, Ph.D., 1977.

ADDRESSES: Home—103 Burgoyne Rd., Richmond, VA 23229. *Office*—Office of the Dean of Arts and Sciences, University of Richmond, Richmond, VA 23173.

CAREER: University of New Hampshire, Durham, assistant professor, 1977-81, associate professor, 1981-87, professor of psychology, history, and humanities, 1987-89, chairperson of department of psychology, 1987-89; University of Richmond, Richmond, VA, professor, 1989—. Fellow at Center for Advanced Study in the Behavioral Sciences, Stanford, CA, 1982-83.

MEMBER: American Psychological Association (fellow; past president of Division of the History of Psychology; past president of the Division of Theoretical and Philosophical Psychology), American Historical Association, Cheiron Society, History of Science Society, Society for the History of Science in America.

AWARDS, HONORS: Grants from National Endowment for the Humanities, 1979, 1982-83, 1991-94, History of Psychology Foundation, 1980, National Science Foundation, 1980-82, 1982-83, and Mellon Foundation, 1986; PSP Award from Association of American Publishers, 1985, for *A Century of Psychology as Science.*

WRITINGS:

(Editor with Sigmund Koch) *A Century of Psychology as Science,* McGraw (New York City), 1985, revised edition, 1992.
(Editor) *Metaphors in the History of Psychology,* Cambridge University Press (Cambridge, MA), 1990.

Contributor to periodicals, including *American Psychological Association Monitor, American Psychologist, History of the Human Sciences, Journal of General Psychology, Journal of the History of Ideas,* and *Journal of Theoretical and Philosophical Psychology.*

WORK IN PROGRESS: Research on the historical relations between psychology and the humanities, especially philosophy, religion, literature, and the arts.

SIDELIGHTS: David E. Leary told *CA:* "I am deeply concerned to understand the influence of culture (especially the humanities) upon psychology, and the influence of psychology upon the humanities and culture. Since many people think of science as independent of the larger context in which it exists, most of the reciprocal influence between psychology and the humanities has been overlooked. Much of this influence has been positive and has contributed to the advancement of both science and culture. However, some of it has had or threatens to have unfortunate consequences—as for instance when psychologists utilize fruitful metaphors drawn from the larger culture, but do so in a simpleminded, reductionistic way. The result is often the creation of psychological myths, promulgated to the public at large as supposedly factual descriptions of psychological phenomena.

"For example, when cognitive psychologists claim that the human mind *is* a computer rather than *like* a computer, they present an oversimplified view of the mind, which suggests and endorses an oversimplified approach to human problem solving. Similarly, when social psychologists speak about human interactions, without qualification, as essentially 'exchanges' in which each actor seeks to maximize 'benefits' and minimize 'costs,' they unwittingly legitimate and reinforce a cultural ideology that might otherwise be subjected to critical scrutiny. No doubt, many people in our culture have been socialized to 'think like a computer' and to approach social situations with a 'market mentality,' but this does not mean that a rationalistic, cost/benefit mentality is an inevitable characteristic of the human condition. To suggest that human mentality or human behavior just *is* that way, and by implication that it *must* be that way, is to corroborate rather than analyze and assess particular patterns of thought and behavior.

"The cumulative effect of broadcasting such convictions as 'the human mind is but a machine' and 'human behavior is always self-interested' can be detected in the transformation of private self-images and in the formulation of many public policies. Although these convictions have been around for a very long time, beginning well before the advent of modern psychology, their endorsement by psychological science has added significant ballast in their favor.

"In summary, although I believe that psychology has the potential to enlighten and enliven us about the human condition, it can also contribute towards the creation of an image of what it means to be human—and thus toward changes in the realities of human life—that I find distasteful at best, and morally repugnant at worst. I hope that my own teaching and writing has encouraged the critical examination and discussion of such matters. *A Century of Psychology as Science,* while having a broader and more diverse set of purposes, contributes generally to this examination and discussion. *Metaphors in the History of Psychology* contributes specifically to it."

Le BARON, Anthony
   See LAUMER, (John) Keith

*   *   *

LEE, (Nelle) Harper   1926-

PERSONAL: Born April 28, 1926, in Monroeville, AL; daughter of Amasa Coleman (a lawyer) and Frances (Finch) Lee. *Education:* Attended Huntington College, 1944-45, and University of Alabama, 1945-49; also attended Oxford University. *Politics:* Republican. *Religion:* Methodist. *Avocational interests:* Golf and music.

*ADDRESSES: Home—*Monroeville, AL.

CAREER: Writer. Airline reservation clerk with Eastern Air Lines and British Overseas Airways, New York, NY, during the 1950s. Member, National Council on the Arts, 1966-72.

AWARDS, HONORS: Pulitzer Prize, 1961, Alabama Library Association award, 1961, Brotherhood Award of National Conference of Christians and Jews, 1961, and *Best Sellers'* Paperback of the Year Award, 1962, all for *To Kill a Mockingbird.*

WRITINGS:

To Kill a Mockingbird (Literary Guild selection, Book-of-the-Month Club alternate, *Reader's Digest* condensed book, British Book Society choice), Lippincott (Philadelphia, PA), 1960.

Contributor to *Vogue* and *McCall's. To Kill a Mockingbird* has been translated into ten languages.

ADAPTATIONS: To Kill a Mockingbird was filmed by Universal in 1962 and adapted as a London stage play by Christopher Sergel in 1987.

SIDELIGHTS: With the enormous popular and critical success of her novel, *To Kill a Mockingbird,* Harper Lee established herself as a leading figure in American literature. Although she has not published any new fiction in over thirty-five years, Lee's reputation is secure. According to Dorothy Jewell Altman in the *Dictionary of Literary Biography, To Kill a Mockingbird,* "a regional novel with a universal message, combines popular appeal with literary excellence, assuring Harper Lee's place in American letters."

To Kill a Mockingbird is narrated by six-year-old Jean Finch, nicknamed "Scout," who, along with her older brother Jem, watch as their father, an attorney, defends a black man accused of raping a white woman. During the three years of the trial, the two children come to an understanding of prejudice as their father stands his ground in defending a man he believes to be innocent. Told with "a rare blend of wit and compassion," according to the critic for *Booklist,* the novel moves "unconcernedly and irresistibly back and forth between being sentimental, tough, melodramatic, acute, and funny," writes the reviewer for the *New Yorker.*

One of the novel's subplots revolves around attempts by the two siblings and their friend Dill Harris to draw out Arthur "Boo" Radley, a local recluse. The children's wild ideas about the unseen Boo—that he eats raw squirrels and wanders the town by night—reflect the town's misconceptions about race. When Boo is revealed as a benefactor to the children, they must reconsider their preconceptions about him. "One of the most interesting features of *Mockingbird,*" writes William T. Going in his collection *Essays on Alabama Literature,* "is the skill with which Miss Lee weaves these two struggles about childhood and the law together into one thematic idea." "The achievement of Harper Lee," Edgar H. Schuster argues in *English Journal,* "is not that she has written another novel about race prejudice, but rather that she has placed race prejudice in a perspective which allows us to see it as an aspect of a larger thing; as something that arises from phantom contacts, from fear and lack of knowledge; and finally as something that disappears with the kind of knowledge or 'education' that one gains through learning what people are really like when you 'finally see them'."

Lee drew upon her own childhood experiences as the daughter of a lawyer in Alabama for the fictional events in *To Kill a Mockingbird.* Together with her brother and their childhood friend Truman Capote, Lee enjoyed many of the small town adventures depicted in the novel. Scout's troubles in school—she is so far advanced in reading that she finds her school work boring—reflects Capote's own childhood boredom with grade school. Lee's older sister, Sook, a recluse who rarely left the family house, shares many of the qualities exhibited by the character Boo. "Although Lee stresses that *To Kill a Mockingbird* is not autobiographical," explains Altman, "she allows that a writer 'should write about what he knows and write truthfully.' The time period and setting of the novel obviously originate in the author's experience."

Lee began writing after leaving college in 1950 just before completing her law studies. While supporting herself in New York City as an airline reservation clerk, she sought the advice of a literary agent about her work. The agent advised her to expand one of the short stories she had written into the novel which became *To Kill a Mockingbird*. The process of writing the novel took several years. During this time Lee quit working, lived in a cold-water flat, and was supported by friends who believed in her work. In 1957 she approached the publishing firm of Lippincott with the manuscript. Although editors criticized the novel's structure, which they felt read like a series of short stories strung together, they saw promise in the book and encouraged Lee to rewrite it. By 1960, with the help of Lippincott editor Tay Hohoff, *To Kill a Mockingbird* was finished.

The book was an immediate popular success, being selected by two major book clubs and condensed in the *Reader's Digest*. In addition, the book won the Pulitzer Prize and several other awards. But critical response to the novel was initially mixed. It was only with the success of the film adaptation in 1962—a winner of two Academy Awards and starring Gregory Peck and Mary Badham—that many critics took a second look at *To Kill a Mockingbird*. Initial reviews had sometimes highlighted the novel's melodramatic qualities or the unlikely nature of the story being narrated by a child of six. Phoebe Adams in *Atlantic Monthly,* for example, finds the story "frankly and completely impossible, being told in the first person by a six-year-old girl with the prose style of a well-educated adult." But later critics were more generous with the novel, citing Lee's storytelling abilities and creation of a believable small town setting. As R. A. Dave writes in *Indian Studies in American Fiction,* Lee "is a remarkable story-teller. The reader just glides through the novel abounding in humour and pathos, hopes and fears, love and hatred, humanity and brutality. . . . We hardly feel any tension between the novelist's creativity and social criticism [while] the tale of heroic struggle lingers in our memory as an unforgettable experience."

Since its initial appearance in 1960, *To Kill a Mockingbird* has been a continuing favorite with high school and college students. But aside from a few short articles for magazines, Lee has published no new work in over thirty-five years. The reason for this extended silence remains a matter of speculation.

Lee has avoided making public comments about her life or her work, although reports at the time *To Kill a Mockingbird* was published describe her as a slow, methodical writer who rewrites constantly. She divides her time between periods of extensive travel and her hometown of Monroeville, Alabama, where her sister, Alice Lee, practices as an attorney.

BIOGRAPHICAL/CRITICAL SOURCES:

BOOKS

Contemporary Literary Criticism, Gale (Detroit), Volume 12, 1980, Volume 60, 1990.
Dictionary of Literary Biography, Volume 6: *American Novelists since World War II,* Gale, 1980.
Going, William T., *Essays on Alabama Literature,* University of Alabama Press, 1975, pp. 9-31.
Johnson, Claudia Durst, *To Kill a Mockingbird: Threatening Boundaries,* Twayne (New York City), 1994.
Johnson, Claudia Durst, *Understanding 'To Kill a Mockingbird': A Student Casebook to Issues, Sources, and Historic Documents,* Greenwood Press (Westport, CT), 1994.
Moates, Marianne M., *A Bridge of Childhood: Truman Capote's Southern Years,* Holt, 1989.
Naik, M. K., S. K. Desai and S. Mokashi, editors, *Indian Studies in American Fiction,* Macmillan (New York City), 1974, pp. 211-323.

PERIODICALS

Alabama Review, April, 1973, pp. 122-36.
America, May 11, 1991, pp. 509-11.
Atlanta Constitution, May 25, 1993, p. A11.
Atlanta Journal & Constitution, May 29, 1988, p. A2; August 26, 1990, p. M1.
Atlantic Monthly, August, 1960, pp. 98-99.
Booklist, September 1, 1960.
Chicago Sunday Tribune, July 17, 1960, p. 1.
Christian Science Monitor, October 3, 1961, p. 6.
Commonweal, December 9, 1960, p. 289.
English Journal, October, 1963, pp. 506-11; December, 1964, pp. 656-61.
Item, March 3, 1991, p. 24.
New Statesman, October 15, 1960, p. 580.
Newsweek, January 9, 1961, p. 83.
New Yorker, September 10, 1960.
New York Herald Tribune, May 3, 1961, p. 16.
New York Herald Tribune Book Review, July 10, 1960, p. 5.
New York Times, June 6, 1993, p. 1.

New York Times Book Review, July 10, 1960, pp. 5, 18; April 8, 1962.

PHYLON: The Atlanta University Review of Race and Culture, June, 1961.

Saturday Review, July 23, 1960, pp. 15-16.

Times Literary Supplement, October 28, 1960.

USA Today, November 5, 1990, p. A3.

Washington Post, August 17, 1990, p. C2.

* * *

LEVY, Faye   1951-

PERSONAL: Born May 23, 1951, in Washington, DC; daughter of Louis (in business) and Pauline (a secretary; maiden name, Dobry) Kahn; married Yakir Levy (a writer), September 28, 1970. *Education:* Attended Hebrew University of Jerusalem, 1969-70; Tel Aviv University, B.A. (magna cum laude), 1973; La Varenne Cooking School, Paris, Grand Diplome, 1977. *Avocational interests:* Travel, gardening.

ADDRESSES: Home and office—5116 Marmol Dr., Woodland Hills, CA 91364. *Agent*—Maureen Lasher Agency, 1210 Tellem Dr., Pacific Palisades, CA 90272.

CAREER: Editorial assistant in Tel Aviv, Israel, 1974-76; La Varenne Cooking School, Paris, France, recipe and cookbook editor, 1976-82; certified cooking teacher and writer, 1982—. Cookbook editor, 1982-84.

MEMBER: International Association of Cooking Professionals, American Institute of Wine and Food, Association of Food Journalists, Southern California Culinary Guild.

AWARDS, HONORS: Faye Levy's Chocolate Sensations was named one of the best books of 1986 by *Publishers Weekly* and won an International Culinary Association Award for best dessert and baking book of the year, 1987; International Association of Culinary Professionals Award for best general and basic book of the year, 1987, for *Classic Cooking Techniques;* International Association of Culinary Professionals Award second prize in the category of veg-

etable books, 1988, for *Fresh from France: Vegetable Creations;* James Beard Cookbook Award in category of Vegetables, Fruits and Grains, 1994, for *Faye Levy's International Vegetable Cookbook.*

WRITINGS:

La Varenne Tour Book, Peanut Butter Publishing (Mercer Island, WA), 1980.

(With Fernard Chambrette) *La Cuisine du poisson* (title means "Fish Cookery"), Flammarion, 1984.

Sefer Hakinuhim: Mivhar Matkonei Tsarfat (title means "The Book of Desserts: The Best Recipes of France"), R. Sirkis (Israel), 1984.

Sefer Haoogot: Mivhar Matkonei Tsarfat (title means "The Book of Cakes: The Best Recipes of France"), R. Sirkis, 1984.

Aruhot Halaviot: Mivhar Matkonei Tsarfat (title means "Meatless Meals: The Best Recipes of France"), R. Sirkis, 1985.

Faye Levy's Chocolate Sensations, HP Books (Tucson, AZ), 1986, revised edition published as *Sensational Chocolate,* 1992.

Classic Cooking Techniques, Ortho Books (San Francisco, CA), 1986.

Fresh from France: Vegetable Creations, Dutton (New York City), 1987.

Fresh from France: Dinner Inspirations, Dutton, 1989.

Sensational Pasta, HP Books, 1989.

Fresh from France: Dessert Sensations, Dutton, 1990.

Faye Levy's International Jewish Cookbook, Warner Books (New York City), 1991.

Faye Levy's International Chicken Cookbook, Warner Books, 1992.

Faye Levy's International Vegetable Cookbook, Warner Books, 1993.

Thirty Lowfat Meals in Thirty Minutes, Warner Books, 1995.

Contributor to *Basic French Cookery, French Regional Cooking,* and *The La Varenne Cooking Course.* Work represented in anthologies, including *The Best of Gourmet* and *More of the Best from Bon Appetit.* Author of "Basics," a column in *Bon Appetit,* 1982-87; nationally syndicated food columnist, *Los Angeles Times* Syndicate, 1990—; food columnist, *Jerusalem Post,* 1990—. Contributor to magazines and newspapers.

WORK IN PROGRESS: A low-fat vegetarian menu book.

SIDELIGHTS: Faye Levy told *CA:* "I first went to Israel when I was seventeen on a six-week summer camp program. I fell in love with the land and the people, in more ways than one—it was on that trip that I met my future husband, Yakir Levy. My interest in cooking came about a year later, when Yakir and I decided to get married. My future mother-in-law was not at all happy with her son's choice, because I did not know how to cook. I decided I had better learn, and I did so by reading cookbooks and following the recipes. I was happy with the results and with the fact that a person like me, who had almost no previous knowledge of cooking, could follow a recipe and produce such delicious food.

"Over the next few years I became more and more intrigued with cooking and with cookbooks, and I decided to try to follow a career in this direction. I contacted Ruth Sirkis, the Julia Child of Israel, and asked to work as her assistant. She hired me and I learned how to write recipes from her. Later my husband and I decided to move to the United States and to visit Europe en route. Since it was clear that many of the best cookbook writers had studied in Paris, I thought it would be a fascinating thing to do. I enrolled in a six-week course at a new Parisian cooking school called La Varenne and soon after worked in exchange for the remaining courses in the program and earned the Grand Diplome of the first graduating class. I took extensive notes on everything the chefs said and how they cooked. On the basis of these notebooks, I became the school's recipe editor and then the cookbook editor. I authored the school's first cookbook and had a major part in researching and writing the school's award-winning cookbooks, *French Regional Cooking, The La Varenne Cooking Course,* and *Basic French Cookery.*"

BIOGRAPHICAL/CRITICAL SOURCES:

BOOKS

Burns, Jim, *Women Chefs,* Aris Books (Berkeley, CA), 1987.
Sims-Bell, Barbara, *Foodwork,* Advocacy Press (Santa Barbara, CA), 1993.

PERIODICALS

Los Angeles Herald Examiner, June 18, 1987.
New York Times, November 11, 1987.

LEWIS, Mervyn K(eith) 1941-

PERSONAL: Born June 20, 1941, in Adelaide, Australia; son of Norman Malcolm (a proofreader) and Valerie (a homemaker; maiden name, Way) Lewis; married Kay Judith Wiesner (a teacher), November 24, 1962; children: Stephanie Jane, Miranda Kay, Alexandra Kim, Antonia Louise. *Education:* University of Adelaide, B.Ec. (with first class honors), 1964, Ph.D., 1978. *Religion:* Church of England.

ADDRESSES: Home—Sarum Chase, 13 Rostrevor Rd., Stirling, South Australia 5152, Australia. *Office*—Department of Economics, University of Nottingham, University Park, Nottingham NG7 2RD, England.

CAREER: Elder Smith and Co. Ltd. (stock agents), Adelaide, Australia, clerk, 1957-58; Commonwealth Trading Bank of Australia, Adelaide, clerk, 1959-64; University of Adelaide, Adelaide, temporary lecturer, 1967, lecturer, 1967-73, senior lecturer, 1973-80, reader in economics, 1980-84; University of Nottingham, Nottingham, England, Midland Bank Professor of Money and Banking, 1985—, director, M.B.A. in Financial Studies, 1990—, member of investment committee. Kingston College of Advanced Education, chairman of finance committee, 1976-79, president of council and chairman of Working Party on Finance, 1978-79; visiting scholar at Bank of England, 1979-80; visiting professor at Flinders University and Cambridge University; member of joint interim committee of Kingston and Murray Park Colleges of Advanced Education.

MEMBER: Royal Economic Society, Academy of Social Sciences in Australia (fellow), Center for Pacific Basin Monetary and Economic Studies, Societe Universitaire Europeenne le Recherches Financieres, American Economic Association.

AWARDS, HONORS: Essay prize, Australian Institute of Bankers, 1963, for article "The Case for Flexible Bank Interest Rates."

WRITINGS:

EDITOR

(With K. T. Davis) *Australian Monetary Economics,* Longman Cheshire, 1981.
(With R. H. Wallace, and contributor) *Australia's Financial Institutions and Markets,* Longman Cheshire, 1985.

(With K. Dowd, and contributor) *Current Issues in Financial and Monetary Economics,* Macmillan (London), 1992.

(With Wallace, and contributor) *The Australian Financial System,* Longman Cheshire, 1993.

Financial Intermediaries, Edward Elger (Cheltenham, England), 1995.

(With Wallace, and contributor) *The Australian Financial System: Evolution, Policy and Practice,* Longman Cheshire, in press.

OTHER

(With Davis) *Monetary Policy in Australia,* Longman Cheshire (Melbourne, Australia), 1980.

(With M. J. Artis) *Monetary Control in the United Kingdom,* Philip Allan (Oxford, England), 1981.

(With Davis and John Foster) *A Member's Guide to Monetarism and Keynesianism,* Legislative Research Service, Parliament of the Commonwealth of Australia, 1983.

(With R. L. Carter and Brian Chiplin) *Personal Financial Markets: An Examination of the Evolving Markets for Personal Savings and Financing in the United Kingdom and the United States,* Philip Allan, 1986.

(With Davis) *Domestic and International Banking,* MIT Press (Cambridge, MA), 1987.

(With Artis) *Money in Britain,* Philip Allan, 1990.

Contributor to numerous books, including *The Australian Capital Market,* edited by R. R. Hirst and R. H. Wallace, Longman Cheshire, 1974; *Inflation and Unemployment: Theory, Experience, and Policymaking,* edited by Victor Argy and J. W. Nevile, Allen & Unwin, 1985; *International Bond Markets,* edited by D. Gowland, Croom Helm, 1991; *New Issues in Financial Services,* edited by R. Kinsella, 1992; *EMU after Maastricht: Transition or Revolution?,* edited by D. Currie and John D. Whitley, Lothian Foundation Press, 1995; and *Selected Readings on Australian Monetary Policy since Deregulation,* edited by M. Freebairn, Swinburne Institute of Technology Press, 1995. Contributor to economic and marketing journals. Coeditor of *Australian Economics Papers,* 1975-84; member of editorial board, *Review of Policy Issues.*

SIDELIGHTS: Mervyn K. Lewis told *CA:* "Financial market developments in the United States during the 1980s—often called the 'financial services revolution'—are most often portrayed by American authors as purely indigenous phenomena. Yet developments in the United Kingdom, Australia, and many other countries are strikingly similar. My recent books explore these parallel trends in terms of the impact of inflation and high interest rates, innovations in financial technology, and the growth of international banking. Working in both the United Kingdom and Australia, along with visits to the United States, helps me to keep abreast of worldwide trends."

M

MATHABANE, Mark 1960-

PERSONAL: First name originally Johannes; name changed, 1976; surname pronounced "mo-ta-bonny"; born in 1960, in Alexandra, South Africa; son of Jackson (a laborer) and Magdalene (a launderer; maiden name, Mabaso) Mathabane; married Gail Ernsberger (a writer), 1987; children: Bianca Ellen, Nathan Phillip, Stanley Arthur. *Education:* Attended Limestone College, 1978, St. Louis University, 1979, and Quincy College, 1981; Dowling College, B.A., 1983; attended Columbia University Graduate School of Journalism, 1984. *Politics:* Humanist, independent. *Religion:* Deist.

ADDRESSES: Home—341 Barrington Park Ln., Kernersville, NC 27284. *Agent*—c/o Kevin McShane, Fifi Oscard Agency, 24 West 40th St., New York, NY 10018.

CAREER: Writer and lecturer, 1985—.

MEMBER: Authors Guild, Writer's Workshop (Asheville, NC; board member).

AWARDS, HONORS: Christopher Award, 1986; nominated for Speaker of the Year Award, National Association of Campus Activities, 1993.

WRITINGS:

Kaffir Boy: The True Story of a Black Youth's Coming of Age in Apartheid South Africa, Macmillan (New York City), 1986, published as *Kaffir Boy: Growing out of Apartheid,* Bodley Head (London), 1987.

Kaffir Boy in America: An Encounter with Apartheid, Scribner (New York City), 1989.

(With wife, Gail Mathabane) *Love in Black and White: The Triumph of Love over Prejudice and Taboo,* HarperCollins (New York City), 1992.

African Women: Three Generations, HarperCollins, 1994.

ADAPTATIONS: Kaffir Boy, Dove Books on Tape, 1988.

SIDELIGHTS: "What television newscasts did to expose the horrors of the Vietnam War in the 1960s, books like *Kaffir Boy* may well do for the horrors of apartheid in the '80s," Diane Manuel determined in a *Chicago Tribune Book World* review of Mark Mathabane's first book. In his 1986 *Kaffir Boy: The True Story of a Black Youth's Coming of Age in Apartheid South Africa,* Mathabane recounts his life in the squalid black township of Alexandra, outside of Johannesburg, where he lived in dire poverty and constant fear until he seemingly miraculously received a scholarship to play tennis at an American college. *Washington Post Book World* critic Charles R. Larson called *Kaffir Boy* "violent and hard-hitting," and Peter Dreyer in the *Los Angeles Times Book Review* found Mathabane's autobiography "a book full of a young man's clumsy pride and sorrow, full of rage at the hideousness of circumstances, the unending destruction of human beings, [and] the systematic degradation of an entire society (and not only black South African society) in the name of a fantastic idea."

Mathabane explained to *CA* his reasons for writing *Kaffir Boy:* "During my senior year in college, I grew convinced that Americans did not understand what the term 'apartheid' meant in human terms. Other black South African students I met in the United States seemed afraid to speak out against apartheid for fear of endangering their families still trapped in South Africa. In my case, however, my urge to expose the horrors of apartheid outweighed my fear of reprisals by South Africa's terrorist regime. I felt compelled to sit down at my typewriter and try to explain to the world, and to myself, all the terrors, struggles, and deprivation I had survived. My friends called me mad for thinking I could write a book. My professors discouraged me from continuing. But once I started writing, the book possessed me wholly. I opened myself to remembering all the painful experiences I had forced myself to forget."

The Alexandra of *Kaffir Boy* is one of overwhelming poverty and deprivation, of incessant hunger, of horrific crimes committed by the government and citizen gangs, and of fear and humiliation. It is a township where one either spends hours at garbage dumps in search of scraps of food discarded by Johannesburg whites or resorts to prostitution to secure a meal—where "children grow up accepting violence and death as the norm," reflected Larson. Mathabane recounts an episode in which he is startled from sleep, terrified to find police breaking into his family's shanty in search of persons who emigrated illegally, as his parents had, from the "homelands," or tribal reserves. His father was imprisoned following one of these raids, and was repeatedly jailed after that. Mathabane recalls in *Kaffir Boy* that his parents "lived the lives of perpetual fugitives, fleeing by day and fleeing by night, making sure that they were never caught together under the same roof as husband and wife" because they lacked the paperwork that allowed them to live with their lawful spouses. His father was also imprisoned—at one time for more than a year with no contact with his family—for being unemployed, losing jobs as a laborer because he once again lacked the proper documents.

"Born and bred in a tribal reserve and nearly twice my mother's age," Mathabane wrote in *Kaffir Boy,* "my father existed under the illusion, formed as much by a strange innate pride as by a blindness to everything but his own will, that someday all white people would disappear from South Africa, and black people would revert to their old ways of living." Mathabane's father, who impressed upon his son tribal laws and customs, was constantly at odds with his wife, who was determined to see her son get an education. Mathabane's mother waited in lines at government offices for a year in order to obtain his birth certificate so that he could attend school, then worked as a launderer for a family of seventeen so that he could continue to study and, with luck, escape the hardships of life in Alexandra. His father burned his son's schoolbooks and ferociously beat his wife in response to her efforts, claiming that an education would only teach Mathabane to be subservient.

Yet those living in the urban ghettos near Johannesburg were more fortunate than people in the outlying "homelands," where black Africans are sent to resettle. "Nothing is more pathetic in this book than the author's description of a trip he takes with his father to the tribal reserve, ostensibly so that the boy will identify with the homelands," stated Larson. "The son, however, sees the land for what it really is—barren, burned out, empty of any meaning for his generation." In *Kaffir Boy* Mathabane depicts the desolation of the Venda tribal reserve as "mountainous, rugged and bone-dry, like a wasteland. . . . Everywhere I went nothing grew except near lavatories. . . . Occasionally I sighted a handful of scrawny cattle, goats and pigs grazing on the stubbles of dry bush. The scrawny animals, it turned out, were seldom slaughtered for food because they were being held as the people's wealth. Malnutrition was rampant, especially among the children." Larson further noted that "the episode backfires. The boy is determined to give up his father's tribal ways and acquire the white man's education."

Although Mathabane had the opportunity to obtain at least a primary education, he nevertheless contemplated suicide when he was only ten years old. "I found the burden of living in a ghetto, poverty-stricken and without hope, too heavy to shoulder," he confesses in his memoir. "I was weary of being hungry all the time, weary of being beaten all the time: at school, at home and in the streets. . . . I felt that life could never, would never, change from how it was for me." But his first encounter with apartheid sparked his determination to overcome the adversities.

His grandmother was a gardener for an English-speaking liberal white family, the Smiths, in an affluent suburb of Johannesburg. One day she took her grandson to work where he met Clyde Smith, an eleven-year-old schoolboy. "My teachers tell us that Kaffirs [blacks] can't read, speak or write English like white people because they have smaller brains, which are already full of tribal things," Smith told

Mathabane, the author recalled in his autobiography. "My teachers say you're not people like us, because you belong to a jungle civilization. That's why you can't live or go to school with us, but can only be our servants." Mathabane resolved to excel in school and even taught himself English—at a time when blacks were allowed to learn only tribal languages—through the comic books that his grandmother brought home from the Smith household. "I had to believe in myself and not allow apartheid to define my humanity," Mathabane points out.

Mrs. Smith also gave Mathabane an old wooden tennis racket. He taught himself to play, then obtained coaching. As he improved and fared well at tournaments, he gained recognition as a promising young athlete. In 1973 Mathabane attended a tennis tournament in South Africa where the American tennis pro Arthur Ashe publicly condemned apartheid. Ashe became Mathabane's hero and inspiration "because he was the first free black man I had ever seen," the author was quoted as saying in the *New York Times*. Mathabane eventually became one of the top South African players and made contacts with influential white tennis players who did not support apartheid. Stan Smith, another American tennis professional, befriended Mathabane, and urged him to apply for tennis scholarships to American schools. Mathabane indeed was awarded one, and *Kaffir Boy* ends with the author boarding a plane headed for South Carolina.

In Mathabane's imagination, the United States was nothing short of the promised land. His illusions quickly faded, however, once he settled into life at Limestone College. He was shocked to find that despite the lack of institutionalized segregation, blacks and whites kept company almost exclusively with those of their own race. Furthermore, he discovered that his serious approach to his studies and lack of interest in drugs and casual sex made him an outcast. He was ridiculed as a homosexual and labeled as one who had turned his back on his own race. These conditions forced Mathabane to transfer to several colleges before graduating.

After discovering the works of Richard Wright and other great black authors, he set his sights on a writing career and began work on *Kaffir Boy*. Yet even as he found a measure of success in the United States, he was tormented by the stories of his family's disintegration in strife-torn South Africa and the knowledge that for political reasons he would never be able to return. In 1989 he published an account of his life in the United States, entitled *Kaffir Boy in America: An Encounter with Apartheid*. This book contains his reflections on the racial divisions in his adopted country, his evolution as a writer, and his eventual reunion with his family, which took place on Oprah Winfrey's television show. Clarence Peterson, in a Chicago *Tribune Books* review, called *Kaffir Boy in America* a book "with a big heart." Lorna Hahn, writing in the *New York Times Book Review,* praised *Kaffir Boy in America* as "an inspiring account of a young man's self-realization and his commitment to the self-realization of others. It provides a better understanding of South Africa, of America—and of being human."

Mathabane had more to say in *Love in Black and White: The Triumph of Love over Prejudice and Taboo,* a book he coauthored with his wife, journalist Gail Ernsberger Mathabane. She is a white American raised in Ohio, Texas, and Minnesota, and the couple has encountered much resistance to their relationship since they met. When they married after a two-year courtship, they did so with profound awareness of the struggle they were taking on as an interracial couple. Their book is both an account of their personal relationship and an examination of interracial marriage in general. "The Mathabanes write well of the sweet, nervous, first days of their love, and they don't flinch from the bad stuff," noted Hettie Jones in the *Washington Post Book World*. She concluded that the Mathabanes' account proves that "all it takes is love, and defending yourself at nearly every turn." Elizabeth Stapler, writing in the *Christian Science Monitor,* pronounced the book "an excellent resource on a subject too long neglected."

Mathabane has said that in order to cope with the difficulties in his life, he strives to cultivate the feminine side of himself because he believes women have greater emotional strength than men. In 1994 he paid tribute to three strong women who greatly influenced him: his mother, sister, and grandmother. Their life stories are related in *African Women: Three Generations*. The narrative shows that although much has changed over the years, still more has remained the same for African women, who are regarded primarily as a source of income and offspring. According to *Washington Post Book World* reviewer Eddy L. Harris, "Mathabane's book reveals the dignity and strength with which women have faced a long-suffering plight and the slow evolution out of it. Now we wait to see what hope the new order of equality will offer the men and women of South Africa, and what lessons have been learned from the lives of African women such as these." Veronica Chambers, reviewing the book for the *New York Times Book Review,* found the three women interesting but did not care for Mathabane's rendering of their stories: "we are always kept at arm's length," she wrote, adding that Mathabane "ultimately condescends" to his subjects. Elizabeth Levitan Spaid commented in the *Christian Science Monitor,* however, that *African Women* "is the kind of book that is difficult to put down, because the women bring the reader into their world quickly, candidly, and vividly."

Although he admits to feeling a great deal of anger and bitterness over conditions in his homeland and racism everywhere, Mathabane commented in the *New York Times:* "If I can turn that anger into something positive, I really am in a very good position to go on with my life." Now he lectures, taking his books "as a springboard to talk about apartheid in human terms." He does want to return to South Africa someday, with hopes of inspiring "other boys and girls into believing that you can still grow up to be as much of an individual as you have the capacity to be," Mathabane was quoted in another article in the *New York Times.* "That is my dream."

Mathabane further explained to *CA* his reasons for writing: "I still base my writing on my convictions, on what James Baldwin called 'the fire in the belly.' I believe that all powerful, moving writing must be totally honest and based on getting at the gist of life's eternal truths. Currently, my writing springs from my strong belief that all of us—regardless of race, gender, creed, or ethnic origin—share a common humanity. I hope my writing and speaking will inspire people to heal the racial divide, respect and celebrate individual differences, communicate better and with more open minds, and work toward building a nation in which diversity is an asset and everyone feels included and valued."

BIOGRAPHICAL/CRITICAL SOURCES:

BOOKS

Mathabane, Mark, *Kaffir Boy: The True Story of a Black Youth's Coming of Age in Apartheid South Africa,* Macmillan, 1986.
Mathabane, Mark, *Kaffir Boy in America: An Encounter with Apartheid,* Scribner, 1989.
Mathabane, Mark, and Gail Mathabane, *Love in Black and White: The Triumph of Love over Prejudice and Taboo,* HarperCollins, 1992.
Mathabane, Mark, *African Women: Three Generations,* HarperCollins, 1994.

PERIODICALS

Chicago Tribune Book World, April 13, 1986.
Christian Science Monitor, May 2, 1986; June 16, 1992, p. 13; April 25, 1994, p. 15.
Los Angeles Times Book Review, March 30, 1986.
New Statesman and Society, March 10, 1995, p. 37.
Newsweek, March 9, 1992.
New York Times, March 2, 1987; September 14, 1987.
New York Times Book Review, April 27, 1986; December 21, 1986, p. 19; March 19, 1987; August 13, 1989, p. 19; July 29, 1990, p. 32; February 16, 1992, p. 18; July 31, 1994, p. 25.
People, July 7, 1986.
Publishers Weekly, February 28, 1986, p. 111; April 28, 1989, p. 66; July 13, 1990, p. 52; December 6, 1991, p. 65.
Time, November 12, 1990, pp. 16-19.
Times Literary Supplement, August 21, 1987.
Tribune Books (Chicago), August 19, 1990, p. 8.
Washington Post Book World, April 20, 1986; May 18, 1989, pp. 3, 11; August 19, 1990, p. 12; February 16, 1992, pp. 1, 10; July 10, 1994, p. 4.

*   *   *

McINTYRE, W(illiam) David   1932-

PERSONAL: Born September 4, 1932, in Hucknall, England; son of John (a minister) and Alice Muriel (Stallard) McIntyre; married Marion Jean Hillyard, December 14, 1957 (died June 20, 1993); married Helen Marcia King, October 16, 1995; children: (first marriage) Jefferson John, Benjamin James, Ruth Margaret, Marcus Edwin, James Maurice. *Education:* Peterhouse, Cambridge, B.A., 1955, M.A., 1959; University of Washington, Seattle, M.A., 1956; School of Oriental and African Studies, London, Ph.D., 1959. *Politics:* "Floating voter." *Religion:* Presbyterian. *Avocational interests:* Architectural history, photographing buildings, cities and railways, reading detective stories.

ADDRESSES: Office—University of Canterbury, Private Bag 4800, Christchurch, New Zealand.

CAREER: University of Nottingham, Nottingham, England, assistant lecturer, 1959-61, lecturer in history, 1961-65; University of Canterbury, Christchurch, New Zealand, professor of history, 1966—, head of department, 1986-96. Occasional broadcaster and commentator on defense and foreign policy issues. Member of executive committee, Paton Theological College, Nottingham, 1963-66. Member of advisory committee, historical branch, New Zealand Department of Internal Affairs, 1967-73, 1988-91, 1995—. *Military service:* British Army, Royal Corps of Signals, 1950-52, became second lieutenant; Territorial Army, 1952-60, became lieutenant.

MEMBER: Royal Commonwealth Society, New Zealand Institute of International Affairs (vice-chair, Christchurch branch, 1967-70), Canterbury Historical Association (president, 1967).

AWARDS, HONORS: Order of the British Empire, 1992.

WRITINGS:

Colonies into Commonwealth, Blandford (Dorset, England), 1966, 3rd edition, 1974, Walker (New York City), 1967.

The Imperial Frontier in the Tropics, 1865-1875, St. Martin's (New York City), 1967.

Britain, New Zealand and the Security of Southeast Asia in the 1970s, New Zealand Institute of International Affairs, 1969.

Neutralism, Non-Alignment and New Zealand, University of New Zealand Press, 1969.

Britain and the Commonwealth since 1907, Heinemann (Melbourne, Australia), 1970.

(With W. J. Gardner) *Speeches and Documents on New Zealand History,* Clarendon Press (Oxford, England), 1971.

The Commonwealth of Nations, 1869-1971: Origins and Impact, University of Minnesota Press (Minneapolis, MN), 1977.

The Rise and Fall of the Singapore Naval Base, 1919-1942, Macmillan (London), 1979.

The Journal of Henry Sewell, 1853-1857, two volumes, Whitcoulls (London), 1980.

(With Len Richardson) *Provincial Perspectives,* University of Canterbury Press (Christchurch, New Zealand), 1981.

New Zealand Prepares for War, 1919-39, University of Canterbury Press, 1988.

The Significance of the Commonwealth 1965-1990, Macmillan, 1991.

Background of the Anzus Pact 1945-1955, Macmillan, 1995.

Contributor to books, including *Malaysia: A Survey,* edited by Wang Gungwu, Pall Mall, 1964; *Australia, New Zealand, and the South Pacific: A Handbook,* Blond (London), 1970; *New Zealand in World Affairs,* edited by A. McIntosh and others, New Zealand Institute of International Affairs, 1977; *New Directions in New Zealand Foreign Policy,* edited by H. Gold, Benton Ross, 1985; *The Oxford Companion to the Second World War,* Oxford University Press (Oxford, England), 1995; and *The Oxford History of the British Empire,* Oxford University Press, in press. Contributor to history, American studies, and international affairs journals. Area organizer for the South Pacific, *Historical Abstracts,* 1966-94.

WORK IN PROGRESS: British Decolonization.

*   *   *

McMAHON, Pat
See HOCH, Edward D(entinger)

*   *   *

MEISLER, Stanley   1931-

PERSONAL: Born May 14, 1931, in New York, NY; son of Meyer (a paperhanger) and Jean (Wolf) Meisler; married Gloria Greenwood, September 28, 1960 (divorced, 1970); married Susan Mitchell, April 15, 1973 (divorced, 1978); married Elizabeth Russell Fox, January 21, 1984; children: (first marriage) Sarah (deceased), Samuel, Joshua; (second marriage) Michael, Michele; (third marriage) Gabriel, Jenaro. *Education:* City College (now of the City University of New York), B.A., 1952; further study at University of California, Berkeley, 1952 and 1961. *Religion:* Jewish.

ADDRESSES: Home—5403 Cromwell Dr., Bethesda, MD 20816-2007. *Office*—*Los Angeles Times,* 1875 I St. NW, Suite 1100, Washington, DC 20006-5482.

CAREER: Middletown Journal, Middletown, OH, writer, 1953-54; Associated Press, New York City, correspondent in New Orleans, LA, 1954-57, and Washington, DC, 1958-64; U.S. Peace Corps,

Washington, DC, evaluation officer, 1964-66, deputy director of Office of Evaluation and Research, 1966-67; *Los Angeles Times,* Los Angeles, CA, correspondent in Nairobi, Kenya, 1967-73, Mexico City, Mexico, 1973-76, Madrid, Spain, 1976-78, Toronto, Ontario, 1978-83, Paris, France, 1983-88, Washington, DC, 1988-90, Barcelona, Spain, 1990, United Nations, 1991—. Consultant, Times Mirror Center, 1990-95; adjunct professor of journalism, Columbia University, 1993—.

MEMBER: United Nations Correspondents Association.

AWARDS, HONORS: Ford Foundation fellow, 1962-63; Korn-Ferry Award, Business Council of the United Nations, 1992 and 1994.

WRITINGS:

United Nations: The First Fifty Years, Atlantic Monthly Press (New York City), 1995.

Contributor to *Africa's Media Image,* 1992, and of articles to *Atlantic, Foreign Affairs, Smithsonian Magazine, Columbia Journalism Review, Progressive, Nation,* and other publications.

SIDELIGHTS: Writing in the *New York Times Book Review* of Stanley Meisler's book *United Nations: The First Fifty Years,* David Callahan finds it to be "an account sprinkled with rich anecdotes and colorful portraits." Callahan believes that in "summing up the record, Mr. Meisler rightly observes that the effectiveness of the United Nations has hinged on strong American leadership."

BIOGRAPHICAL/CRITICAL SOURCES:

PERIODICALS

New York Times Book Review, October 15, 1995, p. 25.

*   *   *

MERWIN, W(illiam) S(tanley)   1927-

PERSONAL: Born September 30, 1927, in New York, NY; son of a Presbyterian minister; grew up in Union City, NJ, and Scranton, PA; married; wife's name, Paula. *Education:* Princeton University, A.B., 1947, one year of graduate study in modern languages.

ADDRESSES: Home—Haiku, HI. *Agent*—c/o Atheneum Publishers, 866 Third Ave., New York, NY 10022-6221.

CAREER: Poet. Tutor in France and Portugal, 1949; tutor of Robert Graves's son in Majorca, 1950; lived in London, England, 1951-54, supporting himself largely by doing translations of Spanish and French classics for the British Broadcasting Corporation Third Programme; returned to the United States in 1956 to write plays for the Poets' Theatre, Cambridge, MA; associated with Roger Planchon's Theatre de la Cite, Lyons, France, ten months, 1964-65.

MEMBER: National Institute of Arts and Letters.

AWARDS, HONORS: Kenyon Review fellowship in poetry, 1954; Rockefeller fellowship, 1956; National Institute of Arts and Letters grant, 1957; Arts Council of Great Britain playwriting bursary, 1957; Rabinowitz Foundation grant, 1961; Bess Hokin Prize, *Poetry* magazine, 1962; Ford Foundation grant, 1964-65; fellowship, Chapelbrook Foundation, 1966; Harriet Monroe Memorial Prize, *Poetry,* 1967; PEN translation prize, 1968; Rockefeller Foundation grant, 1969; Pulitzer Prize for poetry, 1971, for *The Carrier of Ladders;* fellowship, Academy of American Poets, 1973; Guggenheim fellowship, 1973, 1983; Shelley Memorial Award, 1974; Bollingen Prize for poetry, Yale University Library, 1979; Lenore Marshall Poetry Prize, 1994; Tanning Prize, Academy of American Poets, 1994, for outstanding and proven mastery in poetry.

WRITINGS:

POETRY

A Mask for Janus (also see below), Yale University Press (New Haven, CT), 1952.
The Dancing Bears (also see below), Yale University Press, 1954.
Green with Beasts (also see below), Knopf (New York City), 1956.
The Drunk in the Furnace (also see below), Macmillan (New York City), 1960.
(Editor) *West Wind: Supplement of American Poetry,* Poetry Book Society (London), 1961.
The Moving Target (also see below), Atheneum (New York City), 1963.
Collected Poems, Atheneum, 1966.
The Lice (also see below), Atheneum, 1969.

Animae, Kayak (Santa Cruz, CA), 1969.

The Carrier of Ladders (also see below), Atheneum, 1970.

(With A. D. Moore) *Signs,* Stone Wall Press (Washington, DC), 1970.

Asian Figures, Atheneum, 1973.

Writings to an Unfinished Accompaniment (also see below), Atheneum, 1973.

The First Four Books of Poems (contains *A Mask for Janus, The Dancing Bears, Green with Beasts,* and *The Drunk in the Furnace*), Atheneum, 1975.

The Compass Flower, Atheneum, 1977.

Feathers from the Hill, Windhover (New York City), 1978.

Finding the Islands, North Point Press (Berkeley, CA), 1982.

Opening the Hand, Atheneum, 1983.

The Rain in the Trees, Knopf, 1988.

Selected Poems, Atheneum, 1988.

The Second Four Books of Poems (includes *The Moving Target, The Lice, The Carrier of Ladders,* and *Writings to an Unfinished Accompaniment*), Copper Canyon Press (Port Townsend, WA), 1993.

Travels: Poems, Knopf, 1993.

Contributor to numerous anthologies.

PLAYS

(With Dido Milroy) *Darkling Child,* produced, 1956.

Favor Island, produced in Cambridge, MA, at Poets' Theatre, 1957, and on British Broadcasting Corporation Third Programme, 1958.

The Gilded West, produced in Coventry, England, at Belgrade Theatre, 1961.

TRANSLATOR

The Poem of the Cid, Dent, 1959, New American Library (New York City), 1962.

(Contributor) Eric Bentley, editor, *The Classic Theatre,* Doubleday (New York City), 1961.

The Satires of Persius, Indiana University Press (Bloomington), 1961.

Some Spanish Ballads, Abelard, 1961, also published as *Spanish Ballads,* Doubleday Anchor (New York City), 1961.

The Life of Lazarillo de Tormes: His Fortunes and Adversities, Doubleday Anchor, 1962.

(Contributor) *Medieval Epics,* Modern Library (New York City), 1963.

(With Denise Levertov, William Carlos Williams, and others) Nicanor Parra, *Poems and Antipoems,* New Directions, 1968.

Jean Follain, *Transparence of the World,* Atheneum, 1969.

W. S. Merwin: Selected Translations, 1948-1968, Atheneum, 1969.

(And author of introduction) S. Chamfort, *Products of the Perfected Civilization: Selected Writings of Chamfort,* Macmillan, 1969.

Antonio Porchia, *Voices: Selected Writings of Antonio Porchia,* Follett, 1969, revised and enlarged edition published as *Voices: Aphorisms,* Knopf, 1988.

Pablo Neruda, *Twenty Poems and a Song of Despair,* Cape (London), 1969, parallel Spanish and English edition published as *Twenty Love Poems and a Song of Despair,* Chronicle Books (San Francisco), 1993.

(With others) Pablo Neruda, *Selected Poems,* Dell (New York City), 1970.

(With Clarence Brown) Osip Mandelstam, *Selected Poems,* Oxford University Press (New York City), 1973, Atheneum, 1974.

(With J. Moussaieff Mason) *Sanskrit Love Poetry,* Columbia University Press (New York City), 1977, published as *The Peacock's Egg: Love Poems from Ancient India,* North Point Press, 1981, published in limited edition as *Sanskrit Love Poems,* E. Alkazi (London), 1987.

Roberto Juarroz, *Vertical Poems,* Kayak, 1977.

(With George E. Dimock, Jr.) Euripides, *Iphigenia at Aulius,* Oxford University Press, 1978.

Selected Translations, 1968-1978, Atheneum, 1979.

Robert the Devil, Windhover, 1981.

(And author of foreword) *Four French Plays,* Atheneum, 1985.

(And author of foreword) *From the Spanish Morning,* Atheneum, 1985.

(With Soiku Shigematsu) Muso Soseki, *Sun at Midnight: 23 Poems* (limited edition with woodcuts by Antonio Frasconi), Nadja (New York City), 1985.

Juarroz, *Vertical Poetry* (selections in English and Spanish), North Point Press, 1988.

(With Shigematsu) Soseki, *Sun at Midnight: Poems and Sermons,* North Point Press, 1989.

(With Langston Hughes) *Blood Wedding* and *Yerma,* Theatre Communications Group (New York City), 1994.

Also translator of "Eufemia," by Lope de Rueda, in *Tulane Drama Review,* December, 1958; "Crispin," by Lesage, in *Tulane Drama Review;* and *Punishment without Vengeance,* by Lope Felix de Vega Carpio, 1958.

OTHER

The Miner's Pale Children (prose), Atheneum, 1970.

Houses and Travellers (prose), Atheneum, 1977.

Unframed Originals: Recollections (prose), Atheneum, 1982.

Regions of Memory: Uncollected Prose, 1949-82 (prose), University of Illinois Press (Urbana), 1987.

(Selector and author of introduction) Sir Thomas Wyatt, *The Essential Wyatt,* Ecco Press (New York City), 1989.

Poets in Person: W. S. Merwin with James Richardson (sound recording), Modern Poetry Association (Chicago), 1991.

The Lost Upland (short story trilogy; contains "Foie Gras," "Shepherds," and "Blackbird's Summer"), Knopf, 1992.

Contributor to magazines, including *Nation, Harper's, Poetry, New Yorker, Atlantic Monthly, Kenyon Review,* and *Evergreen Review.* Poetry editor, *Nation,* 1962.

The W. S. Merwin Archive in the Rare Book Room of the University Library of the University of Illinois at Urbana-Champaign contains notes, drafts, and manuscripts of published and unpublished work by Merwin from the mid-1940s to the early 1980s.

SIDELIGHTS: W. S. Merwin is a major American writer whose poetry, translations and prose have attracted attention from literary critics since the publication of his first book, *A Mask for Janus,* in 1952. The spare verse comprising the body of Merwin's work has been characterized by many as very difficult reading. Some critics find Merwin's poetry worth whatever extra effort may be required to appreciate it, as does *Yale Review* critic Laurence Lieberman: "This poetry, at its best—and at our best as readers—is able to meet us and engage our wills as never before in the thresholds between waking and sleeping, past and future, self and anti-self, men and gods, the living and the dead." Although Merwin's writing has undergone many stylistic changes through the course of his career, it is unified by the recurring theme of man's separation from nature. The poet sees the consequences of that alienation as disastrous, both for the human race and for the rest of the world. In an interview with *CA,* Merwin affirmed his strong feelings about ecological issues, saying, "It makes me angry to feel that the natural world is taken to have so little importance." He gave an example from his own life: "The Pennsylvania

that I grew up in and loved as a child isn't there . . . it's been strip-mined: it really is literally not there. This happens to a lot of people, but I don't see why one has to express indifference about it. It matters. . . . It's like being told that you can't possibly be mentally healthy."

Merwin's despair over the desecration of nature is strongly expressed in his 1969 collection *The Lice.* "If there is any book today that has perfectly captured the peculiar spiritual agony of our time, the agony of a generation which knows itself to be the last, and has transformed that agony into great art, it is W. S. Merwin's *The Lice,* " writes Lieberman. "To read these poems is an act of self-purification. Every poem in the book pronounces a judgement against modern men—the gravest sentence the poetic imagination can conceive for man's withered and wasted conscience: our sweep of history adds up to one thing only, a moral vacuity that is absolute and irrevocable." His obsession with the meaning of America and its values makes Merwin like the great nineteenth-century poet Walt Whitman, argues L. Edwin Folsom in *Shenandoah.* "Merwin's answer to Whitman is begun in *The Lice,* an anti-song of the self. Here, instead of the Whitmanian self expanding and absorbing everything, naming it in an ecstasy of union, we find a self stripped of meaning, unable to expand, in a landscape that refuses to unite with the self, refuses to be assimilated, in a place alien and unnameable. . . . Instead of expanding his senses, like Whitman, and intensifying his touch, sight, hearing, so that he could contain the multitudes around him, Merwin's senses . . . crumble and fade, become useless. . . . All that is left is silence. . . . Whitman's self sought to contain all, to embody past, present, and future; Merwin's self seeks to contain nothing, to empty itself of a dead past."

Merwin received the Pulitzer Prize in 1971 for his collection *The Carrier of Ladders.* Richard Howard in the *Nation* comments: "Merwin's seventh book of poems is of course his best—of course, because he has made his career what the word means: a course, a passage out, with just those overtones of self-overcoming which bring this book, so rewardingly, in the home-stretch." Denis Donoghue in the *New York Review of Books* argues that "we are to suppose a speaker of these poems, long accustomed to recitations of the beautiful, who is on the brink of discovering that beauty has nothing to do with truth. . . . They are not messages, swiftly delivered from poet to reader, but tokens of fracture; the only hope is to begin again with a recovered ABC of feeling." John

Vernon writes in *Western Humanities Review* that "Merwin has more good poems in [*The Carrier of Ladders*] than most poets manage to accumulate in two or three books." Vernon argues that Merwin's poems are not difficult in a scholarly sense—the problem is the jaded ear of the modern reader: "These are some of the most unacademic poems I have ever read, in the sense that they could never be discussed in a university classroom, since they have no 'meaning' in any usual sense. . . . I think of what Samuel Beckett said about [James Joyce's] *Finnegans Wake:* we are too decadent to read this. That is, we are so used to a language that is flattened out and hollowed out, that is slavishly descriptive, that when we encounter a language as delicately modulated and as finely sensual as this, it is like trying to read braille with boxing gloves on."

The poetic forms of many eras and societies are the foundation for a great deal of Merwin's poetry. According to Vernon Young in *American Poetry Review,* the poems are traceable to "Biblical tales, Classical myth, love songs from the Age of Chivalry, Renaissance retellings; they comprise carols, roundels, odes, ballads, sestinas, and they contrive golden equivalents of emblematic models: the masque, the Zodiac, the Dance of Death." Merwin's versions are so perfectly rendered, says Young, that "were you to redistribute these poems, unsigned, among collections of translated material or of English Poetry Down the Ages, any but the most erudite reader would heedlessly accept them as renderings of Theocritus, Catullus, Ronsard. . . . No stanzaic model was alien to him; no line length was beyond his dexterity." Eric Hartley also comments on the importance of Merwin's background in the *Dictionary of Literary Biography:* "From the first of his career as a poet, Merwin has steeped himself in other cultures and other literary traditions, and he has been praised as a translator. This eclectic background has given him a sense of the presence of the past, of timelessness in time, that comes across emphatically in his poetry. Without some understanding of this background the reader cannot fully appreciate Merwin's poetry. Moreover, without such appreciation one cannot comprehend the thrust of Merwin's poetic and philosophical development."

In 1992, Merwin's semiautobiographical short-story collection *The Lost Upland* also evoked high praise from some reviewers. The stories are set in the Dordogne River valley in southwestern France, an agricultural region where Merwin lived for some time. In *The Lost Upland,* Merwin speaks of the ancient way of life he encountered and the gradual modernization that was changing the area. "Foie Gras" relates the schemes of a penniless nobleman; "Shepherds" tells of an American writer who came to the region and slowly worked his way into the social tapestry there; and "Blackbird's Summer" describes an aging vintner's fruitless search for someone to carry on the time-honored traditions of his business. "As a writer who has specialized in ferreting out hidden regions of both the mythic and the material worlds, Mr. Merwin is eminently qualified to guide us to yet another place he has discovered," states Ginger Danto in the *New York Times Book Review.* Danto finds that at times, Merwin's great love for his subject matter seems to encumber his writing: "Precisely because he invests so much—knowledge, passion and everything else that in his fertile memory must be accounted for—the stories seem overburdened." Yet she praises the character portraits Merwin draws, the sense of timelessness he evokes, and his skill in making a small incident seem extraordinarily meaningful. She singles out "Shepherds" as the best of the three stories, one that reveals "the agile eloquence of an impassioned poet." Chicago *Tribune Books* reviewer Richard Stern credits *The Lost Upland* with exhibiting "an accuracy, concision, humor and beauty of observation and expression that will advance [Merwin's] reputation." Writing in the *Los Angeles Times Book Review,* Richard Eder praises Merwin's prose as "open, lively and inveigling; poetry works inside it as an invisible discipline, making a potent phrase an irreplaceable one."

In 1993, Merwin published his nineteenth collection of poetry, entitled *Travels: Poems.* In a *New York Times Book Review* article, Tom Sleigh calls Merwin's *Travels* "sturdily written [and] extraordinarily entertaining as tales." The verses in the collection were inspired by the poet's journeys around the world; as usual, they incorporate his ecological and social concerns into his descriptions of the regions he visited. The poems frequently relate tales Merwin imagined during his travels. The protagonists of his stories are most often displaced characters who are transformed by their new surroundings—for example, a European rubber tapper who becomes a shaman in a native tribe. "This eccentric gallery of portraits and dramatic monologues provides the poet with subjects rich in human incident and historical reflection," comments Sleigh. "Such material could have degenerated into predictable political allegory (imperialism is bad!). . . . [*Travels*] represents Mr. Merwin doing superbly well what much contemporary poetry attempts to do, but fails. He reveals, with great formal intelligence, the eerie interconnectedness of evil and the minutiae of our day-to-day lives." Judith Kitchen notes in a *Georgia Review* essay that *Travels* is "permeated by a healthy nostalgia for what has been lost to us—a sense of history, an identification with place, a connection between generations, the old forms in art. Everything is seen as though through the window of a passing train, briefly illuminated and then receding into the world of memory." *Poetry* reviewer Ben Howard also remarks on the "mood of regret and the tone of unrequited longing" in the collection. Describing Merwin's imagery as "dense, sensuous, and exact," Howard judges the verses in *Travels* to be among the poet's best work. David St. John, a contributor to the *Los Angeles Times Book Review,* asserts that *Travels* is "one of the most beautiful and moving collections of poetry of [Merwin's] career . . . a book of deep historical resonance and luminous poetic grace. . . . Merwin continues to earn his place as one of our most influential and compelling contemporary poets."

In response to certain literary critics attempting to place Merwin within the group known as the oracular poets, Merwin told *CA:* "I have not evolved an abstract aesthetic theory and am not aware of belonging to any particular group of writers. I neither read nor write much criticism, and think of its current vast proliferation chiefly as a symptom, inseparable from other technological substitutions. . . . I imagine that a society whose triumphs one after the other emerge as new symbols of death, and that feeds itself by poisoning the earth, may be expected, even while it grows in strength and statistics, to soothe its fears with trumpery hopes, refer to nihilism as progress, dismiss the private authority of the senses as it has cashiered belief, and of course find the arts exploitable but unsatisfying."

Merwin added: "I started writing hymns for my father almost as soon as I could write at all, illustrating them. I recall some rather stern little pieces addressed, in a manner I was familiar with, to backsliders, but I can remember too wondering whether there might not be some more liberating mode. In Scranton there was an anthology of *Best Loved Poems of the American People* in the house, which seemed for a time to afford some clues. But the first real writers that held me were not poets: [Joseph] Conrad first, and then [Leo] Tolstoy, and it was not until I had received a scholarship and gone away to the univer-

sity that I began to read poetry steadily and try incessantly, and with abiding desperation, to write it. I was not a satisfactory student; . . . I spent most of my time either in the university library, or riding in the country: I had discovered that the polo and ROTC stables were full of horses with no one to exercise them. I believe I was not noticeably respectful either of the curriculum and its evident purposes, nor of several of its professors, and I was saved from the thoroughly justified impatience of the administration, as I later learned, by the intercessions of R. P. Blackmur, who thought I needed a few years at the place to pick up what education I might be capable of assimilating, and I did in fact gain a limited but invaluable acquaintance with a few modern languages. While I was there, John Berryman, Herman Broch, and Blackmur himself, helped me, by example as much as by design, to find out some things about writing; of course it was years before I began to realize just what I had learned, and from whom . . . . Writing is something I know little about; less at some times than at others. I think, though, that so far as it is poetry it is a matter of correspondences: one glimpses them, pieces of an order, or thinks one does, and tries to convey the sense of what one has seen to those to whom it may matter, including, if possible, one's self."

BIOGRAPHICAL/CRITICAL SOURCES:

BOOKS

Brunner, Edward, *Poetry as Labor and Privilege: The Writings of W. S. Merwin,* University of Illinois Press, 1991.

Byers, Thomas B., *What I Cannot Say: Self, Word, and World in Whitman, Stevens, and Merwin,* University of Illinois Press, 1989.

Christhilf, Mark, *W. S. Merwin, the Mythmaker,* University of Missouri Press (Columbia), 1986.

Contemporary Literary Criticism, Gale (Detroit), Volume 1, 1973, Volume 2, 1974, Volume 3, 1975, Volume 5, 1976, Volume 8, 1978, Volume 13, 1980, Volume 18, 1981, Volume 45, 1987; Volume 88, 1995.

Dickey, James, *Babel to Byzantium,* Farrar, Straus (New York City), 1968.

Dictionary of Literary Biography, Volume 5: *American Poets since World War II,* Gale, 1980.

Hoeppner, Edward Haworth, *Echoes and Moving Fields: Structure and Subjectivity in the Poetry of W. S. Merwin and John Ashbery,* Bucknell University Press (Lewisburg, PA), 1994.

Howard, Richard, *Alone with America: Essays on the Art of Poetry in the United States since 1950,* Atheneum, 1969.

Hungerford, Edward, *Poets in Progress,* Northwestern University Press, 1962.

Nelson, Cary, and Ed Folsom, editors, *W. S. Merwin: Essays on the Poetry,* University of Illinois Press, 1987.

Rexroth, Kenneth, *With Eye and Ear,* Herder, 1970.

Rexroth, *American Poetry in the Twentieth Century,* Herder, 1971.

Rosenthal, M. L., *The Modern Poets: A Critical Introduction,* Oxford University Press, 1960.

Shaw, Robert B., editor, *American Poetry since 1960: Some Critical Perspectives,* Dufour (Chester Springs, PA), 1974.

Stepanchev, Stephen, *American Poetry since 1945,* Harper (New York City), 1965.

PERIODICALS

America, January 29, 1983, pp. 75-76; November 13, 1993, pp. 18-19.

American Poetry Review, January-February, 1978; September-October, 1985, pp. 14-21.

Antioch Review, summer, 1984, pp. 363-74.

Chicago Tribune Book World, December 26, 1982.

Concerning Poetry, spring, 1975.

Exquisite Corpse, May-July, 1984, p. 16.

Furioso, spring, 1953.

Georgia Review, fall, 1993, pp. 582-85.

Hudson Review, winter, 1967-68; summer, 1973.

Los Angeles Times, August 21, 1983.

Los Angeles Times Book Review, August 21, 1983, p. 3; March 22, 1992, pp. 3, 9; December 27, 1992, pp. 2, 9.

Midwest Quarterly, spring, 1986, pp. 277-93.

Modern Age, spring, 1979, pp. 167-77.

Modern Poetry Studies, winter, 1975.

Mundus Artium, Volumes 12-13, 1980-81, pp. 12-14.

Nation, December 14, 1970.

New Mexico Quarterly, autumn, 1964.

New York Review of Books, May 6, 1971; September 20, 1973.

New York Times Book Review, October 18, 1970; June 19, 1977; August 1, 1982, pp. 7, 29; October 9, 1983; July 31, 1988, p. 20; March 29, 1992, pp. 14-15; May 23, 1993, p. 15.

Ontario Review, fall-winter, 1977-78.

Partisan Review, summer, 1958; winter, 1971-72.

Poetry, May, 1953; May, 1961; February, 1963; June, 1964; August, 1974; December, 1984, pp. 167-69; January, 1989, pp. 237-40; December, 1993, pp. 167-70.

Prairie Schooner, fall, 1957; fall, 1962; winter, 1962-63; fall, 1968; winter, 1971-72.

Sewanee Review, spring, 1974.

Shenandoah, spring, 1968; winter, 1970; spring, 1978.

Southern Review, April, 1980.

Southwest Review, winter, 1983, pp. 92-93.

Tribune Books (Chicago), March 29, 1992.

Village Voice, July 4, 1974.

Virginia Quarterly Review, summer, 1973; spring, 1983, p. 62.

Voices, January-April, 1953; May-August, 1957; September-December, 1961.

Wall Street Journal, January 3, 1983, pp. 22.

Washington Post Book World, August 31, 1975; September 18, 1977; August 15, 1982; June 3, 1984.

Western Humanities Review, spring, 1970; spring, 1971.

Western Review, spring, 1955.

World Literature Today, winter, 1984, p. 105; winter, 1985, p. 94; July, 1993, pp. 134-51.

Yale Review, summer, 1961; summer, 1968; summer, 1973.

OTHER

DISCovering Authors Modules (CD-ROM product), Gale (Detroit), 1996.

Poets in Person: W. S. Merwin with James Richardson (sound recording), Modern Poetry Association (Chicago), 1991.*

*   *   *

MIDDLETON, Michael (Humfrey)   1917-

PERSONAL: Born December 1, 1917, in London, England; son of Humfrey (a surveyor) and L. Irene (in publishing; maiden name, Tillard) Middleton; married Julie Harrison, April 10, 1954; children: Humfrey Hugo Sebastian, Kate Augusta Middleton Ellison, Rose Irene Middleton Yates. *Education:* Attended school in Canterbury, England.

ADDRESSES: Home—84 Sirdar Rd., London W11 4EG, England. *Agent*—John Johnson Ltd., 45-47 Clerkenwell Green, London EC1R 0HT, England.

CAREER: Picture Post, London, England, assistant editor and art director, 1949-53; *Lilliput,* London, editor, 1953-54; *House and Garden,* London, editor,

1955-57; Civic Trust, London, deputy director, 1957-69, director, 1969-86; writer, lecturer, consultant, 1986—. Director-general for the United Kingdom, European Architectural Heritage Year, 1975; member of United Kingdom Commission for UNESCO, 1976-78.

MEMBER: Royal Institute of British Architects (honorary fellow), Society of Registered Designers (fellow), Landscape Institute (honorary fellow).

AWARDS, HONORS: John Grierson Award for best short film, British Federation of Film Societies, 1971, for *A Future for the Past*; Silver Wheat-Ear Trophy from Seventh Berlin International Film Festival, First Prize from Fourth Festival of Architectural Films and Eleventh Congress International Union of Architects, Premier Award from British and Scientific Film Association Construction Films Competition, and Silver Award from British Industrial Film Festival, all 1972, all for *A Future for the Past*; Commander of Order of the British Empire, 1975; *Europa Nostra* received the premier award in the United Kingdom Heritage Year Film Awards, 1975; Pro Merito Medal, Council of Europe, 1976.

WRITINGS:

Group Practice in Design, Architectural Press (London), 1967.
A Future for the Past (film), broadcast by British Broadcasting Corp. (BBC-TV), 1971.
Man Made the Town, St. Martin's (New York City), 1987.
Cities in Transition: The Regeneration of Britain's Inner Cities, M. Joseph (London), 1991.

Author of film *Europa Nostra,* released in 1975. Contributor to *Dictionnaire de la peinture moderne, Dictionnaire de la sculpture moderne,* and *Histoire illustree de la peinture.* Contributor to magazines and newspapers in England and abroad. Art critic for *Spectator,* 1946-56.

SIDELIGHTS: Michael Middleton once told *CA:* "Throughout my life, my interests have centered on the visual and the verbal. In my writing I have sought to bring together aspects of the fine and applied arts, architecture, and environmental design and to communicate them to a nonspecialized audience or readership without bringing a hot flush of embarrassment to the cheeks of the specialist. I see environmental quality not as an optional dollop of cream on the cake but as fundamental to the economic and social well-being of communities and nations.

"I have had the good fortune to travel widely (throughout Western Europe, through some thirty of the United States, in South Africa, Australia, Thailand, Nepal, Singapore, and Indonesia), mostly to give papers at conferences and to universities and other groups. I have also served as a consultant on environmental problems. These contacts have brought home to me how great a need there is for a wider sharing of experience in this field."

Middleton later added: "Drawing widely on examples in Europe and America, *Man Made the Town* sought to give an overview of some of the things which go wrong, environmentally, in our towns and cities, and the kind of things we *can* do to enrich and enliven the urban scene. *Cities in Transition* concentrated on the inner city, and the steps that the United Kingdom was taking through the 1980s—through government action, by local authorities, community groups and others—to bring life back to the docklands of London and Liverpool, to run-down sectors of big cities like Glasgow, and even wider areas like Tyneside, South Wales and the Black Country. In my work in Asia and the Pacific rim, I have addressed in particular the problems of planning for tourism, so that it is used to enhance the quality of heritage sites rather than destroying them.

"I am currently engaged on the collation of family papers relating to the Earls of Middleton, the role of the second Earl at the Jacobite Court at St. Germain-en-Laye, and, a hundred years later, Admiral Lord Barham, First Lord of the Admiralty, and his nephew, then a Captain in charge of the Navy Yard in Gibraltar, over the period covering the Battle of Trafalgar and the build up of the Peninsular War."

*　　*　　*

MIKLOWITZ, Gloria D. 1927-

PERSONAL: Surname is pronounced "*mick*-lo-witz"; born May 18, 1927, in New York, NY; daughter of Simon (president of a steamship company) and Ella (Goldberg) Dubov; married Julius Miklowitz (a college professor), August 28, 1948; children: Paul Stephen, David Jay. *Education:* Attended Hunter College (now Hunter College of the City University of New York), 1944-45; University of Michigan, B.A., 1948; New York University, graduate study, 1948. *Politics:* Democrat.

ADDRESSES: Home—5255 Vista Miguel Dr., La Canada, CA 91011.

CAREER: Writer. U.S. Naval Ordnance Test Station, Pasadena, CA, scriptwriter, 1952-57; Pasadena City College, Pasadena, instructor, 1971-81; instructor for Writer's Digest School.

MEMBER: PEN International, Society of Children's Book Writers and Illustrators, California Writer's Guild (member of board of directors), Southern California Council of Literature for Children and Young People.

AWARDS, HONORS: Outstanding Science Books for Children Awards, 1977, for *Earthquake!*, and 1978, for *Save That Raccoon!;* Young Reader Trophy from Western Australia for *Did You Hear What Happened to Andrea?;* Bucks Herald Publisher's Award for Top Teen Fiction, London, England, 1990; Western Australia Young Reader's Book Award, secondary section, 1991; Soaring Eagle Book Award from Wyoming, 1994, for *Desperate Pursuit.*

WRITINGS:

FOR CHILDREN

Barefoot Boy, Follett, 1964.
The Zoo That Moved, Follett, 1968.
The Parade Starts at Noon, Putnam (New York City), 1969.
(With Wesley A. Young) *The Zoo Was My World,* Dutton (New York City), 1969.
The Marshmallow Caper, Putnam, 1971.
Sad Song, Happy Song, Putnam, 1973.
Turning Off, Putnam, 1973.
A Time to Hurt, a Time to Heal, Tempo Books, 1974.
Harry Truman, Putnam, 1975.
Nadia Comaneci, Tempo Books, 1977.
Unwed Mother, Tempo Books, 1977.
Paramedics, Scholastic (New York City), 1977.
Earthquake!, Messner (New York City), 1977.
Ghastly Ghostly Riddles, Scholastic, 1977.
Tracy Austin, Tempo Books, 1978.
Martin Luther King, Jr., Tempo Books, 1978.
Steve Cauthen, Tempo Books, 1978.
Save That Raccoon!, Harcourt (New York City), 1978.

Did You Hear What Happened to Andrea?, Delacorte (New York City), 1979.
Natalie Dunn, Roller Skating Champion, Tempo Books, 1979.
Roller Skating, Tempo Books, 1979.
The Love Bombers, Delacorte, 1980.
Movie Stunts and the People Who Do Them, Harcourt, 1980.
The Young Tycoons, Harcourt, 1981.
Before Love, Tempo Books, 1982.
Close to the Edge, Delacorte, 1983.
The Day the Senior Class Got Married, Delacorte, 1983.
Carrie Loves Superman, Tempo Books, 1983.
After the Bomb, Scholastic, 1985.
The War between the Classes, Delacorte, 1985.
Love Story, Take Three, Delacorte, 1986.
After the Bomb, Week One, Scholastic, 1987.
Goodbye Tomorrow, Delacorte, 1987.
The Emerson High Vigilantes, Delacorte, 1988.
Anything to Win, Delacorte, 1989.
Standing Tall, Looking Good, Delacorte, 1991.
Desperate Pursuit, Bantam (New York City), 1992.
The Killing Boy, Bantam, 1993.
Past Forgiving, Simon & Schuster (New York City), 1995.

Contributor of children's stories to anthologies.

OTHER

Contributor to magazines, including *Sports Illustrated, Hadassah, Writer,* and *Wildlife Conservation.*

Some of Miklowitz's works have been translated into Spanish, Swedish, Japanese, German, Dutch, Danish, and Hebrew.

ADAPTATIONS: Did You Hear What Happened to Andrea? was adapted for an ABC-TV "Afterschool Special," aired in September, 1983; *The Day the Senior Class Got Married* and *The War between the Classes* were adapted for CBS-TV "Schoolbreak Specials," both 1995.

WORK IN PROGRESS: Camouflage, a book about militias.

SIDELIGHTS: Gloria D. Miklowitz told *CA:* "I began writing for children when my own were very young. . . . Before that I wrote documentary films on rockets and torpedoes for the Navy Department.

"In real life I live quite a normal existence, but on paper I have been a boy on drugs, a runaway, unwed mother, a paramedic, a rape victim, a Moonie, a would-be suicide, and more. In a typical book, I may enter the hearts and minds of many people. For example, in the rape novel, *Did You Hear What Happened to Andrea?*, I played the part of victim, rapist, mother, father, sister, brother, boyfriend, and school friends, as well as police officers and doctors. In each book, I try to bring to my readers compassion and understanding for those lives.

"I write for young adults because teenage years are difficult ones and teen problems interest me. Young people are still malleable enough to be influenced to constructive change. I try to offer or suggest alternatives to destructive behavior in my books.

"I do extensive research for each book, including reading and interviewing. To write *The Love Bombers*, for example, I not only read a great deal and interviewed former Moonies and cult specialists, but I stayed with the Moonies for a short time. To write the rape novel, I served on a rape hotline for a year and interviewed victims, psychologists, police, and medical people. It isn't until I've thoroughly understood every aspect of a problem that I feel qualified to write with conviction."

*   *   *

MILLER, Sally M.   1937-

PERSONAL: Born April 13, 1937, in Chicago, IL; daughter of Robert (in business) and Clara (Nixon) Miller. *Education:* University of Illinois, B.A., 1958; University of Chicago, A.M., 1963; University of Toronto, Ph.D., 1966. *Religion:* Jewish.

ADDRESSES: Home—2004 Franklin Ave., Stockton, CA 95204. *Office*—Department of History, University of the Pacific, 3601 Pacific Ave., Stockton, CA 95211.

CAREER: Michigan State University, East Lansing, instructor, 1965-66, assistant professor of American thought and language, 1966-67; University of the Pacific, Stockton, CA, assistant professor, 1967-70, associate professor, 1970-75, professor of history, 1975—. Visiting senior lecturer in history, University of Warwick, 1978-79. Fulbright lecturer, University of Otago, New Zealand, 1986, and University of Turku, Finland, 1996. Founder, Southwest Labor Studies Conference.

MEMBER: American Association of University Professors, American Historical Association, European Labor and Working Class History Study Group, Immigration History Group, Organization of American Historians, Western Association of Women Historians.

AWARDS, HONORS: American Philosophical Society travel grants, 1971, 1976; distinguished faculty award, University of the Pacific, 1976; American Council of Learned Societies travel grant, 1979; California Council for the Humanities grant, 1981; Newberry Library fellow, 1992; Missouri History Book Award, for *From Prairie to Prison: The Life of Social Activist Kate Richards O'Hare*, 1994.

WRITINGS:

EDITOR

Flawed Liberation: Socialism and Feminism, Greenwood Press (Westport, CT), 1981.
(With Philip S. Foner) *Kate Richards O'Hare: Selected Writings and Speeches*, Louisiana State University Press (Baton Rouge, LA), 1982.
John Muir: Life and Work, University of New Mexico Press (Albuquerque), 1993.
(With Daniel Cornford) *American Labor in the Era of World War II*, Greenwood Press, 1995.

OTHER

Victor Berger and the Promise of Constructive Socialism, 1910-1920, Greenwood Press, 1973.
The Radical Immigrant, Twayne (Boston, MA), 1974.
(Contributor) *Socialism and the Cities*, Kennikat (Port Washington, NY), 1975.
The Ethnic Press in the United States, Greenwood Press, 1987.
From Prairie to Prison: The Life of Social Activist Kate Richards O'Hare, University of New Mexico Press, 1993.

Contributor of articles to history journals; during early 1960s contributed fiction to other periodicals.

WORK IN PROGRESS: Autobiographical sketches; fiction.

MILOSZ, Czeslaw 1911-
(J. Syruc)

PERSONAL: Surname is pronounced *"mee*-wosh"; born June 30, 1911, in Szetejnie, Lithuania; came to the West, 1951; immigrated to the United States, 1960, naturalized citizen, 1970; son of Aleksander (a civil engineer) and Weronika (Kunat) Milosz. *Education:* University of Stephan Batory, M.Juris, 1934.

ADDRESSES: Office—Department of Slavic Languages and Literatures, University of California, 5416 Dwinelle Hall, Berkeley, CA 94720.

CAREER: Poet, critic, essayist, novelist, and translator. Programmer with Polish National Radio, 1935-39; worked for the Polish Resistance during World War II; cultural attache with the Polish Embassy in Washington, DC, 1946-50; freelance writer in Paris, 1951-60; University of California, Berkeley, visiting lecturer, 1960-61, professor of Slavic languages and literatures, 1961-78, professor emeritus, 1978—.

MEMBER: American Association for the Advancement of Slavic Studies, American Academy and Institute of Arts and Letters, PEN.

AWARDS, HONORS: Prix Litteraire Europeen, 1953, for novel *La Prise du pouvoir;* Marian Kister Literary Award, 1967; Jurzykowski Foundation award for creative work, 1968; Institute for Creative Arts fellow, 1968; Polish PEN award for poetry translation, 1974; Wandycz Award, 1974; Guggenheim fellow, 1976; Litt.D., University of Michigan, 1977; Neustadt International Literary Prize for Literature, 1978; University Citation, University of California, 1978; Zygmunt Hertz literary award, 1979; Nobel Prize for Literature, 1980; honorary doctorate, Catholic University, Lublin, 1981; honorary doctorate, Brandeis University, 1983; Bay Area Book Reviewers Association Poetry Prize, 1986, for *The Separate Notebooks;* Robert Kirsch Award for poetry, 1990; National Medal of Arts, 1990.

WRITINGS:

Zniewolony umysl (essays), Instytut Literacki (Paris), 1953, translation by Jane Zielonko published as *The Captive Mind,* Knopf (New York City), 1953.
Rodzinna Europa (essays), Instytut Literacki, 1959, translation by Catherine S. Leach published as *Native Realm: A Search for Self-Definition,* Doubleday (New York City), 1968.

Czlowiek wsrod skorpionow: Studium o Stanislawie Brzozowskim (title means "A Man among Scorpions: A Study of St. Brzozowski"), Instytut Literacki, 1962.
The History of Polish Literature, Macmillan (New York City), 1969, revised edition, University of California Press (Berkeley), 1983.
Widzenia and Zatoka San Francisco, Instytut Literacki, 1969, translation by Richard Lourie published as *Visions from San Francisco Bay,* Farrar, Straus (New York City), 1982.
Prywatne obowiazki (essays; title means "Private Obligations"), Instytut Literacki, 1972.
Moj wiek: Pamietnik nowiony (interview with Alexander Wat; title means "My Century: An Oral Diary"), edited by Lidia Ciolkoszowa, two volumes, Polonia Book Fund (London), 1977.
Emperor of the Earth: Modes of Eccentric Vision, University of California Press, 1977.
Ziemia Ulro, Instytut Literacki, 1977, translation by Louis Iribarne published as *The Land of Ulro,* Farrar, Straus, 1984.
Ogrod nauk (title means "The Garden of Knowledge"), Instytut Literacki, 1980.
Dziela zbiorowe (title means "Collected Works"), Instytut Literacki, 1980—.
Nobel Lecture, Farrar, Straus, 1981.
The Witness of Poetry (lectures), Harvard University Press (Cambridge, MA), 1983.
The Rising of the Sun, Arion Press (San Francisco, CA), 1985.
Unattainable Earth, translation from the Polish manuscript by Milosz and Robert Hass, Ecco Press (New York City), 1986.
Beginning with My Streets: Essays and Recollections (essays), translation from the Polish manuscript by Madeline G. Levine, Farrar, Straus, 1992.
Year of the Hunter, translation from the Polish manuscript by Levine, Farrar, Straus, 1994.

POEMS

Poemat o czasie zastyglym (title means "Poem of the Frozen Time"), [Vilnius, Lithuania], 1933.
Trzy zimy (title means "Three Winters"), Union of Polish Writers, 1936.
(Under pseudonym J. Syruc) *Wiersze* (title means "Poems"), published by the Resistance in Warsaw, Poland, 1940.
Ocalenie (title means "Salvage"), Czytelnik (Poland), 1945.
Swiatlo dzienne (title means "Daylight"), Instytut Literacki, 1953.

Trak tat poetycki (title means "Treatise on Poetry"), Instytut Literacki, 1957.

Kontynenty (title means "Continents"), Instytut Literacki, 1958.

Krol Popiel i inne wiersze (title means "King Popiel and Other Poems"), Instytut Literacki, 1962.

Gucio zaczarowany (title means "Bobo's Metamorphosis"), Instytut Literacki, 1965.

Lied vom Weltende (title means "A Song for the End of the World"), Kiepenheuer & Witsch, 1967.

Wiersze (title means "Poems"), Oficyna Poetow i Malarzy (London), 1969.

Miasto bez imienia (title means "City without a Name"), Instytut Literacki, 1969.

Selected Poems, Seabury (New York City), 1973, revised edition published as *Selected Poems: Revised,* Ecco Press, 1981.

Gdzie wschodzi slonce i kedy zapada (title means "From Where the Sun Rises to Where It Sets"), Instytut Literacki, 1974.

Utwory poetyckie (title means "Selected Poems"), Michigan Slavic Publications (Ann Arbor), 1976.

The Bells in Winter, translation by Milosz and Lillian Vallee, Ecco Press, 1978.

Hymn O Perle (title means "Hymn to the Pearl"), Michigan Slavic Publications, 1982.

The Separate Notebooks, translation by Robert Hass and Robert Pinsky, Ecco Press, 1984.

The Collected Poems, 1931-1987, Ecco Press, 1988.

The World, translation by the author, Arion Press, 1989.

Provinces: Poems, 1987-1991, translation by Milosz and Hass, Ecco Press, 1991.

Facing the River: New Poems, translation by Milosz and Hass, Ecco Press, 1995.

NOVELS

La Prise du pouvoir, translation from the Polish manuscript by Jeanne Hersch, Gallimard (Paris), 1953, original Polish edition published as *Zdobycie wladzy,* Instytut Literacki, 1955, translation by Celina Wieniewska published as *The Seizure of Power,* Criterion, 1955, published in England as *The Usurpers,* Faber (London), 1955.

Dolina Issy, Instytut Literacki, 1955, translation by Louis Iribarne published as *The Issa Valley,* Farrar, Straus, 1981.

EDITOR

(With Zbigniew Folejewski) *Antologia poezji spolecznej* (title means "Anthology of Social Poetry"), [Vilnius], 1933.

Piesn niepodlegla (Resistance poetry; title means "Invincible Song"), Oficyna, 1942.

(And translator) Jacques Maritain, *Drogami Kleski,* [Warsaw], 1942.

(And translator) Daniel Bell, *Praca i jej gorycze* (title means "Work and Its Discontents"), Instytut Literacki, 1957.

(And translator) Simone Weil, *Wybor pism* (title means "Selected Works"), Instytut Literacki, 1958.

(And translator) *Kultura masowa* (title means "Mass Culture"), Instytut Literacki, 1959.

(And translator) *Wegry* (title means "Hungary"), Instytut Literacki, 1960.

(And translator) *Postwar Polish Poetry: An Anthology,* Doubleday, 1965, revised edition, University of California Press, 1983.

Lettres inedites de O. V. de L. Milosz a Christian Gauss (correspondence of Milosz's uncle, the French poet Oscar Milosz), Silvaire, 1976.

Founder and editor, *Zagary* (literary periodical), 1931.

TRANSLATOR

(With Peter Dale Scott) Zbigniew Herbert, *Selected Poems,* Penguin (New York City), 1968.

Alexander Wat, *Mediterranean Poems,* Ardi, 1977.

Ewangelia wedlug sw. Marka (title means "The Gospel According to St. Mark"), Znak, 1978.

Ksiega Hioba (title means "The Book of Job"), Dialogue (Paris), 1980.

Also translator of Anna Swir's *Happy as a Dog's Tail,* Harcourt, and, with Leonard Nathan, *With the Skin: Poems of Aleksander Wat.*

SIDELIGHTS: One of the most respected figures in twentieth-century Polish literature, Czeslaw Milosz was awarded the Nobel Prize for Literature in 1980. Born in Lithuania and raised in Poland, Milosz has lived in the United States since 1960. His poems, novels, essays, and other works are written in his native Polish and translated by the author and others into English. Having lived under the two great totalitarian systems of modern history, National Socialism and Communism, Milosz writes of the past in a tragic, ironic style that nonetheless affirms the value of human life. Terrence Des Pres, writing in the *Nation,* states that "political catastrophe has defined the nature of our century, and the result—the collision of personal and public realms—has produced a new kind of writer. Czeslaw Milosz is the perfect example. In exile from a world which no longer exists, a witness to the Nazi devastation of Poland and the Soviet takeover of Eastern Europe, Milosz deals in his poetry with the central issues of our time: the impact of history upon moral being, the search for ways to survive spiritual ruin in a ruined world." Although Milosz writes in several genres, it is his poetry that has attracted the most critical acclaim. Several observers, writes Harold B. Segel in the *Washington Post Book World,* consider Milosz to be "the foremost Polish poet of this century." Similarly, Paul Zweig of the *New York Times Book Review* claims that Milosz "is considered by many to be the greatest living Polish poet." But Joseph Brodsky goes further in his praise for Milosz. Writing in *World Literature Today,* Brodsky asserts: "I have no hesitation whatsoever in stating that Czeslaw Milosz is one of the greatest poets of our time, perhaps the greatest."

Born in Lithuania in 1911, Milosz spent much of his childhood in Czarist Russia, where his father worked as a civil engineer. After World War I the family returned to their hometown, which had become a part of the new Polish state, and Milosz attended local Catholic schools. He published his first collection of poems, *Poemat o czasie zastyglym* ("Poem of the Frozen Time"), at the age of twenty-one. Milosz was associated with the catastrophist school of poets during the 1930s. Catastrophism concerns "the inevitable annihilation of the highest values, especially the values essential to a given cultural system. . . . But it proclaims . . . only the annihilation of certain values, not values in general, and the destruction of a certain historical formation, but not of all mankind," Aleksander Fiut explains in *World Literature Today.* The writings of this group of poets ominously foreshadowed the Second World War.

When the war began in 1939, and Poland was invaded by Nazi Germany and Soviet Russia, Milosz worked with the underground Resistance movement in Warsaw, writing and editing several books published clandestinely during the occupation. One of these books, a collection entitled *Wiersze* ("Poems"), was published under the pseudonym J. Syruc. Following the war, Milosz became a member of the new communist government's diplomatic service and was stationed in Paris, France, as a cultural attache. In 1951, he left this post and defected to the West.

The Captive Mind explains Milosz's reasons for defecting and examines the life of the artist under a communist regime. It is, maintains Steve Wasserman

in the *Los Angeles Times Book Review,* a "brilliant and original study of the totalitarian mentality." Karl Jaspers, in an article for the *Saturday Review,* describes *The Captive Mind* as "a significant historical document and analysis of the highest order. . . . In astonishing gradations Milosz shows what happens to men subjected simultaneously to constant threat of annihilation and to the promptings of faith in a historical necessity which exerts apparently irresistible force and achieves enormous success. We are presented with a vivid picture of the forms of concealment, of inner transformation, of the sudden bolt to conversion, of the cleavage of man into two."

Milosz's break with the government came about when he was recalled to Poland from his position at the Polish embassy. He refused to leave. Joseph McLellan of the *Washington Post* quotes Milosz explaining: "I knew perfectly well that my country was becoming the province of an empire." In a speech before the Congress for Cultural Freedom, quoted by James Atlas of the *New York Times,* Milosz declares: "I have rejected the new faith because the practice of the lie is one of its principal commandments and socialist realism is nothing more than a different name for a lie." Maintaining this stance, Milosz moved to Paris where he worked as a translator and freelance writer. In 1960 he was offered a teaching position at the University of California at Berkeley, which he accepted. He became a United States citizen in 1970.

In *The Seizure of Power,* first published as *La Prise du pouvoir* in 1953, Milosz renders as fiction much of the same material found in *The Captive Mind.* The book is an autobiographical novel that begins with the Russian occupation of Warsaw at the close of the Second World War. That occupation is still a matter of controversy in Poland. As the Russian army approached the Nazi-held city, the Polish Resistance movement rose against the German occupation troops. They had been assured that the Russian army would join the fight the day after their uprising began. But instead, the Russians stood by a few miles outside of the city, allowing the Nazis to crush the revolt unhindered. When the uprising was over, the Russian army occupied Warsaw and installed a communist regime. The novel ends with the disillusioned protagonist, a political education officer for the communists, emigrating to the West.

The Seizure of Power "is a novel on how to live when power changes hands," Andrew Sinclair explains in the London *Times.* Granville Hicks, in an article for the *New York Times Book Review,* sees a similarity between *The Captive Mind* and *The Seizure of Power*. In both books, "Milosz appeals to the West to try to understand the people of Eastern Europe," maintains Hicks. Told in a series of disjointed scenes meant to suggest the chaos and violence of postwar Poland, *The Seizure of Power* is "a novel of ineffable sadness, and a muffled sob for Poland's fate," writes Wasserman. Michael Harrington, in a review for *Commonweal,* calls *The Seizure of Power* "a sensitive, probing work, far better than most political novels, of somewhat imperfect realization but of significant intention and worth."

After living in the United States for a time, Milosz began to write of his new home. In *Native Realm: A Search for Self-Definition* and *Visions from San Francisco Bay,* Milosz compares and contrasts the West with his native Poland. *Native Realm,* Richard Holmes writes in the London *Times,* is "a political and social autobiography, shorn of polemic intent, deeply self-questioning, and dominated by the sense that neither historically nor metaphysically are most Westerners in a position to grasp the true nature of the East European experience since the First War." A series of personal essays examining events in Milosz's life, *Native Realm* provides "a set of commentaries upon his improbable career," as Michael Irwin maintains in the *Times Literary Supplement.* Milosz "has written a self-effacing remembrance composed of shards from a shattered life," believes Wasserman. "He tells his story with the humility of a man who has experienced tragedy and who believes in fate and in destiny. It is a work that reflects the stubborn optimism of his heart, even as it dwells on the pessimism of his intellect." Irving Howe, writing in the *New York Times Book Review,* finds *Native Realm* "beautifully written." Milosz, Howe continues, "tries to find in the chaos of his life some glimmers of meaning."

In *Visions from San Francisco Bay,* Milosz examines his life in contemporary California, a place far removed in distance and temperament from the scenes of his earlier life. His observations are often sardonic, and yet he is also content with his new home. Milosz "sounds like a man who has climbed up, hand over hand, right out of history, and who is both amazed and grateful to find that he can breathe the ahistorical atmosphere of California," Anatole Broyard states in the *New York Times.* The opening words of the book are "I am here," and from that starting point Milosz describes the society around

him. "The intention," notes Julian Symons in the *Times Literary Supplement,* "is to understand himself, to understand the United States, to communicate something singular to Czeslaw Milosz." Broyard takes this idea even further, arguing that Milosz "expresses surprise at 'being here,' taking this phrase in its ordinary sense of being in America and in its other, Heideggerian sense of being-in-the-world."

Although Milosz's comments about life in California are "curiously oblique, deeply shadowed by European experience, allusive, sometimes arch and frequently disillusioned," as Holmes points out, he ultimately embraces his adopted home. "Underlying all his meditations," comments Leon Edel in the *New York Times Book Review,* "is his constant 'amazement' that America should exist in this world—and his gratitude that it does exist." "He is fascinated," explains Symons, "by the contradictions of a society with enormous economic power, derived in part from literally non-human technical achievement, which also contains a large group that continually and passionately indicts the society by which it is maintained." Milosz, P. J. Kavanagh remarks in the *Spectator,* looks at his adopted country with "a kind of detached glee—at awfulness; an ungloomy recognition that we cannot go on as we are—in any direction. He holds up a mirror and shows us ourselves, without blame and with no suggestions either, and in the mirror he himself is also reflected." Edel believes that Milosz's visions "have authority: the authority of an individual who reminds us that only someone like himself who has known tyranny . . . can truly prize democracy."

The story of Milosz's odyssey from tyranny to democracy—from East to West—is also recounted in his poetry. Milosz's "entire effort," Jonathan Galassi explains in the *New York Times Book Review,* "is directed toward a confrontation with experience—and not with personal experience alone, but with history in all its paradoxical horror and wonder." Speaking of his poetry in the essay collection *The Witness of Poetry,* Milosz stresses the importance of his nation's cultural heritage and history in shaping his work. "My corner of Europe," he states, "owing to the extraordinary and lethal events that have been occurring there, comparable only to violent earthquakes, affords a peculiar perspective. As a result, all of us who come from those parts appraise poetry slightly differently than do the majority of my audience, for we tend to view it as a witness and participant in one of mankind's major transformations." "For Milosz,"

Helen Vendler explains in the *New Yorker,* "the person is irrevocably a person in history, and the interchange between external event and the individual life is the matrix of poetry." Writing in *TriQuarterly,* Reginald Gibbons states that Milosz "seems to wonder how good work can be written, no matter how private its subject matter, without the poet having been aware of the pain and threat of the human predicament."

Milosz sees a fundamental difference in the role of poetry in the democratic West and the communist East. Western poetry, as Alfred Kazin of the *New York Times Book Review* writes, is "'alienated' poetry, full of introspective anxiety." But because of the dictatorial nature of communist government, poets in the East cannot afford to be preoccupied with themselves. They are drawn to write of the larger problems of their society. "A peculiar fusion of the individual and the historical took place," Milosz writes in *The Witness of Poetry,* "which means that events burdening a whole community are perceived by a poet as touching him in a most personal manner. Then poetry is no longer alienated."

For many years Milosz's poetry was little noticed in the United States, though he was highly regarded in Poland. Recognition in Poland came in defiance of official government resistance to Milosz's work. The communist regime refused to publish the books of a defector; for many years only underground editions of his poems were secretly printed and circulated in Poland. But in 1980, when Milosz was awarded the Nobel Prize for Literature, the communist government was forced to relent. A government-authorized edition of Milosz's poems was issued. It sold a phenomenal 200,000 copies. One sign of Milosz's widespread popularity in Poland occurred when Polish workers in Gdansk unveiled a monument to their comrades who were shot down by the communist police. Two quotations were inscribed on the monument: one was taken from the Bible; the other was taken from a poem by Milosz.

The Nobel Prize also brought Milosz to the attention of a wider audience in the United States. Since 1980 a number of his earlier works have been translated into English and released in this country, and his new books have received widespread critical attention. Some of this critical attention has focused less on Milosz's work as poetry than "as the work of a thinker and political figure; the poems tend to be considered en masse, in relation either to the condition of Poland, or to the suppression of dissident literature under Communist rule, or to the larger topic of European intellectual history," as Vendler maintains. But most reviewers comment on Milosz's ability to speak in a personal voice that carries with it the echoes of his people's history. Zweig explains that Milosz "offers a modest voice, speaking an old language. But this language contains the resources of centuries. Speaking it, one speaks with a voice more than personal. . . . Milosz's power lies in his ability to speak with this larger voice without diminishing the urgency that drives his words."

This interweaving of the historical and personal is found in all of Milosz's poems. His early works focus on the Lithuania of his childhood and speak of the scenes and people from his own life; Milosz's later poems combine his memories of Europe with the images of his present life in the United States. "Milosz," Harlow Robinson writes in the *Nation,* "has rejected nothing of his long odyssey from the pagan green valleys of Lithuania to the emptying cafes of wartime Europe to the desolate concrete freeways of California." Clarence Brown of the *Village Voice* notes that when reading Milosz, "one has the impression that all his life experience is constantly available to him. . . . [His poetry] fuses the last waking thought with shards of distant or buried experience, foreshortens and warps the space-time of the poem, resulting in a sort of meta-tense, the everlasting now that came into being with Milosz (and thanks to these poems will outlast him)." This synthesis of personal and public, of past and present, is reflected in Milosz's combination of traditional poetic forms with a modern, individual sensibility. Louis Iribarne writes in the *Times Literary Supplement* that "the blending of private and public voices, the imaging of lyrical response to historical events, set off by a distinctly modern irony and a classical strictness of form, established the Milosz style."

Because he has lived through many of the great upheavals of recent history, and because his poetry fuses his own experiences with the larger events in his society, many of Milosz's poems concern loss, destruction, and despair. "There is a very dark vision of the world in my work," he tells Lynn Darling of the *Washington Post.* And yet Milosz goes on to say that he is "a great partisan of human hope." This essential optimism comes from his religious convictions.

Milosz believes that one of the major problems of contemporary society—in both the East and the West—is its lack of a moral foundation. Writing in

The Land of Ulro, Milosz finds that twentieth-century man has only "the starry sky above, and no moral law within." Speaking to Judy Stone of the *New York Times Book Review,* Milosz states: "I am searching for an answer as to what will result from an internal erosion of religious beliefs." Michiko Kakutani, reviewing *The Land of Ulro* for the *New York Times,* finds that "Milosz is eloquent in his call for a literature grounded in moral, as well as esthetic, values. Indeed, when compared with his own poetry, the work of many Westerners—from the neurotic rantings of the Romantics to the cerebral mind games of the avant-gardists—seems unserious and self-indulgent."

Because of his moral vision Milosz's writings make strong statements, some of which are inherently political in their implications. "The act of writing a poem is an act of faith," Milosz claims in *The History of Polish Literature,* "yet if the screams of the tortured are audible in the poet's room, is not his activity an offense to human suffering?" His awareness of suffering, writes Joseph C. Thackery of *Hollins Critic,* makes Milosz a "spokesman of the millions of dead of the Holocaust, the Gulags, the Polish and Czech uprisings, and the added millions of those who will go on dying in an imperfect world."

But Milosz also warns of the dangers of political writing. In a PEN Congress talk reprinted in the *Partisan Review,* he states: "In this century a basic stance of writers . . . seems to be an acute awareness of suffering inflicted upon human beings by unjust structures of society. . . . This awareness of suffering makes a writer open to the idea of radical change, whichever of many recipes he chooses. . . . Innumerable millions of human beings were killed in this century in the name of utopia—either progressive or reactionary, and always there were writers who provided convincing justifications for massacre."

In *The Witness of Poetry* Milosz argues that true poetry is "the passionate pursuit of the Real." He condemns those writers who favor art for art's sake or who think of themselves as alienated. Milosz suggests, as Adam Gussow writes in the *Saturday Review,* that poets may have "grown afraid of reality, afraid to see it clearly and speak about it in words we can all comprehend." What is needed in "today's unsettled world," Gussow explains, are poets who, "like Homer, Dante, and Shakespeare, will speak for rather than against the enduring values of their communities."

This concern for a poetry that confronts reality is noted by Thackery, who sees Milosz searching "for a poetry that will be at once harsh and mollifying, that will enable men to understand, if not to rationalize, the debasement of the human spirit by warfare and psychic dismemberment, while simultaneously establishing a personal *modus vivendi* and a psychology of aesthetic necessity." Des Pres also sees this unifying quality in Milosz's poetry, a trait he believes Milosz shares with T. S. Eliot. "The aim of both Milosz and Eliot," Des Pres states, "is identical: to go back and work through the detritus of one's own time on earth, to gather up the worst along with the best, integrate past and present into a culminating moment which transcends both, which embraces pain and joy together, the whole of a life and a world redeemed through memory and art, a final restoration in spirit of that which in historical fact has been forever lost." Vendler believes that "the work of Milosz reminds us of the great power that poetry gains from bearing within itself an unforced, natural, and long-ranging memory of past customs; a sense of the strata of ancient and modern history; wide visual experience; and a knowledge of many languages and literatures. . . . The living and tormented revoicing of the past makes Milosz a historical poet of bleak illumination."

Upon receiving the Nobel Prize in 1980, Milosz hoped to "continue with my very private and strange occupation," as McLellan quotes him. He has continued to publish books—some new titles and some older books appearing in English for the first time—and has spoken out at meetings of PEN, the international writers' organization, on such topics as censorship and totalitarianism. Darling explains that Milosz lives in Berkeley and writes, "under the benevolent light of the California sun, in a country of easy consummation and temporary passion, poems about the past, about horror, about life in the abyss of the 20th century."

Milosz's place in Polish literature is secure, while his influence and reputation in other nations continues to grow. As Galassi writes, "few other living poets have argued as convincingly for the nobility and value of the poet's calling. Whatever its importance to Polish letters, Mr. Milosz's work, as poetry in English, presents a challenge to American poetry to exit from the labyrinth of the self and begin to grapple again with the larger problems of being in the world." "Milosz has lived through, and participated in, some of the crucial political happenings of our century," Michael Irwin comments in the *Times*

Literary Supplement. "If he had never written a line he would be an intriguing figure merely by virtue of his survival. Since he in fact brought to bear upon his experiences a refined and resilient analytical intelligence, unusually combined with a poet's sensibility, his testimony is of unique importance. Attention must be paid to such a man."

Because Milosz writes of recent Polish history, and decries the nation's political tragedies of the past thirty-five years, his work embodies a spirit of freedom that speaks powerfully to his countrymen as well as to others. "Polish independence exists in this poet's voice," Brodsky maintains in the *New York Times.* "This, at least, is one way to account for the intensity that has made him perhaps the greatest poet of our time." Norman Davies notes in the *New York Times Book Review* that Milosz is one of three Poles who have come to international prominence during the 1980s. Milosz, Pope John Paul II, and Lech Walesa, the leader of the Solidarity trade union challenging the Polish communist government, have "each served in different ways to illuminate the depth and richness of their native Polish culture," Davies writes. In 1981, during his first visit to Poland in thirty years, Milosz met with Walesa and the two men acknowledged their mutual indebtedness. "I told him that I considered him my leader," Milosz recounts to Darling. "He said that he had gone to jail because of my poetry."

With the publication in 1986 of *Unattainable Earth,* Milosz continued to show himself as a poet of memory and a poet of witness. In the prose footnote to "Poet at Seventy" he writes of his continued "unnamed need for order, for rhythm, for form, which three words are opposed to chaos and nothingness." The book uses what Stanislaw Baranczak in *Threepenny Review* calls, a "peculiar structure of a modern *silva rerum*" which "consists in including a number of prose fragments, notes, letters, verses of other poets." *Unattainable Earth* was the first of several lauded collaborative translations between the author and American poet Robert Hass.

A year later, *The Collected Poems, 1931-1987* was published, bringing together *Selected Poems, Bells in Winter, The Separate Notebooks,* and *Unattainable Earth* in one volume. The book contains one hundred and eighty poems ranging in length from two lines to sixty pages. Forty-five poems appear for the first time in English in this edition, of which twenty-six are recently translated older poems and twenty are

new poems. Warren W. Werner in *Southern Humanities Review* calls the work "a big, varied, and important book . . . a feast of poetry." P. J. M. Robertson in *Queen's Quarterly* lauds the collection as "a gift to cherish, for it contains the song of a man . . . passionately affirming the daily miracle of life and its continuity even now on our battered earth" and affirms that the poems "reveal Milosz's answer to the question of the role of poetry and of art in the twentieth century . . . . a responsibility to see and express beauty: that is, the truth about life in its miraculous complexity." *New York Times Book Review* contributor Edward Hirsch finds the volume "one of the monumental splendors of poetry in our age." Baranczak believes that it is a book that can "finally give the English-speaking reader a fairly accurate idea of what [Milosz's] poetry really is, both in the sense of the largeness of its thematic and stylistic range and the uniqueness of his more than half-century-long creative evolution." Don Bogan of *Nation* finds that "with its clarity, historical awareness and moral vision, *The Collected Poems* is among the best guides we have" to help remind us that "poetry can define and address the concerns of an age."

Milosz followed in 1991 with *Provinces: Poems, 1987-1991.* For Milosz, the life in each individual seems made up of provinces, and one new province which he must now visit is the province of old age. He explores getting older in the thirteen-part sequence entitled "A New Province," reporting that "not much is known about that country / Till we land there ourselves, with no right to return." Hirsch finds that these poems about old age have "a penetrating honesty" derived from "a powerful dialectical tension, a metaphysical dispute at work . . . about the conflicting claims of immanence and transcendence, the temporal and the eternal." Ben Howard, in *Poetry,* comments on the inclusion of Milosz's "abiding subjects—the loss of his native Lithuania, the suffering of Eastern Europe, the wrenching upheavals of a long and difficult life" and suggests that the poet through his verse is "asserting his affinity with the common people and his closeness to the soil." *New York Review of Books* contributor Helen Vendler calls *Provinces* a collection of "many of Milosz's central themes—including the strangeness of human life (where in the blink of an eye absurdity can turn to bravery, or tranquillity to war), exile, sensuality, memory, Platonic idealism, and iron disbelief." Bill Marx of *Parnassus* describes *Provinces* as "an inner landscape of clashing contraries and times. Valleys of sensuous admiration for the earth's delights are broken up by notched peaks of traumatic memory; deserts formed by perceptions of nature's indifference are dotted with oases rooted in intimations of the transcendent."

Beginning with My Streets: Essays and Recollections, published in 1992, is a collection of essays, philosophical meditations, literary criticism, portraits of friends and writers, and a genre which Sally Laird in the London *Observer* identifies as "'chatty narratives' in the Polish tradition." Donald Davie in *New Republic* deems the book "more a medley than a collection, with a deceptive air of being 'thrown together'," made up, as Vendler points out, of essays in which Milosz "moves with entire naturalness from Swedenborg to Robinson Jeffers, from Lithuanian scenery to Meister Eckhart, from the Seven Deadly Sins to Polish Marxism." Laird praises in particular the essay "Saligia," in which Milosz takes on two perspectives, those of poet and of engaged historian. The book contains accounts of the poet's childhood in Vilnius and closes with his 1980 Nobel lecture. *Washington Post Book World* contributor Alberto Manguel concludes, "Milosz excels in recounting, in finding the happy phrase for a scene or a concept. The invention of the past, the elusiveness of reality, the fluidity of time, the apparent banality or apparent importance of philosophical inquiries are traditional (some would say intrinsic) poetic fodder, and Milosz arranges the questions on the page with economy and elegance."

A Year of the Hunter, published in 1994, is a journal which Milosz penned between August of 1987 and August of 1988. John Simon in *Washington Post Book World* points out that these entries were "written on airplanes zooming to lecture engagements, poetry readings, literary congresses and the like." Ian Buruma praises the work in the *Los Angeles Times Book Review* as "a wonderful addition to [Milosz's] other autobiographical writing. The diary form, free-floating, wide-ranging . . . is suited to a poet, especially an intellectual poet, like Milosz," allowing for his entries to range from gardening to translating, from Communism to Christianity, from past to present. Indeed, as Michael Ignatieff states in the *New York Review of Books, A Year of the Hunter* is successful "because Milosz has not cleaned it up too much. Its randomness is a pleasure."

In 1995 Milosz produced the poetry collection *Facing the River: New Poems*. This volume includes verse that deals largely with Milosz's return to Vilnius, the city of his childhood, now the capital of the free republic of Lithuania. In returning, Ignatieff

points out, Milosz found himself in an ironic circumstance: "Having been a poet of exile, he had now become the poet of the impossible return of the past." The poet recognized many streets, buildings, and steeples in his homeland, but the people from his past were gone. This left Milosz to "bring the absent dead back to life, one by one, in all their aching singularity," as Ignatieff states. *Facing the River* is not just about Milosz's return to Lithuania and the people that he misses; it also addresses the poet's accomplishments and his views on life. In "At a Certain Age," Milosz declares that old men, who see themselves as handsome and noble, will find: "later in our place an ugly toad / Half-opens its thick eyelid / And one sees clearly: 'That's me.'" *Facing the River,* which ends with Milosz saying, "If only my work were of use to people," leaves Ignatieff speaking for many readers of Milosz when he writes: "Those like myself who see the world differently because of him hope he will continue to stand facing the river, and tell us what he sees."

BIOGRAPHICAL/CRITICAL SOURCES:

BOOKS

Czerni, Irena, *Czeslaw Milosz laureat literackiej nagrody Nobla 1980: katalog wystawy,* Nakl. Uniwersytety Jagiellonskiego (Krakow), 1993.

Contemporary Literary Criticism, Gale (Detroit), Volume 5, 1976, Volume 11, 1979, Volume 22, 1982, Volume 31, 1985, Volume 56, 1989, Volume 82, 1994.

Czarnecha, Ewe, *Prdrozny swiata: Rosmowy z Czeslawem Miloszem, Komentane,* Bicentennial, 1983.

Czarnecha and Alexander Fiut, translation by Richard Lourie, *Conversations with Czeslaw Milosz,* Harcourt (San Diego, CA), 1988.

Dompkowski, Judith Ann, *"Down a Spiral Staircase, Never-ending: Motion as Design in the Writing of Czeslaw Milosz,* P. Lang (New York City), 1990.

Dudek, Jolanta, *Gdzie wschodzi slonce i kedy zapada—europejskie korzenie poezji Czeslawa Milosza,* Nakl. Univwersytetu Jagiellonskiego, 1991.

Fiut, Aleksander, *Rozmowy z Czeslawem Miloszem,* Wydawnictwo Literackie (Kracow), 1981.

Fiut, *The Eternal Moment: The Poetry of Czeslaw Milosz,* University of California Press, 1990.

Gillon, A., and L. Krzyzanowski, editors, *Introduction to Modern Polish Literature,* Twayne (Boston), 1964.

Goemoeri, G., *Polish and Hungarian Poetry, 1945 to 1956,* Oxford University Press (New York City), 1966.

Hass, Robert, *Twentieth Century Pleasures: Prose on Poetry,* Ecco Press, 1984.

Milosz, Czeslaw, *The Captive Mind,* Knopf, 1953.

Milosz, *The History of Polish Literature,* revised edition, University of California Press, 1983.

Milosz, *The Witness of Poetry,* Harvard University Press, 1983.

Milosz, *The Land of Ulro,* Farrar, Straus, 1984.

Mozejko, Edward, *Between Anxiety and Hope: The Poetry and Writing of Czeslaw Milosz,* University of Alberta Press (Edmonton), 1988.

Nathan, Leonard, and Arthur Quinn, *The Poet's Work: An Introduction to Czeslaw Milosz,* Harvard University Press, 1992.

Nilsson, Nils Ake, editor, *Czeslaw Milosz: A Stockholm Conference, September 9-11, 1991,* Kungl. Vitterhets (Stockholm, Sweden), 1992.

Poetry Criticism, Volume 8, Gale, 1994.

Volynska-Bogert, Rimma, and Wojciech Zaleswski, *Czeslaw Milosz: An International Bibliography 1930-80,* University of Michigan Press (Ann Arbor), 1983.

PERIODICALS

America, December 18, 1982; December 15, 1984, p. 409; May 12, 1990, pp. 472-75.

American Book Review, March, 1985, p. 22.

American Poetry Review, January, 1977.

Booklist, April 15, 1988, p. 1387; November 1, 1991, p. 497; January 1, 1992, p. 806; March 1, 1992, p. 1191.

Book Report, November 1988, p. 39.

Books Abroad, winter, 1969; spring, 1970; winter, 1973; winter, 1975.

Book Week, May 9, 1965.

Book World, September 29, 1968.

Boston Globe, October 16, 1987, p. 91; August 28, 1994, p. 62.

Canadian Literature, spring, 1989, pp. 183-84.

Chicago Tribune, October 10, 1980; September 6, 1987, p. 6; December 4, 1989, p. 2; March 15, 1992, p. 6; December 18, 1994, p. 5.

Chicago Tribune Book World, May 31, 1981.

Christian Science Monitor, July 2, 1986, p. 21; October 5, 1990, p. 10; January 17, 1992, p. 14.

Commonweal, July 8, 1955; March 22, 1985, p. 190; November 6, 1992, p. 33-34.

Denver Quarterly, summer, 1976.

Eastern European Poetry, April, 1967.

English Journal, January, 1992, p. 16.

Globe and Mail (Toronto), March 16, 1985.

Guardian Weekly, October 2, 1988, p. 28.

Hollins Critic, April, 1982.

Hudson Review, autumn, 1992, p. 509.

Ironwood, Number 18, 1981.

Journal and Constitution (Atlanta), April 2, 1989, p. N11; April 12, 1992, p. N11; April 23, 1995, p. M13; April 25, 1995, p. B7; April 26, 1995, p. D1.

Journal of Religion, January, 1987, pp. 141-42.

Library Journal, November 15, 1984, p. 2114; April 15, 1986, p. 84; April 15, 1988, p. 83; January, 1989, p. 45; October 15, 1991, p. 80.

Los Angeles Times, January 14, 1987; September 13, 1987, p. 14.

Los Angeles Times Book Review, May 10, 1981; August 22, 1982; June 5, 1983; August 24, 1984; June 24, 1990, p. 12; November 4, 1990, p. 10; August 15, 1993, pp. 19-20; August 14, 1994, p. 3.

Modern Age, spring, 1986, p. 162.

Nation, December 30, 1978; June 13, 1981; December 22, 1984, p. 686; December 19, 1988, pp. 688-91.

New Leader, October 15, 1984, p. 14; September 19, 1988, p. 19.

New Perspectives Quarterly, fall, 1988, p. 55; spring, 1990, p. 44.

New Republic, May 16, 1955; August 1, 1983; October 3, 1988, pp. 26-28; March 16, 1992, pp. 34-37.

New Statesman, October 24, 1980; December 17-24, 1982; August 30, 1985, p. 27.

New Statesman and Society, August 5, 1988, p. 38.

Newsweek, June 15, 1981; October 4, 1982.

New Yorker, November 7, 1953; March 19, 1984; October 24, 1988, p. 122; July 16, 1990, p. 80.

New York Review of Books, April 4, 1974; June 25, 1981; February 27, 1986, p. 31; June 2, 1988, p. 21; August 13, 1992, pp. 44-46; August 11, 1994, p. 41; August 28, 1994, p. 9; March 23, 1995, pp. 39-42; May 11, 1995, p. 15.

New York Times, June 25, 1968; October 10, 1980; September 4, 1982; August 24, 1984; July 26, 1987; June 2, 1988, p. 21.

New York Times Book Review, April 17, 1955; July 7, 1974; March 11, 1979; February 1, 1981; June 28, 1981; October 17, 1982; May 1, 1983; September 2, 1984; October 20, 1985, p. 60; May 25, 1986, p. 2; July 6, 1986; June 2, 1988, p. 21; June 19, 1988, p. 6; December 8, 1988, p. 26; April 26, 1992, p. 20; May 17, 1992, p. 7; May 31, 1992, p. 22; August 28, 1994, p. 9.

New York Times Magazine, January 14, 1990, p. 22.

Observer (London), December 2, 1984, p. 19; August 11, 1985, p. 20; July 24, 1988, p. 42; November 22, 1992, p. 64.

Parnassus, fall, 1983, p. 127; Volume 15, number 2, 1989, p. 67; Volume 18, number 2, 1992, pp. 100-20.

Partisan Review, November, 1953; spring, 1977; fall, 1985, p. 448; spring, 1986, pp. 177-79; Volume 57, number 1, 1990, p. 145.

Poetry, April, 1980; December, 1986, p. 168; January, 1993, pp. 223-26.

Progressive, March, 1985, p. 40.

Publishers Weekly, October 24, 1980; January 31, 1986, p. 362; February 26, 1988, p. 187; January 13, 1992, p. 37; June 6, 1994, p. 49; August 28, 1994, p. 48.

Queen's Quarterly, winter, 1989, pp. 954-56.

Reflections, winter, 1985, p. 14.

San Francisco Review of Books, spring, 1985, p. 22.

Saturday Review, June 6, 1953; May-June, 1983.

Southern Humanities Review, fall, 1989, pp. 382-86.

Spectator, December 4, 1982.

Stand, summer, 1990, p. 12.

Theology Today, January, 1984.

Threepenny Review, summer, 1989, p. 23.

Times (London), July 16, 1981; January 6, 1983; May 19, 1983; February 9, 1985; May 27, 1987.

Times Literary Supplement, December 2, 1977; August 25, 1978; July 24, 1981; December 24, 1982; September 9, 1983; October 3, 1986, p. 1092; September 2-8, 1988, pp. 955-56.

Tribune Books (Chicago), March 15, 1992, p. 6; December 6, 1992, p. 13; December 18, 1994, p. 5.

TriQuarterly, fall, 1983.

Village Voice, May 2, 1974.

Virginia Quarterly Review, spring, 1975; autumn, 1991, p. 125; summer, 1992, p. 99.

Wall Street Journal, July 24, 1992, p. A10.

Washington Post, October 10, 1980; April 29, 1982; September 20, 1989, p. D1; April 26, 1995, p. C1.

Washington Post Book World, June 14, 1981; August 31, 1986, p. 8; December 22, 1991, p. 15; March 8, 1992, p. 9; October 9, 1994, p. 10.

World Literature Today, winter, 1978; spring, 1978, pp. 372-76; winter, 1985, p. 126; winter, 1987, p. 127; summer, 1987, p. 467; autumn, 1991, p. 735; winter, 1993, p. 210.

Yale Review, spring, 1990, p. 467.

OTHER

DISCovering Authors Modules (CD-ROM product), Gale (Detroit), 1996.

* * *

MISTER X
   See HOCH, Edward D(entinger)

* * *

MORGAN, Alison (Mary)   1930-

PERSONAL: Born March 2, 1930, in Bexley, Kent, England; daughter of Geoffrey Taunton (an army officer) and Dorothy Wilson (Fox) Raikes; married John Morgan, April 23, 1960 (deceased); children: Richard, Hugh. *Education:* Somerville College, Oxford, B.A. (second class honors), 1952; University of London, certificate in education, 1953. *Politics:* "Uncommitted." *Religion:* Anglican (Church of Wales). *Avocational interests:* Grandchildren, gardening, community activities, traveling, walking.

ADDRESSES: Home—Talcoed, Llanafan, Builth Wells, Powys, Wales. *Agent*—A. P. Watt, 26/28 Bedford Row, London WC1 R4HL, England.

CAREER: Teacher of English in a secondary modern school in Great Malvern, Worcestershire, England, 1953-54, and in a girls' grammar school in Newtown, Montgomery, Wales, 1954-59; Justice of the Peace, 1964-88; became a C.A.B. adviser and lay reader.

AWARDS, HONORS: Arts Council for Wales literary award, 1973, for *Pete;* Guardian Award for children's fiction runner-up, 1980, for *Leaving Home;* Carnegie Award shortlist, 1984, for *Christabel.*

WRITINGS:

Fish, illustrated by John Sergeant, Chatto & Windus (London), 1971, published as *A Boy Called Fish,* Harper (New York City), 1972.

Pete, Chatto & Windus, 1972, Harper, 1973.

Ruth Crane, Chatto & Windus, 1973, Harper, 1974.

The Raft, illustrated by Trevor Parkin, Abelard Schuman (London), 1974.

River Song, illustrated by John Schoenherr, Harper, 1975.

At Willie Tucker's Place, illustrated by Trevor Stubley, Chatto & Windus, 1975, Elsevier-Nelson (New York City), 1976.

Leaving Home, Chatto & Windus, 1979, published as *All Kinds of Prickles,* Elsevier-Nelson, 1980.

Paul's Kite, illustrated by Vanessa Julian-Ottie, Chatto & Windus, 1981, Atheneum (New York City), 1982.

Christabel, illustrated by Mariella Jennings, MacRae (London), 1984.

Bright-Eye, illustrated by Julian-Ottie, Viking Kestrel (London), 1984.

Staples for Amos, illustrated by Charles Front, MacRae, 1986.

The Eyes of the Blind, Oxford University Press (New York City), 1986.

The Wild Morgans, illustrated by Liz Roberts, Viking Kestrel, 1988.

A Walk with Smudge, MacRae, 1989.

Smudge and the Danger Lion, MacRae, 1989.

The Biggest Birthday Card in the World, MacRae, 1989.

Caroline's Coat, MacRae, 1991.

Smudge, Walker (London), 1992.

Granny and the Hedgehog, MacRae, 1995.

Also author of unpublished short plays produced by various local amateur groups, short stories, radio scripts, and a historical pageant which was produced in Brecon Cathedral. Contributor to *Times Literary Supplement* and other publications.

WORK IN PROGRESS: A historical novel about King David for older readers.

SIDELIGHTS: Alison Morgan set her first four novels, *Fish* (published in the United States as *A Boy Called Fish*), *Pete, Ruth Crane,* and *At Willie Tucker's Place,* in a hypothetical mid-Wales village. Morgan once explained: "Since the age of eight I have lived in the hilly empty heartland of mid-Wales, and my family has had roots in the area ever since my great-grandfather built a house there in the middle of the nineteenth century." It wasn't until her fifth and sixth books, *Leaving Home* (published in the United States as *All Kinds of Prickles*) and its sequel, *Paul's Kite,* that Morgan allowed her characters to venture outside of the Welsh countryside. Both of these stories deal with the adjustments which

have to be made when young characters face change. "In *Leaving Home* and its sequel, *Paul's Kite,*" Morgan explained, "although the main character has come from a mid-Wales setting similar to that of the earlier books, the stories concern his new life, first in a South Wales seaside town and later in London."

Leaving Home is "a penetrating and humane study of a young boy whose roots have been disturbed, if not destroyed," notes a *Junior Bookshelf* reviewer. When Paul Evans' grandfather—his only guardian—dies, Paul is torn from the comfort of small-town life and forced to live with relatives in suburban London. Unable to cope with the transition, Paul runs away back to Wales. In the sequel to *Leaving Home,* Paul is shipped off to London once again, this time to live with the mother who fled when he was an infant. His mother refuses to acknowledge that she could have a son Paul's age, so she passes him off as her nephew or brother. "Morgan neither condemns nor sentimentalizes," remarks a reviewer in the *Bulletin of the Center for Children's Books,* referring to *Paul's Kite.* "She comes between readers and characters as little as it is possible for an author to do, and her well-paced story smoothly fuses the sharply-etched characters." Writing in *Horn Book,* Nancy C. Hammond similarly notes that "the reflective, well-written narrative blends convincing contemporary characters, memorable vignettes of city life, and echoes of Cinderella."

"Writing in any form I have always taken for granted as a form of self-expression essential to me, and always intended to take it up professionally when the opportunity arose," Morgan has explained. "I think I moved from amateur to professional level with *Fish* because writing for children imposed a discipline my work had previously lacked. The best preparation was writing plays for local groups and producing them myself; I learned to prune ruthlessly. I write Welsh countryside books because that is where I live; I am tied domestically, so travel and access to literary material is limited, but staying still in one place one gets to know about people three-dimensionally.

"I live in a bilingual country, but always in an area where English is the normal form of communication, although near enough to the Welsh-speaking districts to be familiar with some of the problems. My children were taught Welsh as a matter of course in the local village school until the age of eleven, but they and their contemporaries always speak English to each other. The country I write about in my books is not a 'real' place but is typical of this sort of upland, sparsely populated English-speaking part of Wales, half-way up, and fairly near the English border. Our house backs onto an afforested hill and faces a patchwork of small fields exclusively inhabited by sheep, or set aside for the hay harvest; behind rises the slope of moorland where sheep and bracken compete for a living on the stony soil, and the army carry out their artillery training on the miles of uninhabited uplands, providing the background for my book *At Willie Tucker's Place.*

"We keep hens and ducks and geese, despite sporadic raids by the foxes that flourish in the fir plantations behind us; we have a large untidy garden and grow our own vegetables. It is a quiet part of the world, just off the tourist beaten track, though we share, to a lesser degree than some areas, the problems of village depopulation and brightly-done-up cottages dotted about the countryside occupied only by fleeting visitors during the summer months. But while the sons and daughters of the old farming families take up jobs as teachers and policemen and bank clerks in the cities, more and more young families come here from the towns, to take up small-holdings or set up pottery or handicraft projects, and so a sort of balance is struck. Change comes gently to the area, but when I look back over the twenty years I have lived in this one place, I realize how much, indeed, has changed."

BIOGRAPHICAL/CRITICAL SOURCES:

PERIODICALS

Best Sellers, November 15, 1973, p. 383; November 15, 1974, p. 378.
Booklist, September 1, 1974, p. 46; November 15, 1975, p. 457; March 1, 1977, p. 1016; March 1, 1980, p. 983; February 1, 1983, p. 725; October 1, 1990, p. 348.
Books for Keeps, September, 1992, p. 10.
Bookshelf, August, 1984, p. 170.
Bulletin of the Center for Children's Books, November, 1973, p. 48; December, 1973, p. 68; February, 1975, p. 97; January, 1981, p. 98; July, 1982, p. 212.
Childhood Education, November, 1973, p. 98; February, 1974, p. 227; January, 1981, p. 172.
Children's Book Review Service, February, 1983, p. 71.
Growing Point, October, 1976, p. 2965; January, 1982, p. 4012; July, 1984, pp. 4280-84; September, 1986, p. 4667; January, 1987, p. 4732; September, 1991, p. 5576.

Horn Book, February, 1974, p. 52; December, 1974, p. 693; February, 1976, p. 52; April, 1980, p. 174; December, 1982, p. 651.
Junior Bookshelf, June, 1980, pp. 145-46; February, 1982, p. 35; October, 1984, p. 210; December, 1986, pp. 233-34; December, 1988, p. 292; April, 1992, pp. 63.
Kirkus Reviews, March 1, 1973, p. 255; November 1, 1974, p. 1162; October 1, 1975, p. 1131; November 1, 1976, p. 1170; May 1, 1980, p. 586; August 1, 1982, p. 868.
Library Journal, March 15, 1973, p. 1006; September 15, 1973, p. 2666; October 15, 1974, p. 2748.
Library Review, autumn, 1972, p. 300; winter, 1974, p. 171; autumn, 1975, p. 137.
Publishers Weekly, June 18, 1973, p. 70; September 15, 1975, p. 60; January 3, 1977, p. 69.
School Librarian, March, 1983, p. 38; June, 1984, pp. 126-27; September, 1984, p. 241; December, 1986, p. 366.
School Library Journal, September, 1975, p. 108; January, 1977, p. 94; September, 1980, p. 76; August, 1982, p. 119; February, 1988, p. 85.
Times Educational Supplement, October 7, 1977, p. 22; November 23, 1979, p. 31; December 14, 1979, p. 21; June 8, 1984, p. 50; October 10, 1986, p. 28.
Times Literary Supplement, December 5, 1975, p. 1448; November 20, 1981, p. 1356; March 30, 1984, p. 337; June 1, 1984, p. 620; September 13, 1991, p. 25.

*   *   *

MUMFORD, Ruth   1919-
(Ruth Dallas)

PERSONAL: Born September 29, 1919, in Invercargill, New Zealand; daughter of Francis Sydney (in business) and Minnie Jane (Johnson) Mumford. *Education:* Attended Southland Technical College, Invercargill, New Zealand.

ADDRESSES: Home—448 Leith St., Dunedin, New Zealand.

CAREER: Poet and children's writer. Writer for children's page of the *Southland Daily News* (now *Southland Times*), 1932.

MEMBER: PEN (New Zealand).

AWARDS, HONORS: New Zealand Literary Fund achievement award, 1963, for *The Turning Wheel;* Robert Burns Fellow at the University of Otago, 1968; New Zealand Book Award in poetry, 1977, for *Steps of the Sun;* Buckland Literature Award, 1977, for *Song for a Guitar and Other Songs;* D.Litt., University of Otago, 1978.

WRITINGS:

CHILDREN'S FICTION; UNDER PSEUDONYM RUTH DALLAS

Ragamuffin Scarecrow, illustrated by Els Noordhof, University of Otago Bibliography Room (Dunedin, New Zealand), 1969.
The Children in the Bush, illustrated by Peter Campbell, Methuen (London), 1969.
A Dog Called Wig, illustrated by Edward Mortelmans, Methuen, 1970.
The Wild Boy in the Bush, illustrated by Campbell, Methuen, 1971.
The Big Flood in the Bush, illustrated by Campbell, Methuen, 1972, Scholastic (New York City), 1974.
The House on the Cliffs, illustrated by Gavin Rowe, Methuen, 1975.
Shining Rivers, illustrated by Gareth Floyd, Methuen, 1979.
Holiday Time in the Bush, illustrated by Gary Hebley, Methuen, 1983.

CHILDREN'S NONFICTION; UNDER PSEUDONYM RUTH DALLAS

Sawmilling Yesterday, illustrated by Juliet Peter, Department of Education (Wellington, New Zealand), 1958.
Curved Horizon: An Autobiography, University of Otago Press (Dunedin, New Zealand), 1991.

POETRY; UNDER PSEUDONYM RUTH DALLAS

Country Road and Other Poems, 1947-1952, Caxton Press (London), 1953.
The Turning Wheel, Caxton Press, 1961.
Experiment in Form, University of Otago Bibliography Room, 1964.
Day Book: Poems of a Year, Caxton Press, 1966.
Shadow Show, Caxton Press, 1968.
Walking on the Snow, Caxton Press, 1976.
Song for a Guitar and Other Songs, edited by Charles Brasch, University of Otago Press, 1976.

Steps of the Sun, Caxton Press, 1979.
Collected Poems, University of Otago Press, 1987.

Contributor to *An Anthology of Twentieth Century New Zealand Poetry,* edited by Vincent O'Sullivan, Oxford University Press (New York City), 1970, and *Ten Modern New Zealand Poets,* Longman (London), 1974. Also contributor to literary quarterlies, including *Landfall, Meanjin,* and *Islands,* and to school journals.

Mumford's manuscripts are collected in the Hocken Library at the University of Otago, Dunedin, New Zealand. Her books have been translated into German, Danish and Swedish.

SIDELIGHTS: Author and poet Ruth Mumford, who writes under the pseudonym Ruth Dallas, is a native New Zealander and was raised on the southern tip of South Island. "We enjoyed the solitary peace of the earth," she has said of her childhood, "and where the sheer magnitude of the sky and sea seemed to dwarf human beings to insignificance." Because there were no children's books set in New Zealand when she was growing up, Dallas decided that she would write her own. Her books are often set in New Zealand's pioneer days, when the islands were first being settled by Europeans, and deal with the country's natural beauty and the lives and customs of its native inhabitants.

In *The Wild Boy in the Bush,* three adventuresome youngsters discover the bones of a moa (an extinct flightless bird), a cave which seems to be the ideal hideout, and, most surprisingly, a wild boy who is living alone in the bush. "By letting an eight-year-old tell the tale, [Dallas] tunes right in, both vocabulary-wise and fictionally, to the wavelength of younger readers," remarks Alice Andrews in *Books and Bookmen.* In *Holiday Time in the Bush* Dallas describes the preparations for Christmas among a group of New Zealand pioneer children. The book is "full of typical happenings of an ordinary family, and this is what makes the story such an acceptable read," notes a *Junior Bookshelf* reviewer. Dallas set *Shining Rivers* in the 1860s, during New Zealand's gold rush. It tells the story of the young boy Johnie, who is lured to try his luck in the New Zealand gold fields before finally returning to the more stable life of a farmer. Johnie is a "boy trying to cope with a man's world and managing to do so remarkably well," observes a *Junior Bookshelf* reviewer.

BIOGRAPHICAL/CRITICAL SOURCES:

BOOKS

Ten Modern New Zealand Poets, Longman, 1974.

PERIODICALS

Books and Bookmen, December, 1971, p. R14.
Growing Point, January, 1980, pp. 3619-24; May, 1983, pp. 4072-76.
Junior Bookshelf, April, 1980, p. 80; August, 1983, p. 161.
Landfall 76, December, 1965.
Review (annual of University of Otago), 1975.
School Librarian, March, 1980, p. 54.*

N-0

NAIPAUL, V(idiadhar) S(urajprasad) 1932-

PERSONAL: Born August 17, 1932, in Chaguanas, Trinidad; son of Seepersad (a journalist and writer) and Dropatie Capildeo Naipaul; married Patricia Ann Hale, 1955. *Education:* Attended Queen's Royal College in Trinidad, 1943-48; University College, Oxford, B.A., 1953.

ADDRESSES: Agent—c/o Aitken & Stone Ltd., 29 Fernshaw Rd., London SW10, England.

CAREER: Writer. Also worked as a freelance broadcaster for the British Broadcasting Corp. (BBC), 1954-56.

MEMBER: Society of Authors, Royal Society of Literature (fellow).

AWARDS, HONORS: John Llewellyn Rhys Memorial Prize, 1958, for *The Mystic Masseur;* grant from government of Trinidad for travel in Caribbean, 1960-61; Somerset Maugham Award, 1961, for *Miguel Street;* Phoenix Trust Award, 1963; Hawthornden Prize, 1964, for *Mr. Stone and the Knights Companion;* W. H. Smith Award, 1968, for *The Mimic Men;* Booker Prize, 1971, for *In a Free State;* D. Litt, St. Andrew's College, 1979, Columbia University, 1981, Cambridge University, 1983, London University, 1988, and Oxford University, 1992; Bennett Award from *Hudson Review,* 1980; T. S. Eliot Award for Creative Writing from Ingersoll Foundation, 1986; knighted, 1990.

WRITINGS:

The Mystic Masseur, Deutsch (London), 1957, Vanguard (New York City), 1959.

The Suffrage of Elvira, Deutsch (London), 1958.
Miguel Street, Deutsch, 1959, Vanguard, 1960.
A House for Mr. Biswas, Deutsch, 1961, McGraw (New York City), 1962.
The Middle Passage: Impressions of Five Societies— British, French and Dutch in the West Indies and South America (nonfiction), Deutsch, 1962, Macmillan (New York City), 1963.
Mr. Stone and the Knights Companion, Deutsch, 1963, Macmillan, 1964.
An Area of Darkness (nonfiction), Deutsch, 1964, Macmillan, 1965.
The Mimic Men, Macmillan, 1967.
A Flag on the Island (short story collection), Macmillan, 1967.
The Loss of El Dorado: A History (nonfiction), Deutsch, 1969, Knopf (New York City), 1970.
(Contributor) Andrew Salkey, editor, *Island Voices: Stories from the West Indies,* new edition, Liveright, 1970.
In a Free State, Knopf, 1971.
The Overcrowded Barracoon and Other Articles, Deutsch, 1972, Knopf, 1973.
Guerrillas, Knopf, 1975.
India: A Wounded Civilization (nonfiction), Knopf, 1977.
The Perfect Tenants and The Mourners, Cambridge University Press (Cambridge, England), 1977.
A Bend in the River, Knopf, 1979.
The Return of Eva Peron (nonfiction), Knopf, 1980.
A Congo Diary, Sylvester & Orphanos (Los Angeles, CA), 1980.
Among the Believers: An Islamic Journey, Knopf, 1981.
Finding the Center, Knopf, 1986.
The Enigma of Arrival, Knopf, 1987.
A Turn in the South, Knopf, 1989.

India: A Million Mutinies Now, Heinemann (London), 1990, Viking (New York City), 1991.
A Way in the World, Knopf, 1994.

Contributor to *New York Review of Books, New Statesman,* and other periodicals. Fiction reviewer, *New Statesman,* 1958-61.

SIDELIGHTS: Born in Trinidad to descendants of Hindu immigrants from northern India and educated at England's Oxford University, V. S. Naipaul is identified by many critics as one of the world's most gifted novelists. As a *New York Times Book Review* critic writes: "For sheer abundance of talent there can hardly be a writer alive who surpasses V. S. Naipaul. Whatever we may want in a novelist is to be found in his books: an almost Conradian gift for tensing a story, a serious involvement with human issues, a supple English prose, a hard-edged wit, a personal vision of things. Best of all, he is a novelist unafraid of using his brains. . . . His novels are packed with thought, not as lumps of abstraction but as one fictional element among others, fluid in the stream of narrative. . . . [He is] the world's writer, a master of language and perception, our sardonic blessing."

The idea of Naipaul as "the world's writer" comes largely, as he has pointed out himself, from his rootlessness. Unhappy with the cultural and spiritual poverty of Trinidad, distanced from India, and unable to relate to and share in the heritage of each country's former imperial ruler (England), Naipaul describes himself as "content to be a colonial, without a past, without ancestors." As a result of this nonattachment to region and tradition, most of his work deals with people who, like himself, feel estranged from the societies they are ostensibly part of and who desperately seek ways to belong or "to be someone." The locales Naipaul chooses for his stories represent an extension of this same theme, for most take place in emerging Third World countries in the throes of creating new national identities from the remnants of native and colonial cultures.

Naipaul's early works explore the comic aspects of these themes. Essentially West Indian variations on the comedy of manners, these works present almost farcical accounts of an illiterate and divided society's shift from colonial to independent status, emphasizing the multiracial misunderstandings and rivalries and various ironies resulting from the sudden introduction of such democratic processes as free elec-

tions. In *The Mystic Masseur, The Suffrage of Elvira,* and *Miguel Street,* Naipaul exposes the follies and absurdities of Trinidadian society; his tone is detached yet sympathetic, as if he is looking back at a distant past of which he is no longer a part. The tragic aspects of the situation are not examined, nor is there any attempt to involve the reader in the plight of the characters. Michael Thorpe describes the prevailing tone of these early books as "that of the ironist who points up the comedy, futility and absurdity that fill the gap between aspiration and achievement, between the public image desired and the individual's inadequacies, to recognize which may be called the education of the narrator: 'I had grown up and looked critically at the people around me.'"

A House for Mr. Biswas marks an important turning point in Naipaul's work; his attention to psychological and social realism foreshadows the intensive character studies of his later works. In addition, *A House for Mr. Biswas* has a universality of theme that the earlier books lacked because of their emphasis on the particularities of Trinidadian society. As a consequence of these "improvements," many critics regard *A House for Mr. Biswas* as Naipaul's masterpiece. Robert D. Hamner wrote in 1973 that with "the appearance in 1961 of *A House for Mr. Biswas,* Naipaul may have published his best fiction. It is even possible that this book is the best novel yet to emerge from the Caribbean. It is a vital embodiment of authentic West Indian life, but more than that, it transcends national boundaries and evokes universal human experiences. Mr. Biswas' desire to own his own house is essentially a struggle to assert personal identity and to attain security—thoroughly human needs."

A *New York Herald Tribune Books* reviewer notes that "Naipaul has a wry wit and an engaging sense of humor, as well as a delicate understanding of sadness and futility and a profound but unobtrusive sense of the tragi-comedy of ordinary living. . . . His style is precise and assured. In short, he gives every indication of being an important addition to the international literary scene. [*A House for Mr. Biswas*] is funny, it is compassionate. It has more than 500 pages and not one of them is superfluous." Paul Theroux, writing in the *New York Times Book Review,* admits that "it is hard for the reviewer of a wonderful author to keep the obituarist's assured hyperbole in check, but let me say that if the silting-up of the Thames coincided with a freak monsoon, causing massive flooding in all parts of South London, the first book I would rescue from my library would be *A House for Mr. Biswas.*"

Michael Thorpe asserts that, "At first sight *Mr. Biswas* seems an abrupt departure from Naipaul's previous fiction: in its concentration upon the life history of a single protagonist it goes far deeper than *The Mystic Masseur* and the mood is predominantly 'serious,' the still pervasive comedy being subordinated to that mood. Yet on further consideration we can see *Mr. Biswas* as the natural and consummate development of themes that ran through the first three books: the perplexing relation of the individual to society, his struggle to impress himself upon it through achievement—or defy its pressures with a transforming fantasy that puts a gloss upon life and extracts order from the rude chaos of everyday existence." In short, Thorpe concludes, "for West Indian literature *A House for Mr. Biswas* forged [the] connexion [between literature and life] with unbreakable strength and set up a model for emulation which no other 'Third World' literature in English has yet equalled."

After the success of *A House for Mr. Biswas,* Naipaul increasingly sought broader geographic and social contexts in which to explore his themes. At the same time, his earlier light-hearted tone gradually faded as he examined the more tragic consequences of alienation and rootlessness through the eyes of various "universal wanderers." As Thomas Lask reports in the *New York Times:* "V. S. Naipaul's writings about his native Trinidad have often enough been touched with tolerant amusement. His is an attitude that is affectionate without being overly kind. . . . These new stories focus on the failure of heart, on the animallike cruelty man exhibits to other men. . . . What the author is saying is that neither customs nor color nor culture seems able to quiet that impulse to destruction, that murderous wantonness that is so much part of our make-up. . . . Mr. Naipaul's style in these stories seems leaner than in the past and much more somber. There is virtually none of the earlier playfulness."

Paul Theroux calls *In a Free State* "a story-sequence brilliant in conception, masterly in execution, and terrifying in effect—the chronicles of a half-a-dozen self-exiled people who have become lost souls. Having abandoned their own countries (countries they were scarcely aware of belonging to), they have found themselves in strange places, without friends, with few loyalties, and with the feeling that they are trespassing. . . . The subject of displacement is one

few writers have touched upon. Camus has written of it. But Naipaul is much superior to Camus, and his achievement—a steady advance through eleven volumes—is as disturbing as it is original. *In a Free State* is a masterpiece in the fiction of rootlessness."

Alfred Kazin, writing in the *New York Review of Books,* claims that "Naipaul writes about the many psychic realities of exile in our contemporary world with far more bite and dramatic havoc than Joyce. . . . What makes Naipaul hurt so much more than other novelists of contemporary exodus is his major image—the tenuousness of man's hold on the earth. . . . Naipaul has never encompassed so much, and with such brilliant economy, with such a patent though lighthanded ominousness of manner, as in [*In a Free State*]." While acknowledging that "one criticism of Naipaul might well be that he covers too much ground, has too many representative types, and that he has an obvious desolation about homelessness, migration, the final placelessness of those who have seen too much, which he tends to turn into a mysterious accusation," Kazin concludes, "Though he is a marvelous technician, there is something finally modest, personal, openly committed about his fiction, a frankness of personal reference, that removes him from the godlike impersonality of the novelist."

With the publication of *Guerrillas,* the novel that established Naipaul's reputation in the United States, many reviewers noted a darkening of Naipaul's outlook. "*Guerrillas* is one of Naipaul's most complex books," Theroux remarks. "It is certainly his most suspenseful, a series of shocks, like a shroud slowly unwound from a bloody corpse, showing the damaged—and familiar—face last. . . . This is a novel without a villain, and there is not a character for whom the reader does not at some point feel deep sympathy and keen understanding, no matter how villainous or futile he may seem. *Guerrillas* is a brilliant novel in every way, and it shimmers with artistic certainty."

Paul Gray of *Time* believes that *Guerrillas* "proves [Naipaul] the laureate of the West Indies. . . . [He] is a native expatriate with a fine distaste for patriotic rhetoric. . . . [The novel] is thus conspicuously short of heroes. . . . The native politicians are corrupt, the foreign businessmen avaricious, and the people either lethargic or criminal. When an uprising does flare, it is nasty and inept. Perhaps no one but Naipaul has the inside and outside knowledge to have turned such a dispirited tale into so gripping a book. . . . *Guer-*

rillas is not a polemic (polemicists will be annoyed) but a Conradian vision of fallibility and frailty. With economy and compassion, Naipaul draws the heart of darkness from a sun-struck land." Charles R. Larson of the *Nation* asserts, "No one writes better about politics in the West Indies than V. S. Naipaul. Nor is there anyone who writes more profoundly about exiles, would-be revolutionaries and their assorted camp followers. Written in a deliberately flat style, *Guerrillas* is a deeply pessimistic novel, telling us that we have seen about as much political change in the West Indian island republics as we are likely to see."

In *A Bend in the River,* Naipaul returns to Africa as a locale (the scene of *In a Free State*) and confirms his basic pessimism. John Leonard comments in the *New York Times:* "This is not an exotic Africa [in *A Bend in the River*]. . . . [The author] despises nostalgia for the colonial past, while at the same time heartlessly parodying . . . the African future. . . . *A Bend in the River* is a brilliant and depressing novel. It is no secret by now, certainly not since *Guerrillas* . . ., that V. S. Naipaul is one of the handful of living writers of whom the English language can be proud, if, still, profoundly uneasy. There is no consolation from him, any more than there is sentiment. His wit has grown hard and fierce; he isn't seeking to amuse, but to scourge."

John Updike, writing in the *New Yorker,* asserts that *A Bend in the River* "proves once more that Naipaul is incomparably well situated and equipped to bring us news of one of the contemporary world's great subjects—the mingling of its peoples." He continues, "In *A Bend in the River,* the alien observer—white bureaucrat or Asian trader—is drawn closer into the rationale of the riots and wars that seethe in the slums or the bush beyond his enclave. The novel might be faulted for savoring a bit of the visiting journalist's worked-up notes: its episodes do not hang together with full organic snugness; there are a few too many clever geopolitical conversations and scenically detailed car rides. . . . [But] the author's embrace of his tangled and tragic African scene seems relatively hearty as well as immensely knowledgeable."

Walter Clemons of *Newsweek* calls *A Bend in the River* "a hurtful, claustrophobic novel, very hard on the nerves, played out under a vast African sky in an open space that is made to feel stifling. . . . Naipaul's is a political novel of a subtle and unusual kind. . . . [It] is about tremors of expectation, shifts

in personal loyalty, manners in dire emergency. . . . As an evocation of place, [the novel] succeeds brilliantly. . . . *A Bend in the River* is by no means a perfected work. . . . But this imperfect, enormously disturbing book confirms Naipaul's position as one of the best writers now at work." "On the surface, *A Bend in the River* emerges mostly as a web of caustic observation, less exciting than its predecessor, *Guerrillas;* but it is a much better and deeper novel, for Naipaul has mastered the gift of creating an aura of psychic and moral tension even as, seemingly, very little happens," Irving Howe writes in the *New York Times Book Review.* He relates this observation to Naipaul's writing style: "A novelist has to be faithful to what he sees, and few see as well as Naipaul; yet one may wonder whether, in some final reckoning, a serious writer can simply allow the wretchedness of his depicted scene to become the limit of his vision. . . . Naipaul seems right now to be a writer beleaguered by his own truths, unable to get past them. That is surely an honorable difficulty, far better than indulging in sentimental or ideological uplift; but it exacts a price. . . . Perhaps we ought simply to be content that, in his austere and brilliant way, he holds fast to the bitterness before his eyes."

Naipaul chose a different setting for his novel *The Enigma of Arrival.* John Thieme explains in the *Dictionary of Literary Biography* that in the years between the publication of *A Bend in the River* and *The Enigma of Arrival,* the author "suffered from a serious illness and was deeply moved by the deaths of his younger sister and his brother, Shiva." *The Enigma of Arrival,* Thieme continues, reflects his somber personal experience and "is pervaded by a sense of personal loss and fragility." The novel examines the impact of imperialism on a native English estate, slowly decaying along with its reclusive landlord, who is suffering from a degenerative disease. "Characteristically for Naipaul," Thieme declares, "the narrator identifies with his landlord's sense of inertia, which is symbolized by his allowing ivy to proliferate and gradually strangle the trees on his grounds. The colonial man has found a haven in a landscape that seems 'benign' to him, but the manor is a semiruin, without the traditional appendages of farms and lands, and the remains of the older management that it represents crumble during the course of the narrative." The decay of the manor and its owner causes the novel's autobiographical narrator to ponder the inevitability of his own death. "The novel is full of intimations of mortality," Thieme concludes, "and ultimately it is as much a generalized lament for human transience and an expression of the writer's all-pervasive sense of vulnerability as an elegy for any particular person or community."

With *A Turn in the South* and *India: A Million Mutinies Now,* Naipaul turned to nonfiction. *A Turn in the South* tells of a journey through the southern United States, ostensibly looking for similarities between Naipaul's own Trinidadian culture and that of the American South. "Consequently 'the race issue' is high on his agenda at the outset," Thieme explains, "but it is increasingly less so as the work proceeds." Instead, Naipaul finds himself drawn deeper and deeper into a description of the culture of the modern American south, including country western music, strict, conservative Christianity, and the enduring fascination with Elvis Presley. *India: A Million Mutinies Now* represents Naipaul's third consideration of his ancestral homeland. Unlike the first two times, in which Naipaul expressed pessimism about India's ability to overcome centuries of religious and ethnic strife, in *India: A Million Mutinies Now* the author "takes heart in what he sees," declares Thomas D'Evelyn in the *Christian Science Monitor.* "As the details accumulate, the reader becomes more deeply involved in a growing appreciation for a life lived under extreme circumstances. Reading Naipaul," D'Evelyn concludes, "one becomes as optimistic about mankind as the author is about India." "His cautious optimism represents the primary value of the book," states Douglas J. Macdonald in *America.* "Pessimism can too easily lead to inertia and despair. . . . Naipaul's message is that despite the problems, despite the obstacles, the Indians, and by extension the rest of us, must continue to try." "Whether or not they know it," asserts *New York Review of Books* contributor Ian Buruma, "the millions of mutineers, wrestling with their fates, are all on the road forever. That is the truth of Naipaul's excellent book."

A Way in the World mixes elements of Naipaul's fiction and nonfiction, merging his Indian and West Indian heritage with the English history and culture he assumed when he immigrated to England at the age of eighteen. "His project is simultaneously to construct his own literary inheritance and the legacy he will leave to the world," explains Philip Gourevitch in *Commentary.* "The book . . . combines memoir, historical scholarship, and imaginative writing in a series of nine independent but thematically interlocking narratives. These narratives accumulate to form a dramatic portrait gallery of people—historical and fictionalized—whose lives have been formed and transformed by their encoun-

ters with Trinidad. And through the echo chamber of their stories there emerges a portrait of the artist, Naipaul himself, at the apex of his literary consciousness." "Now, near the end of his days," declares Caryl Phillips in the *New Republic,* "Naipaul is clearly . . . deliberating over the question of whether he ever left home in the first place, for whatever else it is *A Way in the World* is a beautiful lament to the Trinidad he has so often denigrated."

Naipaul labels each of these early narratives "An Unwritten Story." He includes under that title tales about the sixteenth-century explorer Sir Walter Raleigh travelling down a branch of the Orinoco River in Guyana in search of gold (and not finding it), and a nineteenth century South American revolutionary named Francisco Miranda plotting a Venezuelan revolution that never materializes. However, he also traces the careers of other notable characters—the Trinidadian Marxist revolutionary Naipaul calls Lebrun, for instance, who served as advisor to several independence movements, but was discarded as irrelevant after the regimes were established. "Once in power," declares *Los Angeles Times Book Review* contributor Richard Eder, "[the nationalists] had no use for him; his ideology was good for building up their strength but they had no intention of actually setting up a Marxist regime." Instead, Lebrun found himself exiled to the fringes of society, spending his life in exile, speaking to leftist groups in Great Britain and the United States.

"If there is one thing that unifies the chapters in [*A Way in the World*]," declares Amit Chaudhuri in the *Spectator,* "it is its attempt to explore and define the nature of the colonial's memory." Chaudhuri contrasts Naipaul's fiction in this volume with the work of the British novelist Joseph Conrad, whose work often looked darkly at the spreading colonialism of Great Britain at the end of the nineteenth and the beginning of the twentieth centuries. The reviewer suggests that Naipaul retraces the colonialism that Conrad depicted in his work and shows in *A Way in the World* how British imperialism created not just colonies but colonials—men and women with unique sensibilities and memories. "The river, in these 'stories,' no longer remains simply a Conradian image of Western exploration and territorial ambition," Chaudhuri concludes, "but becomes an emblem of the colonial memory attempting to return to its source."

Naipaul's more recent works have served to confirm his status as one of the English language's most distinguished and perceptive contemporary writers. In his 1976 study of Naipaul, Michael Thorpe offers this overview of the novelist's accomplishments: "While Naipaul is by no means alone in coming from a makeshift colonial society and using the 'metropolitan' language with a native surety, these origins have helped him more than any of his contemporaries from the Commonwealth to develop an inclusive view of many facets of the larger world, a view focussed by his intense sense of displacement from society, race or creed. . . . He has gone beyond local conflicts, isolated instances of the colonial experience, to attempt something approaching a world view. . . . His insights and his manner of conveying them carry a persuasive truth."

As a result, continues Thorpe, "Naipaul has spoken from and to more points within that world [of imperial or social oppression] than any English writer—but his is not a comforting or hopeful voice. . . . Asked if he were an optimist [Naipaul] replied: 'I'm not sure. I think I do look for the seeds of regeneration in a situation; I long to find what is good and hopeful and really do hope that by the most brutal sort of analysis one is possibly opening up the situation to some sort of action; an action which is not based on self-deception.'. . . Yet Naipaul insists that he is hopeful: as one who has not flinched from harsh reality, he has earned the right to our reciprocal hope that he may yet find a way beyond despair."

BIOGRAPHICAL/CRITICAL SOURCES:

BOOKS

Contemporary Literary Criticism, Gale (Detroit), Volume 4, 1975; Volume 7, 1977; Volume 9, 1978; Volume 13, 1980; Volume 18, 1981; Volume 37, 1986.

Dictionary of Literary Biography, Volume 125: *Twentieth-Century Caribbean and Black African Writers, Second Series,* Gale, 1993.

Dictionary of Literary Biography Yearbook: 1985, Gale, 1986.

Dissanayake, Wimal, *Self and Colonial Desire: Travel Writings of V. S. Naipaul,* Peter Lang (New York City), 1993.

Hamner, Robert D., *V. S. Naipaul,* Twayne, 1973.

Kamra, Shashi, *The Novels of V. S. Naipaul: A Study in Theme and Form,* Prestige Books/Indian Society for Commonwealth Studies, 1990.

King, Bruce, *V. S. Naipaul,* St. Martin's (New York City), 1993.

Nixon, Rob, *London Calling: V. S. Naipaul, Postcolonial Mandarin,* Oxford University Press, 1992.

Thorpe, Michael, *V. S. Naipaul,* Longmans, 1976.

Weiss, Timothy, *On the Margins: The Art of Exile in V. S. Naipaul,* University of Massachusetts Press (Amherst), 1992.

PERIODICALS

America, June 15, 1991, pp. 656-57.

Atlantic, May, 1970; January, 1976; July, 1977; June, 1979.

Best Sellers, April 15, 1968.

Books Abroad, winter, 1968; winter, 1969.

Books and Bookmen, October, 1967.

Boston Globe, March 15, 1987; January 22, 1989; December 23, 1990.

Chicago Sunday Tribune, July 12, 1959.

Chicago Tribune Book World, May 13, 1979; April 20, 1980.

Choice, June, 1973.

Christian Science Monitor, July 19, 1962; March 29, 1968; May 28, 1970; February 28, 1991, p. 11.

Commentary, August, 1994, pp. 27-31.

Commonweal, September 9, 1994, pp. 28-29.

Contemporary Literature, winter, 1968.

Economist, July 16, 1977.

Illustrated London News, May 20, 1967.

Kenyon Review, November, 1967.

Listener, May 25, 1967; September 28, 1967; May 23, 1968.

London Magazine, May, 1967.

Los Angeles Times, May 9, 1980; March 15, 1989.

Los Angeles Times Book Review, June 24, 1979; May 22, 1994, pp. 3, 11.

Nation, October 9, 1967; October 5, 1970; December 13, 1975; July 2, 1977; June 30, 1979.

National Review, October 6, 1970; August 29, 1994, pp. 61-62.

New Republic, July 9, 1977; June 9, 1979; June 10, 1991, pp. 30-34; June 13, 1994, pp. 40-45.

New Statesman, May 5, 1967; September 15, 1967; November 7, 1969; October 8, 1971; June 17, 1977.

Newsweek, December 1, 1975; June 6, 1977; May 21, 1979; June 13, 1994, p. 55.

New Yorker, August 4, 1962; August 8, 1970; June 6, 1977; May 21, 1979.

New York Herald Tribune Books, June 24, 1962.

New York Review of Books, October 26, 1967; April 11, 1968; December 30, 1971; May 31, 1979; February 14, 1991, pp. 3-5.

New York Times, December 16, 1967; December 25, 1971; August 17, 1977; May 14, 1979; March 13, 1980; May 17, 1994.

New York Times Book Review, October 15, 1967; April 7, 1968; May 24, 1970; October 17, 1971; November 16, 1975; December 28, 1975; May 1, 1977; June 12, 1977; May 13, 1979; May 22, 1994, pp. 1, 42-43.

Observer (London), April 30, 1967; September 10, 1967; October 26, 1969.

Punch, May 10, 1967.

Saturday Review, July 2, 1960; October 23, 1971; November 15, 1975.

Spectator, September 22, 1967; November 8, 1969; May 14, 1994, p. 36.

Time, May 25, 1970; December 1, 1975; June 20, 1977; May 21, 1979; May 30, 1994, p. 64.

Times Literary Supplement, May 31, 1963; April 27, 1967; September 14, 1967; December 25, 1969; July 30, 1971; November 17, 1972.

Transition, December, 1971.

Washington Post Book World, April 19, 1970; December 5, 1971; November 28, 1976; June 19, 1977; July 1, 1979; May 15, 1994, pp. 1, 14.*

*   *   *

NAPIER, Mary
   See WRIGHT, (Mary) Patricia

*   *   *

NAYLOR, Gloria   1950-

PERSONAL: Born January 25, 1950, in New York, NY; daughter of Roosevelt (a transit worker) and Alberta (a telephone operator; maiden name, McAlpin) Naylor. *Education:* Brooklyn College of the City University of New York, B.A., 1981; Yale University, M.A., 1983.

*ADDRESSES: Office—*One Way Productions, 638 2nd St., Brooklyn, NY 11215.

CAREER: Missionary for Jehovah's Witnesses in New York, North Carolina, and Florida, 1968-75; worked for various hotels in New York City, including Sheraton City Squire, and as telephone operator, 1975-81; writer, 1981—. President, One Way Productions (film production company), New York City,

1990—. Writer in residence, Cummington Community of the Arts, 1983; visiting professor to George Washington University, 1983-84, Princeton University, 1986-87, and Boston University, 1987; cultural exchange lecturer, United States Information Agency, India, 1985; scholar in residence, University of Pennsylvania, 1986; visiting writer, New York University, 1986; Fannie Hurst Visiting Professor, Brandeis University, 1988. Senior fellow, Society for the Humanities, Cornell University, 1988.

AWARDS, HONORS: National Book Award for best first novel, 1983, for *The Women of Brewster Place: A Novel in Seven Stories;* Distinguished Writer Award, Mid-Atlantic Writers Association, 1983; National Endowment for the Arts fellowship, 1985; Candace Award, National Coalition of 100 Black Women, 1986; Guggenheim fellowship, 1988; Lillian Smith Award, 1989.

WRITINGS:

NOVELS

The Women of Brewster Place: A Novel in Seven Stories, Viking (New York City), 1982.

Linden Hills, Ticknor & Fields (New York City), 1985.

Mama Day, Ticknor & Fields, 1988.

Bailey's Cafe (also see below), Harcourt (New York City), 1992.

OTHER

Bailey's Cafe (play; adapted by Naylor from her novel of the same title), produced in Hartford, CT, 1994.

(Editor) *Children of the Night: The Best Short Stories by Black Writers, 1967 to the Present,* Little, Brown (Boston), 1995.

Author of an unproduced original screenplay for Public Broadcasting System's "In Our Own Words," 1985. Contributor to *Centennial,* Pindar Press, 1986. Also author of column, "Hers," *New York Times,* 1986. Contributor of essays and articles to periodicals, including *Southern Review, Essence, Ms., Life, Ontario Review,* and *People.* Contributing editor, *Callaloo,* 1984—.

ADAPTATIONS: Gloria Naylor: Reading and Interview (cassette), American Audio Prose, 1988. *Mama Day* was recorded on audio-cassette, Brilliance, 1989. *The Women of Brewster Place: A Novel in*

Seven Stories was adapted into a miniseries, produced by Oprah Winfrey and Carole Isenberg, and broadcast by American Broadcasting Co. (ABC-TV) in 1989; it became a weekly ABC series in 1990, produced by Winfrey, Earl Hamner, and Donald Sipes.

WORK IN PROGRESS: A screenplay for Zenith Productions, London; a film adaptation of *Mama Day,* to be produced by Naylor's company, One Way Productions, Inc.

SIDELIGHTS: Gloria Naylor's first novel, *The Women of Brewster Place: A Novel in Seven Stories,* which features a cast of seven strong-willed African-American women, won the National Book Award for best first fiction in 1983. Naylor continues her exploration of the black female experience while expanding her fictional realm in her subsequent three novels. In *Linden Hills,* for example, Naylor uses the structure of Dante Alighieri's *Inferno* to create a contemporary allegory about the perils of African-American materialism and the ways in which denying one's heritage can endanger the soul. Naylor's third novel, *Mama Day,* draws on another literary masterpiece—William Shakespeare's *The Tempest*—combining Shakespearean elements with black folkloric strains. Her fourth novel, *Bailey's Cafe,* echoes both the narrative voice and earthiness of Geoffrey Chaucer's *The Canterbury Tales* and the hellish dislocation of Jean Paul Sartre's *No Exit.* By drawing on traditional western sources, Naylor places herself firmly in the literary mainstream, broadening her base from ethnic to American writing. Unhappy with what she calls the "historical tendency to look upon the output of black writers as not really American literature," Naylor told *Publishers Weekly* interviewer William Goldstein that her work attempts to "articulate experiences that want articulating—for those readers who reflect the subject matter, black readers, and for those who don't—basically white middle-class readers."

Naylor's first novel grew out of a desire to reflect the diversity of the African-American experience—a diversity that she feels neither the black nor the white critical establishment has recognized. Naylor commented to Dieter Miller in *Authors and Artists for Young Adults:* "I look back and realize how totally ignorant I was of literature that reflected my experience as a black American. I grew up thinking that black people didn't write books. That benign form of neglect on the part of the educational system was a crime."

The Women of Brewster Place is "organized around the lives of seven women, all of whom live on Brewster Place," summarizes Judith V. Branzburg in *Callaloo.* "Each chapter, or story, is devoted to detailing the circumstances of one of the women's lives." Among the characters of the novel are Mattie Michael, who contends with a son she perceives as having failed her; Etta Mae Johnson and Lucielia Louise Turner, both of whom deal with issues of love; and Kiswana Browne, a young political activist who grew up in the affluent Linden Hills.

Reviewing *The Women of Brewster Place* in the *Washington Post,* Deirdre Donahue writes: "Naylor is not afraid to grapple with life's big subjects: sex, birth, love, death, grief. Her women feel deeply, and she unflinchingly transcribes their emotions. . . . With prose as rich as poetry, a passage will suddenly take off and sing like a spiritual." Donahue concludes that *The Women of Brewster Place* "sings of sorrows proudly borne by black women in America." Despite what Branzburg considers an overemphasis on heterosexual relationships and monetary difficulties in the work, she nonetheless concludes: "taken as part of the whole, these are minor complaints. Naylor's ability to present the pain and love of her characters' lives carries her through."

Naylor often links her novels by utilizing the same characters and settings from one narrative to another. In *The Women of Brewster Place,* for example, Kiswana is from neighboring Linden Hills, an exclusive black suburb. Naylor's second novel, *Linden Hills,* focuses on this affluent community, revealing the material corruption and moral decay that would prompt an idealistic young woman to abandon her home for a derelict urban neighborhood. Though *Linden Hills* approaches the African-American experience from the upper end of the socioeconomic spectrum, it also creates a black microcosm. This book "forms the second panel of that picture of contemporary urban black life which Naylor started with in *Women of Brewster Place,*" writes *Times Literary Supplement* contributor Roz Kaveney. "Where that book described the faults, passions, and culture of the good poor, this shows the nullity of black lives that are led in imitation of suburban whites."

Naylor modeled *Linden Hills,* in part, after Dante's *Inferno,* a complex fourteenth-century Italian masterpiece that describes the nine circles of hell, Satan's imprisonment in their depths, and the lost souls condemned to suffer with him. In Naylor's modern version, notes Catherine C. Ward in *Contemporary Lit-*

erature, "souls are damned not because they have offended God or have violated a religious system but because they have offended themselves. In their single-minded pursuit of upward mobility, the inhabitants of Linden Hills, a black, middle-class suburb, have turned away from their past and from their deepest sense of who they are." Naylor's heroes are two young street poets—outsiders from a neighboring community who hire themselves out to do odd jobs so they can earn Christmas money. "As they move down the hill, what they encounter are people who have 'moved up' in American society . . . until eventually they will hit the center of their community and the home of my equivalent of Satan," Naylor told Goldstein. Naylor's Satan, Luther Needed, is a combination mortician and real estate tycoon, who preys on the residents' baser ambitions to keep them in his sway.

Though *Women's Review of Books* contributor Jewelle Gomez argues that "the Inferno motif . . . often feels like a literary exercise rather than a groundbreaking adaptation," many critics commend Naylor's bold experiment. *San Francisco Review of Books* contributor Claudia Tate, for instance, praises "Naylor's skill in linking together complicated stories in a highly structured but unobtrusive narrative form. In combining elements of realism and fantasy with a sequence of ironic reversals, she sets into motion a series of symbols which become interlinked, producing complex social commentary." Some critics who find the execution flawed nonetheless endorse Naylor's daring. *New York Times Book Review* contributor Mel Watkins comments: "Although Miss Naylor has not been completely successful in adapting the *Inferno* to the world of the black middle class, in *Linden Hills* she has shown a willingness to expand her fictional realm and to take risks. Its flaws notwithstanding, the novel's ominous atmosphere and inspired set pieces . . . make it a fascinating departure for Miss Naylor, as well as a provocative, iconoclastic novel about a seldom-addressed subject." Concludes a reviewer for *Ms.:* "In this second novel, Naylor serves notice that she is a mature literary talent of formidable skill."

The title character of Naylor's third novel, *Mama Day,* is "Mama" or Miranda Day, a wise, old woman with magical powers. This ninety-year-old conjurer makes a walk-on appearance in *Linden Hills* as an illiterate, toothless aunt who hauls about cheap cardboard suitcases and leaky jars of preserves. But it is in *Mama Day* that this "caster of hoodoo spells . . .

comes into her own," according to *New York Times Book Review* contributor Bharati Mukherjee. "The portrait of Mama Day is magnificent," she declares. Mama Day lives on Willow Springs, a wondrous island off the coast of Georgia and South Carolina that has been owned by her family since before the Civil War. The portrayal of slaves as property owners is just one of the ways that Naylor turns the world upside down, according to Rita Mae Brown. Another, continues Brown in the *Los Angeles Times Book Review,* is "that the women possess the real power, and are acknowledged as having it." When Mama Day's grandniece Cocoa brings George, her new husband, to Willow Springs, he learns the importance of accepting mystery. "George is the linchpin of *Mama Day,*" Brown says. "His rational mind allows the reader to experience the island as George experiences it. Mama Day and Cocoa are of the island and therefore less immediately accessible to the reader." George is asked to believe in the powers of Mama Day when Cocoa becomes seriously ill and no doctor is able to visit the island. Only Mama Day has the power to help George save Cocoa's life. She gives him a task, which he bungles because he is still limited by purely rational thinking. Ultimately, George is able to save Cocoa, but only by great personal sacrifice.

Several reviewers have found echoes of works by Shakespeare in the plot twists and thematic concerns of *Mama Day.* "Whereas *Linden Hills* was Dantesque, *Mama Day* is Shakespearean, with allusions, however oblique and tangential, to *Hamlet, King Lear,* and, especially, *The Tempest,*" writes *Chicago Tribune Books* critic John Blades. Mukherjee also believes that *Mama Day* "has its roots in *The Tempest.* The theme is reconciliation, the title character is Miranda (also the name of Prospero's daughter), and Willow Springs is an isolated island where, as on Prospero's isle, magical and mysterious events come to pass." However, Naylor's ambitious attempt to elevate a modern love story to Shakespearean heights "is more bewildering than bewitching," according to Blades. "Naylor has populated her magic kingdom with some appealingly offbeat characters, Mama Day foremost among them. But she's failed to give them anything very original or interesting to do." Mukherjee also acknowledges the shortcomings of Naylor's mythical love story, but asserts, "I'd rather dwell on *Mama Day*'s strengths. Gloria Naylor has written a big, strong, dense, admirable novel; spacious, sometimes a little drafty like all public monuments, designed to last and intended for many levels of use."

Bailey's Cafe was published in 1992 and later adapted for the stage in 1994. Here, Naylor continues to deal with what Donahue calls "life's big subjects" through interlinking stories which echo through the seemingly magical world of Bailey's Cafe, an establishment whose entrance is located on a ghetto street in an unnamed American city and whose back looks out on a void. "Bailey's Cafe is everywhere. It can be entered from the real world at any point," observes Karen Joy Fowler in Chicago *Tribune Books;* "its address is despair." Dan Wakefield writes in the *New York Times Book Review* that Naylor "takes us many keys down, and sometimes back up in this virtuoso orchestration of survival, suffering, courage and humor sounding through the stories" of the patrons of Bailey's Cafe. Sadie is a woman whose dreams of an ideal home are realized only through Five Star liquor—which she acquires by selling her body for the precise amount she needs at any one moment. Jesse Bell, from a strong line of Longshoremen women, turns to heroin as a means of coping with the destruction she endures at the hands of self-hating, bourgeois blacks, symbolized in *Bailey's Cafe* by the character of Uncle Eli. Miss Maple is, in fact, a man who, in his long and futile search for professional employment, "eventually . . . calculates that his chances would be no worse if he wore dresses to his interviews," comments Eder. The characters who frequent Bailey's Cafe make up a chorus whose "emotional outbursts make them universal," contends Roz Kaveney in the *Times Literary Supplement*.

While *Bailey's Cafe* was still in progress, Naylor revealed to Miller that it would have a tie-in with two characters from *Mama Day:* George and his mother. "I expand upon her and the other whores who were with her and deal with the Madonna complex we have in the Western mind when thinking about female sexuality," Naylor explained. However, some critics find Naylor's magical realism less than effective. Kaveney feels "it was a mistake" to set the novel "not in a mundane diner in a particular location, but in a magic diner which is there, in whatever city, for the people who need to find it." Additionally, she argues that the novel lacks the "unifying commitment which kept [*The Women of Brewster Place*] so tightly structured under its apparently loose and flowing surface," for the characters' lives "hardly impinge on each other, yet they share the same grief." *Bailey's Cafe* ends relatively happily, "perhaps too glibly so," finds Eder. As Miriam, who hints at having conceived immaculately, is delivering a baby in the cafe, "someone starts singing a spiri-

tual," notes Wakefield, and "Ms. Naylor has earned the song."

BIOGRAPHICAL/CRITICAL SOURCES:

BOOKS

Authors and Artists for Young Adults, Volume 6, Gale (Detroit), 1991.
Christian, Barbara, editor, *Black Feminist Criticism,* Pergamon Press (Elmsford, NY), 1985.
Contemporary Literary Criticism, Gale, Volume 28, 1984, Volume 52, 1989.
Evans, Mari, editor, *Black Women Writers: 1950-1980,* Doubleday (New York City), 1984.
Gates, Henry Louis, Jr., and K. A. Appiah, editors, *Gloria Naylor: Critical Perspectives Past and Present,* Amistad (New York City), 1993.

PERIODICALS

Callaloo, spring/summer, 1984, pp. 116-19.
Christian Science Monitor, March 1, 1985.
Commonweal, May 3, 1985.
Contemporary Literature, Volume 28, number 1, 1987.
Detroit News, March 3, 1985; February 21, 1988.
Ebony, July, 1989, pp. 76-78.
English Journal, March, 1994, p. 95.
Essence, December, 1989, pp. 48-51; May, 1990.
Life, spring, 1988, p. 65.
Literary Review, spring, 1990, pp. 98-107.
London Review of Books, August 1, 1985.
Los Angeles Times, December 2, 1982.
Los Angeles Times Book Review, February 24, 1985; March 6, 1988; August 30, 1992, pp. 3, 7.
Ms., June, 1985; May, 1986, pp. 56-58.
New Republic, September 6, 1982.
New York Times, February 9, 1985; February 10, 1988, p. C25; May 1, 1990; April 17, 1994.
New York Times Book Review, August 22, 1982; March 3, 1985; November 16, 1986; February 21, 1988; May 14, 1989; October 4, 1992, pp. 11-12.
Publishers Weekly, September 9, 1983; December 18, 1987, p. 54.
San Francisco Review of Books, May, 1985.
Southern Review, summer, 1985, pp. 567-93.
Times (London), April 21, 1983.
Times Literary Supplement, May 24, 1985; July 17, 1992, p. 20.
Tribune Books (Chicago), February 23, 1983; January 31, 1988; October 4, 1992, p. 6.

Washington Post, October 21, 1983; May 1, 1990.

Washington Post Book World, March 24, 1985; February 28, 1988; October 11, 1992.

Women's Review of Books, August, 1985; February, 1993, p. 15.

Yale Review, autumn, 1988; autumn, 1989, pp. 19-31.*

*   *   *

NELSON, Marilyn 1946-
(Marilyn Nelson Waniek)

PERSONAL: Born April 26, 1946, in Cleveland, OH; daughter of Melvin M. (in U.S. Air Force) and Johnnie (a teacher; maiden name, Mitchell) Nelson; married Erdmann F. Waniek, September, 1970 (divorced); married Roger R. Wilkenfeld (a university professor), November 22, 1979; children (second marriage): Jacob, Dora. *Education:* University of California, Davis, B.A., 1968; University of Pennsylvania, M.A., 1970; University of Minnesota, Ph.D., 1979. *Politics:* "Yes." *Religion:* "Yes."

ADDRESSES: Office—Department of English, University of Connecticut, 337 Mansfield Rd., U-25, Storrs, CT 06269-1025.

CAREER: National Lutheran Campus Ministry, lay associate, 1969-70; Lane Community College, Eugene, OR, assistant professor of English, 1970-72; Norre Nissum Seminariam, Norre Nissum, Denmark, teacher of English, 1972-73; Saint Olaf College, Northfield, MN, instructor in English, 1973-78; University of Connecticut, Storrs, assistant professor, 1978-82, associate professor, 1982-88, professor of English, 1988—. Visiting assistant professor, Reed College, 1971-72, and Trinity College, 1982; visiting professor, New York University, 1988, 1994, and XT College, 1991; Elliston Professor, University of Cincinnati, 1994.

MEMBER: Society for the Study of Multi-Ethnic Literature of the United States, Society for Values in Higher Education, Associated Writing Programs.

AWARDS, HONORS: Kent fellow, 1976; National Endowment for the Arts fellow, 1981 and 1990; CT Arts award, 1990; National Book Award finalist, 1991; Annisfield-Wolf award, 1992; Fulbright teaching fellow (France), 1995.

WRITINGS:

POEMS; UNDER NAME MARILYN NELSON WANIEK

For the Body, Louisiana State University Press (Baton Rouge), 1978.

(With Pamela Espeland) *The Cat Walked through the Casserole and Other Poems for Children,* Carolrhoda (Minneapolis, MN), 1984.

Mama's Promises, Louisiana State University Press, 1985.

The Homeplace, Louisiana State University Press, 1990.

Magnificat, Louisiana State University Press, 1994.

OTHER; UNDER NAME MARILYN NELSON WANIEK

(Translator) Pil Dahlerup, *Literary Sex Roles,* Minnesota Women in Higher Education (Minneapolis), 1975.

(Translator with Espeland) Halfdan Rasmussen, *Hundreds of Hens and Other Poems for Children,* Black Willow Press (Minneapolis), 1982.

Contributor to *Gettysburg Review* and *Obsidian II.*

SIDELIGHTS: "Aframerican" poet Marilyn Nelson, who dropped the "Waniek" from her name in 1995, writes in a variety of styles about many subjects. She has also written verse for children and translated poetry from Danish and German. Kirkland C. Jones in the *Dictionary of Literary Biography* calls Nelson "one of the major voices of a younger generation of black poets."

Nelson's first collection, *For the Body,* focuses on the relationships between individuals and the larger social groupings of family, extended family, and society. Using domestic settings and memories of her own childhood, Nelson fashions poetry which "sometimes sings, sometimes narrates," as Jones describes it. In *Mama's Promises,* Nelson continues experimentation with poetic forms in poems about her childhood, her relationship with her mother and daughter, and a woman's role in marriage and society, but she utilizes stanzaic division more than in her previous work. The poems in *Mama's Promises* also seem to bear a cumulative theological weight, as the "Mama" named in each poem is revealed in the last poem to be God.

In *The Homeplace* Nelson turns her attention to the history of her own family, telling their story from the time of her great-great-grandmother to the present in a series of interconnected poems ranging in style from traditional forms to colloquial free-verse. Some critics praised the variety of poetic expression Nelson displays. "The sheer range of Nelson's voice," Christian Wiman writes in *Shenandoah,* "is one of the book's greatest strengths, varying not only from poem to poem, but within individual poems as well." Suzanne Gardinier, reviewing the book for *Parnassus,* finds that through her poems Nelson "reaches back through generations hemmed in on all sides by slavery and its antecedents; all along the way she finds sweetness, and humor, and more complicated truth than its disguises have revealed."

In her poetry for children Nelson also writes of family situations, although in a humorous manner. Her collection *The Cat Walked through the Casserole and Other Poems for Children,* written with Pamela Espeland, contains poems about domestic problems and pleasures. The title poem, for example, tells of the family dog and cat and the trouble they cause throughout the neighborhood, leading the mother to decide that they must go. Such poems as "Grampa's Whiskers," "When I Grow Up," and "Queen of the Rainbow" also focus on family life in a light-hearted manner.

Although biblical allusions appear in even her earliest poems, only with the collection *Magnificat* does Nelson write directly of spiritual subjects. Inspired by her friendship with a Benedictine monk, Nelson tells of her religious awakening to a more profound sense of Christian devotion. Writing in *Multicultural Review,* Mary Walsh Meany finds Nelson's voice— "humorous, earthy, tender, joyous, sorrowful, contemplative, speculative, attached, detached, sometimes silent"—to be what "makes the poems wonderful." The critic for *Publishers Weekly* believes that Nelson's "passion, sincerity and self-deprecating humor will engage even the most skeptical reader."

BIOGRAPHICAL/CRITICAL SOURCES:

BOOKS

Dictionary of Literary Biography, Volume 120: *American Poets since World War II,* Third Series, Gale (Detroit), 1992.

PERIODICALS

Booklist, September 1, 1994, p. 20.
Hudson Review, summer, 1991, p. 346.
Kenyon Review, spring, 1991, p. 179.
Multicultural Review, March, 1995.
Parnassus, Volume 17, number 1, 1992, pp. 65-78.
Publishers Weekly, November 16, 1990, p. 52; August 29, 1994, p. 67.
School Library Journal, June, 1991, p. 137.
Shenandoah, winter, 1992.

*　　*　　*

NEWMAN, Robert (Howard)   1909-1988

PERSONAL: Born June 3, 1909, in New York, NY; died of a brain tumor, December 7, 1988, in Branford, CT; son of Samuel Jerome and Nance (maiden name, Ortman) Newman; married Dorothy Crayder (a writer), 1936; children: Hila Feil. *Education:* Attended Brown University, 1927-28. *Avocational interests:* Field archery, sailing.

CAREER: Freelance writer. Office of War Information, overseas branch, New York, chief of Radio Outpost Division, 1942-44.

MEMBER: PEN, Authors Guild, Radio Writers Guild (council member, 1942-49; vice president of Eastern region, 1945), Writers Guild East.

AWARDS, HONORS: Edgar Allan Poe Award nomination, 1978, for *Night Spell.*

WRITINGS:

JUVENILE FICTION

The Boy Who Could Fly, illustrated by Paul Sagsoorian, Atheneum (New York City), 1967.
Merlin's Mistake, illustrated by Richard Lebenson, Atheneum, 1970.
The Testing of Tertius, illustrated by Richard Cuffari, Atheneum, 1973.
The Shattered Stone, illustrated by John Gretzer, Atheneum, 1975.
Night Spell, illustrated by Peter Burchard, Atheneum, 1977.

"INSPECTOR WYATT" SERIES

The Case of the Baker Street Irregular, Atheneum, 1978.
The Case of the Vanishing Corpse, Atheneum, 1980.
The Case of the Somerville Secret, Atheneum, 1981.
The Case of the Threatened King, Atheneum, 1982.
The Case of the Etruscan Treasure, Atheneum, 1983.
The Case of the Frightened Friend, Atheneum, 1984.
The Case of the Murdered Players, Atheneum, 1985.
The Case of the Indian Curse, Atheneum, 1986.
The Case of the Watching Boy, Atheneum, 1987.

OTHER

The Enchanter, Houghton (Boston), 1962.
The Japanese: People of the Three Treasures (nonfiction), illustrated by Mamoru Funai, Atheneum, 1964.
Corbie (adult fiction), Harcourt (New York City), 1966.
Grettir the Strong (a retelling), illustrated by John Gretzer, Crowell (New York City), 1968.
The Twelve Labors of Hercules (a retelling), illustrated by Charles Keeping, Crowell, 1972.

Also author of radio, television and movie scripts. Contributor of verse and short stories to periodicals.

SIDELIGHTS: Robert Newman began writing children's books after a successful career in radio. His credits included not only adult fiction, but juvenile fantasy and an acclaimed series of detective novels for young readers set in Victorian England. "I began writing books for young people fairly late," Newman once stated. "I think I first became interested in it when my daughter was quite young and I used to read aloud to her."

Raised in New York, Newman studied for two years at Brown University and then went into construction. But he was already writing poetry as a young student, and soon turned his hand to short stories and radio scripts, as well. In 1936 he married and in that same year became a full-time freelance writer. Newman's radio credits included two daytime programs and five mystery shows, including *Inner Sanctum* and *Adventures of the Thin Man.* For television, Newman wrote episodes for the soap opera *Search for Life* and for the popular *Peyton Place.* His first novel appeared in the 1960s and he soon determined that writing books, preferably for children, would be his new career.

Newman's first children's book was a nonfiction title, *The Japanese: People of the Three Treasures.* A history of the Japanese people from legendary times to the seventeenth century, the book employs the three treasures of the imperial family—the Mirror, the Sword, and the Jewel—to explore the Japanese people and their history. With its innovative organization and strong narrative line, *The Japanese: People of the Three Treasures* was dubbed "a distinguished book," by *Horn Book.* *The Boy Who Could Fly* was Newman's first juvenile fiction book. The story is told by Mark, the older brother of a pair of orphans, the younger of which, Joey, has the power to read minds and fly. Mark is faced with hard choices in a "convincing and suspenseful story," according to Ruth Hill Viguers writing in *Horn Book.* Jean Fritz, in *New York Times Book Review,* interpreted the book as a Biblical allusion, with Joey in the role of a potential new messiah, and concluded that the questions raised by Newman's book were "even more haunting than the story itself."

Newman recounted an Icelandic saga in *Grettir the Strong* and a Greek myth in *The Twelve Labors of Hercules.* In response to the tale of Grettir, a tragic hero of Norse legend, cursed by his own strong will, tormented by a ghost, and racked by his enemies, Nancy Farrar in *Library Journal* and *Kirkus Reviews* stated that "Newman's style of writing characterizes very well the life of this legendary hero," further commenting that Newman's was a "firm, concise retelling of the Icelandic saga."

Newman next concentrated on fantasy fiction, writing tales of Merlin and his unwitting apprentice, Tertius, in companion volumes that compress and play with history and provide Camelot with the future knowledge of nuclear reactors and other such twentieth-century science. In *Merlin's Mistake,* two boys, Tertius and Brian, go on an adventurous quest in search of the sorcerer Merlin. Newman intentionally presents an outrageously anachronistic history in this Merlin tale which he tells with "wit and ingenuity and grace," according to Ethel L. Heins in *Horn Book.* "Reaching far beyond mere cleverness, the book has been conceived and executed with care, imagination, and skill," Heins concluded.

Fantasy and mystery blend in the novel *Night Spell,* which was nominated for an Edgar Allan Poe Award. Orphaned 14-year-old Tad Harper is sent to spend the summer at a New England coastal community as the guest of an edgy and disabled recluse, Mr. Gorham. Left to his own devices, Tad befriends the daughter of the lighthouse keeper and together they investigate the drowning death of Gorham's granddaughter the year before and the subsequent disappearance of the girl's mother, Gorham's daughter. Led on by the dream appearance of the ghost of the drowned girl, the two ultimately find the missing woman. A *School Library Journal* reviewer concluded that the "supernatural element is well handled," while a *Kirkus Reviews* critic noted that Newman created "a pleasantly sunlit Gothic."

The Case of the Baker Street Irregular became the first book in Newman's "Inspector Wyatt" series. After realizing that no books had been written about Sherlock Holmes for children, Newman set about fashioning a tale of Holmes's street-urchin helpmates, the Baker Street Irregulars. Ethel L. Heins, writing in *Horn Book,* commented that Newman is "as urbane and fluent as the legendary Mr. Holmes," and that his story moves along with "unflagging energy," while Drew Stevenson concluded in *School Library Journal* that this Holmesian take-off provided the "perfect opportunity for young readers to become acquainted with the famed detective." Newman followed up this initial success with eight further titles between 1980 and 1987. With the second book in the series, *The Case of the Vanishing Corpse,* he introduced the young constable Wyatt as the main character to resolve copyright problems involved with using the character of Sherlock Holmes. Set in Victorian London, the Wyatt books feature, along with Inspector Wyatt, the young Andrew Tillett, another of Newman's orphan protagonists, and Sara Wiggins.

Newman died four months after publication of *The Case of the Watching Boy.* Once commenting on his inspiration for writing, he summarized his career: "I tell stories: stories which I hope will stimulate the imagination by introducing children to places that no longer exist or never existed and to characters and situations that they are not likely to meet in real life but which have some qualities that are recognizable and timeless."

BIOGRAPHICAL/CRITICAL SOURCES:

BOOKS

Holtze, Sally Homes, editor, *Sixth Book of Junior Authors and Illustrators,* H. W. Wilson (New York City), 1989, pp. 206-8.
Twentieth-Century Children's Writers, 3rd edition, St. James Press (Chicago), 1989.

PERIODICALS

America, December 9, 1978.
Booklist, April 15, 1982, p. 1097; September 1, 1986, p. 66.
Bulletin of the Center for Children's Books, March, 1986, p. 134.
Horn Book, June, 1964; April, 1967, p. 208; June, 1970, pp. 298-99; June, 1973, pp. 381-82; October, 1975, p. 465; August, 1978, p. 397; June, 1980, p. 302.
Kirkus Reviews, October 15, 1968, p. 1170; May 15, 1972, p. 585; April 15, 1977, p. 427.
Library Journal, January 15, 1969, p. 314.
Listener, November 11, 1971.
New York Times, June 30, 1978.
New York Times Book Review, April 17, 1966; May 7, 1967, pp. 39-40; November 5, 1967, p. 66; August 27, 1972, p. 24; April 30, 1978, p. 44; January 25, 1981, p. 31.
Observer (London), July 11, 1976.
Publishers Weekly, July 10, 1987, p. 70.
School Library Journal, May, 1977, p. 78; May, 1978, p. 85; December, 1983, p. 86; May, 1984, p. 102; September, 1987, p. 182.
Times Literary Supplement, October 3, 1968, p. 1110; April 2, 1971, p. 390; November 23, 1973, p. 1435.
Voice of Youth Advocates, February, 1987, p. 286.

OBITUARIES:

PERIODICALS

New York Times, December 9, 1988, p. D18.*

* * *

NICOLL, Helen   1937-

PERSONAL: Born October 10, 1937, in Natland, Westmorland, England; married Robert Kime (an antiquarian), 1970; children: Hannah, Tom. *Education:* Attended schools in Bristol, Devon, and London.

ADDRESSES: Home and office—Dene House, Lockeridge, Marlborough, Wiltshire, England. *Agent*—c/o Heinemann Ltd., Michelin House, 81 Fulham Road, London SW3 6RB, England.

CAREER: British Broadcasting Corp. (BBC-TV), London, England, producer and director of children's programs, 1967-71; *Puffin* and *The Egg* magazines, London, editor, 1977-79; Cover to Cover Cassettes, Wiltshire, England, producer, 1983—; writer of children's books.

WRITINGS:

"*MEG AND MOG*" *SERIES; ILLUSTRATED BY JAN PIENKOWSKI*

Meg and Mog, Heinemann (London), 1972, Atheneum (New York City), 1973.
Meg's Eggs, Atheneum, 1973.
Meg at Sea, Heinemann, 1973, Harvey House (New York City), 1976.
Meg on the Moon, Heinemann, 1973, Harvey House, 1976.
Meg's Car, Heinemann, 1975.
Meg's Castle, Heinemann, 1975.
Meg's Veg, Heinemann, 1976.
Mog's Mumps, Heinemann, 1976, Penguin (New York City), 1982.
Meg and Mog Birthday Book, Heinemann, 1979, Puffin (New York City), 1991.
Mog at the Zoo, Heinemann, 1982, Penguin, 1984.
Mog in the Fog, Heinemann, 1984.
Owl at School, Heinemann, 1984, Penguin, 1985.
Mog's Box, Heinemann, 1987.
Owl at the Vet, Penguin, 1992.

OTHER

Quest for the Gloop: The Exploits of Murfy and PHIX, illustrations by Pienkowski, Heinemann, 1980.
(Compiler) *Poems for Seven-Year-Olds and Under*, Kestrel (London), 1983.

Author of *Tom's Home*, 1987.

ADAPTATIONS: David Wood has created four plays for children based on the "Meg and Mog" series, published by Puffin, 1984.

SIDELIGHTS: Helen Nicoll is best known as the creator of Meg, a witch, her cat Mog, and Snowy the Owl. Nicoll's rhyming language is simple enough for the youngest beginning reader, and the trio of witch, cat, and owl have been the focus of a fourteen-book series illustrated by Jan Pienkowski. Nicoll has also produced and directed television and radio broadcasts for children for the British Broadcasting Corporation (BBC) and for a popular series of audio cassettes that accompany her books in the United Kingdom.

Nicoll's witty, minimal text is suitable for the very young and for beginning readers. *Times Literary Supplement* reviewer William Feaver explains that "Meg the wiry witch and Mog her familiar, a black-and-white-striped cat with a tail like a frayed bootlace, are the perfect couple. Meg and Mog stories seize hold. Meg works her magic, Mog reacts and the audience joins in." The Meg and Mog books contain about a line of text per page, "encouraging early reading attempts," writes a reviewer in *Times Literary Supplement*. A reviewer in *School Librarian* states that *Mog at the Zoo* is a "wealth of fun and language learning." The audiocassette series that accompanies the "Meg and Mog" books, produced by Cover to Cover Cassettes, augments the print volumes and provides another learning tool for children. Chris Powling, reviewing the cassettes in *Books for Keeps*, especially recommends *Meg at Sea* and *Meg on the Moon*. Nicoll and Pienkowski have also collaborated on a science fiction book for older children. According to a reviewer in the *British Book News*, *Quest for the Gloop: The Exploits of Murfy and PHIX* "will no doubt please young science fiction addicts" who enjoy puns.

BIOGRAPHICAL/CRITICAL SOURCES:

PERIODICALS

Books for Keeps, January, 1986, p. 12; May, 1986, p. 19; November, 1987, p. 10.
British Book News, spring, 1981, p. 23; March, 1988, p. 7.
Growing Point, May, 1982, p. 3908.
New Statesman, May 21, 1976, pp. 689-90.
Observer Review, April 19, 1987, p. 23.
Publishers Weekly, February 18, 1983, pp. 129-130.
School Librarian, September, 1983, p. 235.
Times Educational Supplement, March 15, 1985, p. 24.
Times Literary Supplement, November 3, 1972, p. 1334; March 29, 1974, p. 331; July 27, 1984, p. 854.*

*   *   *

OCHESTER, Ed(win Frank)   1939-

PERSONAL: Born September 15, 1939, in Brooklyn, NY; son of Edwin Otto (an insurance broker) and Viola (Bachtle) Ochezster; married Clarinda Britton

Horner, June 19, 1965; children: Edwin Hall, Elizabeth Britton. *Education:* Cornell University, B.A., 1961; Harvard University, M.A., 1963; University of Wisconsin, 1963-67.

ADDRESSES: Home—R.D. 1, Box 174, Shelocta, PA 15774. *Office*—Department of English, University of Pittsburgh, Pittsburgh, PA 15260.

CAREER: University of Florida, Gainesville, assistant professor of English, 1967-70; University of Pittsburgh, Pittsburgh, PA, instructor, 1970-74, assistant professor, 1974-77, associate professor, 1977-83, professor of English, 1983—, director of graduate and undergraduate writing program, 1978-83, 1986—. Jemison Professor at the University of Alabama at Birmingham, 1994.

AWARDS, HONORS: Devins Award for Poetry, 1973, for *Dancing on the Edges of Knives;* fellowship for poetry from the National Endowment for the Arts, 1984; Pennsylvania Council for the Arts fellowships in poetry, 1981, 1983, 1985, 1987, 1989, 1991, 1995; Pushcart Prize, 1992.

WRITINGS:

POETRY

We Like It Here, Quixote Press (Houston, TX), 1967.
The Great Bourgeois Bus Company, Quixote Press, 1969.
The Third Express, Quixote Press, 1973.
(Editor) *Natives: An Anthology of Contemporary American Poetry,* Quixote Press, 1973.
Dancing on the Edges of Knives, University of Missouri Press (Columbia), 1973.
The End of the Ice Age, Slow Loris Press (Pittsburgh, PA), 1977.
A Drift of Swine, Thunder City Press (Birmingham, AL), 1979.
Miracle Mile, Carnegie-Mellon University Press (Pittsburgh, PA), 1984.
Weehawken Ferry, Juniper Press (Bangor, ME), 1985.
Changing the Name to Ochester, Carnegie-Mellon University Press, 1988.
Allegheny, Adastra Press (Easthampton, MA), 1995.

OTHER

Work represented in numerous anthologies. Editor of "Pitt Poetry Series," University of Pittsburgh Press,

1978—. General editor of Drue Heinz Literature Prize for short fiction, University of Pittsburgh Press, 1980—. Coeditor of *The Pittsburgh Book of Contemporary American Poetry,* University of Pittsburgh Press, 1993. Contributor to numerous periodicals, including *Poetry, Virginia Quarterly Review, Antioch Review, Ploughshares, North American Review, Paris Review, Southern Review, Georgia Review,* and *American Poetry Review.*

SIDELIGHTS: Ed Ochester told *CA:* "Since 1972 my wife and I have lived on a small farm in Armstrong County, PA, where we raise most of our own food organically and have attempted to return as rapidly as possible to a closer, more satisfying relationship with the earth."

* * *

O'NEILL, Judith (Beatrice)   1930-

PERSONAL: Born June 30, 1930, in Melbourne, Australia; daughter of John Ramsden (a school inspector) and Beatrice (a teacher; maiden name, McDonald) Lyall; married John Cochrane O'Neill (a professor and Presbyterian minister), April 17, 1954; children: Rachel, Catherine, Philippa. *Education:* University of Melbourne, B.A. (with honors), 1950, M.A., 1952; Institute of Education, London, P.G.C.E., 1953.

ADDRESSES: Home—9 Lonsdale Terrace, Edinburgh EH3 9HN, Scotland. *Agent*—A. P. Watt Ltd., 20 John St., London WC1N 2DR, England.

CAREER: University of Melbourne, Victoria, Australia, tutor in English, 1954-55; Open University, England, tutor and counselor, 1971-73; St. Mary's School, Cambridge, England, English teacher, 1974-82; freelance writer, 1982—.

AWARDS, HONORS: Third prize, Rigby Anniversary Literary Contest, Australia, 1982, for *Jess and the River Kids;* shortlist, Children's Book Council Awards, Australia, 1989, for *Deepwater;* shortlist, Carnegie Award, London, 1993, for *So Far from Skye.*

WRITINGS:

FOR CHILDREN

Martin Luther, Cambridge University Press (Cambridge, England), 1975, Lerner Publications (Minneapolis, MN), 1978.

Transported to Van Diemen's Land: The Story of Two Convicts, Cambridge University Press, 1977.
Jess and the River Kids, Hamish Hamilton (London), 1984.
Stringybark Summer, Hamish Hamilton, 1985.
Deepwater, Hamish Hamilton, 1987.
The Message, Hamish Hamilton, 1989.
So Far from Skye, Hamish Hamilton, 1992.

EDITOR; *"READINGS IN LITERARY CRITICISM"* SERIES

Critics on Keats, Allen & Unwin (London), 1967, University of Miami Press (Baltimore, MD), 1968.
Critics on Charlotte and Emily Bronte, Allen & Unwin, 1967, University of Miami Press, 1979.
Critics on Pope, University of Miami Press, 1968.

Critics on Marlowe, Allen & Unwin, 1969, University of Miami Press, 1970.
Critics on Blake, University of Miami Press, 1970.
Critics on Jane Austen, University of Miami Press, 1970.

WORK IN PROGRESS: Hearing Voices, publication expected in 1996; *Spindle River,* publication expected in 1997.

SIDELIGHTS: Judith O'Neill told *CA:* "I am a third-generation Australian and, although I have lived in Britain for over thirty years, my novels for young people are all set in Australia and all in the past. Now that I live in Scotland, I very much enjoy my visits to schools to talk with children about my writing and to encourage their own writing."

P

PAGELS, Elaine Hiesey 1943-

PERSONAL: Born February 13, 1943, in Palo Alto, CA; daughter of William McKinley (a research biologist) and Louise Sophia (van Druten) Hiesey; married Heinz R. Pagels (a theoretical physicist), June 7, 1969 (died July 24, 1988); married Kent Greenawalt (a law professor), June, 1995; children: (first marriage) Mark (died, 1987), Sarah Marie, David van Druten. *Education:* Stanford University, B.A., 1964, M.A., 1965; Harvard University, Ph.D., 1970. *Religion:* Episcopalian.

ADDRESSES: Home—27 West 87th St., New York, NY 10024. *Office*—Department of Religion, Princeton University, Princeton, NJ 08544. *Agent*—John Brockman Associates, Inc., 2307 Broadway, New York, NY 10024.

CAREER: Barnard College, New York City, assistant professor, 1970-74, associate professor, professor of history of religion and head of department, 1974-82; Princeton University, Princeton, NJ, Harrington Spear Paine Professor of Religion, 1982—.

MEMBER: Society of Biblical Literature, American Academy of Religion, Biblical Theologians Club.

AWARDS, HONORS: National Endowment for the Humanities grant, 1972-73; Mellon fellow, Aspen Institute of Humanistic Studies, 1974; Hazen fellow, 1975; Rockefeller fellow, 1978-79; National Book Critics Circle award for criticism, 1979, and National Book Award, 1980, for *The Gnostic Gospels;* Guggenheim fellow, 1979-80; MacArthur Prize fellow, 1981-87.

WRITINGS:

The Johannine Gospel in Gnostic Exegesis: Heracleon's Commentary on John, Abingdon (Nashville, TN), 1973.
The Gnostic Paul: Gnostic Exegesis of the Pauline Letters, Fortress (Philadelphia, PA), 1975.
The Gnostic Gospels, Random House (New York City), 1979.
The Gnostic Jesus and Early Christian Politics, Arizona State University (Tempe), 1981.
Adam, Eve and the Serpent, Random House, 1988.
The Origin of Satan: The New Testament Origins of Christianity's Demonization of Jews, Pagans & Heretics, Random House, 1995.

Member of editorial and translation board, *The Nag Hammadi Library in English,* Harper (New York City), 1978. Contributor to *Nag Hammadi Codex III, 5: The Dialogue of the Savior,* Brill (Leiden), 1984. Contributor to *Harvard Theological Review* and other journals.

WORK IN PROGRESS: Research on degrees of religious participation.

SIDELIGHTS: In 1945, an Egyptian farmer near the town of Nag Hammadi came upon a cache of fifty-two ancient scrolls. Examination by scholars in Cairo showed the scrolls to contain writings by the gnostics, an early heretical sect of Christians. It is surmised that the scrolls, written in the Coptic language, were hidden during the first or second century A.D. to prevent their destruction by the orthodox church as heretical texts. Because the find is one of the few examples of gnostic writing to have survived, it has been compared in importance to the

Dead Sea Scrolls. An international team of scholars, including Elaine Hiesey Pagels, was established to study and translate the writings, which were published in 1978 as *The Nag Hammadi Library in English*. After this publication, Pagels decided to write a popular account of the scrolls to make the gnostic beliefs—often expressed in obscure, mystical language—more easily accessible to a general audience. Her book *The Gnostic Gospels* examines and explains some of the heretical beliefs of the gnostic sect and tells the story of its losing struggle against the orthodox Christian church.

Despite theological differences, Pagels contends that the primary dispute between the gnostics and the orthodox church, and why the gnostics were finally branded as heretics, centered on a political difference. She points out that gnostic church structure was non-hierarchical, democratic, and allowed for the ordination of both men and women into the priesthood. In practice, by emphasizing the individual's relationship with God, the gnostics made any type of church organization virtually irrelevant to spiritual salvation. Gnostic claims of continuing contact with Christ and the apostles disputed the divine authority of the orthodox church and the exclusive validity of its scriptures. The gnostics' rejection of Christ's literal death and resurrection made them unwilling to die as martyrs for the faith, since they saw such a course as unnecessarily extreme. Orthodox believers, on the other hand, considering Christ's death an example to follow, thought the gnostic position insubordinate and cowardly. As Pagels explains in a *Publishers Weekly* interview: "Heresy turns out to be a lot of ideas not helpful in building an orthodox religion. That's really it. If you are constructing an institutional church, there are certain things you don't want Jesus to have said."

Critical reaction to *The Gnostic Gospels* was mixed. John Leonard, writing in the *New York Times,* finds that Pagels' reader is "made to listen to everybody who went sun-crazed out into the Middle Eastern desert and became prophetic." Raymond E. Brown of the *New York Times Book Review* argues that "from [the Nag Hammadi scrolls] we learn not a single verifiable new fact about Jesus' ministry, and only a few new sayings that might plausibly have been his. Professor Pagels recognizes this, for she does use the Coptic works correctly, not to describe Jesus but to describe the struggle within early Christianity."

According to *Times Literary Supplement* reviewer Henry Chadwick, part of Pagels' intent in writing *The Gnostic Gospels* was to undermine what she sees as the Christian tradition's discrimination against women. "[Pagels] approaches gnosticism with very contemporary expectations: notably the hope that in these gnostic documents suppressed by ancient authority we may find an alternative Christianity sympathetic to Eastern and individualist mysticism, unencumbered by historical and miraculous events, emancipated if not from clergymen, at least from the notion that holy orders ought to be a male preserve." However, writes Chadwick, "the new material from Nag Hammadi offers only a few grains of encouragement to liberated women readers," partial evidence, Chadwick feels, of Pagels' failure to demonstrate how the exclusion of gnosticism left Christianity impoverished. From a different angle, Christopher Stead remarks in the *Chicago Tribune* that Pagels' "picture of the Gnostic movement in the early Church is reliable provided always one remembers that it was a minority movement. From the start [Gnosticism] showed features which made for disunion and disintegration. . . . Pagels gives us a fascinating picture of early Christian deviationists." Unlike the activist exponents of gnosticism today, the early gnostics were "mystics, symbolists, quietists . . . who could not have dominated the world of antiquity," offers Stead. For all that Pagels' exegesis may or may not do or be, declares Harold Bloom in the *Washington Post Book World,* it is "always readable, always deeply informed, always richly suggestive of pathways her readers may wish to follow out for themselves."

Pagels continues to pursue the question of the beliefs of the early Christian church in *Adam, Eve and the Serpent* and *The Origin of Satan: The New Testament Origins of Christianity's Demonization of Jews, Pagans & Heretics.* Both works look at the ways in which central beliefs of the Christian Church about sexuality and evil evolved from differing traditions within Christianity. In *Adam, Eve and the Serpent,* for instance, Pagels has tried to "find out how traditional patterns of gender and sexuality arose and how the idea of original sin came to be connected with state power," explains *New York Review of Books* contributor W. H. C. Frend. "How was it that Christianity, which owes so much to Judaism, diverged so strongly from the culture of the Hebrews, to whom procreation and the family stood at the center of its existence?" Pagels, declares James Hitchcock in the *National Review,* "argues that the earliest Christian ideas about sexuality, freedom, and sin have come down to us today only by way of a fair amount of manhandling." The author traces many of these ideas to Church fathers who lived long after the time of Jesus Christ, including Justin Martyr, John Chrysostom, Tertullian, and Saints Jerome, Ambrose, and Augustine. "In our terms," states Thomas D'Evelyn in the *Christian Science Monitor,* "Chrysostom and Pelagius were liberal: They argued for more moderation, some autonomy, freedom of will, and choice—for Christian liberty. On the strength of Augustinian counterargument, both were exiled as heretics." "The author," concludes Frend, "has written a scholarly and challenging work to be set alongside her work on the Gnostic Gospels."

The Origin of Satan was completed after a period of great personal tragedy for Pagels. In 1987, she lost her eldest son, Mark, to a respiratory birth defect. Her husband Heinz died one year later. "*The Origin of Satan* begins with a nakedly personal moment," declares *New Yorker* contributor David Remnick, "a hint of the way Pagels transformed pain into scholarship: 'In 1988, when my husband of twenty years died in a hiking accident, I became aware that, like many people who grieve, I was living in the presence of an invisible being—living, that is, with a vivid sense of someone who had died.'" After the deaths of her son and her husband, Remnick continues, Pagels "wondered how people dealt with catastrophe, where they focussed their anger. 'For people more religious—well, some might get angry at God, but that made no sense to me,' she said. 'In the ancient Church, they got mad at Satan. That seemed to make more sense. And so I had to ask, What is Satan? What's the Devil?'"

The Origin of Satan traces the evolution of a Jewish angel from God's prosecuting attorney to an antagonist of the Almighty himself. Pagels suggests that the character of the Devil was an important uniting factor in the development of Christianity. *Nation* critic Mary Gordon explains: "If the leader of your movement has been ignominiously murdered, Pagels suggests, it is helpful to believe that what seems to be disastrous is in fact chimerical; that the real battle is invisible and has, in fact, already been won." The concept of an evil entity opposed to God (and therefore the Christian community) proved to be a unifying force among the persecuted Christians, allowing them to identify their enemies—first Jews and Romans, then other pagans, and finally their fellow Christians—with the forces of evil and darkness. "In this early and extreme polarization, Pagels contends, sectarian movements came to identify themselves in their siege mentality as 'the good ones' and the others as 'the bad ones,' indeed the 'evil ones,'" declares Brent D. Shaw in the *New Republic*. "Thus, in

her view, began the tragic demonization of 'the other' that was to have such catastrophic effects in Western history." Michiko Kakutani, in the *New York Times,* despite finding that some of Pagel's "interpretations of specific biblical passages are highly debatable," concludes that *The Origin of Satan* makes "familiar concepts disturbingly fresh and provocative."

BIOGRAPHICAL/CRITICAL SOURCES:

PERIODICALS

Atlantic, February, 1980.
Booklist, January 1, 1980.
Books of the Times, January, 1980.
Chicago Tribune, March 13, 1980.
Christian Century, June 9-16, 1976.
Christian Science Monitor, December 3, 1979; September 14, 1988, p. 18.
Commonweal, November 9, 1979.
Critic, February 11, 1980.
Library Journal, June 15, 1988, p. 63; June 1, 1995, p. 123.
Los Angeles Times, April 26, 1980.
Los Angeles Times Book Review, December 23, 1979.
Ms., April, 1980.
Nation, June 26, 1995, pp. 931-33.
National Review, November 7, 1988, pp. 63-65.
New Republic, July 10, 1995, pp. 30-36.
New Statesman & Society, April 20, 1990, p. 37.
New Yorker, January 21, 1980; April 3, 1995, pp. 54-65.
New York Review of Books, June 30, 1988, pp. 27-30.
New York Times, December 14, 1979; June 15, 1995, p. C18.
New York Times Book Review, January 20, 1980; August 21, 1988, pp. 15-16; June 18, 1995, pp. 9-10.
Publishers Weekly, October 15, 1979; July 31, 1995, pp. 59-60.
Rolling Stone, March 6, 1980.
Spectator, March 15, 1980.
Times Literary Supplement, March 21, 1980.
Washington Post Book World, November 25, 1979.*

*   *   *

PANIKER, Raimundo
  See PANIKKAR, Raimon

PANIKKAR, Raimon   1918-
   (Raimundo Paniker, Raymond Panikkar, Raimundo Panikkar)

PERSONAL: Born November 3, 1918, in Barcelona, Spain; citizen of India; came to United States in 1967; son of Ramuni (a chemist) and Carmen (Alemany) Panikkar. *Education:* University of Barcelona, B.A. and B.Sc. (both premio extraordinario), 1935, M.Sc., 1941, M.A., 1942; University of Madrid, Ph.D. (premio extraordinario), 1946, D.Sc., 1958; Lateran University, Th.L. (summa cum laude), 1954, Th.D. (magna cum laude), 1961; also attended University of Bonn for three years.

ADDRESSES: Home—Can Felo, Tavertet 08511, Catalunya, Spain.

CAREER: University of Madrid, Madrid, Spain, assistant to the chair of psychology, 1943-45; Theological Seminary, Madrid, professor of Indian culture and of comparative cultures, 1946-51; Institute of Social Sciences "Leon XIII," Madrid, professor of religious sociology, 1950-51; University of Madrid, Studium Generale, professor of philosophy of history, 1952-53; International University for Social Studies, Rome, Italy, professor of religious sociology, 1962-63; University of Rome, "Libero Docento" for philosophy of religion, 1963—; University of California, Santa Barbara, professor of comparative philosophy of religion and of history of religions, 1971-86, professor emeritus, 1987—. Visiting professor at numerous universities around the world, 1947-73, including International University of Santander, University Hispano-Americana de la Rabida, Equippes Internationales de Renaissance Chretienne, Pontifical University of Pune, University of Montreal, and Harvard University; guest lecturer at more than one hundred universities around the world, 1948-83; lecturer on Indian philosophy, culture, and religion to several Latin American countries, 1965 and 1974; Teape Lecturer, Cambridge University, 1966; honorary professor, United Theological College, Bangalore, India, 1970; Henry Luce Visiting Professor in World Christianity, Union Theological Seminary, 1970; William Noble Lecturer, Harvard University, 1973; lecturer for Cummings Lectureship, McGill University, 1975, Warner Lecture Series, St. Joseph, MN, 1981, Presidential Lecture Series, Duquesne University, 1982, Fifth Annual Thomas Merton Lecture, Columbia University, 1982, and Gifford Lectures, Edinburgh,

1989. *Arbor,* cofounder and vice-director, 1944-52; Colloquium on Oriental Studies, UNESCO, delegate, 1966; International Congress of Philosophy, Barcelona, secretary general, 1984; founder of Spanish Society of Philosophy.

MEMBER: Teilhard Centre for the Future of Man (vice president), Associazione per lo Sviluppo delle Scienze Religiose in Italia, Institut International de Philosophie (Paris), Wissenschaftliche Gesellschaft fuer Theologie (Munich), Permanent People's Tribunal, INODEP (Paris; president), Vivarium (Tavertet), Espanola de Ciencias de la Religion (Madrid), Sociedad de Estudios Indicos y Orientales (Madrid).

AWARDS, HONORS: Prize in Humanities "Menedez y Pelayo," Consejo Superior de Investigaciones Cientificas, Madrid, 1946, for *El concepto de naturaleza: Analisis historico y metafisico de un concepto;* Premio Espanol de Literature (Spanish National Prize of Literature), 1961, for *La India: Gente, cultura, creencias.*

WRITINGS:

F. H. Jacobi y la filosofia del sentimiento, Sapientia (Buenos Aires), 1948.

(Editor) *Actas del Congreso Internacional de Filosofia: Barcelona, 1948,* three volumes, Consejo Superior de Investigaciones Cientificas (Madrid), 1949.

El concepto de naturaleza: Analisis historico y metafisico de un concepto, Consejo Superior de Investigaciones Cientificas, 1951, 2nd edition, 1972.

La India: Gente, cultura, creencias, Rialp (Madrid), 1960.

Patriotismo y cristiandad: Una investigacion teologia-historica sobre el patriotismo cristiano, Rialp, 1961.

Ontonomia de la ciencia: Sobre el sentido de la ciencia y sus relaciones con la filosofia, Gredos (Madrid), 1961.

Humanismo y Cruz, Rialp, 1963.

L'incontro delle religioni de mondo contemporaneo: Morfosociologia dell'ecumenismo, Edizioni Internazional Sociali (Rome), 1963.

Die vielen Goetter und der eine Herr: Beitraege zum oekumenischen Gespraech der Weltreligionen, O. W. Barth (Weilheim), 1963.

Religione e religioni (translated from unpublished English original, *Religion and Religions*), Morcelliana (Brescia), 1964.

The Unknown Christ of Hinduism, Darton, Longman & Todd, 1964, 2nd edition, Orbis Books (Maryknoll, NY), 1981.

Kultmysterium in Hinduismus und Christentum: Ein Beitrag zur vergleichenden Religionstheologie, Karl Alber (Freiburg), 1964.

Maya e Apocalisse: L'incontro dell'Indiusmo e del Cristianesimo, Abete (Rome), 1966.

Kerygma und Indien: Zur heilsgeschichtlichen Problematik der christlichen Begegnung mit Indien, Reich Verlag (Hamburg), 1967.

Offenbarung und Verkuendigung: Indische Briefe (translated from unpublished English original, *Indian Letters*), Herder (Freiburg), 1967.

Tecnica y tiempo: La Tecnocronia, Columba (Buenos Aires), 1967.

La gioia pasquale, La Locusta (Vicenza), 1968.

L'homme qui devient Dieu: La foi dimension constitutive de l'homme, Aubier (Paris), 1970.

La presenza di Dio, La Locusta, 1970.

El silencio del Dios: Un mensaje del Buddha al mundo actual; Contribucion al estudio del ateismo religioso, Guadiana (Madrid), 1970, translation published as *The Silence of God: The Answer of the Buddha,* Orbis Books, 1989.

The Trinity and World Religions: Icon, Person, Mystery, Christian Literature Society (Madras), 1970, revised edition published as *The Trinity and the Religious Experience of Man,* Darton, Longman & Todd, 1973.

Dimensione mariane della vita, La Locusta, 1972.

Cometas: Fragmentos de un diario espiritual de la postguerra, Suramerica (Madrid), 1972.

Worship and Secular Man: An Essay on the Liturgical Nature of Man, Considering Secularization as a Major Phenomenon of Our Time and Worship as an Apparent Fact of All Times; A Study towards an Integral Anthropology, Orbis Books, 1973.

Spiritualita indu: Lineamenti, Morcelliana, 1975.

The Vedic Experience, Mantramanjari: An Anthology of the Vedas for Modern Man and Contemporary Celebration, University of California Press, 1977, revised Indian editions, Pondicherry, 1983, Motilal Banarsidass, 1989, 3rd edition, 1994.

The Intrareligious Dialogue, Paulist Press (Ramsey, NJ), 1978.

Myth, Faith and Hermeneutics, Paulist Press, 1979.

(With others) *Blessed Simplicity: The Monk as Universal Archetype,* Seabury (New York City), 1982.

(Editor with W. Strolz; also contributor) *Die Verantwortung des Menschen fuer eine bewohnbare Welt im Christentum, Hinduismus und Buddhismus,* Herder, 1985.

(Editor with E. Balducci and others) *Pace e disarmo culturale,* Amministrazione Comunale, L'altrapagina (Citta di Castello), 1987.

La torre di Babele: pace e pluralismo, Cultura della Pace (San Domenico di Fiesole), 1990.

Sobre el dialogo intercultural, translated by J. R. Lopez de la Osa, San Esteban (Salamanca), 1990.

Der Weischeit eine Wohnung bereiten, Kosel (Munich), translation published as *A Dwelling Place for Wisdom,* Westminster/John Knox (Louisville, KY), 1993.

La nueva inocencia, Verbo Divino (Estella), 1993.

The Cosmotheandric Experience: Emerging Religious Consciousness, edited by Scott Eastham, Orbis, 1993.

Ecosofia: La nuova saggezza—per una spiritualita della terra, Cittadella (Assisi), 1993.

Paz y Desarme Cultural, Sal Terrae (Santander), 1993.

La experiencia de Dios, PPC (Madrid), 1994.

Cristofania, EDB (Bologna), 1994.

Meinen wir denselben Gott?, Kosel (Munich), 1994.

La nova innocencia II, Llar de Llibre (Barcelona), 1994.

(Editor) *Llenguatge i identitat,* Publicacions de l'Abadia de Montserrat (Barcelona), 1994.

Il "daimon" della politica: Agonia e speranza, EDB, 1995.

Invisible Harmony, Fortress Press (Minneapolis, MN), 1995.

Contributor of hundreds of articles to scholarly journals and periodicals, including *Arbor, Cross-Currents, Diogene, Interculture, FORUM, Jeevadhara, Journal of Ecumenical Studies, Journal of Dharma,* and *Teilhard Review.* Member of editorial board of *Classics of Western Spirituality,* Paulist Press; member of editorial board of journals, including *Concilium, Jeevadhara, Journal of Dharma,* and *Journal of Ecumenical Studies.*

Panikkar's works have been translated into many languages.

WORK IN PROGRESS: Numerous books, including *The Myth of Pluralism, The Christian Predicament,* and *Philosophy and Hermeneutics.*

SIDELIGHTS: Raimon Panikkar is working on what has been called a "Christology for the future." He has published several essays which are to be integrated into *The Supername,* "a 'Christophany' which hopes to help overcome the identity crisis of Western Man," Panikkar told *CA.* At the same time, he is preparing a similar work from an Indian perspective, tentatively entitled *Ramamandala.* He stated that this work "is a study on pure awareness as the central and often forgotten element of human consciousness. It attempts to combine the epoch-making insights of the West with those of India as already adumbrated in the pre-Socratics and the Upanishads." Panikkar is also working on *Muktitattva,* "a Philosophy of Liberation in the Indian context."

Panikkar wrote that his "philosophical life can be summed up under two headings: existential risk and intellectual burden. . . . *Existential risk* applies to a life incarnated in more than one culture and religion, engaged in orthopraxis as much as in orthodoxy. The mutual understanding of the different traditions of the world may be accomplished only by sacrificing one's life in the attempt to sustain the existing tensions without becoming schizophrenic and to maintain the polarities without personal or cultural paranoia. The *intellectual burden* is no lighter than the existential risk. It consists in expressing these basic experiences in an intelligible way. Can the pluralism of one's own experiments and experiences find comprehensible expression?"

Panikkar believes religion to be at the base of culture. "To reduce Man to a mere bundle of psychological or economic needs will not do," he wrote. "Unless we come to a religious understanding of humanity, we will perpetuate destructive tensions, both cultural and ideological."

*   *   *

PANIKKAR, Raimundo
  See PANIKKAR, Raimon

*   *   *

PANIKKAR, Raymond
  See PANIKKAR, Raimon

PELL, Arthur R. 1920-

PERSONAL: Born January 22, 1920, in New York, NY; son of Harry and Rae (Meyers) Pell; married Erica Frost (a music teacher), May 19, 1946; children: Douglas, Hilary. *Education:* New York University, B.A., 1939, M.A., 1944; Cornell University, Professional Diploma, 1943; California Coast University, Ph.D., 1977.

ADDRESSES: Home and office—111 Dietz St., Hempstead, NY 11550.

CAREER: Eagle Electric Manufacturing Co., Long Island, NY, personnel manager, 1946-50; North Atlantic Construction Co., New York City, personnel manager, 1950-53; Harper Associates (personnel consultants), New York City, vice-president, 1953-73; consultant in human resources management in Long Island, 1975—. Professor of management in evening classes at City College of the City University of New York, 1947-67. Adjunct professor of management at New York University, 1960-81, and St. John's University, 1971-77. *Military service:* U.S. Army, 1942-46; became warrant officer.

WRITINGS:

Placing Salesmen, Impact Publishers (San Ramon, CA), 1963.
(With Walter Patterson) *Fire Officers Guide to Leadership,* privately printed, 1963.
Placing Executives, Impact Publishers, 1964.
Police Leadership, C. C. Thomas (Springfield, IL), 1967.
(With Maxwell Harper) *How to Get the Job You Want after Forty,* Pilot Books (Babylon, NY), 1967.
Recruiting and Selecting Personnel, Simon & Schuster (New York City), 1969.
(With Harper) *Starting and Managing an Employment Agency,* U.S. Small Business Administration, 1971.
Advancing Your Career (home study program), Management Games Institute, 1971.
College Graduate Guide to Job Finding, Simon & Schuster, 1973.
Recruiting, Training and Motivating Volunteer Workers, Pilot Books, 1973.
Interviewing and Selecting Sales, Advertising and Marketing Personnel, Personnel Publications, 1974, revised edition, 1981.

Be a Better Employment Interviewer, Personnel Publications, 1974, second revised edition, 1994.

(With Wilma Rogalin) *Women's Guide to Management Positions,* Simon & Schuster, 1975.

(With Albert Furbay) *The College Student Guide to Career Planning,* Simon & Schuster, 1975.

Managing through People, Simon & Schuster, 1975, revised edition, 1987.

Choosing a College Major: Business, McKay (New York City), 1978.

Enrich Your Life the Dale Carnegie Way, Dale Carnegie & Associates, 1979.

Interviewing and Selecting Engineering and Computer Personnel, Personnel Publications, 1980.

(Editor) Dale Carnegie, *How to Win Friends and Influence People,* revised edition (Pell was not associated with previous edition), Simon & Schuster, 1981.

(With George Sadek) *Resumes for Engineers,* Simon & Schuster, 1982.

Interviewing and Selecting Financial and Data Processing Personnel, Personnel Publications, 1982.

How to Sell Yourself on an Interview, Simon & Schuster, 1982.

(With Sadek) *Resumes for Computer Professionals,* Simon & Schuster, 1984.

The Part-Time Job Book, Simon & Schuster, 1984.

Making the Most of Medicare, Prentice-Hall (Englewood Cliffs, NJ), 1987, revised edition, Chronimed, 1990.

How to Be a Successful Supervisor, Dun & Bradstreet (New York City), 1988.

Diagnosing Your Doctor, Chronimed, 1991.

The Supervisor's Infobank, McGraw-Hill (New York City), 1994.

Author of audiocassettes *The Job Finders Program,* Prentice Hall, 1989, and *Getting the Most from Your People,* Prentice Hall, 1990. Also author of "Career Aid Pamphlets" series for Personnel Publications, syndicated monthly feature "The Human Side," published in eighty periodicals, and "The Human Side" monthly series, Dale Carnegie Associates, Inc., 1987-94. Contributor of more than one hundred articles to trade and professional magazines, including syndicated newspaper series, "When Your Husband Loses His Job," 1971.

SIDELIGHTS: Arthur R. Pell told *CA:* "The mission of my writing is to utilize my God-given talents to help others identify, develop and make the most of their capabilities in their work and in their lives."

PETERSON, Levi S(avage) 1933-

PERSONAL: Born December 13, 1933, in Snowflake, AZ; son of Joseph (a teacher of English) and Lydia Jane (an elementary school teacher; maiden name, Savage) Peterson; married Althea Sand (a teacher of Spanish), August 31, 1958; children: Karrin. *Education:* Brigham Young University, B.A., 1958, M.A., 1960; University of Utah, Ph.D., 1965. *Politics:* Democrat. *Religion:* Church of Jesus Christ of Latter-day Saints (Mormons).

ADDRESSES: Home—1561 25th St., Ogden, UT 84401. *Office*—Department of English, Weber University, 1201 University Circle, Ogden, UT 84408-1201.

CAREER: Weber State College, Ogden, UT, assistant professor, 1965-68, associate professor, 1968-72, professor of English, 1972—, chair of department, 1970-73, 1992-96, director of honors program, 1973-82. President of Utah Trails Council, 1977-79.

MEMBER: Association for Mormon Letters (member of board of directors, 1978-82; president, 1981, 1989), Western Literature Association (member of executive council, 1973-75), Rocky Mountain Modern Language Association, Utah Academy of Sciences, Arts and Letters (member of board of directors, 1973-81), Weber County Library (member, board of trustees, 1988—), Kiwanis International, Phi Kappa Phi.

AWARDS, HONORS: First prize from Utah Art Council, 1978, for collection of stories "The Confessions of Augustine," published as *The Canyons of Grace;* first prize from Association for Mormon Letters, 1978, for stories "The Confessions of Augustine" and "Road to Damascus," and 1986, for novel *The Backslider;* first prize from Center for the Study of Christian Values in Literature, 1981, for story "The Gift"; distinguished service award from Utah Academy of Sciences, Arts, and Letters, 1984; first prize from Sunstone Foundation, 1985, for story "Sunswath"; second prize from Utah Art Council, 1985, for manuscript novel *The Backslider;* editorial award from Association for Mormon Letters, 1986, for *Greening Wheat: Fifteen Mormon Short Stories;* second prize from *Dialogue* magazine, 1986, for story "The Third Nephite"; Evans Biography award, 1987, and Mormon History Association's Best Book in Mormon History Award, 1988, for *Juanita Brooks: Mormon Woman Historian.*

WRITINGS:

The Canyons of Grace (stories), University of Illinois Press (Urbana, IL), 1982.
(Editor) *Greening Wheat: Fifteen Mormon Short Stories* (anthology), Signature Books (Midvale, UT), 1983.
The Backslider (novel), Signature Books, 1986.
Juanita Brooks: Mormon Woman Historian, University of Utah Press (Salt Lake City, UT), 1988.
Night Soil (stories), Signature Books, 1990.
Aspen Marooney (novel), Signature Books, 1995.

Contributor to history and western American literature journals. Editor of *Encyclia: Journal of the Utah Academy of Sciences, Arts, and Letters,* 1977-81.

WORK IN PROGRESS: A collection of wilderness essays.

SIDELIGHTS: Levi S. Peterson told *CA:* "I grew up in a Mormon village in northern Arizona. I was a Mormon missionary in Switzerland and Belgium from 1954 to 1957; as a result, I speak French. Intellectually I believe I am a humanist and a citizen of the world; emotionally I still live in the stern ambiance of a frontier Mormon town.

"One of my fictional purposes is to explore the penitential impulse in human beings. Although my characters, as Mormons with rural roots, are fundamental Christians, I hope to reveal universal preoccupations and themes through them. I hope, through a carefully modulated narrative voice, to avoid moralizing or preachment. I am not personally interested in doctrinal or ideological issues; rather I am interested in the tensions which arise among characters who rationalize their lives in doctrinal terms.

"I have engaged in the polemics of liberal Mormonism, especially in my essays. Unlike some of my friends, I have not been excommunicated. In my fiction I continue to be fascinated by Mormons in sin and turmoil. The conflicts of my stories and novels gravitate ineluctably to a guilty conscience. I feel privileged to have spent most of my adult life close to wilderness. I seem never to get enough of the trails and backroads of the West. I am inclined to regret my mortality most keenly on a misty morning in the Uinta Mountains."

BIOGRAPHICAL/CRITICAL SOURCES:

PERIODICALS

Booklist, February 15, 1991, p. 1178.
Chicago Tribune, February 6, 1983.
Publishers Weekly, October 12, 1990, p. 46.
Western American Literature, spring, 1984.
Western Historical Quarterly, November, 1989, p. 452.

*   *   *

PETERSON, Owen M.   1924-

PERSONAL: Born February 17, 1924, in Parker, SD; son of Arthur A. and Grace (Radley) Peterson. *Education:* University of Iowa, B.A., 1946, M.A., 1949, Ph.D., 1952.

ADDRESSES: Home—2100 College Dr., #47, Baton Rouge, LA 70808. *Office*—Department of Speech Communication, Louisiana State University, Baton Rouge, LA 70803.

CAREER: DePauw University, Greencastle, IN, assistant professor of speech, 1952-54; Louisiana State University, Baton Rouge, 1954—, began as instructor, became assistant professor, then associate professor, currently professor of speech communication. Visiting lecturer at Michigan State University, summers, 1952-53, and Wichita State University, summer, 1954.

MEMBER: Speech Communication Association (executive secretary, 1957-60), English Speaking Union, Hansard Society, Southern Speech Communication Association, Delta Sigma Rho.

AWARDS, HONORS: Recipient of Wichelns-Winans special award for distinguished scholarship, Speech Communication Association, 1992.

WRITINGS:

(With Robert C. Jeffrey) *Speech: A Text with Adapted Readings,* Harper (New York City), 1971, 3rd edition, 1980.
(With Jeffrey) *Speech: A Basic Text,* Harper, 1976, 2nd edition, 1982.
(Editor) *Representative American Speeches,* H. W. Wilson (Bronx, NY), Volume 53: *1980-81,*

1981, Volume 54: *1981-82*, 1982, Volume 55: *1982-83*, 1983, Volume 56: *1983-84*, 1984, Volume 57: *1984-85*, 1985, Volume 58: *1985-86*, 1986, Volume 59: *1986-87*, 1987; Volume 60: *1987-88*, 1988; Volume 61: *1988-89*, 1989; Volume 62: *1989-90*, 1990; Volume 63: *1990-91*, 1991; Volume 64: *1991-92*, 1992; Volume 65: *1992-93*, 1993; Volume 66: *1993-94*, 1994; Volume 67: *1994-95*, 1995.

A Divine Discontent: The Life of Nathan S. S. Beman, Mercer University Press (Macon, GA), 1986.

Contributor to books, including *Mississippi in the Confederacy as Seen in Retrospect,* edited by James Silver, Louisiana State University Press (Baton Rouge, LA), 1961; and *Oratory in the Old South, 1828-1860,* edited by W. W. Braden, Louisiana State University Press, 1971. Also contributor to communication and history journals. Editor of *Southern Speech Communication Journal,* 1961-66; associate editor of *Speech Teacher,* 1967-70, and of *Speech Monographs,* 1968-71.

WORK IN PROGRESS: Research on prominent British political, literary, religious, and theatrical speakers who have made lecture tours of the United States and Canada.

SIDELIGHTS: Owen M. Peterson told *CA:* "For many years I have been interested in the effective use of speech by British leaders. I have been particularly impressed by the speaking activities of the British Labour Party in its rise from virtual obscurity at the beginning of this century to its formation of a government in less than twenty-five years. That initial interest led me to a study of the ways that the Fabian Society sought to influence public opinion and promote the new Labour Party through debates, lectures, and pamphlets. From there, it was a short step to consideration of how prominent British speakers have sought to influence public opinion abroad, especially in America."

*   *   *

PETROV, Victor P. 1907-

PERSONAL: Born March 22, 1907, in Harbin, China; naturalized U.S. citizen; son of Porfiry Nicholas (a priest of Russian Orthodox Church) and Catherine (Ryazanov) Petrov; married Elizabeth Onufrieff (a reference librarian), February 6, 1942 (died October 1, 1981); stepchildren: Tatiana B. Tontarski (deceased). *Education:* Attended Institute of Jurisprudence, Harbin, China, 1925-29; American University, B.S., 1951, M.A., 1952, Ph.D., 1954. *Religion:* Russian Orthodox.

ADDRESSES: Home—15524 Pennyroyal Ln., Rockville, MD 20853.

CAREER: U.S. Navy School of Oriental Languages, Boulder, CO, instructor, 1945-46; U.S. Naval Language School, Washington, DC, assistant professor, 1946-50, associate professor, 1950-57, professor of languages and geography, 1957-63; Defense Language Institute, Washington, DC, professor of languages and geography, 1963-65; Shippensburg State College, Shippensburg, PA, professor of geography, 1965-67; National Science Foundation, Washington, DC, assistant program director, foreign science information program, 1967-70; California State University, Los Angeles, professor of geography, 1970-74. Professorial lecturer in geography, George Washington University, 1962-65; visiting professor, University of Victoria, Victoria, British Columbia, 1974-75.

MEMBER: American Association for the Advancement of Slavic Studies.

AWARDS, HONORS: Meritorious award, Congress of Russian Americans, 1981; elected a foreign member of the Center for Studies of Russian America and Russian-American Relations, Institute of World History, Russian Academy of Sciences, 1994; inducted into Hall of Fame of Congress of Russian Americans, 1995.

WRITINGS:

Geography of the Soviet Union, Kamkin, Part IV-B: *Electric Power,* 1959, Part IV: *Soviet Industry,* 1960, Part IV-A: *Energy Resources,* 1962, Part I: *Physical Features,* 1964, Part II: *Geographic Zone,* 1964, Part III: *Population,* 1964, Part V: *Transportation,* 1967.

China: Emerging World Power, Van Nostrand (New York City), 1967, 2nd edition, 1976.

Mongolia: A Profile, Praeger (New York City), 1970.

IN RUSSIAN

Pod Amerikanskim Flagom (title means "Under American Flag"), Malyk & Kamkin (Shanghai), 1933.

Lola (novel), Malyk & Kamkin, 1934.

V Manchzhurii (title means "In Manchuria"), Slovo (Shanghai), 1937.

Albazintsy v. Kitae (title means "Albazinians in China"), Kamkin (Washington, DC), 1956.

Saga Forta Ross (title means "Saga of Fort Ross"), Kamkin, Book I: *Printsessa Elena* (title means "Princess Elena"), 1961, second edition, 1980, Book II: *Konets Mechtam* (title means "End of Dreams"), 1963.

Kitayskie Rasskazy (title means "Chinese Stories"), Kamkin, 1962.

100-Petnyaya Godovschina prihoda russkikh eskadr v. Ameriku (title means "100th Anniversary of the Arrival of Russian Naval Squadrons to America"), Kamkin, 1963.

Rossiyskaya Dukhovnaya missiya v. Kitae (title means "The Russian Ecclesiastical Mission in China"), Kamkin, 1968.

Kolumby Rossiyskie (title means "Russian Columbuses"), Kamkin, 1971.

Kamerger Dvora (title means "Grand Chamberlain of the Court"), Kamkin, 1973.

Zavershenie Tsikla (title means "Completion of a Cycle"), Rodnye Dali, 1975.

Russkaia Amerika (title means "Russian America"), Friends of Fort Ross, 1975, 2nd edition, 1981.

Fort Ross i Ego Kul'turnoe Nasledie (title means "Fort Ross and Its Cultural Heritage"), Friends of Fort Ross, 1977, 2nd edition, 1980.

Kataklizm (title means "Cataclysm"), Russian-American Historical Society, 1982.

Gorod na Sungari (title means "A City on the Sungari"), Russian-American Historical Society, 1984.

Shanhai na Vampu (title means "Shanghai on the Whangpoo"), Russian-American Historical Society, 1985.

Po Sviatoy Zemle (title means "In the Holy Land"), Russian-American Historical Society, 1986.

Po Sledam Inka i Maya (title means "Following the Steps of Inca and Maya"), Russian-American Historical Society, 1987.

Russkie v Istorii Ameriki (title means "Russians in American History"), Russian-American Historical Society, 1988.

Ot Vostochnoy Afriki do Ognennoy Zemli (title means "From East Africa to Tierra del Fuego"), Russian-American Historical Society, 1989.

Russkie v Amerike, XX Vek (title means "Russians in America, Twentieth Century"), Russian-American Historical Society, 1992.

Po Mirovym Prostoram (title means "In the Wide World"), Russian-American Historical Society, 1993.

Izgoy (title means "Expatriate"), Russian-American Historical Society, 1994.

OTHER

Also author of *Sungari Kahan no Machi* (in Japanese; title means "City on the Sungari"), Japan, 1987. Contributor to *Worldmark Encyclopedia of the Nations,* 1971, and to *Encyclopedia Britannica,* 1981. Also contributor of approximately fifty articles on geography of the Soviet Union and China and on astrogeography to professional journals, of four articles in Japanese to *Tokyo Kaiho,* and of more than three hundred articles to Russian language newspapers in the United States and Australia. Contributing editor, *Dictionary of Political Science,* 1964.

WORK IN PROGRESS: An historical research book (in Russian), *Rossiya na Dal'nem Vostoke* (title means "Russia in the Far East").

SIDELIGHTS: Victor P. Petrov is competent in German, Russian, and Chinese and gets along well in several other Slavic languages.

* * *

PHILLIPS, Dewi Zephaniah 1934-

PERSONAL: Born November 24, 1934, in Swansea, Wales; son of D. O. and A. F. (Davie) Phillips; married Margaret Monica Hanford; children: Aled Huw, Steffan John, Rhys David. *Education:* University College of Swansea, University of Wales, B.A. (first class honors in philosophy), 1956, M.A., 1958; St. Catherine's Society, Oxford, B.Litt., 1961. *Religion:* Congregationalist.

ADDRESSES: Home—45 Queen's Rd., Sketty, Swansea, West Glamorganshire, Wales. *Office*—Department of Philosophy, University College of Swansea, University of Wales, Singleton Park, Swansea SA2 8PP, Wales.

CAREER: University of St. Andrews, St. Andrews, Scotland, assistant lecturer in philosophy, 1961-62, lecturer, 1962-63; University of Wales, University College of North Wales, Bangor, lecturer in philosophy, 1962-65, University College of Swansea, Swansea, lecturer, 1965-67, senior lecturer, 1967-70, professor of philosophy, 1971—; Claremont Graduate School, Claremont, CA, Danforth Professor of the Philosophy of Religion, 1992—.

MEMBER: Aristotelian Society, Welsh National Eisteddfod, Welsh Philosophical Society.

WRITINGS:

The Concept of Prayer, Schocken (New York City), 1965.

Faith and Philosophical Enquiry, Routledge & Kegan Paul (London, England), 1970, Schocken, 1971.

Death and Immortality, St. Martin's Press (New York City), 1970.

(With H. O. Mounce) *Moral Practices,* Schocken, 1970.

(With Ilham Dilman) *Sense and Delusion,* Humanities Press (Atlantic Highlands, NJ), 1971.

Religion without Explanation, Basil Blackwell (Oxford, England), 1976.

Through a Darkening Glass, University of Notre Dame Press (Notre Dame and London), 1982.

Belief, Change and Forms of Life, Macmillan (New York City), 1986.

R. S. Thomas: Poet of the Hidden God, Macmillan, 1986.

Faith after Foundationalism, Routledge & Kegan Paul, 1988, Westview Press (Boulder, CO), 1995.

From Fantasy to Faith, Macmillan, 1991.

Interventions in Ethics, Macmillan, 1992.

Wittgenstein and Religion, Macmillan and St. Martin's Press, 1993.

Writers of Wales: J. R. Jones, University of Wales Press (Cardiff, Wales), 1995.

Also author of *Athronyddu Am Greyfydd,* 1974, and *Dramau Gwenlyn Parry,* 1982.

EDITOR

Rush Rhees, *Without Answers,* Schocken Books, 1969.

J. L. Stocks, *Morality and Purpose,* Routledge & Kegan Paul, 1969.

John Anderson, *Education and Inquiry,* Basil Blackwell, 1980.

Jakob Fries, *Dialogue on Morality and Religion,* Basil Blackwell, 1982.

(With Peter Winch) *Wittgenstein: Attention to Particulars: Essays in Honour of Rush Rhees,* Macmillan, 1989.

Editor and author of introduction of *Can Religion Be Explained Away?* and *Religion and Morality* both published by Macmillan.

OTHER

Contributor to books, including *Saith Ysgrif Ar Grefydd,* Gee Press (London), 1967; *Problems of Moral Philosophy,* Dickenson (Belmont, CA), 1972; *The Autonomy of Religious Belief,* edited by Frederick Crosson, University of Notre Dame Press, 1981; *Images in Belief and Literature,* edited by D. Jasper, Macmillan, 1984; Richard H. Bell, *The Grammar of the Heart,* Harper and Row (San Francisco, CA), 1988; R. Douglas Geivett and Brendan Sweetman, *Contemporary Perspectives on Religious Epistemology,* Oxford University Press, 1992; W. J. Rees, *Y Meddwl Cymreig,* University of Wales Press, 1995; and *Philosophy and the Grammar of Religious Belief,* edited by Timothy Tessin and Mario von der Ruhr, Macmillan and St. Martin's Press, 1995. Also contributor to multi-volume works, including *Studies in Ethics and the Philosophy of Religion,* New York Series, Routledge and Kegan Paul and Schocken Books, 1968-74; *Swansea Studies in Philosophy,* Macmillan, 1990—; and *Claremont Studies in the Philosophy of Religion,* Macmillan and St. Martin's Press, 1993—.

Also contributor to proceedings of philosophy societies and to professional journals. General editor, *Values and Philosophical Inquiry,* Basil Blackwell, 1978-86. Editor of *Philosophical Investigations,* 1982—.

WORK IN PROGRESS: Introducing Philosophy, for Blackwell.

*   *   *

PORTER, R. E.
  See HOCH, Edward D(entinger)

*   *   *

PULKINGHAM, Betty Carr   1928-

PERSONAL: Born August 25, 1928, in Burlington, NC; daughter of Leo (a lawyer and judge) and Betty (Knott) Carr; married William Graham

Pulkingham (an Episcopal priest; deceased), September 1, 1951; children: William Graham III, Mary Graham, Nathan Carr, Elizabeth Jane, Martha Louise, David Earle. *Education:* University of North Carolina at Greensboro, B.S. (magna cum laude), 1949; graduate study at Eastman School of Music. *Religion:* Episcopalian.

ADDRESSES: Home and office--722 West Davis St., Burlington, NC 27215.

CAREER: Music theory instructor at University of Texas, 1949-53; Austin High School, Austin, TX, choral music teacher, 1956-57; private piano teacher in Galveston, TX, 1958-60; Church of the Redeemer, Houston, TX, choir director, 1964-71; director of research and development of worship resources for Celebration, 1974-80; director, All Saints Episcopal Choir, Aliquippa, PA, 1987-92.

WRITINGS:

(Arranger and compiler with Oressa Wise) *Songs of Fellowship,* privately printed, 1972, Net Music Co., 1975.

Mass for the King of Glory, G. I. A. Publications (Irving, TX), 1973.

(Compiler with Jeanne Harper) *Sound of Living Waters* (also see below), Eerdmans (Grand Rapids, MI), 1974.

(Compiler with Harper) *Fresh Sounds* (also see below), Hodder & Stoughton (London), 1976.

Mustard Seeds, Hodder & Stoughton, 1977.

(Compiler with Harper) *Sound of Living Waters* [and] *Fresh Sounds,* Hodder & Stoughton, 1977.

Little Things in the Hands of a Big God, Word Publishing (Irving, TX), 1977.

(Editor) *Hosanna in the Highest: Collection of Descants for Traditional Hymns,* Celebration (Nobleboro, ME), 1978.

(Editor with Mimi Farra) *Cry Hosanna,* Hope Publishing (Carol Stream, IL), 1980.

Sing God a Simple Song: Exploring Worship for the Eighties, Marshall Pickering (Basingstoke, England), 1986.

(Composer and editor) *Celebrate the Church Year with Psalms and Canticles,* Cathedral Music Press, 1988.

(Editor with Farra and Kevin Hackett) *Come Celebrate* (hymnal supplement), Cathedral Music Press, 1990.

Freedom Mass (from South African folk songs), Cathedral Music Press, 1990.

(Composer and editor with Hackett) *The Celebration Psalter,* 3 volumes, Cathedral Music Press, 1991.

WORK IN PROGRESS: Completed and seeking a publisher for a cantata based on two early American folk hymns; several chordal arrangements of American hymns; a research project involving ways for children to learn American folk melodies at an early age.

SIDELIGHTS: Betty Carr Pulkingham told *CA:* "Over the years, my primary source of inspiration for writing music has been the worshipping community. Set in the midst of the marketplace, influenced by all the sounds and sights of human commerce, joy and pain, the church-in-the-world draws from me a kaleidoscope of sounds far greater than my own personal musical tastes require. My current quest is to find more ways to enhance the singing of American hymnody which is uniquely ours. While I do not favor nationalism as such, I see every reason to be good stewards of the music which has sprung from our own soil."

*   *   *

PURDY, James (Amos) 1923-

PERSONAL: Born July 17, 1923, in Ohio; son of William and Vera Purdy. *Education:* Attended University of Chicago and University of Puebla, Mexico.

ADDRESSES: Home—236 Henry St., Brooklyn, NY 11201.

CAREER: Writer. Lawrence College (now University), Appleton, WI, faculty member, 1949-53; worked as an interpreter in Latin America, France, and Spain; United States Information Agency lecturer in Europe, 1982.

AWARDS, HONORS: National Institute of Arts and Letters grant in literature, 1958; Guggenheim fellow,

1958, 1962; Ford Foundation grant, 1961; *On Glory's Course* nominated for PEN-Faulkner Award, 1985; received Rockefeller Foundation grant; received Morton Dauwen Zabel Fiction award from American Academy of Arts and Letters, 1993.

WRITINGS:

NOVELS

63: Dream Palace (also see below), William-Frederick, 1956.
Malcolm (also see below), Farrar, Straus (New York City), 1959.
The Nephew (also see below), Farrar, Straus, 1961.
Cabot Wright Begins, Farrar, Straus, 1964.
Eustace Chisholm and the Works, Farrar, Straus, 1967.
Jeremy's Version, Doubleday (New York City), 1970.
I Am Elijah Thrush, Doubleday, 1972.
The House of the Solitary Maggot, Doubleday, 1974.
Color of Darkness [and] *Malcolm* (also see below), Doubleday, 1974.
In a Shallow Grave, Arbor House (New York City), 1976.
Narrow Rooms, Arbor House, 1978.
Dream Palaces: Three Novels (contains *Malcolm, The Nephew,* and *63: Dream Palace*), Viking (New York City), 1980.
Mourners Below, Viking, 1981.
On Glory's Course, Viking, 1984.
In the Hollow of His Hand, Weidenfeld & Nicolson (London), 1986.
Candles of Your Eyes, Viking, 1986.
Garments the Living Wear, City Lights Books (San Francisco, CA), 1989.
Out with the Stars, City Lights Books, 1992.

STORY COLLECTIONS

Don't Call Me by My Right Name and Other Stories, (also see below), William-Frederick, 1956.
63: Dream Palace: A Novella and Nine Stories (contains *63: Dream Palace, Don't Call Me by My Right Name and Other Stories,* and two stories), New Directions, 1957.
Children Is All (stories and plays), New Directions, 1962.
An Oyster Is a Wealthy Beast (a story and poems), Black Sparrow Press, 1967.

Mr. Evening: A Story and Nine Poems, Black Sparrow Press, 1968.
On the Rebound: A Story and Nine Poems, Black Sparrow Press, 1970.
A Day after the Fair: A Collection of Plays and Stories, Note of Hand, 1977.
The Candles of Your Eyes, and Thirteen Other Stories, Weidenfeld & Nicolson (New York City), 1987.
63: Dream Palace: Selected Stories, 1956-1987, Black Sparrow Press (Santa Rosa, CA), 1991.

POEMS

The Running Sun, Paul Waner Press, 1971.
Sunshine Is an Only Child, Aloe Editions, 1973.
Lessons and Complaints, Nadja, 1978.
Sleep Tight, Nadja, 1979.
The Brooklyn Branding Parlors, Contact/II, 1985.
Collected Poems, Athenaeum-Polak & Van Gennep (Amsterdam, Germany), 1990.

Also author of *I Will Arrest the Bird That Has No Light,* 1978, *Don't Let the Snow Fall,* 1985, and *Are You in the Winter Tree?,* 1987.

PLAYS

Cracks, produced in New York City, 1963.
Wedding Finger, New Directions, 1974.
Two Plays (contains *A Day at the Fair* and *True*), New London Press (Dallas, TX), 1979.
Scrap of Paper [and] *The Berrypicker,* Sylvester & Orphanos, 1981.
Proud Flesh, Lord John Press (Northridge, CA), 1981.

Also author of *Mr. Cough and the Phantom Sex,* 1960, *Ruthanna Elder,* 1989, *In the Night of Time and Four Other Plays,* 1992, *Foment,* 1994, *Brice,* 1994, and *Where Quentin Goes,* 1994.

RECORDINGS

Eventide and Other Stories, Spoken Arts, 1968.
63: Dream Palace, Spoken Arts, 1969.

OTHER

Also author of *Dawn* (novel), 1985, and *Kitty Blue* (fairy tale), 1993. Contributor to numerous books, including *New Directions in Prose and Poetry 21,* edited by James Laughlin, New Directions, 1969.

Contributor to magazines, including *Mademoiselle, New Yorker,* and *Commentary.*

ADAPTATIONS: Malcolm was adapted as a play by Edward Albee and published by Dramatists Play Service in 1966; some of Purdy's poems have been set to music by Richard Hundley and Robert Helps; the story "Sleep Tight" was filmed by Inquiring Systems, Inc.; *In a Shallow Grave* was adapted and filmed by Kenneth Bowser in 1988; *63: Dream Palace* was made into an opera by Hans-Jurgen von Bose, published by Ars Viva Verlag (Mainz, France), 1989.

SIDELIGHTS: After his short stories were rejected by every magazine to which he submitted them, James Purdy published his first two books with a subsidy publisher in 1956. He sent copies of these subsidy books—the novel *63: Dream Palace* and the collection *Don't Call Me by My Right Name and Other Stories*—to a number of prominent literary figures, hoping to create some interest in his writing. The resulting interest was far more than he had expected. Dame Edith Sitwell, the English poet, wrote back to Purdy, calling several of his short stories "superb: nothing short of masterpieces" and his novel "a masterpiece from every point of view." Because of her admiration for Purdy's work, Sitwell spoke to the publishing firm of Gollancz and persuaded them to issue a British edition of Purdy's books. The Gollancz edition, combining both of his subsidy books into a single volume entitled *63: Dream Palace: A Novella and Nine Stories,* was well reviewed in England and launched Purdy's literary career. The same material, plus two additional stories, was published in America as *Color of Darkness: Eleven Stories and a Novella* in 1957.

Purdy first made his reputation, a *Times Literary Supplement* reviewer explains, because he wrote "in a style, a tone, that was as direct and natural as someone talking . . . and through eyes that belonged exclusively to him. You may dislike a writer's vision, but if he has one that is unique, you must admit his talent: it is the only sure sign of originality." Purdy's unique vision has been expressed in a variety of ways. As Henry Chupack emphasizes in his book *James Purdy,* he has "created many worlds; and each with its own discernible and distinct features." This variety makes Purdy a difficult writer to categorize. Stephen D. Adams writes in his book *James Purdy* that his "originality and extraordinary talents cannot be neatly inventoried. . . . To portray him as the author of an eccentric body of fiction, as a part of

some movement or fashionable literary trend, or as a novelist who essentially mocks the capacities of art, is to deny the complexities of his individual voice." A continuing concern with the crippling effects of the American family on its children marks all of Purdy's work. His early books portray orphans or runaways who are exploited or abused by older characters, while his more recent novels examine the destructive relationships between family members. The failure of love is behind the failure of the family in Purdy's work, Frank Baldanza writes in *Centennial Review,* resulting in children "who, as adults, pass on the anguished, lonely legacy to their own offspring. . . . Purdy's vision is somber and frightening." This vision is defined by Chupack as being the essence of postwar America. Chupack writes: "Behind [postwar America's] facade of great material wealth lay a vast spiritual wasteland of loveless lives and hellish marriages; from such barren marriages came children who, as a rule, were treated cruelly by their parents and by other adults; rape and homosexuality were engaged in by those who, denied love in their own lives, sought it in antisocial actions; and most ironic of all, the quest for wealth and the possession of it did not result in happiness."

Purdy distances himself from his fictional material while still involving his readers emotionally with his characters. He relates often violent or horrifying events in a flat, ironic prose to create a black comedy that transcends its melancholic subject matter. Writing in the *Village Voice,* Debra Rae Cohen explains that Purdy's narrative voice "cleaves to the rhythms proper to the world it creates, but keeps you aware, by its very pervasiveness, of the bemused, sardonic intelligence behind it all. . . . In the black humor of his artificial America, he seems sometimes as distanced as a puppeteer."

Critical reaction to Purdy's work ranges from high praise from such writers as Gore Vidal, Marianne Moore, Dorothy Parker, and John Cowper Powys to outright dismissal by other observers. A writer for the *Times Literary Supplement* admits that "there has always been a good deal of critical confusion about [Purdy]. As a writer, he has existed at extremes of praise and disparagement." Jerome Charyn also remarks on this critical polarity. Writing in the *New York Times Book Review,* Charyn explains that Purdy "exists in some strange limbo between adoration and neglect," although Charyn judges him to be "one of the very best writers we have." The English writer Francis King, in an article for the *Spectator,* notes the lack of critical acceptance Purdy has received.

"Although," King writes, "he strikes me as a writer of far greater originality and power than [Saul] Bellow, [Philip] Roth, or [John] Updike, James Purdy has only rarely received his due in his native America." Critical reaction in Europe has generally been kinder to Purdy, particularly in France, England, and Italy.

In a letter to *CA,* Purdy states that his literary stature has been determined by the existing literary establishment, which is unsympathetic to his kind of writing. Purdy explains: "Reviewing in America is in a very bad state owing to the fact that there are no serious book reviews, and reputations are made in America by political groups backed by money and power brokers who care nothing for original and distinguished writing, but are bent on forwarding the names of writers who are politically respectable. There are also almost no magazines today which will print original and distinguished fiction unless the author is a member of the 'New York literary establishment.' Reputations are made here, as in Russia, on political respectability, or by commercial acceptability. The worse the author, the more he is known."

Having what Warren French and Donald Pease in the *Dictionary of Literary Biography* call a "haunting, nightmarish quality," Purdy's first novel, *63: Dream Palace,* tells of two orphaned brothers who leave West Virginia to live in Chicago. Living in a big city for the first time, Fenton and Claire unknowingly associate with people who wish to exploit them. In his attempts to support the sickly Claire, Fenton moves from theft to prostitution to drugs, ultimately strangling Claire while under the influence of drugs.

The book was inspired by Purdy's own youth. "I left home at an early age and went to Chicago. It was the first big city I had ever known, and I was unprepared for its overwhelming confusion," Purdy writes in the *Contemporary Authors Autobiography Series* (*CAAS*). But *63: Dream Palace* is "biography . . . transformed into a supreme fiction that sails close-hauled in one direction to out-and-out naturalism, and in the other to surrealistic fable," as Robert K. Morris writes in the *Nation.* Morris concludes by describing the novel as "at once a marvelous and depressing tale, as lucid and total an allegory of despair as one could imagine."

The short stories of Purdy's other early book, *Don't Call Me by My Right Name,* are, Anthony Bailey of *Commonweal* believes, "a novel departure in the

craft of the short story." Bailey finds that Purdy's achievement in these stories makes "the work of many highly skilled writers seem extremely dependent on literary convention and, in doing so, [Purdy] has made fresh contact with moral reality." Similarly, William Bittner of *Nation* thinks Purdy's work "seems to be more what the short story might have been had it developed continuously from [Edgar Allan] Poe, [Nathaniel] Hawthorne, and [Herman] Melville. Purdy, at any rate, is that rare bird in this age of reportorial fiction, a writer who creates."

The critical acclaim for Purdy's work continued with the release of the novel *Malcolm* in 1959. The book tells the story of a fifteen-year-old boy who is abandoned at a posh hotel by his father. Making the acquaintance of an astrologer, Mr. Cox, Malcolm is given a list of addresses of people he should visit and the advice, "Give yourself up to things." The people Malcolm visits, Donald Cook writes in the *New Republic,* try "to use him and to possess him." "The themes of *63: Dream Palace,*" Jean E. Kennard explains in *Number and Nightmare: Forms of Fantasy in Contemporary Fiction,* "are more fully developed in . . . *Malcolm.* Using the picaresque novel pattern of a young man setting out to learn about life through a series of adventures, Purdy ironically tells the story of a young man who is used by everyone he meets and learns nothing." Though Cook admits "there is a great deal of depravity and perversity" in the novel, he believes that Purdy has the "ability to touch upon these things with gentleness and wit, and thereby to provide new illuminations."

Malcolm is eventually pressured into marriage with a nymphomaniac nightclub singer and dies, as Purdy writes in the novel, of "acute alcoholism and sexual hyperaesthesia." Billed as a comic novel by its publisher, *Malcolm* evokes laughter that "sounds a little like the beginning of a death rattle," R. W. B. Lewis writes in the *New York Herald Tribune Book Review.* Lewis places *Malcolm* in the "fine old comic picaresque tradition" and calls Purdy "a writer of exceptional talent, who must be acknowledged in the company, say, of Saul Bellow and Ralph Ellison." Paul Herr of the *Chicago Review* also praises the novel. "With the publication of *Malcolm,*" Herr states, "James Purdy has left no doubt that he is a writer of integrity with a voice of his own."

Kennard argues that *Malcolm* is primarily concerned with "the failure of communication." This failure is dramatized by the contradictory language of Purdy's characters and the self-negating scenes between them. "Characters reply to each other in a series of nonsequitors . . . ," Kennard reports. "Just as individual sentences cancel each other out, so too the action of the novel progressively unmakes itself. All relationships disintegrate. . . . Malcolm is eventually found drifting aimlessly from one place to another." Tony Tanner, writing in *City of Words: American Fiction, 1950-1970,* also sees this process of dissolution in *Malcolm.* "In the world in which . . . Malcolm finds himself," Tanner writes, "sense is continually dissolving in contradictions. There is nothing stable enough or meaningful enough around him to enable him properly speaking to 'begin'. . . . He passes through changing scenes but, instead of thickening into identity and consolidating a real self, his life is really a long fading."

In an article for *Critique: Studies in Modern Fiction,* Charles Stetler finds this dissolution—"the disturbing themes of loneliness and lack of identity in the bizarre nightmare of modern existence," as he calls it—the subject matter of what is essentially a parody. "Without question," Stetler writes, "*Malcolm* is a story of a young man confronting adulthood, for initiation is its central theme. [But Purdy] has offered us a sport on that type, using the genre to satirize it, with a wry approach to form as well as content. Viewed this way, the satire of an already cheerless book is deepened, and the blackness of its humor becomes more pervasive, more complete, and more grim." This parody ultimately extends to the death of Malcolm at book's end. There is some doubt surrounding Malcolm's death, with the coroner and undertaker both claiming there was no body in Malcolm's coffin. "Thus," Stetler writes, "if nothing proves that Malcolm is dead, nothing, likewise, guarantees that Malcolm ever lived, in any sense of the word. Instead of the novel being an allegory of a young everyman, it is more an allegory of no man—the way Purdy sees modern man."

In *The Nephew,* Purdy continues to write of characters who have no fixed identity. This time, though, his primary character never appears in the novel. Cliff Mason, missing in action in the Korean War, becomes the subject of a memorial book being compiled by his Aunt Alma, who raised him after his parents died. Her research into Cliff's life ends inconclusively. As Martin Tucker writes in *Commonweal,* "she discovers she knows almost nothing about the only person she has loved." But her search for Cliff reveals much about the secret sorrows and fears of her neighbors and friends in the small town in which she lives, and what little new

she does discover about Cliff strongly suggests that he was a homosexual. Her search, French and Pease comment, "results not in recovering the boy, but in exposing the banal hidden secrets of her neighbors and leading them to a new apprehension of each other." As in *Malcolm,* where a dissolution takes place in the narrative, "the action of [*The Nephew*] is a movement towards the void. . . . The reader is taken towards nothing as each piece of information gleaned contradicts what has gone before," Kennard writes.

Several observers see *The Nephew* and its story of a search for a dead relative as merely a structure in which Purdy explores small town life, satirizing the conventions of contemporary America. Herbert Gold, writing in the *New Republic,* finds that "the plot is a mere excuse for a curious parody of a Norman Rockwell illustration or an Edgar Lee Masters poem," while French and Pease point out that the town of Rainbow Center in which Alma lives is "a half-American-gothic, half-Ozlike community." "Purdy's aim," Curtis Harnack explains in the *Chicago Sunday Tribune,* "is leveled at America's values and beliefs, at contemporary society itself."

This literary assault utilizes a variety of writing styles and genres, all of which Purdy employs with great skill. "From humor to pathos, from farce to caricature or to straight narrative," William Peden writes in the *Saturday Review,* "Mr. Purdy is in constant control of his material. . . . If any doubts exist concerning Mr. Purdy's unique abilities, this slender, unpretentious, thoroughly admirable novel should dispel them." Calling *The Nephew* "a small work of authentic fictional art," Lewis claims that Purdy "has demonstrated a range and variety in his steadily strengthening talent—one of the most decisive literary talents to have appeared since the last war—to which one happily sees no obvious bounds."

With his next two novels, *Cabot Wright Begins* and *Eustace Chisholm and the Works,* Purdy met with strong opposition from what he calls, in his *CAAS* article, the "essentially stuffy New York establishment." *Cabot Wright Begins* concerns a Wall Street heir who becomes a rapist. After he is captured and imprisoned, Cabot Wright decides to compose his memoirs, hiring a woman writer to help him. But the woman's experiences with the publishing world, which is not interested in the truth of Wright's situation but with a commercial version of it, force her to abandon the project. A third of the novel's length deals with the problems involved in writing Cabot's biography and the reaction the manuscript receives. It is this satirical look at the publishing world, what French and Pease call "Purdy's frontal assault on what he regards as a decadent literary establishment and the vulgarities of a culture shaped by advertising," that inspired, some critics feel, the negative reaction to the novel. A reviewer for the *Times Literary Supplement* asserted, for example, that one of the novel's characters, a critic named Doyley Pepscout, was based on an actual New York critic.

Other reviewers also criticized *Cabot Wright Begins.* Stanley Edgar Hyman writes in *Standards: A Chronicle of Books for Our Time* that "Purdy is a terrible writer, and worse than that, he is a boring writer." Theodore Solotaroff, in his *The Red Hot Vacuum and Other Pieces on the Writing of the Sixties,* finds that "the first two thirds or so of *Cabot Wright Begins* is a cool, mordant, and deadly accurate satire on American values, as good as anything we have had since the work of Nathanael West. . . . But having sprung his indignation, Purdy eventually allows it to get out of hand. Losing the objectivity of his art, he continues to pour it on and pour it on."

Despite such criticism, the book received positive comments from a number of observers. These include Tanner, who states that *Cabot Wright Begins* "gathers together all the themes opened up or touched on in Purdy's earlier work and explores them with a subtlety and humour and power which makes this, to my mind, not only Purdy's most profound novel but one of the most important American novels since the war." A *Times Literary Supplement* critic describes *Cabot Wright Begins* as "not only the most savage of satires on the American way of life . . . [but] also an extremely funny book."

Purdy's next novel, *Eustace Chisholm and the Works,* was again met with derision from "the anaesthetic, hypocritical, preppy, and stagnant New York literary establishment," as Purdy writes in his *CAAS* article. It was the book's sympathetic portrayal of homosexual love that Purdy believes caused the furor. "Such love," he writes in his *CAAS* article, "unless treated clinically or as a documentary cannot be tolerated by the New York literary Powers-That-Be." One negative review was by Nelson Algren who, in *Critic,* finds little merit in *Eustace Chisolm and the Works,* calling it a "fifth-rate *avant-garde* soap opera."

Revolving around Eustace Chisholm, a bisexual would-be poet, the novel tells of several love relationships, including that between Eustace and his wife, Carla, between Daniel Haws and Amos Ratcliffe, and between Maureen O'Dell and Daniel Haws. "Homosexuals comprise most of the characters in *Eustace Chisholm and the Works,*" Robert K. Morris writes in the *Nation,* "but homosexuality is not really the subject. . . . The world of the pervert . . . has been blown up to accommodate the larger themes of alienation, isolation and lovelessness." Similarly, Rachel Trickett of the *Yale Review* calls *Eustace Chisholm and the Works* an "appalling fable of the impossibility of love, with the violent depiction of the frustration and martyrdom of a romantic homosexual passion, and its brutally comic presentation of heterosexual promiscuity and abortion."

Several critics see the novel's early pages as weaker than its conclusion. Wilfred Sheed of the *New York Times Book Review,* for example, finds "the first part of this story [to be] told on a note of shrill facetiousness. . . . But slowly, and one might guess, diffidently, the book becomes a little more serious. . . . The whole last section is a purple feast of sadomasochism. It is also a risky and serious piece of writing, which waives the extenuations of humor, and is possibly the best writing Purdy has ever done." Morris, too, sees a change in the narrative during the course of the novel. "What begins as the whimpering and whining of unrequited lovers moves toward a crescendo of suffering," Morris writes, "and what starts as a vague, troubled dream becomes an excursion in nightmare."

But French, writing in his *Season of Promise,* praises *Eustace Chisholm and the Works* in its entirety. After reading Purdy's earlier fiction, he explains, "I was scarcely prepared for the violently compressed power, the exhausting vehemence, the almost superhuman exorcism of the wanton evil that destroys many innocents that set Purdy's new effort far apart from the whining and the cocktail chatter that often passes for serious fiction. I was staggered by Purdy's tale." Trickett concludes that the novel "is conceived and executed with the most elaborate artistry . . . The book has brilliance and originality."

Since writing *Eustace Chisholm and the Works,* Purdy has turned to stories inspired by the tales he heard as a child from his grandmother and great-grandmother. These stories are set in rural Ohio and concern the farmers and small-town inhabitants of the region. In *Jeremy's Version, The House of the Solitary Maggot, Mourners Below,* and *On Glory's Course,* Purdy transforms his ancestors' remembrances into fiction. This change in subject matter,

French and Pease maintain, is characterized by "less spectacular yet even more frightening tales of the South and Midwest, employing regional vernaculars to present intensive, brooding, in-depth studies of small groups of pathetic figures spotlighted against uncluttered pastoral settings."

Jeremy's Version is set in the small Ohio town of Boutflour and examines the relationships that bind together the Fergus family. "The action is violent, gothic, but mostly kept in the family," a *Times Literary Supplement* reviewer comments. Wilfred Fergus is an irresponsible father; his wife, Elvira, raises their three sons on her own; and the sons are trying to work out their own lives in the stifling atmosphere of their rural community. Though Purdy's subject matter has changed, there is much similarity between this novel and previous ones. As in his previous novels, Purdy remains concerned with the fate of young people abused and exploited by their elders. And as in *The Nephew* and earlier works, he uses a memoirist to relate his story. This time it is a 15-year-old boy who is writing a novel based on the remembrances of an older character and on a diary written by a third character.

Guy Davenport sees Purdy as working in a familiar genre, the American gothic, but using it to express his own vision. "It is a novel which, in a sense, has been written many times before; practically every scene is wonderfully nostalgic rather than new," he writes in the *New York Times Book Review.* "This effect is deliberate and masterfully exploited." The gothic elements in the novel include, the *Times Literary Supplement* reviewer states, "two possible rapes, lost fortunes, drink, fights, 'unspoken of' crimes, lurid revelations about small town sex, scandals, climactic effects, a son's attempt to shoot his mother and a canvas of characters drawn, mostly, in blood." Through these gothic elements, J. R. Lindroth writes in *America,* Purdy "succeeds in evoking the appalling difficulties involved in raising a family in a small town. Financial pressures, sibling rivalries, Oedipal conflicts, dissipate the illusion of a Utopian existence in rural America." Purdy shows that "character is a role written for us by our families; only in loneliness and desperation do we dare leave the stage. . ." Davenport writes. "All the characters . . . are trying to wake up and live . . .; their tragedy is that they do not know what this means, and remain as bewildered as children on a dull afternoon who want something, but do not know what they want."

The House of the Solitary Maggot is set in Prince's Crossing, not far from Boutflour, the setting of *Jeremy's Version.* Prince's Crossing is a place, Purdy explains in the novel, no longer on the maps because it is now too small to constitute a village. It is, writes Irving Malin of the *New Republic,* "a ghostland, . . . filled with people unable to accept the facts of daily life, obsessed by bright visions of glory, fame and love. They are sleepwalkers." The novel is narrated by Eneas Harmond, a hermit who listens to Lady Byethewaite speak into a tape recorder about the history of her family. The tape recording is meant for Lady Byethewaite's great-great-nephew. This narration combines Harmond's story with that of Lady Byethewaite and joins "the voices of past and present" as well, Malin states. The ruin eventually brought upon Byethewaite's three sons—fathered by a Mr. Skegg, a local magnate (pronounced "maggot" by the locals)—is caused by "the irresponsibility of the presumed parents and the inability of the sons to cope with their own emotions," French and Pease write.

Several reviewers find that Purdy's prose transcends the tragedy and squalor of his story. "It has a strange sense of poetry—the poetry of the seedy, the rundown, the decayed and corrupt," writes Douglas Dunn in the *Glasgow Herald.* "The achievement of the book—and I think it is very considerable—is that Purdy's prose and phrase-making elevate the emotional squalor of his story and its characters to a level of effect that is hauntingly beautiful and pure." Calling *The House of the Solitary Maggot* a "mythic and disturbing novel," Malin believes that Purdy transcends his material by using its familiar elements while simultaneously rejecting them. "Purdy," Malin states, "writes a conventional novel but, too shrewd to simply imitate past masters, gives us distinctive, nightmarish patterns, as if . . . he accepts *and* rebels against 'traditional' images."

Mourners Below continues Purdy's interest in Midwestern settings, being set in a nameless location referred to only as "our town" by Purdy. The novel centers on the Bledsoe family: Eugene Bledsoe, his son Duane, and Duane's two half-brothers, Douglas and Justin, recently killed in an unspecified war. Duane is visited by the ghosts of his brothers and comes to feel that Justin, whom he closely resembles, is urging him to carry out his wishes. Before joining the army Justin had an affair with the wealthy Estelle Dumont, and now he wants Duane to rekindle this relationship for him. Duane is first pushed into attending a masquerade at Estelle's home and then, when the party is over, into seducing her. After leaving Estelle the next morning, Duane is set upon by two ruffians who, thinking they are attacking Justin, rape him. "The story that Mr. Purdy is telling," observes King, "is in the nature of a macabre fairy-tale or parable." Similarly, T. O. Treadwell of the *Times Literary Supplement* finds that "the meaning of *Mourners Below* lies on the symbolic, even allegorical level." Writing in the *Chicago Tribune Book World,* Lyle Rexer calls *Mourners Below* "a rural fairy tale, whose fantastic events conceal a psychomythic crisis, in this case the reconciliation of innocence and temporality."

Although there is a mythic level to the novel, King explains that it is "otherwise realistic in its depiction of the life of the small Mid-West town in which all these bizarre, supernatural happenings take place." Julia M. Klein of the *New Republic* believes that Purdy creates "a world where the supernatural merges with the real, [and he] illuminates a reality whose core, if not its contours, matches our own." Because the novel ends with Duane raising the child he has fathered with Estelle, Cohen sees a final twist in the story from the fantastic to the realistic. "Purdy winds up the novel," Cohen writes, "with a deft change of scale; turning, by implication, the small end of the telescope on his characters, he transforms the grotesque and outlandish back into the mundane."

This combination of the real and fantastic parallels Purdy's blending of the comic and bleak as well. "While the grief of *Mourners Below* is very real indeed," Gary Krist writes in the *American Book Review,* "it is touched by an inimitable quality of absurdity and deadpan excess. The morbid background of silence and death is only an instrument of Purdy's essentially comic vision." This view is shared by Klein, who defines the first third of the novel as "a skillful psychological portrait" of Duane's father and the rest of the book as "something wilder and more comic—and finally more terrible."

Krist concludes that *Mourners Below* is "one of [Purdy's] best novels." Klein believes that the novel "recapitulates many of Purdy's concerns—with small-town families in crisis, the explosiveness of contained emotion, the marriage between the dead and the living. Purdy sees to the heart of relations between the sexes. . . . He celebrates the bonds between brothers, between father and son, even as he underlines the near impossibility of intimacy."

On Glory's Course, nominated for the PEN-Faulkner Award in 1985, is set in the Midwestern town of Fonthill during the 1930s. It is a "sexually repressed town," as Michael Dirda describes it in the *Washington Post,* in which Adele Bevington is an elegant and wealthy woman with a "sinful" past. Some thirty years earlier, Adele was forced to give up for adoption her illegitimate son. She has been searching for him ever since, convinced that he is alive and well and still living somewhere in Fonthill.

Marked by a style that attempts to capture the speaking rhythms of the period, *On Glory's Course* has met with some criticism from several reviewers who feel the attempt fails. Robert J. Seidman of the *New York Times Book Review,* for example, thinks the "idiom so ponderous" that Purdy's characters "have trouble speaking their lines." Roz Kaveney of the *Times Literary Supplement* finds the dialogue "wearisomely convoluted and stilted." But Carolyn See of the *Los Angeles Times* argues that the sometimes portentous language is appropriate to the novel's time period. While she admits that at first a reader may believe he is "being made part of an experiment with words," See explains that a more flamboyant speech was common at the time: They "didn't just gossip about you, they resorted to calumny. And people didn't scold or even chide, they were apt to repeat an objuration."

Despite his objections to the novel, Seidman concedes that "Adele, the embattled town rebel, has courage and wit, even stature" and "Purdy does mount a few hilarious comic scenes." Kaveney, too, finds some merit in *On Glory's Course.* "The novel," he writes, "is partly redeemed by the way Purdy keeps the reader turning pages." See maintains that she "recognized a couple of those ironing-board tirades [found in the novel]; others who do may love this book."

Purdy once again combined realism with the fantastic in *Garments the Living Wear,* a tale of New York City's homosexual underworld in the age of AIDS. Bertha Harris, writing in the *New York Times Book Review,* reports that in this novel, "the wit and sauce of a James Purdy drawing room extravaganza collide with the supernatural hyperbole of one of his trademark riffs on the Southern gospel tradition." The story of *Garments* revolves around handsome, extremely desirable Jared Wakeman and his benefactor, the aging drag queen Peg Sawyer. Jared and Peg's social circle is being decimated by AIDS, which is referred to by the characters in the book as "the Pest." Gay theater, a primary concern for both Jared and Peg, is also suffering—both from the loss of its members to the Pest and from lack of funds. Edward Hennings, a wealthy, aging homosexual, appears on the scene to seduce and support Jared. As the story proceeds, it becomes apparent that the mysterious Hennings is able to work miracles. He cures the dying and, in so doing, brings salvation to the damned city of New York; but in the end, he leaves and is later reported to have died in the Caribbean. Those whose lives he touched in New York are grief-stricken by this news, yet, as Harris observes, "they are classic *fin de siecle* characters who will continue to get by in classic *fin de siecle* fashion: on wit and nerve and opportunism." A *Review of Contemporary Fiction* writer calls *Garments the Living Wear* "dramatic, illusory, hallucinatory" and calls Purdy one of "the most interesting novelists we have."

Purdy's 1992 novel, *Out with the Stars,* also delves into the world of New York City's gay artists and musicians; it is set in 1965, however, before AIDS overshadowed that community, and the characters are, for the most part, hiding their homosexuality from the straight world. The plot centers on a composer who finds a libretto describing the stormy marriage of a closet homosexual, but the convoluted storyline involves many liaisons and strange happenings. Like so much of Purdy's work, *Out with the Stars* drew mixed reviews. A contributor to *Review of Contemporary Fiction* rates the book as one of Purdy's best, one that "offers us a cruel *and* comic meditation on the meaning of fame" and is "also concerned with the relationship of art to spiritual longing." Far more reserved is Caroline Moore, who states in *Spectator* that *Out with the Stars* is "a highly-coloured, utterly unbelievable and enjoyable book, which I hesitate to recommend to you."

Reviewing the novel in *Times Literary Supplement,* Firdaus Kanga asserts that "Purdy has certainly never been funnier, his writing never more self-assured"; yet the critic goes on to state that "his book comes to us as one without meaning. . . . He has made his characters into playthings without fitting them into a grand construct." *Boston Globe* writer Richard Dyer labels the book "a curious artifact . . . some of its facets dazzling, polished and reflective, some of them curiously scratched and dull of surface." He praises Purdy's "extraordinary, airy and effortless elegance of style," saying that the work is "suffused with a gay sensibility. There is almost no explicit sexual detail, yet the book is far sexier than the lewdest efforts of younger writers."

Evaluations of Purdy's overall achievement often place him among the finest of American writers. The late Edith Sitwell wrote in the *New York Herald Tribune Book Review* that "James Purdy will come to be recognized as one of the greatest living writers of fiction in our language." Purdy, Chapuck believes, "is a writer of marvelous power, who has made us think deeply and seriously about the human condition." Similarly, Paul Bresnick finds, in an article for the *New York Arts Journal,* that "Purdy has the uncanny ability to compel us to experience emotional states we are thoroughly unfamiliar with. He alerts us to impulses we thought we had successfully murdered or buried. He sensitizes us to new (or rather, submerged) areas of our souls." Charyn calls Purdy "one of the most uncompromising of American novelists," while King feels "that a small, perpetually radioactive particle of genius irradiates the mass of the work he has produced over the years."

Still, Purdy is little known by the American public. As he told *CA* in a letter: "This is an age of exhibitionists, not souls. The press and the public primarily recognize only writers who give them 'doctored' current events as truth. For me, the only 'engagement' or cause a 'called' writer can have (as opposed to a public writer) is his own vision and work. It is an irrevocable decision: he can march only in his own parade."

This approach has gained Purdy a wider readership abroad than in his native America. Speaking of a tour he made for the United States Information Agency in 1982 to Israel, Finland, and Germany, Purdy recalls in his *CAAS* article the welcome he received: "My reception in these countries was enthusiastic beyond my expectations, and it was brought home to me again that my stories reach some deep note in readers who are receptive and open."

BIOGRAPHICAL/CRITICAL SOURCES:

BOOKS

Adams, Stephen D., *James Purdy,* Barnes & Noble (New York City), 1976.

The American Novel: Two Studies, Kansas State Teachers College of Emporia, Graduate Division, 1965.

Chupack, Henry, *James Purdy,* Twayne (Boston), 1975.

Contemporary Authors Autobiography Series, Volume 1, Gale (Detroit), 1984.

Contemporary Literary Criticism, Gale (Detroit), Volume 2, 1974, Volume 4, 1975, Volume 10, 1979, Volume 28, 1984, Volume 52, 1989.

Dictionary of Literary Biography, Volume 2: *American Novelists since World War II,* Gale, 1978.

French, Warren, editor, *The Fifties: Fiction, Poetry, Drama,* Everett/Edwards (DeLand, FL), 1971.

French, Warren, *Season of Promise,* University of Missouri Press (Columbia), 1968.

Hyman, Stanley Edgar, *Standards: A Chronicle of Books for Our Time,* Horizon Press (Dedham, MA), 1966.

Kennard, Jean E., *Number and Nightmare: Forms of Fantasy in Contemporary Fiction,* Archon Books (Hamden, CT), 1975.

Kostelanetz, Richard, editor, *On Contemporary Literature,* Avon (New York City), 1964.

Kumar, Anil, *Alienation in the Fiction of Carson McCullers, J.D. Salinger, and James Purdy,* Guru Nanak Dev University (Amritsar, India), 1991.

Langford, Richard E., editor, *Essays in Modern American Literature,* Stetson University Press, 1963.

Laughlin, James, editor, *New Directions in Prose and Poetry 26,* New Directions, 1973.

Lehmann, John, and Derek Parker, editors, *Edith Sitwell, Selected Letters,* Macmillan (London), 1970.

Malin, Irving, *New American Gothic,* Southern Illinois University Press (Carbondale), 1962.

Moore, Harry T., editor, *Contemporary American Novelists,* Southern Illinois University Press, 1964.

Purdy, James, *Malcolm,* Farrar, Straus (New York City), 1959.

Purdy, James, *63: Dream Palace,* William-Frederick, 1956.

Schwarzschild, Bettina, *The Not-Right House: Essays on James Purdy,* University of Missouri Press, 1969.

Solotaroff, Theodore, *The Red Hot Vacuum and Other Pieces on the Writing of the Sixties,* Atheneum (New York City), 1970.

Tanner, Tony, *City of Words: American Fiction, 1950-1970,* Harper (New York City), 1971.

Waldmeir, Joseph S., editor, *Recent American Fiction: Some Critical Views,* Michigan State University (East Lansing), 1963.

Weales, Gerald, *The Jumping-off Place: American Drama in the 1960's,* Macmillan (New York City), 1969.

PERIODICALS

America, February 27, 1971.
American Book Review, May-June, 1982.
American Literature, November, 1974.
Andy Warhol's Interview, December, 1972.
Antioch Review, spring, 1962; spring, 1971.
Best Sellers, June 15, 1967; June, 1978.
Book Week, October 18, 1964; May 9, 1965; May 28, 1967.
Boston Globe, February 11, 1994, p. A22.
Bulletin of Bibliography, January-March, 1971.
Centennial Review, summer, 1974.
Chicago Review, autumn-winter, 1960.
Chicago Sunday Tribune, October 9, 1960.
Chicago Tribune Book World, August 23, 1981; January 5, 1986.
Commonweal, January 17, 1958; October 16, 1959; October 21, 1960; January 4, 1963.
Contemporary Literature, autumn, 1970; summer, 1974.
Critic, August-September, 1967.
Critique: Studies in Modern Fiction, Volume 14, number 3, 1973.
Glasgow Herald, January 18, 1986.
Interview, April 1, 1988, p. 21.
Kansas Quarterly, spring, 1982, pp. 81-92.
Life, June 2, 1967.
Listener, February 20, 1986, p. 28.
London Magazine, February-March, 1973.
London Review of Books, February 21, 1985, pp. 22-23.
Los Angeles Times, December 18, 1977; March 26, 1984.
Nation, January 11, 1958; November 19, 1960; March 23, 1964; October 9, 1967; June 9, 1969; May 15, 1972.
National Review, February 26, 1963;, September 1, 1972; March 4, 1988, pp. 50-52.
New Republic, November 9, 1959; October 3, 1960; November 17, 1962; October 26, 1974; July 18, 1981.
New Statesman, May 7, 1960; January 17, 1986.
Newsweek, October 12, 1970.
New York Arts Journal, April-May, 1978.
New York Herald Tribune Book Review, December 29, 1957; October 11, 1959; November 6, 1960; November 18, 1962.

New York Review of Books, November 5, 1964.

New York Times, December 29, 1957; January 9, 1966.

New York Times Book Review, October 6, 1957; September 27, 1959; October 9, 1960; May 21, 1967; June 2, 1968; November 15, 1970; February 8, 1976; April 23, 1978; July 26, 1981; February 26, 1984, p. 25; September 6, 1987, p. 23; October 19, 1986, p. 15; October 29, 1989, p. 13; January 16, 1994, p. 24.

Observer (London), May 21, 1989, p. 53.

Partisan Review, fall, 1972.

Penthouse, July, 1974.

Publishers Weekly, June 19, 1981.

Queen's Quarterly, summer, 1962.

Renascence, winter, 1963.

Review of Contemporary Fiction, spring, 1990, p. 327; summer, 1994, pp. 208-209.

San Francisco Chronicle, October 18, 1959.

Saturday Review, January 25, 1958; September 26, 1959; November 26, 1960; November 17, 1962; August 5, 1967; June, 1981.

Southern Review, summer, 1974.

Spectator, April 29, 1960; May 19, 1984; March 1, 1986.

Time, December 9, 1957; October 17, 1960.

Times (London), May 10, 1984.

Times Literary Supplement, May 6, 1960; June 10, 1965; March 28, 1968; June 4, 1971; August 31, 1984, p. 977; March 8, 1985; June 26, 1992, p. 21.

Tri-Quarterly, fall, 1967.

Twentieth Century Literature, April, 1969; fall, 1982.

University of Dayton Review, summer, 1974.

Village Voice, July 22, 1981.

Virginia Quarterly Review, spring, 1963; autumn, 1967; autumn, 1972.

Voice Literary Supplement, September, 1986, pp. 18-19.

Washington Post, August 1, 1981; March 2, 1985; January 12, 1992, pp. 3, 14.

Wilson Library Bulletin, March, 1964.

Wisconsin Studies in Contemporary Literature, summer, 1965.

Yale Review, spring, 1968.

R

RABASSA, Gregory 1922-

PERSONAL: Born March 9, 1922, in Yonkers, NY; son of Miguel and Clara (Macfarland) Rabassa; married Roney Edelstein, July 14, 1956 (marriage ended, 1966); married Clementine C. Christos (a teacher and critic), May 29, 1966; children: Catherine, Clara. *Education:* Dartmouth College, A.B., 1945; Columbia University, M.A., 1947, Ph.D., 1954. *Politics:* Democrat. *Religion:* None.

ADDRESSES: Home—140 East 72nd St., New York, NY 10021. *Office*—Department of Romance Languages, Queens College of the City University of New York, 65-30 Kissena Blvd., Flushing, NY 11367.

CAREER: Columbia University, New York City, assistant professor, 1948-64, associate professor of Spanish and Portuguese, 1964-68; City University of New York, Queens College, Flushing, NY, and Graduate School and University Center, New York City, professor, 1968-85, distinguished professor of Romance languages and comparative literature, 1985—. Democratic committee, New York County, 1956-60. *Military service:* U.S. Army, Office of Strategic Services, 1942-45; became staff sergeant; received Croce al Merito di Guerra (Italy), and special citation from Allied Forces Headquarters, both 1945.

MEMBER: American Association of Teachers of Spanish and Portuguese, American Association of University Professors, American Literature Translators Association, Congreso Internacional de Literatura Iberoamerica, Hispanic Society of America, Latin American Studies Association, Modern Language Association of America, PEN American Center (member of executive board, 1972-77), Renaissance Society of America, Phi Beta Kappa.

AWARDS, HONORS: Fulbright-Hays fellow, Brazil, 1965-66; National Book Award for translation, 1967, for *Hopscotch;* National Book Award nomination for translation, 1971, for *One Hundred Years of Solitude,* and 1977, for *The Autumn of the Patriarch;* American PEN translation prize, 1977, for *The Autumn of the Patriarch;* National Endowment for the Humanities grant, 1980; Alexander Gode Medal, American Translators Association, 1980; Gulbenkian Award, 1981, for translation of *Avalovara;* PEN Medal for Translation, 1982; Litt.D., Dartmouth College, 1982; Professional Staff Congress/City University of New York grant, 1983; New York Governor's Arts Award, 1985; Order of San Carlos, Republic of Colombia, 1985; Guggenheim fellow, 1988-89; Wheatland Prize for Translation, 1988; Presidential Medal for Excellence, Dartmouth College, 1991; Ivan Sandrof Award, National Book Critics Circle, 1993; Literary Lion, New York Public Library, 1993; Mellon Humanities Award, Loyola University, 1995.

WRITINGS:

O Negro na ficcao brasileira (title means "The Negro in Brazilian Fiction"), Tempo Brasileiro, 1965.
(Author of introduction) *The World of Translation,* PEN American Center (New York City), 1987.
A Cloudy Day in Gray Minor (poetry), Cross-Cultural Communications (Merrick, NY), 1992.

TRANSLATOR

Julio Cortazar, *Hopscotch,* Pantheon (New York City), 1966.

Clarice Lispector, *The Apple in the Dark,* Knopf (New York City), 1967.

Miguel Asturias, *Mulata,* Delacorte (New York City), 1967, published in England as *The Mulatta and Mr. Fly,* P. Owen (London), 1967.

Mario Vargas Llosa, *The Green House,* Harper (New York City), 1969.

Juan Goytisolo, *Marks of Identity,* Grove (New York City), 1969.

Afranio Coutinho, *An Introduction to Literature in Brazil,* Columbia University Press (New York City), 1969.

Asturias, *Strong Wind,* Delacorte, 1969.

Manuel Mujica-Lainez, *Bomarzo,* Simon & Schuster (New York City), 1969.

Gabriel Garcia Marquez, *One Hundred Years of Solitude,* Harper, 1970.

Asturias, *The Green Pope,* Delacorte, 1971.

Garcia Marquez, *Leaf Storm and Other Stories,* Harper, 1972.

Cortazar, *Sixty-Two: A Model Kit,* Pantheon, 1973.

Dalton Trevisan, *The Vampire of Curitiba,* Knopf, 1973.

Asturias, *The Eyes of the Interred,* Delacorte, 1973.

Jose Lezama Lima, *Paradiso,* Farrar (New York City), 1974.

Vargas Llosa, *Conversation in the Cathedral,* Harper (New York City), 1975.

Garcia Marquez, *The Autumn of the Patriarch,* Harper, 1976.

Garcia Marquez, *Innocent Erendira and Other Stories,* Harper, 1978.

Cortazar, *A Manual for Manuel,* Pantheon, 1978.

Demetrio Aguilera-Malta, *Seven Serpents and Seven Moons,* University of Texas Press, 1979.

Garcia Marquez, *In Evil Hour,* Harper, 1979.

Osman Lins, *Avalovara,* Knopf, 1980.

Cortazar, *A Change of Light and Other Stories,* Knopf, 1980.

Luis Rafael Sanchez, *Macho Camacho's Beat,* Pantheon, 1981.

Vinicius de Moraes, *The Girl from Ipanema,* Cross-Cultural Communications, 1982.

Juan Benet, *A Meditation,* Persea Books (New York City), 1983.

Cortazar, *We Love Glenda So Much and Other Tales,* Knopf, 1983.

Garcia Marquez, *Chronicle of a Death Foretold,* Knopf, 1983.

Luisa Valenzuela, *The Lizard's Tail,* Farrar, 1983.

Jorge Amado, *Sea of Death,* Avon (New York City), 1984.

Cortazar, *A Certain Lucas,* Knopf, 1984.

(With B. J. Bernstein) Garcia Marquez, *Collected Stories,* Harper, 1984.

Benet, *Return to Region,* Columbia University Press, 1985.

Oswaldo Franca Jr., *The Man in the Monkey Suit,* Ballantine (New York City), 1986.

Amado, *Captains of the Sands,* Avon, 1988.

Amado, *Showdown,* Bantam (New York City), 1988.

Antonio Lobo Antunes, *Fado Alexandrino,* Grove/Weidenfield, 1990.

Jose Donoso, *Taratuta and Still Life with Pipe,* Norton (New York City), 1993.

Jorge Amado, *The War of the Saints,* Bantam, 1993.

OTHER

Contributor of translations, articles, and reviews to numerous periodicals and professional journals, including *Atlantic, Esquire, Nation, New Yorker, New York Times Book Review, Playboy,* and *Saturday Review.* Associate editor, *Odyssey Review,* 1961-63. Latin American editor, *Kenyon Review,* 1978—.

WORK IN PROGRESS: Translations, including *My World Is Not of this Kingdom* by Joao de Melo; *The Sirens, Too, Sang that Way,* by Irene Vilar, for Pantheon; *Fazendas,* by Fernando Tasso Fragoso Pires, for Abbeville Press; and *The Posthumous Memoirs of Bras Cubas* and *Quincas Borba,* both by J. M. Machado de Assis, for Oxford University Press.

SIDELIGHTS: Translator of over forty works, Gregory Rabassa is "a one-man conveyor belt" bringing Latin American fiction to the English speaking world, according to Patrick Breslin in the *Washington Post Book World.* A professor of Romance languages with the City University of New York, Rabassa never intended to become a professional translator. In the early 1960s, however, Rabassa began translating short fiction as part of his work with *Odyssey Review,* a literary quarterly. Shortly after the magazine folded, Rabassa was contacted about writing an English version of Julio Cortazar's *Hopscotch.* "An editor called me up and we had lunch," Rabassa recalled to Edwin McDowell in *Americas.* "I looked through the novel, liked it and gave her a couple of sample chapters. . . . She chose me, and I went to work on it immediately in my spare time. It took about a year working in spurts, and I've been translating ever since."

Cortazar so approved of Rabassa's manuscript that he recommended his work to Gabriel Garcia Marquez, a Colombian writer. Rabassa's rendition of *One Hundred Years of Solitude,* published in 1970, gained widespread attention in the U.S. for both Garcia Marquez's work and that of other Latin American writers. The work also gained attention for Rabassa when Garcia Marquez, the 1982 Nobel laureate, remarked that he preferred the translation to his own work; "Rabassa's *One Hundred Years of Solitude* improved the original," the author remarked to *Time* contributor R. Z. Sheppard. Rabassa comments, however, that the work lent itself to translation because of its quality: "A very good book in its own language goes over more easily into another language than a book that's not so good," he told Jason Weiss in the *Los Angeles Times.* "Part of the quality of the well-written book is that it's easy to translate."

Rabassa takes a reader's approach to his writing, almost always choosing to work with manuscripts that interest him. His translating methods also reflect this interest; in working with *Hopscotch,* "I read it as I translated it," Rabassa remarked to McDowell. "I do that with many books because it's more fun that way, and because translation should be the closest possible reading of the book." Although he commented to Weiss that translation is "lazy man's writing," he sees it as creative work in its own right. "One of the great advantages of translation," he told McDowell, "is that your plots and characters are already written, all you have to do is breathe life into them."

BIOGRAPHICAL/CRITICAL SOURCES:

PERIODICALS

Americas, July-August, 1986.
Los Angeles Times, August 12, 1982.
Time, March 7, 1983.
Washington Post Book World, December 19, 1984.

*　　　*　　　*

RAINE, Craig 1944-

PERSONAL: Born December 3, 1944, in Bishop Auckland, England; son of Norman Edward and Olive Marie Raine; married Ann Pasternak Slater (a professor), August 12, 1974; children: Nina, Isaac,

Moses, Vaska. *Education:* Exeter College, Oxford, honors degree in English language and literature, c. 1965, B.Phil, c. 1968, doctoral study, 1969-71 and 1972-73.

ADDRESSES: Home—Oxford, England. *Office*—New College, Oxford University, Oxford OX1 3BN, England.

CAREER: Oxford University, Oxford, England, lecturer at Exeter College, 1971-72, lecturer at Lincoln College, 1974-75, lecturer at Christ Church, 1976-79; Faber & Faber, London, England, poetry editor, 1981-91; Oxford University, fellow at New College, 1991—. Broadcaster for British Broadcasting Corporation (BBC).

AWARDS, HONORS: First prize, Cheltenham Festival Poetry Competition, 1977, for poem "Flying to Belfast, 1977," and 1978, for poem "Mother Dressmaking"; second prize, National Poetry Competition, 1978, for poem "In the Mortuary"; *New Statesman*'s Prudence Farmer Award, 1979, for poem "A Martian Sends a Postcard Home," and 1980, for poem "Laying a Lawn"; Cholmondeley Award, Society of Authors (Great Britain), 1983.

WRITINGS:

POETRY

The Onion, Memory, Oxford University Press (Oxford, England), 1978.
A Journey to Greece, Sycamore Broadsheets, 1979.
A Martian Sends a Postcard Home, Oxford University Press, 1979.
A Free Translation, Salamander Press (London), 1981.
Rich, Faber (London), 1984.
1953: A Version of Racine's Andromaque, [Boston and London], 1990.
History: The Home Movie, Doubleday (New York City), 1994.

OTHER

The Electrification of the Soviet Union (libretto; based on Boris Pasternak's novella *The Last Summer*), Faber, 1986.
(Editor) *A Choice of Kipling's Prose,* Faber, 1987.
Haydn and the Valve Trumpet (essays), Faber, 1990.

Also author of libretto *Sand Storm* for *Sarajevo* trilogy by Nigel Osborne, 1994. Contributor to *Poetry*

Introduction 4, Faber, 1978, and *The Penguin Book of Contemporary British Poetry,* edited by Blake Morrison and Andrew Motion, Penguin Books (London), 1982. Books editor, *New Review,* 1977-78; editor, *Quarto,* 1979-80; poetry editor, *New Statesman,* 1981.

SIDELIGHTS: "Only occasionally does a poet appear whose voice is instantly and uniquely recognisable, and [Craig] Raine is such a poet," Derek Mahon declared in *New Statesman.* Raine is known for his emphasis on unusual images and metaphors seen from an alien viewpoint and is considered the founder of what critic and poet James Fenton dubbed the Martian School of poets, a group including Christopher Reid and several other of Raine's contemporaries.

The Onion, Memory established Raine's technique of focusing, often humorously, on the external world of objects and phenomena. This approach has been criticized by some reviewers as lacking the human element; according to Mahon, it "wouldn't matter if he didn't sometimes seem a little heartless." Derek Stanford in *Books and Bookmen* compared *The Onion, Memory* to "a bee-hive, a wasps' nest," noting that all "have the power to irritate and sting the literal-minded reader or one with a conservative imagination." Stanford praised Raine's attention to nuances and remarked, "Only an exceptionally agile dealer in language could carry it through with such self-assurance."

A Martian Sends a Postcard Home, perhaps Raine's best-known work, is written from the point of view of an alien visitor who describes Earth to his fellow inhabitants of Mars. *New Statesman* reviewer Andrew Motion was pleased to find "Raine's energy and generosity undiminished." Motion also noticed a change in the poet's willingness to display his emotions. "Once, extraordinarily, [Raine] was accused of heartlessness," Motion noted. "In fact, poem after poem registers a deep affection for what he sees. His way of looking is also a way of baring his heart." Peter Porter in the London *Observer* deemed *A Martian* better than *The Onion, Memory* "because it is a concentration of his talent, and an intensification of his mannerisms. He hasn't set out on new paths after his initial success, but decided to tune a shining engine to perfection."

Raine's collection *Rich* includes the poems published in the pamphlet *A Free Translation* and marks a continuation of a more narrative style in his poetry,

the roots of which are found in *A Martian Sends a Postcard Home.* "The most striking feature of *Rich* is its confirmation of the personal and autobiographical vein in the poet," *Dictionary of Literary Biography* contributor Michael Hulse wrote. "'Inca' and 'A Walk in the Country' join the earlier 'Laying a Lawn' as celebrations of the childhood frailty of his daughter; 'A Hungry Fighter' and 'Plain Song' depict his father as boxer and faith healer, while his mother appears in 'Plain Song' and 'The Season in Scarborough 1923,' and a number of poems persuasively treat of love and sex. Though at times these poems can be too sentimental, or have that inconsequentiality which is the mark of the private in a public place, Raine nevertheless achieves both humanity and precision." *Listener* reviewer Dick Davis described the poet's work at this stage as "a welcome advance on his former work." In discussing the poems of *A Free Translation, Encounter's* Laurence Lerner described Raine as "the most exciting new poet of the decade." Lerner objected, however, to Raine's practice of revealing less than the entire story. "I can see it would be against the spirit of his poems to offer any but the necessary minimum of explanation," Lerner allowed, but he admitted that "sometimes, for my taste, he drops below the minimum." *Hudson Review* contributor Dana Gioia saw *A Free Translation* as a milestone for the poet: "While this small pamphlet may not mark a new stage in his career, it does reflect a difficult maturation. These six new poems . . . are quieter and more somber than his early work. The sharp metaphors are still there but less densely, and they no longer serve as the driving forces of the poem. Most importantly, however, Raine now shows more personal involvement in his material, more humanity in his approach."

History: The Home Movie, described on its dust jacket as an "epic poem," chronicles nearly a century of history—roughly the period of 1905 to 1984—between the Raine and Pasternak families. Comprising dozens of individual parts written in three-line stanzas, the book, which took ten years to complete, "is, on the face of it, the tale of two families, the Pasternaks and the Raines, now brought together by the marriage of Raine and Ann Pasternak-Slater (known as Li), who is Boris Pasternak's great-niece," remarked Sean French in the London *Observer.* Thomas M. Disch commented in the *Washington Post Book World* that Raine "has retooled his copyrighted technique of translating the garage-sale junk of daily life into riddling metaphors and adapted it successfully for epic use. The result is a novel in verse that is both an unputdownable page-turner and a poem distinctively and deliciously Rainean." Several reviewers commented on the work in terms of its subtitle. Writing in *New Statesman and Society,* Carol Rumens declared that Raine's "hand-held camera is an enabling device, like his earlier 'Martian' persona. It permits revelation through apparent incompetence. It is drawn to the erotic and the bizarre. It catches the players off-guard, peers from an odd angle, unembarrassably stares." Disch further claimed: "*History* is, however, an art movie, and suitable only for mature audiences. Younger readers who lack an internalized time chart of 20th-century history may have a hard time assembling the 'plot' in their heads, since Raine doesn't do much backgrounding."

Raine published a collection of critical essays in 1990 entitled *Haydn and the Valve Trumpet.* Sean French observed in a review for the *New Statesman and Society,* "For Raine, a poem or a novel is like a machine. The job of the critic is to get dirty peering among the pistons and cogs establishing how everything fits together." French concluded, "Raine can be infuriating in his rudenesses and his summary dismissals, but he always has the engagement of the practitioner, of the man for whom poetry is an activity and a craft as well as an elevated art form."

BIOGRAPHICAL/CRITICAL SOURCES:

BOOKS

Contemporary Literary Criticism, Volume 32, Gale (Detroit), 1985.
Dictionary of Literary Biography, Volume 40: *Poets of Great Britain and Ireland since 1960,* Gale, 1985, pp. 454-59.
Haffenden, John, *Poets in Conversation,* Faber, 1981.

PERIODICALS

Books and Bookmen, October, 1978, pp. 22-23.
Christian Science Monitor, May 13, 1987.
Critical Quarterly, winter, 1981, pp. 13-21.
Encounter, November, 1978; January, 1982, pp. 56-58.
Hudson Review, spring, 1984, pp. 6-20.
Listener, January 7, 1982, pp. 22-23.
London Review of Books, November 20, 1986, p. 11; June 14, 1990, p. 16; July 12, 1990, p. 11; September 22, 1994, p. 3.

New Statesman, June 23, 1978, p. 852; October 20, 1978; December 14, 1979, pp. 947-48.
New Statesman and Society, June 8, 1990, p. 38; September 9, 1994, p. 37.
New Yorker, December 4, 1989; June 27, 1994, p. 140; July 11, 1994; July 18, 1994, p. 42; August 1, 1994.
New York Times Book Review, December 11, 1994.
Observer (London), January 6, 1980, p. 36; March 18, 1990, p. 63; August 28, 1994, p. 17; September 11, 1994, p. 70.
Poetry Review, January, 1979.
Spectator, December 5, 1984, p. 37; July 21, 1990, p. 33; September 10, 1994, p. 32.
Washington Post Book World, September 7, 1980, p. 5; November 13, 1994, p. 5.
Yale Review, spring, 1988.*

*　　*　　*

RALEIGH, Donald J(oseph)   1949-

PERSONAL: Born November 17, 1949, in Chicago, IL; son of William L. and Lorraine (Plaziak) Raleigh; married Karen Sanders (a banker), December 31, 1971; children: Adam Sanders. *Education:* Knox College, B.A., 1971; Indiana University—Bloomington, M.A., 1972, Ph.D., 1978.

ADDRESSES: Home—1608 Claymore Rd., Chapel Hill, NC 27516. *Office*—Department of History, University of North Carolina at Chapel Hill, Chapel Hill, NC 27599.

CAREER: American Historical Review, Bloomington, IN, editorial assistant, 1976-77; Council for the International Exchange of Scholars, Washington, DC, Fulbright program officer, 1977-78; University of Hawaii at Manoa, Honolulu, assistant professor, 1979-85, associate professor of history, 1985-88; University of North Carolina, Chapel Hill, professor of history, 1988—.

MEMBER: American Historical Association, American Association for the Advancement of Slavic Studies, Western Slavic Association, Study Group on the Russian Revolution.

AWARDS, HONORS: Research grant, University of Hawaii, 1980; translation fellowship, National Endowment for the Humanities, 1983-84, to translate E. N. Burdzhalov's *Second Russian Revolution: The*

February 1917 Uprising in Petrograd; Excellence-in-Teaching Award, University of Hawaii, 1984; Fulbright-Hays Fellowship and IREX Fellowship, Moscow State University, 1986; Title VIII Fellowship, Hoover Institute, 1987; IREX Fellowship, ACLS/Soviet Academy of Sciences, June-July, 1988, May-June, 1990; American Council of Learned Societies Fellowship, 1991; National Humanities Center Fellowship, 1991-92; National Endowment for the Humanities Fellowship, 1992; IREX Short-Term Research Award 1992; ACLS Travel-to-Conference Award, 1994; Honorary Doctorate, Saratov University, Russia, 1994.

WRITINGS:

Revolution on the Volga: 1917 in Saratov, Cornell University Press (Ithaca, NY), 1986, revised and translated into Russian *Politicheskie sud'by rossiiskoi gubernii: 1917 v Saratove,* Slovo (Saratov, Russia), 1995.

Saratov i guberniia v 1917: Sobytiia, partii, liudi (title means "Saratov and Saratov Province in 1917: Events, Parties, People"), Kolledzh (Saratov, Russia), 1994.

Saratov ot avgusta 1914-ogo goda do avgusta 1991-ogo goda: Rossiia glazami amerkantsa (title means "Saratov from August 1914 to August 1991: Russia as Seen by an American") (collection of articles in translation), Izdatel'skii tsentr Saratovskogo ekonomicheskogo instituta (Saratov, Russia), 1994.

EDITOR

(Translator) E. N. Burdzhalov, *Russia's Second Revolution: The February 1917 Uprising in Petrograd,* Indiana University Press (Bloomington), 1987.

(Annotator and author of introduction) *A Russian Civil War Diary: Alexis V. Babine in Saratov, 1917-1922,* Duke University Press (Durham, NC), 1988.

Perestroika and Soviet Historians: The First Phase, M. E. Sharpe, (Armonk, NY), 1989.

(With Kathy S. Transchel, author of introduction with Transchel) Oleg V. Khlevniuk, *In Stalin's Shadow: The Career of "Sergo" Ordzhonikidze,* M. E. Sharpe, 1995.

(With A. A. Iskenderov) *The Emperors and Empresses of Russia: Rediscovering the Romanovs,* M. E. Sharpe, 1996.

OTHER

Contributor of many articles to history and Slavic journals, including *Slavic Review* and *The Maryland Historian.* Also contributor to *Russia at the Barricades: Eyewitness Accounts of the August Coup,* edited by Victoria Bonnel and G. Freiden, M. E. Sharpe, 1994. Editor of *Soviet Studies in History,* 1979-94.

SIDELIGHTS: With *Revolution on the Volga: 1917 in Saratov,* asserted reviewer Tsuyoshi Hasegawa in *American Historical Review,* "[Donald J.] Raleigh has written a major work that should be considered one of the classics on the Russian Revolution." Most previous studies of the revolution concentrated on major urban areas, such as Petrograd, but Raleigh chose to consider the provincial Volga River town of Saratov. In 1917 Saratov was a market town, a significant agricultural administrative center, and a site of military stations. Crowded with refugees from war and tormented by the same shortages that crippled the rest of the country, Saratov provided a ripe atmosphere for political revolution. "Raleigh clearly demonstrates," averred Hasegawa, "that the revolutionary process in Saratov was not a mere echo of the events in Petrograd but rather a violent revolutionary process of its own, which . . . followed the logic of local conditions." Praising the author's research, critic John Keep wrote in the *Times Literary Supplement,* "Raleigh's exemplarily thorough study of . . . published material—he was denied access to Soviet archives—does cast fresh light on the Russian Revolution from an unfamiliar angle, and is welcome for that reason." Hasegawa agreed, adding that "Raleigh's work should thus encourage specialists outside the Soviet Union."

BIOGRAPHICAL/CRITICAL SOURCES:

PERIODICALS

American Historical Review, February, 1987.
Times Literary Supplement, September 12, 1986.

*   *   *

RAO, Raja   1909-

PERSONAL: Born November 21, 1909, in Hassan, Mysore, India; son of H. V. (a professor) and Srimathi (Gauramma) Krishnaswamy; married

Camille Mouly, 1931; married Katherine Jones (a playwright), April, 1966; married Susan Vaught, 1986; children: (second marriage) Christopher. *Education:* Attended Aligarh Muslim University, 1926-27; Nizam College, Hyderabad, University of Madras, B.A., 1929; attended University of Montpellier, 1929-30, and the Sorbonne, 1930-33.

ADDRESSES: Home—1806 Pearl, Austin, TX 78701. *Agent*—Rosalie Siegel, 111 Murphy Drive, Pennington, NJ 08534.

CAREER: University of Texas at Austin, professor of philosophy, 1966-80.

AWARDS, HONORS: Sahitya Academy Award, 1964, for *The Serpent and the Rope;* Padma Bhushan, Government of India, 1970; Neustadt International Prize for Literature, 1988.

WRITINGS:

NOVELS

Kanthapura, Allen & Unwin (London), 1938, New Directions (New York City), 1963.
The Serpent and the Rope, John Murray, 1960, Pantheon (New York City), 1963.
The Cat and Shakespeare: A Tale of India, Macmillan (New York City), 1965.
Comrade Kirillov, Orient (Livingston, NJ), 1976.
The Chessmaster and His Moves, Vision (New Delhi, India), 1978.

SHORT STORIES

The Cow of the Barricades and Other Stories, Oxford University Press (London), 1947.
The Policeman and the Rose, Oxford University Press, 1978.
On Ganga Ghat, Vision, 1989.

EDITOR

(With Iqbal Singh) *Changing India,* Allen & Unwin, 1939.
(With Singh) *Whither India?,* Padmaja (Baroda, India), 1948.
Jawaharlal Nehru, *Soviet Russia: Some Random Sketches and Impressions,* Chetana (Bombay), 1949.

Also contributor to *Pacific Spectator.* Editor, *Tomorrow* (Bombay), 1943-44.

SIDELIGHTS: A novelist, short story writer, essayist, and philosopher, "Raja Rao is perhaps the most brilliant—and certainly the most interesting—writer of modern India," stated Santha Rama Rau in the *New York Times Book Review.* Rao's writings frequently explore the philosophical significance of Indian religions, traditions, and values—especially as they contrast with those of Western society. He is also considered a writer of the metaphysical in that many of his novels abound with symbolism, and he displays a broad knowledge of history and Indian dialects. Born a Brahmin in South India, Rao was educated in Europe as well as India, and taught philosophy for more than a decade in the United States. While several critics have recognized Rao as the finest English-language writer to come out of India, Harish Raizada remarked in *Indo-English Literature: A Collection of Critical Essays* that "Raja Rao is a man of great literary cultures being equally at home in the knowledge of classical Sanskrit and modern European literature, [yet] is basically Indian. His whole approach to life and literature has been outlined against the broad perspective of the Indian philosophy and tradition."

One of Rao's best-known works is his first novel, *Kanthapura,* written when he was only twenty-one years old and published in England eight years later in 1938. Considered by E. M. Forster to be the best novel in English about India, *Kanthapura* describes a young Brahmin who influences a small Indian village to abandon its old ways of acceptance and conformity in order to become involved in the Mahatma Gandhi's non-violence movement for Indian independence from Great Britain. Narrated by a woman of the village, *Kanthapura,* wrote Geoffrey Godsell in the *Christian Science Monitor,* is "a story fascinatingly told, building up . . . to a crashing climax that well-nigh shatters the little village and its traditional organization of society."

A number of critics praised Rao's depiction—in English—of Indian speech patterns and idioms, and of Indian culture and lore. "Written in an elegant style verging on poetry," according to Rama Rau, *Kanthapura* "has all the content of an ancient Indian classic, combined with a sharp, satirical wit and clear understanding of the present." Lois Harley, writing in *America,* called *Kanthapura* "a book of extraordinary veracity in its details of village life in India."

Rao's highly acclaimed second novel, *The Serpent and the Rope,* is the semi-autobiographical tale of the dissolution of the marriage of a Brahmin student,

Ramaswamy, and his French wife, a history teacher. The title represents the schism in the way that husband and wife, or East and West, perceive the world. Ramaswamy believes in the serpent—or imagination—while his wife, Madeleine, remains a believer in the rope—or reality. Richard R. Guzman, writing in the *Virginia Quarterly Review,* observed: "*The Serpent and the Rope* revolves around the question, will one or will one not give up the world?. . . Raja Rao's great achievement is to be able to pursue such questions with an almost manic philosophical drive without robbing them of the passion, pathos, and even sentimentality which must attend questions that threaten the realm of the self."

"I wonder," wrote Gerald Sykes in the *New York Times Book Review,* "if any writer of our time has done such sensitive justice to the minutiae which are the substance of any marriage." Meanwhile, Robert J. Ray, in his article in *Books Abroad,* contended that the psychological and spiritual change that Rao underwent in the twenty years between writing *Kanthapura* and *The Serpent and the Rope* is one of the most profound transformations in contemporary literature. Ray drew attention to the fact that in his second novel, Rao replaced social criticism with a much wider-ranging examination of the human psyche. And yet Ray believes that the most profound change is Rao's use of "paradoxical language patterns that are stunning, subtle, profound, and beautiful." "And this," wrote Ray, "is the change that made *The Serpent and the Rope* Raja Rao's best novel and one of the deepest and most serious literary efforts of the twentieth century."

Rao's *The Chessmaster and His Moves,* the first novel in a projected trilogy, is preoccupied with the question of absolute truth. The protagonist and narrator, Sivarama Sastri, is a mathematician who argues about philosophical ideas, opinions, and love with a large cast of characters. In *World Literature Today,* Edwin Thumboo described the characters in *The Chessmaster and His Moves* as cross-cultural, drawing their identities from India, France, England, Israel, Greece, Senegal, and the Maghreb. "*The Chessmaster,*" Thumboo wrote, "offers perhaps the broadest, deepest internationalism we have in fiction and, in a sense, enables fiction to catch up with life."

Thumboo summed up Rao's literary accomplishments in the ceremony honoring Rao for having been awarded the prestigious Neustadt International Prize for Literature in 1988. Said Thumboo: "Rao's great-est achievement, which I suspect only he can surpass, is the degree to which his works, especially *The Chessmaster,* contain . . . meaning and instruction that enable the individual to achieve, through his own meditations, a better understanding of self through Knowledge and Truth."

BIOGRAPHICAL/CRITICAL SOURCES:

BOOKS

Bhattacharya, P. C., *Indo-Anglian Literature and the Works of Raja Rao,* Atma Ram, 1983.
Contemporary Literary Criticism, Gale (Detroit), Volume 25, 1983, Volume 56, 1989.
Larson, Carles R., *The Novel in the Third World,* Inscape (Washington, DC), 1976.
Naik, M. K., *Raja Rao,* Twayne (New Haven, CT), 1972.
Narasimhaiah, C. D., *Raja Rao: A Critical Study of His Work,* Heinemann (New York City), 1973.
Narayan, Shyamala A., *Rao: The Man and His Works,* Sterling, 1989.
Rao, K. R., *The Fiction of Raja Rao,* Parimal (Aurangabad, India), 1980.
Sharma, K. K., editor, *Indo-English Literature: A Collection of Critical Essays,* Vimal Prakashan, 1977.
Sharma, editor, *Perspectives in Raja Rao,* Vimal (Ghaziabad, India), 1980.
Sharrad, Paul, *Raja Rao and Critical Tradition,* Sterling, 1988.

PERIODICALS

America, February 29, 1964.
Books Abroad, autumn, 1966.
Christian Science Monitor, January 16, 1964.
Commonweal, January 25, 1963; May 15, 1964.
International Fiction Review, summer, 1980.
Los Angeles Times Book Review, August 24, 1986.
Nation, March 16, 1963.
New York Times, January 20, 1965.
New York Times Book Review, April 14, 1963; January 5, 1964; January 17, 1965.
Saturday Review, January 16, 1965.
Time, February 22, 1963.
Virginia Quarterly Review, winter, 1980.
World Literature Today, autumn, 1988.
World Literature Written in English, November, 1973; November, 1975.

—Sketch by Elizabeth Judd

RAWLYK, George Alexander 1935-

PERSONAL: Born May 19, 1935, in Thorold, Ontario, Canada; son of Samuel and Mary (Kautesk) Rawlyk; married August 18, 1959; children: two. *Education:* McMaster University, B.A., 1957; University of Rochester, M.A., 1962, Ph.D., 1966.

ADDRESSES: Office—Department of History, Queen's University, Kingston, Ontario, Canada K7L 3N6.

CAREER: Mount Allison University, Sackville, New Brunswick, Canada, lecturer in history, 1959-61; Dalhousie University, Halifax, Nova Scotia, Canada, assistant professor of history, 1963-66; Queen's University, Kingston, Ontario, Canada, associate professor, 1966-69, professor of history, 1969—. W. P. Bell Professor, Mount Allison University, 1987-88. Scholar in residence, Harvard University, 1982-83 and 1985-86. Researcher for Royal Commission on Bilingualism and Biculturalism, 1965-67.

MEMBER: American Historical Association, Canadian Historical Association, Canadian Political Science Association, Organization of Canadian Historians, Champlain Society.

AWARDS, HONORS: Canada Council fellowship, 1967, senior fellowships, 1971-72, 1981-82; honorary D.C.L., Acadia University, 1995.

WRITINGS:

Yankees at Louisbourg, University of Maine Press (Orono, ME), 1967.
Revolution Rejected, 1775-1776, Prentice-Hall (Englewood Cliffs, NJ), 1968.
(With Ruth Hafter) *Acadian Education in Nova Scotia: An Historical Survey to 1965,* Information Canada, 1970.
(With Gordon Stewart) *A People Highly Favored of God,* Archon Books, 1972.
Nova Scotia's Massachusetts: A Study of Massachusetts-Nova Scotia Relations, 1630-1784, McGill-Queen's University Press (Montreal, Canada), 1973.
(With Bruce W. Hodgins and Richard P. Bowles) *Regionalism in Canada: Flexible Federalism or Fractured Nation?,* Prentice-Hall, 1979.
Streets of Gold, Peter Martin Associates, 1981.
(With Kevin Quinn) *The Redeemed of the Lord Say So,* QTC (Kingston, Ontario, Canada), 1981.

(With M. A. Downie) *Acadian pour de bon* (title means "A Proper Acadian"), Kids Can Press, 1982.
The New Light Letters and Spiritual Songs, Hantsport, 1983.
Ravished By the Spirit, McGill-Queen's University Press, 1984.
Henry Alline, Paulist Press (Ramsey, NJ), 1987.
Wrapped Up in God: A Study of Several Canadian Revivals and Revivalists, McGill-Queen's University Press, 1988.
Champions of the Truth: Fundamentalism, Modernism and the Maritime Baptists, McGill-Queen's University Press, 1990.
The Canada Fire: Radical Evangelism in British North America, 1775-1812, McGill-Queen's University Press, 1994.
Is Jesus Your Personal Saviour?: In Search of Canadian Evangelism in the 1990s, McGill-Queen's, 1996.

EDITOR

(And author of introduction) *Historical Essays on the Atlantic Provinces,* McClelland & Stewart (Toronto), 1967.
Joseph Howe: Opportunist? Man of Vision? Frustrated Politician?, Copp Clark, 1967.
The Atlantic Provinces and the Problems of Confederation, Breakwater Press, 1979.
Canadian Baptists and Christian Higher Education, McGill-Queen's University Press, 1988.

OTHER

Contributor to books, including *Colonists and Canadians,* Macmillan (New York City), 1971, and *Essays on the Left,* McClelland & Stewart, 1971. Also contributor to magazines, including *Queen's Quarterly.*

*   *   *

RAY, N(ancy) L(ouise)   1918-
(Nan Hunt)

PERSONAL: Born September 16, 1918, in Bathurst, New South Wales, Australia; daughter of Edwin (an orchardist) and Katie (a stenographer; maiden name, Hazlewood) Ray; married Walter Gibbs Hunt (a grazier), November 18, 1967 (died December 8, 1975); children: three (stepchildren). *Education:* Educated in Australia. *Religion:* Christian.

ADDRESSES: Home and office—219 Peel St., Bathurst, New South Wales 2795, Australia. *Agent*—Barbara Mobbs, P.O. Box 126, Edgecliff, New South Wales 2027, Australia.

CAREER: Western Stores & Edgleys Ltd., Bathurst, New South Wales, Australia, stenographer, 1935-43; Aeronautical Supply Co. Pty. Ltd., Mascot, Australia, secretary, 1947-48; Briginshow Brothers Pty Ltd., Milsons Point, Australia, secretary, 1948-50; Bowes & Craig (chartered accountants), Sydney, Australia, secretary, 1950-67; writer. *Military service:* Women's Australian Auxiliary Air Force, 1943-46; became sergeant.

MEMBER: Australian Society of Authors, Children's Book Council of Australia.

AWARDS, HONORS: Premier's Literary Award for best children's book from the state of New South Wales, 1982, for *Whistle up the Chimney,* and 1987, for *A Rabbit Named Harris.*

WRITINGS:

JUVENILE NOVELS; UNDER PSEUDONYM NAN HUNT

Roma Mercedes and Fred, Collins (Sydney, Australia), 1978.
The Everywhere Dog, Collins, 1978.
The Pow Toe, Collins, 1979.
There Was This Man Running, Collins, 1979, Macmillan (New York City), 1981.
Nightmare to Nowhere, Collins, 1980.
Never Tomorrow, Collins, 1989.
Track Down, Random House (New York City), 1994.
You Can't See Me, I'm Invisible, Angus & Robertson (North Ryde, New South Wales), 1994.
A Patch of Sunlight, Omnibus, 1995.
Like a Pebble in Your Shoe, Angus & Robertson, 1996.

JUVENILE PICTURE BOOKS; UNDER PSEUDONYM NAN HUNT

Whistle up the Chimney, illustrations by Craig Smith, Collins, 1981.
An Eye Full of Soot and an Ear Full of Steam, illustrations by Smith, Collins, 1983.
Wild and Woolly, illustrations by Noela Hills, Lothian, 1983.
Rain, Hail, or Shine, illustrations by Smith, Collins, 1984.

When Ollie Spat on the Ball, illustrations by Mark David, Collins, 1985.
Prisoner of the Mulligrubs, illustrations by Hills, Collins, 1985.
The Junk Easters, illustrations by Peter Viska, Macmillan, 1987.
A Rabbit Named Harris, illustrations by Bettina Ogden, Collins, 1987.
The Show, illustrations by Ogden, Collins, 1988.
We Got Wheels, Man and Other Things, illustrations by David, Collins, 1988.
Families are Funny, Collins, 1990.
The Whistle Stop Party, illustrations by Smith, Collins, 1990.
The Dove Tree, Random House, 1991.
The Harvest Loaf, Random House, 1992.
Phoenix, Random House, 1994.

OTHER

Contributor to anthologies, including *Beneath the Sun,* edited by Patricia Wrightson, Collins, 1972; *Someone Is Flying Balloons,* compiled by Jill Heylen and Cleia Jellett, Omnibus Press, 1983; *Vile Verse,* compiled by Jane Covernton, Omnibus Press, 1988; *Weird,* compiled by Penny Matthews, Omnibus Press, 1990; *Christmas Crackers,* compiled by Ann Weld, Omnibus Press, 1990; *Can I Keep Him?,* Oxford University Press, 1991; *Hair Raising,* compiled by Matthews, Omnibus Press, 1992; and *Mulligrubs and Friends,* Angus & Robertson, 1992.

SIDELIGHTS: N. L. Ray told *CA:* "I try to give children 'a good read' with dashes of humor. I make no apology for trying to stretch their imaginations, challenge them with the feelings and limitations of adults, or open their eyes to situations of fear and grief, which all come suddenly to many children. I try to be honest.

"Picture-book texts are a difficult discipline. To leave all the adjectives to the artist is the hardest thing I know in writing. Each word must be right."

*   *   *

REDEKOP, Calvin Wall   1925-

PERSONAL: Born September 19, 1925, in Volt, MT; son of Jacob Kasper and Katherine (Wall) Redekop;

married Freda Pellman; children: William Charles, Benjamin Wall, Frederick Jacob. *Education:* Goshen College, B.A., 1949; University of Minnesota, M.A., 1955; University of Chicago, Ph.D., 1959. *Politics:* "Liberal, uncommitted though normally Democratic." *Religion:* Mennonite. *Avocational interests:* Travel, music (piano and flute), biking, tennis, inventions.

ADDRESSES: Office—104 Flint Ave., Harrisonburg, PA 22801-9034.

CAREER: Hesston College, Hesston, KS, professor of sociology, 1954-62; Earlham College, School of Religion, Richmond, IN, associate professor, 1962-67; Goshen College, Goshen, IN, professor of sociology and anthropology, 1967-76; Tabor College, Hillsboro, KS, dean, 1976-79; University of Waterloo, Waterloo, Ontario, professor of sociology, 1979-90. President, Wayne County (Indiana) Anti-Poverty Program, 1962-67; secretary, Richmond Industrial Ministry, 1964-67. Conscientious objector doing civilian peace work, 1950-52.

MEMBER: American Sociological Association, Society for the Scientific Study of Religion, Religious Research Association, Society for the Sociology of Religion.

WRITINGS:

The Old Colony Mennonites: Dilemmas of Ethnic Minority Life, Johns Hopkins University Press (Baltimore, MD), 1969.
The Free Church and Seductive Culture, Herald Press (Scottsdale, PA), 1970.
(With J. R. Burkholder) *Kingdom, Cross, and Community,* Herald Press, 1976.
Reader in Sociology, Herald Press, 1980.
Strangers become Neighbors, Herald Press, 1980.
(With Urie A. Bender) *Who Am I? What Am I? A Christian View of Work,* Zondervan (Grand Rapids, MI), 1988.
(Editor with Samuel Steiner) *Mennonite Identity: Historical and Contemporary Perspectives,* University Press of America (Lanham, MD), 1988.
Mennonite Society, Johns Hopkins University Press, 1989.
Anabaptist/Mennonite Faith and Economics, University Press of America, 1994.
Mennonite Entrepreneurs, Johns Hopkins University Press, 1995.

Also author of several pamphlets published by Mennonites. Contributor to professional and denominational journals.

WORK IN PROGRESS: Research on environment and religion, Mennonites and power; a historical/sociological analysis of the Evangelical Mennonite Brethren Church; research on work, and volunteerism and work.

SIDELIGHTS: Calvin Wall Redekop told *CA:* "Living (aging) brings with it interest in the past. I am now editing some experiences [I had] growing up on the Montana prairies, 'Life on the Prairies.'"

*   *   *

REINHOLD, Meyer   1909-

PERSONAL: Born September 1, 1909, in New York, NY; son of Joseph and Ethel (Rosen) Reinhold; married Diane Roth (an executive medical secretary), September 29, 1939; children: Robert, Helen. *Education:* City College (now City College of the City University of New York), A.B., 1929; Columbia University, A.M., 1930, Ph.D., 1933; American Academy in Rome, F.A.A.R., 1935.

ADDRESSES: Home—63 Sparks St., Cambridge, MA 02138.

CAREER: Brooklyn College (now Brooklyn College of the City University of New York), Brooklyn, NY, 1938-55, began as instructor, became associate professor of classical languages and literature; Richmond Advertising Service, Inc., New York City, vice president, 1955-65; Southern Illinois University at Carbondale, associate professor of Greek, Latin, and ancient history, 1965-67; University of Missouri—Columbia, professor of classical studies, 1967-80, Byler Distinguished Professor of Classical Studies, 1976-80, professor emeritus, 1980—; Boston University, Boston, MA, visiting professor, 1980—, interim chair of department of classical studies, 1985-86, professor emeritus, 1995—, director emeritus, Institute for the Classical Tradition.

MEMBER: International Society for the Classical Tradition (co-president, 1991—), American Association of Ancient Historians, American Philological Association, Vergil Society, Classical Association of New England, Phi Beta Kappa.

WRITINGS:

Marcus Agrippa: A Biography, G. F. Humphrey, 1933, reprinted, L'Erma di Bretschneider (Rome), 1965.
The Classical Drama, Barron's (Woodbury, NY), 1959.
A Simplified Approach to Plato and Aristotle, Barron's, 1964.
Barron's Simplified Approach to Ten Greek Tragedies, Barron's, 1965.
Barron's Simplified Approach to Vergil: Eclogues, Georgics, Aeneid, Barron's, 1966.
Barron's Simplified Approach to "The Iliad": Homer, Barron's, 1967.
Barron's Simplified Approach to "The Odyssey": Homer, Barron's, 1967, revised edition, 1987.
History of Purple as a Status Symbol in Antiquity, Latomus, 1970.
Usurpation of Status and Status Symbols in the Roman Empire, Historia, 1970.
Essentials of Greek and Roman Classics: A Guide to the Humanities, second edition, Barron's, 1971.
Past and Present: The Continuity of Classical Myths, Samuel Stevens (Sarasota, FL), 1972.
The Classics and the Quest for Virtue in Eighteenth-Century America, American Philological Association, 1977.
Classica Americana: The Greek and Roman Heritage in the United States, Wayne State University Press (Detroit, MI), 1984.
From Republic to Principate: An Historical Commentary on Cassius Dio's "Roman History" Books 49-52, American Philological Association, 1988.

EDITOR

(With Naphtali Lewis) *Roman Civilization,* Columbia University Press (New York City), 1951, third edition, Harper (New York City), 1990.
The Classick Pages: Classical Reading of Eighteenth-Century Americans, American Philological Association, 1975, reprinted, Scholars Press (Chico, CA), 1985.
(And translator) *The Golden Age of Augustus,* Samuel Stevens, 1978.
(And translator) *The Jewish Diaspora among Greeks and Romans,* Samuel Stevens, 1981.
(With Louis H. Feldman) *Jewish Life and Thought among the Greeks and Romans: Primary Readings,* Fortress Press (Philadelphia, PA), 1996.

OTHER

Contributor to books, including *Hellas and Rome: The Story of Greco-Roman Civilization,* New American Library (New York City), 1972; *Classical Influences on Western Education, Philosophy and Social Theory, 1650-1870,* Cambridge University Press (New York City), 1978; *The Craft of the Ancient Historian: Essays in Honor of Chester G. Starr,* AMF Press, 1985; and *Thomas Jefferson: A Reference Biography,* edited by Merrill D. Peterson, Scribner (New York City), 1986. Also contributor to American and Italian periodicals, including *Parents' Magazine, Science and Society, Studi italiani di filologia classica,* and *Attidell' VIII Colloquium Tullianum.* Author of "Bibliography of the Classical Tradition," contributed annually to *Classical and Modern Literature,* 1986-92. Co-editor, *International Journal of the Classical Tradition,* 1993—.

WORK IN PROGRESS: Coediting, with Wolfgang Haase, *The Classical Tradition and the Americas,* in six volumes.

*   *   *

**REVELL, J(ohn) R(obert) S(tephen)   1920-
(Jack Revell)**

PERSONAL: Born April 15, 1920, in Tunbridge Wells, Kent, England; son of Clifford Walter (a shopkeeper) and Edith (Wren) Revell; married Patricia M. B. Hiatt, February 23, 1946; children: Barbara, Alison, David John. *Education:* London School of Economics and Political Science, B.Sc., 1950; Cambridge University, M.A., 1960.

ADDRESSES: Home—12 Rustat Road, Cambridge, CB1 3QT England.

CAREER: Cambridge University, Cambridge, England, senior research officer in department of applied economics, 1957-68, fellow and senior tutor of Fitzwilliam College, 1965-68; University College of North Wales, Bangor, professor of economics, 1969-83; University of Wales, professor emeritus, 1985—. Institute of European Finance, Bangor, director, 1973-85, consultant director, 1985—. *Military service:* British Army, 1940-46; became staff sergeant.

MEMBER: Royal Economic Society, European Association of University Teachers in Banking and Finance.

WRITINGS:

(With John Moyle) *The Owners of Quoted Ordinary Shares: A Survey for 1963,* Chapman & Hall (London), 1966.

The Wealth of the Nation: The National Balance Sheet of the United Kingdom, 1957-1961, Cambridge University Press (Cambridge, England), 1967.

Changes in British Banking: The Growth of a Secondary Banking System, Hill, Samuel & Co., 1968.

The British Financial System, Macmillan (London), 1973.

(With C. R. Tomkins) *Personal Wealth and Finance in Wales,* Welsh Office, 1974.

Flexibility in Housing Finance, Organization for Economic Cooperation and Development, 1975.

Solvency and Regulation of Banks, University of Wales Press (Cardiff, Wales), 1975.

Savings Flows in Europe: Personal Saving and Borrowing, Financial Times, 1976.

(Editor) *Competition and Regulation of Banks,* University of Wales Press, 1978.

Inflation and Financial Institutions, Financial Times, 1979.

Costs and Margins in Banking: An International Survey, Organization for Economic Cooperation and Development, 1980.

A Study of the Spanish Banking System, Banco de Vizcaya, 1980.

Banking and Electronic Fund Transfers, Organization for Economic Cooperation and Development, 1983.

Mergers and the Role of Large Banks, Institute of European Finance, 1987.

The Future of Savings Banks, Institute of European Finance, 1989.

Changes in West European Public Banks, Institute of European Finance, 1991.

Also author of *Changes in Spanish Banking,* 1984. Contributor of more than a hundred articles to economic and banking journals.

WORK IN PROGRESS: Research on the future shape of the British financial system; research on the operation of financial institutions.

REVELL, Jack
See REVELL, J(ohn) R(obert) S(tephen)

*   *   *

REYNOLDS, Ann
See BLY, Carol(yn)

*   *   *

RICHARDSON, Joanna

PERSONAL: Born in London, England; daughter of Frederick and Charlotte (Benjamin) Richardson. *Education:* St. Anne's College, Oxford, B.A. (with honors), M.A. *Politics:* Conservative.

ADDRESSES: Agent—Curtis Brown Group, Haymarket House, 28-29 Haymarket, London SW1Y 4SP, England.

CAREER: Biographer and critic.

MEMBER: Royal Society of Literature (fellow; member of council, 1961-86).

AWARDS, HONORS: Chevalier de l'Ordre des Arts et des Lettres, 1987; Prix Goncourt de la biographie, 1989, for the French edition of *Judith Gautier.*

WRITINGS:

Fanny Brawne: A Biography, Vanguard Press (New York City), 1952.

Rachel, Reinhardt (London), 1956, Putnam (New York City), 1957.

Theophile Gautier: His Life and Times, Reinhardt, 1958, Coward, 1959.

Sarah Bernhardt, Reinhardt, 1959.

Edward Fitzgerald, Longmans, Green, 1960.

The Disastrous Marriage: A Study of George IV and Caroline of Brunswick, J. Cape (London), 1960.

My Dearest Uncle: A Life of Leopold I of the Belgians, J. Cape, 1961.

The Pre-Eminent Victorian: A Study of Tennyson, J. Cape, 1962.

(Editor) *Fitzgerald: Selected Works,* Hart-Davis, 1962.

The Everlasting Spell: A Study of Keats and His Friends, J. Cape, 1963.

(Editor) *Essays by Divers Hands: The Transactions of the Royal Society of Literature,* Oxford University Press (Oxford, England), 1963.

(Author of introduction) Victor Hugo, *Things Seen,* Oxford University Press, 1964.

Edward Lear, Longmans, Green, 1965.

George the Magnificent: A Portrait of King George IV, Harcourt (New York City), 1966.

The Bohemians: La Vie de Boheme in Paris, 1830-1914, Macmillan (London), 1969, A. S. Barnes (San Diego, CA), 1971.

Princess Mathilde, Scribner (New York City), 1969.

Verlaine, Viking (London), 1971.

La Vie Parisienne, 1852-1870, Viking, 1971.

Enid Starkie, Macmillan, 1973.

The Regency, Collins (New York City), 1973.

Stendhal, Gollancz (London), 1974.

Louis XIV, Weidenfeld & Nicholson (London), 1974.

(Translator) *Verlaine: Selected Poems,* Penguin (New York City), 1974.

Baudelaire: Selected Poems, Penguin, 1975.

Victor Hugo, St. Martin's (New York City), 1976.

Sarah Bernhardt and Her World, Putnam, 1977.

Zola, St. Martin's, 1978.

Keats and His Circle: An Album of Portraits, Cassell (London), 1980.

Gustave Dore: A Biography, Cassell, 1980.

The Life and Letters of John Keats, Folio Society (London), 1981.

(Translator) Theophile Gautier, *Mademoiselle de Maupin,* Penguin, 1981.

(Editor) *Letters from Lambeth: The Correspondence of the Reynolds Family with J.F.M. Dovaston,* Royal Society of Literature (London), 1981.

Colette, F. Watts (London), 1983.

Judith Gautier, F. Watts, 1987.

Baudelaire, St. Martin's Press, 1994.

SIDELIGHTS: Biographer Joanna Richardson has received critical attention for her biographies of some of nineteenth-century France's most noted writers. Included among these are her portraits of poets Paul Verlaine and Charles Baudelaire and France's famous women of letters, Colette and Judith Gautier.

When Verlaine died in 1896, he was a highly celebrated poet in Europe. For various reasons, his reputation has since diminished, but his life story remains fascinating material. Many reviewers of Richardson's *Verlaine* consider the work adept at exposing the poet's double nature—on the one hand Verlaine was an irascible, violent sort but on the other he was endearing and compassionate. As a *Times Literary Supplement* critic maintains, "with this double nature [Richardson] deals competently. For the most part she is sympathetic without hiding or condoning the vices, and she rightly sees that [Verlaine's] love for Rimbaud . . . was the one great inspiring passion of his life. She has amassed a vast amount of documentation, and is for the most part accurate and level-headed in her use of it without adding any important discoveries of her own." Anna Balakian, a *Saturday Review* contributor, expresses a similar opinion: "Richardson . . . has written a lively, detailed, and factually precise biography of Paul Verlaine. Her materials are not new, her revelations not earthshaking; but out of the medley of confessions, letters, critical and personal comments by Verlaine's contemporaries, she has fashioned a vivid account of the quick rise and protracted degradation of the saturnalian vagabond, who in his last years was designated 'prince of poets.'" *New York Times Book Review* commentator William Beauchamp believes Richardson has relegated Verlaine's poetry to a minor place in her biography, but argues that "the fascination, the drama, the tumult and paradox, the pathos . . . is where . . . Richardson's book excels. . . . It is probably the best, the most convenient introduction to the poet's life now available in either English or French."

Richardson's 1983 account of Colette entitled simply *Colette* is commended by Anatole Broyard in the *New York Times* for concentrating on this scandalous woman without being scandalous itself. According to Broyard, Richardson "approaches the author of *Cheri* with something like Colette's own cosmopolitanism. She is as tasteful as she is thorough, giving us the facts dispassionately. . . . Because almost every writer in Paris seems to have commented on Colette before she died in 1954 at the age of 81, Miss Richardson's book is a ripe and witty anthology of contemporary French criticism." Richardson's objectivity is also what *New York Review of Books* contributor Gabriele Annan values in *Colette:* "The most unexpected and reassuring thing about . . . Richardson's biography is that she does not appear to love Colette unduly. She slots in concise and lucid accounts of the major works, dismissing some, excusing others, admiring most, and not going overboard for any of them. . . . Richardson can be critical . . . but on the whole she remains uninvolved and simply assembles the facts." Though Broyard and Annan congratulate Richardson for keeping a distance between herself and her subject, complaints about the work also arise for this very reason. In the *Detroit News,* Peter Ross claims "Richardson evinces little feel for Colette, and her prose is frankly arid.

She is not an unqualified admirer." Isa Kapp writes in the *New Republic:* "The very least we expect of a Colette biography are high spirits, but starting with its introduction . . . Richardson's book is mystifyingly schoolmarmish and matter-of-fact. She states that it is the first 'full-scale' biography of Colette in English, but its substance is slight and its ambition meager." Kapp concludes that though Richardson's biography is "reliable enough on chronology," it "is erratic about covering Colette's works." Though Ross finds that *Colette* concentrates too heavily on some of the "less-admirable aspects of Colette's life, the overall impression given is of a woman with a genius for appreciation. Anyone who has read Colette on a sunset, on flowers, food, wine, or the delicate love between pet and owner will find enough in this book to increase their joy."

Richardson's 1987 biography focused on another famous French female writer, Judith Gautier, for which she received the Prix Goncourt de la biographie in 1989 (for the French edition). This was the first time this prestigious honor was awarded to a non-French author. As Shelley Temchin in the *New York Times Book Review* notes, Gautier's father Theophile, himself a well-known writer (and of whom Richardson also wrote in 1958), introduced Judith to "a literary milieu that included Baudelaire and Flaubert as casual visitors"; an illustrious beginning for a poet, critic, dramatist, and novelist. Temchin argues that Richardson's biography of Gautier is "engaging and meticulously documented." Rupert Christiansen in the *Spectator* calls *Gautier* "well-intentioned (and on the whole skillfully executed," but finds that Richardson fails to illuminate this "fascinating and little-understood episode in French literature."

In 1994, Richardson focused her work on the formidable topic of the life of Charles Baudelaire. Richardson's *Baudelaire* is criticized by some reviewers for offering no further insight into the complex man deemed "King of Poets" by Rimbaud. Christiansen argues that Richardson fails to focus adequately on Baudelaire's "self-confessed intoxication with the 'aristocratic pleasure of displeasing'" and his political thinking, including his involvement with the revolution in 1848. Christopher Prendergast in the *London Review of Books* remarks: "If in one incarnation [Baudelaire] is the gambler, chancing his arm (in fact his whole body) in a life-consuming encounter with moderninity, in another incarnation he is all withdrawal and retreat." Prendergast finds that Richardson's biography "gives us more 'data', but that's about it," seeing *Baudelaire* as part of "the

culture of biotrash." Christiansen is more forgiving, admiring Richardson's "robust but sensitive approach" to Baudelaire's poetry. Though Christiansen sees *Baudelaire* offering "no revelations and few speculations," he concludes that Richardson's biography will "bring a sharper focus to . . . this strangely unpleasant and disappointing man."

BIOGRAPHICAL/CRITICAL SOURCES:

PERIODICALS

Book World, November 21, 1971.
Detroit News, February 26, 1984.
London Review of Books, March 24, 1994, p. 7.
Nation, February 21, 1972.
New Republic, June 4, 1984.
New Yorker, January 27, 1975.
New York Review of Books, July 18, 1974; April 26, 1984.
New York Times, December 25, 1978; February 25, 1983.
New York Times Book Review, December 11, 1966; October 26, 1969; October 31, 1971; August 18, 1974; April 26, 1987.
Observer (London), April 3, 1994, p. 19.
Saturday Review, September 25, 1971.
Spectator, September 1, 1973; August 1, 1981; June 25, 1983; March 7, 1987, p. 34; March 26, 1994, p. 31.
Times (London), March 5, 1987.
Times Literary Supplement, June 19, 1969; January 15, 1970; June 4, 1971; August 31, 1973; February 21, 1975; March 21, 1980; March 6, 1987; March 25, 1994, p. 10.
Washington Post Book World, June 2, 1974; June 16, 1974; February 20, 1977; February 6, 1979; May 31, 1981.

*   *   *

RIVERS, Elfrida
  See BRADLEY, Marion Zimmer

*   *   *

ROBSON, Lucia St. Clair   1942-

PERSONAL: Surname is pronounced "*Rob*-son"; born September 24, 1942, in Baltimore, MD; daughter of Robert McCombs and Jeanne (Savage) Robson. *Education:* Palm Beach Junior College, A.A., 1962; University of Florida, B.A., 1964; Florida State University, M.L.S., 1974.

ADDRESSES: Agent—Virginia Barber Literary Agency, Inc., 101 Fifth Ave., New York, NY 10003.

CAREER: U.S. Peace Corps, volunteer worker in Caripito, Venezuela, 1964-66; teacher at public school in Brooklyn, NY, 1966-68; Hialeah Public Library, Hialeah, FL, librarian, 1968-69; teacher of English in Japan, 1969-71; Fort Jackson Library, Columbia, SC, librarian, 1971-72; Anne Arundel County Public Library, Annapolis, MD, librarian, 1975-82; writer, 1981—.

MEMBER: American Association of University Women, Western Writers of America, Women Writing the West.

AWARDS, HONORS: America Golden Spur Award for best historical novel, Western Writers of America, 1982, for *Ride the Wind.*

WRITINGS:

HISTORICAL NOVELS

Ride the Wind, Ballantine (New York City), 1982.
Walk in My Soul, Ballantine, 1985.
Light a Distant Fire, Ballantine, 1988.
The Tokaido Road, Ballantine, 1991.
Mary's Land, Ballantine, 1995.

WORK IN PROGRESS: A historical novel set during the Mexican-American War in 1848, for Ballantine.

SIDELIGHTS: Lucia St. Clair Robson told *CA:* "Writing historical fiction is as close as I can come to the career I really would like to pursue—being a time travel agent."

BIOGRAPHICAL/CRITICAL SOURCES:

PERIODICALS

Baltimore Sun, September 14, 1995; October 15, 1995.
Denver Post, March, 1991.
Kirkus Reviews, July 15, 1995.
Library Journal, September 15, 1982; July 15, 1995.
San Francisco Chronicle, April 21, 1991.

Washington Post, July 15, 1985; September 14, 1995 (Maryland edition).

*   *   *

RODMAN, Selden   1909-

PERSONAL: Born February 19, 1909, in New York, NY; son of Cary Selden and Nannie Van Nostrand (Marvin) Rodman; married Eunice Clark, 1933 (divorced); married Hilda Clausen, 1938 (divorced); married Maja Wojciechowska, December 15, 1950 (divorced); married Carole Cleaver, November 7, 1962; children: (third marriage) Oriana; (fourth marriage) Carla Pamela, Van Nostrand. *Education:* Yale University, B.A., 1931.

ADDRESSES: Home—659 Valley Rd., Oakland, NJ 07436.

CAREER: Co-founding editor, *Harkness Hoot,* 1930-31, and *Common Sense* (monthly political magazine), 1932-43; Centre d'Art, Port-au-Prince, Haiti, co-director, 1949-51; Haitian Art Center, New York City, former president and organizer of traveling exhibits; poet, freelance writer, art critic, and art collector. Lecturer at colleges and universities. Member of fine arts committee, New Jersey Tercentenary Commission, 1962-63; chair, New Jersey State Art Commission, 1963. *Military service:* U.S. Army, 1943-45; became master sergeant in foreign nationalities section of Office of Strategic Services.

AWARDS, HONORS: Commander, Haitian Legion of Honor and Merit; honorary doctorate in the arts, Ramapo College of New Jersey, 1995.

WRITINGS:

Mortal Triumph and Other Poems, Farrar & Rinehart, 1932.
Lawrence, the Last Crusade (narrative poem), Viking (New York City), 1937.
The Airmen (narrative poem), Random House (New York City), 1941.
The Revolutionists (play; produced in Port-au-Prince by the government of Haiti, 1941), Duell, Sloan & Pearce, 1942.
Horace Pippin: A Negro Painter in America, Quadrangle, 1947.
The Amazing Year, May 1, 1945-April 30, 1946 (diary in verse), Scribner (New York City), 1947.

Renaissance in Haiti: Popular Painters in the Black Republic, Pellegrini & Cudahy, 1948.

Portrait of the Artist as an American: Ben Shahn, Harper (New York City), 1951.

Haiti: The Black Republic, Devin-Adair (Old Greenwich, CT), 1954, 7th edition, 1973.

The Eye of Man: Form and Content in Western Painting, Devin-Adair, 1955.

Conversations with Artists, Devin-Adair, 1957.

Mexican Journal: The Conquerors Conquered (travel), Devin-Adair, 1958.

The Insiders: Rejection and Rediscovery of Man in the Arts of Our Time, Louisiana State University Press (Baton Rouge), 1960.

(With James Kearns) *The Heart of Beethoven,* Shorewood (New York City), 1962.

Death of the Hero (poem), Shorewood, 1963.

Quisqueya, 1492-1962: A History of the Dominican Republic, University of Washington Press (Seattle), 1964.

The Road to Panama (travel), Hawthorn (New York City), 1966.

The Guatemala Traveler, Meredith (New York City), 1967.

The Peru Traveler, Meredith, 1967.

The Caribbean, Hawthorn, 1968.

The Mexico Traveler, Meredith, 1969.

South America of the Poets, Hawthorn, 1970.

The Colombia Traveler, Hawthorn, 1971.

(With wife, Carole Cleaver) *Horace Pippin: The Artist as a Black American,* Doubleday (New York City), 1972.

The Miracle of Haitian Art, Doubleday, 1974.

Tongues of Fallen Angels (interviews), New Directions (Newton, NJ), 1974.

The Brazil Traveler, Devin-Adair, 1975.

Genius in the Backlands: Popular Artists of Brazil, Devin-Adair, 1977.

Artists in Tune with Their World, Simon & Schuster (New York City), 1981.

Where Art Is Joy: Forty Years of Haitian Popular Art, Ruggles De Latour, 1988.

(With Cleaver) *Spirits of the Night: The Vaudun Gods of Haiti,* Spring Publications (Dallas), 1992.

EDITOR

(With Alfred Mitchell Bingham) *Challenge to the New Deal,* McGraw (New York City), 1935.

A New Anthology of Modern Poetry, Random House, 1938, revised edition, Modern Library (New York City), 1946.

The Poetry of Flight (anthology), Duell, Sloan & Pearce, 1941, reprinted, Books for Libraries, 1969.

(With Richard Eberhart) *War and the Poet,* Devin-Adair, 1945, reprinted, Greenwood Press (Westport, CT), 1974.

One Hundred American Poems, New American Library (New York City), 1948, revised edition, 1972.

One Hundred Modern Poems, Pellegrini & Cudahy, 1949.

One Hundred British Poets, New American Library, 1974.

OTHER

Also author of plays *Hustler of the Gods,* with Cleaver, 1975, *The Liberator Liberated,* 1976, *Saint of the Revolution,* 1978, *The Fool of Passion,* and *Trazom.*

SIDELIGHTS: While working in Haiti during the early 1950s, Selden Rodman fostered a mural painting movement and directed the painting of the Episcopal cathedral in Port-au-Prince by nine primitive artists. His own collection of non-abstract contemporary paintings and sculpture is housed in a gallery in his renovated New Jersey farm home. The gallery's exterior murals were painted by Seymour Leichman from 1961 to 1964. Rodman gave parts of his popular art collection to Ramapo College of New Jersey in 1983 and to Yale University in 1985. Both institutions have printed illustrated catalogues of the collection.

*   *   *

ROGASKY, Barbara   1933-

PERSONAL: Born April 9, 1933, in Wilmington, DE; daughter of Charles (a grocer) and Ida (Rubin) Rogasky. *Education:* Attended University of Delaware, 1950-55. *Politics:* Independent. *Religion:* Jewish. *Avocational interests:* Music, photography.

ADDRESSES: Home—P.O. Box 34, Academy Rd., Thetford Hill, VT 05074. *Agent*—George Nicholson, Sterling Lord Literistic Inc., 1 Madison Ave., New York, NY 10010.

CAREER: Full-time children's books writer and photographer, 1980—. Has held various editorial positions with publishers in New York City, including Macmillan Publishing Co. and Harcourt Brace Jovanovich, 1955-77; part-time freelance editorial consultant, editor, and writer, 1955-79; Pyramid Books, New York City, editor, production editor, managing editor, 1966-74; Harcourt and Jove Books, New York City, senior acquisitions editor and director of special publications, 1974-77.

MEMBER: New England Business Association, League of New Hampshire Craftsmen.

AWARDS, HONORS: In 1988, *Smoke and Ashes: The Story of the Holocaust* was named an American Library Association (ALA) notable children's book, a best nonfiction book for young adults by *Publishers Weekly,* one of the best books of the year by *School Library Journal* and the ALA Young Adult Services Division, and the most outstanding book in secondary social studies by the Society of School Librarians International; "Best of the Best" listing, *School Library Journal,* 1994, for *Smoke and Ashes: The Story of the Holocaust; Winter Poems* was named an ALA notable children's book, 1994; Present Tense/Joel H. Cavior Award for children's literature, American Jewish Committee, for *Smoke and Ashes: The Story of the Holocaust.*

WRITINGS:

FOR CHILDREN

(Reteller) Brothers Grimm, *Rapunzel,* illustrated by Trina Schart Hyman, Holiday House (New York City), 1982.
(Reteller) Brothers Grimm, *The Water of Life,* illustrated by Hyman, Holiday House, 1986.
Smoke and Ashes: The Story of the Holocaust (nonfiction), Holiday House, 1988.
(Photographer) Myra Cohn Livingston, *Light and Shadow,* Holiday House, 1992.
(Compiler and editor) *Winter Poems,* illustrated by Hyman, Scholastic (New York City), 1994.
The Golem: A Version, illustrated by Hyman, Holiday House, 1996.

Also contributor to history books for children, including *From Sea to Shining Sea,* compiled by Amy L. Cohn, Scholastic, 1993; and *Young Reader's Companion to American History,* edited by John A. Garraty, Houghton (Boston), 1994.

WORK IN PROGRESS: A history of U.S. immigration, tentatively titled *Tenement Book,* for Scholastic;

photographs for a collection of Myra Cohn Livingston's poems, tentatively titled *Cloud Poems;* researching a multi-volume history of Jews for teenagers; updating and revising *Smoke and Ashes;* compiling selections for *Fall Poems,* illustrator undecided; *Dybbuk and Gilgul* (working title), new versions of ancient Jewish legends.

SIDELIGHTS: Barbara Rogasky's interests in children's literature include history, poetry, and fairy tales. She once stated: "I was born and raised in Wilmington, Delaware, where I spent most of my time being the typical eyeglasses-wearing, braceshooked, pigtail-encumbered outsider. I was blessed with an older sister who introduced me to good literature and magnificent music. I was also more than blessed by a few—very few—great teachers throughout my school years who encouraged and stimulated me and made me believe that a life in and with the world was possible, after all.

"I moved to what then seemed the Mecca [of publishing,] . . . New York City, right after college. In publishing, which I simply fell into, I worked over the years ranging from 'gopher,' proofreader, production editor, [and] managing editor, to department head and senior acquisitions editor. When the need for sanity became paramount, and [New York City] life seemed on the edge of apocalypse, I moved to New England in 1978. Freelancing full time (which, over the years, had been only part time), I was editorial consultant, content editor, rewriter, [and] 'ghost' for just about every major publisher and many minor ones. Work included much fiction, and nonfiction ranging from fishing guides and cookbooks, to Japanese architecture and biblical history.

"Starting with the retelling of *Rapunzel,* much to my thorough enjoyment—not to mention great surprise— I seem to have found my niche as a writer and photographer of books for children and young adults.

"*Smoke and Ashes: The Story of the Holocaust* will arguably remain the most lasting book of my career. Years after its publication, it remains in print and in use in classrooms and libraries around the country. It is a history of the development of perhaps history's greatest horror, told objectively if not dispassionately. The voices throughout are not only those of the victims, but also those of the perpetrators. Here they are, ranging from Hitler to the lowliest soldier, describing what they will do, what they are doing, what they have already done. In the midst of today's climate of ignorance and the growing clamor to deny the very existence of the Holocaust, the words of the murderers themselves form the barest undeniable truth."

Winning numerous honors, *Smoke and Ashes* was widely praised by critics who admired Rogasky's starkly honest treatment of her subject. Noting what a "formidable literary obligation" it was for the author to write a book about the Holocaust for young readers, Ari L. Goldman said in a *New York Times Book Review* article that Rogasky "rises to both the challenge and the obligation. . . . Aided by a powerful collection of photographs—most of them taken by the Nazi SS and German newspaper photographers—Ms. Rogasky tells the story without dramatizing, moralizing, sensationalizing or even judging." *Voice of Youth Advocates* critic Laura L. Lent further declared that Rogasky's book is more comprehensive than Elie Wiesel's *Night* and is written in language that is more accessible to young readers than Leon Poliakov's *Harvest of Hate.* "I believe any adolescent with even a marginal interest in the Holocaust will find this book fascinating," Lent concluded.

In addition to her interest in history in general and Jewish history in particular, Rogasky has a great love of poetry. She collected twenty-five poems related to the season for *Winter Poems,* sources both ancient and modern. "*Winter Poems* is a perfect combination of some of the things I call most important to me," Rogasky once stated. "It is that unique combination of *language,* and a language that can be *music,* used to convey *images* that can be revealed no other way. Trina Hyman's art reflects that and goes its own wondrous way as well."

BIOGRAPHICAL/CRITICAL SOURCES:

PERIODICALS

Bulletin of the Center for Children's Books, July, 1982, p. 206; November, 1986, p. 49; June, 1988, p. 215.
Five Owls, March, 1988, p. 62; September, 1988, p. 6.
Horn Book, February, 1983, p. 38; March, 1987, p. 229; September, 1988, p. 647; January, 1989, p. 31; November, 1994, p. 761.
Kirkus Reviews, September 15, 1986, p. 1449; May 15, 1988, p. 765.
New York Times Book Review, January 2, 1983, p. 19; November 6, 1988, p. 37.

Publishers Weekly, July 16, 1982, p. 78; August 22, 1986, p. 97; January 9, 1987, p. 52; May 13, 1988, p. 276; January 6, 1989, p. 52; April 26, 1991, p. 60; November 1, 1991, p. 82; October 31, 1994, p. 63.
School Library Journal, May, 1982, p. 62; November, 1986, p. 83; June, 1988, p. 128; December, 1994, p. 26.
Voice of Youth Advocates, December, 1988, p. 254.

*   *   *

ROSE, Wendy   1948-
(Bronwen   Elizabeth   Edwards,   Chiron Khanshendel)

PERSONAL: Born as Bronwen Elizabeth Edwards, May 7, 1948, in Oakland, CA; married Arthur Murata, March 11, 1976. *Education:* Attended Cabrillo College and Contra Costa College; University of California, Berkeley, B.A., 1976, M.A., 1978.

ADDRESSES: Home—41070 Lilley Mountain Dr., Coarsegold, CA 93614.

CAREER: Lowie Museum of Anthropology of University of California, Berkeley, manager of museum bookstore, 1974-79; University of California, Berkeley, lecturer in Native American studies, 1979-83; California University at Fresno, full-time lecturer, 1983-84; Fresno City College, CA, full-time instructor, 1984—. Visual artist with occasional exhibits and shows around the country; designer of postcards, posters, t-shirts, and bookbags, usually in connection with Indian organizations. Member of board of directors, Coordinating Council of Literary Magazines, 1979-82.

MEMBER: American Indian Movement, Native American Writers Association, Poets and Writers, American Federation of Teachers, PEN, Cactus and Succulent Society of America, American Federation of Herpetoculturists, California Indian Education Association.

WRITINGS:

POETRY, EXCEPT AS INDICATED

Hopi Roadrunner Dancing, Greenfield Review Press (New York City), 1973.

Long Division: A Tribal History, Strawberry Press (Bowling Green, NY), 1976, 2nd edition, 1980.

Academic Squaw, Blue Cloud Press, 1977.

Poetry of the American Indian Series: Wendy Rose, American Visual Communications Bank, 1978.

Builder Kachina: A Home-Going Cycle, Blue Cloud Press, 1979.

Aboriginal Tattooing in California (history), Archaeological Research Facility, University of California (Berkeley), 1979.

Lost Copper, Malki Museum Press (Los Angeles, CA), 1980.

What Happened When the Hopi Hit New York, Contact II Press (Bowling Green, NY), 1981.

The Halfbreed Chronicles and Other Poems, West End Press (Minneapolis, MN), 1985.

Going to War with All My Relations: New and Selected Poems, Entrada Press (Flagstaff, AZ), 1993.

Bone Dance: New and Selected Poems, 1965-1993, University of Arizona Press (Tucson), 1994.

Now Poof She Is Gone, Firebrand Books (Ithaca, NY), 1994.

OTHER

Also illustrator of numerous books and journals. Contributor to anthologies, including *Speaking for Ourselves* (under pseudonym Chiron Khanshendel), edited by Barbara Bradshaw and Lillian Faderman, Scott, Foresman (Glenview, IL), 1969, 2nd edition (under name Wendy Rose), 1975; *Time to Greez: Incantations from the Third World,* edited by Mirikitani and others, Glide Press, 1975; *Carriers of the Dream Wheel,* edited by Niatum, Harper (New York City), 1975; *Contemporary California Women Poets,* edited by McDowell, Merlin Press (San Jose, CA), 1977; *The Next World,* edited by Joseph Bruchac, Crossing Press (Trumansburg, NY), 1978; *The Third Woman,* edited by Fisher, Houghton (Boston, MA), 1979; *In Her Own Image: The Lives and Works of Women Artists,* edited by Wendt, Feminist Press (Old Westbury, NY), 1980; *The South Corner of Time,* edited by Evers, Suntracks Press, 1980; and *This Song Remembers,* edited by Katz, Houghton, 1980. Contributor of articles and poems to periodicals, including *Many Smokes, Early American, Contra Costa Advocate, Journal of California Anthropology, San Francisco Bay Guardian,* and *Janus.*

SIDELIGHTS: Born and raised in an urban setting far removed from reservation life and the influence of her Native American relations, Wendy Rose is noted for poetry which examines the experiences of mixed-blood Native Americans estranged from both Native and white societies. Paula Gunn Allen, in *The Sacred Hoop: Recovering the Feminine in American Indian Traditions,* states that "while her enforced distance from her people grieves and angers Rose, she writes poetry that does not fall into suicidal bitterness on the one hand or radical excess on the other. Rather, it hews a clear line toward her understanding of her position, illuminating in that clarity the position of all who are dispossessed." A well-regarded anthropologist and an accomplished visual artist, Rose is additionally known for her ardent support of efforts to establish a place for Native literature within the American literary canon.

In addition to treating ecological and feminist issues, Rose's poetry incorporates her own experiences and those of other mixed-blood Native Americans who, separated from their tribal culture and alienated by the white society in which they live, are searching for a sense of identity and community. For example, in such poems as "The well-intentioned question," from the Pulitzer Prize-nominated *Lost Copper,* Rose documents her feelings of marginalization and her desire to be part of the Native community: "My Indian name listens / / for footsteps / stopping short of my door / then leaving forever." Her experiences in academia—where, she argues, Native writings are viewed as a fad and not serious literature—were first captured in *Academic Squaw,* and her background in anthropology and involvement with various Native American organizations inspires much of the imagery and history employed in her poetry. In *The Halfbreed Chronicles and Other Poems,* written while she was studying anthropology as an undergraduate at Berkeley, Rose's focus on the marginalized mixed-blood Amerindian was expanded to include other minorities, such as Japanese Americans and Native Americans from Mexico.

Rose continues to address environmental, feminist, historical, and Native American concerns in her more recent verse collections, *Going to War with All My Relations: New and Selected Poems* and *Bone Dance: New and Selected Poems, 1965-1993. World Literature Today* reviewer Robert L. Berner states, "*Going to War with All My Relations,* a significant achievement by an important poet, suggests that the revelation of the ambiguities inherent in the historical interrelationship of Indian and European elements in our culture continues to be the great task for American poets." Regarding *Bone Dance, Booklist* reviewer Whitney Scott notes that Rose traces "her evolving linkage not only to Native American issues but to her related concerns on a global level." Darryl Babe Wilson of *American Indian Culture and Research Journal* praises *Bone Dance,* stating that "it is difficult to summarize the power of the thought that emanates from this work. It is a special combination of the study of anthropology guided by the ancient wisdom of two great nations, the Miwok of California and the Hopi of Arizona. But if it is necessary to simmer its contents until only a syrup is left in the bottom of the pail, there will be two words written there by a finger of knowledge: *unique* and *powerful.*"

Rose's poetry has been praised for capturing the pain and confusion of the Native-American experience and for making it accessible to a non-Native audience. Critics note that much of Rose's work employs elements of Native American songs and chants and is preoccupied with spirituality, communion with the natural world, and the encroachment of white culture on Native society. Although some commentators assert that Rose's use of language masks her feelings, others note a sense of urgency and bitterness in her work and maintain that it is fueled by raw, unbridled emotion. Writing in the *American Book Review,* Jamake Highwater comments: "[Rose's] lines are haunted by an unresolved search for a personal as well as a tribal sense of identity. That search gives her words strength and spirit. It dissolves the barrier of race with which she cautiously surrounds [herself], and it gives us access to her pain. In that pain we are all related."

Rose once told *CA:* "Writing is just something that always has been and just is. For everything in this universe there is a song to accompany its existence; writing is another way of singing these songs. Everyone knows the words and tune; it's just that not everyone feels the confidence in themselves to keep their ears open and their senses feeling. Writing just comes from those less afraid of themselves (although possibly more afraid of other-than-themselves). Sometimes the songs are in color; then they become pictures. Sometimes the songs are audible; then they are sung.

"It doesn't really matter how they happen or where they go; they will be, no matter what. Some people have tried to say I sing my songs because I'm half-Hopi; that's not true. . . . I sing them because I hear them. People who think that are just looking for reasons why they don't want to hear them for themselves. I love my songs; I love my people.

"The usual practice in bookstores upon receiving books of poems by American Indians is to classify them as 'Native Americana' rather than as poetry; the poets are seen as literate fossils more than as living, working artists. I have run into this kind of thing too often. Also, there is a great deal of stereotyping of Indian poetry (and Indian art in general); we may be seen as 'nature children' tapping some great earth-nerve and producing poems like pulses. But all art is that way; not just Indian art. There is also the concrete, the abstract, the analytical, the mystical—all components and levels of human understanding and expression. And those qualities stereotypically Indian also exist. The deferential treatment accorded to Indians in artistic and academic settings is just as destructive, ultimately, as out-and-out racism. It is startling to find your book of poems in an anthropology section of a bookstore instead of in the poetry section. . . . My songs are self-conscious when they have to dance alone. You know, I really just want to make people feel good."

BIOGRAPHICAL/CRITICAL SOURCES:

BOOKS

Allen, Paula Gunn, *The Sacred Hoop: Recovering the Feminine in American Indian Traditions,* Beacon Press, 1986.
Coltelli, Laura, *Winged Words: American Indian Writers Speak,* University of Nebraska Press, 1990.
Rose, Wendy, *I Tell You Now: Autobiographical Essays of Native American Writers,* edited by Brian Swann and Arnold Krupat, University of Nebraska Press, 1987.

PERIODICALS

American Book Review, January, 1982, p. 16.
American Indian Culture and Research Journal, 1994, pp. 274-78.
Belles Lettres, fall, 1994, p. 87.
Booklist, September 15, 1977, p. 133.
Choice, May, 1986, p. 1392.
Library Journal, January, 1986, p. 89.
MELUS, fall, 1983, pp. 67-87.
Ms., August, 1986, p. 76.
Nation, December 26, 1994, p. 810.
Publishers Weekly, February 8, 1993, p. 81.
World Literature Today, spring, 1994, pp. 408-09; spring, 1995, p. 410.

ROSENTHAL, M(acha) L(ouis) 1917-

PERSONAL: Born March 14, 1917, in Washington, DC; son of Jacob and Ethel (Brown) Rosenthal; married Victoria Himmelstein (a senior psychiatric social worker), January 7, 1939; children: David Herschel (deceased), Alan, Laura. *Education:* University of Chicago, B.A., 1937, M.A., 1938; New York University, Ph.D., 1949; additional studies at University of Michigan and Johns Hopkins University.

ADDRESSES: Home—17 Bayard Lane, Suffern, NY 10901. *Office*—Department of English, New York University, 19 University Pl., New York, NY 10003.

CAREER: Michigan State University, East Lansing, instructor in English, 1939-45; New York University, New York City, 1945—, began as teaching fellow, professor, 1961—, professor emeritus of English, 1987—; Poetics Institute, founder, 1977, director, 1977-79; Memphis University, first Distinguished Moss Chair of Excellence in English, 1989. Visiting professor, Sir George Williams University, University of Pennsylvania, University of Zurich, and University of Bologna. Guggenheim Foundation, poetry referee, 1961-88; jurist for numerous literary award competitions.

MEMBER: Modern Language Association of America, PEN, American Literature Association, American Association of University Professors, Poetry Society of America (vice president and board member, 1989-91), Yeats Society, Phi Beta Kappa.

AWARDS, HONORS: American Council of Learned Societies fellow, 1941-42, 1951-52; Guggenheim fellowship, 1960-61, 1964-65; finalist, National Book Award, 1967; Distinguished Exchange Scholar, China, 1982; Explicator Literary Foundation Award, 1984; fellow in residence, Rockefeller Foundation Research Center, Bellagio, Italy, 1988; first Golden Apple Award, Yeats Society, 1993, for Yeats scholarship.

WRITINGS:

(With A. J. M. Smith) *Exploring Poetry,* Macmillan (New York City), 1955, 2nd edition, 1973.
The Modern Poets: A Critical Introduction, Oxford University Press (New York City and London), 1960.
A Primer of Ezra Pound, Macmillan, 1960.

Blue Boy on Skates: Poems, Oxford University Press, 1964.
The New Poets: American and British Poetry since World War II, Oxford University Press, 1967.
Beyond Power: New Poems, Oxford University Press, 1969.
The View from the Peacock's Tail: Poems, Oxford University Press, 1972.
Randall Jarrell, University of Minnesota Press (Minneapolis), 1972.
Poetry and the Common Life, Oxford University Press, 1974.
She: A Sequence of Poems, BOA Editions (Brockport, NY), 1977.
Sailing into the Unknown: Yeats, Pound, and Eliot, Oxford University Press, 1978.
Poems, 1964-1980, Oxford University Press, 1981.
(With Sally M. Gall) *The Modern Poetic Sequence: The Genius of Modern Poetry,* Oxford University Press, 1983.
The Poet's Art, Norton (New York City), 1987.
As for Love: Poems and Translations, Oxford University Press, 1987.
Our Life in Poetry: Selected Essays and Reviews, Persea (New York City), 1991.
Running to Paradise: Yeats's Poetic Art, Oxford University Press, 1993.

Also author of introduction to *The Collected Poems of Dilys Laing,* Press of Case Western Reserve University, and *Poems: Selected,* by Charles Sisson, New Directions (New York City), 1996.

EDITOR

Hugh MacDiarmid, *Collected Poems,* Macmillan, 1962.
(And author of introduction) William Butler Yeats, *Selected Poems,* Macmillan, 1962, published as *Selected Poems and Two Plays,* Collier (New York City), 1966, published with corrections and without plays as *Selected Poems,* Franklin Library (Franklin Center, PA), 1979, expanded edition published with new foreword, textual corrections, and revised introduction and notes as *Selected Poems and Three Plays of William Butler Yeats,* Collier, 1986.
(With Gerald De Witt Sanders and John Herbert Nelson) *Chief Modern Poets of England and America,* Macmillan, 1962, 5th edition published as *Chief Modern Poets of Britain and America,* 1970.
(And author of introduction) *The William Carlos Williams Reader,* New Directions, 1966.

(And author of introduction) *The New Modern Poetry: British and American Poetry since World War II*, Macmillan, 1967, published as *The New Modern Poetry: An Anthology of American and British Poetry since World War II*, Oxford University Press, 1969.

(And author of introduction) *100 Postwar Poems: British and American*, Macmillan, 1968.

(And author of introduction) *Poetry in English: An Anthology*, Oxford University Press, 1987.

Also editor of "Lamplighter" series, Persea Books, 1987-92.

OTHER

(Translator and author of afterword) Collodi, *The Adventures of Pinocchio*, Lothrop, Lee, & Shepard (New York City), 1983.

Contributor of poems, articles, and reviews to journals and magazines. Poetry editor, *Nation*, 1956-61, *Humanist*, 1970-78, and *Present Tense*, 1973-90. Editor and author of introduction, *Ploughshares* "Works in Progress" issue, May 15, 1991.

WORK IN PROGRESS: The Present State of Criticism and *The Present State of Poetry*, both for Oxford University Press; *In the World Pub: Selected Poems and Translations*.

SIDELIGHTS: M. L. Rosenthal is a highly acclaimed poet, scholar, and critic of contemporary poetry. His anthology of post-World War II poems, *The New Modern Poetry: British and American Poetry since World War II*, and its companion study, *The New Poets: American and British Poetry since World War II*, form what *New York Times Book Review* critic Robie Macauley called "the first broad view of the new poetry and at the same time the first study that distinguishes and examines the major trends in a satisfactory way." Although a few critics questioned the merit and basis for selection of the poems, others, such as Karl Malkoff, viewed the anthology as yielding "a definition of contemporary poetry as disparate reactions to the agonies of our time." Malkoff concluded that Rosenthal's work "is not simply a work of selection and criticism, but also a creative statement about the nature of our modern world."

With *The Modern Poetic Sequence: The Genius of Modern Poetry*, Rosenthal and coauthor Sally M. Gall "do an inspiringly intelligent and stimulating job simply in noticing a shift in the customary means of arranging the parts of a poem," *Georgia Review* contributor William Harmon asserted. "Like [Robert] Langbaum's ideas [in *The Poetry of Experience*], theirs help to explain the success of certain works and the failure of others." Poet Seamus Heaney, writing in the *New York Times Book Review*, noted that the authors' "survey of more than 40 works by American, British and Irish poets is a cumulative effort to illustrate and define what they mean by their subtitle, 'The Genius of Modern Poetry.' The book starts with [Walt] Whitman, where that genius first abundantly appears; moves on through Emily Dickinson; concentrates its greatest attention on masterworks by Yeats, Eliot, and Pound; and ends with chapters that allocate their places within the development of 'this crucial genre of modern poetic art' to talents as diverse as Wallace Stevens, Hugh MacDiarmid, David Jones, Austin Clarke, Charles Olson, Basil Bunting and Sylvia Plath." *Village Voice* contributor Arthur Krystal found "at least one valuable lesson" in *The Modern Poetic Sequence*: "For those who write or teach poetry, many of the works under discussion may have become with familiarity and the passage of time seamless poems. They're not. They are sequences whose unity depends more on the interplay of metrical and thematic arrangements than on discourse or cohesive argument."

Rosenthal concentrates on William Butler Yeats, Ezra Pound, and T. S. Eliot in *Sailing into the Unknown: Yeats, Pound, and Eliot,* and narrows his focus to Yeats alone in *Running to Paradise: Yeats's Poetic Art*. Fellow poetry critic Robert Langbaum observed in the *New York Times Book Review* that in *Sailing into the Unknown*, the Rosenthal "has chosen to discuss Yeats, Pound and Eliot as founders of modern poetry, because they define their modern voices through close communion with the past and because they conspicuously employ the modern poetic sequence." *Sailing into the Unknown* "reminds us of what we are always inclined to forget: how much a poem can come to," *Times Literary Supplement*'s Theodore Weiss asserted. "[Rosenthal] urges us not to settle for too little, not to be too easily satisfied. Out of his respect for poetry's basic significance to our lives and his refusal to allow critical theorizing to eclipse poems themselves, he is ideally prepared to demonstrate the pertinacy of Yeats, Pound and Eliot in the only way that matters—through their work. We must esteem the intensity of his involvement and his direct but highly discriminating love of that work." Langbaum concluded, "Even where I disagree, I admire the consistency of Mr. Rosenthal's critical judgments, his distrust of anything not genuinely alive in poetry. His readings of poems he loves are so fresh and alive that one of this book's attractions is the chance to discover and rediscover modern masterpieces under the guidance of a critic who makes you realize how marvelous they are."

Reviewing *Running to Paradise* for the *Boston Globe,* Robert Taylor found that "Rosenthal's deeply rewarding consideration of Yeats' lyric poetry and poetic drama emphasizes the interdependence of his artistic and intellectual growth." Edward Engelberg, in a review for *English Literature in Translation,* described the author as "a sensitive reader of poetry" whose "own gifts as a poet help him considerably in providing us with an overall sense of Yeats's accomplishments. Nor is he shy in being critical when he feels it justified. Of course, one might say that such a 'reading' produces more than one subjective opinion, and not all readers of Yeats will agree with certain judgments rendered, either those of approval or disapproval." The critic concluded, "Rosenthal's opinions may not always be unerring simply because they are frankly subjective judgments; but nowhere in this ultimately useful volume do we see any lack of intelligence, sensitivity, and generally good common sense."

Rosenthal's own poems often deal with what Thomas Lask described in the *New York Times* as "the majesty and impersonality of nature and the equal impersonality of history." His first volume, entitled *Blue Boy on Skates: Poems,* was published when Rosenthal was forty-seven, and prompted a number of critics to wonder why the author had switched from criticizing poetry to writing it, according to William B. Thesing in *Dictionary of Literary Biography.* The author fared better with his next volume, *Beyond Power: New Poems,* Thesing observed: "Generally, reviewers were impressed with the new seriousness of this volume: one called it 'a serious attempt to analyze what ails us,' and another noted that 'it is marked by a deeper and more enriched tone.'" A *Times Literary Supplement* reviewer, however, found the work lacking in comparison to Rosenthal's prose: "M. L. Rosenthal's services to modern poetry are important and well known. But his new book, *Beyond Power,* does not match in distinction his work as a scholar or anthologist. The poems are adventurous and in good taste; they convey the impression of a charming, tolerant man, blessed with humour and wisdom. But they do not possess the strength of language, the coherence of

vision, or the marks of individual character that one demands from writers who stir up more than a murmur of polite appreciation."

In his third volume of poetry, *The View from the Peacock's Tail: Poems,* Rosenthal "shows a new command of both form and content," Thesing asserted, and has "discovered the full potentials of his characteristic poetic form—the sequence." Rosenthal explained the form in "We Begin These Sequences Lightly," published in *American Poets in 1976:* "The key to making a sequence is the key of immediacy. It is struck in the quick of the language. It animates ideas and makes them organs of the poem's body. . . . The poetic sequence is our form of both epic and bardic poetry. It embodies cultural tasks and it assumes prophecy. Its protean landmark is the private sensibility, against which we test everything."

Rosenthal continued his exploration of the poetic sequence in *She: A Sequence of Poems,* his next poetry collection. Sally M. Gall, reviewing the work for *Modern Poetry Studies,* described *She* as an "encompassing love poem, a paean to the ability of the human spirit to change despair and desolation into song, and a major addition to the genre of the modern lyric sequence."

With *Poems, 1964-1980,* a collection of new and previously published work, *Library Journal* reviewer Joseph A. Lipari remarked, "Rosenthal displays an impressive range and intelligence," but still demonstrates some imperfections as a poet: "At his best, Rosenthal fuses the personal and universal in a lucid yet suggestive rhetoric. At times, though, stridency and ironic undercutting, mythological and literary allusions, and archaic diction . . . are poor substitutes for vivid emotion." *Booklist* reviewer John Parisi held a similar opinion, finding that "the variety of subjects and tones, the technical skills, the fine perceptions, but also the faults of the poet are well represented" in *Poems, 1964-1980.* "Still," he concluded, "this is a most enjoyable, and accessible, collection from a poet of many tastes and talents."

"Rosenthal's poetry exhibits the qualities of intelligence, energy, variety, and craftsmanship," Thesing concluded. "His poetic vision is sometimes personal, but never private; it is sometimes political, but never inflammatory. The poetic personality that comes through in poem after poem is that of a gentleman blessed with the characteristics of humor and wit, an honesty and generosity of spirit, and a truly humanitarian outlook. His questions are often passionately intense, but his answers are never narrowly dogmatic. In times of suffering and turmoil, his voice of mature wisdom is to be valued."

BIOGRAPHICAL/CRITICAL SOURCES:

BOOKS

Contemporary Authors Autobiography Series, Volume 6, Gale (Detroit), 1987.

Heyen, William, editor, *American Poets in 1976,* Bobbs-Merrill (Indianapolis, IN), 1976.

Dictionary of Literary Biography, Volume 5: *American Poets since World War II,* Gale, 1980, pp. 207-14.

PERIODICALS

American Book Review, February-March, 1992.
American Literature, November, 1976, pp. 426-27.
Antioch Review, summer, 1983, p. 371.
Booklist, November 1, 1981, p. 366.
Boston Globe, December 22, 1993, p. 33.
Choice, September, 1967, p. 676; October, 1967, p. 835; March, 1970, p. 80; May 10, 1973, p. 460; June, 1973, p. 623; September, 1978, p. 874; June, 1983, p. 1458.
Christian Science Monitor, January 12, 1961, p. 7.
Commonweal, May 23, 1975, p. 150.
English Literature in Translation, February, 1995, p. 216.
Georgia Review, spring, 1979, p. 230; spring, 1984, pp. 182-84; winter, 1987, pp. 836-37.
Library Journal, October 1, 1981, p. 1930; May 1, 1991, p. 77; October 1, 1993, p. 95.
Lively Arts and Book Review, May 14, 1961, p. 33.
Los Angeles Times Book Review, July 10, 1983, p. 5.
Modern Poetry Studies, autumn, 1977, pp. 119-33.
Nation, June 14, 1975, pp. 725-26; October 1, 1977, pp. 311-14; October 22, 1977, p. 225; January 21, 1978, pp. 56-9; December 30, 1991, p. 862.
New Leader, April 10, 1967.
New York Review of Books, April 21, 1994, p. 49.
New York Times, April 25, 1967, p. 45M; August 29, 1969, p. 27.
New York Times Book Review, September 10, 1967, p. 6; January 21, 1968; March 2, 1975, p. 4; April 2, 1978, p. 14; August 7, 1983, p. 31; November 20, 1983, p. 3; August 23, 1987, p. 17.
Observer Review, March 19, 1967.
Poetry, March, 1968; March, 1970; April, 1970; September, 1973, pp. 344-50.
Prairie Schooner, spring, 1968.

Publishers Weekly, February 27, 1978, p. 150; May 1, 1987, p. 58; May 10, 1991, p. 264.
Sewanee Review, summer, 1968; October, 1970, p. 698; October, 1978, p. R118; July, 1984, p. 451.
Spectator, September 8, 1967, p. 275.
Times Literary Supplement, April 13, 1967; October 12, 1967, p. 963; December 11, 1970, p. 1436; August 31, 1973, p. 996; February 1, 1980, pp. 124-25; December 30, 1983, p. 1455; August 2, 1991, p. 6.
Village Voice, June 19, 1984, p. 46.
Washington Post Book World, May 12, 1991, p. 11.
Western Humanities Review, autumn, 1978, pp. 364-67.
World Literature Today, spring, 1984, p. 272; autumn, 1988, p. 738; winter, 1992, p. 134.

*   *   *

ROSSNER, Judith (Perelman) 1935-

PERSONAL: Born March 1, 1935, in New York, NY; daughter of Joseph George and Dorothy (Shapiro) Perelman; married Robert Rossner (a teacher and writer), June 13, 1954 (divorced); married Mort Persky (a magazine editor), January 9, 1979 (divorced); children: Jean, Daniel. *Education:* City College (now of the City University of New York), 1952-55.

ADDRESSES: Home—New York City. *Agent*—Wendy Weil, Julian Bach Literary Agency, 747 Third Ave., New York, NY 10017.

WRITINGS:

NOVELS

To the Precipice, Morrow (New York City), 1966.
Nine Months in the Life of an Old Maid, Dial (New York City), 1969.
Any Minute I Can Split, McGraw (New York City), 1972.
Looking for Mr. Goodbar, Simon & Schuster (New York City), 1975.
Attachments, Simon & Schuster, 1977.
Emmeline, Simon & Schuster, 1980.
August, Houghton (Boston), 1983.
His Little Women, Summit (New York City), 1990.
Olivia, or, The Weight of the Past, Crown (New York City), 1994.

OTHER

Also author of short stories for magazines and periodicals.

ADAPTATIONS: Looking for Mr. Goodbar was filmed by Paramount in 1977 and starred Diane Keaton and Richard Gere.

SIDELIGHTS: Since the publication of *To the Precipice* in 1966, Judith Rossner's novels have explored women's fluctuating roles in an era of constantly changing expectations. Prominently featured themes in her work are childbirth and childrearing, love and friendship, ambition, and sexual conflict: "My abiding theme is separations," Rossner told Curt Suplee in a *Washington Post* interview. Her novel *August,* which contrasts a New England teenager undergoing psychoanalysis with her imperfect, middle-aged Manhattan psychologist, has been particularly highly acclaimed, but she is perhaps best known for *Looking for Mr. Goodbar,* a work inspired by the true-life murder of a teacher who haunted singles bars.

Rossner dropped out of college in order to get married. As she once told *CA:* "There wasn't even a particularly defiant quality about my leaving school. It was, well, I'm a writer and I'm a housewife and I have to work at a full-time job, so there's no time for school right now." She worked for a time in the advertising department of *Scientific American,* but ironically, her pleasure in the position sidetracked her from her writing. She considered her next job in a real estate office boring, however, it allowed her the time to begin her first novel. This book was never published and she stopped writing for awhile after the birth of her children. Her next attempt at writing became *To the Precipice,* Rossner's first published novel. But Rossner's interest in writing ran deeper than practicality. As Rossner told Bruce Cook in a *Detroit News* interview, her mother, a schoolteacher, harbored dreams of becoming a writer which she passed along to her daughter: "She kept encouraging me when I was young, and so I just accepted it—this was what I was going to do; I was going to write books. But she never said anything about money or success, so none of that was built into my expectations. Just writing and getting published was enough at first."

To the Precipice is a coming-of-age story about a young Jewish woman, Ruth Kossoff, who is raised in a New York City tenement building in the 1940s and 1950s. The novel relates Ruth's uneasy decision to marry a wealthy gentile instead of the self-made lawyer she grew up with. Though she adapts to her roles as wife and mother, she remains passionately attached to the lawyer. Some critics found the book's plot somewhat formulaic and melodramatic and the heroine unsympathetic, but others praised it more wholeheartedly. *Nation* critic Edward M. Potoker, called it an "ambitious novel," explaining that *To the Precipice* "is a *Bildungsroman,* a psychological novel, a Jewish novel, a woman's novel, a luminous period piece, and a family chronicle with a large, complex canvas that displays many of the author's principle themes and preoccupations." According to Patricia Jewell McAlexander in *Dictionary of Literary Biography, To the Precipice* is dominated by a theme that will be repeated throughout Rossner's books: "the conflict between selfishness and altruism."

Rossner explores these themes again in *Nine Months in the Life of an Old Maid,* a story about a self-absorbed isolated woman who lives in a mansion with her sister. *Saturday Review* critic Cecile Shapiro characterizes it as a tale told "with quiet competence," that "many will read . . . with quiet enjoyment." Despite good reviews, neither *To the Precipice* nor *Nine Months in the Life of an Old Maid* sold particularly well upon publication. Rossner explains her slow progress to Suplee: "my first [published] book took five years to write and I made $1,000 on it and I was in Heaven." *Nine Months in the Life of an Old Maid* "took three years and made $3,000."

In the late 1960s, the Rossners left New York City to begin a free school in New Hampshire. But their marriage began to deteriorate and Rossner felt homesick for New York. She returned to Manhattan in 1971 and began working in the psychiatry department of a hospital. Her third book, *Any Minute I Can Split,* which was written during this period, was published in 1972.

Any Minute I Can Split tells the story of Margaret Adams, a woman pregnant with twins who abandons her husband and stumbles into a 1960s-style commune. She later discovers that life with her wealthy husband, despite his verbal abuse, is preferable to the uncertainty of the commune. Concerned with the nature of the nuclear and the extended family, the book describes communal farm life as fraught with "tension under superficial friendliness . . ." and "a repository for petty squabbles, money problems, lack of communication and lack of privacy," Potoker summarizes. "As the novel's title suggests, all relationships are uneasy and tentative. Margaret begins to recognize the commune as suburbia in disguise."

The book was generally well-received. In *Any Minute I Can Split,* says *New York Times Book Review* critic Martin Levin, Rossner reveals "a sharp eye for the contradictions and paradoxes of her characters." J. D. O'Hara of the *Saturday Review* agrees, stating that Rossner "evokes the commune well," although he maintains that Rossner "is too willing to write about ideas; instead of being incited to thought, we are too often obliged to hear Margaret's expository thinking." O'Hara adds that Rossner's "unpleasant scenes are especially credible," while Thomas Lask indicates in the *New York Times* that the author "has a way of treating even the most outlandish of situations in a cool, almost clinical way. She lets the dialogue carry the nuances in the book." *Any Minute I Can Split* "refuses to exploit its theme for sensational purposes or easy victories," Lask concludes.

After *Any Minute I Can Split* was published, Rossner told Suplee, "I began to feel silly as a secretary. I was 37 years old—it was like being in drag. I wanted to support myself by writing." Rossner was asked to write a story for a women's issue of *Esquire,* and the author suggested a piece about Roseann Quinn, the 27-year-old schoolteacher who had recently been killed by a man she invited home from a bar. The arguably morbid topic suited Rossner's disposition of the time well, as she was recuperating from a car accident that had left her injured as well as depressed.

Esquire eventually killed the story, but Rossner decided to turn it into a novel. McAlexander echoes the sentiments of other reviewers, stating that *Looking for Mr. Goodbar* is "not only the most popular of Rossner's novels but also the best, treating her dominant theme—the conflict between selfishness and altruism—most convincingly." The book begins with the recorded confession of the young drifter who has killed a woman during a bungled attempt at sexual intercourse. The narrative then shifts to Theresa Dunn's upbringing in a lower-middle-class, Irish-Catholic Bronx neighborhood and her painful recovery from poliomyelitis. When an affair with one of her college professors abruptly ends, she transforms herself from a mousy co-ed into a promiscuous barhopper who revels in her newly found, supposedly liberating freedom. According to Caroline Blackwood in the *Times Literary Supplement,* "the real-life testimony that Miss Rossner has used is brutal, bleak and factual. Her imaginary report as

she reconstructs a fictional account of the life of Theresa Dunn leading up to her sordid death, is equally brutal, bleak and factual."

The book reflects its times and can "be read as a long, flat piece of devastating testimony against the destructive and joyless hedonism of New York in the 1960s, the era when everyone realized they were meant to be swinging, to be 'turning on' to grass and acid, to be 'into' music," Blackwood writes. "Rossner's physical descriptions of New York are as desolate as the lives of their New York characters." McAlexander opines that "*Looking for Mr. Goodbar* thus dramatizes the dilemma of many Americans of the time, who were beginning to be disillusioned by the wild sexual experimentation and rejection of past values, but were continuing to hold fast to the narcissistic ideal of sexual fulfillment."

McAlexander explains the morals inherent in Theresa's fate: "the 1960s dream of complete sexual freedom and fulfillment—however much Rossner sympathizes with it—is ultimately an impossible, self-destructive one while traditional morality—however limiting—at least allows one to survive, even to be a credit to family and society." And while Christopher Lehmann-Haupt in the *New York Times* is uncomfortable with the fact that the third person narrator of the book knows so much, *Time* reviewer Martha Duffy refers to *Looking for Mr. Goodbar* as "both a compelling 'page turner' and a superior *roman a clef*." Though the film version brought Rossner wide recognition for her novel, she once told *CA* that she did not care for the adaptation: "Authors are never pleased with the movie."

According to Patricia Jewell McAlexander in the *Dictionary of Literary Biography,* the film version of *Looking for Mr. Goodbar,* the rights of which were sold even before the novel appeared in hardcover, advanced Rossner's standing and increased the sales of her earlier novels, including *Nine Months in the Life of an Old Maid* and *Any Minute I Can Split.* Though Rossner frankly admits that she wrote *Looking for Mr. Goodbar* for money, she told John Askins in a *Detroit Free Press* interview that she "never believed for a minute that I would be able to support myself just by writing for the rest of my life." A divorced mother with two young children, Rossner completed the manuscript while she was working as a secretary and hoped that the novel "might make $40,000 and enable her to quit," a *Time* reporter explains. After receiving an advance she looked forward to a paperback sale with the idea "that I would make just enough money to not be a secretary for a year," Rossner told Suplee.

Rossner followed *Looking for Mr. Goodbar* with several novels about women caught in dramatic circumstances reflecting the conflicts of their gender and era. *Attachments* is a black comedy about two good friends who marry Siamese twins with whom they raise a family. It examines the tension between the need to maintain close, longstanding relationships and the need to establish individuality. And although Jerome Charyn in the *New York Times Book Review* considers the book "an extraordinary leap from the mundane, 'realistic' settings and sexual tableaux" of *Looking for Mr. Goodbar,* other critics objected to the graphic sexuality of the work and perceived it to be a commercial venture. Some simply found the subject matter freakish.

Discussing *Attachments* in the *New Yorker,* a reviewer writes that "though Miss Rossner's writing is fluid and easy to digest, she never fulfills the expectations raised by the oddity of her subject." Conversely, John Leonard of the *New York Times* concedes that *Attachments* "is an ambitious, disturbing novel by a best-selling author who might have written a trashy book, but decided instead to mess up our minds." Charyn concludes that *Attachments* is "funny, sexy and sad, . . . a crazy treatise on 'love' as the ultimate executioner."

Emmeline, a tragic period novel set in the New England of the mid-1800s, is similar to *Looking for Mr. Goodbar* in the fact that it is based on actual events. As Walter Clemons explains in *Newsweek,* in *Emmeline,* Rossner has again "chosen a bizarre catastrophe, which . . . she reveals only near the end, and traced its origins with a steady attention to character and psychological probability." Rossner's story tells of a poor 13-year-old sent to work in the cotton mills of Lowell, Massachusetts, who is seduced and impregnated by her overseer. Emmeline's pregnancy is hushed up, her child is taken from her and adopted, and she returns to her farming village in Maine. Years later during the Civil War, she falls in love and marries a younger man who is passing through town with a road crew. He is later revealed to be her son. When the incestuous nature of her marriage becomes public, Emmeline is ostracized from her community and dies poor and lonely.

According to Anthony Quinton of the London *Times,* *Emmeline* "is a low-keyed, unsensational book, written in pleasant, rather stately prose, that would have been fairly intelligible and even natural at the time of the events recorded." And true or not, points out Lindsay Duguid in the *Times Literary Supplement,* Rossner "has made the most of her material and produced a chilling saga. Her treatment is, in the main, stark; and Emmeline's early sufferings are particularly convincing." Rossner told *CA* that she "was more interested in a complicated tale of good intentions gone wrong than a simple tale of villainy. I didn't want to have a wicked foreman and a bunch of virtuous young girls and so on."

Like *Looking for Mr. Goodbar,* which Blackwood describes as "a morality tale," *Emmeline* contains "themes of religion and punishment of sin," relates Duguid. And like Theresa Dunn, Emmeline "is doomed to repeat her worst mistakes," Nancy Yanes Hoffman says in the *Los Angeles Times.* Conversely, *Village Voice* reviewer Eliot Fremont-Smith contends that no moral can be drawn from the book since Emmeline is obviously a victim. And because the novel is too closely tied to the real-life story from which it is derived, Fremont-Smith argues, neither the protagonist nor her son can be considered tragic characters. They are not given the power to affect their own fate.

Marge Piercy argues in the *Washington Post Book World,* though, that "in *Emmeline,* Judith Rossner has taken on a plot of highly improbable melodrama and come so close to making it believable that the part we cannot swallow scarcely bothers our enjoyment." Piercy considers Emmeline "a fully realized character in her naivete, her courage, her failing piety, her stubborn will, her devotion to her mother and her desperate loneliness." And "only because Emmeline is well drawn and because we identify with her determination to survive difficulties and save her family, we are able to accept a story that is archaic and sensational," adds Piercy. As Susan Fromberg Schaeffer indicates in the *Chicago Tribune Book World,* "this is a novel of rare knowledge and great power, masterfully told, and its last lines descend on the reader with a great cosmic chill. *Emmeline* does what all great novels should do." The book "is built to last," says Clemons, "and its muted ending has the power to haunt our imagination."

Rossner's next novel, *August,* compares the life circumstances of the teenage Dawn Henley to those of her analyst, Lulu Shinfeld—a plot that bears as much resemblance to a real psychoanalysis as a novel does to real life, the author states in the book's preface.

Rossner also pronounced the tale more humorous than her previous novels in a *Los Angeles Times* interview with Mary Schnack. Rossner told *CA* that the idea for the book originated with her readings of Sigmund Freud's case studies and at first involved only Lulu and her affair with one of the characters from *Nine Months in the Life of an Old Maid.* After becoming bored with the manuscript, Rossner began writing about Dawn, Lulu's teenage client. "It was quite extraordinary. It was as though she'd been there all along and I just didn't know it. At that point I began writing several pages a day, or more. It was an astonishment to me," Rossner told *CA.*

After her mother commits suicide and her gay father drowns in a boating accident, Dawn is taken in by her lesbian aunt and her lover, who eventually "divorce." Dawn enters psychoanalysis with Lulu but fears abandonment each August when Lulu goes on vacation. Dawn's psychoanalysis is contrasted with Lulu's own imperfect life, which Dawn craves to know more about.

William A. Henry III of *Time* explains that the novel's "title refers to the month when, in Rossner's flippant vision, all the analysts go on vacation leaving their patients to fret or go crazy. . . . *August* is also a kind of wish fulfillment for patients who want to be the only person in the doctor's life yet long to find out where the analyst goes when the 50-minute-hour is over." *Washington Post Book World* reviewer Suzanne Freeman reports that "throughout the novel, Rossner allows us to shift focus from patient's story to doctor's story and back again. Over the course of five years, we follow the progress of Dawn's therapy and the interludes—Augusts, Christmas vacations—we tune back into Lulu Shinefeld's personal life." In *August,* Freeman says, "Lulu Shinefeld slips into a life that is almost as moving and messy as anything Dawn Henley has to offer."

Together the lives of the two main characters comprise a compelling narrative, according to reviewers. Freeman writes that "the unraveling of Dawn's secrets and the ups and downs of Lulu's life are as absorbing as a good mystery story." Lulu Shinefeld "is a remarkably well-drawn character," Walter Kendrick relates in the *New York Times Book Review,* while Diane M. Ross points out in the *Chicago Tribune Book World* that "being female is itself a major subject of *August.* As in her earlier novels, Judith Rossner here explores the complicated emotional lives of women."

Some reviewers proclaimed *August* Rossner's most mature work. It "turns out to be more careful and more contemplative than any of [Rossner's] earlier works—and, ultimately, far more satisfying," Freeman relates. Kendrick points out that *August* "is absolutely true to its own design; it's a model of rigor and restraint, even when it must take risks." The book is about "pain and maturity," concludes Adam Mars Jones in the *Times Literary Supplement.* "It also proposes affluence and self-obsession as necessary elements of modern life."

Rossner's next novel, *His Little Women,* alludes to Louisa May Alcott's classic *Little Women* in that its central theme concerns an absent father. Another prominent similarity is Rossner's main character, Louisa, a writer who grapples with the age-old tendency to pilfer from the lives of those around her. Narrated by the level-headed Nell, *His Little Women* revolves around the dashing, movie-mogul Sam Pearlstein, whose adoring daughters are devastated by his tendency to abandon those who depend on him. Louisa's latest successful novel utilizes the trials and tribulations of many of her family members, most of whom, in typical Hollywood fashion, do not mind the publicity. A minor relative, however, takes issue with Louisa's disguised depiction of him as a slimy villain and files a libel suit which parlays the book's action into a courtroom drama. Rossner's little women, unlike their literary predecessors, suffer in varying degrees from their father's abandonment. As families blend and mix and half-sisters born of Sam's three wives discover each other, all are affected by their relationship with their father. Louisa, the novelist, is foul-mouthed and strong-willed. Nell, the narrator and lawyer by profession, distances herself from the action and tells the story with an eye toward rationalization.

Michiko Kakutani of the *New York Times* admires Rossner's minor characters, calling them "wickedly funny and well observed," but contends that "the trial seems like a detour from the real subject of Ms. Rossner's novel—namely, the Pearlstein family, Sam's relationship with his four daughters, and their relationships with one another." Cyra McFadden of the *New York Times Book Review* compares the novel to Thackeray's *Vanity Fair,* noting the "crowded and wide-ranging" cast of characters, and compliments Rossner's rejection of literary minimalism: "She doesn't shrink from narrative complexity. Obsessions fascinate her, as do the extremes of behavior." True to the author's style, the tension in the book revolves around the characters' interactions and acceptance of one another, which manifests itself in Louisa's declaration that "the fiction writer always seems to be breaking some contract with reality her friends and relations were sure she'd signed."

McFadden notes that the novel germinated with Rossner's re-reading of *Little Women* and her realization that "the father's absence was the key to the amity among the sisters." Another central idea of Rossner's novel is that truth is relative: "when Nell sets out to tell the truth and nothing but the truth, she can't. Memory is too self-serving. . . . All reinvent their histories and turn them into press releases." Ruth Reichl of the *New York Times Book Review* interprets the novel as "skewered Hollywood with a devastating description of its power-hungry executives, angst-ridden women and failed families." Concentrating on the effect of an absent father upon his four daughters, Joyce Slater states in *Chicago Tribune Book World* that Sam Pearlstein deserts his three wives and four children simply because he does not need them as they need him. The trial, therefore, serves as an opportunity "to explore the issues of truth and responsibility, both in terms of the accountability of family members to one another and the novelist's accountability to her characters." Slater concludes, alluding to Rossner's best-known novel, that "the real threat may not be the dark stranger lurking at the end of the bar. For some women, the most dangerous man they will ever meet is the one they called 'Daddy.'"

Returning to the familiar theme of conflicting expectations, particularly those concerning motherhood, marriage, and career, Rossner's next novel, *Olivia, or, The Weight of the Past,* utilizes the culinary arts as a backdrop to the events in Caroline's life and that of her daughter, Olivia. Feeling ignored by her successful, academic parents, the teenaged Caroline follows the family cook to Italy and soon the college drop-out is married to the roving Angelo Ferrante and running a successful trattoria in Rome. After raising their daughter and toiling for years in the restaurant's kitchen, Caroline is no longer able to tolerate her womanizing husband and returns to New York, leaving the obstinate 12-year-old Olivia behind with the father she adores.

Within two years, Caroline's reinvented life includes a Manhattan loft, a successful cable cooking show, and a steamy romance with a neighboring doctor. Enter Olivia, who escapes her father's new wife for New York and an uneasy reconciliation with her mother. "Few writers are better than Judith Rossner

at describing the agonized ties between mothers and daughters," writes Reichl, who concludes that the book's best scenes are those in which "Caroline and Olivia claw their way to an accommodation." Elaine Kendall of the *Los Angeles Times* concurs, further explaining that "Olivia . . . resists and defies her mother's best efforts. Instead of diminishing, her resentment grows and festers."

Reviewers were split on the success of the novel's gastronomical motif. Reichl laments that "although she treats her classes to long lectures on the history of food, there is not a single scene where she is delighted by the sheer joy of chopping and mixing, so it all feels flat." Conversely, Kendall proclaims that "the intimate, complex connections between food and emotion [is] a theme that allows far more flexibility than you might expect." And a *Kirkus Reviews* writer states that "the importance of traditional meals" sufficiently propels the action.

Rossner continues to live and write in New York City and is a member of the Writers' Room, a place in New York City's Greenwich Village where writers congregate to work and discuss their projects. When asked about the effect of the city upon her writing, Rossner told *CA* that "My ideal is not to sit at a window looking at cows in the pasture. I think that the chaos and the energy bring some rewards, although I don't know that they fuel the work."

BIOGRAPHICAL/CRITICAL SOURCES:

BOOKS

Authors in the News, Volume 2, Gale (Detroit), 1976.
Contemporary Literary Criticism, Gale, Volume 6, 1976, Volume 9, 1978, Volume 29, 1984.
Dictionary of Literary Biography, Volume 6: *American Novelists since World War II,* Gale, 1980.

PERIODICALS

Atlantic, September, 1975.
Chicago Tribune Book World, September 21, 1980; September 11, 1983; May 27, 1990, p. 5.
Detroit Free Press, April 25, 1976.
Detroit News, October 26, 1980; August 10, 1983; August 28, 1983.
Harper's, September, 1983.
Hudson Review, winter, 1975-76.
Kirkus Reviews, May 15, 1994, p. 658.

Los Angeles Times, October 5, 1980; August 21, 1983; September 7, 1983; September 9, 1994, p. 6.

Los Angeles Times Book Review, August 21, 1983.

Ms., June, 1976; September, 1980.

Nation, May 29, 1976.

New Leader, October 6, 1980.

New Republic, October 11, 1980.

Newsweek, May 19, 1975; September 19, 1977; September 29, 1980; August 1, 1983.

New Yorker, July 14, 1975; October 3, 1977.

New York Times, December 22, 1972; May 21, 1975; September 12, 1977; September 25, 1980; July 21, 1983; April 13, 1990, p. C28.

New York Times Book Review, October 26, 1969; July 30, 1972; June 8, 1975; September 18, 1977; September 14, 1980; July 24, 1983; April 22, 1990, p. 11; August 21, 1994, p. 15.

Publishers Weekly, August 22, 1980.

Saturday Review, November 22, 1969; August 5, 1972; October 1, 1977; September, 1980; October, 1983.

Spectator, November 12, 1977.

Time, July 7, 1975; August 22, 1983.

Times (London), January 8, 1981.

Times Literary Supplement, September 12, 1975; March 18, 1977; November 4, 1977; January 25, 1981; November 4, 1983.

Village Voice, September 24-30, 1980; September 6, 1983.

Washington Post, June 1, 1975; September 14, 1980; August 1, 1983.

Washington Post Book World, September 14, 1980; August 14, 1983; September 19, 1994, p. 8.

Washington Star, July 8, 1975.*

*   *   *

ROTH, John K(ing)   1940-

PERSONAL: Born September 3, 1940, in Grand Haven, MI; son of Josiah V. (a Presbyterian minister) and Doris (King) Roth; married Evelyn Austin, June 25, 1964; children: Andrew Lee, Sarah Austin. *Education:* Pomona College, B.A. (magna cum laude), 1962; Yale University, attended Divinity School, 1962-63, M.A., 1965, Ph.D., 1966.

ADDRESSES: Home—1648 Kenyon Pl., Claremont, CA 91711. *Office*—Claremont McKenna College, 850 Columbia Ave., Claremont, CA 91711.

CAREER: Claremont McKenna College, Claremont, CA, assistant professor, 1966-71, associate professor, 1971-76, Russell K. Pitzer Professor of Philosophy, 1976—. Graves fellow in humanities, Harvard University, 1970-71; visiting professor of philosophy, Franklin College, Lugano, Switzerland, spring, 1973; Fulbright lecturer in American studies, University of Innsbruck, 1973-74; fellow, National Humanities Institute, Yale University, 1976-77; visiting professor of philosophy, Doshiva University, 1981-82; fellow, Japan-U.S. Friendship Commission, 1981-83; visiting professor of Holocaust studies, University of Haifa, 1982.

MEMBER: American Academy of Religion, American Philosophical Association, American Studies Association, U.S. Holocaust Memorial Council, Phi Beta Kappa.

AWARDS, HONORS: Named U.S. National Professor of the Year, Council for the Advancement and support of Education and the Carnegie Foundation for the Advancement of Teaching, 1988; L.H.D., Indiana University, 1990; Fulbright scholar in American Studies, Royal Norwegian Ministry of Education, Research and Church Affairs, Oslo, Norway, 1995-96.

WRITINGS:

Freedom and the Moral Life: The Ethics of William James, Westminster (Philadelphia, PA), 1969.

Problems of the Philosophy of Religion, Chandler Publishing (Novato, CA), 1971.

(With Frederick Sontag) *The American Religious Experience,* Harper (New York City), 1972.

American Dreams, Chandler & Sharp (Novato, CA), 1976.

(With Sontag) *God and America's Future,* Consortium (Wilmington, NC), 1977.

A Consuming Fire, John Knox, 1979.

(With Robert H. Fossum) *The American Dream,* British Association for American Studies (Brighton, England), 1981.

(With Richard L. Rubenstein) *Approaches to Auschwitz,* John Knox, 1987.

(With Sontag) *The Questions of Philosophy,* Wadsworth Publishing (Belmont, CA), 1988.

Ethics, Salem Press (Englewood Cliffs, NJ), 1991.

EDITOR

(And author of introduction) *The Moral Philosophy of William James,* Crowell (New York City), 1969.

(And author of introduction) *The Philosophy of Josiah Royce,* Crowell, 1971.

(And author of introduction) *The Moral Equivalent of War and Other Essays,* Harper Torchbooks (New York City), 1971.

(With Sontag) *The Defense of God,* Paragon (Fern Park, FL), 1985.

(With Robert C. Whittemore) *Ideology and American Experience,* Washington Institute for Values in Public Policy (Washington, DC), 1986.

(With Fossum) *American Ground,* Paragon, 1988.

(With Rosenstein) *The Politics of Latin American Liberation Theology,* Washington Institute for Values in Public Policy, 1988.

(With Michael Berenbaum) *Holocaust,* Paragon, 1989.

(With Carol Rittner) *Memory Offended,* Praeger (New York City), 1991.

(With Creighton Pedem) *Rights, Justice, and Community,* Edwin Mellen (Lewiston, NY), 1992.

(With Rittner) *Different Voices,* Paragon, 1993.

American Diversity, American Identity, Henry Holt (New York City), 1995.

*   *   *

ROTHENBERG, Albert 1930-

PERSONAL: Born June 2, 1930, in New York, NY; son of Gabriel (in business) and Rose (Goldberg) Rothenberg; married Elissa Isaacson, September 6, 1953 (divorced, 1969); married Julia C. Johnson (an educational psychologist), June 28, 1970; children: (first marriage) Michael, Mora Ruth, Rina Susannah. *Education:* Harvard University, A.B., 1952; Tufts University, M.D., 1956. *Avocational interests:* Reading, tennis, chess, painting, snorkeling, swimming, walking, travel.

ADDRESSES: Home—52 Pine Ridge Rd., Box 236, Canaan, NY 12029. *Office*—Chatham, NY; Great Barrington, MA; Cambridge Hospital, Cambridge, MA.

CAREER: Pennsylvania Hospital, Philadelphia, intern, 1956-57; Yale University, School of Medicine, New Haven, CT, resident in psychiatry, 1957-60, instructor, 1960-61, 1963-64, assistant professor, 1964-68, associate professor, 1968-74, clinical professor of psychiatry, 1974-84, assistant medical director of Yale Psychiatric Institute, 1964-65, senior staff, Yale Psychiatric Institute, 1964-75, attending

psychiatrist at Yale New Haven Medical Center, 1964-84; University of Connecticut, Farmington, professor of psychiatry, 1975-79; Austen Riggs Center, Stockbridge, MA, director of research, 1979-94. Senior attending physician at Puerto Rico Institute of Psychiatry, 1961-63. Visiting professor at Pennsylvania State University, 1971, Yale University, American Studies Department, 1975-78. *Military service:* U.S. Army, 1961-63; became captain.

MEMBER: American Psychiatric Association (life fellow), American Society for Aesthetics, American Association for the Advancement of Science, Sigma Xi.

AWARDS, HONORS: Research scientist career development program awards from National Institutes of Health, 1964, 1969; Guggenheim fellowship, 1974-75; American College of Psychoanalysts fellow, 1981; Center for Advanced Study in the Behavioral Sciences fellow, 1986-87; Golestan Foundation Award in Psychiatry, 1991, 1992; Netherlands Institute for Advanced Study in the Humanities and Social Sciences, fellow, 1992-93.

WRITINGS:

Comprehensive Guide to Creative Writing Programs in American Colleges and Universities, National Council of Teachers of English (Urbana, IL), 1970.

(With B. R. Greenberg) *The Index of Scientific Writings on Creativity: Creative Men and Women,* Archon, 1974.

The Index of Scientific Writings on Creativity: General, 1566-1974, Archon, 1976.

(With C. R. Hausman) *The Creativity Question,* Duke University Press (Durham, NC), 1976.

The Emerging Goddess: The Creative Process in Art, Science, and Other Fields, University of Chicago Press (Chicago, IL), 1979.

The Creative Process of Psychotherapy, Norton (New York City), 1987.

(Editor) *Adolescence: Psychopathology, Normality, and Creativity,* Saunders (Philadelphia, PA), 1990.

Creativity and Madness: New Findings and Old Stereotypes, Johns Hopkins University Press (Baltimore, MD), 1990.

Contributor to books, including *Explorations in Phenomenology,* edited by D. Carr and E. Casey, Nijhoff, 1973; *Nepalese Short Stories,* edited by V. K. Kar, Gallery Press (Essex, CT), 1975;

Psychologie der Literatur, edited by R. Langner, Weinheim, Psychologie Verlags Union, 1986; *The KeKule Riddle: A Challenge for Chemists and Psychologists,* edited by J. W. Wotiz, Cache River Press, 1992; and *Empirical Perspectives on Object Relations Theory,* edited by J. M. Masling and R. R. Bornstein, American Psychological Association, 1994.

Also contributor to education, philosophy, psychology, medical journals, and periodicals including *Esquire, Psychology Today,* and *Saturday Review.* Member of editorial board, *Creativity Research Journal* and *Journal of Poetry Therapy.* Editorial consultant to *American Journal of Psychiatry, Archives of General Psychiatry, Journal of the American Medical Association, Journal of Nervous and Mental Disease, Journal of Speculative Philosophy,* and *Psychological Reports.*

WORK IN PROGRESS: Scientific Creativity, for Johns Hopkins University Press.

SIDELIGHTS: "I continue to study the creative process," Albert Rothenberg told *CA,* "in the arts, in psychotherapy, and in science. I am gratified about my discoveries and the new knowledge unveiled. Recently, I have been writing a novel, a personal undertaking that is the fulfillment of a long-held goal. I enjoy the writing and sometimes I learn something about my own and others' way of thinking."

*   *   *

ROUNTREE, Owen
   See KRAUZER, Steven M(ark)

*   *   *

ROZMAN, Gilbert Friedell   1943-

PERSONAL: Born February 18, 1943, in Minneapolis, MN; son of David (an accountant) and Celia (a teacher; maiden name, Friedell) Rozman; married Masha Dwosh (a lawyer), June 25, 1968; children: Thea Dwosh, Noah Dwosh. *Education:* Carleton College, B.A., 1965; Princeton University, Ph.D., 1971.

ADDRESSES: Office—Princeton University, 2-N-2 Green Hall, Princeton, NJ 08540.

CAREER: Princeton University, Princeton, NJ, assistant professor, 1970-75, associate professor, 1975-79, professor of sociology, 1979—, Musgrave Professor of Sociology, 1992—, bicentennial preceptor, 1972-75, director, Council on Regional Studies, chairperson, Committee on International Emergence in Undergraduate Education, director, International Studies Program. Member of U.S./U.S.S.R. Binational Commission on Humanities and Social Sciences, 1978-85.

MEMBER: American Sociological Association, American Association for the Advancement of Slavic Studies, Association for Asian Studies.

AWARDS, HONORS: Woodrow Wilson fellow, 1965-66; Foreign Area fellow, 1968-69; grants from National Science Foundation, 1976-79, National Endowment for the Humanities, 1976-79, Social Science Research Council, 1980, 1989, National Council on East European and Soviet Research, 1981-83, 1986-88, and Committee on Scholarly Communication with the People's Republic of China, 1984-85, 1992-95; Guggenheim fellow, 1979-80; Chiang Ching-kuo award, American Council of Learned Societies, 1992-93; U. S. Institute of Peace, 1994-96.

WRITINGS:

Urban Networks in Ch'ing China and Tokugawa Japan, Princeton University Press (Princeton, NJ), 1973.

(With C. E. Black and others) *The Modernization of Japan and Russia,* Free Press (New York City), 1975.

Urban Networks in Russia, 1750-1800, and Premodern Periodization, Princeton University Press, 1976.

Population and Marketing Settlements in Ch'ing China, Cambridge University Press (New York City), 1982.

A Mirror for Socialism: Soviet Criticisms of China, Princeton University Press, 1985.

The Chinese Debate about Soviet Socialism, 1978-85, Princeton University Press, 1987.

Japan's Response to the Gorbachev Era: A Rising Superpower Views a Declining One, Princeton University Press, 1992.

EDITOR

The Modernization of China, Free Press, 1981.

Soviet Studies of China: Assessments of Recent Scholarship, Michigan Publications on China, 1984.

(With Marius B. Jansen) *Japan in Transition: From Tukugawa to Meiji,* Princeton University Press, 1986.

The East Asian Region: Confucian Heritage and Its Modern Adaptation, Princeton University Press, 1991.

Dismantling Communism: Common Causes and Regional Variations, Johns Hopkins Press (Baltimore, MD), 1992.

WORK IN PROGRESS: Editing *Great Power Identities and Regionalism in Northeast Asia* and *The Collapse of Communism and Social Science Theory.*

SIDELIGHTS: Gilbert Friedell Rozman commented: "I chose to approach international affairs as a sociologist able to use the languages of the major countries, concerned about the histories of their peoples, and eager to apply the comparative method of analysis. I often advise students with an interest in international affairs to concentrate on language skills early and to identify an unconventional specialization that is worth pursuing.

"I became interested in foreign areas in high school, when I was a winner in the *Minneapolis Star*'s world affairs contest. In college and graduate school I chose to study societies that were likely to be of greatest importance during the decades ahead. Because scholarship aid was available, I could attend intensive language courses every summer and accelerate my studies. Increasingly, I realized that my background on three countries gave me unique opportunities to study major aspects of social change, including premodern urbanization, modernization, and the impact of communism. In addition, I found that there is a need to examine how people in one country view another country and its people. This new field might be called mutual perceptions among the great powers."

BIOGRAPHICAL/CRITICAL SOURCES:

PERIODICALS

Times Literary Supplement, June 27, 1986.

RUTHVEN, K(enneth) K(nowles) 1936-

PERSONAL: First syllable of surname pronounced "roth"; born May 26, 1936, in Bradford, England; son of Thomas Knowles (a mining deputy) and Freda (Bennett) Ruthven; married Rachel Mary Bainbridge (a secondary school teacher), December 26, 1960; children: Simon, Guy, Patrick. *Education:* University of Manchester, B.A. (honors), 1958, M.A., 1959, Ph.D., 1965. *Politics:* None. *Religion:* None.

ADDRESSES: *Office*—English Department, University of Melbourne, Parkville, Victoria 3052, Australia.

CAREER: University of Canterbury, Christchurch, New Zealand, assistant lecturer, 1961-64, lecturer, 1965-69, senior lecturer, 1969-72, professor of English, 1972-79; University of Adelaide, Adelaide, Australia, professor of English, 1980-85; University of Melbourne, Parkville, Australia, professor of English, 1985—.

MEMBER: Australian Academy of the Humanities (fellow).

WRITINGS:

The Conceit, Methuen (New York City), 1969.

A Guide to Ezra Pound's Personae (1926), University of California Press (Santa Cruz, CA), 1969.

Myth, Methuen, 1976.

Critical Assumptions, Cambridge University Press (New York City), 1979.

Feminist Literary Studies: An Introduction, Cambridge University Press, 1984.

Ezra Pound as Literary Critic, Routledge (London, England), 1990.

Nuclear Criticism, Melbourne University Press (Parkville, Victoria, Australia), 1993.

Contributor to professional journals. General editor of the "Interpretations" series, Melbourne University Press, 1993—. Editor of the *Southern Review* (Adelaide, Australia), 1991-95.

WORK IN PROGRESS: A book on literary forgeries.

BIOGRAPHICAL/CRITICAL SOURCES:

PERIODICALS

Times Literary Supplement, February 22, 1980.

S

SANTOS, Helen
See GRIFFITHS, Helen

*   *   *

SARTOR, Margaret   1959-

PERSONAL: Born August 12, 1959, in Monroe, LA; daughter of Fred Williams (a surgeon) and Tommie Sue (a painter; maiden name, Eaves) Sartor; married Alex Harris (a photographer and professor), December 18, 1982. *Education:* Attended Trinity University, 1977-78, and Southern Methodist University, Paris, France, 1979; University of North Carolina at Chapel Hill, B.A., 1981; graduate study at North Carolina State University, 1983-85.

ADDRESSES: Home—4604 Erwin Rd., Durham, NC 27705; Box 1, El Valle Route, Chamisal, NM 87521. *Office*—Center for Documentary Studies, Duke University, 1317 West Pettigrew Street, Durham, NC 27705.

CAREER: University of North Carolina Press, Chapel Hill, design and production, 1981-82; John Ulmstead Hospital, Butner, NC, special education photography teacher at Children's Psychiatric Institute, 1982-83; Carnegie Corp. of New York City, graphic designer, 1985-86; North Carolina State University, Raleigh, lecturer in photography, 1987—; Duke University, Durham, NC, research associate and lecturer, 1992—, editorial advisor for *DoubleTake* magazine, 1994—. Graphic designer for Duke University, 1982—; guest curator of Interna-

tional Center of Photography, 1983, 1986; photographs exhibited at many shows throughout the United States, 1980—; curator or designer of photographic exhibitions, 1984—.

AWARDS, HONORS: President's Scholar, Trinity University, San Antonio, TX, 1979; design award, *Print Magazine,* 1984; design and production excellence, first place for book design, Rocky Mountain Publishers Association, 1991, for *River of Traps;* North Carolina Visual Arts project grant, 1993.

WRITINGS:

(With husband, Alex Harris) *Gertrude Blom: Bearing Witness,* University of North Carolina Press (Chapel Hill), 1983.
(Editor) *South Africa: The Cordoned Heart,* Norton (New York City), 1986.
(Editor and designer) *Their Eyes Meeting the World: The Drawings and Paintings of Children,* Houghton (Boston), 1992.

OTHER

Also designer and consulting editor for other books, including *River of Traps* by William deBuys and Alex Harris, University of New Mexico Press, 1990, and *Beyond the Barricades: Popular Resistance in South Africa,* Aperture, 1989. Contributor of articles, reviews, poems, and photographs to many publications, including *The New York Times, Carolina Quarterly, Windhover, Cellar Door, DoubleTake,* and *Aperture.*

WORK IN PROGRESS: A photographic documentary of Monroe, Louisiana.

SIDELIGHTS: Margaret Sartor told *CA:* "I work primarily in the field of documentary photography as a teacher, editor, photographer, and designer. In all these roles I feel my work is an attempt to define and refine the concepts and ideas one uses to describe the documentary approach."

*   *   *

SEARLE, John R(ogers)   1932-

PERSONAL: Born July 31, 1932, in Denver, CO; son of George W. (an electrical engineer) and Hester (a physician; maiden name, Beck) Searle; married Dagmar Carboch (a lawyer), December 24, 1959; children: Thomas R., Mark R. *Education:* Attended University of Wisconsin, 1949-52; Oxford University, B.A. (with first class honors), 1955, M.A. and D.Phil., 1959.

ADDRESSES: Home—1900 Yosemite Rd., Berkeley, CA 94707. *Office*—Department of Philosophy, University of California, Berkeley, CA 94720.

CAREER: Oxford University, Christ Church, Oxford, England, lecturer in philosophy, 1956-59; University of California, Berkeley, assistant professor, 1959-64, associate professor, 1964-67, professor of philosophy, 1967—, special assistant to the chancellor, 1965-67, chair of philosophy department, 1973-75. Visiting professor at numerous universities in the United States and Europe, including, University of Michigan, 1961-62, University of Washington, Seattle, 1963, Brasenose College, Oxford, 1967-68, State University of New York at Buffalo, 1971, University of Oslo, 1971, University of Colorado, 1980, University of Frankfurt-am-Main, summer, 1985, Rutgers University, 1986, and University of Venice, 1986; member of visiting committee for linguistics and philosophy, Massachusetts Institute of Technology, 1971-77. Regular panelist, 1970-77, and moderator, 1972-74, of *World Press* weekly program for National Educational Television Network; secretary treasurer, Hanzell Vineyards Ltd., 1975-94.

MEMBER: American Philosophical Association, American Council of Education, American Council of Learned Societies (member of board of directors, 1979-87), American Academy of Arts and Sciences, National Humanities Center (member of board of trustees, 1976-90), American Civil Liberties Union (member of board of directors of California chapter, 1968-71), Aristotelian Society (England), Council on Philosophical Studies (member of board of directors, 1975-80), National Endowment for the Humanities (member of council, 1991—).

AWARDS, HONORS: Rhodes scholar at Oxford University; American Council of Learned Societies research grant, 1963-64; Guggenheim fellowship, 1975-76; honorary doctorate degrees from Adelphi University, 1993, and University of Wisconsin—Madison, 1994.

WRITINGS:

Speech Acts: An Essay in the Philosophy of Language, Cambridge University Press (New York City), 1969, reprinted, 1985.
The Campus War: A Sympathetic Look at the University in Agony, World Publications, 1971.
(Editor and author of introduction) *The Philosophy of Language,* Oxford University Press (New York City), 1971.
Expression and Meaning: Studies in the Theory of Speech Acts, Cambridge University Press, 1979.
(Editor with Ferenc Kiefer and Manfred Bierwisch) *Speech Act Theory and Pragmatics,* D. Reidel, 1980.
Intentionality: An Essay in the Philosophy of Mind, Cambridge University Press, 1983.
Minds, Brains, and Science, BBC Publications, 1984, Harvard University Press (Cambridge, MA), 1985.
(With Daniel Vanderveken) *Foundations of Illocutionary Logic,* Cambridge University Press, 1985.
The Rediscovery of the Mind, MIT Press (Cambridge, MA), 1992.
The Construction of Social Reality, Free Press (New York City), 1995.

Contributor of articles to periodicals. Searle's books have been translated into twenty foreign languages.

BIOGRAPHICAL/CRITICAL SOURCES:

BOOKS

Lepore, E. and R. van Glick, editors, *John Searle and His Critics,* Blackwell (Boston), 1991.

Nolte, Reinhard B., *Einfuhrung in die Sprech-aktttheorie John R. Searle,* Verlag Karl Alber, 1978.

Parret, H. and J. Vershueren, editors, *(On) Searle on Conversation,* John Benjamins (Philadelphia), 1992.

Schaeter, Erich, *Grenzen der kuenstlieher Intelligenz, John R. Searles Philosophie des Geistes,* Verlag W. Kohlhammer, 1994.

Thinkers of the Twentieth Century: A Biographical, Bibliographical and Critical Dictionary, Gale (Detroit), 1983.

PERIODICALS

Best Sellers, June 15, 1971.
Frankfurter Allgemeine Zeitung, July 31, 1992.
Liberation, May 25, 1995.
London Review of Books, July 20, 1995.
New York Review of Books, March 4, 1993.
New York Times Book Review, May 12, 1985.
Spectator, July 12, 1969.
Times Literary Supplement, March 7, 1980; March 2, 1984; December 14, 1984.
Village Voice, June 6, 1995.
Wall Street Journal, July 24, 1995.

*   *   *

SEED, Cecile Eugenie   1930-
(Jenny Seed)

PERSONAL: Born May 18, 1930, in Cape Town, South Africa; daughter of Ivan Washington (a draftsman) and Bessie (Dickerson) Booysen; married Edward Robert Seed (a railway employee), October 30, 1953; children: Anne, Dick, Alan, Robbie. *Religion:* Christian. *Avocational interests:* Tennis, bowling, reading, entertaining, church work.

ADDRESSES: Home—10 Pioneer Cres., Northdene, Kwa Zulu-Natal, Natal, 4093, South Africa.

CAREER: Roads Department, Town Planning Department, Pietarmaritzburg, South Africa, draftsman, 1947-53. Freelance writer, 1965—.

AWARDS, HONORS: M. E. R. Award for Children's Literature in South Africa, 1987, for *Place among the Stones.*

WRITINGS:

FICTION; UNDER PSEUDONYM JENNY SEED

The Dancing Mule, illustrated by Joan Sirr, Nelson, 1964.

The Always-Late Train, illustrated by Pieter de Weerdt, Nasionale Boekhandel, 1965.

Small House, Big Garden, illustrated by Lynette Hemmant, Hamish Hamilton (London), 1965.

Peter the Gardener, illustrated by Mary Russon, Hamish Hamilton, 1966.

Tombi's Song, illustrated by Dugald MacDougall, Hamish Hamilton, 1966, published as *Ntombi's Song,* illustrated by Anno Berry, Beacon Press (Boston), 1989.

To the Rescue, illustrated by Constance Marshall, Hamish Hamilton, 1966.

Stop Those Children!, illustrated by Russon, Hamish Hamilton, 1966.

Timothy and Tinker, illustrated by Hemmant, Hamish Hamilton, 1967.

The River Man, illustrated by MacDougall, Hamish Hamilton, 1968.

The Voice of the Great Elephant, illustrated by Trevor Stubley, Hamish Hamilton, 1968, Pantheon (New York City), 1969.

Canvas City, illustrated by Hemmant, Hamish Hamilton, 1968.

The Red Dust Soldiers, illustrated by Andrew Sier, Heinemann (London), 1968.

Prince of the Bay, illustrated by Stubley, Hamish Hamilton, 1970, published as *Vengeance of the Zulu King,* Pantheon, 1971.

The Great Thirst, illustrated by Stubley, Hamish Hamilton, 1971, Bradbury (Scarsdale, NY), 1973.

The Broken Spear, illustrated by Stubley, Hamish Hamilton, 1972.

Warriors on the Hills, illustrated by Pat Ludlow, Abelard Schuman (New York City), 1975.

The Unknown Land, illustrated by Jael Jordan, Heinemann, 1976.

Strangers in the Land, illustrated by Stubley, Hamish Hamilton, 1977.

The Year One, illustrated by Susan Sansome, Hamish Hamilton, 1981.

The Policeman's Button, illustrated by Joy Pritchard, Human & Rousseau (South Africa), 1981.

Gold Dust, illustrated by Bill le Fever, Hamish Hamilton, 1982.

The New Fire, illustrated by Mario Sickle, Human & Rousseau, 1983.

The 59 Cats, illustrated by Alida Carpenter, Daan Retief, 1983.

The Shell, illustrated by Ann Walton, Daan Retief, 1983.

The Sad Cat, illustrated by Marlize Groenewald, Daan Retief, 1984.

The Karoo Hen, illustrated by A. Venter, Daan Retief, 1984.

The Disappearing Rabbit, illustrated by Walton, Daan Retief, 1984.

Big Boy's Work, illustrated by Paula Collins, Daan Retief, 1984.

The Spy Hill, illustrated by Nelda Vermaak, Human & Rousseau, 1984.

The Lost Prince, illustrated by Walton, Daan Retief, 1985.

Day of the Dragon, illustrated by Collins, Daan Retief, 1985.

Bouncy Lizzie, illustrated by Esther Boshoff, Daan Retief, 1985.

The Strange Blackbird, illustrated by Hettie Saaiman, Daan Retief, 1986.

The Far-Away Valley, illustrated by Joan Rankin, Daan Retief, 1987.

The Christmas Bells, illustrated by Saaiman, Daan Retief, 1987.

Place among the Stones, illustrated by Helmut Starcke, Tafelberg (South Africa), 1987.

The Station-Master's Hen, illustrated by Elizabeth de Villiers, Human & Rousseau, 1987.

The Corner Cat, illustrated by de Villiers, Human & Rousseau, 1987.

Hurry, Hurry, Sibusiso, illustrated by Cornelia Holm, Daan Retief, 1988.

The Big Pumpkin, illustrated by Berry, Human & Rousseau, 1989.

Stowaway to Nowhere, Tafelberg, 1990.

Nobody's Cat, illustrated by Alida Bothma, Human & Rousseau, 1990.

The Wind's Song, illustrated by Rankin, Daan Retief, 1991.

The Hungry People, Tafelberg, 1992.

Old Grandfather Mantis, Tafelberg, 1992.

A Time to Scatter Stones, Macmillan (New York City), 1993.

Eyes of a Toad, Macmillan, 1993.

Run, Run, White Hen, Oxford University Press (New York City), 1994.

Lucky Boy, Excellentia Publishers, 1995.

FOLKTALES; UNDER PSEUDONYM JENNY SEED

Kulumi the Brave: A Zulu Tale, illustrated by Stubley, Hamish Hamilton, World, 1970.

The Sly Green Lizard (Zulu folktale), illustrated by Graham Humphreys, Hamish Hamilton, 1973.

The Bushman's Dream: African Tales of the Creation, illustrated by Bernard Brett, Hamish Hamilton, 1974, Bradbury, 1975.

OTHER

Many of Seed's children's stories have been published in Canada, England, Zimbabwe, New Zealand, and Australia.

ADAPTATIONS: Some of Seed's children's stories have been adapted for broadcasts in countries around the world.

WORK IN PROGRESS: The Strange Large Egg, for Gecko Books.

SIDELIGHTS: Cecile Eugenie Seed, best known under the pseudonym Jenny Seed, writes of her native South Africa, either in stories set in modern times or in historical periods, and retells traditional African folktales as well. Her historical novels portray the experiences and emotions of young characters, both indigenous and immigrant, as they cope with historical situations and events. Seed once explained that she began to write such works for children around the time that she discovered that her own children's history homework was dull. Seed "began to delve into old books" in the Durban reference library and "the past became real" to her. She "found that [history] was not boring at all but tremendously exciting and filled with real and interesting people just waiting to be put into books."

Seed's 1971 book *The Great Thirst,* one of her many historical novels set in the nineteenth century, chronicles the development of a conflict between the Nama Hottentots and the Hereros in West Africa in the 1830s, focusing on a young boy's attempt to avenge his father's murder. A reviewer for *Bulletin of the Center for Children's Books* finds that the characters of *The Great Thirst* possess "vitality" and that "tribal cultures" in the book are "described with dignity." Paul Heins, a critic for *Horn Book*, concludes that Seed's "historical data," "well-sustained narrative," and the "spiritual development of the protagonist" are all "skillfully interwoven."

Seed's retelling of the folktale *Kulumi the Brave: A Zulu Tale* demonstrates her talent for adapting local myths and legends handed down orally for generations. In *Kulumi the Brave,* Kulumi's father, a king, believes that his young son will grow up to defeat and unseat him; he banishes the boy from his kingdom. Kulumi thrives despite this treatment—he bravely faces a dragon, learns to use magic, and successfully challenges an ogress in order to claim his bride. According to Gertrude B. Herman, writing in *Library Journal,* "the use of Zulu words is authentic."

Tombi's Song provides an example of Seed's original fiction for young children. This story follows a six-year-old Zulu girl as she goes to the store for her mother. Tombi tries to be brave, but her neighbors have frightened her with tales of a monster. Nervous, she spills the sugar she has bought at the store when a bus roars by and startles her. Tombi begins to sing a song her mother taught her, and then she begins to dance; in appreciation, a white woman gives Tombi a coin which enables the girl to buy another bag of sugar. Lillian N. Gerhardt asserts in *School Library Journal* that the story "promote[s] at least four attitudes that derogate Negro races." A critic for *Kirkus Reviews* observes that *Tombi's Song* "may be marred for many readers by a semblance of colonial paternalism." Addressing these criticisms, the 1989 version of the book, published as *Ntombi's Song,* features illustrations that present a black tourist couple giving the girl the coin. This revised version of the story moved a critic for *Publishers Weekly* to describe *Ntombi's Song* as "a warm and lovely story of a small triumph," and a critic for *Kirkus Reviews* finds it to be a "happy, long, well-knit story."

Seed once explained that she began writing stories for young people only after she had married and had four children of her own. Nevertheless, she recalled, she had always been interested in writing as a child

growing up in Cape Town, South Africa. "My father was a writer when he was younger, and as a small child I can remember rummaging through his cupboard drawers when I was allowed to play in his room, sorting through piles of his old manuscripts. And then, too, my mother was an excellent reader of stories. My sister Jewel and I would keep her busy with stories until her poor voice was reduced to a croak. It was not surprising then that from the age of about eight I too became interested in the written word and used to enjoy trying to compose little verses."

BIOGRAPHICAL/CRITICAL SOURCES:

PERIODICALS

Bulletin of the Center for Children's Books, May, 1975, p. 155.
Horn Book, April, 1975, pp. 154-55; December, 1975, p. 590.
Junior Bookshelf, February, 1983, p. 49.
Kirkus Reviews, March 1, 1968, p. 262; December 1, 1969, p. 1259; August 1, 1989, p. 1167.
Library Journal, July, 1968, p. 2731; May 15, 1971, p. 1806.
Publishers Weekly, July 28, 1989, p. 220.
School Library Journal, November, 1989, p. 94.
Times Literary Supplement, December 11, 1970, p. 1460; November 3, 1972, p. 1320; April 6, 1973, p. 383.

* * *

SEED, Jenny
See SEED, Cecile Eugenie

* * *

SHIELDS, Carol 1935-

PERSONAL: Born June 2, 1935, in Oak Park, IL; daughter of Robert E. and Inez (Selgren) Warner; married Donald Hugh Shields (a professor), July 20, 1957; children: John, Anne, Catherine, Margaret, Sara. *Education:* Hanover College, B.A., 1957;

University of Ottawa, M.A., 1975. *Politics:* New Democratic Party. *Religion:* Quaker.

ADDRESSES: Home—701-237 Wellington Crescent, Winnipeg, Manitoba, Canada, R3M OA1. *Agent*—Bella Pomer, 22 Shallmar Blvd., Toronto, Ontario, Canada.

CAREER: Canadian Slavonic Papers, Ottawa, Ontario, editorial assistant, 1972-74; freelance writer, 1974—, University of Manitoba, professor, 1980—.

AWARDS, HONORS: Winner of young writers' contest sponsored by Canadian Broadcasting Corp. (CBC), 1965; Canada Council grants, 1972, 1974, 1976; fiction prize from Canadian Authors Association, 1976, for *Small Ceremonies*; CBC Prize for Drama, 1983; National Magazine Award, 1984, 1985; Arthur Ellis Award, 1988; Marian Engel Award, 1990; received Governor General's Award for English-language fiction and National Book Critics Circle Award for fiction, 1994, and Pulitzer Prize for fiction, 1995, all for *The Stone Diaries*. Honorary doctorate, University of Ottawa, 1995.

MEMBER: Writers' Union of Canada, Writers Guild of Manitoba, PEN.

WRITINGS:

Others (poetry), Borealis Press, 1972.
Intersect (poetry), Borealis Press, 1974.
Susanna Moodie: Voice and Vision (criticism) Borealis Press, 1976.
Small Ceremonies (novel), McGraw, 1976.
The Box Garden (novel), McGraw, 1977.
Happenstance (novel), McGraw, 1980, Penguin (New York City), 1994.
A Fairly Conventional Woman (novel), Macmillan (Toronto, Canada), 1982.
Various Miracles (short stories), Stoddart (Don Mills, Canada), 1985, Penguin (New York City), 1989.
Swann: A Mystery (novel), General, 1987, Viking (New York City), 1989.
The Orange Fish (short stories), Random House (Toronto, Canada), 1989, Viking (New York City), 1990.
Departures and Arrivals, Blizzard, 1990.
(With Blanche Howard) *A Celibate Season* (novel), Coteau (Regina, Canada), 1991.
The Republic of Love (novel), Viking (New York City), 1992.

Coming to Canada (poetry), Carleton University Press (Ottawa, Canada), 1992.
The Stone Diaries (novel), Random House, 1993, Viking, 1994.
Thirteen Hands (drama), 1994.
Fashion Power Guilt (drama), 1995.

Author of *The View,* 1982, *Women Waiting,* 1983, and *Face Off,* 1987. Also author with D. Williamson of *Not Another Anniversary,* 1986.

SIDELIGHTS: Carol Shields has had two distinct phases in her writing career. Her first four novels, *Small Ceremonies* (1976), *The Box Garden* (1977), *Happenstance* (1980), and *A Fairly Conventional Woman* (1982), are portrayals of everyday life. Her heros and heroines struggle to define themselves and make human connections in their close relationships. Kathy O'Shaughnessy wrote in *Observer Review* that "*Small Ceremonies* is a novel of ideas: about privacy, knowledge of others, about how we perceive each other, and are perceived by others," while *London Review of Books* writer Peter Campbell, in a review of *Happenstance,* stated that "Shields writes well about decent people, and her resolutions are shrewder than those in the self-help books."

The next phase of Shields's career is marked by risk taking. With her first short story collection, *Various Miracles* (1985), Shields began to experiment more with form by using a variety of voices. She continued, however, to portray ordinary people in everyday situations. *Books Magazine* writer Andrea Mynard asserted that Shields's "robust realism is typical of the growing sorority of Canadian writers, including Margaret Atwood and Alice Munro, who have been gaining a strong reputation. . . . In her accessibly simple and lucid style, Carol intelligently grasps the minutiae of everyday life and illuminates the quirks of human nature. Her observations of contemporary dilemmas are brilliant."

In *Swann: A Mystery* (1987) Shields continued her experimentation by using four distinct voices to tell the story. In this novel she also developed a theme seen in her other work, that of the mysterious nature of art and creation. *Swann,* noted Danny Karlin in *London Review of Books,* "is a clever book, self-conscious about literature, fashionably preoccupied with questions of deconstruction, of the 'textuality' of identity, of the powers and powerlessness of language. This impression is confirmed by its confident and playful manipulation of different narrative modes." Some critics, however, castigated what they considered Shields's simple characterizations. *New York Times Book Review* writer Josh Robins noted that "the characters remain too one-dimensional, often to the point of caricature, to support sporadic attempts at psychological portraiture."

Shields took another risk by attempting the genre of the romance novel in *The Republic of Love* (1992), but she made the form her own by making her main characters wade through the coldness and problems of the twentieth century before reaching the happy ending. "Shields has created a sophisticated [romance] story," stated *Books in Canada* writer Rita Donovan. "And the 'happy ending,' so traditional to the romance novel, is here refurbished, updated, and—most happily—earned."

Shields's early novels were popular but not taken seriously by critics. Some critics argue that in the early part of her career Shields was underestimated as a stylist and her works were dismissed as being naturalistic. Critics generally praised Shields when she began experimenting more with form. Some of her risks were considered failures, however, as in the case of the last section of *Swann,* in which she attempted to bring all four voices together in a screenplay form.

The Stone Diaries (1993) is the fictional biography of Daisy Goodwill Flett, whose life spans eight decades and includes time spent in both Canada and the United States. Written in both the first and third person, the story begins with her birth in 1905 in rural Manitoba, Canada. Daisy's mother, extremely obese and unaware that she is pregnant, dies moments later. Unable to care for his daughter, Cuyler Goodwill convinces his neighbor Clarentine Flett to raise the child. Soon afterward, Clarentine leaves her husband and, taking Daisy with her, travels to Winnipeg, where she moves in with her son, Barker. Cuyler later takes Daisy to Bloomington, Indiana, where he has become a highly successful stonecarver. There, Daisy marries a wealthy young man who dies during their honeymoon. In 1936 she marries Barker, who has become renowned for his agricultural research, and resettles in Canada. In her role as wife and mother, Daisy appears quiet and content, but after her husband dies, she takes over a gardening column for the *Ottawa Recorder,* writing as Mrs. Greenthumb. Her joy—she finds the work incredibly meaningful and fulfilling—is short-lived however, as the editor decides to give the column to a staff writer despite Daisy's protests. She eventually recovers from the disappointment and lives the re-

mainder of her life in Sarasota, Florida, where she amuses herself playing bridge.

Critical reaction to *The Stone Diaries,* which won the Governor General's Award, the National Book Critics Circle Award, and the Pulitzer Prize, and was also short-listed for the Booker Prize, has been overwhelmingly favorable. Commentators have praised Shields for exploring such universal problems as loneliness and lost opportunities and for demonstrating that all lives are significant and important no matter how banal and confined they appear. Others have lauded the novel as a brilliant examination of the divergence between one's inner and outer self, and of the relations between fiction, biography, and autobiography. Allyson F. McGill wrote in *Belles Lettres,* "Shields and Daisy challenge us to review our lives, to try and see life honestly, even while 'their' act of authorship only reveals how impossible it is to see and speak objective truth," while *Canadian Forum* reviewer noted that "Shields demonstrates there are no small lives, no lives out of which significance does not shine. She makes us aware that banality, ultimately, is in the eye of the beholder."

While Shields has been a leading author in Canada for numerous years, she began to attract an international following in the early 1990s, particularly following the American publication of *The Stone Diaries.* Many of her early novels have recently been re-released in the United States and England to much popular and critical acclaim.

BIOGRAPHICAL/CRITICAL SOURCES:

PERIODICALS

Belles Lettres, spring, 1991, p. 56; summer, 1992, p. 20; fall, 1994, pp. 32, 34.

Books in Canada, October, 1979, pp. 29-30; May, 1981, pp. 31-2; November, 1982, pp. 18-9; October, 1985, pp. 16-7; October, 1987, pp. 15-6; May, 1989, p. 32; January/February, 1991, pp. 30-1; April, 1992, p. 40; February, 1993, pp. 51-2; September, 1993, pp. 34-5; October, 1993, pp. 32-3.

Books in Review, summer, 1989, pp. 158-60.

Books Magazine, November/December, 1994, p. 12.

Canadian Forum, July, 1975, pp. 36-8; November, 1993, pp. 44-5; January/February, 1994, pp. 44-5.

Canadian Literature, summer, 1989, pp. 158-60; autumn, 1991, pp. 149-50; spring, 1995.

Christian Science Monitor, December 7, 1990, pp. 10-1.

Kirkus Reviews, May 1, 1976, p. 559.

London Review of Books, September 27, 1990, pp. 20-1; March 21, 1991, p. 20; May 28, 1992, p. 22; September 9, 1993, p. 19.

Los Angeles Times Book Review, August 20, 1989, p. 2; April 17, 1994, pp. 3, 7.

Maclean's, October 11, 1993, p. 74.

New Statesman and Society, August 20, 1993, p. 40.

New York, March 7, 1994.

New York Times, July 17, 1989, p. C15; May 10, 1995.

New York Times Book Review, August 6, 1989, p. 11; August 12, 1990, p. 28; March 14, 1992; March 1, 1992, pp. 14, 16; March 27, 1994, pp. 3, 14.

Observer Review, February 19, 1995, p. 19.

Publishers Weekly, February 28, 1994.

Quill and Quire, January, 1981, p. 24; September, 1982, p. 59; August, 1985, p. 46; May, 1989, p. 20; August, 1993, p. 31.

Scrivener, Spring, 1995.

Spectator, March 21, 1992, pp. 35-6; September 24, 1994, p. 41.

Times Literary Supplement, August 27, 1993, p. 22; February 17, 1995.

West Coast Review, winter, 1988, pp. 38-56 and pp. 57-66.

Women's Review of Books, May, 1994, p. 20.

* * *

SHUCARD, Alan R(obert) 1935-

PERSONAL: Born December 2, 1935, in Brooklyn, NY; son of Jack Donald and Dorothy (Weber) Shucard; married Maureen O'Higgins (an executive secretary), June 23, 1962; children: Sarah Elizabeth. *Education:* Attended University of St. Andrews, 1955-56; Union College, Schenectady, A.B., 1957; University of Connecticut, M.A., 1963; University of Arizona, Ph.D., 1971. *Politics:* "Less naive than formerly." *Religion:* "Corned beef and egg roll worship."

ADDRESSES: Home—72 Woodfield Ct., Racine, WI 53402. *Office*—Department of English, University of Wisconsin—Parkside, Box 2000, Kenosha, WI 53141.

CAREER: Pratt & Whitney Aircraft, East Hartford, CT, technical writer, 1962-63; University of British Columbia, Vancouver, instructor in English, 1965-70; University of Wisconsin—Parkside, Kenosha, assistant professor, 1970-73, associate professor, 1973-86, professor of English, 1986—. Consultant to American Motors, National Endowment for the Humanities, and Holt, Rinehart, Winston, Inc. *Military service:* U.S. Army, Security Agency, 1959-62.

MEMBER: Modern Language Association of America, Society for Values in Higher Education (fellow), American Studies Association, Wisconsin Fellowship of Poets.

AWARDS, HONORS: Canada Council fellow, 1969; Wisconsin Alumni Research Foundation grant, 1972; Fulbright fellow, 1980-81.

WRITINGS:

The Gorgon Bag (poetry), Ladysmith Press, 1970.

The Louse on the Head of a Yawning Lord (poetry), Ladysmith Press, 1972.

Guidebook on Ernest Hemingway, University of Wisconsin Extension, 1978.

(Author of introduction) Carl Linder, *Shooting Baskets in a Dark Gymnasium,* Linwood (Charleston, SC), 1984.

Countee Cullen, Twayne (New York City), 1984.

American Poetry: The Puritans through Walt Whitman, Twayne, 1988.

(Co-author) *Modern American Poetry, 1865-1950,* Twayne, 1989.

Editor of "Poetry in English" section, "History of Poetry" series, Twayne. Contributing editor, *Contemporary Authors,* Gale (Detroit), 1988. Contributor to *Dictionary of Literary Biography, Contemporary Poets, Contemporary Novelists,* and *Writers in English.* Contributor to English and poetry journals, including *Arizona Quarterly, Hawk and Whipoorwill Recalled, Beloit Poetry Journal, Literary Review, Kansas Quarterly, English Quarterly, Library Journal,* and *American Literature.*

WORK IN PROGRESS: We Will Raise a Family, a book of poems for Mellen Poetry Press.

SIDELIGHTS: Alan R. Shucard told *CA:* "My critical writing is motivated by my wish to understand my culture and others as they are illuminated by their literatures; my poetry and fiction are motivated by a determination to survive."

*　　*　　*

SIMMONS, Marc　1937-

PERSONAL: Born May 15, 1937, in Dallas, TX; son of Julian Marion and Lois (Skielvig) Simmons. *Education:* University of Texas, B.A., 1958; University of New Mexico, M.A., 1961, Ph.D., 1965; University of Guanajuato, Spanish study; North Texas Farrier's School, certificate, 1969.

ADDRESSES: Home—P. O. Box 51, Cerrillos, NM 87010.

CAREER: Writer. Former ranch hand in Wyoming, horseshoer in Arizona, movie extra at Warner Brothers, and adobe maker and plasterer; University of New Mexico, Albuquerque, visiting assistant professor of history, 1965-66, 1967-68; St. John's College, Santa Fe, NM, director of Latin American area studies in Peace Corps training program, 1968; Colorado College, Colorado Springs, visiting professor of history, spring, 1975.

MEMBER: Authors Guild, Authors League of America, Western Writers of America, Spanish Royal Order of Isabel la Catolica, Phi Beta Kappa.

AWARDS, HONORS: Woodrow Wilson fellowship; Guggenheim fellowship.

WRITINGS:

(Translator from the Spanish and editor) *Border Comanches,* Stagecoach Press, 1967.
Turquoise and Six Guns: The Story of Cerrillos, Galisteo Press, 1968.
Spanish Government in New Mexico, University of New Mexico Press (Albuquerque), 1968.

Two Southwesterners: Charles Lummis and Amado Chaves, San Marcos Press, 1968.
Yesterday in Santa Fe: Episodes in a Turbulent History, San Marcos Press, 1969.
The Little Lion of the Southwest: A Life of Manuel Antonio Chaves, Swallow Press (Athens, OH), 1974.
Witchcraft in the Southwest: Spanish and Indian Supernaturalism on the Rio Grande, Northland Press (Flagstaff, AZ), 1974.
New Mexico: A Bicentennial History, Norton (New York City), 1977.
(Contributor) Alfonso Ortiz, editor, *Handbook of American Indians North of Mexico,* Smithsonian Institution Press (Washington, DC), 1979.
People of the Sun, University of New Mexico Press, 1979.
(With Frank Turley) *Southwestern Colonial Ironwork,* Museum of New Mexico Press (Santa Fe), 1980.
Albuquerque: A Narrative History, University of New Mexico Press, 1982.
Along the Santa Fe Trail, University of New Mexico Press, 1986.
Murder on the Santa Fe Trail, Texas Western Press (El Paso), 1987.
The Last Conquistador: Juan de Onate and the Settling of the Far Southwest, University of Oklahoma Press (Norman), 1991.
(With Joan Myers) *Santiago, Saint of Two Worlds,* University of New Mexico Press, 1991.
Treasure Trails of the Southwest, University of New Mexico Press, 1994.

Assisted in cataloging the Spanish archives of New Mexico for a guide published by the State Records Center. Contributor to *Encyclopedia Americana.* Contributor to periodicals, including *National Geographic, Journal of the West,* and *El Palacio.*

BIOGRAPHICAL/CRITICAL SOURCES:

PERIODICALS

American Historical Review, April, 1994, p. 636.
Book Talk (New Mexico), September, 1986.
Christian Science Monitor, February 11, 1980.
Kliatt Young Adult Paperback Book Guide, September, 1994, p. 42.
Reviews in Anthropology, February, 1994, p. 115.
Santa Fe New Mexican, November 3, 1968.

SIMON, Sheldon W(eiss) 1937-

PERSONAL: Born January 31, 1937, in St. Paul, MN; son of Blair S. and Jennie (Dim) Simon; married Charlann Scheid (a speech therapist), April 23, 1962; children: Alex Russel. *Education:* University of Minnesota, B.A. (summa cum laude), 1958, Ph.D., 1964; Princeton University, M.A., 1960; additional study at Graduate Institute for International Studies, Geneva, Switzerland, 1962-63. *Politics:* Democrat. *Avocational interests:* Theater and music as a performer (has about eight years of semi-professional musical theater experience).

ADDRESSES: Home—5630 South Rocky Point, Tempe, AZ 85282. *Office*—Political Science Department, Arizona State University, Tempe, AZ 85287-2001.

CAREER: University of Minnesota, Minneapolis, assistant director of Center for International Relations, 1961-62; U.S. Government, Washington, DC, foreign affairs analyst, 1963-66; University of Kentucky, Lexington, assistant professor, 1966-69, associate professor, 1969-74, professor of political science, 1974-75; Arizona State University, Tempe, professor of political science and chair of department, 1975-79, director of Center for Asian Studies, 1980-88. George Washington University, lecturer, 1965-66, research associate of Institute of Sino-Soviet Studies, 1967; visiting professor, University of Hawaii, 1968, University of British Columbia, 1972-73, 1979-80, Carleton University, 1976, American Graduate School of International Management, 1991-92, and The Monteroy Institute of International Studies, 1991, 1996. Visiting lecturer in Asia for the United States Information Service, 1973, 1980-82, 1984, 1986. Acting director, Patterson School of Diplomacy, 1970-71; research associate, American Enterprise Institute for Public Policy Research, 1974. Consultant to Agency for International Development, 1966-75, Research Analysis Corp., Bendix Research Corp., Orkand Corp, and The National Bureau of Asian Research.

MEMBER: International Studies Association, American Political Science Association, Association for Asian Studies, Asia Society, American Association of University Professors, Phi Beta Kappa.

WRITINGS:

The Broken Triangle: Peking, Djakarta, and the PKI, Johns Hopkins Press (Baltimore), 1969.

A Systems Approach to Security in the Indian Ocean Arc, Research Analysis Corp., 1970.
War and Politics in Cambodia, Duke University Press (Durham, NC), 1974.
Asian Neutralism and U.S. Policy, American Enterprise Institute for Public Policy Research (Washington, DC), 1975.
(Editor and contributor) *The Military and Security in the Third World,* Westview (Boulder, CO), 1978.
The ASEAN States and Regional Security, Hoover Institution (Stanford, CA), 1982.
The Future of Asian-Pacific Security Collaboration, Lexington Books (Lexington, MA), 1988.
East Asian Security in the Post-Cold War Era, M. E. Sharpe (Armonk, NY), 1993.

OTHER

Contributor to books, including *Cases in State and Local Government,* edited by R. Frost, Prentice-Hall (Englewood Cliffs, NJ), 1961; *The Great Power Triangle and Asian Security,* edited by Raju Thomas, Heath, 1983; *Role Theory and Foreign Policy Analyses,* edited by Stephen Walker, Duke University Press, 1987; *Security, Strategy, and Policy Responses in the Pacific Rim,* edited by Young Whan Kihl and Lawrence Grinter, Lynn Reinner Publishers (Boulder, CO), 1989; *The Cold War as Cooperation: Regional Patterns and Prospects,* edited by Roger Kanet and Edward Kolodziej, Macmillan (London), 1991; *The End of Superpower Conflict in the Third World,* edited by Melvin Goodman, Westview, 1992; and *The Search for Strategy: Politics and Strategic Vision,* edited by Gary Guertner, Greenwood Press (Westport, CT), 1993. Also contributor to journals of Asian studies and international politics.

WORK IN PROGRESS: "An examination of new multilateral approaches to security and prosperity in the Asia-Pacific."

*   *   *

SINCLAIR, Olga 1923-
(Ellen Clare, Olga Daniels)

PERSONAL: Born January 23, 1923, in Watton, England; daughter of Daniel Robert and Betty (Sapey) Waters; married Stanley George Sinclair (a headmaster), April 1, 1945; children: Michael, Alistair, Jeremy. *Education:* Educated in Norfolk, England. *Religion:* None.

ADDRESSES: Home and office—Dove House Farm, Potter Heigham, Norfolk NR29 5LJ, England.

CAREER: Writer. Justice of the peace in county of Norfolk, England, 1966-93. Auxiliary Territorial Service, pay-clerk, 1942-45.

MEMBER: Society of Authors, Society of Women Writers and Journalists, Romantic Novelists Association, Romance Writers of America.

AWARDS, HONORS: Margaret Rhonda Award from Society of Authors, 1972, for research on Lithuanian immigrants.

WRITINGS:

Children's Games (children's nonfiction), Basil Blackwell (Oxford, England), 1966.
Gypsies (children's nonfiction), Basil Blackwell, 1967.
Night of the Black Tower, Lancer Books, 1968.
Man of the River, R. Hale (London), 1968.
Dancing in Britain, Basil Blackwell, 1970.
The Man at the Manor, Dell (New York City), 1972.
Bitter Sweet Summer, Simon & Schuster (New York City), 1972.
Wild Dreams, R. Hale, 1973.
Toys and Toymaking (children's nonfiction), Basil Blackwell, 1975.
My Dear Fugitive, R. Hale, 1976.
Never Fall in Love, R. Hale, 1977.
Master of Melthorpe, R. Hale, 1979.
Gypsy Girl, Collins (London), 1981.
Orchids from the Orient, R. Hale, 1986.
When Wherries Sailed By, Poppyland (Norfolk, England), 1987.
Gretna Green: A Romantic History, Unwin Hyman, 1989.

UNDER PSEUDONYM OLGA DANIELS

Lord of Leet Castle, Mills & Boon, 1984.
The Gretna Bride, Mills & Boon, 1985.
The Bride from Far Away, Mills & Boon, 1987.
The Untamed Bride, Mills & Boon, 1988.
The Arrogant Cavalier, Mills & Boon, 1991.

UNDER PSEUDONYM ELLEN CLARE

Ripening Vine Mills, Mills & Boon (London), 1981.

WORK IN PROGRESS: "Continuing to work on historical novel with background of Lithuanian immi-

grants. Also still interested in Gypsies. But my main pleasure in writing is in the escapism of the historical romance."

SIDELIGHTS: Olga Sinclair told *CA:* "My nonfiction book, *Gretna Green: A Romantic History,* was received by the media with great acclaim. It is the only book to cover the history of this extraordinary little village—Scotland's gift to lovers—250 years of runaway marriages. There sixteen was old enough for a lad and his lassie to know their own minds and wed if they so wished—whereas almost all the western world said not until they were twenty-one unless their parents consented.

"I have a continuing urge to write and cannot now imagine being without it. Although I have had a very happy life, my writing still has an element of escapism in it—and I hope it also takes my readers away to a land where dreams can come true.

"Most of my books have been translated into foreign languages, I have been published in fifteen different countries, and I have five recorded on cassette and many in large print. Editors are as unpredictable now as they were when I sent out my first pieces thirty years ago. The main thing I have learned is that rejections need not be final. You have to keep on and on. Writing is a constant challenge."

*   *   *

SINGER, Peter (Albert David) 1946-

PERSONAL: Born July 6, 1946, in Melbourne, Australia; son of Ernest (a businessman) and Cora (a doctor; maiden name, Oppenheim) Singer; married Renata Diamond (a teacher), December 16, 1968; children: Ruth, Marion, Esther. *Education:* University of Melbourne, B.A. (with honors), 1967, M.A., 1969; University College, Oxford, B.Phil., 1971. *Politics:* Australian Greens. *Religion:* None.

ADDRESSES: Home—Flat 4, 3-7 The Esplanade, St. Kilda, Victoria, Australia. *Office*—Centre for Human Bioethics, Monash University, Wellington Rd., Clayton, Victoria VIC 3168, Australia.

CAREER: Oxford University, University College, Oxford, England, lecturer in philosophy, 1971-73; New York University, New York City, visiting assistant professor of philosophy, 1973-74; La Trobe

University, Bundoora, Victoria, Australia, senior lecturer in philosophy, 1974-76; Monash University, Clayton, Victoria, professor of philosophy, 1977—; Centre for Human Bioethics, Clayton, Australia, director, 1983-91, deputy director, 1992—. Senate candidate for The Greens, Victoria, at the 1996 Australian federal election.

WRITINGS:

Democracy and Disobedience, Clarendon Press, 1973, Oxford University Press (New York City), 1974.
(Editor with Thomas Regan) *Animal Rights and Human Obligations,* Prentice-Hall (Englewood Cliffs, NJ), 1975, 2nd edition, 1989.
Animal Liberation: A New Ethics for Our Treatment of Animals, Random House (New York City), 1975, 2nd edition, 1990.
Practical Ethics, Cambridge University Press (New York City), 1979, 2nd edition, 1993.
Marx, Oxford University Press, 1980.
The Expanding Circle: Ethics and Sociobiology, Farrar, Straus (New York City), 1981.
(Editor with William Walters) *Test-Tube Babies,* Oxford University Press (Melbourne), 1982.
Hegel, Oxford University Press, 1983.
(With Deane Wells) *The Reproduction Revolution: New Ways of Making Babies,* Oxford University Press, 1984, 2nd edition published as *Making Babies: The New Science and Ethics of Conception,* Scribner's (New York City), 1985.
(Editor) *In Defence of Animals,* Blackwell (New York City), 1985.
(With Helga Kuhse) *Should the Baby Live? The Problem of Handicapped Infants,* Oxford University Press, 1985.
(Editor) *Applied Ethics,* Oxford University Press, 1986.
(With Lori Gruen) *Animal Liberation: A Graphic Guide,* Camden Press (London), 1987.
(With Jim Mason) *Animal Factories,* Harmony Books (New York City), 1990.
(Editor) *Embryo Experimentation,* Cambridge University Press, 1990.
(Editor) *A Companion to Ethics,* Oxford University Press, 1991.
How Are We to Live?, Text (Melbourne, Australia), 1993, Prometheus (Buffalo, NY), 1994.
(Editor) *Ethics,* Oxford University Press, 1994.
(Editor with Paola Cavalieri) *The Great Ape Project: Equality Beyond Humanity,* St. Martin's Press (New York City), 1994.

Rethinking Life and Death, Text, 1994, St. Martin's Press, 1995.
The Greens, Text, 1996.

Coeditor of *Bioethics,* 1986—. Contributor to *New York Review of Books* and to philosophy journals. Also coauthor of *Save the Animals* with Barbara Dover and Ingrid Newkirk in 1991.

WORK IN PROGRESS: Research in ethics, applied ethics, and bioethics.

SIDELIGHTS: While teaching at England's Oxford University in the early 1970s, Peter Singer encountered a group of people who were vegetarians not because of any personal distaste for meat, but because they felt, as Singer later wrote, that "there was no way in which [maltreatment of animals by humans] could be justified ethically." Impressed by their arguments, the young Australian philosopher soon joined their ranks. Out of his growing concern for the rights of animals came the book *Animal Liberation: A New Ethics for Our Treatment of Animals,* a study of the suffering inflicted upon animals in the name of scientific experimentation and food production.

Singer attributes most of this lack of respect for nonhuman life to "speciesism," a concept he defines as "a prejudice or attitude of bias toward the interests of members of one's own species and against those of members of other species." In *Animal Liberation,* explains the *New York Times Book Review*'s C. G. Luckhardt, Singer attempts to prove "only in rare cases" is the speciesism mankind displays "either necessary or moral." For example, says the critic, Singer believes that many of the experiments performed on laboratory animals are unnecessary due to the fact that they often "duplicate experiments already performed,. . . tell us what we already know,. . . cause medical problems in animals that could for the most part be avoided by humans,. . . and create data that are useless because inapplicable to humans." It is also unnecessary for humans to eat meat, the author maintains, especially when it means that animals must suffer during nearly every stage of their lives in order to provide us with protein that can be obtained from other sources. And as Luckhardt concludes in his summary of Singer's position, our treatment of animals is ultimately immoral because "there is every reason to believe, and no good reason to deny, that animals feel pain. . . . Whatever reasons we have for not inflicting pain on innocent and helpless humans extend equally well to animals."

Luckhardt praises Singer for writing a work of philosophy that is so "refreshing and well-argued; as a book intended for the mass market it is quite unhysterical yet engagingly written. [His] documentation is unrhetorical and unemotional, his arguments tight and formidable, for he bases his case on neither personal nor religious nor highly abstract philosophical principles, but on moral positions most of us already accept. The strength of this book lies in shifting the burden of argument to those who would maintain that animals ought to be excluded from our sphere of moral concern."

John Naughton of the *Listener* calls *Animal Liberation* "a sombre, challenging and somewhat harrowing book, which deserves to be widely read and 'inwardly digested,' if that is not too gruesome a phrase. . . . [Singer] is supported in [his] claims, not by the gooey affirmations of little old ladies, but by the sober deliberations of some of the most eminent scientists in Britain." Though Naughton finds that Singer "occasionally rides roughshod over his opponents," he declares that *Animal Liberation* "is one of the most thoughtful and persuasive books that I have read in a long time."

Despite assessments of the book which are otherwise quite favorable, both the *Spectator*'s Nick Totton and the *Village Voice*'s Richard Goldstein detect a hint of naivete in Singer's philosophy. Totton observes: "Mr. Singer's main shortcoming as a propagandist is that he believes in the naked light of human reason. He is a philosopher, and a utilitarian at that; for him, a logical demonstration that meat-eating or vivisection increases the overall quotient of sentient suffering on this planet is conclusive. . . . [His] arguments are lucid, but really quite beside the point: they depend firstly on the axiom that there is a network of ethical values somehow built into the universe, and secondly upon the fond hope that conformity with such values is the primary intention of human beings."

Goldstein also notes a tendency towards what he terms "social obliviousness" in *Animal Liberation*. He contends that Singer ignores considerations such as the major changes that would need to occur in institutions, economics, labor, and individual behavior for people to give up eating meat and the general confusion this would create in our society. Nevertheless, Goldstein concludes, "I am willing to forgive Peter Singer his social obliviousness and more. [*Animal Liberation*] is an important book, first, because it reveals . . . the rough beast of self-interest which motivates all human society. Second, because it offers its solutions . . . in a spirit of mercy so touching and disquieting that one can only marvel at the persistent power of compassion. And third, because it questions, unintentionally perhaps, the sectarian organization of the world's people into competing states, and the brutality we extend to all those (animals, and the people who are denied the protein we feed to animals) beyond the pale."

Singer later turned his interest in ethical behavior to the realm of reproductive technology. In *Making Babies: The New Science and Ethics of Conception*, a book he co-authored with Deane Wells, Singer examines the issue of test-tube babies, surrogate motherhood, sperm banks, and cloning. Praising the authors for their "calm and sensitivity," Lionel Tiger of the *New York Times Book Review* writes, "with almost triumphant sobriety, Mr. Singer and Mr. Wells offer a plausible and practical context within which to approach each general issue . . . without losing sight of a good physician's sense of responsibility to individual patients."

Rae Goodell, reviewing the book for *Washington Post Book World,* comments that while the authors welcome and encourage the unprecedented changes occurring in human reproduction, they cast an unfavorable eye toward unbridled progress and recommended that national bioethics committees be appointed to study and regulate the progress and use of new reproductive technologies. "Singer and Wells ask that each stage of development be carefully evaluated before proceeding to the next, and that basic ethical and environmental standards be set," Goodell writes. Goodell continues that, "the restrictions that Singer and Wells would place on reproduction technologies are relatively few and remarkably lenient, however. Embryos could be harvested for spare organs until the embryos were old enough to be sentient, and cloning would be permitted if limited, say to 'one replica per person.'"

Tabitha Powledge of the *Nation* bemoans the authors' discussion of private and public control of genetic engineering. "It is a mystery why Singer and Wells appear unable to see that the [government] committee's veto power effectively removes the decision from parents, where the authors say it ought to be." Powledge also identifies what she considers another weakness in the work. While congratulating the authors for a "clear, jargon-free model of how to present philosophical arguments to a general audience," Powledge discerns an "insidious" aspect to the book. "It pretends to be a disinterested, dispassionate examination of I.V.F. [in vitro fertilization], although it is actually promulgating a strong utilitarian point of view. . . . It all but ignores the issues of justice and equality which I.V.F. raises."

As a book editor, Singer continues to pursue the issue of animal exploitation. In *The Great Ape Project: Equality beyond Humanity,* he co-edits with Paola Cavalieri the work of more than thirty essayists writing about the treatment of apes in zoos, laboratories, and in the wild as well as the need to consider them equals entitled to the same civil rights as their human cousins. "The diversity of expertise brought to the argument is such that it's hard to believe a more comprehensive book has ever been made," writes Ann Druyan in a review for *Washington Post Book World.* "This book is a powerful work of moral vision that manages to maintain a balance between logic and passion."

In *Rethinking Life and Death: The Collapse of Our Traditional Ethics,* Singer challenges the use of such traditional Judeo-Christian values that uphold the sanctity of human life without regard to quality of life as the basis for making decisions and legislation about life and death. He argues that decisions based on such values are outmoded by twentieth-century advances in medicine and technology and create other moral conflicts such as determining how long to keep someone in a vegetative state alive through technical means. According to *Los Angeles Times* reviewer Judith Gingold, Singer's solution is to discard "the Old Testament account of man as a special being created in God's image, with dominion over the rest of nature. Instead, Singer bases his ethic on a Darwinian view of man as one among other animal species, one who shares many emotional and psychological features with his fellow creatures, and who is a part of nature rather than its conqueror." In this vein, Singer argues that the worth of human and non-human life needs to be examined against items such as self-awareness, rationality, and the conscious desire for life and the ability to enjoy it. He then recommends adding new commandments to the traditional Judeo-Christian set including allowing for a person's will to live or die, bringing only wanted children into the world, and not discriminating

against other species. Singer acknowledges there may be other remedies and encourages people to begin rethinking and searching for solutions.

Rethinking Life and Death received mixed reactions. *Washington Post Book World*'s George Weigel contends that Singer's solutions "would mean nothing less than the end of humanism in either its Judeo-Christian or Enlightenment-secular form." As Weigel views Singer's solutions, "'quality of life' calculations will displace the venerable 'sanctity of life' criterion, and 'responsible decision-making' will replace the immunities once granted to innocent human beings as a first principle of morality." Weigel concludes, "Far from pointing the way out of today's moral dilemmas, Singer's book is a roadmap for driving down the darkest of moral blind alleys, at the end of which, however spiffed-up and genteel, is Dr. Mengele: The embodiment of the triumph of power over principle, in the manipulation of life and death by the fit' at the expense of the 'unworthy.' Read this book, then, not to gain insight into the most profound questions with which men and women must wrestle today; read it to remind yourself of the enormities of which putatively civilized human beings are capable." In contrast, Gingold praises Singer's ideas as "coherent, lucid and fresh, and presented in a non-didactic voice that resonates with good will." And a reviewer for *Publishers Weekly* notes that *Rethinking Life and Death* contains "brilliant essays" and that Singer "makes a forceful case for his new ethic."

BIOGRAPHICAL/CRITICAL SOURCES:

BOOKS

Singer, Peter, *Animal Liberation: A New Ethics for Our Treatment of Animals,* Random House, 1975.

PERIODICALS

Los Angeles Times Book Review, September 24, 1995, p. 2.
Listener, June 17, 1976.
Melbourne Weekly, December 10, 1995, p. 4.
Nation, August 17-24, 1985.
New Republic, May 29, 1976; February 7, 1981.
New York Review of Books, May 15, 1980.
New York Times Book Review, January 4, 1976; March 1, 1981; June 23, 1985.

Publishers Weekly, March 6, 1995, p. 53.
Spectator, June 5, 1976.
Times Literary Supplement, January 15, 1982.
Village Voice, March 22, 1976.
Washington Post Book World, June 7, 1981; August 18, 1985; January 30, 1994; March 26, 1995, pp. 1, 11.

—Sketch by Julie Monahan

* * *

SLEIGH, Barbara 1906-1982

PERSONAL: Born January 9, 1906, in Acock's Green, Worcestershire, England; died February 13, 1982; daughter of Bernard (an artist) and Stella (Phillip) Sleigh; married David Davis (a broadcasting executive), January 29, 1936; children: Anthony, Hilary, Fabia. *Education:* Attended West Bromwich School of Art, Birmingham, England, 1922-25; Clapham High School Art Teacher's Training College, London, England, diploma, 1928. *Religion:* Church of England.

CAREER: Smethwick High School, Staffordshire, England, art teacher, 1928-30; Goldsmiths' College, London, England, lecturer, 1930-33; British Broadcasting Corp. (BBC), London, assistant on radio program *Children's Hour,* 1933-36; writer for children.

WRITINGS:

CHILDREN'S FICTION

Carbonel, illustrated by V. H. Drummond, Parrish (London), 1955, Bobbs-Merrill (New York City), 1958.
Patchwork Quilt, illustrated by Mary Shillabeer, Parrish, 1956.
The Singing Wreath and Other Stories, illustrated by Julia Comper, Parrish, 1957.
The Seven Days, illustrated by Susan Einzig, Parrish, 1958, Meredith, 1968.
The Kingdom of Carbonel, illustrated by D. M. Leonard, Parrish, 1958, Bobbs-Merrill, 1960.

No One Must Know, illustrated by Jillian Willett, Collins (London), 1962, Bobbs-Merrill, 1963.
North of Nowhere: Stories and Legends from Many Lands, illustrated by Victor Ambrus, Collins, 1964, Coward-McCann (New York City), 1966.
Jessamy, illustrated by Philip Gough, Bobbs-Merrill, 1967.
Pen, Penny, Tuppence, illustrated by Meg Stevens, Hamish Hamilton (London), 1968.
The Snowball, illustrated by Patricia Drew, Brockhampton Press, 1969.
West of Widdershins: A Gallimaufry of Stories Brewed in Her Own Cauldron, illustrated by Victor Ambrus, Collins, 1971, published as *Stirabout Stories,* Bobbs-Merrill, 1972.
Ninety-Nine Dragons, illustrated by Gunvor Edwards, Brockhampton Press, 1974.
Funny Peculiar: An Anthology, illustrated by Jennie Garratt, David & Charles (London), 1974.
Charlie Chumbles, illustrated by Frank Franus, Hodder & Stoughton (London), 1977.
Grimblegraw and the Wuthering Witch, illustrated by Glenys Ambrus, Hodder & Stoughton, 1978, revised edition, Penguin (London), 1979.
Carbonel and Calidor, illustrated by Charles Front, Kestrel, 1978.
Winged Magic: Legends and Stories from Many Lands Concerning Things That Fly, illustrated by John Patience, Hodder & Stoughton, 1979.
(Editor) *Broomsticks and Beasticles: Stories and Verse about Witches and Strange Creatures,* illustrated by John Patience, Hodder & Stoughton, 1981.
(Editor) Kenneth Grahame, *The Wind in the Willows,* illustrated by Philip Mendoza, Hodder & Stoughton, 1983.

Also author of radio plays, stories, and talks for children, for the BBC.

OTHER

The Smell of Privet (autobiography), Hutchinson, 1971.

SIDELIGHTS: Barbara Sleigh was well known in her native England as an author and editor of children's fantasy fiction. Her most popular works were those about the character of Carbonel, King of the Cats, who appears in *Carbonel, The Kingdom of Carbonel,* and *Carbonel and Calidor.* Sleigh's characters have been compared to those in the finest tradition of children's literature. As one *Junior Bookshelf* critic stated in a review of *Carbonel and Calidor,* "There is a Nesbit quality about Miss Sleigh's writing as there is in her manipulation of magic. . . . Miss Sleigh is the least prolific of writers, but her books are always well worth waiting for."

Beginning her career as a teacher and later a storyteller on the British Broadcasting Corp.'s *Children's Hour,* Sleigh did not start writing until later in her life, and even then she was never very prolific. Quickly gaining fans with the publication of *Carbonel* in 1955, Sleigh "added a splendidly individual contribution to the long line of fictional felines," according to Geoffrey Trease in the *Times Literary Supplement.* In this first story, the author introduced her famed character as a kitten who is rescued by two children named Rosemary and John from a witch named Mrs. Cantrip. Carbonel is no ordinary cat: he is a king with whom the children can communicate through the use of a magic ring. In addition to the anthropomorphic world of Carbonel and his fellow felines into which Rosemary and John are drawn, there is also much in these books about witchcraft and its colorful practitioners, in particular the "idiosyncratic Mrs. Cantrip," whom Trease called an "unforgettable creation."

After *Carbonel* and *The Kingdom of Carbonel,* Sleigh did not return to this world of witches and intelligent cats for another twenty years, until her 1978 publication of *Carbonel and Calidor.* The central character in this story is actually Calidor, Carbonel's son and heir to the throne. Trouble arises when Carbonel falls in love with Dumpsie—a bright and feisty commoner cat who lives in the dump—and refuses to take Princess Melissa's paw in marriage. "Barbara Sleigh laces adventure with humour and has a casually expert way of twisting everyday settings and events into something bizarre and wholly entertaining," said Margery Fisher in her *Growing Point* assessment of the tale.

In addition to her Carbonel stories, Sleigh's lighthearted style of fantasy can be found in shorter works like *Ninety-Nine Dragons* and *Grimblegraw and the Wuthering Witch,* as well as in her short stories, many of which appear in *West of Widdershins: A Gallimaufry of Stories Brewed in Her Own Cauldron,* published in the United States as *Stirabout Stories.* In *Ninety-Nine Dragons,* Ben and Beth have a problem when the fifty sheep that Beth

has been counting to help her go to sleep are threatened by the dragons that Ben has been dreaming about. *Grimblegraw and the Wuthering Witch* is about a giant who kidnaps people to do his housework. "This stylish tale," Fisher remarked in *Growing Point,* "looks back to Andrew Lang's comic tales of a fairy court as it unwinds."

"My own pleasure in storytelling," Sleigh once commented, "stems from the time when I was a small girl. My father, who among other artistic activities designed stained glass windows, would often use me as a model for an infant angel, or perhaps a young St. John the Baptist. To stop me fidgeting, he would tell me tales which kept me riveted. I write stories in the hope that I may pass on some of this same delight to children today." In a *Twentieth-Century Children's Writers* entry, Sleigh further explained why she chose to write fantasy stories: "I largely write fantasy, but, I hope, of a down-to-earth kind, avoiding mere whimsy. I feel strongly this leads young readers to wider horizons, and later to imaginative adult reading."

BIOGRAPHICAL/CRITICAL SOURCES:

BOOKS

Twentieth-Century Children's Writers, 4th edition, St. James Press (Detroit), 1995.

PERIODICALS

Bulletin of the Center for Children's Books, October, 1967; December, 1969, p. 65; November, 1972, p. 49.

Growing Point, October, 1975, p. 2729; November, 1977, p. 3211; July, 1978, pp. 3354-58; January, 1979, pp. 3435-39.

Junior Bookshelf, February, 1975, pp. 50-51; April, 1978, pp. 93, 195; August, 1978, p. 195; April, 1980, p. 74; February, 1982, p. 30.

Kirkus Reviews, April 1, 1967, p. 416; October 1, 1968, p. 1165; August 15, 1972, p. 941.

Library Journal, May 15, 1967, p. 2024.

New Statesman, October 22, 1971, pp. 559-60; December 4, 1981, p. 18.

Times Educational Supplement, November 20, 1981, p. 34.

Times Literary Supplement, October 22, 1971, p. 1321; December 8, 1972, p. 1499; November 23, 1973, p. 1438; December 6, 1974, p. 1384; July 7, 1978, p. 765; November 25, 1983.

SOMTOW, S. P.
  See SUCHARITKUL, Somtow

*   *   *

SONTAG, Susan   1933-

PERSONAL: Born January 16, 1933, in New York, NY; married Philip Rieff, 1950 (divorced, 1958); children: David. *Education:* Attended University of California, Berkeley, 1948-49; University of Chicago, B.A., 1951; Harvard University, M.A. (English), 1954, M.A. (philosophy), 1955, Ph.D. candidate, 1955-57; St. Anne's College, Oxford, graduate study, 1957-58.

ADDRESSES: Agent—c/o Wylie, Aitken & Stone, 250 West 57th Street, New York, NY 10019.

CAREER: University of Connecticut, Storrs, instructor in English, 1953-54; *Commentary,* New York City, editor, 1959; lecturer in philosophy, City College (now City College of the City University of New York), New York City, and Sarah Lawrence College, Bronxville, NY, 1959-60; Columbia University, New York City, instructor in department of religion, 1960-64; Rutgers University, New Brunswick, NJ, writer in residence, 1964-65; novelist, short story writer, critic, and essayist. Writer and director of the films *Duet for Cannibals,* 1969, *Brother Carl,* 1971, *Promised Lands,* 1974, and *Unguided Tour,* 1983.

MEMBER: PEN American Center (president, 1987-89), American Academy of Arts and Letters, American Academy of Arts and Sciences.

AWARDS, HONORS: Fellowships from American Association of University Women, 1957, Rockefeller Foundation, 1966 and 1974, Guggenheim Memorial Foundation, 1966 and 1975; George Polk Memorial Award, 1966, for contributions toward better appreciation of theater, motion pictures, and literature; National Book Award nomination, 1966, for *Against Interpretation, and Other Essays;* Brandeis University Creative Arts Award, 1975; National Institute and American Academy award for literature, 1976; National Book Critics Circle Award for criticism, 1978, for *On Photography;* named Officier de

l'Ordre des Arts et des Lettres, 1984; fellowship, 1990-95, John D. and Catherine T. MacArthur Foundation; honorary doctorate, Columbia University and Harvard University, both 1993.

WRITINGS:

FICTION

The Benefactor (novel), Farrar, Straus (New York City), 1963.
Death Kit (novel), Farrar, Straus, 1967.
I, etcetera (short stories), Farrar, Straus, 1978.
The Way We Live Now (lithographs by Howard Hodgkin), Farrar, Straus, 1991.
The Volcano Lover: A Romance (novel), Farrar, Straus, 1992.
Alice in Bed: A Play in Eight Scenes, Farrar, Straus, 1993.

Author of the play *A Parsifal,* in *Robert Wilson's Vision,* edited by Trevor Fairbrother, Abrams (New York City), 1991. Contributor of the short story "The View from the Ark" to *Violent Legacies: Three Cantos,* Richard Misrach, Aperture (New York City), 1992.

NONFICTION

Against Interpretation, and Other Essays, Farrar, Straus, 1966.
Styles of Radical Will, Farrar, Straus, 1969.
Trip to Hanoi, Farrar, Straus, 1969.
On Photography, Farrar, Straus, 1977.
Illness as Metaphor, Farrar, Straus, 1978.
Under the Sign of Saturn (essays), Farrar, Straus, 1980.
AIDS and Its Metaphors, Farrar, Straus, 1989.

Author of introductions to *The Temptation to Exist,* by E. M. Cioran, Quadrangle (Chicago), 1968; *The Art of Revolution,* compiled by Dugald Stermer, McGraw (New York City), 1970; *Prose of Maria Tsvetayeva: A Captive Spirit: Selected Prose,* Virago (London), 1983; *Epitaph for a Small Winner,* by Machado de Assis, Farrar, Straus/Noonday, 1990; and *Pedro Paramo,* by Juan Rulfo, Grove (New York City), 1994.

SCREENPLAYS

Duet for Cannibals (produced by Sandrew Film & Teater AB [Sweden], 1969), Farrar, Straus, 1970.

Brother Carl: A Filmscript (produced by Sandrew Film & Teater AB and Svenska Filminstitutet [Sweden], 1971), Farrar, Straus, 1974.

Also author of screenplays for the films *Promised Lands,* 1974, and *Unguided Tour,* 1983.

OTHER

(Editor and author of introduction) *Antonin Artaud: Selected Writings,* Farrar, Straus, 1976.
(Editor and author of introduction) *A Roland Barthes Reader,* Farrar, Straus, 1982.
A Susan Sontag Reader (anthology of fiction and nonfiction), introduction by Elizabeth Hardwick, Farrar, Straus, 1982.
(Editor and author of introduction) Danilo Kis, *Homo Poeticus: Essays and Interviews,* Farrar, Straus, 1995.

Also author of *Literature* (monograph), 1966. Contributor to *Great Ideas Today,* 1966, and *Cage Cunningham Johns: Dancers on a Plane, in Memory of Their Feelings,* Knopf (New York City), 1990. Contributor of short stories, reviews, essays, and articles to numerous periodicals, including *New Yorker, New York Review of Books, Times Literary Supplement, Art in America, Antaeus, Granta, Threepenny Review, Nation, Atlantic Monthly, American Review, Harper's* and *Partisan Review.*

SIDELIGHTS: Susan Sontag is an American intellectual whose works on modernist writing and Western culture form an important modern critical canon. Considered "one of the few bold and original minds to be found among the younger critics," to quote *Partisan Review* contributor William Phillips, Sontag has penned controversial essays on topics ranging from "camp" to cancer, which encompass her views on literature, plays, film, photography, and politics. Though best known for her nonfiction, the author has also written novels and short stories in addition to writing and directing several films; in an introduction to *A Susan Sontag Reader,* Elizabeth Hardwick calls Sontag a "foraging pluralist" who is attracted to "waywardness," "outrageousness," and "the unpredictable, along with extremity." *New York Times Book Review* correspondent David Bromwich notes that her "subjects bear witness to Miss Sontag's range as well as her diligence. She keeps up—appears, at times, to do the keeping-up for a whole generation. . . . From ground to summit, from oblivion to oblivion, she covers the big movements and ideas and then sends out her report, not without

qualms. For the art she most admires, an inward and recalcitrant art, exists in tension with her own role as its advocate." According to Susan Walker in the *Dictionary of Literary Biography,* Sontag's career as a writer "has been marked by a seriousness of pursuit and a relentless intelligence that analyzes modern culture on almost every possible level: artistic, philosophical, literary, political, and moral. . . . Sontag has produced a stimulating and varied body of work which entertains the issues of art while satisfying the rigors of her own intellect."

In a *New Republic* review, Leo Braudy finds a theme that links Sontag's disparate works—that of "the critic/artist in search of an audience that by its understanding will bring him into being." Braudy elaborates: "Since her first essays began appearing in the mid-1960s, all of Sontag's critical writing has focused on the question of intellectual connection: what is the central tradition of Western thought in the 20th century and which writers have contributed most to its creation?" The answer, in the words of *Atlantic Monthly* correspondent Benjamin DeMott, is the modernist sensibility, in its preoccupations with "alienation, deracination, powerlessness, blockage of perception and communication, death of relationship, rage for transformation, search for new consciousness and (no skipping this) the bourgeois West as . . . moral collapse."

Sontag has been a shaper of contemporary criticism through her call for a new formal aestheticism. Michiko Kakutani of the *New York Times* conveys Sontag's argument "that art and morality have no common ground, that it is style, not content, that matters most of all." Likewise, *Saturday Review* contributor Edward Grossman suggests that Sontag takes "distinctions between art and science, between high and low, to be largely, though not entirely, false and irrelevant" and that she also dismisses the "old, mainly literary notion that art is the criticism of life."

From a very early age Sontag nurtured a fascination for literature and philosophy. Born in New York City, she was raised in Tucson, Arizona, and Los Angeles, California. She graduated from high school in 1948, at the age of fifteen, and enrolled at the University of California, Berkeley, the same year. Reminiscing on her youthful ambitions in *Publishers Weekly,* she said she wanted to study medicine—and write in her spare time—until she realized as a teenager that writing should be her only career. "In high school," she said, "I used to buy *Partisan Review* at a newsstand at Hollywood and Vine and read Lionel Trilling and Harold Rosenberg and Hannah Arendt. My greatest dream was to grow up and come to New York and write for *Partisan Review* and be read by 5,000 people." Eventually she fulfilled that dream, after having studied English and philosophy at the University of Chicago, Harvard University, and St. Anne's College, Oxford. Sontag began writing essays and book reviews in the early 1960s, and her first novel, *The Benefactor,* was published in 1963.

Nation reviewer Walter Kendrick suggests that as an American explorer of European artistic trends, Sontag "stands midway between the two continents, in what one might call the Sargasso Sea of thought." Belonging wholeheartedly to neither culture, the critic has taken a position "from which she can see both cultures whole." She therefore seeks to illuminate crucial European modernist sensibilities reacting to the peculiar rigors of twentieth-century life. According to Leon S. Roudiez in *World Literature Today,* her literary essays "almost invariably raise issues that transcend the topic at hand—and that is one reason they are worth preserving. . . . She has tended to write about European (mostly French) authors rather than about American ones; this . . . is what has led her to allow general or even theoretical considerations to intrude—and it has made her essays more interesting. It has also permitted her to act as go-between for European and American traditions." Phillips sees Sontag as a critic who has made "a break with the kind of adaptation to popular taste in the last few decades that made literature so conventional in form and in subject. The effect is to rescue the experimental tradition from its loss of power and the exhaustion of its subject, from its unbearable isolation as it struggled to remain both pure and advanced."

From case studies of neglected artists Sontag moved to theoretical essays on the aims of modern art and the relationship between art and criticism. Her works "encourage, in art and criticism, . . . respect for sensuous surfaces, for feeling, for form, for style," according to *Commentary* writer Alicia Ostriker. A *Times Literary Supplement* reviewer similarly observes that in *Against Interpretation, and Other Essays,* Sontag "is tired of interpretive criticism and mimetic art. . . . She proposes instead an art which is joyously itself and a criticism which enthusiastically dwells on the fact." John S. Peterson elaborates in the *Los Angeles Times:* "Sontag has argued that critical interpretation tends to be stifling and reactionary, and that the job of the critic is not to assign

'meanings' but to show how a work of art is what it is. Her own writings [are] not to be regarded as criticism, strictly speaking, but as case studies for an aesthetic, a theory of her own sensibility." *Nation* essayist Robert Sklar suggests that Sontag makes this aesthetic criticism a form of philosophical inquiry: "Art, particularly the language arts, are themselves caught in the trap of consciousness. When consciousness as we know it is destroyed, art as we know it will also come to an end—art as expression or representation, art as truth and beauty. The 'minimal art' of our own time, in painting, sculpture, the new novel, already aims, in this sense, at the abolition of art." Sklar concludes that Sontag's "form of prophecy and critical insight, this mode of radical will, can be extremely clarifying and stimulating for the willing reader."

Against Interpretation, and Other Essays and *Styles of Radical Will,* both published in the 1960s, assured Sontag a wide and controversial reputation. In the *Atlantic Monthly,* Hilton Kramer describes how the American intellectual community reacted to her works: "Sontag seemed to have an unfailing faculty for dividing intellectual opinion and inspiring a sense of outrage, consternation, and betrayal among the many readers—especially older readers—who disagreed with her. And it was just this faculty for offending respectable opinion that, from the outset, was an important part of her appeal for those who welcomed her pronouncements. She was admired not only for what she said but for the pain, shock, and disarray she caused in saying it. . . . She made criticism a medium of intellectual scandal, and this won her instant celebrity."

A near-fatal case of cancer interrupted Sontag's career in the early 1970s, but as she recovered she wrote two of her best-known works, *On Photography* and *Illness as Metaphor.* In the *Washington Post Book World,* William McPherson describes *On Photography* as "a brilliant analysis of the profound changes photographic images have made in our way of looking at the world, and at ourselves over the last 140 years. . . . *On Photography* merely describes a phenomenon we take as much for granted as water from the tap, and how that phenomenon has changed us— a remarkable enough achievement, when you think about it." William H. Gass offers even stronger praise for the National Book Critics Circle prize-winning work in the *New York Times Book Review.* Every page of *On Photography,* writes Gass, "raises important and exciting questions about its subject and raises them in the best way. In a context of clarity, skepticism and passionate concern, with an energy that never weakens but never blusters, and with an admirable pungency of thought and directness of expression that sacrifices nothing of subtlety or refinement, Sontag encourages the reader's cooperation in her enterprise. . . . The book understands exactly the locale and the level of its argument." *Time* columnist Robert Hughes expresses a similar opinion. "It is hard to imagine any photographer's agreeing point for point with Sontag's polemic," Hughes states. "But it is a brilliant, irritating performance, and it opens window after window on one of the great *faits accomplis* of our culture. Not many photographers are worth a thousand of her words," Hughes concludes.

Illness as Metaphor is not an autobiographical account of Sontag's own experience with cancer but rather an examination of the cultural myths that have developed around certain diseases, which invest sickness with meaning beyond mere physical debilitation. *New Republic* contributor Edwin J. Kenney, Jr., calls the book "a critical analysis of our habitual, unconscious, and even pathological ways of conceptualizing illness and of using the vocabulary of illness to articulate our feelings about other crises, economic, political, and military. Sontag is seeking to go behind the language of the mind to expose and clarify the assumptions and fears the language masks; she wants to liberate us from the terrors that issue not from disease itself, but from our ways of imagining it." Braudy writes: "In *Illness as Metaphor* [Sontag] condemns the way we have used metaphoric language to obscure and mystify the physical and material world, turning diseases into imagery, metamorphosing the final reality of bodily decay and death into the shrouded fantasies of moral pollution and staining sin." DeMott claims that the work "isn't conceived as an act of conversion. It presents itself as an attack on some corrupt uses of language. In a series of ten meditations on the human failure to grasp that sickness is not a metaphor, not a sign standing in for something else, not a symbol of a moral or cultural condition, Miss Sontag develops the thesis that it is therefore wrong to use sickness as a means of interpreting the character of either individuals or nations."

Discussing Sontag's fiction, a *Times Literary Supplement* reviewer writes: "Sontag has had the misfortune (as a novelist) to become well-known for her high, serious, and argumentative mind (as a critic). Much is therefore expected, indeed searched for, in any novel she may write—much, particularly, to do

with technical experiment, learned and subtle allusion, comment on the predicament of the American intellectual today." Technical experiment indeed characterizes much of the author's fiction; in his *Bright Book of Life: American Novelists and Storytellers from Hemingway to Mailer,* Alfred Kazin notes that in Sontag's novels as in her essays, "she is concerned with producing a startling esthetic which her words prolong." Kazin continues: "She is interested in advancing new positions to the point of making her clever, surprisingly sustained novels experiments in the trying-out of an idea." *Washington Post Book World* correspondent John B. Breslin finds Sontag's fiction highly commendable. Breslin states: "At her best, . . . Sontag illuminates our contemporary situation with the peculiar radiance that comes from the fusion of wide learning, precise thinking and deep feeling. Suddenly we see our own face in the mirror and hear our own voice with a shock of recognition all the greater for the restraint with which the revelation is made." In the *Partisan Review,* Tony Tanner contends that Sontag's novels are about a particularly modern theme: "how the head gets rid of the world. . . . The energies of disburdenment—or the fatigues of relinquishment—are very evident."

Despite these general statements about her fiction, Sontag's first two novels, *The Benefactor* and *Death Kit,* have received mixed reviews. Both works "emphasize fiction as a construct of words rather than as a mimesis," to quote Roudiez. In a *New Republic* review, Stanley Kauffmann calls *The Benefactor* "a skillful amalgam of a number of continental sources in fiction and thought" and adds that it contains "a good deal of well fashioned writing." Kauffmann maintains, however, that the book "remains a neat knowledgeable construct, reclining on the laboratory table." Conversely, Kazin feels that the novel "works because its author really sees the world as a series of propositions *about* the world. Her theoreticalness consists of a loyalty not to certain ideas but to life as the improvisation of ideas. She is positive only about moving on from those ideas, and this makes her an interesting fantasist about a world conceived as nothing but someone thinking up new angles to it." *New York Review of Books* essayist Denis Donoghue finds *Death Kit* "an extremely ambitious book" but notes that it is "undermined by the fact that its ideas never become its experience: the ideas remain external, like the enforced correlation of dream and act in *The Benefactor.*" Maureen Howard, on the other hand, praises *Death Kit* in a *Saturday Review* column. "The writing is vigorous, the plot highly imaginative," Howard claims. *Death Kit* "is about the endless and insane demands put upon us to choose coherence and life over chaos and death."

In 1978 Sontag released *I, etcetera,* a collection of eight short stories previously published in periodicals. *New York Times Book Review* correspondent Robert Towers notes that the stories "are not quite the autonomous and self-sufficient verbal constructs that [Sontag's] esthetic position would seem to advocate. They are chock-full of reference to the exhausted world we inhabit; they abound in 'meaning'—meaning that calls not for interpretation but for small, repeated sighs of recognition. All of them bear the impress of an active, questing intelligence that can apply language with neurosurgical skill to isolate and cut away the necrotic tissues of our collective modern consciousness." *Ms.* magazine reviewer Laurie Stone also observes that in *I, etcetera* Sontag "is not so much interested in abstract ideas and experimental styles as she is in revealing human character. . . . Sontag is focused simply (artfully) on the dear, idiosyncratic, alienating behavior of human beings." According to Howard, the stories show a "surrender to imaginative language, a release of [Sontag's] amazing articulateness into a taut, richly associative prose style." The reviewer concludes that *I, etcetera* "is a pleasure to read—inventive, witty, intelligent, of course—but a pleasure."

The Volcano Lover: A Romance, only the third novel in Sontag's career, received much praise for its historically based tale of a lovers' triangle consisting of Admiral Lord Nelson, his plebeian lover Emma, and her husband, Sir William Hamilton, who works as a government official in Naples, Italy. The action takes place in the court of late eighteenth-century Italy in the shadow of Mount Vesuvius, which provides Sontag with a metaphor for exploring her ideas and themes. Considering the author "both epicure and glutton," *Times Literary Supplement* reviewer Jonathan Keates proclaims that "the conviction of *The Volcano Lover* is that of an author who has had a good time."

Sir Hamilton, a subject of the Enlightenment referred to in the book as "the Cavalier," is captivated by Mount Vesuvius and translates his interest into scientific excursions and musings, thus lending one definition to the term "Volcano Lover." Sir Hamilton also likes to collect people and things, most notably his wife, Emma, in an attempt to harness the beauty of the world. This propensity is one of Sontag's

themes; Richard Eder, writing in the *Los Angeles Times Book Review,* explains this obsession with collecting as "essentially a masculine activity. It stems from a man's innate and oddly isolating assurance that he has a place in the world and, conversely, that the world belongs to him." Eder also conveys the book's larger philosophical issues, which he summarizes as concerning "women and their mismanaged fires. . . . men and their vulnerable outrages, about the English character, about the frailty of revolutions and the deadly power of counterrevolutions, about the inhuman aspects of art and power." Emma, the wife and female participant in the triangle, evolves from a downtrodden streetwalker to a self-invented court delight, cultivating the manners, languages, and talents necessary to impress those of her husband's social station. Nelson, a war hero, becomes smitten with Emma, provides the passion she desires and that which makes the novel a romance, and yields to her opinions on political matters even as they grow harsh and conflict with the directives he is given by his superiors.

Many reviewers comment on Sontag's playful nature with the book, despite its immersion in historical figures and events. "She dwells on the great admiration and affection between all three of her principal characters," remarks Gabriele Annan in the *New York Review of Books.* Furthermore, Annan declares that Sontag's novel is "a moral tale" full of "risks," the biggest of which is "to be full of moral fervor, passionate and preachy. The risks pay off because she moves so fast and has such a light and casual touch with language." Other critics are not as consumed by Sontag's style. Calling the novel "as twisty as a mountain road," *New Statesman and Society* writer Harriett Gilbert states that "Sontag's disorienting narrative style—skipping from past to present to past; disrupting the historical narrative with mini-essays and anachronisms—ensures that our *emotional* engagement is never entirely certain." In a *London Review of Books* article, Linda Colley expounds upon the book in a different light: "one should read *The Volcano Lover,* not for its rehearsal of an already well-documented relationship between two men and a woman, but for the snippets it contains of Sontag herself." In the end, though Colley explains British resistance to Sontag in general, she admires the book: "For what could be more piquant than for an author to insert statements of the most unbridled elitism and intellectualism into a book that appears on the surface to be the most populist that she has ever written, a mere historical novel?"

Continuing her interest in historical figures, Sontag published *Alice in Bed,* a play centering on the eccentric writer Alice James, the invalid sister of William and Henry James. Combining Alice's views on life with the absurdist spirit of Lewis Carroll's *Alice in Wonderland,* Sontag forms a hybrid allegory in which the bedridden Alice expounds philosophy while characters envelop her bed with mattresses and which includes a dialogue with other historical figures, including Alice's mother, Margaret Fuller, and poet Emily Dickinson.

Wondering why Sontag offers "no insight into the suffering and invalidism prevalent among intelligent women in the 19th century," *Belles Lettres* writer Tess Lewis concludes that *Alice in Bed*'s afterword is its best attribute because it "explains her intentions so thoroughly that there is no real need for the play at all." Marie Olesen Urbanski of the *Los Angeles Times Book Review,* on the other hand, notes the similarities between Sontag's *Illness as Metaphor,* in which the author "considered tuberculosis . . . the disease for 19th-Century romantics," and *Alice in Bed,* in which "James's retreat into her 'mental prison' of illness was the Victorian lady's archetypal response to anger and grief." In addition, calling James's condition an example of "psychological self-immolation," Urbanski concludes that "Sontag was brave to attempt so challenging a subject. . . . a rare but little-explored reality, from the female experience: a festering rage that causes depression, and perhaps illness—ultimately the 'life force' turned on itself."

AIDS and Its Metaphors is another Sontag work that builds on the premises developed in *Illness and Metaphor.* First appearing as an essay in the *New York Review of Books* in 1988, *AIDS and Its Metaphors* was an early discussion of the widespread social implications of the new disease, acquired immunodeficiency syndrome, that quickly garnered the stigma once reserved for cancer. Wayne Koestenbaum, writing in the *Yale Review,* summarized the book as "the application of principles gleaned from thinking through her own sickness." Through *Illness as Metaphor* and another published work about AIDS, *The Way We Live Now,* Sontag explains how the disease has changed people's social lives and altered communication through both the spoken and the unspoken ramifications of its symptoms, and she notes that by becoming the catastrophe of modern times, it has created a new awareness. She puts forth the notion of AIDS as the cultural plague, or perhaps as a way to "begin again." Koestenbaum

writes that Sontag's "central point—that AIDS has been irresponsibly draped with metaphors—is incontestable," but he also laments that "by mantling AIDS in metaphor [through evasion of specific sexual and medical terms] while striving to disentangle it, she makes it sound fictitious, like a disease in a metaphysical novel." Other critics take issue with Sontag's suggestion that the new epidemic is an opportunity to revise society's morality into one that more greatly respects prudence and monogamy. Koestenbaum also points out the double standard that allows Sontag to decry homophobia while simultaneously describing the rise of gay life in the 1970s as a movement in which the "distinctive folkloric custom was sexual voracity." Conversely, *New York Times* reviewer Christopher Lehmann-Haupt praises the essay as an "edifying . . . study of how people shape reality through language," especially, Lehmann-Haupt adds, "the danger of apocalyptic metaphors and the paralysis in the face of disaster such mental constructs can inspire."

Many reviewers note that Sontag seeks to eliminate military metaphors—such as the concept of disease as an "invasion" that makes the body a "battlefield"—from the dialogue regarding illness, without, as Gregory Kolovakos of the *Nation* argues, "allow[ing] that such thinking can be helpful to people." *The Way We Live Now,* originally published as a short story in the *New Yorker,* discusses AIDS in a more narrative format than *AIDS and Its Metaphors,* as a conversation among friends of a dying victim, although the AIDS victim himself never speaks. Fear and rationalization drive their comments and actions; they wonder if they are at risk, and they watch their friend deteriorate while looking to him for cues on how they should react. Rosemary Dinnage of the *Times Literary Supplement* calls the book a "powerful nexus" that summarizes both of Sontag's previous works on illness, and Roudiez in *World Literature Today* compliments "the eerie uncertainty of [the] narrative that draws one toward death while also refusing to accept the inescapable outcome."

Some critics express reservations about Sontag's work, most notably over her critical stance and her highly erudite presentations. For instance, Kendrick claims that the author's "eminence in American letters is disproportionate to the quality of her thought" because "she perpetuates a tradition of philosophical naivete that has always kept America subservient to Europe and that surely should have run its course by now." *Saturday Review* correspondent James Sloan Allen calls Sontag "a virtuoso of the essay, the

Paganini of criticism," who "has often overwhelmed her subjects and intimidated her readers with intellectual pyrotechniques, pretentious erudition, and cliquish hauteur. Lacking has been the quality of mind that deals in modern but sure understanding rather than bravura." But Harriett Gilbert of *New Statesman and Society* hypothesizes that Sontag's reputation is founded on "her mixture of thoughtfulness, mercury awareness and non-stop internal argument [that] continues to echo long after the voice has stopped."

BIOGRAPHICAL/CRITICAL SOURCES:

BOOKS

Bellamy, Joe David, editor, *The New Fiction: Interviews with Innovative American Writers,* University of Illinois Press (Champaign), 1974.

Contemporary Literary Criticism, Gale (Detroit), Volume 1, 1973, Volume 2, 1974, Volume 10, 1979, Volume 13, 1980, Volume 31, 1985.

Dictionary of Literary Biography, Gale, Volume 2: *American Novelists since World War II,* 1978, Volume 67: *Modern American Critics since 1955,* 1988.

Gilman, Richard, *The Confusion of Realms,* Random House (New York City), 1970.

Kennedy, Liam, *Susan Sontag: Mind as Passion,* St. Martin's, (New York City), 1995.

Poague, Leland, editor, *Conversations with Susan Sontag,* University Press of Mississippi (Jackson), 1995.

Sayres, Sohnya, *Susan Sontag: The Elegaic Modernist,* Routledge (New York City), 1990.

Smith, Sharon, *Women Who Make Movies,* Hopkinson & Blake (New York City), 1975.

Solotaroff, Theodore, *The Red Hot Vacuum,* Atheneum (New York City), 1970.

Vidal, Gore, *Reflections upon a Sinking Ship,* Little, Brown, 1969.

PERIODICALS

Antioch Review, spring, 1978.

Atlantic Monthly, September, 1966; November, 1978; September, 1982.

Belles Lettres, spring, 1993, pp. 2-3, 60; spring, 1994, pp. 25-26.

Best Sellers, April, 1979.

Books, November, 1966.

Book Week, September 22, 1963.

Boston Review, Volume 1, number 1, 1975.

Chicago Tribune Book World, December 10, 1978; October 19, 1980; January 9, 1983.

College English, February, 1986.

Columbia, November, 1981.

Commentary, June, 1966.

Commonweal, February 3, 1978.

Detroit News, January 15, 1967.

Encounter, November, 1978.

Esquire, July, 1968; February, 1978.

Harper's, January, 1979; February, 1983.

Hudson Review, autumn, 1969; summer, 1983.

Listener, February 22, 1979.

London Review of Books, December, 1992, p. 18.

Los Angeles Times, December 22, 1980.

Los Angeles Times Book Review, November 19, 1978; December 12, 1982; August 16, 1992, p. 3; October 10, 1993, p. 8.

Ms., March, 1979.

Nation, October 2, 1967; March 24, 1969; June 2, 1969; October 23, 1982; May 1, 1989, p. 598.

National Review, February 24, 1989, pp. 48-50.

New Boston Review, spring, 1978.

New Leader, August 28, 1967.

New Republic, September 21, 1963; February 19, 1966; September 2, 1967; May 3, 1969; January 21, 1978; July 8, 1978; November 25, 1978; November 29, 1980.

New Statesman and Society, March 24, 1967; March 29, 1991, pp. 23-4; October 2, 1992, pp. 43-4.

Newsweek, December 5, 1977; June 12, 1978; October 11, 1982.

New York Arts Journal, Number 13, 1979.

New York Review of Books, June 9, 1966; September 28, 1967; March 13, 1969; July 20, 1978; January 25, 1979; November 6, 1980; August 13, 1992, pp. 3-6.

New York Times, August 18, 1967; February 4, 1969; May 2, 1969; October 3, 1969; November 14, 1977; January 30, 1978; June 1, 1978; November 11, 1978; October 13, 1980; November 11, 1980; January 16, 1989, p. C18.

New York Times Book Review, September 8, 1963; January 23, 1966; August 27, 1967; July 13, 1969; February 13, 1972; December 18, 1977; July 16, 1978; November 26, 1978; November 23, 1980; September 12, 1982; October 24, 1982.

Observer (London), September 27, 1992, p. 50.

Out, April, 1974.

Partisan Review, summer, 1968; Volume 36, number 3, 1969.

Psychology Today, July, 1978.

Publishers Weekly, October 22, 1982.

Salmagundi, fall, 1975.

Saturday Review, February 12, 1966; August 26, 1967; May 3, 1969; December 10, 1977; October 28, 1978; October, 1980.

Sewanee Review, summer, 1974.

Spectator, March 17, 1979.

Threepenny Review, fall, 1981.

Time, August 18, 1967; December 26, 1977; January 27, 1986.

Times Literary Supplement, March 16, 1967; April 25, 1967; January 8, 1970; March 17, 1978; November 23, 1979; December 10, 1982; March 22, 1991, p. 19; September 25, 1992, p. 24.

Tri-Quarterly, fall, 1966.

Village Voice, August 31, 1967; October 15-21, 1980.

Vogue, August 1, 1971.

Voice Literary Supplement, November, 1982.

Washington Post, March 16, 1982.

Washington Post Book World, February 5, 1978; June 25, 1978; December 17, 1978; October 26, 1980.

World Literature Today, spring, 1983; autumn, 1992, p. 723.

Yale Review, spring, 1989, pp. 466-71.

*   *   *

SPARSHOTT, F. E.
  See SPARSHOTT, Francis (Edward)

*   *   *

SPARSHOTT, Francis (Edward)   1926-
  (F. E. Sparshott; Cromwell Kent, a pseudonym)

PERSONAL: Born May 19, 1926, in Chatham, England; son of Frank Brownley (a teacher) and Gladwys Winifred (Head) Sparshott; married Kathleen Elizabeth Vaughan, February 7, 1953; children: Pumpkin Margaret Elizabeth. *Education:* Corpus Christi College, Oxford, B.A. and M.A., with first-class honors, 1950.

*ADDRESSES: Home—*50 Crescentwood Rd., Scarborough, Ontario, Canada M1N 1E4.

CAREER: University of Toronto, Toronto, Ontario, lecturer in philosophy, 1950-55; Victoria College of the University of Toronto, assistant professor, 1955-62, associate professor, 1962-64, professor of philosophy, 1964-91, chair of department, 1965-70, university professor, 1982-91, university professor emeritus, 1991—. Visiting associate professor, Northwestern University, 1958-59; visiting professor, University of Illinois, 1966; Canterbury Visiting Fellow, University of Canterbury (New Zealand), 1987; external professor, graduate program in dance, York University, 1988-91. *Military service:* British Army, 1944-47; served in Palestine, became sergeant.

MEMBER: American Philosophical Association, American Society for Aesthetics (trustee, 1971-73, 1976-78; president, 1981-82), Aristotelian Society, Canadian Classical Association, Canadian Philosophical Association (president, 1975-76), League of Canadian Poets (president, 1977-78), Royal Society of Canada (fellow, 1977), Society of Dance History Scholars (board of directors, 1986-88).

AWARDS, HONORS: American Council of Learned Societies fellowship, 1961-62; Canada Council fellowship, 1970-71; Killam research fellowship, 1977-78; first prize for poetry, CBC Radio Literary Competition, 1981; Centennial Medal, Royal Society of Canada, 1982; Connaught senior fellowship in the humanities, 1984-85.

WRITINGS:

(Under name F. E. Sparshott) *An Enquiry into Goodness and Related Concepts,* University of Toronto Press (Toronto), 1958.

The Structure of Aesthetics, University of Toronto Press, 1963.

(Under name F. E. Sparshott) *The Concept of Criticism: An Essay,* Oxford University Press (New York City), 1967.

(Under pseudonym Cromwell Kent) *A Book,* privately printed, 1970.

(Under name F. E. Sparshott) *Looking for Philosophy,* McGill Queens University Press (Montreal), 1972.

(Author of introduction) John Stuart Mill, *Collected Works,* Volume XI: *Essays in Philosophy and the Classics,* University of Toronto Press, 1978.

The Theory of the Arts, Princeton University Press (Princeton, NJ), 1982.

Off the Ground, Princeton University Press, 1988.

Taking Life Seriously, University of Toronto Press, 1994.

A Measured Pace, University of Toronto Press, 1995.

POETRY

A Divided Voice, Oxford University Press, 1965.
A Cardboard Garage, Clarke, Irwin (Toronto), 1969.
The Rainy Hills: Verses after a Japanese Fashion, privately printed by Porcupine's Quill (Erin, Ontario), 1979.
The Naming of the Beasts, Black Moss (Windsor, Ontario), 1979.
New Fingers for Old Dikes, League of Canadian Poets (Toronto), 1980.
The Cave of Trophonius and Other Poems, Brick Books (London, Ontario), 1983.
The Hanging Gardens of Etobicoke, Childe Thursday, 1983.
Storms and Screens, Childe Thursday, 1986.
Sculling to Byzantium, Childe Thursday, 1989.
Views from the Zucchini Gazebo, Childe Thursday, 1994.

OTHER

Contributor of essays to periodicals, including *Ethics, Journal of Aesthetic Education,* and *Philosophy and Literature;* contributor of poetry to periodicals, including *Poetry, Nation, Canadian Forum, Literary Review, Fiddlehead,* and *West Coast Review.*

The E. J. Pratt Library at the Victoria College of the University of Toronto houses a collection of Sparshott's manuscripts.

WORK IN PROGRESS: It Occurs to Me Now, "a sort of meditation."

SIDELIGHTS: "Philosopher, critical theorist, and poet, Francis Edward Sparshott has written on a wide range of moral, aesthetic, and intellectual issues," writes Wendy Robbins Keitner in a *Dictionary of Literary Biography* essay. Sparshott's reputation as a philosopher and critical theorist is confirmed by "his series of enquiries into aesthetics, *The Theory of the Arts* . . . a massive, 726-page survey," Keitner explains. *An Enquiry into Goodness and Related Concepts* and *The Structure of Aesthetics* have also received high praise from critics.

In addition to his work as a philosopher and critical theorist, Sparshott's versatility as a poet has also been critically recognized. Describing Sparshott's verse as "traditional and impersonal," Keitner adds that "critics have commented on Sparshott's cerebral poetic style, and his subjects, too, suggest the aca-

demic and the thinker: the nature of reality, memory, perception, change, and unmerited pain."

In his *Contemporary Authors Autobiography Series* essay, Sparshott recalls that he became a philosophy professor because he needed a job and was unqualified to do much of anything else. "Almost no one ever quotes my work or uses my ideas, but I have kept my job and been offered other jobs and never had to apply for a job, so from a practical point of view I must be doing something right," he claims. Of his writing abilities in general, he muses, "Even if I was not meant to be a poet, I was meant to be a writer at any event—novels, philosophical treatises, letters to editors, anything. Prose came naturally to me, colons and all. Observing my academic colleagues shows what a rare blessing this is: after honing their thoughts, they must labor to hammer them into sentences. That is never a problem for me, nor has it ever been a problem to think of something to say, more or less suitable and more or less the right length. True, the outcome strikes me as essentially worthless—but who am I to say?"

Sparshott told *CA:* "On reflection in retirement, it seems to me that my work in philosophy and poetry, as well as my activity as an amateur photographer, has always been animated by a fascination with the ways in which forms emerge in the course of change from the intersection and interruption of disparate processes. My passion is epitomized in a series of photographs I have been taking of balloons, once released in celebration, that have lost their buoyancy over the waters of Lake Huron and washed up on the shore, where they become tangled in weeds or willows, or perish on the limestone until they become mere smears of bright color."

BIOGRAPHICAL/CRITICAL SOURCES:

BOOKS

Contemporary Authors Autobiography Series, Volume 15, Gale (Detroit), 1992.
Dictionary of Literary Biography, Volume 60: *Canadian Writers since 1960; Second Series,* Gale, 1987.
Heath, Jeffrey M., editor, *Profiles in Canadian Literature,* Dundurn Press (Toronto), 1986.

PERIODICALS

Books in Canada, December, 1980, p. 13; June, 1984, p. 24.

Canadian Forum, July, 1969.
Choice, January, 1983, p. 715.
Dance Research Journal, winter, 1988, p. 52.
Modern Language Review, October, 1968, p. 922.
Philosophy and Literature, October, 1993.
Times Literary Supplement, February 16, 1973, p. 190.
Virginia Quarterly Review, summer, 1989, p. 104.

*   *   *

SPENCER, Scott 1945-

PERSONAL: Born September 1, 1945, in Washington, DC; son of Charles (a steelworker and CIO organizer) and Jean Spencer; married Claire Dupuy; children: Celeste, Asher. *Education:* Attended University of Illinois; University of Wisconsin at Madison, B.A., 1969.

ADDRESSES: Office—c/o Janklow Nesbit, 598 Madison Ave., New York, NY 10022. *Agent*—Erica Spellman, William Morris Agency, 1350 Avenue of the Americas, New York, NY 10019.

CAREER: Novelist. Worked variously in an employment agency and as an evaluator for federal education programs.

MEMBER: PEN American Center (member of executive board; member of Freedom to Write Committee).

AWARDS, HONORS: Endless Love was named a notable book of 1979 by the Notable Books Council of the American Library Association's Reference and Adult Services Division and was nominated for an American Book Award in 1981.

WRITINGS:

NOVELS

Last Night at the Brain Thieves Ball, Houghton (Boston), 1973.
Preservation Hall, Knopf (New York City), 1976.
Endless Love, Knopf, 1979.
Waking the Dead, Knopf, 1986.
Secret Anniversaries, Knopf, 1990.
Men in Black, Knopf, 1995.

OTHER

Act of Vengeance (screenplay), Home Box Office (HBO), 1985.

Contributor of stories and articles to periodicals, including *Esquire, Harper's, Film Comment, Ladies' Home Journal, New York Times Book Review, Redbook, Rolling Stone,* and *Vanity Fair.*

ADAPTATIONS: Endless Love was adapted by screenwriter Judith Rascoe as a motion picture for Universal Pictures in 1981. The film was directed by Franco Zeffirelli.

SIDELIGHTS: Noted for the intensity of his prose and his acute understanding of character and situation, Scott Spencer first received widespread critical attention and popularity following the publication of his third novel, *Endless Love.* Writing in the *Dictionary of Literary Biography Yearbook,* Michael Mullen states that "Spencer has said . . . he writes one book at a time; so, while his books do have elements in common, most notably characters whose desires place them in opposition to society, each is unique." The plot and subject matter for Spencer's first novel, *Last Night at the Brain Thieves Ball,* for instance, is a far cry from the story in *Endless Love.* Told in the form of a journal, *Last Night at the Brain Thieves Ball* centers on Paul Galambos, a psychology professor who takes a job with NESTER—a secret company that hopes to use brain implants to control people's desires. Growing dissatisfaction with his employers leads Paul to begin keeping a journal with which he hopes to expose NESTER. Eventually Paul escapes from the company's complex but is returned after being captured. On the day Paul's supervisor releases him from his contract, he informs Paul that his work for NESTER was part of a plan to rehabilitate him, that he was a danger to society, and that all his experiments were fake. The supervisor then cuts off Paul's hand.

"Like Paul Galambos," Mullen writes, "the main character in *Preservation Hall,* Virgil Morgan, is not sure who he is or what his place in the world is, and to learn these things, he must pay a price for them." The main action of the novel takes place at a secluded country house in Maine, where Virgil and his wife are spending the New Year's holiday with Vergil's stepbrother and his stepbrother's girlfriend. While destroying a dresser they plan to burn in the fireplace, Virgil, who despises his father, kills his stepbrother. Mullen states that Virgil's uncertainty over the extent to which his stepbrother's death was accidental forces him "to come to terms with what is good and bad in himself . . . [and] to reevaluate his relationship with his father in an attempt to expiate the guilt he still feels about killing his stepbrother." In a review for the *New York Times Book Review,* Katha Pollitt praises Spencer's characterization of Virgil and his father Earl. "It's a mark of Spencer's skill that although we hear the whole story from Virgil's point of view, ultimately Earl's resentment of his son's success seems less mean-spirited than Virgil's shame at his father's failure. . . . Spencer deserves a good deal of praise for having the imagination to know more about his characters than they do themselves."

Commenting on *Endless Love,* Brigitte Weeks of the *Washington Post Book World* states that "Scott Spencer is becoming a writer of astonishing depth and power." Set in the 1960's, *Endless Love* traces the relationship of seventeen-year-old David Axelrod to sixteen-year-old Jade Butterfield and her pot-smoking, permissive parents. David cherishes the Butterfields' laissez-faire lifestyle and leaves his own parents to live with Jade's family. Although Mr. and Mrs. Butterfield encourage David, who develops an obsessive love for Jade, to sleep with their daughter, they eventually deem the young couple's relationship too intense and banish David from the house, forbidding him to return for thirty days. In his desperation to see the family, David ignites the Butterfields' newspaper on their porch, hoping the small fire will bring the family out of the house where he can see them. The fire, however, rages out of control, and David must rescue the Butterfields from the blazing structure. As punishment for starting the fire, David is sent to a private mental institution for three years, during which time the Butterfield family deteriorates, beginning with the divorce of Jade's parents. After his release from the hospital, David tries to rekindle his relationship with Jade and reunite the Butterfield family, but all his efforts prove futile.

Critics claim that Spencer's book is not concerned so much with the actions of its characters as with the psychological conflicts underlying their actions. Edward Rothstein, writing in the *New York Times Book Review,* notes that "Mr. Spencer has an acute grasp of character and situation. He gives us details that make these often tormented people uncommonly convincing. There are the erotic ties within the Butterfield family that are threatened by David's intrusion; the absence of such ties in his own parents; his mother's confused pain at his obsession; his

father's active interest in it." Rothstein considers David the "true heart of the book," and states: "He tells his story with such ardent conviction that we begin to share his obsession. He constantly surprises us, too, because he takes himself by surprise. . . . But the world in this novel is as unpredictable as David, and just as threatening; unexpected encounters, sudden partings, deaths and punishments assault him. They beset us as well, for we are in the grip of an expert storyteller."

In her *Washington Post Book World* review, Brigitte Weeks writes: "The action doesn't matter. David matters. The striking of the match banishes normalcy for the Butterfields and for David. . . . The reader lives through his emotional maelstroms in a way that is shocking in its intimacy. . . . The sensations aroused by reading this novel are more akin to the legendary thrill of riding some fearsome, swooping, sickening rollercoaster—'What the hell am I doing here?' one moment, and the next a short walk to join the line for another ride. The speed, the fear, the anticipation sharpen the pleasure of walking quietly on solid ground. And that is the joy of *Endless Love.*" And Christopher Lehmann-Haupt warns in the *New York Times:* "If you've ever been wildly and impractically in love, you won't stop to look at it objectively. You'll soar and sink with David, and ache for him. . . . Reading Mr. Spencer's novel, you'll remember for a while when it seemed possible to die of love."

Obsessive love is also a theme in Spencer's next work, *Waking the Dead.* The story centers on Fielding Pierce, a lawyer who loses his girlfriend, Sarah Williams, to a violent act of terrorism. After Fielding has apparently put his life back together and embarked on a promising political career, he begins to imagine that his dead girlfriend has come back to life. His obsession with recapturing his lost love threatens his stability and his nomination as a Congressional candidate.

Critical response to the novel has been ambivalent. A reviewer for the *New Yorker* observes that while Spencer is sometimes "excessive" and has moments of "uncomfortable sentimentality," he is also "a writer of great intensity, of imagery in the Graham Greene manner." For other critics, the novel lacks a narrative coherence that ultimately proves crippling. According to Judith Levine of the *Village Voice,* the trouble starts with the death of Sarah, a left-wing activist from a wealthy family who becomes embroiled in Chilean politics. "The violent event around which much of the action, including Fielding's advancing madness, turns is not all that believable," Levine argues. The reviewer also notes some inconsistencies in how Spencer develops his characters and wonders whether Fielding is meant to be seen as a "a true man of the people," "a naive puppet of the powers that be," or "a self-serving creep using *them.*" Similarly, Michiko Kakutani of the *New York Times* writes: "Given Fielding's calculating nature, we never completely believe in his love for Sarah," and the story's tragic end "seems so arbitrary and unnecessary." Kakutani also notes that the evocative and lyrical prose that marked the speech of *Endless Love*'s teenaged hero becomes awkward and embarrassing for the middle-aged Fielding. "We often have the feeling that Fielding is giving a campaign speech," she comments.

Spencer's next work, *Secret Anniversaries,* pivots on a bold young girl named Caitlin. The action begins in the 1930's, when Caitlin is forced to leave her quiet hometown in rural upstate New York after her employers find her in bed with their son. Caitlin moves to Washington, DC, where she begins working for a pro-German, isolationist Congressman who wants to keep the United States out of World War II. Caitlin's sympathies are torn between loyalty to her boss and love for an investigative reporter who is working to uncover pro-Fascist sympathizers in the government. The culmination of Caitlin's political consciousness, which includes exposure to 1960's radicalism in New York City's Greenwich Village and work for the World Refugee Alliance following World War II, reaches its apogee when she visits the enshrined home of Anne Frank in Amsterdam. "*Secret Anniversaries* is a strange novel, layered, cleverly woven," comments Carol Muske in the *New York Times Book Review*. Kakutani writes that Caitlin is "a finely observed portrait of a woman . . . who has lived most of her life on the margins of conventionality." But, Kakutani laments, *Secret Anniversaries* places its heroine in "such a crudely drawn cartoon world of political villains that it manages to almost completely ruin the reader's sense of credulity."

A lighter tone prevails in Spencer's next work, *Men in Black,* which probes the troubled life of Sam Holland, a serious writer whose literary works have failed to gain a following. Responding to pressure to finally make some money, he gives up his calling and moves to a small rural town to write popular nonfiction on such topics as traveling with a pet and avoiding the hazards of too much salt. To Sam's

astonishment, his book on UFOs brings enormous success and catapults him to the national stage. While his career soars, his family life continues its downward spiral. His wife finds out about his lover, while his son runs away from home and becomes a criminal. Sam also learns that his pseudonym matches the name of an anti-Semitic extremist, whose followers flock to Sam's nationwide book tour.

"Sam's experiences on the road [doing a book tour] are uncommonly hilarious and terrifying, handled with tremendous verve," observes Elaine Kendall in the *Los Angeles Times*. Robert Chatain states in the *Chicago Tribune* that "*Men in Black* is a good story—a speedy time-lapse image of evasive struggle. Its rummage through the debris of a life lived by taking the easier course among available alternatives doesn't uncover much wisdom, merely a talent for survival." The novel loses power, Chatain argues, because Sam is too self-pitying, especially when pondering his fate should his wife discover his infidelity. "His frustrated dreams, his past failures, his old temptations are held up to brooding condemnation, but his close-at-hand present and future actions escape the kind of reasoned weighing of alternatives that is a familiar, even necessary ethical dimension of life," Chatain writes. Christopher Lehmann-Haupt, however, writing in the *New York Times,* finds *Men in Black* "charmingly funny-sad" and argues that "Mr. Spencer . . . has a charming way of capturing the banal side of the antic and the antic side of the banal."

BIOGRAPHICAL/CRITICAL SOURCES:

BOOKS

Contemporary Literary Criticism, Volume 30, Gale (Detroit), 1984.
Dictionary of Literary Biography Yearbook 1986, Gale, 1987, pp. 329-34.
Ruas, Charles, *Conversations with American Writers,* Knopf, 1985, pp. 295-324.

PERIODICALS

Booklist, May 1, 1995, pp. 1553-54.
Chicago Tribune, July 17, 1981; May 11, 1986, p. 39; May 6, 1990, p. 1; May 21, 1995, pp. 3, 5.
Chicago Tribune Book World, September 16, 1979; July 12, 1981.
Los Angeles Times, July 31, 1990, p. E4; May 16, 1995, p. E5.
New York, June 2, 1986, pp. 50-9.

New Yorker, July 21, 1986, pp. 93-4; May 22, 1995, pp. 89-90.

New York Times, September 6, 1979; July 17, 1981; May 7, 1986, p. C28; May 8, 1990, p. C19; April 17, 1995, p. C13.

New York Times Book Review, September 16, 1973; January 2, 1977; September 23, 1979; November 25, 1979; June 8, 1980, pp. 7, 38-9; October 19, 1980; July 22, 1990, p. 12; April 30, 1995, p. 7.

People, June 11, 1990, p. 29.

Publishers Weekly, March 2, 1990, p. 72.

Saturday Review, October 27, 1979.

Time, October 8, 1979.

Times Literary Supplement, February 24, 1978; April 11, 1980.

USA Today, May 16, 1986.

Village Voice, December 16, 1981; June 17, 1986, p. 49.

Wall Street Journal, June 7, 1990, p. A12.

Washington Post, May 6, 1990, p. 3; April 25, 1995, p. D2.

Washington Post Book World, September 16, 1979; December 9, 1979; October 12, 1980.

*   *   *

STEINEM, Gloria   1934-

PERSONAL: Born March 25, 1934, in Toledo, Ohio; daughter of Leo and Ruth (Nuneviller) Steinem. *Education:* Smith College, B.A. (magna cum laude), 1956; University of Delhi and University of Calcutta, India, graduate study, 1957-58.

ADDRESSES: Office—Ms. Magazine, 230 Park Ave., New York, NY 10136.

CAREER: Editor, writer, lecturer. Independent Research Service, Cambridge, MA, and New York City, director, 1959-60; *Glamour* magazine, New York City, contributing editor, 1962-69; *New York* magazine, New York City, co-founder and contributing editor, 1968-72; *Ms.* magazine, New York City, co-founder and editor, 1972-87, columnist, 1980-87, consulting editor, 1988—. Contributing correspondent to NBC's *Today* show. Active in civil rights and peace campaigns, including those of United Farm Workers, Vietnam War, Tax Protest, and Committee for the Legal Defense of Angela Davis. Editorial consultant to Conde Nast Publications, 1962-69,

Curtis Publishing, 1964-65, Random House Publishing, 1988—, and McCall Publishing.

MEMBER: PEN, National Press Club, Society of Magazine Writers, Authors Guild, Authors League of America, American Federation of Television and Radio Artists, National Organization for Women, Women's Action Alliance (co-founder; chairperson, 1970—), National Women's Political Caucus (founding member; member of national advisory committee, 1971—), Ms. Foundation for Women (co-founder; member of board, 1972—), Coalition of Labor Union Women (founding member, 1974), Phi Beta Kappa.

AWARDS, HONORS: Chester Bowles Asian fellow in India, 1957-58; Penney-Missouri journalism award, 1970, for *New York* article "After Black Power, Women's Liberation"; Ohio Governor's journalism award, 1972; named Woman of the Year, *McCall's* magazine, 1972; Doctorate of Human Justice from Simmons College, 1973; Bill of Rights award, American Civil Liberties Union of Southern California, 1975; Woodrow Wilson International Center for Scholars fellow, 1977; Ceres Medal from United nations; Front Page Award; Clarion Award; nine citations from *World Almanac* as one of the twenty-five most influential women in America.

WRITINGS:

The Thousand Indias, Government of India, 1957.

The Beach Book, Viking (New York City), 1963.

(With G. Chester) *Wonder Woman,* Holt (New York City), 1972.

(Author of introductory note) Marlo Thomas and others, *Free to Be . . . You and Me,* McGraw (New York City), 1974.

Outrageous Acts and Everyday Rebellions, Holt, 1983.

Marilyn: Norma Jeane, Holt, 1986.

Bedside Book of Self-Esteem, Little, Brown (Boston), 1989.

Revolution from Within: A Book of Self-Esteem, Little, Brown, 1992.

Moving beyond Words, Simon & Schuster (New York City), 1993.

Contributor to *Running against the Machine,* edited by Peter Manso, Doubleday, New York City, 1969. Writer for television, including series "That Was the Week that Was," NBC, 1964-65. Author of films and political campaign material. Former author of column, "The City Politic," in *New York.* Contributor to periodicals, including *Cosmopolitan, Esquire, Family Circle, Life, Show,* and *Vogue.* Editorial consultant, *Seventeen,* 1969-70, and *Show.*

ADAPTATIONS: "I Was a Playboy Bunny" was produced as an ABC television movie, *A Bunny's Tale,* 1985.

SIDELIGHTS: Gloria Steinem is recognized as one of the foremost organizers of the modern women's movement. Her major contribution, according to Maureen Corrigan in the *New York Times Book Review,* is "her ability to popularize feminist issues to a wide and often wary audience." Her grandmother, Pauline Steinem, was the president of a turn-of-the-century women's suffrage group and was a representative to the 1908 International Council of Women, but Gloria was not substantially influenced by her while growing up in Toledo, Ohio. Her mother and father divorced when she was young, and at the age of ten Gloria was left alone to care for both herself and her mentally ill mother.

Steinem left home when she was seventeen to attend Smith College on a scholarship. Like many women of the era, she was engaged by her senior year but broke her engagement to continue her political science studies in India where she had adjusted quickly, adopting native dress and ways. Because English served as the common language, she was "able to really talk, and tell jokes, and understand political arguments," she told Miriam Berkley in an interview for *Publishers Weekly.* Steinem was also able to freelance for Indian newspapers. She supplemented her university studies by seeking out the company of the activists who were then working for an independent India. As a member of a group called the Radical Humanists, she traveled to southern India at the time of the terrible caste riots there, working as a member of a peacemaking team. Steinem's experiences gave her a deep sympathy for the underclasses as well as an enduring love of India.

When the time came for her to return to the United States, Steinem did so filled with an "enormous sense of urgency about the contrast between wealth and poverty," she told Berkley. Because she "rarely met people who had shared this experience," Steinem related, it became "like a dream. It had no relation to my real, everyday life. . . . I couldn't write about it." Instead, Steinem established a successful freelance career, writing articles about celebrities, fashions, and tropical vacations, while devoting her spare time to work for the civil rights movement.

Berkley describes Steinem's life in the early 1960s as "schizophrenically split between career and conscience." "I was . . . divided up into pieces as a person," the author told Elisabeth Bumiller in the *Washington Post.* "I was working on one thing, and caring about another, which I think is the way a lot of us have to live our lives. I'm lucky it came together."

Steinem's best-known article from her early career is "I Was a Playboy Bunny." Assigned to cover the 1963 opening of the New York City Playboy Club for *Show* magazine, she went undercover to work as a "Bunny," or waitress, for two weeks. The resulting article is an "excellent, ironic, illuminating bit of reporting," claims Angela Carter in the *Washington Post Book Review.* Steinem was instructed by the "Bunny Mother" in techniques for stuffing her bodice and bending over to serve drinks, cautioned against sneezing, which would split the seams of her Bunny costume, presented with a copy of the "Bunny Bible," the lengthy code of conduct for Playboy waitresses, and informed that all new Bunnies were required to have a pelvic examination performed by the club's specially appointed doctor. "I Was a Playboy Bunny" is "hysterically funny," according to Ann Marie Lapinski in the *Chicago Tribune.* It is also as "full of feminist consciousness as some of [Steinem's] later reportage," argues Carter, who comments: "If it is implicit rather than explicit, it is no less powerful for that." Of her experiences in the club, Steinem remarked to *Los Angeles Times* interviewer Elenita Ravicz, "Being a Bunny was more humiliating than I thought it would be. True, it was never the kind of job I would have considered under ordinary circumstances, but I expected it to be more glamorous and better paid than it was. . . . Customers there seemed to be there because they could be treated as superiors. . . . There is a real power difference when one group is semi-nude and the other is fully-clothed."

By the mid-sixties Steinem was getting more substantial writing assignments and earning respect for her pieces on political figures. In 1968 she and Clay Felker founded *New York* magazine, to which Steinem supplied the monthly column "The City Politic" and articles such as "Ho Chi Minh in New York." She was still seen as something of a trendy celebrity by many in the male-dominated world of journalism, however. Bumiller quotes a 1969 *Time* article describing Steinem as "one of the best dates to take to a New York party these days. . . . Writers, politicians, editors, publishers and tuned-in businessmen are all intensely curious about her. Gloria is not only a successful freelance writer and contributing editor of *New York* magazine; she is also a trim, undeniably female, blonde-streaked brunette. . . . She does something for her soft suits and clinging dresses, has legs worthy of her miniskirts, and a brain that keeps conversation lively without getting tricky." Steinem's popularity in such social circles soon waned because of her growing interest in controversial women's issues.

Colleague reaction to a 1969 article she wrote about a New York abortion hearing shocked Steinem. At the hearing Steinem heard testimony from women who had endured illegal abortions, risking injury, possibly ending in sterilization, and sometimes being forced to have sex with the abortionist. She told Ravicz, "I wrote an article about the hearing and my male colleagues, really nice men I got along well with, took me aside one by one and said, 'don't get involved with these crazy women. You've taken so much trouble to establish your reputation as a serious journalist, don't throw it all away.' That was when I realized men valued me only to the extent I imitated them." Instead of abandoning the "crazy women" of the abortion hearing, Steinem followed up her coverage with an extensively researched article on reproductivity and other feminist issues. Her article "After Black Power, Women's Liberation" won her the Penney-Missouri journalism award, but also "unleashed a storm of negative reactions . . . from male colleagues. The response from the publishing establishment, and its reluctance to publish other work on the subject, opened her eyes. She began to pursue not only writing but also speaking engagements and became an active part of the women's movement she had once only observed," relates Berkley.

Steinem came to believe that a magazine controlled by women was necessary if a truly open forum on women's issues was to exist. Accordingly, she and others began working toward that goal. Felker offered to subsidize a sample issue and to include a thirty-page excerpt of the new publication in *New York* magazine. Steinem and the rest of the staff worked without pay and produced the first issue of *Ms.* in January, 1972. "We called it the spring issue," Steinem recalled to Berkley. "We were really afraid that if it didn't sell it would embarrass the women's movement. So we called it Spring so that it could lie there on the newsstands for a long time." Such worries were unfounded—the entire 300,000-copy run of *Ms.* sold out in eight days.

Steinem was suddenly the editor of a very successful monthly magazine, but was somewhat ambivalent about the position: "I backed into [starting *Ms.*]," she admitted to Beth Austin in an interview for the *Chicago Tribune.* "I felt very strongly there should be a feminist magazine. But I didn't want to start it myself. I wanted to be a freelance writer. I'd never had a job, never worked in an office, never worked with a group before. It just happened." Steinem believed that she would turn the editorship of *Ms.* over to someone else as soon as the magazine was squarely on its feet. "I said, 'I'm going to do this two years, that's it.' I kept on saying that until . . . I'd already been doing it for almost seven years. Then I took a fellowship at the Woodrow Wilson Center, which is part of the Smithsonian Institution in Washington [D.C.]. So I was away from the office for the first time for substantial periods of time. . . . I just missed it terribly. And I suddenly realized that, where I thought I'd been delaying life, there *was* life."

As a spokesperson for the women's movement, Steinem has been criticized as subversive and strident by some and as overly tolerant and conservative by others. An overview of the opinions that made her a figurehead of the Woman's Movement during the 1980s is published as *Outrageous Acts and Everyday Rebellions,* a collection representing twenty years of Steinem's writing on a variety of subjects, including politics, pornography, her mother, and Marilyn Monroe. Carter criticizes the book, complaining that Steinem presents only "the acceptable face of feminism" and that she is "straightjacketed by her own ideology." Diane Johnson offers a more favorable appraisal in the *New York Times Book Review:* "Reading Miss Steinem's essays . . . one is struck by their intelligence, restraint and common sense, as well as by the energetic and involved life they reflect. . . . This is a consciousness-raising book. . . . Her views, like her writing itself, are characterized by engaging qualities of unpretentious clarity and forceful expression." Douglas Hill concurs in the Toronto *Globe & Mail:* "Honesty, fairness and consistency gleam in these pages. And Steinem writes superbly. . . . It's her special strength to write as cleanly and affectingly about her mother's mental illness as about the practice of genital mutilation endured by 75 million women worldwide or the inadequacies of William Styron's fiction."

Steinem's next book grew from an essay in *Outrageous Acts* concerning Marilyn Monroe, the actress who became internationally famous as a "sex goddess" in the 1950s and apparently committed suicide in 1962. When photojournalist George Barris decided to publish a series of photographs taken of Monroe shortly before her death, Steinem was asked to contribute the text. While researching *Marilyn: Norma Jeane,* she became aware that although over forty books had already been published about the late film star, only a few were written by women. Most of the biographies focused on the scandalous aspects of Monroe's death and personal relationships, or reinforced her image as the ultimate pin-up. Steinem explained to *Washington Post* interviewer Chip Brown: "I tried to take away the fantasy of Marilyn and replace it with reality. . . . The book doesn't have a thesis so much as an emphasis—an emphasis on Norma Jeane, on the private, real, internal person. I hadn't read a book about Marilyn that made me feel I knew her. My purpose was to try to get to know or to portray the real person inside the public image." Commenting on the ironic fact that Monroe derived little pleasure from her physical relationships, Steinem suggested to Brown that "it's hard for men to admit that a sex goddess didn't enjoy sex. . . . It's part of the desire to believe she was murdered—the same cultural impulse that says if she's a sex goddess she had to have enjoyed sex doesn't want to believe she killed herself, doesn't want to accept her unhappiness."

Brown sees Steinem's *Marilyn* as a feminist rebuttal to Norman Mailer's biography of Monroe: "His book is an extravagant concerto for the 'Stradivarius of sex.' Monroe is the supreme object. . . . [Steinem] stresses the limited choices women had then—and underscores Monroe's struggle for independence, her desire to be taken seriously." London *Times* reviewer Fiona MacCarthy finds fault with Steinem's "passionate involvement with the helpless child in Marilyn," believing that it is an example of "the new phenomenon of women letting women off too lightly. . . . Her sentimental vision of the real Marilyn entrapped in the sex-goddess body sometimes makes one wonder where is now the Gloria Steinem who worked on the campaign trail in the 1960s both as a reporter and an aide to George McGovern. Has she lost all astuteness?" But Diana Trilling argues that *Marilyn: Norma Jeane* is "thoughtful and absorbing." Her *New York Times Book Review* evaluation calls the biography "a quiet book; it has none of the sensationalism that has colored other purportedly serious books about the film star, Norman Mailer's in particular. . . . In writing about Marilyn Monroe, Gloria Steinem for the most part admirably avoids

the ideological excess that we have come to associate with the women's movement—Monroe emerges from her book a far more dimensional figure than she would have been if she had been presented as simply the victim of a male-dominated society."

Bumiller summarizes Steinem's view of the woman's movement in an interview in the *Washington Post:* ". . . it's not dead or even sick, but has instead spread out from the middle class to be integrated into issues like unemployment and the gender gap. [Steinem] sees four enormous goals ahead: 'reproductive freedom, democratic families, a depoliticized culture and work redefined. . . . We are talking about overthrowing, or humanizing—pick your verb, depending on how patient you feel—the sex and race caste systems.'" As the task of meeting these goals was engaged by a new generation of feminists, Steinem turned her energies, and her focus, inward. "I've lived my first 50 years externally, reacting more than acting," she told Molly O'Neill in an interview for the *New York Times* in the year she turned sixty. "I've been much too nice." Steinem's study of her own life became the subject of 1992's *Revolution from Within,* an introspective, circular exploration of the ways in which self-esteem affects everything: handwriting, body language, family relationships, the American system of public education, and world economic policies. Basing her comments on insights drawn from her personal self-exploration as well as her own belief in learning from nature, Steinem provides readers with a "Meditation Guide," suggests means for them to discover and understand their own "inner child," and includes an appendix of self-help books under the heading "Bibliotherapy."

Revolution from Within received mixed reviews, most notably because of the reaction to it from feminist circles. "How can it be," questions Carol Sternhell in *Women's Review of Books,* "after so many years of trying to change the world, that one of our best-known feminists is suddenly advising women to change ourselves instead?" Steinem's focus on self-esteem appeared to many mainstream reviewers to be an attempt to jump aboard the pop-psychology bandwagon, and *Revolution from Within'* s rapid climb to the top of the best-seller lists seemed to bear them out. Feminist critics, however, feared that the book was much more: a sign that this figurehead of the woman's movement had "sold out." Critic Joseph Adelson assures readers that Steinem's "old externalizing mentality is still there, powerful as ever," in his review of *Revolution from Within* for *Commen-*

tary. But, he later notes, "anyone expecting coherent discourse may find much of this book unreadable. It rambles from topic to topic, a mishmash of pseudo-profundities, dubious information, and half-baked opinions." Mary Beard is similarly critical of the work in the *Times Literary Supplement:* "Following in all the worst traditions of popular psychology and self-help manuals, [Steinem] identifies the malaise at the heart of the modern human condition as childhood injury . . . a claim that is so obviously true that it hardly requires the three-hundred page demonstration that she gives it."

Critics view Steinem's next book, *Moving beyond Words*, in a more positive light. Published in 1993, *Moving beyond Words* is a collection of essays—three previously published and three new—that, as Maureen Corrigan contends in the *New York Times Book Review*, demonstrate "that what appears to be 'natural' is, in fact, socially constructed." In one of the book's examples, "What If Freud Were Phyllis?," Steinem performs a fictional sex-change operation on the noted psychotherapist that results in theories of "womb envy" and the like, dramatizing her contention that the basis of many of the late doctor's assumptions lies couched in male superiority. "More than any other brief text I have read, this essay simply revokes, cancels and terminates the reader's ability to take gender inequity for granted," concludes Patricia Limerick in her review for the *Washington Post*. The essay "Sex, Lies and Advertising" takes to task the manipulative practices of magazine advertising, a concern of Steinem's that resulted in *Ms.* magazine's decision to eliminate advertising from its pages in 1990. "Doing Sixty" draws its insights from Steinem's personal exploration of self—similarly recounted in *Revolution from Within*—in its celebration of age as a time to give oneself permission to take risks with fewer worries about social repercussions. In "The Masculinization of Wealth" Steinem contends that wealthy women—who are resented by society and abused by members of their own families to such a point that, even with great financial resources, they are powerless in society—are as much victims of patriarchy as their poorer female counterparts. While also praising the work as a whole, Limerick finds that Steinem fails to adequately address the inequities involved when racial discrimination is coupled with gender discrimination. Limerick declares: "I wanted a chapter on feminism, race and poverty that equalled in power and persuasion the essay on feminism and wealth." Limerick ultimately concludes: "The pleasures and satisfactions of 'being who we really are' prove to be as unequally distributed as income and opportunity. . . . I cannot read [these closing remarks] without thinking that this book, at its end, takes an unexpected turn back to a protected world of white, middle-class privilege and choice." *Moving beyond Words*, finds Susan Cheever in the *Los Angeles Times Book Review*, "is a book that spells out, over and over, the many different direct and subtle ways in which women are reduced to powerlessness in our world."

As the women's movement moves into what many call its second wave, marked by dissent among its ranks and what fellow feminist and author Susan Faludi has termed a social "backlash" in her 1991 book of the same name, Steinem remains positive about the future of feminism. "The first wave was about women gaining a legal identity," she told O'Neill, "and it took 150 years. The second wave of feminism is about social equality. We've come a long way, but its only been 25 years. . . . Women used to say, 'I am not a feminist, but. . . .' Now they say, 'I am a feminist, but. . . .'"

BIOGRAPHICAL/CRITICAL SOURCES:

BOOKS

Heilbrun, Carolyn, *The Education of a Woman: The Life of Gloria Steinem*, Dial (New York City), 1995.

PERIODICALS

Belles Lettres, summer, 1992, p. 26.
Chicago Tribune, October 2, 1983; January 11, 1987.
Commentary, May, 1992, pp. 54-55.
Detroit News, August 28, 1983.
Esquire, June, 1984.
Globe & Mail (Toronto), February 8, 1986.
London Review of Books, April 23, 1992, p. 17.
Los Angeles Times, December 11, 1984; December 10, 1986; May 6, 1987.
Los Angeles Times Book Review, June 19, 1994, p. 2.
National Review, March 2, 1992, pp. 47-48.
New Republic, July 11, 1994, pp. 32-36.
New Statesmen, February 20, 1987, pp. 19-20.
New York Times, April 4, 1987; May 10, 1988; February 9, 1995, pp. C1, 10.
New York Times Book Review, September 4, 1983; December 21, 1986, p. 1; May 22, 1994, p. 37.

People, June 11, 1984; February 25, 1985.
Publishers Weekly, August 12, 1983.
Times (London), February 19, 1987.
Times Literary Supplement, April 24, 1992, p. 11.
Washington Post, October 12, 1983; December 7, 1986.
Washington Post Book World, October 9, 1983; June 26, 1994, p. 1.
Women's Review of Books, June, 1992, pp. 5-6.*

*   *   *

STERNLICHT, Sanford   1931-

PERSONAL: Born September 20, 1931, in New York, NY; son of Irving Stanley (a food manager) and Sylvia (Hilsenroth) Sternlicht; married Dorothy Hilkert, June 7, 1956 (died, 1977); children: David, Daniel. *Education:* State University College of Education (now State University of New York College at Oswego), B.S., 1953; Colgate University, M.A. (with distinction), 1955; Syracuse University, Ph.D., 1962.

ADDRESSES: Home—128 Dorset Rd., Syracuse, NY 13210-3048. *Office*—Department of English, Syracuse University, Syracuse, NY 13244.

CAREER: Colgate University, Hamilton, NY, instructor in remedial reading, 1953-55; State University of New York College at Oswego, instructor, 1959-60, assistant professor, 1960-62, associate professor, 1962, professor of English, 1962-72, professor of theatre, 1972-86, chair of department, 1973-85; Syracuse University, professor of English, 1986—. Leverhulme Foundation visiting fellow, University of York, York, England, 1965-66. Has worked in professional theater, radio, and television. *Military service:* U.S. Navy, active duty with Atlantic and Mediterranean fleets, 1955-59; became lieutenant junior grade. U.S. Navy Reserve, retired as commander.

MEMBER: PEN, Modern Language Association of America, Poetry Society of America (fellow), Shakespeare Association of America.

AWARDS, HONORS: Six prizes from Poetry Society of Norfolk, VA, 1959-64; *Writer* magazine's annual award for a new poet, 1960; State University of New York Research Foundation fellowships for writing, 1963, 1965, 1969, 1970, and grant, 1964.

WRITINGS:

Gull's Way (poetry), Richard R. Smith, 1961.
Uriah Philips Levy: The Blue Star Commodore (biography), Bloch Publishing (New York City), 1961.
Love in Pompeii (poetry), South and West, 1967.

Contributor to books, including *Avalon Anthology,* Different Press, 1960; and *Anthologie de la poesie contemporaine aux Etats-Unis,* Revue Moderne (Paris), 1961. Also contributor of poetry to numerous periodicals, including the *New York Times, Christian Science Monitor, Saturday Evening Post,* and *Poetry Review.*

EDITOR

Selected Stories of Padraic Colum, Syracuse University Press (Syracuse, NY), 1985.
Selected Plays of Padraic Colum, Syracuse University Press, 1986.
Selected Poems of Padraic Colum, Syracuse University Press, 1989.
In Search of Stevie Smith, Syracuse University Press, 1991.

LITERARY CRITICISM

John Webster's Imagery and the Webster Canon, University of Salzburg, 1974.
John Masefield, Twayne (Boston), 1977.
C. S. Forester, Twayne, 1981.
Padraic Colum, Twayne, 1985.
John Galsworthy, Twayne, 1987.
R. F. Delderfield, Twayne, 1988.
Stevie Smith, Twayne, 1990.
Stephen Spender, Twayne, 1992.
Siegfried Sassoon, Twayne, 1993.
All Things Herriot: James Herriot and His Peaceable Kingdom, Syracuse University Press, 1995.

HISTORY

(With E. M. Jameson) *The Black Devil of the Bayous: The Life and Times of the United States Steam-Sloop Hartford,* Gregg (Boston), 1970.
McKinley's Bulldog: The Battleship Oregon, Nelson-Hall (Chicago), 1977.

(With Jameson) *U.S.F. Constellation: Yankee Race-horse,* Liberty Publishing (Cockeysville, MD), 1981.

OTHER

Contributor of articles to numerous periodicals, including *Renaissance Papers, Harvard Magazine, Minnesota Review, Writer's Digest, Journal of Hamlet Studies,* and *Calcutta Review.*

WORK IN PROGRESS: Jean Rhys (literary criticism), for Twayne.

SIDELIGHTS: Sanford Sternlicht told *CA:* "I cut my literary teeth on the poetry of John Masefield and the history of Samuel Eliot Morison. Melville, Conrad, the Navy, and the sea have shaped me."

BIOGRAPHICAL/CRITICAL SOURCES:

PERIODICALS

Choice, December, 1988, p. 649; September, 1990, p. 116; November, 1993, p. 46.
Dalhousie Review, fall, 1992, p. 422.
New York Times Book Review, February 24, 1985.
Reference and Research Book News, December, 1993, p. 46.
Times Literary Supplement, September 6, 1985.

* * *

STEVENS, R. L.
See HOCH, Edward D(entinger)

* * *

STRANGER, Joyce
See WILSON, Joyce M(uriel Judson)

* * *

STRELKA, Joseph P(eter)   1927-

PERSONAL: Listed in some sources as Josef Strelka; born May 3, 1927, in Wiener Neustadt, Austria; came to United States, 1964; son of Josef and Maria (Lisetz) Strelka; married Lucy Zambal, 1951 (divorced, 1957); married Brigitte Vollmer, July 13, 1963; children: Alexandra. *Education:* University of Vienna, Ph.D., 1950.

ADDRESSES: Home—Hope Falls, Northville, NY 12134. *Office*—Department of German, State University of New York, 1400 Washington Ave., Albany, NY 12222.

CAREER: Municipal Office of Cultural Activities, Wiener Neustadt, Austria, director, 1950-51; freelance critic in Vienna, Austria, 1951-64; University of Southern California, Los Angeles, visiting associate professor, 1964, assistant director of program at University of Vienna, 1964-65, professor of German literature, 1965-66; Pennsylvania State University, University Park, professor of German, 1966-71; State University of New York at Albany, professor of German and comparative literature, 1971—. Visiting professor at Free University of Berlin, 1980, University of Augsburg, 1981, University of the Witwatersrand, 1981, and University of Parma, 1983.

MEMBER: International Robert Musil Society (vice president), International Franz Werfel Society (vice president, 1995—) International Association of Germanic Studies, PEN, American Comparative Literature Association, Academia Scientiarum et Artium Europaea, Humboldt Society, Austrian Writers Association (honorary member), Vienna Goethe Society.

AWARDS, HONORS: Theodor Koerner Foundation award, 1955-57; City of Vienna award, 1958; Austrian Institute of Cultural Affairs research fellowship (Paris), 1958-59; Austrian Cross of Honor for the Arts and Sciences, First Class, 1978; Medal of Honor, University of Parma, 1983; Medal of Honor, City of Vienna; two-volume "Festschrift" published by Peter Lang Verlag, Bern, on the occasion of Strelka's sixtieth birthday, 1987.

WRITINGS:

Georg Forsters literarhistorische Bedeutung (title means "Georg Forster's Literary-Historical Significance"), F. Berger, 1955.
Der burgundische Renaissancehof Margarethes von Oesterreich und seine literarhistoriche Bedeutung (title means "The Burgundian Renaissance Court

of Margaret of Austria and Its Literary-Historical Significance"), A. Sexl, 1957.

Kafka, Musil, Broch und die Entwicklung des modernen Romans (title means "Kafka, Musil, Broch, and the Development of the Modern Novel"), Forum Verlag, 1959.

Rilke, Benn, Schoenwiese und die Entwicklung der modernen Lyrik (title means "Rilke, Benn, Schoenwiese, and the Development of Modern Poetry"), Forum Verlag, 1960.

Brecht, Horvath, Duerrenmatt: Wege und Abwege des modernen Dramas (title means "Brecht, Horvarth, Duerrenmatt: Paths and Deviations of Modern Drama"), Forum Verlag, 1962.

Bruecke zu vielen Ufern (title means "Bridges to Many Shores"), Europe Verlag, 1966.

(With Harold von Hofe) *Luegendichtung* (title means "Tall Tales"), Scribner, 1966.

(With von Hofe) *Vorboten der Gegenwart: Marx, Nietzsche, Freud, Einstein* (title means "Precursers to the Present: Marx, Nietzsche, Freud, Einstein"), Holt, 1967.

Vergleichende Literaturkritik (title means "Comparative Literary Criticism"), Francke Verlag (Tuebinhen), 1970.

Die gelenkten Musen (title means "The Bound Muses"), Europa Verlag, 1971.

Auf der Suche nach dem verlorenen Selbst, Francke Verlag, 1977.

Werk, Werkverstaendnis, Wertung, Francke Verlag, 1978.

Methodologie der Literaturwissenschaft, Niemayer, 1978.

Esoterik bei Goethe, Niemayer, 1980.

Stefan Zweig: Freier Geist der Menschlichkeit, Oesterreichischer Bundersverlag, 1981.

Exilliteratur, Peter Lang Verlag (Bern), 1983.

Einfuehrung in die literarische Textanalyse (title means "Introduction into the Anaylysis of Literary Texts"), Francke Verlag, 1989.

Literatur und Politik (title means "Literature and Politics"), Peter Lang Verlag, 1992.

Zwischen Wirklichkeit und Traum. Das Wesen des oesterreichischen in der Literatur, Francke Verlag, 1994.

Austroslvica. Beziehungen zwischen der oesterreichischen Literatur und den slawischen Literaturen (title means "Interrelationships between Austrian Literature and Slavic Literatures"), Stauffenberg Verlag (Tuebinhen), 1996.

Pegasus Austria. Zur Dichtung oesterreichischer Autoren (title means "Pegasus of Austria. About the Works of Austrian Authors"), Boehlau Verlag (Wien-Koeln), 1996.

EDITOR OR COMPILER

Gedichte Margarethe's von Oesterreich (title means "Poems of Margaret of Austria"), A. Sexl, 1954.

(And author of introduction) Felix Grafe, *Dichtungen* (title means "Collected Works"), Bergland Verlag, 1961.

(And author of introduction) *Das zeitlose Wort: Eine Anthologie oesterreichischer Lyrik von Peter Altenberg bis zur Gegenwart* (title means "The Timeless Word: An Anthology of Austrian Verse from Peter Attenberg Up to the Present"), Stiasny Verlag, 1964.

(With Robert Stauffer and Paul Wimmer) *Aufruf zur Wende: Eine Anthologie neuer Dichtung, Ernst Schoenwiese zum 60* (title means "A Call to Change: An Anthology of Modern Literature"), Oesterreichische Verlaganstalt, 1965.

(And author of introduction) Gustav Meyrink, *Der Engel vom westlichen Fenster* (title means "Angel of the Western Window"), Stiasny Verlag, 1966.

(With Walter Hinderer) *Moderne amerikanische Literatur-theorien* (title means "Modern American Theories of Literature"), S. Fischer Verlag, 1970.

Broch heute, Francke Verlag, 1978.

Der Weg war schon das Ziel: Festschrift fuer Friedrich Torberg, Langen-Mueller, 1978.

(With Robert F. Bell and Eugene Dobson) *Protest, Form, Tradition: Essays on German Exile Literature*, University of Alabama Press, 1979.

(With Joerg Jungmayr) *Virtus und Fortuns: Festschrift fuer Hans Gert Roloff*, Peter Lang Verlag, 1983.

Heinrich Heine, *Deutschland: Ein Wintermaerchen*, Insel Taschenbuch Verlag, 1983.

Internationales Georg Trakl Symposium, Peter Lang Verlag, 1983.

Bruno Petzhold, *Goethe und der Mahayana-Buddhismus*, Octobus Verlag, 1983.

(With Marguerite Schlueter) *Versunken in den Traum: Poems of Ernst Schoenwiese*, Limes Verlag, 1984.

Alt-Wiener Geschichten, Insel Taschenbuch Verlag, 1984.

Literary Theory and Criticism: Festschrift fuer Rene Wellek, two volumes, Peter Lang Verlag, 1984.

Ernst Schoenwise: Sein geistigrs Profil und seine literarische Bedeutung, Peter Lang Verlag, 1986.

Psalm und Hawdalah: Zum Werk Paul Celans, Peter Lang Verlag, 1987.

Flucht und Exil. Geschichten und Berichte aus zwei Jahrhunderten (title means "Flight and Exile. Stories and Reports of Two Centuries"), Insel Verlag (Frankfurt), 1988.

Maria von Ebner-Eschenbach, *Dorf-und Schlossgeschichten* (title means "Stories of Villages and Castles"), Insel Verlag, 1991.

Imaginaere Reisen (title means "Imaginary Travels"), Insel Verlag, 1992.

Wien. Ein literarischer Reisefuehrer (title means "Vienna, A Literary Tour Guide"), Insel Verlag, 1995.

(With Ilona Slawinkski) *Bukowina: Verangenheit und Gegenwart* (title means "Bukowina. Past and Present"), Peter Lang Verlag, 1995.

(With Slawinkski) *Viribus Unitis. Oesterreichische Wissenschaft und Kultur im ausland: Impulse und Wechselwirkungen. Festschrift fuer Bernhard Stillfried* (title means "Austrian Scholarship and Culture in Foreign Countries: Impulses and Interrelationships"), Peter Lang Verlag, 1996.

OTHER

Editor of "Yearbook of Comparative Criticism" series, 1968—, and "Penn State Series in German Literature," 1971—, both for Pennsylvania State University Press; editor of "New Yorker Beitraege zur Vergleichenden Literaturwissenschaft" series and "New Yorker Studien zur Neueren Deutschen Literaturgeschichte" series, both 1982—, and "New Yorker Beitrage zur oesterreichischen Literaturgeschichte, 1994—, all for Peter Lang Verlag. Contributor of articles to journals, including *Wort in Zeit* and *German Quarterly,* coeditor, *Deutsche Exilliteratur,* 1976—; member of editorial board, *Colloquia Germanica,* 1971—, *North Carolina Studies in Comparative Literature,* 1972—, *Michigan Germanic Studies,* 1975—, *Modern Austrian Literature,* 1981—, and *Comparative Literature Studies,* 1987—.

SIDELIGHTS: Joseph P. Strelka told *CA* that his reasons for writing include a "search for new information, search for truth, [and] establishing ethical, aesthetic, and religious values in the sense of a universal humanism."

Strelka also told *CA:* "Because of experiences in childhood and youth I am vigorously and actively opposed to any form of totalitarian government regardless of whether from the extreme left or the extreme right. Due to an affinity to mysticism and practice of it, I have practiced 'Mahamudra,' a special yoga technique of Tibetan Buddhism, for decades. One of my most important ideals is intellectual and spiritual freedom and freedom of expression. Though I am a native Austrian and I lecture and write alot about Austria, which I love, I am an American citizen and I am more American-minded than many natives."

*   *   *

SUCHARITKUL, Somtow   1952-
  (S. P. Somtow)

PERSONAL: Surname is pronounced "suture-*writ*-cool"; born December 30, 1952, in Bangkok, Thailand; son of Sompong (an ambassador) and Thaithow Sucharitkul. *Education:* Received B.A. and M.A. from St. Catharine's College, Cambridge.

ADDRESSES: Home—16 Ancell St., Alexandria, VA 22305. *Agent*—Adele Leone Agency, 52 Riverside Dr., Suite 6A, New York, NY 10024.

CAREER: Composer; director of Bangkok Opera Society, 1977-78; conductor of ensembles, including Holland Symphony Orchestra, Cambridge Symphony, Bangkok Opera Society, and Florida Atlantic University New Music Ensemble; writer, 1979—. Representative of Thailand at Asian Composer's Conference-Festival in Kyoto, Japan, 1974, and at International Music Council of UNESCO; artistic director of Asian Composer's Conference-Festival in Bangkok, Thailand, 1978.

MEMBER: Science Fiction Writers of America (secretary, 1980-81), Thai Composers Association (founder and chairman).

AWARDS, HONORS: John W. Campbell Award for best new writer from Science Fiction Research Association, and Locus Award for best first novel from *Locus* magazine, both 1981, both for *Starship and Haiku;* Science Fiction Achievement Award (Hugo) nominations for short fiction from World Science Fiction Society for "Absent Thee from Felicity Awhile" and "Aquila"; Edmond Hamilton Memorial Award, 1982, for short story "The Dust."

WRITINGS:

Starship and Haiku (science fiction novel), Timescape (New York City), 1981.

Mallworld (science fiction stories), illustrations by Karl Kofoed, Starblaze (Norfolk, VA), 1981.

Fire from the Wine-Dark Sea (science fiction stories), Starblaze, 1983.

The Aquiliad (science fiction novel), Timescape, 1983.

(Under name S. P. Somtow) *V: The Alien Swordmaster* (science fiction novel), Pinnacle (London), 1985, published under name Somtow Sucharitkul, Pinnacle Books (New York City), 1986.

The Fallen Country (for children), Spectra (New York City), 1986.

UNDER NAME S. P. SOMTOW

Vampire Junction (horror novel), illustrations by Val Lindahn and Ron Lindahn, Starblaze, 1984.

The Shattered Horses, Tor Books (New York City), 1986.

Forgetting Places, St. Martin's (New York City), 1987.

Symphony of Tenor (for children), Tor Books, 1988.

Aquila and the Iron Horse, Ballantine, 1988.

Aquila and the Sphinx, Ballantine, 1988.

Moondance, Tor Books, 1989.

I Wake from a Dream of a Drowned Star City, Axolotl (Eugene, OR), 1992.

Valentine: The Return to Vampire Junction, Tor Books, 1992.

The Wizard's Apprentice (young adult novel), illustrated by Nicholas Jainschigg, Atheneum, 1993.

Escape from Vampire Junction, Tor Books, 1995.

Jasmine Nights, St. Martin's, 1995.

"INQUESTORS" SCIENCE FICTION SERIES

Light on the Sound, Timescape, 1982.

The Throne of Madness, Timescape, 1983.

Utopia Hunters: Chronicles of the High Inquest, Bantam, 1984.

The Darkling Wind: Chronicles of the High Inquest, Bantam, 1985.

OTHER

Also author of short story collection *The Rainbow King,* and of *Fiddling for Waterbuffalos, Riverrun,* and *Riverrun II.* Work represented in anthologies, including *World's Best SF, the 1980 Annual,* edited by Donald A. Wollheim and Arthur Saha, DAW Books (New York City), 1980. Contributor of short fiction to science fiction periodicals, including *Amazing, Analog Science Fiction-Science Fact, Chrysalis,*

Isaac Asimov's Science Fiction Magazine, and *Other Worlds;* contributor of book reviews to *Washington Post Book World* and of articles on music to *Tempo* and *Musical Newsletter.* Contributing editor and author of monthly column "A Certain Slant of 'I'," *Fantasy Newsletter.* Composer of avant-garde musical works, including "Gongula III," "Cemeteries," "Imaginary Answers," "Music for Violet," "Star Maker," and "Starscapes."

WORK IN PROGRESS: A science fiction novel, *Dreambreak,* for Spectra; an opera, *Doctor Island's Death,* with libretto by novelist Gene Wolfe.

SIDELIGHTS: Somtow Sucharitkul, winner of several literary awards, originally worked in the music field. An avant-garde composer and conductor, he made his conducting debut in a televised performance of the Holland Symphony Orchestra when he was nineteen. He has had compositions performed and broadcast on four continents, and in 1978 he was the subject of a television documentary in Japan.

Sucharitkul began his writing career in 1979, when he published several science fiction short stories. In 1981 he completed his first science fiction novel, *Starship and Haiku,* which earned critical acclaim. The book details a post-holocaust society in which two remaining factions of humanity, both Japanese, deal with their deteriorating world in different ways: one group advocates mass suicide, while the other plans to send starships into space to start a new life. Although W. Warren Wagar, writing in the *Washington Post Book World,* feels that Sucharitkul's imagination might be "too copious for his own good"—employing such diverse elements as Buddhism, telekinetic whales, starships, and concrete poetry—the critic nevertheless concludes that "the waters [the book] probes are deep."

With the 1982 publication of *Light on the Sound* Sucharitkul initiated the "Inquestors" series, a saga of virtually immortal humans who rule their galaxy. *Light on the Sound* follows the experiences of one Inquestor who questions the activities of his caste. Observes Tom Easton of *Analog Science Fiction-Science Fact,* Sucharitkul "writes of worlds and beings just far enough from our lives to feel strange, yet with echoes of a familiar past. He is a mythmaker." *Washington Post Book World* reviewer Orson Scott Card praises both *Light* and *The Throne of Madness,* the second book in the series: "Sucharitkul can create a world with less apparent effort than some writers devote to creating a small room. And yet these tales are as intricately wrought as those hand-carved oriental balls within balls." Easton, who could find only one fault in *Throne*—"lack of restraint"—suggests that Sucharitkul "may yet give us the best SF novel of all time."

Sucharitkul reveals "his wicked sense of humor" in *The Aquiliad,* according to Card. Beginning with the title, which recalls the classical Greek *Iliad* by Homer, Sucharitkul devises a history in which the Romans discovered America and invented the automobile, his heroes an incompetent but honest Roman general and the Sioux chief, Aquila, who repeatedly rescues him. Sucharitkul Latinizes Indian names, geographical names, and names of modern science fiction authors and scatters them throughout the text; he presents Bigfoot as the leader of a group of mutated Jews; and he has "little green men carry off [the] hero in their flying saucer." As Card points out, "Sucharitkul does not want you to take this world seriously at all." Even so, the critic perceives "a perverse elegance" in the story, while Easton finds it "droll, . . . crazy," and "fun." Sucharitkul continues the adventures of Aquila in two young adult novels, *Aquila and the Iron Horse* and *Aquila and the Sphinx.*

In 1984, using the pen name S. P. Somtow, Sucharitkul published *Vampire Junction,* a horror-love-fantasy story that, Theodore Sturgeon reports, confounded those who tried to categorize it. In his *Washington Post* review, Sturgeon praises Sucharitkul for breaking the boundaries of genre, writing that *Vampire Junction* "provokes thought . . . more often than many a contemporary 'serious' novel." Sucharitkul's protagonist, Timothy Valentine, is a two-thousand-year-old vampire and rock star, charismatic and lonely. "Taken alone, he is as intricate a tapestry as all of this story," assesses Sturgeon. Sucharitkul handles such complexity well, the critic judges, packing "a wealth of insight" into the novel with the skillful literary use of such musical devices as tempo and dynamics. Concludes Sturgeon: "It is easy to predict great things for so accomplished and talented a writer as this."

Since the publication of *Vampire Junction,* Sucharitkul has branched into many genres besides science fiction. *Valentine: The Return to Vampire Junction* is a sequel to *Vampire Junction*—"sort of," states Edward Bryant in *Locus.* "This, technically, is a sequel, but author Somtow continues to grow in ambition and accomplishment as a novelist, and

nothing's ever quite as simple as it first appears." *Valentine* is, on one level, a story about the filming of a motion picture based on the life of the departed protagonist of *Vampire Junction.* On another, it is the story of Angel Todd, the unhappy juvenile cast in the role of Timmy Valentine. "The book reads like the novelization of a movie," writes Samantha Hunt in *Voice of Youth Advocates,* "and, indeed, owes a debt not to literature for its style and content but to the 'splatter flick' genre." "Somtow pulls out all the operatic stops," Bryant concludes, "letting the story flip through *The Player*-style cutting satire, viscerally repellant horror, and increasingly seductive character relationships."

Similar to *Vampire Junction* and *Valentine* in theme is *Moondance,* which applies the werewolf legend to the American West. The story begins in 1963, when a young woman named Carrie DuPre travels from her California home to South Dakota to investigate the eighty-year-old story of a relative of hers who might have been a mass murderer. "The secrets she discovers," explains a *Publishers Weekly* reviewer, "connect Austro-Hungarian werewolf immigration and 100 years of Native American wolf-worship, and will change her life forever." She discovers that her ancestor, an Eastern European count and his mentally-disturbed son travelled to the American west in 1880. Both the father and the son are lycanthropes, but so are the local Indians. The "moon dance" of the title is a ritual of the Shungmanitou, who believe that if the son can perform the ritual correctly, they can drive the white men from the American continent and establish a paradise for Native Americans. "What with bloodthirsty white soldiers, sundry slaughters, and two sets of slavering werewolves," declares a *Kirkus Reviews* critic, "the violence is relentless—and Somtow leaves no detail, no matter how unpleasant, to the imagination."

Sucharitkul has also gained a reputation as a young adult novelist. His works for younger readers include *The Wizard's Apprentice* and *Jasmine Nights. I Wake from a Dream of a Drowned Star City* features a young adult protagonist, but deals with themes usually associated with fiction for mature readers. The protagonist in question is Morty Draus, who is the heir of a ruling family that maintains its bloodline by cloning and inbreeding. Morty is initiated into the mysteries of sex by a lower-class fisher girl named Jonellys. When she is taken away by the authorities, Morty resolves to find her. This is Sucharitkul "at his most coy and artful, decadent and depraved, smelling sweetly of rot," declares Tom Easton in *Analog. Locus* reviewer Edward Bryant compares *I Wake from a Dream of a Drowned Star City* to the work of the fantasist Jack Vance, and declares that the story resembles "a classical Greek one-act play."

Both *The Wizard's Apprentice* and *Jasmine Nights* are lighter in tone than *I Wake from a Dream of a Drowned Star City.* They feature modern youths learning to cope with their dysfunctional families and struggling to grow up. Aaron Maguire, the hero of *The Wizard's Apprentice,* is from Southern California. He is fond of skateboarding, ready to date, and dreaming about learning to drive. According to the wizard Anaxagoras, Aaron also has a talent for magic. "While skateboarding," explains a reviewer for the *Wilson Library Bulletin,* "Aaron has unknowingly been defying laws of physics, proving his intuitive genius with magic." However, Aaron is more interested in using his newfound abilities to impress his perfect woman, Penelope Karpovsky. In a series of mishaps, Aaron accidentally summons a dragon who threatens Los Angeles in the form of a cloud of acid rain. "In its shape," the reviewer concludes, "Aaron recognizes his own face, the inner dragon of his rage at his parents." "Overall," writes Donna L. Scalon in the *Voice of Youth Advocates,* "the book is refreshing and funny, and doesn't hit the reader over the head with its message, just as a good fairy tale should." *Jasmine Nights* is set during the Vietnam War, and is the story of Justin, a young Thai boy raised on the outskirts of Bangkok. "Sheltered by his eccentric family," declares *Times Literary Supplement* reviewer Edward Hower, "he has grown up in a fantasy world of trashy American movies and heroic Greek classics." "Justin embarks upon a career as a playwright," declares *Washington Post Book World* contributor Wendy Law-Yone, "even as he receives the irreconcilable truths of the adult world." "*Jasmine Nights* is . . . entertaining, irresistible, gleefully absurd," Law-Yone concludes. "How encouraging that a literary novel can be so much fun."

BIOGRAPHICAL/CRITICAL SOURCES:

PERIODICALS

Analog Science Fiction-Science Fact, September 14, 1981; May, 1982; February, 1983; April, 1984; May, 1984; June, 1984; April, 1985; December, 1985; January, 1993, pp. 303-10.
Chicago Tribune, February 16, 1995, p. 6.
Kirkus Reviews, November 15, 1989, p. 1631; November 1, 1994, pp. 1441-42.
Locus, March, 1990, p. 66; November, 1992, p. 60; December, 1992, p. 19; August, 1993, p. 49; February, 1994, p. 76.
Los Angeles Times Book Review, October 10, 1982.
New York Times, February 7, 1988, p. 22.
New York Times Book Review, February 19, 1995, p. 22.
Publishers Weekly, November 24, 1989, p. 59; November 6, 1995, pp. 84-5.
School Library Journal, August, 1993, p. 189.
Times Literary Supplement, June 3, 1994, p. 24.
Voice of Youth Advocates, April, 1993, p. 46; October, 1993, pp. 235-36.
Washington Post, October 2, 1984; August 28, 1985; April 12, 1990, p. C14; February 5, 1995, p. 2.
Washington Post Book World, October 25, 1981; January 29, 1984; June 24, 1984; September 29, 1985; February 5, 1995, p. 2.
Wilson Library Bulletin, March, 1994, p. 125.

*   *   *

SUGANO, Takuo   1931-

PERSONAL: Born August 25, 1931, in Tokyo, Japan; son of Yoshio (a businessman) and Kazue (Hirano) Sugano; married Nobuko Tako, September 24, 1960; children: Hiroko, Mitsuko. *Education:* University of Tokyo, B.S., 1954, M.S., 1956, Ph.D., 1959.

ADDRESSES: Home—2-2-3 Sakura, Setagaya-ku, Tokyo 156, Japan. *Office*—Office of the President, Toyo University, Tokyo 112, Japan.

CAREER: University of Tokyo, Tokyo, Japan, assistant professor, 1959-60, associate professor, 1960-71, professor of semiconductor electronics, 1971-92; Toyo University, Tokyo, Japan, professor of nanoelectronics, 1992—, president, 1994—.

MEMBER: Japan Society of Applied Physics (president, 1986-87), Institute of Electrical and Electronics Engineers (United States; lifetime fellow), Academy of Science of East Germany.

AWARDS, HONORS: Award from Institute of Electronics, and Communications Engineers of Japan and Matsunaga Foundation, 1974, for outstanding contributions to MOS technologies; Inoue Foundation award, 1984, for outstanding contributions to plasma processes; award from Institute of Electronics and Communications Engineers of Japan, 1985, 1986, and 1992; Tokyo Metropolitan Governors Award, 1983; IEEE Jack A. Morton Award, 1992; Purple Ribbon Prize, Japanese government, 1995.

WRITINGS:

The Physics of Semiconductors, Institute of Electrical Engineers of Japan, 1979.

(Editor) *The Application of Plasma Processes to VLSI Technology,* Sangyo Tosho, 1980.

(Editor with Daniel I. Okimoto and Franklin B. Weinstein) *The Competitive Edge: The Semiconductor Industry in the U.S. and Japan,* Stanford University Press (Stanford, CA), 1984.

(Editor) *High Speed Digital Devices,* Baihukan, 1986.

(Co-author and editor) *Physics of SiMOS Devices,* Corona (San Antonio, TX), 1989.

Semiconductor Integrated Circuits Engineering, Institute of Electronics, Information, and Communication Engineers, 1995.

Contributor to scientific journals.

WORK IN PROGRESS: Research on the physics and technology related to nanoelectronics.

*   *   *

SUGDEN, John   1947-

PERSONAL: Born January 27, 1947, in Kingston-upon-Hull, Yorkshire, England; son of John Henry (in skilled trades) and Lily (Cuthbertson) Sugden. *Education:* Attended Hull College of Commerce, 1967-68; Leeds College, Certificate of Education (with distinction), 1971; University of Leeds, B.Ed. (with honors), 1972; University of Lancaster, M.A., 1974; University of Sheffield, Ph.D., 1981.

ADDRESSES: Home—165 Woodside Ave. S., Coventry CV3 6BJ, West Midlands, England.

CAREER: Master at grammar schools in Pontefract, England, 1972-73, and Rotherham, England, 1974-77; Hereward College, Coventry, England, lecturer in history, director of studies, and tutor for higher education, 1977-93. Member of Working Party on Higher Education, National Bureau for Handicapped Students, 1985-86; public speaker.

MEMBER: American Historical Association, Society for Nautical Research, Nelson Society, Woodland Trust, Grey Owl Society.

AWARDS, HONORS: Arthur W. Thompson Memorial Prize from Florida Historical Society, 1982, for article "The Southern Indians in the War of 1812: The Closing Phase"; Twenty-Seven Foundation Award, 1986; Ford Foundation fellowship, D'Arcy McNickle Center for the History of the American Indian, Newberry Library, 1988-89.

WRITINGS:

Tecumseh's Last Stand, University of Oklahoma Press (Norman), 1985.

The Shawnee in Tecumseh's Time, Abhandlungen der Voelkerkundlichen Arbeitsgemeinschaft, 1990.

Sir Francis Drake, Barrie & Jenkins (London), 1990, Henry Holt (New York City), 1991.

Associate editor of and contributor to *American National Biography,* Oxford University Press, 1990—. Contributor of articles and reviews to history, education, and arts journals, including *Mariner's Mirror, Louisiana History, Florida Historical Quarterly, American Indian Quarterly,* and *Scottish Economic and Social History.*

WORK IN PROGRESS: Tecumseh and His Brothers, for Henry Holt, 1997; a history of the Shawnee Indians.

SIDELIGHTS: John Sugden told *CA:* "At high school I was initially drawn to English literature, but historical research has always been something of a passion. Once my interest has been engaged, my curiosity is almost inexhaustible. After more than twenty-five years intermittently pursuing Tecumseh and his Shawnees through archives and libraries across North America and Europe, I still fret that some relevant document may have escaped scrutiny and that my picture will be incomplete. I always have the feeling that no one else will do this job, so I might as well do it properly.

"Good history is only produced by hard work. I see little virtue in following intellectual fashions, in either my choice of subject matter or my interpretations. There are simply too many writers chasing jobs and contracts by bullying ill-digested historical facts until they conform to preconceived theories. The best foundation for understanding the past comes from a thorough trawl of the available primary sources, a rigorous and open-minded analysis of the catch, and a fearless statement of the conclusions, however convenient or inconvenient they may be. Good, solidly grounded scholarship has a longer life span than cant. There are dangers in ignoring the flow, of course, including the possibility of being marginalized, but I stand with Oscar Wilde when he remarked that if you tell the truth, sooner or later you will be found out.

"If you live long enough you often find unorthodoxies become tomorrow's fetishes. I'm old enough to remember when serious scholars happily wrote American Indians out of history. As a boy I used to comb the pages of the old *Dictionary of American Biography* to find out just how few Indians had been deemed worthy of inclusion. That is why I was glad to work with the new *American National Biography* and to increase the number of Indian biographies and the ratio of eighteenth-century to nineteenth-century figures.

"*Sir Francis Drake,* which drew upon my other academic interest of naval and maritime history, had also been on the back burner for many years. I wanted to question the drift Drake studies had been taking, and in this book also to substitute the arcane language of the scholar for something that might bring up-to-date historical knowledge within the remit of the intelligent lay reader. The reviewers and many correspondents were kind enough to say I succeeded, although in truth it is difficult to write a dull book about Drake. Some of the projects lying up the trail are considerably thornier, but I don't want to be regarded as just a narrow academic historian. You have to address a broader audience than that.

"I was extremely fortunate in growing up with a twin brother, Philip, who shared my enthusiasms and ambitions. We've bounced ideas off each other ever since childhood and are the sternest critics of each other's work. Philip publishes on the history of crime and probably knows more history than I do, and we plan some collaborations. Writing can be a lonely activity, particularly when the author is dealing with subjects that for the most part are outside of people's knowledge, but apart from Philip and a few fellow-scholars I benefit from a rich correspondence. And life isn't all serious research and reflection. I'm partial to the works of Robert Louis Stevenson, western movies, the music of Abba, walks in the countryside, and thinking of old friends."

BIOGRAPHICAL/CRITICAL SOURCES:

PERIODICALS

American Historical Review, Volume 91, 1986, p. 986.
Canadian Historical Review, Volume 67, 1986, pp. 620-21; Volume 73, 1992, pp. 255-57.
History Today, Volume 41, 1991, pp. 56-57.
South Dakota History, Volume 16, 1986, pp. 74-75.

*   *   *

SUPRANER, Robyn   1930-
(Olive Blake, Erica Frost, Elizabeth Warren)

PERSONAL: Born September 14, 1930, in New York, NY; daughter of Mortimer (an insurance broker) and Dorothy (Kalmanowitz) Rubenstein; married Leon Supraner (a photographer), December 16, 1950; children: Keith, Scott, Dennis, Lauren. *Education:* Attended Pratt Institute and Parson's School of Design, 1944-48, and Adelphi University, 1948-51. *Politics:* "Humanist." *Avocational interests:* "I love snorkeling, polishing rocks, hunting for shells, and making good, thick soup."

ADDRESSES: Home—420 Bryant Ave., Roslyn Harbor, NY 11576. *Agent*—Curtis Brown, Ltd., 10 Astor Place, New York, NY 10003.

CAREER: Freelance song writer, 1962-72 (songs have been recorded by popular recording artists, including Chubby Checker, Mel Torme, and Johnny Winter); writer, 1970—; freelance editor. Taught creative dramatics at Roslyn Creative Arts Workshop, 1973-74. Conducts workshops "Writing for Children" and "Writing Poetry"; conducts numerous speaking engagements as a children's book author; gives public poetry readings at various locations in New York.

MEMBER: Authors Guild, Authors League of America, Poetry Society of America.

AWARDS, HONORS: Giggly, Wiggly, Snickety Snick was selected book of the year by Child Study Association, 1978; poetry award from Pen and Brush Club, 1980; *It's Not Fair* was selected classroom choice by International Reading Association.

WRITINGS:

FOR CHILDREN

Draw Me a Circle, illustrated by Evelyn Kelbish, Simon & Schuster (New York City), 1970.

Draw Me a Square, illustrated by Kelbish, Simon & Schuster, 1970.

Draw Me a Triangle, illustrated by Kelbish, Simon & Schuster, 1970.

Would You Rather Be a Tiger?, illustrated by Barbara Cooney, Houghton (Boston), 1973.

Think about It, You Might Learn Something, illustrated by Sanford Kossin, Houghton, 1973.

It's Not Fair! (Junior Literary Guild selection), illustrated by Randall Enos, Warne (New York City), 1976.

Giggly, Wiggly, Snickety-Snick, pictures by Stan Tusan, Parents' Magazine Press (New York City), 1978.

Sam Sunday and the Strange Disappearance of Chester Cats, pictures by Robert Tallon, Parents' Magazine Press, 1979.

(Contributor) *Language Basics Plus,* Harper (New York City), 1979.

Sam Sunday and the Mystery at the Ocean Beach Hotel, illustrated by Will Hillenbrand, Viking (New York City), 1996.

FOR CHILDREN; PUBLISHED BY TROLL (MAHWAH, NJ)

The First Troll Talking Dictionary, 1974.
I Can Read about Witches, 1975.
I Can Read about Weather, 1975.
I Can Read about Baseball, 1975.
I Can Read about Seasons, 1975.
I Can Read about Homonyms: The Mystery of the Hidden Treasure, 1977.
I Can Read about Synonyms and Antonyms: The Case of Strange Aunt Pickles, 1977.
Mrs. Wiggleworth's Secret, illustrated by Paul Harvey, 1979.
Mystery at the Zoo, illustrated by Bert Dodson, 1979.
Mystery of the Witch's Shoes, illustrated by Margot Apple, 1979.
The Case of the Missing Canary, illustrated by Robbie Stillerman, 1979.
The Ghost in the Attic, illustrated by Eulala Conner, 1979.
The Second Troll Talking Dictionary, 1979.
Fun-to-Make Nature Crafts, illustrated by Renzo Barto, 1981.
Fun with Paper, illustrated by Barto, 1981.

Great Masks to Make, illustrated by Barto, 1981.
Happy Halloween: Things to Make and Do, illustrated by Barto, 1981.
Magic Tricks You Can Do!, illustrated by Barto, 1981.
Merry Christmas!: Things to Make and Do, illustrated by Barto, 1981.
(With daughter, Lauren Supraner) *Plenty of Puppets to Make,* illustrated by Barto, 1981.
Quick and Easy Cookbook, illustrated by Barto, 1981.
Rainy Day Surprises You Can Make, illustrated by Barto, 1981.
Science Secrets, illustrated by Barto, 1981.
Stop and Look!: Illusions, illustrated by Barto, 1981.
Valentine's Day: Things to Make and Do, illustrated by Barto, 1981.
Case of the Missing Rattles, illustrated by Joan E. Goodman, 1982.
Mystery of the Lost Ring (with Two Hearts), illustrated by Marsha Winborn, 1982.
The Amazing Mark, 1986.
The Cat Who Wanted to Fly, 1986.
Kitty: A Cat's Diary, 1986.
Molly's Special Wish, 1986.
No Room for a Sneeze!, 1986.

UNDER PSEUDONYM OLIVE BLAKE; FOR CHILDREN; PUBLISHED BY TROLL

The Grape Jelly Mystery, illustrated by Goodman, 1979.
The Mystery of the Lost Letter, illustrated by Kossin, 1979.
The Mystery of the Lost Pearl, illustrated by Ed Parker, 1979.

UNDER PSEUDONYM ERICA FROST; FOR CHILDREN; PUBLISHED BY TROLL

I Can Read about Ballet, 1975.
I Can Read about Good Manners, 1975.
I Can Read about Ghosts, 1975.
Harold and the Dinosaur Mystery, illustrated by Deborah Sims, 1979.
The Mystery of the Runaway Sled, illustrated by Leigh Grant, 1979.
The Mystery of the Midnight Visitors, illustrated by Ann Gamache, 1979.
The Case of the Missing Chick, illustrated by Harvey, 1979.
(With Lauren Supraner) *The Littlest Pig,* 1986.
The Story of Matt and Mary, 1986.
A Kitten for Rosie, 1986.

Mr. Lion Goes to Lunch, 1986.
Jonathan's Amazing Adventure, 1986.

UNDER PSEUDONYM ELIZABETH WARREN; FOR CHILDREN; PUBLISHED BY TROLL

I Can Read about Trees and Plants, 1975.
I Can Read about Bats, 1975.
I Can Read about Indians, 1975.
I Can Read about Baby Animals, 1975.

OTHER

Author of twelve single-concept learning books for Columbia Broadcasting System (CBS), published by Shelley Graphics, 1971, of other learning books published by Shelley Graphics, 1972, and of a sixteen-volume dictionary for children and other learning books, published by Educational Reading Service, 1972—. Also author of books with cassette tapes, under pseudonyms Erica Frost and Elizabeth Warren, for Educational Reading Service, 1975. Contributor to books, including *Under Open Sky: Poets on William Cullen Bryant,* edited by Norbert Krapf, Fordham University Press (Bronx, NY), 1986. Also contributor of over sixty poems to American and Canadian literary journals, including *Prairie Schooner, Ploughshares,*

Unicorn, Xanadu, Beloit Poetry Journal, and *Queen's Quarterly.*

WORK IN PROGRESS: Poetry collection under the working title *Carrying On.*

SIDELIGHTS: Robyn Supraner told *CA:* "Since I was little, I have tried to understand my life by writing things down. Many of my books spring from the bewilderments of my childhood. I was a bewildered child, and now, as a parent, I am a bewildered adult.

"I was almost six when my sister was born. I had wanted a brother. When, in spite of my injunctions, my sister was born, I wept for my lost place and my parents' cruel disregard. It wasn't fair. Some thirty odd years later, still smarting, I wrote *It's Not Fair!*

"Now, I live on a wooded hillside in Roslyn Harbor. My house is large and rambling and has slowly emptied itself of children who are grown."

*   *   *

SYRUC, J.
  See MILOSZ, Czeslaw

T

TANNEHILL, Robert C(ooper)   1934-

PERSONAL: Born May 6, 1934, in Clay Center, KS; son of Francis V. (a clergyman) and Cecelia (Cooper) Tannehill; married Alice I. Hunter (a nursery school teacher), August 13, 1955; children: Grace, Celia, Paul. *Education:* Hamline University, B.A., 1956; Yale University, B.D., 1959, M.A., 1960, Ph.D., 1963; also studied at University of Tuebingen, 1960-61.

ADDRESSES: Home—960 Braumiller Rd., Delaware, OH 43015.   *Office*—Methodist Theological School, Delaware, OH 43015.

CAREER: Ordained Methodist clergyman, 1965; Oberlin School of Theology, Oberlin, OH, instructor in New Testament, 1963-66; Methodist Theological School, Delaware, OH, assistant professor, 1966-69, associate professor, 1969-74, professor of New Testament, 1974—, Harold B. Williams Professor of Biblical Studies and academic dean, 1994—. Visiting professor, Vancouver School of Theology, 1979.

MEMBER: Society of Biblical Literature (co-chair of Literary Aspects of the Gospels and Acts Group, 1991—), Studiorum Novi Testamenti Societas, Eastern Great Lakes Biblical Society (president, 1978-79).

AWARDS, HONORS: Danforth fellowship, 1956-63; Tews Prize, Yale Divinity School, 1957; Two Brothers fellowship, Yale University, 1960-61; Association of Theological Schools faculty fellowship, 1969-70, research award, 1975-76, 1982, 1994; Claremont fellow, Society of Biblical Literature, 1982.

WRITINGS:

Dying and Rising with Christ: A Study in Pauline Theology, Toepelmann (Berlin), 1967.
The Sword of His Mouth: Forceful and Imaginative Language in Synoptic Sayings, Scholars Press (Missoula, MT), 1975.
A Mirror for Disciples: Following Jesus through Mark, Discipleship Resources (Nashville), 1977.
The Narrative Unity of Luke-Acts: A Literary Interpretation, Fortress (Philadelphia), Volume 1: *The Gospel According to Luke,* 1986, Volume 2: *The Acts of the Apostles,* 1990.

Associate editor of "Society of Biblical Literature Monograph Series," 1979-85. Also contributor to *Harper's Bible Dictionary* and *The New Interpreter's Bible.* Contributor to *Anglican Theological Review, Interpretation, Journal of Religion, Journal of Biblical Literature, Semeia, Aufstieg und Niedergang der roemischen Welt.* Member of editorial board, *Journal of Biblical Literature,* 1988-93.

*   *   *

TANNEN, Mary   1943-

PERSONAL: Born June 2, 1943, in New London, CT; daughter of Matthew W. (an educator) and Doris (Beal) Gaffney; married Michael Tannen (a lawyer), June 25, 1965; children: Catherine, Noah. *Education:* Attended William Smith College, 1961-63; Barnard College, B.A., 1965.

ADDRESSES: *Home and office*—90 Riverside Dr., New York, NY 10024.

CAREER: Writer. *Men's Wear,* New York City, copywriter, 1965; *Popular Mechanics,* New York City, in promotion, 1965-66; *Show,* New York City, copywriter, 1966-67; *Avon Products,* New York City, copywriter, 1967-70.

WRITINGS:

JUVENILE

The Wizard Children of Finn, Knopf (New York City), 1981.
The Lost Legend of Finn, Knopf, 1982.
Huntley Nutley and the Missing Link, Knopf, 1983.

NOVELS

Second Sight, Knopf, 1988.
After Roy, Knopf, 1989.
Easy Keeper, Farrar Strauss Giroux (New York City), 1992.
Loving Edith, Riverhead Books (New York City), 1995.

OTHER

Contributor to numerous magazines and newspapers, including *New York Times Magazine, Vogue, Town & Country,* and *Writer.* Contributor of short stories to *New Yorker.*

SIDELIGHTS: In both her juvenile and adult fiction, Mary Tannen spins tales of unlikely adventure and mystery with a flair for memorable and decidedly accessible characters. In *The Wizard Children of Finn,* eleven-year-old Fiona McCool and her eight-year-old brother, Bran, are away from their city home for the summer while their mother, who has hired two Irish women to care for them, is in Los Angeles making a film. During a walk in the woods, the children meet Deimne who tells them he has been raised to avenge his father's death. In a strange twist, the three children are transported to ancient Ireland, where they discover they are Wizard Children with possible roots to the ancient Irish hero, Finn McCool. A reviewer for *Publishers Weekly* notes that Tannen "builds vividly on the epic to create chills as well as laughs at situations handled by the modern children in bafflingly foreign surroundings." Writing in *School Library Journal* Ruth M. McConnell observes that although the book suffers

from "unconvincing dialogue, slang and . . . inconsistencies in character. . .*,* Fiona's flip remarks are sometimes funny or apt."

In *The Lost Legend of Finn,* a sequel to *The Wizard Children of Finn,* Fiona and Bran return to the ancient past to solve the mystery of their father's identity. "As historical fiction, fantasy and a novel of identity, this book is a fine one," writes Ruth K. MacDonald in *School Library Journal.* A reviewer for *Booklist* describes the novel as "smoothly written" and states that Tannen "skillfully weaves history and lore into her well-paced story; and while she sometimes uses magic too casually . . ., the story has enough adventure and tension to hold its audience." While the title character of *Huntley Nutley and the Missing Link* stays in the present, his experience is no less fantastic. During a trek through the snow, Huntley stumbles upon an odd-looking ape that turns out to be the long-sought-after missing link in human evolution. Huntley adopts the animal, whose unsurpassed skill as a video game player helps Huntley resolve his troubles with a gang of bullies at school. Michael Carr writes in *School Library Journal* that Huntley is an "engaging little protagonist who displays both patience and panache."

Tannen made her debut as a writer of adult fiction with *Second Sight,* a novel of "ingenious design," according to a review in the *New Yorker.* Set in a dying factory town in New Jersey, *Second Sight* features Delia Bird, a fortune teller looking for love, and William Appleyard, the son of an affluent local family and a doctoral student whose research into the history of his hometown unearths long-buried secrets. Michiko Kakutani writes in the *New York Times* that "while *Second Sight* occasionally touches on such weighty matters as free will and fate, it is content, for the most part, to skim along the surface, giving us a sad-funny portrait of a family and a town in the guise of an old-fashioned romantic comedy." Tannen "creates a fictional world spacious enough to house the highborn and the lowborn, the rational as well as the mystical" observes Gary Krist in the *New York Times Book Review.* A critic for *Publishers Weekly* writes that Tannen's understanding of human nature and its fallibilities is intuitive; "her characters are engagingly flawed, with eccentricities that fix them memorably in the reader's mind." Krist cautions that Tannen's heavy-handed manipulation of the plot and shifting points of view among too many characters are unfortunate technical flaws, but neither seriously interferes with what he considers an "engaging first novel."

In a *Village Voice* review of *After Roy,* Elizabeth Judd argues that Tannen's strengths as a novelist are based on the same skills she employs in her children's books. "Tannen's writing is spare in the tradition of children's authors who let the adventure speak for itself, and her characters are more often shaped by actions than adjectives." Comparing the book to Tannen's first novel, a *New Yorker* critic writes that *After Roy* "is riskier and more reflective." The story chronicles the lives of four members of a defunct rock band whose divergent paths after their break-up cross again after ten years of separation. The catalyst for the novel's action centers on Maggie, who is in Africa trying to reintroduce tamed chimps to the wild. "The sacrifices Maggie makes to turn herself into a chimp role model grow unsettling as the distinction between woman and chimp disintegrate," observes Judd. What at first appears to be a sentimental portrait of an animal lover, the reviewer notes, transforms into a look at the dark side of fanaticism. Judd writes that "seemingly safe images, like an innocuous-looking curry, grow hotter and harder to swallow."

The counterculture figures prominently in Tannen's next novel, *Easy Keeper.* Set in a small community in Colorado, the story's protagonist is Lily, a sheep rancher and refugee of the turbulent 1960s whose husband dies from cocaine abuse in the novel's opening chapter. The remainder of the story focuses on Lily's reactions to the competing devotions of two men—Dusty, who has loved Lily for years without confessing it, and Foster, a newcomer from New York City. Writing in the *New York Times Book Review,* John Domini notes that the novel displays Tannen's "down-to-earth wit" and her "unembittered sharpness about the day-to-day compromise life requires." A reviewer for *Publishers Weekly* calls the novel "a beguiling but patently overstructured contemporary western romance." Domini argues that while *Easy Keeper* "risks steering close to a conventional romance," the novel is ultimately "about the blurring of imagination and experience, about losing the self in a story."

In *Loving Edith,* Tannen's title character is an enchanting college student who interns for a sophisticated magazine in New York City. Unbeknownst to Edith, who was adopted as an infant, she is working for her real father, the magazine's editor, while her mother, an unstable artist, hovers in the background, wondering if she should reveal herself. "Tannen draws the magazine and art worlds . . . with amusing flair, and she captures ways and customs of a sophis-

ticated urban milieu with wicked ease," comments Diane Cole in a review for the *Chicago Tribune.* "But while Tannen's low-key satire is always on target, she is never mean-spirited."

BIOGRAPHICAL/CRITICAL SOURCES:

PERIODICALS

Booklist, May 15, 1982, p. 1261; July, 1992, p. 1921; April 1, 1995, p. 1379.
Bulletin of the Center for Children's Books, July-August, 1983, p. 219.
Chicago Tribune, February 7, 1988, p. 6; December 10, 1989, p. 5; April 30, 1995, p. 6.
Children's Book Review Service, May, 1982, p. 100.
Kirkus Reviews, April 15, 1981, p. 505; May 1, 1983, pp. 525-26.
Library Journal, April 1, 1995, p. 126.
Los Angeles Times, March 8, 1988, p. 6; December 15, 1989, p. E10; August 9, 1992, p. 6.
New Yorker, April 25, 1988, p. 112; January 1, 1990, p. 84.
New York Times, January 2, 1988, p. A15.
New York Times Book Review, February 7, 1988, p. 15; August 30, 1992, p. 16.
Observer Review, June 12, 1988, p. 43.
People, November 2, 1992, p. 37; May 29, 1995, p. 28.
Publishers Weekly, January 30, 1981, p. 75; November 20, 1987, p. 60; August 25, 1989, p. 49; May 4, 1992, p. 40; February 20, 1995, p. 193.
School Library Journal, September, 1981, p. 131; September, 1983, pp. 128-29; January, 1983, p. 79.
Village Voice, December 19, 1989, p. 12.
Washington Post, December 1, 1989, p. B4.

* * *

TAYLOR, Andrew (McDonald) 1940-

PERSONAL: Born March 19, 1940, in Warrnambool, Victoria, Australia; son of John McDonald (a lawyer) and Margaret (Fraser) Taylor; married Jill Burriss, January 31, 1965 (divorced); married Beate Josephi, 1980; children: Travis, Sarah. *Education:* University of Melbourne, B.A., (with first class honors), 1961, M.A. (with first class honors), 1970; State University of New York at Buffalo, additional graduate study, 1970-71. *Politics:* "Unattached

Left." *Avocational interests:* Travel, gardening, the coastline.

ADDRESSES: Home—19 North St., Mount Lawley, Western Australia 6050, Australia. *Office*—Department of English, Edith Cowan University, Mount Lawley, Western Australia 6050, Australia.

CAREER: British Institute, Rome, Italy, English teacher, 1964-65; University of Melbourne, Melbourne, Australia, Lockie Fellow in Australia Literature, 1965-69; University of Adelaide, Adelaide, Australia, lecturer, 1971-74, senior lecturer in English, 1974-92, associate professor, 1992; Edith Cowan University, Perth, Western Australia, professor of English, 1992—. Member of the literature board of the Australian Council, 1978-81. Helped to organize Adelaide's "Friendly Street" poetry readings; chairman of Writers' Week committee of Adelaide Festival of Arts, 1980 and 1982.

MEMBER: Australian and New Zealand American Studies Association, Association for the Study of Australian Literature, Australian Society of Authors.

AWARDS, HONORS: American Council of Learned Societies fellowship, 1970-71; regional winner of Commonwealth Poetry Prize, 1986, for *Travelling;* Member of the Order of Australia, 1990; Premier's Award for Poetry, 1995, for *Sandstone.*

WRITINGS:

The Cat's Chin and Ears: A Bestiary, Angus & Robertson (Australia), 1976.
Bernie the Midnight Owl (juvenile), Penguin Books (New York City), 1984.
(Translator from German with wife, Beate Josephi) *Miracles of Disbelief,* Leros Press, 1985.
Reading Australian Poetry (essays), University of Queensland Press (Australia), 1987.

POETRY

The Cool Change, University of Queensland Press, 1971.
Ice Fishing, University of Queensland Press, 1973.
The Invention of Fire, University of Queensland Press, 1976.
Parabolas: Prose Poems, Makar Press, 1976.
The Crystal Absences, the Trout, Island Press, 1978.
Selected Poems, University of Queensland Press, 1982.
Travelling, University of Queensland Press, 1986.

Selected Poems: 1960-1985, University of Queensland Press, 1988.
Folds in the Map, University of Queensland Press, 1991.
Sandstone, University of Queensland Press, 1995.

EDITOR

Byron, Selected Poems, Cassell (England), 1971.
Number Two Friendly Street, Adelaide University Union Press (Australia), 1978.
Unsettled Areas (fiction), Wakefield Press, 1986.

OTHER

Also author of opera libretti, "The Letters of Amalie Dietrich" and "Barossa," both first produced in 1988. Author of radio scripts on poetry for Australian Broadcasting Commission. Contributor to magazines and newspapers.

WORK IN PROGRESS: A book of poems; stories; essays.

SIDELIGHTS: Andrew Taylor told *CA:* "Several years living in Europe and several in the U.S.A., Canada, and Mexico have counteracted Australia's isolation, and my involvement with Adelaide Festival of Arts was another attempt at this. But I also like watching plants grow slowly and resolutely in one place, so that despite my travelling, gardening remains a key interest.

"My move to Western Australia in 1992 has brought me back in touch with a sea and beachscape reminiscent of my childhood on the other side of the continent, and this has reformed my recent thinking and poetry."

BIOGRAPHICAL/CRITICAL SOURCES:

PERIODICALS

World Literature Today, winter, 1983.

*   *   *

THELLE, Notto R(eidar) 1941-

PERSONAL: Born March 19, 1941, in Hong Kong; son of Notto Normann (a missionary) and Rannfrid (a missionary and teacher; maiden name, Danielsen)

Thelle; married Mona Irene Ramstad (a psychologist), June 19, 1965; children: Rannfrid Irene, Olav Ramstad, Anne Helene, Notto Johannes, Ellen Mari. *Education:* Attended University of Oslo, 1960-66, University of Sheffield, 1968-69, and Otani University, 1972-73; University of Oslo, Dr. Theol., 1983; attended Modum Bads Nervesanatorium, 1985-86. *Religion:* Lutheran.

ADDRESSES: Home—Skinstadveien, 3370 Vikersund, Norway. *Office*—University of Oslo, P.O. Box 1023, Blindern, Oslo 3, Norway.

CAREER: Scandinavian East Asia Mission, Kyoto, Japan, missionary, 1969-85; National Christian Council Center for the Study of Japanese Religions, Kyoto, associate director, 1974-85; University of Oslo, Oslo, Norway, professor of theology, 1986—.

WRITINGS:

Buddhism and Christianity in Japan, University of Hawaii Press (Honolulu), 1987.
Hvem kan stoppe vinden?, Oslo University Press, 1991.
Mennesket og mysteriet (title means "Humankind and the Mystery"; high school textbook), Samlaget, 1992.
Ditt ansikt soker jag (title means "I Seek Your Face: Texts about Faith"), Oriens Forlag, 1993.

Editor of *Japanese Religions,* 1974-85, and *Norsk Tidsskrift for Misjon,* 1988—.

WORK IN PROGRESS: Research for a book on alternative spirituality and the church.

SIDELIGHTS: Notto R. Thelle told *CA:* "My interest in Japan has especially been the encounter between Christianity and other religions, Buddhist studies, and Japanese studies. As professor of mission studies and ecumenics, I want to motivate students to discover that the center of Christendom is no longer in the West, but in the Third World."

*   *   *

THOMPSON, Sylvia (Vaughn Sheekman)   1935-

PERSONAL: Born June 19, 1935, in Santa Monica, CA; daughter of Arthur (a screenwriter) and Gloria (a film star; maiden name, Stuart) Sheekman; married Gene Thompson (a novelist), June 15, 1955; children: David Oxley, Benjamin Stuart, Dinah Vaughan, Amanda Greenleaf. *Education:* Attended University of California, Berkeley, 1952-55, and Sorbonne, 1954.

ADDRESSES: Home—P.O. Box 145, Idyllwild, CA 92349. *Agent*—Susan Lescher, 67 Irving Pl., New York, NY 10003.

CAREER: Writer. Lord & Taylor, New York, NY, copywriter, 1955-56.

AWARDS, HONORS: International Association of Cooking Professionals Award for *Feasts and Friends: Recipes from a Lifetime.*

WRITINGS:

Economy Gastronomy: A Gourmet Cookbook for the Budget-Minded, Atheneum (New York City), 1963.
The Budget Gourmet, Random House (New York City), 1975.
Woman's Day Crockery Cuisine: Slow-Cooking Recipes for Family and Entertainment, Random House, 1977.
Feasts and Friends: Recipes from a Lifetime, North Point Press, 1988.
The Birthday Cake Book, Chronicle Books (San Francisco), 1993.
The Kitchen Garden: A Passionate Gardener's Comprehensive Guide to Growing Good Things to Eat, Bantam (New York City), 1995.
The Kitchen Garden Cookbook: A Passionate Cook's Recipes to Bring Out the Best in Garden-Fresh Produce, Bantam, 1995.
Festive Tarts, Chronicle Books, 1996.

Author of syndicated newspaper column "Garden Fresh." Contributor of articles to *Vogue, House Beautiful, Gourmet, Woman's Day, Holiday, Family Circle, Travel & Leisure, Good Housekeeping, Harrowsmith,* and *Sphere.*

SIDELIGHTS: Sylvia Thompson told *CA:* "Years ago, when my dear friend and agent Susan Lescher would call and my husband answered the phone, she would ask, 'Is Sylvia working or is she in the garden?' One day, as I was finishing *Feasts and Friends,* I realized that I knew a considerable lot about the garden, and that I could bring my experience and my passion to my work. *The Kitchen Garden* and *The Kitchen Garden Cookbook* took over seven years of gardening, creating recipes, researching, and writing. Conceived as one book, when the stack of pages became unwieldy, my editor, Frances McCullough, Susan Lescher, and I agreed it would best serve readers to divide the work in two. Even so, most of my work on herbs, fruits, edible flowers, and rare vegetables had to be cut for want of space. I very much hope that those pages will also see the light of day.

"Now, after having written about cuisine for over thirty years, I am extremely fortunate to have found a place in both worlds that I love."

BIOGRAPHICAL/CRITICAL SOURCES:

PERIODICALS

Bloomsbury Review, November, 1993, p. 21.
Kirkus Reviews, February 1, 1989, p. 203.
Money, May, 1976.
New York Times, May 9, 1978.
Publishers Weekly, March 10, 1975; October 17, 1977; May 22, 1978.
Time, November 28, 1988, p. 106.
Village Voice, December 22, 1975.
Washington Post Book World, December 4, 1977; December 11, 1988, p. 10.
Wilson Library Bulletin, March, 1989, p. 97.

*   *   *

TILLINGHAST, Richard (Williford)   1940-

PERSONAL: Born November 25, 1940, in Memphis, TN; son of Raymond Charles (a mechanical engineer) and Martha (Williford) Tillinghast; married Nancy Walton Pringle, 1965 (divorced, 1970); married Mary Graves, April 22, 1973; children: (second marriage) three sons, one daughter. *Education:* University of the South, Sewanee, TN, A.B., 1962; Harvard University, A.M., 1963, Ph.D., 1970.

ADDRESSES: Home—1317 Granger Ave., Ann Arbor, MI 48104. *Office*—Department of English, University of Michigan, Haven Hall, Ann Arbor, MI 48109.

CAREER: University of California, Berkeley, assistant professor of English, 1968-73; University of the South, Sewanee, TN, visiting assistant professor, 1979-80; Harvard University, Cambridge, MA, Briggs-Copeland lecturer, 1980-83; University of Michigan, Ann Arbor, associate professor, 1983-92, professor of English, 1992—; formerly affiliated with College of Marin and the college program at San Quentin State Prison. Associate, Michigan Institute for the Humanities, 1989-90, 1993-94; American Research Institute in Turkey fellow, University of the Bosphorus, Turkey, 1990.

AWARDS, HONORS: Woodrow Wilson fellow, 1962-63; Harvard University, Sinclair-Kennedy travel grant, 1966-67; University of California, Berkeley, Creative Arts Institute grant, 1970; National Endowment for the Humanities grant, 1980; Bread Loaf fellowship, 1982; Michigan Arts Council grant, 1985; Millay Colony residency, 1985; Yaddo Writers' Retreat, residency, 1986; Michigan Council for the Arts creative artist grant, 1986; University of Michigan, Horace H. Rackham School of Graduate Study, faculty recognition award, 1990, faculty grant and fellow, 1994-95; Amy Lowell Travel fellow, 1990-91; British Council fellow, 1992, travel grant, 1994; University of Southern California, Ann Stanford Prize for poetry, 1992; Pushcart Prize nomination, 1993-95; Washtenaw Council for the Arts, Annie Award, 1993, 1995.

WRITINGS:

POETRY

Sleep Watch, Wesleyan University Press (Middletown, CT), 1969.
The Knife and Other Poems, Wesleyan University Press, 1980.
Sewanee in Ruins (also see below), drawings by Edward Carlos, University of the South (Sewanee, TN), 1981.
Fossils, Metal, and the Blue Limit, White Creek Press, 1982.
Our Flag Was Still There (includes *Sewanee in Ruins*), Wesleyan University Press, 1984.
The Stonecutter's Hand, David R. Godine (Boston), 1994.

OTHER

Robert Lowell: Damaged Grandeur (criticism), University of Michigan Press (Ann Arbor), 1995.

Contributor to numerous newspapers and periodicals, including *Antaeus, Atlantic Monthly, Boston Globe, Boston Phoenix, Boston Review, Crazy Horse, Critical Quarterly, Georgia Review, Gettysburg Review, Harper's Bazaar, Harvard Advocate, Nation, New Criterion, New Republic, New Yorker, New York Times Book Review, Paris Review, Partisan Review, Ploughshares, Poetry, Sewanee Review, Shenandoah, Southern Review, Washington Post,* and *Yale Review.*

SIDELIGHTS: Richard Tillinghast employs a "quiet, modest, witty [speech] while he talks about the oddness of the ordinary experiences of life," observes *Poetry* contributor Robert Watson. The critic remarks that "the experiences [Tillinghast] presents have the quality of a collage or surrealistic film: waking states of mind shift to dream states, to memories, memories seem to merge with fantasy or vision." Alan Williamson in *Parnassus: Poetry in Review* thinks that the author's work "is poetry carefully made, phrase by phrase, so that it often succeeds in incising itself on one's memory."

In *Our Flag Was Still There,* Tillinghast's 1984 collection, the author "writes with a new confidence, direction, and stylistic maturity," comments Thomas Swiss in the *Sewanee Review.* The focal point of the book is "Sewanee in Ruins," a long poem that combines journals, biographical sources, letters, and Tillinghast's own experiences to deliver a broad portrait of the University of the South. "The poem evolves into an elaborate meditation, beginning with the destruction of the University of the South during the Civil War and finally projecting a vision of a future after nuclear war in the same setting," summarizes Swiss. While *New York Times Book Review* contributor Paul Breslin remarks that the author occasionally "rambles on too long" and "runs the risk . . . of writing an alumni magazine piece," he observes that Tillinghast "escapes that fate by combining his documentary sources to establish a cumulative portrait of a way of life." Swiss also notes, similar to previous criticism of Tillinghast's work, a slow deliberateness to the poet's language: "Tillinghast's habitual listing of images and his linking of adjectives slows the poem, but not often and not in a way that detracts from its impact."

The Stonecutter's Hand, Tillinghast's 1994 collection of poetry, treats a range of historical topics. For Tillnghast, writes Mark Jackson in the *Boston Book Review,* "history . . . has never been a record of events detached from a speaker's current environ-

ment and mood—the past is ever-present in architecture, landscape and the 'inner / Cosmos' of human memory." Jackson finds that the poems of *The Stonecutter's Hand* "view history from a more intimate and self-reflexive perspective" than Tillinghast's earlier poetry and concludes that *The Stonecutter's Hand* "reaffirms [Tillinghast's] status as a major talent."

BIOGRAPHICAL/CRITICAL SOURCES:

BOOKS

Contemporary Literary Criticism, Volume 29, Gale (Detroit), 1984.

PERIODICALS

Boston Book Review, December, 1994.
New York Times Book Review, May 10, 1981; July 22, 1984.
Parnassus: Poetry in Review, fall-winter, 1981.
Poetry, December, 1970.
Sewanee Review, October, 1985.

*   *   *

TOWERS, (Augustus) Robert   1923-1995

PERSONAL: Born January 21, 1923, in Richmond, VA; died May 2, 1995, in New York, NY, of pancreatic cancer; son of A. (in business) and Miriam (a homemaker; maiden name, Reynolds) Towers; married Patricia Locke (a magazine editor), May 13, 1967; children: Sarah. *Education:* Princeton University, A.B. (summa cum laude), 1945, Ph.D., 1952. *Politics:* Democrat.

CAREER: American Consulate, Calcutta, India, viceconsul, 1945-47; Princeton University, Princeton, NJ, instructor in English, 1950-54; Queens College of the City University of New York, Flushing, NY, member of English department, 1954-84; Columbia University, New York City, member of English department and chair of Graduate Writing Division, 1984-89. Director, Corporation of Yaddo, beginning 1980. *Military service:* U.S. Army, 1942-43.

MEMBER: International PEN (director of American Center, 1979-83), National Book Critics Circle.

WRITINGS:

NOVELS

The Necklace of Kali, Harcourt (New York City),
     1960.
The Monkey Watcher, Harcourt, 1964.
The Summoning, Harper (New York City), 1983.

OTHER

Contributor of articles, essays and reviews to periodicals, including *New York Times, New York Review
of Books, Atlantic Monthly,* and *New Republic.*

SIDELIGHTS: Robert Towers published three criti-
cally-praised novels during his career. He also spent
forty years teaching writing at Queens College and
Columbia University and was a frequent book reviewer for such prominent periodicals as the *New
York Times* and *New York Review of Books.*

Towers' first novel, *The Necklace of Kali,* is based
on his own experiences in India as a member of the
diplomatic corps. The story takes place just before
the withdrawal of the British government and the
granting of independence to India. The period was a
time of turmoil between the British and Indians and
between Muslims and Hindus. The novel, wrote M.
J. Tweedy in the *New York Times Book Review,* is
distinguished by "Towers' ability to create memorable word pictures of Calcutta's fabled filth and the
magic of glorious Kanchenjunga." Similarly, Hope
Hale in the *Saturday Review* noted that the book
"presents India in exciting, unforgettable detail. . . .
The Necklace of Kali is an intense and honest effort
to come to terms with the diversities of today's
world."

In his second novel, *The Monkey Watcher,* Towers
turned his attention to an American setting, telling
the story of Arthur Brubeck, a New York art historian. When Brubeck's wife is diagnosed with a fatal
cancer, he begins an affair with a younger colleague.
"The novel has style and shrewdness of observation," wrote the *Times Literary Supplement* critic. "It
also displays a considerable insight into the secret,
aberrant life of the middle-aged male." The aberrant
aspect to the story drew the attention of E. W. Luker
in the *Library Journal,* who stated: "Granted that this
is a sick age. . .but a good novel entertains, releases,
enlightens or otherwise satisfies the reader." Writing
in *Book Week,* Kenneth Lamott found *The Monkey*

Watcher "an honest and workmanlike book of considerable merit. . . . I shall look forward with interest to Mr. Towers' next book."

Towers' next work, *The Summoning,* appeared in
1983. In this novel, Lawrence Hux, a foundation
executive, experiences what may be a religious conversion while searching for the killer of a friend.
Walter Kendrick, writing in the *New York Times
Book Review,* noted that the novel "sets up one conventional expectation after another only to deliver
something surprising each time." Although Kendrick
believed that Towers "takes great risks" with Hux,
he achieves "incomplete success" with the character.
"However," Kendrick concluded, "*The Summoning*
is an absorbing and moving novel, admirable both
for what it achieves and for what it attempts."

In addition to writing three novels, Towers was a
teacher of writing for many years. "[It] was in the 40
years [Towers] spent in the classroom that he made
his most indelible mark," according to Robert McG.
Thomas, Jr., in the *New York Times.* Towers taught
at Queens College in New York City for thirty years
before moving to Columbia University to chair their
Graduate Writing Division. Towers once told *CA:* "I
have combined (not always successfully) a dual career of writing fiction and teaching creative writing,
and I have derived much gratification from both
activities. I have also enjoyed the extensive (possibly
excessive) reviewing that I have done. I have tried
never to repeat myself in my fiction. New ideas keep
bubbling up."

BIOGRAPHICAL/CRITICAL SOURCES:

PERIODICALS

Booklist, October 15, 1960, p. 57.
Book Week, November 8, 1964, p. 28.
Chicago Tribune, November 13, 1960, p. 9.
Kirkus Reviews, July 15, 1960, p. 28.
Library Journal, September 15, 1960, p. 85; Decem-
     ber 1, 1964, p. 89.
New Yorker, November 5, 1960, p. 36; October 17,
     1964, p. 40.
New York Herald Tribune Book Review, October 30,
     1960, p. 13.
New York Review of Books, February 16, 1984, pp.
     40-41.
New York Times, October 6, 1983.
New York Times Book Review, October 2, 1960, p.
     40; October 18, 1964, p. 42; October 16, 1983,
     pp. 11, 33.

Saturday Review, October 15, 1960, p. 43.
Spectator, July 28, 1961, p. 148.
Times Literary Supplement, August 4, 1961, p. 477;
　March 11, 1965, p. 189.
Virginia Quarterly Review, winter, 1965, p. 41.
Washington Post Book World, October 2, 1983, pp.
　3, 14.

OBITUARIES:

PERIODICALS

New York Times, May 4, 1995, p. B15.*

*　　　*　　　*

TURCO, Lewis (Putnam)　1934-
(Wesli Court)

PERSONAL: Born May 2, 1934, in Buffalo, NY; son
of Luigi (a minister) and May (Putnam) Turco; married Jean Houdlette (a music librarian), June 16,
1956; children: Melora Ann, Christopher Cameron.
Education: University of Connecticut, B.A., 1959;
University of Iowa, M.A., 1961.

ADDRESSES: Office—Mathom Press Enterprises,
Box 362, Oswego, NY 13126-0362 (literary and
booking); Mathom Bookshop and Bindery, Box 161,
Dresden, ME 04342-0161 (summer).

CAREER: Cleveland State University, Cleveland,
OH, instructor in English, 1960-64, founder and
director, Cleveland Poetry Center, 1961-64;
Hillsdale College, Hillsdale, MI, assistant professor
of English, 1964-65; State University of New York
at Oswego, assistant professor, 1965-68, associate
professor, 1968-71, professor of English, 1971-96,
founder and director of Program in Writing Arts,
1969-95, poet in residence, 1995-96. Visiting professor, State University of New York at Potsdam, 1968-
69; faculty exchange scholar, State University of
New York system, 1975—; Bingham Poet in Residence, University of Louisville, 1982; Visiting
Writer in Residence, Ashland University, 1991. *Military service:* U.S. Navy, 1952-56.

MEMBER: PEN American Center, Poetry Society of
America, Associated Writing Programs.

AWARDS, HONORS: Yaddo Foundation resident fellow, 1959, in poetry, and 1977, in fiction; Academy

of American Poets prize, University of Iowa, 1960;
Bread Loaf Poetry fellow, 1961; American Weave
Press Chapbook Award, 1962; State University of
New York Research Foundation faculty fellow,
1966, 1967, 1969, 1971, 1973, and 1978, and grant-
in-aid, 1969; *The Davidson Miscellany* fiction prize,
1969; Helen Bullis Prize, *Poetry Northwest,* 1972;
National Endowment for the Arts/PEN Syndicated
Fiction Project award, 1983; First Poetry Award,
Kansas Quarterly/Kansas Arts Commission, 1984-
85, for a poem written under the pseudonym Wesli
Court; State University of New York College at
Oswego President's Award for Scholarly and Cre-
ative Activity and Research, 1985; Chicago Book
Clinic Exhibit Certificate of Award, 1986, for *The
Compleat Melancholick: Being a Sequence of Found,
Composite, and Composed Poems, Based Largely
Upon Robert Burton's 'Anatomy of Melancholy';* se-
lection of *The Compleat Melancholick* included in the
National Endowment for the Arts' New American
Writing Exhibits, International Book Fairs of Frank-
furt and Liber, 1986; Melville Cane Award, Poetry
Society of America, 1986, for *Visions and Revisions
of American Poetry; Silverfish Review* Chapbook
Award, 1989, for *A Family Album;* Cooper House
Chapbook Award, 1990, for *Murmurs in the Walls;*
selected as a participant in the New York Council for
the Humanities Speakers in the Humanities Program,
1992-95; Distinguished Alumnus Award, Alumni
Association of the University of Connecticut, 1992;
installed in the Meriden, Connecticut, Hall of Fame,
1993; Faculty Enhancement Grant, State University
of New York at Oswego, 1995.

WRITINGS:

POETRY

First Poems, Golden Quill Press (Francestown, NH),
　1960.
The Sketches of Lewis Turco and Livevil: A Mask,
　American Weave Press, 1962.
Awaken, Bells Falling: Poems, 1959-1967, Univer-
　sity of Missouri Press (Columbia, MO), 1968.
*The Inhabitant: Poems, with prints by Thom.
　Seawell,* Despa Press (Northampton, MA), 1970.
Pocoangelini: A Fantography & Other Poems, Despa
　Press, 1971.
The Weed Garden, Peaceweed Press (Orangeburg,
　SC), 1973.
A Cage of Creatures, Banjo Press, 1978.
Seasons of the Blood, Mammoth Press (Rochester,
　NY), 1980.

American Still Lifes, Mathom (Oswego, NY), 1981.

The Compleat Melancholick: Being a Sequence of Found, Composite, and Composed Poems, Based Largely Upon Robert Burton's 'Anatomy of Melancholy,' Bieler Press (St. Paul, MN), 1985.

A Maze of Monsters, Livingston University Press (Livingston, AL), 1986.

The Shifting Web: New and Selected Poems, University of Arkansas Press (Fayetteville, AR), 1989.

A Family Album, Silverfish Review Press (Eugene, OR), 1990.

Murmurs in the Walls, Cooper House (Oklahoma City, OK), 1992.

Emily Dickinson, Woman of Letters: Poems and Centos from Lines in Emily Dickinson's Letters, State University of New York Press, 1993.

Legends of the Mists, New Spirit (Kew Gardens, NY), 1993.

NONFICTION

The Book of Forms: A Handbook of Poetics, Dutton (New York City), 1968, expanded edition published as *The New Book of Forms,* University Press of New England (Hanover, NH), 1986.

The Literature of New York: A Selective Bibliography of Colonial and Native New York State Authors, New York State English Council (Rochester, NY), 1970.

Creative Writing in Poetry, State University of New York, 1970.

Poetry: An Introduction through Writing, Reston (Reston, VA), 1973.

Freshman Composition and Literature, State University of New York, 1974.

Visions and Revisions of American Poetry, University of Arkansas Press, 1986.

Dialogue: A Socratic Dialogue on the Art of Writing Dialogue in Fiction, Writers Digest Books (Cincinnati, OH), 1989.

The Public Poet: Five Lectures on the Art and Craft of Poetry, Ashland Poetry Press (Ashland, OH), 1991.

PLAYS

The Dark Man, first produced in Storrs, CT, at the University of Connecticut's Jorgensen Little Theater, May, 1959.

The Elections Last Fall, first produced in Oswego, NY, at the Tyler Hall Experimental Theater, December, 1969.

UNDER PSEUDONYM WESLI COURT

Courses in Lambents: Poems, Mathom, 1977.

Curses and Laments, Song Magazine (Stevens Point, WI), 1978.

Murgatroyd and Mabel (juvenile), illustrated by Robert Michaels, Mathom, 1978.

The Airs of Wales, Poetry Newsletter of Temple University (Philadelphia, PA), 1981.

OTHER

While the Spider Slept (ballet scenario), produced by the Royal Swedish Ballet, Stockholm, June, 1965.

The Fog: A Chamber Opera in One Act (with music by Walter Heckster), Donemus (Amsterdam, Holland), 1987.

Contributor to anthologies and to reference works, including *Dictionary of Literary Biography Yearbook, First Printings of American Authors, Collier's Encyclopedia, Masterplots II: Poetry,* and *The Oxford Companion to Twentieth Century Poetry.* Contributor of poems, stories, essays and reviews to numerous literary journals and periodicals, including *New Yorker, Poetry, Nation, New Republic, Atlantic, Sewanee Review, Hudson Review, Virginia Quarterly Review,* and *Kenyon Review.*

WORK IN PROGRESS: Understanding Post-Modern American Poetry (essays); *A Book of Fears* (poems); *A Book of Leaves* (memoirs); *Voices in an Old House* (poems); *The Museum of Ordinary People* (short stories); *A Book of Proverbs* (poems); *Talk about Poetry* (interviews); *The Salvage Sonnets* (poems); *The Oxford Handbook of Literary Forms* (reference); *The Stranger* (poems); *Guinevere's Quest* (comic novel); *Letters to the Dead* (poems); *Reading and Writing Poetry* (textbook); *Ancient Music* (translations).

SIDELIGHTS: "Those who frequent the small world of the little poetry magazines know Lewis Turco as a champion of the classical virtues of form and craftsmanship," writes David G. McLean in an *Agora* review. Turco, best known as an American poet, is also a critic, playwright, short story writer, and author of children's literature.

Awaken, Bells Falling: Poems, 1959-1967, considered to be one of Turco's strongest early works, is "a full and varied book, showing off the range of Turco's talent and the variety of his mind" comments a *Virginia Quarterly Review* reviewer. In *Concerning*

Poetry, Hyatt H. Waggoner notes that images "of winter, of silence, and of either a cold darkness or a cold whiteness suggest, and sometimes establish, the prevailing mood of *Awaken, Bells Falling.*" Waggoner compares Turco's verse to "early [Wallace] Stevens or early [Robert] Frost, or both at once." William Heyen, in a *Modern Poetry Studies* review, sees the poems in *Awaken, Bells Falling* as "bearers of consciousness, awareness, intelligence. . . . [Turco's] poems . . . are metaphors for what seems to be a developing vision."

The Inhabitant: Poems, with prints by Thom. Seawell, is also generally considered one of Turco's strongest collections of poetry. McLean sees *The Inhabitant* as representing "the American poet caught in the classical vs. romantic crossfire. . . . [This] message is clear, although we do a disservice to *The Inhabitant* if we imply that the book is excessively didactic." McLean concludes that "successful as is the collection as a whole, few, if any, of the individual poems rival the best of Turco's earlier works." Heyen calls *The Inhabitant* "a whole world, not a slice of life, . . . the world [Turco] has opened for himself is dynamic, self-propagating, endless. . . . It seems to me that this is a good test of any aesthetic, any world view: can it take everything into account?" Heyen concludes that much of *The Inhabitant* is "wonderfully realized . . . intelligent and moving."

Writing in the *English Record,* Gene Van Troyer highlights Turco's poetic range and virtuosity as well as "the fantastic element in Turco's work," as evidenced in the collection *A Cage of Creatures.* De Villo Sloan, writing in *Voices in Italian Americana,* argues that Turco's writing moves through a "gothic era" in *A Cage of Creatures:* "All these pieces in some way investigate archetypes of the horrible and fantastic." Van Troyer is also impressed with Turco's diction: "Poetry is sometimes characterized as the means by which the absolute limits of language are tested, and the agency through which new modes of expression are discovered."

Published in 1989, *The Shifting Web: New and Selected Poems* is a retrospective book spanning three decades. De Villo Sloan finds the poems to be "preoccupied with the inherent duality of the western tradition," and "the apparently irreconcilable nature of oppositions." This "rich ambiguity," Sloan continues, "offers many possibilities for specific interpretations." Reviewing *The Shifting Web* in *Voices in Italian Americana,* Elizabeth Blair writes of Turco:

"Despite stylistic idiosyncracies, such as manufactured words and ornate language coupled with deliberately non-visual imagery, his is an honest, intelligent and distinctive voice." Blair concludes that though "these understated yet eerie sketches make us painfully conscious of our own mortality, the absence of human life is too insistent in these poems; birds sing and horses whinny, but no human voice sounds. One wonders whether Turco has carried an interesting idea too far." Turco's *Emily Dickinson, Woman of Letters: Poems and Centos from Lines in Emily Dickinson's Letters* is a book of poems composed by collaging together sentences and fragments from the many letters written by Dickinson. Turco's own words sometimes serve as bridges between the Dickinson quotations or put her words into a particular context. The effect is to create a number of new poems which seem to be written in the famous poet's voice. Sarah Wider commented in the *Emily Dickinson International Society Bulletin:* "The book is a curious one, bound to raise conventional eyebrows." Wider finds that within these poems, readers "will eerily hear Dickinson's voice . . . for the poems themselves are based on her words." Willis Buckingham, writing in *Nineteenth-Century Literature,* praises Turco for steering "well clear of greeting-card banality, retaining Dickinson's verve, haunted complexity, and resonance without clarity. I enjoyed many of these poems." Writing in *Eclectic Literary Forum,* Kevin Walzer finds *Emily Dickinson, Woman of Letters* to be "an unusual contribution to Dickinson scholarship . . . and a strong addition to Turco's own work—a creative homage to another poet." In an overview of Turco's career for the *Hollins Critic,* H. R. Coursen writes that the poet's "individual poems are invariably of high quality, a quality especially remarkable when one considers the virtually complete range of formal approaches that Turco employs."

In addition to his work as a poet, Turco is also known for his writings on poetic form and technique. His *The Book of Forms: A Handbook of Poetics,* written as a handbook for the appreciation of poetry, and its expanded version, *The New Book of Forms,* contain definitions of poetic terms and "a wealth of technical information," says *Booklist* reviewer Penelope Mesick. Turco catalogues examples of verse forms used by poets from many countries and time periods. Mesick notes: "[*The New Book of Forms*] distinguishes itself as a handbook by the inclusion of 'examples of poems written in each form by poets of all periods' and a 'formfinder' that tells the baffled reader exactly what a nine-line, alliterative anapestic stanza *is.*" Morris Rabinowitz, writing in *Kliatt Young Adult Paperback Book Guide,* calls *The New Book of Forms* "the most informative, easy-to-use, and most attractive book about poetics and verse forms that I have seen in 20 years of looking at such texts, both as teacher and librarian."

Turco's critical work *Visions and Revisions of American Poetry,* according to *Times Literary Supplement* contributor Mark Ford, constitutes "a fiercely formalist rejection of organic poetry as it derives from [Ralph Waldo] Emerson." In the ongoing debate between "professionals" and "amateurs," Turco, Ford elaborates, favors poets who master patterns of rhythm, rhyme and syllable count over Walt Whitman and others who use a more relaxed, speech-oriented mode of expression. The reviewer concludes that "it is possible to disagree with everything Turco says and still find this book superbly engrossing." Margaret Dickie, in a review for *American Literature,* argues that as "one poet's testimonial, it draws together more than two decades of thinking about what it means to write and to be devoted to writing." Dickie concludes, however, that *Visions and Revisions* "is too sparse to stand up against its predecessors written by professional scholars." *Visions and Revisions* received the Poetry Society of America 1987 Melville Cane Award.

As a poet, Turco would like readers to see more than formalism in his verse. Turco told *CA:* "Although people believe—because my name is associated with *The Book of Forms*—that I am interested only in traditional ways of writing, such is not the case. I am as interested in experimental writing as in any and all other aspects of the subject. In fact, most of my own poems are written in unrhymed syllabic verse, with which I began experimenting at Yaddo in the summer of 1959. . . . I'm one of those writers who loves to write; I'm never happier than when I'm working on a project. Jim Elledge and Herb Coursen are quite accurate when they say that I'll try anything."

BIOGRAPHICAL/CRITICAL SOURCES:

BOOKS

Contemporary Authors Autobiography Series, Volume 22, Gale (Detroit), 1995.
Contemporary Literary Criticism, Gale, Volume 11, 1979, Volume 63, 1990.
Dictionary of Literary Biography Yearbook: 1984, Gale, 1985.

Dictionary of Literary Biography Yearbook: 1989, Gale, 1990.
Heyen, William, *American Poets in 1976,* Bobbs-Merrill, 1976.
Moore, Marianne, Howard Nemerov, and Alan Swallow, editors, *Riverside Poetry 3,* Twayne, 1958.
Turco, Lewis, *The Book of Forms: A Handbook of Poetics,* Dutton, 1968, expanded edition published as *The New Book of Forms: A Handbook of Poetics,* University Press of New England, 1986.
Turco, *Visions and Revisions of American Poetry,* University of Arkansas Press, 1986.

PERIODICALS

Agora, spring, 1972.
American Literature, March, 1987, pp. 138-39.
Bartleby's Review, fall, 1972, pp. 39-43.
Booklist, January 1, 1987, p. 678.
Centennial Review, spring, 1987, pp. 228-29.
Concerning Poetry, fall, 1969.
Contemporary Poetry, Volume 4, no. 1, 1981, pp. 40-5.
Costerus, Volume 9, 1973, pp. 239-51.
Cream City Review, Volume 8, no. 1-2, 1983, pp. 108-17.
Dusty Dog Reviews, Numbers 14-15, 1994.
Eclectic Literary Forum, fall, 1995, pp. 48-9.
Emily Dickinson International Society Bulletin, May/June, 1993.
English Record, Volume 42, number 2, 1992.
Georgia Review, winter, 1991.
Hollins Critic, December, 1988, pp. 10-11; April, 1991.
Italian Americana, spring, 1975.
Kamadhenu, Volume 2, no. 1-2, 1971.
Kliatt Young Adult Paperback Book Guide, January, 1987, p. 20.
Massachusetts Review, autumn, 1971, pp. 689-708.
Modern Poetry Studies, winter, 1974.
New Review, September/October, 1992.
Nineteenth-Century Literature, June, 1994, pp. 542-43.
Northwest Review, summer, 1970, pp. 127-28.
Oswegonian News, February 9, 1995, p. 7.
Palladium-Times, January 26, 1995, p. 11.
Poetry, December, 1961, pp. 186-87; March, 1969, pp. 423-24; March, 1973.
Times Literary Supplement, May 22, 1987, p. 557.
Virginia Quarterly Review, autumn, 1968.
Voices in Italian Americana, spring, 1990; spring, 1992; spring, 1993.

TWINING, William (Lawrence)   1934-

PERSONAL: Born September 22, 1934, in Kampala, Uganda; son of Edward F. (an administrator) and Helen M. (a doctor; maiden name, DuBuisson) Twining; married Penelope Wall Morris (a surveyor), August 31, 1957; children: Karen, Peter. *Education:* Brasenose College, Oxford, B.A. (with first class honors), 1955, M.A., 1960; University of Chicago, J.D. (cum laude), 1958.

ADDRESSES: Office—Faculty of Laws, University College, University of London, London WC1H 0EG, England.

CAREER: University of Khartoum, Khartoum, Sudan, lecturer in law, 1958-61; University College, Dar es Salaam, Tanganyika (now Tanzania), senior lecturer in law, 1961-65; Queen's University, Belfast, Northern Ireland, professor of jurisprudence and head of department of law and jurisprudence, 1966-72; University of Warwick, Coventry, England, professor of law, 1972-82, chair of School of Law, 1974-75 and 1977-78; University of London, University College, London, England, Quain Professor of Jurisprudence, 1983—. Visiting lecturer at Brasenose College, Oxford, 1960, and University of Chicago, 1964; senior fellow at Yale University, 1965; visiting professor at University of Pennsylvania, 1971, University of Uppsala, 1975, University of Virginia, 1976, Northwestern University, 1978, and Boston College Law School, 1995; visiting fellow at Wolfson College, Oxford, 1982-83, and Australian National University, 1985; distinguished visiting professor at University of Miami, Coral Gables, FL, 1981—. Member of Kenya Council of Legal Education, 1962-65; member of International Legal Center's Committee on Legal Education and Committee on Legal Research, 1972-76; member of Committee on Legal Education in Northern Ireland, 1973; chair of Warwick District Community Relations Council, 1974-76; Bentham Committee, vice-chair, 1976-82, chair, 1982—; consultant to Papua New Guinea Law Reform Commission.

MEMBER: Society of Public Teachers of Law (chair of Working Party on Academic Law Publishing, 1977; president, 1978-79), Commonwealth Legal Education Association (chair, 1983-93).

AWARDS, HONORS: LL.D., University of Victoria, 1980, and University of Edinburgh, 1994; D.C.L., Brasenose College, 1990.

WRITINGS:

The Place of Customary Law in the National Legal Systems of East Africa, University of Chicago Law School (Chicago), 1964.

The Karl Llewellyn Papers: A Guide to the Collection, University of Chicago Law School, 1967, revised edition, 1970.

Karl Llewellyn and the Realist Movement, Weidenfeld & Nicolson (London), 1973, University of Oklahoma Press (Norman), 1985.

(With David Miers) *How to Do Things with Rules,* Weidenfeld & Nicolson, 1976, 3rd edition, 1991.

Theories of Evidence: Bentham and Wigmore, Stanford University Press (Stanford, CA), 1985.

(With Terence Anderson) *Analysis of Evidence,* Little, Brown (Boston), 1991.

Rethinking Evidence, Northwestern University Press (Evanston, IL), 1994.

Blackstone's Tower: The English Law School, Sweet & Maxwell, 1994.

EDITOR

(With Jenny Uglow) *Legal Literature in Small Jurisdictions,* Canadian Law Information Council and Commonwealth Secretariat, 1981.

(With Uglow) *Law Publishing and Legal Information,* Sweet & Maxwell, 1981.

Facts in Law, Franz Steiner Verlag, 1983.

Legal Theory and Common Law, Basil Blackwell (London), 1986.

(With Richard Tur) *Essays on Kelsen,* Oxford University Press (New York City), 1986.

(With Eugene Kamenka and Robert S. Summers) *Sociological Jurisprudence and Realist Theories of Law,* Duncker & Humblot, 1986.

(With Emma Quick) *Legal Records in the Commonwealth,* Dartmouth, 1994.

Editor of series "Law in Context," Butterworth, 1965—, and "Jurists," Weidenfeld & Nicolson/Stanford University Press, 1981—.

SIDELIGHTS: William Twining told *CA:* "As a wandering scholar, pursuing a relatively orthodox academic career, my approach has been interdisciplinary and international. As a writer I have tried to be provocative, clear, and readable. I have succeeded in getting part of one poem broadcast on local radio, but I have so far failed to persuade a publisher to take on a collection of my satirical works."

BIOGRAPHICAL/CRITICAL SOURCES:

PERIODICALS

Melbourne University Law Review, June, 1986.

U

ULAM, Adam B(runo)   1922-

PERSONAL: Born April 8, 1922, in Lvov, Poland; son of Jozef and Anna (Auerbach) Ulam; married Mary Hamilton Burgwin, 1963; children: Alexander Stanislaw, Joseph Howard. *Education:* Brown University, A.B., 1943; Harvard University, Ph.D., 1947. *Politics:* Democrat.

ADDRESSES: Office—Russian Research Center, 1737 Cambridge St., Harvard University, Cambridge, MA 02138.

CAREER: Harvard University, Cambridge, MA, began as teaching fellow, 1947, professor of government, 1959-79, Gurney Professor of History and Political Science, 1979—, Russian Research Center, research associate, 1948—, director, 1973-76 and 1980—. Center for International Studies, Massachusetts Institute of Technology, research associate, 1953-55.

MEMBER: Signet Club (Cambridge).

AWARDS, HONORS: Guggenheim fellow, 1956; Rockefeller fellow, 1957 and 1960.

WRITINGS:

Philosophical Foundations of English Socialism, Harvard University Press (Cambridge, MA), 1951.

Titoism and the Cominform, Harvard University Press, 1952.

(Editor with Samuel Hutchinson Beer) *Patterns of Government,* Random House (New York City), 1958, revised edition, 1979.

The Unfinished Revolution, Random House, 1960.

The New Face of Soviet Totalitarianism, Harvard University Press, 1963.

The Bolsheviks: The Intellectual and Political History of the Triumph of Communism in Russia, Macmillan (New York City), 1965.

Expansion and Coexistence: The History of Soviet Foreign Policy, 1917-1967, Praeger (New York City), 1968, 2nd edition published as *Expansion and Coexistence: Soviet Foreign Policy, 1917 to 1973,* Holt (New York City), 1974.

The Rivals: America and Russia since World War II, Viking (New York City), 1971.

The Fall of the American University, Library Press (LaSalle, IL), 1972.

Stalin: The Man and His Era, Viking, 1973.

Russian Political System, Random House, 1974.

A History of Soviet Russia, Praeger, 1976.

Ideologies and Illusions: Revolutionary Thought from Herzen to Solzhenitsyn, Harvard University Press, 1976.

In the Name of the People: Prophets and Conspirators in Prerevolutionary Russia, Viking, 1977.

Russia's Failed Revolution: From the Decembrists to the Dissidents, Basic Books (New York City), 1981.

Dangerous Relations: The Soviet Union in World Politics, 1970-1982, Oxford University Press (New York City), 1983.

The Kirov Affair (novel), Harcourt (San Diego, CA, and New York City), 1988.

The Communists: The Story of Power and Lost Illusions, 1948-1991, Scribner (New York City), 1992.

Contributor to professional journals.

SIDELIGHTS: Adam B. Ulam's studies of the former Soviet Union focus on the totalitarian nature of the regime at home and its sometimes confrontational relations with foreign powers. Among Ulam's studies are *Stalin: The Man and His Era,* a biography of Soviet leader Joseph Stalin and a history of the communist government from the Russian Revolution in 1917 until Stalin's death in 1953, *In the Name of the People: Prophets and Conspirators in Prerevolutionary Russia,* a look at the various opposition groups in Czarist Russia, *Dangerous Relations: The Soviet Union in World Politics, 1970-1982,* a history of Soviet relations with foreign powers, and *The Communists: The Story of Power and Lost Illusions, 1948-1991,* a look at the events which led to the collapse of the communist regime.

In the *New York Times Book Review,* Paul Avrich comments on *Stalin:* "The character of Stalin's dictatorship is admirably described and analyzed in Ulam's impressive book. . . . But it is much more than a biography of Stalin: it is also a history of the Bolshevik Party, of the Russian Revolution and of the Soviet regime up to Stalin's death in 1953. . . . It is the fullest and most up-to-date biography of Stalin now available, and will make instructive reading for specialist and layman alike."

Ulam's *In the Name of the People* traces, as Theodore Shabad observes in the *New York Times,* "the seeming political inertness of the masses and the conviction of a small minority, whether revolutionary terrorists or Communist functionaries, that it has the right to speak and act for the people 'because history has so ordered'. . . . Ulam has now pulled together the many strands into a coherent, detailed story of the radicals, dissenters, writers and students who sought the overthrow of czarism from the 1860's into the 1880's." Benjamin DeMott, writing in the *New Republic,* claims that Ulam's study "is a solid and illuminating work of historical research. . . . *In the Name of the People* never raises its voice or departs from the honorable norms of its discipline. Yet it does become in its course—movingly, irrefutably, invaluably—a command: *judge the means.* This book is better than history, in a word; it is a shield."

Dangerous Relations is considered a continuation of Ulam's now-classic *Expansion and Coexistence.* In the *New Republic,* David E. Kaiser comments that "*Dangerous Relations* continues Ulam's history of Soviet-American relations. . . . Three themes dominate the book: the changing preoccupations of the Soviet leadership, the gains and losses of detente,

and the significance of recent Soviet advances in the third world. Although . . . Ulam regards the Soviet leaders as prisoners of an expansionist dynamic that they cannot escape, he does not believe that they seek world rule or that they regard nuclear war as a rational means of extending their power."

Following the collapse of the Soviet Union in 1991, Ulam published *The Communists: The Story of Power and Lost Illusions, 1948-1991,* a history of the Soviet Union from the end of the Second World War to its demise.

BIOGRAPHICAL/CRITICAL SOURCES:

PERIODICALS

Commentary, August, 1981.
Harper's, February, 1974.
Los Angeles Times, April 30, 1981; April 13, 1988.
Los Angeles Times Book Review, May 22, 1983; May 22, 1988.
National Review, May 15, 1981.
New Republic, November 2, 1968; June 4, 1977; April 14, 1983.
Newsweek, November 26, 1973; April 11, 1977.
New York Review of Books, November 18, 1971; January 24, 1974; June 23, 1977.
New York Times, July 28, 1974; July 6, 1977.
New York Times Book Review, December 26, 1965; February 23, 1969; January 27, 1974; March 22, 1981; March 27, 1983; June 12, 1988; March 29, 1992.
Saturday Review, November 20, 1965; November 20, 1971; September 4, 1976.
Times Literary Supplement, January 12, 1967; April 3, 1969; February 2, 1973; November 30, 1973; June 14, 1974; October 2, 1981.
Washington Post, June 10, 1988.
Washington Post Book World, November 25, 1973; June 26, 1977; April 19, 1981; April 13, 1983.

*   *   *

UNDERDOWN, David (Edward)   1925-

PERSONAL: Born August 19, 1925, in Wells, Somerset, England; son of John Percival and Ethel (Gell) Underdown; married Mary Ebba Ingholt, 1954 (divorced, 1985); children: Harold D., Peter C., Philip J. *Education:* Exeter College, Oxford, B.A.,

1950, M.A., 1951, B.Litt., 1953; Yale University, M.A., 1952.

ADDRESSES: Office—Department of History, Yale University, P.O. Box 208324, Yale Station, New Haven, CT 06520-8324.

CAREER: Royal Holloway College, London, England, tutorial fellow, 1952-53; University of the South, Sewanee, TN, assistant professor, 1953-58, associate professor of history, 1958-62; University of Virginia, Charlottesville, associate professor of history, 1962-68; Brown University, Providence, RI, professor of history, 1968-85; Yale University, New Haven, CT, professor of history, 1986—, director, Yale Center for Parliamentary History. Visiting Mellon Professor, Institute for Advanced Study, 1988-89; fellow, Exeter College, Oxford, 1990—; visiting fellow, All Souls College, Oxford, 1992. *Military service:* Royal Air Force, 1944-47; became sergeant.

MEMBER: American Historical Association, Conference on British Studies, Royal Historical Society (fellow), British Academy (corresponding fellow).

AWARDS, HONORS: Guggenheim fellow, 1964-65 and 1992-93; American Council of Learned Societies fellow, 1973-74; National Endowment for the Humanities fellow, 1980-81; D.Litt., University of the South, 1981; John Ben Snow Prize, North American Conference on British Studies, and New England Historical Association Book Prize, both 1993, for *Fire from Heaven: Life in an English Town in the Seventeenth Century.*

WRITINGS:

Royalist Conspiracy in England, 1649-1660, Yale University Press (New Haven, CT), 1960.
Pride's Purge: Politics in the Puritan Revolution, Oxford University Press (New York City), 1971.
Somerset in the Civil War and Interregnum, Shoe String (Hamden, CT), 1973.
Revel, Riot and Rebellion: Popular Politics and Culture in England, 1603-1660, Oxford University Press, 1985.
Fire from Heaven: Life in an English Town in the Seventeenth Century, Yale University Press, 1992.

Contributor of articles and reviews to professional journals.

BIOGRAPHICAL/CRITICAL SOURCES:

PERIODICALS

American Historical Review, December, 1987.
English Historical Review, January, 1987.
History Today, August, 1987.
Journal of Interdisciplinary History, summer, 1987.
New York Review of Books, February 26, 1987.
Seventeenth-Century News, spring, 1987.
Sewanee Review, October, 1987.
Times Literary Supplement, July 18, 1986.

*   *   *

UPDIKE, John (Hoyer)   1932-

PERSONAL: Born March 18, 1932, in Shillington, PA; son of Wesley Russell (a teacher) and Linda Grace (an author; maiden name, Hoyer) Updike; married Mary Entwistle Pennington, June 26, 1953 (divorced, 1977); married Martha Bernhard, September 30, 1977; children: (first marriage) Elizabeth Pennington, David Hoyer, Michael John, Miranda; (second marriage) three stepchildren. *Education:* Harvard University, A.B. (summa cum laude), 1954; attended Ruskin School of Drawing and Fine Art, Oxford, 1954-55. *Politics:* Democrat. *Religion:* Christian.

ADDRESSES: Home—Beverly Farms, MA.

CAREER: Novelist, critic, short story writer, poet, essayist, and dramatist. *New Yorker* magazine, reporter, 1955-57. Visited the U.S.S.R. as part of a cultural exchange program of the U.S. Department of State, 1964.

MEMBER: American Academy and Institute of Arts and Letters (secretary, chancellor), American Academy of Arts and Sciences.

AWARDS, HONORS: Guggenheim fellowship in poetry, 1959; American Academy and National Institute of Arts and Letters Richard and Hilda Rosenthal Foundation Award, 1960, for *The Poorhouse Fair;* National Book Award in fiction, 1963, and Prix Medicis Etranger, 1966, both for *The Centaur;* O. Henry Award for fiction, 1966, for short story, "The Bulgarian Poetess"; Fulbright fellow in Africa, 1972; American Book Award nomination, 1980, for *Too Far to Go: The Maples Stories;* Edward MacDowell

Medal for Literature, MacDowell Colony, 1981; Pulitzer Prize for fiction, 1981, American Book Award, 1982, and National Book Critics Circle award for fiction, 1982, all for *Rabbit Is Rich;* National Book Critics Circle award for criticism, 1984, for *Hugging the Shore: Essays and Criticism;* Medal of Honor for Literature, National Arts Club (New York City), 1984; National Book Critics Circle award in fiction nomination, 1986, for *Roger's Version;* PEN/Malamud Memorial Prize, PEN/Faulkner Award Foundation, 1988, for "excellence in short story writing"; National Medal of Arts, 1989; National Book Critics Award and Pulitzer Prize, both 1990, both for *Rabbit at Rest;* Premio Scanno, 1991; Howells medal, American Academy of Arts and Letters, 1995.

WRITINGS:

NOVELS

The Poorhouse Fair (also see below), Knopf (New York City), 1959.
Rabbit, Run (also see below), Knopf, 1960.
The Centaur, Knopf, 1963.
Of the Farm, Knopf, 1965.
The Poorhouse Fair [and] *Rabbit, Run,* Modern Library (New York City), 1965.
Couples, Knopf, 1968.
Rabbit Redux (also see below), Knopf, 1971.
A Month of Sundays, Knopf, 1975.
Marry Me: A Romance, Knopf, 1976.
The Coup, Knopf, 1978.
Rabbit Is Rich (also see below), Knopf, 1981.
Rabbit Is Rich/Rabbit Redux/Rabbit, Run (also see below), Quality Paperback Book Club, 1981.
The Witches of Eastwick, Knopf, 1984.
Roger's Version, Knopf, 1986.
S., Knopf, 1988.
Rabbit at Rest, Knopf, 1990.
Memories of the Ford Administration, Knopf, 1992.
Brazil, Knopf, 1994.
Rabbit Angstrom: The Four Novels (contains *Rabbit Is Rich, Rabbit Redux, Rabbit, Run,* and *Rabbit at Rest*), Knopf/Everymans (New York City), 1995.
In the Beauty of the Lilies, Knopf, 1996.

POETRY

The Carpentered Hen and Other Tame Creatures (also see below), Harper (New York City), 1958, published as *Hoping for a Hoopoe,* Gollancz (London), 1959.

Telephone Poles and Other Poems (also see below), Knopf, 1963.
Verse: The Carpentered Hen and Other Tame Creatures/Telephone Poles and Other Poems, Fawcett (New York City), 1965.
The Angels (poem; limited edition), King and Queen Press (Pensacola, FL), 1968.
Bath after Sailing (poem; limited edition), Pendulum Press (Monroe, CT), 1968.
Midpoint and Other Poems, Knopf, 1969.
Seventy Poems, Penguin (New York City), 1972.
Six Poems (limited edition), Oliphant Press, 1973.
Cunts (poem; limited edition), Frank Hallman, 1974.
Tossing and Turning, Knopf, 1977.
Sixteen Sonnets (limited edition), Halty Ferguson (Cambridge, MA), 1979.
Five Poems (limited edition), Bits Press (Cleveland, OH), 1980.
Spring Trio (limited edition), Palaemon Press (Winston-Salem, NC), 1982.
Jester's Dozen (limited edition), Lord John (Northridge, CA), 1984.
Facing Nature: Poems, Knopf, 1985.
Collected Poems: 1953-1993, Knopf, 1993.
A Helpful Alphabet of Friendly Objects (juvenile poetry; photographs by David Updike), Knopf, 1994.

SHORT STORIES

The Same Door, Knopf, 1959.
Pigeon Feathers and Other Stories, Knopf, 1962.
Olinger Stories: A Selection, Vintage (New York City), 1964.
The Music School, Knopf, 1966.
Bech: A Book, Knopf, 1970.
Museums and Women and Other Stories, Knopf, 1972.
Warm Wine: An Idyll (short story; limited edition) Albondocani Press (New York City), 1973.
Couples: A Short Story (limited edition), Halty Ferguson, 1976.
From the Journal of a Leper (short story; limited edition), Lord John, 1978.
Too Far to Go: The Maples Stories, Fawcett, 1979.
Three Illuminations in the Life of an American Author (short story; limited edition), Targ (New York City), 1979.
Problems and Other Stories, Knopf, 1979.
Your Lover Just Called: Stories of Joan and Richard Maple, Penguin Books (New York City), 1980.
The Chaste Planet (short story; limited edition), Metacom (Worcester, MA), 1980.

People One Knows: Interviews with Insufficiently Famous Americans (limited edition), Lord John, 1980.

Invasion of the Book Envelopes (short story; limited edition), Ewert (Concord, MA), 1981.

Bech Is Back, Knopf, 1982.

The Beloved (short story; limited edition), Lord John, 1982.

Confessions of a Wild Bore (short story; limited edition), Tamazunchale Press, 1984.

More Stately Mansions: A Story (short story; limited edition), Nouveau Press (Jackson, MS), 1987.

Trust Me: Short Stories, Knopf, 1987.

The Afterlife and Other Stories, Knopf, 1994.

ESSAYS

Assorted Prose, Knopf, 1965.

On Meeting Authors (essay; limited edition), Wickford (Newburyport, MA), 1968.

A Good Place (essay; limited edition), Aloe (Atlanta, GA), 1973.

Picked-Up Pieces, Knopf, 1975.

Hub Fans Bid Kid Adieu (essay; limited edition), Lord John, 1977.

Talk from the Fifties (limited edition), Lord John, 1979.

Ego and Art in Walt Whitman (essay; limited edition), Targ, 1980.

Hawthorne's Creed (essay; limited edition), Targ, 1981.

Hugging the Shore: Essays and Criticism, Knopf, 1983.

Emersonianism (essay; limited edition), Bits Press, 1984.

Just Looking: Essays on Art, Knopf, 1989.

Odd Jobs: Essays and Criticism, Knopf, 1991.

Concerts at Castle Hill (music criticism, 1961-65; limited edition), Lord John (Northridge, CA), 1993.

Golf Dreams: Writings on Golf, Knopf, 1996.

AUTHOR OF INTRODUCTION

Henry Green, *Loving, Living, Party Going,* Penguin Books, 1978.

Bruno Schulz, *Sanatorium under the Sign of the Hourglass,* Penguin Books, 1979.

The Art of Mickey Mouse, edited by Craig Yoe and Janet Morra-Yoe, Hyperion (New York City), 1991.

Heroes and Anti-Heroes, Random House (New York City), 1991.

Green, *Surviving,* Viking, 1993.

Edith Wharton, *The Age of Innocence,* Ballantine, 1996.

OTHER

(Contributor of short story) Martin Levin, editor, *Five Boyhoods,* Doubleday (New York City), 1962.

(Adapter with Warren Chappell) *The Magic Flute* (juvenile fiction; adapted from libretto of same title by Wolfgang Amadeus Mozart), Knopf, 1962.

(Adapter with Chappell) *The Ring* (juvenile fiction; adapted from libretto by Richard Wagner), Knopf, 1964.

A Child's Calendar (juvenile poetry), Knopf, 1965.

Three Texts from Early Ipswich (historical pageant; produced in Ipswich, MA, 1968), 17th Century Day Committee of the Town of Ipswich, 1968.

(Adapter) *Bottom's Dream* (juvenile fiction; adapted from William Shakespeare's play *A Midsummer Night's Dream*), Knopf, 1969.

(Editor) David Levine, *Pens and Needles: Literary Caricatures,* Gambit (Ipswich, MA), 1970.

(Contributor of translations) Jorge Luis Borges, *Selected Poems: 1923-1967,* edited by Norman Thomas di Giovanni, Delacorte (New York City), 1972.

A Good Place: Being a Personal Account of Ipswich, Massachusetts, Aloe Editions (New York City), 1973.

Buchanan Dying (play; produced in Lancaster, MA, 1976), Knopf, 1974.

(Author of afterword) Edmund Wilson, *Memoirs of Hecate County,* Nonpareil (Boston, MA), 1980.

(Editor with Shannon Ravenel and author of introduction) *The Best American Short Stories: 1984,* Houghton (Boston, MA), 1984.

Self-Consciousness: Memoirs, Knopf, 1989.

Also author with Gunther Schuller of words and music for *The Fisherman and His Wife,* performed at Savoy Theatre in Boston, MA, by the Opera Company of Boston, May, 1970. Contributor to books, including *The First Picture Book: Everyday Things for Babies,* Fotofolio and Whitney Museum of American Arts (New York City), 1991. "Talk of the Town" reporter, *New Yorker,* 1955-57. Contributor of short stories, book reviews, and poems to the *New Yorker.* Contributor of reviews and short stories to numerous periodicals.

Updike's papers are housed in the Houghton Library, Harvard University.

ADAPTATIONS: Couples was purchased by United Artists in 1969; *Rabbit, Run* was filmed by Warner Bros. in 1970; *Bech: A Book* was adapted for a play entitled, *Bech Takes Pot Luck,* produced in New York at Theatre Guild, 1970; *The Music School* was broadcast by Public Broadcasting System, 1976; *Two Far to Go* was made into a television movie by National Broadcasting Co. in March, 1979, later revised and released for theater distribution by Sea Cliff Productions, 1982; director George Miller's movie *The Witches of Eastwick,* 1987, was loosely based on Updike's novel of the same title; "The Christian Roommates," a short story, was made into a ninety-minute movie for television.

SIDELIGHTS: John Updike "has earned an . . . imposing stance on the literary landscape," writes *Los Angeles Times* contributor Katherine Stephen, "earning virtually every American literary award, repeated bestsellerdom and the near-royal status of the American author-celebrity." Hailed by critics and readers as one of America's great novelists, Updike is considered a premiere chronicler of middle America in all its mundane glory. "A reader would be hard pressed to name a contemporary author other than John Updike who is more in tune with the way most Americans live," writes Donald J. Greiner in a 1994 *Dictionary of Literary Biography* essay. "Man, wife, home, children, job—these . . . concerns have rested at the heart of his art since he published his first book . . . and they have continued to help him dissect, lovingly and clearly, the daily routine of middle America in small town and suburb."

Most critics familiar with Updike have strong opinions about the author's work. As Joseph Kanon explains in *Saturday Review:* "The debate . . . has long since divided itself into two pretty firmly entrenched camps: those who admire the work consider him one of the keepers of the language; those who don't say he writes beautifully about nothing very much." Updike acknowledges this charge but believes the complaint lacks validity. "There is a great deal to be said about almost anything," he explained to Jane Howard in a *Life* magazine interview. "Everything can be as interesting as every other thing. An old milk carton is worth a rose. . . . The idea of a hero is aristocratic. Now either nobody is a hero or everyone is. I vote for everyone. My subject is the American Protestant small town middle class. I like middles. It is in middles that extremes clash, where ambiguity restlessly rules."

Debate about the effectiveness of Updike's writing began in 1957 with publication of *The Poorhouse Fair,* his first novel. As Curt Suplee notes in his *Washington Post* profile of the author: "Updike's fiction is not overburdened by action, and his spare story lines are embellished with a lush and elegantly wrought style that some readers find majestic (John Barth calls him the Andrew Wyeth of American writers) and others intolerable. Norman Podhoretz described his prose in 'The Poorhouse Fair' as 'overly lyrical, bloated like a child who has eaten too much candy.'" Other critics differed: *New York Times* reviewer Donald Barr calls *The Poorhouse Fair* "a work of art," and the *Chicago Sunday Tribune*'s Fanny Butcher cites the work for "the author's brilliant use of words and . . . subtle observations."

"There is one point on which his critics all agree," observes Rachael C. Burchard in *John Updike: Yea Sayings.* "His style is superb. His work is worth reading if for no reason other than to enjoy the piquant phrase, the lyric vision, the fluent rhetoric." In a cover story on Updike, *Time* magazine's Paul Gray claims: "No one else using the English language over the past two and a half decades has written so well in so many ways as he." A reviewer for *Books Abroad* notes, "Critics continually comment on the technical virtuosity of Updike," while in *John Updike* Suzanne Henning Uphaus declares: "In the midst of diversity there are certain elements common to all of Updike's writing. Most important, there is Updike's remarkable mastery of language."

Other commentators fail to see Updike's work in such a favorable light. For example, in her *Partisan Review* commentary on *Couples* Elizabeth Dalton asserts: "In its delicacy and fullness Updike's style seems to register a flow of fragments almost perfectly toned. And yet, after pages and pages of his minutely detailed impressions, the accumulated effect is one of waste." John W. Aldridge writes in *Time to Murder and Create: The Contemporary Novel in Crisis* that the novelist "has none of the attributes we conventionally associate with major literary talent. He does not have an interesting mind. He does not possess remarkable narrative gifts or a distinguished style. He does not create dynamic or colorful or deeply meaningful characters. . . . In fact, one of the problems he poses for the critic is that he engages the imagination so little that one has real difficulty remembering his work long enough to think clearly about it." Updike "has difficulty in reining in his superfluous facility with words," Edward Hoagland complains in the *New York Times Book Review.* "He is too fluent."

Many of the most disparaging reviews of Updike's work have come from critics that object not only to his writing style, but also to the author's subject matter. Commenting on the frenzy of criticism from reviewers that met the 1968 publication of *Couples,* Updike's explicit look at sexual freedom in a small New England town, Robert Detweiler notes in *John Updike:* "As frequently happens, the furor accompanying the depiction of sexual amorality increased the difficulty of judging the novel's artistic quality. Most of the reviews appeared to be impulsive reactions to the subject matter rather than measured assessments." In the case of this novel, negative critical response did little to tone down public enthusiasm for the work; it was on the *Publishers Weekly* bestseller list for thirty-six weeks.

Couples wasn't the first Updike novel to deal with the sexual habits of middle-class America or to receive disapproving reviews from commentators upset by the author's frank language. "Looking back," writes Eliot Fremont-Smith in the *Village Voice,* "it must have been the sexuality that so upset the respectable critics of *Rabbit, Run* in 1960. Their consternation had to do with what seemed a great divide between John Updike's exquisite command of prose . . . and the apparent no-good vulgar nothing he expended it on." *Rabbit, Run* was the first installment in Updike's continuing saga of Harry "Rabbit" Angstrom which would later include *Rabbit Redux,* the highly celebrated *Rabbit Is Rich,* and *Rabbit at Rest.* Published at ten-year intervals, the novels follow the life of "Rabbit" as he tries to leave his marriage, discovers his wife has been unfaithful, finds himself laid off from his blue-collar job, and as he confronts middle-age, ill health, and death. Greiner notes that in the Rabbit tetralogy, Updike "takes a common American experience—the graduation from high school of a star athlete who has no life to lead once the applause diminishes and the headlines fade—and turns it into a subtle expose of the frailty of the American dream. . . . It is now clear that he has written a saga of middle-class America in the second half of the twentieth century."

Both celebrated and vilified for its sexual focus and its deeply ambivalent central character, the Rabbit tetralogy has garnered a number of significant awards. The third volume in the series, *Rabbit Is Rich,* received the Pulitzer Prize, the National Book Critics Circle award, and the American Book Award.

The final volume also earned a Pulitzer and a National Book Critics Award. Anthony Quinton in a London *Times* review argues that the "Rabbit novels are John Updike's best since they give the fullest scope to his remarkable gifts as observer and describer. What they amount to is a social and, so to speak, emotional history of the United States over the last twenty years or more, the period of Rabbit's and his creator's conscious life." Greiner writes: "Like James Fenimore Cooper's Leatherstocking, Hawthorne's Hester, and Mark Twain's Huck, Harry is one of the immortal characters who first absorb and then define a national culture. . . . Personal limitation mirrors national malaise." Greiner concludes: "It is sad to think of death setting its snare for Rabbit Angstrom because, after four decades and four long novels, he has joined the pantheon of American literary heroes. Yet a glimpse of final defeat is the price to be paid for membership in that exclusive club." All four of Updike's Rabbit novels are included in *Rabbit Angstrom: The Four Novels* published in 1995.

In *John Updike and the Three Great Secret Things* George Hunt suggests that sex, religion, and art "characterize the predominant subject matter, thematic concerns, and central questions found throughout [Updike's] adult fiction." According to Greiner in the *Contemporary Authors Bibliographical Series,* Updike criticism has shifted since the 1960s from a consideration of the novelist's style to a focus on his themes and how they interrelate. "Later commentators," Greiner asserts, "are concerned with his intellectually rigorous union of theology and fiction and with his suggestion that sex is a kind of emerging religion in the suburban enclaves of the middle class."

Exploring the interrelatedness of sex and religion in Updike's fiction, Jean Strouse observes in a *Newsweek* review: "Readers and critics have accused Updike of being obsessed with sex. Maybe—but I think he is using Harry Angstrom and Piet Hanema in 'Couples,' and Richard Maple in 'Too Far to Go,' to explore that modern search for 'something behind all this . . . that wants me to find it.' Melville—and many others—may have announced the demise of God, but nobody has managed to excise the desire for something beyond death and daily life, a desire that has in the 20th century shifted its focus from God to sex." The *New York Times*'s Michiko Kakutani offers a similar explanation of the development of what she calls Updike's "favorite preoccupations": "His heroes, over the years, have all suffered from 'the tension and guilt of being human.' Torn between vestigial spiritual yearnings and the new imperatives of self-fulfillment, they hunger for salvation even as they submit to the importunate demands of the flesh."

Updike's 1992 novel, *Memories of the Ford Administration,* centers around a history professor, Alf Clayton, and his contribution to an historical journal concerning the Ford administration. Alf ruminates upon his past and discovers, as Charles Johnson in the *New York Times Book Review* notes, he "can only remember two things—his knot of extramarital affairs and his never-completed opus on the life of President James Buchanan." As Richard Eder comments in the *Los Angeles Times Book Review,* "Alf's struggles with his formless life and time are intercut with his stabs at portraying Buchanan's hapless struggles with his." Nicholas von Hoffman in a *Tribune Books* review finds the layered plots of *Memories* something "only a writer of great technical accomplishment can bring off. . . . While one of the plots pulls us through the sex, the dissolving marital unions, the saturnalian nights of the Ford years, another works its sinuous way into the past and finds an American male unrecognizable to us moderns." Bruce Bawer in the *Washington Post Book World* compares *Memories of the Ford Administration* to Updike's *Rabbit at Rest,* arguing that there "is the same sad sense of life winding down, of the aging eagle stretching his wings; the same fixation on orgasms and grace." Bawer concludes that despite the juxtaposition of Alf and Buchanan offering at times "a touching sense of the isolation and helplessness of the human condition," at other times it "seems sheer contrivance." Hoffman, however, concludes that Updike "has the ability to evoke the micro-epochs that fascinate us." Despite differing appraisals, most critics agree that, as Johnson comments, *Memories* is "quintessential Updike, an exploration of a modern American terrain of desire, guilt and moral ambiguity that he has made distinctly his own."

Breaking with this familiar terrain in 1994, the prolific Updike published his 16th novel, *Brazil*. As Tom Shone discusses in the *Times Literary Supplement, Brazil*'s genre, magic realism, makes for "the most bizarrely uncharacteristic novel Updike has yet written." *Brazil* is the story of two lovers, the poor, black Tristao, and the well-to-do white Isabel living in Rio de Janeiro. The plot, as Caroline Moore summarizes in *Spectator,* is uninhibited: "Isabel invited Tristao to deflower her at their first encounter; they steal from her uncle and flee on the proceeds to a

hotel. . . . They are pursued, recaptured, re-elope, and undergo severe yet picaresque sufferings in the wilds of western Brazil, including starvation and slavery." Both Isabel and Tristao "survive a transformation of identity," as Alexander Theroux comments in *Tribune Books,* "for at one crucial point in the novel there takes place an astonishing role reversal in which she turns black, he white—a piece of fantasy born as much of the ongoing requirements of Updike's parable as of the young lovers' passion."

Brazil received mixed reviews from many critics. Michael Dirda in a *Washington Post Book World* review finds aspects of *Brazil* "that irritate, like the nips of tropical insects," but argues that these are "compensated for by the novel's zesty readability." Michiko Kakutani argues in the *New York Times* that though "there are occasional passages [in *Brazil*] that sparkle with Mr. Updike's patented gift for the lyrical metaphor, his descriptions of Tristao and Isabel's adventures often feel forced and contrived." Rhoda Koenig gives *Brazil* a similarly mixed review in *New York:* ". . . the main characters themselves are not credible, with their mythic passions, expressed in diction more formal and flowery than would ever issue from a boy of the slums and a girl from the world of pampered inanity." Koenig concludes, however, that Updike's *Brazil* "is a novel of endless and astonishing fertility," and is "the most absorbing and unsettling novel, apart from the Rabbit books, that [Updike] has written in some time." Barbara Kingsolver in a review of *Brazil* in the *New York Times Book Review* finds that Updike's "prose is measured, layered, insightful, smooth, as addictive a verbal drug as exists on the modern market. For every tiresome appearance of Tristao's yam, there is also an image or observation that seems, against all odds, to mark the arrival of something new in the English language."

Updike returned to more familiar thematic territory in 1996's *In the Beauty of the Lilies,* a four-generation saga of the spiritual emptiness of modern American life. The novel begins, as Julian Barnes of the *New York Times Book Review* notes, with "a sly misdirection. D. W. Griffith is filming 'A Call to Arms' . . . in the spring of 1910. Mary Pickford, short of sleep and over-costumed for a hot day, faints." Updike then introduces the Reverend Clarence Arthur Wilmot, and never returns to Griffith and Pickford. The novel follows Clarence's loss of faith, his switch from clergyman to encyclopedia salesman, his death, and then follows his family three further generations. When film is mentioned again in the text, Barnes argues, the connection is made by the reader: ". . . religion and the movies: two great illusionary forces, two worlds in which the primal image is of darkness conquered by light." Sybil S. Steinberg in a *Publishers Weekly* interview with Updike paraphrases: "the four generations that *Lilies* depicts . . . are meant to allude to the biblical line from Abraham to Isaac to Joseph and his brothers." Updike told Steinberg that his Sunday school education left him "haunted by that particular [biblical] saga, and the notion that we are members of our ancestors. I wanted to give an American version of that sense." Barnes concludes that *Lilies* is "a novel of accumulated wisdom, with . . . Updike in full control of his subtle, crafty and incessantly observing art." Steinberg also notes Updike's control, finding that his "gift for exact, metaphorical observation binds matters of the soul to the ephemera of daily life."

Like his novels, Updike's short stories, poetry and nonfiction also illustrate his command of language and his deep affection for everyday life in all its banality. "Read as a whole, [Updike's] short-story volumes offer a social commentary on American domesticity since midcentury, and, while the prose is always lyrical and the observations always sharp, a tone of sadness—wistfulness—prevails," writes Greiner in the *Dictionary of Literary Biography*. Reviewing *The Afterlife and Other Stories*, Updike's 1994 short-story collection, Peter Kemp in the Sunday London *Times* finds nearly the entire volume of stories "masterpieces of stead delineation, in which psychological and emotional nuance are traced with as much lucid finesse as the wealth of visual detail." Noting that poetry is not Updike's "primary medium," Mark Ford in the *Times Literary Supplement* nonetheless finds that Updike's verse "evokes with the clarity and precision of his fiction the contours of particular moments and places." Griener finds that the "happy union of lyrical prose and intellectual probing that is the highlight of [Updike's] fiction shows itself everywhere in his nonfiction."

Updike's skill in portraying the anxieties and frustrations of middle-America is considered the outstanding feature of his works. "He is our unchallenged master at evoking the heroic void of ordinary life," Suplee maintains, "where small braveries contend in vain against the nagging entropy of things, where the fear of death drips from a faulty faucet and supermarket daydreams turn to God. With heart-clutching clarity, he transmutes the stubborn banality of middle-class existence into tableaux that shiver with

the hint of spiritual meaning." According to Kakutani, Updike's work "has not only lyrically defined the joys and sorrows of the American middle class, but also gives—as he once wrote of another author—'the happy impression of an oeuvre, of a continuous task carried forward variously, of a solid personality, of a plenitude of gifts explored, knowingly.'" A *Publishers Weekly* reviewer maintains that "one looks forward to the changing perspective (though not changing themes) that each decade brings to this masterful writer's work."

BIOGRAPHICAL/CRITICAL SOURCES:

BOOKS

Aldridge, John W., *Time to Murder and Create: The Contemporary Novel in Crisis,* McKay (New York City), 1966.

Burchard, Rachael C., *John Updike: Yea Sayings,* Southern Illinois University Press (Carbondale, IL), 1971.

Concise Dictionary of American Literary Biography: Broadening Views, 1968-1988, Gale (Detroit, MI), 1989.

Contemporary Authors Bibliographical Series, Volume 1, Gale, 1986.

Contemporary Literary Criticism, Gale, Volume 1, 1973; Volume 2, 1974; Volume 3, 1975; Volume 5, 1976; Volume 7, 1977; Volume 9, 1978; Volume 13, 1980; Volume 15, 1980; Volume 23, 1983; Volume 34, 1985; Volume 43, 1987; Volume 70, 1991.

De Bellis, Jack, *John Updike: A Bibliography, 1967-1993* (foreword by Updike), Greenwood Press (Westport, CT), 1994.

Detweiler, Robert, *John Updike,* Twayne (Boston, MA), 1972, revised edition, 1984.

Dictionary of Literary Biography Documentary Series, Volume 3, Gale, 1983.

Dictionary of Literary Biography Yearbook, Gale, *1980,* 1981, *1982,* 1983.

Dictionary of Literary Biography, Gale, Volume 2: *American Novelists since World War II,* 1978, Volume 5: *American Poets since World War II,* 1980; Volume 143: *American Novelists since World War II, Third Series,* 1994.

Greiner, Donald J., *Adultery in the American Novel: Updike, James, Hawthorne,* University of South Carolina Press (Columbia, SC), 1985.

Greiner, *John Updike's Novels,* Ohio University Press (Athens, OH), 1984.

Hunt, George, *John Updike and the Three Great Secret Things,* Eerdmans (Grand Rapids, MI), 1980.

Luscher, Robert M., *John Updike: A Study of the Short Fiction,* Twayne, 1993.

Neary, John, *Something and Nothingness: The Fiction of John Updike & John Fowles,* Southern Illinois University Press, 1992.

Newman, Judie, *John Updike,* St. Martin's (New York City), 1988.

Plath, James, editor, *Conversations with John Updike,* University Press of Mississippi (Jackson), 1994.

Schiff, James A., *Updike's Version: Rewriting the Scarlet Letter,* University of Missouri Press (Columbia), 1992.

Short Story Criticism, Volume 13, Gale, 1993.

Singh, Sukhbir, *The Survivor in Contemporary American Fiction: Saul Bellow, Bernard Malamud, John Updike, Kurt Vonnegut, Jr.,* B. R. Publishing (Delhi), 1991.

Tallent, Elizabeth, *Married Men and Magic Tricks: John Updike's Erotic Heroes,* Creative Arts (Berkeley, CA), 1981.

Thorburn, David, and Howard Eiland, editors, *John Updike: A Collection of Critical Essays,* G. K. Hall (Boston, MA), 1982.

Trachtenberg, Stanley, editor, *New Essays on Rabbit, Run,* Cambridge University Press (Cambridge, England), 1993.

Updike, John, *Self-Consciousness: Memoirs,* Knopf, 1989.

Uphaus, Suzanne Henning, *John Updike,* Ungar (New York City), 1980.

PERIODICALS

Books Abroad, winter, 1967.

Chicago Sunday Tribune, January 11, 1959.

Christian Science Monitor, February 14, 1994.

Kenyon Review, spring, 1992.

Kirkus Reviews, September 1, 1994, p. 1162.

Life, November 4, 1966.

London Review of Books, March 11, 1993, p. 9.

Los Angeles Times, January 4, 1987.

Los Angeles Times Book Review, November 1, 1992, p. 3.

Modern Fiction Studies, spring, 1974; autumn, 1975.

Newsweek, November 15, 1971, September 28, 1981, October 18, 1982.

New York, January 31, 1994, p. 62.

New York Review of Books, April 11, 1968; August 8, 1974; April 3, 1975; November 19, 1981; November 18, 1982; November 24, 1983; June 14, 1984; December 4, 1986; February 29, 1996, p. 4.

New York Times, January 11, 1959; October 7, 1982; August 27, 1986; January 25, 1994, p. C19.

New York Times Book Review, March 18, 1962; April 7, 1963; April 7, 1968; June 21, 1970; November 14, 1971; September 27, 1981; October 17, 1982; September 18, 1983; May 13, 1984; August 31, 1986; April 26, 1987; November 1, 1992, p. 11; February 6, 1994, p. 1; January 28, 1996, p. 9.

New York Times Sunday Magazine, December 10, 1978.

Partisan Review, winter, 1969.

Publishers Weekly, September 5, 1994, p. 88; January 8, 1996; p. 47.

Saturday Review, March 17, 1962; September 30, 1972.

Spectator, April 9, 1994, p. 25.

Time, April 26, 1968; October 18, 1982; August 25, 1986.

Times (London), January 14, 1982; February 5, 1995.

Times Literary Supplement, January 15, 1982; January 20, 1984; September 28, 1984; October 24, 1986; February 25, 1994, p. 21; April 1, 1994, p. 21.

Tribune Books (Chicago), September 30, 1990, p. 1, 4; November 1, 1992, p. 1, 9; January 30, 1994, p. 1, 9.

Twentieth Century Literature, April, 1966; July, 1967; October, 1971; winter, 1978.

Village Voice, September 30, 1981.

Washington Post, September 27, 1981; April 26, 1982.

Washington Post Book World, November 1, 1992, p. 1, 9; February 13, 1994, p. 1, 14; February 4, 1996, p. 1, 10.

World Literature Today, winter, 1994, p. 128.

OTHER

DISCovering Authors (CD-ROM product), Gale, 1993.

DISCovering Authors Modules (CD-ROM product), Gale, 1996.

*   *   *

URQUHART, Brian (Edward) 1919-

PERSONAL: Born February 28, 1919, in Bridport, England; son of Murray and Bertha (Rendall) Urquhart; married Alfreda Huntington, March 31,

1944 (marriage ended, 1963); married Sidney Damrosch Howard, April 29, 1963; children: (first marriage) Thomas, Katharine, Robert; (second marriage) Rachel, Charles. *Education:* Attended Christ Church, Oxford, 1937-39.

ADDRESSES: Home—50 West 29th St., New York, NY 10001. *Office*—Ford Foundation, New York, NY 10017.

CAREER: United Nations, New York City, personal assistant to executive secretary of Preparatory Commission in London, England, 1945-46, personal assistant to secretary-general, 1945-49, secretary of collective measures committee, 1951-53, member of Office of Undersecretary for special political affairs, 1954-71, assistant secretary-general, 1972-74, undersecretary-general for special political affairs, 1974-86, executive secretary of conferences on peaceful use of atomic energy, 1955 and 1958, worked with emergency force in the Middle East, 1956, deputy executive secretary of Preparatory Commission of International Atomic Energy Agency, 1957, assistant to special representative in the Congo, 1960, representative in Katanga, Congo, 1961-62. Ford Foundation, New York City, scholar in residence, 1986—. *Military service:* British Army, Dorset Regiment and Airborne Forces, 1939-45; served in North Africa, Sicily, and Europe; became major.

MEMBER: Century Association.

AWARDS, HONORS: Member of Order of the British Empire, 1945; Knight Commander of St. Michael and St. George, 1986.

WRITINGS:

Hammarskjold (biography), Knopf (New York City), 1972.
A Life in Peace and War (memoir), Harper (New York City), 1987.
(Editor) W. E. Childers, *A World in Need of Leadership: Tomorrow's United Nations,* Dag Hammarskjold Foundation (New York City), 1990.
Towards a More Effective United Nations, Dag Hammarskjold Foundation, 1992.
Ralph Bunche: An American Life, Norton (New York City), 1993.
Renewing the United Nations System, Dag Hammarskjold Foundation, 1994.

Contributor of articles and reviews to magazines.

SIDELIGHTS: As a memoir, *A Life in Peace and War* focuses primarily on Brian Urquhart's four decades with the United Nations. *Times Literary Supplement* reviewer Richard Falk claims that "Urquhart's book is particularly welcome because it so convincingly develops the positive case for the UN's role in world affairs. . . . What emerges from this highly readable and persuasive account is Urquhart's deep respect for the government and military establishments entrusted with [peacekeeping] missions, often carried out at great risk and under pressure of harsh criticism or unrealistic expectation." Many critics express interest in Urquhart's portrayals of the United Nations's first five leaders. Charles William Maynes remarks in the *New York Times Book Review* that "the portraits are skillfully drawn and honest enough to reveal the strengths of Mr. Urquhart's villains and the weaknesses of his heroes."

Some reviewers detect a degree of caution and reticence on Urquhart's part. According to *Washington Post Book World* contributor Bernard D. Nossiter, "Urquhart has been a professional diplomat too long and is teasingly reticent on some subjects." Additionally, *Los Angeles Times* critic Jonathan Kirsch finds that Urquhart is "oblique in his reminiscences about the great men and women with whom he has contended, and he is guarded about his private life. . . . Even when he confesses his own passions and prejudices, Urquhart is meticulously indirect. . . . Still, Urquhart's perspective on history is compelling, if also sometimes aggravating, and the book is full of fascinating anecdotes and asides." In a more positive light, Clyde Sanger concludes in the Toronto *Globe and Mail* that *A Life in Peace and War* "is a book of fine style and well-argued opinions. . . . It is full of lively descriptions and sharply drawn portraits." Urquhart, he notes, "has a historian's understanding of complex situations, a politician's eye for the essentials and a reporter's gift for storing up the memorable phrase."

BIOGRAPHICAL/CRITICAL SOURCES:

PERIODICALS

Globe and Mail (Toronto), February 27, 1988.
Los Angeles Times, November 6, 1987; December 31, 1987.
New Republic, March 3, 1973.
New York Times Book Review, September 27, 1987.

Time, November 16, 1987.

Times Literary Supplement, April 20, 1973; March 11-17, 1988.

Washington Post Book World, February 4, 1973; September 27, 1987.

*   *   *

USHERWOOD, Elizabeth (Ada) 1923-

PERSONAL: Born July 10, 1923, in London, England; daughter of Walter Edward (a carpenter) and Annie (a homemaker; maiden name, Noonan) Beavington; married Stephen Usherwood (a writer), October 24, 1970. *Religion:* Roman Catholic. *Avocational interests:* Travel, theater.

ADDRESSES: Home—24 St. Mary's Grove, Canonbury, London N1 2NT, England.

CAREER: Central Banker, London, England, bank official, 1941-72; writer, 1972—. Red Cross nurse.

WRITINGS:

(With husband, Stephen Usherwood) *Visit Some London Catholic Churches,* Mayhew McCrimmon, 1982.

(With S. Usherwood) *The Counter-Armada, 1596: The Journal of the "Mary Rose,"* Naval Institute Press, 1983.

(With S. Usherwood) *We Die for the Old Religion,* Sheed & Ward, 1987.

Women First, Sheed & Ward, 1989.

(With S. Usherwood) *A Saint in the Family,* St. Paul's, 1992.

WORK IN PROGRESS: A biography of the first Lord Mansfield, 1705-1793.

SIDELIGHTS: Elizabeth Usherwood told *CA:* "My goal is to reassess history in the light of evidence that my husband and I have collected. *The Counter-Armada, 1596: The Journal of the 'Mary Rose'* describes a ten-week combined naval and military operation by English and Dutch forces against Spain and Portugal, a naval action in the harbor of Cadiz, and the capture of the town, which was held for a fortnight. The *Mary Rose* was one of the largest warships that Queen Elizabeth I sent on the expedition, and the journal kept by her commander, day by day from the beginning to the end of the expedition,

is unique. My husband and I are the first to have studied, transcribed, and published it. Work on the book entailed extensive travel in Spain and the Netherlands.

"Continued work with my husband led to the publication of *A Saint in the Family,* which reassesses the lives of saints through the documentary evidence left by their families and friends, while a solo work, *Women First,* gave me the opportunity to highlight the attributes that enabled women, from the first to the twentieth century, to undertake—without sacrificing their femininity—careers considered in their day the prerogative of men.

"Now I am collecting material for a book on the women whose heroic self-sacrifice contributed so greatly in the nineteenth century to the Christian revival in Britain, known in John Henry Newman's phrase as 'The Second Spring.'"

*   *   *

USTINOV, Peter (Alexander) 1921-

PERSONAL: Born April 16, 1921, in London, England; son of Iona (a journalist; professional name, Klop) and Nadia (a painter and scenic designer; maiden name, Benois) Ustinov; married Isolde Delham, 1940 (divorced, 1950); married Suzanne Cloutier (an actress), 1953 (marriage ended, 1971); married Helen du Lau d'Allemans, June 17, 1972; children: (first marriage) Tamara; (second marriage) Pavla, Igor, Andrea. *Education:* Attended Westminster School, London, England, 1934-37, and London Theatre Studio, 1937-39. *Avocational interests:* Reading voluminously, cars, music, collecting old masters' drawings, lawn tennis, and squash.

ADDRESSES: Office—11 rue de Silly, 92100 Boulogne, France. *Agent*—Margaret Gardner, 17 Onslow Sq., London SW7 3NJ England.

CAREER: Actor and director in theater, films, and television; playwright, film writer, and author. Joint Director, Nottingham Playhouse, 1963—. First rector, University of Dundee, 1968-74. Goodwill ambassador for UNICEF, 1969—. Director of stage productions, including *The Man in the Raincoat, No Sign of the Dove, Photo Finish* (in Paris), and *King Lear* (in Ontario, Canada); director of films, including *The Spies, An Angel Flew over Brooklyn, Schools for Secrets, Vice Versa, Private Angelo, Billy Budd, Lady L, Hammersmith Is Out,* and *Memed My Hawk.*

Actor in stage productions, including *The Wood Demon, The Bishop of Limpopoland, White Cargo, Rookery Nook, Laburnam Grove, First Night, Swinging the Gate, Threshold, Hermoine Gingold Revue, Diversion 1, Diversion 2, Squaring the Circle, Crime and Punishment, Frenzy, Love in Albania, The Love of Four Colonels, Romanoff and Juliet, Photo Finish, The Unknown Soldier and His Wife, The Marriage, Beethoven's Tenth,* and the autobiographical *An Evening with Peter Ustinov.*

Actor in films, including *Mein Kampf, My Crimes, Let the People Sing, One of Our Aircraft Is Missing, The Way Ahead, Private Angelo, Odette, The Goose Steps Out, The True Glory, School for Secrets, Vice Versa, Quo Vadis, Beau Brummel, The Egyptian, Hotel Sahara, We're No Angels, Lola Montez, The Sundowners, Spartacus, Billy Budd, Topkapi, John Goldfarb, Lady L, The Comedians, Blackbeard's Ghost, Hot Millions, Viva Max, Hammersmith Is Out, One of Our Dinosaurs Is Missing, Treasure of Matecumba, Un Taxi Mauve, Logan's Run, The Last Remake of Beau Geste, Death on the Nile, Ashanti, The Thief of Baghdad, Charlie Chan and the Curse of the Dragon Queen, Evil under the Sun, Memed My Hawk, Appointment with Death, The French Revolution,* and *Lorenzo's Oil.*

Writer and actor of television productions, including *The Life of Samuel Johnson,* 1957, *Conversation with Lord North,* 1971, *The Old Curiosity Shop,* 1995, *The Mighty Continent, Jesus of Nazareth,* and *Einstein's Universe.* Host of British Broadcasting Corporation (BBC) series *Peter Ustinov's Russia: A Personal History,* 1986, and of Public Broadcasting Service (PBS) series *The Mozart Mystique with Peter Ustinov,* 1990, and *Inside the Vatican,* 1994. Director of operas with the Royal Opera at Covent Garden, 1962, the Hamburg Opera, 1968, 1985, and 1987, the Edinburgh Festival, 1973, the Paris Opera, 1973, the Berlin Opera, 1978, the Piccola Scala Milan, 1981 and 1982, the Mozarteum, 1987, and the Dresden Opera, 1993. *Military service:* British Army, Royal Sussex Regiment, 1942-46; also served with Royal Army Ordnance Corps and Kinematograph Service.

MEMBER: Royal Society of Arts (fellow), Royal Society of Literature, British Actors' Equity, British League of Dramatists, London Society of Authors, British Film Academy, British Screen Writers' Society, Societe des Auteurs (France), New York Dramatists Guild, Hollywood Screen Actors' Guild, Garrick Club, Savage Club, Royal Automobile Club, Queen's Club.

AWARDS, HONORS: Golden Globe Award for best actor in a supporting role, Hollywood Foreign Press Association, 1952, for *Quo Vadis;* New York Drama Critics Circle Award, 1953, for *The Love of Four Colonels; Evening Standard* Drama Award for best new play, 1956, for *Romanoff and Juliet;* Benjamin Franklin Medal, Royal Society of Arts, 1957; Academy Awards for best supporting actor, Academy of Motion Picture Arts and Sciences, 1960, for *Spartacus,* and 1964, for *Topkapi;* Emmy Award, Academy of Television Arts and Sciences, for best actor in a comedy or drama special, 1958, for *The Life of Samuel Johnson,* 1966, for *Barefoot in Athens,* and 1970, for *Storm in Summer;* Grammy Award for best children's recording, National Academy of Recording Arts and Sciences, 1959, for *Peter and the Wolf;* First prize of Syndicat des journalistes et ecrivains (France), 1964, for *Photo Finish;* Academy Award nomination for best story and screenplay, and British comedy screenplay award from Writers Guild, both 1969, for *Hot Millions;* Doctor of Law, University of Dundee, 1969; Mus.D., Cleveland Conservatory of Music, 1970; D.F.A., La Salle College, 1971; D.Litt., University of Lancaster, 1972; Order of the Smile (for dedication to the idea of international assistance to children), Warsaw, 1974; Commander of British Empire, 1975; Jordanian Independence Medal and UNICEF Award for Distinguished Services, both 1978; Prix de la Butte and Variety Club of Great Britain Award for Best Actor, both 1979; honorary doctorate, University of Toronto, 1984; Commandeur des Arts et des Lettres (France), 1985; elected to Academy of Fine Arts, Institut de France, Paris, 1988; Banff Television Festival Award of Excellence (Canada), 1988; D.H.L., Georgetown University, 1988; Gold Medal of the City of Athens, 1990; Medal of the Greek Red Cross, 1990; D.H.L, University of Ottawa, 1991; Medal of Honour, Charles University (Prague), 1991; D.H.L., University of Durham, 1992; Chancellor, University of Durham, 1992; President, World Federalist Movement, 1992; Britannia Award, British Academy of Film and Television Arts, 1992; Critics' Circle Award, 1993; Ordern Nacional do Cruzerio do Sul (Brazil), 1994; German Cultural Award, 1994; German Bambi, 1994; International Child Survival Award, UNICEF, 1995; honorary doctorate, Pontifical Institute of Medieval Studies, St. Michael's College, University of Toronto, 1995;

Ruldolph Valentino Award for Lifetime Achievement in Motion Pictures, 1995; Doctorate Honoris Causa, Free Flemish University of Brussels, 1995; Norman Cousins Global Governance Award, World Federalist Movement, 1995; also awarded Order of Istiglal of the Hashemite Kingdom of Jordan and the Order of the Yugoslav Flag.

WRITINGS:

Add a Dash of Pity (short stories), Little, Brown (Boston), 1959.

Ustinov's Diplomats (photographs and commentary), Bernard Geis Associates, 1960.

The Loser (novel), Little, Brown, 1960.

We Were Only Human (caricatures), Little, Brown, 1961.

(Illustrator) Paul Marc Henry, *Poodlestan: A Poodle's Eye View of History,* Reynal, 1965.

The Frontiers of the Sea (short stories), Little, Brown, 1966, published as *God and the State Railways,* O'Mara (London), 1993.

The Wit of Peter Ustinov, compiled by Dick Richards, Frewin, 1969.

Krumnagel (novel), Little, Brown, 1971.

Dear Me (autobiography), Little, Brown, 1977.

(Author of introduction) Gordon Forbes, *A Handful of Summers,* Paddington, 1979.

My Russia, Macmillan (London), 1983.

(Author of introduction) Tom Hutchinson, *Niven's Hollywood,* Salem House, 1984.

Peter Ustinov in Russia, Summit Books (New York City), 1988.

The Disinformer: Two Novellas, Arcade (New York City), 1989.

The Old Man and Mr. Smith (novel), O'Mara, 1990, Arcade, 1991.

Ustinov at Large (collected articles), O'Mara, 1991.

Ustinov Still at Large (collected articles), O'Mara, 1993, Prometheus (Buffalo, NY), 1994.

The Quotable Ustinov (compilation), Prometheus, 1995.

PUBLISHED PLAYS

House of Regrets (three-act tragi-comedy; first produced in London at Arts Theatre, 1942), J. Cape (London), 1943.

Beyond (one act; first produced at Arts Theatre, 1943; also see below), English Theatre Guild (London), 1944.

The Banbury Nose (four acts; first produced in London at Wyndham's Theatre, 1944), J. Cape, 1945.

Plays about People (includes *Blow Your Own Trumpet,* first produced in London at Old Vic Theatre, 1943; *The Tragedy of Good Intentions,* first produced in Liverpool at Old Vic Theatre, 1945; *The Indifferent Shepherd,* first produced in London at Criterion Theatre, 1948), J. Cape, 1950.

The Love of Four Colonels (three acts; first produced at Wyndham's Theatre, 1951; also see below), English Theatre Guild, 1951, Dramatists Play Service (New York City), 1953.

The Moment of Truth (four acts; first produced in London at Adelphi Theatre, 1951; also see below), English Theatre Guild, 1953.

Romanoff and Juliet (three-act comedy; first produced in London at Piccadilly Theatre, 1956; produced in New York at Plymouth Theatre, 1957; also see below), English Theatre Guild, 1957, Random House (New York City), 1958, musical version, with libretto by Ustinov, produced as *R Loves J,* at Chichester Festival Theatre, 1973.

Photo Finish: An Adventure in Biography in Three Acts (first produced in London at Saville Theatre, 1962), Heinemann (London), 1962, Little, Brown, 1963, revised acting edition, Dramatists Play Service, 1964.

Five Plays (includes *Romanoff and Juliet, The Moment of Truth, Beyond, The Love of Four Colonels,* and *No Sign of the Dove,* produced in London at Savoy Theatre, 1953), Little, Brown, 1965.

The Unknown Soldier and His Wife (two acts; first produced in New York at Vivian Beaumont Theatre, July 6, 1967), Random House, 1967, published in England as *The Unknown Soldier and His Wife: Two Acts of War Separated by a Trace,* Heinemann, 1968.

Halfway up the Tree (three-act comedy; first produced in New York at Brooks Atkinson Theatre, November 7, 1967), Random House, 1968.

UNPUBLISHED PLAYS

The Bishop of Limpopoland (sketch), produced in London, 1939.

(Translator and adapter from the French) Jean Sarment, *Fishing for Shadows,* produced in London, 1940.

Frenzy (adapted from the Swedish of Ingmar Bergman), produced in London at St. Martin's Theatre, 1948.

The Man in the Raincoat, produced at Edinburgh Festival, 1949.

High Balcony, produced in 1952.

The Empty Chair, produced in Bristol at Old Vic Theatre, 1956.

Paris Not So Gay, produced in Oxford, England, 1958.

The Life in My Hands, produced at Nottingham Playhouse, 1963.

Who's Who in Hell, first produced in New York at Lunt-Fontanne Theatre, December 9, 1974.

Overheard, first produced in London at Haymarket Theatre, May 17, 1981.

The Marriage, produced at Edinburgh Festival, 1982.

Beethoven's Tenth (two-act comedy), first produced in New York at Nederlander Theatre, April 22, 1984.

SCREENPLAYS

(With Eric Ambler) *The Way Ahead,* Twentieth Century-Fox, 1946, also released as *Immortal Battalion.*

School for Secrets, Two Cities, 1946, released as *Secret Flight,* 1951.

Vice Versa, Rank/Two Cities, 1947.

Private Angelo, Pilgrim/ABF-Pathe, 1949.

(With Patricia Chester Moyes) *School for Scoundrels,* Guardsman, 1960.

Romanoff and Juliet, Universal, 1961.

(With Robert Rossen) *Billy Budd,* Allied Artists, 1962.

Lady L, Champion-Concordia/Metro-Goldwyn-Mayer (MGM), 1965.

(With Ira Wallach) *Hot Millions,* Milberg/MGM, 1968.

Hammersmith Is Out, Cinerama, 1972.

Memed My Hawk, Peter Ustinov-Jadran/Focus, 1984.

OTHER

Author of material for revues produced in London, *Diversion 1,* 1940, and *Diversion 2,* 1941. Author of material for BBC radio program, *In All Directions.* Contributor to *Atlantic, Listener,* and other publications.

SIDELIGHTS: Peter Ustinov, once described in the *New Statesman and Nation* as "a tubby character with the affable, slouchy, sulky exterior of a Giant Panda," has enjoyed a remarkable career in show business. Best known as the rotund character actor whose portrayals have earned two Academy Awards, three Emmy Awards, and even a Grammy Award for narration, Ustinov is also esteemed as a playwright, director, and producer. *New York Times* correspon-

dent Leslie Bennets calls Ustinov a "one-man creative industry" who has "won enough honors to furnish a house." John Lahr offers a similar assessment of Ustinov in the *New York Times Book Review,* noting that as "playwright, novelist, short story writer, actor, film director, raconteur, Ustinov has turned his urbane intelligence to all facets of public entertainment and made a good show of it." Indeed, Ustinov's writing and acting careers are often inseparable; for many years he has accomplished the rare feat of performing in plays and films of his own authorship, usually to critical acclaim. A long list of such dual credits includes the movies *Billy Budd,* and *Hot Millions,* and the plays *Romanoff and Juliet, The Unknown Soldier and His Wife,* and *Beethoven's Tenth,* to name only a few. In a *Maclean's* profile, Lawrence O'Toole accords Ustinov a lofty status befitting his vast achievements: "By pluralizing the very concept of career in the way he has, Ustinov qualifies for admission to that august company which avails itself of the royal 'we.'"

Ustinov was born and raised in Great Britain, but his heritage is French and Russian through his widely travelled, artistic parents. "His father," writes a *Forbes* magazine contributor, "was a well-known journalist in London with a gift for storytelling. Smiling, Ustinov recalls Rebecca West's observation 'that I was very good—but not up to my father.'" According to *Dictionary of Literary Biography* contributor Audrey Williamson, this fusion of cultural influences "explains the volatility and range of [Ustinov's] dramatic writings: his multitudinous relatives were concerned both with the arts and diplomacy, and a liberal-minded and at times highly satiric view of politics and international attitudes is evident in his best plays."

This satiric bent was also an element of Ustinov's personality as a youth. His family—if not his schoolteachers—encouraged his attempts to mimic everyone from neighbors to Winston Churchill. "He entered the theater at age 16 after leaving school, which he hated," explains Douglas J. Rowe in the *Chicago Tribune.* "'I hated it,'" Ustinov told Rowe. "'But I knew I hated it at the time. Which helps enormously. I knew I would think about it later. It was the kind of school . . . which trains you to represent one aspect of the truth at the expense of the others.'" Eventually he found work as a professional impersonator in clubs and travelling revues.

From an early age, Ustinov also wrote; he was serving in the Royal Sussex Regiment when his first play, *House of Regrets,* was produced in London in 1942. A study of aging White Russians in exile, the work was well-received by both critics and audiences. Two years later Ustinov scored an even bigger success with *The Banbury Nose,* an examination of generational conflict that Williamson contends is his "most original and effective exercise in dramatic craftsmanship." Thereafter, the ambitious and indefatigable Ustinov acted, wrote, and directed scores of dramas and comedies in England and the United States. His authored works such as *The Love of Four Colonels, Romanoff and Juliet, Photo Finish: An Adventure in Biography in Three Acts,* and *Beethoven's Tenth* found audiences on both sides of the Atlantic.

Ustinov's plays generally explore some political or cultural characteristic in juxtaposition to its polar opposite. In *Romanoff and Juliet,* for instance, a Russian boy and an American girl fall in love while their parents are serving as diplomats in a small neutral nation. *The Unknown Soldier and His Wife* explores soldiering in successive historical periods, and *Beethoven's Tenth* pits the famous composer, returned from the dead, against a stuffy modern music critic. In her essay on his works, Williamson notes that Ustinov, "with a heredity ensuring the overstepping of nationalistic barriers, has always refused to play the power game in politics or to concede either right-wing or left-wing assumptions in his works. Like W. S. Gilbert in another age, his mockery is of all sides and without allegiance, if one excepts allegiance to humanity as a whole." Williamson concludes: "In a world at best maintaining a precarious peace, Ustinov, the traditional serious clown, is a valuable reminder of civilization's most conspicuous and recurring follies. . . . His dramatic career . . . appears remarkable when one assesses it as only one part of a theatrical life which continues to encompass acting and directing for both film and television as well as the stage."

In addition to his numerous plays and screenplays, Ustinov has written short stories, novels, nonfiction collections, and several volumes of memoirs. Critics do not always appreciate Ustinov's efforts in these genres—a *Kirkus Reviews* critic, writing about *Ustinov Still at Large,* calls it "a fine friendship garland of civilized, perishable memories, but nothing worth saving," while a *Publishers Weekly* critic complains that Ustinov's stance in his articles "doesn't always work." Reviewers, however, generally acknowledge Ustinov's skill at storytelling. "It is easy to argue that Ustinov is the world's finest living

raconteur," asserts a *Forbes* magazine contributor. "Along with a lethal gift for mimicry, he is a linguist who lifts accents from everywhere. . . . Talking with Ustinov is like being with a clever friend as he wanders through a costume shop, trying on the masks."

"The trick has always been to write as easily as you talk," notes William Cole in the *Saturday Review.* "Peter Ustinov does just that, and he's the grandest monopolistic talker I've ever stood in a circle around, spellbound." Writing about Ustinov's fable *The Old Man and Mr. Smith,* a *Publishers Weekly* reviewer declares that "within this loquacious novel's cosmic banter, Ustinov offers priceless philosophical nuggets, as well as scathing satirical barbs." His one-man show *An Evening with Peter Ustinov* is described by *Chicago Tribune* writer Sid Smith as "talk-show anecdote raised to art, tripping its way through light-hearted, possibly spurious tattletales" to a broad range of imitations, including a barking dog, crying cat, a flamenco guitar, and "an infant's gastric disturbances." Ustinov is also a gifted musician and historical commentator: his narration of the PBS television special *Inside the Vatican* is, according to Walter Goodman in the *New York Times,* delivered "in orotund tones. . . . It's the classiest interview show of the week." In the two-hour television special *The Mozart Mystique with Peter Ustinov,* a tribute to the Austrian composer, Ustinov "has a kind of avuncular self-awareness that allows you to enjoy his beneficent pomposity as much as he does," declares Daniel B. Wood in the *Christian Science Monitor.* "He can begin one sentence as a raving twit and finish it off with a scowl of unquestionable authority, all in character."

Reflecting on the various facets of his career, Ustinov told the *New York Times:* "Acting is probably much safer than directing or writing. . . . Acting is intrinsically easy. But I've always thought my chief work is what I write. It's much more difficult, and writing for theater is the most difficult of all. In a novel it's enough to know what to write; in theater it's essential to know what not to write." "As an actor you're not dealing entirely with the unknown," Ustinov continued. "Writing is much more mysterious, and more personal. Sitting in front of a white piece of paper and filling it, and then doing that four or five hundred times—it's like a miracle. When writing comes off, it's absolutely thrilling."

Although he is well into his seventh decade, Ustinov expresses no interest in lightening his workload. On the occasion of his seventieth birthday, he tells Rowe, he gathered his family together and said to them, "'I've reached an age that I must, sooner or later, decide what I'm going to do with my life.' And there was a pause and my son said, 'Don't hurry.'" "I like that very much," the author confided to Rowe. "One of the functions of life is that throughout it you discover, sometimes painfully, your limitations." "I have no feeling of achievement at all," he told the *New York Times*. "Every time you do something it's the first time, in a way. . . . I've never got out of the habit of being surprised."

BIOGRAPHICAL/CRITICAL SOURCES:

BOOKS

Authors in the News, Volume 1, Gale (Detroit), 1976.

Cohn, Ruby, *Modern Shakespeare Offshoots,* Princeton University Press (Princeton, NJ), 1976.

Contemporary Literary Criticism, Volume 1, Gale, 1973.

Dictionary of Literary Biography, Volume 13: *British Dramatists since World War II,* Gale, 1982.

Hobson, Harold, *The Theatre Now,* Longmans, Green (London), 1953.

Thomas, Tony, *Ustinov in Focus,* A. S. Barnes (San Diego), 1971.

Trewin, J. C., *A Play Tonight,* Elek (London), 1952.

Ustinov, Peter, *Dear Me,* Little, Brown, 1977.

Warwick, Christopher, *The Universal Ustinov,* Sidgwick & Jackson (London), 1990.

Willians, Geoffrey, *Peter Ustinov,* Copp, 1957, Transatlantic, 1958.

Williamson, Audrey, *The Bristol Old Vic,* Macmillan (New York City), 1957.

Williamson, *Contemporary Theatre, 1953-1956,* Macmillan, 1957.

Williamson, *Theatre of Two Decades,* Rockliff, 1951.

PERIODICALS

Atlantic, July, 1964.

Book World, January 2, 1972.

Chicago Tribune, May 10, 1992, pp. 12-3; May 14, 1992, p. 28; January 15, 1993, p. 7.

Christian Science Monitor, May 17, 1990, p. 11.

Cinema Canada, May, 1986.

Daily Telegraph (London), August 23, 1952.

Drama, summer, 1958.

Forbes, November 22, 1993, pp. 77-8.

Holiday, July, 1958.

Journal of Royal Society of Arts, May 2, 1952.

Kirkus Reviews, July 1, 1989, p. 951; February 1, 1995, p. 153.

Life, April 14, 1958; April 19, 1963.

Listener, February 17, 1966; February 24, 1966.

Look, April 29, 1958.

Los Angeles Times, October 8, 1983.

Maclean's, October 1, 1979.

McCall's, November, 1958.

New Statesman and Nation, December 1, 1951; March 27, 1954.

Newsweek, March 10, 1958; September 19, 1977.

New Yorker, July 15, 1967.

New York Herald Tribune, December 10, 1953; July 10, 1955.

New York Times, January 24, 1965; October 15, 1977; July 30, 1979; March 7, 1982; April 22, 1984; April 23, 1984; May 4, 1987; October 24, 1994, p. C16.

New York Times Book Review, November 28, 1971; September 25, 1977; December 23, 1984; September 17, 1989, p. 30; May 21, 1995, p. 32.

New York Times Magazine, January 29, 1961.

Philadelphia Inquirer, November 17, 1974.

Publishers Weekly, April 19, 1991, pp. 58-9; February 6, 1995, p. 82.

Punch, October 6, 1989, p. 45.

Saturday Review, November 13, 1971; September 3, 1977.

Spectator, August 7, 1971.

Time, March 10, 1958.

Times (London), May 21, 1983; September 15, 1987.

Times Literary Supplement, December 1, 1966; January 9, 1969; July 1, 1983.

Variety, March 13-9, 1995, p. 37.

Vogue, October 1, 1957.

Washington Post, September 21, 1954.

V

van APPLEDORN, Mary Jeanne 1927-

PERSONAL: Born October 2, 1927, in Holland, MI; daughter of John (an insurance man and organist) and Elizabeth (Rinck) van Appledorn. *Education:* University of Rochester, B.M., 1948, M.M., 1950, Ph.D., 1966. *Avocational interests:* Sports.

ADDRESSES: Home—1629 16th St., Apt. 216, Lubbock, TX 79401. *Office*—Department of Composition and Music Theory, Texas Tech University, P.O. Box 42033, Lubbock, TX 79409-2033.

CAREER: Texas Tech University, Lubbock, 1950—, began as instructor, professor of music, 1966—, chairman of department of composition and music theory, 1969-86, Paul Whitfield Horn professor of music, 1989—. Piano debut at Carnegie Hall, New York City, 1957. Annual Symposium of Contemporary Music, founder, 1951, chairman, 1951-81. Musical composition commissions for New Scribner Library, 1960, Texas Federation of Music Clubs, 1980, Inoue Chamber Ensemble, 1988, and North Dakota State University, 1992.

MEMBER: American Society of Composers, Authors, and Publishers, National Association for American Composers and Conductors, American Association of University Professors, College Music Society, Society of Composers, Inc., Mu Phi Epsilon, Alpha Chi Omega, Delta Kappa Gamma.

AWARDS, HONORS: First awards in Mu Phi Epsilon national composition contest, 1951, 1953; international scholarship, Delta Kappa Gamma, 1959-60; selected as one of three most outstanding Texas women composers, 1971; named to Hall of Fame of Texas Composers, 1973; Premier Prix, World Carillon Federation, 1980, for *Suite for Carillon;* Texas Composers Guild Award, 1980, for *Matrices;* Standard Panel Award, American Society of Composers, Authors, and Publishers, 1980-95; Virginia College Band Directors National Association awards, 1981, 1982; Outstanding Researcher Award, Texas Tech University, 1982; first place, keyboards, Composer and Songwriter International Composition, 1986 for *A Liszt Fantasie;* IX Premio Ancona award, 1986, for *Liquid Gold;* Georges Enesco International Composition Contest, 1986, for *Cellano Rhapsody;* First Prize, Texas Composers Guild, 1987, for "Four Duos;" Pacific Composers Forum Competition, 1992, for *Ayre;* Coup de Vents, International Concert Band Competition, 1994, for *A Choreographic Overture.*

WRITINGS:

BOOKS

Keyboard, Singing and Dictation Manual, W. C. Brown, 1968.

MUSICAL COMPOSITIONS

Sonnet for Organ, Galaxy Music Corporation, 1974, recorded by Opus One Records.
Scenes from Pecos County (for piano), Carl Fischer (New York City), 1976, recorded by Vienna Modern Masters, 1991.
West Texas Suite (for chorus, symphonic band and percussion ensemble), performed at Lubbock Bicentennial choral concert, 1976.
Concerto Brevis (for piano and orchestra), Carl Fischer (New York City), 1977.

Set of Five (for piano), Oxford University Press (New York City), 1978, recorded by Northeastern Records, 1982, and by Opus One Records.

Darest Thou Now, O Soul (for women's choir and organ; text by Walt Whitman), Carl Fischer (New York City), 1978.

Cantata: Rising Night after Night (for chorus and orchestra), Carl Fischer (New York City), 1979, recorded by Vienna Modern Masters.

Matrices (for alto saxophone and piano), Dorn (Medfield, MA), 1979, recorded by Golden Crest Records.

Suite for Carillon, Association Bourguignonne Culturelle, La Federation Mondiale de Carillon, 1980, American Carillon Music Editions (Vallejo, CA), 1986.

Elegy for Pepe, E.C. Schirmer (Boston), 1982.

Liquid Gold (for alto saxophone and piano), Dorn (Medfield, MA), 1982, performed by U.S. Navy Concert Band, Nuremburg, Germany, 1982, recorded by Opus One Records.

Cacophony (for wind ensemble, percussion, and toys), Carl Fischer (New York City), 1983, performed by Spring High School Band at Midwest Band and Orchestra Clinic, 1980, recorded by Golden Crest Records.

Lux: Legend of Santa Lucia (for symphonic band), Carl Fischer (New York City), 1983, performed by National Intercollegiate Band at College-Conservatory of Music, University of Cincinnati, 1981, recorded by Century Records.

Missa Brevis (for trumpet and organ), Arsis Press (Washington, DC), 1988, world premiere by Anatoly Selianin, Saratov State Conservatoire, Saratov, U.S.S.R., 1987, American premiere by Robert M. Birch in Washington, DC., recorded by CRS (Contemporary Record Society).

Sonic Mutation (for harp solo), Arsis Press (Washington, DC), 1988, premiered by NACUSA, New York, 1987, recorded by CRS (Contemporary Record Society).

Caprice (for carillon), American Carillon Music Editions (Vallejo, CA), 1988, performed by James Lawson at Riverside Church, New York, 1988.

Set of Seven (ballet), performed by New York City Ballet Company, Lincoln Center, New York, 1988.

Sonatine (for clarinet and piano), Dorn (Medfield, MA), 1989, performed by Edward Gilmore and Kazuko Inoue, Weill Recital Hall at Carnegie Hall, New York, 1988, recorded by Opus One Records.

Concerto for Trumpet and Band Molenaar's Muziekcentrale (The Netherlands), 1991, performed by International Trumpet Guild, Albuquerque, NM, recorded by Opus One Records.

Cornucopia (for solo trumpet), Tromba (Denver, CO), 1991.

Parquet Musique (for clavecin), Arsis Press (Washington, DC), 1992, recorded by Dr. Barbara Harbach, Gasparo Records, 1990.

Tower Music (for carillon), American Carillon Music Editions (Vallejo, CA), 1992.

Incantations (for trumpet and piano), Arsis Press (Washington, DC), 1992, recorded by Willie Strieder, Opus One Records, 1992.

Terrestrial Music (double concerto for violin solo, piano solo, and strings in five movements), world premiere Nagano, Japan, 1992, American premiere, Miller Theatre at Columbia University, New York, 1992.

A Liszt Fantasie (for piano), Arsis Press (Washington, DC), 1992, performed by Dr. William Westney, American Liszt Society Centennial Celebration, Miami, FL, 1986, recorded by North/South Consonance Records and CRS (Contemporary Record Society).

Ayre (for strings, viola da gamba consort, clarinet choir or saxophone choir), Southern Music Company, 1994.

OTHER

Also author of numerous musical compositions, including "A Celestial Clockwork," 1983, and "Four Duos," for viola and violoncello, 1989. Contributor to *New Scribner Music Library,* 1960. Contributor of articles to *College Music Society Journal.*

WORK IN PROGRESS: Form, Style and Analysis, a book for graduate classes.

*   *   *

VAUGHAN, Frances E.   1935-

PERSONAL: Born January 1, 1935, in New York, NY; daughter of Frederick V. and Caroline (Willis) Vaughan; children: Reece Robert Clark, Leslie Elizabeth Clark. *Education:* Stanford University, B.A. (with honors), 1956; California State University, Sonoma, M.A., 1969; California School of Professional Psychology, Ph.D., 1973. *Politics:* Democrat. *Religion:* Episcopalian.

ADDRESSES: Office—10 Millwood St., Suite 3, Mill Valley, CA 94941.

CAREER: California State University, Sonoma, lecturer in psychology, 1969-73; University of California, Extension Division, instructor in psychology at branches in Berkeley, Santa Cruz, Los Angeles, and Riverside, 1973-76; professor of psychology at Institute of Transpersonal Psychology, 1975-84; University of California, Irvine, assistant clinical professor, 1987—. Member of field faculty at Humanistic Psychology Institute, San Francisco, CA, 1973-77; member of faculty at California School of Professional Psychology, 1974-76; adjunct professor at Union Graduate School West, 1979-81. Private practice of psychology, consulting and lecturing, Mill Valley, CA, 1974—; member of board of directors of Transpersonal Institute, 1974-81, International Transpersonal Association, 1981-84, 1989-91, and Interlog, 1983-87.

MEMBER: International Center for Integrative Studies, American Psychological Association Fellow, Association for Humanistic Psychology (president, 1988-89), Association for Transpersonal Psychology (past president), California Psychological Association, Phi Beta Kappa.

WRITINGS:

Awakening Intuition, Anchor Press (New York City), 1979.
The Inward Arc: Healing and Wholeness in Psychotherapy and Spirituality, New Science Library, 1986, 2nd edition, Blue Dolphin (San Diego, CA), 1995.
Shadows of the Sacred: Seeing through Spiritual Illusions, Quest Books (Wheaton, IL), 1995.

EDITOR

(With Roger N. Walsh) *Beyond Ego: Transpersonal Dimensions in Psychology,* J. P. Tarcher, (Los Angeles), 1980.
(With Walsh) *Accept This Gift: Selections from a Course in Miracles,* J. P. Tarcher, 1983.
(With Walsh) *A Gift of Peace: Selections from a Course in Miracles,* J. P. Tarcher, 1986.
(With Walsh) *A Gift of Healing: Selections from a Course in Miracles,* J. P. Tarcher, 1988.
(With Walsh) *Paths Beyond Ego: The Transpersonal Vision,* J. P. Tarcher, 1993.
(With Walsh) *Gifts from a Course in Miracles,* J. P. Tarcher, 1995.

OTHER

Contributor to psychology journals. Member of board of editors of *Journal of Transpersonal Psychology,* 1973—, *Journal of Humanistic Psychology,* and *Re-Vision.*

BIOGRAPHICAL/CRITICAL SOURCES:

PERIODICALS

Virginia Quarterly Review, autumn, 1986.

*   *   *

VECOLI, Rudolph J(ohn)   1927-

PERSONAL: Born March 2, 1927, in Wallingford, CT; son of Giovanni B. (a laborer) and Settima (Palmerini) Vecoli; married Jill Cherrington, June 27, 1959; children: Christopher, Lisa, Jeremy. *Education:* University of Connecticut, B.A., 1950; University of Pennsylvania, M.A., 1951; University of Wisconsin, Ph.D., 1963.

ADDRESSES: Office—Department of History, University of Minnesota, Minneapolis, MN.

CAREER: U.S. Department of State, Washington, DC, foreign affairs officer, 1951-54; instructor in history at Ohio State University, Columbus, 1957-59, and Pennsylvania State University, State College, 1960-61; Rutgers University, New Brunswick, NJ, lecturer and assistant professor of history, 1961-65; University of Illinois at Urbana-Champaign, associate professor of history, 1965-67; University of Minnesota, Minneapolis, professor of history and director of Immigration History Research Center, 1967—. Visiting professor, Uppsala University, spring, 1970, University of Amsterdam, spring, 1988, Marie Curie-Sklodowska University, Lublin, Poland, 1992.

Director, National Endowment for the Humanities Summer Seminars for College Teachers, 1980, and 1983; member, Minnesota Humanities commission, 1983-86. Participant in Project '87 seminar for faculty in immigrants and the Constitution. Member, national committee for preservation of Ellis Island, advisory committee of Ethnic Cultural Center, Minnesota Public Schools, advisory board of Oral History of the American Left, Tamiment Library, New York University. Member of board of directors,

American Immigration and Citizenship Conference, and American Council for Nationalities Service; member of executive council, National Ethnic Studies Assembly; commentator at University of Bremen Conference on American Labor and Immigration History; chair of history committee, Statue of Liberty-Ellis Island Foundation; speaker at various ethnic meetings and festivals. *Military service:* U.S. Navy, 1945-46.

MEMBER: American Historical Association (member of research division, 1984-87), Organization of American Historians, American Association of University Professors, American Italian Historical Association (president, 1966-70; member of council, 1979—), Immigration History Society (vice president, executive council, 1979—; president, 1982-85).

AWARDS, HONORS: Social Science Research Council fellow, 1959-60; Newberry Library fellow, 1964; Rutgers Research Council faculty fellow, 1964-65; American-Scandinavian Foundation fellow, 1970; American Philosophical Society grant, 1970; Medaglia d'oro, Chamber of Commerce, Lucca, Italy, 1971; senior Fulbright-Hays research scholar in Italy, 1973-74; American Council of Learned Societies grant, 1974; U.S. Department of State travel grant, 1977; New Jersey Historical Commission research grant, 1978; City of Ljubljana (Yugoslavia) Medallion, for contributions to the study of the Slovene immigration to the U.S., 1981; made Cavaliere Ufficiale nell 'Ordine al Merito della Reppublica Italiana, 1982; National Endowment for the Humanities fellowship for independent study and research, 1985-86; American Council of Learned Societies grant-in-aid for research, 1986; Immigration History Society Public Service Award, 1988; Academic specialist grant to Brazil, U.S. Information Agency, 1993.

WRITINGS:

The People of New Jersey, Van Nostrand (New York City), 1965.

(Editor with Keith Dyrud and Michael Novak, and contributor) *The Other Catholics,* Arno, 1978.

(Editor and contributor) *Italian Immigrants in Rural and Small Town America,* American Italian Historical Association (Glen Rock, NJ), 1987.

(Editor with Suzanne Sinke) *A Century of European Migrations, 1830-1930* (Statue of Liberty-Ellis Island Centennial Series), University of Illinois Press (Champaign, IL), 1991.

AUTHOR OF INTRODUCTION

Marie Hall Ets, *Rosa: The Life of an Italian Immigrant,* University of Minnesota Press (Minneapolis), 1970.

Jacob A. Riis, *The Children of the Poor,* Johnson Reprint (New York City), 1970.

N. C. Burckel and J. D. Buenker, editors, *Immigration and Ethnicity,* Gale (Detroit), 1977.

Carl Ross, *The Finn Factor in American Labor, Culture, and Society,* New York Mills, 1977.

Maddalena Tirabassi, *Il Faro di Beacon Street,* Franco Angeli (Milan), 1990.

Nadia Venturini, *Nerie Italiani ad Harlem,* Edizioni Lavoro (Rome), 1990.

OTHER

Contributor to many books, including *The State of American History,* edited by Herbert J. Bass, Quadrangle, 1970; *The Reinterpretation of American History and Culture,* edited by William H. Cartwright and Richard L. Watson Jr., National Council for the Social Studies, 1973; *The Rediscovery of Ethnicity,* edited by Sallie TeSelle, Harper, 1974; *Immigrants and Religion in Urban America,* edited by R. M. Miller and T. D. Marzik, Temple University Press (Philadelphia), 1977; *Uncertain Americans,* edited by L. Dinnerstein and F. C. Jaher, Oxford University Press, 1977; *They Chose Minnesota,* edited by June Holmquist, Minnesota Historical Society, 1981; *Italian Americans,* edited by Lydio Tomasi, Center for Migration Studies, 1985; *From "Melting Pot" to Multiculturalism: The Evolution of Ethnic Relations in the United States and Canada,* edited by Valeria Gennaro Lerda, Bulzoni Editori, 1990; *The Lebanese in the World: A Century of Emigration,* edited by Albert Hourani and Nadim Shehadi, The Centre for Lebanese Studies, 1992; *Swedes in America: Intercultural and Interethnic Perspectives on Contemporary Research,* edited by Ulf Beijbom, The Swedish Emigrant Institute, 1993; *The Statue of Liberty Revisited,* edited by Wilton S. Dillon and Neil G. Kotler, Smithsonian Institution Press, 1994; and *Documenting Diversity: The American Catholic Experience,* edited by George Michalek, Nancy Sandleback, and John J. Treanor, Association of Catholic Diocesan Archivists, 1994.

Also general editor of Research Collections on Immigration History, University Publications of America, Inc. Coeditor with Maxine Seller, "Voices of Immigrant Women Series," State University of New York Press. Advisory editor of *International Migration*

Review (formerly *International Migration Digest*); member of editorial boards, *Ethnicity, American History and Life, Studi Emigrazione* (Rome), *Estudios Migratorios Latinoamericanos* (Buenos Aires), *Italian Americana, Revue Francaise d'Etudes Americaines,* (Nancy, France), *Journal of American Ethnic History, Mid-America,* and *Altreitalie* (Turin).

WORK IN PROGRESS: A history of the Italian-American labor and radical movements. Research for a book on Italian-American ethnicity, 1945-95.

BIOGRAPHICAL/CRITICAL SOURCES:

PERIODICALS

Journal of the Canadian Historical Association, 1993, pp. 293-305.

*   *   *

VINCENT, John J(ames)   1929-

PERSONAL: Born December 29, 1929, in Sunderland, England; son of David and Ethel Beatrice Vincent; married Grace Johnston Stafford, December 4, 1958; children: Christopher John, Helen Faith, James Stafford. *Education:* Richmond College, London, B.D. (with first class honors), 1954; Drew University, S.T.M. (summa cum laude), 1955; University of Basel, Dr.Theol. (insigni cum laude), 1960.

ADDRESSES: Home—178 Abbeyfield Rd., Sheffield S4 7AY, England. *Office*—Urban Theology Unit, 210 Abbeyfield Rd., Sheffield S4 7AZ, England.

CAREER: Clergyman of Methodist Church; minister in Manchester, England, 1956-62, and at Rochdale Mission, 1962-69; Urban Theology Unit, Sheffield, England, director, 1970—; Sheffield Inner-City Ecumenical Mission, superintendent minister, 1970—. Harris Franklin Rall Lecturer at Garrett Theological Seminary, spring, 1969; visiting professor at Boston University, autumn, 1969, New York Theological Seminary, spring, 1970, and Drew University, spring, 1977.

MEMBER: British Council of Churches (member of Commission on Defense and Disarmament, 1963-65, 1969-74), Studiorum Novi Testamenti Societas, Campaign for Nuclear Disarmament (member of na-

tional executive committee, 1957-69), Alliance of Radical Methodists (founding member; chairman, 1971-75), Ashram Community Trust (leader, 1967—), Urban Mission Training Association (chairman, 1982—), Association of Centres of Adult Theological Education (member of executive committee, 1984—), Pitsmoor Action Group (chairman, 1970—), British Methodist Church (president, 1989-90), Institute for British Liberation Theology (honorary director, 1994—).

WRITINGS:

Christ in a Nuclear World, Crux Press, 1962, 2nd edition, 1963.
Christ and Our Stewardship: Six Bible Studies, Epworth Press (England), 1963.
Christian Nuclear Perspective, Epworth Press, 1964.
Christ and Methodism: Towards a New Christianity for a New Age, Abingdon (Nashville, TN), 1965, 2nd edition, Epworth Press, 1966.
Here I Stand: The Faith of a Radical, Epworth Press, 1967.
Secular Christ: A Contemporary Interpretation of Jesus, Abingdon, 1968.
The Working Christ: Christ's Ministries through His Church in the New Testament and in the Modern City, Epworth Press, 1968.
The Race Race, Friendship Press, 1970.
The Jesus Thing, Abingdon, 1973.
Stirrings: Essays Christian and Radical, Epworth Press, 1975.
Alternative Church, Christian Journals, 1976.
Starting All over Again, World Council of Churches, 1981.
Into the City, Epworth Press, 1982.
OK, Let's Be Methodists, Epworth Press, 1984.
Radical Jesus, Zondervan (Grand Rapids, MI), 1986.
(With J. D. Davies) *Mark at Work,* Bible Reading Fellowship, 1986.
Britain in the 90's, Methodist Publishing House, 1989.
Discipleship in the 90's, Methodist Publishing House, 1991.
Liberation Theology UK, Urban Theology Unit (Sheffield, England), 1995.

WORK IN PROGRESS: A trilogy on liberation theology, urban theology and discipleship theology.

SIDELIGHTS: John J. Vincent wrote that he is "committed to academic writing within the context of personal lifestyle commitment with deprived inner-city communities and small experimental Christian groups." Vincent also told *CA* that he "sees such communities and groups as prophetic for the coming post-technological, small-scale society."

BIOGRAPHICAL/CRITICAL SOURCES:

PERIODICALS

Books and Bookmen, March, 1968.
Christian Century, June 19, 1968.
Encounter, spring, 1969.

W-Z

WAGNER, Karl Edward 1945-1994

PERSONAL: Born December 12, 1945, in Knoxville, TN; died September 30, 1994, of a burst blood vessel, in Chapel Hill, NC; son of Aubrey Joseph (chair of board of directors of Tennessee Valley Authority) and Dorothea Johanna (Huber) Wagner. *Education:* Kenyon College, A.B., 1967; University of North Carolina, M.D., 1974. *Politics:* Independent.

ADDRESSES: Agent—Kirby McCauley, 60 East 42nd St., New York, NY 10017.

CAREER: Carcosa (publishing house), Chapel Hill, NC, founder and editor, 1972-94; John Umstead Hospital, Butner, NC, resident in psychiatry, 1974; freelance writer, 1975-94. Member of judging panel, World Fantasy Award, 1978.

MEMBER: Science Fiction and Fantasy Writers of America, North Carolina Writers Conference.

AWARDS, HONORS: August Derleth Award, 1975, for short story "Sticks," and 1977, for short story "Two Suns Setting"; World Fantasy Award nomination for short story "Beyond All Measure."

WRITINGS:

"KANE" SERIES; FANTASY

Darkness Weaves with Many Shades (novel), Powell Publications (Reseda, CA), 1970, revised edition published as *Darkness Weaves,* Warner Books (New York City), 1978.
Death Angel's Shadow (short stories), Warner Books, 1973.

Bloodstone (novel), Warner Books, 1975.
Dark Crusade (novel), Warner Books, 1976.
Night Winds (novel), Warner Books, 1978.
The Book of Kane (short stories), Donald M. Grant (West Kingston, RI), 1985.

EDITOR

Robert E. Howard, *The Hour of the Dragon,* Berkley (New York City), 1977.
Howard, *The People of the Black Circle,* Berkley, 1977.
Howard, *Red Nails,* Berkley, 1977.
The Year's Best Horror Stories, Volumes 7-22, DAW Books (New York City), 1980-94.
(And author of introduction) Manly Wade Wellman, *Valley So Low: Southern Mountain Stories,* Doubleday (New York City), 1987.
Echoes of Valor, Tor Books (New York City), Volume I, 1987, Volume II, 1989, Volume III, 1991.
Intensive Scare, DAW Books, 1990.

OTHER

Midnight Sun (story collection), Gary Hoppenstand (Columbus, OH), 1974.
The Sign of the Salamander, Gary Hoppenstand, 1975.
Bran Mak Morn: Legion from the Shadows, Zebra Books (New York City), 1976, published as *Legion from the Shadows,* Baen Books (New York City), 1988.
Conan: The Road of Kings, Bantam (New York City), 1979.
In a Lonely Place, Warner Books, 1983, revised edition, Scream Press (Santa Cruz, CA), 1984.

(With David Drake) *Killer,* Baen Books, 1984.

Why Not You and I? (short stories), illustrated by Ron Lindahn and Val Lakey Lindahn, Dark Harvest (Arlington, IL), 1987.

Where the Summer Ends, Pulphouse Publications (Eugene, OR), 1991.

(Creator of characters and situations with Kent Williams) *Tell Me, Dark,* DC Comics (New York City), 1992.

Also author of *Unthreatened by the Morning Light,* 1989, and of unproduced screenplays *Conan III, The Twist* and *The Horror from the Mound.*

WORK IN PROGRESS: Queen of the Night, a sequel to *Legion from the Shadows; Exorcisms and Ecstasies,* a collection of short stories; *Satan's Gun;* and *The Fourth Seal.*

ADAPTATIONS: The story "Sticks" was adapted and broadcast by National Public Radio, recorded by the ZBS Foundation (Fort Edward, NY) in 1984, and television rights have been sold.

SIDELIGHTS: Although Karl Edward Wagner was a publisher and an author of impressive horror fiction, "when he is remembered—and he will be, by many generations to come—it will be first, as an editor," stated the editors of *Horror: The News Magazine.* Wagner took over DAW Books's anthology *The Year's Best Horror Stories* in 1980 and turned the annual series into a prize collection of new and classic talent in the genre. "I play no favorites with authors," Wagner told Bradley L. Sinor in an interview for *Horror* shortly before his death. "I've run stories by Stephen King, and I've run stories by writers who may have never written another story. I have maintained this attitude for fifteen years as editor: No taboos. No holds barred. No free rides. Excellence required. Whiners piss off." The editors of *Horror* explained that Wagner "became so identified with [the series] that, following his death, DAW canceled the series, rather than allowing it to continue under a different editor."

Wagner came from an unusual background. "My great-great-great uncle was an opera composer named Richard," he told Sinor. "I learned to read from pre-code horror comics; gruesome fairy tales were my favorites. When I was five I distressed my first-grade teacher by drawing horribly violent comic books with dialogue pretty much limited to 'BOOO!' and 'ARRGGHHAA!'" Wagner attended high school in Knoxville, Tennessee. He went to Gambier, Ohio,

to attend Kenyon College and graduated with a degree in history in 1967. He then entered the school of medicine at the University of North Carolina in Chapel Hill but "dropped out for a few years to become a Haight-Ashbury hippie and to write," he told Sinor. He eventually returned to school and earned his M.D. in 1974. For one year he worked as a psychiatrist before turning to writing full time. "Never underestimate the value of a medical education," Wagner told Sinor. "Good for background, good for realism, good for the discipline."

The most popular of Wagner's early works featured a single protagonist, the swordsman known only as Kane. Kane is an immortal wanderer who is cursed to travel the world throughout eternity. "Kane grew out of my childhood fascination for the villain," Wagner confessed to Sinor. "Kane is not a swords and sorcery hero: he is a gothic hero/villain from the tradition of the Gothic novels of the 18th and early 19th centuries. Possibly his single greatest influence was the doomed hero/villain of [nineteenth-century Irish writer Charles Robert] Maturin's *Melmoth the Wanderer,* although there are very many other sources."

In his editorial role, Wagner also worked with other sword-and-sorcery and pulp fiction heroes, including Robert E. Howard's Conan the Barbarian, C. L. Moore's Northwest Smith and Jirel of Joiry, and Manly Wade Wellman's caveman Hok. In the late 1970s, Wagner edited three volumes of Howard's stories and novels, and in 1979 he wrote his own Conan pastiche, entitled *Conan: The Road of Kings.* During the 1980s he presented the best of sword-and-sorcery fiction in three anthologies entitled *Echoes of Valor.* Don Herron wrote in *Nyctalops,* "You're not going to do better than Wagner for rousing, oldtime S[word] and S[orcery] among today's writers."

Besides his "Kane" stories, Wagner also wrote contemporary horror fiction, which was often critically acclaimed. "Wagner," declared Michael A. Morrison in a *Fantasy Review* piece on *In a Lonely Place,* "is a meticulous writer who takes the time to establish mood and a sense of place. . . . Wagner is a sensitive prose stylist, evident on nearly every page." A *Publishers Weekly* reviewer described the stories of *In a Lonely Place* as "praiseworthy," while *Science Fiction Review* contributor Darrell Schweitzer called the book "one of the best horror collections in years. I think what Wagner has managed to do is combine the best elements of the classic supernatural story . . . with the modern variety." Schweitzer concluded, "He's making a definite contribution to a tradition, rather than just aping it."

Wagner's greatest influence on the horror genre, however, was as an editor, not as an author. In 1980 he accepted the position of editor of *The Year's Best Horror Stories* from Gerald Page. "Jerry said he had returned his contract for the *Year's Best Horror: VIII* to DAW because he wanted to devote more time to his own writing," Wagner told Sinor. "That year . . . Don and Elsie Wollheim came up to my room and asked me to take over. Trying not to bite the side out of my glass, I said: 'Sure!' Stepping down as editor? No way. Never. Where do these rumors get started?"

Writing in *Fantasy Newsletter* about why he chose to work in the fantasy and horror genres, Wagner noted: "Ready or not, we're about to live in the age our science fiction prophets warned us about. That's as good an excuse to turn to a fantasy world as you could ask."

BIOGRAPHICAL/CRITICAL SOURCES:

PERIODICALS

Analog Science Fiction/Science Fact, August, 1988, p. 142.
Fantasy Newsletter, March, 1980.
Fantasy Review, March, 1985, p. 14.
Horror: The News Magazine, Number 5, 1995, pp. 11-16.
Kirkus Reviews, October 1, 1989, pp. 1437-38.
Nyctalops, March, 1978.
Publishers Weekly, February 4, 1983, p. 365; October 30, 1987, p. 58; October 6, 1989, p. 85; September 13, 1993, p. 123.
Science Fiction Review, February, 1978; summer, 1983, p. 46.
Washington Post Book World, October 30, 1983, p. 6; December 23, 1984, p. 11; February 22, 1987, p. 13; December 27, 1987, p. 9.

OBITUARIES:

PERIODICALS

Horror: The News Magazine, Number 5, 1995, pp. 5-8.*

—Sketch by Kenneth R. Shepherd

WALLACH, Michael A(rthur) 1933-

PERSONAL: Born April 8, 1933, in New York, NY; son of Max and Wilma (Cheiker) Wallach; married Lise Wertheimer (a psychologist), July 26, 1959; children: Rachel Paula. *Education:* Swarthmore College, B.A. (with highest honors), 1954; Harvard University, Ph.D., 1958.

ADDRESSES: Office—Department of Psychology, Duke University, Durham, NC 27706.

CAREER: Harvard University, Cambridge, MA, instructor in social psychology, 1958-59; Massachusetts Institute of Technology, Cambridge, assistant professor of psychology, 1959-62; Duke University, Durham, NC, associate professor, 1962-66, professor of psychology, 1966-72; University of Chicago, Chicago, IL, William S. Gray Professor of Education, 1972-73; Duke University, professor of psychology, 1973—. Principal or co-principal investigator in research projects for National Institute of Mental Health, 1958-61, U.S. Office of Education, 1961-65, and National Science Foundation, 1961-63 and 1964-67.

AWARDS, HONORS: Cambridge University, Westengard traveling fellow, 1955-56; Social Science Research Council research grant, 1962.

WRITINGS:

(With Nathan Kogan) *Risk Taking: A Study in Cognition and Personality,* Holt (New York City), 1964.
(With Kogan) *Modes of Thinking in Young Children: A Study of the Creativity-Intelligence Distinction,* Holt, 1965.
(With C. W. Wing, Jr.) *The Talented Student: A Validation of the Creativity-Intelligence Distinction,* Holt, 1969.
(With Wing) *College Admission and the Psychology of Talent,* Holt, 1971.
The Intelligence/Creativity Distinction, General Learning Press, 1971.
(With wife, Lise Wallach) *Teaching All Children to Read,* University of Chicago Press (Chicago), 1976.
(With L. Wallach) *The Teaching All Children to Read Kit,* University of Chicago Press, 1976.
Letter Tracing and Drawing Spirit Masters, University of Chicago Press, 1976.

(With L. Wallach) *Psychology's Sanction for Selfishness: The Error of Egoism in Theory and Therapy*, W. H. Freeman (New York City), 1983.

(With L. Wallace) *Rethinking Goodness*, State University of New York Press (Albany), 1990.

Contributor to numerous books. Editor, "Alternatives in Psychology" series, State University of New York Press, 1989—. Contributor of articles to periodicals, including *Journal of Personality and Social Psychology, Contemporary Psychology, American Psychologist, Journal of Social and Clinical Psychology, Developmental Psychology, Psychological Review, Journal of Abnormal and Social Psychology, Psychological Reports, Journal of Consulting Psychology, Journal of Aesthetics and Art Criticism, American Journal of Psychology, American Journal of Psychiatry, American Scientist, Washington Monthly,* and *Harvard Education Review.* Editor of *Journal of Personality,* 1963-72.

*　　*　　*

WALTHAM, Antony Clive   1942-

PERSONAL: Born June 18, 1942, in Birmingham, England; son of Clive (a surveyor) and Mary (Platts) Waltham; married Janet Gore, December 16, 1963 (marriage ended); married Janet Myles, February 20, 1979; children: (first marriage) Sam, Megan. *Education:* B.Sc., D.I.C., and Ph.D. from Imperial College of Science and Technology, London. *Avocational interests:* Travel (has led or joined cave expeditions in Nepal, Iran, Canada, Jamaica, Malaysia, Indonesia, Russia, Brazil, and China, in addition to having visited nearly every country in Europe).

ADDRESSES: Office—Department of Civil Engineering, Trent University, Nottingham NG1 4BU, England.

CAREER: Trent University, Nottingham, England, lecturer in geology, 1968—. University of Nottingham, lecturer in department of adult education, 1971; Open University, Milton Keynes, England, part-time tutor in geology, 1973-76.

MEMBER: British Cave Research Association.

AWARDS, HONORS: Travel fellowship, Winston Churchill Memorial Trust, 1970; Cuthbert Peek Award, Royal Geographical Society, 1981.

WRITINGS:

(Editor) *Limestone and Caves of Northwest England,* David & Charles (North Pomfret, VT), 1974.
Caves, Crown (New York City), 1974.
The World of Caves, Putnam (New York City), 1976.
Catastrophe—The Violent Earth, Crown, 1978.
Caves, Crags and Gorges, Constable (London), 1984.
China Caves, Royal Geographical Society, 1986.
Yorkshire Dales National Park, Webb & Bower, 1987.
Ground Subsidence, Chapman & Hall (London), 1989.
Foundations of Engineering Geology, Chapman & Hall, 1994.
Karst and Caves of Britain, Chapman & Hall, 1996.

Contributor to encyclopedias. Contributor to geology, geography and cave research journals and magazines.

WORK IN PROGRESS: Research on the geomorphology and hydrology of limestone caves and the engineering geology of ground subsidence.

SIDELIGHTS: Antony Clive Waltham told *CA:* "From school-days I was interested in geography and travel but then went to study geology because it seemed more promising careerwise than geography. While at university, I was persuaded to go caving, on the principle of trying anything, but I got hooked on the sport of underground exploration. I drifted into teaching because it was the only occupation to give long summer vacations for travel but then found teaching was my true vocation anyway, and I have developed it along the lines of practical and applied geology, well away from remote academic principles. My parallel interest in caving has developed to include geological research into cave development.

"Caves may appear to be a bit obscure and even unpleasant to many people, but they have kept me occupied for years. I started off exploring them just for the adventure, but once I could be happy and confident in the cave environment, I started to develop my caving. First I was mapping the caves, then studying their geology, and then photographing them more. Now I like to find some application in my cave work, whether it is to contribute to broader landscape studies or to locate usable underground water supplies. I've been to caves almost all around the world, and their variety and contrasts never cease to fascinate me. There's still plenty to see above and below the ground."

BIOGRAPHICAL/CRITICAL SOURCES:

PERIODICALS

Los Angeles Times Book Review, August 23, 1987.

*   *   *

WANIEK, Marilyn Nelson
   See NELSON, Marilyn

*   *   *

WARREN, Elizabeth
   See SUPRANER, Robyn

*   *   *

WARREN, Roland L(eslie) 1915-

PERSONAL: Born June 24, 1915, in Islip, NY; son of Ruy Waverly and Jenny (Simonds) Warren; married Margaret Hodges (a violin maker), June 17, 1938; children: Ursula Washburn, David Hardy, Margaret Robin. *Education:* New York University, B.S., 1935; University of Heidelberg, Ph.D., 1937.

ADDRESSES: Home—R.D. 1, Andover, NY 14806.

CAREER: Hofstra College (now Hofstra University), Hempstead, NY, instructor, 1937-39, assistant professor of social science, 1939-41; Alfred University, Alfred, NY, associate professor, 1941-43, professor of sociology, 1945-58; co-director of Area Study, 1949-58; State Charities Aid Association, New York, NY, director of Social Research Service, 1958-62; American Friends Service Committee, Philadelphia, PA, Quaker international affairs representative for Germany, 1962-64; Brandeis University, Waltham, MA, professor of community theory, 1964-80. Member of National Institute of Mental Health Metropolitan Problems Review Committee, 1969-74, chair,

1972-74. *Military service:* U.S. Naval Reserve, 1943-45.

MEMBER: International Society for Community Development, American Sociological Association (fellow; chair of community section, 1973—), Society for the Study of Social Problems (chair of community research and development committee, 1955-56), Community Development Society.

AWARDS, HONORS: Guggenheim fellowship, 1956-57, to study voluntary citizen participation in community affairs in Stuttgart, Germany; Russell Sage Foundation fellowship, 1958-62; National Institute of Mental Health, research science award, 1964-74; American Sociological Association, Community Section Award, 1982, for outstanding achievements and inspiring contributions to the study of community.

WRITINGS:

Studying Your Community, Russell Sage (New York City), 1955.
(With Joseph S. Roucek) *Sociology: An Introduction,* Rowman, (Totowa, NJ), 1957, revised edition, Littlefield, 1976.
The Community in America, Rand McNally (Chicago), 1963, 3rd edition, 1978.
Social Research Consultation: An Experiment in Health and Welfare Planning, Russell Sage, 1963.
(Editor) *Perspectives on the American Community: A Book of Readings,* Rand McNally, 1966, 3rd edition published as *New Perspectives on the American Community: A Book of Readings,* 1977, 5th edition (with Larry Lyon), 1987.
(Editor) *Politics and the Ghettos,* Atherton, 1969.
Truth, Love, and Social Change: And Other Essays on Community Change, Rand McNally, 1971.
(With Stephen M. Rose and Ann F. Burgunder) *The Structure of Urban Reform: Community Decision Organizations in Stability and Change,* Heath (Lexington, MA), 1974.
Social Change and Human Purpose: Toward Understanding and Action, Rand McNally, 1977.
(With Robert Perlman) *Families in the Energy Crisis: Impacts and Implications for Theory and Policy,* Ballinger (Cambridge, MA), 1977.
An Old Feud and a New House (drama), Nantucket Historical Association (Nantucket, MA), 1986.
Mary Coffin Starbuck and the Early History of Nantucket, Pingry Press, 1987.
Loyal Dissenter: The Life and Times of Robert Pike, University Press of America (Lanham, MD), 1991.

Whittier and the Quaker "Argonauts," Essex Institute Historical Collections (Salem, MA), 1992.

Contributor to numerous books. Correspondent for *Community Development Journal International.* Contributor of more than forty articles to journals, including *Yankee, Community Development Journal, Social Problems, Social Science Quarterly, Community Mental Health Journal, American Sociological Review,* and *Journal of the American Institute of Planners.* Associate editor of *Journal of Voluntary Action Research;* member of editorial committee of *Journal of the Community Development Society;* member of editorial board of *Urban Affairs Quarterly.*

The Community in America has been published in German.

WORK IN PROGRESS: A novel set in seventeenth-century America and entitled *Salem Dynasty;* a study of the Apostle Paul.

SIDELIGHTS: Roland L. Warren told *CA:* "Why the sudden change in nontechnical writing, such as the biography of a seventeenth-century woman? The answer, though easy, is perhaps unusual. I have always felt, to paraphrase a more widely known author, that there was more to life than my sociology. So I retired a few years early and used the time to engage in many activities that were not new, but that had been eclipsed by my major occupation: working in stained glass, composing poetry and music, clarifying my own thoughts about what I believe in the area of religion and what I do not believe. Along the way I became intrigued with the story of the early settlement of Nantucket and with the so-called 'great woman' of that island, Mary Coffin Starbuck: hence the biography, play and *Yankee* article.

"Sociology, like other social and natural sciences, affords a set of concepts and theories (a kit of tools, a pair of glasses) with which to understand *aspects* of reality. It helps to change glasses once in a while and come to participate in other equally fascinating aspects of reality that we might otherwise miss.

"In my more recent research on seventeenth-century Massachusetts I came across the attractive figure of Robert Pike, an early advocate of religious freedom and civil rights and one of the few officials who spoke out against the Salem witchcraft trials while they were still in progress. As a contrast with the biography of Mary Starbuck, in which I interposed many imaginative conversations within the carefully researched background, I decided to limit the Pike biography to words or actions for which there was specific historical documentation. It was quite a discipline, but the voluminous footnotes permit any historian to retrace my steps and check their accuracy."

*   *   *

WASHINGTON, Mary Helen 1941-

PERSONAL: Born January 21, 1941, in Cleveland, OH; daughter of David C. and Mary Catherine (Dalton) Washington. *Education:* Notre Dame College, B.A., 1962; University of Detroit, M.A., 1966, Ph.D., 1976.

ADDRESSES: Office—Department of English, University of Maryland, College Park, MD 20742.

CAREER: High school teacher of English in the public schools of Cleveland, OH, 1962-64; St. John College, Cleveland, instructor in English, 1966-68; University of Detroit, Detroit, MI, assistant professor of English, 1972-75, director of Center for Black Studies, beginning 1975; Boston Harbor College, University of Massachusetts, Boston, associate professor of English, 1980-89; University of Maryland, College Park, MD, professor of English, 1989—.

MEMBER: National Council of Teachers of English, College Language Association, Michigan Black Studies Association.

AWARDS, HONORS: Richard Wright Award for Literary Criticism from *Black World,* 1974.

WRITINGS:

(Editor and author of introduction) *Black-Eyed Susans: Classic Stories by and about Black Women,* Doubleday (New York City), 1975.
(Editor and author of introduction and critical notes) *Midnight Birds: Stories by Contemporary Black Women Writers,* Doubleday, 1980, published in England as *Any Woman's Blues: Stories by Black Women Writers,* Virago Press (London), 1980.
(Editor and author of introduction and critical notes) *Invented Lives: Narratives of Black Women, 1860-1960,* Doubleday, 1987.

(Editor and author of introduction and critical notes) *Memory of Kin: Stories of Family by Black Writers,* Doubleday, 1991.

Contributor of articles and reviews to *Negro Digest* and *Black World.*

SIDELIGHTS: Mary Helen Washington is the editor and author of introductions and critical notes of three valued anthologies containing the work of some of the best black women writers. In reviews of all three books, *Black-Eyed Susans: Classic Stories by and about Black Women, Midnight Birds: Stories by Contemporary Black Women Writers,* and *Invented Lives: Narratives of Black Women, 1860-1960,* reviewers have praised Washington for expertly assembling unique and sensitive stories describing the life and plight of black women.

Black-Eyed Susans, Washington's first anthology, presents the writing of such authors as Toni Cade Bambara, Gwendolyn Brooks, Louise Meriwether, Toni Morrison, Jean Wheeler Smith, and Alice Walker. Joyce Carol Oates writes in *Ms.* that *Black-Eyed Susans* "constitutes an indictment of stereotyped thinking." Oates goes on to state that "no one has been so misunderstood, perhaps, as the black woman: she has been defined by others, whether white writers or black men writers, always seen from the outside, ringed in by convenient stereotypes. . . . What strikes the reader who comes to most of these stories for the first time is the wide range of their humanity. All the protagonists are black women: they are *black* women, black *women,* and fiercely individualistic *persons.* And the fiction that presents them is of a high order, the product of painstaking craftsmanship. There is much anger, and no little despair and heartbreak, but emotion has been kept under control; each of the stories is a work of art, moving and convincing."

Marlene Veach writes in *Best Sellers* that Washington's second book, *Midnight Birds,* "is a collection of stories that revolts against ideologies and attitudes that impress women into servitude. It deals with the real lives and actual experiences of black women, in the hope of demolishing racial and sexual stereotypes." Margaret Atwood writes in a *Harvard Review* of *Midnight Birds* that "this is American writing at its finest, by turns earthy, sinuous, thoughtful, and full of power." Atwood continues to explain that the writers included in this collec-

tion, Toni Cade Bambara, Alexis De Veaux, Gayl Jones, Toni Morrison, Ntozake Shange, Alice Walker, and others, "know exactly whom they are writing for. They are writing for other black American women, and they believe in the power of their words. They see themselves as giving a voice to the voiceless. They perceive writing as the forging of saving myths, the naming of forgotten pasts, the telling of truths."

In *Invented Lives* Washington chose to highlight the work of ten women, including Harriet Jacobs, Frances E. W. Harper, Zora Neale Hurston, and Dorothy West, who wrote between the years of 1860 and 1960. Washington states in a *New York Times Book Review* interview conducted by Rosemary L. Bray that "a lot of people think the tradition of black women writing began in the last 20 years. In fact, black women have been writing about their experiences in America for more than 200 years. . . . I found black women working as domestics, writers, migrant farmers, artists, secretaries—and having economic and personal problems centering around these jobs."

Henry Louis Gates, Jr. comments in the *New York Times Book Review* that in each author's selection "we hear a black woman *testifying* about what the twin scourges of sexism and racism, merged into one oppressive entity, actually *do* to a human being, how the combination confines the imagination, puzzles the will and delimits free choice. What unites these essays, short stories and novel excerpts is their common themes: 'Their literature is about black women; it takes the trouble to record the thoughts, words, feelings, and deeds of black women, experiences that make the realities of being black in America look very different from what men have written.'"

Although the contributors to Washington's anthologies are all of black heritage, their tales can be understood and felt by all women. For example, calling *Midnight Birds* "a book that is difficult to fault," Buchi Emecheta remarks in the *Washington Post* that this collection "speaks through its admirable selection of stories to black women in particular and to all women in general. The message is clear: it is about time we women start talking to each other, the white to the black, the black American to her African sister, ironing out our differences. For as Toni Morrison said, 'Because when you don't have a woman to really talk to, whether it be an aunt or a sister or a friend, that is the real loneliness.'"

BIOGRAPHICAL/CRITICAL SOURCES:

PERIODICALS

America, January 31, 1981.
Belles Lettres, May, 1988, p. 11.
Best Sellers, August, 1980.
Essence, July, 1988, p. 28.
Harvard Review, February, 1981.
Kliatt Young Adult Paperback Book Guide, April, 1990, p. 30.
Library Journal, January 15, 1980.
Modern Fiction Studies, spring, 1988, p. 134; fall, 1993, p. 828.
Ms., March, 1976; July, 1980; January, 1988, p. 76.
Nation, April 30, 1988, p. 615.
New Directions for Women, March, 1988, p. 16.
New York Times Book Review, October 4, 1987.
Publishers Weekly, December 3, 1979.
Times Literary Supplement, October 30, 1981.
Village Voice Literary Supplement, April, 1988, p. 20.
Washington Post, June 3, 1980.
Washington Post Book World, January 7, 1990, p. 12.
Women's Review of Books, February, 1988, p. 15.

*　　*　　*

WATKIN, David (John) 1941-

PERSONAL: Born April 7, 1941, in Salisbury, England; son of Thomas Charles and Vera Mary Watkin. Education: Trinity Hall, Cambridge, B.A. (with first class honors), 1963, Ph.D., 1967.

ADDRESSES: Home—Peterhouse, Cambridge, England. Office—Department of Art History, Cambridge University, Cambridge, England.

CAREER: Cambridge University, Cambridge, England, librarian of the Faculty of Architecture and History of Art, 1967-72, fellow of Peterhouse, 1970—, lecturer in history of art, 1972-93, reader in the history of architecture, 1993—. Member of Historic Buildings Council for England, 1980-84, and Historic Buildings Advisory Committee of the Historic Buildings and Monuments Commission for England, 1984-95.

MEMBER: Society of Antiquaries (fellow), Beefsteak Club, Travellers Club, University Pitt Club.

AWARDS, HONORS: Alice Davis Hitchcock Medallion, Society of Architectural Historians of Great Britain, 1975, for The Life and Work of C. R. Cockerell, R.A.; Litt.D., Trinity Hall, Cambridge, 1994.

WRITINGS:

Thomas Hope, 1769-1831, and the Neo-Classical Idea, J. Murray (London), 1968, Transatlantic (Albuquerque, NM), 1970.
(Editor and author of introduction) Sale Catalogues of Libraries of Eminent Persons, Volume 4: Architects, Mansell, 1972.
The Life and Work of C. R. Cockerell, R.A., A. Zwemmer, 1974.
Morality and Architecture: The Development of a Theme in Architectural History and Theory from the Gothic Revival to the Modern Movement, Oxford University Press (London), 1977, University of Chicago Press (Chicago, IL), 1984.
The Triumph of the Classical, Cambridge Architecture, 1804-34, Cambridge University Press (Cambridge, England), 1977.
English Architecture: A Concise History, Thames & Hudson (London), 1979.
The Rise of Architectural History, Eastview Editions, 1980.
(With Robin Middleton) Neo-Classical and Nineteenth-Century Architecture, Abrams (New York City), 1980.
(With Hugh Montgomery-Massingberd) The London Ritz: A Social and Architectural History, Aurum, 1980.
The English Vision: The Picturesque in Architecture, Landscape and Garden Design, Harper (New York City), 1982.
Athenian Stuart: Pioneer of the Greek Revival, Allen & Unwin (London), 1982.
Regency: A Guide and Gazetteer, Barrie & Jenkins (London), 1982.
The Royal Interiors of Regency England: From Watercolors First Published by W. H. Pyne in 1817-1820, Vendome, 1984.
(With J. D'Ormesson, Montgomery-Massingberd, P. J. Remy, F. Grendel, and M. Walter) Grand Hotel: The Golden Age of Palace Hotels—An Architectural and Social History, Vendome, 1984.
(With A. Ratcliff, N. Thompson, and J. Mills) A House in Town, 22 Arlington Street: Its Owners and Builders, Batsford, 1984.
Peterhouse, 1284-1984: An Architectural Record, Peterhouse, 1984.

A History of Western Architecture, Thames & Hudson, 1986.

(With Tilman Mellinghoff) *German Architecture and the Classical Ideal, 1740-1840,* MIT Press (Cambridge, MA), 1987.

Sir John Soane: Enlightenment Thought and the Royal Academy Lectures, Cambridge University Press, 1996.

Also co-author of *Burke's and Savill's Guide to Country Houses,* Volume 3: *East Anglia,* 1981.

Some of Watkin's works have been translated into Italian, Spanish, German, French, Dutch and Japanese.

BIOGRAPHICAL/CRITICAL SOURCES:

PERIODICALS

Antiquaries Journal, number 2, 1987, p. 428.
Burlington Magazine, January, 1988, p. 42.
Choice, December, 1987, p. 612; March, 1988, p. 1054.
Design Book Review, summer, 1989, p. 33.
New York Times Book Review, December 4, 1969.
Reference and Research Book News, fall, 1987, p. 26.
Spectator, December 31, 1977; November 13, 1982; December 5, 1987, p. 37; February 6, 1988, p. 30.
Times Literary Supplement, August 1, 1975; February 17, 1978; July 25, 1980; January 7, 1983; February 13, 1987.

* * *

WEAVER, William Woys 1947-

PERSONAL: Born March 13, 1947, in West Chester, PA; son of H. William (a business executive) and Alameda (Woys) Weaver; married Lynn Agnes Beebe (an architectural historian), August 29, 1970 (divorced, 1973). *Education:* University of Virginia, B.A., 1969, M.A., 1973; graduate study at International Center for Palladian Studies, Vicenza, Italy, 1971. *Politics:* Independent. *Religion:* Society of Friends. *Avocational interests:* Collecting culinaria, organic gardening, travel, music.

ADDRESSES: P.O. Box 131, Paoli, PA 19301. *Agent*—Blanche Schlessinger, 433 Old Gulph Road, Penn Valley, PA 19072.

CAREER: Dover Publications, Inc., New York City, copy writer, 1972-74; Ametek, Inc. (a manufacturer of industrial components), Paoli, PA, director of product information, 1974-77; writer, 1977—.

MEMBER: International Conference for Ethnological Food Research, American Institute of Wine and Food (board member), Authors Guild, Friends Historical Association (life member), Pennsylvania German Society, Culinary Historians of Boston, Seed Savers Exchange (life member), Historic Foodways Society of the Delaware Valley (president), The Atheneum of Philadelphia, Culinary Historians of New York, Chaine de Rotisseurs.

AWARDS, HONORS: Gold Medal for graphic design from Graphic Arts Association, 1986, for *Thirty-five Receipts from "The Larder Invaded;"* Jane Grigson Award for literary and historical writing, for *Pennsylvania Dutch Country Cooking.*

WRITINGS:

(Contributor) Alexander Fenton and Trefor Owen, editors, *Food in Perspective,* John Donald Publishers, 1981.

(Contributor) Karl Scherer, editor, *Pfaelzer/Palatines: Festschrift fuer Fritz Braun,* Heimatstelle Pfaelz, 1981.

(Editor and author of introduction) *A Quaker Woman's Cookbook: The Domestic Cookery of Elizabeth Ellicott Lea,* University of Pennsylvania Press (Philadelphia), 1982.

Sauerkraut Yankees: Pennsylvania-German Foods and Foodways, University of Pennsylvania Press, 1983.

Thirty-five Receipts from "The Larder Invaded," Library Company of Philadelphia/Historical Society of Pennsylvania, 1986.

America Eats, Museum of American Folk Art/Harper & Row (New York City), 1989.

The Christmas Cook, HarperCollins (New York City), 1990.

Pennsylvania Dutch Country Cooking, Abbeville Press (New York City), 1993.

Epicure with Hoe, Holt (New York City), in press.

Contributor to culinary publications, including *Petits Propos Culinaires, The Pleasures of Cooking,* and *Journal of Gastronomy.*

WORK IN PROGRESS: Food and Drink in Medieval Poland, for University of Pennsylvania Press; *The Painter's Palate;* "three works of fiction, and a book about the deconstructed (!) menu."

SIDELIGHTS: William Woys Weaver described himself to *CA* as "one of only a handful of food historians in the United States—and perhaps the only one who does it full time." A tenth-generation Pennsylvania German, according to Deirdre Bair of the *Pennsylvania Gazette,* Weaver has written extensively about Pennsylvania-German cooking. His *A Quaker Woman's Cookbook: The Domestic Cookery of Elizabeth Ellicott Lea* reprints a long-lost mid-nineteenth-century text by Elizabeth Ellicott Lea. Weaver's edition of Lea's cookbook, with a new introduction and annotated glossary, restores "to the body of American food history a work that should take its place as one of first-rank importance," asserted Grace Kirschenbaum in the *Los Angeles Times.* A *Journal of the American Dietetic Association* reviewer pointed out that *A Quaker Woman's Cookbook* is "one of the first attempts by an American culinary historian to analyze the cookery of a particular social group"; writing in the magazine *Cuisine,* Richard Sax called Lea's collected recipes as presented by Weaver "a valuable folk document." And while Weaver intended his edition of Lea's work to serve as a "source and document for early American food research," according to Kirschenbaum, he nevertheless insists that "anyone with a flair for experimental cookery will soon discover that many of Elizabeth Lea's recipes can be reproduced without difficulty in kitchens today."

Weaver again explored Pennsylvania culinary history in his next book, *Sauerkraut Yankees: Pennsylvania-German Foods and Foodways.* Named one of the best cookbooks of 1983 by *Cuisine, Sauerkraut Yankees* is based on an 1848 Pennsylvania-German cookbook called *Die Geschickte Hausfrau.* Bair wrote that in restoring and expanding this nineteenth-century bestseller, Weaver created "a usable contemporary cookbook, a model of historical accuracy, and a compendium of folklore that is as fascinating to read as a good novel."

Weaver told *CA:* "I always knew I would be a writer, but I came to it in fits and starts. The late Alexandra Tolstoi passed briefly through my life when I was a teenager. She read some of my short stories and urged me to go forward. But as self-identity is the most important part of writing, I had to discover myself before I could discover other things.

"The study of food came as an outgrowth of my interest in architecture and material culture, and also because I am an incurable gardener who loves to eat the things he grows. Since food has so much to do with identity, I found it a fascinating area of exploration. Like architecture, food has structure, but in many ways the subject is a new frontier for American scholarship. That challenge has kept me busy since 1977. Food and the people who eat it will always be an enjoyable scholarly pursuit for me. On the other hand, I will not consider my evolution neatly rounded off until there are also a number of novels behind me. The creative instinct is unshakable."

BIOGRAPHICAL/CRITICAL SOURCES:

PERIODICALS

Americana, January, 1984.
Cuisine, July, 1983.
Early American Life, April, 1984.
Food and Wine, July, 1983.
Journal of the American Dietetic Association, September, 1983.
Los Angeles Times, January 13, 1983.
Pennsylvania Gazette, December, 1983.

*   *   *

WEINSTEIN, Grace W(ohlner)

PERSONAL: Born in New York, NY; daughter of David (chief of property department of New York State Insurance Bureau) and Esther (Lobel) Wohlner; married Stephen D. Weinstein (an architect); children: Lawrence, Janet. *Education:* Cornell University, B.A.

ADDRESSES: Office—8 Brayton St., Englewood, NJ 07631.

CAREER: Freelance writer. Appears frequently on radio and television, including regular weekly *Daytime* show on Hearst/ABC Video Network (cable) as money expert. Member of consumer advisory council, Federal Reserve Board, 1993-96; trustee, Consumer Financial Education Foundation, 1994—; member of board, Copyright Clearance Center, 1995—. Lecturer and consultant on financial topics, including personal money management, children and money and pre-retirement planning.

MEMBER: Society of Magazine Writers (now American Society of Journalists and Authors; vice-president, 1978-79; president, 1979-80, 1980-81), Authors Guild, Authors League of America, Council of Writers Organizations (co-founder; first president, 1979-82).

WRITINGS:

Children and Money: A Guide for Parents, Charterhouse, 1975, revised edition published as *Children and Money: A Parents' Guide,* New American Library/Plume (New York City), 1985.

Retire Tomorrow—Plan Today, Dell (New York City), 1976.

A Teacher's World, McGraw (New York City), 1977.

Money of Your Own, Dutton (New York City), 1977.

People Study People: The Story of Psychology, Dutton, 1979.

Life Plans: Looking forward to Retirement, Holt (New York City), 1979.

The Lifetime Book of Money Management (Book-of-the-Month Club alternate selection), New American Library (New York City), 1983, revised edition, Visible Ink Press (Detroit), 1993.

Men, Women and Money: New Roles, New Rules, New American Library/Plume, 1986.

The Bottom Line: Inside Accounting Today, New American Library, 1987.

Financial Savvy for the Self-Employed, Holt, 1995.

Author of monthly columns, "You and Retirement," *Elks Magazine,* 1975-87, and "Your Money," *Good Housekeeping,* 1979-95; author of column "Grace Weinstein on Your Money," Universal Press Syndicate, 1987-89, and "News for You," *Investor's Business Daily,* 1995—. Contributor of articles to numerous magazines, including *McCall's, Self, Money, House Beautiful, Ladies' Home Journal, Woman's Day, Kiplinger's Personal Finance, Barron's, Parade, Time, Consumer Reports,* and *Parents' Magazine.*

BIOGRAPHICAL/CRITICAL SOURCES:

PERIODICALS

New York Times, September 29, 1985.

Reference and Research Book News, May, 1994, p. 26.

Washington Post Book World, August 26, 1979.

WENDER, Paul H. 1934-

PERSONAL: Born May 12, 1934, in New York, NY; son of Louis (a physician) and Luba (Kibrick) Wender; married Dorothea Schmidt (divorced); married Frances Burger; children: (first marriage) Leslie and Jocelyn (twins), Melissa. *Education:* Harvard University, A.B., 1955; Columbia University, M.D., 1959. *Avocational interests:* Reading, skiing, flute, piano, chess.

ADDRESSES: Office—Department of Psychiatry, University of Utah, College of Medicine, Salt Lake City, UT 84132.

CAREER: Barnes Hospital, St. Louis, MO, intern, 1959-60; Massachusetts Mental Health Center, Boston, resident in adult psychiatry, 1960-62; St. Elizabeth's Hospital, Washington, DC, resident, 1962-63; Johns Hopkins Hospital, Johns Hopkins University, Baltimore, MD, fellow in child psychiatry, 1962-63, instructor in child psychiatry, 1967-68, assistant professor of pediatrics and psychiatry, 1968-73; University of Utah, Salt Lake City, professor of psychiatry, 1973—. Served as a senior surgeon in the U.S. Public Health Service, 1962-64. Research psychiatrist at National Institutes of Health, 1967-73.

MEMBER: American Psychiatric Association, American Academy of Child Psychiatry, American Psychopathological Association, American College of Neuropsychopharmacology, Psychiatric Research Society (president, 1977-78), Utah Psychiatric Association, Phi Beta Kappa, Alpha Omega Alpha.

AWARDS, HONORS: National Institute of Mental Health fellowship, 1964-66; Hofheimer Award from the American Psychiatric Association, 1974, for psychiatric research; University of Utah, Salt Lake City, distinguished professor of psychiatry, 1990.

WRITINGS:

Minimal Brain Dysfunction in Children, Wiley (New York City), 1971.

The Hyperactive Child, Crown (New York City), 1973, revised and enlarged edition (with Esther H. Wender) published as *The Hyperactive Child and the Learning Disabled Child: A Handbook for Parents,* 1978.

(With Donald F. Klein) *Mind, Mood, and Medicine: A Guide to the New Biopsychiatry,* Farrar, Straus (New York City), 1981.

The Hyperactive Child, Adolescent and Adult: Attention Deficit Disorder through the Lifespan, Oxford University Press (New York City), 1987.

(With Klein) *Do You Have a Depressive Illness?,* Plume Press (New York City), 1988.

(With Klein) *Understanding Depression,* Oxford University Press, 1993.

Attention-Deficit Hyperactivity in Adults, Oxford University Press, 1995.

Contributor to books, including, *The Transmission of Schizophrenia,* edited by D. Rosenthal and Seymour S. Kety, Pergamon (Elmsford, NY), 1968; *Genetics and Psychopathology,* edited by Rosenthal, R. Fieve, and H. Brill, Johns Hopkins University Press (Baltimore, MD), 1976; *Origin, Prevention and Treatment of Affective Disorders,* edited by M. Schou and E. Stomgren, Academic Press (New York City), 1979; and Harold I. Kaplan and Benjamin J. Sadock, *Comprehensive Textbook of Psychiatry V,* Williams & Wilkins (Baltimore, MD), 1988. Contributor of articles to numerous journals, including *International Journal of Mental Health, American Journal of Psychiatry, American Journal of Orthopsychiatry, Child Development, Medical Opinion, Life Sciences,* and *Pediatric News.* Member of editorial board of *Psychiatry* and *Psychiatry Research.*

WORK IN PROGRESS: Research on the role of genetics in the development of psychiatric illnesses and on the mechanism and utilization of drugs for the treatment of psychiatric conditions.

SIDELIGHTS: In *Mind, Mood and Medicine: A Guide to the New Biopsychiatry* Paul H. Wender and Donald F. Klein support the contention that many forms of mental illness have a biological base and should therefore be treated with medication rather than relying exclusively on psychotherapy. Among the treatments advocated by the authors is the administration of antidepressant drugs to people suffering from depression and separation anxiety. In *New Republic,* British psychoanalyst Anthony Storr observes that Wender and Klein's position "illustrates an approach to mental illness which, though familiar in Great Britain, is less so in the U.S." "In the U.S.," explains Storr, "psychoanalysis has been the dominant force in psychiatry for over 40 years." In praise of the authors' balanced presentation, Storr comments: "It is one of the virtues of this book that the authors recognize that one or another form of psychotherapy may be the treatment of choice in certain types of mental distress. Moreover, even in those conditions that are best treated initially with drugs,

the authors recognize that psychotherapy may and should play an important subsidiary role."

Wender told *CA:* "Klein and I were prompted to write *Mind, Mood, and Medicine* by a number of motivations, one of which was our awareness of the vast discrepancy between the knowledge of the psychiatric cognoscenti and intelligent laymen, regarding the roll of biological factors in psychological distress. The well-read layman has been led to believe that most human unhappiness results from wrong attitudes, wrong values, and wrong behavior, which in turn are the derivatives of the manner in which he or she was raised. Not so! Current evidence suggests that between 15 and 30 percent of the population has psychological disorders that have genetic contributions and are probably caused through abnormalities in biochemistry. The differences between illnesses so produced and those produced by faulty learning and realistic unhappiness (existential problems) are not widely recognized. As a result, suffering individuals receive inappropriate treatment.

"Our intention in writing the book was to present the intelligent layman with the very powerful evidence that much psychological distress is genetic in origin and biochemically mediated. We wish not only to inform the individual of the status of the field, but, perhaps, to allow him to discriminate between disorder, dislearning, and realistic problems. In addition, we wish him or her to develop a feeling for the way biopsychiatrists think, how their thinking leads to hard scientific experiments, and how this differs from much of the airy philosophical speculation that has beclouded the field."

BIOGRAPHICAL/CRITICAL SOURCES:

PERIODICALS

New Republic, October 31, 1981.
Voice Literary Supplement, October, 1981.

*　　*　　*

WETTENHALL, Roger (Llewellyn) 1931-

PERSONAL: Born February 4, 1931, in Hobart, Australia; son of Ralph Henry (a shipping clerk) and Dorothy Mabel (a dental nurse; maiden name, Rumbold) Wettenhall; married, 1955 (divorced, 1974); remarried; children: Irene, Lynn, Dean. *Edu-*

cation: University of Tasmania, Diploma in Public Administration, 1955, M.A., 1959; Australian National University, Ph.D., 1962.

ADDRESSES: Home—12 Carmichael St., Deakin, Australian Capital Territory 2600, Australia. *Office*—University of Canberra, Belconnen, Australian Capital Territory 2616, Australia.

CAREER: Australian Commonwealth Public Service, personnel cadet in Hobart, 1948-51, personnel officer in Adelaide and Hobart, 1952-59; Australian National University, Canberra, research scholar, 1959-61; University of Tasmania, Hobart, lecturer, 1961-65, senior lecturer, 1966-69, reader in political science, 1969-71; University of Canberra, Belconnen, Australia, head of School of Administrative Studies, 1971-85, 1990-94, college fellow in administrative studies, 1985-90, professor of public administration emeritus, 1994—. Hallsworth research fellow at University of Manchester, 1964-65; visiting scholar at State University of New York at Albany, autumn, 1978, University of Southern California, autumn, 1985, and European Centre for Development Policy Management, 1990-93. Consultant to numerous governmental bodies, including Advisory Council of Intergovernment Relations, Australian Archives, and Royal Commission on Australian Government Administration. External examiner to Universite Brunei Darussalam and University of Hong Kong, 1993—.

MEMBER: International Association of Schools and Institutes of Administration, Royal Institute of Public Administration (national fellow; president of Australian Capital Territory Group, 1973-75; member of national council, 1989-95), Eastern Regional Organization for Public Administration.

AWARDS, HONORS: Haldane Silver Medal from Royal Institute of Public Adminstration, 1965, for essay "The Recoup Concept in Public Enterprise"; Outstanding Public Administrationist Award, Eastern Regional Organization for Public Administration, 1995.

WRITINGS:

Railway Management and Politics in Victoria, 1856-1906, Australian Capital Territory Group, Royal Institute of Public Administration, 1961.

A Guide to Tasmania Government Administration, Platypus Publications, 1968.

The Iron Road and the State: W. M. Acworth as Scholar, Critic, and Reformer, University of Tasmania, 1970.

Bushfire Disaster: An Australian Community in Crisis, Angus & Robertson, 1975.

(Editor with Martin Painter) *The First Thousand Days of Labor,* Canberra College of Advanced Education, 1975.

(Editor with G. R. Curnow) *Understanding Public Administration,* Allen & Unwin, 1981.

(Editor with J. M. Power and J. A. Halligan) *Local Government Systems of Australia,* Australian Government Publishing Service, 1981.

(Editor with A. Kouzmin and J. R. Nethercote) *Australian Commonwealth Administration,* 4 volumes, Canberra College of Advanced Education, 1984-92.

Organising Government: The Problem of Ministries and Departments, Croom Helm, 1986.

Public Enterprise and National Development: Selected Essays, Australian Capital Territory Group, Royal Australian Institute of Public Administration, 1987.

(Editor with C. O Nuallain) *Getting Together in Public Enterprise,* International Institute of Administrative Sciences, 1988.

(Editor with Nuallain) *Public Enterprise: The Management Challenge,* International Institute of Administrative Sciences, 1988.

(Editor with Nuallain) *Public Enterprise Performance Evaluation: Seven Country Studies,* International Institute of Administrative Sciences, 1990.

(Editor with J. Corkery and Nuallain) *Public Enterprise Boards: What They Are and What They Do,* Asian Journal of Public Administration and International Association of Schools and Institutes of Administration, 1994.

Also editor with David Moore of *Keeping the Peace: Police Accountability and Oversight,* University of Canberra and Royal Institute of Public Administration. Contributor to political science, public administration, and current affairs journals. Editor of *Australian Journal of Public Administration,* 1989-95; member of editorial committee of *International Review of Administrative Sciences, Asian Journal of Public Administration,* and *Journal of Indian Institute of Public Enterprise.*

SIDELIGHTS: Roger Wettenhall told *CA:* "As a former public servant with academic preparation mainly in political science, I have been concerned to further the systematic study of public administration, which I believe has too long been relegated to a position of minor importance by the older academic disciplines. Today the need is very great, as forces championing 'the market' and *private* sector methods and traditions are seriously weakening the capacity of public sectors to deliver vital community services."

*   *   *

WHITEFORD, Andrew H(unter)   1913-

PERSONAL: Born September 1, 1913, in Winnipeg, Manitoba, Canada; came to United States, 1923, naturalized citizen, 1928; son of John (a bricklayer) and Janet (Hunter) Whiteford; married Marion Bonneville Salmon, September 2, 1939; children: John Hunter, Michael Bonneville, Linda McMillan Uzell, Laurie Andrea Richards. *Education:* Beloit College, B.A., 1937; University of Chicago, M.A., 1943, Ph.D., 1950. *Religion:* Unitarian.

*ADDRESSES: Home—*447 Camino Monte Vista, Santa Fe, NM 87501.

CAREER: Works Progress Administration, research supervisor, department of anthropology, University of Tennessee, Knoxville, 1938-42; Beloit College, Beloit, WI, 1942-74, began as instructor, became professor of anthropology, George L. Collie Professor of Anthropology, 1955-74, professor emeritus, 1974—, chairman of department, 1944-73, director of Logan Museum of Anthropology, 1946-74; research fellow, committee on social relations, University of Chicago, 1943. Visiting professor, Michigan State University, 1975, 1976, 1979; visiting professor of art history, University of New Mexico, 1980; Faye Laverne Bumpass Lecturer, Texas Tech University, 1981; Research Curator, School of American Research, 1981-84; Wheelwright Museum of the American Indian, research associate, and member of board of trustees, 1982-84; research associate, New Mexico Museum of Indian Art and Culture, 1982—; member of board of directors, Wisconsin Archaeological Survey. Member of advisory board, American Indian Art Magazine, Ellis Museum at Ghost Ranch, NM. Lecturer and consultant on American prehistory for many symposiums and exhibitions at universities and museums throughout the United States.

MEMBER: American Anthropological Association (fellow), Native American Art Study Association, Society for Urban Anthropology, Society for Humanistic Anthropology, Central States Anthropological Society (president, 1964-65), Wisconsin Anthropological Society (first president, board member), Phi Beta Kappa, Sigma Xi, Omicron Delta Kappa, Pi Epsilon Delta, Beta Theta Pi.

AWARDS, HONORS: Research grants from Wenner-Gren Foundation, 1950, 1969-70, 1974, Social Science Research Council, 1951, American Council of Learned Societies-Social Science Research Council, 1962, Cullister Foundation, 1965, and National Institute of Mental Health, 1970; National Science Foundation faculty fellow, 1961, research grant, 1966; Honorary L.L.D. from Beloit College, 1981; Andrew Hunter Whiteford fund established to provide financial aid to students engaged in research, Logan Museum of Anthropology, Beloit College, 1986.

WRITINGS:

(With wife, Marion Whiteford) *How Sandy Squirrel Got His Tail* (juvenile), Follett, 1945.
Folk Music of Colombia (record album and booklet), Folkways Records (New York City), 1954.
Two Cities of Latin America: A Comparative Description of Social Classes (first published as bulletin of Logan Museum of Anthropology), Doubleday (New York City), 1964.
(Editor) *A Reappraisal of Economic Development: Perspectives for Cooperative Research,* Aldine (Hawthorne, NY), 1967.
North American Indian Arts (young adult book), Western Publishing (New York City), 1970, revised, 1990.
An Andean City at Mid-Century: A Traditional Urban Society, Michigan State University (East Lansing, MI), 1977.
(With Barbara Lenssen and Susan McGreevy) *Lullabies from the Earth: Cradles of Native North America,* The Wheelwright Museum of the American Indian (Santa Fe, NM), 1980.
(With McGreevy) *Translating Tradition: Basketry Arts of the San Juan Paiutes,* Wheelwright Museum of the American Indian (Santa Fe, NM), 1985.
Southwestern Indian Baskets: Their History and Their Makers, School of American Research (Santa Fe, NM), 1988.

OTHER

Contributor to numerous books and journals in the field of anthropology, including *American Antiquity,*

Americas, Choice, Christian Century, American Indian Art, and *American Anthropologist.*

WORK IN PROGRESS: "The Southwest" and "California," chapters for the catalog of the Eugene and Clare Thaw collection of American Indian art, Abrams, 1996; "Foliate Designs in Great Lakes Beadwork," for *American Indian Art Magazine.*

*   *   *

WILDE, Larry 1928-

PERSONAL: Surname originally Wildman; born February 6, 1928, in Jersey City, NJ; son of Selig and Gertrude (Schwartzwald) Wildman; married Maryruth Poulos, June 2, 1974. *Education:* University of Miami, B.A., 1952. *Politics:* Liberal. *Religion:* Jewish. *Avocational interests:* Golf, skiing, cooking (with salads as the specialty of the house).

ADDRESSES: Home—25470 Canada Dr., Carmel, CA 93923. *Agent*—Jane Jordan Browne, 410 South Michigan Ave., Chicago, IL 60605.

CAREER: Comedian, performing in night clubs, on stage, and in television. Made professional appearances while attending the University of Miami, has since performed in more than nine hundred cities in forty-nine states, as well as Australia, Canada, the Caribbean, and Europe, sharing the bill with such stars as Vikki Carr, Jack Jones, Diahann Carroll, Ann Margaret, Debbie Reynolds, Pat Boone, and Andy Williams; night club engagements include the Copacabana in New York, Harrah's at Lake Tahoe, Desert Inn in Las Vegas, and Latin Casino in Philadelphia. Has appeared on stage in *One Damn Thing after Another* (revue), *Send Me No Flowers* (comedy play), *Of Thee I Sing* (musical), and *Candide* (musical drama). Has appeared on television programs, including *The Tonight Show, The Today Show, The Merv Griffin Show,* and on situation comedies, including *The Mary Tyler Moore Show* and *Sanford and Son.* Has appeared in commercials for State Farm Insurance, Exxon, Chevrolet, Wrigley Gum, and others. Lecturer on comedy at universities, including University of Southern California, University of California, University of Miami, and New York University. Conducts humor workshops for corporate executives and public speakers. Founder of National Humor Month. *Military service:* U.S. Marine Corps,

Special Services, 1946-48; writer, director, and actor in service musicals and variety shows.

MEMBER: PEN (president, Los Angeles Center, 1981-83), Screen Actors Guild, American Federation of Television and Radio Artists, National Speakers Association.

WRITINGS:

The Great Comedians Talk about Comedy (compendium of taped interviews), Citadel (Secaucus, NJ), 1968, revised edition published as *The Great Comedians,* 1973.
How the Great Comedy Writers Create Laughter, Nelson-Hall (Chicago), 1976.
The Complete Book of Ethnic Humor, Corwin (Los Angeles), 1978.
The Larry Wilde Book of Limericks, Bantam (New York City), 1982.
The Larry Wilde Library of Laughter, Jester Press, 1988.
The Larry Wilde Treasury of Laughter, Jester Press, 1992.
Dimwits, Dweezils and Dumbbells, Pinnacle Books (New York City), 1996.

"OFFICIAL" JOKE BOOKS

The Official Polish/Italian Joke Book, Pinnacle Books, 1973.
The Official Jewish/Irish Joke Book, Pinnacle Books, 1974.
The Official Virgins/Sex Maniacs Joke Book, Pinnacle Books, 1975.
The Official Black Folks/White Folks Joke Book, Pinnacle Books, 1975.
More of the Official Polish/Italian Joke Book, Pinnacle Books, 1975.
The Official Democrat/Republican Joke Book, Pinnacle Books, 1976.
The Official Religious/Not So Religious Joke Book, Pinnacle Books, 1976.
The Official Ethnic Calendar for 1977, Pinnacle Books, 1977.
The Official Smart Kids/Dumb Parents Joke Book, Pinnacle Books, 1977.
The Official Golfers Joke Book, Pinnacle Books, 1977.
The Last Official Polish Joke Book, Pinnacle Books, 1977.
The Official Dirty Joke Book, Pinnacle Books, 1977.
The Official Cat Lovers/Dog Lovers Joke Book, Pinnacle Books, 1978.

The Last Official Italian Joke Book, Pinnacle Books, 1978.

More of the Official Jewish/Irish Joke Book, Pinnacle Books, 1979.

The Official Book of Sick Jokes, Pinnacle Books, 1979.

More of the Official Smart Kids/Dumb Parents Joke Book, Pinnacle Books, 1979.

More of the Official Democratic/Republican Joke Book, Pinnacle Books, 1979.

The Official Bedroom/Bathroom Joke Book, Pinnacle Books, 1980.

The Last Official Jewish Joke Book, Bantam, 1980.

More of the Official Sex Maniacs Joke Book, Bantam, 1981.

The Official Doctors Joke Book, Bantam, 1981.

The Official Lawyers Joke Book, Bantam, 1982.

The Last Official Sex Maniacs Joke Book, Bantam, 1982.

The Last Official Irish Joke Book, Bantam, 1983.

The Absolutely Last Official Polish Joke Book, Bantam, 1983.

The Last Official Smart Kids Joke Book, Bantam, 1983.

The Official Rednecks Joke Book, Bantam, 1984.

The Official Politicians Joke Book, Bantam, 1984.

The Official Book of John Jokes, Bantam, 1985.

The Official Sports Maniacs Joke Book, Bantam, 1985.

The Absolutely Last Official Sex Maniacs Joke Book, Bantam, 1985.

The Official Executives Joke Book, Bantam, 1986.

More of the Official Doctors Joke Book, Bantam, 1986.

The Official All-American Joke Book, Bantam, 1988.

The Official W.A.S.P. Joke Book, Bantam, 1988.

(With Steve Wozniak) *The Official Computer Freaks Joke Book,* Bantam, 1989.

The Official Locker Room Joke Book, Bantam, 1991.

The Official Merriest Christmas Humor Joke Book, Bantam, 1991.

The Official Golf Lovers Joke Book, Bantam, 1992.

"ULTIMATE" JOKE BOOKS

The Ultimate Jewish Joke Book, Bantam, 1986.

The Ultimate Lawyers Joke Book, Bantam, 1987.

The Ultimate Sex Maniacs Joke Book, Bantam, 1989.

The Ultimate Ethnic Humor Joke Book, Bantam, 1989.

The Ultimate Pet Lovers Joke Book, Bantam, 1990.

OTHER

Has recorded albums, including *The Joker Is Wild,* Dot Records, and *The Official Polish/Italian Comedy Album,* Samada Records. Contributor to trade publications, including *Professional Speaker* and to periodicals, including *Coronet, Gallery, Genesis,* and *Penthouse. The Great Comedians Talk about Comedy* has been serialized in *TV Guide* and in newspapers.

WORK IN PROGRESS: A novel; more humor books.

SIDELIGHTS: "You can hardly walk into a bookstore these days without coming upon a new collection of jokes by Larry Wilde," writes Clarence Peterson in the *Chicago Tribune.* Wilde's books have sold over eleven million copies and are available in fifty-three countries. In a *Publishers Weekly* article, Wilde explains his popularity: "Really offensive ethnic jokes may not be exactly tasteful, but from time immemorial this sort of comedy has met a primal need, whether it be for the pure fun of it or because it releases some basic tension and fear in man. The ethnic joke has become America's most popular form of wisecracking." While ethnic humor often comes under attack, Wilde feels it will survive. "Ethnic humor will stay with us in spite of those who think of it as being 'sick, mean-spirited and sacreligious,'" he adds. "We are a nation of many peoples from many lands, and if we have learned anything about the human spirit it is that in order to survive we must laugh at ourselves."

Wilde once told *CA:* "I love humor. Making people laugh has been a significant part of my life for over thirty years. I like hearing that a hospital patient enjoyed one of my joke books or that someone needing a lift got big giggles from some of my gags. When I learn that an aspiring comedian or comedy writer was motivated or influenced by having read one of my serious works on humor it makes me proud. I feel I've made some small contribution to the potential of future professionals."

Wilde's National Humor Month commences each April to "spotlight the importance of laughter in our lives." He lectures to corporations, associations, and healthcare professionals on how humor can overcome stress and tension in the workplace.

BIOGRAPHICAL/CRITICAL SOURCES:

PERIODICALS

Chicago Tribune, July 7, 1987.
Publishers Weekly, November 25, 1983.

*   *   *

WILKINSON, Brenda 1946-

PERSONAL: Born January 1, 1946, in Moultrie, GA; daughter of Malcolm (in construction; deceased) and Ethel (a nurse; maiden name, Anderson) Scott; separated; children: Kim, Lori. *Education:* Attended Hunter College of the City University of New York.

ADDRESSES: Home—123 West 104 St., New York, NY 10023. *Office*—Board of Global Ministries, 475 Riverside Dr., Room 1524, New York, NY 10017.

CAREER: Poet and author of books for children. Gives poetry readings.

MEMBER: Authors Guild of Authors League of America.

AWARDS, HONORS: National Book Award nomination, 1976, for *Ludell; Ludell and Willie* was named one of the outstanding children's books of the year by the *New York Times* and a best book for young adults by the American Library Association, both 1977.

WRITINGS:

BOOKS FOR CHILDREN

Ludell (first book in trilogy), Harper (New York City), 1975.
Ludell and Willie (second book in trilogy), Harper, 1976.
Ludell's New York Time (third book in trilogy), Harper, 1980.
Not Separate, Not Equal, Harper, 1987.
Jesse Jackson: Still Fighting for the Dream, Silver Burdett (Morristown, NJ), 1990.
Definitely Cool, Scholastic, Inc. (New York City), 1993.

OTHER

Also contributor of poetry and short stories to periodicals.

SIDELIGHTS: Brenda Wilkinson's "Ludell" trilogy has been praised for its accurate, yet sensitive and compassionate portrayal of rural black life. These books—*Ludell, Ludell and Willie,* and *Ludell's New York Time*—follow the life of a poor, young, black child growing up in Waycross, Georgia, in the late 1950s and early 1960s.

In the first volume of this trilogy, Ludell Wilson is left in the care of her grandmother after her mother moves to New York City in search of a better life. L. W. Lindsay writes in the *Christian Science Monitor* that *Ludell* is a "beautiful little novel about a sensitive young girl whose individuality and talent blossom in spite of the abyssmal circumstances under which she has to live and go to school." Addison Gayle notes in the *Nation* that "the universe of this novel is alive with innocence, which emanates from the community . . . and it is highlighted by the love and care that each black person exhibits toward the other—characteristics of black life from the days of slavery until the present time." "Unlike many novels of the South, 'Ludell' is not a tragedy in any sense, not any angry book, nor is it soft-centered," remarks Cynthia King in the *New York Times Book Review.* "By the end of the book I liked Ludell. I was glad to have known her and her friends."

Wilkinson's second book, *Ludell and Willie,* tells the story of Ludell's teenage years, when she falls in love, starts to plan for the future, and experiences the death of her grandmother. Ludell must leave her love, Willie, and her home in Georgia and live with her mother in New York City. *Publishers Weekly* calls *Ludell and Willie* "a brilliant novel." In the *New York Times Book Review,* Georgess McHargue comments that "we should be grateful to Ludell and Willie, their families and friends, for living and talking like themselves, thus transcending weighty generalizations about black teen-agers, Southern mores or social justice. I'm looking forward to the next book about Ludell."

Ludell's New York Time, the last book in Wilkinson's trilogy, finds Ludell unhappily trying to cope with her separation from her love, while getting reacquainted with her mother, and adjusting to her vastly different life in New York City. "Wilkinson has crafted a special kind of love story with wideranging appeal," believes Jerrie Norris. Writing in the *Christian Science Monitor*, Norris comments that "the clash of Ludell's Waycross background with the Harlem of the '60s reveals the social fabric of both places. [Wilkinson writes] with a keen eye for detail and a carefully paced presentation of events to totally involve us with Ludell and her life."

BIOGRAPHICAL/CRITICAL SOURCES:

PERIODICALS

Christian Science Monitor, November 5, 1975; April 14, 1980.
Ms., August, 1980.
Nation, April 17, 1976.
New York Times Book Review, February 22, 1976; August 3, 1980.
Publishers Weekly, February 7, 1977.

* * *

WILLEY, Margaret 1950-

PERSONAL: Born November 5, 1950, in Chicago, IL; daughter of Foster L. (an artist) and Barbara (Pistorius) Willey; married Richard Joanisse (a professor), 1980; children: Chloe. *Education:* Grand Valley State College, B.Ph., B.A., 1975; Bowling Green State University, M.F.A., 1979.

ADDRESSES: Home—431 Grant, Grand Haven, MI 49417.

CAREER: Writer.

AWARDS, HONORS: American Library Association best books for young adults listings, 1983, for *The Bigger Book of Lydia*, 1986, for *Finding David Dolores*, 1988, for *If Not for You*, and 1990, for *Saving Lenny;* Creative Artist Grant, Michigan Arts Council, 1984, 1988, and 1995; Recommended Books for Reluctant YA Readers selection, Young Adult Services Division, 1989, for *If Not for You;* Best of the Best for Children listing, American Library Association, 1993, for *Finding David Dolores.*

WRITINGS:

YOUNG ADULT FICTION

The Bigger Book of Lydia, Harper (New York City), 1983.
Finding David Dolores, Harper, 1986.
If Not for You, Harper, 1988.
Saving Lenny, Bantam (New York City), 1990.
The Melinda Zone, Bantam, 1993.
Facing the Music, Delacorte (New York City), 1996.

Also contributor of short stories to *Redbook, Good Housekeeping, Quarry West, Sou'wester, Heresies,* and literary journals.

SIDELIGHTS: "The success of Margaret Willey's books for young adults is due at least in part to her skill at presenting totally believable characters who must struggle to resolve their problems in her coming-of-age dilemmas," remarks Jan Tyler in *Twentieth-Century Young Adult Writers.* "Hers are distinctly drawn personalities with a wide range of conflicts: problems with parents; troubles with boyfriends; breeches of loyalty between best friends; school woes; and particularly, always, the struggle to find and to be oneself."

Willey published her first novel for teenagers, *The Bigger Book of Lydia*, in 1983. The plot introduces a double conflict: Lydia wishes she was not so tiny, and Michelle wishes she was not so large. Nasty schoolyard nicknames hurt Lydia deeply, for she believes herself to be strong and independent. Due to her embarrassment and lack of support from teachers, she begins to withdraw from her classmates. With caution, lonely Michelle befriends Lydia and, as trust enters the friendship, Michelle reveals to Lydia her problem with anorexia nervosa. The two friends work together to solve their predicaments.

Willey followed *The Bigger Book of Lydia* with other novels addressing serious issues, including *The Melinda Zone*, which is about a fourteen-year-old girl's personal struggles with her parents' divorce. "Diverse though the works and characters of this . . . ALA Best Book awardee certainly are," concludes Tyler, "it is easy to recognize a common thread: the attempt of the protagonist to strike a balance in the chaotic blend of relationships that so often characterizes adolescence."

Willey once told *CA:* "I have always been concerned with the transformation from childhood to adulthood, especially for women. I love writing for and about teenagers. My books have touched on such adolescent concerns as anorexia nervosa, the death of a parent, aversion to school, depression, sexism in school, the need for creative outlets, and mother-daughter dynamics."

BIOGRAPHICAL/CRITICAL SOURCES:

BOOKS

Twentieth-Century Young Adult Writers, St. James Press (Detroit), 1994.

PERIODICALS

Booklist, January 15, 1993.
Kirkus Reviews, November 1, 1983, p. 210; January 1, 1993, p. 69.
Publishers Weekly, December 9, 1983, p. 50; January 18, 1993.
School Library Journal, December, 1983, p. 78; March, 1993, p. 224.
Voice of Youth Advocates, April, 1984, p. 36.

*   *   *

WILLIAMS, David Ricardo   1923-

PERSONAL: Born February 28, 1923, in Kamloops, British Columbia, Canada; son of Humphrey David (a banker) and Mary Elizabeth (Cassady) Williams; married Laura Ella-Belle Bapty, May 29, 1948; children: Bruce, Suzanne, Harry, Owen, Jonathan. *Education:* University of British Columbia, B.A., 1948, LL.B., 1949. *Politics:* Conservative. *Religion:* Anglican.

ADDRESSES: Home—3355 Gibbins Rd., R.R. 2, Duncan, British Columbia, Canada V9L IN9.

CAREER: Author-researcher in Duncan, British Columbia, 1949—. Writer in residence at University of Victoria, 1980-90. Became Queen's Counsel, 1969. Member of board of governors of Queen Margaret's School; past member of board of governors of University of British Columbia. Past president of Duncan Chamber of Commerce; past chair of British Columbia Forest Museum and King's Daughters'

Hospital. *Military service:* Canadian Army, 1943-45; became lieutenant.

MEMBER: Writers Union of Canada, Foundation for Legal Research (fellow), Oregon Historical Society.

AWARDS, HONORS: Medal for Canadian biography from University of British Columbia, 1978, for *The Man for a New Country: Sir Matthew Baillie Begbie;* biography award from Association for Canadian Studies, 1979; British Columbia Book Prize, 1985, for *Duff: A Life in the Law;* Crime Writers of Canada Award for best true crime book, 1994, for *With Malice Aforethought: Six Spectacular Canadian Trials.*

WRITINGS:

One Hundred Years at St. Peter's Quamichan, Cowichan Leader, 1966, 2nd edition, 1977.
The Man for a New Country: Sir Matthew Baillie Begbie, Gray's Publishing, 1977.
Matthew Baillie Begbie, Fitzhenry & Whiteside (Toronto), 1980.
Trapline Outlaw: Simon Peter Gunanoot, Sono Nis Press (Victoria, BC), 1982.
Duff: A Life in the Law, University of British Columbia Press, 1984.
Mayor Gerry: The Remarkable Gerald Grattan McGeer, Douglas & McIntyre (Toronto), 1986.
Ace of Pentacles (novel), Sono Nis Press, 1990.
Pioneer Parish: The Story of St. Peter's Quamichan, St. Peter's Church (Duncan, BC), 1991.
Yesterday, Today and Tomorrow: A History of Vancouver's Terminal City Club, Terminal City Club (Vancouver, BC), 1992.
With Malice Aforethought: Six Spectacular Canadian Trials, Sono Nis Press, 1993.
Just Lawyers: Seven Portraits, University of Toronto Press (Toronto) and Osgoode Society for Canadian Legal History, 1995.

Contributor to books, including *Biographical Dictionary of the Common Law,* Butterworths, 1984; and *Law and Justice in a New Land,* edited by Louis Knafla, Carswell, 1986. Contributor to numerous periodicals.

WORK IN PROGRESS: Call in Pinkerton's: American Detectives at Work in Canada.

SIDELIGHTS: Lawyer and historian David Ricardo Williams often chronicles the lives of famous Canadians. In *Mayor Gerry: The Remarkable Gerald*

Grattan McGeer, he relates the career of the early twentieth-century Vancouver mayor Gerald Grattan McGeer. Using sources culled from McGeer's private papers—including letters to his wife—Williams "has written a well-researched and entertaining book," writes Allan Levine in the Toronto *Globe and Mail.* He continues, "His prose is readable and concise, accompanied by the right amount of analysis. . . . The author is generally sympathetic to his subject, but is critical when a tough judgment of McGeer is warranted. In short, Williams' account of Gerry McGeer's unusual career is popular history at its best."

Williams once told *CA:* "My field of interest is biography and history, related in some way to law, lawyers or judges. You might say I am a legal biographer. My experience as a practising lawyer has been helpful when it comes to researching material for biographies (lawyers, after all, are supposed to deal in facts). Assembling the facts in a readable fashion is another matter. I find writing to be extremely hard work. I tend to write on impulse rather than by adhering to a fixed schedule of so many words a day, but impulsiveness in writing may lead to unevenness of style. It is also rather difficult in writing in a rather esoteric field to reach the general reader, which is what I try to do. However . . . I firmly intend on continuing."

BIOGRAPHICAL/CRITICAL SOURCES:

PERIODICALS

Globe and Mail (Toronto), February 21, 1987.

*   *   *

WILLIAMS, John A(lfred)   1925-
(J. Dennis Gregory)

PERSONAL: Born December 5, 1925, in Jackson, MS; son of John Henry (a laborer) and Ola Mae Williams; married Carolyn Clopton, 1947 (divorced); married Lorrain Isaac, October 5, 1965; children: (first marriage) Gregory D., Dennis A.; (second marriage) Adam J. *Education:* Syracuse University, A.B., 1950, graduate study, 1950-51. *Avocational interests:* Travel (has visited Belgium, Cameroon, the Caribbean, Congo, Cyprus, Denmark, Egypt, Ethiopia, France, Germany, Ghana, Great Britain, Greece, Israel, Italy, Mexico, the Netherlands, Nigeria, Portugal, Senegal, Spain, the Sudan, and Sweden), tennis.

ADDRESSES: Home—693 Forest Ave., Teaneck, NJ 07666.

CAREER: Writer. Case worker for county welfare department, Syracuse, NY; public relations department, Doug Johnson Associates, Syracuse, NY, 1952-54, and later with Arthur P. Jacobs Co.; Columbia Broadcasting System (CBS), Hollywood, CA, and New York City, staff member for radio and television special events programs, 1954-55; Comet Press Books, New York City, publicity director, 1955-56; *Negro Market Newsletter,* New York City, publisher and editor, 1956-57; Abelard-Schuman Ltd., New York City, assistant to the publisher, 1957-58; American Committee on Africa, New York City, director of information, 1958; European correspondent for *Ebony* and *Jet* (magazines), New York City, 1958-59; Station WOV, New York, special events announcer, 1959; *Newsweek,* New York City, correspondent in Africa, 1964-65.

Lecturer in writing, City College of the City University of New York, 1968; lecturer in Afro-American literature, College of the Virgin Islands, summer, 1968; guest writer at Sarah Lawrence College, Bronxville, NY, 1972; regents lecturer, University of California, Santa Barbara, 1972; distinguished professor of English, La Guardia Community College, 1973-74, 1974-75; visiting professor, University of Hawaii, summer, 1974, and Boston University, 1978-79; Rutgers University, professor of English, 1979-90, Paul Robeson Professor of English, 1990-93; Exxon Professor of English, New York University, 1986-87; Band Center Fellow, Bard College, 1994-95. National Education Television, narrator and co-producer of programs, 1965-66, interviewer on *Newsfront* program, 1968. *Military service:* U.S. Naval Reserve, pharmacist's mate, active duty, 1943-46; served in the Pacific.

MEMBER: Authors Guild, Authors League of America, PEN, Rabinowitz Foundation (member of board of directors), Coordinating Council of Literary Magazines (chair, 1984), New York State Council on the Arts (member of board of directors).

AWARDS, HONORS: Award from National Institute of Arts and Letters, 1962; centennial medal for outstanding achievement from Syracuse University, 1970; Lindback Award, Rutgers University, 1982, for distinguished teaching; American Book Award,

Before Columbus Foundation, 1983, for *!Click Song;* LL.D. from Southeastern Massachusetts University, 1978, and from Syracuse University, 1995.

WRITINGS:

NOVELS

The Angry Ones, Ace Books (New York City), 1960, published as *One for New York,* Chatham Bookseller (Madison, NJ), 1975.
Night Song, Farrar, Straus (New York City), 1961.
Sissie, Farrar, Straus, 1963, published in England as *Journey out of Anger,* Eyre & Spottiswoode (London), 1965.
The Man Who Cried I Am, Little, Brown (Boston), 1967.
Sons of Darkness, Sons of Light: A Novel of Some Probability, Little, Brown, 1969.
Captain Blackman, Doubleday (New York City), 1972.
Mothersill and the Foxes, Doubleday, 1975.
The Junior Bachelor Society, Doubleday, 1976.
!Click Song, Houghton (Boston), 1982.
The Berhama Account, New Horizons Press (Chico, CA), 1985.
Jacob's Ladder, Thunder's Mouth (New York City), 1987.

NONFICTION

Africa: Her History, Lands, and People, Cooper Square (Totowa, NJ), 1962, 3rd edition, 1969.
(Under pseudonym J. Dennis Gregory, with Harry J. Anslinger) *The Protectors: The Heroic Story of the Narcotics Agents, Citizens and Officials in Their Unending, Unsung Battles against Organized Crime in America and Abroad,* Farrar, Straus, 1964.
This Is My Country Too, New American Library (New York City), 1965.
The Most Native of Sons: A Biography of Richard Wright, Doubleday, 1970.
The King God Didn't Save: Reflections on the Life and Death of Martin Luther King, Jr., Coward (New York City), 1970.
Flashbacks: A Twenty-Year Diary of Article Writing, Doubleday, 1973.
(Author of introduction) *Romare Bearden,* Abrams (New York City), 1973.
Minorities in the City, Harper (New York City), 1975.

(With son, Dennis A. Williams) *If I Stop I'll Die: The Comedy and Tragedy of Richard Pryor,* Thunder's Mouth, 1991.

EDITOR

The Angry Black (anthology), Lancer Books, 1962, 2nd edition published as *Beyond the Angry Black,* Cooper Square, 1966.
(With Charles F. Harris) *Amistad I,* Knopf (New York City), 1970.
(With Harris) *Amistad II,* Knopf, 1971.
Yardbird No. 1, Ishmael Reed (Berkeley, CA), 1979.
The McGraw-Hill Introduction to Literature, McGraw (New York City), 1985, 2nd edition, 1994.
Bridges: Literature across Cultures, McGraw, 1994.
Approaches to Literature, McGraw, 1994.

OTHER

The History of the Negro People: Omowale—The Child Returns Home (television script; filmed in Nigeria), National Education Television, 1965.
The Creative Person: Henry Roth (television script; filmed in Spain), National Education Television, 1966.
Sweet Love, Bitter (screenplay), Film 2 Associates, 1967.
Last Flight from Ambo Ber (play; first produced in Boston, 1981), American Association of Ethiopian Jews, 1984.

Contributor to numerous anthologies and of numerous stories and articles to newspapers and magazines, including *Negro Digest, Yardbird, Holiday, Saturday Review, Ebony, Essence, Emerge, Nation,* and *New York.* Member of editorial board, *Audience,* 1970-72; contributing editor, *American Journal,* 1972—.

ADAPTATIONS: The Junior Bachelor Society was adapted for television by National Broadcasting Corp. (NBC) as *Sophisticated Gents* in 1981.

WORK IN PROGRESS: Colleagues and *Trio: Clifford's Blue,* both novels; *Flashbacks II: A Forty-year Diary of Article Writing.*

SIDELIGHTS: John A. Williams, says *Dictionary of Literary Biography* contributor James L. de Jongh, is "arguably the finest Afro-American novelist of his generation," although he "has been denied the full degree of support and acceptance some critics think his work deserves." Part of the reason for this,

Williams believes, may be because of racial discrimination. In 1961, for instance, he was awarded a grant to the American Academy in Rome based on the quality of his novel *Night Song,* but the grant was rescinded by the awarding panel. Williams felt that this happened because he was black and because of rumors that he was about to marry a white woman, which he later did. However, Alan Dugan, "the poet who eventually was awarded the prize, courageously made public the issue at the presentation ceremony," explains Jeffrey Helterman, another *Dictionary of Literary Biography* commentator, and the resulting scandal caused the American Academy to discontinue its prize for literature for a time.

Williams's first three novels trace the problems facing blacks in a white society. The books *The Angry Ones, Night Song,* and *Sissie* relate attempts by black men and women to come to terms with a nation that discriminates against them. In *The Angry Ones,* for instance, the protagonist Steve Hill "struggles with various kinds of racial prejudice in housing and employment, but the focus [of the novel] is on his growing realization of the way his employers at Rocket Press destroy the dreams of would-be authors," explains Helterman. Like Williams himself, Hill perceives that he is being exploited by a white-dominated industry in which a black artist has no place. Williams has said that "the plain, unspoken fact is that the Negro is superfluous in American society as it is now constructed. Society must undergo a restructuring to make a place for him, or it will be called upon to get rid of him."

The Man Who Cried I Am, a novel that brought Williams international recognition, further explores the exploitation of blacks by a white society. The protagonist, Max Reddick, is a black writer living in Europe, as did Williams for a time. Max is married to a Dutch woman, and he is dying of colon cancer. His chief literary rival and mentor is one Harry Ames, a fellow black author, but one who "packages racial anger and sells it in his books," according to Helterman. While in Paris to attend Harry's funeral Max learns that Harry has in fact been murdered because he had uncovered a plot by the Western nations to prevent the unification of black Africa. Max himself unearths another conspiracy: America's genocidal solution to the race problem—code-named "King Alfred"—which closely resembles Hitler's "Final Solution." Finally Max, and a Malcolm X-like figure called Minister Q, are captured by the opposing forces and put to death.

The Man Who Cried I Am escapes the protest novel format of most black literature by putting the situation on an epic scale. Jerry H. Bryant describes the book in *Critique: Studies in Modern Fiction* as "Williams's adaptation of the rhetoric of black power to his own needs as a novelist," calling it "in a sense Williams's *Huckleberry Finn.* It reflects his deep skepticism over the capacity of America to live up to its professed ideals, and a development of deep pessimism about whites in particular and man in general." "What purpose does the King Alfred portion of the novel serve?" asks Robert E. Fleming in *Contemporary Literature.* "In one sense, black people have been systematically killed off in the United States since their first introduction to its shores. Malnutrition, disease, poverty, psychological conditioning, and spiritual starvation have been the tools, rather than military operations and gas chambers, but the result has often been the same. King Alfred is not only a prophetic warning of what might happen here but a fictional metaphor for what has been happening and is happening still," he concludes.

The Man Who Cried I Am includes a character named Paul Durrell, who is obviously based on civil rights leader Martin Luther King. Durrell is presented in a negative light, and Williams's unfavorable opinion of Durrell's real-life counterpart became all the more evident in his 1970 nonfiction book, *The King God Didn't Save: Reflections on the Life and Death of Martin Luther King, Jr.* In this unflattering biography, Williams portrays Dr. King as a man who allowed himself to be manipulated by high-ranking federal agents and as a leader who was badly out of touch with the community he influenced so strongly. In addition to *The King God Didn't Save,* Williams published another biography in 1970. Intended for reading by a young adult audience, *The Most Native of Sons: A Biography of Richard Wright* relates the life of the radical black author whose work profoundly influenced Williams.

Williams states in his *Contemporary Authors Autobiography Series* entry that he considers *!Click Song* to be his "very best novel." Like *The Man Who Cried I Am,* the book details the careers of two writers, in this case Paul Cummings and Cato Caldwell Douglass, friends who attended school on the GI Bill after World War II. Cummings is Jewish; it is his reaffirmation of his Jewishness that provides the theme for his novels, and his suicide opens the book. Douglass, on the other hand, is black; his problem, as Jervis Anderson indicates in the *New York Times Book Review,* is to overcome racism in the publishing industry. *Chicago Tribune Book World* contributor Seymour Krim compares the two characters: Cummings "was a more successful competitor, a novelist who had won a National Book Award and all the attention that goes with it, while Cato was forced to lecture for peanuts before Black Studies groups. A further irony is the fact that Cummings was a 'passed' Jew who had only recently declared his real name, Kaminsky, in an effort to purge himself. Purge or not, his writing has gone downhill since his born-again declaration, while his earnings have gone up." Roy Hoffman, writing for the *Washington Post Book World* points out, however, that "as Paul's career skyrockets, his private life goes to shambles. As Cato's career runs into brick walls, his personal life grows ever more fulfilled, ever more radiant."

"*!Click Song* is at least the equal of Williams's other masterpiece, *The Man Who Cried I Am,*" states de Jongh. "The emotional power, the fluid structuring of time, the resonant synthesis of fiction and history are similar. But the novelist's mastery is greater, for Williams's technique here is seamless and invisible," the reviewer concludes. Other critics also celebrate Williams's work; says Krim, "Unlike a James Baldwin or an Amiri Baraka, Williams is primarily a storyteller, which is what makes the reality of Black Rage become something other than a polemic in his hands. . . . Before [Cato Douglass's] odyssey is ended, we know in our bones what it is like to be a gifted black survivor in America today; we change skins as we read, so to speak, and the journey of living inside another is so intense that no white reader will ever again be able to plead ignorance."

Although Williams's writing explores racial themes, he has stated that he dislikes being categorized as a black author. In his view, that label only facilitates the segregation of black writers and their work from the rest of American literature. In an interview with Shirley Horner, published in the *New York Times,* he confessed that he was "pessimistic" about the possibility that racial tensions in modern American society could ever be resolved. He added, however, that "it's the kind of pessimism that would be delighted to be proved wrong, absolutely wrong." Commenting specifically on relations between blacks and Jews, he stated: "I don't think those days of black-Jewish cooperation were ever that glorious; its nice to think that they were. . . . Blacks and Jews in 1993 are even less willing to learn from each other, so few people try." He explained that he and his wife, who

is Jewish, had moved to Teaneck, New Jersey, because they thought that "the town would not be inhospitable to a mixed marriage." Asked if they had suffered many slights because of their marriage, Williams acknowledged: "We've had our share, as we expected we would. I'm sure that there are lots of things that go on because of our marriage that I'm totally unaware of. . . . In such a marriage, you both have to be strong in ways that are sometimes not very visible. A sense of humor helps."

BIOGRAPHICAL/CRITICAL SOURCES:

BOOKS

Cash, Earl A., *Evolution of a Black Writer,* Third Press, 1975.
Contemporary Authors Autobiography Series, Volume 3, Gale (Detroit), 1986.
Contemporary Literary Criticism, Gale, Volume 5, 1976, Volume 13, 1980.
Dictionary of Literary Biography, Gale, Volume 2: *American Novelists since World War II,* 1978, Volume 33: *Afro-American Fiction Writers after 1955,* 1984.
Gayle, Addison, Jr., editor, *Black Expression: Essays by and about Black Americans in the Creative Arts,* Weybright and Talley, 1969, pp. 365-72.
Muller, Gilbert H., *John A. Williams,* Twayne (New York City), 1984.
O'Brien, John, editor, *Interviews with Black Writers,* Liveright (New York City), 1973, pp. 225-43.

PERIODICALS

Black Literature Forum, spring/summer, 1987, pp. 25-42.
Black World, June, 1975.
Bloomsbury Review, January/February, 1988, p. 10; October/November, 1991, p. 13.
Chicago Tribune Book World, April 18, 1982; November 17, 1985.
Contemporary Literature, spring, 1973.
Critic, April, 1963.
Critique: Studies in Modern Fiction, Volume 16, number 3, 1975.
Detroit News, June 6, 1982.
Library Journal, November 1, 1961; September 15, 1967.
Los Angeles Times Book Review, May 9, 1982; November 29, 1987.
Nation, September 18, 1976.
New Yorker, August 16, 1976.

New York Times, June 13, 1993.

New York Times Book Review, May 6, 1973, pp. 34-35; July 11, 1976; April 4, 1982; October 18, 1987; November 15, 1987.

Prairie Schooner, spring, 1976.

Publishers Weekly, November 11, 1974.

Studies in Black Literature, spring, 1972, pp. 24-32.

Time, April 12, 1982.

Washington Post Book World, March 23, 1982; October 4, 1987.

* * *

WILLIAMS, Pete
See FAULKNOR, Cliff(ord Vernon)

* * *

WILSON, Joyce M(uriel Judson)
(Joyce Stranger)

PERSONAL: Born May 26 in London, England; daughter of Ralph (an advertising manager) and Beryl Judson; married Kenneth Wilson, February 28, 1944; children: Andrew Bruce, Anne Patricia and Nicholas David (twins). *Education:* University College, B.Sc., 1942. *Religion:* Church of England.

ADDRESSES: Agent—Aitken, Stone & Wylie, 29 Fernshaw Rd., London SW10 0TG, England.

CAREER: Imperial Chemical Industries, Manchester, England, research chemist, 1942-46. Lecturer and writer on dog training.

MEMBER: Society of Authors, Institute of Journalists, United Kingdom Registry of Canine Behaviourists, Society for the Study of Companion Animals, Canine Concern (honorary president), People and Dogs Society (honorary president).

WRITINGS:

CHILDREN'S BOOKS; UNDER PSEUDONYM JOYCE STRANGER

Wild Cat Island, illustrated by Joe Acheson, Methuen (London), 1961.

Circus All Alone, illustrated by Sheila Rose, Harrap (London), 1965.

Jason—Nobody's Dog, illustrated by Douglas Phillips, Dent (London), 1972.

The Honeywell Badger, illustrated by Phillips, Dent, 1972.

Paddy Joe, Collins (London), 1973.

The Hare at Dark Hollow, illustrated by Charles Pickard, Dent, 1973.

Trouble for Paddy Joe, Collins, 1973.

The Secret Herds: Animal Stories, illustrated by Douglas Reay, Dent, 1974.

Paddy Joe at Deep Hollow Farm, Collins, 1975.

The Fox at Drummer's Darkness, illustrated by William Geldart, Dent, 1976, Farrar, Straus (New York City), 1977.

The Wild Ponies, illustrated by Robert Rothero, Kaye & Ward, 1976.

Joyce Stranger's Book of Hanak's Animals (poetry), illustrated by Mirko Hanak, Dent, 1976.

Paddy Joe and Thomson's Folly, Pelham, 1979.

The Curse of Seal Valley, Dent, 1979.

Vet on Call, Carousel, 1981.

Double Trouble, Carousel, 1981.

Vet Riding High, Carousel, 1982.

No More Horses, Carousel, 1982.

Dial V.E.T., Carousel, 1982.

Marooned!, Kaye & Ward, 1982.

The Hound of Darkness, Dent, 1983.

Shadows in the Dark, Kaye & Ward, 1984.

The Family at Fools' Farm, Dent, 1985.

Spy, the No-Good Pup, Dent, 1989.

Midnight Magic, Lions, 1991.

Animal Park Trilogy, Lions, 1992.

The Runaway, Lions, 1992.

The Secret of Hunter's Keep, Lions, 1993.

The House of Secrets Trilogy, Lions, 1994.

ADULT BOOKS; UNDER PSEUDONYM JOYCE STRANGER

The Running Foxes, Hammond, 1965, Viking, 1966.

Breed of Giants, Hammond, 1966, Viking, 1967.

Rex, Harvill Press, 1967, Viking, 1968.

Casey, Harvill Press, 1968, published as *Born to Trouble,* Viking, 1968.

Rusty, Harvill Press, 1969, published as *The Wind on the Dragon,* Viking, 1969.

One for Sorrow, Corgi, 1969.

Zara, Viking, 1970.

Chia, The Wildcat, Harvill Press, 1971.

Lakeland Vet, Viking, 1972.

Walk a Lonely Road, Harvill Press, 1973.

A Dog Called Gelert and Other Stories (short stories), Corgi, 1973.

Never Count Apples, Harvill Press, 1974.

Never Tell a Secret, Harvill Press, 1975.

Flash, Harvill Press, 1976.

Khazan, the Horse That Came Out of the Sea, Harvill Press, 1977.

A Walk in the Dark, Joseph, 1978.

The January Queen, Joseph, 1979.

The Stallion, Joseph, 1981.

The Monastery Cat and Other Stories (short stories), Corgi, 1982.

Josse, Joseph, 1983.

The Hounds of Hades, Joseph, 1985.

The Hills are Lonely, Souvenir, 1993.

Thursday's Child, Souvenir, 1994.

A Cry on the Wind, Souvenir, 1995.

OTHER; UNDER PSEUDONYM JOYCE STRANGER

Kym: The True Story of a Siamese Cat, M. Joseph, 1976, Coward McCann, 1977.

Two's Company, M. Joseph, 1977.

Three's a Pack, M. Joseph, 1980.

All about Your Pet Puppy, Pelham, 1980.

How to Own a Sensible Dog, Corgi, 1981.

Two for Joy, M. Joseph, 1982.

Stranger Than Fiction: The Biography of Elspeth Bryce-Smith, M. Joseph, 1984.

A Dog in a Million, M. Joseph, 1984.

Dog Days, M. Joseph, 1986.

Double or Quit, M. Joseph, 1987.

ADAPTATIONS: Jason was filmed by Walt Disney Productions; *The Fox at Drummers' Darkness* was filmed as *The Wild Dog; The Honeywell Badger* and *The Hare at Dark Hollow* were adapted for television by the British Broadacasting Corp.

SIDELIGHTS: Joyce M. Wilson has written about animals for over thirty years under the pseudonym of Joyce Stranger. She studied to be a biologist, specializing in animal behavior. It is no surprise, therefore, that she calls the animal material in her books "autobiographical," written about animals she has known—horses she used to ride, hares that lived near her house, or dogs she has owned. Stranger's books all promote the rewards of partnerships between human and animals. She comments in *Twentieth-Century Children's Writers* that "for many people, an animal can provide a harmony lacking in day-to-day relationships with people."

Many of her books, including *Jason—Nobody's Dog, Walk a Lonely Road,* and *Spy, the No-Good Pup,* explore the theme of friendship between humans and animals. Other books tell of humans who, intentionally or otherwise, mistreat animals. *The Honeywell*

Badger, for instance, is the story of two young children who are so set upon having a badger for a pet that they ignore the consequences of trying to tame such an animal. In the 1973 book, *Trouble for Paddy Joe,* it is Paddy Joe's poor training of his pet Alsatian, Storm, that causes the animal to become lost in the Scottish wilderness.

Several of Stranger's books are told from the animal's point of view. *The Hare at Dark Hollow,* for example, is the story of how a hare adapts to changes in its natural surroundings. "*The Hare at Dark Hollow* came from a hare that lived near us in the middle of a housing estate," Stranger once explained. "She reared her family on a tiny playing field and fed in the gardens. There were hares there until we moved to Anglesey, yet the field was only about an acre in size. Another hare was on our caravan site and used to lurk and watch stock car racing. There are hares all over Manchester airport."

One of Stranger's literary strengths is her ability to appeal to a wide audience of adults and children. A reviewer in *Junior Bookshelf* of *The Hound of Darkness* not only praises Stranger's "deep feeling for wild country and for nature in its harshest moods," but notes that it is "by no means a book for children alone, or even for them particularly."

Although Stranger's books concentrate on deepening her readers' understanding of animals and their needs, she does not go to extremes in defending animal rights. In *The Family at Fools' Farm,* for example, eighteen-year-old Jan is hampered in her attempts to keep her family together and make the farm profitable by the irresponsible activities of a group of animal rights activists. A critic in *Growing Point* calls the book an "absorbing and stirring narrative," while a reviewer in *Junior Bookshelf* states that the book gives "an honest picture of what farming really means in daily repetitive hard work and disappointment when crops fail or animals are sick," but it also shows the joys and pleasures of "the fruition of plans followed out against all odds."

In *Midnight Magic,* Stranger writes of twelve-year-old Mandy, who has been thrown from a horse and is now afraid to ride again. Stranger incorporates much information about horses and horse training into the story as Mandy takes riding lessons from Kristy, an elderly horsewoman who helps Mandy conquer her fear and learn to respond to each horse as an individual. In *Twentieth-Century Children's Writers,* Gwen Marsh calls the book "a remarkable *tour de force* even from a writer whose feeling for animals has always been her greatest strength."

Stranger once told *CA:* "My animal books work because I watched the animals and studied animal behavior. I knew where the foxes laired and bred their cubs; where the hare hid, and watched her as she moved around and when she was caught by a fox or dog; I listened to a goose on an island as it died when the fox caught it. I hid in trees to watch badgers; I ride horses and I am in daily contact with many dogs. Farm animals are all around me—I can see sheep and cattle as I write. The world beyond the human is vastly exciting; it has much to reveal to us."

BIOGRAPHICAL/CRITICAL SOURCES:

BOOKS

Twentieth-Century Children's Writers, 4th edition, St. James Press (Detroit), 1995.

PERIODICALS

Booklist, April 15, 1969, p. 944; July 15, 1977, p. 1731.
Growing Point, November, 1985, p. 4524.
Junior Bookshelf, October, 1983, p. 215; December, 1985, p. 281; October, 1989, p. 245.
Kirkus Reviews, March 1, 1967, p. 300.
Magpies, September, 1992, p. 31.
New York Times Book Review, May 1, 1977, p. 44.
Publishers Weekly, March 28, 1977, p. 79.
School Librarian, June, 1986, p. 174; February, 1992, p. 21.
Times Educational Supplement, January 18, 1980, p. 41; July 17, 1981, p. 26.
Times Literary Supplement, November 23, 1973, p. 1430.

* * *

WIRTH, John D(avis)   1936-

PERSONAL: Born June 17, 1936, in Dawson, NM; son of Cecil W. (a school administrator) and Virginia (Davis) Wirth; married Nancy Farwell Meem, June 22, 1960; children: Peter Farwell, Timothy Corbin, Nicholas Newhall. *Education:* Harvard University, B.A., 1958; Stanford University, Ph.D., 1966. *Politics:* Democrat. *Religion:* Episcopalian.

ADDRESSES: Home—37 Park Dr., Atherton, CA 94027. *Office*—Department of History, Stanford University, Stanford, CA 94305.

CAREER: Stanford University, Stanford, CA, assistant professor, 1966-72, associate professor, 1971-77, professor of history, 1977—, director of Center for Latin American Studies, 1975-83, chairman of department of Spanish and Portuguese, 1985-87, vice-provost for academic planning and development, 1988-91, Gildred Professor of Latin American Studies, 1991—. *Military service:* U.S. Army Reserve, 1958-64.

MEMBER: American Historical Association, Conference on Latin American History, Latin American Studies Association, Society for Environmental History, Commission for Environmental Cooperation in Montreal.

AWARDS, HONORS: Social Science Research Council fellowship, 1969-70, 1972; Bolton Memorial Prize, 1971; Pacific Coast Council on Latin American Studies Prize, 1971; Fulbright scholar, 1980.

WRITINGS:

The Politics of Brazilian Development, 1930-1954, Stanford University Press (Stanford, CA), 1970.
Minas Gerais in the Brazilian Federation, 1889-1937, Stanford University Press, 1977.
(Editor with Robert L. Jones) *Manchester and Sao Paulo: Problems of Rapid Urban Growth,* Stanford University Press, 1978.
The Inca and Aztec States, 1400-1800, Academic Press (San Diego, CA), 1982.
(Editor) *Latin American Oil Companies and the Politics of Energy,* University of Nebraska Press (Lincoln, NE), 1985.
State and Society in Brazil: Continuity and Change, Westview (Boulder, CO), 1987.
(Editor with Robert L. Earle) *Identities in North America: The Search for Community,* Stanford University Press, 1995.

WORK IN PROGRESS: Smelter Smoke in North America.

SIDELIGHTS: John D. Wirth once told *CA:* "With my first book translated into Portuguese, I am proud to be one of the Brazilianists, a small group which is privileged to interpret one of the world's most fascinating societies, contemporary Brazil."

WOLFE, Christopher (F.)   1949-

PERSONAL: Born March 11, 1949, in Boston, MA; son of W. Brewster (a physician) and Margaret (a homemaker; maiden name, Conway) Wolfe; married Anne McGowan (a homemaker), June 17, 1972; children: Julia, Jared, Rebecca, Thomas, Stephen, Trevor, Patrice, Elena, Marisa. *Education:* University of Notre Dame, B.A. (summa cum laude), 1971; Boston College, Ph.D. (with highest distinction), 1978. *Politics:* Republican. *Religion:* Roman Catholic.

ADDRESSES: Home—11637 West Layton Ave., Greenfield, WI 53228. *Office*—Department of Political Science, Marquette University, Box 1881, Milwaukee, WI 53201-1881.

CAREER: Assumption College, Worcester, MA, instructor in political science, 1975-78; Marquette University, Milwaukee, WI, assistant professor, 1978-84, associate professor, 1985-92, professor of political science, 1992—. Founder, American Public Philosophy Institute, 1990.

MEMBER: American Political Science Association, Fellowship of Catholic Scholars, Federalist Society, Phi Beta Kappa.

AWARDS, HONORS: Woodrow Wilson fellowship, 1971; grants from Institute for Educational Affairs, 1982, 1983, and Bradley Foundation, 1986; National Endowment for the Humanities fellow, 1994.

WRITINGS:

The Rise of Modern Judicial Review: From Constitutional Interpretation to Judge-Made Law, Basic Books (New York City), 1986, revised edition, Rowman & Littlefield (Totowa, NJ), 1994.
Faith and Liberal Democracy, University Press of America (Lanham, MD), 1987.
Judicial Activism: Bulwark of Freedom or Precarious Security?, Brooks/Cole (Monterey, CA), 1991.
(Editor with John Hittinger) *Liberalism at the Crossroads,* Rowman & Littlefield, 1994.
How to Interpret the Constitution, Rowman & Littlefield, 1996.

Contributor of articles and reviews to political science journals and other magazines, including *Crisis.*

WORK IN PROGRESS: Liberalism, Natural Law, and American Public Philosophy.

SIDELIGHTS: Christopher Wolfe told *CA:* "The main concern in my scholarly activity is to bring the insights derived from the study of classical and medieval political thought to bear upon our understanding of our own regime, with a special concentration on the political thought of America's founders. Another major concern is to point out that our liberal democracy cannot be too consistently liberal if it wants to remain healthy. Liberal democracies are kept relatively sound by relying on certain nonliberal elements, including religion and traditional family morality.

"I initially brought these general concerns to a critical study of the evolution of judicial review. I have, with my completion of my project on judicial review, shifted the focus of my study to liberal legal philosophy and American public philosophy. In particular, I find that contemporary liberal political theory (post-Rawls) undermines essential conditions for healthy liberalism. Liberal societies such as the United States have, in a sense, been parasitic on natural law thought, and with the 'purification' of American law by removing its more traditional elements, the importance of these elements (such as the conditions for stable family life and for epistemological realism) can be seen more clearly. In 1990 I founded the American Public Philosophy Institute, with a view to giving natural law thought (broadly conceived) a stronger voice in contemporary discussions of political and legal theory."

BIOGRAPHICAL/CRITICAL SOURCES:

PERIODICALS

National Review, November 21, 1986.

*   *   *

WOODSIDE, Alexander Barton   1938-

PERSONAL: Born February 5, 1938, in Toronto, Ontario, Canada; son of Moffatt (a teacher) and Eleanor (an actress; maiden name, Barton) Wadset. *Education:* University of Toronto, B.A., 1960; Harvard University, A.M., 1962, Ph.D., 1968.

ADDRESSES: Office—Department of History, University of British Columbia, Vancouver, British Columbia, Canada.

CAREER: Harvard University, Cambridge, MA, 1968-75, began as assistant professor, became professor of history; University of British Columbia, Vancouver, professor of history, 1975—.

MEMBER: Canadian Association for the Study of Asia, Association for Asian Studies.

AWARDS, HONORS: Guggenheim fellow, 1984-85; elected fellow, Royal Society of Canada, 1990.

WRITINGS:

Vietnam and the Chinese Model, Harvard University Press (Cambridge, MA), 1971.
Community and Revolution in Modern Vietnam, Houghton (Boston), 1976.
(With D. Steinberg, D. Wyatt, D. Chandler, and others) In Search of Southeast Asia: A Modern History, University of Hawaii Press (Honolulu), 1987.
(With B. Elman) Education and Society in Late Imperial China, University of California Press (Berkeley), 1995.

BIOGRAPHICAL/CRITICAL SOURCES:

PERIODICALS

American Historical Review, April, 1972; December, 1976.
Virginia Quarterly Review, summer, 1971.

*   *   *

WOSMEK, Frances   1917-
(Frances Brailsford)

PERSONAL: Born December 16, 1917, in Popple, MN; daughter of Frank J. (a farmer) and Rebecca Mabel (Fenton) Wosmek; married Paul Brailsford, November 18, 1949 (divorced); children: Brian, Robin. Education: Attended Wadena Teachers Training College, Wadena, MN, and Meinzinger's Art School, Detroit, MI. Religion: "Somewhere outside the limitations of any special creed."

ADDRESSES: Home—44 Lexington Ave., Gloucester, MA 01930-3973.

CAREER: School teacher in rural Minnesota; designer of greeting cards for American Greetings,

Cleveland, OH, and Rustcraft, Boston, MA; has done layout and advertising art; freelance designer of toys, children's products, and textiles; teacher of creative writing and writer.

AWARDS, HONORS: A Brown Bird Singing was named a Notable Book in the Social Sciences by the Children's Book Council of New York, 1986, was on the Sequoyah Book Award Committee's MasterList in Oklahoma, 1988-89, and was nominated for the South Carolina Book Award by the South Carolina Association of School Librarians, 1988-89; three first prizes for adult short stories; special Edgar Allan Poe Award, Mystery Writers of America, for Mystery of the Eagle's Claw.

WRITINGS:

FOR CHILDREN; SELF-ILLUSTRATED

Sky High, John Martin's House, 1949.
Twinkle Tot Tales, Lowe, 1949.
Cuddles and His Friends, Lowe, 1949.
A Bowl of Sun, Children's Press (Chicago, IL), 1976.
The ABC of Ecology, May Davenport (Los Altos Hills, CA), 1981.
It's Nice to Be Nice, Kiddie Products, 1983.

FOR CHILDREN

Little Dog, Little Dog, Rand McNally (Chicago, IL), 1963.
(Under name Frances Brailsford) In the Space of a Wink, illustrations by Ati Forberg, Follet, 1969.
Never Mind Murder, Westminster (Philadelphia, PA), 1977.
Mystery of the Eagle's Claw, Westminster, 1979.
Let's Make Music, Houghton (Boston, MA), 1981.
A Brown Bird Singing, Lothrop (New York City), 1986.
Neighbors, Font & Center Press, 1993.

ILLUSTRATOR

Edith May Lowe, Throughout the Day, John Martin's House, 1949.
Rosemary Smith Fitzgerald, Bobby and Buttons, Garden City Books, 1949.
Josephine Van Dolzen Pease, One, Two, Cock-a-Doodle-Do, Rand McNally, 1950.
Helen Earle Gilbert, Go to Sleep Book, Rand McNally, 1969.

OTHER

Acknowledge the Wonder, Theosophical Publishing House (Wheaton, IL), 1988.

Contributor of poems to *Christian Science Monitor* and *North Shore Examiner.*

WORK IN PROGRESS: Children's books.

SIDELIGHTS: "My career has been an attempt to be as true to who I am in as honest an expression as I am able," Frances Wosmek told *CA.* "It has not always been easy. We live in a materialistic society that believes itself to be a practical and 'down-to-earth' one, impatient with those who persist in straying beyond the bounds of the proven and provable. However, some of us remain convinced that even the most rigid forms of a generally accepted reality are produced and supported from within by the same living spirit that is the source of an artist's inspiration. Science, itself, may be drawing very near to the same conclusion."

*   *   *

WRIGHT, (Mary) Patricia   1932-
    (Mary Napier)

PERSONAL: Born May 10, 1932, in Surrey, England; daughter of Roy (a company chairperson) and Violet Mary (Wilkinson) Matthews; married Richard M. Wright (an engineer), April 25, 1959; children: Katherine Mary, Penelope Diana. *Education:* Royal Institution of Chartered Surveyors, A.R.I.C.S., 1957; Chartered Land Agents' Society, Q.A.L.A.S., 1958; University of London, degree (with first class honors), 1966. *Politics:* "A liberal if the liberals were any good, which they aren't, so usually a conservative." *Religion:* "Church of-England—up to a point." *Avocational interests:* Travel (Western Europe and the Soviet Union), local government, environment, history.

ADDRESSES: *Home*—Whitehill House, Frant, Sussex, England. *Agent*—Lavinia Trevor, 6 The Glasshook, 49A Goldhawk Rd., London W1Z 8QP, England.

CAREER: Writer, 1959—. Hughes & Wilbraham, Exeter, England, agricultural surveyor and agent, 1955-57; Alsop & Co., London, England, salesperson, 1957-59; Turnbridge Wells Grammar School for Girls, Turnbridge Wells, England, part-time teacher of history and economics, 1966-80. Elected county councillor for East Sussex, 1981, re-elected, 1985, 1989, 1993. Lecturer.

AWARDS, HONORS: Georgette Heyer Historical Novel Prize, 1987, for *I Am England.*

WRITINGS:

NOVELS

Space of the Heart, Doubleday (New York City), 1976, new edition published as *Ilena,* Fontana, 1978.
Journey into Fire, Doubleday, 1977.
Shadow of the Rock, Doubleday, 1979.
Storm Harvest, Collins (London), 1979, also published as *Heart of the Storm,* Doubleday, 1980.
This, My City, Collins, 1981.
The Storms of Fate, Doubleday, 1981.
While Paris Danced, Doubleday, 1982.
I Am England, St. Martin's (New York City), 1987.
That Near and Distant Place, St. Martin's, 1988.

UNDER PSEUDONYM MARY NAPIER

Women's Estate (humor), Hart-Davis, 1959.
The Waiting (romantic thriller), Bantam, 1979.
Blind Chance, Collins, 1980.
Forbidden Places (romantic thriller), Coward, 1981.
State of Fear, Hutchinson (East Sussex, England), 1984.
Heartsearch, Fawcett, 1988.
Powers of Darkness, Severn House (London), 1990.

OTHER

Conflict on the Nile (study of the Fashoda incident, 1898-1901), Heinemann (London), 1971.
The Strange History of Buckingham Palace, Alan Sutton (Gloucester, England), 1996.

Contributor to *History Today.*

SIDELIGHTS: Patricia Wright told *CA:* "Although no diehard in politics—in fact rather sceptical of all politicians and in favour of a pragmatic approach to problems—I am very concerned about all issues of personal freedom and how easily it can be lost. I am also concerned about how easily we can destroy our most precious possessions of beauty and continuity. This has been the chief motive for my writings over the past several years."

BIOGRAPHICAL/CRITICAL SOURCES:

PERIODICALS

Washington Post Book World, December 11, 1987.

* * *

YOUCHA, Geraldine 1925-

PERSONAL: Born September 24, 1925, in Suffern, NY; daughter of Joseph (a storekeeper) and Hilda Shavelson; married Isaac Z. Youcha (a psychoanalyst), August 31, 1950; children: Victoria, Sharon, Joseph. *Education:* Northwestern University, B.S., 1946. *Avocational interests:* Travel, potting, reading, sailing.

ADDRESSES: *Home*—New City, NY. *Agent*—Fox Chase Agency, Inc., Public Ledger Bldg., Room 930, Independence, PA 19106.

CAREER: *Coronet,* New York City, member of editorial staff, 1946-52; writer, 1952—. Member of board of directors of Family Service Association of Rockland County, 1972-73, and Rockland County Center for the Arts.

WRITINGS:

A Dangerous Pleasure: Alcohol from the Woman's Perspective, Hawthorn (New York City), 1978, revised edition published as *Women and Alcohol: A Dangerous Pleasure,* Crown (New York City), 1986.
(With Judith S. Seixas) *Children of Alcoholism: A Survivor's Manual,* Crown, 1985.
(With Seixas) *Drugs, Alcohol, and Your Children: How to Keep Your Family Substance-Free,* Crown, 1989.
Minding the Children: Childcare in America from Colonial Times to the Present, Scribner (New York City), 1994.

Author of weekly column "As I Was Saying" in *Rockland County Journal News.* Contributor of articles to periodicals, including *Good Housekeeping, Redbook,* and *New York Daily News.*

WORK IN PROGRESS: A social history of the breast.

SIDELIGHTS: *Drugs, Alcohol, and Your Children: How to Keep Your Family Substance-Free,* coauthored by Geraldine Youcha and Judith S. Seixas, is a "commonsense guide" for parents whose children are using addictive substances, according to a *Publishers Weekly* reviewer. Addressed to parents of preadolescents and teens, the book identifies warning signals indicative of possible drug use by children, and recommends actions parents can take, including communication strategies, when faced with actual drug and/or alcohol abuse. Kim Banks writes in *Library Journal* that Youcha strives to help parents "understand how addictions occur and to suggest how to prevent a child from becoming addicted."

Minding the Children: Childcare in America from Colonial Times to the Present explores the historical roots of current day care trends and circumstances. Ann Babits Grice remarks in *Library Journal* that Youcha "presents a fascinating historical account" of American child care. By use of diaries, letters, books, and other primary source materials, Youcha identified numerous child care systems in place at various times in American history. Applying psychological and sociological analysis to her research, she concludes that mothers have always had help in looking after their children, whether they be "working" or "full-time" mothers. A *Publishers Weekly* reviewer comments that Youcha "argues that the concept of full-time motherhood is a 'myth' because other women, as well as male relatives and servants, have always helped care for offspring." Susan Salter Reynolds observes in the *Los Angeles Times Book Review,* that "Women have always helped each other raise . . . babies," and concerning this, Youcha "writes almost proudly." Youcha describes many different caregiving situations including wet nurses and nannies, Christian communities, and government-funded programs. Kathryn Carpenter notes in *Booklist,* Youcha's "readable, fascinating history of a concern central to Americans . . . provides both essential insights for parents struggling with childcare choices and historical context for national policy decisions."

Youcha once told *CA:* "In writing, my aim has been to say simply what seems complicated, whether I am dealing with the effects of alcohol on women or the juvenile justice system. Freelance writing is also the perfect occupation for a dilettante, which is how I see myself."

BIOGRAPHICAL/CRITICAL SOURCES:

PERIODICALS

Booklist, January 1, 1995, p. 789.
Kirkus Reviews, January 1, 1989, p. 43.
Library Journal, March 15, 1989, p. 79; March 15, 1995, p. 87.
Los Angeles Times Book Review, January 22, 1995, p. 6.
Publishers Weekly, January 20, 1989, p. 130; November 21, 1994, p. 61.*

*   *   *

ZEITLIN, Maurice   1935-

PERSONAL: Born February 24, 1935, in Detroit, MI; son of Albert Joseph and Rose (Goldberg) Zeitlin; married Marilyn Geller, March 1, 1959; children: Michelle, Carla, Erica. *Education:* Wayne State University, B.A. (cum laude), 1957; University of California, Berkeley, M.A., 1960, Ph.D., 1964. *Politics:* Democrat. *Religion:* Jewish.

ADDRESSES: Home—Los Angeles, CA. *Office*—Department of Sociology, University of California, Los Angeles, CA 90024.

CAREER: Princeton University, Princeton, NJ, instructor in sociology and anthropology, 1961-64, research associate at Center of International Studies, 1962-64; University of Wisconsin—Madison, assistant professor, 1964-67, associate professor, 1967-70, professor of sociology, 1970-77, director of Center for Social Organization, 1974-76; University of California, Los Angeles, professor of sociology, 1977—, research associate at Institute of Industrial Relations, 1979—. Visiting professor, University of California, Santa Barbara, 1970-71, and Hebrew University of Jerusalem, 1971-72. Madison Citizens for a Vote on Vietnam, founder, chairman, 1967-68; American Committee for Chile, founder, chairman, 1973-75; member of executive board of U.S. Committee for Justice to Latin American Political Prisoners, 1977-84; member of executive board of California Campaign for Economic Democracy, 1983-86; founder of Faculty for Peace, 1967.

MEMBER: American Sociological Association (member of council, 1977-80), Latin American Studies Association, Monthly Review Associates, American Historical Association, American Civil Liberties Union.

AWARDS, HONORS: Woodrow Wilson Foundation fellowship in sociology, 1959-61; Ford Foundation postdoctoral fellowship in Latin American studies, 1965-67; Louis M. Rabinowitz Foundation grant, 1969-70; Ford Foundation research fellowship and American Philosophical Society grant, 1970-71; article "Who Owns America? The Same Old Gang" received National Media Project award from Sonoma State University, and was named one of the "ten best censored stories of 1978" by a prominent print media panel; article "How We Got into this [Economic] Mess, and How to Get Out" was named the top censored story of 1981 by a prominent print media panel; Guggenheim fellowship, 1981-82; National Science Foundation grant, 1981-82; Distinguished Contribution to Scholarship Award in political sociology, Sociological Association, 1992, for article "'Red' Unions and 'Bourgeois' Contracts."

WRITINGS:

(With Robert Scheer) *Cuba: Tragedy in Our Hemisphere,* Grove (New York City), 1963, revised edition published as *Cuba: An American Tragedy,* Penguin (New York City), 1964.
Revolutionary Politics and the Cuban Working Class, Princeton University Press (Princeton, NJ), 1967, augmented edition, Harper (New York City), 1970.
(With James Petras) *El radicalismo politico de la clase trabajadora chilena,* Centro Editor de America Latina, 1969, revised edition, 1970.
Propiedad y control: La Gran corporacion y la clase capitalista, edited and translated by Lluis Argemi and Luis Rodriguez Zuniga, Editorial Anagrama, 1976.
The Civil Wars in Chile (or the bourgeois revolutions that never were), Princeton University Press, 1984.
(With Richard E. Ratliff) *Landlords and Capitalists: The Dominant Class of Chile,* Princeton University Press, 1988.
The Large Corporation and Contemporary Classes, Rutgers University Press (New Brunswick, NJ), Polity Press, 1989.
(With Judith Stepan-Norris) *Talking Union,* University of Illinois Press (Champaign, IL), in press.

OTHER

(Editor and translator with Petras) *Latin America: Reform or Revolution?*, Fawcett (New York City), 1968.

(Editor and author of introduction) *American Society, Inc.: Studies of the Social Structure and Political Economy of the United States*, Markham, 1970, 2nd revised edition, Rand McNally (Chicago, IL), 1977.

(Editor and author of introduction) *Father Camilo Torres: Revolutionary Writings*, Harper, 1972.

(Editor and author of introduction) *Classes, Class Conflict, and the State: Empirical Studies in Class Analysis*, Little, Brown (Boston, MA), 1980.

(Editor) *How Mighty A Force? Workers' Consciousness and Organization in the United States*, University of California (Berkeley, CA), 1983.

(Editor and author of introduction) *Insurgent Workers: The Origins of Industrial Unionism in the United States*, University of California, 1987.

Member of editorial board of New Critics Press, 1969-73, Bobbs-Merrill series of studies in sociology, 1969-75, and International Sociological Association's "Sage" series in international sociology, 1977-81; editor-in-chief, *Political Power and Social Theory: A Research Annual*, Volumes 1-7, 1980-88. Contributor to numerous books, including *Intercorporate Relations: The Structural Analysis of Business*, edited by M. Mizruchi and M. Schwartz, Cambridge University Press (New York City), 1987; *Development and Social Change in the Chilean Countryside*, edited by C. Kay and P. Silva, Center for Latin American Research and Documentation (Amsterdam, The Netherlands), 1992; *Reexamining Democracy: Essays in Honor of S. M. Lipset*, edited by L. Diamond and G. Marks, Sage (Beverly Hills, CA), 1992. Contributor of articles and reviews to newspapers and periodicals, including *Los Angeles Times, New York Times, American Journal of Sociology, Politics and Society, American Sociological Review, Nation, Ramparts,* and *Progressive.* Contributing editor, *Canadian Dimension*, 1966-69; *Ramparts*, contributing editor, 1967-68, Latin American editor, 1971-73; associate editor, *American Sociologist*, 1968-71, and *Journal of Political and Military Sociology*, 1975-87; member of board of advisors, *Third World Review*, 1974-76.

SIDELIGHTS: Maurice Zeitlin told *CA:* "The questions addressed in my works could not have been asked or answers to them sought, in the way I sought them, if I had simply accepted the then conventional conception of what a sociological problem is (antiseptic, 'value neutral'), and how it should be posed and solved (*a*historically). Rather, I have tried through my writings to *engage* some of the momentous questions of our time, on class domination and class conflict, on reform and revolution. Only such questions, which touch the essential and whose answers reveal dangerous truths, are worth asking and worth trying to answer."

Some of Zeitlin's work has been translated into Japanese, Spanish, Swedish, German, Portuguese, Arabic, Persian, and other languages.

BIOGRAPHICAL/CRITICAL SOURCES:

PERIODICALS

American Historical Review, June, 1985.
American Journal of Sociology, September, 1989.
Americas, April, 1986; July, 1989.
Choice, February, 1985.
Contemporary Sociology, May, 1991.
Critical Sociology, summer-fall, 1989.
Hispanic American Historical Review, August, 1989.
International Review of Social History, number 1, 1990.
Journal of Politics, November, 1985.
Journal of Social History, number 23, 1989.
Latin American Research Review, Volume 47, number 2, 1986.
Network, March, 1990.
Perspective, April, 1985.
Queen's Quarterly: A Canadian Review, summer, 1985.
Review of Social History, number 1, 1990.
Social Science Quarterly, December, 1989.
Sociology, August, 1989; November, 1990.
South Eastern Latin Americanist, September-December, 1985.
Times Higher Education Supplement (London), February 8, 1985.
Transformations, number 3, 1987.
Work, Employment & Society, September, 1989.
World Development, number 17, 1989.